AMERICA AND ITS PEOPLES

3rd edition
AMERICA AND ITS PEOPLES

A Mosaic in the Making

Volume 2 - from 1865

James Kirby Martin
University of Houston

Randy Roberts
Purdue University

Steven Mintz
University of Houston

Linda O. McMurry
North Carolina State University

James H. Jones
University of Houston

LONGMAN

An imprint of Addison Wesley Longman, Inc.

New York • Reading, Massachusetts • Menlo Park, California • Harlow, England
Don Mills, Ontario • Sydney • Mexico City • Madrid • Amsterdam

Executive Editor: Bruce Borland
Developmental Editor: Betty Slack
Project Editor: Brigitte Pelner
Design Manager: Mary Archondes
Text and Cover Designer: Mary Archondes
Cover Art: Michael Staats
Art Studio: Bur Mar
Maps: Mapping Specialists, Ltd.
Collage Art: Michael Staats
Photographer, Collage Art: Keith Tishken
Photo Researchers: Ellen Behrman/Leslie Coopersmith
Electronic Production Manager: Valerie A. Sawyer
Desktop Administrator: Joanne DelBen
Manufacturing Manager: Helene G. Landers
Electronic Page Makeup: ComCom, An RR Donnelley & Sons Company
Printer and Binder: RR Donnelley & Sons Company
Cover Printer: The Lehigh Press, Inc.

ISBN 0-673-98073-1 (single volume)
ISBN 0-673-98324-2 (instructor's edition)
ISBN 0-673-98074-X (volume 1)
ISBN 0-673-98075-8 (volume 2)
12345678910—DOW—99989796

FOR OUR STUDENTS

BRIEF CONTENTS

Detailed Contents   ix
Maps   xvii
Tables and Figures   xix
Preface   xxi
About the Authors   xxix
Comparative Chronologies   xxx

16 THE NATION RECONSTRUCTED: NORTH, SOUTH, AND THE WEST, 1865–1877   524

17 EMERGENCE AS AN ECONOMIC POWER   562

18 THE RISE OF AN URBAN SOCIETY AND CITY PEOPLE   604

19 END-OF-THE-CENTURY CRISIS   646

20 IMPERIAL AMERICA, 1870–1900   680

21 THE PROGRESSIVE STRUGGLE, 1900–1917   716

22 THE UNITED STATES AND WORLD WAR I   756

23 MODERN TIMES, 1920–1929   790

24 THE AGE OF ROOSEVELT   822

25 THE END OF ISOLATION: AMERICA FACES THE WORLD, 1920–1945   856

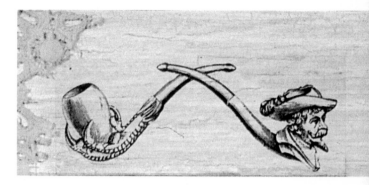

26 WAGING PEACE AND WAR   898

27 IKE'S AMERICA   930

28 POWER SHIFTS: THE EMERGENCE OF THE SOUTH AND WEST   966

29 VIETNAM AND THE CRISIS OF AUTHORITY   998

30 THE STRUGGLE FOR A JUST SOCIETY   1034

31 AMERICA IN OUR TIME   1082

Appendix   A-1
Credits   C-1
Index   I-1

DETAILED CONTENTS

Maps   xvii

Tables and Figures   xix

Preface   xxi

About the Authors   xxix

Comparative Chronologies   xxx

16 THE NATION RECONSTRUCTED: NORTH, SOUTH, AND THE WEST, 1865–1877   524

Postwar Conditions and Issues   527
The War's Impact on Individuals•Unresolved Issues

Presidential Reconstruction   531
Lincoln's Plan•Johnson's Plan•Black Codes in the South

Congressional Reconstruction   537
"Radical" Reconstruction•Black Suffrage

Reconstruction in the South   543
Carpetbaggers, Scalawags, and Black Republicans•Character of Republican Rule•Black and White Economic and Social Adaptation• Violent White Resistance

Reconstruction in the North and West   550
Northern Shifts in Attitudes•Western Expansion, Racism, and Native Americans• Final Retreat from Reconstruction

Conclusion   558

Chronology of Key Events   559

Suggestions for Further Reading   560

SPECIAL FEATURE ESSAY:
THE AMERICAN MOSAIC   532
DAY OF JUBILO: SLAVES CONFRONT EMANCIPATION

17 EMERGENCE AS AN ECONOMIC POWER   562

America: Land of Plenty   565
Mineral and Geographic Possibilities•Technological Change•An Expanding Railroad Network

Creating a Favorable Climate: The Role of Ideology, Politics, and Finance   570
Social Darwinism and the Gospel of Wealth• Laissez-Faire in Theory and Practice•Corporations and Capital Formation

The Rise of Big Business   574

Controlling Competition•New Managerial Styles and an Expanding Middle Class•Mass Marketing, Assembly Lines, and Mass Production•The Power of Bigness

Varieties of Economic Change in the West and South   580

Western Expansion and Exploitation•The Changing Nature of Farming•The New South

Working in Industrial America   590

Conditions of Work•Worker Discontent•Early Labor Violence•Unorganized and Organized Labor

Conclusion   599

Chronology of Key Events   600

Suggestions for Further Reading   600

SPECIAL FEATURE ESSAY:
POPULAR PROTEST   582
THE WILD WEST

18   THE RISE OF AN URBAN SOCIETY AND CITY PEOPLE   604

The New Immigrants   607

"Birds of Passage"•In Search of a New Home

Nativism: The Anti-Immigrant Reaction   611

Sources of Conflict•Closing the Golden Door

New Cities and New Problems   615

City Technology•The Segregated City•The Problems of Growth•From Private City to Public City

City Culture   623

Night Life and Day Life•From the Genteel Tradition to Realism and Naturalism•Describing the Urban Jungle•Painting Urban Reality•The Sounds of the City

Entertaining the Multitudes   630

Of Fields and Cities•"I Can Lick Any Sonofabitch in the House"•The Excluded

Americans•From Central Park to Coney Island•The Magic of the Flickering Image•The Agony of Painless Escape

Conclusion   641

Chronology of Key Events   642

Suggestions for Further Reading   641

SPECIAL FEATURE ESSAY:
SPORTS AND LEISURE   632
COLLEGE FOOTBALL WARS

19   END-OF-THE-CENTURY CRISIS   646

Equilibrium and Inertia: The National Political Scene   650

Divided Power: The Parties and the Federal Government•Subtle Differences: The Bases of Party Loyalty•The Business of Politics: Party Organization•The Struggle for Inclusion: Women and Politics

Style over Substance: Government in the Gilded Age, 1877–1892   655

Hayes and the "Money Question"•Garfield, Arthur, and the Patronage Issue•Cleveland, the Railroads, and Tariffs•Harrison and Big Business•Legislative Activity on Minority Rights and Social Issues

Revolt of the West and South   662

Grievances: Real and Imagined•The Farmers Organize•The Agrarian Agenda•Emergence of the Populist Party

Depression and Turbulence in the 1890s   668

The Roots and Results of the Depression•Expressions of Worker Discontent•Deteriorating Race Relations•The Tide Turns: The Election of 1896

Chronology of Key Events   676

Conclusion   677

Suggestions for Further Reading   677

SPECIAL FEATURE ESSAY:
THE AMERICAN MOSAIC   674
"RISE, BROTHERS!": THE BLACK RESPONSE TO JIM CROW

20 IMPERIAL AMERICA, 1870–1900   680

Congressional Control and the Reduction of American Power   683

Trimming the State Department•Reducing the Military•Seward's Dream

The Spirit of American Greatness   685

American Exceptionalism•Sense of Duty•Search for Markets•The New Navy•Shaping Public Opinion

The Emergence of Aggression in American Foreign Policy   690

Confronting the Germans in Samoa•Teaching Chile a Lesson•Plucking the Hawaiian Pear•Facing Down the British

The War for Empire   695

The Spirit of the 1890s•The Cuban Revolution•The Yellow Press•The Spanish-American War•Freeing Cuba•The Imperial Debate•The War to Crush Filipino Independence•Keeping the Doors Open

Chronology of Key Events   712

Conclusion   713

Suggestions for Further Reading   713

PRIMARY SOURCE ESSAY   701

WILLIAM RANDOLPH HEARST AND THE SINKING OF THE *MAINE*

SPECIAL FEATURE ESSAY:
THE AMERICAN MOSAIC   706
THEODORE ROOSEVELT AND THE ROUGH RIDERS

21 THE PROGRESSIVE STRUGGLE, 1900–1917   716

The Progressive Impulse   719

America in 1901•Voices for Change•The Muckrakers

Progressives in Action   725

The Drive to Organize•Urban Beginnings•Reform Reaches the State Level

Progressivism Moves to the National Level   736

Roosevelt and New Attitudes Toward Government Power•Taft and Quiet Progressivism•Wilson and Moral Progressivism

Progressivism in the International Arena   744

Big Stick Diplomacy•Dollar Diplomacy•Missionary Diplomacy

Progressive Accomplishments, Progressive Failures 748

The Impact of Legislation•Winners and Losers

Chronology of Key Events 752

Conclusion 753

Suggestions for Further Reading 753

SPECIAL FEATURE ESSAY:
MEDICINE AND THE ARTS 726
THE WHITE PLAGUE

22 THE UNITED STATES AND WORLD WAR I 756

The Road to War 759

The Guns of August•American Neutrality•Allied Violations of Neutrality•Submarine Warfare•Preparedness Campaign•The Election of 1916•The End of Neutrality

American Industry Goes to War 770

Voluntarism•"Hooverizing"•Peace with Labor•Financing the War

The American Public Goes to War 772

Selling the War•Political Repression•Wartime Reform•African Americans and the Great Migration

The War Front 777

The War at Sea•Raising an Army•The Defeat of Germany

Social Unrest After the War 779

Mounting Racial Tension•Labor Unrest and the Red Scare

The Treaty of Versailles 781

The Fourteen Points•Discord Among the Victors•The Struggle for Ratification•The Election of 1920

Conclusion 787

Chronology of Key Events 787

Suggestions for Further Reading 788

SPECIAL FEATURE ESSAY:
THE HUMAN TOLL OF COMBAT 764
THE FIRST DAY OF THE SOMME

23 MODERN TIMES, 1920—1929 790

The Emergence of Modern America 793

Urban Growth•The Rise of a Consumer Economy

The Formation of Modern American Culture 797

Mass Entertainment•Spectator Sports•Low-Brow and Middle-Brow Culture•The Avant-Garde•The Sex Debate

The Clash of Cultures 804

The New Woman•Prohibition•The Scopes Trial•Xenophobia and Restricting Immigration•The Ku Klux Klan•African-American Protests•The Harlem Renaissance

The Republican Restoration 811

Handsome Harding•Silent Cal•The Twilight of Progressivism•The Election of 1928

The Great Crash 814

Speculative Manias•The Market Crashes•Why It Happened

Chronology of Key Events 818

Conclusion 819

Suggestions for Further Reading 819

SPECIAL FEATURE ESSAY:
ASPECTS OF FAMILY LIFE 802
THE SEXUAL REVOLUTION OF THE EARLY 1900S

24 THE AGE OF ROOSEVELT 822

The Great Depression in Global
Perspective 825

The Human Toll 826
The Dispossessed•Private and Public Charity

President Herbert Hoover Responds 828
Conservative Responses•Government Loans

Franklin Roosevelt and the First
New Deal 830
The Election of 1932•The First 100 Days•The
New Dealers•The Farmers' Plight•The National
Recovery Administration•Jobs Programs•
Roosevelt's Critics

The Second New Deal 842
The Wagner Act•Social Security•The Election of
1936

The New Deal, Women, and Minority
Groups 844
Women•African Americans•Mexican
Americans•Native Americans

The New Deal in Decline 848
Court Packing•The Depression of 1937

Popular Culture During the Great
Depression 850
Artistic and Literary Endeavors•Hollywood Dur-
ing the Great Depression

Conclusion 851

Chronology of Key Events 852

Suggestions for Further Reading 853

PRIMARY SOURCE ESSAY 833

THE FIRST "FIRESIDE CHAT"

SPECIAL FEATURE ESSAY:
MEDICINE AND RACE 846
THE TUSKEGEE SYPHILIS STUDY

25 THE END OF ISOLATION: AMERICA FACES THE WORLD, 1920—1945 856

Diplomacy Between the Wars 859
American Diplomacy During the 1920s•United
States Policy Toward Latin America•The Isola-
tionist Mirage

The Coming of World War II 861
Conflict in the Pacific•Italy•Germany•The
American Response to Hitler•War Begins•"The
Arsenal of Democracy"•A Collision Course in
the Pacific•Pearl Harbor

America Mobilizes for War 871
Mobilizing the Economy•Taming Inflation•
Election of 1944•Molding Public Opinion

Social Changes During the War 874
Women•African Americans•Mexican Americans
Fear of Enemy Aliens•Internment of Japanese
Americans

The War in Europe 880
The Grand Alliance•Early Axis Victories•
Stemming the German Tide•Liberating Europe•
The Yalta Conference

The War in the Pacific 886
Island Hopping•The Dawn of the Atomic Age•
The Manhattan Project•Hiroshima and Nagasaki

Conclusion 892

Chronology of Key Events 894

Suggestions for Further Reading 895

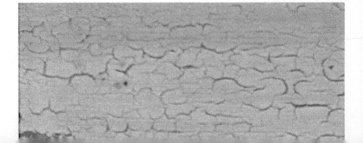

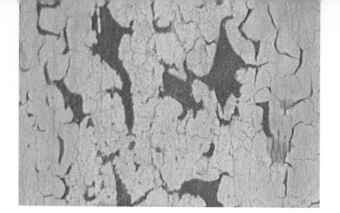

MAP ESSAY
LANDINGS ON D-DAY   884
The Longest Day

SPECIAL FEATURE ESSAY:
THE HUMAN TOLL OF COMBAT   890
HIROSHIMA AND NAGASAKI

26 WAGING PEACE AND WAR   898

Containing the Russian Bear   902
Origins of the Cold War•A World Divided•
Tough Talk•The Truman Doctrine•The Marshall
Plan: "Saving Western Europe"

The Containment Policy   908
Berlin Test•Troubling Times•The Korean War

The Cold War at Home   915
Adjusting to Peace•Confronting the Demands of
Labor•Failure of the Fair Deal•Searching for the
Enemy Within•The Rise and Fall of Joseph
McCarthy

The Paranoid Style   924
HUAC Goes to Hollywood•"What's Wrong with
Our Kids Today?"

Conclusion   926

Chronology of Key Events   927

Suggestions for Further Reading   928
SPECIAL FEATURE ESSAY:
POPULAR PROTEST   922
THE KEFAUVER CRIME COMMITTEE

27 IKE'S AMERICA   930

Quiet Changes   934
"I Like Ike"•"Dynamic Conservatism"•A Coun-
try on Wheels•Ike, Dulles, and the World•A
New Face in Moscow•1956: The Dangerous
Year•The Troubled Second Term•*Sputnik* and
Sputtering Rockets•Third-World Challenges•
Not with a Bang, But a Whimper

We Shall Overcome   946
Taking Jim Crow to Court•A Failure of Leader-
ship•The Word from Montgomery

The Sounds of Change   955
"Father Knows Best"•The Other Side of the
Coin•The Meaning of Elvis•A Different Beat

Conclusion   963

Chronology of Key Events   963

Suggestions for Further Reading   964

PRIMARY SOURCE ESSAY   957
EDWARD R. MURROW AND THE FUNCTION OF
TELEVISION

SPECIAL FEATURE ESSAY:
SPORTS AND LEISURE   948
INTEGRATION IN SPORTS

28 POWER SHIFTS: THE EMERGENCE OF THE
SOUTH AND WEST   966

The Emergence of the Southern Rim   970
From the Long Hot Summer to the Sunbelt•A
Shift in Race Relations•The Business of the South
Is Business

The Myth and Reality of the West   975
Packaging the West•Washington and the West•
The Problems and Benefits of Growth

Politics Western Style   984
An Aberration or an Omen?•Shifting Party Loy-
alties•The Politics of Liberation

Conclusion   994

Chronology of Key Events   994

Suggestions for Further Reading   995

SPECIAL FEATURE ESSAY:
MEDICINE AND MORALITY   990
AIDS: A MODERN PLAGUE

29 VIETNAM AND THE CRISIS OF
   AUTHORITY   998

The Illusion of Greatness   1001
Television's President•The "Macho" Presidency•
Something Short of Camelot•*Cuba Libre* Revisited

Vietnam: America's Longest War   1008
A Small Corner of a Bigger Picture•Kennedy's
Testing Ground•Texas Tough in the Gulf of
Tonkin•Lyndon's War•To Tet and Beyond•The
Politics of a Divided Nation

The Tortuous Path Toward Peace   1022
Outsiders on the Inside•Vietnamization: The
Idea and the Process•A "Decent Interval"•The
Legacy of the War

Chronology of Key Events   1030

Conclusion   1031

Suggestions for Further Reading   1031

MAP ESSAY
LOGISTICS IN A GUERILLA WAR   1016
The Longest War

SPECIAL FEATURE ESSAY:
THE HUMAN TOLL OF COMBAT   1004
MY LAI AND THE QUESTION OF WAR ETHICS

30 THE STRUGGLE FOR A JUST SOCIETY
   1034

The Struggle for Racial Justice   1037
Freedom Now•To the Heart of Dixie•
"Bombingham"•Kennedy Finally Acts•The
March on Washington•The Civil Rights Act of
1964•Voting Rights•Black Nationalism and
Black Power•The Civil Rights Movement Moves
North•The Great Society and the Drive for
Equality•White Backlash•The Struggle
Continues

The Youth Revolt   1055
The New Left•The Making and Unmaking of a
Counterculture

Liberation Movements   1059
Women's Liberation•Sources of Discontent•
Feminism Reborn•Radical Feminism•The
Growth of Feminist Ideology•The Supreme
Court and Sex Discrimination•The Equal Rights
Amendment•Impact of the Women's Liberation
Movement•*¡Viva La Raza!*•The Native-American
Power Movement•Gay and Lesbian
Liberation•The Earth First

Conclusion   1077

Chronology of Key Events   1078

Suggestions for Further Reading   1079

PRIMARY SOURCE ESSAY   1041
MARTIN LUTHER KING, JR., AND THE "LETTER
   FROM THE BIRMINGHAM JAIL"

SPECIAL FEATURE ESSAY:
THE AMERICAN MOSAIC   1062
CÉSAR CHÁVEZ AND *LA CAUSA*

3I AMERICA IN OUR TIME   1082

Crisis of Political Leadership   1086
Restraining the Imperial Presidency•New-Style
Presidents

Wrenching Economic Transformations   1088
The Age of Inflation•Oil Embargo•Foreign Com-
petition and Deindustrialization•Whipping
Stagflation

A New American Role in the World   1092
Détente•Foreign Policy Triumphs•No Island of
Stability

The Reagan Revolution   1097
The Gipper•Reaganomics•The Celebration of
Wealth•The Reagan Doctrine•A Remarkable
Ideological Turnaround•The Reagan Revolution
in Perspective

The Bush Presidency   1103
A Kinder, Gentler Nation•Collapse of Commu-
nism•Economic and Foreign Policy•Enter Bill
Clinton

A New Covenant   1111

Conclusion   1112

Chronology of Key Events   1113

Suggestions for Further Reading   1114

SPECIAL FEATURE ESSAY:
AMERICA AND THE WORLD   1106
THE END OF TWO ERAS

MAP ESSAY
THE FIRST CRISIS OF THE POST-COLD
   WAR ERA   1108
The Persian Gulf War

APPENDIX   A-I

The Declaration of Independence   A-2

The Constitution of the United States of America   A-4

Amendments to the Constitution   A-10

Presidential Elections   A-14

Vice Presidents and Cabinet Members by Administration   A-17

Supreme Court Justices   A-25

Admission of States to the Union   A-27

U.S. Population, 1790–1990   A-28

Regional Origins of Immigration   A-29

Credits   C-I

Index   I-I

MAPS

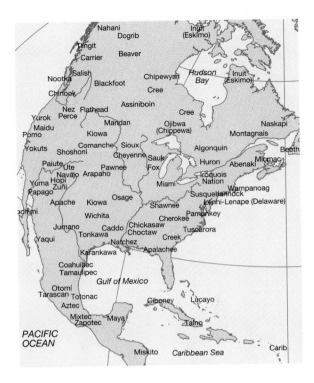

Page

547	Reconstruction and Redemption
554	Indian Battles and Reservations
558	Election of 1876
587	Rise of Tenancy
596	The Great Railroad Strike, 1877
608	Immigration, 1880–1889 and 1900–1909
682	Area of Grant's Expansionist Scheme
691	Hawaii and Samoa
705	Spanish-American War, Cuban Theater
708	American Empire
730	Women's Suffrage
737	National Parks and Forests
742	Election of 1912
745	Panama Canal
748	American Interventions in the Caribbean
760	European Alliances and Battlefronts
778	United States Participation on the Western Front
783	American Military Forces in Russia, 1918
785	Europe After World War I
794	Growth of Chicago
795	African-American Population, 1910 and 1950
831	Electoral Shift, 1928 and 1932
863	Axis Takeovers in Europe, 1936–1939
878	Location of Nazi Concentration and Death Camps
879	Location of Internment Camps for Japanese Americans
882	World War II, European Theater
885	**Map Essay** Landings on D-Day: The Longest Day
887	World War II, Pacific Theater
905	Europe After World War II
913	Korean War
914	Marine Breakout from Chosin Reservoir

Page

936	United States Interstate Highway System
937	Suburban Growth
974	Migration to the Sunbelt, 1970–1981
983	Damming Western Waters
987	Election of 1964
988	Election of 1968
989	Population Shifts, 1980–1986
1010	Vietnam and Southeast Asia
1015	Vietnam Conflict, 1964–1975
1017	**Map Essay** Logistics in a Guerrilla War: The Longest War
1094	Conflict in the Middle East
1101	U.S. Involvement in Central America and the Caribbean
1109	**Map Essay** The First Crisis of the Post–Cold War Era: The Persian Gulf War
A-27	Admission of States to the Union
Following the index: Political and Physical Map of the United States; The World	

TABLES AND FIGURES

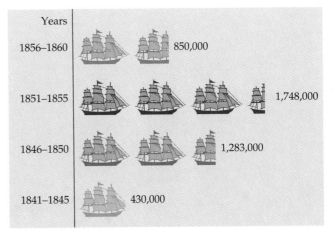

Page

538   Table 16.1   Reconstruction Amendments, 1865–1870

539   Figure 16.1   Composition of State Constitutional Conventions Under Congressional Reconstruction

569   Figure 17.1   Railroad Construction, 1861–1920

574   Figure 17.2   Index of U.S. Manufacturing Production, 1864–1914

577   Figure 17.3   Iron, Steel, and Coal Production, 1870–1900

579   Figure 17.4   Distribution of Wealth, 1890

616   Figure 18.1   Urban and Rural Population, 1870–1920

653   Figure 19.1   Voter Participation in Presidential Elections, 1876–1920

664   Figure 19.2   Price Indexes for Consumer and Farm Products, 1865–1913

739   Table 21.1   Progressive Era Legislation and Amendments

769   (Chap. 22)   Road to War: World War I

772   Figure 22.1   Labor Union Membership, 1897–1920

781   Table 22.1   Woodrow Wilson's Fourteen Points, 1918: Success and Failure in Implementation

805   Figure 23.1   Women in the Workforce, 1900–1940

827   Figure 24.1   Unemployment, 1929–1942

828   Table 24.1   Depression Shopping List, 1932–1934

832   Figure 24.2   Bank Failures, 1929–1933

832   Table 24.2   Legislation Enacted During the First Hundred Days, March 9–June 16, 1933

843   Table 24.3   Later New Deal Legislation

893   (Chap. 25)   Road to War: World War II

907   Figure 26.1   National Defense Budgets, 1940–1964

939   Figure 27.1   Defense Expenditures, Armed Forces Strength, 1945–1990

956   Table 27.1   Population of Metropolitan Areas, by Region, Size, and Race, 1950–1970

956   Figure 27.2   American Birthrate, 1940–1960

1026   Figure 29.1   U.S. Troop Levels in Vietnam

Page

1037   Table 30.1   High School Graduates (Percentage of Population Ages 25–29)

1038   Table 30.2   Income Distribution of African Americans, Other Nonwhites, and Whites 1960, 1969

1038   Figure 30.1   Unemployment, 1950–1970

1049   Table 30.3   Black Voter Registration Before and After the Voting Rights Act of 1965

1052   Figure 30.2   Federal Spending on Social Programs, Excluding Social Security

1052   Figure 30.3   Federal Aid to Education, 1964–1970

1060   Figure 30.4   Percentage of Females in Selected Occupations

1061   Figure 30.5   American Birthrate, 1960–1985

1068   Table 30.4   Occupation by Gender, 1972, 1980, and 1989 (Percentage)

1069   Table 30.5   Ratio of Divorces to Marriages, 1890–1987

1090   Figure 31.1   Consumer Price Index, 1960–1990

1097   Figure 31.2   Inflation, 1960–1990

1099   Figure 31.3   U.S. Budget Deficits, 1940–1990

1100   Figure 31.4   Weekly Earnings, 1980–1990

Appendix

A-28   U.S. Population, 1790–1990, Urban and Rural

A-28   U.S. Population, 1790–1990, White and Nonwhite

A-29   Regional Origins of Immigration

PREFACE

mericans are of two minds about history. Popular history fascinates Americans. Many of Hollywood's most popular films—from *Birth of a Nation* to *Pocahontas*—draw on history for their themes, characters, and drama. From *Roots* to public television's Civil War series, a surprising share of our favorite television shows take their subject matter from history. Nothing underscores this fascination with history better than the fact that more Americans visit historical sites and museums like Colonial Williamsburg or the Smithsonian Institution than attend major league baseball games.

Academic history is far less popular, however. At colleges and universities, the number of history majors and enrollment in history courses has fallen at an alarming rate. At the high-school level, history requirements have increasingly been replaced by courses in social studies. A recent poll found that high-school students consider history the least relevant subject that they study.

We have designed *America and Its Peoples* to convey American history's excitement and drama. The story that we tell is fraught with conflict, suspense, and controversy, and we have sought to recapture this excitement by writing a book built around vivid character sketches, colorful anecdotes, a strong narrative pulse, and a wide-angle view that allows us to examine such subjects as crime, disease, the family and sexuality, and sports.

A history textbook, in our view, need not be dull, humorless, or lifeless. Rather, it should bring the past back to life in all of its complexity and ambiguity, underscoring history's continuing fascination and relevance in our daily lives. The issues addressed in this book—colonialism, revolution, the origins of racial prejudice, the costs and benefits of industrialization and urbanization—are anything but trivial or irrelevant; they remain very much alive today.

Nor do we think that a textbook should insulate readers from controversy. One of history's greatest benefits is that it allows us to "second guess" the decisions and choices made in the past, to reassess the meaning of past events, and to reevaluate real-life heroes and villains. History, we believe, is the ideal laboratory for critical thinking; by engaging the past, we can learn now to identify significant evidence, draw causal connections, and evaluate conflicting interpretations. This textbook seeks to demonstrate that history is an arena of debate and contention as exciting as any other.

Each generation must create a history that addresses the concerns of its own time. In writing *America and Its Peoples*, we have sought to fashion a history of the United States that speaks to the realities of a changing America. Today, the United States is the most ethnically diverse nation in the world. Over the past four centuries, 45 million people have arrived in America from Africa, Asia, and Europe. In *America and Its Peoples* we recount the histories of the diverse ethnic, religious, and racial groups that make up our society; we underscore the pivotal role that ethnicity, race, and religion have played in our nation's social, cultural, and political development. From its earliest settlement, America has been a multicultural society, and by placing ethnicity, race, gender, and class at the very heart of our narrative, we have sought to present a new perspective on how our multifaceted culture and politics functioned through time.

Contemporary American society perceives itself as beset by unprecedented problems—of ethnic and racial tension, economic stagnation and inequality, crime, family upheaval, and environmental degradation. In *America and Its Peoples*, we have made a special point of uncovering the historical roots of the problems confronting American society today. One of history's values is that it can show how previous generations confronted the controversial issues of their times, allowing us to assess their achievements and failures.

Americans are an optimistic, forward-looking people who, in the course of everyday life, care little about the past. More than two centuries ago, Thomas Jefferson gave pointed expression to this attitude when he declared that "the earth belongs to the living and not the dead." But as William Faulkner once observed, "the past is never dead. It's not even past." We are convinced that the very worst forms of bigotry, fanaticism, and racism are ultimately grounded in historical ignorance and mythology. History reminds us that our values, our identities, and our most pressing social problems are rooted in our historical experience. Thus, in writing this book, we have not simply sought to create an encyclopedic compendium of names, dates, events, and concepts; we have conceived of American history as a dramatic story: a story involving contention, struggle, compromise, and, above all, conflicting visions of the nation's dominant values.

Today, many Americans are wary about the future and uneasy about the state of their society. In *America and Its Peoples* we have written a textbook that emphasizes historical contingency—the idea that different decisions and choices in the past would have created a very different world today. Ours is a history that emphasizes the importance of personal choice and collective action; a history that stresses peoples' capacity to shape their destiny. As America enters the twenty-first century, we believe that this is a historical lesson with profound implications for the nation's future.

Besides structuring the book's contents to encourage student involvement, we have worked to keep the needs of history faculty members very much in mind. The text's structure conforms to the course outlines used by most history instructors. *America and Its Peoples* also places a premium on chronological flow, an essential organizational element for college students grappling with the complexities of U.S. history. It also provides a clear narrative rendering of essential political, diplomatic, cultural, social, intellectual, and military history and concisely identifies major historical concepts and themes.

Finally, we have taken great care to present a text offering both breadth and balance. We have found that the often-expressed dichotomies between political and diplomatic history and social and cultural history disappear when history is people-centered from its inception. Materials on ethnicity, gender, and race belong at the core of the historical narrative, not as adjunct information, and we have attempted to include the important findings and insights of both traditional and newer historical subjects. It is our hope that we have achieved a sensitive and compelling presentation.

FEATURES

The book's structure is organized to heighten and sustain student interest. To borrow a phrase associated with computers, we have aimed at the production of a "user-friendly" text. Each chapter begins with an outline of contents and a carefully selected anecdote or incident that frames the chapter's themes while drawing students into the material. A chronological and topical narrative follows, building toward a chapter conclusion highlighting and reinforcing essential points. In addition, each chapter contains a chronology of key events; a bibliography of suggested readings; and a special feature essay designed to offer students an in-depth look at a significant topic in one of the following people-oriented categories that illustrate change over time: Aspects of Family Life, Sports and Leisure, The American Mosaic, Medicine, The Human Toll of Combat, and Popular Protest. Also included in this edition are eight Primary Source Essays, that provide an in-depth look at a selected document in detail, examining its context, purpose, historical importance, and contemporary relevance.

Other features of the text include an extensive **full-color map** and **photo program,** completely redesigned **figures and charts,** five full-page battlefield **picture maps** with accompanying essays, new **"Road to War" tables** summarizing events leading up to the outbreak or declaration of major wars, a **multidimensional timeline** at the front of the book that is replete with high-interest items; and valuable tables, charts, graphs, and maps in the **Appendix.**

NEW TO THIS EDITION

As authors we are grateful for the extremely positive reception accorded the first and second editions of *America and Its Peoples.* As with all books, however, there is always room for improvement, and we have worked very hard to make our text even more balanced in this new edition. In addition to numerous small revisions throughout to clarify certain points and to update our interpretations according to the latest findings in particular subfields, we cite the following major revisions:

- new bibliography for every chapter, featuring annotated listings of four or five major works for each chapter
- Chapter 1: new material on the Maya social order
- Chapter 3: new section "Allies as Enemies: Making War on the Cherokees" deals with the Cherokee War of 1759–1761
- Chapter 7: retitled "The Formative Decade"; new opening vignette on James Thomson Callender; new section "The Roots of American Economic Growth"; a revised and condensed section "Alexander Hamilton's Financial Program"; new section "Clearing the Ohio Country of Native Americans"
- Chapter 11: retitled "America's First Age of Reform"; new opening vignette on Sojourner Truth; new section "Social Problems on the Rise"; new section "Religious Diversity"; new section "Ethnic Voices" examines the writings of African, Mexican, Native Americans, and Irish immigrants, and includes new information on antebellum women writers; new section

"Forms of Popular Entertainment" features discussions of P. T. Barnum, popular humor, the tall tale, theater, and oratory
- Chapter 12: additional information on Irish and German immigrant groups
- Chapter 13: retitled "Cultures Collide in the Far West"; new opening vignette on Juan Cortina; expanded discussion of Spanish America; new section "The Fate of Mexican Americans" discusses the fate of these people following the Mexican-American War
- Chapter 16: new section "Western Expansion, Racism, and Native Americans" covers Native Americans in the West, cultural differences, and U.S. government policies and practices for dealing with Native Americans: confrontation, annihilation, ethnocide, and assimilation
- Chapter 17: section "Western Expansion and Exploitation" includes discussion of the competition for resources in the West; new section "Working in Industrial America" (from the former chapter 18) so that the rise of the new economic order and industrialization are now covered in the same chapter
- Chapter 18: combines material from former chapters 18 and 19 so that immigration and urbanization of the late nineteenth and early twentieth centuries are now covered in the same chapter
- Chapter 21: includes information on African-American women among the Progressive era reformers; additional material on Theodore Roosevelt's conservation policies, especially with regard to land in the West; section "Missionary Diplomacy" has been expanded to include additional discussion of the Mexican Revolution
- Chapter 22: new section "The Guns of August" discusses German military strategies and offensives, the military stalemate, the Easter Uprising in Ireland, and the beginning of the Russian Revolution; section "Political Re-

pression" has been expanded to include more examples of government action against dissenters

- Chapter 23: new section "The Emergence of Modern America" deals with urban growth and the rise of a consumer economy; new section "The Formation of Modern American Culture" discusses mass entertainment (radio, the phonograph, new forms of music), spectator sports (baseball, football), low-brow and middle-brow culture (parlor games, pulp fiction, "confession" magazines), the avant-garde (literature, drama, music, poetry, and the lost generation); new section "The New Woman"; section "The Great Crash" revised to include discussion of Charles Ponzi and "Ponzi" schemes
- Chapter 24: new section "The Great Depression in Global Perspective" discusses international experiences of and responses to the Depression; new section "The Human Toll" examines the personal suffering wrought by the Depression; new section "The Dispossessed" discusses the Depression's effects on African and Mexican Americans in particular; new section "The New Dealers" examines the differences between Progressive era reformers and New Deal officials and advisors; new section "Popular Culture During the Great Depression" discusses literature, photojournalism, and movies of the era
- Chapter 25: new opening vignette on Auschwitz concentration camp; new section "American Diplomacy During the 1920s" includes discussion of disarmament proposals and the Kellogg-Briand Pact; revised section "The Isolationist Mirage" discusses disillusionment and antiwar sentiment among Americans; revised section "The Coming of World War II" features additional material on Hitler and the beginning of the war and the Battle of Britain; new section "The Manhattan Project" discusses U.S. development of the atomic bomb; new section "Hiroshima and Nagasaki" focuses on the devastation wrought by the bomb; new conclusion discusses the controversy over the proposed *Enola Gay* exhibit at the Smithsonian Institution's Air and Space Museum

- Chapter 28: entirely new chapter for this edition; discusses the South and the West in the twentieth century, the rise of the Sunbelt, the shift of political and economic power from North and East to South and West, the role of the government in developing industry and harnessing power in the South and West
- Chapter 29: new special feature essay on the My Lai incident of the conflict in Vietnam
- Chapter 30: new section "*¡Viva La Raza!*" discusses Mexican Americans in the twentieth century; new section "Gay and Lesbian Liberation" discusses the rise of activism among homosexual groups; new section "The Earth First" discusses the rise of the environmentalist movement; chapter now includes the special feature essay on César Chávez (formerly in chapter 29)
- Chapter 31: new section "Enter Bill Clinton" discusses Clinton's election and administration; new picture map essay on the Persian Gulf War; new special feature essay on the end of the Cold War

SUPPLEMENTS

A comprehensive and up-to-date supplements package accompanies *America and Its Peoples*.

For Instructors

Instructor's Resource Manual This extensive resource by Mark Newman of the University of Illinois, Chicago, begins with essays on teaching history through maps, film, and primary sources. Each chapter contains a synopsis, sample discussion questions, lecture supplements, and instructional flowcharts. The manual includes a reproducible set of map exercises by James Conrad of Nichols College, designed to teach basic geographic literacy.

America Through the Eyes of Its People: A Collection of Primary Sources, Revised Edition

This one-volume collection of primary documents reflects the rich and varied tapestry of American life. It contains documents by Native Americans, women, African Americans, Hispanics, and others who helped to shape the course of U.S. history. The documents and accompanying student exercises are designed to be duplicated by instructors for student use. This revised edition includes more social history and regional documents and has been reformatted so that it is easier to use than the previous edition.

Reading the West: A Collection of Primary Sources

This collection of primary sources developed by James Olsen of Sam Houston State University is devoted exclusively to the history and peoples of the West and Southwest. It is filled with the crucial documents that describe the contributions and life experiences of the diverse people of this region. The sources are accompanied by contextual headnotes and critical thinking questions.

Comprehensive American History Transparency Set

This vast collection of American history map transparencies will soon become a necessary teaching aid. This set includes over 200 map transparencies ranging from the first Native Americans to the end of the Cold War, covering wars, social trends, elections, immigration, and demographics. Included are a reproducible set of student map exercises, teaching tips, and correlation charts. This fresh and extensive map package provides *complete* geographic coverage of American history.

Discovering American History Through Maps and Views

Created by Gerald Danzer, University of Illinois, Chicago, the recipient of the AHA's 1989 James Harvey Robinson Award for his work in the development of map transparencies, this set of 140 four-color acetates is a unique instructional tool. It contains an introduction on teaching history through maps and a detailed commentary on each transparency. The collection includes cartographic and pictorial maps, views and photos, urban plans, building diagrams, and works of art.

A Guide to Teaching American History Through Film

Created by Randy Roberts of Purdue University, this guide provides instructors with a creative and practical tool for stimulating classroom discussions. The sections include a historian's perspective on American film, a list of films for specific periods in American history, practical suggestions, and a bibliography.

Video Lecture Launchers

Prepared by Mark Newman of the University of Illinois at Chicago, these video lecture launchers (each two to five minutes in duration), cover key issues in American history from 1877 to the present. The launchers are accompanied by an Instructor's Manual.

American Impressions: A CD-ROM for U.S. History

This unique and groundbreaking CD-ROM for the U.S. history course is organized in a thematic framework that allows in-depth coverage. Hundreds of photos, maps, documents, works of art, graphics, and historical film clips are organized into narrated vignettes and interactive activities. This rich tool is useful for professors and students. The first volume includes four segments: "The Encounter Period," "Revolution to Republic," "A Century of Labor and Reform," and "The Struggle for Equality." A Guide for Instructors provides teaching tips and suggestions for using advanced media in the classroom. The CD-ROM is available in both Macintosh and Windows formats.

Visual Archives of American History, Second Edition

This two-sided video laser-disc is an encyclopedic chronology of U.S. history from the meeting of three cultures to the present—with hundreds of photographs and illustrations; a variety of source and reference maps, several of which are animated, and 50 minutes of video. For ease in planning lectures, a manual listing bar codes for scanning and frame numbers is available.

"This Is America" Immigration Video Produced by the Museum of Immigration, these two 20-minute videos tell the story of immigrant America and the personal stories and accomplishments of immigrants. The videos explore the ways in which America's strength derives from the ethnically and culturally diverse backgrounds of its citizens by showing the contributions of millions of immigrants to American culture.

Text Map Transparencies A set of 30 four-color transparencies from the maps in *America and Its Peoples.*

Test Bank Created by Ken Weatherbie of Del Mar College, this test bank features approximately 45 multiple-choice, 10 essay, and 5 map items per chapter. Multiple-choice items are referenced by topic, text page number, and type (factual or interpretive).

TestMaster Computerized Testing System This flexible, easy-to-use computerized test bank includes all the test items in the printed test bank. The TestMaster software allows you to edit existing questions and add your own items. Tests can be printed in several different formats and can include figures such as graphs and tables. Available for DOS and Macintosh.

QuizMaster This new program enables you to design TestMaster generated tests that your students can take on a computer. QuizMaster is available separately from TestMaster and can be obtained free through your sales representative.

Grades A grade-keeping and classroom management software program that maintains data for up to 200 students.

For Students

Study Guide and Practice Tests Each chapter of this study guide by Ken Chiaro of Pima Community College is designed to provide students with a comprehensive review of text material and to encourage application and critical analysis of the material. Each chapter contains a student introduction, reading comprehension and geography exercises, and true-false, completion, and multiple-choice practice tests.

Learning to Think Critically: Films and Myths About American History Randy Roberts and Robert May of Purdue University use well-known films such as *Gone with the Wind* and *Casablanca* to explore some common myths about America and its past. Many widely held assumptions about our country's past come from or are perpetuated by popular films. Which are true? Which are patently not true? And how does a student of history approach documents, sources, and textbooks with a critical and discerning eye? This short handbook subjects some popular beliefs to historical scrutiny to help students develop a method of inquiry for approaching the subject of history in general.

SuperShell Computerized Tutorial This interactive program for DOS helps students learn major facts and concepts through drill and practice exercises and diagnostic feedback. SuperShell provides immediate correct answers and the text page number on which the material is discussed. Missed questions appear with greater frequency; a running score of the student's performance is maintained on the screen throughout the session.

Mapping American History: Student Activities Written by Gerald Danzer of the University of Illinois, Chicago, this free map workbook for students features exercises designed to teach students to interpret and analyze cartographic materials as historical documents. The instructor is entitled to a free copy of the workbook for each copy of the text purchased from Longman.

Timelink Computer Atlas of American History This atlas, compiled by William Hamblin of Brigham Young University, is an introductory software tutorial and textbook companion. A Macintosh program, it presents the historical geography of the continental United States from colonial times to the settling of the West and the admission of the last continental state in 1912. The program covers territories in different time periods, provides quizzes, and includes a special Civil War module.

ACKNOWLEDGMENTS

Any textbook project is very much a team effort. We would like to thank the many individuals who have worked with us on this project, beginning with the talented historians who have served as reviewers and whose valuable critiques greatly strengthened the final product: Larry T. Balsamo, Western Illinois University; James Banks, Cuyahoga Community College; Robert A. Becker, Louisiana State University; Larry K. Burke, Dodge City Community College; Ballard C. Campbell, Northeastern University; Berry Craig, Paducah Community College; Thelma Epstein, DeAnza College; John Findlay, University of Washington; Ronald H. Fritze, Lamar University; Sam W. Haynes, University of Texas at Arlington; J. David Hoeveler, University of Wisconsin—Milwaukee; Steven R. Hoffbeck, Minot State University; Tim Koerner, Oakland Community College; Barbara E. Lacey, Saint Joseph College; Irene Ledesma, University of Texas—Pan American; Ann E. Liston, Fort Hays State University; M. Catherine Miller, Texas Tech University; Barbara J. Oberlander, Santa Fe Community College; Peter L. Petersen, West Texas A&M University; Randall Rosenberg, University of Northern Alabama; James G. Ryan, Texas A&M University at Galveston; David P. Shriver, Cuyahoga Community College; Jason Silverman, Winthrop University; Larry Steck, Lake Michigan College; Gary E. Thompson, Tulsa Junior College; Jose Torres, Mesa Community College; Eddie Weller, San Jacinto College South; Larry C. Wilson, San Jacinto College Central.

We are also indebted to the reviewers of the first and second editions: Joe S. Anderson, Azusa Pacific University; Larry Balsamo, Western Illinois University; Lois W. Banner, University of Southern California; Robert A. Becker, Louisiana State University; Delmar L. Beene, Glendale Community College; Nancy Bowen, Del Mar College; Blanche Brick, Blinn College; Larry Burke, Dodge City Community Junior College; Frank L. Byrne, Kent State University; Colin G. Calloway, Dartmouth College; Albert Camarillo, Stanford University; Clayborne Carson, Stanford University; Jay Caughtry, University of Nevada at Las Vegas; Raymond W. Champagne, Jr., University of Scranton; John P. Crevelli, Santa Rosa Junior College; Shannon J. Doyle, University of Houston, Downtown; David Glassberg, University of Massachusetts; James P. Gormly, Washington and Jefferson College; Elliott Gorn, Miami University; Neil Hamilton, Brevard Community College; Nancy Hewitt, Duke University; Alphine W. Jefferson, Southern Methodist University; David R. Johnson, University of Texas at San Antonio; Ellen K. Johnson, Northern Virginia Community College; George W. Knepper, University of Akron; Steven F. Lawson, University of South Florida; Barbara LeUnes, Blinn College; Myron Marty, Drake University; James McCaffrey, University of Houston, Downtown; James McMillan, Arizona State University; Otis Miller, Belleville Area College; William Howard Moore, University of Wyoming; Peter Myers, Palo Alto College; Roger L. Nichols, University of Arizona; Michael Perman, University of Illinois at Chicago; Paula Petrik, University of Maine; Robert Pierce, Foothill College; George Rable, Anderson College; Max Reichard, Delgado Community College; Leonard R. Riforgiato, Pennsylvania State University, Shenango Valley Campus; Marilyn Rinehart, North Harris County College; John Ray Skates, University of Southern Mississippi; Sheila Skemp, University of Mississippi; Kathryn Kish Sklar, State University of New York at Binghamton; James Strandberg, University of Wisconsin—Stout; Robert Striplin, American River College; J. K. Sweeney, South Dakota State University; Alan Taylor, Boston University; Phillip Vaughn, Rose State College; Peter H. Wang, Cabrillo Community College; Valdenia Winn, Kansas City Kansas Community College; Bill Worley, Sterling College; Eli Zaretsky, University of Missouri.

The dedicated staff at Longman provided us with great support and expert guidance. From the beginning, Bruce Borland has been a very special friend to this project. We also wish to thank Betty Slack, Adina Popescu, Lily Eng, Jim Strandberg, Leslie Coopersmith, Brigitte Pelner, and Mary Archondes. To all of them, we offer our sincere gratitude and appreciation.

Each author received invaluable help from friends, colleagues, and family. James Kirby Martin thanks Larry E. Cable, Don R. Gerlach, Joseph T. Glatthaar, Karen Guenther, David M. Oshinsky, Cathy Patterson, Jeffrey T. Sammons, Hal T. Shelton, and Karen Martin, whose talents as an editor and critic are too often overlooked. Randy Roberts thanks Terry Bilhartz and Joan Randall, and especially James S. Olson and Suzy Roberts. Steven Mintz thanks Susan Kellogg for her encouragement, support, and counsel. Linda O. McMurry thanks Joseph P. Hobbs, John David Smith, Richard McMurry, and William C. Harris. James H. Jones thanks James S. Olson, Terry Rugeley, Laura B. Auwers, and especially Linda S. Auwers, who contributed both ideas and criticisms. All of the authors thank Gerard F. McCauley, whose infectious enthusiasm for this project has never wavered. And above all else, we wish to thank our students to whom we have dedicated this book.

ABOUT THE AUTHORS

JAMES KIRBY MARTIN is a member of the Department of History at the University of Houston. A graduate of Hiram College in Ohio, he earned his Ph.D. degree at the University of Wisconsin in 1969, specializing in Early American history. His interests also include American social and military history. Among his publications are *Men in Rebellion* (1973), *In the Course of Human Events* (1979), *A Respectable Army* (1982), and *Drinking in America: A History*, rev. ed. (1987), the latter two volumes in collaboration with Mark E. Lender. Martin serves as general editor of the *American Social Experience* series, New York University Press. He recently was a senior fellow at the Philadelphia Center for Early American Studies, University of Pennsylvania, as well as scholar-in-residence at the David Library of the American Revolution, Washington Crossing, Pennsylvania. He is completing a biography of Benedict Arnold.

RANDY ROBERTS earned his Ph.D. degree in 1978 from Louisiana State University. His specializations include modern U.S. history and the history of sports and films in America. He is a faculty member at Purdue University, where he has won both the Murphy Award for outstanding teaching and the Society of Professional Journalists Teacher of the Year. His books include *Jack Dempsey: The Manassa Mauler* (1979), *Papa Jack: Jack Johnson and the Era of White Hopes* (1983), *Heavy Justice: The State of Indiana v. Michael G. Tyson* (1994), and, in collaboration with James S. Olson, *Winning Is the Only Thing: Sports in American Society Since 1945* (1989), *Where the Domino Fell: America and Vietnam, 1945–1995* (1991, 1996), and *John Wayne: American* (1995). Roberts serves as the co-editor of the *Sports and Society* series, University of Illinois Press, and is on the editorial board of the *Journal of Sports History*.

STEVEN MINTZ graduated from Oberlin College in Ohio before earning his Ph.D. degree at Yale University in 1979. A specialist in pre-Civil War America, he is also a leading authority on the history of the family. He is the author or editor of eight books including *Domestic Revolutions: A Social History of the American Family* (1988), *A Prison of Expectations: The Family in Victorian Culture* (1983), and most recently, *Moralists and Modernizers: America's Pre-Civil War Reformers* (1995). A professor of history at the University of Houston, he has also taught at Oberlin College, Pepperdine University, and Yale University, and been a visiting scholar at Harvard University's Center for European Studies. He is an editor of New York University Press's *American Social Experience* series and has served as a consultant in family history to the Smithsonian Institution's National Museum of American History.

LINDA O. McMURRY is a member of the Department of History at North Carolina State University. She completed her undergraduate studies at Auburn University, where she also earned her Ph.D. degree in 1976. Her fields of specialization include nineteenth- and twentieth-century U.S. history with an emphasis on the African-American experience and the New South. A recipient of a Rockefeller Foundation Humanities fellowship, she has written *George Washington Carver: Scientist and Symbol* (1981), and *Recorder of the Black Experience: A Biography of Monroe Nathan Work* (1985). McMurry has been active as a consultant to public television stations and museums on topics relating to black history, and is currently completing a study of biracial organizations in the South from the Reconstruction era to World War II.

JAMES H. JONES earned his Ph.D. degree at Indiana University in 1972. His areas of specialization include modern U.S. history, the history of medical ethics and medicine, and the history of sexual behavior. A member of the Department of History at the University of Houston, Jones has been a senior fellow of the National Endowment for the Humanities, a Kennedy fellow at Harvard University, a senior research fellow at the Kennedy Institute of Ethics, Georgetown University, and a Rockefeller fellow at the University of Texas Medical Branch, Galveston. His published writings include *Bad Blood: The Tuskegee Syphilis Experiment* (1981), and he is currently finishing a book on Alfred C. Kinsey and the emergence of scientific research dealing with human sexual behavior.

COMPARATIVE CHRONOLOGIES

Political/Diplomatic	Social/Economic	Cultural
30,000 B.C.— 1450		
300–900 Mayan civilization flourishes in present-day Mexico and Guatemala. **c.900** Toltecs rise to power in the Valley of Mexico and later conquer the Maya. **c.1000** Vikings led by Leif Ericson reach Labrador and Newfoundland. **1095** European Christians launch the Crusades to capture the Holy Lands from Muslims. **c.1100** Inca civilization emerges in what is now Peru.	**30,000–20,000 B.C.** First people arrive in North America from Asia across what is now the Bering Straits. **8000–5000 B.C.** Central American Indians begin to practice agriculture.	**1271** Marco Polo begins a 20-year journey to China. **1347–1353** "Black Death" kills one-third of Europe's population. **1420S** Prince Henry of Portugal sends out mariners to explore Africa's western coast. **c.1450** Johannes Gutenberg, a German printer, develops movable type, the basis of modern printing.
1450–1550		
1494 Treaty of Tordesillas divides the New World between Portugal and Spain. **1497–1498** John Cabot's voyages to Newfoundland and Cape Breton Island lay the basis of English claims to North America. **1519** Hernán Cortés and 600 Spanish conquistadores begin the conquest of the Aztec empire. **1531** Francisco Pizarro and 180 Spanish soldiers start the conquest of the Inca empire.	**1492** Columbus makes the first of his voyages to the Americas. **1496** Columbus introduces cattle, sugarcane, and wheat to the West Indies. **1501** Spain authorizes the first shipment of African slaves to the Caribbean. **1507** The New World is named America after Florentine navigator Amerigo Vespucci. **1508** First sugar mill is built in the West Indies. **1517** Coffee is introduced in Europe. **1542** Spain outlaws the *encomienda* system and the enslavement of Indians.	**1517** Martin Luther's public protest against the sale of indulgences (pardons of punishment in purgatory) marks the beginning of the Protestant Reformation. **1518** Bartolomé de Las Casas proposes that Spain stop exploiting native laborers in America. **1527** Henry VIII of England begins to sever ties with the Roman Catholic church. **1539** First printing press in the New World is established in Mexico City.
1550–1650		
1607 English adventurers establish first permanent English settlement at Jamestown in Virginia. **1608** Samuel de Champlain claims Quebec for France. **1610** Spanish found Santa Fe, New Mexico. **1619** First representative assembly in English North America meets in Jamestown. **1620** Pilgrims arrive at Cape Cod on the *Mayflower* and establish a colony at Plymouth.	**1553** Europeans learn about the potato. **1576** Some 40,000 slaves are brought to Latin America. **1585–1587** Sir Walter Raleigh sponsors England's first North American settlements at Roanoke Island, along the coast of present-day North Carolina. **1616** Chicken pox wipes out most New England Indians.	**1584** Richard Hakluyt's *Discourse of Western Planting* encourages English exploration, conquest, and colonization. **1613** Pocahontas becomes the first Indian in Virginia to convert to Christianity. **1636** Harvard College founded. **1637–1638** Anne Hutchinson is convicted of heresy in Massachusetts and flees to Rhode Island.

Political/Diplomatic	Social/Economic	Cultural
		1550-1650
1624 New York is settled by the Dutch and named New Netherland.	**1617** England begins transporting criminals to Virginia as punishment.	**1640** The first book is published in the colonies, the *Bay Psalm Book*.
1630 The Puritans establish Massachusetts Bay Colony.	**1619** Cargoes of Englishwomen begin to arrive in Virginia.	**1647** Massachusetts Bay Colony adopts the first public school law in the colonies.
1632 Maryland, the first proprietary colony, is established as a refuge for Roman Catholics.	**1619** A Dutch ship brings the first Africans to Virginia.	**1649** Maryland's Act of Toleration affirms religious freedom for all Christians in the colony.
1638 Delaware is settled by Swedes and is named New Sweden.	**1624** Cattle are introduced into New England.	
1649 Charles I of England is beheaded.	**1630** Colonial population totals about 5700.	
		1650-1750
1660, 1663 Parliament passes Navigation Acts to ensure that the colonies trade exclusively with England.	**1670** Colonial population totals about 114,500, including 4535 slaves.	**1650** Anne Bradstreet, New England's first poet, publishes *The Tenth Muse*.
1664 Dutch settlers in New Netherlands surrender to the English, who rename the colony New York.	**1673** Regular mail service between Boston and New York begins.	**1692** Witchcraft scare in Salem, Massachusetts, results in the execution of 20 men and women.
1676 Bacon's Rebellion in Virginia.	**1699** Parliament outlaws the export of woolen products from the colonies.	**1731** Benjamin Franklin founds first circulating library in Philadelphia.
1681–1682 William Penn founds Pennsylvania as a "holy experiment" in which diverse groups can live together in harmony.	**1714** Tea is introduced in the colonies.	**1732** Benjamin Franklin begins publishing *Poor Richard's Almanac*.
1688–1689 The English drive James II from the throne in the Glorious Revolution and replace him with William and Mary.	**1739** Stono slave uprising occurs in South Carolina.	**1735** John Peter Zenger acquitted on charge of seditious libel on ground that truth can be no libel.
1733 Georgia founded as a haven for debtors and a buffer against Spanish Florida.	**1749** Benjamin Franklin invents the lightning rod.	**1739** George Whitefield begins preaching tours, turning local revivals into the Great Awakening.
		1750
1750 Parliament passes the Iron Act, which prohibits colonists from expanding the production of finished iron or steel products.	**1750** The flatboat and the Conestoga wagon appear in Pennsylvania.	**1755** A British army surgeon, Dr. Richard Schuckburg, composes *Yankee Doodle* during the French and Indian War.
1754 Albany Congress draws up a plan to unite the 13 colonies under a single government.	**1756** Stagecoach line is established between New York and Philadelphia.	**1756** Wolfgang Amadeus Mozart born in Salzburg, Austria.
1754–1763 French and Indian War.		
1759 British forces under General James Wolfe conquer Quebec.		

Political/Diplomatic	Social/Economic	Cultural

1760

1760 George III becomes king of England.	**1760** Colonial population numbers about 1.6 million, including 325,000 slaves.	**1759** Touro Synagogue in Newport, Rhode Island, is designed. It is the first synagogue in the 13 colonies.
1763 Pontiac leads an unsuccessful Indian rebellion on the western frontier.	**1763** English surveyors Charles Mason and Jeremiah Dixon set the boundary between Pennsylvania and Maryland—the Mason-Dixon line.	**1761** *The Complete Housewife*, a cookbook, is published in New York City.
1763 The Proclamation of 1763 forbids white settlement west of the Appalachian Mountains.	**1765** The first medical school in the colonies is established in Philadelphia.	**1766** Robert Rogers writes the first play on a Native American subject, *Ponteach, or the Savages of America*.
1764 The Sugar Act levies new duties on coffee, indigo, sugar, and wine.	**1766** Mastodon bones are discovered along the Ohio River.	
1764 Currency Act prohibits colonial governments from issuing paper money and requires all taxes and debts to British merchants to be paid in British currency.	**1767** Daniel Boone undertakes his first exploration west of the Appalachian Mountains.	
1765 Quartering Act requires colonists to provide barracks, candles, bedding, and beverages to soldiers stationed in their area.		
1765 Stamp Act—which requires stamps to be affixed to all legal documents, almanacs, newspapers, pamphlets, and playing cards, among other items—provokes popular protests.		
1766 Parliament repeals the Stamp Act, but asserts its authority to tax the colonists in the Declaratory Act.		
1767 Townshend Duties Act imposes taxes on imported glass, lead, paint, paper, and tea to defray the cost of colonial administration.		

1770

1770 The Boston Massacre leaves five colonists dead and others wounded.	**1770** Colonial population is about 2.2 million.	**1771** Historical painter Benjamin West renders *Death of Wolfe* and *Penn's Treaty with the Indians*.
1770 Townshend Duties are repealed, except the tax on tea.	**1773** Harvard College announces that it will no longer rank students in order of social prominence.	**1773** Phillis Wheatley, the slave of a Boston merchant, publishes *Poems on Various Subjects*.
1772 Parliament declares that the crown will pay the salaries of royal governors and colonial judges.	**1774** Mother Ann Lee, founder of the Shakers in America, lands in New York City.	**1776** Thomas Paine publishes *Common Sense*, urging immediate separation from England.
1773 Tea Act allows the East India Company to sell tea directly to American retailers.		
1773 Boston Tea Party occurs when a band of "Indians" boards three British vessels and dumps 342 chests of tea into Boston Harbor.		
1774 The Coercive Acts close the port of Boston; modify the Massachusetts charter; provide for trials outside colonies when royal officials are accused of serious crimes; and call for billeting of troops in unoccupied private homes.		

Political/Diplomatic	Social/Economic	Cultural
		1770
1775 The shot "heard 'round the world"—the first military clashes between British troops and patriots take place at Lexington and Concord. 1775 George III issues declarations that a state of rebellion exists in the colonies. 1776 Continental Congress adopts the Declaration of Independence. 1778 Benjamin Franklin negotiates an American alliance with France.		
		1780
1781 Lord Cornwallis surrenders to George Washington at Yorktown. 1781 The states approve the nation's first constitution, the Articles of Confederation. 1783 The Treaty of Paris is signed, ending the American Revolution. 1787 Congress passes the Northwest Ordinance, forever barring slavery north of the Ohio River. 1787 Constitutional convention convenes in Philadelphia. 1788 Constitution is ratified. 1789 Electoral college names George Washington the first president.	1780 U.S. population is about 2,780,400. 1783 Benjamin Franklin invents bifocals. 1784 The *Empress of China* inaugurates sea trade with China. 1786 Western Massachusetts farmers, led by Daniel Shays, close county courthouses to protest low farm prices and high state taxes. 1787 Levi Hutchins, a Concord, New Hampshire, clockmaker invents the alarm clock.	1782 J. Hector St. John de Crèvecoeur publishes *Letters from an American Farmer.* 1786 Virginia legislature enacts separation of church and state. 1786 Charles Willson Peale opens the first art gallery in Philadelphia. 1789 William Hill Brown's *The Power of Sympathy* is the first novel published in the United States.
		1790
1790 Congress adopts Hamilton's proposal to fund the national debt at full value and to assume state debts from the Revolutionary War. 1791 Bank of the United States established. 1791 The Bill of Rights becomes part of the Constitution. 1794 General Anthony Wayne defeats an Indian alliance at the Battle of Fallen Timbers, opening Ohio to white settlement. 1796 Washington issues a Farewell Address, warning against political factionalism and foreign entanglements. 1798 Congress adopts the Alien and Sedition acts. 1798–1799 Kentucky and Virginia resolutions declare the Alien and Sedition acts unconstitutional.	1790 U.S. population is 3,929,214. 1790 Samuel Slater opens the first textile factory in the United States. 1793 Eli Whitney invents the cotton gin. 1794–1795 The Whiskey Rebellion, protesting the federal excise tax on whiskey, is put down.	1793 Louis XVI of France sent to the guillotine. 1794 Thomas Paine publishes *The Age of Reason.* 1798 Charles Brockden Brown publishes *Wieland.*

Political/Diplomatic	Social/Economic	Cultural

1800

1801 House of Representatives selects Thomas Jefferson as third president.

1801 Jefferson sends eight ships to enforce a blockade of Tripoli.

1803 Thomas Jefferson purchases Louisiana Territory from Napoleon for $15 million or 4 cents an acre.

1803 *Marbury* v. *Madison* upholds the principle of judicial review.

1804 Vice president Aaron Burr kills Alexander Hamilton in a duel.

1807 Jefferson imposes a trade embargo in order to pressure Britain and France to respect American rights.

1807 Congress votes to prohibit the African slave trade.

1809 Embargo Act repealed.

1809 Non-Intercourse Act prohibits trade with Britain and France.

1800 U.S. population is 5,308,483, including 896,849 slaves.

1800 John Chapman, better known as Johnny Appleseed, passes out religious tracts and apple seeds throughout the Ohio Valley.

1804 Lewis and Clark expedition sets out from St. Louis to explore the Louisiana Purchase.

1807 Seth Thomas and Eli Terry begin to manufacture clocks out of interchangeable parts.

1807 Robert Fulton proves the practicality of the steamboat by sailing the *Clermont* from New York City to Albany in 32 hours.

1800 Mason Locke Weems publishes his *Life of Washington*, the source of the legend about Washington chopping down the cherry tree.

1806 Noah Webster's *Compendious Dictionary of the English Language* is published.

1810

1812 Congress declares war against Britain.

1813–1814 Creek War.

1814 United States and Britain sign Treaty of Ghent, which ends the War of 1812.

1816 Second Bank of the United States chartered.

1818 United States and Britain agree to joint occupation of Oregon.

1819 Spain cedes Florida to the United States.

1819 "A Firebell in the Night." A crisis over slavery erupts after Missouri applies for admission to the Union as a slave state.

1810 U.S. population is 7,239,881.

1814 The first totally mechanized factory producing cotton cloth from raw cotton opens in Waltham, Massachusetts.

1817 American Colonization Society is founded to colonize free blacks in Africa.

1819 Panic of 1819.

1819 An asylum for the deaf, dumb, and blind opens in Hartford, Connecticut, inaugurating a new era of humanitarian concern for the handicapped.

1819 The *Savannah* becomes the first steamship to cross the Atlantic.

1819 *Dartmouth* v. *Woodward* upholds the sanctity of contracts. *McCulloch* v. *Maryland* upholds the constitutionality of the second Bank of the United States.

1814 Francis Scott Key writes the lyrics to "The Star-Spangled Banner" during the British assault on Fort McHenry, Maryland.

1818 Washington Irving publishes *Rip Van Winkle*.

1819 William Ellery Channing helps found American Unitarianism.

Political/Diplomatic	Social/Economic	Cultural

1820

1820 Missouri Compromise prohibits slavery in the northern half of the Louisiana Purchase; Missouri enters the union as a slave state and Maine as a free state.
1821 Mexico declares independence from Spain.
1823 President James Monroe opposes any further European colonization or interference in the Americas, establishing the principle now known as the Monroe Doctrine.

1820 U.S. population is 9,638,453.
1820 Land Act reduces the price of public land to $1.25 per acre.
1822 Stephen F. Austin founds the first American colony in Texas.
1822 Liberia is founded as a colony for free blacks.
1825 Erie Canal opens.
1829 The first U.S. school for the blind opens in Boston.

1821 Emma Willard founds the Troy Female Seminary, one of the first academies to offer women a higher education.
1823 John Howard Payne and Henry Bishop compose the song "Home, Sweet Home."
1823 James Fenimore Cooper publishes *The Pioneers*, the first of his Leather-stocking tales.
1827 James Audubon publishes *Birds of America*, consisting of 435 lifelike paintings of birds.
1827 *Freedom's Journal*, the first black newspaper, begins publication in New York City.
1828 The *Cherokee Phoenix*, the first Indian newspaper, begins publication.
1829 David Walker issues his militant "Appeal to the Colored Citizens of the World."

1830

1830 Indian Removal Act provides funds to purchase Indian homelands in exchange for land in present-day Oklahoma and Arkansas.
1832 Jackson vetoes the bill to recharter the second Bank of the United States.
1832 South Carolina nullifies the federal tariff.
1836 Texans under Sam Houston defeat the Mexican army at the Battle of San Jacinto.
1839 Liberty party founded.

1830 U.S. population is 12,866,020.
1830 America's first commercially successful steam locomotive, the *Tom Thumb*, loses a race against a horse.
1831 William Lloyd Garrison begins publishing militant abolitionist newspaper *The Liberator*.
1831 Nat Turner's slave insurrection occurs in Southampton County, Virginia.
1832 Samuel F. B. Morse invents the telegraph.
1837 Horace Mann becomes Massachusetts' first superintendent of education.
1837 Panic of 1837 begins.
1838 Sarah Grimké publishes *Letters on the Equality of the Sexes and the Condition of Women*, one of the earliest public defenses of sexual equality.
1839 Charles Goodyear successfully vulcanizes rubber.

1830 Joseph Smith, Jr., founds the Church of Jesus Christ of Latter-Day Saints.
1831 Samuel Francis Smith composes the words to the song "America."
1831 Oberlin College opens its doors as the nation's first coeducational college. In 1835, it becomes the first American college to admit blacks.
1834 *A Narrative of the Life of David Crockett* is published.
1835 The Liberty Bell cracks as it tolls the death of Chief Justice John Marshall.
1836 William Holmes McGuffey publishes his first and second *Reader*

Political/Diplomatic	Social/Economic	Cultural

1840

1846 Britain and the United States divide Oregon along the 49th parallel.	**1840** U.S. population is 17,069,453.	**1841** Edgar Allan Poe publishes "Murders in the Rue Morgue," the first modern detective story.
1846 The United States declares war on Mexico.	**1841** The first wagon train arrives in California.	**1843** New word *millionaire* coined to describe Pierre Lorillard, tobacco magnate.
1848 Treaty of Guadalupe Hidalgo ends the Mexican War.	**1842** The Massachusetts Supreme Court upholds workers' right to organize.	**1848** Karl Marx and Friedrich Engels publish the *Communist Manifesto.*
	1845 A potato blight strikes Ireland.	
	1846 Elias Howe patents the first reliable sewing machine.	
	1846 William Morton, a Boston dentist, uses an anesthetic for the first time during a surgical operation.	
	1846–1847 Brigham Young leads the Mormons to the Great Salt Lake Valley.	
	1848 Alexander T. Stewart opens the first department store in New York City.	
	1848 Gold is discovered at Sutter's Mill in California.	
	1848 The first women's rights convention is held in Seneca Falls, New York.	
	1849 Elizabeth Blackwell becomes the first woman physician in the United States.	

1850

1850 Compromise of 1850 is enacted.	**1850** U.S. population is 23,191,876.	**1850** Nathaniel Hawthorne publishes *The Scarlet Letter.*
1854 Stephen A. Douglas introduces the Kansas-Nebraska Act. Opponents of the act form the new Republican party.	**1850** U.S. Navy outlaws flogging.	**1851** Herman Melville publishes *Moby Dick.*
1854 Commodore Matthew Perry negotiates a treaty opening Japan to American trade.	**1851** The Young Men's Christian Association opens its first American chapter in Boston.	**1852** Harriet Beecher Stowe's *Uncle Tom's Cabin* sells a million copies in its first year and a half.
1859 John Brown's raid fails at Harpers Ferry.	**1854** Abolitionist William Lloyd Garrison publicly burns the U.S. Constitution, calling it an "agreement with hell and a covenant with death."	**1854** Henry David Thoreau publishes *Walden.*
	1857 Elisha Graves Otis installs the first passenger elevator in a New York City department store.	**1855** Walt Whitman publishes *Leaves of Grass.*
	1859 Edwin L. Drake drills the first commercial oil well at Titusville, Pennsylvania.	**1859** Charles Darwin publishes *Origin of Species.*

Political/Diplomatic	Social/Economic	Cultural
		1860

1860 Abraham Lincoln is elected sixteenth president.

1860 South Carolina secedes from the Union.

1861 Confederate States of America formed.

1863 President Lincoln signs the Emancipation Proclamation.

1865 John Wilkes Booth assassinates President Lincoln at Ford's Theater in Washington, D.C.; Andrew Johnson becomes seventeenth president.

1865 Thirteenth Amendment ratified, abolishing slavery.

1867 Russia sells Alaska to the United States for $7.2 million, or less than 2 cents an acre.

1868 House of Representatives impeaches Andrew Johnson; he escapes conviction in the Senate by one vote.

1860 U.S. population is 31,443,321.

1860 The Pony Express begins carrying mail between St. Joseph, Missouri, and Sacramento, California.

1862 To help raise revenue for the Civil War, the first federal income tax goes into effect.

1863 New York City draft riots.

1865 The Ku Klux Klan is founded in Pulaski, Tennessee.

1866 The potato chip is invented by a Saratoga, New York, chef.

1866 Cyrus W. Field lays the first permanent trans-Atlantic telegraph cable.

1867 Christopher Latham Sholes and Carlos Glidden invent the first practical typewriter.

1869 William Finley Semple of Mount Vernon, Ohio, receives a patent for chewing gum.

1869 First transcontinental railroad is completed.

1860 Erastus and Irwin Beadle issue the first dime novels, featuring such figures as Daniel Boone and Kit Carson.

1865 Mark Twain publishes his first story, "The Celebrated Jumping Frog of Calaveras County."

| | | **1870** |

1870 Senator Hiram R. Revels of Mississippi becomes the first black U.S. senator.

1875 Civil Rights Act forbids racial discrimination in public accommodations and public transportation and guarantees African Americans the right to serve on juries.

1877 Electoral Commission awards disputed electoral votes to Republican Rutherford Hayes, who is inaugurated nineteenth president.

1877 Hayes withdraws the last federal troops from the South, ending Reconstruction.

1878 Bland-Allison Act requires the U.S. Treasury to buy $2 to $4 million of silver each month in order to inflate the currency.

1879 Congress votes to allow women to argue cases before the Supreme Court.

1870 U.S. population is 39,818,449.

1871 Great Chicago fire claims 300 lives, destroys 17,500 buildings, and leaves 100,000 people homeless.

1873 Comstock Act bans obscene materials, including rubber prophylactics, from the mails.

1876 Custer's Last Stand.

1876 Twenty-nine-year-old Alexander Graham Bell patents the telephone.

1876 The nation celebrates its centennial with a $10 million exposition in Philadelphia.

1879 Thomas Edison, 32, invents the light bulb.

1879 Frank W. Woolworth establishes his first successful 5-and-10-cent store in Lancaster, Pennsylvania.

1871 P. T. Barnum opens his circus, which he calls "The Greatest Show on Earth."

1871 James Whistler paints *Arrangement in Gray and Black No. 1*, better known as *Whistler's Mother*.

1875 Mary Baker Eddy publishes *Science and Health*, the basic text of Christian Science.

1875 The first Kentucky Derby.

1876 Mark Twain publishes *The Adventures of Tom Sawyer*.

1876 Baseball's National League founded.

1879 Henry George publishes *Progress and Poverty*.

Political/Diplomatic	Social/Economic	Cultural

1880

Political/Diplomatic	Social/Economic	Cultural
1881 President James A. Garfield mortally wounded at a Washington train station; Chester Arthur becomes twenty-first president. **1882** Chinese Exclusion Act suspends Chinese immigration for ten years; extended in 1892 and 1902. **1883** Civil Service Act classifies approximately 15,000 federal jobs as civil service positions to be awarded only after a competitive examination. **1883** Supreme Court declares Civil Rights Act of 1875 unconstitutional. **1887** Congress establishes the Interstate Commerce Commission, the first federal regulatory commission, to regulate railroads. **1887** Dawes Allotment Act subdivides all Indian reservations into individual plots of land of 160 to 320 acres and opens "surplus" land to white settlers.	**1880** U.S. population is 50,155,783. **1881** Clara Barton founds the American Red Cross. **1883** U.S. railroads adopt four standard time zones. **1886** Supreme Court extends protection of due process to corporations. **1886** The American Federation of Labor founded in Columbus, Ohio. **1886** Pharmacist James S. Pemberton invents Coca-Cola. **1888** The first incubators are used for premature infants. **1889** The Johnstown flood kills almost 2300 people.	**1881** Helen Hunt Jackson publishes *A Century of Dishonor* describing mistreatment of Native Americans. **1883** "Buffalo Bill" Cody organizes his first Wild West Show. **1884** Mark Twain publishes *The Adventures of Huckleberry Finn.* **1886** The Statue of Liberty is unveiled. **1888** Edward Bellamy publishes *Looking Backward*, describing life in Boston in the year 2000.

1890

Political/Diplomatic	Social/Economic	Cultural
1890 Congress passes the Sherman Antitrust Act, forbidding restraints on trade. **1891** Separate Federal Courts of Appeal are created to relieve the Supreme Court's case load. **1896** William McKinley defeats William Jennings Bryan for the presidency. **1897** President Cleveland vetoes a literacy requirement for adult immigrants. **1898** Spanish-American War begins. **1898** United States acquires Guam, the Philippines, and Puerto Rico, and annexes Hawaii. **1899** Emilio Aguinaldo leads a rebellion against the United States to win Philippine independence. **1899** United States annexes Wake Island.	**1890** U.S. population is 62,947,714. **1890** The U.S. Bureau of the Census announces that the western frontier is closed. **1890** Sequoia and Yosemite National parks in California established. **1892** Ellis Island opens as a center to screen immigrants. **1893** Chlorine is first used to treat sewage in Brewster, New York. **1895** *Pollack* v. *Farmers Loan and Trust Company* declares a federal income tax unconstitutional. **1896** *Plessy* v. *Ferguson* decision rules that the principle of "separate but equal" does not deprive blacks of civil rights guaranteed under the Fourteenth Amendment. **1897** A high-society ball, costing $370,000, is held at New York's Waldorf Astoria Hotel despite a serious economic depression.	**1890** Jacob A. Riis publishes *How the Other Half Lives.* **1891** Basketball is invented by Dr. James A. Naismith in Springfield, Massachusetts. **1896** The first comic strip appears in Joseph Pulitzer's *New York World.* **1896** Billy Sunday begins his career as an evangelist. **1899** Composer Scott Joplin's "Maple Leaf Rag" helps popularize ragtime. **1899** In *The School and Society*, John Dewey outlines his ideas about "progressive education."

Political/Diplomatic	Social/Economic	Cultural
		1900
1902 Oregon, South Dakota, and Utah become first states to adopt initiative and recall. **1903** Wisconsin becomes the first state to adopt primary elections. **1904** Construction of Panama Canal begins. **1907** President Theodore Roosevelt dispatches 16 battleships ("the great white fleet") on an around-the-world cruise.	**1900** U.S. population is 75,994,575. **1900** Great Galveston, Texas, hurricane kills 6000. **1903** The Wright Brothers make the first piloted flight in a powered airplane. **1904** The ice-cream cone and iced tea are introduced at the St. Louis World's Fair. **1906** The Great San Francisco earthquake leaves 452 people dead and 225,000 homeless. **1908** Henry Ford introduces the Model T. **1909** The National Association for the Advancement of Colored People formed to press for equal rights for black Americans. **1909** Explorers Robert E. Peary and Matthew Henson reach the North Pole.	**1900** Theodore Dreiser publishes his first novel, *Sister Carrie*. **1900** L. Frank Baum publishes *The Wonderful Wizard of Oz*. **1903** W. E. B. Du Bois publishes *The Souls of Black Folk*, declaring that "the problem of the twentieth century is the color line." **1903** Edwin S. Porter's *The Great Train Robbery* is the first American film to tell a story. **1906** Upton Sinclair's *The Jungle* exposes unsanitary conditions in the meat-packing industry. **1908** Jack Johnson becomes the first black heavyweight boxing champion.
		1910
1913 Sixteenth Amendment gives Congress the power to levy an income tax. **1914** World War I begins in Europe. **1917** United States enters the war. **1917** Jeannette Rankin becomes first woman elected to Congress.	**1910** U.S. population is 91,972,266. **1911** Female garment workers (145) lose their lives in a fire at New York's Triangle Shirtwaist Company. **1912** The *Titanic* sinks on its maiden voyage, and 1500 of the ship's 2200 passengers drown. **1915** Margaret Sanger is arrested in New York City for teaching methods of contraception. **1918** Influenza epidemic claims more than 20 million lives worldwide.	**1913** The first crossword puzzle appears in a U.S. newspaper. **1914** Edgar Rice Burroughs publishes *Tarzan of the Apes*. **1914** President Wilson proclaims the first Mother's Day. **1918** Post Office confiscates copies of *The Little Review* on grounds of obscenity. It contains a part of James Joyce's *Ulysses*.

Political/Diplomatic	Social/Economic	Cultural

1920

Political/Diplomatic	Social/Economic	Cultural
1920 Palmer Raids to arrest suspected Communists.	**1920** U.S. population is 105,710,620.	**1920** F. Scott Fitzgerald publishes his first novel, *This Side of Paradise*.
1920 National Prohibition begins.	**1920** A Chicago grand jury indicts eight Chicago "Black Sox" players for throwing the 1919 World Series.	**1921** The first bathing beauty pageant is held in Atlantic City, New Jersey.
1920 Nineteenth Amendment grants women the right to vote.	**1923** Colonel Jacob Schick receives patent for first electric shaver.	**1922** Tomb of Egyptian Pharaoh Tutankhamen ("King Tut") discovered.
1920 The Panama Canal declared officially opened.	**1924** Clarence Birdseye develops the first packaged frozen foods.	**1926** National Broadcasting Company becomes the first nationwide radio network.
1928 Kellogg-Briand Treaty renounces war "as an instrument of national policy."	**1925** Scopes trial, the celebrated "Monkey Trial," involving the teaching of evolution in public schools, takes place in Tennessee.	**1927** The first talking motion picture, *The Jazz Singer*, starring Al Jolson, opens.
	1927 Charles Lindbergh completes 33-hour solo flight from New York to Paris.	**1928** Walt Disney releases first Mickey Mouse cartoon.
	1929 Stock market crashes.	

1930

Political/Diplomatic	Social/Economic	Cultural
1933 Adolf Hitler is appointed Chancellor of Germany.	**1930** U.S. population is 122,775,046.	**1931** CBS inaugurates the first regular schedule of TV broadcasts.
1933 Twenty-first Amendment repeals prohibition.	**1934** Public Enemy Number One, John Dillinger, is shot and killed by FBI agents at a Chicago movie theater.	**1935** Charles Darrow, an unemployed engineer, markets a new board game, Monopoly.
1935 Italy invades Ethiopia.	**1935** Wagner Act guarantees workers' right to bargain collectively.	**1936** Jesse Owens wins four gold medals at the Berlin Olympics.
1935 Huey Long is assassinated.	**1936** The last public hanging in the United States takes place in Owenboro, Kentucky.	**1938** Action Comics #1 presents the Man of Steel, Superman.
1936 Civil War breaks out in Spain.	**1937** The German zeppelin *Hindenberg* bursts into flames at Lakehurst, New Jersey, killing 35 passengers.	**1938** Orson Welles broadcasts reports of a Martian invasion.
1938 Munich Pact hands over a third of Czechoslovakia to Nazi Germany.	**1937** Following a 44-day sit-down strike, General Motors recognizes the United Automobile Workers.	**1939** John Steinbeck publishes *The Grapes of Wrath*.
1939 Soviet Union and Germany sign a non-aggression pact.	**1938** Patent issued for nylon.	**1939** Movies *Gone with the Wind* and *The Wizard of Oz* released
1939 World War II begins following Germany's invasion of Poland.		

Political/Diplomatic	Social/Economic	Cultural

1940

Political/Diplomatic

1941 Japan attacks Pearl Harbor, killing nearly 2000 U.S. soldiers and sailors.

1942 Nazis begin their "final solution" to the Jewish problem.

1942 President Franklin D. Roosevelt authorizes internment of 112,000 West Coast Japanese Americans.

1944 D-Day.

1945 V-E Day.

1945 Atomic bombs dropped on Hiroshima and Nagasaki, Japan.

1945 V-J Day.

1946 Winston Churchill declares that "an iron curtain" had descended across Europe.

1948 State of Israel is proclaimed.

1949 Mao Tse-tung's Communist forces win China's civil war.

Social/Economic

1940 U.S. population is 131,669,275.

1942 Physicist Enrico Fermi sets off the first atomic chain reaction.

1942 Gasoline rationing goes into effect.

1943 A race riot in Detroit leaves 25 blacks and 9 whites dead.

1944 GI Bill of Rights provides educational benefits for veterans.

1945 The transistor is invented.

1946 ENIAC, the first electronic computer, begins service.

1947 Air Force Captain Charles Yeager becomes the first pilot to fly faster than the speed of sound.

1947 Twenty-eight-year-old Jackie Robinson becomes the first black player in major league baseball.

1948 The first successful long-playing record is developed.

Cultural

1940 Richard Wright publishes *Native Son.*

1942 Irving Berlin writes "White Christmas."

1943 Rodgers and Hammerstein musical *Oklahoma!* opens in New York.

1946 Joe Louis successfully defends his heavyweight boxing title for 23rd time.

1947 *The Diary of Anne Frank* is published.

1948 Alfred Kinsey publishes *Sexual Behavior in the Human Male,* followed five years later by *Sexual Behavior in the Human Female.*

1949 French fashion designers introduce the bikini bathing suit.

1950

Political/Diplomatic

1950 North Korean troops cross the 38th parallel, beginning the Korean War.

1950 Senator Joseph McCarthy claims that 205 State Department employees are members of the Communist party.

1951 Ethel and Julius Rosenberg are convicted of espionage and executed.

1954 The French garrison at Dien Bien Phu falls to Vietnamese nationalists led by Ho Chi Minh.

1954 *Brown* v. *Board of Education* decision holds that "separate educational facilities are inherently unequal."

1959 Fidel Castro leads Cuban revolution against the regime of Fulgencio Batista.

Social/Economic

1950 U.S. population is 150,697,361.

1952 United States detonates the first hydrogen bomb.

1954 Dr. Jonas Salk develops a vaccine against polio.

1955 The birth control pill is invented.

1955 Black seamstress Rosa Parks refuses to give up her seat on a Montgomery, Alabama, city bus, sparking a year-long bus boycott.

1957 Nine black students enter Central High School in Little Rock, Arkansas, under the protection of 1000 army paratroopers.

1957 Soviet Union rockets *Sputnik,* the first artificial satellite, into space.

1958 European Common Market is formed.

Cultural

1950 Charles Schulz creates the cartoon strip "Peanuts."

1951 J. D. Salinger publishes *Catcher in the Rye.*

1952 Ralph Ellison publishes *The Invisible Man.*

1956 Elvis Presley's first hit, "Heartbreak Hotel," is released.

1957 Jack Kerouac's *On the Road* is published.

1957 Dr. Seuss publishes *The Cat in the Hat.*

Political/Diplomatic	Social/Economic	Cultural

1960

1960 U-2 spy plane is shot down over the Soviet Union.

1961 Cuban exiles stage abortive invasion of Cuba at Bay of Pigs.

1961 Cuban missile crisis erupts.

1963 United States and Soviet Union agree to ban nuclear tests in the atmosphere.

1963 President Kennedy is assassinated; Lyndon Johnson becomes thirty-sixth president.

1964 Civil Rights Act bans discrimination in jobs and public facilities.

1965 United States begins regular bombing missions over North Vietnam and sends American ground combat troops into South Vietnam.

1968 Martin Luther King, Jr., and Robert F. Kennedy are assassinated.

1960 U.S. population is 179,323,175.

1960 First civil rights sit-in takes place in Greensboro, North Carolina.

1961 Russian cosmonaut Yuri Gagarin becomes the first human to orbit the earth.

1962 Second Vatican Council opens in Rome.

1964 Martin Luther King, Jr., receives the Nobel Peace Prize.

1965 Congress requires cigarette packages and ads to carry health warnings.

1969 Astronaut Neil Armstrong becomes the first person to walk on the moon.

1960 A House subcommittee accuses disk jockeys of accepting "payola" to play certain records on the air.

1961 FCC Chairman Newton Minow describes TV as a "vast wasteland."

1962 Rachel Carson publishes *Silent Spring*.

1963 Betty Friedan publishes *The Feminine Mystique*, helping launch a new feminist movement.

1967 The musical *Hair* with its nudity brings controversy to the Broadway stage.

1969 Half a million young people attend a four-day rock concert near Woodstock, New York.

1970

1971 Twenty-sixth Amendment gives 18-year-olds the right to vote.

1972 Five burglars are arrested for breaking into Democratic National Headquarters at Washington's Watergate Office Complex.

1973 United States ends direct military involvement in Vietnam.

1973 Vice President Spiro Agnew pleads no contest to a charge of income tax evasion and resigns his office.

1974 Richard Nixon becomes the first president to resign from office.

1975 Vietnam War ends as Communist troops occupy Saigon.

1978 Jimmy Carter mediates Egyptian-Israeli peace settlement.

1979 Iranian militants seize American hostages.

1979 Soviet Union invades Afghanistan.

1970 U.S. population is 203,235,175.

1972 Eleven Israeli athletes are killed in a terrorist attack at the Summer Olympic Games in Munich, Germany

1973 U.S. Supreme Court legalizes abortion in *Roe* v. *Wade* decision.

1973 Arab oil embargo begins; oil prices quadruple.

1977 United States ends a ten-year moratorium on capital punishment.

1977 Massive blackout hits New York City, leaving 9 million people without electricity for $4\frac{1}{2}$ to 25 hours.

1979 The nation's most serious nuclear power accident occurs at Pennsylvania's Three Mile Island nuclear plant.

1979 Oil price climbs from $10 to $20 a barrel.

1970 Satirical comic strip *Doonesbury* begins appearing in 30 newspapers.

1971 Controversial situation comedy "All in the Family" debuts.

1977 Record television audiences watch the dramatization of Alex Haley's black family history *Roots*.

1977 The film *Saturday Night Fever* popularizes disco dance music.

1978 Karol Wojtyla (Pope John Paul II) is first non-Italian elected pope in 456 years.

Political/Diplomatic	Social/Economic	Cultural
		1980
1981 Ronald W. Reagan inaugurated as fortieth president; minutes later, Iran releases American hostages after 444 days of captivity. **1981** Sandra Day O'Connor becomes the first female Supreme Court Justice. **1984** Democrats make Geraldine Ferraro the first female vice-presidential nominee of a major party. **1985** Mikhail S. Gorbachev becomes leader of the Soviet Union. **1985** United States begins secret arms-for-hostages negotiations with Iran. **1986** Profits from Iranian arms sales are diverted to Nicaraguan contras. **1988** George Bush is elected forty-first president. **1989** Prodemocracy demonstration crushed in Beijing, China. **1989** Communist regimes collapse in Eastern Europe.	**1980** U.S. population is 226,545,805. **1980** Trade union Solidarity is founded in Poland. **1981** Doctors diagnose the first cases of AIDS. **1981** President Reagan dismisses 15,000 striking air traffic controllers. **1982–1983** The nation's worst post-World War II recession raises unemployment to 10.2 percent; but reduces inflation and interest rates. **1983** 230 U.S. soldiers are killed in a terrorist attack in Beirut, Lebanon. **1986** Space shuttle *Challenger* explodes shortly after takeoff, killing all aboard. **1987** The Dow Jones Industrial Average plummets a record 509 points in a single day.	**1987** *Platoon*, a highly sympathetic account of the plight of U.S. troops in Vietnam, wins the Academy Award for best picture. **1987** The publication of Allan Bloom's *The Closing of the American Mind* triggers widespread debate about American education. **1987** Baby M case raises moral and ethical issues involved in surrogate parenting. **1989** Berlin Wall comes down
		1990
1990 Iraqi troops invade and occupy Kuwait. **1990** Germany is reunited **1991** U.S., Western European, and Arab forces eject Iraq from Kuwait by force. **1992** Bill Clinton is elected forty-second president. **1992** Soviet Union is dissolved. **1993** Palestine Liberation Organization and Israel sign peace accord. **1994** Nelson Mandela elected president of South Africa. **1995** Israeli Prime Minister Yitzhak Rabin assassinated.	**1990** U.S. population is 248,709,873. **1991** Confirmation hearings of Clarence Thomas for the Supreme Court focus attention on the issue of sexual harassment. **1992** Riots erupt in Los Angeles following the "not guilty" verdict in the Rodney King case. **1993** Terrorist bomb explodes in New York City's World Trade Center, killing 6. **1994** Great Flood hits nine midwestern states, leaving 50 dead, 70,000 homeless, and causing an estimated $12 billion in property damage. **1995** Terrorist bomb explodes in Alfred P. Murrah Federal Building in Oklahoma City, killing 169.	**1990** Soviet President Mikhail S. Gorbachev wins the Nobel Peace Prize for promoting political liberalization in Eastern Europe and ending the Cold War. **1990** Emperor Akihito is enthroned in Japan, the 125th occupant of the Chrysanthemum Throne. **1993** Toni Morrison wins Nobel Prize for Literature, the first African American to do so.

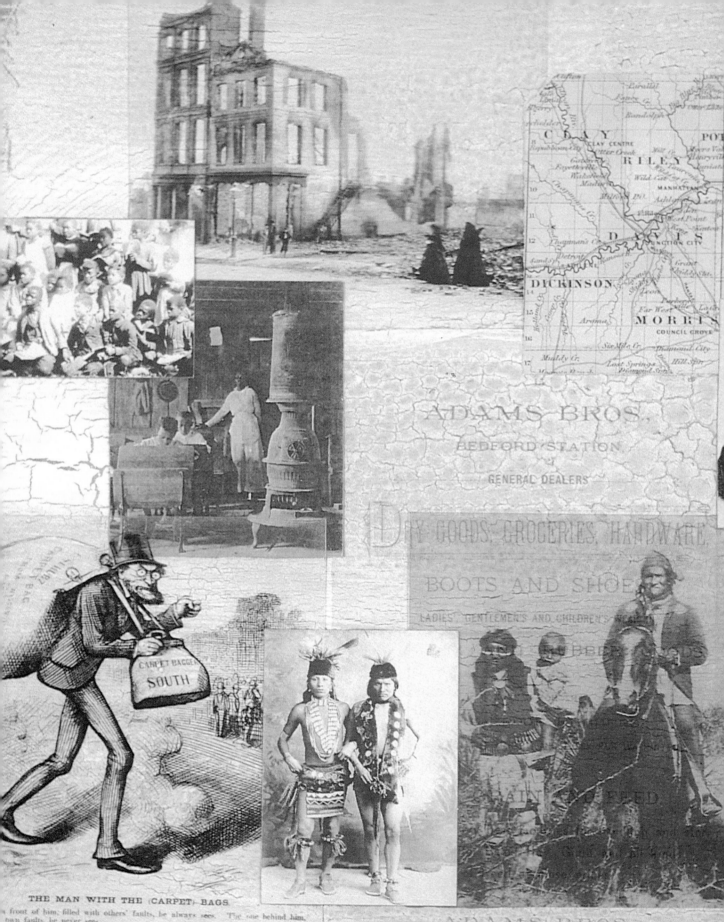

ADAMS BROS.

BEDFORD STATION

GENERAL DEALERS

DRY GOODS, GROCERIES, HARDWARE,

BOOTS AND SHOES

LADIES, GENTLEMEN'S AND CHILDREN'S

CARPET BAGS
SOUTH

THE MAN WITH THE (CARPET) BAGS.

ADAMS BROS.

CHAPTER 16
THE NATION RECONSTRUCTED:
NORTH, SOUTH, AND THE WEST,
1865–1877

POSTWAR CONDITIONS AND ISSUES
   The War's Impact on Individuals
   Unresolved Issues

PRESIDENTIAL RECONSTRUCTION
   Lincoln's Plan
   Johnson's Plan
   Black Codes in the South

CONGRESSIONAL RECONSTRUCTION
   "Radical" Reconstruction
   Black Suffrage

RECONSTRUCTION IN THE SOUTH
   Carpetbaggers, Scalawags, and Black
      Republicans
   Character of Republican Rule
   Black and White Economic and Social
      Adaptation
   Violent White Resistance

**RECONSTRUCTION IN THE NORTH
AND WEST**
   Northern Shifts in Attitudes
   Western Expansion, Racism, and
      Native Americans
   Final Retreat from Reconstruction

As Thomas Pinckney approached El Dorado, his plantation on the Santee River in South Carolina, he felt a quiver of apprehension. Pinckney, a captain in the defeated Confederate army, had stayed the night with neighbors before going to reclaim his land. "Your negroes sacked your house," they reported, "stripped it of furniture, bric-a-brac, heirlooms, and divided these among themselves. They got it in their heads that the property of whites belongs to them." Pinckney remembered the days when his return home had been greeted with slaves' chants of "Howdy do, Master! Howdy do, Boss!" Now he was welcomed with an eerie silence. He did not even see any of his former slaves until he went into the house. There, a single servant seemed genuinely glad to see him, but she pleaded ignorance as to the whereabouts of any others. He lingered about the house until after the dinner hour. Still no one appeared, so he informed the servant that he would return in the morning and expected to see all his former slaves.

On his ride back the next day, Pinckney nostalgically recalled his days as a small boy when the slaves had seemed happy to see him as he accompanied his mother on her Saturday afternoon rounds. He could not believe he had any reason to fear his "own people" whom he "could only remember as respectful, happy and affectionate." He probably mistook their previous displays of submissiveness as expressions of a genuine affection that would not be altered by freedom. Yet he was armed this time, and after summoning his former slaves, he quickly noticed that they too were armed. Their sullen faces reflected their defiant spirits.

Pinckney told them, "Men, I know you are free. I do not wish to interfere with your freedom. But I want my old hands to work my lands for me. I will pay wages." They remained silent as he gave further reassurances. Finally one responded, "O yes, we gwi wuk! We gwi wuk fuh ourse'ves. We ain' gwi wuk fuh no white man." Pinckney was confused and asked how they expected to support themselves and where they would go. They quickly informed him that they intended to stay and work "right here on de lan' whar we wuz bo'n an' whar belongs tuh us." One former slave, dressed in a Union army uniform, stood beside his cabin, brought his rifle down with a crash, and declared, "I'd like tuh see any man put me outer dis house."

Pinckney had no intention of allowing the former slaves to work the land for themselves. He joined with his neighbors in an appeal to the Union commander at Charleston, who sent a company of troops and addressed the blacks himself. They still refused to work under his terms, so Pinckney decided to "starve" them into submission. He denied them access to food and supplies. Soon his head plowman begged food for his hungry family, claiming he wanted to work, "But de other niggers dee won' let me wuk." Pinckney held firm, and the man returned several days later saying, "Cap'n, I come tuh ax you tuh lemme wuk fuh you, suh." Pinckney pointed him to the plow and let him draw his rations. Slowly, his other former slaves drifted back to work. "They had suffered," he later recalled, "and their ex-master had suffered with them."

All over the South this scenario was acted out with variations, as former masters and former slaves sought to define their new relationships. Whites tried to keep the blacks a dependent labor source; African Americans struggled to win as much independence as possible. Frequently Union officials were called upon to arbitrate; the North had a stake in the final outcome. At the same time the other sections of the nation faced similar problems of determining the status of heterogeneous populations whose interests were sometimes in conflict with the majority. The war had reaped a costly harvest of death and hostility, but at the same time it accelerated the modernization of the economy and society. Western expansion forced Americans to deal with the often hostile presence of the Plains Indians; the resumption of large-scale immigration raised issues of how to adapt to an increasingly pluralistic society made up of many different ethnic and religious groups. More and more the resolution of conflicting interests became necessary: farmer versus industrialist, whites versus blacks, Republicans versus Democrats, Indians versus settlers, North versus South, management versus la-

Although former slaves hoped that emancipation would release them from supervised gang labor in cotton fields, many were forced to sign yearly labor contracts and work under conditions similar to what they had endured under slavery.

bor, immigrant versus native born, men versus women, one branch of government versus another. Complicating these issues were unresolved questions about federal authority, widespread racial prejudice in both North and South, and strongly held beliefs in the sanctity of property rights.

Reconstruction offered an opportunity to balance conflicting interests with justice and fairness. In the end, however, the government was unwilling to establish ongoing programs and permanent mechanisms to protect the rights of minorities. As on Pinckney's plantation, economic power usually became the determining factor in establishing relationships. Northerners were distracted by issues related to industrialization and Westerners by conflicts with the Plains Indians. Authorities sacrificed the interests of both African Americans and the Indians of the West to the goals of national unity and economic growth. In 1865 a planter predicted the outcome, using a reference to the black Shakespearean character Othello. "Where shall Otello go? Poor elk—poor buffaloe—poor Indian—poor Nigger—this is indeed a white man country." Yet in the ashes of failure were left two cornerstones on which the future could be built—the Fourteenth and Fifteenth amendments to the Constitution.

POSTWAR CONDITIONS AND ISSUES

General William T. Sherman proclaimed, "War is all hell." Undoubtedly it was for most soldiers and civilians caught up in the actual throes of battle and for the families of the 360,000 Union and 258,000 Confederate soldiers who would never return home. The costs of war, however, were not borne equally. Many segments of the North's economy were stimulated by wartime demands, and with the once powerful southern planters no longer there, Congress enacted programs to aid industrial growth. Virtually exempt from the devastation of the battlefield, the North built railroads and industries and increased agricultural production at the same time that torn-up Southern rails were twisted around trees, Southern factories were put to the torch, and Southern farmland lay choked with weeds.

In 1865 Southerners were still reeling from the bitter legacy of total war. General Philip Sheridan announced that after his troops had finished in the Shenandoah Valley even a crow would have to carry rations to fly over the area. One year after the war, Carl Schurz noted that along the path of Sherman's march the countryside still "looked for many miles like a broad black streak of ruin and desolation." Southern cities suffered the most. A northern reporter described Columbia, South Carolina, as a "wilderness of ruins . . . blackened chimneys and crumbling walls." Atlanta, Richmond, and Charleston shared the same fate. Much of what was not destroyed was confiscated, and emancipation divested Southerners of another $2 billion to $4 billion in assets. The decline of southern wealth has been estimated at more than 40 percent during the four years of war.

The War's Impact on Individuals

Returning soldiers and their wives had to reconstruct relationships disrupted by separation—and the assumption of control by the women on farms and plantations. War widows envied them that adjustment. While the homeless wandered, one plantation mistress moaned, "I have not one human being in the wide world to whom I can say 'do this for me.'" Another noted, "I have never even so much as washed out a pocket handkerchief with my own hands, and now I have to do all my work." Southerners worried about how to meet their obligations; Confederate currency and bonds were worthless except as collectors' items—and even as collectors' items, they were too plentiful to have much value. One planter remarked dryly that his new son "promises to suit the times, having remarkably large hands as if he might one day be able to hold plough handles." Many white Southerners, rich and poor, suffered a self-induced paranoia. They imagined the end of slavery would bring a nightmare of black revenge, rape, and pillage unless whites retained social control.

For four million former slaves, emancipation had come piecemeal, following the course of the Northern armies. It was not finalized until the ratification of the Thirteenth Amendment in December 1865. By then most border states had voluntarily adopted emancipation, but the amendment destroyed the remnants of slavery in Delaware and Kentucky. Most slaves waited patiently for the day of freedom, continuing to work the plantations but speaking up more boldly. Sometimes the Yankees came, proclaimed them free, and then left them to the mercy of their masters. Most, therefore, reacted cautiously to test the limits of their new freedom.

Many African Americans had to leave their plantations, at least for a short time, to feel liberated. A few were confused as to the meaning of freedom and thought they would never have to work again. Soon, most learned they had gained everything—and nothing. As Frederick Douglass, the famous black abolitionist, noted, the freedman "was free from the individual master but a slave of society. He had neither money, property, nor friends. He was free from the old plantation, but he had nothing but the dusty road under his feet. He was free from the old quarter that once gave him shelter, but slave to the rains of summer and the frosts of winter. He was turned loose, naked, hungry, and destitute to the open sky."

The wartime plight of homeless and hungry blacks as well as whites impelled Congress to take unprecedented action, establishing on March 3, 1865, the Bureau of Refugees, Freedmen, and Abandoned Lands, within the War Department. The bureau was to provide "such issues of provisions, clothing, and fuel" as were needed to relieve "destitute and suffering refugees and their wives and children." Never before had the national government assumed responsibility for relief. Feeding and clothing the population had not been deemed its proper function. Considered drastic action, warranted only by civil war, the bureau was supposed to operate for just a year.

Under Commissioner Oliver O. Howard, the bureau had its own courts to deal with land and labor disputes. Agents in every state provided rations and medical supplies and helped to negotiate labor contracts between former slaves and landowners. The quality of the service rendered to the former slaves depended on the ability and motivation of the individual agents. Some courageously championed the former slaves' cause; others sided with the former masters. One of the most lasting benefits of the Bureau was the schools it established, frequently in cooperation with such Northern agencies as the American Missionary Association. During and after the war, African Americans of all ages flocked to these schools to taste the previously forbidden fruit of education. The former slaves shrewdly recognized the keys to the planters' power—land, literacy, and the vote. The white South had legally denied all three to African Americans in slavery, and now many former slaves were determined to have them all.

Some former bondsmen had a firmer grasp of reality than their "liberators." Southern whites had long claimed to "know our Negroes" better than outsiders could. Ironically, this was proven false, but the reverse *was* true. Ex-slaves knew their ex-masters very well. One freedman pleaded, "Gib us our own land and we can take care ourselves; but widout land, de ole massas can hire us or starve us, as dey please." The events on Pinckney's

plantation proved the wisdom of that statement.

Later generations have laughed at the widespread rumor among former slaves that they were to receive "forty acres and a mule" from the government, but the rumor did have some basis. During the war, General Sherman was plagued with swarms of former slaves following his army, and in January 1865 he issued Special Field Order 15 setting aside a strip of abandoned coastal lands from Charleston, South Carolina, to Jacksonville, Florida, for the exclusive use of former slaves. African Americans were to be given "possessory titles" to 40-acre lots. Three months later, the bill establishing the Freedmen's Bureau gave the agency control of thousands of acres of abandoned and confiscated lands to be rented to "loyal refugees and freedmen" in 40-acre plots for three-year periods with an option to buy at a later date. By June 1865, 40,000 African Americans were cultivating land. In the Sea Islands and elsewhere, they proved they could be successful independent farmers. Yet land reform was not a popular cause among whites. Although a few congressmen continued to advocate land confiscation and redistribution, the dream of "forty acres and a

Freed persons realized that education was a key to real freedom and flocked to schools opened by the Freedmen's Bureau, the American Missionary Association, and other groups.

mule" was a casualty of the battle for control of Reconstruction when Andrew Johnson's pardons returned most confiscated lands. Indeed, the issue of economic security for the former slaves was obscured by other questions that seemed more important to whites.

Unresolved Issues

At war's end some issues had been settled, but at a terrible cost. As historian David Potter noted, "slavery was dead, secession was dead, and six hundred thousand men were dead." A host of new problems had arisen from the nature of civil war and the results of that war as well as the usual postwar dislocations. Many questions remained unanswered. Reconstruction was shaped by the unresolved issues.

The first of these concerned the status of the former slaves. They were indeed free, but were they citizens? The Dred Scott decision (1857) had denied citizenship to all African Americans. Even if it were decided that they were citizens, what rights were conferred by that citizenship? Would they be segregated as free blacks in the antebellum North had often been? Also, citizenship did not automatically confer suffrage; women were proof of that. Were the freedmen to be given the ballot? These weighty matters were complicated by racial prejudice as well as constitutional and partisan questions.

The Constitution had been severely tested by civil war, and many felt it had been twisted by the desire to save the Union. Once the emergency was over, how were constitutional balance and

Republican Representative Thaddeus Stevens of Pennsylvania was among those who thought that the Southern states had forfeited their rights. He believed they should revert to the status of territories and be required to reapply for statehood in the Union.

limits to be restored? Except during the terms of a few strong presidents, Congress had been the most powerful branch of government during the nation's first 70 years. Lincoln had assumed unprecedented powers, and Congress was determined to regain its ascendancy. The ensuing battle directly influenced Reconstruction policies and their implementation.

Secession was dead, but what about states' rights? Almost everyone agreed that a division of power between the national and state governments was crucial to the maintenance of freedom. The fear of centralized tyranny remained strong. There was reluctance to enlarge federal power into areas traditionally controlled by the states, even though action in some of those areas was essential to craft the kind of peace many desired. Hesitation to reduce states' rights produced timid and compromised solutions to such issues as suffrage. Also troubling many was federal action in the realm of social welfare—an idea so new that it failed to win lasting acceptance by that generation.

Another constitutional question concerned the status of the former Confederate states and how they were to be readmitted to the Union. There was no constitutional provision for failed secession, and many people debated whether the South had actually left the Union or not. The query reflected self-interest rather than an intellectual inquiry. Ironically, Southerners and their Democratic sympathizers now argued that the states had never legally separated from the rest of the nation, thus denying validity to the Confederacy in order to quickly regain their place in the Union. Extremists on the other side— Radical Republicans—insisted that the South had reverted to the status of conquered territory, forfeiting all rights as states. Under territorial governments, Representative Thaddeus Stevens declared, Southerners could "learn the principles of freedom and eat the fruit of foul rebellion." Others, including Lincoln, believed that the Confederate states had remained in the Union but had forfeited their rights. This constitutional hair-splitting grew out of the power struggle between the executive and legislative branches to determine which had the power to readmit the states and on what terms. It also reflected the hostility of some Northerners toward the "traitorous rebels" and the unwillingness of some Southerners to accept the consequences of defeat.

Lingering over all these questions were partisan politics. Although not provided for in the Constitution, political parties had played a major role in the evolving American government. The road to war had disrupted the existing party structure—killing the Whig party, dividing the Democratic party, and creating the Republican party. The first truly sectional party, the Republican party had very few adherents in the South. Its continued existence was dubious in the face of the probable reunion of the Northern and Southern wings of the Democratic party. Paradoxically, the political power of the South, and in turn the Democratic party, was increased by the abolition of slavery. As slaves, only three-fifths of African Americans had been counted for representation; with the end of slavery, all African Americans would be counted. Thus the Republican party's perceived need to make itself a national party also colored the course of Reconstruction.

PRESIDENTIAL RECONSTRUCTION

Early in the conflict, questions regarding the reconstruction of the nation were secondary to winning the war—without victory there would be no nation to reconstruct. Nonetheless, Lincoln had to take some action as Union forces pushed into the South. Authority had to be imposed in the reclaimed territory, so the president named military governors for Tennessee, Arkansas, and Louisiana in 1862 after federal armies occupied most of those states. He also began formulating plans for civilian government for those states and future Confederate areas as they came under the control of Union forces. The result was a Proclamation of Amnesty and Reconstruction issued in December 1863 on the constitutional basis of the president's power to pardon.

Lincoln's Plan

Called the 10 percent plan, Lincoln's provisions were incredibly lenient. Rebels could receive presidential pardon by merely swearing their future allegiance to the Union and their acceptance of the end of slavery. In other words, former Confederates were not required to say they were sorry—only to promise they would be good in the future. A few people were excluded from pardons: Confederate military and civilian officers; United States judges, congressmen, and military officers who had resigned their posts to serve the Confederacy; and those accused of failing to treat captured black Union soldiers as prisoners of war. Nevertheless, Lincoln did not require the new state governments to bar such people from future voting or officeholding. Moreover after only 10 percent of the number who had voted in 1860 had taken the oath, a state could form a civilian government. When such states produced a constitution outlawing slavery, Lincoln promised to recognize them as reconstructed. He did not demand any provisions for protecting black rights or allowing black suffrage.

Tennessee, Arkansas, and Louisiana met Lincoln's requirements and soon learned they had only cleared the first barrier in what became a long obstacle course. Radical Republicans, such as Representative Thaddeus Stevens of Pennsylvania and Senator Charles Sumner of Massachusetts, were outraged by the president's generosity. They thought the provisions did not adequately punish Confederate treason, restructure Southern society, protect the rights of African Americans, or aid the Republican party. The Radicals were in a minority, but many moderate Republicans were also dismayed by Lincoln's leniency, and shared the Radical view that Reconstruction was a congressional, not a presidential, function. As a result Congress recognized neither the three states' elected congressmen nor their electoral votes in the 1864 election.

After denying the president's right to reconstruct the nation, Congress drew up a plan for reconstruction: the Wade-Davis Bill. Its terms were much more stringent, yet not

DAY OF JUBILO: SLAVES CONFRONT EMANCIPATION

ROOTED in Africa, the oral tradition became one of the tools slaves used to maintain a sense of self-worth. Each generation heard the same stories, and story-telling did not die with slavery. The day that slaves first learned of their emancipation remained vivid in their own minds and later in those of their descendants. The great-grandchildren of a strong-willed woman named Caddy relished the family account of her first taste of freedom:

> Caddy threw down that hoe, she marched herself up to the big house, then she looked around and found the mistress. She went over to the mistress, she flipped up her dress and told the white woman to do some thing. She said it mean and ugly. This is what she said: *Kiss my ass!*

Caddy's reaction was not typical. There was no typical response. Reminiscences of what was called the "Day of Jubilo" formed a tapestry as varied as the range of personality. Some, however, seem to have occurred more frequently than others. Many former slaves echoed one man's description of his and his mother's action when their master announced their emancipation: "Jes like tarpins or turtles after 'mancipation. Jes stick our heads out to see how the land lays."

Caution was a shrewd and realistic response. One of the survival lessons in slavery had been not to trust whites too much. This had been reinforced during the war when Union troops moved through regions proclaiming emancipation only to depart, leaving blacks at the mercy of local whites. One elderly slave described the aftermath to a Union correspondent. "Why, the day after you left, they jist had us all out in a row and told us they was going to shoot us, and they did hang two of us; and Mr. Pierce, the overseer, knocked one with a fence rail and he died the next day. Oh, Master! we seen stars in de day time."

Environment played a role in slaves' reactions to the Day of Jubilo. Urban slaves frequently enjoyed more freedom than plantation slaves. Even before emancipation such black social institutions as schools and churches emerged in many cities. When those cities were liberated, organized celebrations occurred quickly. In Charleston 4000 black men and women paraded before some 10,000 spectators. Two black women sat in one mule-drawn cart while a mock auctioneer shouted, "How much am I offered?" In the next cart a black-draped coffin was inscribed with the words "Slavery is Dead." Four days after the fall of Richmond blacks there held a mass rally of some 1500 people in the First African Church.

Knowledge of their freedom came in many forms to the slaves. Rural slaves were less likely to enjoy the benefits of freedom as early as urban slaves. Many heard of the Emancipation Proclamation through the slave grapevine or from Union soldiers long before its words became reality for them. Masters sometimes took advantage of the isolation of their plantations to keep their slaves in ignorance or to make freedom seem vague and frightening. Their ploys usually failed, but learned patterns of deference made some former slaves unwilling to challenge their former masters. Months after emancipation one North Carolina slave continued to work without compensation, explaining to a northern correspondent, "No, sir; my mistress never said anything to me that I was to have wages, nor yet that I was free; nor I never said anything to her. Ye see I left it to her honor to talk to me about it, because I was afraid she'd say I was insultin' to her and presumin', so I wouldn't speak first. She ha'n't spoke yet." There were, however, limits to his patience; he intended to ask her for wages at Christmas.

Numerous blacks described the exuberance they felt. One elderly Virginia man went to the barn, jumped from one stack of straw to another, and "screamed and screamed!" A Texan remembered, "We all felt like horses" and "everybody went wild." Other blacks recalled how slave songs and spirituals were updated, and "purty soon ev'ybody fo' miles around was singin' freedom songs."

Quite a few slaves learned of freedom when a Union officer or Freedmen's Bureau agent read them the Emancipation Proclamation—often over the objections of the master. "Dat one time," Sarah Ford declared, "Massa Charley can't open he mouth, 'cause de captain tell him to shut up, dat he'd do the talkin'." Some masters, however, still sought to have the last word. A Louisiana planter's wife announced immediately after the Union officer departed, "Ten years from today I'll have you all back 'gain."

Fear did not leave all slaves as soon as their bondage was lifted. Jenny Proctor of Alabama recalled that her fellow slaves were stunned by the news. "We didn' hardly know what he means. We jes' sort of huddle 'round together like scared rabbits, but after we knowed what he mean, didn' many of us go, 'cause we didn' know where to of went." James Lucas, a former slave of Jefferson Davis, explained, "folks dat ain' never been free don' rightly know de *feel* of bein' free. Dey don' know de meanin' of it."

Former slaves quickly learned that one could not eat or wear freedom. "Dis livin' on liberty," one declared, "is lak young folks livin' on love after they gits married. It just don't work." They searched for the real meaning of liberty in numerous ways. Some followed the advice of a black Florida preacher, "You ain't none 'o you, gwinter feel rale free till you shakes de dus ob de Ole Plantashun offen you feet," and moved. Others declared their independence by legalizing their marriages and taking new names or publicly using surnames they had secretly adopted while in slavery. "We had a real sho' nuff weddin' wid a preacher," one recalled. "Dat cost a dollar." When encouraged to take his old master's surname, a black man declared, "Him's nothing to me now. I don't belong to he no longer, an' I don't see no use in being called for him." Education was the key for others. "If I nebber does do nothing more while I live," a Mississippi freedman vowed, "I shall give my children a chance to go to school, for I considers education next best ting to liberty."

Most came to a good understanding of the benefits and limits of their new status. One explained, "Why, sar, all I made before was Miss Pinckney's, but all I make now is my own." Another noted, "You could change places and work for different men." One newly freed slave wrote his brother, "I's mighty well pleased tu git my eatin' by de 'sweat o' my face, an all I ax o' ole masser's tu jes' keep he hands off o' de Lawd Almighty's property, fur *dat's me*." A new sense of dignity was cherished by many. An elderly South Carolina freedman rejoiced, "Don't hab me feelins hurt now. Used to hab me feelins hurt all de times. But don't hab em hurt now, no more." Charlie Barbour exulted over one thing: "I won't wake up some mornin' fer fin' dat my mammy or some ob de rest of my family am done sold." Most agreed with Margrett Millin's answer when she was asked decades later whether she had liked slavery or freedom better. "Well, it's dis way. In slavery I owns nothin'. In freedom I's own de home and raise de family. All dat cause me worryment and in slavery I has no worryment, but I takes de freedom."

unreasonable. A majority, rather than 10 percent, of each states' voters had to declare their allegiance in order to form a government. Only those taking "ironclad" oaths of their past Union loyalty were allowed to participate in the making of new state constitutions. Barely a handful of high-ranking Confederates, however, were to be permanently barred from political participation. The only additional requirement imposed by Congress was the repudiation of the Confederate debt; Northerners did not want Confederate bondholders to benefit from their "investment in treason" at a cost to loyal taxpayers. Congress would determine when a state had met these requirements.

Constitutional collision was postponed by Lincoln's pocket veto of the bill and his assassination on April 14, 1865. While most of the nation mourned, some Radicals rejoiced at the results of John Wilkes Booth's action. Lincoln had been a formidable opponent and had articulated his position on the South in his second inaugural address. Calling for "malice toward none" and "charity for all," he proposed to "bind the nation's wounds" and achieve "a just and lasting peace." His successor, Andrew Johnson, on the other hand, had announced, "Treason is a crime, and crime must be punished." Johnson was a Tennessee Democrat and Unionist; he had been the only Southerner to remain in the Senate after his state seceded. Placed on the 1864 Republican "Union" ticket as a gesture of unity, Johnson's political affiliation was less than clear, but some considered him a weaker opponent than Lincoln. Radical Senator Benjamin Wade proclaimed, "By the gods there will be no trouble now in running this government."

Radicals found comfort in, but miscalculated, Johnson's hatred of the planters. He hated them for their aristocratic domination of the South, not for their slaveholding. Born of humble origins in Raleigh, North Carolina, and illiterate until adulthood, Johnson entered politics in Tennessee as a successful tailor. A champion of the people, he called the planters a "cheap purse-proud set . . . not half as good as the man who earns his bread by the sweat of his brow." Favoring free public education and a homestead act, Johnson was elected mayor, congressman, governor, and senator,

North Carolina–born Andrew Johnson, a former governor of Tennessee and a U.S. senator from that state, was the only senator from a seceding state to remain loyal to the Union. In 1862 Lincoln appointed him military governor of Tennessee, and in 1864 Johnson was selected as Lincoln's running mate.

before being appointed military governor of Tennessee and then becoming vice president. Although he shared the Radicals' hatred and distrust of the planters, he was a firm believer in black inferiority and did not support the Radical aim of black legal equality. He also advocated strict adherence to the Constitution and strongly supported states' rights.

Johnson's Plan

In the end Johnson did not reverse Lincoln's lenient policy. Congress was not in session when Johnson became president so he had about eight months to pursue policies without congressional interference. He issued his own proclamation of amnesty in May 1865 that barred everyone with taxable property worth more than $20,000. Closing one door, he opened another by providing for personal presidential pardons for excluded individuals. By year's end he had issued about 13,000 pardons. The most important aspect of the pardons was Johnson's claim that they restored all rights, including property rights. Thus many former slaves with crops in the ground suddenly found their masters back in charge—a disillusioning first taste of freedom that foreclosed further attempts at widespread land redistribution.

Johnson's amnesty proclamation did not immediately end the Radicals' honeymoon period with him, but his other proclamation issued on the same day caused deep concern. In it, he announced plans for the reconstruction of North Carolina—a plan that would set the pattern for all southern states. A native Unionist was named provisional governor with the power to call a constitutional convention elected by loyal voters. Omitting Lincoln's 10 percent provision, Johnson did eventually require ratification of the Thirteenth Amendment, repudiation of Confederate debts, and state constitutional provisions abolishing slavery and renouncing secession. He also recommended limited black suffrage, primarily to stave off congressional attempts to give the vote to all black males.

The presidential plan fell short of the Radicals' hopes, but many moderates might have accepted it if the South had complied with the letter and the spirit of Johnson's proposals. Instead, Southerners seemed determined to ignore their defeat, even to make light of it. The state governments, for the most part, met the minimum requirements (Mississippi and South Carolina refused to repudiate the debt and Mississippi declined to ratify the Thirteenth Amendment). Their apparent acceptance, however, grew out of a belief that very little had actually changed, and Southerners proceeded to show almost total disregard for northern sensibilities. Presenting themselves, like prodigal sons, for admission to Congress were four Confederate generals, six Confederate cabinet officials, and as the crowning indignity, Confederate Vice President Alexander H. Stephens. Most Northerners were not exceedingly vindictive. Although Union soldiers had sung, "We'll hang Jeff Davis in a sour apple tree," he, and only he, served more than a few months in prison, and the only execution was not for treason,

but for alleged war crimes at the Confederate prison camp in Andersonville, Georgia. Still the North did expect some sign of change and hoped for some indication of repentance by the former rebels.

Black Codes in the South

At the very least, Northerners expected adherence to the abolition of slavery, and the South was blatantly forging new forms of bondage. African Americans were to be technically free, but Southern whites expected them to work and live as they had before emancipation. To accomplish this, the new state governments enacted a series of laws known as the Black Codes. This legislation granted certain rights denied to slaves. Freedmen had the right to marry, own property, sue and be sued, and testify in court. Complex legalisms, however, often took away what was apparently given. Black Codes in all states prohibited racial intermarriage. Some forbade freedmen to own certain types of property, such as alcoholic beverages and firearms. Most so tightly restricted black legal rights that they were practically nonexistent. Black Codes imposed curfews on African Americans, segregated them, and outlawed their right to congregate in large groups.

Black Codes and vagrancy laws sharply curtailed the freedom of former slaves. In this sketch the provost guard in New Orleans is rounding up vagrant blacks in 1864.

The Black Codes did more than merely provide means of racial control; they also sought to fashion a labor system as close to slavery as possible. Some required that African Americans obtain special licenses for any job except agricultural labor or domestic service. Most mandated the signing of yearly labor contracts, which sometimes required African Americans to call the landowner "master" and allowed withholding wages for minor infractions. To accomplish the same objective, Mississippi prohibited black ownership or even rental of land. Mandatory apprenticeship programs took children away from their parents, and vagrancy laws allowed authorities to arrest blacks "wandering or strolling about in idleness" and use them on chain gangs or rent them out to planters for as long as a year.

When laws failed, some southern whites resorted to violence. In Memphis, whites resented the presence of black troops at nearby Fort Pickering. A local paper asserted "the negro can do the country more good in the cotton field than in the camp" and chastised "the dirty, fanatical, nigger-loving Radicals of this city." In May 1866 a street brawl erupted between white policemen and recently discharged black soldiers. That night, after the soldiers had returned to the fort, white mobs attacked the black section of the city, with the encouragement of the police and local officials, one of whom urged the mob to "go ahead and kill the last damned one of the nigger race." The reign of terror lasted over 40 hours and left 46 blacks and 2 whites dead. This and other outbreaks of violence disgusted northern voters.

Most Northerners would not have insisted on black equality or suffrage, but the South had regressed too far. Some Black Codes were even identical to the old slave codes, with the word negro substituted for slave. At the same time, reports of white vio-

Southern whites frequently vented their frustration on blacks. Following a Radical Republican meeting in New Orleans on July 30, 1866, rioting erupted; 37 blacks and 3 white sympathizers were killed in the fighting.

lence against blacks filtered back to Washington. It is no wonder that upon finally reconvening in December 1865, Congress refused to seat the representatives and senators from the former Confederate states and instead proceeded to investigate conditions in the South.

CONGRESSIONAL RECONSTRUCTION

To discover what was really happening in the South, Congress established the Joint Committee on Reconstruction, which conducted inquiries and interviews that provided graphic and chilling examples of white repression and brutality toward African Americans. Prior to the committee's final report, even moderates were convinced that action was necessary. In early 1866 Congress passed a bill to extend the life of the Freedmen's Bureau. The bill also granted the agency new powers to establish special courts for disputes concerning former slaves and to promote black education. Johnson vetoed it, claiming that the bureau was constitutional only in wartime conditions. Now, he claimed, the country had returned "to a state of peace and industry."

At first Johnson prevailed; his veto was not overridden. Then he made a mistake. In an impromptu speech on Washington's birthday, Johnson launched into a bitter attack on the Joint Committee on Reconstruction. Even moderates were offended. In mid-March 1866 Congress passed the Civil Rights Act. It declared that "all persons born in the United States and not subject to any foreign power, excluding Indians not taxed," were citizens and entitled to "full and equal benefit of all laws." Congress was responding to the Black Codes, but Johnson deemed the bill both unconstitutional and unwise. He vetoed it. This time, however, Congress overrode the veto. It then passed a slightly revised Freedmen's Bureau bill in July and enacted it over Johnson's veto. Even though the South had ignored much of Johnson's advice, such as granting limited suffrage to blacks, he stubbornly held to his conviction that reconstruction was complete and labeled his congressional opponents as "traitors."

His language did not create a climate of cooperation. Congress was concerned about the constitutional questions he raised and his challenge to congressional authority. To protect its handiwork and establish an alternate program of reconstruction, it drafted the Fourteenth Amendment. Undoubtedly the most significant legacy of Reconstruction, the first article of the amendment defined citizenship and its basic rights. Every person born in the United States and subject to its jurisdiction is declared a citizen. It also forbids any state from abridging "the privileges and immunities" of citizenship, from depriving any person of "due process of law," and from denying citizens the "equal protection of the laws." Although 100 years passed before its provisions were enforced as intended, the amendment has been interpreted to mean that states as well as the federal government are bound by the Bill of Rights—an important constitutional change that paved the way for the civil rights decisions and laws of the twentieth century.

The remaining four sections of the amendment spelled out Congress's minimum demands for postwar change and was the South's last chance for a lenient peace. A creation of the congressional moderates, the amendment did not require black suffrage but reduced the "basis of representation" proportionately for those states not allowing it. Former Confederate leaders were also barred from holding office unless pardoned by Congress—not the president. Finally, neither Confederate war debts nor compensation to former slaveholders were ever to be paid. The amendment, which passed Congress in June 1866, was then sent to the states for ratification.

President Johnson bridled at this assault on his perceived powers and urged the southern states not to ratify the amendment. All but Tennessee decided to take his advice and wait for further congressional action. They and Johnson miscalculated; both hoped that the public would repudiate the amendment in the 1866 congressional elections. Johnson hit the campaign trail, urging people to oust the Radicals.

Table 16.1 RECONSTRUCTION AMENDMENTS, 1865–1870			
Amendment	Main Provisions	Congressional Passage ($^2/_3$ majority in each house required)	Ratification Process ($^3/_4$ of all states including ex-Confederate states required)
13	Slavery prohibited in United States	January 1865	December 1865 (27 states, including 8 southern states)
14	1. National citizenship 2. State representation in Congress reduced proportionally to number of voters disfranchised 3. Former Confederates denied right to hold office	June 1866	Rejected by 12 southern and border states, February 1867 Radicals make readmission of southern states hinge on ratification Ratified July 1868
15	Denial of franchise because of race, color, or past servitude explicitly prohibited	February 1869	Ratification required for readmission of Virginia, Texas, Mississippi, Georgia Ratified March 1970

His "swing around the circle" was met with heckling and humiliation. The campaign was vicious, characterized by appeals to racial prejudice by the Democrats and charges of Democratic treason by the Republicans. Although few elections are referenda on any single issue, the Republicans won overwhelming victories, which they interpreted as a mandate for congressional reconstruction.

"Radical" Reconstruction

The election results along with the South's intransigence finally gave the Radicals an upper hand. In 1867 Congress passed the Military Reconstruction Act that raised the price of readmission. The act declared all existing "Johnson governments," except Tennessee's, void and divided the South into five military districts headed by military governors granted broad powers to govern. Delegates to new constitutional conventions were to be elected by all qualified voters—a group that by congressional stipulation included black males and excluded former Confederate leaders. Following the ratification of a new state constitution providing for black suffrage, elections were to be held and the state would be required to ratify the Fourteenth Amendment. When that amendment became part of the Constitution and Congress approved the new state constitutions, the states would be granted representation in Congress once again.

Obviously, Johnson was not pleased with the congressional plan; he vetoed it, only to see his veto overridden. Nevertheless, as commander in chief he reluctantly appointed military governors, and by the end of 1867 elections had been held in every state except Texas. Because many white Southerners boycotted the elections, the South came under the control of Republicans supported by Union forces. In a way, however, Southerners had brought more radical measures upon themselves by their inflexibility. As the *Nation* declared in 1867,

Six years ago, the North would have rejoiced to accept any mild restrictions upon the spread of slavery as a final settlement. Four years ago, it would have accepted peace on the basis of gradual emancipation. Two years ago, it would have been con-

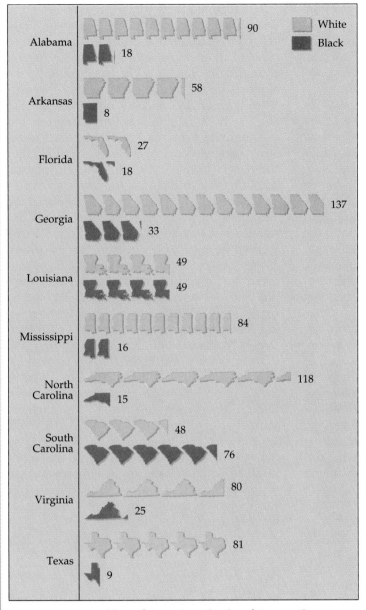

FIGURE 16.1 Composition of State Constitutional Conventions under Congressional Reconstruction

tent with emancipation and equal civil rights for the colored people without the extension of suffrage. One year ago, a slight extension of the suffrage would have satisfied it.

Congress realized the plan it had enacted was unprecedented and subject to challenge by the other two branches of government. To check Johnson's power to disrupt, Congress took two other actions on the same day it passed the Military Reconstruction Act. The Command of the Army Act limited presidential military power. The Tenure of Office Act required Senate consent for the removal of any official whose appointment had required the Senate's confirmation. It was meant in part to protect Secretary of War Edwin M. Stanton, who supported the Radicals.

The Supreme Court had also shown its willingness to challenge Reconstruction actions in two important cases of 1866. In *Ex parte Milligan* the justices struck down the conviction of a civilian by a military tribunal in an area where civil courts were operating. Another decision ruled as void a state law barring former Confederates from certain professions on the basis that the act was *ex post facto*. Nevertheless, other decisions reflected a hesitation to tackle some of the thornier issues of Reconstruction. Important cases were pending, and Congress acted in March 1868 to limit the court's power to review cases. Because the congressional action was clearly constitutional, the Supreme Court acquiesced and in *Texas* v. *White* (1869) even acknowledged congressional power to reframe state governments.

President Johnson was not so accommodating. He sought to sabotage military reconstruction by continuing to pardon former Confederates, removing military commanders who were Radical sympathizers, and naming former Confederates to federal positions. Congress was angry but could not find adequate grounds for impeachment. Johnson did not attempt to mend fences. In August 1867, during a congressional recess, he tried to replace Secretary of War Stanton with Ulysses S. Grant. When the Senate refused confirmation, however, Grant returned the office to Stanton. Johnson did not surrender; on February 21 he named Lorenzo Thomas to the cabinet position. Stanton also refused to surrender and barricaded himself in his office. On February 24, the House voted impeachment.

Andrew Johnson was the only president of the United States to be impeached. His successful defense centered on the legitimate uses of his executive powers.

The Senate was given 11 articles of impeachment for its trial of the president. Eight related to the violation of the Tenure of Office Act and another to a violation of the Command of the Army Act. Only the last 2 reflected the real reasons for congressional action. Those articles accused Johnson of "inflammatory and scandalous harangues" against Congress and of "unlawfully devising and contriving" to obstruct congressional will. The heated and bitter trial lasted from March 5 to May 26. Johnson did not attend, but his lawyers made a good legal case that he had not technically violated the Tenure of Office Act since Stanton had been appointed by Lincoln. They tried to keep the trial focused on indictable offenses. Radical prosecutors continued to argue that Johnson had committed "high crimes and misdemeanors," but they also asserted that a president could be removed for political reasons, even without being found legally guilty of crimes—a position James Madison had supported during the drafting of the Constitution.

The vote for conviction fell one short of the required two-thirds majority, when seven Republicans broke ranks and voted against conviction. This set the precedent that a president must be guilty of serious misdeeds to be removed from office. The outcome was a political blow to the Radicals, costing them some support. The action, however, did make Johnson more cooperative for the last months of his presidency.

Black Suffrage

In the 1868 presidential election, the Republicans won with Ulysses S. Grant, whose Civil War victories made his name a household word. He ran on a platform that endorsed congressional reconstruction, urged repayment of the national debt, and defended black suffrage in the South as necessary but supported the right of each northern state to restrict the vote. His slogan, "Let us have peace," was appealing, but his election was less than a ringing endorsement for Radical policies. The military hero who had seemed invincible barely won the popular vote in several key states.

While Charles Sumner and a few other Radicals had long favored national black suffrage, only after the Republicans' electoral close call in 1868 did the bulk of the party begin to consider a suffrage amendment. Many were swayed by the political certainty that the black vote would be theirs and might give them the margin of victory in future close elections. Others were embarrassed by the hypocrisy of forcing black suffrage on the South while only 7 percent of northern African Americans could vote. Still others believed that granting African Americans the vote would relieve whites of any further responsibility to protect black rights.

Suffrage supporters faced many objections to such an amendment. One was based on the lack of popular support. At that time only seven northern states granted blacks the right to vote, and since 1865, referendum proposals for black suffrage in eight states had been voted down. In fact, only in Iowa and Minnesota (both containing minuscule black populations) had voters supported the extension of the vote. The amendment was so unpopular that, ironically, it could never have won adoption without its ratification by the southern states, where black suffrage already existed.

A more serious challenge was the question of whether Congress could legislate suffrage at all. Before Reconstruction the national government had never taken any action regarding the right to vote; suffrage had been considered not a right but a privilege which only the states could confer. The Radical answer was that the Constitution expressly declared that "the United States shall guarantee to every State in this Union a republican form of government." Charles Sumner further asserted that "anything for human rights is constitutional" and that black rights could only be protected by black votes.

Senator George Vickers sarcastically asked, "does not the doctrine of human rights asserted by the senator apply as well to females as to males?" Although he was "no advocate for woman suffrage," he noted that "if the Congress of the United States had been composed exclusively of women we should have had no civil war. We might have had a war of words, but that would have been all." When one senator did propose female suffrage, a colleague informed him that "to extend the right of suffrage to negroes in this country I think is necessary for their protection; but to extend the right of suffrage to women is not necessary."

Some women, such as Elizabeth Cady Stanton and Susan B. Anthony, did not want to rely upon their fathers, brothers, or husbands to protect their rights. As leaders of the Women's Loyal League, both had worked hard for the adoption of the Thirteenth Amendment, only to be rewarded by inclusion of the word *male* in the Fourteenth Amendment of the Constitution—the first time that word appears. Some women, such as Lucy Stone of the American Woman Suffrage Association, accepted the plea of long-time woman suffrage supporter Frederick Douglass that it was the "Negro's hour," and worked for ratification. Anthony, however, vowed "[I will] cut off this right arm of mine before I will ever work for or demand the ballot for the Negro and not the woman." Such differences played a role in splitting the women's movement in 1869 between those working for a national suffrage amendment and those who concentrated their efforts on the state level. Anthony and Stanton founded the National Woman Suffrage Association to battle for a constitutional amendment and other feminist reforms. Others became disillusioned with that approach and established the American Woman Suffrage Association, which focused on obtaining suffrage on a state-by-state basis.

Actually, women did not lose much by not being included in the Fifteenth Amendment. To meet the various objections, compromise was necessary. The resulting amendment did not grant the vote to anyone. It merely stated that the vote could not be denied "on account of race, color, or previous condition of servitude." Suffrage was still essentially to be controlled by the states, and other bases of exclusion were not deemed unconstitutional. These loopholes would eventually allow white Southerners to make a mockery of the amendment.

Although congressional reconstruction was labeled "Radical," compromise had instead

Susan B. Anthony (left) moved from temperance work to join with Elizabeth Cady Stanton in 1869 to form the National Woman Suffrage Association.

produced another essentially moderate plan. What Congress did *not* do is as important as what it did. It did not even guarantee the right to vote. There was only one execution for war crimes and only Jefferson Davis was imprisoned for more than a few months. For all but a handful, former Confederates were not permanently barred from voting or holding office. By 1872 only about 200 were still denied the right to hold office. Most local Southern governments were undisturbed. Land as well as rights were restored to former rebels, eliminating the possibility of extensive land redistribution. Most areas that had traditionally been the states' domain remained so, free from federal meddling. For example, no requirements were placed on the states to provide any education to former slaves. The only attempt by the national government to meet the basic needs of its citizens was the temporary Freedmen's Bureau—justified only as an emergency measure. The limited nature

of Reconstruction doomed it as an opportunity to provide means for the protection of minority rights.

Such congressional moderation reflected the spirit of the age. Enduring beliefs in the need for strict construction of the Constitution and in states' rights presented formidable barriers to truly radical changes. Property rights were considered sacrosanct—even for "traitors." Cherished ideals of self-reliance and the conviction that a person determined his or her own destiny led many to support Horace Greeley's so-called root, hog, or die approach to the black problem. By ending the threat of slavery, he argued, "we may soon break up our Freedmen's Bureaus and all manner of coddling devices and let the negroes take care of themselves." Few agreed with Charles Sterns who argued that even a hog could not root without a snout—that there could be no equality of opportunity where one group had long been allowed an unfair advantage. Many instead sided with an editorialist for the *New York Herald* who wrote of the bill to extend the life of the Freedmen's Bureau: "The bill ought to be called an act to support the negroes in idleness by the honest labor of white people, or an act to establish a gigantic and corrupt political machine for the benefit of the radical faction and a swarm of officeholders." Clearly the idea of affirmative action or even equal opportunity had less support then than it did 100 years later.

Tainting every action was the widespread conviction that African Americans were not equal to whites. Many Northerners were more concerned with keeping blacks in the South than with abstract black rights. In 1866, for example, New York Senator Roscoe Conkling catered to the northern fear of black immigration while calling for support of the Fourteenth Amendment:

Four years ago mobs were raised, passions were aroused, votes were given, upon the idea that emancipated negroes were to burst in hordes upon the North. We then said, give them liberty and rights in the South, and they will stay there and never come into a cold climate. We say so still, and we want them let alone, and that is one thing that this part of the amendment is for.

Even Radical Representative George Julian admitted to his Indiana constituents, "the real trouble is that we hate the negro. It is not his ignorance that offends us, but his color."

The plan for Reconstruction evolved fitfully, buffeted first one way and then another by the forces of the many issues unresolved at war's end. If permanent changes were very limited, nonetheless precedents had been set for later action, and for a brief time congressional reconstruction brought about the most democratic governments the South had ever seen—or would see for another hundred years.

RECONSTRUCTION IN THE SOUTH

Regardless of the specific details hammered out in Washington, any dictated peace would probably have been unpalatable to Southern whites. They were especially leery of any action that seemed to threaten white supremacy—whether or not that was the intended result. Even before the war, suspicion greeted every Northern move. Southerners continued to see a radical abolitionist behind every bush.

The Freedmen's Bureau established during the last year of the war operated for five years in the South. Most Southerners criticized and condemned the bureau from its first day to its last. Many believed its agents were partial to African Americans. As one Mississippi planter declared, "The negro is a sacred animal. The Yankees are about negroes like the Egyptians were about cats." Actually there was a great diversity in the background and goals of bureau agents. Some were idealistic young New Englanders who, like the Yankee schoolmarms, came south to aid in the transition to freedom. Others were army officers whose first priority was to maintain order—often by siding with the landowners. All were overworked, underpaid, and under pressure.

The results of bureau actions were mixed in regard to conditions for African Americans. The agents helped to negotiate labor contracts that African Americans were forced to sign to obtain rations. Frequently the wages were well below the rate at which slaves had been hired out by their owners before the war. While it should be remembered that money was scarce at the time, these contracts helped to keep African Americans on the farm—someone else's farm. On the other hand, between 1865 and 1869 the bureau issued over 21 million rations, of which about 5 million went to whites. Thus it showed that the government could establish and administer a massive relief program, as it would again do during the depression of the 1930s. The bureau also operated more than 40 hospitals, opened hundreds of schools, and accomplished the Herculean task of resettling some 30,000 people displaced by the war.

Carpetbaggers, Scalawags, and Black Republicans

Until the passage of the Reconstruction Acts in 1867, Southern governments were much the same as they had been before the war. Afterwards however, Republican officeholders joined bureau agents in directing the course of Reconstruction. Despised by many whites, these men, depending on their origins, were derisively labeled "carpetbaggers," "scalawags," and "nigrahs." Opponents considered all three groups despicable creatures whose "black and tan" governments were tyrannizing native whites, while engaged in an orgy of corruption. Myths created about Southern Republicans lingered long after the restoration of Democratic party rule.

Northerners who came to the South during or after the war and became engaged in politics were called carpetbaggers. They supposedly arrived with a few meager belongings in their carpetbags, which would expand to hold ill-gotten gains from looting an already devastated South. Probably what most infuriated whites was the carpetbaggers' willingness to cooperate with African Americans. Calling them "a kind of political dry-nurse for the negro population," native whites accused the carpetbaggers of cynically exploiting former slaves for their own gain.

Northerners who engaged in politics in the South before or after the war were called carpetbaggers. This cartoon shows Grant and Union soldiers propping up carpetbag rule with bayonets, while the "Solid South" staggers under the weight.

Many agreed with the charge that the carpetbaggers were standing "right in the public eye, stealing and plundering, many of them with both arms around negroes, and their hands in their rear pockets, seeing if they cannot pick a paltry dollar out of them."

White Southerners who voted for Republicans were labeled scalawags. The term, said to be derived from Scalloway, "a district in the Shetland Islands where small, runty cattle and horses were bred," had been used previously as a "synonym for scamp, loafer, or rascal." Thus southern white Republicans were depicted as people "paying no taxes, riding poor horses, wearing dirty shirts, and having no use for soap." Such men were said to have "sold themselves for office" and become a "subservient tool and accomplice" of the carpetbaggers.

Most detested by white Southerners were the black Republicans. Having long characterized African Americans as inferior creatures dependent on white management for survival,

Southerners loathed the prospect of blacks in authority. They feared that the former slaves would exact payment for their years of bondage. Democrats also knew that racism was their best rallying cry to regain power. Thus Reconstruction governments were denounced for "Ethiopian minstrelsy, Ham radicalism in all its glory." Whites claimed ignorant freedmen, incapable of managing their own affairs, were allowed to run the affairs of state with disastrous results. A former governor of South Carolina observed, "All society stands now like a cone on its Apex, with base up."

Such legends persisted for a long time, despite contrary facts. Southern whites had determined even before Reconstruction began that it would be "the most galling tyranny and most stupendous system of organized robbery that is to be met with in history." The truth was, as W. E. B. Du Bois later wrote, "There is one thing that the white South feared more than negro dishonesty, ignorance, and incompetency, and that was negro honesty, knowledge, and efficiency." To a surprising degree they got what they most feared.

Black voters were generally as fit to vote as the millions of illiterate whites enfranchised by Jacksonian democracy. Black officials as a group were as qualified as their white counterparts. In South Carolina two-thirds of them were literate, and in all states most of the acknowledged leaders were well educated and articulate. They usually had been members of the Northern or Southern free black elite or part of the slave aristocracy of skilled artisans and household slaves. Hiram Revels, a U.S. senator from Mississippi, was the son of free blacks who had sent him to college in the North. James Walker Hood, the presiding officer of the North Carolina constitutional convention of 1867, was a black carpetbagger from Pennsylvania who came to the state as an African Methodist Episcopal Zion missionary. Some, such as Francis Cardoza of South Carolina, were the privileged mulatto sons of white planters. Cardoza had been educated in Scottish and English universities. During Reconstruction 14 such men served in the U.S. House of Representatives and 2 in the Senate. By 1901, 6 others were elected to the House, before

Southern black political power was effectively demolished.

Even if black Republicans had been incompetent, they could hardly be held responsible for the perceived abuses of so-called black reconstruction. Only in South Carolina did African Americans have a majority of the delegates to the constitutional convention provided for by the Reconstruction Acts. Neither did they dominate the new governments; only for a two-year period in South Carolina did blacks control both houses of the legislature. None were elected governor, although P. B. S. Pinchback, the lieutenant governor of Louisiana, did serve as acting governor for a short time. When the vote was restored to ex-Confederates, African Americans comprised only one-third of the voters of the South, and only in two states did they have a majority.

Actually, carpetbaggers dominated most Republican governments to an extent not warranted by their numbers. They accounted for less than 1 percent of the party's voters but held a third of the offices. Their power was especially obvious in the higher offices. Over half of the South's Republican governors and almost half of the Republican congressmen and senators were former Northerners. Although some carpetbaggers did resemble their stereotypes, most did not. Many had

In a historic first, seven African Americans were elected to the Forty-first and Forty-second Congresses. Between 1869 and 1901, two African Americans became senators and 20 served in the House.

come south before black enfranchisement and could not have predicted political futures based on black votes. Most were Union veterans whose wartime exposure to the region convinced them that they could make a good living there without having to shovel snow. Some brought with them much needed capital for investment in their new home. A few came with a sense of mission to educate blacks and reform southern society.

Obviously, if African Americans constituted only a third of the population and carpetbaggers less than 1 percent, those two groups had to depend on the votes of a sizable number of native white Southerners to obtain office in some regions of the South. Those men came from diverse backgrounds. Some scalawags were members of the old elite of bankers, merchants, industrialists, and even some planters who, as former Whigs, favored the "Whiggish" economic policies of the Republican party and hoped to control and use the black vote for their own purposes. On discovering their inability to dominate the Republican governments, most of these soon drifted into alliance with the Democrats. The majority of southern white Republican voters were yeoman farmers and poor whites from areas where slavery had been unimportant. They had long resented planter domination and had opposed secession.

To win their vote the Republicans appealed to class interests. In Georgia they proclaimed, "Poor White men of Georgia: Be a Man! Let the Slave-holding aristocracy no longer rule you. Vote for a constitution which educates your children free of charge; relieves the poor debtor from his rich creditor; allows a liberal homestead for your families; and more than all, places you on a level with those who used to boast that for every slave they were entitled to three-fifths of a vote in congressional representation." Many accepted such arguments and joined African Americans to put Republicans into office. The coalition, however, was always shaky, given the racism of poor whites. The scalawags actually represented a swing vote that finally swung toward the Democratic party of white supremacy later in the 1870s.

Character of Republican Rule

While the coalition lasted, the Republican governments became the most democratic that the South had ever had. More people could vote for more offices, all remaining property requirements for voting and office holding were dropped, representation was made fairer through reapportionment, and more offices became elective rather than appointive. Salaries for public officials made it possible to serve without being wealthy. Most important, universal male suffrage was enacted with the support of black legislators. Ironically, by refusing to deny southern whites what had been denied to them—the vote—African Americans sowed the seeds of their own destruction.

The Republican state constitutions, which brought the South firmly into the mainstream of national reform, often remained in effect years after the end of Reconstruction. Legislatures abolished automatic imprisonment for debt and reduced the use of the death penalty. More institutions for the care of the indigent, orphans, mentally ill, deaf, and blind were established. Tax structures were overhauled, reducing head taxes and increasing property taxes to relieve somewhat poorer taxpayers. At the same time, southern railroads, harbors, and bridges were rebuilt.

Reforms also affected the status of women, increasing their rights in the possession of property and divorce. Although giving women legal control of their property was mainly intended to protect the families of their debt-ridden husbands, African Americans in particular pushed for more radical changes. When William Whipper's motion to give South Carolina women the vote did not receive a second, he persevered and declared:

However frivolous you may think it, I know the time will come when every man and woman in this country will have the right to vote. I acknowledge the superiority of woman. There are large numbers of the sex who have an intelligence more than equal to our own. Is it right or just to deprive these intelligent beings of the privileges which we enjoy? The time will come when you will have to meet this question. It will continue to be agitated until it must ultimately triumph.

However derisively we may treat these noble women, we shall yet see them successful in the assertion of their rights.

The area in which black legislators had the most success was laying the foundations for public education. Antebellum provisions for public schools below the Mason-Dixon line were meager to nonexistent. In every state African Americans were among the main proponents of state-supported schools, but most accepted segregated facilities as necessary compromises. Some black parents did not even desire integration; they believed their children could not flourish in environments tainted by white supremacy. By 1877 some 600,000 blacks were in schools, but only the University of South Carolina and the public schools of New Orleans were integrated.

As desirable as many of the new social services were, they required money and money was scarce. The war had destroyed not only railroads and bridges but also much of

African Americans eagerly participated in politics when allowed. As depicted in this sketch of the 1867 election in the nation's capital, they served as polling place judges and lined up as early as 2 A.M. to vote.

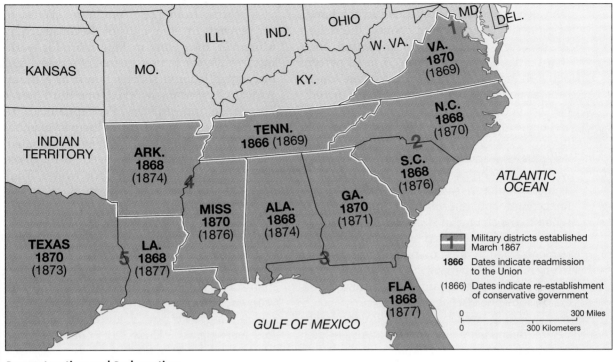

Reconstruction and Redemption

the southern tax base. The necessary tax increases were bound to be unpopular, as were soaring state debts. Both were blamed on corruption, with some justification. Louisiana governor Henry C. Warmouth netted some $100,000 in a year in which his salary was only $8000. A drunken South Carolina governor signed an issue of state bonds for a woman in a burlesque show. One black man was paid $9000 to repair a bridge with an original cost of only $500. Contracts for rebuilding and expanding railroads, subsidies to industries, and bureaucracies for administering social services offered generous opportunities for graft and bribery. When these occurred, southern whites loudly proclaimed that they knew it would happen if shifty former slaves were given the keys to the till.

Actually, although African Americans received a large share of the blame, they received little of the profit. A smaller percentage of blacks than whites were involved in the scandals. Also the corruption that the Democrats denounced at every turn was rather meager compared with the shenanigans of such contemporary northern Democratic regimes as the Boss Tweed Ring of New York. There seemed to be an orgy of national corruption that infected both parties. Indeed, in the South a Democratic state treasurer who came to office after Reconstruction deserves the dubious distinction of being the largest embezzler of the era.

The "tyranny" that so distressed southern whites did not include wholesale disfranchisement or confiscation of their lands. In fact, the demands of most African Americans were quite reasonable and moderate. Their goals were expressed by the declarations of the many postwar black conventions, such as a Virginia one in 1865 that declared, "All we ask is an *equal chance* with the white *traitors* varnished and japanned with the oath of amnesty."

Black and White Economic and Social Adaptation

Just as the former slaves on Thomas Pinckney's plantation had learned, blacks everywhere soon realized that the economic power of whites had diminished little. If anything, land became more concentrated in the hands of a few. In one Alabama county, the richest 10 percent of landowners increased their share of landed wealth from 55 to 63 percent between 1860 and 1870. Some African Americans, usually through hard work and incredible sacrifice, were able to obtain land. The percentage of blacks owning property increased from less than 1 to 20 percent. Indeed, African Americans seemed to fare better than poor whites. One observer noted, "The negro, bad as his condition is, seems to me, on the whole, to accommodate himself more easily than the white to the change of situation." The truth of his assertion is reflected in the fact that the percentage of whites owning land dropped from 80 to 67 percent. Increasingly, poor blacks and whites became agricultural laborers on someone else's land.

The black landless farmers, like the slaves before them, were not mere pawns. If they could not control their destinies, at least they could shape them. As one northern observer wrote, "They have a mine of strategy to which the planter sooner or later yields." Through strikes and work slowdowns, African Americans resisted contract and wage labor because working in gangs under white supervision smacked too much of slavery. When they could not own land, they preferred to rent it, but the few who had the cash to do so found few southern whites would risk the wrath of their neighbors by breaking the taboo against renting to blacks.

Sharecropping emerged both as a result of blacks' desire for autonomy and whites' lack of cash. Landowners gave blacks as well as poor whites a plot of land to work in return for a share of the crops. Freedom from white supervision was so desirable to former slaves that they sometimes hitched mule teams to their old slave cabins and carried them off to their assigned acres. To put distance between themselves and slavery, many black men would not allow their wives and children to work in the fields.

Sharecropping at first seemed to be a good bargain for African Americans because they frequently negotiated their way to a half-share of the crops. Their portion of the profits from southern agriculture, including all pro-visions, rose from 22 percent under slavery to 56 percent by the end of Reconstruction. Moreover, they were making more for working less. Fewer family members worked and black men labored shorter hours; as a group African Americans worked one-third fewer hours than under slavery. Per capita black income increased quickly after the war to about one-half that of whites, but then it stagnated.

Sharecropping later proved to be disastrous for most blacks and poor whites. They needed more than land to farm; they also required seeds, fertilizers, and provisions to live on until they harvested their crops. To obtain these they often borrowed against their share of the crops. Falling crop prices, high credit rates, and sometimes cheating by creditors left many to harvest a growing burden of debt with each crop. In many states, when the Democrats regained power, laws favoring creditors were passed. These led to debt peonage for many sharecroppers.

If most former slaves did not win economic freedom, they benefited from freedom in other ways. It was no longer illegal to learn to read and write, and African Americans pursued education with much zeal. Many even paid as much as 10 percent of their limited incomes for tuition. They began to learn the fundamentals, and a growing number also sought higher education. Between 1860 and 1880 over 1000 African Americans earned college degrees. Some went north to college, but most went to 1 of the 13 southern colleges established by the American Missionary Association or by black and white churches with the assistance of the Freedmen's Bureau. Such schools as Howard and Fisk were a permanent legacy of Reconstruction.

African Americans were also able to enjoy and expand their rich cultural heritage. Religion was a central focus for most, just as it had been in slavery. Withdrawing from white congregations with segregated pews and self-serving sermons on the duty of servants to their masters blacks everywhere established separate black churches. The membership in such antebellum denominations as the African Methodist Episcopal soared. In essence, black Christians declared their religious independence, and their churches became centers of political and social activities as well as religious ones. As one carpetbagger noted, "The colored preachers are *the great power* in controlling and uniting the colored vote." The churches also functioned as vehicles for self-help and sources of entertainment.

Most African Americans desired racial intermingling no more than whites. Many could not feel free until they had removed themselves and their children as far as possible from white arrogance. They created separate congregations and acquiesced to segregated schooling. Nevertheless, they did not want to be publicly humiliated by such measures as separate railroad cars. They frequently used their limited political power to protect civil rights through clauses in state constitutions and legislation, as well as by appeals for the enforcement of national laws. Consequently, black Southerners did enjoy the use of public facilities to a greater degree than they would during the 75 years following Reconstruction.

The very changes that gave African Americans hope during Reconstruction distressed poor whites. Black political equality rankled them, but much more serious was their own declining economic status. As their landownership declined, more whites became dependent on sharecropping and low-wage jobs, primarily in the textile industry. Even these meager opportunities were eagerly greeted; as one North Carolina preacher proclaimed, "Next to God, what this town needs is a cotton mill." Economic competition between poor whites and blacks was keen, but their common plight also favored cooperation based on class interest. The economic pressures applied by the white elite frequently hurt both groups as well as middle-class yeoman farmers, and for brief periods during Reconstruction they warily united in politics. Invariably, however, these attempts were shattered by upper-class appeals to white supremacy and racial unity.

Ironically, although poor whites were perceived by nearly everyone as the group most hostile to blacks, the two shared many aspects of a rich Southern cultural heritage. Both groups developed colorful dialects. For each, aesthetic expression was based on utility—reflecting their need to use wisely what little they had. Their quilts were not merely func-tional but often quite beautiful. In religion and recreation, their experiences were similar. At camp meetings and revivals, poor whites practiced a highly emotional religion, just as many black Southerners did. Both groups spun yarns and sang songs that reflected the perils of their existence and provided folk heroes. They also shared many superstitions as well as useful folk remedies. Race, however, was a potent wedge between them that upper-class whites frequently exploited for their own political and economic goals.

Planters no longer dominated the white elite; sharecropping turned them and others into absentee landlords. The sons of the old privileged families joined the growing ranks of lawyers, railroad entrepreneurs, bankers, industrialists, and merchants. In some ways, the upper and middle classes began to merge, but in many places the old elite and their sons still enjoyed a degree of deference and political leadership. Their hostility toward African Americans was not as intense, largely because they possessed means of control. When their control slipped, however, they also became ranting racists.

So strongly were all southern whites imbued with a belief in white superiority that most could not imagine total black equality. A Freedmen's Bureau agent reported in 1866 that "a very respectable old citizen . . . swore that, if he could not thrash a negro who insulted him, he would leave the country." White attitudes toward blacks were as irrational as they were generalized. Most whites exempted the blacks they knew from such generalizations. As an Alabama planter declared in 1865, "If all were like some of mine I wouldn't say anything. They're as intelligent and well behaved as anybody. But I can't stand free niggers anyhow!"

Violent White Resistance

Large numbers of whites engaged in massive resistance to Reconstruction. Unlike the resistance of southern blacks 100 years later, however, this brand of resistance was not passive but very aggressive. In 1866, some bored young men in Pulaski, Tennessee, organized a social club with all the trappings of fraternal orders—secret rituals, costumes, and practical jokes. They soon learned that their antics intimidated African Americans; thenceforth the Ku Klux Klan grew into a terrorist organization, copied all over the South under various names. A historian of the Klan asserts that it "whipped, shot, hanged, robbed, raped, and otherwise outraged Negroes and Republicans across the South in the name of preserving white civilization." A major goal of the Klan was to intimidate Republican voters and restore Democrats to office. In South Carolina, when blacks working for a scalawag began to vote, Klansmen visited the plantation and "whipped every nigger man they could lay their hands on." The group's increasing lawlessness alarmed many people and led to congressional action. The Klan was broken up by three Enforcement Acts (1870–1871) that gave the president the right to suspend habeas corpus against "armed combinations" interfering with any citizen's right to vote. In 1871 Grant did so in nine South Carolina counties. Disbanding the Klan, however, did little to decrease southern violence or the activities of similar terrorist groups.

The Ku Klux Klan and other white terrorist groups used violence to eliminate black gains. This 1874 cartoon and others like it helped arouse the public to demand action against the Klan.

Some black Southerners were probably never allowed to vote freely. At the peak of Reconstruction, fewer than 30,000 federal troops were stationed in the entire South—hardly enough to protect the rights of 4.5 million African Americans. As troops were being withdrawn, Democrats sought to regain control of their states. They made appeals to white supremacy and charged the Republicans with corruption. Without secret ballots landowners could threaten sharecroppers with eviction for "improper" voting. In addition to economic intimidation, violence against African Americans escalated in most states as the Democrats increased their political power. When victory seemed close, Democrats justified any means to the desired end that they called "redemption." A South Carolina Democratic campaign plan in 1876 urged, "Never threaten a man individually. If he deserves to be threatened, the necessities of the times require that he should die. A dead Radical is very harmless." One Democratic candidate for governor in Louisiana proclaimed, "We shall carry the next election if we have to ride saddle-deep in blood to do it." In six heavily black counties in Mississippi such tactics proved highly successful—reducing Republican votes from more than 14,000 in 1873 to only 723 in 1876. Beginning with Virginia and Tennessee in 1869, by 1876 all but three states—Louisiana, Florida, and South Carolina—had Democratic "Redeemer" governments. The final collapse of Reconstruction became official the following year with the withdrawal of federal troops from the three unredeemed states.

RECONSTRUCTION IN THE NORTH AND WEST

In the end, the South could be said to have lost the war but won the peace. After 1877 Southern whites found little resistance to their efforts to forge new institutions to replace both the economic benefits and racial control of slavery. By 1910 they had devised a system of legalized repression that gave whites many of the benefits of slavery without all the responsibilities. Surely this was not what the North had envisioned after Appomattox. How did it happen? Much of the answer is found in events occurring in the North and West.

Northern Shifts in Attitudes

The basic cause for the decline of Reconstruction can be seen in an 1874 conversation between two northern Republicans during which one declared that the people were "tired out with this wornout cry of 'Southern Outrages!!!' Hard times and heavy taxes make them wish the . . . 'everlasting nigger' were in [hell] or Africa. . . . It is amazing the change that has taken place in the last two years in the public sentiment." A shifting political climate, economic hard times, increasing preoccupation with other issues, and continued racism combined to make most Northerners wash their hands of the responsibility for the protection of black rights.

When Grant won the presidency in 1868, the nation appeared to reject the Democratic charge that the Republican Congress had "subjected ten states, in the time of profound peace, to military despotism and Negro supremacy." In reality the voters had chosen a war hero who had no political record or experience. They voted not so much for a program, but for Grant's campaign slogan: "Let us have peace."

The victorious general proved to be a poor choice for the presidency. Not only was he politically inexperienced, but he also lacked a taste for politics. Haunted by a fear of failure and socially insecure, Grant was too easily influenced by men of wealth and prestige. He made some dismal appointments and remained loyal to individuals who did not merit his trust. The result was a series of scandals. Grant was not personally involved, but his close association with the perpetrators blemished both his and his party's image. The first major scandal surfaced in 1872; it involved Credit Mobilier, a dummy construction company used to milk money from railroad investors in order to line the pockets of a few insiders, including Vice President Schuyler Colfax and a number of other prominent Republicans. Later, bribes and kickback schemes surfaced that involved Indian trading posts, post office contracts, and commissions for tax collection. Such revelations as well as the corruption in some southern Republican governments did little to enhance the public image of the party, and Democrats were quick to make corruption a major issue in both the North and the South.

Although by the 1872 presidential election, there had only been a hint of scandal, some Republicans were disenchanted. In that election the Republican party was split; a number, calling themselves Liberal Republicans, formed a separate party. They supported their own candidate, *New York Tribune* editor Horace Greeley, rather than Grant. Among Greeley's campaign pledges was a more moderate southern policy. Even with the Democrats also nominating Greeley, Grant easily won reelection, but the fear of disgruntled Republicans merging with Democrats remained. By 1874 Republicans were becoming aware that the black vote would not save them. That year Democrats captured the House and gained in the Senate, following further revelations of Republican corruption.

At least as detrimental to Republican political fortunes was a depression that followed the Panic of 1873, which was caused by overinvestment in railroads and risky financial deals. Lasting six years, it was the most serious economic downturn the nation had yet experienced. Whatever their cause, depressions usually result in "voting the rascals out." Democratic fortunes were bound to rise as the people's fell. Yet economic distress had an even wider impact on Reconstruction. People's attention became focused on their pocketbooks rather than on abstract ideals of equality and justice. Economic scrutiny brought such issues as currency and tariffs to the forefront. As the depression deepened, many questioned Republican support for "sound money" backed by gold and the retirement of the legal tender "greenback" paper money that had been issued during the war.

Those greenbacks had increased the money supply needed to finance postwar economic expansion. Yet many Republicans were suspicious of any money not backed by specie—that is, gold or silver. One of the last actions of the Republican-controlled Congress was to pass the Resumption Act of 1875. It provided for the gradual redemption of greenbacks in gold. The resulting deflation favored creditors over debtors because debtors were forced to repay loans with money that was worth more than it had been when they borrowed it. Many Americans, especially farmers, were in debt, and deflation coupled with a depression brought economic distress.

Actually, the Panic of 1873 merely brought into clearer focus the vast changes occurring in the North during Reconstruction. The South had never had the undivided attention of the rest of the nation. Such events as the completion of the first transcontinental railroad in 1869 often overshadowed reports of "Southern outrages." The United States was experiencing the growing pains of economic modernization and western expansion. The Republican platform of 1860 had called for legislation favoring both of these as well as stopping the expansion of slavery. Comprised of diverse interest groups, the party went through a battle for its soul during Reconstruction. For a while the small abolitionist faction had gained some ascendancy due to postwar developments. By the late 1870s, however, the Republican party had forsaken its reformist past to become a protector of privilege rather than a guarantor of basic rights. In effect, Republicans and Democrats joined hands in conservative support of railroad and industrial interests.

Western Expansion, Racism, and Native Americans

The major reason for the decline of Reconstruction was the pervasive belief in white supremacy. There could be little determination to secure equal rights for those who were considered unequal in all other respects. Reconstruction became a failed opportunity to resolve justly the status of one minority, and the climate of racism almost ensured failure for others as well. Western expansion not only diverted attention from Reconstruction but also raised the question of what was to be done about the Plains Indians. They, too, were considered inferior to whites. William H. Seward, who later became secretary of state, spoke for most white Americans when in 1860 he described blacks as "a foreign and feeble element like the Indians, incapable of assimilation." Indeed, while Reconstruction at first offered hope to African Americans, for Native Americans hope was fading.

In the end, African Americans were oppressed; Native Americans were exterminated or separated into shrinking reservations. From the white viewpoint the reason was obvious. As a so-called scientific treatise of the 1850s explained, "The *Barbarous* races of America . . . although nearly as low in intellect as the Negro races, are essentially untameable. Not merely have all attempts to civilize them failed, but also every endeavor to enslave them. Our Indian tribes submit to extermination, rather than wear the yoke under which our negro slaves fatten and multiply." Because most Africans, like Europeans, depended on agriculture rather than hunting, they adapted more easily to agricultural slavery. Black labor was valuable, if controlled; Native Americans were merely barriers to expansion.

Cultural Differences When settlers first began moving onto the Great Plains, they encountered about 250,000 Plains Indians and 13 million buffalo. Some groups, including the Zuni, Hopi, Navaho, and Pawnee, were fairly settled and depended on gardening and farming. Others, such as the Sioux, Apache, and Cheyenne, however, were nomadic hunters who followed the buffalo herds over vast tracts of land. These herds played a crucial role in most Plains Indians' culture—providing almost all the basic necessities. Indians ate the buffalo meat, made clothing and teepees out of the hides, used the fats for cosmetics, fashioned the bones into tools, made thread from the sinews, and even burned dried buffalo droppings as fuel. To settlers, however, the buffalo were barriers to western expansion. The herds interfered with construction, knocked over telegraph poles and fences, and could derail trains during stampedes.

Other cultural differences caused misunderstandings between settlers and Native Americans. Among Anglo-Americans, capitalism fostered competition and frontier living promoted individualism. On the other hand, Plains Indians lived in tribes based on kinship ties. As members of an extended family that included distant cousins, Indians were taught to place the welfare of the group over the interests of the individual. The emphasis within a tribe was on cooperation rather than competition. Some tribes might be richer than other tribes, but there was seldom a large gap between the rich and the poor within a tribe.

Power as well as wealth was usually shared. Tribes were loosely structured rather than tightly organized. Chiefs seldom had much individual power. The Cheyenne, for example, had a council of 44 to advise the chief. Instead of having a lot of political power, chiefs were generally religious and ceremonial leaders. Anglo-Americans did not always understand their limited power. Whites incorrectly believed that an individual Indian could make decisions and sign agreements that would be considered legal by their fellow Indians.

Another major cultural difference between the newly arriving settlers and the Plains Indians was their attitudes toward the land. Most Native Americans had no concept of private property. Chief Joseph of the Nez Percé eloquently expressed the view: "The earth was created by the assistance of the sun, and it should be left as it was. . . . The country was made without lines of demarcation, and it is no man's business to divide it."

Native Americans refused to draw property lines and borders because of how they viewed the place of people in the world. Whites tended to see land, plants, and animals as resources to be exploited. Native Americans, on the other hand, stressed the unity of all life—and its holiness. As Chief Joseph said, "The earth and myself are of one mind." Thus people were not meant to dominate the rest of nature; they were a part of it.

Most of the Plains Indians believed that land could be utilized, but never owned. The idea of owning land was as absurd as owning the air people breathed. To some, the sacredness of the land made farming against their religion. Chief Somohalla of the Wanapaun explained why his people refused to farm. "You ask me to plow the ground! Shall I take a knife and tear my mother's bosom? . . . You ask me to cut grass and make hay and sell it, and be rich like white men! But how dare I cut off my mother's hair?"

Chief Joseph of the Nez Percé expressed the views of Native Americans who had no concept of owning the earth. He proclaimed, "The earth and myself are of one mind."

Indians had great reverence for all land. In addition, some particular pieces of land were considered especially sacred or holy. Certain bodies of water were seen as sources of healing and sites for worship. Some areas were burial grounds, where the spirits of ancestors were believed to reside. White settlers had little understanding of or respect for such Indian sentiments. The results could be tragic where interests collided.

From the white viewpoint, the most significant characteristic of many of the Plains Indian tribes, such as the Cheyenne, Sioux, and Arapaho, was their ability as mounted warriors. Using horses introduced by the Spanish, they had resisted white encroachment for two centuries. Most had no desire for assimilation; they merely wanted to be left alone. "If the Indians had tried to make the whites live like them," one Sioux declared, "the whites would have resisted, and it was the same way with the Indians."

Although some tribes could coexist peacefully with settlers, the nomadic tribes had a way of life that was incompatible with miners, railroad developers, cattle ranchers, and farmers. To Anglo-Americans the Indians were barriers to expansion. They agreed with Theodore Roosevelt that the West was not meant to be "kept as nothing but a game reserve for squalid savages." Thus U.S. Indian policy focused on getting more territory for white settlement. Prior to Reconstruction this was done by signing treaties that divided land between Native Americans and settlers and restricted the movement of each on the lands of the other. Frequently Indian consent was fraudulently obtained, and white respect for Indian land depended on how desirable it was for settlement. As the removal of the Southern Cherokees to Oklahoma had shown in the 1830s, compatibility of cultures did not protect Native Americans from the greed of whites.

During the Civil War, Sioux, Cheyenne, and Arapaho braves rejected the land cessions made by their chiefs. Violence against settlers erupted as frontier troop strength was reduced to fight the Confederacy. The war also provided an excuse to nullify previous treaties and pledges with the Native Americans resettled in Oklahoma under Andrew Jackson's Indian removal policy. Some did support the Confederacy, but all suffered the consequences of Confederate defeat. Settlers moved into the most desirable land, pushing the Indians farther south and west. Some Native Americans began to resist.

Confrontation and Annihilation   By the close of the Civil War, Indian hostility had escalated, especially after an 1864 massacre. The territorial governor of Colorado persuaded most of the warring Cheyennes and Arapahos to come to Fort Lyon on Sand Creek, promising them protection. Colonel J. M. Chivington's militia, however, attacked an Indian camp flying a white flag and the American flag and killed hundreds of Native-American men, women, and children. The following year Congress established a committee to investigate the causes of conflict. Its final report in 1867 led to the creation of an Indian Peace Commission charged with negotiating settlements. At two conferences in 1867 and 1868, Indian chiefs were asked to restrict their tribes to reservations in the undesirable lands of Oklahoma and the Black Hills of the Dakotas in return for supplies and assistance from the government.

Most Indians did not consider the offer very generous. Some acquiesced and others resisted, but in the end federal authorities subdued or killed them all. Several factors made their resistance unsuccessful. Railroads

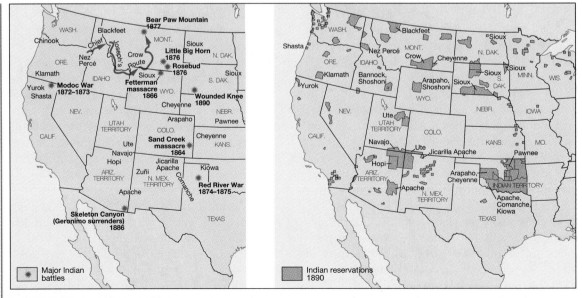

Indian Battles and Reservations

A Native-American watercolor rendering of the Battle of Little Bighorn depicts its aftermath. As Sitting Bull and others stand watching, Sioux and Cheyenne warriors ride horseback over the corpses of Custer (left center) and his troops.

had penetrated the West, bringing in both settlers and federal troops more rapidly. Most important, however, was the destruction of the buffalo herds. Just as modern Americans would be helpless without oil or electricity, the Plains Indians' culture could not survive the near extinction of the buffalo by professional and sport hunters. In 1872 the Indian commissioner accurately forecasted that in a few years the "most powerful and hostile bands of today" would be "reduced to the condition of suppliants for charity."

In 1876, the final year of Reconstruction, Lieutenant Colonel George A. Custer's defeat at Little Bighorn called attention to the "Indian problem." The stage was set for this confrontation with Chief Sitting Bull's Sioux warriors and their Cheyenne allies two years earlier when gold was discovered in the Black Hills. The territory suddenly became tempting, and miners began pouring into the lands guaranteed to the Indians only five years before. "The white man is in the Black Hills just like maggots," one Indian lamented.

Despite Sitting Bull's victory, the die had been cast during Reconstruction. All that remained were "mopping up" exercises. Federal authorities solved the Indian problem by reducing the number of Native Americans to a level that posed no threat. Still, white Americans would not leave the Indians alone to practice their religion and culture. The last major bloody confrontation occurred during the cold December of 1890 on the Pine Ridge Reservation (Sioux) in South Dakota. Poorly fed and supplied on the reservation, dissatisfied with their present, and longing for the glories of their past, members of the Teton Sioux took up the "Ghost Dance," a harmless ritual that promised the faithful the mystical disappearance of the whites and the return of their lands. An inept government agent overreacted, calling in troops to suppress the Ghost Dance and arrest the Sioux leader Sitting Bull, who the government considered the focal point of Indian resistance. When Indian police killed Sitting Bull, some Sioux took up arms and left the reservation. Near Wounded Knee Creek, U.S. soldiers, armed with rapid-fire Hotchkiss guns, attempted to disarm the Indians. When one Indian resisted, soldiers opened fire, killing more than 300 men, women, and children. The Battle of Wounded Knee, which resembled more a slaughter than a battle, ended the violent era of Indian and white relations.

The violent confrontations, however, convinced most Americans that to solve the Indian problem most of the Indians had to be removed from rich American land. An editor for the *New York Herald* claimed, "It is inconsistent with our civilization and with common sense to allow the Indian to roam over a country as fine as that around the Black Hills, preventing its development in order that he may shoot game and scalp his neighbors. That can never be. The region must be taken from the Indian." Others had even more radical solutions. L. Frank Baum, who in 1900 became famous for writing *The Wizard of Oz,* noted in the Aberdeen *Saturday Pioneer* in 1890 that the "nobility of the Redskin is extinguished" and that the whites "are masters of the American continent." To end any lingering problems, Baum proposed "the total annihilation of the few remaining Indians.... Their glory has fled, their spirits broken, their manhood effaced; better that they should die than live the miserable wretches that they are."

Ethnocide and Assimilation By the time of Wounded Knee, the U.S. government had adopted a policy that emphasized ethnocide rather than genocide. An assault on tribalism, ethnocide—the calculated destruction of a culture—was an attempt by white Americans to force Native Americans to assimilate into their culture. Although not as bloody as the Indian wars, ethnocide was even more destructive to Native-American societies.

At the heart of this new policy was the destruction of the reservation system. Reservations encouraged tribal unity, and, as such, distinctiveness from white American society. Congress believed that the solution was to treat Indians less like members of individual tribes and more like autonomous individuals. As a first step, in 1871 Congress had ruled that no Indian tribe "shall be acknowledged or recognized as an independent nation, tribe or power, with whom the United States may contract by treaty." Then in an attempt to de-

stroy Indian culture, in 1887 Congress passed the Dawes Severalty Act, which authorized the president to divide tribal lands and redistribute the lands among tribal members, giving 160 acres to each head of a family and lesser amounts to bachelors, women, and children. Although the plots would be held in trust for 25 years to prevent Indians from immediately selling the land, the object of the legislation was to make Indians individual landowners. In addition, all Native Americans receiving land grants were also made citizens of the United States.

Dawes was motivated by what he believed were the best interests of the Native Americans. Like other reformers, he believed that the most effective solution to the Indian problem was to assimilate Indians into mainstream white American culture. To this end, other reformers opened Indian schools to teach Indian children to be mechanics and farmers and to train them for citizenship. Richard Pratt, an army officer who founded the Carlisle Indian Industrial School in Pennsylvania in 1879, maintained that the fastest and surest way to assimilate Indians was to remove Indian children from reservations and send them to boarding schools in the East. By 1905 there were 25 boarding schools patterned after Carlisle. The schools emphasized ruthless assimilation. The "Rules for Indian Schools" called for compulsory observation of the Christian Sabbath, all formal and casual conversation in English, and instruction in "the sports and games enjoyed by white youth, such as baseball, hopscotch, croquet, marbles, bean bags, dominoes, checkers." Even more boarding schools were established on reservations to serve the same ends. What surprised reformers the most, however, was the failure of these schools to break tribal loyalties or destroy Indian culture.

While the reformers opened schools, Congress continued its efforts to break up the reservations. The Curtis Act of 1898 ended tribal sovereignty in Indian Territory, voiding tribal control of mineral rights, abolishing tribal laws and courts, and imposing the laws and courts of the United States on the Indians. The Dead Indian Act (1902) permitted Indians to sell allotted lands they had inherited, thereby circumventing the 25-year trust period imposed by the Dawes Act. Four years later, Congress continued its assault on the trust period with the Burke Act, which eliminated the trust period altogether and allowed the secretary of interior to decide when Indians were competent to manage their own affairs. Finally, in 1924 Congress enacted the Snyder Act, which granted all Indians born in the United States full citizenship. As far as Congress was concerned, the United States had now assimilated its true natives.

Reformers believed that these acts would end the tribal system and lead to assimilation. The legislation, however, served only the land interests of white Americans. By 1932 the allotment program had taken 90 million acres of land away from tribal control. Far from being assimilated, Indians saw their own culture attacked and partially destroyed, while at the same time they were never fully accepted into the dominant American culture.

Final Retreat from Reconstruction

The exact nature of the Native Americans' status, like that of African Americans, was determined after Reconstruction was over. The treatment of both, as well as of immigrants, would be justified by the increasingly virulent racism of whites, which was given "scientific" support by the scholars of the late nineteenth century. The patriotism engendered by the 1876 centennial of the Declaration of Independence also fostered a desire for unity among white Americans at the expense of nonwhites.

By 1876, fewer Americans championed black rights than had at the close of the war. Neither could Northerners who believed that the only good Indian was a dead Indian condemn southern whites for their treatment of African Americans. Some of the old abolitionist Radicals had grown tired of what had become a protracted and complex problem. They therefore justified their withdrawal from the fight by the failures of some southern Reconstruction governments. Those least likely

to do so, such as Thaddeus Stevens and Charles Sumner, were dead. Until his death in 1874, Sumner had struggled to get Congress to pass a civil rights act that would spell out more specifically the guarantees of the Fourteenth Amendment. He proposed that segregation of all public facilities, including schools, be declared illegal and the right of African Americans to serve on juries specified. After his death, in part as a tribute to him but mostly as one provision of a larger political bargain, Congress enacted the Civil Rights Act of 1875. The act did not include Sumner's clause on schools and did not provide any means of enforcement. For African Americans it was a paper victory that marked an end of national action on their behalf. Never effectively enforced, the act was rendered totally impotent by Supreme Court decisions of the late nineteenth century.

By 1876 all the elements were present for a national retreat on Reconstruction: the distraction of economic distress, a deep desire for unity among whites, the respectability of racism, a frustrated weariness with black problems by former allies, a growing conservatism on economic and social issues, a changing political climate featuring a resurgence of the Democratic party, and finally a general public disgust with the failure of Reconstruction. The presidential election of that year sealed the fate of Reconstruction and brought about an official end to it.

Corruption was a major issue in the 1876 election and the Democrats chose Samuel J. Tilden, a New Yorker whose claim to fame was breaking up the notorious Boss Tweed Ring. The Republicans nominated Rutherford B. Hayes, a man who had offended few—largely by doing little. Although Hayes had been elected governor of Ohio three times, to one observer he was "a third rate nonentity, whose only recommendation is that he is obnoxious to no one." As would become typical of most elections during the decades following Reconstruction, the campaign did not focus on any burning issues. The Democrats ran against Republican corruption. The Republicans ran against Democratic violence in the South. "Our strong ground," Hayes wrote, "is

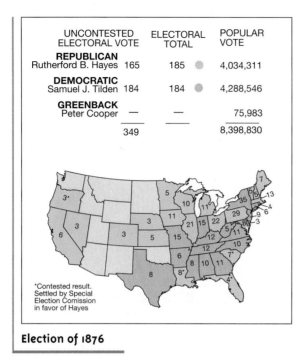

UNCONTESTED ELECTORAL VOTE	ELECTORAL TOTAL	POPULAR VOTE
REPUBLICAN Rutherford B. Hayes 165	185	4,034,311
DEMOCRATIC Samuel J. Tilden 184	184	4,288,546
GREENBACK Peter Cooper —	—	75,983
349		8,398,830

*Contested result. Settled by Special Election Comission in favor of Hayes

Election of 1876

the dread of a solid South, *rebel rule,* etc., etc. . . . It leads people away from 'hard times'; which is our deadliest foe."

The election itself was so riddled with corruption and violence that no one can ever know what would have happened in a fair election. One thing is certain. The Democrats gained strength. Tilden won the popular vote and led Hayes in undisputed electoral votes 184 to 165. However, 185 votes were needed for election, and 20 votes were disputed—19 of them from Louisiana, Florida, and South Carolina. They were the only Southern states still under Republican rule with the backing of federal troops. In each, rival election boards sent in different returns.

With no constitutional provision for such an occurrence, the Republican Senate and Democratic House established a special commission to decide which returns were valid. The 15-member Electoral Commission had 5 members each from the House, the Senate, and the Supreme Court. At first it was evenly divided with 7 Republicans and 7 Democrats; politically independent Supreme Court Justice David Davis was the swing vote. Illinois Democrats then made a mistake and selected

Davis as their senator. Thus, a Republican justice was appointed to replace him on the Electoral Commission, which proceeded to vote along party lines, 8 to 7, to give all the disputed votes to Hayes. Democrats were outraged, and a constitutional crisis seemed in the making if a united Democratic front in the House voted to reject the commission's findings.

A series of agreements between Hayes's advisors and Southern Democratic congressmen averted the crisis. In what came to be called the "Compromise of 1877," Hayes agreed to support federal aid for Southern internal improvements, especially a transcontinental railroad. He also promised to appoint a southern Democrat to his cabinet and to allow southern Democrats a say in the allocation of federal offices in their region. Most important, however, was his pledge to remove the remaining federal troops from the South. In return southern Democrats promised to protect black rights and to support the findings of the Electoral Commission. On March 2, the House voted to accept the report and declare Hayes the presidential winner by an electoral vote of 185 to 184. After taking office, Hayes removed the troops, and the remaining Republican governments in the South soon collapsed.

Scholars once considered the Compromise of 1877 an important factor in the end of Reconstruction. Actually, its role was more symbolic than real; it merely buried the corpse. The battle for the Republican party's soul had been lost by its abolitionist faction well before the election of 1876. The Democratic party had never sought to extend or protect blacks' rights. The Supreme Court began to interpret the Fourteenth and Fifteenth amendments very narrowly, stripping them of their strength. Thus African Americans were left with a small number of allies, and one by one many of their rights were lost during the next four decades.

CONCLUSION

As the Civil War ended, many unresolved issues remained. The most crucial involved the status of the former slaves and of the former

CHRONOLOGY OF KEY EVENTS

1863	Lincoln proclaims 10 percent plan for Reconstruction, which requires states to abolish slavery and have 10 percent of the citizens who had voted in the 1860 election subscribe to an oath to support the Constitution and the Union
1864	Lincoln vetoes Wade-Davis Bill on grounds that it imposes too severe conditions on the readmission of the seceded states; Sand Creek Massacre of Indians in Colorado
1865	Congress establishes Freedmen's Bureau to aid former slaves and refugees; Confederate army surrenders at Appomattox; John Wilkes Booth assassinates Lincoln at Ford's Theater in Washington, D.C.; Andrew Johnson becomes seventeenth president; Thirteenth Amendment is ratified, abolishing slavery
1866	Civil Rights Act provides that all persons born in the United States are citizens and possess equal legal and property rights; Fourteenth Amendment is proposed
1867	Reconstruction Act, passed over Johnson's veto, divides the South into five military districts, each governed by an army general. It requires each state to adopt a constitution disqualifying former Confed-

	erate officials from holding office to grant black citizens the right to vote, and to ratify the Fourteenth Amendment
1868	House of Representatives impeaches President Johnson; he escapes conviction in the Senate by one vote; Fourteenth Amendment is ratified; it guarantees citizenship to black Americans; Indian peace conference leads to establishment of reservations in Oklahoma and the Black Hills of the Dakotas; Ulysses S. Grant is elected eighteenth president
1870	Fifteenth Amendment is ratified; outlaws the exclusion from voting on the basis of race
1870–1871	Ku Klux Klan Acts are passed, which outlaw use of force to prevent people from voting and authorize use of federal troops to enforce the laws; Tweed Ring in New York City is exposed
1872	Credit Mobilier scandal is exposed
1876	Custer is defeated at Little Bighorn; disputed presidential election between Tilden and Hayes
1877	Electoral Commission awards disputed ballots to Republican Rutherford B. Hayes, who becomes nineteenth president

Confederate states. The destinies of both were inextricably intertwined. Anything affecting the status of either influenced the fate of the other. Quick readmission of the states with little change would doom black rights. Enforced equality of African Americans under the law would create turbulence and drastic change in the South. This difficult problem was further complicated by constitutional, economic, and political considerations, ensuring that the course of Reconstruction would be chaotic and contradictory.

Presidential Reconstruction under both Lincoln and Johnson favored rapid reunification and white unity more than changes in the racial structure of the South. The South, however, refused to accept a meaningful end of slavery, as was blatantly demonstrated by the Black Codes. Congressional desire to reestablish legislative supremacy and the Republican need to build a national party combined with this southern intransigence to unite Radical and moderate Republicans on the need to protect black rights and to restructure the South. What emerged from congressional reconstruction were Republican governments that expanded democracy and enacted needed reforms but were deeply resented by many southern whites. At the core of that resentment was not disgust over incompetence or corruption but hostility to black political power in any form.

Given the pervasiveness of racial prejudice, what is remarkable is not that the Freedmen's Bureau, the constitutional amendments, and the civil rights legislation did not produce permanent change but that these actions were taken at all. Cherished ideas of property rights, limited government, and self-reliance, as well as an almost universal belief in black inferiority, almost guaranteed that the experiment would fail. The first national attempt to resolve fairly and justly the question of minority rights in a pluralistic society was abandoned in less than a decade. After Native American populations had been decimated, the government sought to eradicate all elements of their culture that differed from that of the dominant society. Indians, blacks, and women saw the truth of the Alabama planter's words of 1865: "Poor elk—poor buffaloe—poor Indian—poor Nigger—this is indeed a white man country." However, less than a century later seeds planted by the amendments would finally germinate, flower, and be harvested.

SUGGESTIONS FOR FURTHER READING

Richard Nelson Current, *Those Terrible Carpetbaggers* (1988). Refutes the longstanding myth that northerners in the South after the Civil War were ill-educated people whose only goal was private gain.

Eric Foner, *Nothing But Freedom: Emancipation and Its Legacy* (1983). Compares and contrasts the postemancipation experience of African Americans with that of former slaves in the Caribbean.

Eric Foner, *Reconstruction: America's Unfinished Revolution, 1863–1877* (1988). Comprehensive history of the period, which emphasized African-Americans' central role in defining the period's political and social agenda.

Leon Litwack, *Been in the Storm So Long: The Aftermath of Slavery* (1979). Examines the varied responses of African Americans in the South to emancipation.

Mark W. Summers, *The Era of Good Stealings* (1993). Investigates political corruption during the Reconstruction period.

Joel Williamson, *The Crucible of Race* (1984). Explores the evolution of Southern race relations after reconstruction.

Overviews and Surveys

Eric Anderson and Alfred A. Moss, Jr., *The Facts of Reconstruction: Essays in Honor of John Hope Franklin* (1992); Mary Francis Berry and John W. Blassingame, *Long Memory: The Black Experience in America* (1982); Eric Foner and Olivia Mahoney, *America's Reconstruction: People and Politics After the Civil War* (1995); W. E. B. DuBois, *Black Reconstruction in America, 1860–1880* (1935); Jay R. Mandle, *Not Slave, Not Free: The African-American Experience Since the Civil War* (1992); James McPherson, *Ordeal by Fire* (1982); James G. Randall and David Donald, *The Civil War and Reconstruction,* 2d ed. (1969); Kenneth M. Stampp, *The Era of Reconstruction, 1865–1877* (1965).

Postwar Conditions and Issues

Herman Belz, *Emancipation and Equal Rights: Politics and Constitutionalism in the Civil War Era* (1976); John H. and La Wanda Cox, *Politics, Principles, and Prejudice* (1963); John Hope Franklin, *Reconstruction After the Civil War,* 2d. ed. (1994); Peter Kolchin, *First Freedom: The Responses of Alabama's Blacks to Emancipation and Reconstruction* (1972); J. Morgan Kousser and James McPherson, eds., *Region, Race, and Reconstruction* (1982); Rembert W. Patrick, *Reconstruction of the Nation* (1967); James Roark, *Masters Without Slaves* (1977); Willie Lee Rose, *Rehearsal for Reconstruction* (1964); James Sefton, *The United States Army and Reconstruction, 1865–1877* (1967); Ted Tunnell, *Crucible of Reconstruction* (1984).

Presidential Reconstruction

Richard H. Abbott, *The Republican Party and the South, 1855–1877: The First Southern Strategy* (1986); Michael Les Benedict, *A Compromise of Principle* (1974); William R. Brock, *An American Crisis* (1963); LaWanda Cox, *Lincoln and Black Freedom* (1981); David Donald, *The Politics of Reconstruction* (1965); William B. Hesseltine, *Lincoln's Plan of Reconstruction* (1960); Peyton McCrary, *Abraham Lincoln and Reconstruction* (1978); Eric McKitrick, *Andrew John-*

son and Reconstruction (1960); James M. McPherson, *The Struggle for Equality: Abolitionists and the Negro in the Civil War and Reconstruction* (1964); Patrick W. Riddleberger, *1866: The Critical Year Revisited* (1979); Hans L. Trefousse, *The Radical Republicans* (1969).

Congressional Reconstruction

Michael Les Benedict, *The Impeachment of Andrew Johnson* (1973); Ellen DuBois, *Feminism and Suffrage* (1978); William Gillette, *The Right to Vote* (1969); Harold M. Hyman, *A More Perfect Union* (1973); Joseph James, *The Framing of the Fourteenth Amendment* (1956); Stanley I. Kutler, *The Judicial Power and Reconstruction Politics* (1968); Hans L. Trefousse, *The Impeachment of a President* (1975).

Reconstruction in the South

Dan T. Carter, *When the War Was Over: The Failure of Self-Reconstruction in the South, 1865–1867* (1985); Stephen J. DeCanio, *Agriculture in the Postbellum South* (1974); Paul D. Escott, *Many Excellent People* (1985); Barbara Jeanne Fields, *Slavery and Freedom on the Middle Ground: Maryland During the Nineteenth Century* (1985); Eric Foner, *Nothing But Freedom* (1983); Herbert G. Gutman, *The Black Family in Slavery and Freedom* (1976); Steven Hahn, *The Roots of Southern Populism* (1983); William C. Harris, *The Day of the Carpetbagger* (1979); Thomas Holt, *Black over White* (1977); Gerald Jaynes, *Branches Without Roots: Genesis of the Black Working Class in the American South, 1862–1882* (1986); Jay R. Mandle, *The Roots of Black Poverty* (1978); William E. Montgomery, *Under Their Own Vine and Fig Tree: The African-American Church in the South, 1865–1900* (1993); Robert C. Morris, *Reading, 'Riting and Reconstruction* (1981); Otto H. Olsen, ed., *Reconstruction and Redemption in the South* (1980); Michael Perman, *The Road to Redemption: Southern Politics, 1869–1879* (1984); Lawrence N. Powell, *New Masters: Northern Planters During the Civil War and Reconstruction* (1980); Howard Rabinowitz, *Race Relations in the Urban South* (1978); George C. Rable, *But There Was No Peace: The Role of Violence in the Politics of Reconstruction* (1984); Peter J. Rachleff, *Black Labor in the South: Richmond, Virginia, 1865–1890* (1984); Roger L. Ransom and Richard Sutch, *One Kind of Freedom: The Economic Consequences of Emancipation* (1977); Edward Royce, *The Origins of Southern Sharecropping* (1993); Joe Gray Taylor, *Louisiana Reconstructed* (1974); Allen Trelease, *White Terror* (1971); Ted Tun-

nell, *Crucible of Reconstruction* (1984); Jonathan M. Wiener, *Social Origins of the New South: Alabama, 1860–1885* (1978); Sarah Woolfolk Wiggins, *The Scalawag in Alabama Politics* (1977); Joel Williamson, *After Slavery: The Negro in South Carolina During Reconstruction* (1965), and *A Rage for Order: Black-White Relations in the American South Since Emancipation* (1986).

Reconstruction in the North and West

Ralph K. Andrist, *The Long Death: The Last Days of the Plains Indians* (1964); Robert F. Berkhofer, *The White Man's Indian* (1978); Eugene H. Berwanger, *The West and Reconstruction* (1981); George Pierre Castile and Robert L. Bee, eds., *State and Reservation: New Perspectives on Federal Indian Policy* (1992); Charles Fairman, *Reconstruction and Reunion*, 2 vols. (1971–1987); David A. Gerber, *Black Ohio and the Color Line, 1860–1915* (1976); William Gillette, *Retreat from Reconstruction* (1979), and *The Right to Vote* (1969); Norris Handley, Jr., ed., *The American Indian* (1974); Nell Irvin Painter, *The Exodusters* (1977); Keith Ian Polakoff, *The Politics of Inertia* (1973); Francis Paul Prucha, *American Indian Policy in Crisis* (1975); David Roberts, *Once They Moved Like the Wind: Cochise, Geronimo, and the Apache Wars* (1993); Nina Silber, *The Romance of Reunion: Northerners and the South, 1865–1900* (1993); Mark W. Summers, *Railroads, Reconstruction and the Gospel of Prosperity* (1984); Orlan J. Svingen, *The Northern Cheyenne Indian Reservation, 1877–1900* (1993); Ronald T. Takaki, *Iron Cages* (1979); Wilcomb E. Washburn, *The Indian in America* (1975), and *Red Man's Land/White Man's Law* (1971); C. Vann Woodward, *Reunion and Reaction* (1951).

Biographies

Fawn M. Brodie, *Thaddeus Stevens* (1959); David Donald, *Charles Sumner and the Rights of Man* (1970); Erik S. Lunde, *Horace Greeley* (1980); William S. McFeely, *Yankee Stepfather: General O. O. Howard and the Freedmen* (1968), *Grant: A Biography* (1981), and *Frederick Douglass* (1990); Sally M. Miller, ed., *John Muir: Life and Work* (1993); John G. Neihardt, *Black Elk Speaks* (1932); Michael F. Steltenkamp, *Black Elk: Holy Man of the Oglala* (1993); Hans L. Trefousse, *Andrew Johnson* (1989); Robert M. Utley, *The Lance and the Shield: The Life and Times of Sitting Bull* (1993).

CHAPTER 17
EMERGENCE AS AN ECONOMIC POWER

AMERICA: LAND OF PLENTY
Mineral and Geographic Possibilities
Technological Change
An Expanding Railroad Network

CREATING A FAVORABLE CLIMATE: THE ROLE OF IDEOLOGY, POLITICS, AND FINANCE
Social Darwinism and the Gospel of Wealth
Laissez-Faire in Theory and Practice
Corporations and Capital Formation

THE RISE OF BIG BUSINESS
Controlling Competition
New Managerial Styles and an Expanding Middle Class
Mass Marketing, Assembly Lines, and Mass Production
The Power of Bigness

VARIETIES OF ECONOMIC CHANGE IN THE WEST AND SOUTH
Western Expansion and Exploitation
The Changing Nature of Farming
The New South

WORKING IN INDUSTRIAL AMERICA
The Conditions of Work
Worker Discontent
Early Labor Violence
Unorganized and Organized Labor

On a cold winter night in December 1900, 75 of the richest, most influential American businessmen gathered at the New York University Club for a dinner to honor Charles Schwab, president of Carnegie Steel Company. Seated to the honoree's right was J. P. Morgan, the powerful investment banker and consolidator of industry. He had been placed there so that he would not miss a word of Schwab's speech. When Schwab finally spoke, what he delivered was a veiled threat instead of a speech. With pretended innocence he rhapsodized over a bright future of stability and low prices for the steel industry. This future was to be ushered in by the formation of a scientifically integrated firm—one that combined all phases of the industry from the production of raw steel to the manufacture of finished products.

Morgan did not miss the point. Previously, Carnegie Steel had limited its operations to making raw steel. For several years before this dinner Morgan and others had been busily creating trusts among the producers of such finished steel products as tubes and wire. Trusts, which were often-successful attempts to unite smaller competing firms in order to control markets and raise prices, often used this combined power to put remaining competitors out of business. The steel products trusts, however, had a problem. Andrew Carnegie's company was the largest supplier of raw steel and he hated trusts.

When American Tin Plate Company threatened to cancel its orders with Carnegie Steel unless he refused to sell to its competitors, Carnegie decided to beat them at their own game. He joined several informal arrangements to fix prices, known as "pools," only to sabotage them from within. Morgan and his cohorts soon realized that depending on Carnegie for raw steel would doom their consolidation schemes. Consequently, in July 1900 National Tube, American Steel and Wire, and American Hoop canceled all contracts with Carnegie. They were going to produce their own steel or buy it from others—and put Carnegie out of business.

Rather than surrender, Carnegie continued his policy of spending money to make money. He telegraphed instructions to his company's officers: "Crisis has arrived, only one policy open; start at once hoop, wire, nail mills. . . . Extend coal and coke roads, announce these; also tubes. . . . Have no fear as to result, victory certain. Spend freely for finishing mills, railroads, boat lines." Carnegie knew he could produce superior products at cheaper prices. After Schwab assured him that they could manufacture tubes at a price $10 a ton cheaper than National Tube, he decided to pay no dividends on common stock and announced plans to build a $12-million tube plant.

The antiquated and scattered plants of his competitors would have been no match for Carnegie's new ones. Panicked promoters scurried to J. P. Morgan in the weeks before the testimonial dinner. Few doubted Federal Steel president Elbert Gary's assertion that Carnegie could "have driven entirely out of business every steel company in the United States." Carnegie, however, wanted to retire. Schwab's speech was aimed at producing a bargain, not a war. After the dinner Morgan fired dozens of questions at Schwab. Later they held an all-night session at Morgan's house. In the early hours of the next day Morgan finally said, "Well, if Andy wants to sell, I'll buy. Go find his price."

Schwab approached Carnegie on the golf course, where he might be more inclined to cooperate. Carnegie listened, then asked Schwab to return the next day for an answer. At that time Carnegie handed him a slip of paper with his asking price of $480 million written in pencil. When Schwab gave Morgan the offer, he glanced at it and replied, "I accept the price." A few days later Morgan stopped by Carnegie's office, shook hands on the deal and stated, "Mr. Carnegie, I want to congratulate you on being the richest man in the world."

Two of the best had locked in combat, and both emerged victors. Carnegie had his millions to endow libraries, and anything else that struck his fancy. Morgan was able to found United States Steel Corporation which became a colossus even among the existing giants of American industry. It was capitalized at $1.4 billion, a figure three times larger than the annual budget of the United States gov-

Lavish displays of wealth were common in the business world, as exemplified by this 1901 dinner meeting of officials of the Carnegie Steel Company to celebrate the formation of United States Steel.

ernment. These outcomes for Carnegie and Morgan reflected momentous changes occurring after the Civil War. The United States moved out of the ranks of second-rate industrial powers and became the leader. By 1900 its manufacturing output exceeded the combined totals of Great Britain, France, and Germany. The speed with which this happened seems more suited to fairy tales than reality. As Andrew Carnegie exclaimed in 1886, "The old nations of the earth creep on at a snail's pace; the Republic thunders past with the rush of an express."

Many yardsticks supported his assertion. Between 1870 and 1914 U.S. railroad mileage increased from 53,000 to 250,000—more than the combined railroad mileage of the rest of the world. Almost every sector of the economy grew in multiples of two or more from the 1860s to 1900. Land under agricultural production doubled; the gross national product was six times larger; the amount of manufactured goods per person tripled.

This phenomenal growth had resulted from the foundations laid by antebellum industrial development, the abundance of the land and its people, technological breakthroughs, and a favorable business climate—ideologically, financially, legally, and politically. The rapidity of change first produced

chaotic conditions, which eventually led to new managerial styles and finally to economic consolidation and the rise of such supercorporations as United States Steel.

Forces of economic change swept through all sections and all segments of the economy. The profound alterations of the social order that resulted touched virtually every aspect of life. Much of what is now commonplace—electric lights, petroleum products, the telephone, the skyscraper, the handheld camera, the typewriter—was largely unknown prior to the Civil War. The natures of work and marketing were drastically transformed, affecting all social relationships. The new order produced a few big winners, such as Carnegie and Morgan, but there were more losers.

AMERICA: LAND OF PLENTY

In 1847 Walt Whitman boasted, "Yankeedoodledom is going ahead with the resistless energy of a sixty-five-hundred-horse-power steam engine. . . . Let the Old World wag on under its cumbersome load of form and conservatism; we are of a newer, fresher race and land. And all we have to say is, to point to fifty years hence and say, 'Let those laugh who win.'" By 1897 Americans were laughing. Their victory was facilitated by the abundance of the nation's new land, new people, and new ideas. Western expansion, increasing immigration, and numerous inventions ushered in a new era.

Mineral and Geographic Possibilities

Explorers and early settlers in what would become the United States were disappointed not to find the same abundance of gold and silver that had enriched their Spanish neighbors to the south. It wasn't until the nineteenth century that Americans began to realize the vast wealth that their expansion had brought. Most spectacular was the discovery of gold in California in the 1840s. That discovery sparked frenzied prospecting all through the West. Each new discovery led to "rushes," creating mining towns almost overnight. Between 1850 and the 1880s thousands of men and women of almost every ethnic background helped create makeshift social institutions whenever and wherever strikes were made.

Wherever it moved, the mining frontier tended to follow the same pattern. Adventurous optimists would search for the elusive glint of precious metals. After living weeks or months at subsistence level, many would go home poorer. Although a few did strike it rich, inexpensive and inefficient mining methods quickly exhausted the more easily obtainable supplies of precious metals. Extracting ore from beneath the ground and in veins of quartz was expensive. It required large amounts of capital best raised by mining syndicates. Frequently financed by Eastern and European investors, these syndicates bought prospectors' claims for a fraction of their value.

As mining became an organized business, its focus moved to less exotic but more useful minerals such as copper, lead, talc, zinc, and quartz. These fed the growing demands of Eastern industries. By the 1880s mining no longer represented easy riches for pioneering individuals; it had become an integrated part of the nation's modern industrial economy.

Emerging basic industries such as steel and petroleum, and those producing electric power, depended on large supplies of various minerals, which seemed to become available as needed. New deposits were sometimes found; at other times new uses spurred the mining of known deposits.

Prior to the Civil War iron was used extensively for plows and other implements, but it was not durable. Then new technology developed by Andrew Carnegie and others led to the production of large quantities of relatively cheap and durable steel. New manufacturing vistas were thus opened, and between 1870 and 1900 steel output rose from 850,000 tons to over 10.5 million tons.

The same pattern developed in the mining of other minerals. Copper, first used for

The first oil well, called "Drake's folly," was drilled in Titusville, Pennsylvania, in 1859. Edwin Drake (in top hat) got his inspiration from watching salt-well drilling operations.

household commodities, became a key product in such new fields as oil refining, electrical generation and conduction, and telephone communications. Most went into the miles and miles of wiring that electrified the cities. Similarly, the increased use of coal-burning steam engines to power machinery and locomotives sparked a spectacular rise in coal mining. As late as 1869 almost half of all power used in manufacturing was produced by water wheels; by 1900 coal-burning steam engines supplied 80 percent of such power.

Even more dramatic was the rise in the importance of petroleum. Many people were aware of large oil reserves in Pennsylvania because it seeped into streams and springs. Early demand was mainly for making patent medicines of dubious value. Encouraged by reports of its potential use as a lighting source and lubricating oil, Pennsylvania businessman George Bissell funded the first drilling efforts. In 1859 his employee, Edwin L. Drake, tapped the first oil well, in Titusville, Pennsylvania. Commonly labeled "Drake's folly," the well marked the beginning of another new industry. Oil was indeed needed to lubricate the increasing number of machine parts, and in the 1870s about 20 million barrels were being produced annually. John D. Rockefeller and others built refineries to refine the oil into kerosene, which was used as a popular form of illumination, displacing candles before it itself was replaced by electricity. (An officer in Rockefeller's Standard Oil Company is reputed to have volunteered to drink all the oil ever found outside of Pennsylvania. Fortunately no one held him to his word.)

The growing demand led to the search for "liquid gold" in the Southwest. In 1901 a well at Spindletop, Texas, shot a 160-foot stream of oil into the air. New sources of oil led to the development of the gasoline engine in the twentieth century, exemplifying how abundant natural resources and technology often interacted—each shaping the evolution of the other.

Technological Change

Seldom has technology so dramatically transformed so much of people's lives in a single generation. Bewildering as the changes sometimes were in the late nineteenth century, the public generally welcomed new inventions with wide-eyed wonder and nationalistic pride. Many public events were like mass rituals to the new god of technology. Parades and thanksgiving services as well as the ringing of the Liberty Bell greeted the completion of the first transcontinental railway at Promontory Point, Utah, in May 1869. Awed sightseers crammed expositions celebrating "progress." At the 1876 Philadelphia Centennial Exposition, visitors saw for the first time the Corliss engine, bicycles, the typewriter, the elevator, Alexander Graham Bell's telephone, and even the "floor covering of the future"—linoleum. By the time of the World's Columbian Exposition at Chicago in 1893, the Corliss engine was obsolete, and many of the miracles of 1876 were commonplace "necessities." The impact of new inventions was enormous. Whereas only 276 inventions were recorded during the Patent Office's first decade, 22,000 patents were issued in the year 1893.

The Columbian Exposition of 1893 in Chicago celebrated the enormous technological progress of the late nineteenth century. In the Palace of Electricity many visitors saw their first electric lamp.

Technological change during the era affected the lives of individuals far more than any political or philosophical development. Offices became mechanized with the invention of the typewriter in 1867 and the development of a practical adding machine in 1888. As clerical work became more necessary and required less skill, it became classed as women's work with lower pay scales. New machines drastically altered the nature of housework, but higher standards of cleanliness kept housewives as busy as ever. Numerous inventions revolutionized railroad transportation, including George Westinghouse's airbrake, which made longer, faster trains possible. Later, electric streetcars profoundly changed the character of urban development by accelerating the move to the suburbs.

Innovations in communication unified a collection of island communities into a nation. The completion of a telegraphic cable across the Atlantic in 1866 increased the nation's links with the rest of the world. New inventions in printing made popular newspapers with wide circulations a reality—along with mass advertising. Photographic advances culminated in George Eastman's Kodak handheld camera in 1888. However, few, if any, inventions rivaled the impact of Alexander Graham Bell's 1876 "toy." Telephones rapidly became necessities—more than one and one-half million were installed by 1900.

The new inventions increasingly relied on cheap and efficient sources of electricity. The names of Thomas Edison and George Westinghouse stand above the rest in this area. Edison began his career peddling candy and newspapers on trains, but he soon became a telegrapher and invented various improvements to it. The success of his ideas convinced him to go into the "invention business." Establishing a research lab at Menlo Park, New Jersey, in 1876, he promised to produce "a minor invention every ten days and a big thing every six months or so." In 1877 he invented the phonograph and in 1879 the incandescent light bulb, as well as hundreds of other de-

vices over the years, such as a better telephone, the dictaphone, the mimeograph, the dynamo, motion pictures, and an electric distribution for lighting transmission. With backing from banker J. P. Morgan, he created the first electric company in 1882 in New York City, and formed the Edison General Electric Company in 1888 to produce light bulbs.

Edison's only serious mistake was his choice of direct electrical current, which limited the range of transmission to a radius of about two miles. George Westinghouse developed an alternating current system in 1886 that soon supplanted direct current, forcing even Edison's companies to make the switch. Westinghouse also acquired and improved an electric motor that had been invented by Croatian immigrant Nikola Tesla in 1888.

An Expanding Railroad Network

Americans developed a love/hate relationship with the railroads. The same locomotive that inspired Walt Whitman's rhapsody to its "fierce throated beauty" was described by Frank Norris in 1901 as "the leviathan, with tentacles of steel clutching into the soil, the

In his Menlo Park, New Jersey, laboratory, Thomas Edison, who eventually obtained over 1000 patents, aimed at practicality in his inventions. He is shown listening to his phonograph in 1888.

soulless Force, the iron-hearted Power, the Master, the Colossus, the Octopus." Despite differing visions, no one doubted the importance of the railroads. They played a crucial role in forging a new society, transforming a continent of isolated communities into a unified nation with an interdependent economy. Rails brought raw materials to population centers, making possible large factories that mass-produced goods. Those goods were then shipped to national markets over the same rails.

Early railroads were strictly local affairs, however. Although there were already 35,000 miles of rails by 1865, few lines linked up in any rational way. Having 11 different rail gauges meant that both goods and passengers had to be unloaded from one set of cars and reloaded onto another set—sometimes at a depot on the opposite side of town. Between New York and Chicago, for example, cargo had to be unloaded and reloaded as many as six times. (In some cases the inefficiency was intentional; many small ante-bellum railroads purposely adopted different gauges and conflicting schedules to avoid being swallowed up by larger, more powerful competitors.)

Unlike many European rail systems, American railroads grew with little advance planning or government regulation, sprouting like weeds in populous areas where immediate profits could be made. In the antebellum South especially, too many small lines serviced the same places—400 companies sprang up, each with an average track length of a mere 40 miles. Twenty competing lines provided service between Atlanta and St. Louis!

While too many railroads served some sections in the East, prior to 1869 there were no transcontinental lines linking the East and West coasts due to the high cost of construction. Large amounts of capital were required in the East but a return on the investment came quickly. In the West railroads often preceded settlement and, therefore, demand for their lines. Transcontinental routes were needed, however, and land grants became the solution. Contemporary and later analysts

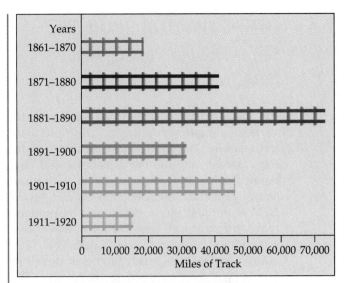

FIGURE 17.1 Railroad Construction, 1861–1920
By 1865 there were 35,000 miles of railroad, but few lines connected in any logical way to provide direct routes from one location to another.
Source: U.S. Bureau of the Census, 1975.

have questioned the size of those grants, but they undoubtedly had the desired effect. By the turn of the century there were five transcontinental routes.

At the same time, after some fierce competitive battles, a few eastern railroad companies gained control of many of the local lines. When the dust settled, there were four main trunklines in the Northeast and five in the Southeast. The average track length of a railroad grew from a mere 100 miles in 1865 to over 1000 miles two decades later. Gauges were also standardized, and a more efficient rail system emerged.

America's "newer, fresher race and land" provided the material basis for economic expansion. The "land of plenty" produced resources, people, and machinery in seemingly inexhaustible amounts, and railroads tied them together. Nevertheless, even such wealth does not adequately explain the phenomenal mushrooming of American industry or the rise of large corporations. Less tangible factors also nurtured the fantastic growth rate.

CREATING A FAVORABLE CLIMATE: THE ROLE OF IDEOLOGY, POLITICS, AND FINANCE

An abundant harvest requires good soil, favorable climatic conditions, and adequate fertilization. Materials and machinery were the "seeds" of industrialization, but the bountiful economic harvest of the late nineteenth century depended first on the "good soil" of popular support fostered by intellectual and cultural justifications. Favorable government policies created a desirable, "climate," while legal and financial developments provided the needed "fertilizer." The combination produced not only more but also larger industries.

Social Darwinism and the Gospel of Wealth

Expanding economic opportunities fostered cutthroat competition from which fewer and fewer winners emerged. The road to wealth taken by the new captains of industry was strewn with the bodies of ruined competitors and broken labor movements. Ruthlessness not only seemed to become increasingly necessary, it was also transformed into a virtue by the twin ideologies of Social Darwinism and the "Gospel of wealth."

For men like Andrew Carnegie the writings of Social Darwinists Herbert Spencer and William Graham Sumner helped relieve unwelcome guilt. "I remember that light came as in a flood and all was clear," Carnegie noted, after reading Spencer's writings. Spencer and his followers applied the biological concepts of Charles Darwin to the workings of society. Natural selection allowed the fittest individuals to survive and flourish in the marketplace. Survival of the fittest supposedly enriched not only the winners but also society as a whole. Human evolution would produce what Spencer called "the ultimate and inevitable development of the ideal man" through a culling process. "If [individuals] are suffi-

ciently complete to live, they do live," he wrote, "and it is well that they should live. If they are not sufficiently complete to live, they die and it is best they should die."

According to the Social Darwinists, poverty and slums were as inevitable as the concentration of wealth. Spencer pleaded that "there should not be a forcible burdening of the superior for the support of the inferior." His disciple Sumner declared, "If we do not like the survival of the fittest, we have only one possible alternative, and that is the survival of the unfittest." Both argued that governmental or charitable intervention to improve the conditions of the poor interfered with the functioning of natural law and prolonged the life of "defective gene pools" to the detriment of society as a whole.

The so-called fittest naturally greeted "scientific" endorsement of their elite positions with eagerness. John D. Rockefeller told his Baptist Sunday school class, "The growth of large business is merely the survival of the fittest. This is not an evil tendency in Business. It is merely the working out of a law of nature and a law of God." The captains of industry relied on religion as well as science to justify themselves and their wealth. Some who found the ruthlessness of Social Darwinism unpalatable sought their justification in religious rationales. Since colonial times, the Protestant work ethic had denounced idleness and viewed success as evidence of being among the "elect"—God's chosen people. Building upon this base, apologists constructed the gospel of wealth.

Some simply and boldly announced God's sanction of their wealth: Rockefeller asserted, "God gave me my riches." Carnegie produced a written, logically argued rationale: "Not evil, but good, has come to the race," he wrote, "from the accumulation of wealth by those who have the ability and energy that produces it." The masses would waste any extra income "on the indulgence of appetite." "Wealth, passing through the hands of the few," Carnegie wrote, "can be a much more potent force for the elevation of our race than if it had been distributed in small sums to the people themselves." In other words, the "fittest" could best decide what other people needed. In Carnegie's case, he took that responsibility seriously, distributing over $300 million to such philanthropic causes as the founding of libraries and the Carnegie Foundation.

Among the most effective apologists for the wealthy were religious leaders of the era. In 1901 Bishop William Lawrence, for example, proclaimed, "Godliness is in league with riches." Not only did the elite deserve their riches, but the poor were responsible for their low status. The eminent preacher Henry Ward Beecher argued that "no man suffers from poverty unless it be more than his fault—unless it be his sin." Perhaps the most popular evangelist for the gospel of wealth was the lawyer and Baptist minister Russell Conwell, who delivered his celebrated "Acres of Diamonds" speech approximately 6000 times between 1861 and 1925. In it he declared that "it is your duty to get rich." To those preaching sacrifice and vows of poverty, Conwell proclaimed, "It is a mistake of these pious people to think you must be awfully poor in order to be pious." Instead he asserted,

Money is power, and you ought to be reasonably ambitious to have it. You ought because you can do more good with it than you could without it. Money printed your Bible, money builds your churches, money sends your missionaries, and money pays your preachers. . . . The man who gets the largest salary can do the most good with the power that is furnished to him.

Thus, according to both scientific and religious thought, the maldistribution of wealth was not only inevitable but also desirable. Probably more important, though, was the support for this idea provided by popular culture. *McGuffey Readers* stressed the virtue of hard work and its inevitable rewards in poems such as "Try, Try Again." Novelist Horatio Alger penned many stories in which the heroes rose from poverty to comfortable middle-class status through a combination of diligence and good luck. Popular literature reinforced the idea that success always came to those who deserved it, in America, the land of opportunity.

Laissez-Faire in Theory and Practice

The prevailing economic theory also lent respectability to greed and to the idea that government should not intervene in the economy. In 1776 Adam Smith presented arguments in *The Wealth of Nations* that would long be used to explain the workings of a free economy and to prescribe government's role in that economy. Smith asserted that the market was directed and controlled by an "invisible hand" composed of a multitude of individual choices. If government did not meddle, competition would naturally lead to the production of desired goods and services at reasonable prices—the natural laws of supply and demand. In short, if everyone were free to act according to self-interest, the resulting economy would be best suited to meet society's needs.

Acceptance of the "invisible hand" of supply-and-demand economic theory naturally led to a policy called "laissez-faire." Government properly was to leave the economy alone so as to not disrupt the operation of these natural forces. Business leaders naturally endorsed the theory's rejection of governmental regulation, yet they saw no contradiction in asking for government aid and subsidies to foster in-dustrialization. And to a large extent the industrialists got what they wanted—a laissez-faire policy that left them alone, except for help when they wanted it. Ironically, this distortion of theory helped produce an economy where business consolidation wreaked havoc

Popular culture at the turn of the century reinforced the American Dream. In the Horatio Alger stories, the hero always escapes poverty through hard work and good fortune and joins the middle class.

Following the Civil War, government did little to regulate business. As a result, no laws protected consumers from fraudulent services or products like this patent medicine.

upon the very competition needed for natural regulation of the economy.

Absolute free enterprise never really existed, however. There was plenty of governmental activity—just not in the area of regulation. Business freedom of action boggles the modern mind. No laws protected the consumer from adulterated foods, spurious claims for ineffective or even dangerous patent medicines, the sale of stock in nonexistent companies, or unsafe and overpriced transportation services. No national regulating agency of any kind existed prior to the establishment of the Interstate Commerce Commission in 1887. The proclamation "Let the buyer beware" asked people to make decisions and choices without enough information to protect their interests.

While denying support and protection to consumers or workers, government at all levels aided businesspeople. Alexander Hamilton's vision of an industrializing nation fostered by favorable governmental action, which had never entirely died, was rejuvenated by the Republican party. In 1860 the party pledged to enact higher tariffs, to subsidize the completion of a transcontinental railroad, and to establish a stable national banking system. The Republican victory undoubtedly helped create a favorable environment for rapid industrialization. There was no sharp break with the past, however, nor did business gain a great victory over agriculture. The pattern of governmental aid to business was, as one historian has noted, "like certain kinds of embroidery . . . boldly

visible but not of simple design." No form of aid was without antebellum precedents and most had wide public support. Both the motives behind many actions and their results were mixed. At the same time, agriculture was far from unrepresented and powerless, as can be seen by the passage of the Homestead and Morrill Land Grant acts, which provided free land to settlers and financed agricultural education.

Another government aid to business was the tariff. Tariffs had a long history. Two days before Lincoln took office, in 1861, Democratic President Buchanan signed the Morrill Tariff, marking the first tariff increase since 1842 and beginning a practically uninterrupted rise in tariff rates for the remainder of the century. At first, such American industries as steel needed to be protected from European competition to survive. Yet even after Carnegie greatly reduced the cost of steel production, the tariff remained. Without foreign competition, businesspeople were able to make higher profits by charging higher prices, which consumers came to resent. Tariffs were nevertheless widely viewed as serving the national interest by fostering economic independence.

Additional forms of subsidy were also meant to serve the public good. Dwarfing all others were the land grants to railroads. During the 1860s Congress granted 20 square miles of public land in alternating sections to the Union Pacific and Central Pacific railroads for each mile of track laid by the two railroads, to spur completion of a transcontinental route. Only the scale of these grants was new—railroads had already received nearly 20 million acres of federal land prior to the war. By the time the grants ended, railroad developers had received a total of 130 million acres of federal land, and some 51 million acres of state land (although it was still less than 7 percent of the national domain in the West). Congress gave all those acres to a handful of people—creating some of America's wealthiest families. In return the government paid only half fare to move troops and supplies, the value of the remaining land increased, and the uniting of the

East and West aided the entire economy. Only a decade after the grants ceased were they denounced.

Business also benefited from favorable labor and financial legislation and low-interest loans. Individuals exploited these policies for personal gain, and the results were not uniformly positive. Although never unlimited or unrestricted, aid to business enjoyed wide public support at first. Indeed, nationalism and patriotism accompanied the process of industrialization. Many Americans took pride in the nation's growing economic power. When John D. Rockefeller explained his business activities by saying, "I wanted to participate in the work of making our country great," his words fell on sympathetic ears. Only after the problems of industrialization became more apparent did the public begin to cry "foul."

Corporations and Capital Formation

Such governmental aid as high tariffs, land grants, low-interest loans, and lack of regulation provided rich fertilizer for economic expansion. The harvest brought both blessings and problems as did the rise of the corporation and decline of individual ownership and partnerships.

Although corporations were certainly not new, changes dating from the Jacksonian period paved the way for their postwar domination of the economy. Businesspeople had once been required to apply to a state legislature for a charter; by the 1830s they could incorporate on their own, provided they met certain standards. Following the Civil War, courts also began to affirm the principle of limited liability. Previously, bankruptcy could bring not only the loss of one's investment but also seizure of personal property by creditors. A corporation's liability eventually became limited to its assets—making investment a safer and more desirable venture. One knew just how much could be lost.

In *Santa Clara County* v. *The Southern Pacific Railroad* (1886) the Supreme Court perverted the Fourteenth Amendment by ruling that a corporation was a legal "person" and therefore entitled to all the protections granted by the amendment. States could not deny corporations equal protection of the law or deprive them of their rights or property without due process of the law. Corporations were also eventually granted the "right" to "reasonable" profits—to be determined by the courts, not the state.

Corporations not only received "equal protection," they became privileged "persons." Real human beings whose rights were protected by the Constitution were also held responsible for illegal activities. There were no handcuffs or jail cells large enough for "corporate persons." Punishing individuals for corporate crimes was difficult because corporate directors were considered to be merely employees of the company. A popular saying noted that a corporation had "neither a soul to be damned nor a body to be kicked." Such advantages helped spur the growth of corporations—by 1904 almost 70 percent of all manufacturing employees worked for corporations.

Perhaps the greatest advantage of corporations was their ability to raise large amounts of capital. The expansion of industry in the late nineteenth century required big infusions of money. Farmers needed new machinery to increase productivity; manufacturers needed new plants to utilize the latest technology; cities needed new construction to service the needs of the urban population.

From where was all this money to come? Some, of course, was generated by the rising gross national product—the total value of goods and services produced in one year—which grew from $225 per person in 1870 to nearly $500 in 1900. New technology increased productivity and put "extra" money into the hands of middle and upper class people—money not required to meet physical needs. Many chose to use the extra money, or capital, to make more money by investing it. This "capital deepening" meant an increasing

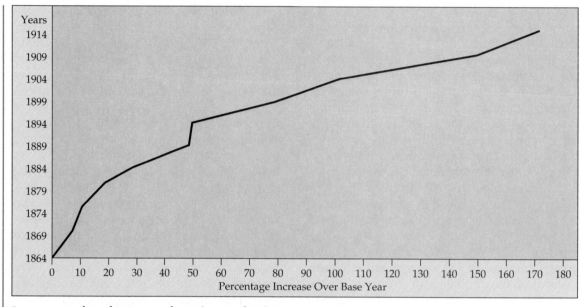

FIGURE 17.2 **Index of U.S. Manufacturing Production, 1864–1914**

share of the national income was invested rather than spent for personal consumption, capital formation almost doubling by the 1880s.

Increasing amounts of this capital were invested in manufacturing partly because investment bankers such as J. P. Morgan marketed corporate stocks and bonds. Foreign investment was also important; by 1900 Europeans had $3.4 billion invested in the United States, which represented approximately one-third of the almost $10 billion invested in manufacturing. This was indeed rich fertilizer for growth.

The net result of the favorable conditions of the late nineteenth century was the industrial supremacy of the United States. Vast mineral wealth, technological breakthroughs, population changes, growth of railroads, popular support, beneficial government policies, liberal corporation laws, and the availability of capital fostered this transformation and Americans reveled in it. At first these favorable conditions worked like overfertilized land—too many plants were produced for the available space and resources. This overgrowth created chaos until such entrepreneurs as Andrew Carnegie found ways to prune away their rivals.

THE RISE OF BIG BUSINESS

"You might as well endeavor to stay the formation of clouds, the falling of rains, the flowing of streams, as to attempt . . . to prevent the organization of industry." These words of John D. Rockefeller's attorney described what he considered to be the inevitable domination of entire industries by large corporations. Over the years in industry after industry men like Rockefeller, Morgan, and Carnegie eliminated competitors and controlled markets. The impact of this consolidation of industry was enormous. As companies grew larger, new management styles and more white-collar workers were needed. Mass production increased—profoundly changing the nature of work for industrial laborers. Giant corporations thus amassed great power over production, people, and politics.

Controlling Competition

Most business leaders did not really advocate free enterprise fueled by competition. To them competition meant chaos, and they sought to eliminate it. J. P. Morgan, one historian wrote, "felt that the American economy should ideally be like a company organizational chart, with each part in its proper place, and the lines of authority clearly designated. He did not really believe in the free enterprise system, and like most ardent socialists, he hated the waste, duplication, and clutter of unrestrained competition."

As America's first big business, the railroad industry was also the first to confront the problems of competition. In some regions too many companies were after the same traffic. Some railroads desperately wooed shippers by giving lower rates for bulk shipments and long hauls. They also gave "rebates"—secret kickbacks below their published prices—to some preferred customers. They then sought to make up for that lost revenue by overcharging smaller shippers.

Such tactics did not solve the railroads' problems, however, especially when rate wars broke out. In the 1870s some railroad managers tried cooperation as a cure for competition. They formed "pools," regional federations to divide traffic equitably and to raise rates to increase profits. Pools were not legally enforceable, however, and greed frequently doomed many.

For the railroads, consolidation—often through ruthless tactics—rather than cooperation became the key to controlling competition. The former shipping magnate Cornelius Vanderbilt gained control of the New York Central Railroad in 1867 by buying two key lines that connected with it. He then refused to accept any rail cars going to or from the Central. In response to criticism Vanderbilt replied, "Can't I do what I want with my own?" Elsewhere other buyouts and mergers eventually reduced the number of competitors—especially after the economic depressions of the 1870s and 1890s.

Like the railroads, the oil industry suffered from the proliferation of small companies and dramatically fluctuating prices. John D. Rockefeller, founder of the Standard Oil Company, lamented that "the butcher, the baker, and the candlestick maker began to refine oil." Rockefeller first tried a combination of pooling and rebates to deal with this problem. In 1872 he organized the South

After a period of intense competition in the railroad industry, a few rail barons consolidated lines often by using unscrupulous methods, seemingly to carve up the nation at will, as illustrated by this cartoon.

Improvement Company—a combine of oil refiners and railroad directors aimed at dividing the oil carriage trade between the railroads. In return for a guaranteed share of the shipments, Rockefeller convinced the railroads to give rebates. Eventually Rockefeller was able to obtain rebates not only on the oil he shipped but also on the shipments of his competitors. Thus Rockefeller could undersell his competitors, whom he often bought out during times of economic depression.

Although such techniques allowed Rockefeller to ultimately control 90 percent of the oil business, legal problems arose from Standard Oil's far-flung holdings. His solution was the *trust*. In 1882 he convinced the major stockholders in a number of refineries to surrender their stock to a board of nine trustees. In return the stockholders received trust certificates that entitled them to a share of the joint profits of all the refineries. Because pools had no legal standing, they could be manipulated by some members to the detriment of other members. In a trust, however, competitive actions were of no benefit. Everyone shared all losses and gains. Soon trusts began popping up throughout the economy.

Andrew Carnegie disliked pools and trusts, but he found other ways to gain a competitive edge. One of these was *vertical integration*—buying the sources of his raw materials (iron ore and coke) and later many of the transportation facilities needed to distribute his product. He thus was able to bring down his costs and control his supply and shipping costs, resulting in lower final product prices.

The key to Carnegie's success was his ability to cut costs without lowering quality. He used such traditional measures as wage cuts and increased hours for workers, but he also constantly explored new methods of increasing produc-

Andrew Carnegie rose from an immigrant bobbin-boy in a textile mill to control the U.S. steel industry.

tivity. When told that a plant had broken all records the previous week, he replied "Congratulations! Why not do it every week?" He did not focus only on short-term profits, but was willing to invest in expensive new technology to lower long-term costs of production. He reportedly opened one board meeting with the question, "Well, what shall we throw away this year?"

Carnegie often boasted that he knew almost nothing about making steel—he hired experts to do that. He did know how to run a company and make money. By effectively using all the economies of scale available to large firms, Carnegie was able to undersell and destroy most of the steel companies that had sprung up in response to the increased demand from railroads and industry. He also was a master at exploiting downturns in business cycles. Most of his acquisitions were made during economic depressions, when prices were lower.

Although competitors and labor movements suffered from Carnegie's actions, the result was better steel at cheaper prices. As Carnegie once noted, "Two pounds of ironstone mined upon Lake Superior and transported nine hundred miles to Pittsburgh; one pound and one half of coal, mined and manufactured into coke, and transported to Pittsburgh; a small amount of manganese ore mined in Virginia and brought to Pittsburgh . . . these four pounds of materials [are] manufactured into one pound of steel, for which the consumer pays one cent." And cheap steel aided the expansion of the railroads and the rise of other industries.

Of course, Carnegie was well-paid for providing these benefits—receiving around $350 million dollars when he sold Carnegie Steel to J. P. Morgan. That sale illustrates another factor in consolidation: bankers. Morgan and other bankers often stepped in during economic panics to reorganize bankrupt companies. They chewed up failing companies and railroads and spat them out as single supercorporations. The result was a more orderly economy and increased production, but at the price of centralizing vast economic power into the hands of a few unelected individuals. One wit quipped when

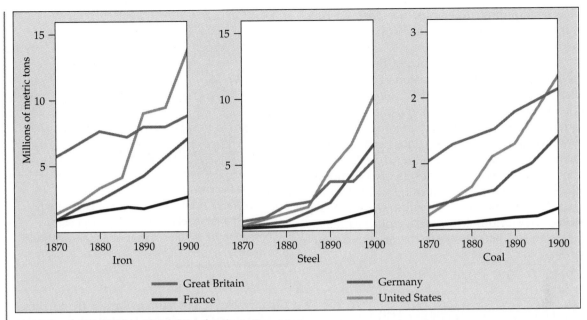

FIGURE 17.3 Iron, Steel, and Coal Production, 1870–1900
Source: Carl N. Degler, The Age of Economic Revolution. Copyright © 1977 by Scott, Foresman and Co.

U.S. Steel was formed: "God created the world in 4004 B.C. and J. P. Morgan reorganized it in 1901."

New Managerial Styles and an Expanding Middle Class

Consolidation into giant corporations created the need for new management techniques, and again the railroads pioneered. As railroad companies grew larger, their activities covered hundreds of miles and employed thousands of workers. Safety and market conditions required that the entire system operate as a single unit under a tight schedule, which caused managerial problems. In the beginning, as one railroad expert wrote, "management had been personal and autocratic; the superintendent, a man gifted with energy and clearness of perception, molded the property to his own will. But as the properties grew, he found himself unable to give his personal attention to everything. Undaunted, he sought to do everything and do it well. He ended by doing nothing."

Railroad management thus required a division of responsibilities and a level of coordination previously unknown in business. Erie Railroad employee Daniel McCallum created the first organizational table for an American company in the 1850s. It had a chain of command moving from local train agents to the president and board of directors, and responsibilities were divided on a functional basis, with top management separate from daily operations. Since railroads also needed better accounting procedures to keep track of the monies collected and paid out, management and accounting of funds became the function of the controller's office. A cost-accounting system was adopted to provide accurate data to judge the performance of the various lines.

Other large businesses began to adopt the accounting methods, hierarchical administrative structures, and divisions of responsibilities pioneered by the railroads. "Middle management" was thus created to coordinate the operations of far-flung local plants and bring reports to top executives. Big businesses were now run by bureaucracies staffed by white-collar workers, who had no role in founding the companies they served but who began to work their way up the bureaucratic ladder.

A profound consequence of the new economic order was the expansion of the middle class. Corporations needed accountants, middle managers, clerical workers, and sales representatives. Urban growth created demands for professionals, shopkeepers, and government employees. Between the Civil War and the 1890s the average earnings of the middle class rose nearly 30 percent. By 1900 more than a third of urban families owned their homes. The middle class clearly derived benefits from and had a stake in the new economic order.

Because the emergence of gigantic trusts concentrated economic power into relatively few hands, many people saw the trusts as the real "bosses of the Senate," as shown in this political cartoon.

Mass Marketing, Assembly Lines, and Mass Production

Some economic historians contend that of all the factors spurring industrial growth none was more important than the rise of an American mass market. Both the urban population boom and the transportation revolution created markets unparalleled in vastness and accessibility. But such markets would not have inevitably led to mass production and mass marketing without the public's acceptance of standardized goods. Several factors made Americans more receptive than Europeans to such goods. Class distinctions, although not absent, were more blurred and became increasingly so with the availability of ready-made clothing. Also, physical mobility broke down many of the local loyalties so prevalent in Europe. These factors created opportunities that modern mass advertising was quick to exploit. Nowhere were changes greater than in the food industry.

Food processors originally only produced limited quantities for nearby markets. When transportation advances widened distribution areas, producers used wholesale merchants and agents to sell their goods to the public. Then the communication revolution transformed the marketing of consumer goods. Manufacturers could now peddle their wares

directly to the consumer. Rather than selling nonperishable foods by the barrel to wholesalers, they now packaged them in smaller containers of standard size and weight. By 1900, they were spending $90 million annually to convince Americans of the advantages of specific brand names—modern advertising had embarked on its unending quest to shape public tastes.

Meanwhile the same drastic transformation was taking place in the meat-packing business. The railroads again played a key role by opening up the grazing ranges of the Great Plains. Because of its rail network, Chicago quickly became the major funnel through which cattle were distributed from West to East. Cattle were shipped from its Union Stock Yards, to abattoirs, or slaughterhouses, on the outskirts of eastern cities. The meat was then distributed through local butchers to city residents.

There were several problems with such a distribution system, chief of which was stock deterioration during long train journeys. Until the advent of the refrigerated car, however, the only alternative was pickling or curing meat—processes that had made Chicago the pork-packing center but were not as well suited to beef.

Gustavus Swift, a Boston cattle buyer who had moved to Chicago, hired an engineer to design a refrigerated train car for safely shipping fresh meat long distances, with the first successful shipment in 1877. Swift also recognized the possibilities of centralized slaughtering, one of which was using all waste products (horns into buttons, hooves into glue, for example) and thus increasing profits. Eventually he formed glue, fertilizer, soap, and glycerin factories. People said that he used every part of the pig except the squeal.

Swift also pioneered assembly-line mass production. He subdivided the slaughtering and packing process into numerous distinct jobs as carcasses moved along on overhead conveyor belts. There was little wasted motion, and, as one of Swift's superintendents noted, "If you need to turn out a little more, you speed up the conveyor a little and the men speed up to keep pace."

In meat packing, machinery did not replace workers—their work was merely subdivided to increase efficiency. In other industries, machines were created to replace hand labor after the work had been broken down into simple, repetitive tasks. Mass production by machine worked best when the products were made from standardized, interchangeable parts. Such parts had been used before the Civil War, but early part-cutting machines were not very precise. Workers still had to hand-file most metal pieces before they were fit together. New inventions improved the machine tool industry; for example, the turret lathe automatically made a series of complex cuts in metal with great speed and accuracy. The stage was now set to mass produce large numbers of standardized goods.

The Power of Bigness

The creation of the gigantic U.S. Steel Corporation was not an isolated occurrence. By 1904 a single firm in each of 50 different industries accounted for 60 percent or more of the total output in that industry. Such concentrations of economic power alarmed many Americans, although competition was never entirely eliminated, and consolidation brought such benefits as lower prices. The transition from local, independently owned shops and factories to giant national corporations with impersonal boards of directors dramatically altered the work and leisure time of the American people. For individuals the transition was often painful, and the economy experienced a frightening cycle of boom and bust. Periodic depressions rocked the nation, causing widespread unemployment and business failures.

Big business also created a class of millionaires who flaunted ostentatious homes and lavish life-styles. For example, during the 1897 depression Mr. and Mrs. Bradley Martin gave a costume ball to which they invited most of the richest people in New York. The Waldorf-Astoria Hotel was redecorated to resemble the palace at Versailles in France. The hostess was dressed as Mary, Queen of Scots and wore an enormous ruby necklace that had once adorned Queen Marie Antoinette. One guest came in a $10,000 suit of armor inlaid with gold. Those few hours of entertainment cost the Marins $369,000.

In 1890 about 11 million of the 12.5 million families in the United States averaged less than $380 a year in income, so it is obvious that all did not share equally in the economic expansion of the era. Wealth had always been concentrated and industrialization only continued the trend. In 1890 the bulk of wealth was concentrated in less than 10 percent of the population, while 0.03 percent of the population controlled 20 percent of the wealth. Many

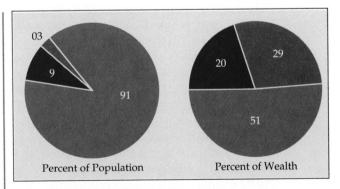

FIGURE 17.4 **Distribution of Wealth, 1890**
The bulk of the wealth was concentrated in less than 10 percent of the population, while 0.03 percent of the population controlled 20 percent of the wealth.
Source: George K. Holmes, "The Concentration of Wealth," Political Science Quarterly, vol. 8, no. 4, December 1893, p. 593.

This portrait of the family of William Astor illustrates the lavish life-style of the rich. Their parties were especially ostentatious—at one, guests smoked cigarettes rolled in one hundred dollar bills after drinking coffee.

people resented or envied the life-styles such wealth provided, and they feared the power it produced.

Government and organized labor remained relatively small while big business grew. Business leaders wielded enormous power over many phases of American life. Some of their actions benefited the nation but were taken in a high-handed manner. For example, to simplify schedules, in 1883 railroad owners established four time zones—without consulting any branch of government. And some of the freewheeling railroad barons only aggravated the fears such arbitrary power raised. Vanderbilt once remarked, "What do I care about the law? Hain't I got the power?" Another time a member of the Pennsylvania legislature reportedly said, "Mr. Speaker, I move we adjourn unless the Pennsylvania Railroad has some more business to conduct."

The railroad industry pioneered the accumulation and use of economic power, but others followed in their footsteps, often corrupting politics. Popular outcries eventually forced congressional action to curb their excesses (see Chapter 19).

VARIETIES OF ECONOMIC CHANGE IN THE WEST AND SOUTH

Although most industrialization occurred in the Northeast, all regions of the country experienced profound changes as a national, interdependent economy emerged. Some of the forces feeding the growth of industry also fueled agricultural expansion. Rural population kept growing, although not as rapidly as urban population. Even as the number of farms and farmers more than doubled, farmers became a minority of the population. Most of the new farmers were in the West, where new settlers competed with existing populations to exploit the region's economic potential. Demand by urban dwellers for food sparked a farming revolution made possible by mechanization and scientific agriculture. For a variety of reasons, the South failed to keep pace with the rest of the nation. Despite numerous efforts to forge a "New South," the region's economy failed to keep pace with the rest of the nation.

Western Expansion and Exploitation

The transcontinental railroads were laid across what was called the "Great American Desert" in order to link the East and West coasts, not to "open up" the West. The perceived worthlessness of the Plains was reflected in the willingness at first to give much of it away—first to Native Americans and later to the railroads.

Confrontations between miners—the first actors in the drama of western expansion— and Native Americans foreshadowed the eventual expulsion of the American Indians from land that had been "given" to them "forever." But "forever" lasted only until the white men realized the region's true value. From then on, competition for resources among a diverse number of populations marked the history and culture of the West, creating a distinctly American mosaic. Anglo-Americans came to dominate Western economic development, but their lives and how they worked were shaped by earlier Native American and Hispanic societies as well as by African-American and Asian immigrants.

In addition to mineral wealth, the region had two other plentiful resources: grass and cattle. The railroads played a significant role in exploiting the new land by getting the cattle to eastern cities that wanted more meat. Western ranching was born.

At first, ranching, like placer mining (in which loose ore was washed from gravel), did not require much capital. Both the cows and grass were free. By 1860, there were some five million head of wild Texas longhorn descendants of cattle imported by Spanish colonists. They replaced the buffalo that were being hunted to virtual extinction. Although cattle were so plentiful that they were considered almost worthless in the West, steers sold for $30 to $50 a head in Chicago. All that was needed was a way to get them there. Joseph G. McCoy realized the potential for profit and established the first "cowtown" at Abilene, Kansas, where he built stock pens and loading chutes. Cowboys would "drive" cattle there for shipment by rail to Chicago. Other cowtowns arose as some six million head of cattle were driven to such sites between 1866 and 1888.

Since longhorns were not easily captured or herded on foot, settlers used methods of the

In the heyday of the open range, hundreds of thousands of wild cattle were rounded up to be driven to cowtowns for shipment to Chicago.

The Wild West

AT 6 P.M. or April 5, 1892, a mysterious train, its shades tightly drawn, pulled out of Cheyenne, Wyoming, the state capital, bound for Casper, 200 miles to the northwest. Aboard the train were 46 vigilantes heavily armed with an impressive array of weapons including army rifles, dynamite, and strychnine. The train had been chartered by Wyoming's cattle kings. The vigilantes' mission: kill Johnson County settlers suspected of cattle rustling.

For more than two decades, the cattlemen had accused homesteaders of land grabbing and cattle theft. Juries refused to convict the small stockmen, so the cattle barons responded by taking the law into their own hands. In one incident, on the night of July 20, 1889, ten cattlemen captured two homesteaders and hanged them from a stunted pine tree. Altogether six or seven suspected rustlers were shot or hanged. Despite lynchings and shootings, the rustling continued. In the summer of 1891, the cattle barons decided to launch an armed invasion of Johnson County and kill the most notorious rustlers. The Wyoming Stock Growers' Association, asked to provide names of suspected rustlers, compiled a list of 70 purported cattle thieves. The invasion was scheduled for the following spring.

On Saturday, April 9, 1892, the vigilantes killed two suspected rustlers at K C Ranch near the southern edge of Johnson County. Word quickly spread to Buffalo, Wyoming, the county seat, 46 miles to the north. There, 200 small stock-

men formed a posse to avenge the murders. They caught up with the vigilantes at the T A Ranch, 14 miles south of Buffalo, and surrounded them.

Before they could be captured, however, the cavalry rode to the rescue early on Wednesday, April 13. Wyoming's acting governor and the state's senators had sent frantic telegrams to President Benjamin Harrison declaring that a state of insurrection existed in Johnson County and asking that the U.S. cavalry be sent in to quell the disturbances. The invaders, who included several federal marshals and state officials, were escorted out of Johnson County. Although they charged with first-degree murder, the charges were late dropped. The Johnson County war was over.

Today it is commonly assumed that the roots of violence in Ameri-

can society lie in our frontier heritage of violence and lawlessness. According to popular mythology—disseminated by dime novels, pulp newspapers, and television and movie westerns—the frontier was a lawless land populated by violent men: outlaws, stagecoach robbers, gunslingers, vigilantes, claim jumpers, cattle rustlers, horse thieves, Indian fighters, border ruffians, and mule skinners.

But how violent was the Wild West? Certain forms of violence and lawlessness were indeed common: warfare between Native Americans and whites, attacks on Chinese and Mexican minorities, vigilantism, rowdyism, drunkenness, opium addiction, gambling, vigilante executions, stagecoach robberies, and gunfights. Racially motivated acts of brutality represented the ugliest side of frontier violence. In 1871, in one of the most

ers averaged over 65 hours a week, steelworkers over 66, and canners nearly 77. Even as late as 1920, skilled workers still averaged 50.4 hours a week and the unskilled 53.7 hours. Before the 1930s, workers regarded an 8-hour day or even a 10-hour day as an unattainable dream.

The new ideals of industrial America created even more work for women. The increased emphasis on cleanliness led to a demand for tidier homes. As a result, women now devoted more time to cleaning, dusting, and scrubbing. New washable cotton fabrics increased the amount of laundering. And more varied diets meant women spent more time plucking feathers from chickens, soaking and blanching hams, roasting coffee beans, grinding whole spices and sugar, and cooking meals. By 1900 the typical housewife worked six hours a day on just two tasks:

Factory owners demanded standards of work, behavior, and punctuality that left the industrial worker little leisure time or energy. Workers campaigned unsuccessfully for an eight-hour workday during the late nineteenth century.

meal preparation and cleaning—in addition to the time she already spent on other household tasks.

Worker Discontent

Although workers complained regularly about wages and hours, they were equally disturbed by several other aspects of industrialization. The late-nineteenth-century industries differed from the preindustrial workshop in four important areas: size, discipline, mechanization, and displacement of skill. The huge new factories, employing hundreds or even thousands of laborers, needed an organized, disciplined workforce. Workers were carefully regulated to ensure maximum productivity. Work itself became formalized and structured, and several levels of bureaucrats separating the owner from workers emerged. There was an incredible boom in productivity, and the informal preindustrial workshop, with its handful of employees, was an inevitable casualty.

Mechanization also caused an erosion of certain skilled trades. Newly invented machines performed tasks previously done by skilled artisans. For example, once a single tailor took a piece of cloth, cut it, fashioned it, and sewed it into a pair of pants; by 1859 a Cincinnati clothing factory had divided the process into 17 different semiskilled jobs. This replacement of highly skilled by semiskilled workers was characteristic of the factory system. By the end of the century, it appeared to many observers that *all* work was being mechanized and moving toward a factory mode. Even farmers followed the mechanization march. By the early 1880s, one Dakota Territory wheat farm—or "food factory" as a critic called it—stretched over 30,000 acres, used 20 reapers and 30 steam-powered threshers, and employed 1000 field hands. Workers did not know their bosses, but this impersonality was offset by a remarkable increase in output.

In the long run, industrialization brought much to many. From a worker's perspective, however, industrialization was often an inhumane process. Factory labor tended to be monotonous, and machines made work more dangerous. Industrial accidents were alarmingly common—careless or tired workers sacrificed fingers, hands, arms, and sometimes even lives. Frequent production speedups increased the chances of injury. In one year at Armour's meat-packing plant in Chicago, 22,381 workers were injured or became ill. Conditions were much the same at Swift's meat-packing plant.

To make matters even worse, owners concerned with production quotas and cost efficiency, often assumed an uncaring attitude toward their laborers. Many were indeed insensitive. One factory manager even proclaimed, "I regard my people as I regard my machinery. So long as they can do my work for what I choose to pay them, I keep them, getting out of them all I can. What they do or how they fare outside my walls I don't know, nor do I consider it my business to know. They must look out for themselves as I do myself."

Where once it was workers who determined their production and work pace, factory managers with stopwatches now made laborers account for their time by seconds.

Workers particularly resented scientific time-motion experts who strove to get the maximum production out of every laborer. Frederick W. Taylor, the father of "scientific management," believed that his ideas benefited labor as well as management. Instead, his aim "to induce men to act as nearly like machines as possible" promoted monotony and displaced workers—especially skilled ones.

Workers did not passively accept industrialization and the changes it caused. They resisted change at almost every step and they had formidable weapons at their disposal. On one level, resistance entailed a simple, individual decision not to change completely. Despite demanding a steady, dependable workforce, factory managers were plagued by chronic absenteeism. Immigrant workers refused to labor on religious holidays, and in some towns factories had to shut down on the day the circus arrived. Across America, heavy drinking on Sunday led to "blue Monday," a euphemism for absenteeism.

Another form of individual protest was quitting. Most industrial workers changed jobs at least every three years, and in many in-

Workers at Swift's meat-packing plant wield huge cleavers as they impassively go about their tasks. A slip of the cleaver could mean the loss of a limb or even a life.

dustries the annual turnover rate was over 100 percent. Some quit because they were bored, "forced to work too hard," or because they were struck by spring wanderlust and simply wanted to move on. Others quit because of severe discipline, unsafe working conditions, or low wages. This compulsive quitting was a clear indication that perhaps 20 percent of the workforce never came to terms with industrialization.

Workers were similarly quick to take collective action. The late nineteenth century witnessed the most sustained and violent industrial conflict in the nation's history. Strikes were as common as political corruption during the period—Bureau of Labor Statistics estimated that 9668 strikes and lockouts occurred between 1881 and 1890. Although most of these conflicts were relatively peaceful, some were so violent that citizens across the nation feared that America was moving toward another revolution.

Early Labor Violence

An early, violent conflict occurred in the anthracite coal region of eastern Pennsylvania. During the depression of the mid-1870s, mine owners agreed to cut wages and increase workloads in the mines. This sort of oppression was nothing new to the Irish, and they responded much as they had in the Old Country, Ireland. While the Workingmen's Benevolent Association (WBA) battled owners at the negotiating table, the Ancient Order of Hibernians, a secret fraternal society of Irish immigrants, and its inner circle, the Molly Maguires, waged a violent guerrilla war in the coalfields in 1877. They disrupted the operation of several mines and attacked a handful of mining officials.

The mine owners infiltrated the group with a secret agent, James McParlan, who agreed to inform on his fellow Irishmen for the Pinkerton agency. While McParlan was gathering information, the WBA went on strike. Disorder and violence followed. Through the local press, management convinced much of the community that there was a direct link between the WBA, the Mollies,

and the bloodshed. The tactic worked and the strike was broken. A short time later, McParlan's testimony was used to destroy both the Mollies and the WBA. Altogether, 20 Mollies were convicted and executed after sensational trials. It was a scenario that industrialists would use again and again. Their greatest weapon against strikers was the community's fear of violence.

The same depression that convulsed the Pennsylvania coalfields shook the rest of the country. To keep from going under, many businessmen cut rates and attempted to recoup their losses by reducing labor costs. This was true especially in the highly competitive railroad business. Workers, most often unskilled, suffered repeated wage cuts. Workingmen, one railroad worker declared in 1877, "know what it is to bring up a family on ninety cents a day, to live on beans and cornmeal week in and week out, to run in debt at the stores until you cannot get trusted any longer, to see the wife breaking down under privation and distress, and the children growing up sharp and fierce like wolves day after day because they don't get enough to eat." That knowledge drove many workers to desperate lengths.

During the dog days of mid-July 1877, the Baltimore and Ohio Railroad (B&O) announced its third consecutive 10 percent wage cut. Angry, frustrated, hot, and hungry railroad workers along the line, led by the new Trainmen's Union, went on strike. When trouble followed, B&O workers seized an important junction at Martinsburg, West Virginia. The state militia and local sheriffs sympathized with the workers but could not end the strike. President Rutherford B. Hayes sent in federal troops to protect an army of strikebreakers.

From Martinsburg the strike spread. Railroad workers walked off their jobs, and trains sat unused. The strike paralyzed transportation in the Midwest and much of the industrial Northeast. Violence and destruction seemed to be everywhere. In Baltimore the state militia shot into a mob and killed ten persons; in Pittsburgh rioters burned 2000 freight cars, looted stores, and torched railroad buildings; in Buffalo, Chicago, and

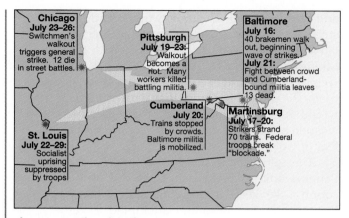

The Great Railroad Strike, 1877
During the spontaneous uprising that followed the railroad strike of 1877 two-thirds of the nation's track was paralyzed for two weeks and millions of dollars worth of railroad property was destroyed.

Indianapolis workers and police engaged in bloody battles.

When local police and state militiamen failed to control the situation, President Hayes ordered more federal troops in to do the job. Eventually, superior force restored peace and the trains started rolling again, but not before more than a hundred strikers were killed. Like most spontaneous strikes, the Great Strike of 1877 failed. But the anger it revealed frightened America. Although some authorities labeled the disturbances as the work of communist agitators, more thoughtful observers knew workers had legitimate grievances. For owners and workers alike, the strike was a lesson. Owners learned that workers were not merely passive partners in the industrial process. Labor learned that when pressed, the federal government was not neutral—it would side with capital.

At the same time, economic consolidation increased the power of industrialists such as Carnegie, Rockefeller, and Swift. Men who believed that they knew what was best for themselves and their workers, their confidence bred arrogance. A sense of superiority and self-righteousness ran through their public statements. For example, one textile company manager confidently declared, "There is such a thing as too much education for working people . . . I have seen cases where young people were spoiled for labor by being educated to a little too much refinement."

The power of industrialists can be seen in the famous Haymarket Square riot of 1886. In 1885, skilled molders at McCormick Harvester Machine Company in Chicago won a 15 percent pay increase after a strike. Reacting angrily to the union's activities, McCormick introduced pneumatic molders that could be run by unskilled workers. The skilled workers went on strike again in 1886, but with different results. The combination of McCormick's forces and local police ensured the safety of an army of strikebreakers and the plant's output continued until the strike was broken.

Tempers, however, remained high, and violence resulted. In May, after the strike ended, police and workers clashed once again, and a number of laborers were killed and wounded. Disturbed by the violence used by police in defense of industrialists' positions, August Spies, a Chicago anarchist and labor agitator who edited the radical newspaper *Arbeiter Zeitung*, called for a protest meeting in Haymarket Square, a location that could hold 20,000 persons. On the evening of May 4, a small and generally unenthusiastic crowd of about 3000 labor supporters gathered in the rain. The speeches were dull and the listeners were peaceful. But as the meeting was breaking up, local police unexpectedly charged the crowd. Then somebody—to this day no one knows who—threw a bomb into the melee, killing both police and protesters. Surrounded by a fog of confusion and anger, the police opened fire, shooting protesters and even, accidentally, each other.

Industrialists, city officials, ministers, and the local press convinced a bewildered public that the bombing was a prelude to anarchistic revolution. Police arrested eight local radicals, including Spies, and charged them with conspiracy. Despite no real evidence against them, the eight were tried and convicted, and seven were sentenced to be hanged. One man committed suicide in his cell and three were eventually pardoned, but Spies and three others were executed. For radicals, labor agitators, and unionists, the message was clear: Police and public opinion were on the side of the industrialists.

The excessive violence of the Molly Maguires, the Great Strike of 1877, and the Haymarket Square riot were not necessarily typical of disputes between labor and management. Although labor violence continued in the 1890s, with such dramatic episodes as the Homestead strike and the Pullman strike (see Chapter 19), late-nineteenth-century labor disputes often were settled peacefully. In most cases, however, management was the winner. Only in small towns, where prolabor and anti-industrial sentiment knew no class

lines, did labor battle management on anything approaching even terms.

Unorganized and Organized Labor

Historians have used the term *robber barons* to characterize late-nineteenth-century industrialists. Whether "robber" is accurate or not is debatable, but "baron" is a fitting description. They controlled their industries as medieval barons ruled their fiefs. Their word was usually final, and such a modern concept as democracy did not find a sympathetic environment inside factory walls. A Pennsylvania coal miner described the situation accurately: "They

The famous Haymarket Square riot of 1886 began as a peaceful protest meeting. The arrest and conviction of eight local radicals without any real evidence against them sent a message to workers: police and public opinion side with the industrialists.

find monopolies as strong as government itself. They find capital as rigid as absolute monarchy. They find their so-called independence a myth, and that their subjection to power is as complete as when their forefathers were part and parcel of the baronial estate."

In the last third of the nineteenth century, labor was unable to form an organization powerful enough to deal with capital on equal terms. Before 1900, most unions were weak, with goals that were often out of touch with the changing American economy. In addition, the labor force itself was divided along ethnic, racial, gender, and craft lines. During this period, however, labor attempted to overcome its own divisions and fumble its way toward a clearer vision of what were its own best interests.

Before the 1870s most American unions were locally rooted, craft-based organizations. They were geared to the small workshop of Jacksonian America, not to the large modern factory. The first union to attempt to organize all workers was the short-lived National Labor Union (NLU), founded in Baltimore in 1866. Besides shorter work hours and higher wages, the NLU supported the rights of women and African Americans, monetary reform, and worker-owned industries. As one of their leaders said, the "only way by which the toiling masses can protect themselves against the unjust claims and soul-crushing tyranny of capital" was for "themselves to become capitalists." Rich in ideas and solutions, the NLU was poor in organization and finances, and it died during the depression of the mid–1870s.

The NLU's was carried on by the Noble and Holy Order of the Knights of Labor. Begun in 1869 as a secret fraternal order as well as a union, the Knights remained small and unimportant until 1878 when it went public. Led by Terence V. Powderly, a machinist and former mayor of Scranton, Pennsylvania, in 1881 the Knights opened its membership not only to "any person working for wages but to anyone who had at any time worked for wages." The Knights excluded only bankers, lawyers, liquor dealers, speculators, and stockbrokers, whom they viewed as money manipulators and exploiters.

Complete worker solidarity was the Knights' goal. "An injury to one is an injury to all," they proclaimed. They welcomed and spoke for all laborers—women and men, black and white, immigrant and native, unskilled and skilled. Like the NLU, the Knights rejected industrial capitalism and favored cooperatively owned industries. "The aim of the Knights of Labor," Powderly emphasized, "is to make each man his own employer." Although critics at the time labeled the Knights "wild-eyed, utopian visionaries," they are best understood in the context of exploited workers searching for a less exploitive alternative to industrial capitalism. If their statements were extreme, their suffering was real.

An able leader, Powderly called for reforms of the currency system, the abolition of child labor, regulation of trusts' and monopolies, an end to alien contract labor networks, and government ownership of public utilities. By nature a diplomatic, good-natured man, he favored peaceful arbitration of labor disputes and opposed strikes. He also opposed the formation of narrow trade unions, instead advocating that skilled workers should assist the unskilled. Harmony and fellowship ultimately dominated his vision of America's future. Consensus, not conflict, was his goal.

The Knights' rhetoric found receptive listeners among American workers, and membership rolls grew during the early 1880s. Then came 1884, the beginning of what labor historians have called "the great upheaval." Strikes erupted in the coalfields of Pennsylvania and Ohio and the railroad yards of Missouri and Illinois. The labor conflicts continued into 1885 and 1886. Labor won some, but by no means all, of the strikes. Although its role was small, the Knights were associated with several important labor victories. By mid–1886 perhaps 750,000 workers had joined the Knights.

From that high point, however, the Knights declined rapidly. From the start, they could not weld together the diverse rank and file. Administrative and organizational problems surfaced, and Powderly's relatively conservative leadership was opposed by more radical members, who fully accepted strikes and conflict. The Haymarket Square bombing in 1886 branded all unions as un-American and violent in the public mind. By 1893, when Powderly was driven from office, the Knights' membership had declined alarmingly. Weakened and divided, it failed to survive the depression of the mid-1890s.

Unlike the NLU and the Knights, the American Federation of Labor (AFL) did not aspire to remake society. Its leaders accepted industrial capitalism and rejected partisan politics and the dreams of radical visionaries. Instead they concentrated on practical, reachable goals—higher wages, shorter workdays, and improved working conditions. Most importantly, they only recruited skilled laborers, recognizing that easily replaceable unskilled workers were in a poor position to negotiate with employers.

Formed in 1886 by the coming together of skilled-trade unions, the AFL was led ably by Samuel Gompers, a Jewish immigrant from England who had been the president of a New York cigar makers' union. Like many cigar makers, Gompers was well, if informally, educated. Cigar-rolling was a quiet job, and the rollers often employed one of their number as a reader. As a boy Gompers not only learned a skill, but he absorbed the leading political, economic, and literary ideas of his day. "In fact," Gompers later wrote, "these [readings and] discussions in the shops were more like public debating societies . . . 'labor forums.'"

As the head of the AFL for almost 40 years, Gompers used his considerable "moral power" and organizational ability to fight for *achievable* goals. American laborers were divided over religious, racial, ethnic, gender, and political issues, but they all desired higher wages, more leisure time, and greater liberty. Working out of his eight-by-ten-foot office, and using tomato boxes for filing cases, Gompers battled for those unifying issues. He focused on the world around him, not on the best of all possible worlds. Once effectively organized, he maintained, labor could deal with capital on equal terms.

Gompers's approach toward working with capital and organizing labor proved successful in the long run. Before 1900, however, the AFL was not more successful than the Knights or the NLU. In fact, workers benefited little from unions before the turn of the century. Fewer than 5 percent of American workers joined trade unions, and the major areas of industrial growth were the least unionized. Nevertheless, the experimentation during the late nineteenth century taught workers valuable lessons: to combat the power of capital, labor needed equal power. During the twentieth century labor would move closer to that power.

CONCLUSION

In one generation the United States became the economic colossus of the world. After a heated period of intense competition, mergers forged supercorporations that controlled the majority of their industries. This economic expansion and consolidation provided many benefits. In some cases people were able to buy superior goods at cheaper prices. (As Edwin Atkinson noted in 1886, "Did Vanderbilt keep any of you down by saving you two dollars and seventy-five cents on a barrel of flour, while he was making fourteen cents?") And social mobility did increase. Although some skilled artisans slipped downward on the social ladder, upward mobility rates usually doubled the downward rates. Of course not all shared equally. Few duplicated Andrew Carnegie's transition from rags to riches.

Average annual incomes rose steadily for almost all classes of workers, although wage increases rarely equaled the rising cost of living. Nevertheless, most families' standard of living improved because more members of the family worked for wages. Items that had been considered luxuries soon became viewed as necessities.

Individuals, however, paid huge social costs for these advances. Some paid a disproportionate share. Patterns of working and living changed dramatically. Many workers' new status imperiled their independence. Personal relationships were being replaced by impersonal, contractual arrangements. Workers confronted the changes, and some sought to organize themselves to offset the overwhelming advantages enjoyed by management. In short, all of the late nineteenth century is the story of profound transformation

CHRONOLOGY
OF KEY EVENTS

1856	Bessemer steelmaking process is invented
1859	Edwin Drake drills the first commercial oil well in Titusville, Pennsylvania
1861	Morrill Tariff is passed; first of a series of high protective tariffs
1862	Homestead Act gives 160 acres of free public land to those who will cultivate it for five years; Morrill Land Grant Act establishes many technical and agricultural colleges
1866	National Labor Union is founded in Baltimore; Cyrus W. Field lays the first successful transatlantic telegraph cable
1869	First transcontinental railroad is completed on May 10
1870	John D. Rockefeller founds Standard Oil Company
1873	Timber Culture Act awards 160 acres of public land to anyone who will plant trees on a quarter of the land
1876	Alexander Graham Bell invents the telephone
1877	Thomas Edison invents the phonograph; Desert Land Act grants 640 acres at $1.25 per acre to anyone who will irrigate the land; Great Strike paralyzes railroad transportation from Midwest and most of Northeast; 20 Molly Maguires are convicted and executed for terrorism in Pennsylvania coalfields

1879	Edison invents the incandescent lightbulb
1883	Railroad companies divide country into time zones
1885	George Westinghouse introduces alternating current for transmitting electricity
1886	*Santa Clara County* v. *Southern Pacific Railroad* decision rules that a corporation is a legal entity entitled to constitutional protection; Haymarket Square riot erupts in Chicago; American Federation of Labor is founded in Columbus, Ohio, by Samuel Gompers
1888	George Eastman produces the first handheld camera
1892	Homestead, Pennsylvania, steelworkers strike
1894	Pullman strike by railroad workers leads to nationwide boycott railroad
1895	Booker T. Washington's "Atlanta Compromise" speech advocates that African Americans focus on achieving economic success as a basis for social and political equality
1896	*Plessy* v. *Ferguson* decision rules that the principle of "separate but equal" does not deprive African Americans of civil rights guaranteed under the Fourteenth Amendment
1901	Andrew Carnegie sells his steel company for almost $500 million to a group that is forming U.S. Steel

as well as and adaptation and adjustment to a new social and economic order.

SUGGESTIONS FOR FURTHER READING

Walter Licht, *Industrializing America: The Nineteenth Century* (1995). Presents an up-to-date interpreta-

tion of the growth of industry and its consequences for American workers.

David Montgomery, *The Fall of the House of Labor: The Workplace, The State, and American Labor Activism, 1865–1925.* (1987). Examines labor's responses to the growth of industry.

Carroll W. Pursell, *The Machine in America: A Social History of Technology* (1995). Provides a thorough examination of the growth of mechanization in U.S. industry.

Ronald Takaki, *A Different Mirror: A History of Multicultural History* (1993). Retells American history from the perspective of ethnic and minority groups.

Alan Trachtenberg, *The Incorporation of America: Culture and Society in the Gilded Age* (1982). Explores intellectual and artistic responses to late nineteenth-century industrialization.

Ricahrd White, *"It's Your Misfortune and None of My Own": A History of the American West* (1991). Stresses the federal government's role in Western development.

Overviews and Surveys

Sean Dennis Cashman, *America in the Gilded Age: From the Death of Lincoln to the Rise of Theodore Roosevelt* (1988); Carl N. Degler, ed., *The Age of the Economic Revolution, 1876–1900* (1977); John A. Garraty, *The New Commonwealth, 1877–1890* (1968); Ray Ginger, *The Age of Excess: The United States From 1877 to 1914*, 2d ed., 1975; Morton Keller, *Affairs of State: Public Life in Late Nineteenth Century America* (1977); Jacqueline Jones, *The Dispossessed: America's Underclasses from the Civil War to the Present* (1992); Edward C. Kirkland, *Industry Comes of Age: Business, Labor, and Public Policy, 1860–1877* (1961); William Leach, *Land of Desire: Merchants, Power, and the Rise of a New American Culture* (1993); Nell Irvin Painter, *Standing at Armageddon: The United States, 1877–1919* (1987); Robert Wiebe, *The Search for Order, 1877–1920* (1967).

America: Land of Plenty

George H. Daniels, *Science in American Society: A Social History* (1971); Sigfried Giedion, *Mechanization Takes Command: A Contribution to Anonymous History* (1948); Samuel P. Hays, *The Response to Industrialism, 1885–1914*, 2d ed. (1995); Robert Higgs, *The Transformation of the American Economy* (1971); Leo Marx, *The Machine in the Garden: Technology and the Pastoral Ideal in America* (1964); Elting E. Morison, *From Know-How to Nowhere: The Development of American Technology* (1974), and *Men, Machines, and Modern Times* (1966); D. F. Noble, *America by Design: Science, Technology, and the Rise of Corporate Capitalism* (1977); Nathan Rosenberg, *Technology and American Economic Growth* (1972).

A Favorable Climate: The Role of Ideology, Politics, and Finance

Robert Bannister, *Social Darwinism: Science and Myth in Anglo-American Social Thought* (1979); W. Elliot Brownlee, *Dynamics of Ascent: A History of the American Economy*, 2d ed. (1988); Thomas C. Cochran, *Business in American Life: A History* (1972); Sidney Fine, *Laissez-faire and the General Welfare State: A Study of Conflict in American Thought* (1956); Milton Friedman and Anna J. Schwartz, *Monetary History of the United States, 1867–1960* (1963); Louis Galambos, *The Public Image of Big Business in America, 1880–1940: A Quantitative Study in Social Change* (1975); Richard Hofstadter, *Social Darwinism in American Thought*, rev. ed. (1992); T. Jackson Lears, *No Place of Grace: Antimodernism and the Transformation of American Culture, 1880–1920* (1981); Robert McCloskey, *American Conservatism in the Age of Enterprise, 1865–1910: A Study of William Graham Sumner, Stephen J. Field, and Andrew Carnegie* (1951); Daniel T. Rodgers, *The Work Ethic in Industrial America, 1850–1920* (1978); Martin Sklar, *The Corporate Reconstruction of American Capitalism, 1890–1916: The Market, the Law, and Politics* (1988); John L. Thomas, *Alternative America: Henry George, Edward Bellamy, Henry Demarest Lloyd, and the Adversary Tradition* (1983); Christopher L. Tomlins, *The State and the Unions: Labor Relations, Law, and the Organized Labor Movement in America, 1880–1960* (1985); James Weinstein, *The Corporate Ideal in the Liberal State, 1900–1918* (1968).

The Rise of Big Business

Alfred D. Chandler, *The Visible Hand: The Managerial Revolution in American Business* (1977); Thomas Cochran, *Railroad Leaders, 1845–1890* (1953); Francis L. Eames, *The New York Stock Exchange* (1894); Jonathan Hughes, *The Vital Few: American Economic Progress and Its Protagonists* (1966); Matthew Josephson, *The Robber Barons: The Great American Capitalists, 1861–1901* (1962); Maury Klein, *The Flowering of the Third America: The Making of an Organizational Society, 1850–1920* (1993); Daniel Nelson, *Managers and Workers: Origins of the New Factory System in the United States, 1880–1920* (1975); Glenn Porter, *The Rise of Big Business, 1865–1920*, 2d ed. (1992); George R. Taylor and Irene D. Neu, *The American Railroad Network, 1861–1890* (1956); Peter Temin, *Iron and Steel in Nineteenth-Century America* (1964); Daniel Yergin, *The Prize: The Epic Quest for Oil, Money and Power* (1991); Olivier Zunz, *Making America Corporate, 1870–1920* (1990).

Varieties of Economic Change in the West and South

Blake Allmendinger, *The Cowboy: Representations of Labor in an American Work Culture* (1992); Gunther Barth, *Instant Cities: Urbanization and the Rise of San Francisco and Denver* (1975); Ray A. Billington, *Westward Expansion,* 5th ed. (1982); Allan G. Bogue, *From Prairie to Corn Belt: The Life of the Social Activist Kate Richards O'Hare* (1963); Orville Vernon Burton and Robert C. McMath, Jr., eds., *Toward a New South?: Studies in Post–Civil War Southern Communities* (1982); David L. Carlton, *Mill and Town in South Carolina, 1880–1920* (1982); Thomas D. Clark, *Frontier America: The Story of the Westward Movement,* 2d ed. (1969), with Albert D. Kirwan, *The South Since Appomattox: A Century of Regional Change* (1967); William C. Culberson, *Vigilantism: Political History of Private Power in America* (1990); Edward E. Dale, *The Range Cattle Industry, 1865 to 1925,* rev. ed. (1969); Pete Daniel, *Breaking the Land: The Transformation of Cotton, Tobacco, and Rice Cultures Since 1880* (1985); David Dary, *Cowboy Culture: A Saga of Five Centuries* (1981); Everett Dick, *The Sod-House Frontier, 1854–1890: A Social History of the Northern Plains From the Creation of Kansas & Nebraska to the Admission of the Dakotas* (1937); Philip Durham and E. L. Jones, *The Negro Cowboys* (1965); Robert R. Dykstra, *The Cattle Towns* (1968); Paul Gaston, *The New South Creed* (1970); P. W. Gates, *History of Public Land Law Development* (1968); Dewey Grantham, Jr., *The Democratic South* (1963); Melvin Greenhut and W. Tate Whitman, eds., *Essays in Southern Economic Development* (1964); William S. Greever, *Bonanza West: The Story of the Western Mining Rushes, 1848–1900* (1963); Steven Hahn, *The Roots of Southern Populism: Yeoman Farmers and the Transformation of the Georgia Upcountry, 1850–1890* (1983); Katherine Harris, *Long Vistas: Women and Families on Colorado Homesteads* (1993); Robert Higgs, *Competition and Coercion: Blacks in the American Economy, 1865–1914* (1977); Robert V. Hine, *The American West,* 2d ed. (1984); W. Eugene Hollon, *Frontier Violence: Another Look* (1974); Julie Roy Jeffrey, *Frontier Women: The Trans-Mississippi West, 1840–1880* (1979); Terry G. Jordan, *Trails to Texas: Southern Roots of Western Cattle Ranching* (1981); J. Morgan Kousser, *The Shaping of Southern Politics: Suffrage Restriction and the Establishment of the One-Party South, 1880–1910* (1974); Howard R. Lamar, *The Far Southwest, 1846–1912: A Territorial History* (1966); Patricia Nelson Limerick, *The Legacy of Conquest: The Unbroken Past of the American West* (1987); Roger D. McGrath, *Gunfighters, Highwaymen, and Vigilantes: Violence on the Frontier* (1984); Melton A. McLaurin, *Paternalism and Protest: Southern Cotton Mill Workers and Organized Labor* (1971); Earl Pomeroy, *The Pacific Slope: A History of California, Washington, Idaho, Utah, and Nevada* (1965); Roger Ransom and Richard Sutch, *One Kind of Freedom: The Economic Consequences of Emancipation* (1977); R. M. Robbins, *Our Landed Heritage: The Public Domain, 1776–1936* (1942); Duane A. Smith, *Rocky Mountain Mining Camps: The Urban Frontier* (1967); Henry Nash Smith, *Virgin Land: The West as Symbol and Myth* (1978); Frederick Jackson Turner, *The Frontier in American History* (1920); Carroll Van West, *Capitalism on the Frontier: Billings and the Yellowstone Valley in the Nineteenth Century* (1993); C. Vann Woodward, *Origins of the New South, 1877–1913* (1951), and *The Strange Career of Jim Crow,* 3d ed. (1974); Gavin Wright, *Old South, New South: Revolutions in the Southern Economy Since the Civil War* (1986).

Working in Industrial America

Paul Avrich, *The Haymarket Tragedy* (1984); James R. Barrett, *Work and Community in the Jungle: Chicago's Packinghouse Workers, 1894–1922* (1987); Susan Porter Benson, *Counter Cultures: Saleswomen, Managers, and Customers in American Department Stores, 1890–1940* (1986); John Bodnar, *Immigration and Industrialization: Ethnicity in an American Mill Town* (1977); Jeanne Boydston, *Home and Work: Housework, Wages, and the Ideology of Labor in the Early Republic* (1990); David Brody, *Steelworkers in America* (1960); Wayne G. Broehl, Jr., *The Molly Maguires* (1964); Robert V. Bruce, *1877: Year of Violence* (1959); John R. Commons, et al., *History of Labor in the United States,* 4 vols. (1918–1935); Ruth Schwartz Cowan, *More Work for Mother: The Ironies of Household Technology From the Open Hearth to the Microwave* (1983); Melvyn Dubofsky, *Industrialism and the American Worker,* 2d ed. (1985), and *We Shall Be All: A History of the Industrial Workers of the World,* 2d ed. (1988); Leon Fink, *Workingmen's Democracy: The Knights of Labor and American Politics* (1983); Victor Greene, *The Slavic Community on Strike: Immigrant Labor in Pennsylvania Anthracite* (1968); Gerald Grob, *Workers and Utopia* (1961); Herbert Gutman, *Work, Culture, and Society in Industrializing America* (1976); Jacqueline Hall, et al., *Like a Family: The Making of a Southern Cotton Mill World* (1987); Tamara Hareven and Randolph Langenbach, *Amoskeag: Life and Work in an American Factory City* (1979) and Hareven, *Family and Industrial Time: The Relationship Between the Family and Work in a New*

England Industrial Community* (1982); Alice Kessler-Harris, *Out to Work: A History of Wage-Earning Women in the United States* (1982); William H. Harris, *The Harder We Run: Black Workers Since the Civil War* (1982); Victoria C. Hattam, *Labor Visions and State Power: The Origins of Business Unionism in the United States* (1993); David Katzman, *Seven Days a Week: Women and Domestic Service in Industrializing America* (1978); Stuart B. Kaufman, *Samuel Gompers and the Origins of the AFL* (1973); Susan Kennedy, *If All We Did Was to Weep at Home: A History of White Working-Class Women in America* (1979); S. J. Kleinberg, *The Shadow of the Mills: Working-Class Families in Pittsburgh, 1870–1907* (1989); Susan Levine, *Labor's True Woman: Carpet Weavers, Industrialization, and Labor Reform in the Gilded Age* (1984); Glenna Matthews, *"Just a Housewife": The Rise and Fall of Domesticity in America* (1987); David Montgomery, *Beyond Equality: Labor and the Radical Republicans* (1967) and *Workers' Control in America: Studies in the History of Work Technology and Labor Struggles* (1979); Stephen H. Norwood, *Labor's Flaming Youth: Telephone Operators and Worker Militancy, 1878–1923* (1990); Annegret S. Ogden, *The Great American Housewife: From Helpmate to Wage Earner, 1776–1986* (1986); Daniel T. Rodgers, *The Work Ethic in Industrial America, 1850–1920* (1978); Gerald Rosenblum, *Immigrant Workers: Their Impact on American Labor Radicalism* (1973); Roy A. Rosenzweig, *Eight Hours for What We Will: Workers and Leisure in an Industrial City, 1870–1920* (1983); David Shannon, *The Socialist Party of America: A History* (1955); Peter Shergold, *Working-Class Life: The American Standard in Comparative Perspective, 1899–1913* (1982); Susan Strasser, *Never Done: A History of American Housework* (1982); Sharon Hartman Strom, *Beyond the Typewriter: Gender, Class, and the Origins of Modern American Office Work, 1900–1930* (1992); Leslie W. Tentler, *Wage-Earning Women: Industrial Work and Family Life in the United States, 1900–1930* (1979); Daniel J. Walkowitz, *Worker City, Company Town: Iron and Cotton-Worker Protest in Troy and Cohoes, New York, 1855–84* (1978); Norman Ware, *The Labor Movement in the United States, 1860–1895* (1929).

Biographies

Andy Adams, *Log of a Cowboy: A Narrative of the Old Trail Days* (1927); Frederick Lewis Allen, *The Great Pierpont Morgan* (1949); Robert V. Bruce, *Bell: Alexander Graham Bell and the Conquest of Solitude* (1973); Julius Grodinsky, *Jay Gould, His Business Career, 1867–1892* (1957); Louis R. Harlan, *Booker T. Washington: The Making of a Black Leader, 1856–1901* (1972), and *Booker T. Washington: The Wizard of Tuskegee, 1901–1915* (1983); David F. Hawke, *John D.: The Founding Father of the Rockefellers* (1950); Maury Klein, *The Life and Legend of Jay Gould* (1986); Harold c C. Livesay, *Andrew Carnegie and the Rise of Big Business* (1975) and *Samuel Gompers and Organized Labor in America* (1978); Linda O. McMurry, *George Washington Carver: Scientist and Symbol* (1981); Allan Nevins, *Study in Power: John D. Rockefeller, Industrialist and Philanthropist*, 2 vols. (1953); Raymond B. Nixon, *Henry W. Grady: Spokesman of the New South* (1943); Nick Salvatore, *Eugene V. Debs, Citizen and Socialist* (1982); Andrew Sinclair, *Corsair: The Life of J. Pierpont Morgan* (1981); Robert M. Utley, *Billy the Kid: A Short and Violent Life* (1989); Joseph F. Wall, *Andrew Carnegie* (1970), and *Alfred I. du Pont: The Man and His Family* (1990); George Wheeler, *Pierpont Morgan and Friends* (1973).

CHAPTER 18
THE RISE OF AN URBAN SOCIETY AND CITY PEOPLE

THE NEW IMMIGRANTS
"Birds of Passage"
In Search of a New Home

NATIVISM: THE ANTI-IMMIGRANT REACTION
Sources of Conflict
Closing the Golden Door

NEW CITIES AND NEW PROBLEMS
City Technology
The Segregated City
The Problems of Growth
From Private City to Public City

CITY CULTURE
Night Life and Day Life
From the Genteel Tradition to
    Realism and Naturalism
Describing the Urban Jungle
Painting Urban Reality
The Sounds of the City

ENTERTAINING THE MULTITUDES
Of Fields and Cities
"I Can Lick Any Sonofabitch in the
    House"
The Excluded Americans
From Central Park to Coney Island
The Magic of the Flickering Image
The Agony of Painless Escape

PLUMBERS & ARCHITE

HARRISON'S

HARR

PATENT T HAN

BASIN

FOR HOTELS, PUBLIC BUILDINGS,

SIMPLE—DURA

We make a full line
the same principle for Uri
Pantry Sinks.

MANUFA

CHARLES HARRISON & CO.,
NO. 16 WEST FOURTH ST.   NEW YORK.

FLUSHING-RIM AND VENTILATOR.
CIALLY ADAPTED FOR

Andrew Borden had, as the old Scotch saying goes, short arms and long pockets. He was cheap not because he had to be frugal but because he hated to spend money. He had dedicated his entire life to making and saving money, and tales of his unethical and parsimonious business behavior were legendary in his home town of Fall River, Massachusetts. Local gossips maintained that as an undertaker he cut off the feet of corpses so that he could fit them into undersized coffins that he had purchased at a very good price. Andrew, however, was not interested in rumors or the opinions of other people; he was more concerned with his own rising fortunes. By 1892 he had amassed over half a million dollars, he controlled the Fall River Union Savings Bank, and he served as the director of the Globe Yard Mill Company, the First National Bank, the Troy Cotton and Manufacturing Company, and the Merchants Manufacturing Company.

Andrew was rich, but he did not live like a wealthy man. Instead of living alongside the other prosperous Fall River citizens in the elite neighborhood known as the Hill, Andrew resided in an area near the business district called the Flats. He liked to save time as well as money, and from the Flats he could conveniently walk to work. For his daughters Lizzie and Emma, whose eyes and dreams focused on the Hill, life in the Flats was an intolerable embarrassment. Their house was a grim, boxlike structure lacking both comfort and privacy. Since Andrew believed that running water on each floor was a wasteful luxury, the only washing facilities were a cold-water faucet in the kitchen and a laundry room water tap in the cellar. Also in the cellar was the only toilet in the house. To make matters worse, the house was not connected to the Fall River gas main. Andrew preferred to use kerosene to light his house. Although it did not provide as good light or burn as cleanly as gas, it was less expensive. To save even more money, he and his family frequently sat in the dark.

The Borden home was far from happy. Lizzie and Emma, ages 32 and 42 in 1892, strongly disliked their stepmother Abby and resented Andrew's penny-pinching ways. Lizzie especially felt alienated from the world around her. Although Fall River was the largest cotton-manufacturing town in America, it offered few opportunities for the unmarried daughter of a prosperous man. Society expected a woman of Lizzie's social position to marry, and while she waited for a proper suitor, her only respectable social outlets were church and community service. So Lizzie taught a Sunday School class and was active in the Woman's Christian Temperance Union, the Ladies' Fruit and Flower Mission, and other organizations. She kept herself busy, but she was not happy.

In August 1892, strange things started to happen in the Borden home—after Lizzie and Emma learned that Andrew had secretly changed his will. Abby became violently ill. In time so did the Borden maid Bridget Sullivan and Andrew himself. Abby told a neighborhood doctor that she had been poisoned, but Andrew refused to listen to her wild ideas. Shortly thereafter, Lizzie went shopping for prussic acid, a deadly poison, that she said she needed to clean her sealskin cape. When a Fall River druggist refused her request, she left the store in an agitated state. Later in the day, she told a friend that she feared an unknown enemy of her father's was after him. "I'm afraid somebody will do something," she said.

On August 4, 1892, Bridget awoke early and ill, but she still managed to prepare a large breakfast of johnnycakes, fresh-baked bread, ginger and oatmeal cookies with raisins, and some three-day-old mutton and hot mutton soup. After eating a hearty meal, Andrew left for work. Bridget also left to do some work outside. This left Abby and Lizzie in the house alone. Then somebody did something very grisly. As Abby was bent over making the bed in the guest room, someone moved into the room unobserved and killed her with an ax.

Andrew came home for lunch earlier than usual. He asked Lizzie where Abby was, and she said she did not know. Unconcerned, Andrew, who was not feeling well, lay down on the parlor sofa for a nap. He never awoke. Like Abby, he was slaughtered by someone with an ax. Lizzie "discovered" his body, still lying on the sofa. She called Bridget, who had taken the back stairs to her attic room: "Come down quick; father's dead; somebody came in and killed him."

Experts have examined and reexamined the crime, and most have reached the same conclusion: Lizzie killed her father and stepmother. In fact, Lizzie was tried for the gruesome murders. Despite a preponderance of evidence, however, an all-male jury found her not guilty, a verdict arrived at without debate or disagreement. A woman of Lizzie's social position, they affirmed, simply could not have committed such a terrible crime.

Even before the trial began, newspaper and magazine writers had judged Lizzie innocent for the same reason. As historian Kathryn Allamong Jacob, an expert on the case, noted, "Americans were certain that well-brought-up daughters could not commit murder with a hatchet on sunny summery mornings." Criminal women, they believed, originated in the lower classes and even looked evil. A criminologist writing in the *North American Review* commented, "[The female criminal] has coarse black hair and a good deal of it. . . . She has often a long face, a receding forehead, overjutting brows, prominent cheek bones, an exaggerated frontal angle as seen in monkeys and savage races, and nearly always square jaws." They did not look like round-faced Lizzie and did not belong to the Ladies' Fruit and Flower Mission.

Jurors and editorialists alike judged Lizzie according to their preconceived notions of Victorian womanhood. They believed that such a woman was gentle, docile, and physically frail, short on analytical ability but long on nurturing instincts. "Women," wrote an editorialist for *Scribner's*, "are merely large babies. They are shortsighted, frivolous and occupy an intermediate stage between children and men." Too uncoordinated and weak to accurately swing an ax and too gentle and unintelligent to coldly plan a double murder, a woman of Lizzie's background simply had to be innocent because of her basic innocence.

Even as Lizzie was being tried and found innocent, Victorian notions were being challenged elsewhere. In the larger cities of America, a new culture based on freedoms, not restraints, was taking form. Anything was possible, or at least so some people claimed. Immigrants could become millionaires and women could vote and hold office. Rigid Victorian concepts crumbled under the weight of new ideas, but the price of the new freedoms was high. In both the cities and the culture that flourished within them, a new order had to be constructed out of the chaos of freedom.

Preconceived notions of Victorian womanhood saved Lizzie Borden from being convicted of murdering her father and stepmother.

THE NEW IMMIGRANTS

On October 28, 1886, President Grover Cleveland traveled to New York Harbor to watch the unveiling of the Statue of Liberty. A gift from France, Frederic Auguste Bartholdi's grand statue was meant to symbolize solidarity between the two republics, but for Americans and incoming immigrants, it was a simple symbol of welcome, the statue's torch lighting the path to a better future.

In popular theory, the promise of America exerted a powerful pull on Europe and Asia. The United States stood for political freedom, social mobility, and economic opportunity. Since the first settlers landed in Jamestown, millions of immigrants had responded to the American magnet. At no time was immigration as great as in the late nineteenth and early twentieth centuries. Between 1860 and 1890, more than 10 million immigrants arrived on America's shores; between 1890 and 1920 over 15 million more arrived.

Seen in a worldwide context, however, the United States' pull was less powerful than Europe's push. Almost every European country—from Ireland in the northwest to Greece in the southeast—experienced a dramatic population increase during the nineteenth century. Advances in medicine and public health standards reduced infant mortality rates and increased life expectancies, but available land and food supplies did not increase to meet the new population demands. Twenty or so years later, when the "baby boomers" reached maturity, emigration increased sharply. (The United States was not the only country to lure immigrants from Europe—millions more emigrated to Australia, New Zealand, South Africa, Canada, Brazil, Argentina, and other underpopulated areas of the globe.)

Historians have divided immigration to the United States into two categories: old and new. The source of the "old" immigration was for the most part northern and western Europe—England, Ireland, France, Germany, and Scandinavia. Immigrants were mostly Protestants (except for the Irish Catholics) and always white; a majority were literate and had

lived under constitutional forms of government. Assimilation for them was relatively easy. But this pattern fundamentally changed beginning in the 1880s. The next wave of immigration came from eastern and southern Europe—Greeks, Poles, Russians, Italians, Slavs, Turks. These people found assimilation more difficult; politically, religiously, and culturally, they differed greatly from both the earlier immigrants and native-born Americans.

More than geography differentiated the new immigrants. Their reasons for leaving Europe, their visions of America, and their settlement patterns in the United States varied dramatically. Conditions in southern and eastern Europe were right for the push to America at this time.

With the abolition of serfdom, peasants were free to emigrate; and with the rise in population, young men faced job, land, and food shortages. Too, railroads and steamships made travel faster and less expensive. During the 1880s, British and German steamships car-

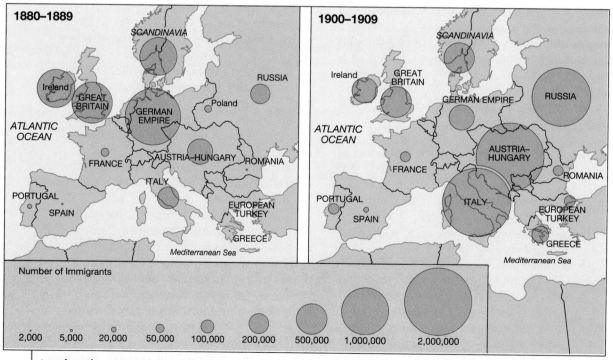

Immigration, 1880–1889 and 1900–1909

The source of old immigration was primarily northern and western Europe—England, Ireland, Germany, and Scandinavia. By the 1890s a wave of new immigrants began to arrive from eastern and southern Europe.

ried immigrants across the Atlantic for as little as $8, and by the turn of the century the trip took only five and a half days.

"Birds of Passage"

Essentially there were two types of immigrants—permanent immigrants and migrant workers. The people in the second group, often called birds of passage, never intended to make the United States their home. Unable to earn a livelihood in their home countries, they came to America, worked and saved, and then returned home. Most were young men in their teens and twenties. They left behind their parents, young wives, and children, indications that their absence would not be too long. Before 1900, an estimated 78 percent of Italian immigrants and 95 percent of Greek immigrants were men. Many traveled to America in the early spring, worked until late fall, and returned to the warmer climates of their southern European homes for the winter. Some fully intended to return home, but for one reason or another—love, hardship, early death—did not. Overall, 20 to 30 percent of all immigrants did return home.

Italian immigration patterns are a good example of the activity of the birds of passage. Beginning in the 1870s, Italian birthrates rose and mortality rates fell. Population pressure became severe, especially in *Il Mezzogiorno,* the southern and poorest provinces of Italy. The central government, dominated by northerners and concerned only with northern interests, seemed unconcerned about the impoverished southern provinces. Heavily taxed and hurt by high protective tariffs on northern industrial goods, Italians in southern Italy sank deeper into poverty.

Then even nature joined the opposition. Natural disasters rocked southern Italy during the first decade of the twentieth century. Earthquakes caused untold devastation in the provinces of Basilicata and Calabria. Vesuvius erupted and buried a town near Naples. Then Etna erupted. The cruelest blow came in 1908 when an earthquake and tidal wave swept through the Strait of Messina between Sicily and the Italian mainland and killed hundreds of thousands of people.

Many immigrants who looked on their stay in the United States as temporary sought jobs that might have paid a little better but were dangerous and physically demanding.

The jobs that Italian men sought reflected their attitude toward America. They did not look for careers; occupations that provided opportunity for upward economic mobility were alien to them. Unlike most earlier immigrants, they did not want to farm in America or even own land, both of which implied a permanence that did not figure in their plans. Instead, Italians headed for the cities, where labor was needed and wages were relatively good. Few jobs were beneath them. Expecting their stay in America to be short, they lived as inexpensively as possible under conditions that native-born families considered intolerable.

Italians were particularly attracted to heavy construction jobs. One study of Italians in America noted in 1905 that Italians gravitated toward "work that is simple and monotonous . . . that can be performed by men disposed in a gang, under the more or less military supervision of a foreman, so that the worker becomes himself like a part of a machine." Contracted out by professional labor brokers known as a *padrones,* Italians supplied the muscle that dug tunnels and canals, laid railroad tracks, and constructed bridges and roads. So important were they to the construction business that in 1905 the Industrial Commission concluded that "it would be a difficult thing . . . to build a railroad of any considerable length without Italian labor."

While they received good wages, they seldom forgot their homes in Italy. One nostalgic Italian admitted, "Doctor, we brought to America only our brains and our arms. Our hearts stayed there in the little house in the beautiful fields of our Italy." For women, adjustment to America was even more difficult. They often wore black clothing, an old-country practice that symbolized self-sacrifice, misery, and determination.

The same feelings of loneliness and alienation were also felt by many Chinese immigrants in the United States. Beginning in the mid-1860s, they emigrated to America to work building the Central Pacific railroad, and when that project was completed they sought jobs in western mining towns and cities. Normally only men emigrated, and they lived frugally and sent much of their wages to their families back in China. Their dream was almost always to return home, not to forge a new life in America.

Italians and Chinese were not the only birds of passage. The same forces that had initiated their flight—population pressure, unemployment, hunger, and the breakdown of agrarian societies—sent Greeks, Slavs, Japanese, Mexicans, French Canadians, and inhabitants of scores of other nations to the United States. Seeking neither permanent homes nor citizenship, they desired only an opportunity to work for a living, hoping to save enough money to return to a better life in the country of their birth. Always the land *they* coveted was some distant home, not in the United States.

In Search of a New Home

In contrast to the birds of passage were the permanent immigrants, for whom America offered political and religious freedom as well as economic opportunity. The promise of America was especially appealing to members of ethnic and religious minorities who were persecuted, abused, and despised in their homelands. Germans from Slavic countries, Greeks from Romania, Serbs from Hungary, Turks from Bulgaria, Poles from Russia—for these men and women home held few warm associations.

Czarist Russia, for example, was a country notoriously and historically inhospitable to many minorities. In 1907, 250,000 "Russians" emigrated from Russia. But who were these Russians? More than 115,000 were Jews, and another 73,000 were Poles. Others were Finns, Germans, and Lithuanians. Only a small percentage were of Russian ethnic stock. In short, emigration from Russia was generally an alternative for minorities, not Russians.

The Jews were the prototypical new immigrants. Like the Irish Catholics a generation before, they fled nearly unbearable hardships. Historically, from the thirteenth century, millions of Jews had maintained a relatively stable communal life in Poland. Then during the eighteenth century Russia, Prussia, and Austria conquered and divided Poland. Most of the Polish Jews lived under Russian rule, and the quality of their lives took an immediate and drastic downward turn. Russian authorities drove Jews out of commerce and forced them into an area known as the Pale of Settlement, home to over 90 percent of Russian Jews. There they toiled as farmers on the poor soil of the steppes or earned a living as artisans or craftsmen in impoverished villages. There, too, Russian officials burned their books, disrupted their religious practices, and occasionally even broke up their families.

Starting in 1881, when the liberal Russian Czar Alexander II was assassinated, conditions for Jews in Russia went rapidly from bad to worse to intolerable. Laws restricted Jewish businesses, prevented Jewish land ownership, and limited Jewish education. Pogroms, legally sanctioned mob attacks against Jews, killed and injured thousands. Sometimes at the whim of authorities, Russian Cossacks burned Jewish houses and destroyed Jewish possessions.

For Jews, then, emigration offered a chance for a far better life than that in the Pale of Settlement. Dr. George M. Price, one of the several million Jews who left Russia for America during the late nineteenth century, expressed the feelings of these immigrants for their homeland. In his diary he wrote: "Sympathy for Russia? How ironical it sounds! Am I not despised? Am I not urged to leave? Do I not hear the word zhid (Jew) constantly? Can I even think that some consider me a human

Hester Street on New York City's Lower East Side, in a photograph from 1907, was home to thousands of Jewish immigrants from Russia and eastern Europe. The immigrants crowded into the tenements lining the street, which bustled with peddlers and pedestrians.

capable of thinking and feeling like others? Do I not rise daily with the fear lest the hungry mob attack me? . . . It is impossible . . . that a Jew should regret leaving Russia." He voiced his feelings for America, his new home, in his booklet *Yidn in America* (1891) where he described the Atlantic crossing as "a kind of hell that cleanses a man of his sins before coming to the land of Columbus." Compared to Russia, the United States seemed like heaven to Price.

Because these Jewish immigrants came to the United States to stay, their form of immigration differed substantially from that of the generally young, male birds of passage. Jews, like other permanent immigrants, tended to come to America in family units, men and women, young and old. They brought their life savings and most valuable possessions with them, never expecting to see again what they left behind. The move to America thus was financially and physically taxing, and once in America, whole families had more expenses than the young male birds of passage.

Since America was now their home, Jewish men looked for jobs that offered future op-portunities rather than simply work for wages. They were not drawn to unskilled labor in the steel mills and mines or even in construction. Many Jews had skills, for the uncertain life of the Russian Pale had taught them not to depend on land or commerce. In the Pale a Jew's greatest possession was the ability to do something that could not be taken away, a skilled craft. First in the Pale and then in America, Jews were tailors and seamstresses, cigar makers and toy makers, tanners and butchers, carpenters, joiners, roofers, and masons, coppersmiths and blacksmiths. They had the knowledge and ability to perform the thousands of skilled tasks needed in an urban environment.

NATIVISM: THE ANTI-IMMIGRANT REACTION

In American cities, where native-born citizens and new immigrants now confronted each other, tensions often ran high. An isolated event, by itself historically unimportant, can illuminate like a flash of lightning the social landscape and beliefs of a particular time. This was true with the Hennessy case in 1891. In 1890 a feud between gangs on the New Orleans docks turned violent, and Joe and Pete Provenzano were arrested and tried for attempting to massacre the rival gang. The trial took a sensational turn when David Hennessy, the New Orleans superintendent of police, asserted in 1891 that he had evidence that a secret Sicilian organization known as the Mafia was involved in the affair. Shortly after Hennessy made his bold charges, he was gunned down by five armed men. Before he died, Hennessy was heard to say, "The dagos shot me."

The crime raised a hue and cry against Sicilians. Local police, urged on by Mayor Joseph Shakespeare to "arrest every Italian you come across, if necessary," arrested scores. Eleven Sicilians were brought to trial, but a jury failed to convict them. A local mob promptly took matters into its own hands and shot or clubbed to death nine suspects and hanged the other two. As far as most natives of New Orleans were concerned, justice had been done.

Many other Americans seemed to agree. Editorial writers praised the mob action and damned the vile "un-American" Italians. The affair sent ripples across diplomatic waters. Italy protested the mob assault, but Washington refused to take any action. Across the country anti-Italian rhetoric became ugly, and wild rumors ricocheted like bullets. Some said that the Italian fleet was headed toward America's east coast; others claimed that uniformed Italians were going through military drills in the streets of New York City. One thing was clear, noted an editorial writer in the *Review of Reviews*, Congress had to pass immigration legislation to keep out "the refuse of the murder-breeds of Southern Europe."

Although the Hennessy case soon faded from the front pages of American newspapers, the emotions it generated and revealed were very real. Native-born Americans harbored deep suspicion of and resentment toward immigrants, especially those from Asia and southern and eastern Europe. American industrialists saw in the immigrants a bottomless pool of dependable, inexpensive labor,

but other Americans saw something far different and much less promising. Workers saw competition. Protestants saw Catholics and Jews. Educators saw illiterate hordes. Politicians saw peasants, unfamiliar with the workings of republicanism, democracy, and constitutionalism, and—even worse—perhaps contaminated by a belief in socialism, communism, or anarchism. Social Darwinists saw a mass of dark-skinned, thick-browed, bent-backed people who were far "below" northern and western Europeans on the evolutionary ladder. In short, native-born Americans, heirs of a different culture, religion, and complexion, saw something alien and inferior, perhaps even dangerous, in these new immigrants.

They reacted accordingly. They posted signs: "No Jews or Dogs Allowed." They called the Chinese "coolies," and the Mexicans "bean heads." Overall, they created an atmosphere of hostility that too often spilled over into open violence. In 1891 in a New Jersey mill town, 500 tending boys in a glassworks rioted when the management hired 14 young Russian Jews. During an 1895 labor conflict in the southern Colorado coal fields, American miners killed 6 Italians. When Slavic coal miners went on strike in 1897 in eastern Pennsylvania, local citizens massacred 21 Polish and Hungarian workers. On the West Coast, Chinese workers were subject to regular and vicious attacks. Especially during economic hard times, native-born Americans lashed out against the new immigrants.

Sources of Conflict

Nativism, as this anti-immigrant backlash was called, took many forms. Racial nativism, the subject of thousands of books and articles, is the best remembered. University professors such as Wisconsin's Edward Alsworth Ross and popular writers such as Madison Grant decried the new immigrants as biologically less advanced than the Americans who traced their ancestry back to northern and western Europe. Using such criteria as complexion, size of cranium, length of forehead, and slope of shoulders, the immigrants from southern and eastern Europe were judged inferior to most native-born Americans. That university professors and scientists accepted such theories of innate racial and ethnic inferiority gave credibility to these notions. And popular writers readily accepted the stereotypes. Jacob Riis, a Danish immigrant who became an urban reformer in America and wrote the popular book *How the Other Half Lives* (1890), characterized Italians as "born gamblers" who lived destitute and disorderly lives, Chinese as secretive and addicted to every vice, and Jews as "enslaved" by their pursuit of gold as well as living amidst filth.

Religious differences reinforced ethnic variations. Overwhelmingly Catholic and Jewish, the new immigrants challenged the Protestant orthodoxy in America. Anti-Catholicism, noted a leading student of nativism, "blossomed spectacularly" during the late nineteenth century. Many Americans regarded the pope as the anti-Christ and Catholics as his evil minions. And it was widely believed that the authoritarian bent of the Catholic mind made it incompatible with democratic institutions.

Native-born Americans viewed Jews with even greater suspicion, attributing the characteristics of Shakespeare's Shylock to Jews as a whole. "Money is their God," wrote Jacob Riis. Other writers commented that Jews were tactless, tasteless, and pushy. Eventually many social clubs, country clubs, hotels, and universities excluded Jews, arguing that money alone could not purchase respectability.

The Leo Frank case painfully demonstrated the ubiquitous anti-Semitism in American society. Frank, a Cornell University graduate and a son of a wealthy New York merchant, managed an Atlanta pencil factory. In 1914 one of the factory hands, Mary Phagan, was found murdered on the premises. Frank was tried and convicted on flimsy evidence, but the case soon became an international cause célèbre. After reviewing the case, the governor of Georgia commuted Frank's death sentence to life imprisonment. The decision outraged native Georgia whites. They boycotted Jewish merchants and clamored for Frank's blood. Finally, a group of citizens from Mary Phagan's home town took Leo Frank from a state prison, transported him 175 miles across the state, and coldly hanged him. As news of the hanging

spread, people gathered to gaze at the sight and shout "Now we've got you! We've got you now!" In the 1980s, new evidence in the Phagan case proved Frank innocent, and Georgia's Board of Pardons granted him a posthumous pardon. But dispassionate justice was scarce in the weeks after Frank's death.

Orators used the Frank case as an object lesson. Tom Watson, the fiery Georgia politician, warned listeners, "From all over the world, the Children of Israel are flocking to this country, and plans are on foot to move them from Europe *en masse* . . . to empty upon our shores the very scum and dregs of the *Parasite Race.*" Watson believed that Congress should stop the flow of immigrants before America was flooded by the waves of eastern and southern Europeans.

Many congressmen agreed. They too harbored strong suspicions of the new immigrants. For them, political fears mixed naturally with racial and religious misgivings. They tended to equate immigration with radicalism and suspected that every boat that docked at Ellis Island contained a swarm of socialists, communists, and anarchists prepared to foment revolution. As unfounded as their fears were, they could always point to isolated cases of radicalism among immigrants. They drew attention, for example, to Leon Czolgosz, born only months after his eastern European parents arrived in America. After embracing anarchism, Czolgosz shot and killed President William McKinley on September 6, 1901.

The new immigrants were most strongly resented, however, for purely economic reasons. American workers, particularly the unskilled, believed that the immigrants depressed wages by their willingness to "work cheap" An iron worker complained: "Immigrants work for almost nothing and seem to be able to live on wind—something which I cannot do." Even skilled workers maintained that the birds-of-passage immigrants were unwilling to support any union efforts to improve working conditions in America. Samuel Gompers, himself an immigrant and head of the American Federation of Labor, said that the immigration problem in America was "appalling." He believed that the immigrants from eastern and southern Europe and from Asia were ignorant, unskilled, and unassimilable. Calling for strong restrictive legislation, he said, "Some way must be found to safeguard America."

In the 1890s, a terrible depression disrupted the normal economic and social course of America, and the new immigrants became a convenient scapegoat for the nation's myriad ills. People elevated racial prejudice and rumors to universal truths. Native-born Americans blamed crime on Italians and prostitution on the Chinese; they claimed that the social ills of America's expanding cities—corruption, poor sanitation, violence, crime, disease, pollution—were the fault of the new immigrants. And they looked to the federal government for relief and protection.

Closing the Golden Door

The first immigrants attacked were those who were the most different from native-born Americans and the most unskilled—the Chinese. The more than 160,000 Chinese who entered the United States between 1868 and 1882, laid down railroad tracks and mined for gold, silver, and coal. Unlike native-born Americans and most members of other immigrant groups, they did not consider cooking, washing, and ironing as "women's work," and in these areas they were particularly successful. Perhaps too successful.

Lee Chew, who as a boy in China dreamed of obtaining wealth in "the country of the American wizards," immigrated as a young man to the United States. In America he found opportunity. He worked and saved and sacrificed. In America he also discovered that the Chinese were subject to the worst forms of exploitation and abuse. As they did with African Americans in the South and Native Americans in the West, white Americans cheated and sometimes violently attacked the Chinese. "Americans are not all bad," Lee noted, "nor are they wicked wizards. Still . . . their treatment of us is outrageous."

During the depression of the mid-1870s the Chinese came under increasingly bitter and violent attack. Labor and political leaders, especially in California, demanded an end to Chinese immigration. But the provisions of the Burlingame Treaty (1868) with China encouraged the Chinese to immigrate to America and establish citizenship.

Eventually Congress responded to the pressure for restriction. In 1880, China gave the United States Congress the right "to regulate, limit or suspend," though not to prohibit, the immigration of Chinese workers to the United States. The golden door quickly slammed shut. In 1882 the Chinese Exclusion Act suspended Chinese immigration for ten years and drastically restricted the rights of the Chinese already in the United States. In 1892 Congress extended the act for another ten years, and then in 1902 extended it indefinitely.

The legislation established a precedent for the future exclusion of other immigrants. By the 1890s most Americans agreed that the country should restrict "undesirable" immigrants. But how, for example, could Congress close America's door to southern and eastern Europeans while still leaving it open for northern and western Europeans? Politicians came up with the idea of a literacy test. As early as the late 1880s economist Edward W. Bemis proposed that the United States exclude all male adults who could not read and write their own language. He maintained that such a law would effectively stop the flow of eastern and southern Europeans into America. The idea soon had the backing of the influential Republican Senator Henry Cabot Lodge of Massachusetts and the equally important Immigration Restriction League.

In 1896 Lodge pushed through Congress a literacy test bill that would have excluded any adult immigrant unable to read 40 words in his own language. Lodge's timing was poor. The bill reached the desk of Democratic President Grover Cleveland two days before his second term expired. Cleveland promptly vetoed the measure, suggesting that the bill tested prior opportunities and that America stood for open opportunities.

Cleveland's veto did not end the demand for restrictive legislation, nor did it even kill the idea of a literacy test. Subsequent presidents William Howard Taft and Woodrow Wilson also vetoed similar pieces of legislation. In 1917, on the eve of America's entry into

World War I, Wilson vetoed a literacy test bill on the grounds that it was "not a test of character, of quality, or of personal fitness." Congress nevertheless passed the act over Wilson's veto.

World War I made even chillier the already cold climate for immigrants from southern and eastern Europe. Those born in the polyglot Austro-Hungarian Empire were now considered the enemy, and others were watched with deep suspicion. This was especially true after the 1917 Bolshevik Revolution in Russia. Once again American authorities regarded Jews from Russia as potential revolutionaries. Responding to this fear, in 1918 and 1920 Congress passed legislation to exclude or deport anarchists and other "dangerous radicals."

The generation-long battle over restriction was to end with a clear victory for nativism. In the early 1920s Congress discovered its own solution: the quota system. The Emergency Quota Act (1921) limited immigration according to a nation-based quota system—no more than 3 percent of any given nationality in America in 1910 could annually immigrate to the United States. In 1924 the National Origins Act lowered the quota to 2 percent of each nationality residing in America in 1890. By using 1890 as the base year, the act was clearly aimed at restricting eastern and southern Europeans, for there were far fewer of the new immigrants in America in 1890 than in 1910. Although in 1927 the base year was changed to 1920, the National Origins Act had achieved its desired result. America's doors were no longer fully open to eastern and southern Europeans, and it was completely closed to Asians. An important era in American history had ended.

Despite the prejudice against them, immigrants contributed greatly to the growth of industrial America. They and their fellow workers—native-born white and black Americans—built the railroads that crisscrossed the country; mined the gold and silver that made other men rich; and labored in the oilfields, steel mills, coal pits, packing plants, and factories that made such names as Rockefeller, Carnegie, Swift, and Westinghouse famous. Without these men and their companions, there would have been no industrialization. In the process they made the

This political cartoon depicts the 1882 Chinese Exclusion Act, which barred Chinese laborers from entering the United States for ten years.

United States an ethnically rich nation, as well as help to transform the country into an increasingly urban nation.

NEW CITIES AND NEW PROBLEMS

The physical layout of the mid-nineteenth-century city was strikingly different from its twentieth-century counterpart. In an age before reliable mass transportation, when only the rich could afford carriages, the majority of city dwellers walked to and from work. This simple fact dictated the type of cities that emerged—compact and crowded, their sizes normally limited to about a two-mile radius from center city, or the distance a person could walk in half an hour. Even America's largest cities—New York, Philadelphia, and Boston—conformed to these standards.

Inside the cities, houses, businesses, and factories were strewn about willy-nilly. Tightly packed near the waterfront were shops, banks, warehouses, and business offices, and not far away were the residences of the people who owned those enterprises or worked in them. There was little residential segregation. The rich may have occupied the finest houses in the center city, but the poor lived in the alleys and dirty streets close by. People dealt with people in a congested, highly personalized world. Rich and poor, native-born and immigrant, black and white—they all walked along the same streets and worked in the same area.

During the last third of the century, however, booming industrialization and immigration shattered this arrangement. Industrialists built their new plants in or near existing cities, and urban growth accelerated at an alarming rate. Like twin children, factories and cities each helped the other to reach its physical potential. In 1860, before America's industrial surge, 20 percent of the population lived in cities. By 1900 almost 40 percent of the population lived in cities or towns, and that figure climbed to over 50 percent in 1920. The numbers of large cities (those with a population of over 100,000) increased at an even faster rate. In 1860, America had only 9 large cities, in 1900 there were 38 and 68 in 1920.

Immigrant and native sources fueled the urban explosion. Most of the late-nineteenth-century immigrants came from rural communities, but they settled in America's industrial heartland. In 1920, 87 percent of Irish immigrants, 89 percent of Russians, 84 percent of Italians and Poles, 80 percent of Hungarians, and 75 percent of Austrians, British, and Canadians lived in cities. For every industrial worker who moved to the countryside, 20 farmers moved to urban America. As in Europe and Asia, rural opportunities in the United States were dwindling at the same time that the population was growing. Thus, for each farm son who became a farm owner, 10 farm sons moved to the cities.

Black migration from the rural South to the urban North further expanded the labor pool in the industrial cities. Slowly at first, blacks left the land of their bondages determined to forge a better life for themselves and their families in the northern cities. Between 1897 and 1920 almost one million African Americans left the South, and 85 percent of those settled in the urban North.

City Technology

Even the largest of the "walking" cities was unprepared to meet the demands the newcomers placed on it. Cities were already crowded, and construction technology was not yet sufficiently advanced to accommodate new arrivals. In time, however, engineers and scientists discovered ways to expand cities. Horizontal and vertical growth changed the skyline and living conditions of urban America during the half-century after 1870.

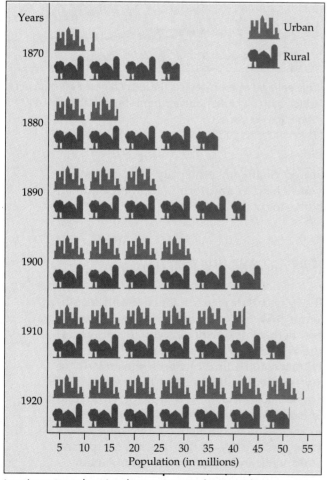

Immigrants and native-born migrants from rural areas contributed to the urban population explosion in this 50-year span.

During the early decades of the twentieth century, hundreds of thousands of African Americans left the rural South for the cities of the industrial North.

Better transportation facilities solved the most basic limitation of the walking city, although at first only the wealthy and those with some money benefited. As early as the 1830s, the horse-drawn omnibus permitted a handful of wealthier urbanites to escape life in the crowded center city. Usually pulled by one or two horses, an omnibus carried 12 to 20 passengers along a fixed route for between 6 and 12 cents. Faster than walking, it was also expensive, certainly beyond the means of an unskilled laborer who earned less than one dollar a day. Similarly the commuter railroads, which also dated back to the 1830s and 1840s and cost between 12 and 25 cents to ride, served only the wealthier classes. Constructed and owned by entrepreneurs, omnibuses and commuter railways existed only for the comfort of people who could pay.

The horse railway expanded the city for the middle-class urbanites, white-collar workers, and skilled workers. For 5 cents, these horse-drawn omnibuses carried passengers over steel rails at a speed of 6 to 8 miles per hour. In southern and border towns, mules, which tended to live longer, pulled the omnibuses. By the 1880s, over 300 American cities and towns had constructed horsecar lines, which significantly expanded the size of cities. Now a person could live 5 miles from his or her place of work and still be there in less than an hour. The age of walking was almost over.

The horsecar was not always as safe or as comfortable as its developers planned. Travelers complained about pickpockets, tobacco juice, and overcrowding. Describing the activity of pickpockets, one passenger suggested, "Before boarding a car, prudent persons leave their purses and watches in the safe deposit company and carry bowie knives and derringers." Entrepreneurial conductors often overloaded their cars, occasionally packing 80 persons into a car designed for 25, a situation that made the pickpocket's task easier.

Drivers and horses suffered even worse fates. Underfed, overworked horses struggled day after day until they dropped from exhaustion, at which point they were unhitched and left to die. Drivers fared only a little better. In New York City during the early 1880s they worked 16-hour days for $12 a week. Exposed to the weather in the front or rear of the cars, they suffered terribly in the winter as cold winds whipped their faces and froze their fingers around the reins. One streetcar conductor, hardened by years of work, remarked, "I feel that I could almost digest cobblestones."

For hillier cities like San Francisco and Pittsburgh, the cable car, introduced during the 1870s, proved a blessing for humans and horses alike. Utilizing steam power, cable cars were faster and cleaner than horse-drawn transportation. Even relatively flat cities such as Kansas City and Chicago installed cable cars. Because it was pulled by a moving underground cable, engineers believed it would be the public transportation of the future—but its problems were considerable. Expensive to install and quick to break down, the cable car soon gave way to the electric trolley, which was cheaper to run and more dependable.

In 1888, former naval engineer Frank Sprague converted the horsecar network of Richmond, Virginia, to electricity. Employing electrical current in overhead wires, these trolleys could operate in stop-and-go traffic and travel at average speeds of 10 to 12 miles per hour. American cities quickly climbed aboard the electric bandwagon. By 1902, 97 percent of urban transit mileage had been electrified, and trolleys connected not only city with suburb, but also city with city. By 1920 a person could travel from Boston to New York entirely by trolleys known as interurbans.

Called "one of the most rapidly accepted innovations in the history of technology," trolleys were not without their problems: overhead wires gave cities a weblike appearance; in winter the electric wires snapped from the cold and created dangerous situations; and they sometimes frightened horses, thus aggravating traffic problems. By the 1890s, the mixture of horsecars, cable cars, and trolleys jostling each other and pedestrians on city streets created immense traffic jams. English

science fiction writer H. G. Wells found Chicago streets in 1906 "simply chaotic—one hoarse cry for discipline."

Engineers searching for other solutions to clogged streets designed electric-powered elevated railway lines and underground subways. Each helped ease mass transportation. The Chicago "el" (elevated railway) and the New York City subway satisfied the urban traffic engineers and even occasionally stirred the souls of artists. W. Louis Sonntag, Jr.'s beautiful watercolor captured New York City's Bowery in 1896, in which, illuminated by electric lights, an electric el and trolley pass in the night.

Mass transportation allowed cities to spread miles beyond their cores, but steel and glass permitted cities to reach for the sky. At midcentury, few buildings were higher than five stories, and church spires still dominated the urban skyline. Buildings, like cities themselves, were personal; they did not dwarf the individual. That, however, was soon to change. As a real-estate columnist wrote in the *Chicago Tribune* in 1888: "In real estate calculations, Chicago has thus far had but three directions, north, south, and west, but there are indications now that a fourth is to be added and that it is to cut a larger figure in the coming decade than all the others. The new direction is zenithward. Since water hems in the business center on three sides and a nexus of railroads on the south, Chicago must grow upward."

Architects could not design buildings much higher than ten stories, using traditional brick-and-masonry construction. In 1885 New York architect William LeBaron Jenney solved this problem by using light masonry over an iron and steel skeleton. Although only ten stories high his Home Insurance Building in Chicago was the first true skyscraper in history. Steel, light masonry, and eventually glass, revolutionized building construction, and the use of electric elevators made tall buildings functional.

Skyscrapers changed the profile of American cities as surely as industrialism altered the American landscape. Returning to America from Europe in 1906, novelist Henry James observed "the multitudinous skyscrapers stand-

This watercolor of New York City's Bowery at night by W. Louis Sonntag, Jr., shows how steam, steel, and electricity played a major part in transforming cities.

ing up to the view . . . like extravagant pins in a cushion already overplanted, and stuck in as in the dark, anywhere and anyhow." What disturbed James's sensibilities excited most Americans. Their reasoning was that the skyscraper was America out to prove that its reach did not exceed its grasp. In fact, businesspeople and industrialists even used skyscrapers to glorify their own accomplishments. Bigger was better, and the race to the sky was on. In 1913, President Woodrow Wilson pressed the button that lit up the Woolworth Building. At 792 feet, it was the largest building in America, a monument to five-and-ten-cents king Frank Woolworth. This hauntingly beautiful structure, which freely adapted aspects of Gothic and Moorish construction, truly was "the Cathedral of Commerce."

The Segregated City

With the outward and upward growth of cities came an end to the more personal walking city. Mass transportation freed the upper and middle classes from having to live in the city core. Voicing their decision with their

feet, they scampered for the "streetcar suburbs," where, popular theory held, the water was purer, the trees fuller, and the air fresher. They commuted to work and no longer mixed daily with their economic inferiors.

The working class moved into the areas and even houses deserted by wealthier families. In New York City the large stately brownstone homes that had served the upper classes were divided into small apartments that satisfied the new demand for inexpensive housing. Of course, the houses had not been designed to be used as multiunit apartments, and there were numerous problems. Heatless, sunless, and poorly ventilated rooms became increasingly common.

Ethnic groups and races, like economic classes, tended to stake out particular neighborhoods in the new larger cities, and real-estate brokers and landlords restricted blacks and immigrants to specific areas. Black ghettos emerged in the major northern cities for the first time. And in Chicago, New York, Boston, and Philadelphia, English became a foreign language in ethnic neighborhoods, which reproduced in their finer details Old World conditions. Familiar faces, foods, churches, and speech patterns comforted lonely immigrants.

Since members of the ethnic working class were too poor for even moderately priced mass transit, they tended to settle close to their places of work. Only on a bitterly cold winter day would workers pay the nickel or dime it cost to ride a streetcar or a horse-pulled omnibus. In New York City, Jews and Italians lived within walking distance of the Lower East Side garment factories. In Chicago, the Poles and Lithuanians who worked in the meat-packing industry awoke in the morning and went to sleep at night hearing the sounds of dying animals and smelling the stench of the stockyards.

Just as new residential trends separated rich and poor, prices for real estate in the central business district shot up at an incredible rate, sometimes as much as 1000 percent a decade in the late nineteenth century. Only businesses and industries could afford the new prices, so the central cities were turned over to high-income businesses, banks, warehouses, railroad terminals, and the recently developed department stores. It became an area where money was made, not where people lived.

The Problems of Growth

By the 1890s, British observers despaired over what had become of the once small American cities. The uncontrolled growth, they suggested, had created ugliness on an almost unprecedented scale. English traveler Charles Philips Trevelyan graphically described the horrors of industrial Pittsburgh:

A cloud of smoke hangs over it by day. The glow of scores of furnaces light the river banks by night. It stands at the junction of two great rivers, the Monongahela which flows down in a turbid yellowish stream, and the Allegheny which is blackish. . . . All nations are jumbled up here, the poor living in tenement dens or wooden shanties thrown up or dumped down with little reference to roads or situation, whenever a new house is wanted. It is the most chaotic city, and as yet there is no public spirit or public consciousness to make conditions healthy or decent.

Numerous American observers echoed Trevelyan's observations. American cities were unprepared for the incredible growth they experienced during the late nineteenth century. Housing, clean water, competent police, and adequate public services were all in short supply. Health standards were low everywhere and scientists had barely begun to study the problems and diseases created by crowded urban conditions. To make matters worse, the people who moved to the cities usually came from rural areas and were not familiar with city life.

Crime plagued rich and poor. Pickpockets, robbers, con artists, and violent gangs roamed the streets and alleyways of American cities. Urban police forces had been established in the 1830s and 1840s. In the 1850s, police were outfitted with uniforms and badges and allowed to carry clubs and revolvers, but the police still could not control or seriously curtail urban crime. In fact, during this earlier period, police were often expected to clean streets, inspect boilers, or run poorhouses as well as prevent crime and maintain public order. In addition, police corruption was as common as purse snatchings. Police took bribes from saloon keepers and streetwalkers to overlook illegal activities, and it was not uncommon to find policemen serving the ends of robbers or intimidating voters on election day. They owed their loyalty to the political boss who appointed them, not to some abstract public. Not until the end of the century would attempts to bring professionalism and civil service reform to police departments be successful.

Housing presented an even more pressing problem. Immigrants disembarking at the ports of entry and farmers arriving by train had to have some place to live, which created opportunities as well as problems. The building industry was one of the great urban boom industries, and its leaders largely determined the shape and profile of the modern city. Equipped with a lofty disregard for public opinion, like other businesspeople they worked in an essentially unregulated economic world and were bent on maximizing their profits.

When it came to urban housing money talked. In large cities from New York to San Francisco the rich built stately homes, in which high ceilings, European furnishings, and spacious rooms were common. Even the apartments of the upper classes were designed and constructed by gifted architects and artisans. The beautiful Dakota Apartments, Central Park West at Seventy-second Street, still stands as one of the architectural triumphs of the period.

On the other hand, undermaintained tenements—built to minimal codes but designed to cram the largest number of people into the smallest amount of space—greeted urban newcomers without money. Like skyscrapers, the tenements made use of vertical space by piling family upon family into small, poorly lit, badly ventilated apartments. By 1900 portions of the Jewish Tenth Ward in New York City's Lower East Side had reached population density levels of 500,000 people per one square mile and as many as one person per square foot of land in the most crowded areas. To be in the land of tenements, noted writer William Dean Howells, "is to inhale the stenches of the neglected streets, and to catch the yet fouler and dreadfuller poverty-smell which breathes from the open doorways. . . . It is to see the work-worn look of mothers, the squalor of the babies, the haggish ugliness of the old women, and the slovenly frowziness of the young girls."

Dumbell tenements—with a dumbbell-shaped indentation in the middle to allow better ventilation—were the most notorious examples of exploitative urban housing. Architectural critic Lewis Mumford claimed they "raised bad housing into an art." Although they conformed to the Tenement Reform Law of 1879, which required all rooms to have access to light and air, they made maximum use

Tenement apartments on the Lower East Side of New York were overcrowded, filthy, and dangerous. City life could be quite luxurious for the wealthy, however, as this room from Alexander T. Stewart's Fifth Avenue mansion shows..

of standard 25- by 100-foot urban lots. Although the problems inherent in the dumbbell tenement were obvious from the first, the design was not outlawed in New York until 1901. Their use, in fact, spread east to Boston and west to Cincinnati and Cleveland.

Street conditions, unlike housing, were more democratic in that they plagued rich and poor alike. People dumped trash and horses unloaded their own pollution onto dirty city thoroughfares. Spring rains turned the streets into fetid quagmires, and winter freezes left them with hard deep ruts. Well into the 1870s, pigs roamed the streets of most cities, rooting for food in the garbage and further polluting the environment. When trolleys began to replace horses as the primary form of urban transportation, editorialists predicted that air pollution would soon come to an end. As late as 1900, however, there were still 150,000 horses in New York City, each producing between 20 and 30 pounds of manure a day.

Waste not dumped onto the streets often found its way into the rivers that flowed through the major cities or into the harbors that bordered them. By the turn of the century, 13 million gallons of sewage were emptied each day into the Delaware River, the major source for Philadelphia's drinking water. In Baltimore, according to writer H. L. Mencken, the bay smelled like a "billion polecats." But this paled in comparison to Pittsburgh's rivers: The Golden Triangle, where the Allegheny and Monongahela rivers meet to form the Ohio River, could have just as aptly been dubbed the black triangle because of the industrial waste poured into it.

The establishment of dump sites did little to solve the terrible garbage problem. The Reverend Hugh Miller Thompson described the conditions in a New Orleans dump to a meeting of the American Public Health Association in 1879: "Thither were brought the dead dogs and cats, the kitchen garbage and the like, and duly dumped. This festering rotten mess was picked over by rag-pickers and wallowed over by pigs, pigs and humans contesting for a living in it, and as the heaps increased, the odors increased also, and the mass lay corrupting under a tropical sun, dispersing the pestilential fumes where the winds carried them."

The garbage problem grew worse between 1880 and 1914. According to a 1905 study, Americans produced more trash than any other people. An American city dweller, for example, produced an average 860 pounds of mixed rubbish each year, compared to 450 pounds per capita in English cities and 319 pounds in German cities.

The overcrowded housing, polluted streets and rivers, and uncollected garbage contributed to the notoriously unhealthy urban environment. Unfortunately, advances in medicine and public health to cope with the consequences of such problems lagged behind technological and industrial progress. Diseases ranging from yellow fever and smallpox to diphtheria and typhoid claimed thousands of victims. In 1878 a yellow fever epidemic moved along the Mississippi River—5150 people died in Memphis, another 3977 in New Orleans. Known as the American Plague, the disease struck without warning and often led to a rapid, painful death. Walter Reed's discovery in 1900 that the disease was carried by the *Aedes aegypti* mosquito led to a cure for this dreaded scourge.

The smallpox virus proved more persistent. Although not as deadly as yellow fever, it struck more people and left millions of pockmarked faces. Like diphtheria and scarlet fever, smallpox flourished in the overcrowded and garbage-strewn cities. During the late nineteenth century, health wardens were unsuccessful in limiting the diseases, mostly because they were party hacks who owed their jobs to political loyalty rather than knowledge of public health.

Death, suffering, and massive inconvenience eventually prodded city officials to move toward a more systematic approach to their problems. Slowly political appointees were replaced with trained experts. During the late nineteenth century remarkable progress was made, particularly after the development of the germ theory in the 1880s linked contagious disease to environmental conditions.

Health officials and urban engineers vigorously attacked the sewage and water problems. Discussing the importance of a good sewer system, one Baltimore engineer noted in 1907 that Paris is "the center of all that is best in art, literature, science, and architecture, and is both clean and beautiful. In the evolution of this ideal attainment, its sewers took at least a leading part." Without good sewers and clean drinking water, urban civilization was almost a contradiction of terms. Cities replaced cesspools and backyard privies with modern sewer systems, and most large cities turned to filtration and chlorination to assure a supply of pure water.

From Private City to Public City

In the areas of housing, pure water, and clean streets, the battle lines in most cities were drawn between individual profits and public need. Individual entrepreneurs had shaped the modern American city. They laid the horsecar and trolley lines; constructed the skyscrapers, apartments, and tenements; and provided water for the growing urban population. They worked, planned, and invested, fully expecting to earn huge profits. Because their pocketbooks came before their civic responsibilities, they provided good housing and services for only those city dwellers who could pay for it.

Historians have called this type of city the "private city." Using the profit motive to determine urban growth created numerous problems. It led to waste and inefficiency, for example competing trolley lines, where promoters could turn a profit; and such inconveniences as poorly cleaned streets, from which little money was to be made. But most important, it was contrary to planned urban growth. Urban entrepreneurs, generally unconcerned about the city as a whole, regarded parks as uneconomic use of real estate and battled against the idea of zoning. In the end, they contributed to the ugliness and problems of Pittsburgh, New York, Chicago, and other American cities.

By the turn of the century, however, urban engineers and other experts began calling for planned urban growth and more concern for city services. Advocates of the "public city," their aim was efficient, clean, healthy cities where rich and poor could enjoy a decent standard of life. Most urban planning advocates were college-educated professionals who brought knowledge, administrative expertise, and a taste for bureaucracy to government service. After 1900 they would increasingly dominate the quest for better services and more public responsibility, but in many cities their voices were heard too late. The scars of the private city remained on the urban landscape.

CITY CULTURE

It was almost like magic. At 3:00 P.M. on September 4, 1882, Thomas Edison's chief electrician threw the switch at the inventor's Pearl Street station in New York City. Four hundred electric lights went on. For the first time Wall Street buildings were illuminated by the brightest and clearest of all artificial lighting. "It was not until 7 o'clock, when it began to be dark that the electric light made itself known and showed how bright and steady it was," commented a *New York Times* reporter. In the *Times* offices, where 52 Edison lights illuminated the night, "it seemed almost like writing by daylight." Just as trolleys spelled the end for the horse car, electric lights eventually replaced gaslights, candles, and kerosene and oil lamps.

Night Life and Day Life

Electricity soon bathed America's leading cities in white light, making night day. In the rural regions life revolved around the sun. Farmers awoke with the sun, labored during the daylight hours, and went to sleep soon after the sun disappeared over the horizon. Although one's labor changed depending on the season, the order of one's day was changeless. In cities and industries, however, night became more than just a time to rest. Labor and leisure soon claimed their share of the night.

Nighttime labor proved a plague for the working class, but nighttime leisure animated the lives of the wealthy. For Broadway's "fast set," the real fun began after the theaters closed. They moved down the Great White Way, stopping at an exclusive restaurant for a late-night dinner, dining on shrimp Mornay, beef marguery, canape of crab meat, bisque de crème, and other such exotic dishes. At now-famous restaurants like Delmonico's, eating became a refined pleasure, not just a physical necessity.

City dwellers' eating habits also demonstrated the yawning gap between the values of an older rural America and those of the merging urban society. In 1840, critics of presidential candidate Martin Van Buren attacked him for his eating habits. William Henry Harrison, his opponent who subsisted on "raw beef without salt," ridiculed Van Buren's taste for strawberries, raspberries, celery, cauliflower, and French cooking, claiming that democratic virtue thrived only on crude, tasteless food. But the American diet had expanded along with the nation's cities. Lorenzo Delmonico, the Swiss immigrant who founded New York's most famous restaurant, popularized ices and green vegetables and made meals that rivaled the best in Paris.

Not only did city dwellers consume different types of food, the middle and upper classes consumed more of everything. This shift in consumption patterns signaled a break with the past. The traditional Victorian ethos emphasized production and values—thrift, self-control, delayed gratification, and hard work—that encouraged production. But with industrial success came a general fear of overproduction. Increasingly, advertisers and economic advisors in various ways attempted to transform Americans from "savers" to "spenders." They told people to abandon the traditional laissez-faire economic thinking (which viewed scarcity as an inevitable and fundamental fact of life) and to give in to their desire for luxury.

This new attitude was fostered in large American cities by department stores and hotels. John Wanamaker in Philadelphia, Marshall Field in Chicago, and Rowland H. Macy in New York opened department stores that catered to and pampered the middle and upper classes by offering an unequaled range of products and quality service. The architecture and interior decoration of the department stores, with their grand entrances, marble staircases, chandeliers, stained glass, plush carpets, and wood paneling, inspired extravagance. Spending came easily when the shopper was made to feel like royalty. Grand ho-

Late in the century, the widespread use of electricity and steel began to alter the face of American cities. With electric lights illuminating the streets, urban nightlife flourished, as in this scene of *Washington Street, Indianapolis at Dusk* (c. 1900) by Theodore Groll.

tels like the Waldorf Astoria in New York and the Palmer House in Chicago provided the same luxury. The austerity doctrines of the early nineteenth century were easily forgotten amidst such splendor.

It is difficult to imagine the impression electric lights, fruit salads, department stores, and grand hotels made on the people who lived in or visited American cities. They underscored a style of life clearly different from what existed in rural America. City life presented a strange new world that produced in American writers, painters, and musicians feelings of excitement and revulsion. This ambivalence formed the basis of a new urban culture, which combined the energies and experiences of all city people—black and white, male and female, immigrant and native-born.

From the Genteel Tradition to Realism and Naturalism

Frank Norris was born in Chicago, grew up in San Francisco, and lived for a time in Paris.

Restlessly moving about the world looking for action, he traveled to Cuba to report on the Spanish-American War, and to South Africa to chronicle the Boer War. In his journalism and novels, he told the truth, feeding his readers bloody slices of the real world. He battled "false views of life, false characters, false sentiments, false morality, false history, false philosophy, false emotions, false heroism." Shortly before he died at 32 of appendicitis in 1902, he boasted, "I never truckled. I never took off the hat to fashion and held it out for pennies. I told them the truth. They liked it or they didn't like it. What had that to do with me? I told them the truth."

The truth. How literature had changed from the previous generation! At the end of the Civil War, American literary tradition had little to do with harsh truth. Controlled by a literary aristocracy in Boston, literature conformed to the "genteel tradition." Great writers endeavored to reinforce morality, not portray reality. Real life was too sordid, corrupt, and mean; far too coarse, violent, and vulgar. These arbiters decided that literature should transcend the real and anchor to the ideal. James Russell Lowell spoke for other genteel writers when he commented that no man should describe any activity that would make his wife or daughter blush. Sex, violence, and passion were taboo.

Out of rural America came the first challenge to this genteel tradition. Local colorists like Bret Harte, who set his stories in the rough mining camps of the West, emphasized regional differences and used regional dialects to capture the flavor of rural America. In their own way, however, the local colorists were just as confined by their literary approaches. Although their characters used real American speech, they were hardly realistically presented. Humor and innocence were the hallmarks of local colorists.

Mark Twain, whose real name was Samuel Langhorne Clemens, was the only one to transcend the genre. Like a local colorist, he used regional dialects, humor, and sentimentality in all his novels, but he also explored the darker impulses of human nature. His classic, *The Adventures of Huckleberry Finn* (1884), exposed the greed, violence, corruption, alcoholism, and racism in American society. As

Huck and runaway slave Jim travel down the Mississippi River toward freedom, they encounter a society based on a perversion of Christian ethics and the Golden Rule. Nowhere is Twain more insightful than when he deals with American racism. In one scene, Huck invents a story about a riverboat explosion. A woman asks if anyone was injured. "No'm," Huck responds. "Killed a nigger." Relieved, she replies, "Well, it's lucky; because sometimes people do get hurt."

Mark Twain never outgrew his obsession with life on the Mississippi River. Except perhaps in *A Connecticut Yankee in King Arthur's Court,* the impact of industrialism and city life on the American character did not much interest Twain. It did, however, fascinate most of the other great writers of his generation. Equipped with camera eyes and critical minds, they wanted to show American life in all its harsh and sordid reality. The realism movement soon replaced the genteel sentimentality of the previous generation. Defined

Samuel Langhorne Clemens, better known as Mark Twain, wrote humorous and insightful novels about problems in nineteenth-century America.

by its leader William Dean Howells as "the truthful treatment of material," realism depicted average individuals dealing with concrete ethical choices in realistic circumstances. Even style became secondary. "Who cares for a fine style," Norris wrote in 1899. "Tell your yarn and let your style go to the devil. We don't want literature, we want life."

As realism matured in the largely unregulated and highly competitive cities, it turned into the more pessimistic naturalism, which was influenced by the writings of Charles Darwin, Karl Marx, and Sigmund Freud. The individual was seen as a helpless victim in a world in which biological, social, and psychological forces determined his or her fate. Naturalists were particularly interested in the effect of the uncaring forces of industrialization and urbanization on people's lives.

Describing the Urban Jungle

The premier naturalistic writer was Theodore Dreiser. Unlike most earlier American novelists, he was not Protestant, Anglo-Saxon, or respectable middle-class. His German-Catholic immigrant father's life was the flip side of the American success story. After a promising beginning, the family slid deeper and deeper into poverty. Dreiser knew what it was like to subsist on potatoes and fried mush, and all his life he dreaded winter, which reminded him of his most painful days of poverty. Sympathetic to those who suffered similarly, he wrote, "Any form of distress—a wretched, down-at-heels neighborhood, a poor farm, an asylum, a jail, or an individual or group of individuals anywhere that seemed to be lacking in the means of subsistence or to be devoid of the normal comforts of life—was

Novelist Theodore Dreiser, writing in the naturalist style, described urban social problems, often portraying characters as helpless victims of their environment.

sufficient to set up in me thoughts and emotions, which had a close kinship to actual and severe physical pain."

Dreiser left his home in Indiana at 16 and went to Chicago, where he became first a journalist and then a novelist. Unlike better-educated writers, Dreiser had no genteel tradition to shed or rebel against. With his plodding style and atrocious English, Dreiser lacked every writing tool except genius. His first novel, *Sister Carrie* (1900), unflinchingly describes the effect of modern urban society on the lives of one woman and one man. Carrie travels to Chicago from the countryside in search of happiness, which she equates with material possessions, but she discovers only poverty, exploitation, and hardship. The likable, friendly Carrie sinks ever deeper into physical and moral despair.

Frank Norris praised the novel, but it shocked most readers, who were accustomed to the genteel tradition. Doubleday, Page and Company published *Sister Carrie* but did not advertise it. As a result it sold only 456 copies, and Dreiser's royalties amounted only to a depressing $68.40. Americans did eventually recognize Dreiser's genius and interpreted his novels as realistic treatments of modern industrial society.

Like Dreiser, Stephen Crane was also interested in the effects of poverty and urban life on individual character. In his first novel, *Maggie: A Girl of the Streets* (1893), a girl raised in a New York City slum loses, in rapid order, her innocence, her virginity, and her life. It was not a story of a character being rewarded or punished—Maggie was an honest, cheerful person—but rather being a victim of her environment. Poverty determined Maggie's, and later Carrie's, fate.

Naturalistic writers challenged the traditional idea that individuals had the power to control their own destinies. The cherished frontier ideal of rugged individualism seemed poor protection against the forces of urban poverty and industrial exploitation. Carrie was no match for the sweatshop owner, and Maggie's innocence was merely a target in her environment. Neither book was a blueprint for reform, but they did suggest a pressing need for change.

Painting Urban Reality

Nationalistic Americans began to develop a truly national culture during the 1830s and 1840s. Unlike Europe, America did not have proud literary, artistic, or musical traditions—no Parthenon, no Rembrandt, no Beethoven. America's asset was land, thousands of square miles of wild land, and it became the basis of American culture. Writers wrote about it. Artists painted it. James Fenimore Cooper created Natty Bumppo, the virtuous frontier hero. Artist Thomas Cole endowed the American wilderness with a religious quality. Indeed, after visiting Europe, Cole reported that plowed fields and mountain castles had ruined the Old World landscape. "American scenery," he wrote, "has features, and glorious ones, unknown to Europe. The most distinctive, and perhaps the most impressive, characteristic of American scenery is its wildness."

American artists shared with American writers and social critics a general aesthetic and philosophical dislike of the city. As Americans moved west, artists continued to focus on the landscape. Albert Bierstadt exaggerated the drama of the Rocky Mountains, but his pictures thrilled eastern and western Americans alike. Even the great, late-nineteenth-century realists—Winslow Homer, Thomas Eakins, and John LaFarge—harbored a suspicion, if not an outright fear, of the city. To be sure, Eakins's work demonstrated a profound respect for the machine, but his admiration did not extend to the city.

By the end of the century, however, the varied urban landscape began to intrigue artists. Steel bridges; colorful immigrant costumes; smoke-filled, congested streets; clashing boxers; washed clothes hanging between tenements; pigeons soaring over flat apartment roofs—each demonstrated the everyday beauty of the city. The energy, conflict, and power of the city seemed to explode with artistic possibilities. When a critic noted that the fighters' faces in George Bellows's *Stag at Starkey's* were hidden, Bellows replied, "Who cares what a prize fighter looks like. It's his muscles that count."

Appropriately enough, the center of this new movement was New York City. The leader of the school—often called Ashcan because of its urban orientation—was Robert Henri, an artistic and political radical. Skyscrapers thrilled him, and he saw beauty in the most squalid slum. He was joined by other artists who shared his love of city life and political radicalism. Generally impressionistic in style, the paintings used unmixed primary colors and quick brush strokes to produce a general impression of a scene. But they were more concerned with content than technique. As George Luks sneered at a critic, "Technique, did you say? My slats! Say, listen, you—it's in you or it isn't. Who taught Shakespeare technique? Guts! Guts! Life! Life! That's my technique."

Like Theodore Dreiser, who admired the Ashcan school, Henri and his followers used their talent to show problems in the growing cities. Bellows's *Cliff Dwellers* portrayed teeming life but also overcrowded tenement conditions; *Steaming Streets* underscored the problems of urban traffic. And George Luks's *Hester Street* illuminated the excitement but also the packed conditions of the Jewish section of Lower New York.

Maturing along with the Ashcan painters was a second school of artists who also drew inspiration from the urban landscape. Labeled modernists, they championed the pure freedom of nonrepresentational abstract painting. Their intellectual leader was Alfred Stieglitz, whose studio at 291 Fifth Avenue in New York was used to exhibit the modernist paintings. The modernists were also drawn to the conflict and power of the city. Painter John Marin observed, "I see great forces at work, great movements, the large buildings and the small buildings, the warring of the great and the small. . . . While these powers are at work . . . I can hear the sound of their strife, and there is great music being played."

In 1913 the Ashcanners and the modernists participated in the most important art exhibition in American history. Held at the Sixty-ninth Regiment Armory in New York City, the show also included works by Cézanne, Van Gogh, Picasso, Marcel Duchamp, Georges Braque, and Juan Gris, the leaders of the European post-impressionists. The Armory Show drew some sharp criticism; Duchamp's cubist

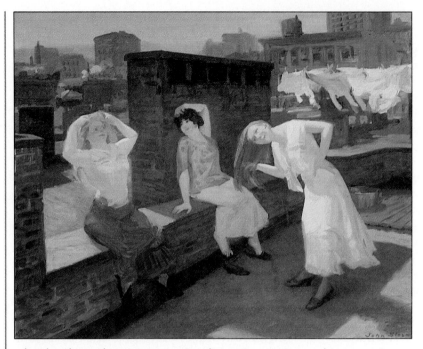

John Sloan's *Sunday, Women Drying Their Hair,* 1912, is an urban portrait typical of the Ashcan school. The school got its name because the artists preferred to paint the unglamorous, everyday aspects of city life.

Nude Descending a Staircase, for example, was called "an explosion in a shingle factory." Other critics and collectors maintained that the exhibition marked a new age for American art. "The members of this association have shown you that American artists—young American artists, that is—do not dread . . . the ideas or the culture of Europe," noted leading collector John Quinn. "This exhibition will be epoch-making." Its most important result was to fuse European and American art movements. It further signaled the ascendancy of the modernists, who would dominate the next generation of American art.

The Sounds of the City

Before the nineteenth century, music critics regarded American music as decidely inferior to European music; America had produced no great classical composers in the European tradition. Modern American music, uninfluenced by those traditions, was from the very first the language of the oppressed. American blacks adapted the rhythms and melodies of Africa to meet American conditions. Out of the marriage came the work songs of Mississippi slaves, the street cries of Charleston fish and fruit vendors, and spirituals, deeply emotional religious songs. Unlike European music, which was based on a 12-note scale, African music centered on rhythmic complexity with notes that did not conform to the standard scale. Repetition, call and response, and strong beat became the hallmarks of African-American music.

The two music traditions, African and European, existed independently in the United States until the 1890s. At that time they were thrown together in New Orleans as a result of the Jim Crow laws that legally and forcefully separated the races in that city. This process had unexpected results for American music. Before the 1890s wealthy half-white, half-black Creoles who followed European musical traditions lived in the affluent downtown section of New Orleans. Segregation, however, forced them uptown, where the poorer blacks who followed African musical traditions lived. Although the two groups did not mix socially, they did forge a new musical style–jazz.

This musical form, based on improvisation within a structured band format, used both the African and European traditions. Such early New Orleans jazz bands as Buddy Bolden's Classic Jazz Band and Joe "King" Oliver's Creole Jazz Band pioneered the style. Bolden was considered particularly talented. Even before segregation he had lived in the uptown region, where Baptist churches stood next to voodoo parlors and music provided the background for prayer, work, and play. Bolden's style was characterized by a powerful, moody grace that mesmerized audiences. But his music came from the soul of a troubled man. Plagued by syphilis and alcoholism, in 1907 he went berserk during a street parade and spent the rest of his life in a mental hospital.

In Storyville, the New Orleans red-light district, the jazz musicians, freed from manual labor during the day, honed their musical skills and explored the possibilities of their instruments. Charlie "Sweet Lovin'" Galloway,

Ferdinand "Jelly Roll" Morton, Robert "Baby" Dodds, Bunk Johnson, Sidney Bechet, Alphonse Picou, and especially Louis Armstrong, entertained Storyville customers. This section may have been the "Gibraltar of commercialized human degradation and lust," but it was also the mecca of jazz musicians. On an average night, 50 musicians played in Storyville; during carnival season as many as 75.

African-American musicians who worked in Storyville earned far more than even skilled laborers. Alphonse Picou recalled the days before Storyville was officially closed with fond nostalgia: "Those were happy days, man, happy days. Buy a keg of beer for one dollar and a bag of food for another. . . . Talking 'bout wild and wooly! There were two thousand registered girls and must have been ten thousand unregistered. And all crazy about clarinet blowers."

Ragtime and the blues also flourished in Storyville. Ragtime, a syncopated piano style that needed only one performer, was popular as café and bordello entertainment. Tony Jackson, Scott Joplin, and Jelly Roll Morton played ragtime piano with style and grace. Joplin, a Texas-born African American who

Jazz combined European and African musical styles into a new musical form. Here King Oliver's Creole Jazz Band poses for a rare picture.

had formal musical training, wrote several scores of popular rags, and his "Maple Leaf Rag" (1899) probably sold a million copies in sheet music form. Morton also advanced ragtime, developing the piano swing beat. Blues musicians—mostly African Americans from the Mississippi Delta region raised outside of European music traditions—performed in cheap saloons and expressed the pain of life in a hostile world.

During World War I, government officials closed Storyville, charging it was a health hazard. As the houses of prostitution closed their doors, the talented black musicians headed north—to St. Louis, Chicago, Memphis, Kansas City, and New York. They continued to play jazz and it continued to evolve. White musicians, trained in the European tradition, also contributed to this new American musical form. Bix Beiderbecke from Davenport, Iowa, for example, who formed a Chicago-based jazz band, used more instruments, replaced the African banjo with the guitar, and moved away from improvisation.

The larger jazz bands that dominated music during the next generation were an outgrowth of the New Orleans sound, the result of the mixture of European and African musical traditions. It could only have happened in the fertile atmosphere of the cities, where old and new, black and white, immigrant and native-born combined to create new literary, artistic, and musical forms.

ENTERTAINING THE MULTITUDES

City sports, like city music, were loud and raucous. They moved to the beat of the trolley cars, steel wheels on steel tracks, not horses' hooves on dusty farm roads. Before the urbanization of the late nineteenth century, American sports and games tended to be informal and participant-oriented. Rules varied from region to region, and few people even considered the standardization of rules desirable. By 1900 this cozy informality had all but disappeared. Entertainment became a major industry, and specialized performers competed for the right to entertain the multitudes.

The emergence of commercialized entertainment was the result of changes in both American technology and values. Transportation improvements allowed professional entertainers and sports teams to move across America more easily and cheaply, and technological advances in the popular press, telegraph, and telephone allowed the results of games and entertainment news to quickly spread throughout the country. Also the Victorian notion that entertainment was somehow suspect began to decline. Drawing on Puritan criticisms of play and recreation and a Republican ideology that was hostile to luxury, hedonism, and extravagance, the Victorians had tended to associate theaters, dance halls, circuses, and organized sports with such vices as gambling, swearing, drinking, and immoral sexual behavior. Popular entertainments were judged guilty by association.

In the second half of the nineteenth century, however, these prejudices were challenged. Members of the Victorian counterculture revered play, gratification, and revelry more than the virtues of hard work, punctuality, delayed gratification, and self-control. At first, members of the counterculture tended to be immigrants and bachelors. Irish, German, and eastern and southern European immigrants brought with them a culture at odds with Victorian notions of work and play. In addition, immigrants tended to marry later than native-born Americans; even at midcentury 40 percent of men between the ages of 25 and 35 were unmarried. These men thus formed a "bachelor subculture" that revolved around saloons, gambling halls, race tracks, boxing rings, billiard rooms, and cockpits. As the Victorian economic and social order began to crumble toward the end of the century, upper-class and then middle-class Americans became interested in the activities of the bachelor subculture. The result: a new attitude toward sports and leisure.

Of Fields and Cities

"Baseball," wrote Mark Twain, "is the very symbol, the outward and visible expression of the drive and push and struggle of the raging, tearing, booming nineteenth century." Baseball captured the bustle and hustle of city life. More than any other sport of the period, baseball was an urban game. All of the early professional teams were located in cities and most of the paid players were products of the cities.

The mythology of the sport, however, still lingers—that Abner Doubleday "invented" baseball in 1839, when he laid out the first baseball diamond in the pastoral village of Cooperstown, New York. The United States Post Office gave semiofficial recognition to the myth in 1939 when it issued a commemorative stamp honoring the centennial anniversary of the event. In fact, however, if anyone can be said to have invented a sport that actually evolved, it was Alexander J. Cartwright, Jr., a New York City stationery-bookstore owner who in 1845 set down the first written rules for the game.

The symbols of the game also recalled America's rural past. Unlike most modern sports, no clock governed the pace of a baseball game. In crowded, dirty cities, baseball was played on open, grassy fields with such bucolic names as Sportsman Park, Ebbets Field, and the Polo Grounds. (Yankee Stadium, opened in 1923, was the first baseball enclosure to veer from the rural tradition.) The field even had fences and bullpens, and the game was played during the planting and harvesting seasons of spring, summer, and fall.

If the symbols and mythology of baseball were rural, the game itself was very urban. Team managers, like their industrialist counterparts, preached the values of hard work, punctuality, thrift, sobriety, and self-control to their players. Baseball, they emphasized, was like modern life, ruthlessly competitive and demanding sacrifice for the "good of the team." As Mr. Clayton, a character in an 1891 baseball novel, explained, "We can't work and we can't play, we can't learn and we can't make money without getting some of other people's help." Like modern corporate society, then, modern sports reinforced the idea of teamwork.

During the last third of the nineteenth century, as men like Rockefeller and Carnegie struggled to bring order to their industrial empires, modern baseball took form. Rules were standardized, for one thing. In the early years of baseball, a base runner could be

Baseball was the leading sport of the late nineteenth century. It brought a sense of America's rural past into the country's urban present.

thrown out by hitting him with the ball as he ran between the bases. Organizers outlawed such violent relics of the past. Then owners attempted to make the sport suitable for the urban middle class. They banned the spitball, arranged games to fit the urban professionals' schedules, fined players for using profanity, and encouraged women to attend the games.

Most important, the owners formed competitive professional leagues centered in the industrial cities of America. In 1869 Harry Wright took his all-professional Cincinnati Red Stockings on a barnstorming tour. Traveling on the recently completed transcontinental railroad, they played teams from New York City to San Francisco and compiled a record of 57 wins, no losses, and 1 tie. Over 23,000 fans watched their 6-game series in New York, and almost 15,000 spectators attended a single game they played in Philadelphia. In that year the team traveled 11,877 miles by rail, stage, and boat, and entertained more than 200,000 spectators.

The Cincinnati club taught the rest of America, as one journalist commented, that "steady, temperate habits and constant training are all conditions precedent to all first class professional organizations." It also demonstrated to entrepreneurs that there was money to be made in professional sports. In 1876 William A. Hulbert and several associates formed the National League, which was organized around owners and clubs, not players. In business

SPORTS AND LEISURE

COLLEGE FOOTBALL WARS

ALTHOUGH the year was 1905, the story is hauntingly familiar: colleges, football, corruption. Henry Beach Needham in an article in *McClure's* charged that college football had become a professional endeavor, that players were paid performers who cared little for their studies. One example was James J. Hogan, Yale's team captain and star player who knew how to make the most out of an "amateur" sport. At the age of 27, he agreed to play football for Yale. In return, Yale paid his tuition, gave him a $100-a-year scholarship, housed him in rooms at its most luxurious dormitory, and fed him at the University Club. In addition, Hogan and two other players received all the profits from the sale of game programs; Hogan was also appointed the American Tobacco Company's agent in New Haven and received a commission on every package of cigarettes sold in the area. Finally, after each season—but during the school term—Hogan was given a ten-day vacation trip to Cuba.

Hogan was by no means unique. In an age of unregulated football competition, it was each school for itself, each player for himself. Money talked and school spirit was for the students in the stands. Players were more mercenaries than students; their loyalty was constantly on the auction block. Andrew Smith demonstrated this principle in 1902. On October 4, Smith played an exceptional game for Pennsylvania State

University against a powerhouse Penn team. The next Monday he had transferred schools and was practicing with Penn, a college that had also "drafted" players from Middlebury, Colorado College, Lafayette, and Peddie. Lafayette College had little cause for complaint. Fielding H. Yost, who coached the University of Michigan for three decades, was an undergraduate at West Virginia at that time. During one season, an undefeated Lafayette "hired" Yost to play against the also unbeaten Penn. After the game, Yost "transferred" back to West Virginia.

Critics charged that football was undermining the very ethics that college professors were laboring to instill into students. As early as 1893, E. L. Godkin, editor of the influential *Nation,* noted that the leading colleges were losing their educational orientation and becoming "huge training grounds for young gladiators, around whom as many spectators roar as roared in the Flavian amphitheatre." More

than a decade later, Charles W. Eliot, president of Harvard, complained bitterly that each fall undergraduates at his university seemed totally obsessed by football, talking about or thinking about little else. Godkin and Eliot found an unlikely kindred spirit in John S. Mosby, who had led the Confederate Mosby's Raiders during the Civil War. Although he had been suspended from the University of Virginia in 1853 for shooting a fellow student, Mosby continued to think of the school as his alma mater. In 1909 the old Raider wrote, after a tragic accident there, "I do not think football should be tolerated where the youth of the country are supposed to be taught literature, science and humanity. The game seems to overshadow everything else at the University."

By the turn of the century, the number of athletes killed or injured in football games had reached an alarming level. In 1909 Virginia halfback Archer Christian died shortly after being injured in a

632

game against Georgetown. Mosby asked, "I believe that cock-fighting is unlawful in Virginia: Why should better care be taken of a game chicken than a school boy?"

Other critics pondered the same question—during the 1909 season 30 boys were killed and 216 seriously injured in football games. The most publicized death of that season was Army's captain Eugene Byrne. He was fatally injured in a game against Harvard. The event was so shocking that the game was immediately halted, and the Army-Navy game of that year was canceled. Byrne was buried with full military honors, while thousands mourned his senseless death and questioned the place of college football in American society.

The nature of football emphasized brutality and violence. Today the team with the ball has four plays to make a 10-yard first down, but during the late-nineteenth and early-twentieth centuries the offensive team had three plays to make a 5-yard first down, and passing was severely restricted, both by the rules and by tradition. As a result, coaches emphasized "mass plays" that directed the maximum amount of force against one isolated player or point on the field. The flying wedge was the most notorious mass play. It entailed players grouping themselves in a V formation and starting to run before the ball was put into play. At the last moment the ball was snapped and passed to a player within the wall of the wedge. The wedge of runners then crashed into their station-ary opponents. Given that equipment was crude—players often played without helmets and no helmet had a facemask—this use of a massed brute force injured hundreds of players each year.

If such plays were not bad enough, referees rarely enforced rules against slugging, kicking, and piling on. Victory was the supreme object; and any method seemed justified in the pursuit of that goal. One Princeton player confessed to a reporter that he and his teammates were coached to eliminate dangerous opponents during the early minutes of a game. A writer for the *Nation* believed this ruthless drive for victory illustrated a fundamental American characteristic: "The spirit of the American youth, as of the American man, is to win, 'to get there,' by fair means or foul; and the lack of moral scruple which pervades the struggles of the business world meets with temptations equally irresistible in the miniature contests of the football field."

By the end of the particularly brutal 1905 season many educators, journalists, and politicians had decided that college football served no educational good and did considerable harm. Professor Shailer Mathews of Chicago's Divinity School labeled football "a social obsession—a boy-killing, education-prostituting, gladiatorial sport." President Theodore Roosevelt stepped in and tried to clean up the game, and officials altered the rules of the sport, but a number of universities chose to drop football from their athletic programs. Columbia, Union, Northwestern, Stanford, and the University of California led the abolitionist movement.

Critics continued to level charges of brutality, commercialism, and corruption against football between 1905 and 1910. The 1905 rules had not lessened the violence, and deaths continued to shock concerned Americans. In 1910 the rules of football were once again altered. In the most important change, the forward pass as we know it today was legalized. Although football conservatives continued for several years to ignore the new offensive weapon, the pass came into its own in 1913. That year a highly regarded Army team filled an open date in its schedule with a small Indiana school called Notre Dame. During the game Notre Dame quarterback Charley Dorais threw perfectly timed passes to his favorite end Knute Rockne. The result was a 35–13 upset by the Irish of Notre Dame. By the end of the season other teams had adopted the new tactic and passes filled the autumn air. The age of the mass play was over.

Passing made football even more exciting, and after 1913 criticism of the sport generated little support. Continuing scandals over, brutality, commercialism, and corruption led more to attacks on individual schools than against football as a college sport. Indeed, by 1917 football reigned unrivaled as college's supreme sport and public spectacle.

terms, the league was a loosely organized cartel designed to eliminate competition among franchises for players. League officials eventually devised the "reserve clause," which effectively bound a player to the team that held the rights to him and further undermined his ability to negotiate for higher salary. Although the National League was known as a "rich man's" league because it charged a 50-cent admission price, it was certainly not a rich player's league.

In 1890 the players revolted and formed the Players' League. Headed by lawyer and star player John Montgomery Ward, the Players' League was an experiment in workers' control of an industry. In words similar to those used by workers in industry, the players' "manifesto" of 1889 claimed, "There was a time when the [National] League stood for integrity and fair dealing. Today it stands for dollars and cents.... Players have been bought, sold, and exchanged, as though they were sheep, instead of American citizens . . . by a combination among themselves, stronger than the strongest trusts, they [the owners] were able to enforce the most arbitrary measures, and the player had either to submit or get out of the profession in which he had spent years in attaining a proficiency." Although lofty in ideals, the Players' League was badly managed and lasted only one year.

With its failure, the National League increased its control over professional baseball. It either crushed rival leagues or absorbed them. In 1903, for example, after a short business war the National League entered into a partnership with the American League. The only losers were the players, whose salaries decreased with the absence of competition. Nevertheless, the sport's popularity soared. By 1909, when President William Howard Taft established the practice of the president opening each season by throwing out the first ball, baseball had become the national pastime.

"I Can Lick Any Sonofabitch in the House"

Only boxing rivaled baseball in popularity during the late nineteenth century. Like baseball, boxing began as a largely unstructured

sport, but by 1900 entrepreneurs had reorganized the activity into a profitable business. Although it remained illegal in most parts of America, it produced some of the first national sports heroes.

Bare-knuckle boxing, the forerunner of modern boxing, was a brutal, bloody sport. Two men fought bare-fisted until one could not continue. A round lasted until one of the men knocked or threw down his opponent. At that point both men rested for 30 seconds and then started to fight again. Fights could and often did last over 100 rounds and as long as 7 or 8 hours. After such a fight it took months for the fighters to recover.

Boxers, unlike baseball players, were often from poor immigrant families. Irish-Americans dominated the sport during the late nineteenth century, and they used boxing as a means of social mobility. Such men as John Morrissey, James C. Heenan, and John L. Sullivan became national legends during the period. Morrissey, for instance, was born in Ireland, lived in poverty in Troy, New York, gained fame as a prizefighter, and eventually became a leading New York gambler and politician. By the time he died, he had served two terms in Congress and made a fortune.

The Great John L. (John L. Sullivan), however, eclipsed Morrissey in popularity. He became the best-known American athlete of the nineteenth century. "Excepting General Grant," one newspaperman wrote, "no American has received such ovations as Sullivan." Born in Boston of Irish immigrant parents, Sullivan was a loud, boastful man who loved to fight. He often walked into a saloon and claimed he could outfight and outdrink "any sonofabitch in the house." After he won the bare-knuckle world heavyweight title in 1882, tales of his punching power and his unrestrained attacks on Victorian morality spread across the country. Politicians, actors, writers, and merchants avidly followed his exploits, but Sullivan never lost touch with his immigrant, working-class origin. In Irish Boston, Sullivan's elevated standing went unquestioned. Comparing the Boston of old and new America, one poet wrote:

Just fancy what mingled emotions
Would fill the Puritan heart
To learn what renown was won for his town
By means of the manly art!
Imagine a Winthrop or Adams
In front of the bulletin board,
Each flinging his hat at the statement that
The first blood was by Sullivan scored.

During the 1880s, Sullivan watched his sport move toward greater respectability. Boxing, like baseball, underwent a series of reforms. The traditional challenge system of arranging fights was replaced by modern promotional techniques pioneered by New Orleans athletic clubs. Fighters deserted barefisted combat and started wearing gloves. Most important of all, professional boxers adopted the Marquis of Queensberry Rules, which standardized a round at three minutes, allowed a one-minute rest period between rounds, and outlawed all wrestling throws and holds. The new rules also replaced the fight to the finish with a fight to a decision over a specified number of rounds. Although the new rules did not reduce the violence, they did provide for more orderly bouts.

With the advent of the Queensberry Rules, the factory system effectively invaded boxing. Just as workers lost control of the pace of work, fighters no longer could determine the pace of the action. Under the old rules prizefighters could tacitly agree to slow down the action in order to catch their breath or simply exchange boasts and oaths. Now a bell and a referee told them when to fight and when to rest.

John L. Sullivan won the last bare-knuckle championship contest. In 1889 he defeated Jake Kilrain in a fight held near Richburg, Mississippi. It was an illegal fight, but it attracted spectators from all social classes. Bat Masterson, the gunfighter and gambler, served as timekeeper, and he was joined at ringside by wealthy sons of southern aristocrats, gamblers, and sporting men of every variety. The fight lasted for 75 rounds, and both boxers drank whiskey between rounds. After winning the epic fight, Sullivan gained even greater fame.

In 1892 Sullivan lost the title to James J. Corbett in a legal gloved contest fought in New Or-leans. Nicknamed "Gentleman Jim," Corbett's scientific boxing style and smooth manners outside the ring demonstrated that boxing had gained some respectability. In fact, by the 1890s boxing was no longer a working-class sport. Like baseball, it had become an organized, structured, and profitable business. All that was left of the older sport was the legend of the Great John L.—the boisterous, crude, lovable, man-child. As he told future novelist Theodore Dreiser shortly after the Corbett fight: "I'm ex-champion of the world, defeated by that little dude from California, but I'm still John L. Sullivan—ain't that right. Haw! Haw! They can't take that away from me, can they? Haw! Haw! Have some more champagne, boy."

The Excluded Americans

Although promoters talked about the democratic nature of sports, this was far from the case. To be sure, a number of Irish and German men—often immigrants or sons of immigrants—prospered in professional sports, but far more Americans were excluded from the world of sports.

In large cities the lines between social classes tended to blur, much to the discomfort of the wealthy who struggled to separate themselves from the hoi polloi. The rich moved to the suburbs and employed other methods of residential segregation to isolate themselves. Another tactic to protect their exclusive status was to allow their children only to marry within their narrow group of acquaintances. They also used sports and athletic clubs to set themselves apart. "Gentlemen and ladies," as they styled themselves, they only wanted to compete against opponents of similar dress, speech, education, and wealth.

One way to exclude the masses was to engage in sports that only the very rich could play. Yachting and polo, for example, demanded nearly unlimited free time, expensive equipment, and a retinue of hired helpers.

In 1884 the New York Yacht Club was founded, quickly gaining as members a "succession of gentlemen ranking high in the social and financial circles" in the city. By the

1890s every major eastern seaboard city had its exclusive yacht club, and each summer the richest yacht owners sailed their splendid vessels to Newport, Rhode Island, the most exclusive of the summer colonies.

Athletic clubs devoted to track and field, golf, and tennis were similarly exclusive. The members of Shinnecock Hills, one of the oldest golf clubs in America, prided themselves not only on the beauty of their course, but on their social standing. Such exclusive clubs also had elaborate social calendars filled with dress balls and formal dinners. When sporting events were scheduled, participation and even the privilege of watching were normally on an invitation-only basis.

Wealthy patrons also advocated the code of amateurism to separate the greedy professionals—who often came from the poorer classes—from more prosperous athletes who participated in a sport simply for the love of the game. The constitution of the British Amateur Rowing Association, for example, defined an amateur as a person who had never rowed for a stake or money; who had never knowingly rowed with or against a professional; who had never taught any form of athletics for money; who had never "been employed in or about boats, or in manual labour, for money or wages"; and who was not "by trade or employment for wages a mechanic, artisan or labourer, or engaged in any menial duty." The revival of the Olympic Games in 1896 strengthened the amateur code. (When it was discovered, for example, that Jim Thorpe, an Oklahoma Indian who had attended the Carlisle Indian School and who won the decathlon and the pentathlon in the 1912 Stockholm Games, had played baseball for a minor league professional team during the summer of 1909, the International Olympic Committee stripped him of his medals.)

Although amateurism was a subtle attack on the working class, sports leaders moved more forcefully against African Americans. During the 1870s and 1880s, blacks and whites competed against each other on a fairly regular basis. A number of blacks even rose to become world champions. Marshall W. "Major" Taylor was hailed as the "Fastest Bicycle Rider in the World"; Isaac Murphy rode to three Kentucky Derby victories; and George Dixon and other blacks won boxing titles. During the 1890s, however, most sports became segregated.

Jim Crow laws came to boxing during this period. John L. Sullivan steadfastly refused to fight African-American boxers. In 1892 he issued his famous challenge to fight all contenders: "In this challenge I include all fighters—first come, first served—who are white. I will not fight a Negro. I never have and I never shall." True to his word, the Boston Strong Boy never did. The same year, lightweight champion George Dixon administered a terrible beating to white challenger Jack Skelly in New Orleans. After the fight, the editor of the *New Orleans Times-Democrat* wrote that it was "a mistake to match a negro and a white man, a mistake to bring the two races together on any terms of equality, even in the prize ring." After 1892 the number of "mixed bouts" declined rapidly.

Organized baseball also excluded African Americans during the 1890s. Several owners integrated their professional baseball teams during the 1880s, but the trend toward segregation that led to the landmark court case, *Plessy* v. *Ferguson* (1896), overtook baseball. In 1889 baseball's *Sporting News* announced that "race prejudice exists in professional baseball ranks to a marked degree, and the unfortunate son of Africa who makes his living as a member of a team of white professionals has a rocky road to travel." The observation was accurate. By 1892 major league baseball was all white, to remain so until Jackie Robinson broke the "color barrier" in 1946.

Cultural expectations and stereotypes also limited the development of women athletes. Scientists spoke confidently about women's "arrested evolution." Compared to men, women were considered weak and uncoordinated, athletically retarded because of their narrow sloping shoulders, broad hips, underdeveloped muscles, and short arms and legs. Women might ride a bicycle or gently swing a croquet mallet, but men ridiculed women who were interested in serious competitive athletics. The cult of domesticity, which idealized women as nurturers and maintained that women's proper sphere was the home, also militated against female participation in competitive sports.

Even during the 1890s, when the tall, commanding Gibson Girl was the physical ideal and women were becoming more interested in sports and exercise, women's athletics developed along different lines than men's. Male and female physical educators considered women to be noncompetitive and decided that women's sports should promote a woman's physical and mental qualities and thus make her more attractive to men. They also believed that sports and exercise would sublimate female sexual drives. As renowned physical educator Dudley A. Sargent noted: "No one seems to realize that there is a time in the life of a girl when it is better for her and for the community to be something of a boy rather than too much of a girl."

But tomboyish behavior had to stop short of abrasive competition. Lucille Eaton Hill, director of physical training at Wellesley College, urged women to "avoid the evils which are so apparent . . . in the conduct of athletics for men." She and other female physical educators encouraged widespread participation rather than narrow specialization. Spectator and professional sports were left to the men. It was not until 1924 that women were allowed to compete in Olympic track and field events, and even then on a limited basis.

From Central Park to Coney Island

Like sports, parks changed to satisfy new urban demands. Uneasy about the urban environment, mid-nineteenth-century park designers saw in parks an antidote for the tensions and anxieties caused by city living. Frederick Law Olmsted, the most famous park architect, believed cities destroyed community ties and fostered ruthless competition. He designed Central Park to serve as a rural retreat in the midst of New York City. Surrounded by trees, streams, and ponds, city dwellers would be moved toward greater sociability. "No one who has closely observed the conduct of the people who visit [Central] Park," Olmsted declared, "can doubt that it

exercises a distinctly harmonizing and refining influence upon the most unfortunate and most lawless classes of the city—an influence favorable to courtesy, self-control, and temperance." But Olmsted was occasionally upset by the behavior of a "certain class" of visitors who believed "that all trees, shrubs, fruit and flowers are common property" and who refused to behave according to Olmsted's ideal.

Other leaders of Victorian culture shared Olmsted's vision. They believed that culture and leisure activities should smooth the rough edges of the urban masses. They built parks, libraries, and museums. Both the Metropolitan Museum of Art in New York and the Museum of Fine Arts in Boston opened in 1870. Visitors to these repositories of culture were expected to behave in an orderly, respectful manner. Museum officials frowned upon laughing, talking, coughing, shouting, and loud demonstrations of enthusiasm.

Many urbanites, however, wanted more excitement than the quiet world of Central Park and the new museums. This was clearly seen at the World's Columbian Exposition of 1893 in Chicago. The most popular area of the World's Fair was the Midway, the center of commercial amusements. Visitors eagerly rode the Ferris wheel, frequented the "40 Ladies from 40 Nations" exhibition, and watched "Little Egypt" perform her exotic dances. Parks and entertainment that amused, not soothed, attracted the most people.

Entrepreneurs were quick to recognize and satisfy the public's desire for entertainment. During the 1890s a series of popular amusement parks opened in Coney Island, New York. Unlike Central Park, which was constructed as a rural retreat, the Coney Island parks glorified the sense of adventure and excitement of the cities, and offered exotic, dreamland landscapes; wonderful, novel machines; and a free and loose social environment. Men could remove their coats and ties, and both sexes could enjoy a rare personal freedom. As one immigrant claimed, for the young, "privacy could be had only in public."

Coney Island also exemplified new values. If Central Park reinforced self-control, sobriety, and delayed gratification, Coney Island

Coney Island provided a temporary escape from the pressures of urban life. Its sense of informality and sheer excitement attracted people of every class.

stressed the emerging consumer-oriented values of extravagance, gaiety, abandon, revelry, and instant gratification. It attracted working-class Americans who longed for at least a taste of the "good life." A person might never own a mansion in Newport, but he could for a few dimes experience the exotic pleasures of Luna Park or Dreamland Park.

Even the rides in the amusement parks were designed to create illusions and break down reality. Mirrors distorted people's images, and rides threw them off balance. At Luna Park, the Witching Waves simulated the bobbing of a ship in high seas, and the Tickler featured spinning circular cars that threw riders together. "Such rides," wrote a student of Coney Island, "served in effect as powerful hallucinogens, altering visitors' perceptions and transforming their consciousness, dispelling everyday concerns in the intense sensations of the present moment. They allowed customers the exhilaration of whirlwind activity without physical exertion, of thrilling drama without imaginative effort."

A leading cultural critic of the period, James Gibbons Huneker, feared the surrender of reason and repression that Coney Island encouraged. "Unreality," he commented, "is as greedily craved by the mob as alcohol by the dipsomaniac; indeed, the jumbled night-mares of a morphine eater are actually realized at Luna Park." And Maxim Gorky, the Russian writer and revolutionary who visited America in 1906, suggested that mass amusement acted as an opiate of the people.

The Magic of the Flickering Image

Coney Island showed workers that machines could liberate as well as enslave. The motion picture industry, in turn, offered a less expensive, more convenient escape. During the early twentieth century the motion picture developed into a major popular culture form, one that reflected the hopes and ambitions, fears and anxieties of an urban people.

In 1887 when Thomas Edison moved his research laboratory from Menlo Park to Orange, New Jersey, he gave William K. L. Dickson, one of his leading inventors, the task of developing a motion picture apparatus. Edison envisioned a machine "that should do for the eye what the phonograph did for the ear." Working closely with Edison, Dickson developed the Edison kinetophonograph, a machine capable of showing film in synchronization with a phonograph record. The idea of talking pictures, however, was not as popular as the moving pictures themselves. Further refinements by Edison and other inventors made silent moving pictures a commercial reality.

The first movies, as the new form was soon called, presented brief vaudeville turns or glimpses of everyday life. Such titles as *Fred Ott's Sneeze, Chinese Laundry, The Gaiety Girls Dancing, Dentist Scene,* and *Highland Dance* tell the full content of each 3- or 4-minute film. Filmmakers soon began to experiment with such techniques as editing and intercutting separate "shots" to form a dramatic narrative. In 1903 Edwin S. Porter's *The Great Train Robbery,* the first western and the first film to exploit the violence of armed robbery, fully demonstrated the commercial possibilities of the movie. The 12-minute film mesmerized audiences.

During the early twentieth century, movies developed a strong following in ethnic, working-class neighborhoods. Local entrepreneurs converted stores and saloons into nickelodeons and introduced immigrants to a silent world of promise, inexpensive and short escapes from the grimmer realities of urban life. Describing the experience of visiting a nickelodeon, Abraham Cahan, editor of the *Jewish Daily Forward,* wrote in 1906: "People must be entertained and five cents is little to pay. A movie lasts half an hour. If it isn't too busy you can see it several times. They open in the afternoon and customers, mostly men and women, eat fruit and have a good time." In addition, since the movies were silent, knowledge of English was not required for enjoyment.

Ministers, politicians, and other guardians of traditional Victorian morality were quick to criticize the new form of entertainment. Their fears were summarized by Nebraska's superintendent of schools Joseph R. Fulk. Movies, he said, "engendered idleness and cultivated careless spending" at the "expense of earnest and persistent work." Worse yet, they stirred "primitive passions," encouraged "daydreaming," and fostered "too much familiarity between boys and girls." Soon local boards of censorship formed to protect innocent boys and girls, and some not-so-innocent men and women, from being corrupted by movies.

In the cities, censorship movements ultimately failed. Attempts by white, native-born American entrepreneurs to control the new industry similarly failed. Ironically, while films were beginning to attract middle-class audiences, control of the industry began to shift to immigrant entrepreneurs, most of whom were Jews from eastern Europe who proved better able than native-born businessmen to develop the possibilities of the medium. The immigrants emerged from a culture that valued laughter, cooperation, and entertainment, which allowed them to make movies that appealed to Americans.

They were committed to giving the people what they wanted, not to the traditional Victorian code of morality. As Samuel Goldwyn, one of the best immigrant filmmakers, observed, "If the audience don't like a picture, they have a good reason. The public is never wrong. I don't go for all this thing that when I have a failure, it is because the audience doesn't have the taste or education, or isn't sensitive enough. The public pays the money. It wants to be entertained. That's all I know." Film moguls started producing feature-length

Early nickelodeons were cramped and uncomfortable, but they provided endless leisure enjoyments for both immigrants and native-born Americans.

films and moved the industry from the East Coast to sunny Hollywood, where they could shoot outdoors and, incidentally, escape union difficulties. While such "stars" as Charlie Chaplin, Douglas Fairbanks, and Mary Pickford captured the hearts of America, producers such as Adolph Zukor, William Fox, Louis B. Mayer, Carl Laemmle, and Harry Warner forged a multimillion-dollar industry.

The Agony of Painless Escape

At the same time as popular culture was exploring the theme of mechanized instant gratification, however, Americans were seeking escape in other, more ominous forms. Like the whirring machines at Coney Island and the flickering images on the silent silver screen, the mindless escape of narcotics attracted millions

Swashbuckling hero Douglas Fairbanks and "America's Sweetheart" Mary Pickford in a scene from *The Taming of the Shrew,* a United Artists film of 1929. In 1919, Fairbanks and Pickford, who married the following year, joined Charlie Chaplin and D. W. Griffith to form United Artists Corporation.

of Americans. During the late nineteenth and early twentieth centuries, as the nation underwent the trauma of industrialization and urbanization, Americans took drugs in unprecedented amounts. Apologists blamed this development on the Civil War, claiming that soldiers became addicted to morphine after using it as a painkiller. Yet France, Germany, Great Britain, Russia, and Italy also fought wars in the second half of the nineteenth century, and their drug addiction rates were far below those of the United States.

Part of the problem was that before 1915 there were few restrictions on the importation and use of opium, its derivatives, and cocaine. Physicians routinely prescribed opiates for a wide range of ailments, and patent medicine manufacturers used morphine, laudanum, cocaine, or heroin in their concoctions. William Hammond, former surgeon general of the army, swore by cocaine and drank a glass of a cocaine drink with each meal. The Hay Fever Association officially recommended cocaine as an effective remedy. Coca-Cola used cocaine as one of its secret ingredients, and the Parke-Davis Company produced coca-leaf cigarettes, cheroots, and a Coca Cordial. Vin Mariani, a wine product containing cocaine and endorsed by Pope Leo XIII, was advertised as "a perfectly safe and reliable diffusable stimulant and tonic; a powerful aid to digestion and assimilation; admirably adapted for children, invalids, and convalescents."

Cocaine in particular was regarded as a wonder drug. One manufacturer claimed that it could take "the place of food, make the coward brave, the silent eloquent, free the victims of the alcohol and opium habits from their bondage, and, as an anesthetic, render the sufferer insensitive to pain." But by the late 1890s its harmful effects had become obvious. Journalists and government officials linked it to urban crime and racial unrest in the South. Eventually, angry citizens and the federal and state governments launched the first great American crusade against cocaine. It culminated with the Harrison Anti-Narcotic Act in 1914, which controlled the distribution of opiates and cocaine; but drug addiction remained a problem in cities well into the 1920s.

Robert Louis Stevenson's *Dr. Jekyll and Mr. Hyde,* which he wrote while under the influence of cocaine, described the dangers of challenging society's standards and altering one's personality, but in America's cities a new culture had taken shape. Advocates of this culture opposed Victorian restraints, glorified the freedoms of urban life, and at the same time worried about the implications of a liberated life-style. Social, as well as economic, freedom came with a price. By the 1890s many Americans believed that some new form of regulation was needed to check the social and economic freedom unleashed in urban America.

CONCLUSION

On January 17, 1906, Marshall Field, the dry-goods merchant and founder of the large Chicago department store that bears his name, died. "The first as well as the richest citizen" in Chicago, noted the *New York Sun,* Field left his children over $140 million. Americans questioned how one man could accumulate such a fortune. "No man could earn a million dollars honestly," said politician William Jennings Bryan. Another critic suggested that Field's fortune was made at the expense of his more than 10,000 employees, 95 percent of whom earned $12 dollars a week or less: "The female sewing-machine operators, who make the clothes which are sold in the Field establishment, get $6.75 per week.... The makers of socks and stockings are paid: finishers, $4.75 per week of fifty-nine working hours ... knitters, $4.75 per week of fifty-nine and one-half working hours."

Most Americans, however, focused more on what Field offered shoppers than what he paid his employees. Marshall Field, A. T. Stewart, Rowland H. Macy, John Wanamaker—their very names conjured visions of miles and miles of consumer goods. These men brought order to shopping and emphasized standardization of products. In their department stores in New York, Chicago, and Philadelphia, customers could purchase ready-made clothes, jewelry, toys, sheet music, cutlery, and a wide

range of other products. Serving urban markets and satisfying urban desires, they also provided a safe haven for urban shoppers. Inside one of the great department stores, consumers were isolated from the garbage in the streets, the filth in the air, and the sounds of traffic and commerce that dominated the outside world. They chose not to think about the workers who made the goods they purchased.

The orderly world of the department store and the chaotic one of the streets were both products of the urban entrepreneurs who fashioned the modern cities. In pursuit of profits they were capable of producing dazzling monuments to commerce and terrible tributes to greed. The same spirit that built the Woolworth Building and the Dakota Apartments also constructed dumbbell tenements, but by 1900, their days of absolute dominance were numbered. Although they would remain a vital part of American capitalism, in the future they would be rivaled by governmental planners—people who wanted to extend the smooth, efficient order of the department store to the outside streets.

The emergence of the great cities changed American life, and more than just economically. Eventually they came to dominate the American imagination. In the cities, the clash of ideas and beliefs, of peoples and traditions created an exciting, new heterogeneous culture. The result was evident at places such as Coney Island and at the Armory Show; it was visible in many of the movies, and it was audible at a New Orleans jazz café. As the nineteenth century drew to a close, a new culture was clearly emerging. It would add a new element to the new century.

SUGGESTIONS FOR FURTHER READING

Lois W. Banner, *American Beauty* (1983). Charts changing standards of beauty in America.

John Bodnar, *The Transplanted: A History of Immigrants in Urban America* (1985). Rejects an older interpretation that viewed immigrants as peasants whose cultures were uprooted in the course of migration.

Roger Daniels, *Coming to America: A History of Immigration and Ethnicity in American Life* (1990). Of-

CHRONOLOGY
OF KEY EVENTS

Year	Event	Year	Event
1869	First professional baseball team, the Cincinnati Red Stockings, begins a barnstorming tour of America	1892	James J. Corbett wins heavyweight boxing title from John L. Sullivan; Stephen Crane publishes his first novel, *Maggie: A Girl of the Streets*
1870	The Metropolitan Museum of Art in New York and the Museum of Fine Arts in Boston open	1896	President Cleveland vetoes literacy requirement for adult immigrants
1871	Great Chicago fire claims 300 lives, destroys 17,500 buildings, and leaves 100,000 people homeless	1899	Scott Joplin composes "Maple Leaf Rag"
1873	Cable car is introduced in San Francisco	1900	Theodore Dreiser publishes his first novel, *Sister Carrie*
1878	Yellow fever epidemic causes 5150 deaths in Memphis and 3977 in New Orleans	1903	Edwin S. Porter's *The Great Train Robbery* is the first American film to tell a story
1879	New York City adopts Tenement Reform Law, requiring all rooms to have access to light and air	1912	Jim Thorpe, an Oklahoma Indian, wins the decathlon and pentathlon at the 1912 Olympic Games in Stockholm
1882	Chinese Exclusion Act suspends Chinese immigration for ten years; extended in 1892 and 1902; electric lighting comes into widespread use for the first time in New York City	1913	Artists from the Ashcan and modernist schools participate in the Armory Show in New York City
1884	Mark Twain's *The Adventures of Huckleberry Finn* is published	1914	Harrison Anti-Narcotic Act controls the distribution of opiates and cocaine
1885	William LeBaron Jenney erects the Home Insurance Building in Chicago, the first true skyscraper	1921	Emergency Quota Act provides that no more than 3 percent of a nationality already in America in 1910 could immigrate annually to the United States
1886	Statue of Liberty is unveiled	1924	National Origins Act lowers the immigration quota to 2 percent of each nationality already residing in the United States in 1890
1887	W. K. L. Dickson and Thomas Edison develop motion pictures		
1888	Richmond, Virginia, introduces the electric-power trolley		

fers a thorough history of immigrants to the United States.

Leonard Dinnerstein, *The Leo Frank Case* (1968). Case history of anti-Semitism and violence in America.

Caroline Golab, *Immigrant Destinations* (1977). Study of immigrant work in industrial America.

John F. Kasson, *Amusing the Millions: Coney Island at the Turn of the Century* (1978). Uses Coney Island to illustrate changes in American values from agrarian, to industrial, to consumption.

Lawrence W. Levine, *Highbrow/Lowbrow: The Emergence of Cultural Hierarchy in America* (1988). Demonstrates that popular culture can be fascinating without being trivialized.

Kerby A. Miller, *Emigrants and Exiles: Ireland and the Irish Exodus to North America* (1985). First-rate study of why many Irish left Ireland and how they were received in America.

Robert H. Wiebe, *The Search for Order, 1870–1920* (1967). Classic synthesis of major historical trends in turn-of-the-century America.

Overviews and Surveys

Thomas J. Archdeacon, *Becoming American: An Ethnic History* (1983); Leonard Dinnerstein, *Natives and Strangers: Blacks, Indians, and Immigrants in America* (1990); John Garraty, *The New Commonwealth* (1968); Charles N. Glaab and A. Theodore Brown, *A History of Urban America*, 3d ed. (1983); David R. Goldfield and Blaine A. Brownwell, *Urban America: From Downtown to No Town* (1979); Oscar Handlin, *The Uprooted*, 2d ed. (1973); Samuel Hays, *The Response to Industrialism, 1885–1914* (1957); Jacqueline Jones, *The Dispossessed: America's Underclasses from the Civil War to the Present* (1992); Maldwyn Allen Jones, *American Immigration*, 2d ed. (1992); Alan M. Kraut, *The Huddled Masses* (1982); Raymond A. Mohl, *The New City: Urban America in the Industrial Age, 1860–1920* (1985); Lewis Mumford, *The City in History: Its Origins, Its Transformations, and Its Prospects* (1961); Gerald Sorin, *A Time for Building: The Third Migration, 1880–1920* (1992); Jon C. Teaford, *Twentieth-Century American City*, 2d ed. (1993); Rudolph J. Vecoli and Suzanne M. Sinke, eds., *A Century of European Migrations, 1830–1930* (1991); Sam Bass Warner, Jr., *The Urban Wilderness* (1972).

THE NEW IMMIGRANTS

Rodolfo Acuña, *Occupied America: A History of Chicanos* (1988); Josef J. Barton, *Peasants and Strangers: Italians, Rumanians, and Slovaks in an American City, 1890–1950* (1975); John W. Briggs, *The Italian Passage: Immigrants to Three American Cities, 1890–1930* (1978); Jack Chen, *The Chinese of America* (1980); Hasia R. Diner, *Erin's Daughters in America: Irish Immigrant Women in the Nineteenth Century* (1983); John Duff, *The Irish in the United States* (1971); David M. Emmons, *The Butte Irish* (1989); Elizabeth Ewen, *Immigrant Women in the Land of Dollars: Life and Culture in the Lower East Side* (1985); Richard Gambino, *Blood of My Blood: The Dilemma of the Italian-Americans* (1974); Mario García, *Desert Immigrants: The Mexicans of El Paso, 1880–1920* (1981); Susan A. Glenn, *Daughters of the Shtetl: Life and Labor in the Immigrant Generation*

(1990); Yuji Ichioka, *The Issei: The World of the First Generation Japanese Americans, 1885–1924* (1988); Thomas Kessner, *The Golden Door: Italian and Jewish Immigrant Mobility in New York City, 1880–1915* (1977); Harry Kitano, *Japanese Americans*, 2d ed. (1976); Helena Znaniecka Lopata, *Polish Americans: Status Competition in an Ethnic Community* (1976); Joseph Lopreato, *Italian Americans* (1970); Ande Manners, *Poor Cousins* (1972); Charles C. Moskos, Jr., *Greek Americans: Struggle and Success*, 2d ed. (1989); Cecyle S. Neidle, *America's Immigrant Women* (1975); Humbert S. Nelli, *Italians in Chicago, 1880–1930: A Study in Ethnic Mobility* (1970), and *The Business of Crime: A Documentary Study of Organized Crime in the American Economy* (1976); Walter Nugent, *The Great Transatlantic Migrations, 1870–1914* (1993); William Petersen, *Japanese Americans* (1971); Andrew F. Rolle, *The Immigrant Upraised* (1968), and *The Italian Americans* (1980); Theodore Saloutos, *The Greeks in the United States* (1964); Henry Tsai Shih-shan, *China and the Overseas Chinese in the United States, 1868–1911* (1983); Stephan Thernstrom, *Poverty and Progress: Social Mobility in a Nineteenth-Century American City* (1964), and *The Other Bostonians* (1973); Maurice Biolette, *The Franco Americans* (1976); Sydney Weinberg, *The World of Our Mothers: Lives of Jewish Immigrant Women* (1988); Mark Wyman, *Round-Trip to America: The Immigrants Return to Europe, 1880–1930* (1993); Virginia Yans-McLaughlin, *Family and Community: Italian Immigrants in Buffalo, 1880–1930* (1977); Olivier Zunz, *The Changing Face of Inequality: Urbanization, Industrial Development, and Immigrants in Detroit* (1982).

Nativism: The Anti-immigrant Reaction

David H. Bennett, *The Party of Fear: From Nativist Movements to the New Right in American History* (1988); Robert Carlson, *The Americanization Syndrome: The Quest for Conformity* (1987); Mark Haller, *Eugenics* (1963); Leo Hershkowitz, *Tweed's New York: Another Look* (1977); John Higham, *Strangers in the Land*, 2d ed. (1988); Gerd Korman, *Industrialization, Immigrants, and Americanizers* (1967); Richard M. Linkh, *American Catholicism and European Immigrants, 1900–1924* (1975); Seymour Mandelbaum, *Boss Tweed's New York* (1965); Paul McBride, *Culture Clash* (1975); Stuart C. Miller, *The Unwelcome Immigrant: The American Image of the Chinese, 1785–1882*

(1969); Thomas J. Pavlak, *Ethnic Identification and Political Behavior* (1976); Diane Ravitch, *The Great School Wars: A History of New York City Public Schools* (1974); Alexander Saxton, *The Indispensable Enemy: Labor and the Anti-Chinese Movement in California* (1971).

New Cities and New Problems

Elaine S. Abelson, *When Ladies Go A-Thieving: Middle-Class Shoplifters in the Victorian Department Store* (1989); John M. Allswang, *Bosses, Machines and Urban Voters*, rev. ed., (1986); Andrew Alpern, *Apartments for the Affluent: A Historical Survey of Buildings in New York* (1975); Nelson M. Blake, *Water for the Cities* (1956); Charles W. Cheape, *Moving the Masses: Urban Public Transit in New York, Boston, and Philadelphia, 1800–1912* (1980); Howard P. Chudacoff, *Mobile Americans: Residential and Social Mobility in Omaha, 1880–1920* (1972); Michael H. Ebner, *Creating Chicago's North Shore: A Suburban History* (1988); Dean R. Esslinger, *Immigrants and the City: Ethnicity and Mobility in a Nineteenth-Century Midwestern Community* (1975); Phillip J. Ethington, *The Public City: The Political Construction of Urban Life in San Francisco, 1850–1900* (1994); David M. Fine, *The City, The Immigrant and American Fiction, 1880–1920* (1977); Robert M. Fogelson, *Big-City Police* (1977); Kenneth Fox, *Better City Government: Innovation in American Urban Politics, 1850–1937* (1977); Clifton Hood, *722 Miles: The Building of the Subways and How They Transformed New York* (1993); Maury Klein and Harvey A. Kantor, *Prisoners of Progress: American Industrial Cities, 1850–1920* (1976); Roger Lane, *Policing the City: Boston, 1822–1885* (1967), and *Violent Death in the City* (1979); Peter McCaffery, *When Bosses Ruled Philadelphia: The Emergence of the Republican Machine, 1867–1933* (1993); Blake McKelvey, *American Urbanization: A Comparative History* (1973); Clay McShane, *Technology and Reform* (1974); Harold M. Mayer and Richard C. Wade, *Chicago* (1969); Martin V. Melosi, *Garbage in the Cities: Refuse, Reform, and the Environment* (1982), and (ed.) *Pollution and Reform in the American Cities, 1870–1930* (1980); Gilbert Osofsky, *Harlem: The Making of a Ghetto* (1966); Harold L. Platt, *The Electric City: Energy and the Growth of the Chicago Area, 1880–1930* (1991); Bradley R. Rice, *Progressive Cities* (1977); Christine M. Rosen, *The Limits of Power: Great Fires and the Process of City Growth in America* (1986); Martin J. Schiesl, *The Politics of Efficiency: Municipal Administration and Reform in America, 1800–1920* (1977); Carl Smith, *Urban Disorder and the Shape of Belief: The Great Chicago Fire, the Haymarket Bomb, and the Model Town of Pullman* (1994); Allan H. Spear, *Black Chicago: The Making of a Negro Ghetto, 1890–1920* (1967); John Stilgoe, *Borderland: Origins of the American Suburb, 1820–1939* (1988); Jon C. Teaford, *The Unheralded Triumph: City Government in America, 1870–1900* (1984); David Ward, *Poverty, Ethnicity, and the American City, 1840–1925: Changing Conceptions of the Slum and the Ghetto* (1989); William S. Worley, *J. C. Nichols and the Shaping of Kansas City* (1990).

City Culture

Gunther Barth, *City People: The Rise of Modern City Culture in Nineteenth-Century America* (1980); Susan P. Benson, *Counter Cultures: Saleswomen, Managers, and Customers in American Department Stores, 1890–1940* (1986); Edward Berlin, *Ragtime: A Musical and Cultural History* (1980); Burton J. Bledstein, *The Culture of Professionalism: The Middle Class and the Development of Higher Education in America* (1976); Stuart Blumin, *The Emergence of the Middle Class: Social Experience in the American City, 1760–1900* (1989); Paul Boyer, *Urban Masses and Moral Order in America, 1820–1920* (1978); Susan Curtis, *Dancing to a Black Man's Tune: A Life of Scott Joplin* (1994); Blanche H. Gelfant, *The American City Novel*, 2d ed. (1970); James Gilbert, *Perfect Cities: Chicago's Utopias of 1893* (1991); Martin Green, *New York, 1913: The Armory Show and the Paterson Strike Pageant* (1988); Neil Leonard, *Jazz and the White Americans* (1962); Walter Benn Michaels, *The Gold Standard and the Logic of Naturalism: American Literature at the Turn of the Century* (1987); William L. O'Neill, *Divorce in the Progressive Era* (1967); David J. Pivar, *Purity Crusade: Sexual Morality and Social Control, 1868–1900* (1973); W. J. Rorabaugh, *The Alcoholic Republic: An American Tradition* (1979); Sheila M. Rothman, *Woman's Proper Place: A History of Changing Ideals and Practices, 1870 to the Present* (1978); Lewis O. Saum, *The Popular Mood of America, 1860–1890* (1990); William J. Schafer and Johannes Riedel, *The Art of Ragtime* (1973); David Shi, *Facing Facts: Realism in American Thought and Culture, 1850–1920* (1994); Thomas J. Schlereth, *Victorian America: Transformations in Everyday Life, 1876–1915* (1991); Vincent Scully, *American Architecture and Urbanism* (1969).

Entertaining the Multitudes

Melvin L. Adelman, *A Sporting Time: New York City and the Rise of Athletic Culture* (1986); Robert C. Allen, *Horrible Prettiness: Burlesque and American*

Culture (1991); Reid Badger, *The Great American Fair: The World's Columbian Exposition and American Culture* (1979); David F. Burg, *Chicago's White City of 1893* (1976); Dominick Cavallo, *Muscles and Morals: Organized Playgrounds and Urban Reform, 1880–1920* (1981); John E. DiMeglio, *Vaudeville U.S.A.* (1973); Perry Duis, *The Saloon: Public Drinking in Chicago and Boston, 1880–1920* (1983); Lewis A. Erenberg, *Steppin' Out: New York Nightlife and the Transformation of American Culture, 1890–1930* (1981); Charles E. Funnell, *By the Beautiful Sea: The Rise and High Times of That Great American Resort, Atlantic City* (1975); Warren Goldstein, *Playing for Keeps: A History of Early Baseball* (1989); Elliott Gorn, *The Manly Art: Bare-Knuckle Prize Fighting in America* (1986); Stephen Hardy, *How Boston Played: Sport, Recreation, and Community, 1865–1915* (1982); T. J. Jackson Lears, *No Place of Grace: Antimodernism and the Transformation of American Culture, 1880–1920* (1981); Lary May, *Screening Out the Past: The Birth of Mass Culture and the Motion Picture Industry* (1980); Donald J. Mrozek, *Sport and American Mentality, 1880–1910* (1983); James D. Norris, *Advertising and the Transformation of American Society, 1865–1920* (1990); Kathy Peiss, *Cheap Amusements: Working Women and Leisure in Turn-of-the-Century New York* (1986); Steven A. Riess, *Touching Base: Professional Baseball and American Culture in the Progressive Era* (1980); Roy Rosenzweig, *Eight Hours for What We Will: Workers and Leisure in an Industrial City, 1870–1920* (1983); Robert Sklar, *Movie-Made America*, rev. ed. (1994).

Biographies

Marianne Doezema, *George Bellows and Urban America* (1992); Neil Harris, *Humbug: The Art of P. T. Barnum* (1973); Michael T. Isenberg, *John L. Sullivan and His America* (1988); Peter Levine, *A. G. Spalding and the Rise of Baseball* (1985); Randy Roberts, *Papa Jack: Jack Johnson and the Era of White Hopes* (1983), and *Jack Dempsey: The Manassa Mauler* (1979); Laura Wood Roper, *FLO: A Biography of Frederick Law Olmsted* (1973); Elizabeth Stevenson, *Park Maker: A Life of Frederick Law Olmsted* (1977).

CHAPTER 19

End-of-the-Century Crisis

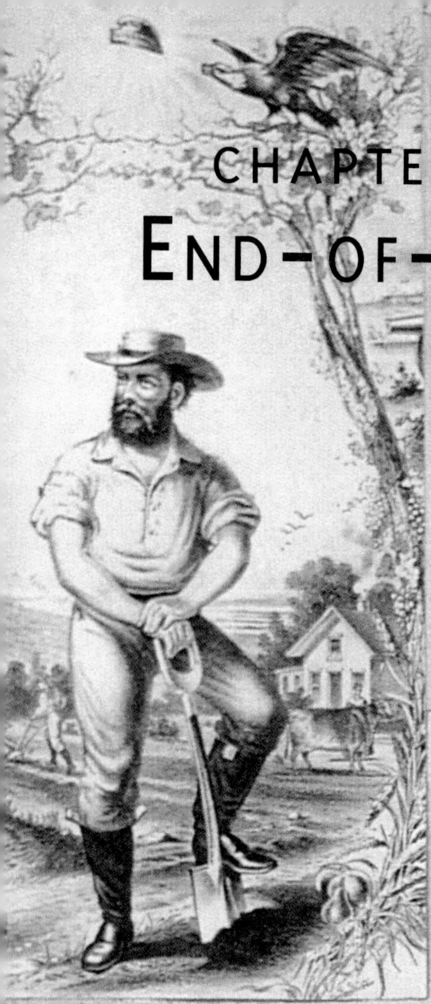

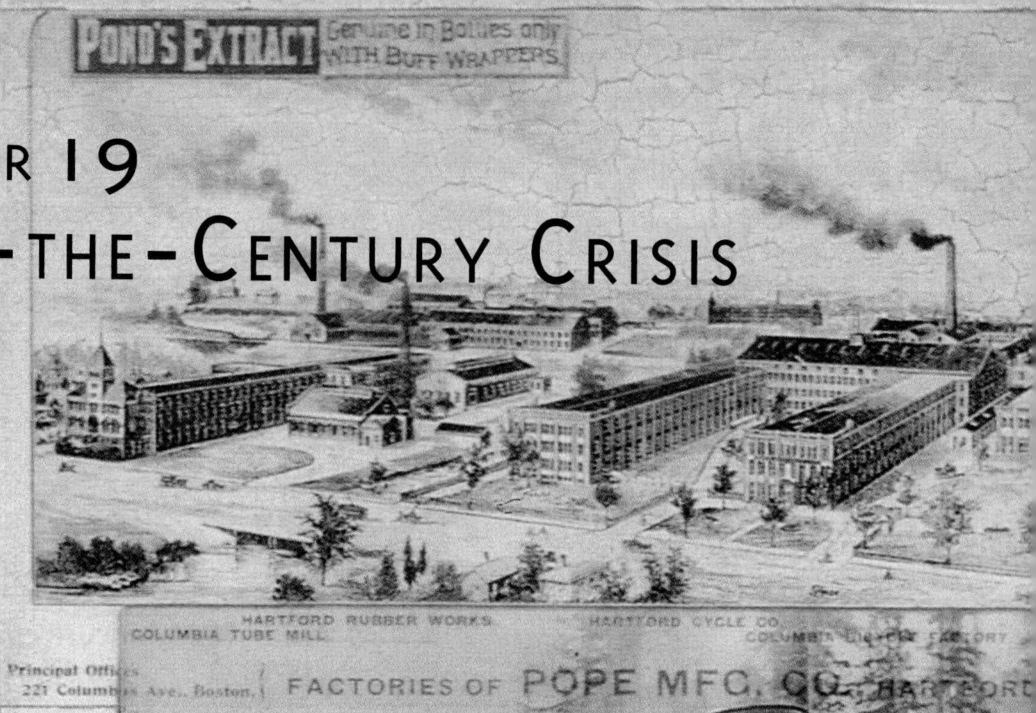

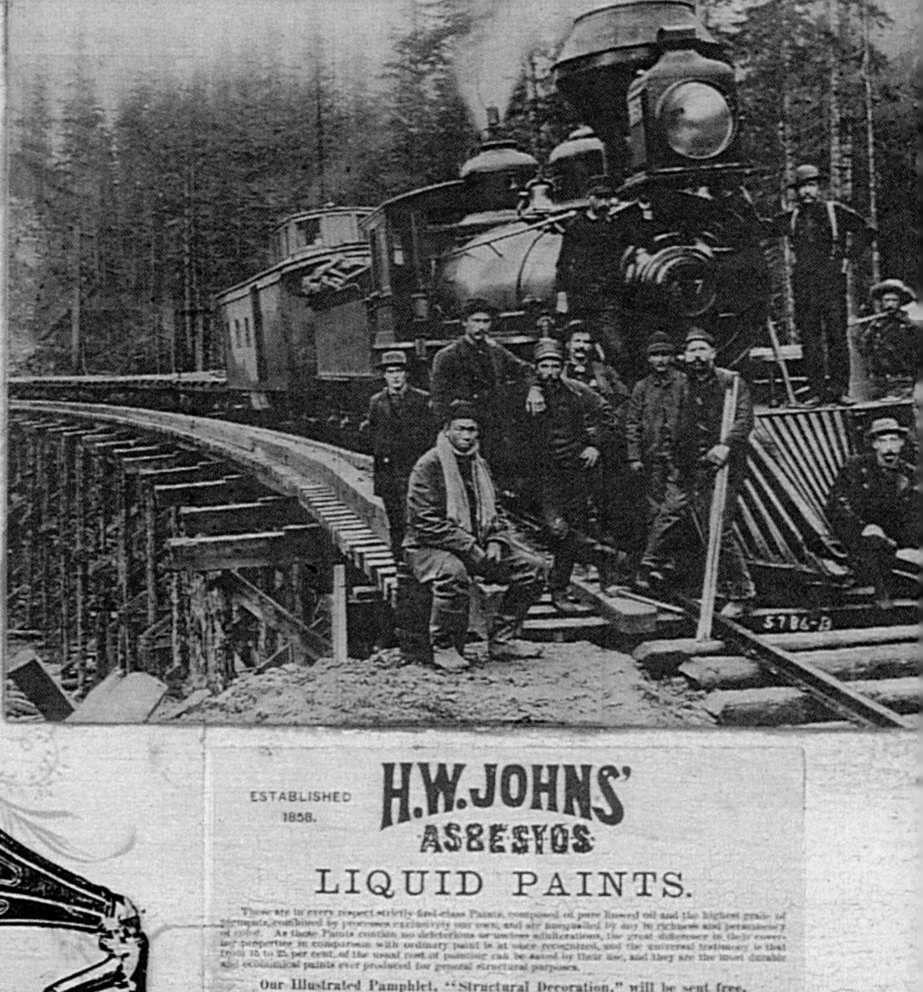

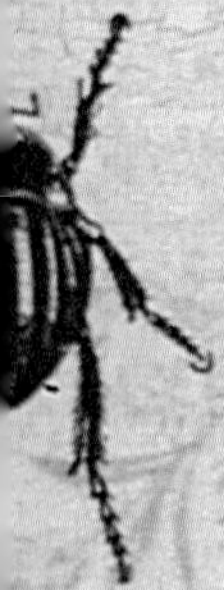

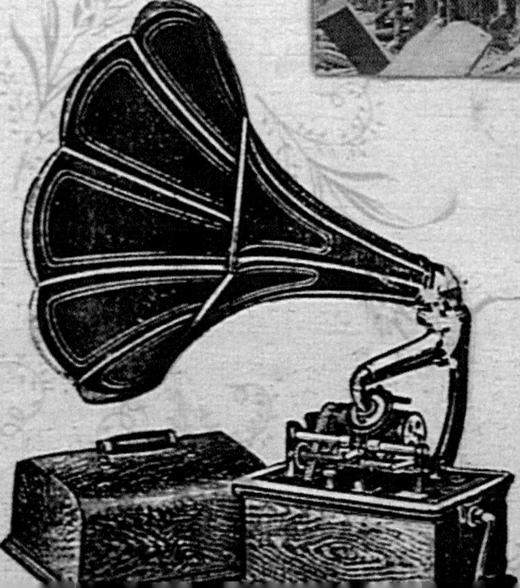

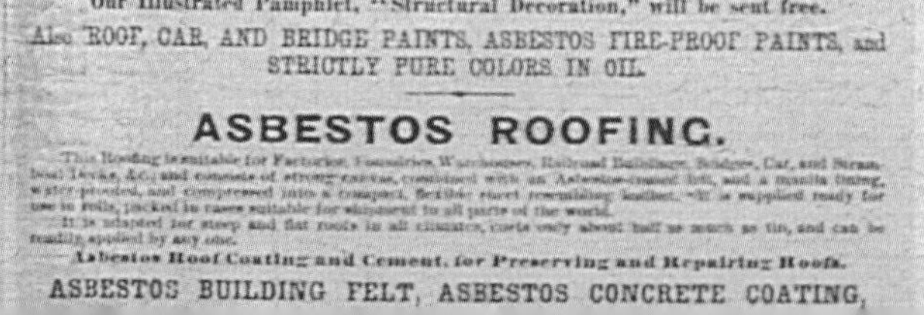

DECKER
BROTHERS'
MATCHLESS
PIANOS
33 Union Square, N.Y.

EQUILIBRIUM AND INERTIA: THE NATIONAL POLITICAL SCENE
Divided Power: The Parties and the Federal Government
Subtle Differences: The Bases of Party Loyalty
The Business of Politics: Party Organization
The Struggle for Inclusion: Women and Politics

STYLE OVER SUBSTANCE: GOVERNMENT IN THE GILDED AGE, 1877–1892
Hayes and the "Money Question"
Garfield, Arthur, and the Patronage Issue
Cleveland, the Railroads, and Tariffs
Harrison and Big Business
Legislative Activity on Minority Rights and Social Issues

REVOLT OF THE WEST AND SOUTH
Grievances: Real and Imagined
The Farmers Organize
The Agrarian Agenda
Emergence of the Populist Party

DEPRESSION AND TURBULENCE IN THE 1890s
The Roots and Results of the Depression
Expressions of Worker Discontent
Deteriorating Race Relations
The Tide Turns: The Election of 1896

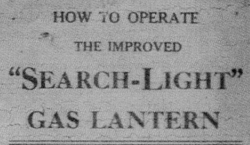

HOW TO OPERATE
THE IMPROVED
"SEARCH-LIGHT"
GAS LANTERN

BRIDGEPORT BRASS COMPANY
BRIDGEPORT   CONNECTICUT

Hale's Honey of Horehound and Tar

EPPS' COCOA.
Grateful & Comforting
Only Boiling Water or Milk needed.

STANDARD THERMOMETERS.

Organ & Piano

Franklin Square
Song Collection

BUY AMERICAN UNION LABEL GOODS AND SERVICES

On July 9, 1896, William Jennings Bryan rose to speak to the delegates at the Democratic National Convention in Chicago. "I thought I had never seen a handsomer man," a reporter wrote, "young, tall, powerfully built, clear-eyed, with a mane of black hair which he occasionally thrust back with his hand." Thirty-six-year-old Bryan was the son of a circuit court judge who was a Baptist deacon; his mother was a devout Methodist. Bryan, elected to Congress from Nebraska in 1890, was thus steeped in both religion and politics from an early age.

As the cry for "free silver" swept the rural areas of the West and South, Bryan took up the cause. "I don't know anything about free silver," he admitted. "The people of Nebraska are for free silver and I am for free silver. I will look up the arguments later." In the 1890s the slogan referred to expanding the amount of money in circulation by coining more silver dollars. Farmers believed that such inflation of the currency would raise crop prices and alleviate their heavy debt burdens. Many rural residents felt the national government had not been responsive to their needs—that both political parties had been captured by industrialists, railroad owners, and bankers. In 1896 silver was a symbol for popular grievances—it represented rural values, the common people, and a growing discontent with northeastern political domination.

By the time of the Democratic convention the Republicans had nominated William McKinley and adopted a platform calling for the gold standard (or currency backed entirely by gold supplies in the federal treasury). The Democrats were divided between the "silverites" and the "Gold Democrats," monetary conservatives who supported President Grover Cleveland. Control of the party by northeasterners was being challenged by southern and western delegates when Bryan finally rose to speak.

Called "the Great Commoner," Bryan voiced the frustrations of farmers with the failure of traditional politicians to meet their needs. "We have petitioned," he cried, "and our petitions have been scorned; we have entreated, and our entreaties have been disregarded; we

have begged, and they have mocked when our calamity came. We beg no longer; we entreat no more; we petition no more. We defy them!"

He enthralled the crowd from the beginning, but his closing words created pandemonium. "We will answer the demand for a gold standard," he roared, "by saying to them: 'You shall not press down upon the brow of labor this crown of thorns, you shall not crucify mankind upon a cross of gold hair.'" As he spoke his fingers first traced the course of imaginary trickles of blood from his temples. He closed with his arms outstretched as if he were nailed to a cross. When he dropped his arms, he had won the Democratic nomination and cinched the victory of the party's silverites.

Cleveland supporters were unwilling to accept Bryan's "foul pit of repudiation, socialism, [and] anarchy," as one declared. Another said, "I am a Democrat still—very still." Because many party regulars deserted him and nearly half the Democratic newspapers opposed him, Bryan was able to raise only the meager sum of about $500,000. Low on funds he took his campaign directly to the people, appealing to sectional and class animosities: "Probably the only passage in the Bible read by some financiers is that about the wise men of the East. They seem to think that wise men have been coming from that direction ever since."

Bryan relied on his oratorical genius and electrifying charisma rather than money. Between August and November he traveled more than 18,000 miles, visiting 27 states and giving 600 speeches. His youth sustained him as he made his own travel arrangements, bought his own tickets, carried his own bags, rode in public cars, and walked from train stations to hotels late at night. He was often called upon to give unscheduled speeches—when one Indiana crowd awakened him, he spoke in his nightshirt.

With a Republican campaign fund of more than $3.5 million, McKinley had no need to follow Bryan's course. "I might just as well put up a trapeze in my front lawn and compete with some professional athlete as to go out speaking against Bryan," he said. Between June and November, McKinley left his home in Canton, Ohio, for only three days.

In the 1896 election, Republicans sought to convince voters that William Jennings Bryan (left) was a radical who threatened American values and institutions, while William McKinley (shown in the campaign poster on the right) would guarantee stability, order, and integrity.

Railroads provided cheap excursion rates to Canton, so every day except Sunday, crowds of up to 50,000, thronged to McKinley's lawn, from where he conducted his "front porch" campaign. The gatherings were hardly spontaneous, however. His staff organized the groups by occupation or interest, screened each delegation's remarks, and planned each event in detail, right down to brass bands and banners.

In contrast to Bryan's speeches, McKinley's were calm and dispassionate, stressing national unity rather than division. "We are all dependent on each other, no matter what our occupation may be," he declared. "All of us want good times, good wages, good markets; and then we want good money always." From his front porch he addressed some 750,000 people from 30 states. The Republicans also spent more for printing than Bryan raised for his entire campaign. By the campaign's end Republicans had sent 200 million pamphlets in several languages to 15 million voters, and some 250 paid speakers toured 27 states.

On election day Bryan and his wife rose at 6:30 A.M. and voted at a local fire station in Omaha, Nebraska. He then gave seven speeches in his hometown before collapsing,

exhausted, in bed that evening. McKinley walked to his polling place and stood in line to vote. He then returned home to wait for the returns—his lawn and porch in worse shape than he was. All over the nation politicians and just plain people waited to find out which man and party would preside over the dawning of the twentieth century.

The 1896 election occurred near the end of a decade of turbulence that saw violence toward the labor movement, rising racial tensions, militancy among farmers, and discontent among the unemployed—all of which had intensified after a major depression began in 1893. The social fabric seemed to be unraveling rapidly, which is why this election was considered so important. For the first time since the 1870s voters were given a clear choice between two very different candidates and platforms.

Following Reconstruction, national politics were colorful but not very significant. No important policy differences separated the two major parties at the national level; the campaigns revolved around personalities, gimmicks, emotional slogans, and local issues. As elections were trivialized, they became a major source of entertainment, and voters turned out in record numbers. For its triumph of style over substance in politics as well as culture the era is known as the "Gilded Age," a term taken from the title of a novel by Mark Twain and Charles Dudley Warner. By 1890 both the Democratic and Republican parties had lost touch with the sentiments of large blocks of voters—especially those in the West and South. The losers in the great national race toward economic modernization began to question its assumptions. They raised their voices in the 1890s but, unable to unite around a workable agenda they failed to win many battles at that time. The issues they raised, however, appeared regularly on political agendas in the twentieth century.

EQUILIBRIUM AND INERTIA: THE NATIONAL POLITICAL SCENE

American politics have often seemed odd to Europeans. Never was this more true than in the closing decades of the nineteenth century. Commenting on American politics in his 1898 book, *The American Commonwealth,* Lord James Bryce wrote that "neither party has any principles, any distinctive tenets. Both have traditions. Both claim to have tendencies. Both have certainly war cries, organizations, interests enlisted in their support. But those interests are in the main the interests of getting or keeping the patronage of government. . . . All has been lost, except office or the hope of it."

Patronage, or the granting of political favors and offices, became more important than issues to the two major parties for many reasons. In close elections the parties had to be careful not to alienate potential supporters. Most people also believed in limited government. Political parties were therefore organized more to win offices than to govern. The result was a failure by government to deal effectively with the enormous changes wrought by industrialization and urbanization.

Divided Power: The Parties and the Federal Government

Both the Democratic and Republican parties emerged from Reconstruction with sizable

and stable constituencies. For the 20 years between 1876 and 1896 they shared a rare equality of political power. Elections were so close that until 1896 no president won office with a majority of the popular vote—The average popular vote margin was 1.5 percent. Two (Hayes and Harrison) even entered the presidency without a plurality. Republicans occupied the White House for 12 years, Democrats for 8. During only three two-year periods did the same party control the presidency and both houses of Congress—Democrats once and Republicans twice. Most of the time Congress itself was split, with Democrats generally taking the House and the Republicans the Senate. Very few seats shifted parties in any given election.

The party division of Congress inevitably weakened the presidents of the era. None was elected to consecutive terms. Calling them "the lost Americans," one observer noted that "their gravely vacant and bewhiskered faces mixed, melted, swam together" in the public mind. Lord Bryce claimed none of them "would have been remembered had he not been President." To be fair, all were competent men, most with considerable public service, and some with distinguished war records. One reason they were so forgettable was the era's concept of the presidency. Many agreed with Cleveland's assertion that the office "was essentially executive in nature." "I did not come here to legislate," he said. Presidents were only supposed to implement efficiently and honestly laws passed by Congress—occasionally vetoing ill-advised legislation. Even though these presidents did turn back many of the encroachments on presidential authority that began in Andrew Johnson's term, none considered it his duty to propose legislation.

Some found the office frustrating. After James Garfield moved from leadership roles in the House of Representatives to the presidency, he lamented, "I have heretofore been treating of the fundamental principles of government, and here I am considering all day whether A or B should be appointed to this or that office." Even representatives and senators were frequently frustrated, however, because congressional action was often stalemated. In the House, outdated and complex rules hampered action. Party discipline was practically impotent in both houses, and since neither controlled both houses for more than a two-year term, there was little possibility of formulating and enacting any coherent legislative program.

The lack of legislative action did not seem a serious problem at the start of the Gilded Age. Most people rejected the idea of an activist government—widely accepted doctrines of laissez-faire and Social Darwinism limited what people expected of government. The Social Darwinist William Graham Sumner once proclaimed that government had "at bottom . . . two chief things . . . with which to deal. They are the property of men and the honor of women. These it has to defend against crime." Both parties basically accepted a narrow vision of federal responsibility. When vetoing a small appropriation for drought relief in Texas, Democrat Cleveland asserted that "though the people support the Government, the Government should not support the people." Republican Senator Roscoe Conkling of New York claimed that the only duty of government was "to leave every class and every individual free and safe in the exertions and pursuits of life."

Such antigovernment sentiment tended to increase the power of the judicial branch. Many saw the courts as a bastion against governmental interference in the economy, and the courts certainly fulfilled that role. On the basis of the Fourteenth Amendment, judges were especially active in striking down state laws regulating business. The courts narrowly interpreted the Constitution on federal authority—ruling that the power to tax did not extend to personal incomes and that the power to regulate interstate commerce applied only to trade, not manufacturing. Congress indirectly gave judges more power by enacting vague laws that relied upon the courts for both definition and enforcement.

Subtle Differences: The Bases of Party Loyalty

One consequence of the equality of power shared by the Democrats and Republicans was the reluctance of either party to chance losing voters by taking clear positions on most contemporary issues. This reluctance may also have been based on the memories of the divisive 1860 election and its devastating impact on party and national unity. In addition, there was widespread agreement on many issues. Few members of either party questioned the pace or cost of industrialization; neither saw any need for federal action to regulate the economy. When a Democratic president replaced a Republican one in 1893, one of Andrew Carnegie's managers wrote the industrialist, "I cannot see that our interests are going to be affected one way or another by the change in administration." Business leaders had so little to fear from either party that they contributed generously to both.

Until 1896 the parties did share numerous similarities. Both were led by wealthy men but still tried to appeal to wage earners and farmers as well as merchants and manufacturers. Most members of both parties believed in protective tariffs and "sound currency." Both rejected economic radicalism and activist programs to aid workers. Presidents of both parties sent federal troops to break up strikes.

Ironically, for all their similarities the parties evoked fierce loyalty from a heterogeneous mix of people. One reason party platforms were so innocuous as to be interchangeable is that both parties were composed of factions and coalitions of "strange bedfellows." Because of its past abolitionist connections the Republican party retained the support of many activist reformers, idealists, and African Americans. Yet most Republicans came from established, "old stock" families. The more wealth a man had, the more likely he was to vote Republican. The party therefore was a curious combination of "insiders" and "outsiders."

The Democrats were even more mixed. The party's constituents sometimes seemed united mainly by opposition to the Republicans on various grounds. One Republican leader complained, "The Republican party does things, the Democratic party criticizes; the Republican party achieves, the Democratic party finds fault." Several generations later humorist Will Rogers quipped, "I don't belong to an organized party; I'm a Democrat."

His words were certainly true of the Democratic party of the Gilded Age. The party contained such disparate elements as Southern whites, immigrants, Catholics, and Jews.

For historical and cultural reasons, party loyalty was frequently determined by the three factors of region, religion, and ethnic origin. The regional factor was most evident in the support white Southerners gave to the Democratic party. To vote for the party of abolition and Reconstruction was considered treason and a threat to white supremacy. Republicans could count on heavy support from New England for the opposite reasons. To New Englanders, the Democrats were members of the party of traitorous rebellion against the Union. Because they had little hope of winning southern white votes, Union loyalty was one issue the Republicans did not need to tiptoe around. They frequently "waved the bloody shirt," reminding Northerners that the Democrats had caused the Civil War. In 1876 one Republican declared, "Every man that tried to destroy this nation was a Democrat. . . . Soldiers, every scar you have on your heroic bodies was given you by a Democrat."

For various reasons immigrants had long gravitated toward the Democratic party. Many were members of the poorest classes, which traditionally voted Democratic. In the 1850s anti-immigration Know Nothing party members joined the Republican ranks, reinforcing immigrants' ties to the Democrat party. Most of the "new immigrants" of the Gilded Age settled in cities controlled by Democratic political machines that won immigrants' loyalty by meeting their needs. As immigration swelled, increasing Democratic strength, Republicans became more and more restrictionist. In fact, immigration policy was one of the very few substantive issues on which the parties took clearly different stands.

Religious affiliations also helped determine party loyalty—partly because of the positions on immigration. Many of the late-nineteenth-century immigrants were Catholics and Jews who were suspicious of the Protestant-dominated Republican party. There were also fundamental differences in the religious orientation of most Republicans and Democrats. Republicans tended to belong to *pietistic* sects that

based salvation on good works and moral behavior. Democrats, on the other hand, leaned toward *ritualistic* religions that emphasized faith and observance of church rituals above adherence to strict codes of moral conduct.

Pietistic Republicans frequently sought to legislate morality, supporting prohibition of alcohol and enforcement of Sunday blue laws, which barred various activities on the Sabbath—including baseball. Many Democrats did not believe that personal morality could or should be a matter of state concern. A Chicago Democrat explained, "A Republican is a man who wants you t' go t' church every Sunday. A Democrat says if a man wants t' have a glass of beer on Sunday he can have it."

The roots and constituencies of the parties thus created differences in their outlooks. The Republicans became the "party of morality," the Democrats the "party of personal liberty." Democrats not only rejected government interference in their personal life; in the nineteenth century, they were also more suspicious of government action of any sort. Some quoted Democrat Albert Gallatin's dictum: "We are never doing as well as when we are doing nothing."

Because of their mixed constituencies, however, the differences and divisions *within* parties were as great, and sometimes greater, than those between the parties. Democrats could count on the South for all its electoral votes, but southern Democrats frequently broke party ranks when voting on legislation. They sometimes voted with western Republicans on acts favorable to farmers. They were, however, fundamentally conservative men of Whiggish tendencies who usually voted with northern Republicans on financial and economic issues, as well as on immigration restriction. In a bizarre political arrangement, southern Democrats also voted with northern Republicans at times in order to receive a share of the patronage.

The Republicans were even more deeply divided into factions. One group, led by Roscoe Conkling, was labeled the "Stalwarts." Followers of James G. Blaine of Maine were called "Half-breeds." The only significant item of dispute between the two was who would receive the numerous jobs the president could make appointments to. Because the distribution of patronage was a prime function of both parties of the era, the division was bitter. When Conkling was asked if he intended to campaign for Blaine for president in 1884, he snapped that he did not engage in criminal activities.

One faction of the Republican party, however, did have some ideological basis. It was composed of reformers whose primary concern was honest and effective government. They had bolted the party in 1872 because of the corruption of the Grant regime, and they bolted again in 1884, supporting Democratic candidate Grover Cleveland for president. Party regulars ridiculed them, calling them "goo-goos" for their idealistic good government crusade. They were finally labeled "Mugwumps"—a joke that asserted they had their "mugs" on one side of the fence and their "wumps" on the other.

The divisions in the Republican party reflected the fact that the politicians of the day were less concerned with issues and ideology than with winning office and distributing patronage. Lord Bryce observed that American politicians could be differentiated from European ones by the fact "that their whole time is frequently given to political work, that many of them draw an income from politics . . . that . . . they are proficient in the acts of popular oratory, of electioneering, and of party management."

The Business of Politics: Party Organization

Gilded Age politicians were very serious about their careers. They worked hard at both "party management" and "electioneering." The result was the largest voter turnout in the nation's history. In the elections from 1860 to 1900 an average of 78 percent of eligible voters cast ballots. Outside of the South (where African Americans were increasingly prevented from voting and where the Democratic nomination determined the general election), the turnout sometimes reached 90 percent.

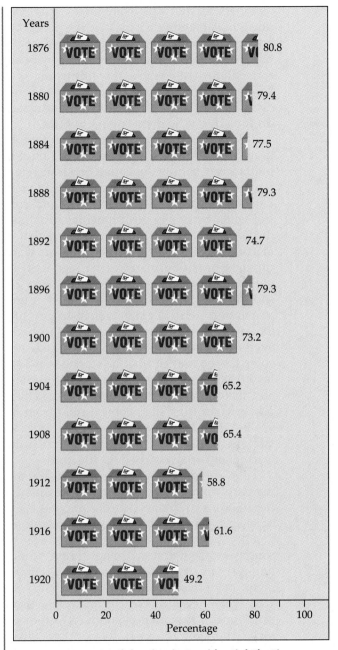

FIGURE 19.1 **Voter Participation in Presidential Elections, 1876–1920**

Party organization was geared to getting out the vote. The parties were structured like pyramids: at the base were ward or precinct meetings, which all party members could attend. There they generally elected representatives to county committees, which then sent members to the state committees that conducted the ongoing business of the party and nominated state candidates for office. At the top were the national committees. National conventions, at which representation was based on the electoral votes of the states, met every four years to select national candidates, draft platforms, and vote on party rules.

There was one main difference in Republican and Democratic party organization. Republicans generally depended on strong state organizations, while Democrats tended to rely on urban political machines to win and control votes. Since city governmental structures did not keep pace with the huge population increases, political machines based on ward captains provided many of the services for which government would later be held responsible. This machine also helped immigrants and rural migrants adjust to city life. One ward boss noted: "There's got to be in every ward somebody that any bloke can come to—no matter what he's done—and get help. Help, you understand, none of your law and justice, but help." Politicians took their pay in votes from the people, bribes from legal and illegal businesses, and graft from contractors. The system worked so well that the Democrats usually carried the big cities.

For both parties, recruiting and maintaining party voters was a game for professionals. Republicans in Pennsylvania compiled a list of 800,000 voters with notations as to their reliability as party loyalists. Politics was a rough and sometimes corrupt game. Conkling warned, "Parties are not built by deportment, or by ladies' magazines, or gush." In 1888 when newly elected Benjamin Harrison proclaimed, "Providence has given us the victory," Republican party boss Matt Quay snorted, "Providence hadn't a damn thing to do with it." Quay then added that Harrison "would never know how close a number of men were impelled to approach the gates of the penitentiary to make him president." Electoral corruption was not limited to one party. In the same year a Mississippi Democrat admitted: "It is no secret that there has not been a full vote and a fair count in Mississippi since 1875, that we have been preserving the ascendancy of white people by

revolutionary methods. In other words, we have been stuffing ballot boxes, committing perjury, and here and there in the state carrying the elections by fraud and violence."

Gilded Age politics was not dull. One could almost claim that the business of politics was entertainment. One observer remarked, "What the theatre is to the French, or the bull fight . . . to the Spanish . . . [election campaigns] and the ballot box are to *our* people." The drama of emotional tent meetings rivaled circuses, and the pageantry of parades provided excitement. Almost everyone got caught up in the elections, frequently displaying such paraphernalia as buttons, handkerchiefs, hats, banners, and posters emblazoned with their party's symbol or slogan. In 1888 one tobacco company enclosed in its packages pictures similar to baseball cards of the 25 presidential hopefuls. Politics was undoubtedly a prime form of mass entertainment.

Many politicians surely must have enjoyed their status as "media stars" and folk heroes. For some whose ethnic or class backgrounds closed conventional doors of opportunity, politics provided a vehicle of upward social mobility, similar to professional entertainment and athletics or trade union leader-

Gimmicks in Gilded Age political campaigns, such as this Bryan donkey, stirred public interest, resulting in the highest voter turnouts in the nation's history.

ship. Yet politics as a vocation offered other rewards. Elected and appointed officials not only received salaries but many also openly accepted gifts from lobbyists and free passes from railroads. They sometimes used their governmental status to promote their private interests. James G. Blaine of Maine expressed no qualms about accepting stock concessions from an Arkansas railroad that he had aided in getting a federal land grant. One quip claimed that the United States had the best Congress money could buy.

The Struggle for Inclusion: Women and Politics

Politics could be a rough and dirty business—one many considered inappropriate for women. Increasingly women disagreed. After an 1869 split in the suffrage movement, the National Woman Suffrage Association (NWSA), led by Elizabeth Cady Stanton and Susan B. Anthony, fought for the vote on the national level through the courts and a proposed constitutional amendment. At the same time the American Woman Suffrage Association (AWSA), headed by Lucy Stone and Julia Ward Howe, sought victories at the state level.

Up to the point in 1890 when the groups merged to form the National American Woman Suffrage Association (NAWSA), the victories of both groups had been limited. NWSA lost an 1874 Supreme Court decision in a suit filed by Virginia Minor against a St. Louis registrar for denying her the right to vote. The Court ruled that citizenship did not automatically confer the vote and that suffrage could be denied specific groups, such as criminals, the insane, and women. In 1878 Anthony did succeed in getting a constitutional amendment introduced into the Senate that stated that "the right to vote shall not be denied or abridged by the United States or by any state on account of sex." It continued to be submitted for the next 18 years, but it was usually killed in committee and only rarely reached the Senate floor.

There was more success on the state and local level. By 1890 19 states allowed women to vote on school issues, and 3 states extended

In 1869 Wyoming became the first territory to allow women to vote in all territorial elections. It later refused to enter the Union without women's suffrage.

women the franchise on tax and bond issues. Referenda were held in 11 states, but only the territory of Wyoming had granted women full political equality. After three states—Colorado, Utah, and Idaho—adopted women's suffrage during the 1890s, the movement seemed to lose steam. As male resistance mounted, no other state acted on the issue until 1910. Many men agreed with a Texas senator that "equal suffrage is a repudiation of manhood."

STYLE OVER SUBSTANCE: GOVERNMENT IN THE GILDED AGE, 1877–1892

Politics provided great entertainment, but there were always people who wanted more. Local political activity was often considerably more vibrant than the political inertia at the national level. Many problems were first tackled on the city, county, and state levels before becoming a part of the national agenda. Such issues as the currency and tariffs could only be solved at the national level, but others, such as demands for clean government, were undertaken at all levels. On the whole, the states responded more vigorously than the national government to the problems created by economic changes—only to have the Supreme Court sometimes tie their hands. Out of frustration, people began to look to Washington for solutions, but the presidents and Congress responded timidly. National elections still focused mainly on trivial issues. When backed to the wall, Congress would enact laws to quiet popular cries for action, but such laws were often limited in scope and unenforceable. As the nation struggled to find appropriate governmental responses to sweeping economic change, style often triumphed over substance, and many problems remained unsolved.

Hayes and the "Money Question"

After the disputed election of 1876 almost created a constitutional crisis, the presidency was snatched from Democrat Samuel J. Tilden and given to Rutherford B. Hayes. A series of bargains was needed for the acceptance of the 8 to 7 vote of the electoral commission that named Hayes president. His administration was thus from the start tainted with snide references to him as "His Fraudulence" and "Old 8 to 7." He was actually honest and competent, and did much to establish the Republican party as the "party of morality" after the corruption of the Grant regime. His wife also helped to link Republicans with morality by her refusal to serve strong drinks—earning her the label of "Lemonade Lucy." One guest at a White House party remarked in disgust that "the water flowed like champagne."

Hayes is now probably best remembered for removing the remaining federal troops from the South—marking the end of Reconstruction. At the time, however, economics rather than race relations occupied the public's mind. Hayes came into office more than three years into an economic depression that began with the panic of 1873. That depression raised the "money question," which continued to crop up for more than two decades.

At the root of this issue—as complex as it was heated—was a long period of deflation following the Civil War. Price levels dropped because the production of goods was growing faster than the supply of money. Farmers are not necessarily hurt by a general deflation if all prices fall equally and the farmers debt levels are low. Wheat, corn, and cotton prices, however, declined more than other prices in the late nineteenth century, and farmers had also borrowed heavily to expand production. They were thus caught in a debt squeeze—their mortgage payments remained high while the prices they received fell. For example, a farmer who borrowed $1000 with a 25-year mortgage to buy a farm in 1868 had to produce over twice as much cotton to make the mortgage payment in 1888. The farmer received virtually nothing for doubled efforts, but the creditor received not only interest for the use of the money but also an additional bonanza—dollars now worth twice as much as those lent.

Debtors in all occupations began blaming their problems on deflation and saw inflation of the currency as the cure—for them it was a moral issue, a question of justice. One way to inflate currency was to increase the number of legal tender paper "greenbacks" first issued during the war. Supporters of that solution organized the Greenback party in 1874. Instead, two years before Hayes entered the White House, Congress enacted the Resumption Act of 1875 to eliminate paper money not backed by gold or silver.

After the Resumption Act, some inflationists turned their attention to silver. The nation had been on a bimetallic standard since the 1790s. The dollar was based on both gold and silver, and for years dollars were coined at a 16 to 1 mint ratio—16 times as much silver as gold. By the 1870s this ratio did not reflect the market prices of the metals. Silver prices got so high that producers sold it on the open market rather than take it to the mint to be coined. Unable to buy silver at that ratio, Congress passed the Coinage Act of 1873, which halted the minting of silver dollars.

Soon after, the discovery of large deposits of silver drove prices down again. Then it was in the interest of both silver miners and infla-

In this Greenback party cartoon from the 1870s, a gold-nosed government octopus puts a stranglehold on U.S. farmers, laborers, and small businesses. The Greenbackers wanted to distribute more money to more of the American people and opposed specie (gold) payments on bonds.

tionists to return to the coining of silver at 16 to 1. The two groups formed a large lobby that wrested minor concessions from Congress. The Bland-Allison Act of 1878 required the government to buy between $2 and $4 million worth of silver each month. Like much of the legislation of the Gilded Age, the Bland-Allison Act proved to be a cosmetic answer to popular demands. It neither raised silver prices nor inflated the currency significantly. Inflationists remained unhappy, and the Greenback party nominated former Union general James B. Weaver of Iowa for president in the 1880 election.

Garfield, Arthur, and the Patronage Issue

As in earlier elections neither of the two major parties focused on substantial issues in the 1880 election, but instead relied on slogans and gimmicks to win votes. The battle for the Republican nomination was between the Half-Breed and Stalwart factions. Although Hayes had sought to set some standards for federal officeholders, his actions mainly alienated fellow Republicans, and he refused to run for a second term in 1880. Stalwarts hoped to run Grant again, but the Republican con-

vention became deadlocked. On the thirty-sixth ballot the party picked James A. Garfield, a veteran but relatively unknown Ohio congressman. To conciliate the Stalwarts, Chester A. Arthur, a Conkling henchman, became the vice-presidential nominee.

The Democrats nominated an even more obscure figure, General Winfield Scott Hancock, whose only claim to fame was being a hero of the Battle of Gettysburg. He was described as "a good man weighing 250 pounds." Garfield was also bland, but he had the advantage of a log cabin birth and a brief career on a canal towpath—giving rise to a popular Republican campaign slogan: "From the towpath to the White House." The 1880 election was one of the closest of the century in popular vote. Garfield received a mere 39,000 vote plurality out of almost 10 million ballots cast. Greenback nominee Weaver came in a distant third, gaining only 3.4 percent of the popular vote.

Returning prosperity and a tragic event focused attention on the issue of patronage, overshadowing the currency question. Four months after Garfield's inauguration he was shot twice by a deranged office-seeker, Charles Guiteau, who exclaimed, "I am a Stalwart. Arthur is now President of the United States." A native of Vermont, Arthur attended Union College, became an abolitionist lawyer, and then held a series of appointed offices. Considered by many to be a party hack, Arthur surprised them by becoming a champion of governmental reform.

The Mugwumps and others had become increasingly concerned with corruption in government. In the 1873 novel that gave the era its label of the Gilded Age, Mark Twain and Charles Dudley Warner wrote, "The present era of indelible rottenness is not Democratic, it is not Republican, it is national. Politics are not going to cure more ulcers like these, nor the decaying body they fester upon." Because of the pervasiveness of the corruption, some saw no way out. "All being corrupt together," E. L. Godkin, editor of *The Nation*, wrote, "what is the use of investigating each other?"

Some reformers believed that one answer to the problem of corruption was the reformation of the "spoils system" of patronage. Since the early 1800s government jobs had been considered the "spoils" of political victory, to be awarded to loyal party workers regardless of their qualifications. Between 1865 and 1891

problems grew as federal positions tripled from 53,000 to 166,000. Indeed, presidents of the era spent much of their time making some 100,000 appointments—most of which were in the postal service. That number of jobs provided incentives to precinct and ward bosses to get out the vote, but such inventions as the typewriter began to make it necessary for government workers to have skills other than getting people to vote.

Hayes's actions to improve the quality of political appointees had lost him his party's support, and it was not until after Garfield's assassination that Congress finally took action. With the support and encouragement of President Arthur, Congress enacted the Pendleton Act in 1883, which outlawed political contributions by appointed officeholders. It also established competitive examinations for federal positions, to be given by the Civil Service Commission. The rather timid act only applied to about 10 percent of government employees, and some self-serving motives contributed to its passage. Since it

Charles Guiteau shoots President Garfield as Secretary of State Blaine looks on in horror. After suffering for two and a half months, the President died on September 19, 1881. Guiteau, whose behavior during his trial suggested insanity, was convicted on January 25, 1882, and hanged on June 30.

was to apply only to future appointees and protected incumbents, the Democrats called it "a bill to perpetuate in office the Republicans who now control the patronage of the Government." In the same manner, every president elected after its enactment increased the number of positions protected from political removal—usually to prevent his appointees from being removed. The political system thus was becoming modernized, but some questioned whether it was being improved.

Cleveland, the Railroads, and Tariffs

By the time of the 1884 election, Arthur's actions had won more favor from the public than from his party. The Republicans bypassed him and nominated James G. Blaine, who was far from bland. He was so handsome and charismatic that a colleague's wife once remarked, "Had he been a woman, people would have rushed off to send expensive flowers." Indeed, Blaine had almost all the qualities of a successful presidential candidate: a phenomenal memory for names and faces, eloquent oratory, and a quick wit. He was, however, tainted politically. While in Congress he had become very rich without any visible means of outside income. Letters circulated that implied Blaine was up for sale to the railroads. He was more than the Mugwumps could stomach; they could not support him.

Realizing the potential advantage of a Mugwump defection, the Democrats selected Grover Cleveland, a reform governor of New York. Neither physically attractive nor charismatic, he did have one appealing quality. He was honest. As one supporter explained, "We love him for the enemies he has made." Cleveland and Blaine did not disagree on the major issues, so their campaign revolved around personalities and became one of the most scurrilous in the nation's history.

Blaine's tainted past was obvious fodder for the Democrats' campaign. At torchlit rallies Democrats chanted: "Blaine! Blaine! James G. Blaine! Continental liar from the state of Maine!" Unable to find a shred of evidence to challenge Cleveland's honesty, Republicans publicized a more personal scandal. Cleveland, a bachelor, had supported an illegitimate child since 1874, even though his paternity was questionable. Thus Republicans countered Democratic chants with "Ma! Ma! Where's my pa? Going to the White House? Ha! Ha! Ha!" In the end Cleveland's victory may have been due to an indiscretion by a Blaine supporter, who had labeled the Democrats as the party of "rum, Romanism, and rebellion." Even though Blaine's mother was Catholic, Democrats were able to rally Catholic voters to win key states.

The major legislation of Cleveland's first presidency resulted from public pressure and court actions. The power and discriminatory rates of the railroads frightened and angered many Americans, and actions to regulate the railroads had started at the state level. Beginning with the establishment in 1869 of a regulatory commission in Massachusetts, by 1880 there were railroad commissions in 14 states. The most active advocate of regulation was the Patrons of Husbandry—a farmers' group organized into local chapters called "granges." The "Grangers" and their allies, especially in the Midwest, got stronger legislation enacted that set maximum rates and charges within their states.

In this cartoon, Grover Cleveland's alleged illegitimate child is used to impugn "Grover the Good's" well-known political integrity.

The railroad men naturally attacked these so-called Granger laws through the courts. At first they lost. In the 1877 *Munn* v. *Illinois* decision, the Supreme Court ruled that when "private property is affected with a public interest it . . . must submit to be controlled by the public for the common good." Nevertheless, states had difficulty regulating railroads chartered by other states and doing business across state lines. Then in the 1886 *Wabash, St. Louis & Pacific Railway Company* v. *Illinois* case the Supreme Court took away the rights of states to even try by ruling that only Congress had the right to regulate interstate commerce.

Pressure began to build for federal action, and Congress finally responded to the demands by passing the Interstate Commerce Act, which Grover Cleveland signed into law in February 1887. It prohibited pools, rebates, and rate discriminations; provided that all charges by the railroads should be "reasonable and just"; and established the Interstate Commerce Commission (ICC). Although significant as the first federal regulatory agency, the commission's power was woefully limited. It could investigate charges against the railroads and issue "cease and desist" orders, but these could only be enforced by the courts.

Conservative courts soon nullified 90 percent of the commission's orders; between 1887 and 1905 the Supreme Court decided against the ICC in 15 of 16 cases. By 1892 railroad attorney Richard S. Olney wrote, "The Commission, as its functions have now been limited by the Courts, is, or can be made of great use to the railroads. It satisfies the popular clamor for a government supervision of railroads, at the same time that such supervision is almost entirely nominal. . . . It thus becomes a sort of protection against hasty and crude legislation hostile to railroad interests. . . . The part of wisdom is not to destroy the Commission but to utilize it." One railroad executive admitted, "There is not a road in the country that can be accused of living up to the rules of the Interstate Commerce Commission."

The Interstate Commerce Act temporarily satisfied "popular clamor" without alienating railroad owners, so it did not become a partisan issue for either party. However, during

Public anger over railroad power, as expressed in this political cartoon, finally pushed Congress to pass the Interstate Commerce Act in 1887.

Cleveland's term, a major issue on which Democrats and Republicans actually differed emerged: the tariff. Although both parties supported these taxes on imports both to raise revenue and to protect American products from being undersold by foreign competitors, the difference lay in how high these tariffs should be. Regardless of party, congressmen voted their constituents' interests, which made few of them consistent on the issue. "I am a protectionist for every interest which I am sent here by my constituents to protect," one Democratic senator explained. Supporters of protectionism were those who sold on the domestic markets; opponents depended on foreign markets. There were some farmers and manufacturers from every region in both groups.

Like most Democrats, Cleveland had long been less enthusiastic about high tariffs than Republicans. While in office he found that existing tariff rates were producing treasury surpluses that were tempting congressmen to propose programs and appropriations that he considered dangerous expansions of federal activities. A moralistic man, Cleveland was deeply opposed to governmental involvement in the economy and social issues. He thus became an advocate of tariff reduction. In 1887, at his urging, the Democratic House enacted moderate reductions, but the Republican Senate blocked the bill. Cleveland then proceeded to make the tariff a focus of his reelection bid in 1888.

Harrison and Big Business

In 1888 the Democrats renominated Cleveland and wrote tariff reduction into their platform. The Republicans chose Benjamin Harrison and cheerfully picked up the gauntlet—denouncing Cleveland's "free trade" as unpatriotic. They also promised generous pensions to veterans. Voters at last were given some choice on a real issue. The result was a viciously corrupt and close election. Harrison's campaign chairman, Matt Quay, proceeded to "put the manufacturers of Pennsylvania under the fire and fry all the fat out of them." He asked them to make large contributions to the Republican party as insurance against lowered tariff rates. When Cleveland lost, many blamed his defeat on his taking too clear a stand on an issue. Republicans erroneously interpreted his narrow defeat as a mandate for protectionism. Congress then enacted the McKinley Tariff, which raised average duties to the highest level yet, but the Republicans misread public sentiment. The McKinley Tariff was very unpopular.

Both high tariffs and trusts were becoming distasteful to many Americans. Popular demand for legislative action against trusts had been growing during the 1880s. Again action started on the state level; 15 southern and western states had passed antitrust legislation by the mid-1880s. Of course, companies simply incorporated in more sympathetic states. The laws were ineffective and likely to be overturned by federal courts, but they did reflect popular distaste for the monopolies. Congress responded to these rumblings by enacting the Sherman Antitrust Act in 1890. On the surface it seemed to doom the trusts, prohibiting any "contract, combination in the form of trust or otherwise, or conspiracy in restraint of trade or commerce." As with the Interstate Commerce Act, appearances were deceiving, though not to all the congressmen who passed it. One senator explained that Congress had wanted to pass "some bill headed 'A bill to Punish Trusts' with which to go to the country" to aid their reelection.

Until 1901 the act was virtually unenforced—the Justice Department had instituted only 14 suits and failed to get convictions in most of them. The Supreme Court also emasculated the law in *United States* v. *E. C. Knight Co.* (1895), ruling that it applied to commerce but not manufacturing. Thus, the subject of that suit, a sugar trust controlling 98 percent of the industry, was not held in violation. Indeed, the only effective use made of the act in its first decade was as a tool to break up labor strikes by court injunctions.

The Sherman Antitrust Act of 1890 was designed to quiet "public clamor." In that same year popular pressure also led to further action on the currency question. Following the Bland-Allison Act of 1878, the money supply continued to grow too slowly for the expanding economy. By 1890 pressure to coin more silver was growing. Congress responded with the Sherman Silver Purchase Act, which required the government to buy 4.5 million ounces of silver each month at the unrealistic ratio of 16 to 1. Paper money to pay for the purchases was redeemable in gold or silver, keeping the inflationary impact minimal. The act was a compromise that satisfied no one; the silver issue grew more heated in the 1890s.

During Harrison's presidency Congress was more active than previously—passing the McKinley Tariff, the Sherman Antitrust Act, the Sherman Silver Purchase Act, and the first billion-dollar budget. At the same time the Republican party was alienating itself from its abolitionist past and becoming more closely tied to big business.

Legislative Activity on Minority Rights and Social Issues

To African Americans the Republicans remained the party of black rights, but after the election of 1876 the party did less and less to earn that label. By 1890, however, increasing southern assaults on African-American voting rights finally moved some Republicans to action. Senator Henry Cabot Lodge and others drafted the Lodge Bill, a federal elections bill that sought to protect voter registration and guarantee fair congressional elections by establishing mechanisms to investigate charges of voting fraud and to deal with disputed elections.

Southern white response was rapid and bitter. The *Florida Times-Union* charged: "The gleam of federal bayonets will again be seen in the South." The *Mobile Register* warned that the bill "would deluge the South in blood." Northern Democrats lent their support to southern outrage. Cleveland exclaimed, "It is a dark blow at the freedom of the ballot." Although in 1890 Republicans controlled both houses of Congress, they finally bartered away the Lodge Election Bill to gain support for the McKinley Tariff. Protection of manufacturers was more important to them than the protection of African Americans.

In that same year Republicans also let the Blair Education Bill die. This bill would have provided federal aid to schools, mostly African American, that did not get a fair share of local and state funds. The Blair Bill marked the last glimpse of the party's dying abolitionist roots as well as the loss of party idealism. The Fifty-first Congress wanted to alleviate treasury surpluses to protect tariffs, but in the end the only group to receive substantial aid was Union Army veterans, who were voted pensions by the so-called Billion-Dollar Congress in 1890.

Other measures of the era affected minorities—but usually in a negative way. Southern white Democrats enacted discriminatory legislation against African Americans at the local and state level. A movement for immigration restriction, usually initiated by Republicans, led to the Chinese Exclusion Act of 1882 and other legislation that banned certain categories of immigrants and gave the federal government control of overseas immigration. The 1887 Dawes Act attacked the roots of American Indian culture by trying to make Native Americans homesteading farmers, which resulted, unintentionally, in making them dependent wards of the state.

Although most social issues received short shrift at the federal level, some received passionate attention at the local and state level. The two main ones—education and prohibition—were essentially Republican issues. An Iowa Republican slogan called for "a school house on every hill, and no saloon in the valley." Many people were alarmed by the increased use of alcohol—annual consumption of beer rose from 1.6 to 6.9 gallons per capita from 1850 to 1880. Republicans moved beyond the educational focus of the temperance movement to attempt to make drinking alcohol a crime. They also sought to increase compulsory school attendance, but these efforts were often linked to moves to undermine parochial schools and schools that taught immigrants in their native tongues. In most areas these Republican actions backfired, losing more voters than they gained. For example, Republicans had once predicted "Iowa will go Democratic when Hell goes Methodist," but in 1890 the state fell to their opponents.

By 1890 very little effective national legislation had been adopted to deal with the problems of a pluralistic society experiencing rapid social and economic change. Resulting partly from a political equilibrium that bred inertia, concepts of the limited nature of governmental responsibility also did not provide impetus for action. Public demands for change were nevertheless growing. No group challenged the status quo more than the farmers.

REVOLT OF THE WEST AND SOUTH

Cries for change naturally came from the losers in the new economic order, and among the greatest losers were American farmers. Their failure to thrive in the expanding economy convinced many that the cards had been stacked against them. After seeking various other solutions to their problems, farmers turned to politics—taking up Populist leader Mary E. Lease's cry "to raise less corn and more hell." Their success was limited, but they did lead the first American mass movement to reject Social Darwinism and laissez-faire. They also promoted the "radical" idea that "it is the duty of government to protect the weak, because the strong are able to protect themselves." Some even questioned basic tenets of industrial capitalism.

Grievances: Real and Imagined

In 1887 North Carolina editor Leonidas L. Polk summed up the views of many farmers: "There is something radically wrong in our industrial system. There is a screw loose. . . . The railroads have never been so prosperous, and yet agriculture languishes. The banks have never done a better . . . business, and yet agriculture languishes. Manufacturing enterprises never made more money, . . . and yet agriculture languishes. Towns and cities flourish and 'boom,' . . . and yet agriculture languishes."

The basic cause of the farmers' problems was the decline of agricultural prices—primarily because of overproduction. Farmers had a hard time believing, however, that they were producing too much. Kansas governor Lorenzo Dow Lewelling wondered how "there were hungry people . . . because there was too much bread" and "so many . . . poorly clad . . . because there was too much cloth."

Overproduction was an abstract, invisible enemy, so many farmers sought more tangible, personal villains—the railroads, bankers, and monopolists. As "Sockless" Jerry Simpson claimed, "It is a struggle between the robbers and the robbed." Farmers believed they were being robbed by high freight and credit costs, an unfair burden of taxation, middlemen who exploited their marketing problems, and an inadequate currency.

By the late 1880s many farmers were already suffering from severe economic dislocation. In this 1889 cartoon a poor, hungry farmer gazes at a banquet being enjoyed by tariff-gorged industrialists; in the back Congressman McKinley is pouring whiskey.

Although there was no conspiracy by the "monopolists" to fleece the farmers, there was a germ of truth in farmers' grievances. Freight rates were higher for western farmers because of the long distances to markets and the scattered and seasonal nature of grain shipments. Although these farmers generally paid the same interest rates as easterners, they were more dependent on mortgages to finance their operations than were the corporations, who could market stocks and bonds to raise needed capital. Southern farmers also had to pay dearly, through higher credit prices for goods obtained by crop liens. Large debts increased all farmers' marketing problems. All the crops in a region were usually harvested at the same time, and farmers had to sell them immediately to pay off loans. Middlemen took advantage of the glutted markets—buying the crops at low prices and selling them when prices rose. Sometimes their profit margin was greater than that of the farmer who had gotten up before dawn every day and worked long hours to produce the goods. The unfairness of this galled farmers, living as they did isolated from the excitement and modern conveniences of the city. (The isolation was especially hard on the women, who were, as one writer noted, "not much better than slaves. It is a weary, monotonous round of cooking and washing and mending and as a result the insane asylum is 1/3d filled with wives of farmers.")

Governmental policy seemed to hurt more than help. Property taxes hit farmers hard because they had a lot of land but little income. The tariffs affected most farmers both by raising the prices they paid for goods and by making it harder for them to sell their crops on the international market. The deflationary policy of the federal government especially hurt because of the farmers' great indebtedness. Every economic downturn brought a wave of farm foreclosures and frustration. Thousands of dreams died slowly, as one Kansas farmer's letter reveals.

At the age of 52 years, after a long life of toil, economy and self-denial, I find myself and family virtually paupers. With hundreds of cattle, hundreds of hogs, scores of good horses, and a farm that rewarded the toil of our hands with 16,000 bushels of golden corn, we are poorer by many dollars than we were years ago. What once seemed a neat little fortune and a house of refuge for our declining years . . . has been rendered valueless.

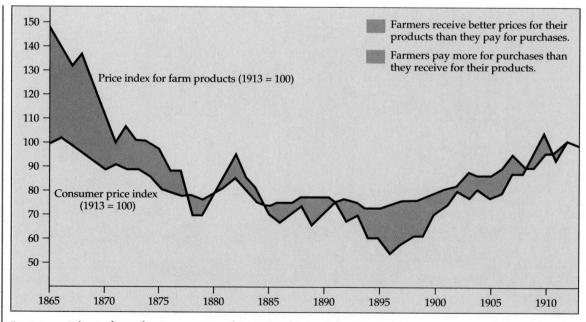

FIGURE 19.2 Price Indexes for Consumer and Farm Products, 1865–1913

The Farmers Organize

In this age of economic consolidation farmers realized early the need to unite and cooperate. Unfortunately they were never able to do so as effectively as the industrialists and railroad magnates because of greater geographic separation and their frontier-bred individualism. A national farm organization, the Patrons of Husbandry, was founded in 1867 by Oliver Kelley. This U.S. Department of Agriculture employee's action illustrated that the federal government was not totally insensitive to farm problems. Local granges sponsored lectures, dances, and picnics, fulfilling a deep hunger for social interaction, and membership in the organization grew to more than one million by 1874.

The Grangers, as they were called, soon moved beyond their social functions to address the economic grievances of the farmers. Focusing their actions on railroad regulation and cooperatives, they had some success in both areas. They were responsible for numerous state laws that established railroad commissions to oversee and regulate railroad operations. Grangers also viewed buying cooperatives as one solution to the problem of high prices paid *by* farmers and the low prices paid *to* farmers. Cooperatives were formed to purchase in bulk directly from manufacturers, eliminating retail markups. In some places granges established cooperative banks, grain elevators, cotton gins, insurance companies, processing plants, and even plants to manufacture farm implements. Sales cooperatives aimed at increasing crop prices by joint marketing.

Granger victories and successes were generally short-lived and limited. The Supreme Court nullified the Granger laws that regulated railroads in the *Wabash* case of 1886. Most cooperatives were short on capital and skilled management and were hampered by the continued individualism of many farmers. They were no match for the unrelenting attacks by private business. In the late 1870s the granges began to decline, reverting to rural social clubs, but they did continue to operate some cooperative stores.

Economic grievances remained, however, and farmers' organizational efforts shifted to the Alliance movement. Milton George, the editor of the Chicago-based *Western Rural,* organized a northwestern Alliance in 1880. Never very effective, by the late 1880s it

A grange meeting at a schoolhouse in Illinois. The grange worked for farmers' interests by opposing monopolies, advocating lower standard freight and passenger rates on railroads, urging the founding of agricultural schools, and forming buying cooperatives.

Kansas homesteader and radical activist Mary E. Lease urged farmers to "raise less corn and more hell."

was mainly a paper organization. The Alliance movement in the South was more radical and more successful. Started in 1877 as a frontier farmers' club in Lampasas County, Texas, it grew into the Grand State Alliance in 1879. Beginning in 1886, under the new leadership of Dr. Charles W. Macune, the southern Alliance spread rapidly by organizing new locals and absorbing existing farm groups in the South and other regions. At the same time a separate Colored Alliance was established. By 1890 the southern Alliance was a national organization with about 1.5 million members—with an additional 1 million members in its African-American affiliate.

Like the Grangers, Alliancemen sought to establish cooperatives, mostly without long-term success. They also conducted wider social and educational programs and boasted about 1000 affiliated newspapers. Self-help, however, proved inadequate, so in 1890 they turned to political action. In the 1890 elections southern Alliancemen tried to capture their state Democratic parties rather than supplant them. Because Northwest and Great Plains farmers were not burdened with such intense party loyalty or the complication of the racial issue, they established independent third parties. Regardless of the form of the organization, Alliancemen sought political solutions to their problems.

The Agrarian Agenda

The demands of the farmers mixed rhetoric, radicalism, and realism. Their words expressed an anger that was flaring white-hot after years of smouldering resentment. No one voiced that anger better than Kansas homesteader Mary E. Lease.

Wall Street owns the country. It is no longer a government of the people, by the people and for the people, but a government of Wall Street, by Wall Street and for Wall Street. The great common people of this country are slaves, and monopoly is the master. The West and South are bound and prostrate before the manufacturing East. . . . Our laws are the output of a system which clothes rascals in robes and honesty in rags. The parties lie to us and the political speakers mislead us. We were told two years ago to go to work and raise a big crop, that was all we needed. We went to work and plowed and planted; the rains fell, the sun shone, nature smiled, and we raised the big crop that they told us to; and what came of it? Eight-cent corn, ten-cent oats, two-cent beef and no price at all for butter and eggs—that's what came of it.

Farmers' words rang with a rejection of aspects of capitalism that in retrospect seems radical. The language used divided the nation into "haves" and "have-nots." "There are but two sides," one manifesto proclaimed. "On the one side are the allied hosts of monopolies, the money power, great trusts and railroad corporations. . . . On the other are the farmers, laborers, merchants and all the people who produce wealth. . . . Between those two there is no middle ground." To farmers, government either stood by idly or actively aided the monopolists as the "fruits of the toil of millions are stolen to build up colossal fortunes for a few." The result was that from "the same prolific womb of governmental injustice we breed the two great classes—tramps and millionaires." They also saw a division between the toiling masses who produced wealth and the parasitic capitalists who exploited it. In response they proclaimed that "wealth belongs to him who creates it."

Their rhetoric earned scorn from critics, who labeled the leaders "hayseed socialists." To be fair, there were some unsavory aspects to the movement: A few agrarians espoused simplistic and often anti-Semitic conspiracy theories, and some flamboyant demagogues— such as "Pitchfork Ben" Tillman of South Carolina—exploited rural anger for personal political ambitions. With a mixture of contempt and fear, critics called the rural reformers "crackpot radicals."

By Gilded Age standards the farmers' demands *were* radical—even though most were adopted in the twentieth century. Their most socialistic ideas called for government ownership and operation of the railroads and the telegraph and telephone, although they did not desire state ownership of all productive property. As landowners, farmers rejected socialism, but some did believe that these transportation and communication facilities were "natural monopolies" that could only be run efficiently under centralized management and were, besides, too important to the public welfare to be in the hands of private monopolies for profit.

The remainder of the agrarian political agenda reflected a realistic and moderate response to the farmers' problems. To ease their credit crisis they advocated an inflated, more flexible currency and the subtreasury plan. Considered by the Alliancemen to be the keystone of their program, subtreasuries (federal warehouses) were to be constructed as places where farmers could store their crops and receive treasury notes amounting to 80 percent of the crops' market value. Relieved from the pressure to sell immediately, farmers could wait for prices to rise to sell their crops and then pay back their subtreasury advances plus small interest and storage fees. Farmers saw the plan as a solution to the twin evils of the crop lien and depressed prices at harvest time. To finance government programs farmers called for a graduated income tax based upon the ability to pay.

Farmers believed that many of their ailments could be relieved by a more responsive, activist government. They therefore proposed political changes to "restore the government of the Republic to the hands of 'the plain people,' with which class it originated." Among the proposed changes were initiative and referendum, direct primaries, the direct election of United States senators, and the use of a secret ballot.

Initiative and referendum would allow people to propose legislation through petitions and enact laws by popular vote—thereby bypassing the state legislatures that seemed unwilling to act on their grievances. Direct primaries would let "the people" vote on political party candidates rather than having party leaders pick the candidates. In the same manner, people would directly elect senators instead of allowing state legislatures to select them. All of these proposals were intended to give citizens more control over their government. To make those changes effective a secret ballot was needed to protect voters from economic intimidation by employers and creditors or physical intimidation by threats of violence.

Although the farmers did not address the fundamental problem of overproduction, adoption of the agrarian demands could have relieved somewhat the agricultural distress fueling their anger. Thus it was that farmers became increasingly involved in political organization.

Emergence of the Populist Party

In 1890 Alliancemen entered politics in the West and the South with remarkable success. Under independent party banners, western Alliancemen elected a governor in Kansas, gained control of four state legislatures, and elected U.S. senators from Kansas and Nebraska. Working through the existing Democratic state parties, southern Alliancemen elected four governors, 44 congressmen, and several senators.

Western Alliancemen interpreted this success as a mandate to establish a national third party. At a May 1891 meeting in Cincinnati they failed to convince the southern Alliancemen to join them. By 1892, however, the Southerners were disillusioned with Alliance-backed Democrats who failed to support the subtreasury system. Overcoming their apprehension of third parties, the Alliances joined hands in St. Louis to create the People's, or Populist, party. In July 1892 the Populist party's national convention in Omaha drafted a platform and gave its presidential nomination to James B. Weaver, the former Union general who had been the Greenback party nominee in 1880. To symbolize the unity of the party they nominated former Confederate officer James G. Field for vice president. The Populist platform included all the agrarian agenda:

the subtreasury plan; an income tax; free coinage of silver to inflate the currency; government ownership of railroads, telephone, and telegraph; and the political reforms intended to restore government to "the hands of the people;" as well as restrictions on immigration and an eight-hour workday.

Most Populists were small-scale farmers in the South and West whose farms were minimally mechanized. Most relied on a single cash crop, had unsatisfactory access to credit, and lived in social isolation some distance from towns and railroads. In other words, their existence was marginal in all respects. The majority owned some land, but sizable numbers of sharecroppers and tenant farmers joined the party. Prosperous, large-scale, diversified farmers found little appeal in the party's platforms or activities.

Because the Populists realized the need to broaden the base of their constituency, the Omaha platform included planks to appeal to urban workers. They advocated an eight-hour

A PARTY OF PATCHES.
Grand Balloon Ascension—Cincinnati, May 20th, 1891.

The Populist party was a coalition of western and southern farm organizations, urban laborers, Grangers, and Greenbackers. This hostile cartoonist ridiculed as lunacy the Populist platforms.

day, immigration restriction, and the abolition of the Pinkerton system that supplied strikebreakers to management. One plank promised "fair and liberal" pensions to veterans. In the South some Populists, such as Tom Watson of Georgia, sought to woo African-American voters. "You are kept apart," he told audiences of black and white farmers, "that you may be separately fleeced of your earnings. You are made to hate each other because upon that hatred is rested the keystone of the arch of financial despotism which enslaves you both."

The Populists conducted colorful campaigns, which one Nebraska Democrat called a blend of "the French Revolution and a western religious revival." Their anger fostered a revolutionary spirit that appealed to large numbers of farmers. In 1892 Weaver became the first third-party candidate to win over one million votes. He carried Kansas, Colorado, Idaho, and Nevada for a total of 22 electoral votes. Populist strength in such mining states as Colorado reflected the appeal to silver miners of the party's demand for inflation by means of the free and unlimited coinage of silver at 16 to 1. On the other hand, the Populists failed to carry a single southern state, largely because of voting fraud, Democratic cries of white supremacy, and economic intimidation of many African-American voters. Nevertheless, it was a remarkable showing for a new party, revealing the extent of popular discontent. The next year brought the panic of 1893, which produced even more discontent and gave the Populists great hopes for the election of 1896.

DEPRESSION AND TURBULENCE IN THE 1890S

Social harmony became somewhat strained in the late 1880s with such violent episodes as the Haymarket Square riot of 1886. Economic "losers," mainly workers and farmers, were already becoming restless. The depression following the panic of 1893 intensified their suffering. Naturally, turbulence increased, setting the stage for an attempt to unite the losers in a quest for political power in the election of 1896.

The Roots and Results of the Depression

While the Populists made their bid for office in the election of 1892, the two major parties were involved in a rerun of the 1888 election. Once again Cleveland and Harrison faced each other over the issue of the tariff. The presence of the unpopular McKinley Tariff created a different outcome, and Cleveland entered the White House—just in time for the panic of 1893.

The depression started in Europe and spread to the United States as overseas buyers reduced their purchases of American goods as well as their American investments. Their unloading of some $300 million of investments caused American gold to leave the country to pay for these securities. Thus supplies of currency dropped, which led to rapidly falling prices. There had also been serious overexpansion of the economy, especially in railroad construction. Confidence faltered, the stock market crashed, and banks failed.

During the depression that followed, unemployment reached 20 percent of the work force, farm prices dropped to new lows; and farm foreclosures reached new highs. Sharp wage cuts and massive layoffs took place in virtually every industry. Historian Henry Adams lamented, "Men died like flies under the strain, and Boston grew suddenly old, haggard, and thin." Still opposed to direct federal aid, President Cleveland responded to the suffering by repealing the Sherman Silver Purchase Act and selling lucrative federal bonds to a banking syndicate headed by J. P. Morgan in an effort to protect the nation's gold reserves.

The Democrats did act on their campaign issue, passing the Wilson-Gorman Tariff that reduced rates by 10 percent. Reformers were disappointed with the moderate cuts but were appeased by a provision placing a 2 percent tax on incomes. That provision, however, was declared unconstitutional in *Pollock* v. *The Farmer's Loan and Trust Co.* in 1895. In the face of massive suffering, many people wanted the government to do more.

Expressions of Worker Discontent

Violence had begun to escalate in labor-management relations in the late 1880s and continued into the 1890s. In 1892 Andrew Carnegie and the Amalgamated Association of Iron and Steel Workers clashed at Carnegie's Homestead plant outside of Pittsburgh. In an effort to crush the union, Carnegie had slashed wages and—expecting a confrontation—had fortified his steel mills, hired strikebreakers, and employed the Pinkerton Agency to protect them. This done, Carnegie departed for Scotland on a fishing trip and left his manager, Henry Clay Frick, to do battle with the union.

On July 5, strikers and Pinkerton agents fought their first battle. Smoke from cannons, rifles, dynamite, and burning oil filled the hot summer air. Ten men were killed and another 70 were wounded, as the strikers won the first engagement. When Frick appealed to the governor of Pennsylvania for help, the governor dispatched 8000 militiamen to Homestead "to protect law and order"—a phrase normally synonymous with defense of industrialists' property.

The fighting continued until late July when an anarchist from Chicago named Alexander Berkman took matters into his own hands. He went to Frick's office, shot the manager twice, and stabbed him seven times before being subdued. Frick lived and police arrested Berkman. Although Berkman had no connection with the steel union, the local and national press linked unionism with radicalism. Shortly afterward, strikebreakers went to work—the union was defeated and destroyed by the powerful forces of capital, government, and press.

During the depression, employers frequently cut wages to preserve profits. In 1894,

Striking workers from Carnegie's Homestead steel plant outside Pittsburgh used guns and dynamite to try to keep Pinkerton guards from approaching the plant on barges from a nearby river.

for example, the workers in the Pullman plant at Chicago had their wages reduced several times while their rent for company-owned housing remained the same. When management refused to negotiate with the union, members of the American Railway Union (ARU) refused to handle any cars made in the Pullman plant. The boycott totally disrupted railroad traffic in the Midwest. Railroad executives appealed to Illinois governor John Altgeld for help, but the liberal politician refused to interfere. The executives then turned to U.S. Attorney General Richard Olney, a former railroad corporation lawyer. Olney and President Cleveland responded quickly, using the excuse of protecting the mails to come to the aid of the railroad managers. Over Altgeld's protest, the government sent 2000 troops to the Chicago area, and a federal court issued a blanket injunction that virtually ordered union leaders to discontinue the strike. When ARU president Eugene V. Debs defied the injunction, he was imprisoned. Only after federal troops arrived did violence occur. Within two days, bitter fighting had broken out, railcars were burned, and over $340,000 worth of damage had been done to railroad property. Force—absolute, final, and fed-

eral—crushed the Pullman strike. Such unified repressive force drove some workers to the political left.

Prior to 1894, the badly divided Socialist Labor party, led by the abrasive Daniel DeLeon, had a minuscule membership. After the Pullman strike Eugene V. Debs emerged from prison a socialist and made socialism more respectable. Born in Indiana in 1855, the balding Debs had the common touch and delivered with a Hoosier twang a version of socialism based upon distinctly American values. The movement thus acquired a fiery and effective orator. "Many of you think you are competing," Debs would declare. "Against whom? Against Rockefeller? About as I would if I had a wheelbarrow and competed with the Santa Fe [railroad]." Around the nucleus of his personality the larger and stronger Socialist Party of America began to form and directly challenge unrestrained capitalism.

The mass suffering during the depression also provoked some to ask the federal government to provide work for the unemployed. Jacob S. Coxey, a short, quiet Ohio businessman, was one who advocated putting men to work on the roads. They were

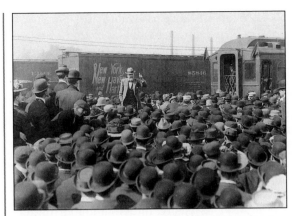

Eugene V. Debs was the Socialist Party of America's presidential nominee four times. Here Debs addresses a crowd of railroad workers during one of his campaigns.

to be paid by the printing of $500 million in legal tender paper money, which would also help to inflate the currency. He organized the Army of the Commonwealth of Christ to march to Washington and demand action. When about 500 of the marchers straggled into the capital on May 1, 1894, their leader was arrested for walking on the grass. Federal authorities beat and arrested his "troops." Although "Coxey's Army" fell far short of his dream of a demonstration of 400,000 jobless workers, their actions did get the attention of the public. Forty-three newspaper reporters accompanied them, reporting almost every detail of the march. One journalist quipped, "Never in the annals of insurrection has so small a company of soldiers been accompanied by such a phalanx of recording angels."

Deteriorating Race Relations

The turbulent 1890s was also one of the worst decades of racial violence in the nation's history. It stemmed from class as well as race conflict. Following Reconstruction, white southern "Redeemer" Democrats in some states had forged a rather strange alliance with black Republicans. In return for the protection of the Redeemers and a share of the lesser offices, African Americans helped those conservative, elitist whites to beat back challenges from lower-class whites, who called the Redeemer Democrats "Bourbons," after the French royal line. Tom Watson was right when he told black and white farmers that the Bourbons were using race as a wedge to keep them apart.

The Bourbon-black alliance could work only so long as it was in the interests of upper-class whites to support African-American rights and votes. But there were few external pressures to do so as the Republican party and all three branches of government deserted African Americans. Although the Populists failed to unite blacks and whites on the basis of class interests, the attempt led to considerable bloodshed. Whites shed white blood, but more frequently they spilled black blood. Lynching became a tool for controlling both black votes and actions. Under the pretext of "maintaining law and order," vigilante mobs hanged, mutilated,

Businessman Jacob S. Coxey is shown leading his army of unemployed workers into Washington, D.C., where he was arrested and his army dispersed by club-wielding police.

and burned African Americans in increasing numbers. During the 1890s an average of two to three black Southerners were lynched each week.

It is probably not coincidental that attempts to limit African-American voting began in earnest precisely at the time that farmer unrest arose. Mississippi led the way in finding ways to skirt the Fifteenth Amendment. Without mentioning "race, color, or previous condition of servitude," the 1890 Mississippi constitution established poll taxes, literacy tests, and residency requirements, all aimed at reducing black voting. A key element of the literacy tests was the requirement that voters be able to explain what they read to the satisfaction of the voter registrars—African Americans found registrars extremely hard to satisfy. The Supreme Court displayed its disregard for black rights by upholding the so-called Mississippi Plan in *Williams* v. *Mississippi,* and other states soon adopted similar measures. Later, to woo lower-class white voters, grandfather clauses were added—providing exemptions from these requirements based on voting eligibility prior to the Reconstruction Acts. These clauses applied to all adult white males and to no African Americans.

Once whites stripped away black political power other black rights toppled. With no need to cater to African-American voters, whites soon began to pass discriminatory legislation. Most wanted to use segregation as a means of racial control, but the Fourteenth Amendment raised constitutional questions. The Supreme Court removed that barrier. After several rulings that limited constitutional protection of black rights, in the 1896 *Plessy* v. *Ferguson* decision the Court finally ruled that public accommodations for blacks could be "separate but equal." With segregation now legalized, for the next two decades southern states frantically passed legislation—known as "Jim Crow" laws—to make legal the separation of the races. When the frenzy stopped, some states had even passed laws prohibiting interracial checker playing and requiring textbooks used in African-American schools to be stored in separate rooms from those used in white schools.

Segregation and the exclusion of African Americans from public facilities had long existed in a haphazard way based on custom. As this informal and inconsistent arrangement was converted into a legalized system of repression, violence erupted, and no one stepped in to protect African Americans. The popularity of Booker T. Washington's 1895 "Atlanta Compromise," with its plea for racial cooperation, is easily understandable under the conditions it was delivered. Both whites and blacks were eager to find a way out of the bloodshed. More militant black voices, however, such as that of Memphis newspaper editor Ida B. Wells, insisted on federal action to prevent lynching.

Fissures seemed to be opening up along a number of the seams in American society. The turbulence was enough to provoke the Democratic party to respond to popular demands for economic relief and political reform in 1896, creating a dilemma for the Populists.

The Tide Turns: The Election of 1896

After the Republicans nominated William McKinley and the Democrats chose William Jennings Bryan, the Populists were left with an impossible choice. When Bryan and the Democrats endorsed silver, the Populists had their thunder stolen. They had hoped to ride silver to power because of the growing popularity of the issue. William H. Harvey's pro-silver book *Coin's Financial School* had become a best-seller in 1894. Instead of picking up silverite bolters from the major parties as they had expected to do, the Populists were now faced with a real problem. To nominate someone else would split the silver votes and ensure a victory for McKinley. Yet to nominate Bryan meant a loss of their identity and momentum.

Many Populists argued fervently against "fusion" with the Democrats, who focused almost exclusively on silver at the expense of the rest of the Populist demands. Watson

In the 1896 *Plessy* v. *Ferguson* decision, the U.S. Supreme Court ruled that enforced separation of the races and "separate but equal" public facilities for African Americans were not discriminatory, as prohibited by the Fourteenth Amendment. Facilities were certainly separate, as shown in this African-American school near Henderson, Kentucky, but rarely equal.

and others viewed the obsession with silver as "a trap, a pitfall, a snare, a menace, a fraud, a crime against common sense and common honesty." In the end Populists bit the bullet and nominated Bryan for president but chose Tom Watson for vice president rather than the Democratic choice, Arthur Sewall.

"God's in his Heaven, all's right with the world!" Republican campaign manager Mark Hanna wired McKinley when he learned of the Republican victory. McKinley carried the popular vote 7.1 million to 6.5 million and the electoral votes 271 to 176. The defeat of Bryan and the silver forces brought an end to political equilibrium. Millions of Democrats left their party, and the Republican party became the majority party. Republicans then won the presidency in seven of the nine contests between 1896 and 1928, and controlled both houses of Congress 17 of the next 20 sessions. One basic reason for the Republican victory of 1896 was the bad luck of the Democrats to be in power when the depression came. Republicans gleefully noted in 1894, "We were told in the old times that the rich were getting richer and the poor were getting poorer. To cure that imaginary ailment our political opponents have brought on a time when everybody is getting poorer."

The Populists, of course, suffered the most from the election results: Their party disappeared. The attempt to unite farmers and labor, blacks and whites, failed. Like the Socialists and other radicals, the Populists were never able to recruit organized labor in order to forge a broadly based working-class movement. American Federation of Labor president Samuel Gompers and other labor

"RISE, BROTHERS!": THE BLACK RESPONSE TO JIM CROW

AFRICAN Americans had long struggled against white prejudice and repression. During Reconstruction constant vigilance was needed to protect and expand newly won rights. Some efforts were in vain, but a few successes had helped curb the growth of segregation. For example, African Americans in Savannah, Georgia, succeeded in desegregating their city's streetcar system in 1872 by boarding the so-called white cars, threatening legal action, and boycotting the Jim Crow cars. Beginning in the 1890s, however, a rising tide of virulent white racism eventually confounded black attempts to resist being made into second-class citizens. With a new determination white Southerners stripped African Americans of their voting rights, passed segregation laws, and lynched those who refused to cooperate.

Once whites had won the battle and the smoke had cleared from the battlefields, the mythology of African-American submission and acceptance began to prevail. Booker T. Washington became a symbol of black cooperation and accommodation. Selected passages of his 1895 Atlanta address, the "Atlanta Compromise," were heralded as the "will of blacks." Other voices were ignored. Few quoted the words of John Hope, a professor at a black college in Nashville, the next year. Hope exhorted African Americans:

> Rise, Brothers! Come let us possess this land. Never say "Let well enough alone." Cease to console yourself with adages that numb the moral sense. Be discontented. Be dissatisfied. . . . Be restless as the tempestuous billows on the boundless sea. Let your dissatisfaction break mountain-high against the walls of prejudice and swamp it to the very foundation. Then we shall not have to plead for justice nor on bended knee crave mercy; for we shall be men. Then and not until then will liberty in its highest sense be the boast of our Republic!

Many African Americans responded to the new wave of discrimination by employing every available tactic to protest the loss of their rights. Before disfranchisement was completed, black officeholders made impassioned speeches and lobbied their white colleagues to oppose to discriminatory legislation. Activists organized local "Negro Rights," "Emancipation," and "Colored Uplift" groups that wrote strongly worded resolutions and organized petition drives. Individuals and groups launched legal challenges in the courts. Some tested the new laws by breaking them. Protest meetings were held. Boycotts of newly segregated facilities occurred in New Orleans, Savannah, Jacksonville, Richmond, and other southern cities. The black press often fearlessly attacked white actions; a Bay Minette, Alabama, paper counseled, "The best remedy for lynching is a good Winchester rifle." Finally, a few engaged in the ultimate protest—armed resistance.

Two very different examples illustrate the nature and results of African-American protest at the turn of the century. The first, a Savannah streetcar boycott in 1906, had many similarities to the Montgomery bus boycott of 1955—the main exception being the outcome. The second, the story of Robert Charles, demonstrates that this early civil rights movement had its share of martyrs.

At the beginning of the twentieth century both whites and blacks of Savannah were proud that their city had been immune to the lynching virus. In 1906 it was also one of the few southern cities without a single Jim Crow law on its books. Race relations were better than average, though not ideal. Of the city's 72,000 residents 54 percent were African American, but the white minority exercised a firm, if benevolent, control. There were only three black public officials, and they held positions allotted to blacks by law. Nevertheless, the black community had spawned a leadership class that commanded some respect from the white establishment and enjoyed a measure of political clout. They had thus been able to turn back all previous attempts to enact segregation.

The year 1906, however, brought increased racial tension throughout the South, with several outbreaks of violence, including those in Brownsville, Texas, and in Georgia where the bitter gubernatorial campaign of Hoke Smith aroused white prejudice. Savannah whites began to urge city leaders to get into the "new order of things" and exclude African Americans from both politics and social contact with whites. On September 12, 1906, the city adopted a law that required separate seating in streetcars and empowered the police to arrest anyone sitting in the wrong place.

The African-American elite— leading ministers, physicians, and businessmen—had already formed a committee to lobby against the ordinance. Once the law was passed, they immediately organized a boycott. In the churches, ministers urged compliance with the boycott and the black *Savannah Tribune* declared: "Let us walk! walk! and save some nickels. . . . Do not trample on your pride by being 'jim crowed.' Walk!" Black hackmen reduced their fares for boycotters from 25 cents to 10 cents. One group attempted to form the United Transportation Company to compete with white lines. Those rich enough to own wagons drove themselves and friends to town.

Many who could get no other transportation heeded the words of their leaders and walked. It was reported that the mayor's secretary had given his maid carfare to bring two large suitcases from his home to city hall. When she arrived late and soaked with perspiration, he discovered that she had followed her minister's advice and refused to ride the streetcar. The local white paper noted that trolley after trolley went by with the back seats vacant. The boycott was almost total.

City authorities responded much as Montgomery authorities did in 1955. They cracked down on unlicensed hacks and harassed licensed ones. African Americans remained firm for some time—even after it became apparent that the boycott was not going to change white minds. As late as May 1908, two years after the start of the boycott, the streetcar line admitted that no more than 80 percent of blacks had returned to the cars. Without action by the federal government, even economic loss could not persuade whites to abandon segregation.

Savannah blacks suffered inconvenience to protest the infringement of their rights, but Robert Charles paid a much higher price. A quiet, intense young man in his twenties who worked at odd jobs, he supported black emigration to Africa as a response to white prejudice in the South. He read a lot and collected weapons but broke no laws. One night in July of 1900 he sat on a front porch in New Orleans talking quietly with a friend. Near midnight three police officers arrived with drawn pistols and flailing billy clubs to arrest him.

Charles responded to the attempted arrest by drawing his own gun and shooting one of the officers. Wounded himself, he then fled—not to safety but to rearm with a rifle. Charles then moved from one hiding place to another, leaving a trail of five dead police officers and a dozen wounded ones. A mob of over a thousand whites joined police in the manhunt, frequently firing indiscriminately into the African-American community. Finally surrounded, Charles was burned out of his hiding place and immediately riddled with bullets. As was customary, the mob then badly mutilated the body. They killed the man but not the spirit. African-American newspaper woman Ida Wells-Barnett investigated the incident and ended her report with the words: "The white people of this county may charge that he was a desperado, but to the people of his own race Robert Charles will always be regarded as the 'hero of New Orleans.'" Later, his willingness to fight police brutality with retaliatory violence would be renewed by the Black Panthers in the 1960s.

Even heroic actions failed to protect African-Americans' rights from the onslaught of discrimination at the dawn of the new century. Nevertheless these men and women added to the heritage of protest that would reap rewards a half-century later—when the media were more sympathic and the federal government finally decided that it was in the national interest to protect the rights of all citizens.

CHRONOLOGY OF KEY EVENTS

1867	The Grangers, first national farmers' organization, is founded
1873	"Crime of '73": Coinage Act declares that gold alone would be minted to back paper money
1877	Southern Farmers' Alliance is founded in Texas; *Munn* v. *Illinois* upholds the constitutionality of state regulation of railroads
1878	Bland-Allison Act requires the U.S. Treasury to buy $2 to $4 million of silver a month in order to inflate the currency
1881	President James A. Garfield mortally wounded at a Washington, D.C., train station, Chester Arthur becomes twenty-first president
1883	Pendleton Act classifies approximately 15,000 federal jobs as civil service positions to be awarded only after a competitive examination
1886	*Wabash, St. Louis, & Pacific Railway Company* v. *Illinois* reverses *Munn* v. *Illinois* and states that only Congress can regulate commerce between states
1887	Congress establishes the Interstate Commerce Commission, the first federal regulatory commission, to regulate railroads
1890	National Woman Suffrage Association and American Woman Suffrage Association merge to form the National American Woman Suffrage Association; Congress passes Sherman Antitrust Act, forbidding restraints on trade; Sherman Silver Purchase Act increases amount of silver that had to be purchased annually and allows the Treasury to issue paper money based on silver; Mississippi becomes first southern state to adopt poll taxes, literacy tests, and residency requirements to restrict African-American voting
1892	Populist party is formed and receives over a million votes in presidential race; violent-Homestead, Pennsylvania, steel strike erupts
1893	Severe economic depression begins
1894	Pullman workers strike; Coxey's Army marches on Washington, D.C., to protest unemployment and to urge a public works program to relieve unemployment
1895	*United States* v. *E. C. Knight Co.* weakens Sherman Antitrust Act by stating that law does not apply to companies that operate exclusively in one state; *Pollock* v. *Farmer's Loan and Trust Co.* declares a federal income tax unconstitutional
1896	*Plessy* v. *Ferguson* decision rules that the principle of "separate but equal" does not deprive blacks of civil rights guaranteed under the Fourteenth Amendment; Republican William McKinley defeats Democrat William Jennings Bryan to become the twenty-fifth president
1900	Gold Standard Act places the nation on the gold standard

leaders argued that farmers were capitalists, not wage earners, and that their goals were not compatible with labor's interests. For example, the inflation that farmers wanted would raise food prices to the detriment of workers already living close to the margin. In the South race proved to be more important than class, and many disillusioned white Populists such as Tom Watson became anti-black activists following their defeat. They joined gladly with the Bourbons to curtail African-American suffrage. The Bourbons had stirred up the issue of racism to defeat the Populists and then were unable to put the genie back into the bottle. In many states they were replaced by less elitist, bigoted demagogues.

Americans had come to a turning point in 1896 and chose the conservative path. The Republican administration quickly raised duties with the Dingley Tariff of 1897. Three years later the Gold Standard Act officially put the nation on the gold standard by requiring all money to be redeemable in gold. Ironically, new discoveries of gold and more efficient extracting methods brought the inflation that farmers had sought from silver. Prosperity began to return, and the Republicans could point with pride to their slogan, "The Full Dinner Pail." That prosperity sapped the strength of the agrarian movement as rising farm prices eased farmers' economic distress. And such inventions and services as the telephone and rural free delivery of mail decreased farmers' isolation—especially after mail-order catalogs began to arrive from Montgomery Ward's and Sears, Roebuck.

CONCLUSION

After Reconstruction, national politics entertained the masses and voter turnout reached all-time highs. At the same time, the emerging problems of industrialization challenged the traditional roles of state and federal governments. The failure of either major party to dominate the federal government created some degree of political inertia. Competing for voters, the parties differed little in their laissez-faire support of business or their primary concern with the spoils of office. Most people supported the government's nonintervention in the economy and society until problems escalated for farmers, workers, and minorities. State and local governments made efforts to solve emerging problems, but many ills seemed to require federal action. Political inertia in Washington bred crisis after crisis as problems remained unresolved.

Finally, in the West and South a challenge to unrestrained capitalism arose from the losers in the race toward industrialism and economic expansion. Led by disgruntled farmers, the Populist party sought to unite large segments of the American population on the basis of class interest. In 1896 the Democratic party responded by nominating William Jennings Bryan. As a result, the presidential election of that year provided a real choice for American voters. The victory of conservative William McKinley brought about the death of Populism, but many of the problems the farmers addressed in the 1890s continued into the twentieth century. Time vindicated the farmers' demands. A large number of their rejected solutions were adopted in the first two decades of the new century, and most of their remaining agenda was enacted in modified form during the New Deal of the 1930s.

SUGGESTIONS FOR FURTHER READING

Ed Ayers, *The Promise of the New South: Life After Reconstruction* (1992). Provides a thorough examination of diverse aspects of Southern culture following Reconstruction.

Sean Dennis Cashman, *America in the Gilded Age: From the Death of Lincoln to the Rise of Theodore Roosevelt*, 3d ed. (1993). A thorough account of politics and society during the late nineteenth century.

Lawrence Goodwyn, *Democratic Promis: The Populist Moment in America* (1976). An interpretation that focuses on the Populists' attempt to expand democracy.

William F. Holmes, ed., *American Populism* (1994). Comprehensive collection of significant interpretations of the Populist movement.

Michael Kazin, *The Populist Persuasion: An American History* (1995). Analyzes the various functions that Populism has served in American politics.

Robert C. McMath, *American Populism: A Social History, 1877–1898* (1993). Presents an up-to-date account of Populism and its supporters.

Overviews and Surveys

Vincent P. DeSantis, *The Shaping of Modern America, 1877–1916* (1973); Harold U. Faulkner, *Politics, Reform, and Expansion, 1890–1900* (1959); John A. Garraty, *The New Commonwealth, 1877–1890* (1968); Ray

Ginger, *The Age of Excess: The United States From 1877 to 1914* (1965); John D. Hicks, *The Populist Revolt: A History of the Farmers' Alliance and the People's Party* (1931); Richard Hofstadter, *The Age of Reform* (1955); Alan Trachtenberg, *The Incorporation of America: Culture and Society in the Gilded Age* (1982).

Equilibrium and Inertia: The National Political Scene

John Allswang, *Bosses, Machines, and Urban Voters* (1977); William R. Brock, *Investigation and Responsibility* (1984); John M. Dobson, *Politics in the Gilded Age: A New Perspective on Reform* (1972); J. Rogers Hollingsworth, *The Whirligig of Politics: The Democracy of Cleveland and Bryan* (1963); Richard Jensen, *The Winning of the Midwest: Social and Political Conflicts, 1888–1896* (1971); Morton Keller, *Affairs of State: Public Life in Nineteenth Century America* (1977); Paul Kleppner, *The Cross of Culture: A Social Analysis of Midwestern Politics, 1850–1900* (1970), and *The Third Electoral System, 1853–1892* (1979); Michael E. McGerr, *The Decline of Popular Politics: The American North, 1865–1928* (1986); Robert D. Marcus, *GOP: Political Structure in the Gilded Age, 1880–1896* (1971); Horace S. Merrill, *Bourbon Democracy in the Middle West, 1865–1896* (1953); H. Wayne Morgan, *From Hayes to McKinley* (1969); David J. Rothman, *Politics and Power: The United States Senate, 1869–1901* (1966); Leonard D. White, *The Republican Era, 1869–1901* (1958); R. Hal Williams, *Years of Decision: American Politics in the 1890s* (1978).

Style Over Substance: Government in the Gilded Age, 1877–1892

Ballard C. Campbell, *Representative Democracy* (1980); Justus D. Doenecke, *The Presidencies of James A. Garfield & Chester A. Arthur* (1981); Eleanor Flexner, *Century of Struggle: The Women's Rights Movement in the United States*, rev. ed. (1975); Margaret Forster, *Significant Sisters: The Grassroots of Active Feminism, 1839–1939* (1984); Lewis L. Gould, *The Presidency of William McKinley* (1980); Stanley P. Hirshson, *Farewell to the Bloody Shirt: Northern Republicans and the Southern Negro* (1962); Ari A. Hoogenboom, *Outlawing the Spoils: The Civil Service Reform Movement* (1961); Aileen Kraditor, *The Ideas of the Woman's Suffrage Movement, 1890–1920* (1965); Gerald W. McFarland, *Mugwumps, Morals, and Poli-

tics 1884–1920* (1975); Arnold M. Paul, *Conservative Crisis and the Rule of Law: Attitudes of Bar and Bench, 1887–1895* (1969); Theda Skocpol, *Protecting Soldiers and Mothers: The Political Origins of Social Policy in the United States* (1992); John G. Sproat, *The Best Men: Liberal Reformers in the Gilded Age* (1968); Mark Wahlgren Summers, *The Era of Good Stealings* (1993); Tom E. Terrill, *The Tariff, Politics, and American Foreign Policy, 1874–1901* (1973); Allen Weinstein, *Prelude to Populism: Origins of the Silver Issue, 1867–1878* (1970).

The Farmers Revolt

Peter H. Argersinger, *Populism and Politics: William Alfred Peffer and the People's Party* (1974); Allan G. Bogue, *Money at Interest: The Farm Mortgage on the Middle Border* (1955); Paul W. Glad, *McKinley, Bryan, and the People* (1964); Sheldon Hackney, *Populism to Progressivism in Alabama* (1969); Steven Hahn, *The Roots of Southern Populism: Yeomen Farmers and the Transformation of the Georgia Upcountry, 1850–1890* (1983); Robert McMath, Jr., *Populist Vanguard: A History of the Southern Farmers' Alliance* (1975); Walter T. K. Nugent, *The Tolerant Populists: Kansas Populism and Nativism* (1963); Jeffrey Ostler, *Prairie Populism: The Fate of Agrarian Radicalism in Kansas, Nebraska, and Iowa, 1880–1892* (1993); Bruce Palmer, *Man over Money: The Southern Populist Critique of American Capitalism* (1980); Norman Pollack, ed., *The Populist Mind* (1967); Barton C. Shaw, *The Wool-Boys: Georgia's Populist Party* (1984).

Depression and Turbulence in the 1890s

John P. Diggins, *The American Left in the Twentieth Century* (1973); Robert F. Durden, *The Climax of Populism: The Election of 1896* (1965); Charles Hoffmann, *The Depression of the Nineties: An Economic History* (1970); Stanley L. Jones, *The Presidential Election of 1896* (1964); J. Morgan Kousser, *The Shaping of Southern Politics: Suffrage Restriction and Establishment of the One-Party South, 1880–1910* (1974); Paul Krause, *The Battle for Homestead, 1880–1892* (1992); Charles Lofgren, *The Plessy Case: A Legal-Historical Interpretation* (1987); Donald L. McMurry, *Coxey's Army: A Study of the Industrial Army Movement of 1894* (1929); Samuel T. McSeveney, *The Politics of Depression* (1972); Howard N. Rabinowitz, *Race Relations in the Urban South, 1865–1890* (1978); William G. Ross, *A Muted Fury: Populists, Progressives, and

Labor Unions, 1890–1937 (1994); C. Vann Woodward, *The Strange Career of Jim Crow*, rev. ed. (1974).

Biographies

Paolo Coletta, *William Jennings Bryan: Political Evangelist* (1964); Ray Ginger, *Bending Cross: A Biography of Eugene Victor Debs* (1949); Paul W. Glad, *The Trumpet Soundeth: William Jennings Bryan and His Democracy* (1960); Louis Koenig, *Bryan: A Biography of William Jennings Bryan* (1971); Allan Nevins, *Grover Cleveland: A Study in Courage* (1932); Allan Peskin, *Garfield: A Biography* (1978); Thomas Reeves, *Gentleman Boss: The Life of Chester Alan Arthur* (1975); Martin Ridge, *Ignatius Donnelly: The Portrait of a Politician* (1962); Nick Salvatore, *Eugene V. Debs: Citizen and Socialist* (1982); Charles Morrow Wilson, *The Commoner: William Jennings Bryan* (1970); C. Vann Woodward, *Tom Watson: Agrarian Rebel* (1938).

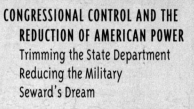

CONGRESSIONAL CONTROL AND THE REDUCTION OF AMERICAN POWER
Trimming the State Department
Reducing the Military
Seward's Dream

THE SPIRIT OF AMERICAN GREATNESS
American Exceptionalism
Sense of Duty
Search for Markets
The New Navy
Shaping Public Opinion

THE EMERGENCE OF AGGRESSION IN AMERICAN FOREIGN POLICY
Confronting the Germans in Samoa
Teaching Chile a Lesson
Plucking the Hawaiian Pear
Facing Down the British

THE WAR FOR EMPIRE
The Spirit of the 1890s
The Cuban Revolution
The Yellow Press
The Spanish-American War
Freeing Cuba
The Imperial Debate
The War to Crush Filipino
   Independence
Keeping the Doors Open

Dreams of expansion came easily to Americans during the nineteenth century. For most of the century they expanded westward, moving into Texas and Kansas, pushing across the Great Plains, and occupying California and the Pacific Northwest. But they did not restrict their dreams to the millions of acres between Mexico and Canada. They cast covetous eyes toward Central America and the islands of the Caribbean and the Pacific. Plans to annex Nicaragua, Cuba, Santo Domingo, the Virgin Islands, Hawaii, and Samoa fired politicians' imaginations. Before the Civil War, the debate over slavery blocked these larger expansionist efforts. Once the Union was preserved, however, expansionists returned to their plans with revived energy and enthusiasm.

President Ulysses S. Grant had a pet expansionist project of his own—the Dominican Republic, the eastern two-thirds of the Caribbean island of Santo Domingo. Annexation, he maintained, would benefit the United States in a number of ways. The island was rich in mineral resources, possessed an important natural harbor, and its inhabitants were eager to buy American products. Most importantly for Grant, who was ever mindful of America's race problem, the Dominicans were black. The island could serve as a frontier for black Americans, a retreat from Ku Klux Klan harassment.

With so much to gain, Grant put his full political weight behind annexation. His conduct was less than presidential. First, he sent his personal secretary and close friend Orville Babcock to Santo Domingo on a "fact-finding" mission. Unimpressed by the islanders, Babcock reported: "The people are indolent and ignorant. The best class of people are the American Negroes who have come here from time to time." But Babcock was convinced that the Dominican Republic was a commercial and strategic prize worthy of annexation. What was more, Bue-

Area of Grant's Expansionist Scheme

naventura Baez, the unscrupulous president of the republic, was eager to sell his country. With the money he would make from the transaction, Baez hoped to establish residence in Paris or Madrid, because, as Babcock noted, the Dominican Republic was "a dull country."

Unrest around him added fuel to Baez's willingness to sell. Both neighboring Haiti and a strong force of Dominican rebels threatened his government. So difficult was Baez's position that Babcock had to order a United States Navy ship to protect the Baez government during the annexation negotiations, which were completed in the late fall of 1869. The promise of American dollars had convinced Baez that his country should belong to the United States.

Grant was pleased. The treaty of annexation, however, would have to be ratified by the Senate, a body more difficult to satisfy than Baez's government. An informal man, Grant decided to forgo presidential protocol and personally visit Charles Sumner, the chairman of the Senate Foreign Relations Committee. On the evening of January 2, 1870, Grant made an unannounced call at Sumner's Washington home on Lafayette Park. Sumner recalled later that Grant was drunk at the time. Drunk or sober, Grant was certainly in earnest. He energetically discussed the need to annex the Dominican Republic. Sumner listened, then replied: "Mr. President, I am an Administration man, and whatever you do will always find in me the most careful and candid consideration." Grant departed for his short walk back to the White House believing he had won Sumner's full support. In fact, he had only won the powerful Massachusetts senator's "candid consideration."

After consideration and considerable investigation, Sumner decided that the entire annexation scheme was distasteful. He was disturbed by Babcock's and Baez's unethical financial dealings and was enraged that the United States Navy had been used to keep the Dominican president in power. Sumner was not a man to mince words. Labeled "probably the most intolerant man that American history has ever known," he accused Grant of being "a colossus of ignorance." Finally, by a vote of 5 to 2, the Foreign Relations Committee voiced its disapproval of the treaty of annexation.

Grant was furious. His son later recalled, "I never saw Father so grimly angry." Known for his bulldog tenacity during the Civil War, Grant was not about to quit. He hinted that if the United States did not take the Dominican Republic, one of the European powers would; he even reported the results of a rigged plebiscite in which the Dominicans supposedly supported annexation by the suspiciously lopsided vote of 15,169 to 11. Grant's efforts failed. On June 30, 1870, the Senate rejected the treaty. Defining America's duty toward the island, Sumner said, "Our duty is as plain as the Ten Commandments. Kindness, beneficence, assistance, aid, help, protection, all that is implied in good neighborhood, these we must give freely, bountifully, but their independence is as sacred to them as is ours to us."

The failed attempt to annex the Dominican Republic is important for the themes it underscored. It demonstrated both the desire for expansion by the president and his advisers and the power of Congress in foreign affairs. For the remainder of the century the scenario would be repeated again and again, often with differing results. Gradually presidents wrested more control over foreign affairs from Congress. And Congress, for its part, accepted a more expansionist foreign policy. As presidents and Congress found common ground, America expanded outward into the Caribbean and the Pacific, although the expansion took different forms. Sometimes the United States annexed countries outright; other times it was content to exercise less forceful control over nominally independent countries. The results were the same. The United States ultimately acquired an overseas empire and expanded its influence over the Western Hemisphere.

CONGRESSIONAL CONTROL AND THE REDUCTION OF AMERICAN POWER

In 1869, when Grant took office, congressmen and other Americans held the State Department and the diplomatic service in low esteem. No majestic building housed the State Department—it was headquartered in a former orphan asylum. Nor was the post of secretary of state as great a prize as it had been. Once regarded as a stepping-stone to the presidency, politicians increasingly viewed the post as a reward for outstanding party men or the refuge for defeated presidential aspirants. Even the diplomats themselves did not escape criticism. One newspaper editor said the diplomatic service was too often used as "gilt edged pigeon holes for filing away Americans, more or less illustrious, who are no longer particularly wanted at home."

Trimming the State Department

The irreverent treatment of the State Department reflected a congressional and national mood. Concerns over the currency, civil service reform, Reconstruction, taxation, the tariff, Indian fighting, and railroad building dwarfed interest in foreign affairs. As late as 1889, Henry Cabot Lodge, whose interest in foreign affairs was great, could write: "Our relations with foreign nations today fill but a slight place in American politics, and excite . . . a languid interest. We have separated ourselves so completely from the affairs of other people." During the 1870s and 1880s, when a powerful Congress largely dictated foreign policy, the spirit of Washington's Farewell Address and the Monroe Doctrine guided the country. Washington had counseled America to steer clear of foreign entanglements and Monroe had made isolationism from Europe a national obsession. Separated from a powerful Europe by the cold North Atlantic, Congress saw no reason to spend time or money on the State Department or foreign affairs.

Using its control over the budget as a sword, Congress trimmed the State Department to the bone. In 1869, Congress allowed the State Department a paltry 31 clerks; by 1881 presidential efforts had succeeded in raising that number to a still inadequate 50. Politicians who considered the foreign service "a nursery of snobs" viewed diplomats as an expensive, nearly useless luxury. A few reformers even advocated the abolition of the foreign service. They argued that two oceans protected

During the turn of the century, the United States increasingly tried to influence the affairs of the Americas. Here, Uncle Sam assumes a forceful attitude.

America and that international lawyers could be hired to handle serious international crises.

Reducing the Military

The sword that trimmed the State Department was also used to pare the United States army and navy. When the Civil War ended and peace returned, Congress quickly reduced the country's military might, making the United States a weaker country. In 1865 the United States had the largest and perhaps the most powerful navy in the world, with 971 vessels. To be sure, it was a ragtag navy, composed of just about any vessel that would float ranging from the powerful *Monitor*-class ironclads to modest yachts. Within nine months of Appomattox, the fleet had been reduced to 29.

As Congress watched unconcerned, the navy declined intellectually as well. To begin with, there were far too many officers. Although after the post–Civil War reductions the United States navy was less than one-tenth as large as Great Britain's, it contained over half as many officers. With promotions based strictly upon length of service, any officer who lived long enough could become an admiral. This system of promotion almost guaranteed poor leadership. The world's best navies converted to steel and steam, but U.S. naval leaders remained tied to wood and sails. As one U.S. officer from the period recalled, "To burn coal was so grievous an offense in the eyes of the authorities that for years the coal-burning captain was obliged to enter in the logbook in *red ink* his reasons for getting up steam and starting the engines." The U.S. navy quickly became a joke. In 1881 authorities claimed, with some justification, that a single modern ship of the Chilean navy could destroy the entire United States fleet.

The men appointed as the secretaries of the navy did nothing to help matters. They were mostly political appointees who knew little and cared less about ships. One historian noted that Richard W. Thompson of Indiana, whom Rutherford B. Hayes appointed secretary of the navy, was "so densely ignorant of naval affairs as to express surprise upon learning that ships were hollow."

The power and effectiveness of the army were similarly reduced. On May 23, 1865, with the Civil War just ended, Union bluecoats marched down Pennsylvania Avenue in a victory parade. There were over 100,000 soldiers. It took an hour for General Meade's cavalry to pass the reviewing stand. "Marching twelve abreast, the general's infantry consumed another five hours." The next day thousands of General Sherman's men repeated the performance, marching briskly "like the lords of the world!"

The sight would not be repeated for over 50 years. Demobilization occurred quickly and haphazardly. In May 1865 the army contained 1,034,064 volunteers; by November 1866 only 11,043 remained in uniform. Eventually Congress slashed the number of even the regular troops. By the end of Reconstruction, Congress had reduced the army to a distant echo of its former self. In 1876 maximum strength stood at 27,442 troops.

Certainly, in 1876 the United States did not need an active foreign service and a powerful army and navy to secure its borders. No countries threatened America. Geography defended the United States, and the European balance of power discouraged European designs on any part of the Western Hemisphere. At the same time, the relative weakness of America's foreign service, army, and navy discouraged the United States from attempting to extend its influence beyond its own borders. All in all, most congressmen were entirely happy with the situation.

Seward's Dream

Not everyone in government agreed with congressional leadership in foreign affairs. Regularly during the 1860s and 1870s, presidents or their secretaries of state called for a more forceful, expansionist foreign policy. William Henry Seward of New York, who served as secretary of state for Lincoln and Johnson, was such a man. A cold and vain man with a weak chin and a prominent nose, Seward dreamed of an American empire that would dominate the Pacific and Caribbean basins. During his term as secretary of state, he advocated a vigorous expansionism. He negotiated with Denmark to purchase the Danish West Indies (Virgin Islands), with Russia to buy Alaska, and with Santo Domingo for the Dominican harbor of Samana Bay. In addition, his plan for an American empire encompassed Haiti, Cuba, Iceland, Greenland, Honduras's Tigre Island, and Hawaii.

Congress, not sharing Seward's vision, balked. During Seward's term, America did acquire the Midway Islands in the middle of the Pacific Ocean, but few Americans even noticed the addition. The purchase of Alaska in 1867 drew more comments, most of them negative. Congressmen grumbled over the treaty. Some senators claimed that $7.2 million was too much money for a frozen wasteland that only Eskimos and seals could love. Others cracked jokes about "Johnson's Polar Bear Garden" and "Frigidia." But in the end the Senate, influenced by a few well-placed bribes, reluctantly ratified the treaty.

Congress and most Americans did not share Secretary of State William Henry Seward's expansionist ambitions. Only a few well-placed bribes convinced the Senate to purchase Alaska in 1867. The purchase became known as "Seward's Folly."

Articulate and aggressive anti-imperialists blocked the remainder of Seward's dreams. During the late 1860s and the 1870s congressional power was at high tide. Seward and President Andrew Johnson were no match for Sumner and Thaddeus Stevens and their colleagues in Congress. Congressmen consistently found other issues more pressing than foreign affairs. Some pushed for money to enact a fair Reconstruction policy. Others freely gave money to railroad construction companies and Union veterans, such gifts contributing significantly to their reelection. But they drew America's purse strings tight when confronted with most expansionist schemes.

THE SPIRIT OF AMERICAN GREATNESS

Although Congress was reluctant to endorse expansionist schemes, during the last third of the nineteenth century many other citizens had become convinced that the United States had to adopt a more aggressive and forceful foreign policy. Their reasons varied. Some believed expansion would be good for American business. Others felt America had a duty to spread its way of life to less fortunate countries. Still others maintained that economic and strategic security required that the country acquire overseas bases. Behind all the arguments, however, rested a common assumption: The United States was a great and important country, and it should start acting the part.

American Exceptionalism

For many Americans it started with God's plan. The idea of American exceptionalism—that the nation houses God's chosen people—has deep roots in the country's history. Puritan concepts of "a city upon a hill" mixed easily with talk of the greatness of republicanism and democracy and the manifest destiny of America. The teachings of Social Darwinists added "scientific proof" to the concept of American exceptionalism. With such Darwinian phrases as "natural selection" and "survival of the fittest," American intellectuals praised the course of American history. Even Charles Darwin himself was not immune to the lure of American exceptionalism. In *The Descent of Man* (1871), he wrote: "There is apparently much truth in the belief that the wonderful progress of the United States, as well as the character of the people, are the results of natural selection; the more energetic, restless, and courageous men from all parts of Europe have emigrated during the last ten or twelve generations to that great country."

Such ideas found a warm reception in America. There was, however, a dark side to American exceptionalism, and too many Americans were quick to endorse it: If white Anglo-Saxon Americans were biologically superior, then other races and other nations had to be inferior. During the late nineteenth century, such Social Darwinists as Herbert Spencer in England and John Fiske in the United States helped make racism intellectually acceptable. Catering to Anglo-Saxon audiences, Social Darwinists advanced one pseudoscientific theory after another to "prove" the superiority of Anglo-Saxons.

From the idea of superiority to the acceptance of domination was a short step. If Americans were God's and Darwin's chosen people, why shouldn't they dominate and uplift less fortunate countries and peoples? This was the question that advocates of a more aggressive American foreign policy asked their audiences. Senator Albert J. Beveridge of Indiana spoke for many Americans when he told Congress,

God has not been preparing the English-speaking and Teutonic peoples for a thousand years for nothing but vain and idle self-admiration. No! He has not made us the master organizers of the world to establish a system where chaos reigns. . . . He has given us the spirit of progress to overwhelm the forces of reaction throughout the earth. He has made us adept in government that we may administer government among savage and senile peoples.

Sense of Duty

Religious leaders also noted the duty that American exceptionalism implied. Talk of the "white man's burden" and the duty of "advanced" peoples was rife during the period. Protestant missionaries carried their faith and beliefs to the far corners of the world, but the benefits of their message extended well beyond preaching salvation and saving souls.

Many foreign missionaries sought to unite the people of the world by extolling the virtues of American civilization. White missionaries are shown meeting with blacks in Africa.

They also extolled the virtues of American civilization, which included everything from democracy and rule by law to sanitation, material progress, sewing machines, and cotton underwear. Defining good and bad, progress and savagery by American standards, they attempted to alter native customs and beliefs to conform to a single American model.

Popular writer and religious leader Reverend Josiah Strong voiced what other missionaries and true believers acted upon. In 1885 Strong published *Our Country: Its Possible Future and Present Crisis,* a book that quickly sold 170,000 copies and was translated into dozens of languages. "The Anglo-Saxon," Strong wrote, "is the representative of two great ideas . . . civil liberty [and] a pure *spiritual* Christianity." These two ideas, he added, are destined to elevate all mankind, and "the Anglo-Saxon . . . is divinely commissioned to be . . . his brother's keeper." He firmly believed that it was America's destiny and duty to expand and spread its influence. Quoting the Bible while speaking to Anglo-Saxon Americans, he intoned, "Prepare ye the way of the Lord!"

Search for Markets

Strong's message was not lost on the business leaders of America. They fully agreed that missionaries should preach the benefits of American material progress as well as the glories of the Protestant faith. Looking south toward Latin America and west toward Asia, American businesspeople and farmers saw vast virgin markets for their industrial and agricultural surpluses as well as endless sources of raw materials. Sensing that American markets, filled with low-paid workers, offered few new opportunities, they entertained fabulous visions of hungry Latin Americans and shoeless Chinese. They fully agreed with the able American diplomat John A. Kasson who warned the readers of the *North American Review* in 1881: "We are rapidly utilizing the whole of our continental territory. We must turn our eyes abroad, or they will soon look inward upon discontent."

Kasson's words seemed particularly apt during the late nineteenth century. Although the United States became the leading industrial and agricultural country in the world, domestic consumption did not keep pace with the galloping production. In addition, throughout the period the government pursued tight-money policies, and laborers' real income only modestly grew. The result was a boom-and-bust economy: spectacular growth and severe depressions. In fact, in the 25 years after 1873, the country suffered through three depressions: 1873 to 1878, 1882 to 1885, and 1893 to 1897.

In part, the United States was a victim of its own spectacular success. Increased production without increased consumption led to glutted markets and falling prices. For example, in 1870 Americans produced 4.3 million bales of cotton; by 1891 that figure had grown to 9 million. In 1871 a pound of cotton sold for 18 cents; by 1891 the price had dropped to 7 cents. The story was the same for wheat, meat, tobacco, and corn. Increasingly, farmers—and industrialists—looked toward foreign markets. Too often, export trade spelled the difference between prosperity and bankruptcy. Although American businesspeople and bankers had yet to develop overseas marketing networks and foreign branch banks to market their goods and finance sales, they clearly saw the need for such additions. The future of the United States, many economic leaders believed, would be determined by the government's ability to find and secure overseas trade.

During depression years, foreign trade seemed a necessity. Depressions meant farm foreclosures and industrial unemployment, problems that led to social unrest. The Grange and Populist movements, the two largest agrarian revolts, originated in cotton and wheat areas during depression years. And such labor confrontations as the violent railroad strikes of 1877, Chicago's Haymarket riot of 1886, and the Pullman strike of 1894 occurred during lean economic times. For many Americans the issue was simple: The United States had to acquire foreign markets or face economic hardship and revolution at home.

As one industrial spokesman put it: The time has come for the United States to pursue "an intelligent and spirited foreign policy," one in which the government would "see to it" that the country had adequate foreign markets. If force proved necessary, then so be it.

The State Department was in full agreement. William Henry Seward and Hamilton Fish, Johnson's and Grant's secretaries of state, believed firmly that America needed new markets. Seward called the potentially bottomless markets of Asia "the prize," and he wanted the United States to acquire islands in the Pacific as stepping-stones toward that prize. He similarly believed that the United States should extend its economic control to include Canada and Latin America. Hamilton Fish agreed with the hoarse-voiced, cigar-chewing Seward. Although, like Seward, he had to contend with a cautious, isolationist Congress, Fish made several important strides toward the Asia markets. During his term as secretary of state, the United States signed treaties and established more formal relations with Hawaii and Samoa, two Pacific island groups that would later become part of the American empire.

During the late 1870s and 1880s, economic hard times quickened the search for new markets. Rutherford B. Hayes's secretary of state, William Evarts, who valued a good story, once told a British minister that George Washington had been able to throw a dollar across the Rappahannock River because a dollar went farther in those days. Evarts also valued dollars, and he felt Americans needed far more of them. As secretary of state, he worked toward an American commercial empire. He hoped that unexploited Asian and Latin American markets would guarantee continual economic growth and social tranquillity for all Americans.

James G. Blaine and Frederick T. Frelinghuysen, who served as secretaries of state for James Garfield and Chester Arthur, concentrated their efforts on Latin American markets. Blaine later recounted that during his short stay in the State Department in 1881 he followed two principles: "first, to bring about peace . . . ; second, to cultivate such friendly commercial relations with all American coun-tries as would lead to a large increase in the export trade of the United States." When Blaine was forced out of office after Garfield's assassination, Frelinghuysen continued his policies. He successfully negotiated bilateral reciprocity treaties with many Latin American countries, which lowered tariffs and thus stimulated trade between the United States and Latin America.

By the mid-1880s, expansion efforts combined with economic and social problems at home convinced Congress to reevaluate its isolationist policies. The West was settled, the Native Americans defeated, the Union reconstructed, and the railroads built. It was now time to look at our oceans not as defensive barriers but as paths toward new markets and increased prosperity. There was one final problem: America's navy and merchant marine seemed woefully unfit for the challenge.

The New Navy

By 1880 the United States Navy was a sad joke. Ill-informed officers commanded obsolete wooden ships—both should have been retired years before. British writer and wit Oscar Wilde was close to the truth when he had one of his fictional characters reply to an American woman who complained that her country had no ruins and no curiosities: "No ruins! No curiosities! You have your Navy and your manners!"

If America hoped to compete for world markets, it had to upgrade its navy. During the 1880s and early 1890s advocates of a "New Navy" moved Congress to action. The transformation from a "heterogeneous collection of naval trash" to a great navy occurred in two stages. The face-lift began in 1883, during the administration of Chester A. Arthur. Prodded by the president, Congress passed an act providing for three small cruisers and a dispatch boat, the beginning of the famous White Squadron. More vessels soon followed. Under the direction of President Grover Cleveland and his able secretary of the navy, William Whitney, the White Squadron grew in size, and naval bureaucracy and fleet personnel improved.

By 1890 great gains had been made, but there were still serious problems. The White Squadron was not a world-class navy. Its ships were lightly armored, fast cruisers, ideal for hit-and-run missions but inadequate for any major naval engagement. While Britain and Germany were building large, heavily armored battleships capable of bombarding and damaging coastal cities, the United States continued to think of naval warfare in terms of commerce raiding.

Benjamin F. Tracy, Benjamin Harrison's secretary of war, was determined to change American naval thinking. Although careful to note that he wanted a fleet not for "conquest, but defense," Tracy had a very modern view of what defense entailed. To adequately defend America's interests, Tracy called for ships that could "raise blockades" and attack an enemy's coast, "for a war, though defensive in principle, may be conducted most effectively by being offensive in its operations." In fact, Tracy maintained that proper defense might even include shooting first: "The nation that is ready to strike the first blow will gain an advantage which its antagonist can never offset." Such a first-strike definition of defense meant one thing: The United States needed to build modern, armored battleships. Tracy wanted two battleship fleets, one for the Atlantic and another for the Pacific.

Personal tragedy momentarily sidetracked Tracy. In February 1890 his wife and youngest daughter burned to death in a fire that destroyed Tracy's Washington home. But Tracy's program was kept alive in Congress by such "Big Navy" advocates as Senator Eugene Hale of Maine and Representative Henry Cabot Lodge of Massachusetts. They found Congress in the mood to act. As one senator said, "You can not negotiate without a gun." In 1890, Congress appropriated money for the construction of three first-class battleships and a heavy cruiser. It was the beginning of a new, very much offensive navy for the United States. Reviewing his accomplishments in 1891, Tracy boasted: "The sea will be the future seat of empire. And we shall rule it as certainly as the sun doth rise."

Talk of empire, navy, trade, and national greatness came together in 1890 in the publication of a monumentally important book, *The Influence of Sea Power upon History*, by Captain Alfred Thayer Mahan. Mahan, who was attached to the Naval War College, was more comfortable around books than on ships. Although he had served throughout the world, he had the look, temperament, and inclinations of a college don. His masterpiece set forward the simple thesis that naval power was the key to national greatness. Taking Greece, Rome, and England as examples, he attempted to demonstrate that countries rise to world power through expanding their foreign commerce and protecting that commerce with a strong navy. Without a powerful navy, Mahan emphasized, a nation can never enjoy full prosperity and security. Without a strong navy, in short, no nation could ever hope to be a world power.

Shaping Public Opinion

Mahan's writings and Tracy's proposal were applauded by American politicians and businesspeople who felt it was time for the United States to assume the rights and responsibilities of world-power status. These were important citizens—men of wealth, education, and influence. Some like Whitelaw Reid, editor of the *New York Tribune*, helped shape public opinion through their editorials. Others like Henry Cabot Lodge, Theodore Roosevelt, Albert J. Beveridge, and John Hay were powerful politicians and administrators. They were vocal nationalists who believed that the United States was destined to be the greatest of world powers. Increasingly after 1890, these and other men of like mind dominated and shaped America's foreign policy, and "public opinion" followed their lead. "After all," noted Secretary of State Walter Q. Gresham in 1893, "public opinion is made and controlled by the thoughtful men of the country."

These expansionists often shared common experiences and beliefs. Most were prosperous Republicans from old-line American families, and most had traveled abroad widely. Anglo-Saxon by heritage, they tended to be ardent Anglophiles, full of praise for Great Britain's imperial efforts. They believed that the United States should join "Mother England" in administering to the "uncivilized" corners of the globe. As Beveridge noted, without the work of Anglo-Saxons "the world would relapse into barbarism and night. . . . We are trustees of the world's progress, guardians of its righteous place."

Lodge and other expansionists called for a bold foreign policy, what they called the "large policy." They advocated the construction of a canal through Central America to allow American ships to move between the Atlantic and Pacific oceans more rapidly. To protect the canal, the United States would have to exert control over Cuba and the other strategically located Caribbean islands. Next America would have to acquire coaling stations and naval bases across the Pacific. Secure bases in Hawaii, Guam, Wake Island, and the Philippines would allow the United States to exploit the seemingly limitless Asian market. Finally, a powerful navy would have to protect the entire American empire.

In the end, then, all of their plans were rooted in the theme of a strong navy. Like his friend Mahan, Lodge was a student of history. "It is the sea power which is essential to the greatness of every splendid people," he said. It had enabled Rome to crush the Carthaginians, England to defeat Napoleon, and the North to win the Civil War. Without the power of a strong navy, Lodge believed that America could never experience real peace and security: "All the peace the world has ever had has been obtained by fighting, and all the peace that any nation . . . can ever have, is by readiness to fight if attacked." For Lodge as for Tracy, thoughts of peace and war often ran together and appeared in the same sentences.

THE EMERGENCE OF AGGRESSION IN AMERICAN FOREIGN POLICY

Proponents of the New Navy and the "large policy" talked loudly about peace. But their talk of peace, like their foreign policy and naval ambitions, was couched in aggressive language. "To be prepared for war is the most effectual means to promote peace," said Theodore Roosevelt. The more such politicians talked about peace, the closer war seemed. It is not coincidental that the United States launched a more belligerent foreign policy at the same time it was building and launching more powerful ships. The two developments originated from the same source: a ready acceptance of force as the final arbiter of international disputes. Before the turn of the century, the acceptance of force would lead to the Spanish-American War of 1898; and between 1885 and 1897, during the presidencies of Benjamin Harrison and Grover Cleveland, the same attitudes almost caused several other wars. The Spanish-American War was not an aberrant event. Rather it was the result of a more aggressive American foreign policy, one aimed at acquiring both world respect and an empire.

Confronting the Germans in Samoa

Changing American attitudes toward foreign policy first became apparent in relation to Samoa, a group of 14 volcanic islands lying

MORE BLUSTER THAN BLOOD.

America's attempt to gain the Samoan islands as coaling stations along the route to Australia led to a diplomatic crisis with Germany.

4000 miles from San Francisco along the trade route to Australia. Throughout the nineteenth century, American whalers stopped in Samoa, and its two splendid natural harbors, Apia and Pago Pago, had often provided refuge for ships caught in Pacific storms. If the Samoans were quarrelsome among themselves, they were exceptionally friendly with Americans.

American interest in Samoa was decidedly mercenary. In 1872 an American negotiated a treaty with a tribal chief to grant the United States rights to a naval station at Pago Pago. Although an antiexpansionist Senate took no action on the treaty, expansionists kept trying. In 1878 the Senate did ratify a similar treaty, which formally committed the United States to Samoa. Unfortunately for the United States, Germany and England were also determined to influence events on the islands.

America's chief rival for Samoa was Germany. Like the United States, Germany was just beginning to think in terms of empire. German Chancellor Otto von Bismarck decided that Samoa should belong to Germany, and as a result of the intricacies of European politics, England sided with the "iron chancellor." President Cleveland and his secretary of state, Thomas F. Bayard, firmly disagreed with the Europeans. Germany and the United States were set on a collision course.

When a conference between the three countries held in Washington in 1887 failed to solve the problem, war seemed closer still. Neither Germany nor the United States had much money invested in the islands, but both felt their national pride was at stake. "We must show sharp teeth," remarked Bismarck. Cleveland decided to show part of America's new White Squadron. He dispatched three warships to Samoa. Nature, however, had the most powerful weapon. On the morning of March 16, 1889, a typhoon swept across Samoa, destroying both American and German warships anchored in Apia harbor.

The violent winds seemed to calm the ruffled emotions of the United States and Germany. "Men and nations," wrote the *New York World,* "must bow before the decrees of nature." The same year as the typhoon, Germany, the United States, and England met for another conference, this one in Berlin. With-

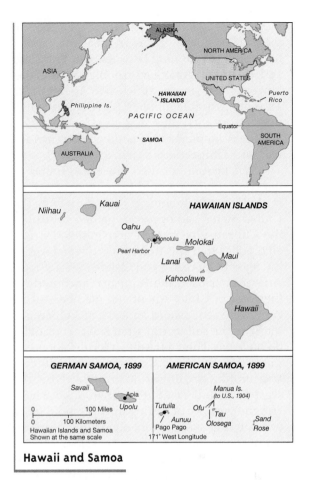

Hawaii and Samoa

out consulting the Samoans, they decided to partition the islands. Everyone seemed satisfied—except the Samoans, who were deprived of their independence and saddled with an unpopular king. The plan lasted until 1899, when Germany and the United States ended the facade of Samoan independence and officially made colonies of the islands. The United States was granted Tutuila, with the harbor of Pago Pago, and several smaller islands. Many expansionists believed that America's aggressive stand against Germany had paid handsome dividends.

Teaching Chile a Lesson

American expansionists had something to gain from their confrontation with Germany over Samoa. Pago Pago was, after all, "the most perfectly landlocked harbor that exists in the Pacific Ocean." It was an ideal coaling station for ships running between San Francisco and Australia. American troubles with Chile, however, are more difficult to understand. Trade and strategic policy played only small roles. More than anything else, touchy pride and jingoism pushed the United States toward war with Chile.

Had people not died, the background to the confrontation would have been amusing. In 1891 a revolutionary faction, which the United States had opposed, gained control of the Chilean government and initiated a foreign policy that was unfriendly toward America. Shortly thereafter, on October 16, 1891, an American cruiser, the *Baltimore,* anchored off the coast of Chile. About 100 members of its crew were sent ashore on leave at Valparaiso. Many of the sailors did what sailors normally do on leave: They retired to a local saloon—in this particular case, the True Blue Saloon—and drank. An officer who arrived on the scene later said that the men had gone ashore "for the purpose of getting drunk" and that by evening they were "probably drunk, properly drunk." As the men left the saloon, a riot broke out. An angry, anti-American mob attacked the sailors, killing 2 and injuring 16. To make matters worse, the Chilean police, who had done nothing to halt the fighting, carried the surviving Americans off to jail.

It was an unfortunate affair, and the United States loudly protested, demanding a formal apology and "prompt and full reparation." The Chilean government refused. President Harrison, a former Union general who prided himself on his patriotism and was easily swayed by jingoism, a form of chauvinistic patriotism, threatened to break off diplomatic relations—a serious step toward war—unless the United States received an immediate apology. When his secretary of state, James G. Blaine, tried to counsel moderation, Harrison angrily replied, "Mr. Secretary, that insult was to the uniform of United States sailors."

Public opinion sided with Harrison. The *New York Sun* commented that "we must teach men who will henceforth be called snarling whelps of the Pacific that we cannot be snapped at with impunity." And angry young Theodore Roosevelt insisted, "For two nickels he would declare war himself . . . and wage it sole." Finally the Chilean government backed down, apologizing for the attack on the sailors and paying an indemnity of $75,000.

The threat of force had again carried the day. Advocates of the New Navy and aggressively nationalistic Americans cheered Harrison's actions. The foreign policy of the United States was becoming increasingly belligerent and strident. Few Americans heeded Edwin L. Godkin, editor of the *Nation,* who wrote, "The number of men and officials in this country who are now ready to fight somebody is appalling. Navy officers dream of war and talk and lecture about it incessantly. The Senate debates are filled with predictions of impending war and with talk of preparing for it at once. . . . Most truculent and bloodthirsty of all, jingo editors keep up a din day after day about the way we could cripple one country's fleet and destroy another's commerce, and fill heads of boys and silly men with the idea that war is the normal state of a civilized country."

Plucking the Hawaiian Pear

Throughout the late nineteenth century, Hawaii figured prominently in American foreign policy planning. Earlier in the century, the islands had been a favorite place for American missionaries. Many went to Hawaii to spread Christianity and ended up settling and raising their families in the tropical paradise. More important still was the islands' location. Not only were they ideally situated along the trade routes to Asia, but they offered a perfect site for protecting the Pacific sea lanes to the American west coast and to the potential locations of an isthmus canal. In Hawaii, missionary, economic, and strategic concerns met in complete harmony.

By the mid-1880s, Congress was willing to accept expansionists' dreams for Hawaii. In 1884 a treaty between Hawaii and the United States set aside Pearl Harbor for the exclusive use of the American navy. After some debate the Senate ratified the treaty in 1887, and Hawaii officially became part of American strategic planning. By that time the islands were already economically tied to the United States. An 1875 treaty had allowed Hawaiians to sell their sugar in the United States duty-free, giving them a two-cents-per-pound advantage over other foreign producers. The legislation encouraged American speculators to invest in Hawaiian sugar and to import Chinese and Japanese laborers to the islands to work on the large plantations. The investments returned incredibly high dividends, and for a time business boomed.

Problems arose suddenly in 1890. The McKinley Tariff Act removed all tariffs on foreign sugar and protected domestic sugar producers by awarding American sugar a bounty of two cents per pound. Hawaiian sugar prices plummeted. The American minister in Honolulu estimated that the McKinley Tariff cost Hawaiian producers $12 million. And in

Queen Liliuokalani assumed the Hawaiian throne in 1891. Strongly nationalistic, she sought to purge white influence from Hawaii. She was overthrown by white islanders with the aid of American sailors and marines.

1891 the government of the islands changed. Queen Liliuokalani ascended the throne. A poet and a composer interested in humanitarian work, she nevertheless initiated a strongly anti-American policy. She wanted to purge American influences in Hawaii and disfranchise all white men except those married to native women.

The white population in Hawaii reacted quickly. On January 17, 1893, three days after the queen dismissed the legislature and proclaimed a new constitution, white islanders overthrew her government. Supported by the American minister in Honolulu, John L. Stevens, and aided by American sailors and marines, the revolution was fast, almost bloodless, and successful. Stevens then proclaimed Hawaii an American protectorate and wired his superiors in Washington that "the Hawaiian pear is now fully ripe, and this is the golden hour for the United States to pluck it."

The revolutionaries in Hawaii favored prompt American annexation of the islands. In Washington, the Harrison administration, which was due to leave office on March 4, agreed. It negotiated a treaty of annexation with "indecent haste" and sent it to the Senate for ratification. Public sentiment cheered Harrison's actions.

Before the Senate could ratify the treaty, Cleveland took office. An anti-imperialist, Cleveland had grave misgivings about the revolution, America's reaction, and the treaty. Five days after his inauguration, he recalled the treaty from the Senate and sent a special agent, James H. Blount of Georgia, to Hawaii to investigate the entire affair. After a careful investigation, Blount reported to Cleveland that the majority of native Hawaiians opposed annexation and that on moral and legal grounds the treaty was unjustified. Cleveland accepted Blount's report and killed the treaty.

The controversy, however, was not over. A white American minority continued to govern Hawaii. To correct the situation, Cleveland sent another representative, Albert S. Willis, to Hawaii to convince the new government to step down and allow Queen Liliuokalani to return to the throne. Willis failed in his mission. "Queen Lil" refused to promise full amnesty for the revolutionaries if she were returned to power. "My decision would be," she said, "as the law directs, that such persons should be beheaded." In addition, newly elected President Sanford B. Dole, head of a large Hawaiian pineapple corporation, refused to leave office. In the end, Cleveland washed his hands of the entire matter, and the revolutionaries proclaimed an independent Hawaiian republic on July 4, 1894. Four years and three days later, during the Spanish-American War, the United States finally annexed Hawaii.

Facing Down the British

Potentially the most serious conflict America faced during the 1890s originated in a dispute over a strip of land in a South American jungle. Venezuela and British Guiana shared a common border; the dispute was over exactly where that border was located. Both sides claimed land the other side said was theirs. For almost 50 years this dispute remained peacefully unsettled, but the discovery of gold in the region in the 1880s increased the importance of the issue. It was a rich deposit—the largest nugget ever discovered, 509 ounces, was found there—and both Britain and Venezuela wanted it. In response to Venezuelan requests for help, the United States several times offered to arbitrate the matter, and each time Britain refused the offer.

By June 1895 Cleveland and his new secretary of state, Richard Olney, two short-tempered men, had decided that Britain's actions violated the spirit, if not the letter, of the Monroe Doctrine. (Ever since a cancer operation had left him with an artificial jaw of vulcanized rubber, Cleveland had been irritable.) Olney, who had persuaded Cleveland to use federal troops to put down the Pullman strike in Chicago the year before, was a man of strong ideas who did not shrink from the use of force. In a strongly worded message to Great Britain, Olney demanded that Britain submit the dispute to arbitration, hinting that the United States might intervene militarily if its wishes were not honored.

Lord Salisbury, Britain's prime minister, foreign secretary, and consummate aristocrat, did not reply to Olney's note for four months; he then answered, in effect, that the dispute did not involve either the United States or the Monroe Doctrine and would America kindly mind its own business. Olney was furious. Americans throughout the country felt insulted. Cleveland, who was duck hunting in North Carolina when Salisbury's response was received in Washington, returned to the capital, read the message, and became "mad clean through." In a special message to Congress, he asked for funds to establish a commission to determine the actual Venezuelan boundary. He also insisted that he would use force if necessary to maintain that boundary against any aggressors. Both houses of Congress unanimously approved Cleveland's request. The excitement of war was in the air. Although he was in London during much of the controversy, Senator Henry Cabot Lodge captured the mood of America when he wrote a friend, "War is a bad thing no doubt, but there are worse things both for nations and for men."

The violence of America's reaction surprised Salisbury and British officials. England certainly did not want war, particularly at that time, when it was becoming involved in a conflict in South Africa. Salisbury reversed his position and allowed a commission to arbitrate the dispute. In the end, the arbitral tribunal gave Britain most of the land it claimed.

America, however, felt it was the real winner. Cleveland had faced the British lion and won. The Monroe Doctrine and American prestige soared to new heights. More important for the future, Cleveland's actions, coupled with his handling of the Hawaiian revolution, significantly increased the power of the president over foreign affairs. Relations between the United States and Britain would quickly improve, and relations between America and Venezuela would rapidly deteriorate, but future presidents would not soon relinquish their control over foreign policy.

THE WAR FOR EMPIRE

During the Venezuela crisis many Americans seemed to invite and look forward to the prospect of war. Theodore Roosevelt, who was determined to atone for the failure of his father to fight in the Civil War and to be the first in war even if he were the last in peace, wrote: "Let the fight come if it must; I don't care whether our sea coast cities are bombarded or not; we would take Canada." For Roosevelt, war would be an ennobling experience. It would test and validate American greatness. "All the great masterful races," Roosevelt wrote, "have been fighting races; and the minute that a race loses the hard fighting virtues, then . . . it has lost its proud right to stand as the equal of the best."

The Spirit of the 1890s

Throughout the 1890s other Americans echoed Roosevelt's war cries. Viewed as a whole, it was a decade of strident nationalism and aggressive posturing. It was also a troubled and violent decade. Racked by the depression of 1893, frustrated by the problems created by monopolies and overproduction, and plagued by internal strife, Americans turned on each other, often with violent results. Strikes in Pullman, Illinois, and Homestead, Pennsylvania, saw laborers battle federal and state authorities. Populist protest dramatized the widening gulf between city and country, rich and poor. Anarchists and socialists talked about the need for violent solutions to complex problems.

Popular culture in America reflected this aggressive mood. As Roosevelt denounced "the soft spirit in the cloistered life" and "the base spirit of gain," Americans looked to arenas of conflict for their heroes. They glorified boxers like the great John L. Sullivan, who held the heavyweight championship of the world between 1882 and 1892. They cheered as violence increased on the Ivy League football fields. They admired bodybuilders like Bernard Macfadden and Eugene Sandow, who was heralded as the most perfectly developed man in the world. In the first issue of *Physical Culture,* Macfadden declared, "Weakness Is a Crime." In saloons across the country, Sullivan defiantly boasted, "I can lick any sonofabitch in the house." And in the parlors of the wealthy, Roosevelt stressed, "Cowardice in a race, as in an individual, is the unpardonable sin." Between Sullivan and Roosevelt, and the Americans that admired both men, was a bond forged by the love of violence and power.

This attitude led to the glorification of war and jingoistic nationalism. During the mid-1890s a remarkable interest in Napoleon gripped the nation—between 1894 and 1896 28 books were written about the Corsican general. In public schools throughout the country, administrators instituted daily flag salutes and made the recitation of the new pledge of allegiance mandatory. Even the popular music of the day had a particularly martial quality. Such marches as John Philip Sousa's "Stars and Stripes Forever" (1897) and "A Hot Time in the Old Town Tonight" (1896) captured the aggressive, patriotic, and boisterous mood of the country.

As the disputes with Germany, Chile, and Great Britain demonstrated, neither the American people nor its leaders feared war. The horrors of the Civil War were dying with the generation that had known them. A younger generation of men, filled with romantic and idealized conceptions of battle and heroism, now openly sought a war of their own. In Washington some politicians even began to view war as a way to unite the country, to quell the protests of angry farmers and laborers.

The Cuban Revolution

Oftentimes the mood of a nation governs the reaction to and interpretation of events. Such was the case with America's attitude toward the Cuban Revolution. In 1895, while Sousa was writing energetic marches and Americans were cheering new boxing heroes, an independence revolt broke out in Cuba. It was not the first time the Cubans took up arms in pursuit of independence. During the Ten Years' War (1868–1878) Cuban patriots had unsuccessfully fought for independence from their Spanish rulers. The war was bloody and violent, and Cubans actively sought American support; but the United States, guided by a policy of isolationism, steered clear.

By 1895, however, cautious isolationism was out of step with Sousa's and Roosevelt's aggressive tempo. From the start of this revolution, Americans expressed far more than casual interest in the rebellion. To be sure, American business was concerned: Americans had invested over $50 million in Cuba and the annual trade between the two countries totaled almost $100 million. Once the revolution started, insurgents burned crops in the fields, and the trade between Cuba and the United States slowed to a trickle. Overall, however, economics played a relatively unimportant role in forming America's attitude toward the revolution.

Humanitarianism was a far more important factor. Americans cheered the underdog. In Cuba's valiant fight, they saw a reenactment of their own war for independence. And the resourceful Cubans made sure that Americans stayed well supplied with stories of Spanish atrocities and Cuban heroism. The Cuban junta—central revolutionary committee—established bases in New York City and Tampa, Florida, and daily provided American newspapers with stories aimed at sympathetic American hearts.

Not all the stories were false. The Cuban—and Spanish—suffering was real enough. Unable to defeat the Spanish army in the field, Cuban revolutionaries resorted to guerilla tactics. They burned sugarcane fields and blew up mills. They destroyed railroad tracks and bridges. They vowed to win their independence or destroy Cuba in the process. One of their leaders, General Maximo Gomez, aptly stated the guerrillas' and Cuba's position: "The chains of Cuba have been forged by her own richness, and it is precisely this which I propose to do away with soon." Supported by the populace, the guerillas succeeded in turning Cuba into an economic and military nightmare for Spanish officials.

In 1896 Spain sent Governor-General Valeriano Weyler y Nicolau to Cuba to crush the rebellion. A man of ruthless clarity, he understood the nature of guerilla warfare. Guerrillas could not be defeated by conventional engagements. Their generals did not imitate the tactics of Napoleon; they were not concerned with flanking maneuvers and cavalry charges. Their weapons were patience and endurance and popular support. Weyler knew this, and he decided to fight the guerrillas on their own terms.

His first plan was to rob the guerrillas of their base of support, the rural villages and the sympathetic peasants. He divided the island into military districts and relocated Cubans into guarded camps. It was a policy that the United States would later use to fight guerrillas in the Philippines and Vietnam, but Weyler was brutal in his execution of it. He forced over a half million Cubans from their homes and crowded them into shabbily constructed and unsanitary camps. The food was bad, the water worse. Disease spread with frightful speed and horrifying results. Perhaps 200,000 Cubans died in the camps as Weyler earned the sobriquet "the Butcher." After inspecting the camps, Senator Renfield Proctor of Vermont reported on the plight of the Cuban people to Congress: "Torn from their homes, with foul earth, foul air, foul water, and foul food or none, what wonder that one-half have died and that one-quarter of the living are so diseased that they cannot be saved? . . . Little children are still walking about with arms and chest terribly emaciated, eyes swollen, and abdomens bloated to three times the natural size."

The Yellow Press

In the United States reports of the suffering Cuban masses filled the front pages of newspapers. In New York City, William Randolph Hearst's *New York Journal* and Joseph Pulitzer's *New York World* used the junta's lurid stories as ammunition in a newspaper war. Newspaper reporters freely engaged in "yellow journalism," exaggerating conditions that were in truth already depressingly sad and inhumane. Most stories had a sensational twist. One particularly incendiary drawing by Frederic Remington, the famous western artist sent to Cuba by Hearst, pictured three leering Spanish officials searching a nude Cuban woman. Hearst ran the picture five columns wide on the second page of the *Journal,* and the edition sold close to one million copies, the largest newspaper run in history until then. Neither the picture nor the story, however, mentioned that Spanish women—not men—conducted the search, although men had conducted other such searches. Such coverage biased American opinion against Spain. It also sold newspapers. When Hearst bought the *Journal* in 1895 it had a daily circulation of 77,000 copies; by the summer of 1898 sales had increased to over 1.5 million daily.

"Yellow journalism" and the more sober coverage of the standard press persuaded many Americans to call for U.S. intervention in the Cuban Revolution. Grover Cleveland,

This *New York Journal* sketch by Frederic Remington of Spanish officials searching a Cuban woman on an American steamer shocked the nation. Such "yellow journalism," or exaggeration of the facts, played an important role in persuading Americans to call for intervention in the Cuban Revolution.

however, was not easily moved by newspaper reports. His administration wanted to protect American interests in Cuba but was dead set against any sort of military intervention in the conflict. Without recognizing the revolutionaries, he worked to convince Spain to grant "home rule." Spain remained unconvinced. But Cleveland was not prepared to move beyond vague warnings. When he left office in early 1897, the revolution in Cuba was raging as violently as ever. Cleveland passed the Cuban problem to his successor William McKinley. Like Cleveland, McKinley deplored war. He had fought bravely in the Civil War, and he knew the horrors of war firsthand. For McKinley, arbitration was the civilized way to settle disputes—war was a poor and wasteful alternative. Before he would even consider military intervention, McKinley was determined to exhaust every peaceful alternative.

McKinley displayed strength and patience. As many influential Americans called for U.S. intervention, McKinley worked diplomatically to end the fighting. Rather than inflame public opinion, he attempted to remove the issue from public debate. In his inaugural address, for example, he did not even mention Cuba. For a time it appeared that his efforts would succeed. In October 1897 a new government in Spain moved toward granting more autonomy to Cuba. It removed Weyler and promised to end his hated reconcentration program. Spain, said McKinley, was following "honorable paths." Patience and cool heads, he hoped, would carry the day.

Spain moved with glacial slowness. Some of its reforms were half-hearted, others were merely designed to calm American emotions. In Cuba the bloodshed continued. As Spanish officials and Cuban revolutionaries ignored or denounced Spain's "honorable paths," pressure on McKinley to take stronger action mounted. In May 1897 he dispatched his trusted political friend William J. Calhoun of Ohio to Cuba to provide him with an independent report on the conditions on the island. Calhoun's report confirmed the grim picture presented in American newspapers. "The country outside of the military posts was practically depopulated," Calhoun noted. "Every house had been burned, banana trees cut down, cane fields swept with fire, and everything in the shape of food destroyed. . . . I did not see a house, a man, woman or child; a horse, mule or cow, not even a dog; I did not see a sign of life, except an occasional vulture or buzzard sailing through the air. The country was wrapped in the stillness of death and the silence of desolation." By January of 1898 the president looked as defeated as his diplomatic efforts. He had to take drugs to sleep, his skin was pasty, and his dark eyes seemed to be sinking farther back into his head. Two events in February would end any hope of a diplomatic solution and lead to the Spanish-American War.

William Randolph Hearst had often told his reporters: "Don't wait for things to turn up. Turn them up!" He did just that in early February 1898. With the help of the Cuban junta, Hearst acquired a private letter from Enrique Dupuy de Lôme, the Spanish minister in the United States, to a Spanish friend of his in Cuba. The letter contained de Lôme's unguarded and undiplomatic opinion of McKinley. Reprinted on the front page of the *Journal* on February 9, 1898, Hearst labeled the letter: "Worst insult to the United States in Its History." De Lôme called McKinley "weak and a bidder for the admiration of the crowd." He accused the American president of being a hypocrite and a "would-be politician." Even worse, de Lôme suggested that Spain's new peace policy was mere sham and propaganda.

The letter hit the American public like a bombshell. Although de Lôme resigned, America was in no mood to forgive and forget. Former Secretary of State Richard Olney wrote his old boss Grover Cleveland, "I confess [that] some expressions of his letter stagger me and, if they . . . mean that Spain has been tricking us as regards autonomy and other matters incidental to it, I should have wanted the privilege of sending him his passports before he had any chance to be recalled or resign." Olney expressed the mood of the nation. As one of the leaders of the Cuban junta noted, "The de Lôme letter is a great thing for us."

Less than a week later a second event rocked America. On the still evening of February 15, an explosion ripped apart the *Maine,* a U.S. battleship anchored in Havana harbor. The ship quickly sank, killing over 250 officers and men. An 1898 investigation ruled that an external explosion had sunk the *Maine.* In a 1976 study, Admiral Hyman G. Rickover, however, blamed the sinking on an internal explosion. In truth, no one knows the who, how, and why answers. Americans at the time, however, were not in an impartial or philosophical mood. They blamed Spain. One diplomatic historian commented, " 'Remember the *Maine!*' became a national watch word. . . . In a Broadway bar a man raised his glass and said solemnly, 'Gentlemen, remember the *Maine!*' Through the streets of American cities went the cry, 'Remember the *Maine!* To Hell with Spain!' "

War was in the air, and it is doubtful if McKinley or any other president could have long preserved peace. Congress was ready for war. On March 6, McKinley told a leading congressman, "I must have money to get ready for war." Congress responded on March 8 by passing the "Fifty Million Bill" (the amount of McKinley's request) without a single dissenting vote. Although McKinley continued to work for a diplomatic solution to the crisis, his efforts lacked his earlier energy and optimism. By early April, diplomacy had reached its end.

On April 11, an exhausted McKinley sent a virtual war message to Congress. He asked for authority to use force to end the Cuban war. His message mixed talk of commerce with lofty humanitarianism. America must take up the "cause of humanity," he wrote, and stop the "very serious injury to the commerce, trade, and business of our people, and the wanton destruction of property."

On April 19 Congress officially acted. It proclaimed Cuba's independence, called for Spain's evacuation, and authorized McKinley to use the army and navy to achieve those ends. In the Teller Amendment, Congress added that the United States had no intention of annexing Cuba for itself. As Senator John C. Spooner of Wisconsin said, "We intervene not for conquest, not for aggrandizement, not be-

The sinking of the *Maine* was one of the major events leading to the Spanish-American War. It is still uncertain who or what caused the explosion that sank the ship.

cause of the Monroe Doctrine; we intervene for humanity's sake." For some Americans it was a great and noble decision. Senator Albert Beveridge, one of the great speakers of his day, intoned: "At last, God's hour has struck. The American people go forth in a warfare holier than liberty—holy as humanity." For the men and boys who would have to fight the battles, the war would soon seem considerably less noble.

The Spanish-American War

There is no simple explanation for the Spanish-American War. Economics and imperial ambitions certainly played a part, but no more so than did humanitarianism and selfless concern for the suffering of others. McKinley tried to find a peaceful solution, but he failed. Some

historians and many of his contemporaries have viewed McKinley as a weak, hollow president, a messenger boy for America's financial community. A Washington joke in the late 1890s ran, "Why is McKinley's mind like a bed?" Answer: "Because it has to be made up for him every time he wants to use it." Such was not the case. McKinley did have a vision—a peaceful vision—of America's role in world affairs. But the unpredictability of events and the mood of the nation were more powerful than the president.

In theory America had prepared for war with Spain. In 1897 the Navy Department had drawn up contingency plans for a war against Spain for the liberation of Cuba. It had envisioned a war centered mainly in the Caribbean, but the navy had plans to attack the Philippine Islands, which belonged to Spain, and even the coast of Spain, if necessary. In the Caribbean, the plan was to blockade Cuba and assist an army invasion of the island. On paper, neatly written and soundly reasoned, America was well prepared for a war that seemed more of a military exercise than a deadly struggle.

In reality, the military was not physically ready for war. The process of mobilizing troops was chaotic and the training given volunteers was inadequate. In addition, the army faced severe supply shortages, with volunteers suffering the most. They were herded into camps, often without such basic equipment as tents and mess kits. Long before they ever faced enemy guns or even saw Cuba, they battled wet uniforms, bad food, and deadly sanitary conditions. Far more volunteers died in stateside camps than were killed by Spanish bullets.

For African-American troops, regular and volunteers, racism aggravated already difficult conditions. They too were plagued by spoiled beef, thick wool uniforms, and unsanitary conditions. Also, since most of the large camps were located in the South—in places such as Tampa, New Orleans, Mobile, and Chickamauga Park, Tennessee—they had to battle Jim Crow laws and other forms of racial hostility. They saw signs that proclaimed "Dogs and niggers not allowed" and were pelted by rocks. Once in the camps, they were

All black troops fighting in Cuba were commanded by white officers, much to the dissatisfaction of the black soldiers.

given the lowest military assignments. George W. Prioleau, a black chaplain, noted: "Talk about fighting and freeing poor Cuba and of Spain's brutality; of Cuba's murdered thousands, and starving reconcentradoes. Is America any better than Spain?"

While the agony of mobilization was taking place, the navy moved into action. During the tense weeks before the United States went to war against Spain, Theodore Roosevelt, then acting secretary of the navy, joyfully followed McKinley's orders and wired his friend Commodore George Dewey, leader of America's Asiatic Squadron: "KEEP FULL OF COAL, IN THE EVENT OF DECLARATION OF WAR [WITH] SPAIN, YOUR DUTY WILL BE TO SEE THAT THE SPANISH SQUADRON DOES NOT LEAVE THE ASIATIC COAST, AND THEN OFFENSIVE OPERATIONS IN PHILIPPINE ISLANDS." Dewey had been anxiously waiting just that order. He was a warrior, and he looked forward to war. One historian remarked that "Dewey looked like a resplendent killer falcon, ready to bite through wire, if necessary, to get at a prey."

Biting through wire was not necessary. He only had to sail to Manila Bay. At the break of light on the morning of May 1, 1898, he struck. In a few hours of fighting, he destroyed Spain's Asiatic fleet. It was a stunning victory. Only one American died, from heat prostration manning a ship's overworked boiler. "You have made a name for the nation, and the Navy, and yourself," Roosevelt wrote Dewey. Americans rejoiced in the quick victory. Newspapers were filled with stories of American heroics and poems praised Dewey. One not-very-accomplished poet captured the public mood:

Oh, dewey was the morning
Upon the first of May,
And Dewey was the Admiral,
Down in Manila Bay.
And dewey were the Spaniard's eyes,
Them orbs of black and blue;
And dew we feel discouraged?
I do not think we dew.

Not every victory came so easily. Closer to home, in the Caribbean theater, the war was much more prosaic. The main Spanish forces in Cuba controlled the strategically important

PRIMARY SOURCE ESSAY

WILLIAM RANDOLPH HEARST AND THE SINKING OF THE *MAINE*

If William Randolph Hearst (1863–1951) did not invent "yellow journalism," he certainly perfected the genre. The only child of wealthy parents, Hearst started life with every advantage. Throughout his life, his primary goal was the acquisition of power; the newspaper world offered him his first taste of it. In 1887 he became the proprietor of his father's *San Francisco Examiner*. His style became readily apparent. He bought the best equipment, hired the best writers, and emphasized sensationalism and emotionalism in reporting the news. "Truth in the news," Hearst's leading biographer noted, "was never of great importance" to him; "he was essentially a showman and propagandist, not a newsman." But if he was not a great newsman, he was a powerful one. In 1895 he bought the *New York Journal* and used yellow journalism to build its circulation. In later years he extended his publishing empire to Chicago, Boston, Los Angeles, Atlanta, Omaha, Pittsburgh, Rochester, and other cities. He also bought magazines as well as newspapers. It seems clear that Hearst planned to use his strength in publishing to support his political ambitions. But he was never a successful politician. Bashful in public, his high-pitched voice and cold eyes gave him a weak public presence. And his tempestuous private life was a decided political disadvantage. Nevertheless, his publishing empire gave him power, and if it could not make him president, it could make him a feared political enemy.

William Randolph Hearst. This photo was taken in 1906, when Hearst was a member of Congress.

NEW YORK JOURNAL, FEBRUARY 17, 1898

ONE WORD WOULD PRECIPITATE WAR.

Nation Awaits a Verdict on the Great Disaster.

TREACHERY SUPECTED

General Belief That the Spaniards Blew Up the Maine.

WAS THERE A TORPEDO?

Officials Generally Believe That the Awful Wreck Was the Result of One.

The clearest report from Havana indicates that the explosion was too far forward for boilers, or coal bunkers, or magazines; that the vessel seemed to lift in the front and then its forecastle was filled with flames.

A Submarine Mine Probably Did the Work.

All theories of accident, explosion from within, having been discussed, we will now take up the external causes.

THE HARBOR OF HAVANA IS UNDOUBTEDLY MINED AND PLOTTED OUT IN SQUARES SO THAT ALL THAT IS NECESSARY TO DESTROY A VESSEL IS TO SEE WHAT SQUARE SHE IS IN, MAKE NECESSARY CONNECTION AND PRESS A BUTTON, THE TORPEDO DOES THE REST. The vessel, swinging to the tide may have accidentally fouled a submarine mine, which exploded.

As the marine sentry, on the forecastle, did not see any boat, none but a submarine torpedo could have approached her without being observed. Either one of these could have done the deed.

A bomb, disguised to look like a lump of coal, might have been used, but the explosion was evidently far forward of the boilers.

This method caused the loss of the steamer Sultana, on the Mississippi River in 1865. This vessel's boilers were exploded by a bomb placed in the fuel, and hundreds of Iowa soldiers, who had just been released from Andersonville Prison, were killed, maimed and drowned. The vessel blew up, and then burned just like the Maine.

Where the explosion came from, can be settled when divers examine the wreck. If the plates are bulged in, the explosion came from without. If they are bulged out, the explosion came from within.

How a Spanish Submarine Mine May Have Destroyed the Maine and Many of Her Crew.

It was an easy matter for the Spaniards to have destroyed the Maine. She lay not far from a magazine in Havana, and wires from the shore to a hidden mine, filled with high explosive could easily have been arranged. The utmost vigilance of the American officers could not have guarded against a concealed mine . . . .

On the evening of February 15, 1898, the *Maine*, a 24-gun battleship, rested quietly in Havana harbor. Captain Charles D. Sigsbee, commander of the ship, sat in his cabin writing a letter to his wife. At 9:40 P.M., an explosion rocked the ship. Sigsbee was unhurt, but 260 of the ship's 350 officers and men died in the explosion. As survivors jumped off the side of the *Maine*—and the ship sank into the mud of Havana harbor—Spaniards in Havana helped Americans in the dangerous rescue efforts.

That same evening William Randolph Hearst had enjoyed the nightlife—theater and late dinner—of New York. When he returned to Worth House, his fashionable Twenty-fifth Street residence, his valet was waiting up for him with a message. Hearst was to telephone his *New York Journal* offices at once. It was over the phone that his editor told him that the *Maine* had sunk. "Good heavens, what have you done with the story?" Hearst asked. "We have put it on the first page, of course," his editor replied. "Have you put anything else on the front page?" "Only the other big news." "There is not any other big news," Hearst responded. "Please spread the story all over the page. This means war."

Without knowing the facts of the episode, Hearst knew the slant his paper would take on the news: Spain sank the *Maine*. To this day there is no evidence that Spain was at fault. Indeed during the previous year Spain had gone to great lengths, accepted painful na-

The *New York Journal*'s inflammatory but unsubstantiated reports on the sinking of the *Maine* fueled anti-Spanish sentiment and catapulted the United States into war.

tional insults, in order to avoid conflict with the United States. It is inconceivable that Spain would have destroyed the *Maine* as an act of national policy. It is inconceivable that a poor nation of 18 million people would have courted war with a prosperous nation of 75 million citizens.

But truth and political realities were of marginal interest to Hearst. He was determined to use the sinking of the *Maine* to push the United States toward war. During the week after the tragedy the *New York Journal* ran headlines that were total lies. On February 17, for example, the *Journal*'s headline read: THE WARSHIP MAINE WAS SPLIT IN TWO BY AN ENEMY'S SECRET INFERNAL MACHINE. This was pure fabrication. There was no infernal machine (underwater mine), no secret enemy plot. But such stories captured the imagination of the *Journal*'s readers and moved America closer to war. In less than a month President McKinley reluctantly asked Congress for a declaration of war. Hearst labeled the conflict "the *Journal*'s war," and W. A. Swanberg, Hearst's biographer, asserts that "there would have been no war" had Hearst not inflamed public opinion.

Santiago Bay. To defeat the Spanish would require the combined efforts of the army and the navy. With this in mind, McKinley ordered Major General William R. Shafter, commander of the 5th Corps, from Tampa to Santiago. The trip to Cuba set the tone for the entire expedition. Delays, confused orders, and other problems slowed the process. Some 17,000 American troops were forced to spend 19 days on crowded transports, sweating in their woolen uniforms, eating unappetizing travel rations, and thinking about what lay ahead. Finally, toward the end of June, and with the help of Cuban rebels, American troops landed at the ports of Daiquiri and Siboney.

From there they moved toward Santiago. The distance was not great—Santiago Bay was only about 15 miles from the coastal town of Siboney. But the road to Santiago was little more than a rutted, dirt trail. When it rained, wagons became mired in the mud, streams swelled and made fording treacherous, and the troops suffered in the jungle humidity. Slowly the army moved forward, more concerned with broken wagons and tropical diseases than Spanish soldiers.

On July 1, American soldiers learned firsthand the horrors of battle. Between the American position and Santiago were Spanish troops in the tiny hamlet of El Caney and along the San Juan Heights, a ridge to the east of Santiago. From the first, American plans broke down in the face of stiff Spanish opposition. There were no romantic charges, no idealized warfare. The American troops that struggled up Kettle and San Juan hills moved very slowly and suffered alarming casualties. Although outnumbered more than ten to one, Spanish soldiers made U.S. troops pay for every foot they advanced. After America finally secured the enemy positions, correspondent Richard H. Davis wrote, "Another such victory as that of July 1 and our troops must retreat."

General Shafter was frankly worried and even considered retreat. Grossly overweight and gout-ridden, Shafter had neither the disposition nor the ability to lead an energetic campaign. Fortunately for him, Spain's forces in Cuba were even less ready to fight. In Santiago, Spanish soldiers faced shortages of food, water, and ammunition. On July 3, the Spanish squadron tried to break an American blockade and force its way out of Santiago Bay. The act was a suicidal move. American guns destroyed the Spanish fleet and killed some 500 Spanish sailors. Only one American died in the decisive engagement. When his men broke out in a yell of joy, Captain Philip of the *Texas* said, "Don't cheer, men, the poor devils are dying."

Little fighting remained. On July 17 the leading Spanish general in Cuba surrendered to Shafter. Timid in war, Shafter was petty in victory. He refused to permit any naval officers to sign the capitulation document, nor would he allow any Cubans to participate in the surrender negotiations and ceremonies. It was a sad moment. The Cubans who had fought so long and bravely for their independence were denied the glory of their success.

Before the full Spanish surrender, the United States extended its influence in the Caribbean. In late July, General Nelson A. Miles invaded Puerto Rico, Spain's other Caribbean colony. Without any serious resistance, U.S. forces took the island. Finally, on August 12, Spain surrendered, granting Cuban independence and ceding Puerto Rico and Guam to the United States. Both countries agreed to settle the fate of the Philippines at a postwar peace conference to be held in Paris.

For America, it had been a short, successful war. Spanish bullets killed only 379 Americans, the smallest number in any of America's declared wars. Disease and other problems cost over 5000 more lives. If the army's mobilization had been chaotic, its troops had performed heroically under fire. And the navy, which took most of the credit for winning the war, demonstrated the wisdom of its planners. Finally, the war served to bring the North and South closer together as the two sections fought alongside each other rather than against each other. All in all, many Americans agreed with U.S. Ambassador to England John Hay that it had been a "splendid little war."

There was nothing little about the consequences of the war. With the Spanish-American War the United States became an imperial power. The war also increased

America's appetite for overseas territories. The McKinley administration used the war to annex Hawaii and part of Samoa. In addition, at the Paris Peace Conference the United States wrested the Philippines, Puerto Rico, and Guam from Spain. Although the United States paid Spain $20 million for the Philippines, there was no question that Spain was forced to negotiate under duress. These new imperial possessions gave the United States strategic bases in the Caribbean and along the trade routes to Asia.

Freeing Cuba

Many Americans favored the annexation of Cuba. In the land grab that ended the war, the idealism of the Teller Amendment and the war's beginning was all but forgotten. When the war ended, U.S. troops stayed in Cuba, and the country was ruled by an American-run military government. Particularly under General Leonard Wood, the military government helped Cuba recover from its terrible conflict with Spain. Wood restored the Cuban economy and promoted reforms in the legal system, education, sanitation, and health care. Neither Wood nor McKinley, however, was willing to grant Cuba its immediate independence. In his annual message of December 1898, McKinley noted that American troops would stay in Cuba until "complete tranquility" and a "stable government" existed on the island.

The United States finally recognized Cuban independence in 1903. But it was a limited independence. According to the Platt Amendment to the Army Appropriation Bill of 1901, Cuba could exercise self-government, but it could sign no treaties that might limit its independence. The amendment also gave the United States the right to maintain two naval bases on Cuba. Should, in the judgment of the United States, Cuban independence ever be threatened, the Platt Amendment authorized the United States to intervene in Cuba's internal and external affairs. The amendment was also written into the 1901 Cuban constitution. In short, for Cuba, independence had the look and feel of an American protectorate.

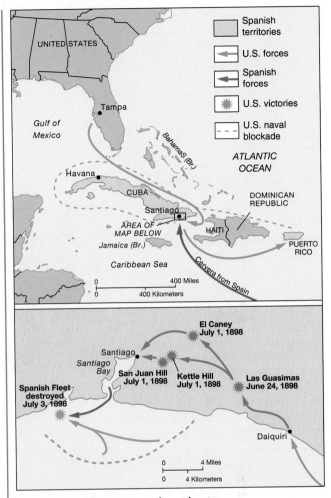

Spanish-American War, Cuban Theater

The Imperial Debate

Compared to the Philippines, Cuba was a minor problem. McKinley's decision to annex the Philippines pleased some Americans and angered many more. Businessmen who dreamed of the rich Asian markets applauded McKinley's decision. Naval strategists similarly believed it was a wise move. They argued that if the United States failed to take the Philippines, then one of the other major powers probably would. Germany, Japan, and England had already expressed interest in the strategically located islands. Finally, Protestant missionaries favored annexation to facilitate their efforts to Christianize the Filipinos. That the Filipinos already favored Roman

THEODORE ROOSEVELT AND THE ROUGH RIDERS

ABOARD the *Yucatan*, anchored off the coast of Cuba, Theodore Roosevelt (TR) received the news on the evening of June 21, 1898. He and his men, a volunteer cavalry regiment dubbed the Rough Riders, had received their orders to disembark from the safety of the ship and join the fighting ashore. It was a welcomed invitation, celebrated with cheers, war dances, songs, boasts, and toasts. "To the Officers—may they get killed, wounded or promoted," urged one toast that captured the mood aboard the ship.

Roosevelt and many men of his generation looked forward to war, greedily anticipating the chance to prove their mettle in battle. They had been raised on stories of the Civil War, stories that over the years had taken on the golden gloss of time. Tales of Shiloh, Chancellorsville, Antietam, and Gettysburg; of Robert E. Lee, Ulysses S. Grant, and Stonewall Jackson; of battles won and causes lost had fired their imaginations. The Spanish-American War was their chance to experience first-hand what they had long only heard about from their fathers' and uncles' lips.

Few men wanted the war more than Roosevelt. Son of a wealthy New York family, he was competitive by nature and enjoyed all physical sports. He also loved history, writing books about American wars and heroic deeds. And for Roosevelt there was perhaps even a deeper motivation. During the Civil War his father, the man he admired above everyone else, had hired a substitute soldier to serve for him. Thousands of other wealthy men had done the same, but for Theodore such a course was unmanly. During a war, he believed, able-bodied men should be in a uniform, not dressed in mufti. He would not repeat his father's mistake. When the Spanish-American War was declared, TR quickly resigned his post as assistant secretary of the navy and joined the fray. In his own mind, he could do nothing else. In *The Rough Riders*, his memoirs of the war, he quoted a poem by Bret Harte, whose last verse was:

> "But when won the coming battle,
> What of profit springs therefrom?
> What if conquest, subjugation,
> Even greater ills become?"
> But the drum
> Answered, "Come!"

And come Roosevelt did.

The men who followed him were kindred spirits. They were rough riders, the men who with Roosevelt formed the First United States Volunteer Cavalry regiment. Some were Ivy Leaguers from Harvard, Yale, and Princeton who belonged to the most exclusive clubs in Boston and New York City. Many had been college athletes, stars in football, tennis, and track and field, men for whom war was a grand playing field. Others were Westerners—cowboys, hunters, frontier sheriffs, Indian fighters, Texas Rangers, prospectors—"a splendid set of men," wrote Roosevelt, "tall and sinewy, with resolute, weather-beaten faces, and eyes that looked a man straight in the face without flinching." Such men were accustomed to riding horses, shooting rifles, and living off the land.

Bucky O'Neill was something of a Rough Rider ideal. Indian fighter and sheriff of Prescott, Arizona, Bucky could shoot with the hunters, exchange stories with the prospectors, and philosophize with the college graduates. Roosevelt once overheard Bucky and Dr. Robb Church, the former Princeton football player who served as the surgeon for the Rough Riders, "discussing Aryan word roots together, and then sliding off into a review of the novels of Balzac, and a discussion as to how far Balzac could be said to be the founder of the modern realistic school of fiction." Once when Bucky and Roosevelt were leaning on the ship's railing searching the Caribbean sky for the Southern Cross, the old Indian fighter asked, "Who would not risk his life for a star?" TR agreed that great risk was part of greatness.

Brimming with enthusiasm, perhaps a bit innocent in their naïveté, the Rough Riders viewed Cuba as a land of stars, a place to win great honors or die in the pursuit. Like many of his men, TR believed "that the nearing future held . . . many chances of death, of honor and renown." And he was ready. Dressed in a Brooks Brothers uniform made especially for him and with several extra pairs of spectacles sewn in the lining of his Rough Rider hat, Roosevelt prepared to meet his destiny.

In a land of beauty, death often came swiftly. As the Rough Riders and other soldiers moved inland toward Santiago, snipers fired on them. The high-speed Mauser bullets seemed to come out of nowhere, making a *z-z-z-z-z-eu* as they moved through the air or a loud *chug* as they hit flesh. Since the Spanish snipers used smokeless gunpowder, no puffs of smoke betrayed their positions.

On their first day in Cuba, the Rough Riders experienced the "blood, sweat, and tears" of warfare. Dr. Church looked "like a kid who had gotten his hands and arms into a bucket of thick red paint." Some men died, and others, dying, lay where they had been shot. The reality of war strikes different men differently. It horrifies some, terrifies others, and enrages still others. Sheer exhilaration was the best way to describe Roosevelt's response to the death and danger. Even sniper fire could not keep TR from jumping up and down with excitement.

On July 1, 1898, the Rough Riders faced their sternest task. Moving from the coast toward Santiago along the Camino Real, the main arm of the U.S. forces encountered an entrenched enemy. Spread out along the San Juan Heights, Spanish forces commanded a splendid position. As American troops emerged from a stretch of jungle, they found themselves in a dangerous position. Once again the sky seemed to be raining Mauser bullets and shrapnel. Clearly, the Heights had to be taken. Each hour of delay meant more American casualties.

The Rough Riders were deployed to the right to prepare to assault Kettle Hill. Once in position, they faced an agonizing wait for orders to charge. Most soldiers hunched behind cover. Bucky O'Neill, however, casually strolled up and down in front of his troops, chain-smoked cigarettes, and shouted encouragement. A sergeant implored him to take cover. "Sergeant," Bucky remarked, "the Spanish bullet isn't made that will kill me." Hardly had he finished the statement when

a Mauser bullet ripped into his mouth and burst out of the back of his head. Even before he fell, Roosevelt wrote, Bucky's "wild and gallant soul had gone out into the darkness."

Finally the orders came. On foot the Rough Riders moved up Kettle Hill toward the Spanish guns. It was a slow, painful, heroic charge. Bullets, sounding "like the ripping of a silk dress," cut down a number of Roosevelt's men. But unable to stop the push of the American forces, the Spanish gave way, leaving their fortified positions and running for safety.

From the heights of Kettle Hill, Roosevelt watched another U.S. attack on nearby San Juan Hill. Once again feeling the wolf rising in his heart, he led his men toward the new objective. Again the fighting was difficult. Again the Spanish gave way. By the end of the day, American forces had taken the San Juan Heights. Before them was Santiago and victory. "The great day of my life," as TR called it, was over.

"Another such victory like that of July 1," wrote Richard Harding Davis, "and our troops must retreat." Indeed, casualties ran high, and the Rough Riders suffered the heaviest losses. But the fighting helped to break the Spanish resistance. It was the last really difficult day of fighting in the war. Perhaps more importantly, the day made Roosevelt a national hero. Aided by his ability at self-promotion, TR used the event as a political stepping-stone. "I would rather have led the charge," he later wrote, "than served three terms in the U.S. Senate."

CHRONOLOGY OF KEY EVENTS

1867	Russia sells Alaska to the United States for $7.2 million, or less than 2 cents an acre
1870	Senate rejects President Grant's attempt to annex the Dominican Republic
1889	Britain, Germany, and the United States agree to share control of Samoa
1890	Captain Alfred Thayer Mahan's *The Influence of Sea Power upon History* asserts that naval power is the key to national greatness
1893	Americans organize the overthrow of Queen Liliuokalani of Hawaii and, with the help of U.S. marines, set up a new government
1895	Venezuela border dispute; Cuban revolt against Spain intensifies
1898	The battleship *Maine* explodes in Havana harbor; Spanish-American War begins; Dewey sinks Spanish fleet in Manila Bay; Battle of San Juan Hill; destruction of Spanish fleet in Santiago harbor ends Spanish resistance in Cuba; U.S. annexes Hawaii
1899	Aguinaldo leads a rebellion against the United States to win Philippine independence; John Hay, McKinley's secretary of state, issues an Open Door note to prevent further partitioning of China by European powers and to protect the principle of free trade
1900	Boxer Rebellion, a Chinese nationalist revolt against foreigners, erupts
1901	Platt Amendment gives the United States the right to maintain two naval stations on Cuba and to send troops to the island to preserve order
1902	United States finally crushes Philippine revolt

duties and closing no ports within their spheres of influence. Although most European countries expressed little interest in Hay's Open Door Policy—which, after all, benefited the United States the most—in 1900 Hay announced that the European powers had accepted his proposal.

The Chinese themselves had other plans. In the late spring of 1900 a group of Chinese nationalists, known as Boxers, besieged the Legation Quarter in Peking, calling for the expulsion or death of all westerners in China. The Boxers, whose Chinese name better translates as "Righteous and Harmonious Fists," were a quasi-religious organization that believed deeply in magic and maintained that all its members were impervious to western bullets. As a joint European and American rescue force proved, bullets could and would kill Boxers. By late summer, 1900, westernizers had crushed the Boxer Rebellion.

Additional troops in China threatened Hay's Open Door Policy, On July 3, 1900, during the tensest moment of the Boxer Rebellion, he issued a second Open Door note, calling on all western powers to preserve "Chinese territorial and administrative entity" and uphold "the principle of equal and impartial trade with all parts of the Chinese Empire." Once again, few European countries paid attention to Hay's Open Door Policy. Mutual distrust and the fear of provoking a general European war—more than any American plan—prevented the major European powers from dismembering China. Out of Hay's Open Door Policy notes came the idea, held mostly in America, that the United States was China's protector. It was another example of the increasingly active role the United States had taken in world affairs.

CONCLUSION

Thirty-two years separated the inauguration of Ulysses S. Grant and the assassination of William McKinley, but during that generation, America and the presidency changed radically. Part of the change can be attributed to growth—industry boomed, the population swelled, agricultural production increased. The growth was also psychological. Perhaps a more appropriate term would be maturation. During those years many Americans achieved a new sense of confidence, and their vision broadened. After 250 years of looking westward across America's seemingly limitless acres of land, they began to look toward the oceans and consider the possibilities of a new form of expansion. They also began to follow the imperial examples of England, France, Italy, and Germany. Talk of world power, world outlook, world responsibilities colored their rhetoric.

This outward thrust was accompanied and enhanced by the growth of presidential power. Grant worked hard for the annexation of the Dominican Republic, but Congress blocked his efforts. By the turn of the century, however, Congress clearly expected the president to lead the nation in the area of foreign affairs. Harrison, Cleveland, and McKinley, as well as their advisers, firmly guided America's foreign affairs. Although the presidents pursued different policies, they agreed that America should have a greater influence in world affairs. None questioned the fundamental fact that the United States was and should be a world power.

Many questions, nevertheless, remained unanswered. What were the rights of a world power? What were its responsibilities? What were its duties? Neither Harrison, Cleveland, nor McKinley gained much experience in running a colonial administration. The limits and possibilities of American power had yet to be

defined and explored. The next three presidents—Roosevelt, Taft, and Wilson—would help define how America would use its new power.

SUGGESTIONS FOR FURTHER READING

Michael Hunt, *Ideology and U.S. Foreign Policy* (1987). Examines the issue of race in American imperialism.

Gerald F. Linderman, *The Mirror of War: American Society and the Spanish-American War* (1974). Relates patterns of war to patterns in American culture.

Stuart C. Miller, *"Benevolent Assimilation": The American Conquest of the Philippines, 1899–1903* (1982). Classic study of war in the Philippines.

H. Wayne Morgan, *America's Road to Empire* (1967). Short but interesting history of the origins of the American war with Spain.

David F. Trask, *The War with Spain in 1898* (1981). Most detailed study of the Spanish-American War.

William A. Williams, *The Tragedy of American Diplomacy*, 2d ed. (1972). Pioneering but controversial study of economic motives in American imperialism.

Overviews and Surveys

William H. Becker and Samuel F. Wells, Jr., eds., *Economics and World Power: An Assessment of American Diplomacy Since 1789* (1984); Robert L. Beisner, *From the Old Diplomacy to the New, 1865–1900* (1975), and *Twelve Against Empire: The Anti-Imperialists, 1898–1900* (1968); Charles S. Campbell, Jr., *Transformation of American Foreign Relations, 1865–1900* (1976); Warren I. Cohen, ed., *New Frontiers in American-East Asian Relations* (1983); B. Franklin Cooling, *Gray Steel and Blue Water Navy: The Formative Years of America's Military Industrial Complex* (1979); Arthur Power Dudden, *The American Pacific: From the Old China Trade to the Present* (1992); David F. Healy, *U.S. Expansionism: Imperialist Urge in the 1890s* (1970), and *Drive to Hegemony: The United States in the Caribbean* (1988); Michael Hunt, *The Making of a Special Relationship: The United States and China to 1914* (1983); Walter LaFeber, *The New Empire: An Interpretation of American Expansion* (1963), and *The American Search for Opportunity, 1865–1913* (1993); Tenant S. McWilliams, *The New South Faces the World* (1988); Thomas G. Paterson, et al., *American Foreign*

Policy, 2 vols., 3d ed. (1988), and Paterson and Stephen C. Rabe, *Imperial Surge: The United States Abroad* (1992).

Congressional Control and The Reduction of American Power

Paul Holbo, *Tarnished Expansion: The Alaska Scandal, the Press, and Congress, 1867–1871* (1983); Henry E. Mattox, *The Twilight of Amateur Diplomacy* (1989); Allan R. Millett and Peter Maslowski, *For the Common Defense: A Military History of the United States of America* (1984); David Pletcher, *The Awkward Years: American Foreign Relations under Garfield and Arthur* (1963); Tom E. Terrill, *The Tariff, Politics, and American Foreign Policy, 1874–1901* (1973).

The Spirit of American Greatness

Henry Blumenthal, *France and the United States: Their Diplomatic Relation, 1789–1914* (1970); Alexander E. Campbell, *Great Britain and the United States, 1895–1903* (1960); Richard Challener, *Admirals, Generals, and American Foreign Policy, 1889–1914* (1973); Kenton J. Clymer, *Protestant Missionaries in the Philippines, 1898–1916: An Inquiry Into the American Colonial Mentality* (1986); Warren I. Cohen, *America's Response to China*, 3d ed. (1990); John Dobson, *America's Ascent: The United States Becomes a Great Power, 1880–1914* (1978); James A. Field, Jr., *America and the Mediterranean World, 1776–1882* (1969); Thomas J. McCormick, *China Market: America's Quest for Informal Empire, 1893–1901* (1967); Bradford Perkins, *The Great Rapprochement: England and the United States, 1895–1914* (1968); James Reed, *The Missionary Mind and American East Asia Policy* (1985); Emily Rosenberg, *Spreading the American Dream: American Economic and Cultural Expansion, 1890–1945* (1982); Marilyn B. Young, *Rhetoric of Empire: American-China Policy, 1895–1901* (1968).

The Emergence of Aggression in American Foreign Policy

David Anderson, *Imperialism and Idealism: American Diplomats in China, 1861–1898* (1985); Phillip Darby, *Three Faces of Imperialism: British and American Approaches to Asia and Africa, 1870–1970* (1987); R. P. Gilson, *Samoa 1830 to 1900* (1970); Kenneth J. Hagan, *American Gunboat Diplomacy and the Old Navy,* *1877–1889* (1973); Walter R. Herrick, *The American Naval Revolution* (1966); Akira Iriye, *Across the Pacific* (1967); Paul M. Kennedy, *The Samoa Tangle: A Study in Anglo-German-American Relations, 1878–1900* (1974); John L. Offner, *An Unwanted War: The Diplomacy of the United States and Spain over Cuba, 1895–1898* (1992); Thomas J. Osborne, *Empire Can Wait: American Opposition to Hawaiian Annexation, 1893–1898* (1981); William A. Russ, Jr., *The Hawaiian Revolution, 1893–94* (1959); Thomas D. Schoonover, *The United States in Central America, 1860–1911: Episodes of Social Imperialism and Imperial Rivalry in the World System* (1991); Merze Tate, *The United States and the Hawaiian Kingdom* (1965).

The War for Empire

Jules R. Benjamin, *The United States and the Origins of the Cuban Revolution* (1990); H. W. Brands, *Bound to Empire: The United States and the Philippines* (1992); Frank Freidel, *The Splendid Little War* (1958); John M. Gates, *Schoolbooks and Krags: The United States Army in the Philippines, 1898–1902* (1973); Willard B. Gatewood, Jr., *"Smoked Yankees" and the Struggle for Empire* (1971), and *Black Americans and the White Man's Burden, 1898–1903* (1975); Lewis L. Gould, *The Presidency of William McKinley* (1980); David Healy, *U.S. Expansionism: The Imperialist Urge in the 1890s* (1970); Lester D. Langley, *The Banana Men: American Mercenaries and Entrepreneurs in Central America, 1880–1930* (1995); Ernest R. May, *Imperial Democracy: The Emergence of America as a Great Power* (1961), and *American Imperialism*, rev. ed. (1991); Glenn May, *Battle for Batangas* (1991); H. Wayne Morgan, *From Hayes to McKinley* (1969), and ed. *The Gilded Age*, rev. ed. (1970); Louis Pérez, Jr., *Cuba under the Platt Amendment, 1902–1934* (1986), and *Cuba Between Empires, 1878–1902* (1983); Julius W. Pratt, *Expansionists of 1898* (1936); Goran Rystad, *Ambiguous Imperialism* (1975); Daniel B. Schirmer, *Republic or Empire* (1972); E. Berkeley Tompkins, *Anti-Imperialism in the United States* (1970); Richard E. Welch, Jr., *Response to Imperialism: The United States and the Philippine-American War, 1899–1902* (1979); Leon Wolff, *Little Brown Brother: How the United States Purchased and Pacified the Philippines* (1961).

Biographies

Howard Beale, *Theodore Roosevelt and the Rise of America to World Power* (1956); Kenton J. Clymer, *John Hay: The Gentleman as Diplomat* (1975); David

Donald, *Charles Sumner and the Rights of Man* (1970); John A. Garraty, *Henry Cabot Lodge* (1953); Lewis J. Gould, *The Presidency of Theodore Roosevelt* (1991); H. Wayne Morgan, *William McKinley and His America* (1963); Allan Nevins, *Grover Cleveland* (1932), and *Hamilton Fish,* rev. ed. (1957); Ernest N. Paolino, *The Foundations of the American Empire: William Henry Seward and U.S. Foreign Policy* (1973); Ronald Spector, *Admiral of the New Empire: The Life and Career of George Dewey* (1974); John M. Taylor, *William Henry Seward* (1991); Richard W. Turk, *The Ambiguous Relationship: Theodore Roosevelt and Alfred Thayer Mahan* (1987); Richard E. Welch, Jr., *The Presidencies of Grover Cleveland* (1988); William C. Widenor, *Henry Cabot Lodge and the Search for an American Foreign Policy* (1980).

CHAPTER 21
THE PROGRESSIVE STRUGGLE, 1900–1917

THE PROGRESSIVE IMPULSE
America in 1901
Voices for Change
The Muckrakers

PROGRESSIVES IN ACTION
The Drive to Organize
Urban Beginnings
Reform Reaches the State Level

PROGRESSIVISM MOVES TO THE NATIONAL LEVEL
Roosevelt and New Attitudes Toward Government Power
Taft and Quiet Progressivism
Wilson and Moral Progressivism

PROGRESSIVISM IN THE INTERNATIONAL ARENA
Big Stick Diplomacy
Dollar Diplomacy
Missionary Diplomacy

PROGRESSIVE ACCOMPLISHMENTS, PROGRESSIVE FAILURES
The Impact of Legislation
Winners and Losers

Times had changed by 1902 when George F. Baer declared "anthracite mining is business and not a religious, sentimental or academic proposition." Those tough-minded words might have won public approval at an earlier time, but many believed that Baer, spokesperson for mine owners in Pennsylvania, was merely being pigheaded. His words were in response to a request by John Mitchell of the United Mine Workers (UMW) for arbitration of a labor dispute. There was an unusual amount of support for the coal miners' position. Exposés had increased popular awareness of miserable working conditions, and the union's demands seemed reasonable: a 9-hour day, recognition of the union, a 10 to 20 percent increase in wages, and a fair weighing of the coal mined. Mitchell repeatedly stated the miners' willingness to accept arbitration, both before and after 50,000 miners walked out of the pits in May 1902.

Skillfully led, the coal miners stood firm month after month. By September, coal reserves were running short and prices were rising. With winter approaching, empty coal bins began multiplying, even in schools and hospitals. Baer remained stubborn. "The rights and interests of the laboring man," he declared, "will be protected and cared for— not by the labor agitators, but by the Christian men to whom God in his infinite wisdom has given the control of property interests in this country." This proclamation of the Gospel of Wealth fell on deaf ears. Newspaper after newspaper expressed disgust with the mine owners, and some tentatively suggested government ownership of the mines.

On October 3, President Theodore Roosevelt, temporarily in a wheelchair as a result of an accident, presided over a conference at the White House. Attending were Mitchell, Baer, Attorney General Philander C. Knox, and other labor leaders and mine operators. Baer was not in a mood to be cooperative. "We object to being called here to meet a criminal," he told a reporter, "even by the President of the United States." Refusing to speak directly to Mitchell, Baer urged Roosevelt to prosecute UMW leaders under the Sherman Antitrust Act and to use federal troops to break the strike, just as Cleveland had done in the 1894 Pullman strike. While Mitchell "behaved like a gentleman" according to Roosevelt, Baer was obstinate, concluding one diatribe against unions by calling "free government . . . a contemptible failure if it can only protect the lives and property and secure comfort of the people by compromise with violators of law and instigators of violence and crime."

Irritated with Baer, Roosevelt declared, "If it wasn't for the high office I hold I would have taken him by the seat of the breeches and the nape of the neck and chucked him out of that window." When the owners returned to Pennsylvania, they took actions that indicated they might use force to break the strike. Roosevelt's response was to begin preparations to send 10,000 federal troops to take over and operate the mines. This action jolted opponents of state socialism, who induced banker J. P. Morgan to get involved. Serving as a broker, Morgan was able to patch together a compromise under which the miners returned to work and Roosevelt appointed a commission to arbitrate the dispute.

The commission and its findings illustrate a number of aspects of the turn-of-the-century reforms labeled "progressivism." Originally, the commission was to consist of an army engineer, a mining engineer, a businessperson "familiar with the coal industry," a federal judge, and an "eminent sociologist"—reflecting a progressive tendency to call upon "experts" to conduct public affairs. Its composition was also decidedly probusiness, and even the addition of two other members and the appointment of a labor leader as the "eminent sociologist" did not redress this imbalance. As a result, its findings were essentially conservative: a 10 percent wage increase and reduction of working hours to 8 a day for a handful of miners and to 9 for most. The union did not receive recognition, and the traditional manner of weighing coal was continued. The commission also suggested a 10 percent increase in the price of coal. Business influence on other progressive responses to social problems generally produced similar moderate solutions that frequently brought industrialists as many benefits as losses.

President Theodore Roosevelt, surrounded here by coal miners after their 1902 strike, set a precedent by threatening the use of force against management rather than labor.

Nevertheless, Roosevelt's actions did add some new rules to the game. For the first time, a president did not give knee-jerk support to business. Government became not merely a champion of the status quo, but also an arbiter of change. Demands from the middle class and from workers motivated this retreat from laissez-faire. By 1902 many middle-class citizens had rejected management's heavy-handed tactics, which had often ended in chaos and conflict. They sought a more orderly, stable, and just society through government intervention. Workers also began to flex their political muscles, electing sympathetic mayors in a number of cities. Like the coal miners, Americans of all classes were learning the limits of individualism and the benefits of joining together in organizations to accomplish their goals. National leaders such as Roosevelt began to recognize the need for change in order to preserve stable government and the capitalistic system. Roosevelt justified his actions in 1902 as a way to save "big propertied men . . . from the dreadful punishment which their folly would have brought upon them." He stood, he declared,

"between them and socialistic action." For a variety of motives, a plethora of legislation was enacted—sometimes with unintended results.

THE PROGRESSIVE IMPULSE

Americans exalted progress as a basic characteristic of their nation's distinctiveness. Technology was reshaping the human environment in dramatic ways. The pace of change was dizzying. Then in the late 1890s, people seemed to stop, catch their breath, and look around at their brave, new world. Much filled them with pride, but some of what they saw seemed outmoded or disruptive. Problems, however, appeared eminently solvable. Modern minds were explaining and harnessing natural forces. Could they not also understand and control human behavior? Could they not eliminate conflict and bring harmony to competing interests through some simple adjustments in the system? Americans increasingly answered "Yes" and called themselves "progressives." Many agreed with Thomas Edison's observation, "We've stumbled along for awhile, trying to run a new civilization in old ways, but we've got to start to make this world over."

America in 1901

The twentieth century opened with a rerun of the 1896 election between William Jennings Bryan and William McKinley. Although the outcome was the same, much was different. "I have never known a Presidential campaign so quiet," Senator Henry Cabot Lodge noted. By 1900 the crises of the 1890s had largely passed. Prosperity had returned and was shared by many. The nation also reveled in its new-found international power following the Spanish-American War. The social fabric seemed to be on the mend, but memories of the depression still haunted Americans, and society's blemishes appeared more and more intolerable to many.

As the nation reached adulthood, a number of ugly moles and warts had indeed come to the surface. Unequal distribution of wealth and income persisted. One percent of American families possessed nearly seven-eighths of its wealth. Four-fifths of Americans lived on a subsistence level, while a handful lived in incredible opulence. In 1900, Andrew Carnegie's income was $23 million, the average working man earned $500. The wealth of a few was increased by the exploitation of women and children. To feed their families women worked for wages as low as $6 a week. The sacrifice of the country's young to the god of economic growth was alarming. One reporter undertook to do a child's job in the mines for one day and wrote, "I tried to pick out the pieces of slate from the hurrying stream of coal, often missing them; my hands were bruised and cut within a few minutes; I was covered from head to foot with coal dust, and for many hours afterwards I was expectorating some of the small particles of anthracite I had swallowed."

Working conditions were equally horrifying in other industries, and for many

Americans housing conditions were as bad or worse. One investigator described a Chicago neighborhood, remarking on the "filthy and rotten tenements, the dingy courts and tumble-down sheds, the foul stables and dilapidated outhouses, the broken sewer pipes, the piles of garbage fairly alive with diseased odors." At the same time the Vanderbilts summered in a "cottage" of 70 rooms, and wealthy men partied in shirts with diamond buttons.

The middle class did not experience either extreme. Its members did have their economic grievances, however. Prosperity increased the cost of living by 35 percent in less than a decade, while many middle-class incomes remained fairly stable. Such people were not poor, but they believed they were not getting a fair share of the prosperity. Many came to blame the monopolies and watched with alarm as trusts, proving to be immune from the Sherman Act, proliferated rapidly. Nearly three-fourths of all trusts in 1904 had been created since 1898. Decreasing competition seemed to threaten America's status as the land of opportunity.

People came to believe that they had to find political solutions to the nation's problems. To achieve that goal they had to wrest government from the hands of a few and return it to the "people." The great democratic experiment seemed to have run awry. Wealthy industrialists bought state and federal legislators; urban political machines paid for votes with money from bribes; Southern elections had become both bloody and corrupt.

Most problems were not new in 1901; neither were the proposed solutions. What came to be called progressivism was rooted in the Gilded Age. Whereas reform had been a sideshow earlier, it now became a national preoccupation. Progressivism was more broadly based and enjoyed greater appeal than any previous reform movement. The regional differences of the North, South, and West shaped reformers' concerns but not their intensity. The entire nation had experienced war or depression, never reform. One reason it did so now was the diversity and

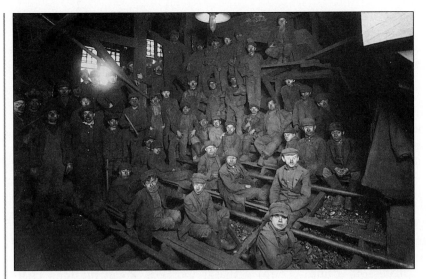

Breaker boys employed by the mines worked in dirty, dismal, and dangerous surroundings that robbed them of their childhood.

pervasiveness of the voices calling for change.

Voices for Change

By 1900, Americans had done nothing less than reinterpret their understanding of their world. Under the old, classical interpretation, the universe was governed by absolute and unchangeable law. There was divine logic to all and truth was universal—the same at all times and in all places. Humanity's chore was to discover these truths, not to devise new ones. Under this vision, public policy should be aligned with natural laws; to attempt to change the course of those laws through man-made law was to court disaster. Such logic justified the concentration of wealth as well as the lack of governmental regulation of business and assistance to the poor and weak.

Social Darwinism, laissez-faire economics, and the Gospel of Wealth never enjoyed total acceptance. Throughout the Gilded Age, challenges and alternative visions chipped away at their bases of support. The earlier challengers, however, either offered rather radical or simplistic alternatives. In 1879

Henry George wrote *Progress and Poverty.* As the title implies, he early recognized the unequal distribution of the fruits of economic growth. His solution was a "single tax" on the "unearned increment" of land values. He wanted to tax those who benefited from land speculation and rising property values without producing anything. In essence he attacked the premise of capitalism that said that one could use money to make more money without providing other goods or services. In *Looking Backward* (1888) Edward Bellamy provided a glimpse of a utopian society based upon a state-controlled economy propelled by cooperation rather than competition. Such writings profoundly influenced the Populists, the Socialists, and many who called themselves progressive.

Although critics dismissed the likes of George as crackpots, some respectable voices arose from the worlds of arts and literature, academia, the law, organized religion, and journalism. Realist writers described the world as it was, not as it should be. Instead of romantic heroes battling for abstract ideals, their characters were ordinary people dealing with concrete problems. The naturalists portrayed the powerlessness of the individual against the uncaring forces of urbanization and industrialization. Artists of the Ashcan school painted urban scenes teeming with problems as well as life. Art and literature thus became mirrors of social concerns (see Chapter 18).

A revolution was also taking place in the academic world. Two important changes were the democratization of higher education and the revolt against formalism. From 1870 to 1910 the number of colleges and universities nearly doubled, and their enrollment grew from 52,000 in 1870 to 600,000 in 1920. Higher education became less elitist, white, religious, and male, as women came to account for 47.3 percent of students in 1920 and African-American enrollment grew to over 20,000. Increasingly, their professors came from the middle class as well. Such students and teachers had little interest in supporting the status quo.

Also undermining the status quo was the revolt against formalism. Previous academics had sought to explain the world by formulating abstract, universal theories. The new scholars, especially in the emerging social sciences, turned this approach on its head.

They began instead by collecting concrete data. In field after field that data did not support the so-called natural laws propounded by their predecessors. Knowledge, philosopher and educator John Dewey proclaimed, was "no longer an immobile solid; it has been liquefied."

Theories had prescribed limits to human action; facts became weapons for change. Classical economists asserted earlier that self-interested economic decisions by individuals in a freely competitive economy naturally regulated markets through the laws of supply and demand. The new economists, calling themselves "institutional economists," conducted field research to learn how the economy actually worked. Their findings challenged the laissez-faire doctrines of the classicists on two levels: (1) that free competition existed and (2) that human decisions were based on purely economic motivations. To continue policies based on competition was absurd, they argued, in an economy dominated by monopolies. In *Theory of the Leisure Class* (1899) and *The Instinct of Workmanship* (1914), economist Thorstein Veblen demon-

These women in a physics class illustrate the growing presence of women in college during the Progressive Era.

strated the power of noneconomic motives. For example, vanity prompted the newly rich to indulge in "conspicuous consumption" well beyond their economic needs. For many economists "natural laws" were, in the words of Richard T. Ely, "used as a tool in the hands of the greedy."

A group of sociologists, calling themselves "Reform Darwinists," rejected Spencer's Social Darwinism as another tool of exploitation. They accepted evolutionary principles and the influence of environment but denied that people were merely pawns manipulated by natural forces. Human intelligence was an active force that could control and change the environment, especially when people worked together. A leading Reform Darwinist, Lester Frank Ward, proclaimed, "The individual has reigned long enough. The day has come for society to take its affairs into its own hands and shape its own destinies."

Ward's call for "rational planning" and "social engineering" in his *Dynamic Sociology* (1883) was echoed by Frederick W. Taylor, an efficiency advisor to management. His time and motion studies led to lowered production costs, and he asserted, "The fundamental principles of scientific management are applicable to all kinds of human activities." The goal of most such social scientists was a more orderly society, as was expressed by journalist Walter Lippmann, who called on society "to introduce plan where there has been clash, and purpose into the jungles of disordered growth."

Legal scholars joined the assault on formalism in both books and court decisions. During the Gilded Age, courts had read laissez-faire principles into their interpretation of the Constitution. Decisions striking down regulatory and reform legislation invoked such abstract principles as the sanctity of property rights and contracts. In theory all such rights were equal before the law; reality was a different matter. For example, in *Lochner* v. *New York* (1905) the Supreme Court struck down a New York law limiting bakers' working hours. The law, the Court ruled, violated the bakers' rights to bargain freely and to make contracts. Most workers, however, had no real power to bargain, and maintaining that myth merely increased management's already overwhelming advantage.

A new breed of jurists challenged laissez-faire justice. Dean Roscoe Pound of the Harvard Law School advocated "sociological jurisprudence," calling for "the adjustment of principles and doctrines to the human conditions they are to govern rather than assumed first principles." Supreme Court Justice Oliver Wendell Holmes, Jr., rejected the idea that laws had ever been the logical result of pure, universal principles. "The life of the law has not been logic"; he wrote, "it has been experience." Laws had been and should be based on "the felt necessities of the time." Lawyer Louis D. Brandeis successfully argued these ideas in 1908. That year the Supreme Court upheld a law in *Muller* v. *Oregon* that set a ten-hour workday for women working in Oregon laundries, primarily because social research documented the damage done to women's health by long hours of work.

As Americans began to reject absolute truths and universal principles, the question remained of how to determine right from wrong and good from bad. Philosopher William James with his doctrine of pragmatism provided an answer. "The ultimate test for us of what a truth means," he wrote, "is the conduct it dictates or inspires." Inherited ideas and principles needed scientific scrutiny before being accepted as guides to social development. As a distinctly American philosophy, pragmatism found many adherents. One of them, John Dewey, applied its principles to education. Requiring rote memorization of a static body of facts, he believed, did not meet the needs of individuals in a dynamic, changing environment. Instead, education should be based on experience to prepare students to assume personally fulfilling roles in society. In schools modeled after Dewey's Laboratory School at the University of Chicago, students engaged in activities that taught problem solving by doing rather than reading.

The literary and intellectual currents of the era helped to set the stage for reform by combining optimism, idealism, and a tough-minded practicality. Yet the educated elite were probably reflecting rather than shaping public

In 1889 Jane Addams founded Hull House, a social settlement in Chicago. A "Social Gospeler," Addams turned to Christian ideals to solve social problems.

opinion. Priests and preachers influenced far more people than professors. The impact of organized religion on progressivism was profound. It was no coincidence that Teddy Roosevelt's supporters marched around the hall singing "Onward Christian Soldiers" at the 1912 convention.

The confrontation between the church and the city produced the Social Gospel movement. Urban clergymen saw ravaged bodies that needed to be healed before souls could be saved. As a young Baptist minister in the dismal New York neighborhood "Hell's Kitchen," Walter Rauschenbusch described the poor coming to his church for aid. "They wore down our threshold, and they wore away our hearts . . . one could hear human virtue cracking and crunching all around." Following the lead of William Graham Taylor at the Chicago Theological Seminary, theology schools added courses in Christian sociology to teach "the application of our common Christianity to . . . social conditions." Social Gospelers used the tools of scientific inquiry to root out and solve human problems in order to usher in the "Kingdom of God on Earth." Many settlement house workers, such as Jane Addams, sought to put their faith into action for "the joy of finding the Christ that lieth in man, but which no man can unfold save in fellowship." The Social Gospelers advocated a kind of sacred humanism.

Progressivism was dominated by, but not limited to, Protestantism. The 1891 encyclical, *Rerum Novarum,* by Pope Leo XIII, inspired such Catholic priests as Father John A. Ryan to declare "a small number of very rich men have been able to lay upon the masses of people a yoke little better than slavery itself" and "no practical solution of this question will ever be found without the assistance of the church." Such Catholics as Alfred E. Smith and Robert F. Wagner became prominent progressive politicians. Others such as Jewish lawyer Louis Brandeis illustrated that the reform sentiment was not exclusively Christian.

The Muckrakers

A final spark that ignited public interest in reform was popular journalism. The expansion of education and cities provided a mass audience for low-priced magazines. Such journals as *Collier's* and *McClure's* sold for only 10 cents and could only succeed if large numbers of people bought them. Their editors quickly rediscovered people's fascination with evil. Investigative reporters peered beneath all sorts of rocks and brought to light corruption in almost every facet of society. Their vivid, indignant accounts sold magazines but appalled some of the elite. Teddy Roosevelt compared the writers to the character in John Bunyan's *The Pilgrim's Progress,* who was too engrossed in raking muck to look up and accept a celestial crown. Thus these chroniclers came to be called muckrakers.

Most of their exposés came out serially in magazines; others were published as books, but all titillated the public. John Spargo wrote on child labor, "Statistics cannot express the withering of child lips in the poisoned air of factories; the tired strained look of child eyes that never dance to the glad music of souls tuned to Nature's symphonies." The U.S. Senate, according to David Graham Phillips, "betrayed the public to that cruel and vicious spirit of Mammon [money] which has come to dominate the nation." Further, he argued, "The United States Senate is a larger factor than your labor and intelligence, you average American, in determining your income. And the Senate is a traitor to you!" State legislatures were little better, as was shown by journalist William Allen White's investigation in Missouri. "The legislature met biennially, and enacted such laws as the corporations paid for and such as were necessary to fool the people." In *Following the Color Line* journalist and author Ray

Stannard Baker exhorted, "Whether we like it or not the whole nation . . . is tied by unbreakable bonds to its Negroes, its Chinamen, its slum-dwellers, its thieves, its murderers, its prostitutes. We cannot elevate ourselves by driving them back either with hatred, violence or neglect; but only by bringing them forward: by service." Ida Tarbell called Standard Oil "one of the most gigantic and dangerous conspiracies ever attempted." In similar, stirring words Lincoln Steffens denounced urban politics in *The Shame of the Cities,* and the socialist Upton Sinclair described the horrifying conditions in the meat-packing industry in *The Jungle.*

One might believe these men and women were cynical mudslingers, but that was not how they saw themselves: "We muckraked," said Baker, "not because we hated our world, but because we loved it. We were not hopeless, we were not cynical, we were not bitter." The public sometimes missed the intended message. Sinclair's goal in *The Jungle* was a socialist critique of the exploitation of labor in the meatpacking industry, but as he ruefully noted, "I aimed at the nation's heart and hit it in the stomach." After a few years, muckraking tended to degenerate into sloppy research and wild, unsubstantiated charges. Yet the publishers of the more than 2000 muckraking books and articles who aimed at the nation's pocketbooks hit a number of Americans in the heart.

Ida Tarbell became one of the most influential muckrakers after the 1904 publication of her *History of the Standard Oil Company.*

PROGRESSIVES IN ACTION

Voices of change echoed a genuine transformation of popular sentiment. Americans of all classes began calling themselves "progressives" and sought to reform whichever social evil captured their attention. Most believed problems could be legislated away; their typical response to injustice or sin was "There ought to be a law." At the same time they rejected the individualism of Social Darwinism and believed that progress would come through cooperation rather than competition. Thus they organized themselves by droves into groups that shared their own particular vision of human progress.

The diversity of new organizations reflected the breadth of reform activity. Indeed, so varied were the aims of people calling themselves progressive that to call progressivism a single movement is a mistake. The only unity lay in the idea that people could improve society. Most progressives, however, were middle-class moderates who abhorred radical solutions. Motivated by a fear and hatred of class conflict, such progressives sought to save the capitalists from their own excesses and thereby salvage the system. Their goal was an orderly and harmonious society.

The Drive to Organize

Organizing was a major activity at the turn of the century. Such professional groups as the American Medical Association (AMA) and the American Historical Association emerged in their modern form. These groups reflected the rise of a new professionalism that helped to create a body of "experts" to be tapped by progressives wanting to impose order and efficiency on social institutions. The organizations themselves also acted to bring change. The AMA was reorganized in 1901, and by 1910 its membership had increased from 8400 to more than 70,000. Its major goal was to improve professional standards. Governments assisted by enacting laws that required licenses to practice medicine. In 1910 a Carnegie Foundation study recommended minimum standards for medical education. Widespread acceptance

THE WHITE PLAGUE

DURING the Progressive Era, the rise of scientific ways of thinking cleared the way for reformers and health officers to launch a campaign against the disease most identified with industrialization—tuberculosis (TB). During the nineteenth century, TB was aptly called "the Captain of All the Men of Death." It killed more people and caused more sickness than any other disease in the western world. Its very name conjures up images of fetid sweatshops and sulfurous mills where long working hours and physical exhaustion broke the health of men, women, and children; of urban slums and overcrowded tenements rotten with disease; and, finally, of emaciated, ghostlike wretches, feverish with infection, gasping for breath, coughing up mouthfuls of blood, and staring hollow-eyed into space waiting for death.

In a sense, TB mirrors the complexity of the industrial revolution, for just as the transformation of the economy was multifaceted, TB is not one but many diseases. TB is merely the generic name for a host of infections caused by tubercle bacilli, isolated in 1882 by Robert Koch, the famous German scientist. The most common (and most feared) is pulmonary tuberculosis, a chronic, debilitating disease of the lungs; it can kill its victims in a few months but usually requires several years to complete the task. Other common forms of the disease include meningeal TB, which produces an inflammation of the membranes surrounding the brain; TB of the spine, which causes a hunchback deformity of the spine; lupus,

TB of the skin; and miliary TB, a generalized infection that occurs when the tubercle bacilli are distributed by the bloodstream throughout the body, producing small nodules on most organs.

Because the term *tuberculosis* did not appear in print until around 1840, most Americans knew the disease as consumption, which seemed the perfect metaphor since victims of the disease gradually wasted away from debilitating fever, weight loss, night sweats, chronic cough, and copious sputum decorated toward the end with the bright red blood spots that denoted advanced pulmonary tuberculosis.

In less polite society, consumptives were called *lungers,* a term of derision. Throughout the nineteenth century, many people associated TB with poverty and attached a social stigma to the dis-

ease. Others believed that TB was caused by some hereditary defect; for them, the perplexing problem was why the disease hit some families harder than others. In Ralph Waldo Emerson's family, for example, he and three of his brothers suffered from the disease, while his fellow transcendentalist, Henry David Thoreau, lost his father, a sister, and a grandfather to TB before dying from the disease himself.

Paradoxically, despite its dreadful symptoms and terrifying ability to wipe out entire families, TB was romanticized on both sides of the Atlantic. For many writers, it became a metaphor for comparing decay in nature to disease in man. Thus, Henry Thoreau, upon seeing the first splashes of red in the green maple leaves of autumn, could write in 1852 in his *Journal Intime:* "Decay and disease are often beau-

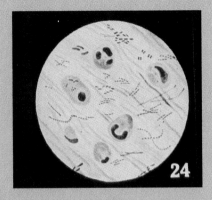

tiful, like . . . the hectic glow of consumption."

In fact, the Age of Romanticism's much heralded "doom and gloom" may have derived at least in part from the sadness and melancholy caused by the deaths of loved ones from TB—especially the death of young adults, for whom the disease had a special affinity. John Keats, the quintessential romantic poet, succumbed to TB at 26; Emily Brontë, author of the powerful *Wuthering Heights,* was cut down tragically at 30. The novels of the day, Charles Dickens's *David Copperfield,* for one, are positively littered with the corpses of people killed in the bloom of youth by the "White Plague."

The disease also broke its share of hearts in the theater and at the opera. Alexander Dumas lamented the death from TB of a beautiful heroine in *La Dame aux Camelias,* which in its English translation became the play, *Camille, or the Fate of a Coquette,* later adapted by Verdi for the opera as *La Traviata.* An identical fate befell the heroine in the play, *La Bohème,* which inspired Puccini's opera of the same name.

Under the spell of this heart-wrenching romanticism, writers, poets, and artists created a new and profoundly twisted ideal of feminine beauty: the dying angel, smitten by consumption, whose physical appeal was somehow enhanced by her malady. One gravely ill woman confided to her diary, "I cough continually! But for a wonder, far from making me look ugly, this gives me an air of languor that is very becoming." As depicted by writers, the dying female consumptive was, to her fingertips, an exquisitely fragile creature, the very embodiment of both the romantic and the Victorian ideal of frail feminine beauty. Her languid pallor was rendered even more pale by the generous application of whitening powders; and her slender body, with its swanlike neck and elongated limbs, was adorned in thin, sheer white clothing of cotton or linen, giving her an ethereal quality, as a spirit not quite of this earth.

Numerous artists struggled to capture this image on canvas, including Gabriel Rossetti of the Pre-Raphaelite school, who idealized tall, slender women "with cadaverous bodies and sensual mouths." Reducing this image to a word portrait, Henry James described Janet Burden, one of the leading Pre-Raphaelite models, as "strange, pale, livid, gaunt, silent, and yet in a manner graceful and picturesque." To another observer the same woman looked "as if she had walked out of an Egyptian tomb at Luxor."

As the nineteenth century drew to a close, however, the romantic view of life gradually lost its hold on the public's imagination. Instead of celebrating TB, writers, joined by health reformers, saw TB through the lens of realism. They linked the disease to poverty, unsafe working conditions, overcrowded housing, poor diet, and the failure of government to safeguard the public's health. Rather than glorifying consumptives, this change in attitude depicted them as the victims of a cruel, punishing illness. TB was no longer something to spark the artistic imagination; it was now a microbial insult to mankind and an indictment against the society that tolerated it.

of its report closed dozens of marginal medical schools, several of which trained minority doctors. Professionalization thus reduced the number of practitioners. Although this did help weed out incompetents, it also increased the incomes of the remaining practitioners and often reduced minority participation. Order, stability, and improved standards came at the cost of decreased opportunity for some.

Given the religious bent of progressive thought, a number of church-related organizations also arose. One of the most important was the Federal Council of Churches of Christ in America. Founded in 1908, it was an interdenominational group that advocated safer working conditions, the abolition of child labor, shorter workweeks, higher wages, workmen's compensation, old-age pensions, and "the most equitable division of the products of industry that can ultimately be devised."

To a large extent, middle-class women led in the organization of reform. Technology and domestic help lessened the burdens of running a home for these women, but a stigma remained on paid employment. Women's clubs provided an outlet for the energies and abilities of many competent and educated women. Local organizations flourished and in 1890 joined to form the General Federation of Women's Clubs. In the next two decades, reform groups founded and led mainly by women sprang up.

The majority of activist, middle-class women became involved in movements closely linked to their assigned social roles as guardians of morality and nurturers of the family. Many worked through such religious groups as the Young Women's Christian Association. Numerous others joined in a resurgence of prohibitionism. The Woman's Christian Temperance Union, led by Frances Willard, revived a flagging prohibition movement and by 1898 had 10,000 local branches. It was assisted by the Anti-Saloon League (organized in 1893) and such church organizations as the Temperance Society of the Methodist Episcopal church.

Some of the prohibitionists were Protestant fundamentalists who considered the consumption of alcohol a sin; others were concerned with its social impact. Urban reformers constantly saw the consequences of alcohol abuse in domestic violence, accidents, and pauperism. Alcohol was the root of so many social problems that to ignore it was like "bailing water out of a tub with the tap turned on; letting the . . . liquor traffic run full blast while we limply stood around and picked up the wreckage." The physically devastating effects of alcoholism were reported by the AMA. Many in the Anti-Saloon League were also dismayed by the part played by drinking establishments in machine politics.

The idea of legislating morality for the good of society spilled over into the sexual sphere. A major area of concern was prostitution, and its opponents had a variety of motivations. Some stressed its role in the spread of venereal disease; others deplored the exploitation of women and the double standard that allowed only men sexual freedom. For some it was morally wrong; to others it was just one more social evil—a product of environment rather than original sin. Many linked it with immigration as they did alcohol abuse. The crusade against this age-old problem had deep roots, but at the turn of the century it followed a typically progressive path. Muckraking journalists enraged the public with lurid accounts of "white slavery" rings that kidnapped young women and forced them into prostitution. The next step was to pressure local governments to establish commissions to study the issue. Most reports stressed the economic roots. One prostitute asked an investigator, "Do you suppose I am going back to earn five or six dollars a week in a factory, when I can earn that amount any night and often much more?"

Some people believed prostitution was merely a symptom of a larger disease, and they became "purity crusaders." Dr. Will K. Kellogg wrote "The exorbitant demands of the sexual appetites encountered among civilized people are not the result of a normal instinct, but are due to the incitements of an abnormally stimulating diet, including alcohol, the seduction of prurient literature and so-called art, and the temptations of impure associations." After a national Purity Congress in 1895, the purity crusaders lobbied not only for the prohibition of alcohol and prostitution but also for such things as censorship and the regulation of narcotics.

Progressive social reform had two aims: control and justice. Women were deeply involved in social justice as well as control movements like prohibition. Middle-class women had long dominated humanitarian work, but during the 1890s their work took on a new aggressiveness. Women came to believe that aid to the poor was an inadequate response to society's ills; they wanted to attack the causes of poverty. They sought to improve wages and working conditions, especially for women, and to protect children from exploitation. To this end, they started several organizations. The National Consumers League, led by former Illinois factory inspector Florence Kelly, lobbied for protective legislation for women and children as well as better working and living conditions for all. Kelly became a leading advocate of child labor laws and was joined in this cause by Alabama clergyman Edgar Gardner Murphy, who proposed the formation of the National Child Labor Committee in 1904. Like most progressives, child labor reformers gathered data and photographs to document horrors for legislators at the local, state, and finally federal level.

African-American women were among the most active of the reformers. The growing black middle class produced increasing numbers of educated women. Unlike their white counterparts, most engaged in paid employment. More than financial need alleviated the stigma of employment for African-American women. They were expected to play a larger role in society. Journalist Lucy Wilmot Smith explained that although the white woman "has had to contest with her brother every inch of the ground for recognition; the Negro man, having had his sister by his side on plantations and in rice swamps, keeps her there, now that he moves in other spheres." In addition to working, black women engaged in reform. Ida B. Wells (later Wells-Barnett) launched an antilynching campaign that resulted in the expulsion of both her and her newspaper, the *Free Speech,* from Memphis, Tennessee, in 1893. In 1895 she joined with other clubwomen to form what became the National Association of Colored Women.

Some reformers were not content to be merely advocates for the poor and the weak; they wanted to become directly involved with such people to educate and organize them to help themselves. Here again middle-class women played a key role. Foremost among such activities was the settlement house movement. Following the lead of Jane Addams of Hull House in Chicago, many young college-educated women moved into slum neighborhoods to live and work with those they sought to help. "From the first," Addams wrote, "it seemed understood that we were ready to perform the humblest neighborhood services. We were asked to wash the newborn babies, and to prepare the dead for burial, to nurse the sick, and to 'mind the children.' "

More than unselfishness motivated such women. One worker confessed that settlement houses gratified her "thirst to know how the other half lives." Some educated women wanted more freedom than marriage and part-time volunteer work seemed to offer. One appeal of settlement work was that men did not control it. A result was a growing social feminism that cut across class lines. An example was the founding of the National Women's

Alarmed by the unhealthy child-care practices of many immigrants, visiting nurses went to immigrant homes to teach such things as the proper bathing of babies.

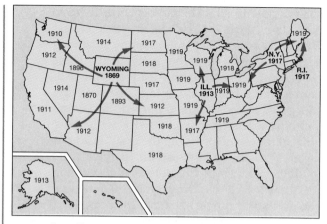

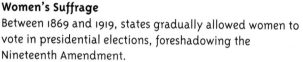

Women's Suffrage

Between 1869 and 1919, states gradually allowed women to vote in presidential elections, foreshadowing the Nineteenth Amendment.

Trade Union League in 1905. Through it, wealthy supporters organized women workers, joined their strikes, and trained leaders.

At first such activity seemed to draw attention away from the suffrage movement. Women's roles in progressive reforms, however, did eventually convince many people that women not only deserved the right to vote but also that their political participation would be socially beneficial. Jane Addams asserted, "If women have in any sense been responsible for the gentler side of life which softens and blurs some of its harsher conditions may they not have a duty to perform in our American cities?" Arguments based on women's "special role," however, cut both ways. In articles with such titles as "Famed Biologist's Warning on the Peril in Votes to Women," writers charged that voting was so "unnatural" for women that pregnant women would miscarry and nursing mothers' milk would cease to flow. As during the fight for ratification of the Equal Rights Amendment in the 1970s, not all opponents were male. Mrs. A. J. George of the National Association Opposed to Woman Suffrage declared, "The Woman-suffrage movement is an imitation-of-man movement, and as such, merits the condemnation of every normal man and woman."

In the face of such opposition, suffragists began to escalate their demands for the vote.

Many became convinced that only national action would be effective. Thus the National American Woman Suffrage Association, led by Carrie Chapman Catt after 1915, began a broad-based campaign for an amendment to the U.S. Constitution. More militant women followed the young Quaker, Alice Paul, who founded the National Woman's party in 1914. She preferred the tactics of British suffragists who had picketed, gone on hunger strikes, and actively confronted both politicians and police.

Another group in the social justice movement sought to improve relations between blacks and whites. White Southerners had continued to devise forms of racial control to replace slavery. Their solution became a three-legged stool: legal segregation, disfranchisement, and violence. From the beginning, African Americans resisted white efforts to suppress them. In city after city, they utilized every tool and tactic that would prove successful in the 1960s. They marched, they lobbied legislative bodies, they petitioned, they challenged discriminatory legislation in courts, and they boycotted segregated streetcars. Under the leadership of Booker T. Washington, they also tried conciliation. Nothing stemmed the rising tide of racism.

As conditions worsened Washington seemed to grow even more accommodating, at least in public. His influence with white politicians and philanthropists as well as his control of much of the black press gave him incredible power, which he used ruthlessly on occasion. Behind the scenes, he supported protest activities, using code names and secret funds. Educated African Americans, however, became increasingly disenchanted with his public performance. They also resented his suppression of dissent by fellow blacks. The so-called anti-Bookerite radicals found their spokesperson in W.E.B. Du Bois. Unlike Washington, who had been born into slavery and educated at an industrial school, Du Bois was born to free parents in Massachusetts and became the first African American to receive a doctorate from Harvard.

Gifted with staggering intellectual brilliance, Du Bois expressed the frustrations and dreams of his fellow blacks in *The Souls of Black Folks* (1903). Of being black in America, he wrote, "one ever feels his twoness—an American, a Negro, two souls, two thoughts, two unreconciled strivings, two warring ideals in one dark body." In that book he also penned a polite but devastating critique of Washington's leadership. He objected to Washington's failure to recognize the importance of the vote, his emphasis on industrial education at the expense of higher education, his reluctance to criticize as well as praise white actions, and his willingness to give up previously won rights.

Relations between the two men deteriorated steadily after 1903, even though only immediate methods and not ultimate goals separated them. Both wanted the full acceptance of African Americans as first-class citizens. To Washington, the best route was self-help and educating the masses. To these ends, he made Tuskegee Institute into an impressive institution staffed entirely by blacks. Du Bois, on the other hand, was more integrationist and believed the key to black advance-

ment was in cultivating what he called the "Talented Tenth." To him, more of the limited education funds should go to train the ablest 10 percent of African Americans for leadership through liberal arts and professional schooling. Although most African Americans saw value in both approaches, the dispute became bitter and divisive.

In 1905 Du Bois joined William Monroe Trotter in forming the Niagara Movement, an organization devoted to two main objectives: opposition to Washington's leadership and demands for "full manhood rights." Only about 50 educated African-American men— mainly Northerners—joined, and the movement struggled to exist in the face of unrelenting sabotage by Washington. It played an important role, however, in convincing northern white progressives that an alternative to Washington was desirable. When a white mob in Springfield, Illinois, went on a rampage against African Americans, concerned whites joined with Du Bois and Ida B. Wells to

Women employed a variety of tactics in their fight for the vote. Here Dr. Anne Shaw and Carrie Chapman Catt lead 20,000 marchers down Fifth Avenue in New York City.

found the National Association for the Advancement of Colored People (NAACP) in 1909. At first the group was led and dominated by whites; Du Bois was the only African American to hold a responsible position, as editor of its journal *The Crisis*. The organization became more black over time, but the focus of its activities remained essentially the same: education and propaganda, court challenges to discrimination, and lobbying for such legislation as a federal antilynching law.

Immigration policy became another source of organizational activity. The American Protective Association (1887) sought to control and limit the access of the "teeming masses yearning to breathe free." Members lobbied for literacy tests and quotas. One described a boatload of immigrants, saying "in every face there was something wrong—lips thick, mouth coarse, upper lip too long, cheek bones too high, chin poorly formed, the bridge of the nose hollowed, the base of the nose tilted, or else the whole face prognathous." While many Americans recoiled from the nation's pluralistic nature, others welcomed it. One wrote, "our dream of the United States ought not to be a dream of monotony," but instead an "orchestration of mankind." Thus some progressives formed the North American League for Immigrants to "protect the newcomers from unscrupulous bankers, steamship captains and fellow countrymen."

Although most were middle class, progressives came from all classes, and within classes there was a diversity of responses to the changes at the turn of the century. Many businesspeople organized to fight regulatory and labor legislation in such groups as the National Association of Manufacturers and the American Anti-Boycott Association. Others, however, joined such moderate reform groups as the Reform Municipal Voters League and the Chamber of Commerce. Some viewed labor unionism as more desirable than government regulation. The National Civic Federation was founded in 1901 with wealthy Republican politician Mark Hanna as president and labor leader Samuel Gompers as vice president. The group accepted unionization and sought to bring together employers, employees, and the general public to discuss industrial problems.

The drive to organize pervaded all of society, creating such diverse groups as the Boy Scouts of America (1910), the Rotary Club (1915), the National Collegiate Athletic Association (1906), the National Birth Control League (1915), and even the Aero Club of America (1905) to popularize "ballooning as a sport, especially among the more wealthy class." Americans came to believe in cooperative efforts to reach goals. In unprecedented numbers they also began to look to government for answers—starting at the city level and moving up to Washington.

W.E.B. Du Bois, shown here in the editorial offices of *The Crisis* at the New York headquarters of the NAACP, was at first the only African American to hold a significant office in the organization.

Urban Beginnings

Progressivism was a response to emerging problems and confronted the most visible ones, many of which were found in the cities. Incredibly rapid increases in urban populations outpaced the ability of "small-town" governments to meet the challenges. Political machines provided needed services but came under attack in the 1890s as inefficient and corrupt. Progressivism began to emerge in cities even while most attention was still focused on the rural-based Populists. Middle- and upper-class reformers demanded that governments operate "on a strict business basis" and be run "not by partisans, [n]either Republican nor Democratic, but by men who are skilled in business management and social service."

Urban reformers' victories included the secret ballot and voter registration in some cities. Then in 1900, a model for efficient, nonpartisan city government emerged from the chaos created when a devastating hurricane killed more than 6000 people in Galveston, Texas. Local government broke down and the state legislature appointed a five-man commission to run the city. The idea had spread to over 400 cities by World War I. A refinement was added in 1913, when in the wake of a disastrous flood, the government of Dayton, Ohio, hired a city manager to run the city on a day-to-day basis.

The cost of efficiency was decreased democracy. Indeed, some urban reformers were openly antidemocratic. One wrote in 1901, "Ignorance should be excluded from control. City business should be carried on by trained experts selected on some other principle than popular suffrage." The ward system, under which aldermen were elected by district, was seen as a problem because, as a Chicago businessman noted in 1911, "Men of successful experience and ability large enough to do justice to public affairs will seldom live and bring up families in the poorer wards." The reformers naively sought to take politics out of government, but by "politics" they often meant the voice of people not like themselves. Nevertheless, these goals contradicted broader support for democracy, and by 1914 most city commissioners were required to run for election—although often, in at-large elections rather than by district.

Middle-class progressives sometimes found their will thwarted by lower-class voters. Breaking up urban machines often destroyed the informal welfare networks that met the needs of the poor. When that happened, the poor rejected the new efficiency. In 1901, the Tammany Hall machine recaptured New York with the campaign slogan "To hell with reform." Poor immigrants did not accept that their ignorance and "foreign ways" were at the root of urban problems. "It is not so much the under crust," one declared, "as the upper crust that endangers the interests of the people."

In a number of cities, voters elected mayors who sympathized with working-class desires. Tom L. Johnson, elected mayor of Cleveland in 1901, rejected efforts to impose middle-class morality on the poor. "I am not trying to enforce Christianity," he proclaimed, "only make it possible." To this end he expanded social services and brought about the public ownership of the waterworks, gas and electric utilities, and public transportation, thereby reducing their costs to the poor. After his election in 1899, Mayor Samuel "Golden Rule" Jones sought to establish the "Cooperative Commonwealth, the Kingdom of Heaven on Earth," in Toledo, Ohio. Until his death in 1904, he worked to provide free kindergartens, free playgrounds, free golf courses, and free concerts. He also reformed the police department, substituting light canes for the heavy clubs carried by patrolmen and prohibiting the jailing of people without charges. He made some powerful enemies and once declared, "Everyone is against me but the people." Most urban liberals depended on working-class voters.

The move toward public ownership of utilities was most avidly supported by the Socialists, who showed growing strength on the local level. In 1910 a Socialist was elected mayor of Milwaukee, and in the next year 70 other socialists were elected in towns and cities across the nation. By 1912 about 1000 held offices in 33 states and 160 cities. Their rising power, however, helped trigger a backlash by middle-class voters, who favored regulatory commissions to public ownership of utilities.

Urban progressivism was obviously not a coherent, unified movement. Different groups at different times succeeded in different cities. Social services were cut to lower business taxes in some cities and expanded in others. In most cities the evils of overcrowded, unhealthy tenements were attacked with varying degrees of success with such measures as building codes. By the turn of the century, however, more and more people began to look to the states to solve problems.

Reform Reaches the State Level

Regardless of their objectives, many urban reformers eventually dabbled in state politics. The city had little power and the federal government seemed too remote. Thus the states became major battlegrounds for reform. The form and leadership of state progressivism were as diverse and complex as urban progressivism. In the South, most progressives worked through the Democratic party; in the Midwest and on the Pacific Coast, progressives captured the Republican party. In the industrial Northeast, progressives emerged in both major parties, but the Democrats were the more successful. In some cases progressive governors, such as Al Smith of New York, were the products of urban machines that embraced reform to hold onto their electorates. Others, such as Robert La Follette of Wisconsin, were Republican regulars who bypassed party leaders to ride reform to power. In the South, reform governors were elected by startlingly diverse constituencies. In Mississippi, small-town lawyer and editor James K. Vardaman was elected by poor farmers, the "redneck" vote. In Georgia, the urban middle class was the main support of Hoke Smith, publisher of the *Atlanta Journal.*

State progressives pursued four major goals: (1) providing "direct democracy," (2) protecting the public by regulating the economy, (3) increasing state services, and (4) establishing social control. Reformers passed many laws, but the impact of legislation was not always what they expected. One progressive creed was dramatically stated by writer and journalist William Allen White: "The voice of the people is indeed the will of God." By World War I many states had adopted political procedures designed to give the people a more direct say in running the government. An initiative allowed voters to propose legislative changes, usually by petition; a referendum gave the public a mechanism for voting directly on controversial legislation; recall provided a way to remove elected officials. Many states also established direct primaries. Other states adopted measures to cleanse electoral procedures, including the secret ballot, voter registration, and corrupt practices legislation. The drive for direct democracy culminated in the Seventeenth Amendment to the Constitution (1913), which substituted the popular election of senators for their election by state legislatures.

The victories of women suffragists at the state level also expanded democracy—especially in the West. In that region the relatively barren environment and the frontier conditions endured by early settlers caused husbands and wives to work together as partners to survive. The Anglo conflict with existing Hispanic and Native American cultures may have also fostered a unity that created more equality. At any rate, Washington state gave women the vote in 1910. California did so the next year, and four other western states had followed suit by 1916. That year Jeannette Rankin was elected to Congress from Montana. These victories encouraged efforts to obtain a constitutional amendment allowing women to vote.

Progressive actions by states to protect the public and regulate the economy took many forms. In the West the emphasis was on regulating railroads and utilities, reflecting the region's Populist heritage. The region was also especially vulnerable to rate discrimination because of its remoteness and the long distances to markets. Legislatures created commissions to regulate the rates charged by both railroads and utilities. At the same time, taxes on corporations were increased. For example, after La Follette's election as governor of Wisconsin in 1900, state revenues from taxes on railroads grew from $1.9 million to $3.4 million.

In the industrialized states, workmen's compensation became a major goal. Horror stories about industrial accidents had long abounded, and muckrakers further inflamed the public. Then in 1911 a major tragedy chilled the hearts of Americans. A fire broke out at the Triangle Shirtwaist Company in New York just 30 minutes before closing time. The doors were locked to prevent the women who worked there from leaving early, and many fire escape ladders were either broken

Born on a Montana ranch in 1880 and a 1902 graduate of the University of Montana, Jeannette Rankin was elected to Congress in 1916.

or missing. By the time the flames were doused, 147 workers, mainly women and girls, had lost their lives—47 had jumped to their deaths, littering the street with bodies. The Triangle fire was the worst example of escalating industrial accidents. The only recourse for most maimed workers or their widowed spouses was to sue the company, which for many was not a realistic option. Some did get large settlements, however, which represented an unpredictable cost to businesses. Gradually, the idea of mandatory insurance grew in popularity, with the support of many factory owners. Between 1910 and 1916, 32 states enacted workmen's compensation laws.

The work of the National Child Labor Committee and other organizations moved states to legislate protection for women and children. Progressives gathered evidence of the harm done to both by long working hours and unsafe, unhealthy conditions. State action was necessary, they argued, for two reasons: Women and children could not protect themselves and the nation's future depended on the health of both. By 1916, 32 states had laws regulating the hours worked by women and children, 11 had specified minimum wages for women, and every state regulated child labor in some manner. Other protective legislation included building and sanitary codes, which benefited all workers.

A number of states also expanded social services. Because of lobbying by settlement house workers, by 1914 some 20 states had provided mother's pensions to widows or abandoned wives with dependent children. The sums paid were meager, however, ranging from $2 to $15 a month for the first child and lesser amounts for the rest. Funding for education also increased. A major area of reform was the expansion of compulsory education to the high school level. Support often came from businesses, which saw public education as a means of preparing individuals for life in an industrial society. As a result, very few public schools were modeled on John Dewey's progressive educational doctrines. Instead of promoting personal development, education, in the industrialists' minds, should inculcate discipline and punctuality. Hence school bells trained one for factory whistles and letter grades taught the value of individual initiative. Governments also made school organization more businesslike, with increased power given to school superintendents and principals, who were expected to be trained in management techniques.

The flip side of state social justice legislation was increased efforts at social control. Prohibitionists won many victories in the states, especially in the South. That region provided fertile soil for prohibitionists because of the strength of Protestant fundamentalism and the so-called race problem. One southern prohibitionist argued that African Americans were "a child race in the South, and if drunkenness causes three-fourths of the crime ascribed to it, whiskey must be taken out of the Negro's hands," and that it was the duty "of the stronger race to forego its own personal liberty for the protection of the weaker race." Between 1907 and 1909 Georgia, Mississippi, North Carolina, Tennessee, and Alabama adopted state prohibition; 14 other states had joined them by 1916.

The move toward social control infected all regions. Between 1907 and 1917, 16 states passed laws authorizing sterilization of various categories of allegedly unfit individuals. Social control measures were usually directed at minorities, so the South naturally offered the most extreme examples, but California progressives excluded Asians almost as ruthlessly. Southern whites trumpeted segregation as a reform, and they had the approval of many northern progressives. Even race relations muckraker Ray Stannard Baker wrote, "As for the Jim Crow laws in the South, many of them, at least, are at present necessary to avoid clashes between the ignorant of both races." Segregation was often enacted under progressive governors—a paradox only if the general progressive tendency toward social control is ignored.

In most ways, southern progressivism was for whites only. Increased school funding was common, but the bulk went to educating white children. The discrepancies between the amounts spent accelerated, making even more of a lie of the *Plessy* v. *Ferguson* (1896) formula of "separate but equal" facilities. In 1919 southern states spent an average of $12.16 per white student and $3.29 per black student. Racism remained a potent force. As governor of Mississippi from 1903 to 1907, James K. Vardaman pursued progressive reforms in such areas as convict-lease (a system by which states rented out their prisoners to private interests to provide a cheap labor source), school funding, and railroad regulation. At the same time he defended lynching, saying "We would be justified in slaughtering every Ethiopian on earth to preserve unsullied the honor of one Caucasian home."

The legacy of progressivism in the states was mixed, as were the motives of reformers. Regardless of their goals, most came to look to the federal government for help. One reformer expressed their frustration. "When I was in the city council . . . fighting for a shorter work day, [my opponents] told me to go to the legislature; now [my fellow legislators] tell me to go to Congress for a national law. When I get there and demand it, they will tell me to go to hell."

PROGRESSIVISM MOVES TO THE NATIONAL LEVEL

When McKinley was reelected in 1900, few expected a national reform leader, and but for a quirk of fate they would have been right. As the 1900 Republican convention rolled around, party leaders realized they had a problem. Theodore Roosevelt had become a national hero in the wake of the Spanish-American War, but he had angered party regulars by supporting regulatory legislation as governor of New York. When they decided to "bury" Roosevelt in the vice presidency, presidential adviser and politician Mark Hanna warned, "Don't you realize that there's only one life between that madman and the White House?" On September 6, 1901, anarchist Leon Czolgosz shot McKinley. Eight days later that one life was gone, and Roosevelt was president. It was not immediately apparent, however, that he would usher in reform. Many remembered that during the Pullman strike Roosevelt had suggested shooting the strikers. Most therefore did not expect the action he took in the 1902 coal strike. That year, however, became the first in a decade and a half of snowballing reform that would result in a massive amount of legislation and four constitutional amendments by 1920.

Roosevelt and New Attitudes Toward Government Power

Roosevelt became the most forceful president since Abraham Lincoln, but few men have looked or sounded less presidential. He was short, nearsighted, beaver-toothed, and talked in a high-pitched voice. A frail, asthmatic child, he seemed intent on proving his manliness from childhood on. His life became a robust adventure of sports, hunting, and camping. Once while president he took a foreign diplomat skinny-dipping in the Potomac. His exuberance, vitality, and wit captivated most Americans. They called him "Teddy" and named a stuffed bear after him. To understand him, an observer declared, one had to remember "the president is really only six years old." He was not a simple man, however. His hobbies included writing history books, and he displayed a keen intellect that he had honed at Harvard.

Born into an aristocratic Dutch family in New York, Roosevelt rejected a leisurely life for the rough and tumble world of politics, which his friends declared was an occupation for saloonkeepers and such. "I answered," he wrote in his autobiography, "that if this were so it merely meant that the people I knew did not belong to the governing class, and that I intended to be one of the governing class." His privileged background made him an unlikely candidate for a reformer, yet he ended up making reform both fun and respectable. He saw himself as a conservative but declared, "The only true conservative is the man who resolutely sets his face toward the future." To preserve what was vital, one had to reform. The conservatives of his time, however, rejected his call for change and continued to insist on laissez-faire policies and limited government.

Roosevelt, on the other hand, shared two progressive sentiments. One was that government should be efficiently run by able, competent people. The other was that industrialization had created the need for expanded governmental action. "A simple and poor society," he observed, "can exist as a democracy on the basis of sheer individualism. But a rich and complex society cannot so exist." As a result of these two sentiments, Roosevelt reorganized and revitalized the executive branch, modernized the army command structure and the consular service, and pursued the federal regulation of the economy that has characterized twentieth-century America.

Although he was later remembered more for his "trust-busting" and "Square Deal," Roosevelt considered conservation his greatest domestic accomplishment. It was the topic of his first presidential address. "We are prone to think of the resources of this country as inexhaustible, this is not so," he later warned Congress. Roosevelt used presidential

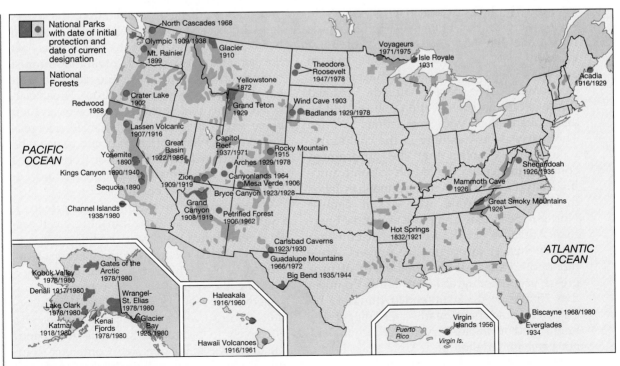

National Parks and Forests

Under the presidency of Theodore Roosevelt, who considered conservation his most important domestic achievement, millions of acres of land were set aside for national parks and forests.

power to add almost 150 million acres to national forests and to preserve valuable coal and water sites for national development. With his ally, Chief Forester Gifford Pinchot, he sponsored a National Conservation Congress in 1908. Roosevelt's actions won both praise and condemnation.

The conservation movement, then as well as later, divided into two camps. Naturalist John Muir and the Sierra Club (formed in 1892) wanted to preserve the scenic beauty and biological diversity of the West. Most businesspeople and Westerners wanted government action only to promote orderly economic exploitation of resources. In 1902 they supported the Newlands Reclamation Act, which began many years of federally sponsored irrigation and reclamation projects (for details of this and other federal legislation see Table 21.1). Furious, however, about the withdrawal from sale of so many acres of federal land, they led a move to limit presidential authority to do so. Western and business influences usually prevailed in such disputes. For the West a scarcity of water was the main ecological problem, and its solution was a regional priority. In 1913 the city of San Francisco won a dispute over a dam that had flooded one of the most beautiful areas of Yosemite National Park in order to solve the city's water shortage.

Some businesspeople already disliked Roosevelt for his conservation policies, but he aggravated others with two actions in 1902. The first was his handling of the coal strike, which served notice that the government could no longer be counted on to come automatically to the aid of management in labor disputes. The second was a suit against Northern Securities Company under the Sherman Antitrust Act. Roosevelt's trust-busting was an answer to progressive prayers. Antimonopoly was a strong component of progressivism. Most agreed with Louis Brandeis that "if the Lord had intended things to be big, he would have made men bigger—in brains and character." Antitrust action had not been undertaken on a large scale in the cities and states only because federal action seemed necessary.

Northern Securities, a highly unpopular combination of northwestern railroad systems

engineered by such heavyweights as James J. Hill and J. P. Morgan, was a wise choice for action. Its unpopularity reflected the West's concern for railroad regulation. The suit infuriated Hill, who complained, "It seems hard that we should be compelled to fight for our lives against the political adventurers who have never done anything but pose and draw a salary." In 1904 the Supreme Court ordered the company's dissolution. That same year, in a case against the major meat packers, the Court also reversed the *E. C. Knight* ruling that exempted manufacturing from federal antitrust law.

The rulings pleased Roosevelt, who rejected the Court's earlier narrow, strict interpretations of the Constitution. Instead, he believed that the Constitution "must be interpreted not as a straight-jacket . . . but as an instrument designed for the life and healthy growth of the Nation." In his desire to expand federal power, he was once credited with asking "What's the Constitution between friends?" Yet Roosevelt was not a complete convert to trust-busting.

"This is an age of combination," he wrote, "and any effort to prevent all combination will be not only useless, but in the end vicious." At the same time he believed "of all the forms of tyranny the least attractive and the most vulgar is the tyranny of mere wealth." Thus he attacked trusts that abused their power and left alone trusts that acted responsibly. He preferred to negotiate differences, and to do so he established in 1904 a Bureau of Corporations within the Department of Commerce and Labor, created the year before.

Campaigning on the promise to provide a "Square Deal" to all Americans, Roosevelt easily defeated the Democratic candidate Alton B. Parker in the 1904 presidential election. Now elected in his own right, he launched into expanding the regulatory power of the federal government. His top priority, over the objections of conservative Republican senators, was effectively to control the railroads by expanding the power of the Interstate Commerce Commission (ICC). Although the Elkins Act, passed in 1903, had already eliminated rebates, Roosevelt wanted to go further and give the ICC the power to set rates. Through shrewd politi-

Table 21.1 PROGRESSIVE ERA LEGISLATION AND AMENDMENTS

Year	Act	Provisions
1902	Newlands Reclamation	Set aside proceeds from the sale of federal land for irrigation and reclamation projects
1903	Elkins	Outlawed rebates to favored shippers; federal courts could issue injunctions to stop rate discrimination
1906	Pure Food and Drug	Made it a crime to sell adulterated foods or medicine; required correct labeling of the contents of certain substances
1906	Meat Inspection	Required governmental approval of sanitary conditions in meat-packing plants; prohibited use of dangerous chemicals or preservatives; government paid inspection costs
1906	Hepburn	Gave ICC the power to set railroad rates, subject to court review
1909	Payne-Aldrich Tariff	Raised most tariff rates, while reducing or eliminating the rates for very few products
1910	Mann-Elkins	Extended jurisdiction of the ICC to telephone & telegraph companies; gave ICC further power to suspend rate increases; rulings were still subject to court review
1910	Mann	Outlawed the transportation of women across state lines for "immoral purposes"
1913	Sixteenth Amendment	Gave Congress the right to impose an income tax
1913	Seventeenth Amendment	Provided for the direct election of senators by the people rather than by state legislatures
1913	Underwood-Simmons Tariff	Substantially reduced tariff rates; levied an income tax rising from 1 percent on incomes over $4000 to 4 percent on incomes over $100,00
1913	Federal Reserve	Reformed the banking and currency system; created 12 regional banks that were privately owned but responsible to the Federal Reserve Board, which was appointed by the president; the Board had the ability to regulate the amount of currency (federal reserve notes) through its transactions with the regional banks
1914	Federal Trade Commission	Created FTC, composed of 5 members, to oversee business transactions; could publicize infractions and issue cease and desist orders, which were subject to court review
1914	Clayton Antitrust	Outlawed unfair business practices that reduced competition; held company officials liable for actions; specifically exempted farm and labor groups from its provisions, limited the use of court injunctions against strikers
1914	Harrison Anti-Narcotic	Listed "controlled substances" that could only be sold with a doctor's prescription; required manufacturers to keep records of the manufacture and sale of such substances
1916	Federal Farm Loan	Provided farmers with cheap credit through 12 farm loan boards
1916	Keating-Owen	Outlawed the sale of goods made by children from interstate commerce
1916	Adamson	Provided for an eight-hour workday for workers on interstate railroads
1916	Workman's Compensation	Established a workmen's compensation system for federal employees

cal maneuvering he got this with the Hepburn Act of 1906, although he had to give up his demand for limited court review of rate decisions.

The publication of Upton Sinclair's *The Jungle* in that same year caused a consumer uproar for regulation of the food and drug industries. A chemist in the Agriculture Department, Harvey W. Wiley had long been analyzing food products for chemical adulteration by testing additives on volunteers known as the "Poison Squad." His data were supplemented by an investigation of the meat-packing industry ordered by Roosevelt, which proved the truth of Sinclair's charges of filth and contamination. As a result, Congress passed the Pure Food and Drug Act and the Meat Inspection Act on the same day in 1906. By 1908 Roosevelt had left his indelible mark on the nation and decided not to run for reelection. He cast his support to William Howard Taft, who easily defeated William Jennings Bryan, the Democratic nominee and loser for the third time. Roosevelt then retired and went to hunt lions in Africa, a move that led J. P. Morgan to toast "Health to the Lions."

Taft and Quiet Progressivism

William Howard Taft brought to the presidency a distinguished record of public service.

An Ohio lawyer, he had served as a federal judge, the first civil governor of the Philippines, and secretary of war. He did not, however, look presidential; he weighed more than 350 pounds, which led to rumors that a special bathtub was to be installed in the White House. Unlike his predecessor, he was far from charismatic and indeed quite shy. Legalistic and precise, he was neither a fiery writer nor speaker. In short, he was incapable of rallying public support for any cause, and reformers were especially skeptical about him. As a judge he had been called the "injunction standard bearer" by labor leaders. When soldiers shot into the crowd at the Haymarket riot, he confided, "they have only killed six as yet. This is hardly enough to make an impression."

Taft was indeed more conservative than Roosevelt, especially in his view of governmental power. "The lesson must be learned," he argued, "that there is only a limited zone within which legislation and governments can accomplish good." Further, he declared, "We can, by passing laws which cannot be enforced, destroy that respect for laws . . . which has been the strength of people of English descent everywhere." On the other hand, his respect for the law extended to the Sherman act. "We are going to enforce that law or die in the attempt," he promised, and his administration prosecuted far more cases than Roosevelt's had.

Without federal regulation, meat packers exploited workers and allowed rats and other contaminants to be processed with meat in making sausages.

At his inauguration in 1909, William Howard Taft did not realize the challenges he would face in Congress from a divided Republican party.

In his own quiet way Taft was as sympathetic to reform as Roosevelt. He supported the eight-hour workday and favored legislation to improve mine safety. He also urged passage of the Mann-Elkins Act of 1910 to increase the power of the ICC. The Sixteenth and Seventeenth amendments were initiated under his presidency. Purity crusaders also won a victory in 1910 with the passage of the Mann Act against prostitution.

Nevertheless, Taft was not forceful enough to effectively overcome the growing divisions within the Republican party. The conservatives, led by powerful Senator Nelson W. Aldrich of Rhode Island, were determined to draw the line against further reform. At the same time, progressive Republicans such as Robert La Follette of Wisconsin and George Norris of Nebraska were growing rebellious. Conflict came on several fronts. One was the tariff. In his campaign Taft had promised a lower tariff, but in the end he accepted the much compromised Payne-Aldrich Tariff. While placing many nonessential items on the duty-free list, it actually raised some key duties. It disappointed reformers immensely. Listing such duty-free items as silkworm eggs, canary birdseed, hog bristle, leeches, and

skeletons, the political humorist Finley Peter Dunne had his fictional bartender, Mr. Dooley, proclaim, "The new tariff puts these familyer commodyties within the reach iv all." Taft had suffered a defeat but foolishly did not admit it. He called the tariff the "best" ever passed. In reality he backed down on his pledges because he believed the president should not interfere unduly with the legislative branch. And he simply had an accommodating personality. One Republican griped, "The trouble with Taft is that if he were Pope he would think it necessary to appoint a few Protestant Cardinals."

Caught in the middle of several conflicts, Taft eventually alienated the progressive wing of his party as well as Teddy Roosevelt. He first supported and then abandoned party insurgents who challenged the power of conservative Speaker of the House "Uncle Joe" Cannon of Illinois. Later, when Gifford Pinchot protested a sale of public lands by Secretary of the Interior Richard A. Ballinger, Taft fired Pinchot from his position as chief of the Forest Service, which infuriated both conservationists and Roosevelt. The latter was also irritated by Taft's antitrust prosecutions. He believed that a case had been pursued against U.S. Steel to embarrass him: The investigation

Robert La Follette in Cumberland, Wisconsin, in 1897. La Follette, known for progressive reforms as governor of and U.S. senator from Wisconsin, was on the progressive side of the split in the Republican party between progressives rebelling against Taft and conservatives opposing further reforms.

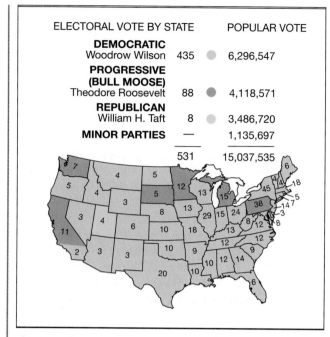

ELECTORAL VOTE BY STATE		POPULAR VOTE
DEMOCRATIC Woodrow Wilson	435	6,296,547
PROGRESSIVE (BULL MOOSE) Theodore Roosevelt	88	4,118,571
REPUBLICAN William H. Taft	8	3,486,720
MINOR PARTIES	—	1,135,697
	531	15,037,535

Election of 1912

Woodrow Wilson did not receive a majority of the popular vote, but the split in the Republican party gave him the majority of the votes in the electoral college.

exposed a deal Roosevelt had made with J. P. Morgan in 1907 in return for the banker's aid in stemming a financial panic.

By 1912 progressive Republicans were ready to bolt the party if Taft were renominated, and Roosevelt declared his intention to run. The fight for the nomination became bitter. Taft called Roosevelt's supporters "political emotionalists or neurotics." Roosevelt labeled Taft's people as "men of cold heart and narrow mind, who believe we can find safety in dull timidity and dull inaction." As president, Taft was able to control the convention. The defeated Roosevelt walked out with his supporters and formed a third party, known as the Progressive or Bull Moose party.

Many leading reformers attended the Progressive convention, which often resembled a religious revival, with hymn singing and marches. Its platform endorsed such wide-ranging reforms as abolition of child labor; federal old-age, accident, and unemployment insurance programs; an eight-hour workday; and women's suffrage. At Roosevelt's request,

however, a plank supporting equality for African Americans was deleted. Calling the major parties "husks with no real soul," he accepted the third party's nomination.

With the Republicans divided, Democratic chances of recapturing the White House increased. A former Republican senator lamented that his party's only unanswered question was "Which corpse gets the most flowers?" The scent of victory led to a hard fight for the Democratic nomination, which New Jersey's progressive governor, Woodrow Wilson, won on the forty-sixth ballot. The Socialist party nominated Eugene V. Debs, making it a four-way race.

As soon became apparent, the real battle was between Wilson and Roosevelt. It was marked by an unusually high level of debate over the proper role of government in a modern, industrialized society. Wilson declared, "What this country needs above everything else is a body of laws which will look after the men who are on the make rather than the men who are already made." Labeling his program "New Freedom," his aim was the restoration of competition and his tool was to be trust-busting.

Roosevelt, on the other hand, believed that big business was not necessarily bad, but he proclaimed, "Somehow or other we shall have to work out methods of controlling the big corporations without paralyzing the energies of the business community." His answer was "New Nationalism"—the expansion of federal regulatory activities to control rather than dismantle the trusts. Big government would offset the power of big business. Their rhetoric differed sharply, but in their presidencies both Roosevelt and Wilson practiced a little of both "New Nationalism" and "New Freedom."

The split in the Republican party enabled the Democrats to capture not only the White House but also the Senate. Democrats also consolidated their control of the House, so Wilson entered the presidency with his party solidly in power. Nevertheless, Wilson did not receive a majority of the popular vote. He got 6.3 million votes, Roosevelt 4.1 million, Taft 3.5 million, and Debs nearly 1 million. In the electoral college, however, Wilson won an impressive 435 votes to Roosevelt's 88 and a mere 8 for Taft.

Wilson and Moral Progressivism

As the third progressive-era president, Woodrow Wilson differed from his predecessors in both appearance and leadership style. He looked very much like the moralistic professor he was. The son and grandson of Presbyterian ministers, Wilson was raised in the South and practiced law in Atlanta before receiving his doctorate from Johns Hopkins University in Baltimore. His book *Congressional Government* was published in 1895, and he became president of Princeton University in 1902 before being elected governor of New Jersey. His religion was an important factor in his personality. "My life would not be worth living," he declared, "if it were not for the driving power of religion."

Wilson was not the kind of man whom people named stuffed animals after or gave nicknames. His self-righteousness was not endearing. One politician noted that when Wilson "said something to me . . . I didn't know whether God or him was talking." Although much less charismatic, Wilson did resemble Roosevelt in being a better speaker than Taft and in his view of the role of the president.

A distinguished professor, Woodrow Wilson brought both competence and a grim moral determination to the presidency.

Roosevelt had called the presidency a "bully pulpit," and Wilson agreed that the president should be the "political leader of the nation" because "his is the only national voice in politics." Unlike Taft, he argued that the president must be "as much concerned with the guidance of legislation as with the just and orderly execution of the laws."

Wilson's activism coincided with growing demands for further reform. Investigations and amendments launched earlier came to fruition during his presidency. The result was an outpouring of legislation. In 1913, his first year in office, the Sixteenth Amendment was ratified, allowing the imposition of a federal income tax. It appeared as a provision of the Underwood Tariff, which was passed in a special session of Congress that year. Wilson called the session to redeem a campaign pledge to lower duties as part of the New Freedom goal of restoring competition. During the tariff hearings, lobbyists were so plentiful that Wilson complained, "a brick wouldn't be thrown without hitting one of them." This time, however, they did not all prevail. Congress significantly lowered duties for the first time since the Civil War. To recoup lost revenues, a graduated tax of from 1 to 6 percent was placed on personal incomes of $3000 and over.

Congress passed banking reform the same year. Following the panic of 1907, congressional investigations were launched into its causes. Everyone, including bankers, had come to believe the nation's banking system needed to be stabilized by governmental action. The question was *how* to do it. Wall Street wanted a centralized system owned and controlled by bankers. Others wanted a more decentralized system owned or controlled by the government. The Federal Reserve Act of 1913 was a compromise. It established the Federal Reserve System of 12 regional banks owned by bankers but under the control of a presidentially appointed Federal Reserve Board.

Prohibitionists won their first national victory with the Webb-Kenyon Act of 1913, which increased the power of states to enforce their own prohibition laws. The next year those concerned with the large amounts of narcotics in patent medicines rejoiced over the passage of the Harrison Narcotic Act. It required a doctor's prescription for the sale of any drug on a list of controlled substances. In 1914 Congress took action to deal with monopolies and to regulate business. In September it established the Federal Trade Commission to replace the Bureau of Corporations. The five-person body was charged with investigating alleged violations of antitrust law and could issue cease and desist orders against corporations found guilty of unfair trade practices. The next month the Clayton Antitrust Act sought to close some of the loopholes of the Sherman act and limit court actions against labor unions.

At that point Wilson believed he had accomplished his agenda. He was not a supporter of further labor legislation or farmcredit plans. A firm opponent of paternalism, he said, "The old adage that God takes care of those who take care of themselves is not gone out of date. No federal legislation can change that thing. The minute you are taken care of by the government you are wards, not independent men." As the election of 1916 approached, however, progressives reminded Wilson of the importance of the farm and labor vote. Legislation to win those votes soon followed. Farmers were given the Federal Farm Loan Act and federal supplemental funding for agricultural specialists in each county; labor leaders got the Keating-Owen Child Labor Act; railroad workers got the Adamson Act to limit their work hours; and federal employees got the Workman's Compensation Act. Progressives were also pleased by Wilson's appointment of Louis Brandeis to the Supreme Court. All of these actions helped ensure Wilson's victory over the Republican nominee Charles Evans Hughes in 1916.

PROGRESSIVISM IN THE INTERNATIONAL ARENA

Many progressives did not believe that progress was limited by national boundaries. In their eyes, human beings had the capacity to create a more just and orderly society both at home and abroad. The progressive spirit was optimistic, and progressive victories on the home front expanded Americans' confidence in their ability to solve problems—even on the international level. This confidence was further bolstered by the nation's economic growth and victory in the Spanish-American War.

Everyone agreed that by 1900, America's status in the world had changed. How to respond to those changes was the question. Just as people differed over what alterations, if any, were required in domestic policies, various visions of a new American foreign policy also emerged. For some, progressivism simply redefined and reinvigorated the old ideas of manifest destiny. The United States would solve its problems at home and then remake the world in its own image. Such a new world order would also open up new markets for America's industrial and agricultural surpluses. Other progressives believed that democratic principles required that all people, even foreigners, be free to determine their own destinies. Order and justice were two progressive goals that sometimes conflicted, and that conflict was also apparent in the international arena.

Big Stick Diplomacy

Theodore Roosevelt's foreign policy reflected the same vigor he displayed in everything else he did. His "macho" foreign policy emerged from his belief that a man's mission was to "work, fight, and breed." He believed progress and order could benefit the world as well as the nation, He also asserted that Congress was "not well fitted for the shaping of foreign policy" and expanded presidential power in the conduct of diplomacy. It was his destiny to deal with the legacies of increased power and influence from the Spanish-American War. Order having been restored in Cuba and the Philippines by 1903, Roosevelt launched the United States into the role of policeman. His doctrine was to "speak softly and carry a big stick," but he really only lived up to the second half of the slogan.

Possession of the Philippines caused concern over turbulent Asian politics. Most alarming was the emergence of Japan as a power after its unexpected victories in the

Russo-Japanese War (1904–1905). Often playing the role of arbiter at home, Roosevelt now shifted his arena and mediated an end to the war at a Portsmouth, New Hampshire, conference in August 1905—an action that won him a Nobel Peace Prize. Japan remained a formidable rival, however, and agreements were later reached to respect each other's Asian interests. In the Pacific, Roosevelt displayed his "big stick" by sending a fleet of 16 battleships, called the "Great White Fleet," on a 1907 to 1909 around-the-world tour with conspicuous stops in the Pacific, including Japan. His intent was to intimidate the Japanese, but he failed to halt their growing power.

Within the Western Hemisphere, Roosevelt was even less reluctant to threaten or use force. In 1906 he responded to Cuban demonstrations against the Platt Amendment and insurrection by sending in marines, who stayed until 1909. "I am doing my best," he declared, "to persuade the Cubans that if only they will be good, they will be happy. I am seeking the very minimum of interference necessary to make them good." The marines could be very persuasive.

Progress and strategic considerations also demanded that a canal in Central America link the Atlantic and Pacific oceans. Roosevelt was determined to make it happen. There were two possible routes: one through Nicaragua and one across the Panamanian isthmus, which belonged to Colombia. A French company had made a start in Panama, but it ran out of funds and was reorganized as the New Panama Canal Company. The new company's major asset was its concession from Colombia that extended to 1904.

Three commissions appointed to determine the route recommended Nicaragua, primarily because the New Panama Canal Company demanded $190 million for its rights, property, and previous work. The company's stockholders, however, mainly Americans, were frantic to convince Congress to choose the Panamanian route. They dropped their demand to $40 million, contributed profusely to campaign funds, and hired a full-time lobbyist—Philippe Bunau-Varilla, the French chief engineer of the original company. In June 1902,

Congress authorized efforts to secure the rights to a Panamanian canal. The Hay-Herrán Treaty provided the United States with rights to a 6-mile-wide zone in return for a $10 million payment to Colombia and an annual rental fee of $250,000. As in America, ratification required the consent of the Colombian senate, which in August 1903 rejected the treaty

Panama Canal
The Panama Canal provided a strategic shipping and military link between the Atlantic and the Pacific oceans.

unanimously. Its motive was probably to delay the treaty until 1904, when the New Panama Canal Company's concession expired and Colombia might receive some of the $40 million originally earmarked for the company.

Roosevelt was furious. "The blackmailers of Bogota," he roared, should not be allowed "permanently to bar one of the future highways of civilization." He drafted a message to Congress proposing to take the canal zone by force but never delivered it. A different solution was found, Bunau-Varilla engineered a Panamanian revolution by providing people with a national constitution, flag, and anthem as well as assurances that the United States would not let their revolt fail. He was right. Most Colombian troops were prevented from even getting to the so-called revolution by the USS *Nashville*. Three days after its start, Roosevelt recognized the independence of the Republic of Panama. U.S. Secretary of State John Hay and the French citizen Bunau-Varilla, who had demanded to be made ambassador to the United States, then quickly drafted the Hay–Bunau-Varilla Treaty with essentially the same terms as the Hay-Herrán Treaty—only now the payment went to the rebels, not Colombia.

American actions enraged people all over the world. At first Roosevelt denied any part in the revolution, but he eventually admitted, "I took the Canal Zone and let Congress debate; and while the debate goes on the Canal does also." In 1914, the canal, a monument to both progress and Yankee imperialism, was completed. It was a big investment, one that required protection from foreign military vessels.

At the same time, Latin American countries sometimes fell behind in debt payments to such European powers as Britain and Germany. As a result those two nations blockaded Venezuela in 1902 to 1903. A year later, Roosevelt announced that the United States would assume the responsibility of seeing that the nations of the Caribbean behaved themselves and paid their debts. European intervention, therefore, would not be necessary. Known as the Roosevelt Corollary to the Monroe Doctrine, this policy justified U.S. intervention in such places as the Dominican Republic, Nicaragua, and Haiti. Roosevelt's "big stick" diplomacy established America as the "police of the Western Hemisphere"—a role that would last long into the twentieth century.

Dollar Diplomacy

Before becoming president, William Howard Taft had served as governor-general in the Philippines and as Roosevelt's troubleshooter in Cuba. These experiences had convinced Taft of two principles. The first was the need for order and stability, the second was the limited capacity of armed force for solving problems. He also realized that the United States had a new source of power—its economic clout. From 1898 to 1909, American overseas investments had risen from about $800 million to more than $2.5 billion.

Called "dollar diplomacy," Taft's approach was to use dollars instead of bullets to ensure stability and order. He wanted American capital to replace European capital in Latin America in order to increase U.S. influence there. When British bondholders wanted to collect their debts from Honduras in 1909, Taft asked American financiers to assume the debt. In 1910 he convinced New York bankers to take over the assets of the National Bank of Haiti. When needed, however, Taft also wielded a big stick. He refused to recognize a revolution in Nicaragua until the leaders agreed to accept

American credits to pay off British debts and sent marines to punctuate his point.

Missionary Diplomacy

As in domestic policies, Woodrow Wilson's foreign policy differed more in style than substance from his predecessors. Wilson's moralism did not stop at national boundaries. Indeed his sermonistic foreign policy has sometimes been called "missionary diplomacy." His gospel was American-style democracy. "When properly directed," he declared, "there is no people not fitted for self-government." That direction was to come from the United States. He spoke of "releasing the intelligence of America for the service of mankind" and proclaimed "every nation needs to be drawn into the tutelage of America."

The rhetoric was different from his predecessors, but the results were the same. Renouncing both big stick and dollar diplomacy, Wilson nevertheless used similar measures to maintain stability and order in the Caribbean. He sent marines to the Dominican Republic and Haiti and kept them in Nicaragua. His interventionism ran into more trouble in Mexico, where the overthrow of long-time dictator Porfirio Díaz in 1911 began a cycle of revolution.

General Porfirio Díaz ruled Mexico with an iron hand from the early 1870s to 1910. As dictator, he brought order to his nation and opened Mexico to foreign investors. Under his protective hand a flood of foreign businesspeople rushed in to tap Mexico's rich mineral wealth, build railroads, and exploit the agricultural sector of its economy. On the eve of World War I, American businesspeople valued their holdings in Mexico at $1 billion. Yet only a handful of wealthy Mexicans benefited from their nation's economic development, and the political stability Díaz brought to Mexico was bought at the expense of individual liberties. He crushed political opposition and turned a deaf ear to pleas for land reform.

In 1910, his opponents revolted and to the world's amazement Díaz proved to be a paper tiger. Unable to extinguish a series of small revolts that sprang up across Mexico, he fled the country. Mexico's new leader was Francisco I. Madero, an idealist who championed the middle class's aspirations for democracy and the peasant class's demands for land reform. Madero had hardly settled into the presidency before new revolts broke out, plunging Mexico into chaos. On February 22, 1913, less than two weeks before William Howard Taft's term as president ended, Madero and his vice president were assassinated by federal troops under the command of General Victoriano Huerta, who immediately proclaimed himself Mexico's new ruler. Despite the urgent recommendations of his ambassador to Mexico, President Taft did not extend diplomatic recognition to Huerta's government, leaving the issue to be resolved by the president-elect, Thomas Woodrow Wilson.

President Wilson refused to recognize Huerta's government, calling it a "government of butchers." Wilson regarded Mexico's new strong man as a murderer and a usurper, a ruler who symbolized all that was wrong with Latin American governments. To Wilson's legalistic mind, diplomatic recognition implied moral approval, and he could never sanction a government that had seized power by substituting bullets for ballots. He wrote one diplomat, "The United States intends not merely to force Huerta from power but to exert every influence it can to secure Mexico a better government under which all contracts and business concessions will be safer than they have ever been." Americans considered protection of contracts and concessions very important—American businesses controlled 75 percent of Mexico's mines, 60 percent of its oil, and 70 percent of its rubber.

Huerta's claims to power were shaky. Following Madero's assassination, several political factions in Mexico revolted against Huerta. Emiliano Zapata led an army against federal troops in Morelos, a mountainous state in southern Mexico. In the north, Venustiano Carranza, the governor of Coahuila, declared himself the first chief of the Constitutionalist forces and won the allegiance of several powerful regional leaders, including Pancho Villa, Alvaro Obregón, and Pablo González.

Because Huerta was not able to defeat his opponents in battle, his claim to controlling

Mexico was suspect; and his apparent weakness only strengthened President Wilson's decision to withhold diplomatic recognition. American policy was designed to aid Huerta's opponents, particularly Carranza. As the self-proclaimed first chief of the Constitutionalist forces, Carranza appealed strongly to Wilson, who was anxious to find a tool for restoring democracy to Mexico. As Wilson confided to a British diplomat, "I am going to teach the South American republics to elect good men."

However noble his ambition, Wilson allowed his animus against Huerta to trigger an American invasion of Mexico. In April 1914, Mexican officials arrested several American sailors in Tampico, a seaport on Mexico's east coast; detained a mail courier; and delayed an official Department of State dispatch. Wilson used these minor incidents to precipitate a showdown with Huerta's government—less than two weeks later American troops invaded the port city of Veracruz. At least 200 Mexicans died in the fighting that followed and another 300 were wounded, most of them noncombatant civilians. American troops remained in Veracruz for six months.

None of Mexico's warring factions approved the invasion and subsequent occupation of Veracruz. In fact, no issue has produced more bitterness in Mexico against the United States—not even the Mexican-American War. To Mexicans their defeat in the 1840s inflicted a serious wound to their national pride, but they saw the war as a lesson in power politics. Manifest destiny was a harsh policy, but Mexicans could understand the motives from which it sprang. Americans wanted American land, and they took it. What made the invasion of Veracruz so galling was that President Wilson clothed American aggression, in the words of one historian, "with the sanctimonious raiment of idealism." Because he insisted his acts were moral, Wilson "aroused both the hatred and the scorn of the Mexicans—hatred over the invasion but a deep scorn for what they saw as his hypocrisy."

In one sense, Wilson got what he wanted in Mexico. Huerta's government collapsed in 1915, and Carranza became the new president. In the larger sense, however, the United States

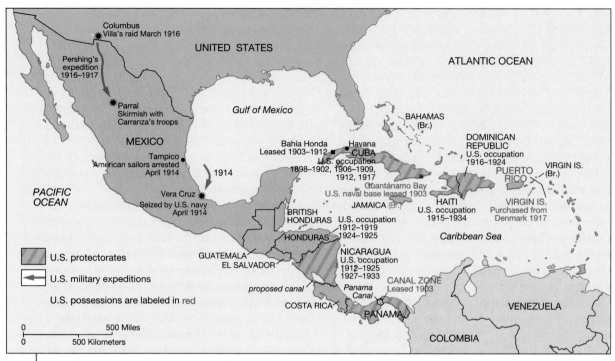

American Interventions in the Caribbean
Early in the twentieth century, the United States took it upon itself to police the Western Hemisphere and often took action when it judged Latin American countries were not running their affairs properly.

was the big loser. Mexicans deeply resented Wilson's arrogant assumption that he had the right to intervene in their internal affairs. Even after Huerta was overthrown, civil war continued between Carranza's government forces and rebels led by Pancho Villa. In an attempt to draw America into the fracas, Villa launched a raid into New Mexico in March 1916. The tactic worked. Wilson sent an expedition led by General John Pershing to capture Villa. American troops failed to find him, but soon were 300 miles deep into Mexican territory, and, as a result, in January 1917 on the brink of war with Carranza's government. By then, however, America was being drawn into World War I, and Wilson decided to withdraw the troops. Although Wilson eventually got the kind of government he wanted for Mexico, Mexicans continued to believe that their government was their business and deeply resented the American intervention.

American involvement in World War I diverted attention from more than Mexico. Do-

mestic reform took a back seat to "making the world safe for democracy." Yet war always brings changes on the home front. The nation shifted gears, but progressivism did not entirely die. Indeed prohibitionists, woman suffragists, and immigration restrictionists won their greatest victories in the wake of war.

PROGRESSIVE ACCOMPLISHMENTS, PROGRESSIVE FAILURES

The twentieth century began with great optimism about the power of human beings to shape their destinies. Progress, people believed, could be legislated. Efficient, noncorrupt government could provide order and stability, promote social justice, and improve personal morals. Groups organized to promote their goals, and more and more of them began to win their objectives. In the 1920s, however, some began to realize that legislation had not always had its desired effect, that not everyone had benefited equally, and that change had been far from radical.

The Impact of Legislation

Measured by direct results most progressive reforms proved disappointing. In some cases unintended consequences actually worked against the intended goals of laws. This often occurs when ideals confront reality. Solving one problem frequently creates another. Nevertheless, progressives established important precedents that opened doors to later, more effective reform.

Attempts to promote direct democracy were among the least effective. Direct election of senators did not seem to alter the kinds of people elected. Initiative, referendum, and recall were rarely used, and then not by people in general. The expense and organization needed for petition drives were beyond the reach of any but well-financed pressure groups. An unintended result of democratization was to increase the power of urban machines. Bosses may have had to work a little harder, but most were still able to dominate primaries as well as elections. The move toward popular voting increased the political power of populous cities and the machines that controlled them. The greatest failing of the movement was a dramatic drop in voter participation. Nevertheless, in some states, such as Wisconsin, government did become more responsive to public needs, and urban machines often adopted reform measures to maintain power.

Other kinds of urban reforms had varying results. In some, government did indeed become more efficiently and economically run. The competency and honesty of officials generally increased. An occasional consequence, however, was decreased social services in less affluent neighborhoods. This was more likely to happen where the commissioner-manager system was adopted—usually in midsize cities without a tradition of machine politics. In other cities municipally owned utilities lowered rates, providing some real relief for the poor.

Attempts to regulate the railroads on either the state or national level rarely produced dramatic benefits for the general public. The chief advocates and beneficiaries of railroad regulation were frequently large shipping interests that did not share lower costs with consumers. With the Hepburn Act, Roosevelt did accomplish his primary goal of giving the ICC the power to set rates. The provision allowing court review of its decisions, however, made the act more significant as a precedent for expanded governmental power than as an immediate solution to problems. The courts ruled in favor of the railroads in most rate disputes.

Antimonopoly actions also did not always produce the intended results. For example, the breakups of Standard Oil and the American Tobacco Company did not increase competition or lower prices. Perhaps the only legislation to fulfill the promise of New Freedom was the Underwood Tariff, and it was reversed by the tariff legislation of the 1920s. The Clayton Antitrust Act was widely, and correctly, considered too vague for effective enforcement. The general counsel of the American Anti-Boycott Association analyzed the provision to exempt labor organizations from antitrust legislation; he declared that the law "makes few changes in existing law as relating to labor unions, injunctions and contempts of court, and those are of slight practical importance." Later court decisions proved his assessment accurate.

The Federal Trade Commission (FTC) did not become an aggressive watchdog either. One of Wilson's cabinet members reported that the president viewed it as "a counsellor and friend to the business world," rather than as a "policeman to wield a club over the head of the business community." His appointments were fairly probusiness, and appointments made in the 1920s were even more so. In the end, the FTC proved beneficial to big business by protecting firms from unexpected suits and by outlawing many "unfair trade practices," many of which had promoted competition at the expense of stability. On the other hand, the FTC was also an important precedent for the regulation of business.

Proclaimed victories for labor frequently turned out to be more symbolic than real. In the arbitration of the 1902 coal strike, for example, what the United Mine Workers did not receive is very significant: The union did not win recognition. As the 1920s would show, organized labor did not emerge from the progressive era any stronger. Yet symbolism can be important. The precedent that the government would not automatically support the demands of management was later built upon during the New Deal of the 1930s.

Some labor legislation did bring benefits but also produced unintended results. Child labor laws in combination with compulsory education legislation decreased the number of children from ages 10 to 15 who were working for wages, from 1 in 5 in 1900 to 1 in 20 by 1930. During those same years, the number of students enrolled in secondary education increased by 800 percent. Both were desirable results, but in the short run at least, it was a mixed blessing for the poor. The incomes of a family's children were often crucial to its welfare, and no alternatives were provided. As one historian noted, "Child labor laws treated the symptoms and made the disease—poverty—worse." Much the same can be said about limits imposed on women's working hours. Laws establishing minimum wages for women helped somewhat to offset earning losses resulting from child labor legislation. In any event, laws such as the Child Labor Act were declared unconstitutional in the 1920s.

Workmen's compensation laws were an improvement over existing procedures but were not an unqualified victory of labor over management. Indeed, businesspeople eventually welcomed the relief from the growing number of suits instituted by hungry lawyers on a contingency-fee basis. By agreeing to take a percentage of any damage awards and to charge no fee for lost cases, attorneys made it possible for poor workers to take legal action. The award schedule in most compensation plans provided payments far below what some lawyers had been winning in court. Workers, however, were guaranteed at least some compensation. For the industrialists, a predictable premium replaced the uncertainty of court actions, decreasing risks and increasing stability in the cost of doing business.

The establishment of the Federal Reserve System also enhanced order and stability.

Everyone benefited from the maintenance of cash reserves for emergencies, a more flexible currency, and national check-clearing facilities. The banking system became more resistant to panics but, as 1929 would prove, not immune to them. Wall Street was not a big loser here. Three of the five seats on the Federal Reserve Board went to large bankers, and the New York Federal Reserve bank quickly came to dominate the system. The new system, in other words, was a significant improvement, but far from a radical change.

From the consumer's point of view, the Pure Food and Drug Act and the Meat Inspection Act were great victories. After the advent of mass production and mass marketing, only federal action could provide adequate protection from adulteration of the nation's foodstuffs. Unintended beneficiaries, however, were the large drug and meat-packing companies, which could more easily afford the increased expenses of meeting required production standards. The effect was thus anticompetitive. Lobbying by the big meat packers also affected the final form of the legislation. Their victories included government payment of inspection costs and the deletion of the requirement to date canned meat. Like much progressive legislation, the final act did provide protection for consumers, but in a way agreeable to big business. Swift, one of the largest meat packers, even endorsed its passage in an advertisement declaring, "It is a wise law."

Other progressive legislation left mixed legacies. Roosevelt's conservation measures prevented wanton squandering of resources but also aided the larger lumber companies. Morality legislation made undesirable activities illegal but at the same time more profitable for organized crime. It also fostered widespread disrespect for the law. With a maximum rate of 6 percent, the income tax did little to redistribute the huge fortunes of such men as J. P. Morgan but did establish an important tool for later use. A significant precedent was set by the Adamson Act, through which the federal government first dabbled in wage and hour legislation. Many other progressive reforms were illusory or short-lived. In the 1920s, lax enforcement and hostile court decisions reversed many of them. Nevertheless, laissez-faire had suffered an irreversible blow.

That was a major accomplishment and perhaps as much as many progressives wanted.

Winners and Losers

Before the era ended, people from almost every class and occupation had sought to take advantage of the climate of change to promote their interests. Obviously not all were equally successful. Few were unqualified winners or losers, but some gained far more than others, and some lost more than they gained. Clearly, large corporations were among the biggest winners. One historian labeled the movement "the triumph of conservatism." Given the basic moderation of all three presidents and most congressmen, as well as the resources and influence of big business, this may have been inevitable. It was not, however, the original intention of all legislation. To label most progressives as conservative is a gross mistake. They rejected the strict laissez-faire principles of nineteenth-century conservatives and embraced a vision of a more activist government.

Other winners included members of the growing body of middle-class technocrats. At all levels of government the search for orderly, efficient management created new job opportunities for engineers, health professionals, trained managers, and other experts. Reforms that diminished the influence of political parties also increased the power of special-interest groups working for particular social and economic goals. Consumers of all classes shared benefits from government regulation.

In general most of the winners were white, urban, Protestant, and middle class. This was true even though working-class ethnic groups won victories in some cities and states. They and small businesspeople were among those who both lost and gained. African Americans came closest to being unqualified losers. For them, the only lasting advances came from establishing organizations. The NAACP survived to become an important force later in the century, and self-help organizations provided aid to many. Other victories were mainly token; the defeats were concrete.

In the South, and often in the North as well, African Americans were clearly losers on the local level. At the same time black relations with the federal government also deteriorated. Of the three presidents, Roosevelt was the most sympathetic. In 1901, he invited Booker T. Washington to dine at the White House, consulted with him on some southern appointments, and named a few African Americans to federal positions. His actions hardly reflected an acceptance of black equality, however. He believed, "as a race and in the mass they are altogether inferior to whites." One of his speeches to Congress seemed to condone lynching. Most disturbing to African Americans was his handling of an incident in Brownsville, Texas, in 1906. There, white townspeople and black soldiers met in a shoot-out. No one could determine exactly what had happened, but that did not deter Roosevelt from ordering dishonorable discharges for 167 black soldiers without court-martial.

Theodore Roosevelt gave the appearance of supporting African Americans when he invited Booker T. Washington to the White House, but like many white leaders, he did not promote equality between blacks and whites.

CHRONOLOGY
OF KEY EVENTS

1879 Henry George's *Progress and Poverty* proposes a tax on land as a means of controlling illegitimate profits

1888 Edward Bellamy's *Looking Backward* depicts a utopian society guided by cooperation rather than competition

1889 Jane Addams founds Hull House

1901 President William McKinley is assassinated; Theodore Roosevelt becomes the twenty-sixth president

1902 Oregon, South Dakota, and Utah become first states to adopt initiative and recall; Roosevelt threatens to use troops to run coal mines when owners refuse to negotiate; Roosevelt charges Northern Securities with violating the Sherman Antitrust Act, and in 1904, the U.S. Supreme Court orders the company's breakup

1903 In *The Souls of Black Folks,* W.E.B. Du Bois attacks Booker T. Washington for abandoning the goal of equal rights; Wisconsin becomes the first state to adopt primary elections; Elkins Act bars railroad rebates

1904 Lincoln Steffens's *Shame of the Cities* exposes corruption in city government; United States obtains right to build the Panama Canal; announcement of Roosevelt Corollary to the Monroe Doctrine, asserting the right of the United States to exercise international police power in the Caribbean

1905 Roosevelt helps negotiate an end to a war between Russia and Japan, and wins a Nobel Peace Prize for his efforts

1906 Upton Sinclair's *The Jungle* exposes unsanitary conditions in the meat-packing industry; Meat Inspection Act enforces health and sanitary standards in meat-packing industry; Pure Food and Drug Act prohibits the use of harmful additives and misleading advertisements of drugs; Hepburn Act gives the Interstate Commerce Commission the right to set maximum freight rates

1907 Roosevelt dispatches 16 battleships (the Great White Fleet) on an around-the-world cruise

1908 Staunton, Virginia, hires the first city manager

1909 National Association for the Advancement of Colored People (NAACP) is founded to protect the rights of black Americans

1910 Mann-Elkins Act allows Interstate Commerce Commission to regulate railroad rates even without complaints from shippers

1912– 1917 12 states adopt minimum wage laws for women; 30 states adopt workmen's compensation insurance (industrial accident insurance)

1912 Roosevelt and his supporters launch the Progressive ("Bull Moose") party; Democrat Woodrow Wilson is elected the twenty-eighth president

1913 Sixteenth Amendment gives Congress the power to levy an income tax; Underwood-Simmons Tariff substantially lowers duties on imports and imposes a graduated income tax; Seventeenth Amendment requires direct election of senators; Federal Reserve System is created to supervise banking system and regulate money supply

(continued)

(continued)

1914	Federal Trade Commission is established to preserve economic competition by preventing unfair business practices; Clayton Antitrust Act prohibits interlocking corporate directorates and predatory pricing policies; U.S. Navy captures Mexican port of Veracruz	**1915**	U.S. marines are dispatched to Haiti
		1916	U.S. troops enter Mexico to search for Pancho Villa; U.S. marines are sent to Dominican Republic
		1919	Eighteenth Amendment prohibits manufacture and sale of liquor
		1920	Nineteenth Amendment grants women the right to vote

When Taft became president, he approved of southern disfranchisement and appointed white-supremacist Republicans to federal jobs. These actions by the two Republicans convinced some African Americans, including W.E.B. Du Bois, to support Wilson in 1912. That was a mistake. The influence of Wilson's southern upbringing and advisers became apparent when he allowed his cabinet to segregate federal employees and to demote black officeholders, especially those "who boss white girls." Jim Crow moved to Washington, and Wilson's defense of these actions indicated the blindness and paternalism of many white progressives on race:

It is true that the segregation of the colored employees in the several departments was begun upon the initiative and at the suggestion of the heads of departments, but as much in the interest of the negroes as for any other reason, with the approval of some of the most influential negroes I know, and with the idea that the friction, or rather the discontent and uneasiness, which had prevailed in many departments would thereby be removed. It is as far as possible from being a movement against the negroes. I believe it to be in their interest.

It seems that white progressives often seemed to feel they knew the best interests of those not like them, at home and abroad.

CONCLUSION

At the start of the new century, Americans confronted the urban squalor, poverty, powerful monopolies, corrupt and inefficient government, disorder, and despair that had accompanied rapid industrialization and urbanization. They were determined to do something to achieve more social justice and stability. Numerous solutions were proposed and victories won. In the end, however, Americans rejected radicalism and ignored major problems.

Once again the nation resolutely refused to come to terms with its ethnic and cultural diversity. Rather than protect minorities, most actions infringed on their personal liberties and sought to control rather than accommodate their differences. Women won some victories, but the majority of Americans did not accept the radical feminists' vision of true equality. Socialists' dreams of a peaceful, democratic redistribution of the country's wealth fell on deaf ears. In the end, there was no significant change in the distribution of either wealth or power. The United States had weeded and tidied up its social garden, not replanted it. Although that garden produced bitter fruit for some people, many Americans benefited. Also, the vigor and diversity of progressive actions brought to light many problems and provided later generations with a body of experience in dealing with them.

SUGGESTIONS FOR FURTHER READING

John Whiteclay Chambers, *The Tyranny of Change: America in the Progressive Era, 1890–1920,* 2d ed. (1992). Offers a thorough and up-to-date history of Progressivism.

John Milton Cooper, *The Warrior and the Priest: Woodrow Wilson and Theodore Roosevelt* (1983). Examines the lives, philosophies, and actions of the key Progressive presidents.

Morton Keller, *Regulating a New Society: Public Policy and Social Change in America, 1900–1933* (1994). Assesses government responses to the social problems of the early twentieth century.

James T. Kloppenberg, *Uncertain Victory: Social Democracy and Progressivism in European and American Thought, 1870–1920* (1986). Places the major thinkers of the Progressive era in comparative perspective.

Martin J. Sklar, *The Corporate Reconstruction of American Capitalism, 1890–1916: The Market, the Law and Politics* (1988). Analyzes relationships between business and government during the Progressive era.

Overviews and Surveys

Paul Boyer, *Urban Masses and Moral Order in America, 1820–1920* (1978); Robert M. Crunden, *Ministers of Reform: The Progressives' Achievement in American Civilization* (1982); Arthur Ekrich, *Progressivism in America* (1974); Lewis L. Gould, *Reform and Regulation: American Politics from Roosevelt to Wilson* (1986); Richard Hofstadter, *The Age of Reform* (1955); Gabriel Kolko, *The Triumph of Conservatism* (1963); Arthur S. Link and Richard L. McCormick, *Progressivism* (1983); Robert Wiebe, *The Search for Order* (1967).

The Progressive Impulse

Richard Abrams, *The Burdens of Progress* (1978); Jerold S. Auerbach, *Unequal Justice: Lawyers and Social Change in Modern America* (1976); Harold U. Faulkner, *The Quest for Social Justice, 1898–1914* (1931); Andrew Feffer, *The Chicago Pragmatists and American Progressivism* (1993); Louis Filler, *The Muckrakers*, rev. ed. (1976); Samuel Haber, *Efficiency and Uplift: Scientific Management in the Progressive Era* (1964); Thomas Haskell, *The Emergence of Professional Social Science* (1977); William R. Hutchison, *The Modernist Impulse in American Protestantism* (1976); Samuel Konefsky, *The Legacy of Holmes and Brandeis* (1956); David W. Marcell, *Progress and Pragmatism: James, Dewey, Beard, and the American Idea of Progress* (1974); David W. Noble, *The Progressive Mind*, rev. ed. (1981); Frank Tariello, *The Reconstruction of American Political Ideology* (1982); John L. Thomas, *Alternative America: Henry George, Edward Bellamy, Henry Demarest Lloyd, and the Adversary Tradition* (1983); Laurence Veysey, *The Emergence of the American University* (1970); James Weinstein, *The Corporate Ideal in the Liberal State, 1900–1918* (1968); Morton White, *Social Thought in America: The Revolt Against Formalism* (1975); Harold S. Wilson, *McClure's Magazine and the Muckrakers* (1970).

Progressives in Action

Mansel G. Blackford, *The Lost Dream: Business and City Planning on the Pacific Coast, 1890–1920* (1993); John D. Buenker, *Urban Liberalism and Progressive Reform* (1973); Norman H. Clark, *Deliver Us From Evil: An Interpretation of Prohibition* (1976); Allen F. Davis, *Spearheads for Reform: The Social Settlements and the Progressive Movement, 1890–1914* (1967); Rene J. Dubos, *The White Plague: Tuberculosis, Man, and Society* (1952); Nancy S. Dye, *As Equals and Sisters: Feminism, the Labor Movement, and the Women's Trade Union League of New York* (1980); Dewey Grantham, *Southern Progressivism: The Reconciliation of Progress and Tradition* (1983); Sheldon Hackney, *Populism to Progressivism in Alabama* (1969); Melvin G. Holli, *Reform in Detroit: Hazen S. Pingree and Urban Politics* (1969); Charles F. Kellogg, *NAACP: A History of the National Association for the Advancement of Colored People* (1967); Maury Klein, *The Flowering of the Third America: The Making of an Organizational Society, 1850–1920* (1993); Regina G. Kunzel, *Fallen Women, Problem Girls: Unmarried Women and the Professionalization of Social Work, 1890–1945* (1993); Elisabeth Lasch-Quinn, *Black Neighbors: Race and the Limits of Reform in the American Settlement House Movement, 1890–1945* (1993); Ellen Condliffe Lagemann, *A Generation of Women: Education in the Lives of Progressive Reformers* (1979); William A. Link, *The Paradox of Southern Progressivism, 1880–1930* (1992); Roy Lubove, *The Progressives and the Slums, 1890–1917* (1962); Richard L. McCormick, *From Realignment to Reform: Political Change in New York State, 1893–1910* (1981); August Meier, *Negro Thought in America, 1880–1915* (1963); George E. Mowry, *California Progressives* (1951); Bradley R. Rice, *Progressive Cities: The Commission Government Movement* (1977); Ruth Rosen, *The Lost Sisterhood: Prostitution in America, 1900–1918* (1982); Bruce M. Stave, *Urban Bosses, Machines, and Progressive Reformers*, 2d ed. (1984); Edward A. Stettner, *Shaping Modern Liberalism: Herbert Croly and Progressive Thought* (1993); David P. Thelen, *The New Citizenship: Origins of Progressivism in Wisconsin* (1972); James H. Timberlake, *Prohibition and the Progressive Movement* (1963); Walter I. Trattner, *Crusade for the Children* (1970);

Irwin Yellowitz, *Labor and the Progressive Movement in New York State* (1965).

Progressivism Moves to the National Level

John D. Buenker, *The Income Tax and the Progressive Era* (1985); Paolo E. Coletta, *The Presidency of William Howard Taft* (1973); James Holt, *Congressional Insurgents and the Party System* (1969); James Penick, Jr., *Progressive Politics and Conservation: The Ballinger-Pinchot Affair* (1968); James Oliver Robertson, *No Third Choice: Progressives in Republican Politics, 1916–1921* (1983); Robert Stanley, *Dimensions of Law in the Service of Order: Origins of the Federal Income Tax, 1861–1913* (1993).

Progressivism in the International Arena

P. Edward Haley, *Revolution and Intervention: The Diplomacy of Taft and Wilson with Mexico, 1910–1917* (1970); Walter LaFeber, *The Panama Canal*, rev. ed. (1989); Lester Langley, *The United States and the Caribbean* (1980); Dana G. Munro, *Intervention and Dollar Diplomacy in the Caribbean, 1900–1921* (1964); Whitney Perkins, *Constraints of Empire: The United States and Caribbean Interventions* (1981); Robert E. Quirk, *An Affair of Honor: Woodrow Wilson and the Occupation of Veracruz* (1962); John Womack, *Zapata and the Mexican Revolution* (1968).

Progressive Accomplishments, Progressive Failures

Paul D. Casdorph, *Republicans, Negroes, and Progressives in the South, 1912–1916* (1981); John Dittmer, *Black Georgia in the Progressive Era, 1900–1920* (1977); Jack Temple Kirby, *Darkness at the Dawning: Race and Reform in the Progressive South* (1972); Robert Wiebe, *Businessmen and Reform* (1962).

Biographies

Howard K. Beale, *Theodore Roosevelt and the Rise of America to World Power* (1956); John M. Blum, *The Republican Roosevelt*, 2d ed. (1977), and *Woodrow Wilson and the Politics of Morality* (1956); Allen F. Davis, *American Heroine: Jane Addams* (1973); William Harbaugh, *The Life and Times of Theodore Roosevelt*, rev. ed. (1963); Louis R. Harlan, *Booker T. Washington: The Making of a Black Leader, 1856–1901* (1972), and *The Wizard of Tuskegee, 1901–1915* (1983); Arthur S. Link, *Wilson*, 5 vols. (1947–1965), and *Woodrow Wilson and the Progressive Era* (1954); Daniel Nelson, *Frederick W. Taylor and the Rise of Scientific Management* (1980); David Riesman, *Thorstein Veblen* (1953); Elliott M. Rudwick, *W. E. B. Du Bois* (1960); David P. Thelen, *Robert La Follette and the Insurgent Spirit* (1976).

CHAPTER **22**
THE UNITED STATES AND WORLD WAR I

THE ROAD TO WAR
The Guns of August
American Neutrality
Allied Violations of Neutrality
Submarine Warfare
Preparedness Campaign
The Election of 1916
The End of Neutrality

AMERICAN INDUSTRY GOES TO WAR
Voluntarism
"Hooverizing"
Peace with Labor
Financing the War

THE AMERICAN PUBLIC GOES TO WAR
Selling the War
Political Repression
Wartime Reform
African Americans and the Great
  Migration

THE WAR FRONT
The War at Sea
Raising an Army
The Defeat of Germany

SOCIAL UNREST AFTER THE WAR
Mounting Racial Tension
Labor Unrest and the Red Scare

THE TREATY OF VERSAILLES
The Fourteen Points
Discord Among the Victors
The Struggle for Ratification
The Election of 1920

Disillusioned writers of the 1920s honored Randolph Silliman Bourne as "the intellectual hero of World War I," yet his appearance was anything but heroic. Theodore Dreiser called Bourne "as frightening a dwarf as I had ever seen." An unusually messy forceps delivery crushed one side of Bourne's skull at birth, leaving him with a misshapen ear, a partially paralyzed face, and a mouth permanently askew in a horrible grimace. Then, when he was four, an attack of spinal tuberculosis twisted his frame and left him a hunchback dwarf.

Bourne's brain, however, was razor sharp. He started reading at the age of two, and by the time he entered school, he had finished entire books, including the Bible. A brilliant student, Bourne attended Columbia University where he studied under Franz Boaz, the father of cultural anthropology; John Dewey, the famed educator and apostle of pragmatism; and Charles A. Beard, the historian who stressed the economic motives of the founding fathers.

Bourne left college on the eve of World War I determined to become a writer. Drawn by the intense intellectual ferment of the day, he settled in New York's Greenwich Village, where self-styled literary radicals had declared war on the smugness and optimism of American culture. He contributed to new magazines, such as *The New Republic, The Seven Arts,* and *The New Masses.* While Bourne's interests ranged wide and far, he made his reputation as a critic of America's entrance into World War I.

Bourne loathed President Woodrow Wilson, but he directed his choicest barbs at fellow intellectuals who supported Wilson's policies. In effect, he accused them of not doing their job as thinkers—of not subjecting the president's high-sounding rhetoric to the fierce scrutiny required to sharpen public debate. Instead of questioning Wilson's policies, they had betrayed their duty by "opening the sluices and flooding the public with the sewage of the war spirit." When his colleagues accused Bourne of not understanding the realities of war, he replied; "In a time of faith, skepticism is the most intolerable of all insults."

Bourne refused to endow the war with lofty purposes. Hardly a knee-jerk pacifist, he knew that some wars were unavoidable, perhaps even necessary. In his judgment, however, World War I was not a struggle to make the world safe for democracy; it was nothing more than "frenzied mutual suicide." To those who argued that this war would be different, that this war could somehow be converted into an instrument of progress and democracy, Bourne replied that World War I would unleash "all the evils that are organically bound up with it." America's allies would reject Wilson's call for a "peace without victory," Bourne cautioned, because "war determines its own end—victory." Eschewing a just peace, they would try to win the war and "then grab what they can."

On the home front, warned Bourne, there would be "clumsily levied taxes and the robberies of imperfectly controlled private enterprises," the suppression of civil liberties, and the growth of big government. "War is the health of the State," he declared in one of his most famous lines. "It automatically sets in motion throughout society those irresistible forces for uniformity, for passionate cooperation with the Government in coercing into obedience the minority groups and individuals which lack the larger herd sense."

Like many of his contemporaries, Bourne feared the state. During wartime the state's power grew exponentially, making it "the inexorable arbiter and determinant of men's businesses and attitudes and opinions." The individual would lose every conflict with the state. Bourne denied that America could rely on "individual offerings of good will and enterprise" to conduct the war. "It will be coercion from above that will do the trick rather than patriotism from below," he warned.

Most alarming of all, the war would kill reform by diverting public attention from the unfinished work of progressivism. It would "leave the country spiritually impoverished because of the draining away of sentiment into the channels of war." Finally, Bourne rejected the charge that opposition to the war was unpatriotic. Patriotism, he opined, was "merely the emotion that fills the herd when it imagines itself engaged in massed defense or massed attack."

This drawing of American critic, essayist, and pacifist Randolph Silliman Bourne was done by Arthur G. Dove from the death mask by James Earle Fraser.

A few days after the Armistice was signed in 1918, Bourne died, a victim of the influenza epidemic that killed 500,000 Americans that winter—five times the number that died in World War I. Although he had no visible impact on Wilson's administration, Bourne raised important questions about the relationship between the individual and the state during wartime, and many of his fears proved prophetic. In the end, the United States had little choice but to enter the conflict on the side of the Allies, but the war itself was a terrible human tragedy. World War I did not make "the world safe for democracy" or serve as the "war to end all wars" as President Wilson promised. Rather, World War I sowed the seeds of World War II.

THE ROAD TO WAR

World War I killed more people—more than 9 million soldiers, sailors, and flyers and another 5 million civilians—involved more countries—28—and cost more money—$186 billion in direct costs and another $151 billion in indirect costs—than any previous war in history. It was the first war in which parties used airplanes, tanks, long-range artillery, submarines, and poison gas. It left at least 7 million men permanently disabled.

World War I probably had more far-reaching consequences than any other preceding war. Politically, it resulted in the downfall of four monarchies—in Russia in 1917, in Austria-Hungary and Germany in 1918, and in Turkey in 1922. It contributed to the Bolshevik rise to power in Russia in 1917 and the triumph of fascism in Italy in 1922.

Economically, the war severely disrupted European economies and allowed the United States to become the world's leading creditor and industrial power. The war also had vast social consequences, including the mass murder of Armenians in Turkey and an influenza epidemic that killed over 25 million people worldwide.

The event that triggered World War I was the assassination of Archduke Franz Ferdinand, the heir to the Austro-Hungarian throne. On June 28, 1914, Gavrilo Princip, a Serbian nationalist, assassinated the archduke while Ferdinand and his wife were riding through Sarajevo, the provincial capital of Bosnia in the

Within weeks of the assassination of Archduke Franz Ferdinand—shown here with his wife Sophie—Germany, Turkey, Italy, and Austria-Hungary were at war with England, France, and Russia.

Balkans. The assassination provoked outrage in Austria-Hungary, which wanted to punish Serbia for the assassination and intimidate other minority groups whose independence struggles threatened the empire's stability.

A complicated system of military alliances transformed the Balkan crisis into a full-scale European war. After consulting with its ally Germany, Austria-Hungary sent Serbia an ultimatum. Serbia accepted most of Austria-Hungary's demands and agreed to mediate the rest, but Austria-Hungary was unwilling to compromise and on July 28, declared war on Serbia. Meanwhile, Russia, vowing to defend Serbia if it was attacked, began to mobilize, while France, in turn, promised to support Russia. Germany demanded that Russia halt its military buildup; Russia refused. Germany responded by declaring war on Russia on August 1, and on France two days later.

World War I caught most people by surprise. Lulled by a century of peace (Europeans had not seen a large-scale war since the defeat of Napoleon in 1815), many observers had come to regard armed conflict as an anachronism, a dead relic rendered unthinkable by human progress. Convinced that the major powers had advanced too far morally and materially to fight, these optimists believed that nation states would settle disputes through diplomacy. And for a time, it looked as though the world had outgrown war. By the end of the century, peace societies abounded on both sides of the Atlantic, nurturing visions of a world without war, and the Hague Conferences of 1899 and 1907 seemed to bear out these hopes by codifying international law in order to establish procedures for the peaceful resolution of conflict. World War I shattered these dreams, demonstrating that death and destruction had not yet been banished from human affairs.

The Guns of August

Faced by Russia to the east and France to the west, Germany believed that its only hope for victory was to strike first. The German mili-

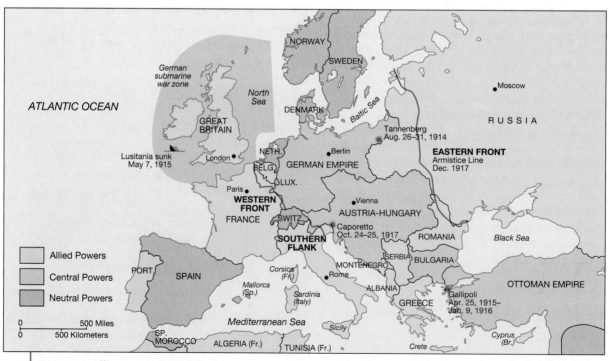

European Alliances and Battlefronts

Life in the trenches, as seen in this photograph of British soldiers in 1916, was often cramped, uncomfortable, and miserable. Many men tried to make the best of it by surrounding themselves with personal effects.

tary plan, originally devised by General Alfred von Schlieffen in 1905, called for a small force to defend Germany's eastern border, while a much larger German army raced across Belgium into France.

Germany's plan involved a violation of international law. Belgium was a neutral country, and Britain was committed to its defense. Thus a German invasion was certain to bring Britain into the war. Germany asked for permission to move its troops through Belgium, but King Albert, the country's monarch, refused, saying "Belgium is a nation, not a road." Germany decided to press ahead anyway; its forces invaded Belgium on August 3.

The German military strategy worked better on paper than it did in practice. While fierce resistance by 200,000 Belgian soldiers did not stop the German advance, it did give Britain and France time to mobilize their forces. Meanwhile, Russia mobilized faster than expected, forcing Germany to divert 100,000 troops to the eastern front. German hopes for a quick victory were dashed at the first battle of the Marne in September 1914, when a retreating French army launched a powerful counterattack, assisted by 6000 troops transported to the front by 1200 Parisian taxicabs.

After the Allies halted Germany's massive offensive through France and Belgium at the Marne River, the Great War bogged down into trench warfare and a ghastly stalemate ensued. Congealed lines of men, stretching from the English Channel to the Swiss border, formed an unmovable battle front across northern France. Four million troops burrowed into trenches that were 6 to 8 feet deep and wide enough for two men to pass, and which stretched for 450 miles. The soldiers of both sides, ravaged by tuberculosis and plagued with lice and rats, stared at each other across barren expanses called "no man's land," fighting pitched battles over narrow strips of blood-soaked earth.

To end the stalemate, Germany introduced several military innovations in 1915, but none proved decisive. Germany dispatched submarines to prevent merchant ships from reaching Britain; it added poison chlorine gas to its military arsenal at the second battle of Ypres in northern France; and it dropped incendiary bombs over London from a zeppelin. Other innovations that distinguished World War I from previous conflicts were airplanes, tanks, and hand grenades. But it was the machine gun that did most of the killing. The grim cycle repeated itself countless times: officers cried "Attack!"; men rose in waves; and the opposing forces opened fire with machine guns, spewing out death at the rate of eight bullets per second. In minutes, thousands of men lay wounded or dead, savage evidence of how efficiently military technology and insane tactics could slaughter a generation of young men. When the war ended, Germany had lost 1,800,000 men; Russia, 1,700,000; France, 1,385,000; Austria-Hungary, 1,200,000; and Great Britain, 947,000.

In a fateful attempt to break the deadlock, German forces adopted a new objective in 1916; to kill so many French soldiers that France would be forced to sue for peace. The German plan was to attack the French city of Verdun, a psychologically important town in northeastern France, and bleed the French dry. The battle, the war's longest, lasted from February 21, 1916 through July, and engaged 2 million soldiers. When it ended, Verdun had become a symbol of wartime futility. France had suffered 315,000 casualties, Germany 280,000. The town was destroyed, but the front had not moved.

With fighting on the western front deadlocked, action spread to other arenas. A British soldier and writer named T. E. Lawrence (better known as "Lawrence of Arabia"), organized revolts against the Ottoman territories in Syria, Palestine, Iraq, and the Arabian peninsula. With Germany preoccupied in Europe, Japanese and British commonwealth forces seized German islands in the Pacific, while British forces conquered German colonies in Africa.

The military stalemate produced political turmoil across Europe. On Easter Monday, 1916, some 1500 Irish Catholics seized buildings in Dublin and declared Ireland an independent republic. Fighting raged for a week before British forces suppressed the rebellion. British reprisals created great sympathy for the rebels. In 1919, renewed fighting broke out between British forces and supporters of Irish independence.

In Czarist Russia, wartime casualties, popular discontent, and shortages of food, fuel, and housing touched off revolution and civil war. In March 1917 strikes and food riots erupted in the Russian capital of Petrograd. Soldiers called in to quell the strikes joined the uprising; and on March 15, Czar Nicholas II abdicated. The czarist regime was replaced by a succession of weak provisional governments which tried to keep Russia in World War I. On November 7 communist Bolsheviks led by V. I. Lenin overthrew the provisional government, promising "Peace to the army, land to the peasants, ownership of the factories to the workers."

In 1917, after two and a half years of fighting, 5 million troops were dead and the western front remained deadlocked. This was the situation that awaited the United States in 1917.

American Neutrality

Like the combatants, Americans did not see the war coming. As one North Carolinian wrote in November 1914, the war struck "as lightning out of a clear sky." Most Americans felt relieved when President Woodrow Wilson issued an official declaration of neutrality on August 4, 1914. Many citizens did not believe their nation's interest and security hinged on the war's outcome. Mindful of the wisdom embodied in Washington's Farewell Address, steeped in a long tradition of isolation from Europe's wars, and shielded from the hostilities by the Atlantic Ocean, they hoped to escape the insanity. As a *New York Sun* editorial declared, "It would be folly for the country to sacrifice itself to the frenzy of dynastic politics and the clash of ancient hatreds which is urging the Old World to destruction."

Two weeks after the official declaration of neutrality Wilson asked his countrymen to remain impartial "in thought as well as in action." Yet the president himself could not meet this standard. Privately, his sympathies lay with the Allies, especially Great Britain, whose culture and government he had long admired. "England is fighting our fight," he told his private secretary shortly after the war erupted; "she is fighting for her life and the life of the world." Moreover, with the notable exception of William Jennings Bryan, his first secretary of state, Wilson's closest advisers all favored Great Britain. Robert Lansing, who succeeded Bryan as secretary of state; Walter Hines Page, ambassador to the Court of St. James; and Colonel Edward House, Wilson's alter ego, pushed the president to side with England and her Allies. Yet Wilson saw the war's causes as complicated and obscure; simple prudence dictated that the United States avoid taking sides.

Internal divisions underscored the wisdom of neutrality. Wilson knew his countrymen felt deeply divided over the war. Ties of language and culture prompted many Americans to side with the Allies, and, as the war progressed, the British adeptly exploited these bonds with anti-German propaganda. After the German invasion of neutral Belgium, for example, British propagandists depicted the Germans as sadistic brutes who committed atrocities against civilians. Yet the Central Powers had their sympathizers, too. Approximately one-third of the nation, 32 million people, were either foreign-born or the children of immigrants, and the roots of more than 10 million of these were the nations of the Central Powers. Furthermore, millions of Irish Americans sided with the Central Powers because they hated the English.

Domestic politics reinforced Wilson's determination to remain neutral. In 1914 the United States stood at the end of two decades of bitter social and political debate. Labor unrest, corporate growth, trust-busting, and the arrival of 12 million new immigrants since the turn of the century had opened deep fissures in American society. As Wilson struggled to correct these problems through legislation, he feared his domestic program would be endangered if neutrality failed. "Every reform we have won will be lost if we go into this war," declared Wilson in 1914.

Allied Violations of Neutrality

Because German armies held the edge in the land war, Great Britain had no choice but to press its naval superiority. Like Thomas Jefferson and James Madison a century earlier, President Wilson confronted a Great Britain bent upon ruling the waves, and no less than his predecessors in the White House, Wilson fought to protect neutral rights. During the early part of the war, British efforts to control the seas repeatedly posed threats to Anglo-American relations.

Immediately after war erupted, the British navy attempted to blockade Europe. In February 1915 British ships mined the North Sea and started seizing American vessels bound for neutral countries, often without offering compensation. The British captured not only war materiel, but also noncontraband items, including food and cotton, bound for neutral nations such as Holland for reshipment to Germany. In 1916 Britain blacklisted some 87 American companies accused of trading with Germany and censored the mail coming from Europe to the United States.

These actions, coupled with England's ruthless suppression of the Irish Rebellion in 1916, infuriated Wilson. In retaliation, the State Department bombarded England with a flurry of firm protests. These objections were consistently undermined, however, by Walter Hines Page, the pro-British American ambassador at the Court of St. James. On one occasion, for example, Page delivered a long dispatch to Sir Edward Grey, the British foreign secretary, and declared: "I have now read the dispatch but I do not agree with it; let us consider how it should be answered." Although the British interpreted Wilson's ardent defense of neutral rights as petty, legalistic quibbling, they realized they could not push Wilson too far, since they needed American trade to survive.

Wilson could have ended the controversy over neutral rights by clamping an embargo on trade with the belligerents, but he refused to take this action because wartime trade was stimulating the American economy. The United States had been in a recession when Wilson entered office in 1913, and the war had quadrupled its exports to the Allied nations.

The huge volume of trade quickly exhausted the Allies' cash reserves, forcing them to ask the United States for credit. Secretary of State William Jennings Bryan, a near pacifist

THE FIRST DAY OF THE SOMME

DURING the American Civil War Richard J. Gatling hoped to become wealthy by selling the Union army his hand-cranked precursor to the machine gun, the Gatling gun. It could unleash up to 200 rounds a minute, as compared to the 2 to 3 rounds a minute from a rifled musket being loaded and fired by a well-trained soldier. Gatling considered his weapon "providential," the ultimate device, he wrote to Abraham Lincoln, for "crushing the rebellion." After the war Gatling even spoke of social benefits. His gun would ease the pain and suffering of war. Only one soldier would be needed "to do as much battle duty as a hundred" because of its "rapidity of fire." His weapon would "supersede the necessity of large armies, and consequently exposure to battle and disease would be greatly diminished."

Hiram Maxim, another inventor, offered a major improvement to Gatling's weapon in 1884 when he demonstrated a mechanism that would permit the gun to fire automatically, simply by depressing the trigger—the modern rapid-firing machine gun was born. Because of such technological breakthroughs, water-cooled machine guns capable of shooting 600 rounds a minute were commonplace in the arsenal of weapons used by the armies engaged in World War I. The Maxim guns, as they were generically known, could spray an area with bullets and easily destroy companies of soldiers trained well enough to fire their breechloading rifles only 15 times a minute. The machine gun proved to be an effective killing weapon.

More sophisticated weapons did not, as Richard Gatling had assured his customers, result in any reduction in the size of wartime armies. During Europe's Age of Industrialization the major powers built up ever-larger military forces, as if only huge masses of troops could defeat the enhanced firepower of new weapons such as the machine gun.

When the armies of Europe first collided in August 1914 after Germany's penetration through Belgium, a stark reality became clear. Firepower, both in the form of small arms and large artillery, was so overwhelming that neither side could defeat the other without virtual annihilation. What emerged were opposing lines of trenches along what was called the western front, running without interruption south from the North Sea all the way through France to the border of Switzerland. For the next three years combat became a horrible contest in which one side or the other periodically tried to break through these trench lines.

The Battle of the Somme was in many ways typical of trench warfare. Up until June 1916 this sector in northeastern France was inactive. German divisions had been present since September 1914 and had constructed three defensive lines of trenches running back from "no man's land," an area some 500 to 1000 yards wide on the other side of which were trenches manned by the Allies—the British to the north and the French to the south of the Somme River. Because of a fearsome struggle occurring far to the south at Verdun, the Allied high command, after preliminary planning, decided in May 1916 to mount a massive offensive in the Somme sector.

If German lines could be permanently ruptured, then it would be possible to roll up enemy divisions on their flanks. German soldiers would face surrender or retreat, thus breaking the military deadlock in favor of the Allies. To breech the German trenches in coordinated fashion along a stretch of 50 miles involved detailed planning, considering the thousands of troops and massive firepower that the Allies faced. Further, surprise attacks were impossible. German artillery and machine-gun operators could obliterate waves of soldiers trying to cross no man's land, even before they reached the barbed wire placed in front of the German trenches. The alternative was to prepare the way with an extended artillery bombardment.

The Battle of the Somme was launched with a seven-day cannonade. During the last week of June some 50,000 British artillerists fired 2,960,000 rounds at the German trenches. By evening of the second day, wrote an observer, "some sectors of the German front line were already unrecognizable and had become crater fields." The next day the British started releasing clouds of chlorine gas, hoping that it would seep down into dugouts 20 or more feet belowground where German soldiers were at that moment living, surviving, and listening carefully for the climactic fury of the bombardment, a sure sign that the infantry assault was to begin.

At 6:30 A.M., on July 1, 1916, one hour before infantry troops were to advance, the cannonade reached "an intensity as yet unparalleled . . . along the whole front." German soldiers noticed the difference and knew that the moment of reckoning was near. The whole course of the battle would depend on their ability to get back aboveground, set up their machine guns, and begin firing before enemy infantry overran them. It was a moment for which they had repeatedly trained.

As zero hour approached, thousands of British and French soldiers made final preparations in their trenches. Their assignment was to secure control of the second German line by the end of the day. Soon they would climb up scaling ladders and jump over the top, then listen for the sounds of whistles from their platoon leaders to guide them across no man's land. Most found themselves "sweating at zero hour," supposedly from "nervous excitement." Many had attended church services the previous day. Explained one British soldier, "I placed my body in God's keeping, and I am going into battle with His name on my lips." Everyone received a warm breakfast and a healthy ration of rum to settle their jittery nerves.

Promptly at 7:30 A.M., the race began. "Over the top" went hundreds of thousands of British and French troops. Up out of their dugouts came German soldiers. In most areas the Germans were ready with time to spare. Their machine gun and artillery fire cut a third of the British battalions to shreds before they reached what remained of the first German trenches.

British soldiers who survived witnessed unbelievable sights. One watched as "two men suddenly rose into the air vertically, 15 feet perhaps," as a German shell hit the ground ahead of him. "They rose and fell with the easy, graceful poise of acrobats," he noted, as they died. Another saw men "falling forward," stating that it was "some time before I realized they were hit." In one company only three soldiers made it to the German barbed wire. Their leader, a lieutenant, looked around in amazement and said: "God, God, where's the rest of the boys?"

Hardly over the top, a British sergeant heard the "patter, patter" of German machine guns. "By the time I'd gone another ten yards," he explained, "there seemed to be only a few men left around me; by the time I had gone twenty yards, I seemed to be on my own. Then I was hit myself." This sergeant was among the fortunate. In some sectors, British soldiers who evaded machine-gun fire and reached the other side "were burned to death by [German] flame throwers."

From the British perspective, the fighting went poorly that day. By evening they had not captured the German second line, but they had suffered 60,000 casualties, including 21,000 dead. By comparison, the Germans, who got most of their machine guns up and operating, experienced only 6000 casualties.

The battle, however, had just begun. It would rage in fits and starts until November 18, 1916, when the Allies decided that a breakthrough in the Somme sector was not attainable. By that time the British had suffered 420,000 casualties, the French an estimated 200,000. No one knows exactly how many soldiers the Germans lost, but a fair guess would be in the 500,000 to 600,000 range. Yet virtually no ground had been lost or gained by either side.

It is not surprising, then, that the Allies rejoiced when the Americans finally entered the war. They needed more than loans and war goods to achieve total victory. Field Marshal Joseph Joffre, the former French commander-in-chief, said it all when he arrived in the United States after Congress declared war in April 1917. Declared Joffre with his usual bluntness: "We want men, men, men."

and the only member of Wilson's cabinet who supported strict neutrality, opposed their requests. After hesitating several months, Wilson agreed in October 1915 to permit loans to belligerents, a decision that favored Great Britain and France far more than Germany. By 1917 American loans to the Allies had soared to $2.25 billion; loans to Germany stood at a paltry $27 million. The United States became a creditor nation for the first time, giving Americans a strong economic interest in an Allied victory.

Submarine Warfare

Given Britain's overwhelming naval superiority, Germany decided to rely on a new weapon, the submarine, and on February 4, 1915, Germany proclaimed a "war zone" around the British Isles. Henceforth, they declared, all enemy merchant ships that entered the zone would be torpedoed without warning, and neutral ships would not be guaranteed safe passage. Germany was bluffing. It had only four submarines in the area, but Germany intended to use the threat of submarine warfare to terrorize and intimidate its enemies until it could build enough ships to enforce its threats.

A new development in naval technology, the submarine posed serious challenges to international law. The law required ships that attacked other vessels on the high seas to warn their intended victims, allow time for passengers to reach lifeboats, and then rescue survivors after the sinking. Moreover, merchant vessels suspected of transporting contraband had to be "visited and searched" before being attacked. By its very nature, the submarine could not abide by these regulations. A silent assassin whose effectiveness depended on the element of surprise, it had to strike from below the surface in violation of international law.

Wilson's approach to foreign affairs was both legalistic and moralistic. He expected nation-states to behave like gentlemen; and, above all, that meant living up to the letter of international law and respecting the rights of every nation. To Wilson, German submarines were committing criminal acts. In contrast to British violations of American neutrality,

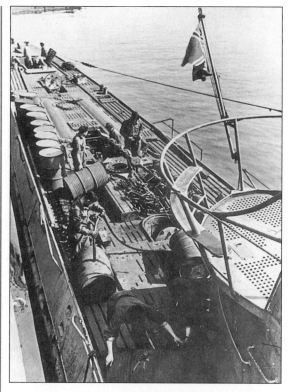

The German U-boat (*Unterseeboot*) violated the international law that required a warship to warn a passenger or merchant vessel before it attacked. The U-boat struck silently and without warning.

which merely resulted in property losses, submarine warfare threatened to kill innocent civilians. In unusually blunt language, he warned Berlin that it would be held "strictly accountable" for American lives lost to submarine attacks. While international law did not guarantee the safety of neutrals who traveled on belligerent ships, Wilson acted as though it did.

On March 28, 1915, a German submarine torpedoed the *Falaba*, a British liner, killing 104 passengers, including one American. "PIRACY," "SHOCKING BLOODTHIRSTINESS," "BARBARISM RUN MAD," screamed the American press in banner headlines. Wilson was furious, but Secretary of State Bryan reminded the president of numerous British violations of American neutrality in her attempt to blockade Germany. "Why be shocked at the drowning of a few people," asked Bryan, "if there is no objection to the starving of a nation?"

On May 1, the German Embassy took out ads in New York newspapers warning Americans not to travel on Allied ships. Undeterred, 197 Americans sailed for the British Isles on board the *Lusitania,* the queen of the British-owned Cunard fleet. On May 7, 1915, a German submarine torpedoed the *Lusitania* off the coast of Ireland. The ship sank in 18 minutes, killing 1198 persons, 128 of them Americans. The public was shocked and outraged. The *New York Nation* called the sinking "wholesale murder on the high seas," and a small minority of Americans, led by Theodore Roosevelt, demanded war. It did not seem to matter that the *Lusitania* (like the *Falaba*) was transporting munitions in her hull and had secret orders to ram submarines on sight.

In a sharply worded dispatch, Wilson ordered Germany to apologize for the sinking, compensate the victims, and pledge to stop attacking merchant ships. When Berlin equivocated, Wilson sent a second *Lusitania* note repeating his demands. This time the Germans met him halfway, expressing regret over the *Lusitania* and agreeing to pay an indemnity. However, the Imperial Government refused to stop sinking merchant ships without warning, explaining that Germany's survival depended on full use of the submarine.

Convinced that Wilson's policies would lead to war, Bryan resigned from the cabinet to protest what he saw as a dangerous tilt toward Great Britain in American policy. For his part, Wilson knew that the issue of submarine warfare had not been resolved. "I can't keep the country out of war," he admitted privately. "Any little German lieutenant can put us into war at any time by some calculated outrage."

Events soon showed how right he was. On March 24, 1916, a German submarine attacked the *Sussex,* an unarmed French passenger ship, killing more than 80 and severely wounding 7 Americans. Wilson threatened to sever diplomatic relations unless Germany promised to stop sinking all merchant and passenger ships without warning. Anxious to keep the United States neutral, Berlin agreed. The so-called *Sussex* pledge reduced tensions between the United States and Germany for the remainder of 1916, but the fragile peace depended solely on German restraint.

Preparedness Campaign

As the submarine threatened to draw the United States into the fighting, the American people and their leaders debated whether or not to make ready for war. Initially, Wilson's policy toward preparedness was cautious. In December 1914 he told Congress, "We never have had, and while we retain our present principles and ideals we never shall have, a large standing army."

Many Americans saw the issue differently. Wilson increasingly found himself assailed by prominent and highly vocal critics who insisted that the best way to preserve peace was to prepare for war. The pugnacious Theodore Roosevelt called the president "the popular pacifist hero," while another critic growled that the Germans were "standing by their torpedoes, the British by their guns, and Wilson by strict accountability." As Tin Pan Alley produced songs with titles such as "I Did Not Raise My Boy to Be a Coward," the National Security League, headed by General Leonard Wood, organized volunteer military training programs across the country.

Yet Wilson also felt pressured by groups opposed to war. Socialists such as Eugene V. Debs dismissed the war as a struggle for assets among capitalist nations. Radicals such as anarchist Emma Goldman and "Big Bill" Haywood, head of the Industrial Workers of the World, shared this view and advocated violent resistance to preparedness. Liberal reformers such as Randolph Bourne feared that war would destroy the spirit of progressivism. Pacifists such as social worker Jane Addams opposed the war on moral grounds. Most troubling of all, Wilson had to worry about opposition from within his own party. Speaking for the peace Democrats, former Secretary of State William Jennings Bryan warned that a preparedness campaign would transform the United States into "a vast armory with skull and crossbones above the door."

In the end, Wilson shifted ground and threw his support behind a moderate preparedness program. Throughout January and February 1916, he stumped the country demanding a military force powerful enough to protect the nation's honor. In June 1916, Congress increased the army from 90,000 to

175,000 men, and a few months later appropriated more than $500 million for new ships. Though of small importance militarily (Teddy Roosevelt dismissed the measures as a "shadow program" of "half preparedness"), both acts drew fire from those who predicted that armaments would lead to war.

At the height of the preparedness controversy, Wilson had to beat back a serious challenge to his control of American foreign policy. During the early months of 1916, Congress considered separate resolutions sponsored by Senator Thomas Gore of Oklahoma and Representative Jeff McLemore of Texas. Fearing that Wilson's defense of neutral rights would draw the United States into the conflict, the Gore and McLemore resolutions sought to prevent future incidents by prohibiting Americans from traveling on ships owned by belligerent nations and by prohibiting American vessels or neutral vessels from transporting American citizens and contraband "at one and the same time." Both resolutions enjoyed strong support in Congress, and for a while their passage appeared inevitable, but Wilson threw his power and prestige into a furious attack on both measures, insisting that if the United States accepted any abridgment of neutral rights "many other humiliations would follow." In the end, Congress accepted his argument and the Gore and McLemore resolutions went down in defeat.

The Election of 1916

Despite his own support for military preparedness, Wilson decided to make peace the key issue in his bid for reelection in 1916. The Republicans chose Charles Evans Hughes, a former governor of New York and a Supreme Court justice who had earned a solid reputation as a liberal. His nomination demonstrated the GOP's determination to regain progressive support and avoid the split that had put Wilson in the White House four years earlier. Wilson labeled the Republicans "the party of war" and charged that Hughes's election would plunge the United States into Europe's madness. "He kept us out of war" became the Democrats' rallying cry.

The race was extremely close. On election eve the *New York Times* and the *New York World* both awarded victory to Hughes, who went to bed believing he had won. He ran well in traditional Republican strongholds such as the Midwest (he won Illinois, Indiana, and Michigan) and the large eastern states. However, Wilson won in the electoral college by a vote of 277 to 254, with a popular vote margin of 9.1 million to Hughes's 8.5 million.

A careful analysis of Wilson's victory reveals that the Democrats won because they managed to fuse progressivism with the cause of peace. Wilson carried the Solid South, Ohio, Maryland, and New Hampshire, but he owed his victory to voters west of the Mississippi River, where he took every state except Oregon, Iowa, South Dakota, and Minnesota. This was the section of the country where peace sentiment ran highest and the opposition to preparedness was strongest.

The End of Neutrality

Interpreting his reelection as a vote for peace, Wilson attempted to mediate an end to the war. In 1917, Wilson urged both sides to embrace his call for "peace without victory," but neither welcomed his overtures. Randolph Bourne was right. Above all else, the belligerents wanted victory.

Any hope for a negotiated settlement ended when Germany announced that after February 1, 1917, all vessels caught in the war zone, neutral or belligerent, armed or unarmed, would be sunk without warning. Driven to desperation by the British blockade and unable to break the impasse on land, Germany had decided to risk everything on a furious U-boat campaign designed to starve Britain into submission. The German high command expected the United States to declare war in retaliation, but they believed their submarines could deliver a knockout blow before America could mobilize.

Members of his cabinet pressed Wilson to declare war, but he broke diplomatic relations instead. Though critics accused the president of shaking first his fist and then his finger, Wilson refused to budge, largely because he viewed war as a defeat for reason. For weeks he seemed indecisive and confused, unable to accept the fact that "strict accountability" de-

ROAD TO WAR
WORLD WAR I

1914	**Archduke Franz Ferdinand assassinated**	After the murder of the Crown Prince of Austria, Austria-Hungary declares war on Serbia; other war declarations follow; real war erupts when Germany invades Belgium.
	American neutrality	President Woodrow Wilson urges Americans to be "impartial in thought as well as action."
1915	**Submarine warfare**	President Wilson warns Germany that he will hold it responsible for the loss of American lives and property resulting from submarine warfare.
	***Lusitania* sunk**	A British passenger liner is sunk without warning by a German submarine; 128 Americans are among the 1198 fatalities.
1917	**U.S.-German relations chill**	President Wilson breaks diplomatic relations with Germany, citing the resumption of unrestricted submarine warfare.
	The Zimmermann telegram	Sent from the German foreign minister to the German ambassador in Mexico, it proposes that Mexico enter the war in return for Arizona, New Mexico, and Texas.
	Merchant ships armed	President Wilson authorizes the arming of American merchant ships.
	Declaration of war	President Wilson asks Congress to declare war, stating that "the world must be made safe for democracy."

manded war once the Germans started sinking American ships.

The Zimmermann telegram snapped Wilson out of his daze. In January, British cryptographers had intercepted a secret message from Arthur Zimmermann, the German foreign minister, to the German ambassador to Mexico, proposing an alliance between Germany and Mexico in the event Germany went to war with the United States. Germany promised to help Mexico recover the territory it had lost in the 1840s, roughly the present-day states of Texas, New Mexico, California, and Arizona. The British revealed the scheme to Wilson in late February, hoping to draw the United States into the war.

The Zimmermann telegram convinced Wilson and millions of Americans that Germany would stop at nothing to satisfy her ambitions—goals that posed a serious danger to America's rights and security. Late in February, Wilson asked Congress for permission to arm American merchant ships. The House ap-

proved, but 11 pacifists in the Senate filibustered against the bill. Dismissing his Senate opponents as "a little band of willful men, representing no opinion but their own," Wilson issued an executive order on March 12, arming merchant ships and instructing them to shoot submarines on sight.

At this critical juncture, with the United States and Germany virtually at war, the Russian Revolution erupted. Suddenly, the czar's government was swept away, and in its place stood the provisional government of a Russian Republic, complete with a representative parliament. Given his penchant for framing issues in moral terms, Wilson could now view the Allies in a new light: With the only autocratic regime among the Allies transformed overnight into a fledgling democracy, the war truly seemed to pit the forces of democracy against the forces of despotism.

Pale and solemn, Wilson delivered his war message to Congress on April 2. The United States "had no quarrel with the

German people," he insisted, but their "military masters" had to be defeated in order to make the world "safe for democracy." The next day the Senate approved the war resolution, 82 to 6; the House followed on April 6, 373 to 50. The president signed the declaration on April 7, 1917, and America was at war.

For more than two years Wilson had worked frantically to keep the United States at peace: why did he now lead the nation to war? True, cultural ties with Great Britain predisposed the United States to favor the Allies, and enormous volumes of trade and loans strengthened those ties. Yet cultural bonds and money did not decide the issue. Wilson, reluctantly, drew the sword, because he concluded that German submarines violated international law and made a mockery of America's long-standing commitment to freedom of the seas. His strong defense of neutral rights left him no choice but to declare war once Germany resumed its attacks on American ships.

One additional factor carried great weight for Wilson—his desire to help shape the peace. By entering the war, the United States would be guaranteed a place at the peace table. "I hate this war," an anguished Wilson confided to one of his aides, "and the only thing I care about on earth is the peace I am going to make at the end of it."

Most Americans supported Wilson's call to arms. John Dewey, the famed educator, spoke for progressives when he described war as an ugly reality that had to be converted into an instrument for benefiting mankind. Randolph Bourne disagreed. "If the war is too strong for you to prevent," he asked pointedly, "how is it going to be weak enough for you to control and mold to your liberal purposes?"

AMERICAN INDUSTRY GOES TO WAR

The United States entered the Great War unprepared. The problem went far beyond the puny size of the military forces. Americans had no idea of what the war would ask of them as a society. Decisions had to be made about mobilization, but the public had not yet

formed a consensus on the proper role of government in society, especially during wartime. As a result, Wilson hesitated to place the economy on a wartime footing by decree. Instead, he tried to create a system of economic incentives that would encourage Americans to support the war in a spirit of voluntary cooperation.

Voluntarism

It took nearly a year to organize an effective war administration. Wilson established a war cabinet with six key boards, conferring broad power on the central government. The War Industries Board (WIB), organized early in 1918 under the leadership of Bernard M. Baruch, a Wall Street financier, assumed the task of managing the economy by fixing prices, setting priorities, and reducing waste. To increase production, the WIB appealed to the profit motive, permitting earnings to triple during the war. One steel executive confessed: "We are all making more money out of this war than the average human being ought to."

The Fuel Administration, the War Trade Board, the Shipping Board, and the U.S. Railroad Administration adopted similar policies. Under the slogan "Mine More Coal," the Fuel Administration increased production by two-fifths and conserved supplies through voluntary "lightless nights" and "gasless Sundays." By spending $500 million on new equipment and repairs, offering large profits to railroads and high wages to workers, the Railroad Administration established an efficient rail system under national control.

"Hooverizing"

Agricultural production came under the jurisdiction of the Food Administration headed by Herbert Hoover, a mining engineer and self-made millionaire who had served with distinction as director of relief operations in Belgium. Appealing to the spirit of patriotism, he preached "the gospel of the clean plate." Americans "Hooverized" with wheatless

Mondays and Wednesdays, meatless Tuesdays, and porkless Thursdays and Saturdays.

No foe of profits, Hoover set farm prices at high levels to encourage production, stabilized the grain market by guaranteeing farmers a minimum price, and purchased raw sugar and then sold it to refineries at a fixed rate. The policies worked. Overall, real farm incomes rose 30 percent during the war, food production increased by one-quarter, domestic food consumption fell, and America's food shipments to the Allies tripled.

Peace with Labor

The government also made concessions to labor. Wilson addressed the American Federation of Labor (AFL) convention in November 1917, the first time a president had so honored the trade union movement. Important policy shifts followed. Gradually, Wilson recognized labor's right to organize and engage in collective bargaining, and he sanctioned other key demands, including the eight-hour workday. To settle labor disputes, Wilson created the National War Labor Board (WLB). Though it lacked legal authority, the WLB had the president's backing and a commitment from industry and labor to accept its decisions. During the war the WLB heard 1241 cases affecting 711,500 workers.

While Wilson embraced the AFL, his administration opposed the militant Industrial Workers of the World (IWW, also called "Wobblies"). From the textile mills of New England to the logging camps of the Pacific Northwest and steel companies in between, the Wobblies demanded higher wages and better working conditions, and they went out on strike to win them. Because the Wobblies frequently employed the rhetoric of class

Wilson's administration opposed militant labor unions like the Industrial Workers of the World (IWW), shown here striking against Oliver Steel in Pennsylvania. Such strikes did little to help the war effort at home.

warfare to dramatize their demands, their strikes frightened many Americans who feared social revolution. Businessmen played upon these fears to demand suppression of the so-called radical unions. The Wobblies were "traitors," they sneered, and the IWW stood for "I Won't Work."

The AFL shrewdly separated its union from these more militant workers, pledging not to strike for the duration of the war. The AFL supported the war and joined the administration's attack on socialist critics. In return, the AFL won a voice in home-front policy. Union men occupied seats in wartime agencies, where they pushed for the 8-hour workday and staved off pressure from employers bent on preserving the open shop. Real income of manufacturing workers and coal miners rose by one-fifth between 1914 and 1918, hours were reduced (by 1919 half the labor force had achieved a 48-hour workweek), and AFL membership jumped from 2.7 million in 1916 to 4 million in 1919.

Financing the War

By 1920 the war had cost the nation $33.5 billion—33 times the federal government's revenues in 1916. Conservatives favored a regressive tax policy: consumption taxes, borrowing, and, if necessary, a slight increase in income taxes. Reformers and radicals demanded a progressive tax policy: inheritance and excess profits taxes coupled with higher income taxes. Wilson walked the middle ground, but the heaviest burdens fell on the wealthy, through taxes on large incomes, corporate profits, and estates. By 1919 the tax burden in the highest income brackets had risen to 77 percent.

World War I brought an important change in the sources of federal tax revenues. Before the war nearly three-quarters of federal revenues had come from excise and customs taxes. After the war, America's tax structure shifted from taxing consumption to taxing wealth, proof that progressives had won an important victory in the struggle to make upper-income groups pay a large share of the cost of government. On the tax issue Randolph Bourne was wrong.

THE AMERICAN PUBLIC GOES TO WAR

Although Wilson preferred to rely on voluntary efforts rather than mandated government interference, federal powers were greatly expanded during World War I. Wilson's decision to substitute voluntarism for statutory controls on industry placed the burden of supporting the war on the profit motive and the public's sense of patriotism. This policy avoided a clash between Wilson and industry that would have resulted from strict government control over the economy, but it did so at a huge cost to civil liberties.

Selling the War

Throughout the war the government directed its coercion at people rather than industries, largely through the Committee on Public Information (CPI). Ably led by George W. Creel, the CPI created America's first propaganda agency. Creel immediately drafted a voluntary censorship agreement with newspapers to keep sensitive military information out of print. The CPI hired hundreds of musicians,

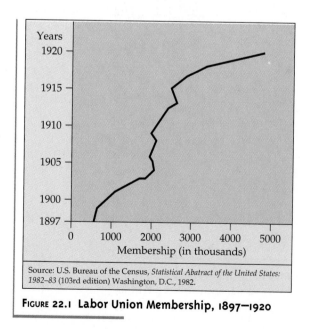

Source: U.S. Bureau of the Census, *Statistical Abstract of the United States: 1982–83* (103rd edition) Washington, D.C., 1982.

FIGURE 22.1 Labor Union Membership, 1897–1920

Hollywood and Tin Pan Alley did their parts to encourage patriotism by putting out a multitude of war films and a large number of music pieces like the one shown here.

writers, and artists to stage a patriotic campaign, sponsored 75,000 speakers who delivered four-minute war pep talks in vaudeville and movie theaters across the country, and got movie stars to sell war bonds.

Indeed, the CPI found a powerful ally in Hollywood. Quick to perceive the link between patriotism and profits, studio moguls cranked out scores of crude propaganda films with titles such as *The Prussian Cur*, *The Claws of the Hun*, and *To Hell with the Kaiser*, which reduced World War I to a conflict between good and evil, Allied heroes and Central Powers villains. Songwriters did their best to foster patriotism by pumping out a series of catchy tunes with titles like "Keep the Home Fires Burning" and "Over There."

Popular culture reflected the CPI's influence. Suddenly, dissent meant treason, Germans devolved into Huns, and all German Americans spied for the fatherland. It did not matter that the vast majority of German Americans supported the United States; the CPI consistently attacked their loyalty. At its best the CPI may have sold war bonds, discouraged war stoppages, and convinced the public to support the war; at its worst the CPI fostered a witch-hunt.

In the name of patriotism, musicians no longer played Bach and Beethoven, and schools stopped teaching the German language. Americans renamed sauerkraut "liberty cabbage"; dachshunds, "liberty hounds"; and German measles, "liberty measles." Cincinnati, with its large German-American population, even removed pretzels from the free lunch counters in saloons. More alarming, vigilante groups attacked anyone suspected of being unpatriotic. Workers who refused to buy war bonds often suffered harsh retribution, and attacks on labor protesters were nothing short of brutal. The legal system backed the suppression. Juries routinely released defendants accused of violence against individuals or groups critical of the war. German Americans became favored victims of mob violence. In one appalling instance, Robert Paul Praeger, a baker from Colinsville, Illinois, was lynched. Before the mob hanged him, they let him write a last note, which read: "Dear Parents, I must this day the fourth of April 1918 die. Please dear parents pray for me." A jury acquitted the lynch mob in less than half an hour, while a band played patriotic songs in the courthouse.

Political Repression

The government fueled the hysteria. In June 1917 Congress passed the Espionage Act, which gave postal officials the authority to ban newspapers and magazines from the mails and threatened individuals convicted of obstructing the draft with $10,000 fines and 20 years in jail. Congress passed the Sedition Act of 1918, which made it a federal offense to use "disloyal, profane, scurrilous, or abusive language" about the Constitution, the government, the American uniform, or the flag. The government prosecuted over 2100 people under these acts. Randolph Bourne's prediction that civil rights would fall victim to the power of the state rang true.

Political dissenters bore the brunt of the repression. Eugene V. Debs, who urged socialists to resist militarism, went to prison for nearly three years. Another Socialist, Kate Richards O'Hare served a year in prison for stating that the women of the United States were "nothing more nor less than brood sows, to raise children to get into the army and be made into fertilizer."

Labor radicals offered another ready target for attack. In July 1917 in Cochise County, Arizona, armed men, under the direction of a local sheriff, rounded up 1186 strikers at the Phelps Dodge copper mine. They placed these workers, many of Mexican descent, on railroad cattle cars without food or water, and left them in the New Mexico desert, 180 miles away. The *Los Angeles Times* editorialized: "The citizens of Cochise County have written a lesson that the whole of America would do well to copy."

The IWW never recovered from government attacks during World War I. In September 1917 the Justice Department staged massive raids on IWW officers, arresting 169 of its veteran leaders. The administration's purpose was, as one attorney put it, "very largely to put the IWW out of business." Many observers thought the judicial system would protect dissenters, but the courts handed down stiff prison sentences to the Wobblies.

Radicals were not the only ones to suffer harassment. Robert Goldstein, a motion picture producer, had made a movie about the American Revolution called *The Spirit of '76,* before the United States entered the war. When he released the picture after the declaration of war, he was accused of undermining American morale. A judge told him that his depiction of heartless British redcoats caused Americans to question their British allies. He was sentenced to a 10-year prison term and fined $5000.

The Supreme Court later approved the attacks on civil liberties. Oliver Wendell Holmes, the court's leading champion of civil liberties, upheld the Espionage Act in *Schenck* v. *United States* (1919), ruling that the conviction of Charles T. Schenck for distributing leaflets urging draftees to oppose the war did not violate Schenck's free speech rights. Holmes delivered the famous "clear and present danger" doctrine, which held that there are circumstances (like "a man falsely shouting fire in a theater") that pose such a threat to public order that First Amendment protections do not apply. In *U.S.* v. *Debs* (1919), the court, with Holmes's support, again approved the Espionage Act, upholding the conviction of Eugene Debs, the Socialist Party leader, who opposed the war. In a third case, *Abrams* v. *United States* (1919), Holmes reversed himself, returning to his support for "free trade in ideas," but he was outvoted seven to two. The American Civil Liberties Union (ACLU) was founded during World War I to defend the First Amendment.

World War I did not *cause* repression, it merely intensified old fears. Many Americans clung to the image of the United States as a strong, isolated country, inhabited by old stock, white, middle-class Protestants. Their vision no longer reflected reality, but the war offered them a chance to lash out at those who had changed America. Immigrants, radical labor organizers, socialists, anarchists, Communists, and critics of any kind became victims of intolerance.

Wartime Reform

The war hysteria bred a curious alliance between superpatriots and old-style reformers. Prohibitionists had little difficulty turning World War I to their advantage. They had been winning victories at the state level since the middle of the nineteenth century, but they did not enjoy any success at the federal level until 1917 when Congress prohibited the use of grain for the production of alcoholic beverages, insisting that foodstuffs must be used to feed America's soldiers and Allies. Prohibitionists joined the anti-German craze, warning that German Americans controlled the nation's breweries. Congress passed the Eighteenth Amendment in 1917 and the final state ratified the amendment two months after the Armistice. The Volstead Act, which banned the manufacture, transportation, and sale of alcoholic beverages, took effect in 1920.

Like prohibition, women's suffrage benefited from the emergency atmosphere of World War I. Although radical suffragists, led by Alice Paul of the National Women's Party, refused to back the war as long as women could not vote, most women's organizations supported the war effort. Wilson appointed suffragists Carrie Chapman Catt and Anna Howard Shaw as directors of the Women's Committee of the Council of National Defense. As blue-collar female workers started pouring into defense industries, middle-class women showed support for the war by volunteering to help the sick and the wounded. Thousands of women joined the Red Cross and the American Women's Hospital Service and served overseas as nurses, physicians, clerks, and ambulance drivers. Thousands more enlisted after the army established the Army Corps of Nurses in 1918.

Suffragists demanded the vote in return for their support of the war. Wilson had long opposed women's suffrage, but political reality ultimately forced his hand. Most western states had granted women the vote before he entered the White House. When Illinois fell in line in 1914, followed by Rhode Island and New York in 1917, pressure started building for national action. Alice Paul pressed the issue by organizing around-the-clock picketing in front of the White House. Determined to prevent women's suffrage from becoming a political issue in the congressional elections of 1918, Wilson told the Senate that the vote for women "is vital to the winning of the war." In 1919, shortly after the Armistice, Congress

During the war, many women took jobs previously held by men. Here a group of women assemble an automobile in a factory.

passed the Nineteenth Amendment, granting women the right to vote. Ratification followed in the summer of 1920.

Apart from voting rights, World War I brought few permanent changes for women. Women had hoped the war would open new jobs for them. Instead, employment opportunities proved meager and brief. Of the one million women who found work in war-related industries, the majority had held jobs before the war. Labor unions opposed hiring women and tolerated their presence solely as a wartime necessity. As the Central Federated Union of New York put it: "the same patriotism which induced women to enter industry during the war should induce them to vacate their positions after the war." Fewer than half of the women who took jobs in heavy industry during the war still held them in 1919, and the number of women who remained in the workforce in 1920 dropped below the 1910 figures.

African Americans and the Great Migration

Like women, African Americans wanted to use the war to improve their status. While the government had given African Americans little reason to shed their blood, most African-American newspapers backed the war. W.E.B. Du Bois urged African Americans to "close

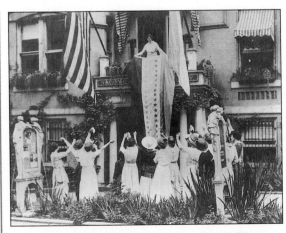

Members of the National Woman's Party, led by Alice Paul (on the balcony), celebrate their right to vote at their headquarters in Washington, D.C., in 1920.

ranks" with whites, declaring, "If this is our country, then this is our war." Du Bois hoped that by demonstrating patriotism and bravery, African Americans could win public respect and earn better treatment after the war.

At first military leaders denied African Americans even the right to fight for their country. The marines accepted no African Americans; the navy used them only as mess workers; and the army planned to make them laborers and stevedores. When the National Association for the Advancement of Colored People (NAACP) and other African-American organizations protested, however, the army agreed to compromise. Following the Civil War example, the army created black regiments commanded almost exclusively by white officers. Black regiments committed to battle fought bravely, but most African-American soldiers in Europe never got the chance to prove their valor. Instead, they were assigned to move supplies. While two-thirds of the American Expeditionary Force saw combat, only one-fifth of African-American troops did so. Even so, 14.4 percent of African-American soldiers lost their lives, compared with 6.3 percent of white soldiers. African-American soldiers faced segregation and humiliation. When the war ended, they were denied the right to march in the victory parade down Paris's Champs-Elysées boulevard, even though Africans from European colonies were permitted to do so.

Back home the record was equally mixed. In the decades following the Civil War a steady trickle of African Americans had left the South to search for jobs in northern cities. During World War I the trickle became a flood. Plagued by the boll weevil, low cotton prices, and unrelenting white repression, sharecroppers longed for change. When labor agents appeared in 1916 promising jobs in the North, they responded eagerly. By November 1918 the "Great Migration" had brought half a million southern African Americans to the "Land of Hope."

Many found jobs in northern factories and packing houses. The labor force in Chicago's packing houses had been 97 percent white in 1901, but by 1918 they employed 10,000 African Americans—over 20 percent of the workforce. The labor force in the northern steel industry had been virtually all white in

The 369th Infantry Regiment returned from the war in February 1919. They were awarded the *Croix de Guerre* (war cross) for bravery in the Meuse-Argonne campaign.

1900, but by 1920 African Americans held 10 percent of those jobs. Still, regardless of the industry, discrimination forced many to the bottom of the ladder, where they took over the menial, backbreaking jobs that had been vacated by Slavic and Italian workers, the prior most recent wave of immigrants.

The Great Migration angered many southerners. The price of cotton tripled during the war, southern planters, fearing the loss of their labor force, resorted to intimidation and mob violence to stop the exodus. A mob in Mississippi, for example, derailed a train to prevent blacks from leaving. Like their ancestors who had taken the underground railroad to freedom, many African Americans who moved to the North during World War I had to travel under cover of darkness.

Northern whites opposed the Great Migration, too. Manufacturers welcomed the cheap labor (especially as strikebreakers), but most Northerners felt threatened by the newcomers. Middle-class whites feared changes in the racial composition of their society, while immigrants resented the competition for jobs and housing. Increasingly, Northerners turned to segregation, discrimination, and violence; and African Americans, hoping for a better life in the North, fought back. Race riots erupted in 26 cities in 1917, with the most serious violence occurring in East St. Louis, where at least 39 African Americans died in the fighting.

Clearly, World War I meant different things to different groups: for the administration, a test of the limits of voluntarism; for businessmen and technocrats, a chance to pull the levers of government; for nativists and superpatriots, an excuse to lash out at "undesirable" elements; for radicals and dissenters, repression and hardship; for manufacturers and farmers, high profits; for reformers, victories on women's suffrage and prohibition; for trade unions, the right to organize for better pay; and for African Americans, a chance to escape from southern poverty.

THE WAR FRONT

The United States entered World War I without a large army or the ships to transport one to Europe. Six weeks before Congress declared war, the army had not even drafted plans to organize a large military force. At first confident the Allies were winning, Wilson hoped to limit America's contribution to supplies, financial credit, and moral support. In truth, the Allies were ready to collapse. The French army was in the throes of mutiny. Soldiers were tired of suicidal assaults ordered by inept generals, and the submarine offensive had reduced Britain to a six-week supply of food.

The War at Sea

With the allies ready to collapse due to huge casualties, low morale, and dwindling food supplies, Wilson ordered the United States Navy to act immediately. American ships relieved the British of patrolling the Western Hemisphere while another portion of the fleet steamed to the north Atlantic to combat the submarine menace. Six destroyers reached Ireland on May 4; 35 ships had arrived by July; and 343 ships were patrolling the seas surrounding England by the war's end.

To cut down losses of merchant ships, which in April alone totaled 881,027 tons, the Americans proposed a convoy system—using warships to escort merchant ships to Great Britain. By December the convoy system had cut losses in half.

Raising an Army

Wilson's choice to lead the American Expeditionary Force (AEF) was Major General John J. "Black Jack" Pershing. Despite urgent requests from Allied commanders, Pershing refused to send raw recruits to the front, and he rejected demands that American units be integrated into British and French regiments. Instead, Pershing insisted on keeping American troops as independent units under his command. To bolster Allied morale while the army trained, the War Department hurriedly dispatched the First Division to France, where it marched through Paris on July 4, 1917, to the cheers of thousands.

A bitter debate erupted over how to raise the troops. Despite heavy pressure from Theodore Roosevelt and others who favored a volunteer army, Wilson insisted on conscription. Critics, like Congressman Champ Clark of Missouri, opposed the draft as unnecessary and undemocratic, insisting: "There is precious little difference between a conscript and a convict." Congress passed the Selective Service Act on May 18, 1917. More than 23 million men registered during World War I, and 2,810,296 draftees served in the armed forces.

To assign soldiers to the right military tasks, the army launched an ambitious program of psychological testing. "If the Army machine is to work smoothly and efficiently," declared Robert M. Yerkes, the man who presided over the effort, "it is as important to fit the job to the man as to fit the ammunition to the gun." Yerkes saw the war as an opportunity to establish the academic legitimacy of psychology by providing a vital service to the nation.

Though the tests supposedly measured native intelligence, in reality they favored men with the most schooling, and thus reinforced the class structure of American society. Native-born whites, who possessed academic skills, achieved the highest scores, while recent immigrants consistently scored lowest.

Apart from selecting officers, the army made little use of the test data. Ordinary soldiers were not assigned tasks on the basis of

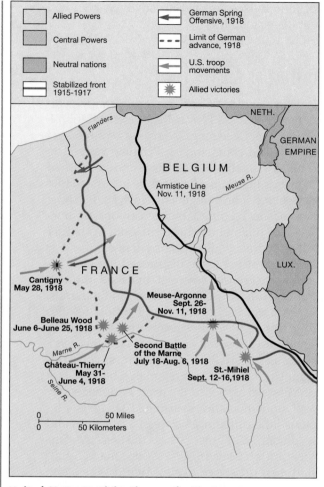

Legend:

- Allied Powers
- Central Powers
- Neutral nations
- Stabilized front 1915-1917
- German Spring Offensive, 1918
- Limit of German advance, 1918
- U.S. troop movements
- Allied victories

NETH.

GERMAN EMPIRE

Flanders

BELGIUM

Armistice Line Nov. 11, 1918

Meuse R.

LUX.

FRANCE

Cantigny May 28, 1918

Meuse-Argonne Sept. 26-Nov. 11, 1918

Belleau Wood June 6-June 25, 1918

Marne R.

Second Battle of the Marne July 18-Aug. 6, 1918

Château-Thierry May 31-June 4, 1918

St.-Mihiel Sept. 12-16, 1918

Seine R.

0   50 Miles
0   50 Kilometers

United States Participation on the Western Front

test scores. After the war, however, Yerkes boldly proclaimed that mental testing had "helped to win the war." All it really accomplished was to sell the public on the idea of mental testing and lay the groundwork for a thriving peacetime industry. After the war, numerous businesses adopted mental tests to screen personnel, and many colleges began requiring them for admission. Few legacies of the war had a more lasting or widespread impact on American society.

The Defeat of Germany

As the American army trained, the situation in Europe deteriorated. Mutiny within the French army was spreading (ten divisions were now in revolt); the eastern front dissolved in March when the Bolsheviks, who had seized power in Russia in November, accepted Germany's peace terms; and German and Austrian forces all but routed the Italian armies. In fact, by late 1917 the war had come down to a race between American mobilization and Germany's war machine.

On March 21, 1918, the Germans launched a massive offensive on the western front in the Valley of the Somme in France. For a time, it looked as though the Germans would succeed. Badly bloodied, the Allied forces lost ground. But with German troops barely 50 miles from Paris, Marshal Ferdinand Foch, the leader of the French army, assumed command of the Allied forces. Foch's troops, aided by 85,000 American soldiers, launched a furious counteroffensive, hitting the Germans hard in a series of bloody assaults. By the end of October the German army had been pushed back to the Belgian border.

During the final months of fighting, American troops hit Europe like a tidal wave. In June 279,000 American soldiers crossed the Atlantic; in July over 300,000; in August, 286,000. All told, 1.5 million American troops arrived in Europe during the last six months of the war.

Fresh and battle-ready, Pershing's forces made the crucial difference in the war. Germany had enjoyed numerical superiority when American troops first arrived, but by the end of the war the Allies could field 600,000 more men than the Germans. Buoyed by the fresh manpower, the Allies pressed their advantage. Their furious offensive in the summer of 1918 broke the opposition, and within a few months the Central Powers faced certain defeat. The Austro-Hungarian Empire asked for peace; Turkey and Bulgaria stopped fighting; and Germany requested an armistice. In a direct slap at the kaiser, Wilson announced that he would negotiate only with a democratic regime in Germany. When the military leaders and the kaiser wavered, a brief revolution forced the kaiser to abdicate, and a civilian regime assumed control of the government.

Germany's new government immediately accepted the armistice and agreed to negotiate a treaty. At 11:00 A.M., November 11, 1918, the guns stopped. Throughout the Western world, crowds filled the streets to celebrate peace.

On November 11, 1918, American troops celebrated the news of the Armistice on the western front, while the Western world rejoiced at home.

SOCIAL UNREST AFTER THE WAR

Peace did not restore stability to the United States. Jubilation over the Armistice quickly dissolved into fear, unleashing the forces of conformity, vigilantism, and repression. Attacks centered on African Americans, organized labor, and political dissidents—the very groups old-stock citizens blamed for the changes in American society that they found most threatening. The Wilson administration led the attacks or did nothing to stop them, as government officials found new enemies at home to replace those abroad. Echoing Bourne's earlier warnings, Frederick Howe, the commissioner of immigration under President Wilson, later confided: "I became distrustful of the state. It seemed to want to hurt people; it showed no concern for innocence; it aggrandized itself and protected its powers by unscrupulous means."

Mounting Racial Tension

Race relations deteriorated badly after the war, as tensions rose in the North because of competition for jobs and housing. In the South, whites felt threatened by the return of 400,000 African-American veterans, many of whom had been trained in the use of firearms, even if they had not seen actual combat. Moreover, many of the veterans had served in France, where they were treated as equals, and southern whites feared they would demand the same treatment at home. Determined to keep African Americans down, southern whites instituted a reign of terror. In 1919, 10 African-American veterans were lynched (several still in uniform); 14 were burned at the stake. All told, 70 lynchings occurred in the first year of peace.

As the heat of summer brought tensions to a boil, race riots broke out in 25 cities. The worst violence erupted on a Chicago beach where 17-year-old Eugene Williams strayed into waters claimed by whites. A rock-throwing mob kept him from reaching shore, and Williams drowned. Fighting broke out when police refused to arrest his killers. Thirteen days of street violence followed, leaving 38 dead, 578 injured, and 1000 families homeless. Racial injustice remained a defining feature of American life throughout the Progressive Era, despite American efforts abroad to make the world "safe for democracy."

Labor Unrest and the Red Scare

Labor was another trouble spot. Most workers had demonstrated their patriotism by not striking during the war, but the Armistice ended their truce with management. High inflation, job competition from returning veterans, and government policies all contributed to labor's discontent. Of the three, inflation hit workers the hardest. Food prices more than doubled between 1915 and 1920; clothing costs more than tripled. Wilson had made peace with trade unions only as a wartime necessity. After the fighting stopped, he removed wartime controls on industry, and business leaders closed ranks to roll back wartime concessions to workers.

The first strike came four days after the Armistice, when textile workers in New York walked out for a 15-percent wage hike and a 44-hour workweek. To the surprise of most observers, the workers won. Many more strikes occurred in the months that followed. Strikers ranged from clothing workers to actors. A general strike paralyzed Seattle; in the steel industry 365,000 steelworkers staged the biggest strike the nation had ever seen; even the Boston police force walked out. By the end of 1919 more than 4 million workers (a staggering 20 percent of the workforce) had staged over 3600 strikes nationwide.

The strikes, however, left the labor movement in shambles. Well-established unions affiliated with the AFL came through the turmoil in good shape, but unions made up of unskilled workers in the mass production industries, such as the United Mine Workers or the steelworkers, went down for the count. Overall, labor unions lost 1.5 million members by 1920. The message was clear: without government backing, organized labor could not win against the united strength of antiunion employers.

The strikes frightened middle- and upper-class Americans, who feared the country might be swept by revolution. The government made matters worse by blaming the strikes on Communists. In 1919, Russian Bolsheviks called for socialists and workers in Europe and the United States to seize their governments and join the worldwide revolution. When Communist revolts erupted in eastern Europe, Americans braced themselves for trouble at home.

A bomb scare brought public fears to a head. On the eve of May 1 (May Day), 1919, authorities discovered 20 bombs in the mail of prominent capitalists, including John D. Rockefeller and J. P. Morgan, Jr., as well as government officials like Supreme Court justice Oliver Wendell Holmes. A month later, bombs exploded in eight American cities. Anarchists were probably responsible, but the public blamed the Communists.

Fear sparked by the labor unrest, communism, and the bombings plunged the United States into the "Red Scare." Every threat to national security, real or imagined, fed the public's anxiety. In Washington, D.C., in May 1919, a man who refused to stand during the Star Spangled Banner at a victory pageant was shot by an enraged sailor while the crowd cheered; in Hammond, Indiana, in February 1919, a jury took two minutes to acquit a man who had killed an immigrant for yelling "To Hell with the United States."

Vigilantism flourished as juries across the country acquitted individuals accused of violent acts against Communists. In the Washing-ton lumber town of Centralia, American Legionnaires stormed the IWW office on Armistice Day. Four attackers died in the fight, and townspeople lynched an IWW member in reprisal. Federal officials then moved to break the IWW's back by prosecuting 165 Wobblie leaders, who received prison sentences of up to 25 years.

Congress joined the attack on radicalism. In May 1919 the House refused to seat Victor Berger, a Milwaukee Socialist, after he was convicted of sedition. The House again denied him his seat following a special election in December 1919. Not until his reelection in 1922, after the government had dropped its charges, did Congress seat him.

Attorney General A. Mitchell Palmer led the attack on radicalism. Determined to become president in 1920, Palmer hoped to ride a wave of public hysteria against radicalism into the White House. To root out sedition, he created a General Intelligence Division (the precursor of the Federal Bureau of Investigation) in the Justice Department under the direction of J. Edgar Hoover. Hoover collected the names of thousands of known or suspected Communists and made plans for a coordinated government attack on their headquarters.

In November 1919 Palmer struck with lightning speed at radicals in 12 cities. The raids netted 250 arrests, a small taste of what was to follow. A second series of raids in 33 cities came in January. This time Palmer's men arrested more than 4000 alleged Communists, many of whom were jailed without bond, beaten, and denied food and water for days. Local authorities freed most of them in a few weeks, except for 600 aliens, who were deported.

Palmer insisted he was ridding the country of the "moral perverts and hysterical neurasthenic women who abound in communism." To cooler heads, however, his tactics gave off the unmistakable odor of a police state. Charles Evans Hughes denounced the raids as "violations of personal rights which savor of the worst practices of tyranny." Suddenly on the defensive, Palmer tried to rally public support by predicting a second wave of terrorist attacks on May Day, 1920. Federal troops went on alert, and police braced them-

THE TREATY OF VERSAILLES

selves in cities across the country, but May Day came and went without incident. Suddenly Palmer looked more like dead wood than presidential timber. His bid for the White House fizzled, and the Red Scare faded into memory.

THE TREATY OF VERSAILLES

Long before the war's military outcome became clear, the Allies started planning for peace, signing secret treaties and plotting harsh peace terms for Germany. Their schemes made a mockery of Wilson's call for "peace without victory." Wilson felt a punitive treaty would sow the seeds of future wars. He repeatedly elaborated his ideas on the interdependence of democracy, free trade, and liberty, and on January 8, 1918, he unveiled the Fourteen Points, his personal peace formula.

The Fourteen Points

Among other things, Wilson called for "open covenants openly arrived at," freedom of the seas, free trade, arms reduction, and self-determination. Other points demanded partial or full independence for minorities and a recognition of the rise of nationalist sentiments. The fourteenth point, which Wilson considered the heart of his plan, called for a League of Nations, an international organization to promote world peace by guaranteeing the territorial integrity of all nations.

Economically, the Fourteen Points projected Wilson's vision of liberal capitalism onto a world stage. His call for freedom of the seas and free trade was designed to protect free-market capitalism from monopolistic restrictions and open huge markets to booming American industries. Self-determination would offer independence to Europe's minorities and thereby delight millions of recent immigrants back in the

---

Table 22.1 WOODROW WILSON'S FOURTEEN POINTS, 1918: SUCCESS AND FAILURE IN IMPLEMENTATION

1. Open covenants of peace openly arrived at	Not fulfilled
2. Absolute freedom of navigation upon the seas in peace and war	Not fulfilled
3. Removal of all economic barriers to the equality of trade among nations	Not fulfilled
4. Reduction of armaments to the level needed only for domestic safety	Not fulfilled
5. Impartial adjustment of colonial claims	Not fulfilled
6. Evacuation of all Russian territory; Russia to be welcomed into the society of free nations	Not fulfilled
7. Evacuation and restoration of Belgium	**Fulfilled**
8. Evacuation and restoration of all French lands; return of Alsace-Lorraine to France	**Fulfilled**
9. Readjustment of Italy's frontiers along lines of Italian nationality	Compromised
10. Self-determination for the former subjects of the Austro-Hungarian Empire	Compromised
11. Evacuation of Rumania, Serbia, and Montenegro; free access to the sea for Serbia	Compromised
12. Self-determination for the former subjects of the Ottoman Empire; secure sovereignty for Turkish portion	Compromised
13. Establishment of an independent Poland, with free and secure access to the sea	**Fulfilled**
14. Establishment of a League of Nations affording mutual guarantees of independence and territorial integrity	Not fulfilled

Source: Data from G. M. Gathorne-Hardy, *The Fourteen Points and the Treaty of Versailles* (Oxford Pamphlets on World Affairs, no. 6, 1939), pp. 8–34; Thomas G. Paterson et al., *American Foreign Policy, A History Since 1900,* 2d ed., Vol. 2, pp. 282–93.

United States, most of whom were drifting into the Democratic party. The League of Nations would enable the world to police aggression and spare the United States that responsibility.

When the tide of war turned in favor of the Allies in 1918, peace forces within Germany agreed to surrender on the basis of the Fourteen Points. They overthrew the kaiser's regime, paving the way for Wilson to make good on his promise of peace without victory.

Wilson's personal prestige peaked with the Armistice. Europeans saw him as the moral leader of the Western democracies, and his authority rested not only on words but on might. Economically, the United States was now the most powerful nation on earth. It had been spared the devastation of war; its economy was booming; and its armed forces, in sharp contrast to Europe's exhausted armies, had barely geared up for battle.

Yet Wilson proved to be his own worst enemy in marshaling support for his peace plans. His first mistake was in asking voters to support Democratic candidates at the polls in 1918 if they wished him to continue as their "unembarrassed spokesman." His request offended the Republicans who had faithfully supported the administration throughout the war. When voters gave Republicans a narrow majority (primarily reflecting local issues), Wilson looked as if he had lost a national referendum on his leadership.

The American Peace Commission's composition further alienated Congress. Wilson elected to take personal responsibility for negotiating the peace, a role no previous president had assumed. In addition, he named only one Republican to the five-man commission; the other three men were loyal Democrats. The failure to include a prominent Republican senator, such as Henry Cabot Lodge of Massachusetts, the newly elected chairman of the powerful Senate Committee on Foreign Relations, was a serious tactical error. The treaty had to be approved by two-thirds of the Senate, and Republicans picked up five new Senate seats in

the congressional elections of 1918, giving them a two-vote majority.

Discord Among the Victors

The delegates, who arrived in Europe early in January 1919, confronted three basic issues: territory, reparations, and future security. On each of these issues, Wilson and the Allies disagreed. Early in the war the Allies had decided to divide Germany's territorial possessions among themselves, but the Fourteen Points called for self-determination. Devastated by the war, the Allies (especially France) wanted to saddle Germany with huge reparations to pay for the war. The Fourteen Points rejected punishment, arguing it would only lead to future wars. On the issue of security, France wanted Germany dismembered while the other Allies favored treaties and alliances.

Only five nations played an important role in the proceedings (the Allies refused to allow Russia's Communist government to participate). Prime Minister David Lloyd George of Great Britain proved to be Wilson's staunchest ally, yet he also defended Britain's colonial ambitions and insisted on reparations. Premier Georges Clemenceau of France was determined to break up the German empire and bleed the German people dry in order to rebuild France. He wryly remarked, "God gave us the Ten Commandments and we broke them. Wilson gave us his Fourteen Points—we shall see."

Premier Vittorio Orlando of Italy was bent on pressing Italy's territorial ambitions in the Tyrol and on the Adriatic. When Wilson refused to sanction Italy's sovereignty over the largely Yugoslav population near Fiume, Orlando stormed out of the peace conference in disgust. The final important negotiator was Count Nobuaki Makino, the spokesman for Japan, who demanded control over German interests in the Far East. He also insisted upon a statement of racial equality in the League of Nations charter—a demand the Allies rejected.

The Russians were conspicuous by their absence at Versailles. Allied leaders, furious at

At the January peace conference in Paris, Wilson met with British Prime Minister David Lloyd George, Italian Premier Vittorio Orlando, and French Premier Georges Clemenceau. Not pictured is Count Nobuaki Makino of Japan, the fifth nation to play an important role in the proceedings.

the Bolsheviks for negotiating a separate peace with Germany at Brest-Litovsk in March 1918, refused to assign V. I. Lenin's "Red" government a place at the peace conference. Indeed, the Allies had earlier decided to intervene militarily in the Russian Revolution, and even as their spokesmen met in Versailles, Allied armies were fighting in Russia on the side of the "White," or anti-Communist, forces.

Personally, Wilson despised the Bolsheviks, and, in keeping with his response to Huerta's regime in Mexico, he refused to extend diplomatic recognition to Lenin's government. Moreover, much as he had with Mexico, Wilson did not stop to ponder how Russians would react to finding American soldiers on their soil. To help rescue Czech troops trapped by the Germans in northern Russia, Wilson sent 5000 American soldiers to the Soviet Union in 1918, where they joined British troops. The following year Wilson sent 9000 American troops to Siberia to help evac-

uate Czech troops through Vladivostok. Wilson hoped American troops in Russia would save the Czechs and discourage any Japanese designs on Siberia. In addition, he wanted this show of force to bolster the anti-Communist forces in Russia by weakening the Bolsheviks' claims to power. Consequently, the United States dragged its feet and did not withdraw its last troops from Russia until 1920.

The Bolsheviks deeply resented these heavy-handed efforts to undermine their regime. Yet the invasion of Russian soil by American troops was not the only reason for the intense hatred that developed between Lenin and Wilson. As the architect of

American Military Forces in Russia, 1918

the Bolshevik Revolution, Lenin emerged as Wilson's chief rival for world leadership. Where Wilson offered liberal democracy and limited social change, Lenin championed communism, social revolution, and swift changes. Wilson was determined to see his vision of the future, not Lenin's, carry the day at Versailles.

To achieve any treaty at all, Wilson had to compromise. Though he fought gallantly, he could not overcome the combined strength of his opponents. In the end he tried to scale down their demands and pinned his hopes on the League of Nations. Under the territorial compromise, the Allies gained control of Germany's colonies as "mandates" under the League of Nation's supervision. Japan acquired Germany's Pacific islands under mandate and assumed Germany's economic interest in China's Shantung peninsula. In eastern Europe, the delegates created the nation states of Poland, Yugoslavia, Czechoslovakia, Estonia, Latvia, Lithuania, and Finland. Europe's political map for the first time roughly resembled its linguistic and cultural map.

Security proved more difficult to negotiate. Over the misgivings of most delegates, Wilson insisted on making the League of Nations an integral part of the final treaty. Dubious that any international organization could protect its borders, France demanded a buffer zone. To satisfy Clemenceau, the delegates gave France control over Alsace-Lorraine for 10 years and placed the coal-rich Saar Basin under the League of Nations for 15 years. After Wilson and Lloyd George both signed security treaties guaranteeing these arrangements, France grudgingly agreed to join the League of Nations.

Despite promises of a just peace, the treaty imposed a harsh settlement on Germany, saddling the country with a $34-billion reparations bill, far more than Germany could pay. In addition, Germany lost territories that contained German people: Alsace-Lorraine to France, the Saar Basin to a League protectorate, a corridor containing the port of Danzig to Poland, and Upper Silesia to Czechoslovakia. Moreover, under the terms of

the war guilt clause in the reparations bill, Germany accepted the blame for World War I, agreed to dismantle its war machine, and pledged not to rearm in the future. Germany felt betrayed. Clearly, this was not a peace based upon the Fourteen Points. Rather, it brought to life Bourne's prediction of victors who "grab what they can."

Wilson derived no joy from the Treaty of Versailles. He accepted the treaty's territorial and punitive provisions in order to ensure the adoption of the League of Nations, which he hoped would secure world peace and eventually redress the treaty's inequities. The League consisted of a general assembly that included all member states and an executive council composed of the United States, Great Britain, France, Italy, Japan, and four other states to be elected by the assembly. But the heart of the League was clearly Article 10, which pledged all members "to respect and uphold the territorial integrity and independence of all members of the League." It embodied Wilson's dream of an international organization that would keep the peace by giving all nations (large and small) equality and protection.

The Struggle for Ratification

Wilson knew the treaty faced stiff opposition back home. In February 1919, 39 Senate Republicans had signed a petition warning they would not approve the League in its present form. To court domestic support, Wilson persuaded the delegates in Europe to acknowledge the Monroe Doctrine, omit domestic issues from the League's purview, and permit member states to withdraw after two years' notice. Though he worked to include provisions the Senate wanted, Wilson refused to separate the League from the treaty.

Senate opposition broke into three groups. The first, 14 "irreconcilables," were staunch isolationists who opposed the League of Nations in any form. Though their attack was broad-based, they concentrated their fire on Article 10, which called for the mutual protection of the territorial integrity of all member states. Critics charged that the article gave the League the authority to commit American troops to foreign military actions.

Henry Cabot Lodge of Massachusetts spoke for the second group of critics, the "strong reservationists." Parodying Wilson's "Fourteen Points," Lodge offered 14 amendments, called the "Lodge" reservations. The most important decreed that the United States "assumes no obligation" to protect the independence or territory boundaries of any other nation, or to send American troops for such purposes unless Congress should so order. Lodge and his followers were basically in favor of the treaty and could have been won over if Wilson had agreed to their modifications.

The third group of opponents, the "limited reservationists," could have been assuaged by relatively minor alterations. They approached international affairs as cautious nationalists, favoring an independent foreign policy as the best tool for protecting American interests. With their backing and the support of Senate Democrats, the treaty would have passed easily.

As Wilson sailed back to the United States, polls suggested that most Americans favored the League in some form. All he had to do was compromise and the treaty would pass. Instead, Wilson descended on Washington in July itching for a fight. Dismissing his opponents as "blind and little provincial people," he declared that the "Senate must take its medicine." His use of a medical metaphor was telling, for Wilson's health had deteriorated under the strain of the war. In fact, in Paris he had suffered what doctors diagnosed as a severe bout of indigestion. In all probability, however, the attack was a mild stroke.

Fearing Senate debate had eroded popular support for the treaty, Wilson decided to take his case directly to the people. Against his doctor's advice, he launched a nationwide tour in September 1919, covering 8000 miles in 33 days and delivering 32 major addresses. He started in the Midwest where opposition to the treaty was strongest, grad-

Europe After World War I

ually moving west where he met cheering crowds. Totally exhausted, Wilson collapsed on September 25 in Pueblo, Colorado. Four days after returning to Washington, he suffered a severe stroke that paralyzed the left side of his body. In all probability, Wilson sustained enough neurological damage to affect his personality and impair his judgment. Unable to work, he did not meet with his cabinet for more than six months. Since the law made no provision for removing an incapacitated president, Wilson's second wife, Edith Bolling Wilson, assisted by a few close aides, ran the government, operating under a cloak of silence about the president's condition.

As the Senate vote on the treaty drew near, Wilson remained intransigent, telling his wife: "Better a thousand times to go down fighting than to dip your colors to dishonorable compromise." He ordered all Democrats to vote against the treaty if it contained any changes. On November 19, the Senate defeated the revised version of the treaty, 55 to 39; a few minutes later the Senate defeated the treaty without changes, 39 to 53.

The Senate's failure to reach a compromise must be blamed on Wilson. When the treaty's supporters tried again in March, many of the Democrats disobeyed the president and voted for a revised version. But 23 Democrats followed Wilson's orders, and the treaty fell 7 votes short of adoption. It would be wrong, however, to interpret the treaty's defeat as an endorsement of isolationism. In essence, the Senate rejected both isolationism and Wilsonian internationalism in favor of preserving a nationalistic foreign policy that would allow the United States to act independently.

The Election of 1920

Unable to accept defeat, Wilson decided to make the election of 1920 a "solemn referendum" on the League: the election of a Democrat would signify approval of the treaty; a Re-

publican victory would mean the treaty's death. At best the president's proposal offered a dubious test of the public's support for the treaty. National elections rarely turn on a single issue. Instead, they involve a myriad of issues, most of which are quite local in character.

When the Democratic convention met in San Francisco, the delegates ignored Wilson's pathetic anglings for a third term and nominated Governor James M. Cox of Ohio. To round out the ticket, they selected the assistant secretary of the navy, Franklin D. Roosevelt, for vice president, largely to capitalize on the magic Roosevelt name. The Republicans nominated Senator Warren G. Harding of Ohio. A stalwart party regular on domestic issues, Harding had voted for the Treaty of Versailles with the Lodge reservations.

While Cox barnstormed the country, campaigning unequivocally for the League of Nations and the Treaty of Versailles, Harding waffled on the issue. Tired of foreign crusades, the people wanted to repudiate Wilson's ardent internationalism, and they did just that, giving Harding 61 percent of the popular vote. (Eugene V. Debs, the Socialist candidate, won 919,799 votes, even though he was then serving a prison term for opposing American involvement in the war.) In the electoral college, Harding trounced Cox 404 to 127.

Wilson's fragile coalition of 1916 had collapsed. Many Democrats, disillusioned by the costs of the war, either stayed at home or switched parties. Angered by the Treaty of Versailles, ethnic Americans (Germans, Italians, and the Irish in particular) abandoned the Democrats in droves. Their defection cost Democrats the nation's urban centers. Western states and the Midwest went Republican as well, for despite their wartime prosperity, many farmers believed that Wilson's agricultural policies had favored cotton growers in the South over grain producers of the Midwest. The Solid South remained a bastion of Democratic strength, but it did not have nearly enough votes to elect a president.

Harding interpreted his victory as a mandate to reject the League. America never joined the League of Nations, opening the way for those who later blamed the United States for the rise of fascism in Italy and

The refusal of the Senate to ratify the Treaty of Versailles and join the League of Nations is satirized in this political cartoon.

CHRONOLOGY OF KEY EVENTS

1914	World War I begins in Europe
1915	U.S. marines are dispatched to Haiti; German submarine sinks the British passenger ship *Lusitania*, killing 1198 passengers, including 128 Americans
1916	Germany promises to suspend unannounced submarine attacks in *Sussex* pledge
1917	Germany resumes submarine attacks; Zimmermann telegram, secret note to German ambassador in Mexico, proposing Mexico and Japan join Central Powers if the United States enters the war in Europe; United States enters the war; Espionage Act passed, imposing fines and jail sentences for aiding the enemy or obstructing recruitment; Russian Revolution begins;

	War Industries Board is created to coordinate industrial production
1918	Wilson's Fourteen Points outline a plan for peace; National War Labor Board is created to arbitrate disputes between labor and management; Sedition Act passes, punishing any expression of disloyalty to the American government or flag; Germany surrenders
1919	Treaty of Versailles ends World War I
1920	In raids authorized by Attorney General Palmer many suspected Communists are arrested; Senate rejects Treaty of Versailles; Nineteenth Amendment grants women the right to vote; Republican Warren Harding is elected twenty-ninth president

Nazism in Germany. Critics, including a number of later historians, went so far as to claim that America's failure to join the League caused World War II. If the United States had only joined, they insisted, the League would have been able to deter German and Japanese aggression by presenting a united front. Instead of peace without victory, the war's main legacy turned out to be bitterness and suspicion.

CONCLUSION

World War I made Randolph Bourne a prophet. The changes in American life between 1914 and 1919 bore out his fear that war obliterates idealism and brings out the dark side of the human spirit. World War I accelerated social and economic changes, expanded the power of the federal government, and unleashed extraordinary fears that led to attacks on labor unions, African Americans, immigrants, Socialists, and Communists. Similar confusion gripped America's foreign policy. The United States emerged from the Great War as the premier economic power on earth, with global interests requiring protection. Those responsibilities terrified a country that had been lulled into a sense of security by three centuries of geographic isolation. Tired and disillusioned, Americans attempted to flee their responsibilities rather than make global political commitments commensurate with their new economic interests.

The result was an upsurge in isolationist sentiment in the United States during the 1920s and 1930s that made it very difficult for America's leaders to respond strongly to the rise of despotic governments in Europe and the Far East. The Great War did not make the world "safe for democracy." It left humankind a legacy of bitterness, hatred, and suspicion, creating rich soil for the seeds of future conflicts.

In 1920, however, most Americans felt too tired and too disillusioned to give much thought to the future. Harding's promise of a return to "normalcy" struck a responsive chord. Millions of Americans thought he meant resurrecting rural villages and a small farm economy, restoring Anglo-Protestant culture, and forgetting about the rest of the world. The 1920s proved they were in for a surprise.

SUGGESTIONS FOR FURTHER READING

Lloyd Ambrosus, *Woodrow Wilson and the American Diplomatic Tradition* (1988). Presents a comprehensive account of American diplomacy during and after the war.

Robert H. Ferrell, *Woodrow Wilson and World War I, 1917–1921* (1985). Thoroughly analyzes the president's responses to the conflict.

Martin Gilbert, *The First World War* (1994). Discusses the conflict's causes and fighting.

David M. Kennedy, *Over Here: The First World War and American Society* (1980). Examines the war's impact on the homefront.

Michael J. Lyons, *World War I* (1994). Offers a comprehensive account of the conflict.

Herbert F. Margulies, *The Mild Reservations and the League of Nations Controversy in the Senate* (1989). Explores the reasons the Senate rejected American membership in the League of Nations.

Arthur Walworth, *Wilson and His Peacemakers: American Diplomacy at the Paris Peace Conference* (1986). Examines the contentious debates surrounding the Treaty of Versailles.

OVERVIEWS AND SURVEYS

Randolph S. Bourne, *War and the Intellectuals: Collected Essays, 1915–1919* (1964); Foster R. Dulles, *America's Rise to World Power, 1898–1954* (1955); Modris Eksteins, *Rites of Spring: The Great War and the Birth of the Modern Age* (1989); Robert H. Ferrell, *Woodrow Wilson and World War I, 1917–1921* (1985); Lloyd C. Gardner, *Safe for Democracy: The Anglo-American Response to Revolution, 1913–1923* (1984); Otis L. Graham, Jr., *The Great Campaigns: Reform and War in America, 1900–1928* (1971); Ellis W. Hawley, *The Great War and the Search for a Modern Order: A*

History of the American People and Their Institutions, 1917–1933 (1979); William E. Leuchtenburg, *The Perils of Prosperity, 1914–32* (1958); Emily S. Rosenberg, *Spreading the American Dream: American Economic and Cultural Expansion 1890–1945* (1982); Bernadotte Schmitt and Harold C. Vedeler, *The World in the Crucible: 1914–1919* (1984); Daniel M. Smith, *The Great Departure: The United States and World War I, 1914–1920* (1965).

The Road to War

John M. Cooper, Jr., *The Vanity of Power: American Isolationism and the First World War, 1914–1917* (1969) and *The Warrior and the Priest: Woodrow Wilson and Theodore Roosevelt* (1983); Patrick Devlin, *Too Proud to Fight: Woodrow Wilson's Neutrality* (1974); Ross Gregory, *The Origins of American Intervention in the First World War* (1971); George F. Kennan, *The Decision to Intervene* (1958) and *Russia Leaves the War* (1956); N. Gordon Levin, Jr., *Woodrow Wilson and World Politics: America's Response to War and Revolution* (1968); Arthur S. Link, *Woodrow Wilson: Revolution, War and Peace* (1979); Ernest R. May, *The World War and American Isolation, 1914–1917* (1959); Barbara Tuchman, *The Guns of August* (1962).

American Industry Goes to War

William J. Breen, *Uncle Sam at Home, 1917–1919* (1984); Valerie Jean Conner, *The National War Labor Board: Stability, Social Justice, and the Voluntary State in World War I* (1983); Robert D. Cuff, *The War Industries Board: Business-Government Relations During World War I* (1973); Charles Gilbert, *American Financing of World War I* (1970); Maurine Weiner Greenwald, *Women, War, and Work: The Impact of World War I on Women Workers in the United States* (1980); Stephen Skowronek, *Building a New American State: The Expansion of National Administrative Capacities, 1877–1920* (1982); Stephen L. Vaughn, *Holding Fast the Inner Lines: Democracy, Nationalism, and the Committee on Public Information* (1980); Neil A. Wynn, *From Progressivism to Prosperity: World War I and American Society* (1986).

The American Public Goes to War

Rodolfo Acuña, *Occupied America*, 3d ed. (1988); Arthur E. Barbeau and Florette Henri, *The Unknown Soldiers: Black American Troops in World War I* (1974); Allan M. Brandt, *No Magic Bullet: A Social*

History of Venereal Disease in the United States Since 1880 (1985); John Whiteclay Chambers II, *To Raise an Army: The Draft Comes to Modern America* (1987); Wayne Cornelius, *Building the Cactus Curtain: Mexican Migration and U.S. Responses from Wilson to Carter* (1980); Maurine W. Greenwald, *Women, War, and Work: The Impact of World War I on Women Workers* (1980); James R. Grossman, *Land of Hope: Chicago, Black Southerners, and the Great Migration* (1989); David M. Kennedy, *Over Here: The First World War and American Society* (1980); K. Austin Kerr, *Organized for Prohibition: A New History of the Anti-Saloon League* (1985); Daniel J. Kevles, *In the Name of Eugenics: Genetics and the Uses of Human Heredity* (1985); Frederick C. Luebke, *Bonds of Loyalty: German-Americans and World War I* (1974); Carole Marks, *Farewell—We're Good and Gone: The Great Black Migration* (1989); John F. McClymer, *War and Welfare: Social Engineering in America, 1890–1925* (1980); Paul L. Murphy, *World War I and the Origin of Civil Liberties in the United States* (1979); Gerald W. Patton, *War and Race: The Black Officer in the American Military* (1981); H. C. Peterson and Gilbert C. Fite, *Opponents of War 1917–1918* (1957); William Preston, Jr., *Aliens and Dissenters: Federal Suppression of Radicals, 1903–1933* (1963); John A. Thompson, *Reformers and War: American Progressive Publicists and the First World War* (1987); Stephen L. Vaughn, *Holding Fast the Inner Lines: Democracy, Nationalism, and the Committee on Public Information* (1980).

The War Front

Arthur E. Barbeau and Florette Henri, *The Unknown Soldiers: Black American Troops in World War I* (1974); Edward M. Coffman, *The War to End Wars: The American Military Experience in World War I* (1968); Harvey DeWeerd, *President Wilson Fights His War: World War I and the American Intervention* (1968); Russell F. Weigley, *The American Way of War: A History of United States Military Strategy and Policy* (1973).

Social Unrest After the War

Wesley M. Bagby, *The Road to Normalcy: The Presidential Campaign and Election of 1920* (1962); David Brody, *Labor in Crisis: The Steel Strike of 1919* (1965); Richard C. Cortner, *A Mob Intent on Death: The NAACP and the Arkansas Riot Cases* (1988); Paul Fussell, *The Great War and Modern Memory* (1975); Christine A. Lunardini, *From Equal Suffrage to Equal Rights: Alice Paul and the National Woman's Party, 1910–1928* (1986); Robert K. Murray, *The Red Scare: A Study in National Hysteria, 1919–1920* (1955); Burl Noggle, *Into the Twenties: The United States from Armistice to Normalcy* (1974); Francis Russell, *A City in Terror: 1919, the Boston Police Strike* (1975); Arthur M. Schlesinger, Jr., *The Crisis of the Old Order, 1919–1933* (1957); William Tuttle, Jr., *Race Riot: Chicago and the Red Summer of 1919* (1970).

The Treaty of Versailles

Thomas A. Bailey, *Woodrow Wilson and the Great Betrayal* (1945), and *Woodrow Wilson and the Lost Peace* (1944); Warren F. Kuehl, *Seeking World Order: The United States and International Organization to 1920* (1969); N. Gordon Levin, Jr., *Woodrow Wilson and World Politics: America's Response to War and Revolution* (1968); Herbert F. Margulies, *The Mild Reservationists and the League of Nations Controversy in the Senate* (1989); Arno J. Mayer, *Politics and Diplomacy in Peacemaking: Containment and Counterrevolution at Versailles, 1918–1919* (1967) and *Wilson vs. Lenin: Political Origins of the New Diplomacy, 1917–1918* (1959); Ralph A. Stone, *The Irreconcilables: The Fight Against the League of Nations* (1970); William C. Widenor, *Henry Cabot Lodge and the Search for an American Foreign Policy* (1980).

Biographies

Robert W. Cherny, *A Righteous Cause: The Life of William Jennings Bryan* (1985); Kendrick A. Clements, *William Jennings Bryan, Missionary Isolationist* (1982); Stanley Coben, *A. Mitchell Palmer: Politician* (1963); Lawrence W. Levine, *Defender of the Faith: William Jennings Bryan, The Last Decade, 1915–1925* (1965); Arthur S. Link, *Wilson*, 5 vols. (1947–1965); James R. Vitelli, *Randolph Bourne* (1981); Edwin A. Weinstein, *Woodrow Wilson: A Medical and Psychological Biography* (1981).

CHAPTER 23
MODERN TIMES, 1920–1929

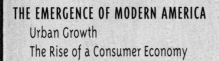

THE EMERGENCE OF MODERN AMERICA
Urban Growth
The Rise of a Consumer Economy

THE FORMATION OF MODERN AMERICAN CULTURE
Mass Entertainment
Spectator Sports
Low-Brow and Middle-Brow Culture
The Avant-Garde
The Sex Debate

THE CLASH OF CULTURES
The New Woman
Prohibition
The Scopes Trial
Xenophobia and Restricting
  Immigration
The Ku Klux Klan
African-American Protests
The Harlem Renaissance

THE REPUBLICAN RESTORATION
Handsome Harding
Silent Cal
The Twilight of Progressivism
The Election of 1928

THE GREAT CRASH
Speculative Manias
The Market Crashes
Why It Happened

In 1898 the Physicians Club of Chicago held a symposium on "sexual hygiene" to give its members some practical tips on marriage counseling. To those married women who wanted information on birth control, Chicago physicians were to offer this advice: "Get a divorce and vacate the position for some other woman, who is able and willing to fulfill all a wife's duties as well as to enjoy her privileges."

Most Americans shared this view. They did not believe sex should be separated from procreation. To the male custodians of morality, birth control challenged patriarchy. It would lead to sexual promiscuity and an epidemic of venereal diseases, they charged, and weaken the family by raising the divorce rate. Many women condemned birth control just as soundly. Taught from childhood to embrace the cult of domesticity, they accepted childbearing as their "biological duty" and rejected birth control as immoral and radical.

Yet by 1950 most Americans regarded birth control as a public virtue rather than a private vice. The person most responsible for this amazing transformation was Margaret Sanger, a tireless crusader who possessed an iron will and the soul of a firebrand. Sanger's mother, Margaret Higgins, bore 11 children, all weighing ten pounds or more; Michael Higgins, her father, worked as a stonecutter. Her mother died of pulmonary tuberculosis at 43; her father lived to 84. For the rest of her life, Sanger blamed her mother's suffering on the absence of effective family planning.

An unhappy marriage also pushed Sanger toward reform work. While still in nursing school, she married William Sanger, an architect and would-be artist. After bearing three children in rapid succession, Sanger overcame her own struggle with tuberculosis, finished school, and began a nursing career. Feeling trapped by married life and determined to achieve her own identity, Margaret plunged into New York's labor movement. As her marriage to William slowly dissolved, she devoted herself to the working poor.

Convinced that large families placed a terrible economic burden on poor people, Sanger came to regard family planning as the most important issue of her day because it could make abortion, as well as unwanted babies, unnecessary. When male labor leaders refused to add contraception to their reform agenda, Sanger left the labor movement, resolving to make birth control her life's work.

From 1914 to 1937 Sanger campaigned to make birth control morally acceptable. She built a network of clinics where women could get accurate information about contraception and obtain inexpensive, reliable birth control devices. After World War II she helped organize the international planned parenthood movement and played a key role in the development of "the pill." Through her birth control work, Margaret Sanger probably had a greater influence on the world than any other American woman of her day.

Sanger played a key role in the transition to modern times. By promoting birth control, she helped alter American sexual behavior, redefine women's role in society, and redistributed power within the family. But the birth control movement represented just one symp-

Margaret Sanger, a nurse who had watched many women suffer from unwanted births and die from illegal abortions, was one of the founders of the modern American birth control movement. After spending a year studying medical literature and learning about contraceptives, Sanger began publishing the journal *The Woman Rebel*.

tom of a society in flux, one in which urban growth, ethnic diversity, and economic development set the stage for controversy.

The 1920s was a decade of exciting social changes and deep cultural conflicts. The most obvious signs of change were the growth of cities, with their huge ethnic populations; the rise of a consumer-oriented economy, evident in the spread of cars, electricity, and a host of new appliances; and the spread of mass entertainment, such as spectator sports, radio, and the movies. But a deeper transformation was also under way, a "revolution in morals and manners." Sexual mores and gender roles underwent dramatic shifts.

For many Americans, these changes represented a liberation from the restrictions of the country's Victorian past. But for others, especially those who lived in the more rural and provincial parts of the country, morals seemed to be decaying and the United States seemed to be changing in undesirable ways. The result was a thinly veiled "cultural civil war," in which a pluralistic society clashed bitterly over such issues as foreign immigration, evolution, and race.

Wets battled drys, Darwinists ridiculed fundamentalists, nativists denounced the "new immigrants," and rural folks denounced the dubious morals of city dwellers. None of these disputes was new. Each was a continuing, if sharpening, controversy that had been building for decades. At bottom, these conflicts were the unavoidable growing pains of a nation struggling to come to grips with cultural pluralism and changing values.

THE EMERGENCE OF MODERN AMERICA

Americans in the 1920s were the first to wear ready-made, exact-sized clothing, the first to play electric phonographs or use electric vacuum cleaners or listen to commercial radio broadcasts or drink fresh orange juice year round. In countless ways, large and small, American life was transformed during the 1920s, at least in the nation's growing towns and cities, where the majority of Americans now lived. Cigarettes, cosmetics, and syn-

thetic fabrics such as rayon became staples of American life. Public opinion polling, sex education, newspaper gossip columns, illuminated billboards, commercial airplane flights—all were novelties during the 1920s. In that decade, the United States became a modern consumer society.

Urban Growth

For more than four decades, the Empire State Building was the largest building in the world, rising 102 stories above New York City's Fifth Avenue. Today, only Chicago's Sears Tower and New York's World Trade Center are taller. Assembly-line construction techniques allowed crews to erect a floor a day—five times faster than had been possible a decade before. The 1454-foot-high building cost nearly $41 million to erect, but when it was finished in 1930, it stood half-empty—a symbol of a decade's broken dreams.

For over a decade, architects had designed buildings to reach higher into the sky. In 1907, New York's 700-foot-high Metropolitan Life Insurance Building became the world's tallest. In 1913, it was surpassed by the 800-foot-high Woolworth Building. In 1929, a 185-foot spire placed atop the Chrysler Building gave it the title of the world's tallest structure. A year later, it lost the title to the Empire State Building. In less than a decade, the average height of a New York skyscraper rose ten stories.

All across America, urban skylines were transformed. Urban growth drove up land values and reshaped the skyline of America's cities, especially in central business districts, where office space more than doubled during the 1920s. Skyrocketing land prices forced architects to build "up" instead of "out," launching the first great era of skyscrapers. In Miami, art deco hotels and office buildings, with bold outlines and streamlined forms, rose up along the city's stunning beachfront. By 1929, the United States had 377 buildings with more than 20 stories.

According to the census of 1920 more Americans dwelled in cities than in the country. For the first time in its history, the United

States became a predominantly urban society. Most urbanites lived in small towns and cities, but a surprising number resided in rapidly growing large cities, like Chicago, of 50,000 or more.

America's cities attracted large numbers of new immigrants from southern and eastern Europe. These immigrants poured into the industrial cities of the Northeast and Midwest, filling them with new sights, sounds, and smells that many old-stock Americans found offensive. World War I briefly stopped the flow of immigrants, but after the armistice another 3.2 million immigrants poured into the United States before the country restricted entry.

The racial composition of the nation's cities also underwent a decisive change. In 1910, urban areas outside the South were overwhelmingly white; three out of every four African Americans lived on farms and nine out of ten lived in the South. World War I changed that profile. Hoping to escape tenant farming, sharecropping, and peonage, 1.5 million southern African Americans moved to cities in the 1920s. Some went to southern cities, but most settled in major northern metropolises such as New York, Philadelphia, Cleveland, and Chicago. In 1890, African-Americans made up just one percent of Manhattan's population, in 1930, 11 percent. During the 1910s and 1920s, Chicago's African-American population grew 148 percent, Cleveland's by 307 percent, Detroit's by 611 percent.

During this massive movement of people, competition for available housing became a major source of friction. In city after city, whites closed ranks against African Americans, blocking access to white neighborhoods. Cities passed municipal residential segregation ordinances; white realtors refused to show houses in white areas to African Americans; and white property owners formed "neighborhood improvement associations," largely in order to keep African Americans out. After the Supreme Court declared municipal resident segregation ordinances unconstitutional in 1917, whites resorted to the restrictive covenant, a formal deed restriction that bound white property owners in a given neighborhood to sell only to whites. Those who broke such agreements could be sued by "damaged" neighbors. Not until 1948 did the Supreme Court strike down restrictive covenants. Zoning laws offered an even more subtle way of segregating cities. Originally designed to keep businesses and industry out of residential neighborhoods, zoning restrictions had become the tool of choice for segregating people on the basis of wealth by the 1930s.

Racial animosity, restrictive covenants, and zoning restrictions confined African Americans to certain neighborhoods. The decade following World War I saw the development of scores of American cities within cities. The largest was Harlem, in upper Man-

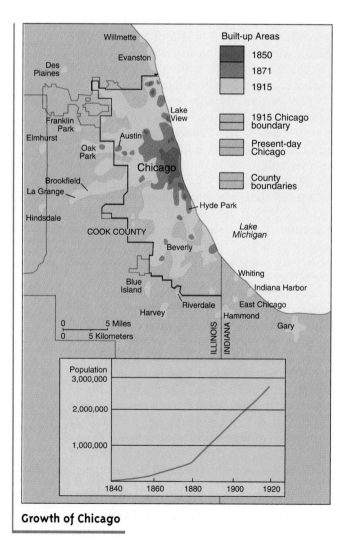

Growth of Chicago

hattan; 200,000 African Americans lived in a neighborhood that had been virtually all white fifteen years before. These "black metropolises" resembled the ethnic ghettoes of the late nineteenth and early twentieth centuries, with one major difference—racial prejudice made it all but impossible for their residents to escape.

While a growing number of African Americans migrated to central cities, many white members of the country's new middle class of white-collar employees moved to fast-growing suburbs, which new forms of transportation had made possible. For much of the nation's history, cities could not grow larger because workers had to live within walking distance of their jobs. After the Civil War, trolleys and streetcars permitted workers to move beyond the walking radius of the factories. During the 1920s, the automobile opened up vast new regions for housing, giving people numerous options about where to live. Once the exclusive domain of the well-to-do, the suburbs were now widely accessible.

Yet optimists who hoped to escape the city's congestion by moving to the suburbs were too optimistic. The sharp rise in road construction following the Federal Highway Act of 1916 produced complicated lateral traffic flows within cities, and traffic congestion got worse. City planners counterattacked with traffic circles, synchronized stoplights, and divided dual highways, but nothing could free motorists from rush hour and holiday traffic jams.

The Rise of a Consumer Economy

Two automotive titans—Henry Ford and Alfred Sloan—symbolized the profound transformations that took place in American industry during the 1910s and 1920s. In 1913, the 50-year-old Ford revolutionized American manufacturing by introducing the automated assembly line. By using conveyor belts to bring automobile parts to workers, he reduced the assembly time for a Ford car from 12½ hours in 1912 to just 1½ hours in 1914. Declining production costs allowed

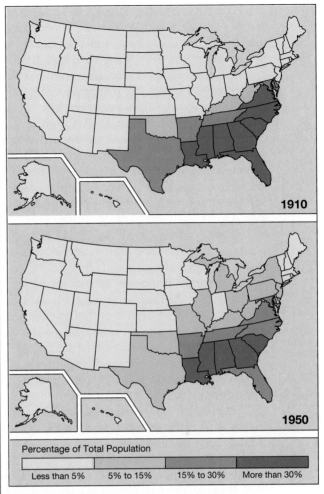

African-American Population, 1910 and 1950

Ford to cut prices—six times between 1921 and 1925, reducing a new Ford's cost to just $290. This was less than three months wages for an average American worker, and it made cars affordable for the average family. To lower employee turnover and raise productivity, Ford also introduced a minimum daily wage of $5 in 1914—twice what most workers earned—and shortened the workday from nine hours to eight. Twelve years later, Ford reduced his workweek from six days to five. Ford demonstrated the logic of mass production: expanded production allows manufacturers to reduce costs and therefore increase the number of products sold, and higher wages allow workers to buy more products.

Alfred Sloan, the president of General Motors from 1923 to 1941, built his company into the world's largest automaker not by refining the production process but by adopting new approaches to advertising and marketing. Sloan summed up his philosophy with these blunt words: "The primary object of the corporation was to make money, not just to make cars." Unlike Ford, a farmer's son who wanted to produce an inexpensive, functional vehicle with few frills (he said that his customers could have any color that they wanted as long as it was black), Sloan was convinced that Americans were willing to pay extra for luxury and prestige. He advertised his cars as symbols of wealth and status, and in 1927 introduced the yearly model change, to convince motorists to trade in old models for newer ones with flashier styling. He also developed a series of divisions that were differentiated by status, price, and level of luxury, with Chevrolets less expensive than Buicks or Cadillacs. To make his cars affordable, he set up the nation's first national consumer credit agency in 1919. If Henry Ford demonstrated the efficacy of mass production, Sloan revealed the importance of merchandising in a modern consumer society.

Cars were the symbol of the new consumer society that emerged in the 1920s. In 1919, there were just 6.7 million cars on American roads. By 1929, there were more than 27 million—nearly one car for every household in the United States. In that year, 1 American in every 5 had a car—compared to 1 in every 37 English and 1 in every 40 French. With car manufacturers and banks encouraging the public to buy the car of their dreams on credit, the American love affair with the car truly began. A quarter of all American families purchased a car in 1929. About 60 percent bought it on credit, often paying interest rates of 30 percent or more.

Cars revolutionized the American way of life. Enthusiasts claimed the automobile promoted family togetherness through evening rides, picnics, and weekend excursions. Critics decried squabbles between parents and teenagers over use of the automobile, and an apparent decline in church attendance resulting from Sunday outings. Worst of all, charged critics, automobiles gave young people freedom and privacy, serving as "portable bedrooms" that couples could take anywhere.

The automobile also transformed the American landscape, quickly obliterating all traces of the horse and buggy past. During the 1920s, the country doubled its system of roads and highways. The nation spent over $2 billion annually building and maintaining roads; by 1929 there were 852,000 miles of roads in the United States, compared to just 369,000 in 1920. The car also brought with it pollution, congestion, and nearly 30,000 traffic deaths a year.

The automobile industry provided an enormous stimulus for the national economy. By 1929, the industry produced 12.7 percent of all manufacturing output, and employed 1 out of every 12 workers. Automobiles in turn stimulated the growth of steel, glass, and rubber industries, along with gasoline stations, motor lodges, campgrounds, and the hotdog stands that dotted the nation's roadways.

Other emblems of the consumer economy were the telephone and electricity. By 1930, two-thirds of all American households had electricity and half had telephones. As more and more of America's homes received electricity, new appliances followed—refrigerators, washing machines, vacuum cleaners, and toasters quickly took hold. Advertisers claimed that "labor-saving" appliances would ease the sheer physical drudgery of housework, but they did not shorten the average housewife's workweek. Women now had to do more because standards of cleanliness kept rising. Sheets had to be changed weekly; the house had to be vacuumed daily. In short, social pressure expanded household chores to keep pace with the new technology. Far from liberating women, appliances imposed new standards and pressures.

Ready-to-wear clothing was another important innovation in America's expanding consumer economy. During World War I, the federal government defined standard clothing sizes to help the nation's garment industry meet the demand for military uniforms. Standard sizes meant that it was now possible to mass-produce ready-to-wear clothing. Since there was no copyright on clothing designs until the 1950s, garment manufacturers could pirate European fashions and reproduce them using less expensive fabrics.

Even the public's eating habits underwent far-reaching shifts, as Americans began to consume fewer starches (like bread and potatoes) and more fruit and sugar. But the most striking development was the shift toward processed foods. Instead of preparing certain foods from scratch at home (plucking chickens, roasting nuts, or grinding coffee beans), an increasing number of Americans purchased foods that were ready to cook. Important innovations in food processing occurred during World War I, as manufacturers learned how to efficiently can and freeze foods. Processed foods saved homemakers enormous amounts of time in peeling, grinding, and cutting.

Accompanying the rise of new consumer-oriented businesses were profound shifts in the ways that business operated. To stimulate sales and increase profits, businesses expanded advertising, offered installment credit, and created the nation's first regional and national chains.

The nation's first million-dollar advertising campaign was for Uneeda Biscuits and its patented waterproof box, demonstrating the power of advertising. Before the 1920s, most advertisements consisted of vast expanses of print. Absent were brand names, pictures, or catchphrases. During the 1920s, advertising agencies hired psychologists (including John B. Watson, the founder of behaviorism, and Edward Bernays, Sigmund Freud's nephew) to design the first campaigns. They touted products by building up name-brand identification, creating memorable slogans, manipulating endorsements by doctors or celebrities, and appealing to consumers' hunger for prestige and status. By 1929, American companies were spending $3 billion annually to advertise their products, five times more than in 1914.

The use of installment credit soared during the 1920s. Banks offered the country's first home mortgages, while manufacturers of everything from cars to irons allowed consumers to pay "on time." About 60 percent of all furniture and 75 percent of all radios were purchased on the installment plan. In contrast to a Victorian society that had placed a high premium on thrift and saving, the new consumer society emphasized spending and borrowing.

A fundamental shift took place in the American economy during the 1920s. The nation's families spent a declining proportion of their income on necessities—food, clothing, and utilities—and an increasing share on appliances, recreation, and a host of new consumer products. As a result, older industries, such as textiles, railroads, and steel, declined, while newer industries, such as appliances, automobiles, aviation, chemicals, entertainment, and processed foods, surged ahead rapidly.

During the 1920s, the chain-store movement revolutionized retailing. Chains like Woolworth's, the five-and-dime store chain, multiplied across the country. The largest grocery chain, A&P, had 17,500 stores by 1928. Besides drugstore and cigar-store chains, there were also interlocking networks of banks and utility companies. These banks and utilities played a critical role in promoting the financial speculation of the late 1920s that would become one of the causes of the Great Depression.

THE FORMATION OF MODERN AMERICAN CULTURE

Many of the defining features of modern American culture emerged during the 1920s. The best-seller, the book club, the record chart, the radio, the talking picture, and spectator sports all became popular forms of mass entertainment. But the primary reason the 1920s stand out as one of the most important periods in American cultural history is because the decade produced a generation of artists, musicians, and writers who were among the most innovative and creative in the country's history.

Mass Entertainment

Of all the new appliances to enter the nation's homes during the 1920s, none had a more revolutionary impact than radio. Sales soared from $60 million in 1922 to $426 million in 1929. The first commercial radio station began broadcasting in 1919, and during the 1920s, the nation's airwaves were filled with musical variety shows and comedies.

Radio drew the nation together by bringing news, entertainment, and advertisements to more than ten million households. Radio blunted regional differences and imposed similar tastes and lifestyles. No other media had the power to create heroes and villains so quickly; when Charles Lindbergh became the first person to fly nonstop across the Atlantic from New York to Paris in 1928, the radio brought his incredible feat into American homes, transforming him into a celebrity overnight.

Radio also brought the nation decidedly unheroic images. The nation's most popular radio show, "Amos 'n Andy," which first aired in 1926 on Chicago's WMAQ, spread vicious racial stereotypes into homes whose white occupants knew little about African Americans. Other minorities fared no better. The Italian gangster and the tightfisted Jew became stock characters in radio programming.

The phonograph was not far behind the radio in importance. The 1920s saw the record player enter American life in full force. Piano sales sagged as phonograph production rose from just 190,000 in 1923 to 5 million in 1929.

The popularity of jazz, blues, and "hillbilly" music fueled the phonograph boom. Novelist F. Scott Fitzgerald called the 1920s the "Jazz Age"—and the decade was truly jazz's golden age. Duke Ellington wrote the first extended jazz compositions; Louis Armstrong popularized "scat" (singing of nonsense syllables); Fletcher Henderson pioneered big band jazz; and trumpeter Jimmy McPartland and clarinetist Benny Goodman popularized the Chicago school of improvisation.

The blues craze erupted in 1920, when a black singer named Mamie Smith released a recording called "Crazy Blues." The record became a sensation, selling 75,000 copies in a month and a million copies in seven months. Recordings by Ma Rainey, the "Mother of the Blues," and Bessie Smith, the "Empress of the Blues," brought the blues, with its poignant and defiant reaction to life's sorrows, to a vast audience.

"Hillbilly" music broke into mass culture in 1923, when a Georgia singer named "Fiddlin' John" Carson sold 500,000 copies of his recordings. Another country artist, Vernon Dalhart, sold 7 million copies of a recording of "The Wreck of Old 97." "Country" music's appeal was not limited to the rural South or West; city people, too, listened to country songs, reflecting a deep nostalgia for a simpler past.

The single most significant new instrument of mass entertainment was the movies. Movie attendance soared, from 50 million patrons a week in 1920 to 90 million weekly in 1929. Americans spent 83 cents of every entertainment dollar going to the movies—and three-fourths of the population went to a movie theater every week.

During the late teens and 1920s, the film industry took on its modern form. In cinema's earliest days, the film industry was based in the nation's theatrical center—New York. By the 1920s, the industry had relocated to Hollywood, drawn by cheap land and labor, the ready accessibility of varied scenery, and a climate ideal for year-round filming. (Some filmmakers moved to avoid lawsuits from individuals like Thomas Edison, who owned patent rights over the filmmaking process.) Each year, Hollywood released nearly 700 movies, dominating worldwide film production. By 1926, Hollywood had captured 95 percent of the British and 70 percent of the French markets.

A small group of companies consolidated their control over the film industry and created the "studio system" that would dominate film production for the next thirty years. Paramount, 20th-Century Fox, MGM, and other studios owned their own production facilities, ran their own worldwide distribution networks, and controlled theater chains committed to showing their companies' products. In addition, they kept certain actors, directors, and screenwriters under contract.

The popularity of the movies soared as films increasingly featured glamour, sophistication, and sex appeal. New kinds of movie stars appeared: the mysterious sex goddess, personified by Greta Garbo; the passionate hot-blooded lover, epitomized by Rudolph Valentino; and the flapper, with her bobbed hair and skimpy skirts. New film genres also debuted, including swashbuckling adventures, sophisticated comedies, and tales of flaming youth and the new sexual freedom. Americans flocked to see Hollywood spectacles such as Cecil B. DeMille's *Ten Commandments* (1923) with its "cast of thousands" and dazzling special effects. Comedies, such as the slapstick masterpieces starring Charlie Chaplin and Buster Keaton enjoyed great popularity as well.

Like radio, movies created a new popular culture, with common speech, dress, behavior, and heroes. And like radio, Hollywood did its share to reinforce racial stereotypes by denigrating minority groups. The radio, the electric phonograph, and the silver screen all molded and mirrored mass culture.

Spectator Sports

Spectator sports attracted vast audiences in the 1920s. The country yearned for heroes in an increasingly impersonal, bureaucratic society, and sports, as well as the film industry, provided them. Prize fighters like Jack Dempsey became national idols. Team sports flourished, but Americans focused on individual superstars, people whose talents or personalities made them appear larger than life. Knute Rockne and his "Four Horsemen" at Notre Dame spurred interest in college football, and professional football began during the 1920s. In 1925, Harold "Red" Grange, the "Galloping Ghost" halfback for the University of Illinois, attracted 68,000 fans to a professional football game at Brooklyn's Polo Grounds.

Baseball drew even bigger crowds than football. The decade began with the sport mired in scandal. In 1920, three members of the Chicago White Sox told a grand jury that they and five other players had thrown the 1919 World Series. As a result of the "Black Sox" scandal, eight players were banished from the sport. But baseball soon regained its popularity, thanks to George Herman ("Babe") Ruth, the sport's undisputed superstar. Up until the 1920s Ty Cobb's defensive brand of baseball, with its emphasis on base hits and stolen bases, had dominated the sport. Ruth transformed baseball into the game of the home-run hitter. In 1921, the New York Yankee slugger hit 59 home runs—more than any other team combined. In 1927, the "Sultan of Swat" hit 60.

Low-Brow and Middle-Brow Culture

"It was a characteristic of the Jazz Age," novelist F. Scott Fitzgerald wrote, "that it had no interest in politics at all." What, then, were Americans interested in? Entertainment was Fitzgerald's answer. Parlor games like Mah Jong and crossword puzzles became enormously popular during the 1920s. Contract bridge became the most durable of the new pastimes, followed closely by photography. Americans hit golf balls, played tennis, and bowled. Dance crazes like the fox trot, the Charleston, and the jitterbug swept the country.

New kinds of pulp fiction found a wide audience. Edgar Rice Burroughs' *Tarzan of the Apes* became a runaway best-seller. For readers who felt concerned about urbanization and industrialization, the adventures of the lone white man in "dark Africa" revived the spirit of frontier individualism. Zane Grey's novels, such as *Riders of the Purple Sage,* enjoyed even greater popularity, with their tried but true formula of romance, action, and a moralistic struggle between good and evil, all in a western setting. Between 1918 and 1934, Grey wrote 24 books and became the best-known writer of popular fiction in the country.

Other readers wanted to be titillated, as evidenced by the boom in "confession magazines." Urban values, liberated women, and Hollywood films had all relaxed Victorian standards. Confession magazines rushed to fill the vacuum, purveying stories of romantic success and failure, divorce, fantasy, and adultery. Writers survived the censors' cut by

Spectator sports became popular in the 1920s. Heroes of the day included men like "Red" Grange (left) of the University of Illinois and "Babe" Ruth (right) of the New York Yankees.

placing moral tags at the end of their stories, in which readers were advised to avoid similar mistakes in their own lives.

Readers too embarrassed to pick up a copy of *True Romance* could read more urbane magazines such as *The New Yorker* or *Vanity Fair,* which offered entertainment, amusement, and gossip to those with more sophisticated tastes. They could also join the Book-of-the-Month Club or the Literary Guild, both of which were founded during the decade.

The Avant-Garde

Few decades have produced as many great works of art, music, or literature as the 1920s. At the decade's beginning, American culture stood in Europe's shadow. By the decade's end, Americans were leaders in the struggle to liberate the arts from older canons of taste, form, and style. It was during the twenties that Eugene O'Neill, the country's most talented dramatist, wrote his greatest plays, and that William Faulkner, Ernest Hemingway, F. Scott Fitzgerald, and Thomas Wolfe published their first novels.

American poets of the 1920s—such as Hart Crane, e.e. cummings, Countee Cullen, Langston Hughes, Edna St. Vincent Millay, and Wallace Stevens—experimented with new styles of punctuation, rhyming, and form. Likewise, artists like Charles Demuth, Georgia O'Keeffe, and Joseph Stella challenged the dominant realist tradition in American art and pioneered nonrepresentational and expressionist art forms.

The 1920s marked America's entry into the world of serious music. It witnessed the founding of fifty symphony orchestras and three of the country's most prominent music conservatories—Julliard, Eastman, and Curtis. The decade also produced America's first great classical composers—including Aaron Copland and Charles Ives—and witnessed George Gershwin create a new musical form by integrating jazz into symphonic and orchestral music.

World War I had left many American intellectuals and artists disillusioned and alienated. Neither Wilsonian idealism nor Progressive reformism appealed to America's postwar writers and thinkers, who believed that the crusade to end war and to make the world safe for democracy had been a senseless mistake. "Here was a new generation," wrote F. Scott Fitzgerald, ". . . grown up to find all Gods dead, all wars fought, all faith in man shaken."

During the 1920s, many of the nation's leading writers exposed the shallowness and narrow-mindedness of American life. The United State was a nation awash in materialism and devoid of spiritual vitality, a "wasteland," wrote the poet T. S. Eliot, inhabited by "hollow men." No author offered a more scathing attack on middle-class boorishness and smugness than Sinclair Lewis, who in 1930 became the first American to win the Nobel Prize for Literature. In *Main Street* (1920) and *Babbitt* (1922) he satirized the narrow-minded complacency and dullness of small-town America, while in *Elmer Gantry* (1922) he exposed religious hypocrisy and bigotry.

As editor of *Mercury* magazine, H. L. Mencken wrote hundreds of essays mocking practically every aspect of American life. Calling the South a "gargantuan paradise of the fourth rate," and the middle class the "booboisie," Mencken directed his choicest barbs at reformers, whom he blamed for the bloodshed of World War I and the gangsters of the 1920s. "If I am convinced of anything," he snarled, "it is that Doing Good is in bad taste."

The writer Gertrude Stein defined an important group of American intellectuals when she told Ernest Hemingway in 1921, "You are all a lost generation." Stein was referring to the expatriate novelists and artists who had participated in the Great War only to emerge from the conflict convinced that it was an exercise in futility. In their novels, F. Scott Fitzgerald and

Members of the "Lost Generation" of writers felt disillusioned with an American culture obsessed with money and devoid of spiritual vitality. Two of the Lost Generation's most prominent members were Ernest Hemingway (left) and F. Scott Fitzgerald (right).

Hemingway foreshadowed a philosophy now known as "existentialism"—which maintains that life has no transcendent purpose and that each individual must salvage personal meaning from the void. Hemingway's fiction lionized toughness and "manly virtues" as a counterpoint to the softness of American life. In *The Sun Also Rises* (1926) and *A Farewell to Arms* (1929) he emphasized meaningless death and the importance of facing stoically the absurdities of the universe. In the conclusion of *The Great Gatsby* (1925), Fitzgerald gave pointed expression to an existentialist outlook: "so we beat on, boats against the current, borne back ceaselessly into the past."

The Sex Debate

"If all girls at the Yale prom were laid end to end, I wouldn't be surprised," sighed Dorothy Parker, the official wit of New York's smart set. Parker's quip captured the public's perception that America's morals had taken a nosedive. Practically every newspaper featured articles on prostitution, venereal disease, sex education, birth control, and the rising divorce rate.

City life nurtured new sexual attitudes. With its crowded anonymity, urban culture

ASPECTS OF FAMILY LIFE

THE SEXUAL REVOLUTION OF THE EARLY 1900S

DURING the 1800s, public sexual attitudes in the United States were rooted in a moral code known as "civilized sexual morality." This sexual code condemned public discussion of sexual matters, held that sexual relations outside marriage were the blackest of sins, and declared that the only legitimate purpose of sexual relations was reproduction. Foreign travelers were invariably struck by Americans' sexual prudery. In the United States, they reported, a chicken breast was called a bosom and a piano leg was called a limb and was covered with lace trousers.

This strict sexual code drew support from a large medical literature that declared that any violation of the tenets of civilized morality would be detrimental to a person's health. Respected physicians insisted that loss of semen through masturbation or excessive sexual intercourse would produce "urinary difficulties, disorders of the genital organs, spinal diseases, weakness of the brain, loss of memory, epilepsy, insanity, apoplexy, abortions, premature births, and extreme feebleness, morbid predispositions, and an early death of offspring." Medical authorities also warned that women were too frail physically and too sensitive spiritually to engage in frequent intercourse and that "the majority of women (happily for them) are not very much troubled with sexual feelings of

any kind." Above all, physicians warned that individuals who had sexual relations outside of marriage ran a high risk of contracting incurable venereal diseases.

The Victorian sexual code was a public ideal, not an accurate description of reality. Prostitution flourished in turn-of-the-century America. Every large city had at least one red-light district. In New York, there was the Tenderloin; in Chicago, the Levee; in New Orleans, Storyville; in San Francisco, the Barbary Coast. Early-twentieth-century vice commissions estimated that there were "not less" than a quarter of a million prostitutes in the country. In Chicago, an estimated quarter of the city's males visited prostitutes annually, and paid them $15 million a year. Pornography was also widespread.

Nor were nineteenth-century women necessarily the prudish, asexual, sexually ignorant figures popularized in Victorian mythology. An early sexual survey of the attitudes of 45 well-educated women, mainly born before 1870, reported that most enjoyed intercourse and experienced orgasm.

Nevertheless, the values of civilized sexual morality dominated polite society and received strong public backing from the broad-based crusade to suppress vice. A

"purity crusade" had arisen in the 1860s and 1870s in response to proposals to legalize and regulate prostitution. In almost every major city in the country, former abolitionists like William Lloyd Garrison, feminists like Susan B. Anthony, temperance advocates, and ministers joined forces to defeat legalized prostitution. Prostitution, they argued, was a menace "to the chastity of our women and the sanctity of the home." It exploited poor women to satisfy male lust and endangered respectable women, who were often infected with syphilis and gonorrhea by their husbands.

In later years, the purity forces broadened their aims. In addition to fighting prostitution, they also sought to protect the family by outlawing abortion, restricting the sale of alcohol, stamping out pornography, censoring nudity in the arts, enforcing the Sabbath through enactment of "blue laws," suppressing the use of narcotics, and stopping the flow of birth control information through the mails.

The self-appointed leader of the purity forces was a staunch crusader named Anthony Comstock. Born on a farm in New Canaan, Connecticut, Comstock, as a youth, had been so upset by an impulse to masturbate that he feared he might be driven to commit suicide. While serving with a Connecticut regiment in the Civil War he had been appalled by the pornographic French postcards circulated among soldiers. After the war he moved to New York, where he became active in the Young Men's Christian Association, and was shocked by the prevalence of prostitutes and of vendors selling obscene books.

In 1873, Comstock persuaded Congress to pass a federal law banning from the mails "every obscene, lewd, lascivious or filthy book, pamphlet, paper, letter, writing, print or other publication of an indecent character." Comstock was then appointed special agent of the Post Office and made responsible for arresting those who used the mail in violation of the law. "Morals, not art or literature," was Comstock's motto. He took credit for hounding 16 persons to their deaths.

By 1910, Comstock and the purity forces had achieved many of their legislative goals. They had successfully pushed for state laws to restrict divorce; raised the age of consent for sexual intercourse (from 7, in some states, to 18); imposed tests for venereal disease prior to marriage; and criminalized abortion. The purity crusaders also won passage of a federal statute that defined the mailing of birth control information a felony.

The years just before World War I witnessed a series of sharp challenges to the nineteenth-century code of sexual purity. Radical new ideas about marriage were publicized and debated. Swedish feminist Ellen Key preached a scheme of "unwed motherhood"; Edith Ellis, wife of British sex researcher Havelock Ellis, advocated trial marriage and "semi-detached marriage" in which each spouse occupied a separate domicile; still others advocated "serial marriage" and easier divorce. Greenwich Vil-

lage bohemians and political radicals advocated, and to some extent practiced, free love. Psychologists, including Havelock Ellis, G. Stanley Hall, and Sigmund Freud, attacked the notion that women lacked sexual impulses.

Sexual conduct was also changing rapidly. The first scientific sex surveys indicated that women who came to maturity after the turn of the century were much more likely than their mothers to engage in sex before marriage and outside it. Women who were born around 1900 were two to three times as likely to have premarital intercourse compared to women born before 1900. They were also more likely to experience orgasm. Among men, premarital sexual experience did not increase, but it occurred less often with prostitutes and more frequently with other women.

Public alarm over the changes occurring in American sexual experience culminated in the first decade of the 1900s in an explosion of concern over "white slavery"—prostitution—and the "black plague"—venereal disease. Many lurid books appeared—with such titles as *The Traffic in Souls, The House of Bondage,* and *The Shame of a Great Nation*—that explained how innocent young girls were seduced by panderers and, through the use of a chloroformed cloth, a hypodermic needle, or a drugged drink, forced into prostitution. Congress attacked the problem of "white slavery" in 1910 by adopting the Mann Act, which made it a crime to transport women across state lines for immoral purposes. During World War I, Congress provided states with federal funds to set up facilities to detain and rehabilitate women apprehended as prostitutes. Fifteen thousand women were detained during the war. Sex was becoming a subject of open public debate and direct government involvement.

During the 1920s, the drift toward sexual liberalization continued. Journalists wrote in bewilderment about a new social phenomenon, the flapper, the independent, assertive, pleasure-hungry, young woman, "making love lightly, boldly, and promiscuously." Systematic sex surveys showed that the incidence of premarital intercourse was continuing to rise and that an increasing number of young women had slept with men other than their future husbands. Half of the women born in the first decade of the twentieth century and two-thirds of those born in the second decade had engaged in intercourse before marriage. Meanwhile, contraceptive practices were also changing dramatically. Instead of relying heavily on douching or coitus interruptus as a form of birth control, younger women were using the more effective and less disruptive diaphragm.

This growing sexual permissiveness evoked a sharp reaction. Purity forces renewed their crusade to discourage indecent styles of dancing, immodest dress, and impure books and films. Religious journals denounced popular dance styles as "impure, polluting, corrupting, debasing, destroying spirituality, [and] increasing carnality." A bill was introduced in the Utah state legislature to fine and imprison women who wore, on the streets, skirts "higher than three inches above the ankle." In the Ohio legislature it was proposed that cleavage be limited to two inches and that the sale of any "garment which unduly displays or accentuates the lines of the female figure" be prohibited. Four states and many cities established censorship boards to review films, and many other cities broke up red-light districts and required licenses for dance halls. But despite these efforts, a sexual revolution had begun that has continued to this day.

eroded sexual inhibitions by relaxing community restraints on individual behavior. Cities also promoted secular, consumer values, and city people seemed to tolerate, if not welcome, many forms of diversity.

While cities provided the ideal environment for liberalized sexual values, Sigmund Freud provided the ideal psychology. A Vienna physician, Freud revolutionized academic and popular thinking about human behavior by arguing that unconscious sexual anxieties cause much of human behavior. Freud also explained that sexual desires and fears develop in infancy and stay with people throughout their lives. During the 1920s, Freud's theories about the sexual unconscious were widely debated by physicians, academics, advice columnists, women's magazine writers, and preachers.

The image of the "flapper"—the liberated woman who bobbed her hair, painted her lips, raised her hemline, and danced the Charleston—personified the public's anxiety about the decline of traditional morality. In the 1950s Alfred C. Kinsey, a sex researcher at Indiana University, found that women born after 1900 were twice as likely to have had premarital sex as their mothers, with the most pronounced changes occurring in the generation reaching maturity in the early 1920s.

Sexual permissiveness had eroded Victorian values, but the "new woman" posed less of a challenge to traditional morality than her critics feared. Far from being promiscuous, her sexual experience before marriage was generally limited to one or two partners, one of whom she married. In practice, this narrowed the gap between men and women and moved society toward a single standard of morality. Instead of turning to prostitutes, men made love with their sweethearts, who in many instances became their wives.

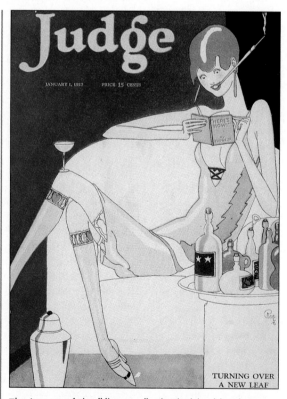

The image of the "flapper," who bobbed her hair, bared her knees, and smoked and drank in public, alarmed a public still clinging to Victorian codes of morality.

THE CLASH OF CULTURES

The 1920s was a decade of intense cultural conflict. No longer a nation of farms and villages, the United States had become a nation of factories and cities. The Protestant culture of rural America was being undermined by the secular values of an urban society. Country against city, native against immigrant, Protestant against Catholic and Jew, fundamentalist against liberal, conservative against progressive, wet against dry—bitter confrontations erupted as the United States underwent a colossal identity crisis as it struggled to come to terms with secular values and cultural pluralism. The chief battlegrounds in this "cultural civil war" were gender, immigration, prohibition, and the teaching of evolution in public schools.

The New Woman

In 1920, after 72 years of struggle, American women received the right to vote with the passing of the Nineteenth Amendment. Reformers talked about female voters uniting to clean up politics, improve society, and end discrimination.

At first, male politicians moved aggressively to court the women's vote, passing legislation guaranteeing women's right to serve on juries and hold public office. Congress also passed legislation to set up a national system of women's and infant's health care clinics as well as a constitutional amendment prohibiting child labor, a measure supported by many women's groups.

But the early momentum quickly dissipated, as the women's movement divided from within and faced growing hostility from without. The major issue that split feminists during the 1920s was a proposed Equal Rights Amendment to the Constitution outlawing discrimination based on sex. The issue pitted the interests of professional women against those of working class women, many of whom feared that the amendment would prohibit "protective legislation" that stipulated the minimum wages and maximum work hours of female workers.

The women's movement also faced mounting external opposition. During the Red Scare following World War I, the War Department issued the "Spider Web" chart that linked feminist groups to foreign radicalism. Many feminist goals went down to defeat in the mid-1920s. Opposition from many southern states and from the Catholic church defeated the proposed constitutional amendment outlawing child labor. The Supreme Court struck down a minimum wage law for women workers, while Congress failed to fund the system of health care clinics.

Women also did not win new opportunities in the workplace. Although the American workforce included eight million women in 1920, more than half were African American or foreign-born. Domestic service remained the largest occupation, followed by secretarial work, typing, and clerking—all low-paying jobs. The American Federation of Labor (AFL) remained openly hostile to women because it did not want females competing for men's jobs. Female professionals, too, made little progress. They consistently received less pay than their male counterparts. Moreover, they

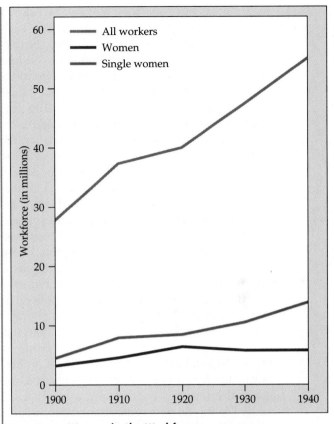

FIGURE 23.1 **Women in the Workforce, 1900–1940**
Although the number of women in the workplace rose from 1900 to 1940, they were mostly concentrated in only a few fields.

were concentrated in traditionally "female" occupations such as teaching and nursing.

Prohibition

Prohibition exposed deep fissures in American society. The issue turned on the class, ethnic, and religious makeup of individual communities.

At first prohibition's apparent success muted its critics. Distilleries and breweries shut down, saloons locked their doors, arrests for drunkenness declined, and alcohol-related deaths all but disappeared. Compliance, however, had less to do with piety and public support than the law of supply and demand: since illegal liquor remained in short supply, its price rose beyond the average worker's means.

Private enterprise filled the void. Smugglers supplied wealthy imbibers, but the less affluent had to rely on small-time operators who produced for local consumption. Much of this liquor ran the gamut from swill to poison. According to one story, a potential buyer who sent a liquor sample to a laboratory for analysis was shocked when the chemist replied, "Your horse has diabetes." For others the problem of "killer batches" was no laughing matter. Hundreds, perhaps thousands, died from drinking these illegal concoctions.

Neither federal nor state authorities had enough funds to enforce prohibition. New York's mayor estimated that it would require a police force of 250,000 to enforce prohibition—and another 250,000 to police the police. In fact, only about 2200 agents across the country enforced the law. Lax enforcement, coupled with huge profits, enticed organized crime to enter bootlegging. Long a fixture of urban life, with gambling and prostitution as its base, organized crime had operated on a small, local scale. Liquor, however, demanded production plants, distribution networks, and sales forces. Bootlegging turned into a gold mine for organized crime. By the late 1920s liquor sales generated revenue in excess of $2 billion annually. Chicago's Al Capone had a gross income of $60 million in 1927. A ruthless figure accused of ordering numerous gangland killings, he preferred to think of himself as a businessman.

From the outset, cynics had insisted that prohibition could not be enforced. They were right. Particularly in large cities, people openly defied the law. In New York City, 7000 arrests for liquor law violations resulted in 17 convictions. A newspaper sports article on baseball's spring training featured the headline: "Yankees Train on Scotch." On more than one occasion journalists saw President Warren G. Harding's bootlegger deliver cases of liquor to the White House in broad daylight.

In 1923 New York became the first state to repeal its enforcement law, and by 1930 six more states had followed suit. Others remained firmly committed to prohibition. After a presidential commission reported prohi- bition could not be enforced, Congress finally repealed it in 1933, making liquor control a state and local matter.

The campaign to outlaw cigarette smoking was closely allied to the prohibition movement. Opposition to tobacco was not new. During the nineteenth century the anti-tobacco campaign remained an appendage of the temperance movement. After the introduction of machine-made cigarettes in the 1880s, however, opponents concentrated their fire specifically on the "little white slavers."

As early as the Civil War, a few cities had banned smoking in restaurants, theaters, public buildings, trolleys, and railway cars. After antismokers organized the National Anti-Cigarette League in 1903, scores of prominent leaders joined the crusade. By 1923, 14 states had outlawed the sale of cigarettes, prompting calls for a constitutional amendment for national prohibition. By the end of the decade, however, every state had repealed its law against cigarette sales. A national consensus had not formed against tobacco, and the tobacco industry opposed every effort to restrict the sale of cigarettes, spending millions of dollars on advertisements. Thus smokers had no difficulty defending their right to smoke—at least for the present.

The Scopes Trial

During the late nineteenth century, Charles Darwin's theory of evolution produced a momentous split within the ranks of American Protestantism. Earlier in the century, virtually all American Protestant denominations were united in the belief that the findings of science confirmed the teachings of religion. But Darwin's theory shattered that consensus. Religious liberals argued that religion had to accommodate to the teachings of modern science. Religious fundamentalists sought to preserve the basic tenets of Protestant faith against liberal criticisms.

The split between religious liberals and fundamentalists widened in the early twentieth century. A religious revival in Topeka, Kansas, in 1901, marked the beginning of Pentecostalism, a movement that emphasizes the spiritual gifts conferred by the Holy Spirit, including the ability to "speak in tongues" (an unknown, but divinely inspired language) and the power of prayer to heal the sick. By arguing that the Biblical age of miracles had not ended, Pentecostals directly challenged the ideas of religious modernists. *The Fundamentals,* 12 volumes by anonymous authors published between 1910 and 1915, argued that there were certain Christian doctrines that must be accepted without question, including the infallibility of the Bible, the authenticity of the miracles described in the Scriptures, and the virgin birth of Jesus Christ. Although the fundamentalist and Pentecostal movements began in the North, they attained their greatest support in the South.

During the 1920s, conflict erupted between fundamentalists and liberals over the teaching of evolution in public schools, a clash that culminated in the celebrated "Monkey Trial." In 1925 the Tennessee legislature passed a bill that prohibited the teaching of evolution in public schools. Immediately afterwards, a 24-year-old science teacher, John Scopes, from Dayton, Tennessee, provoked a test case by declaring publicly that he taught biology from an evolutionary standpoint.

Scopes was brought to trial in the summer of 1925. William Jennings Bryan, rural America's defender of the faith, agreed to join the team of prosecutors, and Clarence Darrow, the celebrated trial lawyer and self-proclaimed agnostic, volunteered his services to defend Scopes.

The trial opened on July 10, 1925. As "Holy Rollers" from the surrounding regions held revivals and religious zealots exhorted people to read their Bibles, huge crowds poured into Dayton to watch Bryan and Darrow do combat. Near the end of testimony the defense surprised everyone by asking Bryan to take the stand as an expert witness on the Bible. His simple, direct answers to Darrow's sarcastic questions revealed an unshakable faith in the literal truth of the Bible. Bryan insisted "it is better to trust in the Rock of Ages than to know the ages of rocks."

The outcome was never in doubt. Scopes admitted he had broken the law. He was con-

GATHERING DATA FOR THE TENNESSEE TRIAL

When biology teacher John Scopes taught evolutionary theory to his class, the state of Tennessee brought him to trial. The well-publicized trial emphasized the split between religious fundamentalists and those who advocated scientific and academic freedom.

victed and fined $100. (Tennessee's supreme court later rescinded the fine on a technicality.) What gave the trial its drama was the clash between Bryan and Darrow and the opposite images of America they represented. Bryan, who died five days after the trial ended, left the courtroom believing he had carried the day. His opponents, however, thought he had been humiliated and they proclaimed the Scopes trial a victory for academic freedom. In the end, the Scopes trial merely illustrated how little tolerance secular and fundamentalist groups had for each other.

Xenophobia and Restricting Immigration

Cultural fears unleashed a new wave of nativism in the 1920s. Organized labor, bent upon protecting high wages, resented competition from cheap labor; staunch nativists and superpatriots warned that foreign influences would corrupt the American character; and assorted businessmen denounced immigrants as dangerous radicals.

To protect the United States these groups demanded drastic changes in the nation's immigration policy. Congress passed the National Origins Act of 1924, establishing an annual immigration quota of 2 percent of each national group counted in the 1890 census, and barring Asians entirely. Since southern and eastern Europeans did not begin arriving in large numbers until the turn of the century, the law gave western and northern Europeans a big edge over the "new immigrants."

Hostility to immigrants also surfaced in the Sacco and Vanzetti case. On April 15, 1920, two unidentified gunmen robbed a payroll messenger from a shoe factory in South Braintree, Massachusetts, killing a paymaster and a guard. Two Italian immigrants, Nicola Sacco and Bartolomeo Vanzetti, both avowed anarchists, were arrested and charged with the crime. Although the state failed to prove its case, prosecutors succeeded in parading before the jury the radical political views of both men. On July 14, 1921, Sacco and Vanzetti were convicted and sentenced to death.

The trial and conviction brought a storm of protest from Italian-Americans, liberals, and civil rights advocates. Despite lengthy appeals, the conviction was upheld, and Sacco and Vanzetti, asserting their innocence to the end, went to the electric chair on August 23, 1927.

The Ku Klux Klan

Fear of political radicals and ethnic minorities found its most strident voice during the 1920s in the rebirth of the Ku Klux Klan. The secret organization, led by Colonel William Joseph Simmons, stood for "100 percent pure Americanism" and limited its membership to white, native-born Protestants. Membership remained modest until Simmons hired two advertising specialists, Edward Young Clarke and Elizabeth Tyler, to market the Klan nationwide.

Clarke and Tyler hired an army of organizers to canvas the country selling memberships in the Klan. (Membership cost $10; the

Many people felt that Italian-born, self-admitted anarchists Sacco and Vanzetti, shown here in handcuffs in a painting by Ben Shahn, were persecuted for their immigrant status and radical views rather than for any real crime. Their trial became an important symbol in the fight for civil liberties and brought about violent protest in America and abroad. (Ben Shahn, *Bartolomeo Vanzetti and Nicola Sacco* (1931–32). Tempera on paper over composition board, $10\frac{1}{2} \times 14\frac{1}{2}$". Gift of Mrs. John D. Rockefeller, Jr./The Museum of Modern Art, New York.)

sheet was $4 extra.) Working on commission and molding their pitch to match their clientele, the salesmen enjoyed astounding success. By 1921 the Klan had become a national organization with over 90,000 paying members; by 1925 it claimed a membership of five million. The Klan was strongest in the South, but it had a large following in the Southeast, the Far West, and the Midwest. Its natural habitat was not the countryside, but middling towns and small cities as well as larger cities like Chicago and Detroit. Philadelphia reportedly had 30,000 members. Most members were not "poor white trash," but members of the lower middle class from old-stock, respectable families.

In the mid-1920s the Klan was a political force to reckon with. It influenced the election of several governors and members of state legislatures. The Klan also sought to intimidate individuals, using night ridings, cross burnings, tar and featherings, public beatings, and lynching as forms of coercion. The Klan did not limit its wrath to ethnic and religious "offenders," but also lashed out against wife-beaters, drunkards, bootleggers, gamblers—anyone who violated time-honored standards of morality.

In the end poor leadership and the absence of a political program destroyed the Klan. Once they attained office, Klan-supported officials offered no constructive legislation. Even more damaging, several Klan leaders became involved in sex scandals, and several more were indicted for corruption. By 1930 the white sheets and cross burnings had vanished from public view, only to return again a few decades later when the civil rights movement challenged white supremacy.

African-American Protests

Many African Americans believed that the sacrifices of African-American soldiers during World War I would be repaid when the war was over. In the words of one Texan, "our sec-ond emancipation will be the outcome of this war." It was not to be. The federal government denied African-American soldiers the right to participate in the victory march down Paris's Champs-Elysées boulevard. In the 25 race riots that took place in 1919, 10 of the 70 African-American victims were veterans of World War I.

African Americans did not respond passively to these outrages. Already, in the 1910s, they had stepped up their protests against discrimination. Closely identified with Booker T. Washington's conciliatory approach to race relations, the National Urban League, organized in 1911 by social workers, white philanthropists, and conservative African-American leaders, concentrated on finding jobs for urban African Americans. Despite the nation's postwar prosperity, African Americans made scant progress on the job front during the 1920s.

Leaving economic issues to the Urban League, the National Association for the Advancement of Colored People (NAACP),

The Ku Klux Klan exploited postwar confusion and fear of things "un-American." Although the Klan had originally flourished in small, rural towns across the South, during the 1920s it spread to working-class and middle-class neighborhoods of large cities, where people felt threatened by the influx of African-American and immigrant workers.

formed in 1909, concentrated on civil rights and legal action. The NAACP won important Supreme Court decisions against the grandfather clause (1915) and restrictive covenants (1917). The NAACP also fought school segregation in northern cities during the 1920s, and lobbied hard, though unsuccessfully, for a federal antilynching bill. Though progress on these fronts was not made until after World War II, the NAACP became the nation's leading civil rights organization.

African-American radicals dismissed the Urban League and the NAACP as too conservative. A. Philip Randolph, the editor of the Socialist monthly the *Messenger* called for a "New Negro" who would meet violence with violence to end discrimination and achieve racial equality. Randolph urged African-American workers to seek admission to trade unions.

No black leader was more successful in touching the aspirations and needs of the mass of African Americans than Marcus Garvey. A flamboyant and charismatic figure from Jamaica, Garvey rejected integration and preached racial pride and self-help. He declared that Jesus Christ and Mary were black and he exhorted his followers to glorify their African heritage and revel in the beauty of their skin. "We have a beautiful history," he told his followers, "and we shall create another one in the future."

In 1917 Garvey moved to New York, where he organized the American branch of the Universal Negro Improvement Association (UNIA), the first mass movement in African-American history. Convinced that African Americans would never achieve full equality in the United States, Garvey called on

Marcus Garvey, a charismatic Jamaican, encouraged black pride. His Universal Negro Improvement Association (UNIA) included one million members worldwide.

blacks to regard Africa as their homeland. By the mid-1920s, Garvey's organization had 700 branches in 38 states and the West Indies and published a newspaper with as many as 200,000 subscribers. The UNIA operated grocery stores, laundries, restaurants, printing plants, clothing factories, and a steamship line.

In the mid-1920s, Garvey was charged with mail fraud, jailed, and finally deported. Still, the "Black Moses" left behind a rich legacy. At a time when magazines and newspapers overflowed with advertisements for hair straighteners and skin lightening cosmetics, Garvey's message of racial pride struck a responsive chord in many African Americans.

The Harlem Renaissance

The movement for African-American pride found its cultural expression in the Harlem Renaissance—the first self-conscious literary and artistic movement in African-American history.

For over three decades, African Americans had shown increasing interest in African-American history and folk culture. As early as the 1890s, W.E.B. Du Bois, Harvard's first African-American Ph.D., began to trace African-American culture in the United States to its African roots; Fisk University's Jubilee Singers introduced Negro spirituals to the general public; and the American Negro Academy, organized in 1897, promoted African-American literature, arts, music, and history. A growing spirit of racial pride was evident, as a group of talented writers, including Charles Chestnut, Paul Lawrence Dunbar, and James Weldon Johnson, explored life in African-American communities; as the first Negro dolls appeared; and as all-Negro towns were founded in Whitesboro, New Jersey, and Allensworth, California.

Signs of growing racial consciousness proliferated during the 1910s. Fifty new African-American newspapers and magazines appeared in that decade, bringing the total to 500. The Associated Negro Press, the first national African-American press agency, was founded in 1919. In 1915, Carter Woodson, a Harvard Ph.D., founded the first permanent Negro his-

Artist Archibald Motley, Jr., one of the black painters of the 1920s Harlem Renaissance, celebrated the energy and excitement of the era there in *Black Belt* (1934).

torical association—the Association for the Study of Negro Life and History—and began publication of the *Journal of Negro History.*

During the 1920s, Harlem, in upper Manhattan, became the capital of black America, attracting African-American intellectuals and artists from across the country and the Caribbean as well. Soon, the Harlem Renaissance was in full bloom. The poet Countee Cullen eloquently expressed black artists' long-suppressed desire to have their voices heard: "Yet do I marvel at a curious thing: To make a poet black, and bid him sing!"

Many of the greatest works of the Harlem Renaissance sought to recover links with African and folk traditions. In "The Negro Speaks of Rivers," the poet Langston Hughes reaffirmed his ties to an African past: "I looked upon the Nile and raised the pyramids above it." In "Cane" (1923), Jean Toomer—the grandson of P.B.S. Pinchback, who served briefly as governor of Louisiana during Re-

construction—blended realism and mysticism, poetry and prose, to describe the world of the black peasantry in Georgia and in the ghetto of Washington, D.C. Zora Neale Hurston, a Columbia University–trained anthropologist, incorporated rural folklore and religious beliefs into her stories.

A fierce racial consciousness and a powerful sense of racial pride animated the literature of the Harlem Renaissance. The West Indian–born poet Claude McKay expressed the new spirit of defiance and protest with militant words: "If we must die—oh let us nobly die . . . dying, but fighting back!"

THE REPUBLICAN RESTORATION

The Republican party dominated American politics in the 1920s. When Republican leaders promised to restore prosperity, most

Americans embraced the conservative rhetoric, hoping to find in politics the stability they found lacking in their culture. Talk about trust-busting and regulating big business gave way in New Era politics to calls for a partnership between government and industry, one that would promote the interests of American corporations at home and abroad.

Handsome Harding

By and large the presidents of the New Era were mediocre figures. Senator Warren G. Harding of Ohio, who led off the decade, suited the times perfectly. Handsome enough to be a movie star, he not only looked great, but promised voters what they wanted: a return to "normalcy." He appeared to be a moderate, responsible leader who would avoid extremes and guide the country into a decade of prosperity.

Harding, a fun-loving man who liked to play poker, drink whiskey, and shoot the breeze with old pals, left government to his cabinet members and to the Supreme Court. Political conservatives all, they equated the people's interests with those of big business, championing American business interests abroad, denouncing government regulation, and slashing taxes on the rich.

Business leaders had contributed $8 million to the GOP's campaign chest in 1920; in return they expected the federal government to roll back the gains organized labor had made during World War I. They were not disappointed. Under the leadership of Chief Justice William Howard Taft, the Court took a narrow view of federal power, assigning the responsibility for protecting individual citizens to the states. During the 1920s the Court outlawed picketing, overturned national child labor laws, and abolished minimum wage laws for women.

The decade's most capable figure was Herbert Hoover, secretary of commerce under both Harding and his successor, Calvin Coolidge. A successful engineer, Hoover abhorred destructive competition and waste in the economy, which he proposed to eliminate through "associationism." Hoover called for voluntary trade associations to foster cooperation in industry and agriculture through commissions, trade practice controls, and ethical standards. By 1929 more than 2000 trade associations were busily at work implementing Hoover's vision of a stable and prosperous economy. No other Harding appointment matched Hoover's talent and vision.

In fact, several of Harding's appointees proved to be disasters. Harding found it difficult to say "no" to old friends and cronies, members of the so-called Ohio Gang, when they asked for government jobs. In the end this motley assortment of political hacks and hangers-on plunged his administration into disgrace, as major scandals involving bribes and kickbacks erupted in the Justice Department and in the Veterans Bureau. Shortly after these disclosures, Harding died of a cerebral embolism, on August 2, 1923. Immediately after his death, more misdeeds came to light. In the infamous Teapot Dome oil scandal, Secretary of the Interior Albert B. Fall was convicted of accepting $360,000 in bribes in exchange for leasing drilling rights on federal naval oil reserves, the first cabinet member in American history convicted for crimes in office. Attorney General Harry Daugherty, accused of accepting payoffs for selling German chemical patents controlled by the Alien Property Office, was forced to resign in disgrace.

Silent Cal

The election of 1924 symbolized, in a variety of ways, the tensions and concerns of the 1920s. Despite the Harding scandals, President Calvin Coolidge remained extremely popular, largely because of the nation's prosperity. Deeply divided over such issues as immigration, prohibition, and the Ku Klux Klan, the Democrats balloted 103 times before nominating a compromise candidate, John W. Davis, a Wall Street attorney.

A coalition of labor leaders, social workers, and former progressives bolted both major parties and formed the Progressive party, which nominated Wisconsin Senator Robert La Follette for president. Their platform called for government ownership of natural re-

Harding's administration was fraught with scandals involving bribes and kickbacks within his cabinet and inner circle, as illustrated in this political cartoon.

sources, abolition of child labor, elimination of monopolies, and increased taxes on the rich. In the end, no issue could match the GOP's prosperity crusade. Coolidge won the election by a comfortable margin.

Coolidge was a stern-faced, tight-lipped New Englander, Born in Plymouth Notch, Vermont, where five generations of Coolidges had worked the same family farm, he epitomized the rural values threatened by immigration, urbanization, and industrialization. As governor of Massachusetts, Coolidge had crushed a police strike in Boston in 1919 by calling out the National Guard, prompting the Republicans to give him the number two slot on their ticket in 1920.

Coolidge had no desire to be a strong president in the tradition of a Teddy Roosevelt or a Woodrow Wilson. A firm believer in the wisdom of inactivity, Coolidge slept ten hours a night, napped every afternoon, and seldom worked more than four hours a day. A staunch conservative, Coolidge was positively consumed by his reverence for the corporate elite. "The man who builds a factory builds a temple," said Coolidge. "The man who works there, worships there." Government, he be-

lieved, should do everything in its power to promote business interests. While Coolidge set the tone for his administration, he left it to his cabinet members, the courts, and Congress to devise strategies for consummating the marriage between business and government.

The Twilight of Progressivism

The government's tilt toward business signaled a retreat from progressivism. With the Democrats in disarray and Teddy Roosevelt's wing of the GOP all but dead, conservative Republicans were riding high. Still, the reform impulse did not disappear entirely during the 1920s. A small band of beleaguered reformers, led by Robert La Follette of Wisconsin and George Norris of Nebraska, kept progressivism alive in Congress, where they worked for farm relief, child labor laws, and regulation of wages and working hours for women.

In keeping with their historic pattern, progressives had better luck at the state and local level than at the federal level, where they ran into stiff opposition from Congress or from Coolidge himself. Social workers and women's groups spearheaded campaigns which sponsored a broad range of welfare legislation. By 1930, 43 states had passed laws providing assistance to women with dependent children, and 34 states had adopted workers' compensation laws. Under the leadership of Governor Alfred Smith, New York granted women a 40-hour workweek and instituted the nation's first public housing program.

Welfare opponents counterattacked, arguing labor reforms would increase production costs and leave states that passed welfare legislation at a competitive disadvantage with states without such laws. Asked to choose between social welfare programs and jobs, Congress, along with most states, opted for jobs.

The Election of 1928

After Coolidge announced his retirement from politics in 1928, the Republicans nominated Herbert Hoover, while the Democrats turned to Alfred E. Smith. Since both parties adopted nearly identical platforms, the election turned on personalities and images. Few elections have pitted opponents who better defined the two faces of America—one rural, the other urban.

A native of Iowa, Hoover depicted himself as a simple farmboy who, through hard work and pluck, had grown up to become wealthy and famous. Orphaned as a boy and cared for by a variety of relatives, Hoover worked his way through Stanford University, earning a degree in mining engineering. Brilliant and hard-working, he was a millionaire 12 years after landing his first engineering job. As a self-made man, Hoover presented a portrait of a safe, reassuring world.

Yet Hoover was also a spokesman for the future. He thought the federal government had a responsibility to coordinate the competing interests of a modern economy. He accepted the reality of industrialization, technology, governmental activism, and global markets, and in contrast to Harding and Coolidge, Hoover believed the president should lead the nation. According to Hoover, technology and expertise would make economic prosperity a permanent feature of American life.

The son of immigrants, Smith was an Irish Catholic from Hell's Kitchen in New York City. He had started public life with nothing and had climbed the political ladder as a faithful son of the New York Democratic machine. Smith also represented the future, not so much in terms of science, technology, and organization, but in terms of cultural pluralism and urbanization. America's future lay with her cities, and the cities contained large groups of ethnic Americans struggling for acceptance and their share of the good life.

Herbert Hoover, the consummate self-made man, was in office only a few months when the stock market crashed.

Aided by prosperity, Hoover coasted to an easy victory. Smith was hurt by his failure to bridge the North-South, urban-rural split in the Democratic party; by anti-Catholic sentiment; and by his opposition to prohibition. The Democrats were so divided that six states from Dixie abandoned the Solid South and defected to Hoover. Yet even in defeat, Smith's campaign revealed the most significant political change of the 1920s—the growing power of urban and ethnic voters and the shrinking influence of the rural element within the Democratic party.

Herbert Hoover's election marked the climax of New Era politics. As president he advocated total cooperation between government and business. Optimistic businesspeople, bankers, and stockbrokers applauded Hoover's promises, predicting a future of prosperity and progress. Ironically, the stock market crashed before their cheers had stopped echoing.

THE GREAT CRASH

Few people ever see their name enter the English language, but Charles Ponzi did. A "Ponzi scheme" has become synonymous with wild speculation. In September 1919, Ponzi was a 42-year-old former vegetable dealer with just $150 to his name. He promised to return $15 to anyone who lent him $10 for 90 days. His plan, he explained, was to buy foreign currencies at low prices and sell them at higher prices. After newspapers reported his scheme, dollars began to pour in—$1 million a week. An admirer described him as the greatest Italian of all time. "Columbus discovered America . . . but you discovered money."

It was too good to be true. Ponzi took in $15 million in eight months—and less than $200,000 was ever returned to investors.

Speculative Manias

Ponzi symbolized the "get-rich-quick" mentality that infected the public during the 1920s. A vivid example was the Florida land boom. During the 1920s, sun-worshipping northerners discovered Florida's warm winter climate and its sun-drenched beaches. Could there be a safer investment? Real estate promoters—including the former presidential candidate William Jennings Bryan—offered seafront lots to investors for 10 percent down. Investors snapped up the properties—much of which turned out to be swamp and scrub land. Prices skyrocketed. A lot 40 miles from Miami sold for $20,000. A beach lot sold for $75,000. Ponzi himself sold lots "near Jacksonville"—actually 65 miles west of the city; he divided each acre into 23 lots.

In the fall of 1926 the bubble burst. Two hurricanes ripped through Florida, killing more than 400 people. Property valued at $1 billion in 1925 dropped to $143 million in 1928.

A wave of similar stock swindles and business frauds took place during the 1920s. But the most striking manifestation of the decade's speculative frenzy was the stock market boom of 1928 and 1929. After rising steadily during the 1920s, stock prices began to soar in March 1928. Between March 3, 1928, and September 3, 1929, AT&T rose from $179\frac{1}{2}$ to $335\frac{5}{8}$, General Motors from $139\frac{3}{4}$ to $181\frac{7}{8}$, and Westinghouse from $91\frac{5}{8}$ to 313. By the beginning of the fall of 1929, stock prices were four times higher than five years before.

Brokerage houses lured investors into the market by selling stock on margin, requiring investors to only put down 10 or 20 percent of the stock's price in cash and borrowing the rest. By 1929, 1.5 million Americans had invested in securities.

Boosters like John Jacob Raskob, the chairman of the Democratic Party, encouraged ordinary people to invest in stocks. In an article in the *Ladies' Home Journal* entitled "Everybody Ought to be Rich," he explained that a person who invested $15 a month in the stock market for 20 years would have a nest egg of $80,000. Leading economists encouraged investors to believe that the stock market would continue to rise. Irving Fisher of Yale University announced: "Stock prices have reached what looks like a permanently high plateau." At the end of October 1929, the seemingly endless surge in stock prices came to a crashing halt.

The Market Crashes

On Thursday, October 24, 1929, an unprecedented wave of sell orders shook the New York Stock Exchange. Stock prices tumbled, falling $2, $5, and even $10 between trades. As prices fell, brokers required investors who had bought stock on margin to put up money to cover their loans. To raise money, many investors dumped stocks for whatever price the stocks could fetch. During the first three hours of trading, stock values plunged by $11 billion.

At noon, a group of prominent bankers met at the offices of J. P. Morgan and Company. To stop the hemorrhaging of stock prices, the bankers' pool agreed to buy stocks well above the market. At 1:30 P.M. they put their plan into action. Within an hour, U.S. Steel was up $15 a share, AT&T up $22, General Electric up $21, Montgomery Ward up $23.

Even though the market recovered its morning losses, public confidence was badly shaken. Rumors spread that 11 stock speculators had killed themselves and that government troops were surrounding the exchange to protect traders from an angry mob. President Hoover sought to reassure the public by declaring that the "fundamental business of the country . . . is on a sound and prosperous basis."

Prices held steady on Friday, then slipped on Saturday. Monday, however, brought fresh disaster. Eastman Kodak plunged $41 a share, AT&T went down $24, New York Central Railroad, $22. The worst was yet to come—Black Tuesday, October 29, the day the stock market experienced the greatest crash in its history.

As soon as the stock exchange's gong sounded, a mad rush to sell began. Trading volume soared to an unprecedented 16,410,030 shares, and the average price of a share fell 12 percent. Stocks were sold for whatever price they would bring. White Sewing Machine had reached a high of $48 a share. One purchaser—reportedly a messenger boy—bought a block of the stock for $1 a share.

The bull market of the late 1920s was over. By 1932, the index of stock prices had fallen

This newspaper headline from Friday, October 25, 1929, tried to reassure the public that the economy was fundamentally sound, only four days before Black Tuesday. The economy's downward spiral continued through 1932, when prices were 80 percent below their 1929 highs.

from a 1929 high of 210 to 30. Stocks were valued at just 12 percent of what they had been worth in September 1929. Altogether, between September 1929 and June 1932, the nation's stock exchanges lost $179 billion in value.

The great stock market crash of October 1929 brought the economic prosperity of the 1920s to a symbolic end. For the next ten years, the United States was mired in a deep economic depression. By 1933, unemployment had soared to 25 percent of the workforce, up from just 3.2 percent in 1929. Industrial production declined by 50 percent. In 1929, before the crash, investment in the U.S. economy totaled $16 billion. By 1933, the figure had fallen to $340 million, a decrease of 98 percent.

Why It Happened

Why did the seemingly boundless prosperity of the 1920s end so suddenly? And why, once an economic downturn began, did the Great Depression last so long?

Economists have been hard pressed to explain why "prosperity's decade" ended in financial disaster. In 1929, the American economy appeared to be extraordinarily healthy. Employment was high and inflation was virtually nonexistent. Industrial production had risen 30 percent between 1919 and 1929 and per capita income had climbed from $520 to $681. The United States accounted for nearly half the world's industrial output. Still, the seeds of the Depression were already present in the "boom" years of the 1920s.

For many groups of Americans, the prosperity of the 1920s was a cruel illusion. Even during the most prosperous years of the Roaring Twenties, most families lived below what contemporaries defined as the poverty line. In 1929, economists considered $2500 the income necessary to support a family. In that year, more than 60 percent of the nation's families earned less than $2000 a year, the income necessary for basic necessities; and over 40 percent of all families earned less than $1500 annually. Although labor productivity soared during the 1920s because of electrification and more efficient management, wages stagnated or fell in mining, transportation, and manufacturing. Hourly wages for coal miners sagged from 84.5 cents in 1923 to just 62.5 cents in 1929.

Prosperity bypassed specific groups of Americans entirely. A 1928 report on the condition of Native Americans found that half earned less than $500 and that 71 percent lived on less than $200 a year. Mexican Americans, too, had failed to share in the prosperity. During each year of the 1920s, 25,000 Mexicans migrated to the United States. Most lived in conditions of extreme poverty. In Los Angeles, the infant mortality rate was five times that for other Americans and most homes lacked toilets. A survey found that a substantial minority of Mexican Americans had virtually no meat or fresh vegetables in their diet; 40 percent said that they could not afford to give their children milk.

The farm sector had been mired in depression since 1921. Farm prices had been depressed ever since the end of World War I, when European agriculture revived and grain from Argentina and Australia entered the world market. Strapped with long-term debts, high taxes, and a sharp drop in crop prices, farmers lost ground throughout the 1920s. In 1910, a farmer's income was 40 percent of a city worker's. By 1930, it had sagged to just 30 percent.

The decline in farm income reverberated throughout the economy. Rural consumers stopped buying farm implements, tractors, automobiles, furniture, and appliances. Millions of farmers defaulted on their debts, placing tremendous pressure on the banking system. Between 1920 and 1929, more than 5000 of the country's 30,000 banks failed.

Because of the banking crisis, thousands of small businesspeople failed because they could not secure loans. Thousands more went bankrupt because they had lost their working capital in the stock market crash. A heavy burden of consumer debt also weakened the economy. Consumers built up an unmanageable amount of consumer installment and mortgage debt, taking out loans to buy cars, appliances, and homes in the suburbs. To re-

pay these loans, consumers cut back sharply on discretionary spending. Drops in consumer spending then led inevitably to reductions in production and subsequent worker layoffs. Unemployed workers then spent less, and the cycle repeated itself.

A poor distribution of income compounded the country's economic problems. During the 1920s, there was a pronounced shift in wealth and income toward the very rich. Between 1919 and 1929, the share of income received by the wealthiest 1 percent of Americans rose from 12 percent to 19 percent, while the share received by the richest 5 percent jumped from 24 percent to 34 percent. Over the same period, the poorest 93 percent of the nonfarm population actually saw its disposable income fall. Because the rich tend to spend a high proportion of their income on luxuries—such as large cars, entertainment, and tourism—and save a disproportionately large share of their income, there was insufficient demand to keep employment and investment at a high level.

Even before the onset of the Depression, business investment had begun to decline. Residential construction boomed between 1924 and 1927, but in 1929 housing starts fell to less than half the 1924 level. A major reason for the depressed housing market was the 1924 immigration law that had restricted foreign immigration. Soaring inventories also led businesses to reduce investment and production. During the mid-1920s, manufacturers expanded their productive capacity and built up excessive inventories. At the decade's end, they cut production back sharply, directing their surplus funds into stock market speculation.

The Federal Reserve, the nation's central bank, played a critical, if inadvertent, role in weakening the economy. In an effort to curb stock market speculation, the Federal Reserve slowed the growth of the money supply, then allowed that supply to fall dramatically after the stock market crash, producing a wrenching "liquidity crisis." Consumers found themselves unable to repay loans, while businesses did not have the capital to finance business operations. Instead of actively stimulating the economy by cutting interest rates

CHRONOLOGY OF KEY EVENTS

1914	Marcus Garvey organizes the Universal Negro Improvement Association (UNIA), in Jamaica, to promote black migration to Africa, with first U.S. UNIA branch in Harlem in 1917
1915	Ku Klux Klan is revived and claims 4 million members by 1924
1917–1925	Some 600,000 black Americans migrate to northern industrial cities
1919	Labor unrest includes a nationwide steel strike, a coal miners' strike, a general strike in Seattle, and a police strike in Boston; race riots erupt in over 20 cities; Eighteenth Amendment bans the manufacture and sale of alcoholic beverages
1920	Palmer raids arrest suspected Communists; Massachusetts trial of two Italian anarchists, Nicola Sacco and Bartolomeo Vanzetti, begins on charges of murder, and they are executed in 1927; Sinclair Lewis's *Main Street* exposes the complacency of small-town life
1921	Warren Harding's inauguration as the twenty-ninth president begins 12 years of Republican control of the presidency; Revenue Act slashes taxes on higher incomes;

	European immigration is restricted to a quota of 3 percent of the population of a nationality living in the United States in 1910
1922	Fordney-McCumber Tariff raises duties on imports
1923	President Harding dies; Calvin Coolidge becomes the thirtieth president
1924	Congress reduces immigration quota to 2 percent of the population of a nationality living in the United States in 1890; Senate committee begins an investigation of Teapot Dome oil-leasing scandal
1925	Scopes trial, the celebrated "Monkey Trial," attacks the teaching of evolution in public schools; F. Scott Fitzgerald's *The Great Gatsby* criticizes the American success ethic
1926	New revenue act further reduces tax rates on high incomes
1929	Herbert Hoover is inaugurated as the thirty-first president; annual quota of immigrants is reduced to about 152,000; stock market crashes
1930	Hawley-Smoot Tariff raises import duties to unprecedented levels

and expanding the money supply—the way monetary authorities fight recessions today—the Federal Reserve allowed the country's money supply to decline by 27 percent between 1929 and 1933.

Finally, Republican tariff policies damaged the economy by depressing foreign trade. Anxious to protect American industries from foreign competitors, Congress passed the Fordney-McCumber Tariff of 1922 and the Hawley-Smoot Tariff of 1930, raising tariff rates to unprecedented levels. American tariffs stifled international trade, making it diffi-

cult for European nations to pay off their debts. As foreign economies foundered, those countries imposed trade barriers of their own, choking off U.S. exports. By 1933, international trade had plunged 30 percent.

All these factors left the economy ripe for disaster. Yet the depression did not strike instantly; it infected the country gradually, like a slow-growing cancer. Measured in human terms, the Great Depression was the worst economic catastrophe in American history. It hit urban and rural areas, blue- and white-collar families alike. In the nation's cities, unemployed men took to the streets to sell apples or shine shoes. Thousands of others hopped freight trains and wandered from town to town, looking for jobs or handouts.

Unlike most of Western Europe, the United States had no federal system of unemployment insurance. The relief burden fell on state and municipal governments working in cooperation with private charities, such as the Red Cross and the Community Chest. Created to handle temporary emergencies, these groups lacked the resources to alleviate the massive suffering created by the Great Depression. Poor southerners, whose states had virtually no relief funds, were particularly hard-hit.

Urban centers in the North fared little better. Most city charters did not permit public funds to be spent on work relief. Adding insult to injury, several states disqualified relief clients from voting, while other cities forced them to surrender their automobile license plates. "Prosperity's decade" had ended in economic disaster.

CONCLUSION

In 1931, a journalist named Frederick Lewis Allen published a volume of popular history that did more to shape the popular image of the 1920s than any book ever written by a professional historian. Entitled *Only Yesterday*, it depicted the 1920s as a cynical, hedonistic interlude between the Great War and the Great Depression, a decade of dissipation, of jazz bands, raccoon coats, bathtub gin, flappers, flagpole sitters, bootleggers, and marathon dancers. Allen argued that World War I shattered Americans' faith in reform and moral crusades. The younger generation proceeded to rebel against traditional taboos while their elders engaged in an orgy of speculation.

In fact, however, the twenties present a much more complicated picture than that summed up by such catchphrases as "The Jazz Age" or "The Age of Flaming Youth." Janus, the two-faced god of antiquity, offers a more accurate symbol for America in the 1920s. The nation's image was divided, with one profile looking optimistically to the future and the other staring longingly at the past. Caught between the disillusionment of World War I and the economic malaise of the Great Depression, the 1920s witnessed a gigantic struggle between an old and a new America. Immigration, race, alcohol, evolution, gender politics, sexual morality—all became major cultural battlefields during the twenties. But what World War I started, the Great Depression interrupted. The intense cultural upheavals of the 1920s gave way to the equally intense economic debates of the 1930s and cultural politics took a back seat to the politics of survival.

SUGGESTIONS FOR FURTHER READING

Stanley Coben, *Rebellion Against Victorianism: The Impetus for Cultural Change in 1920s America* (1991). Analyzes social and intellectual changes during the 1920s.

Ann Douglas, *Terrible Honesty: Mongrel Manhattan in the 1920s* (1995). Examines the intellectual and artistic ferment in New York City.

John A. Garraty, *The Great Depression* (1986). Discusses the causes of the depression.

Ellis W. Hawley, *The Great War and the Search for Modern Order: A History of the American People and Their Institutions, 1917–1933*, 2d ed. (1992). Presents an interpretive overview of the period.

Roderick Nash, *The Nervous Generation: American Thought, 1917–1930* (1970). Analyzes intellectual and artistic innovations from World War I to the Great Depression.

Geoffrey Perrett, *America in the Twenties* (1982). Offers an overview of social and cultural developments of the decade.

Overviews and Surveys

Frederick Lewis Allen, *Only Yesterday: An Informal History Of the Nineteen-Twenties* (1931); Paul A. Carter, *Another Part of the Twenties* (1977), and *The Twenties in America,* 2d ed. (1975); Ellis Hawley, *The Great War and the Search for Modern Order: A History of the American People and Their Institutions, 1917–1933,* 2d ed. (1992); John D. Hicks, *Republican Ascendancy, 1921–1933* (1960); William E. Leuchtenburg, *The Perils of Prosperity, 1914–32* (1958); Geoffrey Perrett, *America in the Twenties* (1982).

The Emergence of Modern America

Erik Barnouw, *A Tower of Babel: A History of Broadcasting in the United States to 1933* (1966); Robert Crunden, *From Self to Society, 1919–1941* (1972); James J. Flink, *The Car Culture* (1975); Lewis F. Fried, *Makers of the City* (1990); Kenneth T. Jackson, *Crabgrass Frontier: The Suburbanization of the United States* (1985); Peter J. Ling, *America and the Automobile: Technology, Reform, and Social Change* (1990); Fred J. MacDonald, *Don't Touch That Dial! Radio Programming in American Life, 1920–1960* (1979); Roland Marchand, *Advertising the American Dream: Making Way for Modernity, 1920–1946* (1985); John B. Rae, *The Road and the Car in American Life* (1971).

The Formation of Modern American Culture

Loren Baritz, ed., *The Culture of the Twenties* (1970); Lynn Dumenil, *The Modern Temper: American Culture and Society in the 1920s* (1995); Paula Fass, *The Damned and the Beautiful: American Youth in the 1920s* (1977); Frederick Hoffman, *The Twenties: American Writing in the Postwar Decade,* rev. ed. (1962); Roderick Nash, *The Nervous Generation: American Thought, 1917–1930* (1970); Kathy J. Ogren, *The Jazz Revolution: Twenties America and the Meaning of Jazz* (1989); Daniel Pope, *The Making of Modern Advertising* (1983); Robert Sklar, *Movie-Made America: A Cultural History of American Movies* (1975).

The Clash of Values

Houston A. Baker, Jr., *Modernism and the Harlem Renaissance* (1987); Dorothy M. Brown, *Setting a Course: American Women in the 1920s* (1987); Susan D. Becker, *The Origins of the Equal Rights Amendment* (1981); Kathleen M. Blee, *Women of the Klan: Racism & Gender in the 1920s* (1991); Albert Camarillo, *Chicanos in a Changing Society* (1979); William H. Chafe, *The American Woman: Her Changing Social, Economic, and Political Role* (1972); David Chalmers, *Hooded Americans: The First Century of the Ku Klux Klan, 1865–1965* (1965); Mark Thomas Connelly, *The Response to Prostitution in the Progressive Era* (1980); Nancy Cott, *The Grounding of Modern Feminism* (1987); Robert A. Divine, *American Immigration Policy, 1924–1952* (1957); John D'Emilio and Estelle B. Freedman, *Intimate Matters: A History of Sexuality in America* (1988); Peter G. Filene, *Him/Her/Self Sex*

Roles in Modern America (1986); David H. Fischer, *Growing Old In America* (1978); Ellen Fitzpatrick, *Endless Crusade: Women Social Scientists and Progressive Reform* (1990); Norman Furniss, *The Fundamentalist Controversy, 1918–1931* (1954); Ray Ginger, *Six Days or Forever? Tennessee* v. *John Thomas Scopes* (1958); Penina Migdal Glazer and Miriam Slater, *Unequal Colleagues: The Entrance of Women into the Professions, 1890–1940* (1987); Robert A. Goldberg, *Hooded Empire* (1981); Linda Gordon, *Woman's Body, Woman's Right: A Social History of Birth Control in America* (1976); Vivian Gornick, *The Romance of American Communism* (1977); John Higham, *Strangers in the Land: Patterns of American Nativism, 1860–1925* (1955); John B. Holway, *Black Diamonds: Life in the Negro Leagues From the Men Who Lived It* (1989); Nathan Huggins, *Harlem Renaissance* (1971); Kenneth T. Jackson, *The Ku Klux Klan in the City* (1967); Ira Katznelson, *Black Men, White Cities: Race Politics and Migration in the United States, 1900–30, and Britain, 1948–68* (1973); Don S. Kirshner, *City and Country: Rural Responses to Urbanization in the 1920s* (1970); Kenneth Kusmer, *A Ghetto Takes Shape: Black Cleveland, 1870–1930* (1976); J. Stanley Lemons, *The Woman Citizen: Social Feminism in the 1920s* (1973); David Levering Lewis, *When Harlem Was in Vogue* (1981); Leonard Moore, *Citizen Klansmen* (1991); Gilbert Osofsky, *Harlem: The Making of a Ghetto: Negro New York, 1890–1930,* 2d ed. (1971); James Reed, *From Private Vice to Public Virtue: The Birth Control Movement and American Society* (1978); Ricardo Romo, *East Los Angeles: History of a Barrio* (1983); Ruth Rosen, *The Lost Sisterhood: Prostitution in America, 1900–1918* (1982); Ernest Sandeen, *The Roots of Fundamentalism* (1970); Andrew Sinclair, *Prohibition* (1962); Leslie W. Tentler, *Wage-Earning Women: Industrial Work and Family Life in the United States, 1900–1930* (1979); Theodore Vincent, *Black Power and the Garvey Movement* (1971); Winifred D. Wandersee, *Women's Work and Family Values, 1920–1940* (1981); Nancy Weiss, *The National Urban League, 1910–1940* (1974); William Young and David E. Kaiser, *Postmortem: New Evidence in the Case of Sacco and Vanzetti* (1985).

The Republican Restoration

Gary Alchon, *The Invisible Hand of Planning: Capitalism, Social Science, and the State in the 1920s* (1985); LeRoy Ashby, *The Spearless Leader: Senator Borah and the Progressive Movement in the 1920s* (1972); Gary Dean Best, *The Politics of American Individualism: Herbert Hoover in Transition, 1918–1921* (1976); David Burner, *The Politics of Provincialism: The Democratic Party in Transition, 1918–1932* (1968);

Clarke Chambers, *Seedtime of Reform, 1918–1932* (1963); Douglas B. Craig, *After Wilson: The Struggle for the Democratic Party* (1992); Paula Eldot, *Governor Alfred E. Smith: The Politician as Reformer* (1983); John D. Hicks and Theodore Saloutos, *Twentieth-Century Populism: Agricultural Discontent in the Midwest, 1900–1939* (1951); Allan Lichtman, *Prejudice and the Old Politics: The Presidential Election of 1928* (1979); Robert K. Murray, *The Harding Era: Warren G. Harding and His Administration* (1969) and *The Politics of Normalcy* (1973); Burl Noggle, *Teapot Dome: Oil and Politics in the 1920s* (1962); Thomas B. Silver, *Coolidge and the Historians* (1982); Robert H. Zieger, *Republicans and Labor, 1919–1929* (1969).

The Great Crash

William J. Barber, *From New Era to New Deal: Herbert Hoover, the Economists, and American Economic Policy, 1921–1933* (1985); Irving Bernstein, *The Lean Years: A History of the American Worker, 1920–1933* (1960); David Brody, *Workers in Industrial America: Essays on the Twentieth-Century Struggle* (1980); Alfred Chandler, *Strategy and Structure: Chapters in the History of the Industrial Enterprise* (1962); Martin L. Fausold, *The Presidency of Herbert Hoover* (1985); John Kenneth Galbraith, *The Great Crash, 1929* (1955); Ellis W. Hawley, *The Great War and the Search for a Modern Order: A History of the American People and Their Institutions, 1917–1933,* 2d ed. (1992); Sanford M. Jacoby, *Employing Bureaucracy: Managers, Unions, and the Transformation of Work in American Industry* (1985); David C. Jones, *Empire of Dust: Settling and Abandoning the Prairie Dry Belt* (1987); C.P. Kindleberger, *The World in Depression, 1929–1939* (1973); Jim Potter, *The American Economy Between the World Wars,* rev. ed. (1985); James Prothro, *The Dollar Decade: Business Ideas in the 1920s* (1954); Albert U. Romasco, *The Poverty of Abundance: Hoover, the Nation, and the Depression* (1965); Jordan A. Schwarz, *Interregnum of Despair: Hoover, Congress, and the Depression* (1970); Robert Sobel, *The Great Bull Market: Wall Street in the 1920s* (1968); George Soule, *Prosperity Decade: From War to Depression, 1917–1929* (1947); Peter Temin, *Did Monetary Forces Cause the Great Depression?* (1976).

Biographies

David Burner, *Herbert Hoover: A Public Life* (1979); Ellen Chesler, *Woman of Valor: Margaret Sanger and the Birth Control Movement in America* (1992); William Harbaugh, *Lawyer's Lawyer: The Life of John W. Davis* (1973); Matthew Josephson and Hannah Josephson, *Al Smith: Hero of the Cities* (1969); David Kennedy, *Birth Control in America: The Career of Margaret Sanger* (1970); Lawrence Levine, *Defender of the Faith: William Jennings Bryan, 1915–1925* (1965); Richard Lowitt, *George W. Norris* (1971); Manning Marable, *W.E.B. Du Bois: Black Radical Democrat* (1986); Donald R. McCoy, *Calvin Coolidge: The Quiet President* (1967); George Nash, *The Life of Herbert Hoover—The Engineer* (1983); Randy Roberts, *Jack Dempsey: The Manassa Mauler* (1979); Francis Russell, *The Shadow of Blooming Grove: Warren G. Harding in His Times* (1968); Andrew Sinclair, *The Available Man: The Life Behind the Masks of Warren Gamaliel Harding* (1965); Richard N. Smith, *An Uncommon Man: The Triumph of Herbert Hoover* (1984); David P. Thelen, *Robert M. La Follette and the Insurgent Spirit* (1976); William Allen White, *A Puritan in Babylon: The Story of Calvin Coolidge* (1938).

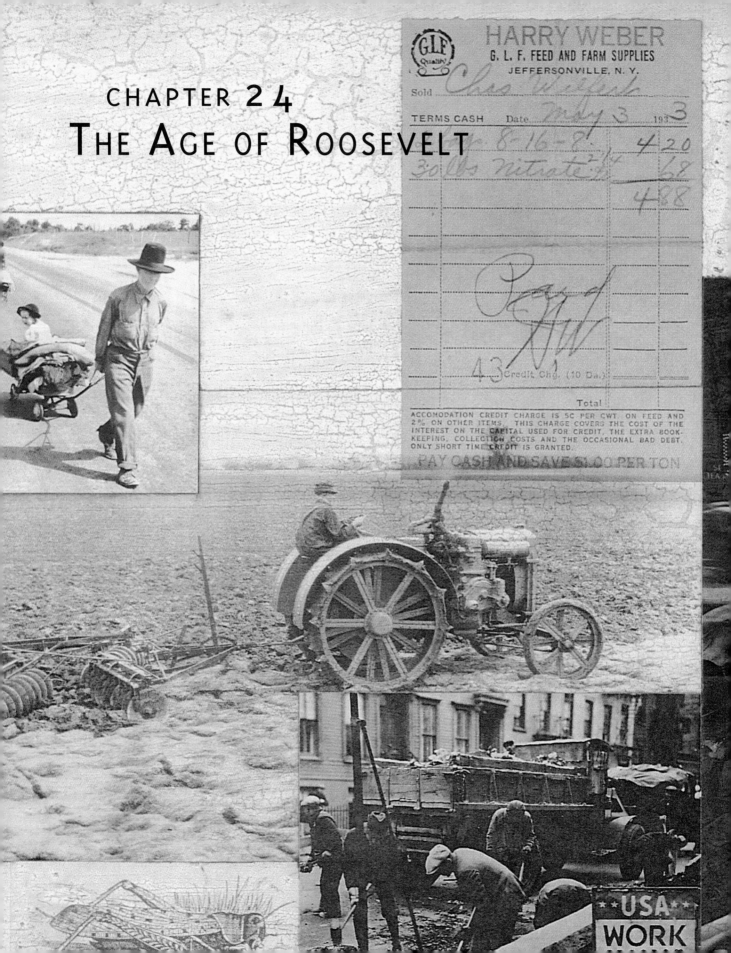

CHAPTER **24**
THE AGE OF ROOSEVELT

THE GREAT DEPRESSION IN GLOBAL PERSPECTIVE

THE HUMAN TOLL
The Dispossessed
Private and Public Charity

PRESIDENT HERBERT HOOVER RESPONDS
Conservative Responses
Government Loans

FRANKLIN ROOSEVELT AND THE FIRST NEW DEAL
The Election of 1932
The First 100 Days
The New Dealers
The Farmers' Plight
The National Recovery Administration
Jobs Programs
Roosevelt's Critics

THE SECOND NEW DEAL
The Wagner Act
Social Security
The Election of 1936

THE NEW DEAL, WOMEN, AND MINORITY GROUPS
Women
African Americans
Mexican Americans
Native Americans

THE NEW DEAL IN DECLINE
Court Packing
The Depression of 1937

POPULAR CULTURE DURING THE GREAT DEPRESSION
Artistic and Literary Endeavors
Hollywood During the Great Depression

To fans of authentic folk music, Woodrow Wilson "Woody" Guthrie was a "Shakespeare in overalls," the finest American frontier balladeer of the twentieth century. His nasal, high-pitched singing voice was definitely an acquired taste, but Guthrie's lyrics were at once simple and penetrating. He sang of vagabonds who wandered in search of work, of union men who saw their comrades on the picket lines knocked to the ground by company goons, and of farmers who watched with horror as their land dried up and turned into a dust bowl. In short he put to music the hardships and struggles of working-class Americans trapped in the Great Depression.

Guthrie drew his material from his life. Born in 1912, Woody grew up in Oklahoma and the Texas Panhandle in a family star-crossed by disasters. When he was still a boy his older sister died from setting herself on fire; his father, once a prosperous land speculator, sank into alcoholism; and his mother slipped slowly into madness and had to be committed to the state mental hospital.

In the face of these tragedies the Guthrie household simply dissolved, leaving Woody pretty much on his own. He passed the time by learning to play the guitar and harmonica. Eventually, he dropped out of school and became a drifter, driven by an internal restlessness that kept him on the road for the rest of his life.

Guthrie spent the Great Depression riding the rails, playing his music, and visiting "his" people, in the boxcars, hobo jungles, and migrant camps from Oklahoma to California. He saw families sleeping on the ground and children with distended bellies who cried from hunger while guards hired to protect the orchards prevented them from eating fruit that lay rotting on the ground. Over time a quiet anger began to eat at him and he blamed the nation's "polli-Tish-uns" for not doing more to relieve the people's suffering.

By 1940 Guthrie had recorded several albums of Dust Bowl ballads and union protest songs. His home-grown radicalism made him an instant hit with socialist and communist intellectuals and entertainment figures who saw his music as a powerful weapon in the class struggle. They saw Guthrie as an authentic folk hero, the very embodiment of the proletarian artist. In truth, Guthrie held more radical political views than most Americans, but he aptly fulfilled his role as the "voice of the people" by putting to music the most important themes to emerge in American life during the 1930s—the common man's defiant pride, his will to survive in the face of adversity, and the extraordinary love Americans felt for their country.

In "God Blessed America" (which later generations of Americans would recognize by its first line, "This land is your land, this land is my land"), Guthrie sang of "endless skyways," "golden valleys," "diamond deserts," and "wheat fields waving," evoking the country's grandeur with a poet's sense of beauty. What gave the song its power, however, was the idea that America belonged to the people; every verse closed with the refrain, "God blessed America for me."

Even in the depths of the Great Depression, Guthrie found much of enduring value in America. In ballad after ballad, he celebrated the fortitude and dignity of the American people. They provided the glue that held things together while President Franklin D. Roosevelt experimented with policies and programs designed to promote relief, recovery, and reform.

Woody Guthrie often inscribed the phrase "This machine surrounds hate and destroys it" on his guitars.

THE GREAT DEPRESSION IN GLOBAL PERSPECTIVE

Unlike previous economic downturns, which generally were confined to a handful of nations or specific regions, the Great Depression was a global phenomenon. Africa, Asia, Australia, Europe, and North and South America all suffered from the economic collapse. International trade fell 30 percent, as most nations tried to protect their industries by raising tariffs on imported goods. These "beggar-thy-neighbor" trade policies were a major reason why the depression persisted as long as it did. By 1932, an estimated 30 million people around the world were unemployed.

Also, in contrast to the relatively brief economic "panics" of the past, the Great Depression dragged on with no end in sight. As it deepened, the depression had far-reaching political consequences. One response to it was military dictatorship—a response found in Argentina and many countries in Central America. Western industrialized countries cut back sharply on the purchase of raw materials and other commodities. The price of coffee, cotton, rubber, tin, and other commodities dropped 40 percent. The collapse in raw material and agricultural commodity prices led to social unrest, resulting in the rise of military dictatorships that promised to maintain order.

A second response to the depression was fascism and militarism—a response found in Germany, Italy, and Japan. In Germany, Adolf Hitler and his Nazi party promised to restore the country's economy and rebuild its military. After becoming chancellor in 1932, Hitler outlawed labor unions, restructured German industry into a series of cartels, and, after 1935, instituted a massive program of military rearmament that ended high unemployment. In Italy, fascism arose under the leadership of Italian dictator Benito Mussolini even before the depression's onset. In Japan, militarists seized control of the government during the 1930s. In an effort to relieve the depression, Japanese military officers conquered Manchuria, a region rich in raw materials, in 1931, and coastal China in 1937.

A third response to the depression was totalitarian communism. In the Soviet Union, the Great Depression helped solidify Joseph Stalin's grip on power. In 1928, Stalin instituted a planned economy. His first Five-Year Plan called for rapid industrialization and "collectivization" of small peasant farms under government control. To crush opposition to his program, which required peasant farmers to give their products to the government at low prices, Stalin exiled millions of peasants to labor camps in Siberia, instituting a program of terror called the Great Purge. Historians estimate that as many as 20 million Soviets died during the 1930s as a result of famine and deliberate killings.

A fourth and final response to the depression was welfare capitalism, which could be found in countries such as Canada, Great Britain, and France. Under welfare capitalism, the government assumed ultimate responsibility for promoting a reasonably fair distribution of wealth and power and providing security against the risks of bankruptcy, unemployment, and destitution.

The economic decline brought on by this depression was steeper and more protracted in the United States than in other industrialized countries. The unemployment rate rose higher and remained higher longer than in any other western society. While European countries significantly reduced unemployment by 1936, as late as 1939, when World War II began in Europe, the American jobless rate still exceeded 17 percent, not dropping below 14 percent until 1941.

The Great Depression transformed the American political and economic landscape. It produced a major political realignment, creating a coalition of big-city ethnics, African Americans, and Southern Democrats committed, to various degrees, to interventionist government. It strengthened the federal presence in American life, spawning such innovations as national old-age pensions, unemployment compensation, aid to dependent children, public housing, federally subsidized school lunches, insured bank deposits, the minimum wage, and stock market regulation. It fundamentally altered labor relations, producing a revived labor movement and a national labor

policy protective of collective bargaining. It transformed the farm economy by introducing federal price supports and rural electrification. Above all, the Great Depression produced a fundamental shift in public attitudes. It led Americans to view the federal government as their agency of action and reform and the ultimate protector of public well-being.

THE HUMAN TOLL

Even after more than half a century, images of the Great Depression remain firmly etched in the American psyche—breadlines, soup kitchens, tin-can shanties and tarpaper shacks known as "Hoovervilles," penniless men and women selling apples on street corners, and gray battalions of "Arkies" and "Okies" packed into Model A Fords heading out to California.

The economic collapse was staggering in its dimensions. Unemployment jumped from less than 3 million in 1929 to 4 million in 1930, 8 million in 1931, and 12½ million in 1932. By 1932, a quarter of the nation's families did not have a single employed wage earner. Even those fortunate enough to have jobs suffered drastic pay cuts and reductions in hours. Only one company in ten failed to cut pay, and in 1932, three-quarters of all workers were on part-time schedules, averaging just 60 percent of the normal workweek.

Appalling in dimension, the collapse was terrifying in its scope and impact. By 1933 average family income had tumbled 40 percent, from $2300 in 1929 down to just $1500 four years later. In the Pennsylvania coalfields, three or four families crowded together in one-room shacks and lived on wild weeds. In Arkansas, families were found inhabiting caves, and in Oakland, California, whole families lived in sewer pipes.

Vagrancy shot up as many families were evicted from their homes for nonpayment of rent. The Southern Pacific Railroad boasted that it threw 683,000 vagrants off its trains in 1931. Free public flophouses and missions in Los Angeles provided beds for 200,000 of the uprooted.

Many families sought to cope by planting gardens, canning food, buying day-old bread, and using cardboard and cotton for shoe soles. Despite a steep drop in food prices, many families did without milk or meat. In New York City, milk consumption dropped a million gallons a day. To save money, families neglected medical and dental care.

President Herbert Hoover declared, "Nobody is actually starving. The hoboes are better fed than they have ever been." But in New York City in 1931 there were 20 known cases of starvation; in 1934, there were 110 deaths from hunger. There were so many accounts of people starving in New York that the West African nation of Cameroon sent $3.77 in relief.

The Great Depression had a powerful impact on families. It forced couples to delay marriage and drove the birthrate below the replacement level for the first time in American history. The divorce rate fell—for the simple reason that many couples could not afford to maintain separate households or pay legal fees. But rates of desertion soared—by 1940, 1.5 million married women were living apart from their husbands. More than 200,000 vagrant children wandered the country because of the breakup of their families.

The depression inflicted a heavy psychological toll on jobless men. With no wages to reinforce their authority, many men lost power as primary decision makers. Large numbers of men lost their self-respect, became immobilized, and stopped looking for work, while others turned to alcohol or became self-destructive or abusive to their families.

In contrast to the men, many women saw their status rise during the depression. To supplement the family income, married women entered the workforce in large numbers. Although most women worked in menial occupations, the fact that they were employed and bringing home paychecks elevated their position within the family and gave them a say in family decisions.

Despite the hardships it inflicted, the Great Depression drew some families closer together. As one observer noted, "Many a family has lost its automobile and found its soul." Families had to devise strategies for getting through hard times because their survival depended on

it. They pooled their incomes, moved in with relatives in order to cut expenses, and did without. Many families drew comfort from their religion, sustained by the hope things would turn out well in the end, while others placed their faith in themselves, in their own dogged determination to survive that so impressed observers like Woody Guthrie. But many Americans no longer believed the problems could be solved by people acting alone or through voluntary associations. Increasingly, they looked to the federal government for help.

The Dispossessed

Economic hardship and loss visited all sections of the country. One-third of the Harvard class of 1911 confessed that they were hard up, on relief, or dependent on relatives. Doctors and lawyers saw their incomes fall 40 percent. But no groups suffered more from the depression than African Americans and Mexican Americans.

A year after the stock market crashed, 70 percent of Charleston's black population and 75 percent of Memphis's was unemployed. In Macon County, Alabama, home of Booker T. Washington's famous Tuskegee Institute, most black families lived in homes without wooden floors, windows, or sewage disposal and subsisted on salt pork (pork fat cured in salt), hominy grits, corn bread, and molasses. Income averaged less than a dollar a day.

Conditions were also distressed in the North. In Chicago, 70 percent of all black families earned less than a $1000 a year, far below the poverty line. In Chicago and other large northern cities, most African Americans lived in "kitchenettes." Six-room apartments, previously rented for $50 a month, were divided into six kitchenettes renting for $8 dollars a week, assuring landlords of a windfall of an extra $142 a month. Buildings that previously held 60 families now contained 360.

The depression hit Mexican-American families especially hard. Mexican Americans faced serious opposition from organized labor, which resented competition from Mexican workers as unemployment rose. Bowing to union pressure, federal, state, and local authorities "repatriated" more than 400,000 people of Mexican descent to prevent them from applying for relief. Since this group included

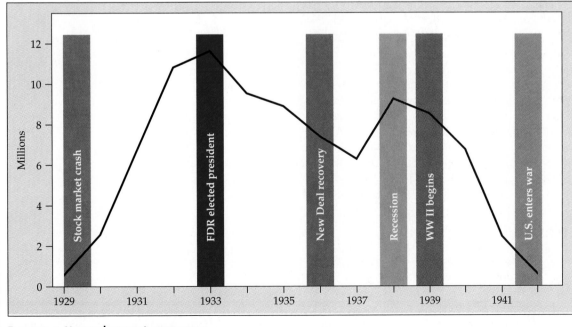

Figure 24.1 **Unemployment, 1929–1942**

many United States citizens, the deportations constituted a gross violation of civil liberties.

Private and Public Charity

The economic crisis of the 1930s overwhelmed private charities and local governments. In south Texas, the Salvation Army provided a penny per person each day. In Philadelphia, even though private and public charities distributed $1 million a month in poor relief, this provided families with only $1.50 a week for groceries. In 1932, total public and private relief expenditures amounted to $317 million—$26 for each of the nation's 12½ million jobless.

PRESIDENT HERBERT HOOVER RESPONDS

When the Great Depression struck, most political and economic leaders had regarded recessions as inevitable, a natural part of the business cycle. The prevailing economic theory held that government intervention was both

Table 24.1 DEPRESSION SHOPPING LIST: 1932–1934

Automobiles		Household Items		Toys	
Pontiac Coupe	$ 585.00	Silverplate flatware,		Doll carriage	$ 4.98
Chrysler Sedan	995.00	26 pieces	$4.98	Sled	1.45
Dodge	595.00	Double-bed sheets	.67	Tricycle	3.98
Studebaker	840.00	Bath towel	.24	Bicycle	10.95
Packard	2150.00	Wool blanket	1.00	Fielder's glove and	
Chevrolet ton pick-up		Wool rug (9'×12')	5.85	ball	1.25
truck	650.00				

Clothing		Appliances		Food	
Women's		Electric iron	$ 2.00	Sirloin steak/lb.	$.29
Mink coat	$585.00	Electric coffee		Rib roast/lb.	.22
Leopard coat	92.00	percolator	1.39	Bacon/lb.	.22
Cloth coat	6.98	Electric mixer	9.95	Ham/lb.	.31
Wool dress	1.95	Vacuum cleaner	18.75	Chicken/lb.	.22
Wool suit	3.98	Electric washing		Pork chops/lb.	.20
Wool sweater	1.69	machine	47.95	Salmon (16 oz can)	.19
Silk stockings	.69	Gas stove	23.95	Milk (quart)	.10
Leather shoes	1.79	Electric sewing		Butter/lb.	.28
		machine	24.95	Eggs (dozen)	.29
				Bread (20 oz loaf)	.05
Men's		**Furniture**		Coffee/lb.	.26
Overcoat	$11.00	Dining room set,		Sugar/lb.	.05
Wool suit	10.50	8-piece	$ 46.50	Rice/lb.	.06
Trousers	2.00	Lounge chair	19.95	Potatoes/lb.	.02
Shirt	.47	Double bed and		Tomatoes (16 oz.	
Pullover sweater	1.95	mattress	14.95	can)	.09
Silk necktie	.55	Mahogany coffee		Oranges/dozen	.27
Stetson hat	5.00	table	10.75	Cornflakes (8 oz.	
Shoes	3.85	Chippendale sofa	135.00	box)	.08
		Louis XV walnut dining			
		table	124.00	**Air Travel**	
		Wing chair	39.00	New York to Chicago,	
		Grand piano	395.00	round trip	$ 86.31
				Chicago to Los Angeles,	
				round trip	207.00

unnecessary and unwise. Previous financial panics had failed to elicit much response from government; and many economists in 1929 continued to extol the virtues of inaction, arguing that the economy would recover by itself. President Herbert Hoover disagreed. Though Hoover saw the Great Crash as a temporary slump in a fundamentally healthy economy, he believed the president should try to facilitate economic recovery.

Conservative Responses

First, Hoover resorted to old-fashioned "jawboning." Shortly after the stock market crashed, he summoned business and labor leaders to the White House. Industrial leaders promised to maintain prices and wages, and labor spokesmen pledged not to strike or demand higher wages. While Hoover remained hopeful voluntary measures would suffice, businesses struggled to survive, forcing employers to lay off workers.

Next, the president tried cheerleading. The contrast between Hoover's speeches and conditions in the country was jarring. According to Hoover, the economy in 1930 was fundamentally sound, and recovery was just around the corner. His rosy pronouncements prompted critics to accuse Hoover of being insensitive to the unemployed and the dispossessed. Cynics called the shantytown slums on the edges of cities "Hoovervilles." Newspapers became "Hoover blankets" and empty pockets turned inside out, "Hoover flags."

Neither cruel nor insensitive, Hoover was tormented by the suffering of the poor. Yet he could not bring himself to sanction large-scale federal public works programs because he honestly believed that recovery depended on the private sector, because he wanted to maintain a balanced budget, and because he feared federal relief programs would undermine individual character by making recipients dependent on the state.

Government Loans

When jawboning and cheerleading failed to revive the economy, Hoover reluctantly adopted other measures. In 1932 Congress created the Reconstruction Finance Corporation (RFC) and authorized it to loan $2 billion to banks, savings and loan associations, railroads, and life insurance companies. Blaming the depression on tight credit, Hoover believed federal loans would enable businesses to increase production and hire workers. The same principle applied to the Federal Home Loan Bank System (FHLBS), created by Congress in July 1932 to lend up to $500 million to savings and loan associations to revive the construction industry.

Yet by early 1933 Hoover's agencies had failed to make a dent in the Great Depression. The real problem was not tight credit but the soft demand for goods, a problem that flowed both from the chronic low wages paid to the bulk of American workers and the massive layoffs following the Great Crash. It was a vicious cycle. Unemployed workers could not buy goods, so businesses cut back production and laid off additional workers. Businesspeople did not ask banks for working capital loans, which the RFC and FHLBS were created to provide, because they had no interest in increasing production.

Bank failures wiped out the life savings of many prudent Americans.

FRANKLIN ROOSEVELT AND THE FIRST NEW DEAL

In June 1932, Franklin D. Roosevelt received the Democratic presidential nomination. At first glance he did not look like a man who could relate to other peoples' suffering, for Roosevelt had spent his entire life in the lap of luxury. A fifth cousin of Teddy Roosevelt, he was born in 1882 to one of New York's oldest and wealthiest families. No fewer than 16 of his ancestors had come over on the Mayflower. Roosevelt enjoyed a privileged youth. He attended Groton, an exclusive private school, then went to Harvard University and Columbia Law School. After three years in the New York state senate, Roosevelt was tapped by President Wilson to serve as assistant secretary of the navy in 1913. His status as the rising star of the Democratic party was confirmed when James Cox chose Roosevelt as his running mate in the presidential election of 1920.

The Election of 1932

Handsome and outgoing, Roosevelt seemed to have a bright political future. Then disaster struck. In 1921 he was stricken with polio, which left him paralyzed from the waist down and confined to a wheelchair for the rest of his life. Instead of retiring, however, Roosevelt labored diligently to return to public life. "If you had spent two years in bed trying to wiggle your toe," he later declared, "after that anything would seem easy."

Buoyed by an exuberant optimism and devoted political allies, Roosevelt won the governorship of New York in 1928, one of the few Democrats to survive the Republican landslide. Surrounding himself with able advisers, Roosevelt labored to convert New York into a laboratory for reform, involving conservation, old-age pensions, public works projects, and unemployment insurance.

In his acceptance speech before the 1932 Democratic convention in Chicago, Roosevelt promised "a New Deal for the American peo-

Roosevelt was charming and charismatic, and many people felt he was genuinely interested in their concerns. Here Roosevelt meets with a miner during his 1932 campaign.

Members of the Bonus Army poured into Washington, D.C., from every part of the country during the spring and summer of 1932.

ple." Although his speech contained few concrete proposals, Roosevelt radiated confidence, giving many desperate voters hope. He even managed during the campaign to turn his lack of a blueprint into an asset, promising to experiment. "It is common sense to take a method and try it," he declared, "if it fails, admit it frankly and try another."

The Republicans stuck with Hoover. Dejected and embittered, he projected despair and failure. What little chance he had for reelection was dashed by his callous treatment of the "Bonus Army." A bedraggled collection of unemployed veterans and their families, the Bonus Army marched on Washington in the spring of 1932 to ask Congress for immediate payment of their war service bonuses, which did not come due until 1945. More than 15,000 strong, they erected a shantytown, camped out in vacant lots, and occupied empty government buildings. Though the House voted to give them what they wanted, the Senate killed the bill after Hoover lobbied against it.

Most of the veterans then left Washington, D.C., but a few thousand stayed behind because they had no place to go. At Hoover's request, Congress appropriated $100,000 to help the remaining veterans return home. When police tried to evict some of the marchers in late July, a riot broke out in which two policemen and two marchers died.

Hoover then ordered General Douglas MacArthur to use federal troops to remove them from government buildings. Exceeding his orders, MacArthur used tanks and tear gas to drive the veterans from the city. Newsmen captured the melee in vivid photographs which papers carried the next day.

Although Hoover was appalled by what happened, he publicly accepted the responsibility and endorsed MacArthur's charge that the bonus marchers included dangerous radicals who wanted to overthrow the government. Most Americans were outraged by the government's harsh treatment of the Bonus Army, and Hoover encountered resentment everywhere he campaigned.

Upon learning of the Bonus Army incident, Franklin D. Roosevelt remarked: "Well, this will elect me." Roosevelt was correct—he buried Hoover in November, winning 22,809,638 votes to Hoover's 15,758,901, and 472 to 59 electoral votes. The Democrats also won commanding majorities in both houses of Congress.

Roosevelt appealed to a wide range of voters, wooing southerners back into the Democrat fold and attracting new groups of voters, including young people, women, and ethnic Americans. Urban Catholics, Jews, and members of the Eastern Orthodox Church voted overwhelmingly for Roosevelt. The 1932 election was the first of many in which these groups would support strongly the Democratic party.

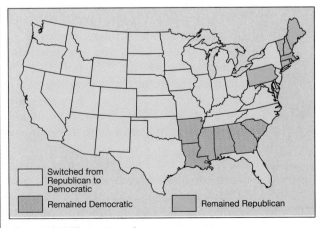

Electoral Shift, 1928 and 1932

Table 24.2 Legislation Enacted During the First Hundred Days March 9—June 16, 1933	
March 9	Emergency Banking Relief Act
March 20	Economy Act
March 22	Beer-Wine Revenue Act
March 31	Unemployment Relief Act
March 31	Civilian Conservation Corps Act
May 12	Agricultural Adjustment Act
May 12	Federal Emergency Relief Act
May 18	Tennessee Valley Authority Act
May 27	Securities Act of 1933
June 5	Gold Repeal Joint Resolution
June 13	Home Owners' Refinancing Act
June 16	Farm Credit Act
June 16	Banking Act of 1933
June 16	Emergency Railroad Transportation Act
June 16	National Industrial Recovery Act

The First 100 Days

The nation's plight on March 4, 1933, the day Franklin Roosevelt assumed the presidency, was desperate. A quarter of the nation's workforce was jobless. A quarter-million families had defaulted on their mortgages the previous year. About 9000 banks, holding the savings of 27 million families, had failed since 1929—1456 in 1932 alone. Farm foreclosures were averaging 20,000 a month. The public was frantic for action. Hamilton Fish, a conservative Republican Congressman from New York, promised the president that Congress would "give you any power that you need."

In his inaugural address, Roosevelt expressed confidence that his administration could end the depression. "The only thing we have to fear," he declared, "is fear itself." The president promised decisive action. He called Congress into special session and demanded "broad executive power to wage a war against the emergency, as great as the power that would be given me if we were in fact invaded by a foreign foe." Across the nation people held their breaths waiting to see what the new president would do. In his first hundred days in office, the president pushed 15 major bills through Congress, which would reshape every aspect of the economy, from banking and industry to agriculture and social welfare.

He attacked the bank crisis first, declaring a national bank holiday, which closed all banks. In just four days, his aides drafted the Emergency Banking Relief Act, which permitted solvent banks to reopen under government supervision, and allowed the RFC to buy the stock of troubled banks and keep them open until they could be reorganized. The law also gave the president broad powers over the Federal Reserve System. The law radically reshaped the nation's banking system; it passed Congress in eight hours.

To generate support for his program, Roosevelt appealed directly to the people. On March 12, eight days after he took office, he conducted the first of many radio "fireside chats." Using the radio the way later presidents would exploit television, he explained what he had done in plain, simple terms and told the public to have "confidence and courage." When the banks reopened the following day, people demonstrated their faith by making more deposits than withdrawals. One of Roosevelt's key advisers did not exaggerate when he later boasted, "Capitalism was saved in eight days."

The president quickly pushed ahead on other fronts. The Federal Emergency Relief

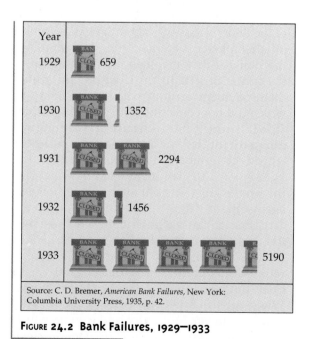

Source: C. D. Bremer, *American Bank Failures*, New York: Columbia University Press, 1935, p. 42.

Figure 24.2 Bank Failures, 1929—1933

Primary Source Essay

THE FIRST "FIRESIDE CHAT"

On the eve of Franklin D. Roosevelt's inauguration, America's banking system was in shambles. In the first three years following the Great Crash some 5500 banks had closed, and only a handful of those that remained open were solvent. With less than $6 billion in cash against $41 billion in deposits, banks were vulnerable to a wholesale run. If depositors demanded their money, banks would be forced to sell their assets (securities and mortgages) at a fraction of their former value to raise funds.

In the weeks before Roosevelt took office, the run began. Warned that Detroit's Union Guardian Trust Company was about to collapse and drag other banks down with it, Michigan governor William A. Comstock declared a banking moratorium throughout the state on February 14, 1933. As news of Michigan's horrors spread, long lines of depositors demanding their money appeared in banks across the country. Banks in Indiana, Ohio, and Kentucky tried to weather the storm by limiting withdrawals to 5 percent of balances, but many states followed Michigan's lead. By March 1, only two weeks later, 17 states had declared so-called banking holidays. During the next two days every bank in Kansas and Minnesota closed its doors, and the closings quickly spread into North Carolina and Virginia. On the eve of Roosevelt's inauguration, rumors spread that the largest banks in New York City and Chicago were teetering. With its two most important financial strongholds in jeopardy, the nation's financial system was truly on the brink of disaster.

Within days after taking office, Roosevelt moved to restore the public's confidence in banks. The first bill he sent to Congress addressed the nation's banking crisis, and on March 12, 1933, Roosevelt held his first "Fireside Chat" to explain his actions directly to the American people. He spoke not as some remote politician in an ivory tower but as a straightforward man who understood the public's concerns and could relate to their fears. Above all, he spoke in simple language and with profound confidence. When the banks reopened the following morning, the long lines disappeared as people demonstrated their confidence by returning far more money to their accounts than they withdrew. In the Federal

President Franklin Delano Roosevelt, Jr., used the relatively new broadcast medium of radio to deliver a message of reassurance to the American public.

Reserve districts alone, deposits outstripped withdrawals by more than $10 million dollars in a single day.

In the following excerpts from the president's speech, note his word choice, his gift for simplifying complicated issues, and his ability to banish "the phantom of fear" from people's hearts:

bank puts your money to work to keep the wheels of industry and of agriculture turning around.   A comparatively small part of the money you put into the bank is kept in currency—an amount which in normal times is wholly sufficient to cover the cash needs of the average citizen.   In other words the total amount of all the currency in the country is only a ~~comparatively~~ small ~~proportion~~ fraction of the total deposits in all of the banks.

What, then, happened during the last few days of February and the first few days of March?   Because of undermined confidence on the part of the public, there was a general rush by a large portion of our population to turn bank deposits into currency or gold. — A rush so great that the soundest banks could not get enough currency to meet the demand.   The reason for this was that on the spur of the moment it was, of course,

Reproduced here is the actual radio script FDR used in his fireside chat of March 12, 1933. Note the handwritten changes made to simplify the address even further.

I want to talk for a few minutes with the people of the United States about banking—with the comparatively few who understand the mechanics of banking but more particularly with the overwhelming majority who use banks for the making of deposits and the drawing of checks. I want to tell you what has been done in the last few days, why it was done, and what the next steps are going to be. . . .

First of all, let me state the simple fact that when you deposit money in a bank the bank does not put the money into a safe deposit vault. It invests your money in many different forms of credit—bonds, commercial paper, mortgages and many other kinds of loans. . . . In other words, the total amount of all the currency in the country is only a small fraction of the total deposits in all of the banks.

What, then, happened during the last few days of February and the first few days of March? Because of undermined confidence on the part of the public, there was a general rush by a large portion of our population to turn bank deposits into currency or gold—a rush so great that the soundest banks could not get enough currency to meet the demand. . . .

By the afternoon of March 3d scarcely a bank in the country was open to do business. . . .

It was then that I issued the proclamation providing for the nationwide bank holiday and this was the first step in the Government's reconstruction of our financial and economic fabric.

The second step was the legislation promptly and patriotically passed by the Congress confirming my proclamation and broadening my power so that it became possible in view of the requirement of time to extend the holiday and lift the ban of that holiday gradually. . . .

The third stage has been the series of regulations permitting the banks to continue their functions to take care of the distribution of food and household necessities and the payment of payrolls. . . .

A question you will ask is this: why are all the banks not to be reopened at the same time? The answer is simple. Your Government does not intend that the history of the past few years shall be repeated. We do not want and will not have another epidemic of bank failures.

As a result, we start tomorrow, Monday, with the opening of banks in the twelve Federal Reserve Bank cities—those banks which on first examination by the treasury have already been found to be all right. This will be followed on Tuesday by the resumption of all their functions by banks already found to be sound in cities where there are recognized clearing houses. . . .

On Wednesday and succeeding days banks in smaller places all through the country will resume business, subject, of course, to the Government's physical ability to complete its survey. . . .

The success of our whole great national program depends, of course, upon the cooperation of the public—on its intelligent support and use of a reliable system. . . .

It has been wonderful to me to catch the note of confidence from all over the country. . . .

. . . Confidence and courage are the essentials of success in carrying out our plan. You people must have faith; you must not be stampeded by rumors or guesses. Let us unite in banishing fear. We have provided the machinery to restore our financial system; it is up to you to support and make it work.

It is your problem no less than it is mine. Together we cannot fail.

Few political speeches have enjoyed more success than President Roosevelt's first "Fireside Chat." Before he addressed the nation, there were over $7.5 billion in circulation; the figure declined by $1.25 billion during the remainder of March. The money returned to banks derived from hoarded funds rather than general circulation, since most deposits came in larger bills ($50 or over), which were not generally used in day-to-day transactions.

The flow of money back into banks saved them. Three days after the banking holiday ended, 4507 national banks and 567 state banks reopened for business, an impressive 76 percent of all the member banks of the Federal Reserve System. By the middle of April, 7400 nonmember banks (approximately 72 percent of the total of such banks) had been licensed by state authorities. By the end of 1933, the banks that had reopened had been strengthened with new capital, either from local interests or funds supplied by the Reconstruction Finance Corporation. The U.S. banking system had survived its greatest challenge in history, thanks in no small part to the superb communication skills and resolute action of President Roosevelt.

Act pumped $500 million into state-run welfare programs. The Homeowners Loan Act provided the first federal mortgage financing and loan guarantees. By the end of Roosevelt's first term it had provided more than a million loans totaling $3 billion. The Glass-Steagall Act provided a federal guarantee on all bank deposits under $5000, (with creation of the Federal Deposit Insurance Corporation), separated commercial and investment banking, and strengthened the Federal Reserve's ability to stabilize the economy.

In addition, Roosevelt took the nation off the gold standard, devalued the dollar, and ordered the Federal Reserve System to ease credit. Other important laws passed during the 100 days included the Agricultural Adjustment Act, the nation's first system of agricultural price and production supports; the National Industrial Recovery Act, the first major attempt to plan and regulate the economy; and the Tennessee Valley Authority Act, the first direct government involvement in energy production.

The New Dealers

Franklin Roosevelt brought a new breed of government officials to Washington. Previously, most government administrators were wealthy patricians, businessmen, or political loyalists. Roosevelt, however, looked to new sources of talent, bringing to Washington a team of Ivy League intellectuals and New York State social workers. Known as the "brain trust," these advisers provided Roosevelt with economic ideas and oratorical ammunition.

The New Dealers were strongly influenced by the Progressive reformers of the early twentieth century, who believed that government had not only a right but a duty to intervene in all aspects of the economy in order to improve the quality of American life. In one significant respect, however, the New Dealers differed decisively from the Progressives. Progressive reform had a strongly moral dimension; many reformers wanted to curb drinking, regulate sexual behavior, and reshape human character. In comparison, the New Dealers were much more pragmatic—an attitude vividly illustrated by an incident that took place during World War I. One of the most intense policy debates during the war was whether to provide American troops with condoms. The secretary of the navy, Josephus Daniels, rejected the idea, fearing that it would corrupt the troops' morals. "It is wicked," he declared, "to seem to encourage and approve placing in the hands of the men an appliance which will lead them to think they may indulge in practices which are not sanctioned by moral . . . law." While Daniels was on vacation, however, his undersecretary, Franklin Roosevelt, authorized prophylactics for sailors. Moral reform would not drive the New Deal.

Apart from their commitment to pragmatism, the New Dealers were unified in their rejection of laissez-faire orthodoxy—the idea that the federal government's responsibilities were confined to balancing the federal budget and providing for the nation's defense. The New Dealers did, however, disagree profoundly about the best way to end the depression, offering three alternative prescriptions for rescuing the nation's economy. The "trust-busters," led by Thurman Arnold, called for vigorous enforcement of antitrust laws to break up concentrated business power. The "associationalists" wanted to encourage cooperation between business, labor, and government by establishing associations and codes supported by the three parties. The economic planners, led by Rexford Tugwell, Adolph Berle, and Gardiner Means, wanted to create a system of centralized national planning.

The Farmers' Plight

Roosevelt moved aggressively to address the crisis facing the nation's farmers. No group was harder hit by the depression than farmers and farm workers. At the start of the depression, a fifth of all American families still lived on farms, but they were in deep trouble. Farm income fell a staggering two-thirds during the depression's first three years. A bushel of wheat that sold for $2.94 in 1920 dropped to $1 in 1929 and 30 cents in 1932. In one day, a quarter of Mississippi's farm acreage was auctioned off to pay debts.

The farmers' problem, ironically, was that they grew too much. Worldwide crop production soared—a result of more efficient farm machinery, stronger fertilizers, and improved plant varieties—but demand fell, as people ate less bread, Europeans imposed protective tariffs, and consumers replaced cotton with rayon. The glut caused prices to fall. To meet farm debts in 1932, farmers had to grow 2.5 times as much corn as in 1929, 2.7 times as much wheat, and 2.4 times as much cotton.

As farm incomes fell, farm tenancy soared; two-fifths of all farmers worked on land that they did not own. The Gudgers, a white southern Alabama sharecropping family of six, illustrated the plight of tenants, who were slipping deeper and deeper into debt. Each year, their landlord provided them with 20 acres of land, seed, an unpainted one-room house, a shed, a mule, fertilizer, and $10 a month. In return, they owned him half their corn and cotton crop and 8 percent interest on their debts. In 1934 they were $80 in debt; by 1935, their debts had risen another $12.

Nature itself seemed to have turned against farmers. In the South, the boll weevil devoured the cotton crop, while on the Great Plains, the top soil literally blew away, piling up in ditches like "snow drifts in winter." The Dust Bowl produced unparalleled human tragedy, but it had not occurred by accident. Although the Plains had always been a harsh, arid, inhospitable environment, a covering of tough grass-roots called sod allowed the land to retain moisture and support vegetation. During the 1890s, however, overgrazing by cattle severely damaged the sod. Then, during World War I, farmers driven by the demand for wheat, used gasoline-powered tractors to plow large sections of the prairie for the first time. The fragile skin protecting the prairie was stripped away. When, beginning in 1930, drought struck and temperatures soared (to 108° in Kansas for weeks on end), the wind began to blow the soil away. One Kansas county, in which 3.4 million bushels of wheat

were produced in 1931, harvested just 89,000 bushels in 1933.

Tenant farmers found themselves evicted from their land. By 1939, a million Dust Bowl refugees and other tenant farmers left the Plains to work as itinerant produce pickers in California. Whole counties were depopulated as a result. In one part of Colorado, 4333 homes were abandoned.

The New Deal attacked farm problems through a variety of programs. Rural electrification programs meant that for the first time, Americans in Appalachia, the Texas hill country, and other areas would have the opportunity to share in the benefits of electric light and running water. As late as 1935 more than 6 million of America's 6.8 million farms had no electricity. Unlike their sisters in the city, farmwomen had no washing machines, refrigerators, or vacuum cleaners. Nor did private utility companies intend to change things. Private companies insisted that it would be prohibitive to provide electrical service to rural areas.

Roosevelt disagreed. He wanted to break the private monopoly of electric power in rural areas, envisioning a future in which electric power would serve broader goals, including flood control, soil conservation, reforestation, diversification of industry, and a general improvement in the quality of life for rural Americans. Settling on the 40,000-square-mile valley of the Tennessee River as a test site, Roosevelt decided to put the government into the electric business.

Two months after he took office Congress passed a bill creating the Tennessee Valley Authority (TVA). The bill authorized the TVA to build 21 dams to generate electricity for tens of thousands of farm families. In 1935 Roosevelt signed an executive order creating the Rural Electrification Administration (REA) to bring electricity generated by government dams to America's hinterland. Between 1935 and 1942 the lights came on for 35 percent of America's farm families.

Nor was electricity the only benefit the New Deal bestowed on farmers. The Soil Conservation Service helped farmers battle erosion; the Farm Credit Administration provided some relief from farm foreclosures, and the Commodity Credit Corporation permitted farmers to use stored products as collateral for loans. Roosevelt's most ambitious farm program, however, was the Agricultural Adjustment Act (AAA).

The AAA, led by Secretary of Agriculture Henry Wallace, sought a partnership between the government and major producers. Together the new allies would raise prices by reducing the supply of farm goods. Under the AAA, the large producers, acting through farm cooperatives, would agree upon a "domestic allotment" plan that would assign acreage quotas to each producer. Participation would be voluntary. Farmers who cut production to comply with the quotas would be paid for land left fallow.

Unfortunately for its backers, the AAA got off to a horrible start. Because the 1933 crops had already been planted by the time Congress established the AAA, the administration ordered farmers to plow their crops under, paying them over $100 million to destroy 10 million acres of cotton. The government also purchased and slaughtered six million pigs, salvaging only one million pounds for the needy. The public neither understood nor forgave the agency for destroying food while jobless people went hungry.

Overall, the AAA's record was mixed. It raised farm income, but did little for sharecroppers and tenant farmers, the groups hardest hit by the agricultural crisis. Farm incomes doubled between 1933 and 1936, but those with large farms reaped most of the benefits. Many large landowners used government payments to purchase tractors and combines allowing them to mechanize farm operations, increasing crop yields and reducing the need for sharecroppers and tenants. One Mississippi planter, for example, bought 22 tractors with his payments and subsequently evicted 160 tenant families. An unintentional consequence of the New Deal farm policies was to force at least 3 million small farmers off the land. For all its inadequacies, however, the AAA established the precedent for a system of farm price supports, subsidies, and surplus purchases that continues more than half a century later.

The National Recovery Administration

To help industry and labor, Roosevelt asked for—and Congress passed—the National Industrial Recovery Act (NIRA), which authorized establishment of the National Recovery Administration (NRA). The NRA sought to revive industry through rational planning. Representatives of business, labor, and government would establish codes of fair practices that would set prices, production levels, minimum wages, and maximum hours within each industry. The NRA also supported workers' right to join labor unions. By ending ruinous competition, overproduction, labor conflicts, and by deflating prices, the NRA sought to stabilize the economy.

Led by General Hugh Johnson, the new agency got off to a promising start. By midsummer 1933, over 500 industries had signed codes covering 22 million workers. (In New York City, burlesque show strippers' agreed on a code limiting the number of times that they would undress each day.) By the end of the summer the nation's ten largest industries had been won over, as well as hundreds of smaller businesses. All across the country businesses displayed the Blue Eagle, the insignia of the NRA, in their windows. Thousands participated in public rallies and spectacular torchlight parades.

The NRA's success was short-lived, however. Johnson proved to be an overzealous leader who alienated many businesspeople. Instead of creating a smooth-running corporate state, Johnson presided over a chorus of endless squabbling. The NRA boards, dominated by representatives of big business, drafted codes that favored their interests over those of small competitors. Moreover, even though they controlled the new agency from the outset, many leaders of big business resented the NRA for interfering in the private sector. Many quipped that the NRA stood for "national run-around."

For labor the NRA was a mixed blessing. On the positive side, the codes abolished child labor and established the precedent of federal regulation of minimum wages and maximum hours. Under the National Industrial Recovery Act, union membership was expanded by the drawing of large numbers of unskilled workers into unions. On the negative side, however, the NRA codes set wages in most industries well below what labor demanded, and large occupational groups, such as farm workers, fell outside the codes' coverage.

Jobs Programs

Harry Hopkins, one of Roosevelt's most trusted advisers, asked why the federal government could not simply hire the unemployed and put them to work. Reluctantly, Roosevelt agreed, and the first major program to attack unemployment through public works was the Public Works Administration (PWA). It was supposed to serve as a "pump-primer," providing people with money to spend on industrial products. In six years the PWA spent $6 billion, building such projects as Brownsville, Texas's port, the Grand Coulee Dam, and Chicago's sewer system. Unfortunately, the man who headed the program, Harold Ickes, was so concerned about potential graft and scandal that the PWA did not spend enough money to significantly reduce unemployment.

One of the New Deal's most famous jobs programs was the Civilian Conservation Corps (CCC). By mid-1933, 300,000 jobless young men between the ages of 18 and 25 went to work in the nation's parks and forests. For $30 a month, CCC workers planted saplings, built fire towers, restocked depleted streams with fish, and restored historic battlefields. Workers lived in wilderness camps, earning money that they passed along to their families. By 1942, when the program ended, 2.5 million men had served in Roosevelt's "Tree Army." Despite its immense popularity, the CCC failed to make a serious dent in depression unemployment. It excluded women, imposed rigid quotas on African Americans, and offered employment to only a small number of the young people who needed work.

Far more ambitious was the Civil Works Administration (CWA), established in No-

vember 1933. Under the energetic leadership of Harry Hopkins, the CWA put 2.6 million men to work in its first month. Within two months it employed 4 million men building 250,000 miles of road, 40,000 schools, 150,000 privies, and 3700 playgrounds. In March 1934, however, Roosevelt scrapped the CWA because he (like Hoover) did not want to run a budget deficit or create a permanent dependent class.

John L. Lewis, one of the nation's most influential labor leaders, expanded the membership of the United Mine Workers Union (UMW) under the National Industrial Recovery Act.

Roosevelt badly underestimated the severity of the crisis. As government funding slowed down and economic indicators leveled off, the depression deepened in 1934, triggering a series of violent strikes. The climax came on Labor Day, 1934, when 500,000 garment workers launched the single largest strike in the nation's history. All across the nation, critics attacked Roosevelt for not doing enough to combat the depression, charges that did not go unheeded in the White House.

Following the congressional elections of 1934, in which the Democrats won 13 new House seats and 9 new Senate seats, Roosevelt abandoned his hopes for a balanced budget, deciding that bolder action was required. He had lost faith in government planning and the proposed alliance with business. This left only one other road to recovery—government spending. Encouraged by the CCC's success, he decided to create more federal jobs for the unemployed.

In January 1935 Congress passed the Emergency Relief Appropriation Act, which created the Works Progress Administration (WPA), Roosevelt's program to employ 3.5 million workers at a "security wage"—twice the level of welfare payments but well below union scales. To head the new agency, Roosevelt again turned to Harry Hopkins. Since the WPA's purpose was to employ men

MEDICINE AND RACE

THE TUSKEGEE SYPHILIS STUDY

THE South in the 1930s was the section of the United States that most resembled the underdeveloped nations of the world. Its people (white and black) remained mostly rural; they were less well-educated than other Americans; and they made decidedly less money.

As a group, African Americans in the South were among the poorest of the poor—virtual paupers, chronically unemployed, without benefit of sanitation, adequate diet, or the rudiments of hygiene. They suffered from a host of diseases, including tuberculosis, syphilis, hookworm, pellagra, rickets, and rotting teeth; and their death rate far exceeded that of whites.

Despite their evident need, few blacks received proper medical care. In fact, many African Americans lived outside the world of modern medicine, going from cradle to grave without ever seeing a doctor. There was a severe shortage of black physicians, and many white physicians refused to treat black patients. In addition, there were only a handful of black hospitals in the South, and most white hospitals either denied blacks admission or assigned them to often overcrowded segregated wings.

But poverty as much as racism was to blame for the medical neglect of African Americans. Medical care in the United States was offered on a fee-for-services basis, and the simple truth was that many African Americans were too poor to be able to afford medical care.

To combat this and other problems, the federal government in 1912 united all its health-related activities under the Public Health Service (PHS). Over the next few decades, the PHS distinguished itself by launching attacks on hookworm, pellagra, and a host of other illnesses. In no field was it more active than in its efforts to fight venereal diseases.

Health reformers knew that not only was syphilis a killer, but it was also capable of inflicting blindness, deafness, and insanity on its victims. Furthermore, they saw the disease as a serious threat to the family because they associated it with prostitution and loose morals in general, thus adding a moral dimension to their medical concerns.

Taking advantage of the emergency atmosphere of World War I, progressive reformers pushed through Congress in 1918 a bill to create a special Division of Venereal Diseases within the PHS. The PHS officers who launched this

new offensive against syphilis began with high motives, and their initial successes were impressive. By 1919, they had established over 200 health clinics, which treated over 64,000 patients who could not otherwise have afforded health care.

In the late 1920s, the PHS joined forces with the Rosenwald Fund (a private philanthropic foundation based in Chicago) to develop a syphilis control program for African Americans in the South. Most doctors assumed that blacks suffered a much higher infection rate than whites because blacks abandoned themselves to sexual promiscuity. And once infected, the argument went, African Americans remained infected because they were too poor and too ignorant to seek medical care.

To test these theories, the PHS selected communities in six different southern states, examined the local African-American populations to ascertain the incidence of syphilis, and offered free treatment to those who were infected. This pilot program had hardly gotten underway, however, when the stock market collapse forced the Rosenwald Fund to terminate its support. The PHS was left without sufficient funds to follow up its syphilis control work among African Americans in the South.

Macon County, Alabama, was the site of one of those original pilot programs. Its county seat, Tuskegee, was the home of the famed Tuskegee Institute. It was in and around Tuskegee that the PHS had discovered an infection rate of 35 percent among those tested, the highest incidence in the six communities studied. In fact, despite the presence of the Tuskegee Institute, which boasted a well-equipped hospital that might have provided low-cost health care to African Americans in the region, Macon County was home to the worst poverty and the most sickly residents the PHS discovered anywhere in the South. It was precisely this ready-made laboratory of human suffering that prompted the PHS to return to Macon County in 1932. Since they could not afford to treat syphilis, the PHS decided to document the damage inflicted on its victims by launching a scientific study of the effects of untreated syphilis on African-American males. Many white Southerners (including physicians) believed that although practically all blacks had syphilis, it did not harm them as severely as it did whites. PHS officials knew that syphilis was a serious threat to the health of African Americans, and they intended to use the results of the study to pressure southern state legislatures into appropriating funds for syphilis control work among rural blacks.

Armed with these good motives, the PHS launched the Tuskegee Study in 1932. It involved approximately 400 African-American males who tested positive for the disease and 200 nonsyphilitic black males to serve as controls. In order to secure cooperation, the PHS told the local residents that they had returned to Macon County to treat the ill men. The PHS did not inform them that they had syphilis. Instead, the men were told that they had "bad blood," a catch-all phrase rural blacks used to describe a host of ailments.

The PHS had not intended to treat the men, but state health officials demanded, as the price of their cooperation, that the men be given at least enough medication to render them noninfectious. Consequently, all of the men received a little treatment. No one worried much about the glaring contradiction of offering treatment in a study of supposedly untreated syphilis (the reasoning being that the men had not received enough treatment to cure them). Thus, the experiment was scientifically flawed from the outset.

Although the original plan called for only a one-year experiment, the Tuskegee Study continued until 1972—partly because many of the health officials became fascinated by the scientific potential of a long-range study of syphilis. No doubt others rationalized the study by telling themselves that the men were too poor to afford proper treatment, or that too much time had passed for treatment to be of any benefit. Some health officials may even have seen the men as clinical material rather than human beings.

At any rate, the Tuskegee Study killed approximately 100 African-American men, who died as a direct result of syphilis; scores went blind or insane, and still others endured lives of chronic ill health from syphilis-related complications. Throughout their suffering, the PHS made no effort to treat the men, and on several occasions even took steps to prevent them from getting treatment on their own. As a result, the men did not receive penicillin when that "wonder drug" became widely available after World War II.

During those same four decades civil protests raised America's concern for the rights of African Americans, and the ethical standards of the medical profession changed dramatically. These changes had no impact on the Tuskegee Study, however. PHS officials published no fewer than 13 scientific papers on the experiment (several appearing in the nation's leading medical journals), and the PHS routinely presented sessions on it at medical conventions. The Tuskegee Study only ended in 1972 because a "whistle-blower" in the PHS named Peter Buxtun leaked the story to the press. Health officials at first tried to defend their actions, but public outrage quickly silenced them, and they agreed to end the experiment. As part of an out-of-court settlement, the survivors were finally treated for syphilis, and the men, and the families of the deceased, received small cash payments.

The 40-year deathwatch had finally ended, but its legacy can still be felt today. In the wake of its hearings, Congress enacted new legislation to protect the subjects of human experiments. The Tuskegee Study left behind a host of unanswered questions about the social and racial attitudes of the medical establishment in the United States. It served as a cruel reminder of how class distinctions and racism could negate ethical and scientific standards.

his bills if he tried to fight them on the race question.

Yet the New Deal did record a few gains in civil rights. Roosevelt named Mary McLeod Bethune, a black educator, to the advisory committee of the National Youth Administration (NYA), and thanks to her efforts, African Americans received a fair share of NYA funds. The WPA was colorblind, and blacks in northern cities benefited from its work relief programs. Harold Ickes, a strong supporter of civil rights who had several African Americans on his staff, poured federal funds into black schools and hospitals in the South. Most blacks appointed to New Deal posts, however, served in token positions as advisers on black affairs. At best they achieved a new visibility in government.

Mexican Americans

Like African Americans, most Mexican Americans reaped few benefits from the New Deal. Affected in much the same way as sharecroppers and tenant farmers, many Mexican-American migrant workers lost their jobs due to AAA acreage reductions or competition in the fields from unemployed whites.

Still, the New Deal offered Mexican Americans a little help. The Farm Security Administration established camps for migrant farm workers in California, and the CCC and WPA hired unemployed Mexican Americans on relief jobs. Many, however, did not qualify for relief assistance because, as migrant workers, they did not meet residency requirements. Furthermore, agricultural workers were not eligible for benefits under workers' compensation, Social Security, and the National Labor Relations Act.

Native Americans

The so-called Indian New Deal was the only bright spot in the administration's treatment of minorities. In the late nineteenth century, American Indian policy had begun to place a growing emphasis on erasing a distinctive Native American identity. To weaken the authority of Native American leaders, Congress in 1871 ended the practice of treating Indian groups as sovereign nations. To undermine

traditional Native American justice systems, Congress, in 1882, created a Court of Indian Offenses, to try Native Americans who violated government laws and rules. Native American schools took Native American children away from their families and sought to strip them of their heritage. Schoolchildren were required to trim their hair and speak English and were prohibited from practicing Native American religions.

The culmination of these policies was the 1887 Dawes Act, which allocated reservation lands to individual Native Americans. The purpose of the act was to encourage Native Americans to become farmers, but the plots were too small to support a family or to raise livestock. Government policies further reduced Native American–owned lands from 155 million acres to just 48 million acres in 1934.

When Roosevelt became president in 1933, he appointed John Collier, a leading reformer, as Commissioner of Indian affairs. At Collier's request, Congress created the Indian Emergency Conservation Program (IECP), a CCC-type project for the reservations that employed more than 85,000 Native Americans. Collier also made certain that the PWA, WPA, CCC, and NYA hired Native Americans.

Collier had long been an opponent of the 50-year-old government allotment program that had broken up and distributed Native American lands. In 1934 he persuaded Congress to pass the Indian Reorganization Act, which terminated the allotment program of the Dawes Severalty Act of 1887; provided funds for Native American groups to purchase new land; offered government recognition of Native American constitutions; and repealed prohibitions on Native American languages and customs. That same year, federal grants were provided to local school districts, hospitals, and social welfare agencies to assist Native Americans.

THE NEW DEAL IN DECLINE

In his second inaugural address in early 1937, Franklin Roosevelt promised to press for new social legislation. "I see one-third of a nation ill-housed, ill-clad, ill-nourished," he told the country. Yet instead of pursuing new reforms, he allowed his second term to bog down in political squabbles. And he wasted his energies on an ill-conceived battle with the Supreme Court and an abortive effort to purge the Democratic party.

Court Packing

On "Black Monday," May 27, 1935, the Supreme Court struck down a basic part of Roosevelt's program of recovery and reform. A kosher chicken dealer sued the government, charging that the NRA was unconstitutional. In its famous "dead chicken" decision, *Schechter Poultry Corporation* v. *United States,* the court agreed, declaring that Congress had delegated excessive authority to the president and had improperly involved the federal government in regulating interstate commerce. Complained Roosevelt, "We have been relegated to the horse-and-buggy definition of interstate commerce."

In June 1936, the court ruled another of the measures enacted during the 100 days—the Agricultural Adjustment Act—unconstitutional. Then, six months later, the high court declared invalid a New York state minimum-wage law. Roosevelt was aghast. The court, he charged, had established a "'no-man's land' where no Government—State or Federal—can function." Roosevelt feared that every New Deal reform—such as the prohibition on child labor or regulation of wages and hours—was at risk. In 1936, his supporters in Congress responded by introducing over a hundred bills to curb the judiciary's power.

After his landslide reelection in 1936, the president proposed a controversial "court-packing scheme." In an effort to make his opponents on the Supreme Court resign so he could replace them with justices more sympathetic to his policies, Roosevelt announced a plan to add one new member to the Supreme Court for every judge who had reached the age of 70 without retiring (six justices were over 70). To offer a carrot with the stick, Roosevelt also outlined a generous new pension program for retiring federal judges.

The court-packing scheme was a political disaster. Conservatives and liberals alike denounced Roosevelt for attacking the separation of powers, and critics accused him of trying to become a dictator. Fortunately, the Court itself ended the crisis by shifting ground. In two separate cases the Court upheld the Wagner Act and approved a Washington state minimum-wage law, furnishing proof that it had softened its opposition to the New Deal.

Yet Roosevelt remained too obsessed with the battle to realize he had won the war. He lobbied for the court-packing bill for several months, squandering his strength on a struggle that had long since become a political embarrassment. In the end, the only part of the president's plan to gain congressional approval was the pension program. Once it passed, Justice Willis Van Devanter, the most obstinate New Deal opponent on the Court, resigned. By 1941 Roosevelt had named five justices to the Supreme Court. Few legacies of the president's leadership proved more important, for the new "Roosevelt Court"

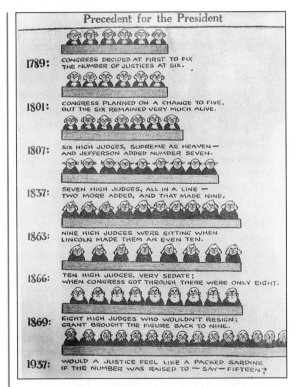

Precedent for the President

1789: CONGRESS DECIDED AT FIRST TO FIX THE NUMBER OF JUSTICES AT SIX.

1801: CONGRESS PLANNED ON A CHANGE TO FIVE, BUT THE SIX REMAINED VERY MUCH ALIVE.

1807: SIX HIGH JUDGES, SUPREME AS HEAVEN— AND JEFFERSON ADDED NUMBER SEVEN.

1837: SEVEN HIGH JUDGES, ALL IN A LINE— TWO MORE ADDED, AND THAT MADE NINE.

1863: NINE HIGH JUDGES WERE SITTING WHEN LINCOLN MADE THEM AN EVEN TEN.

1866: TEN HIGH JUDGES, VERY SEDATE; WHEN CONGRESS GOT THROUGH THERE WERE ONLY EIGHT.

1869: EIGHT HIGH JUDGES WHO WOULDN'T RESIGN; GRANT BROUGHT THE FIGURE BACK TO NINE.

1937: WOULD A JUSTICE FEEL LIKE A PACKED SARDINE IF THE NUMBER WAS RAISED TO — SAY — FIFTEEN?

Fearful that the Supreme Court would invalidate the Social Security Act and other measures, Roosevelt proposed in 1937 that he be allowed to appoint an additional justice for every court member over the age of 70, up to a total of six.

significantly expanded the government's role in the economy and in civil liberties.

The Depression of 1937

The sweeping Democratic electoral victory in 1936 was followed by a deep economic relapse known as the "Roosevelt Recession." In just a few months, industrial production fell by 40 percent; unemployment rose by 4 million; stock prices plunged 48 percent.

Several factors contributed to the "little depression," of which the most important was a blunder in fiscal policy. Secretary of the Treasury Henry Morgenthau urged Roosevelt to cut federal spending in an effort to balance the federal budget and restore business confidence. Reassured by good economic news in 1936, Roosevelt slashed government spending the following year. The budget cuts knocked the economy into a tailspin. Roosevelt's virulent attacks on "economic royalists" also undermined business confidence.

By the end of 1938 the reform spirit was gone. A conservative alliance of southern Democrats and northern Republicans in Congress blocked all efforts to expand the New Deal. In the congressional elections of 1938, Roosevelt campaigned against five conservative senators who opposed the New Deal; but all won reelection. The failed purge intensified the conservative-liberal split within the Democratic party by showing conservatives they could defy the president with impunity. (And it weakened the Democratic coalition at a time when Roosevelt badly needed conservative support for military preparedness to meet the growing threat to peace in Europe.) Roosevelt may not have been able to pass any new measures, but his opponents could not dismantle his programs. The New Deal ended in stalemate, but several reforms had been ensconced as permanent features of American politics.

POPULAR CULTURE DURING THE GREAT DEPRESSION

The popular culture of the 1930s was fraught with contradictions. It was, simultaneously, a decade of traditionalism and of modernist experimentation, of sentimentality and "hard-boiled" toughness, of longings for a simpler past and fantastic dreams of the future.

It was a decade in which many Americans grew increasingly interested in tradition and folk culture. Under the leadership of Alan Lomax, the Library of Congress began to collect folk songs, while folk singers like Woody Guthrie and Pete Seeger attracted large audiences.

Henry Ford, who had revolutionized the American landscape through the mass production of cars, devoted his energies and fortune to a new project: Greenfield Village, a collection of historic homes and artifacts, located near Detroit. At the same time, the Rockefeller family began restoring colonial Williamsburg in Virginia.

Beset by deep anxieties and insecurities, many Americans in the 1930s hungered for heroes. Popular culture offered many: superheroes like Superman and Batman, who appeared in the new comic books of the 1930s; tough, hard-boiled detectives in the fiction of Dashiell Hammett and Raymond Chandler; and radio heroes like "The Lone Ranger" or "The Shadow."

Artistic and Literary Endeavors

Seeing modern society as excessively individualistic and fragmented, many prominent intellectuals of the time looked to the past. Eleven leading white southern intellectuals, known as the Southern Agrarians, issued a manifesto titled *I'll Take My Stand*, urging a return to an agrarian way of life. Another group of distinguished intellectuals known as the New Humanists, led by Irving Babbitt and Paul Elmer More, extolled classical civilization as a bulwark against modern values. One of the decade's leading social critics was Lewis Mumford. In volumes like *Technics and Civilization* (1934), he examined how the values of a pre-machine culture could be blended into modern capitalist civilization.

And yet, for all the emphasis on tradition, the 1930s was also a decade in which modernism in the arts and architecture became increasingly pronounced. Martha Graham developed American modern dance. William Faulkner experimented with "stream-of-consciousness" in *As I Lay Dying* (1930) and other novels, while John Dos Passos's avant-garde trilogy, *U.S.A.,* combined newspaper headlines, capsule biographies, popular song lyrics, and fiction to document the disintegration of depression-era society. The architect R. Buckminster Fuller and the industrial designer Walter Dorwin Teague employed curves and streamlining to give their projects a modern appearance. Nothing better illustrated the concern with the future than the 1939 New York World's Fair, the self-proclaimed "Fair of the Future," which promised to show fairgoers "the world of tomorrow."

The depression was, in certain respects, a powerful unifying experience. A new phrase, "the American way of life," entered the language—as did public opinion polls and statistical surveys that gave the public a better sense of what the "average American" thought, voted, and ate. The new photojournalism that appeared in new magazines like *Life* helped create a common frame of reference. Yet regional, ethnic, and class differences occupied an important place in the literature of the 1930s. The great novels of the decade successfully combined social criticism and rich detail about the facets of American life in specific social settings. In his novels of fictional Yoknapatawpha County, William Faulkner explored the traditions and history of the South. James T. Farrell's *Studs Lonigan* trilogy (1932–1935) analyzed the impact of urban industrial decay on Catholic youth, while Henry Roth's *Call It Sleep* (1934) traced the assimilation of Jewish youth into American life. John Steinbeck's *Grapes of Wrath* (1939) examined the struggle of a poor Oklahoma farming family migrating to California. Richard Wright's classic *Native Son* (1940) discussed the ways that poverty and prejudice in Chicago drove a young African American to crime.

Hollywood During the Great Depression

During the Great Depression, Hollywood played a valuable psychological role, providing reassurance to a demoralized nation. Even at the depth of the depression, 60 to 80 million Americans attended movies each week.

During the depression's earliest years, movies reflected a despairing public's mood, as Tommy-gun toting gangsters, haggard prostitutes, and sleazy backroom politicians and lawyers appeared on the screen. Screen comedies released in these years expressed an almost anarchistic disdain for traditional institutions and values. The Marx Brothers spoofed everything from patriotism to universities; W. C. Fields ridiculed families; and Mae West used sexual innuendo to poke fun at the middle-class code of sexual propriety.

A renewed sense of optimism generated by the New Deal combined with industry self-censorship to produce new kinds of films during the second half of the depression. G-men, detectives, western heroes, and other defenders of law and order replaced gangsters. Audiences enjoyed Frank Capra comedies and dramas in which little men stood up against corruption and restored America to itself. A new comic genre—the screwball comedy—presented a world in which rich heiresses wed impoverished young men, keeping alive a vision of America as a classless society.

In the face of economic disaster, the fantasy world of the movies sustained a traditional American faith in individual initiative, in government, and a common American identity transcending social class.

CONCLUSION

At the end of 1938, Harry Hopkins observed that the American people had become "bored with the poor, unemployed, and insecure." The New Deal was over. From a purely economic perspective, the New Deal barely made a dent in the Great Depression. Roosevelt's programs suffered from poor planning and moved with considerable caution. By 1939 national productivity had barely reached 1929 levels, and ten million men and women remained unemployed. Roosevelt simply could not bring himself to support huge federal budgets. As a result, government expenditures stayed below $10 billion a year, not nearly enough to fuel economic recovery. World War II, not the New Deal, snapped

CHRONOLOGY
OF KEY EVENTS

1928	Herbert Hoover is elected thirty-first president
1929	Stock market crashes
1930	Hawley-Smoot Tariff raises import duties to unprecedented levels
1932	Congress creates Reconstruction Finance Corporation to lend money to banks, railroads, and insurance companies; Bonus Army, a group of veterans demanding immediate payment of World War I bonuses, is dispersed by federal troops in Washington, D.C.; to revive the construction industry, Congress creates the Federal Home Loan Bank System to lend money to savings and loan associations; Franklin Roosevelt is elected thirty-second president
1933	Emergency Banking Relief Act addresses banking crisis; Roosevelt conducts the first of many "fireside chats" over national radio; Civilian Conservation Corps puts young people to work conserving natural resources; Federal Emergency Relief Act provides relief payments to the unemployed through local and state welfare agencies; Civil Works Administration offers employment to over 4 million people; Agricultural Adjustment Act sets up a system of farm price supports and production limits; National Industrial Recovery Act authorizes industrial codes regulating production, prices, and working conditions and provides funds for public works projects; Tennessee Valley Authority constructs dams and hydroelectric plants in the Tennessee River valley; Twenty-first Amendment repeals prohibition; Glass-Steagall

Act creates the Federal Deposit Insurance Corporation to insure savings accounts against bank failure; Farm Credit Administration provides low-interest loans for farmers.

1934	Dr. Francis Townsend proposes a $200 monthly pension for every citizen over 60; former supporter, "radio priest" Father Charles Coughlin, breaks with Roosevelt and forms the National Union for Social Justice; Senator Huey Long of Louisiana announces his "Share Our Wealth" program to provide every American family with a guaranteed annual income; Indian Reorganization Act provides funds for tribes to purchase land, offers recognition of tribal constitutions, and repeals prohibitions on Native American customs
1935	*Schechter Poultry Corporation* v. *United States* declares National Industrial Recovery Act unconstitutional; Emergency Relief Appropriation Act creates Works Progress Administration and National Youth Administration; National Labor Relations Act guarantees workers' right to organize and bargain collectively; Public Utility Holding Company Act is passed to prevent monopolies in gas and electricity distribution; Social Security Act creates a federal system of old-age pensions and state-run unemployment compensation programs
1937	Roosevelt proposes his "court-packing" scheme
1938	Fair Labor Standards Act bans child labor and establishes minimum wages and maximum hours

America out of the depression, for then and only then did unemployment disappear.

Whatever its shortcomings, the New Deal did blunt the worst effects of the Great Depression. By means of economic reforms and public works projects Roosevelt managed to preserve the public's faith in capitalism and in democratic government at a time when both seemed on the verge of collapse. Roosevelt accomplished this, in large measure, by reaching out to groups that Washington had largely neglected in the past. The Social Security program, while it ignored many, made the government responsible for old-age pensions and welfare payments to citizens who could not support themselves. The NIRA and the Wagner Act encouraged the growth of unions; minimum wage laws benefited many workers; and the Fair Labor Standards Act finally abolished child labor in industry (though it remained in agriculture). While the New Deal stopped far short of providing equal treatment under the law for minorities, it offered them a measure of relief from the depression.

The New Deal encouraged Americans to look to the White House for strong executive leadership. Roosevelt responded to situations with decisive action, and the public increasingly expected the other branches of government to support presidential initiatives. Roosevelt's administrative style—creating special agencies to handle specific problems and placing people in charge who answered directly to him—further enhanced presidential power. On a purely partisan level, the New Deal enabled Roosevelt to forge a Democratic coalition of diverse groups—labor, African Americans, urban ethnics, intellectuals, and southern whites—that helped shape American politics for the next several decades.

Above all, the New Deal made the federal government responsible for safeguarding the nation's economic health. Prior to the 1930s, if people were asked how the government affected them, they probably thought in terms of state or even local government. The New Deal, however, made the federal government such a daily presence in peoples' lives that they now expected Washington to involve itself in everything from farm subsidies to the sale of stocks and securities.

SUGGESTIONS FOR FURTHER READING

Alan Brinkey, *The End of Reform: New Deal Liberalism in Recession and War* (1995). Analyzes the reasons for the New Deal's decline.

Kenneth S. Davis, *FDR: The New York Years* (1985), *FDR: The New Deal Years* (1986), *FDR: Into the Storm* (1993). Recent biographies of the president.

Melvyn Dubovsky and Stephen Burnwood, eds., *Women and Minorities During the Great Depression* (1990). Examines issues confronting women and minority groups during the depression.

Mario T. Garcia, *Mexican-American Leadership, Ideology, and Identity* (1989). Analyzes the Depression's impact on Mexican-Americans and the conmmunity's responses.

William E. Leuchtenburg, *The Supreme Court Reborn: The Constitutional Revolution in the Age of Roosevelt* (1995). Explores the impact of the Depression on constitutional law.

Robert S. McElvaine, *The Great Depression: America, 1929–1941* (1984). Offers a thorough treatment of the United States during the Depression.

Michael E. Parrish, *Anxious Decades: America in Prosperity and Depression* (1992). Provides insights into America during the 1930s.

Lois Scharf, *To Work and to Wed: Female Employment and Feminism in the Great Depression* (1980). Examines the impact of the Depression on women.

Harvard Sitkoff, ed., *Fifty Years Later: The New Deal Evaluated.* (1985) Offers recent assessments of various aspects of the New Deal.

T. H. Watkins, *The Great Depression: America in the 1930s* (1993). Offers an up-to-date account of the Depression decade.

Overviews and Surveys

Michael Bernstein: *The Great Depression: Delayed Recovery and Economic Change in America, 1929–1939* (1988); Roger Biles, *A New Deal for the American People* (1991), and *The New Deal and the South* (1995); James M. Burns, *Roosevelt: The Lion and the Fox* (1956); Sean Dennis Cashman, *America in the Twenties and Thirties* (1989); Paul K. Conkin, *The New Deal*, 2d ed. (1975), and *The Southern Agrarians* (1988); Peter Fearon, *War, Prosperity, and Depression: The U.S. Economy, 1917–1945* (1988); Otis L. Graham, Jr., *The New Deal: The Critical Issues* (1971); Robert L. Heilbroner and Aaron Singer, *The Economic Transformation of America* (1977); Jack Temple Kirby, *Rural*

Worlds Lost: The American South, 1920–1960 (1987); William E. Leuchtenburg, *Franklin D. Roosevelt and the New Deal* (1963), and *The Perils of Prosperity, 1914–32* (1958); Albert U. Romasco, *The Politics of Recovery: Roosevelt's New Deal* (1983); Page Smith, *Redeeming the Time: A People's History of the 1920s and the New Deal* (1987); Studs Terkel, *Hard Times: An Oral History of the Great Depression* (1970).

The Human Toll

Robert S. McElvaine, ed., *Down and Out in the Great Depression: Letters from the "Forgotten Man"* (1983); James H. Jones, *Bad Blood: The Tuskegee Syphilis Experiment, A Tragedy of Race and Medicine*, 2d ed. (1992); Robin D. G. Kelly, *Hammer and Hoe: Alabama Communists During the Great Depression* (1990); Steven Mintz and Susan Kellogg, *Domestic Revolutions: A Social History of American Family Life* (1983); Bernard Sternsher, *Hitting Home: The Great Depression in Town and Country* (1989); Nan Elizabeth Woodruff, *As Rare as Rain: Federal Relief in the Great Southern Drought of 1930–31* (1985).

Herbert Hoover Responds

William J. Barber, *From New Era to New Deal: Herbert Hoover, the Economists, and American Economic Policy* (1985); Roger Daniels, *The Bonus March: An Episode of the Great Depression* (1971); Mark Dodge, *Herbert Hoover and the Historians* (1989); Glen H. Elder, Jr., *Children of the Great Depression: Social Change in Life Experience* (1974); Martin L. Fausold, *The Presidency of Herbert Hoover* (1985); Donald J. Lisio, *Hoover, Blacks, and Lily-Whites* (1985), and *The President and Protest: Hoover, Conspiracy, and the Bonus Riot* (1974); Albert U. Romasco, *The Poverty of Abundance, Hoover, the Nation, the Depression* (1965); Jordan A. Schwarz, *Interregnum of Despair: Hoover, Congress, and the Depression* (1970); Gene Smith, *The Shattered Dream: Herbert Hoover and the Great Depression* (1984); Winifred D. Wandersee, *Women's Work and Family Values, 1920–1940* (1981); Joan Hoff-Wilson, *Herbert Hoover: Forgotten Progressive* (1975).

Franklin Roosevelt and the First New Deal

Sue Bridwell Beckham, *Depression Post Office Murals and Southern Culture* (1989); Bernard Bellush, *The Failure of the NRA* (1975); Donald R. Brand, *Corporatism and the Rule of Law: A Study of the National Recovery Administration* (1988); David E. Conrad, *The Forgotten Farmers: The Story of the Sharecroppers in the New Deal* (1965); Frank Freidel, *Franklin D. Roosevelt: Launching the New Deal* (1973); James N. Gregory, *American Exodus: The Dust Bowl Migration and Okie Culture in California* (1989); Robert F. Himmelberg, *The Origins of the National Recovery Administration* (1976); R. Douglas Hurt, *The Dust Bowl: An Agricultural and Social History* (1981); Jerre Mangione, *The Dream and the Deal: The Federal Writers' Project, 1935–1943* (1972); Robert S. McElvaine, *The Great Depression: America, 1929–1941* (1984); Joseph P. Lash, *Dealers and Dreamers: A New Look at the New Deal* (1988); David Milton, *The Politics of U.S. Labor: From the Great Depression to the New Deal* (1982); Michael Parrish, *Securities Regulation and the New Deal* (1970); Elliot Rosen, *Hoover, Roosevelt, and the Brain Trust* (1984); John Salmond, *The Civilian Conservation Corps, 1933–1942: A New Deal Case Study* (1967); James E. Sargent, *Roosevelt and the Hundred Days* (1981); Ronald W. Schatz, *The Electrical Workers: A History of Labor at General Electric and Westinghouse, 1923–1960* (1983); Bonnie Schwartz, *The Civil Works Administration* (1984); Paul S. Taylor, *On the Ground in the Thirties* (1983); Graham White and John Maze, *Harold Ickes and the New Deal* (1985); Donald Worster, *Dust Bowl: The Southern Plains in the 1930s* (1979).

The Second New Deal

Irving Bernstein, *A Caring Society: The New Deal, the Worker, and the Great Depression* (1985); Alan Brinkley, *Voices of Protest: Huey Long, Father Coughlin, and the Great Depression* (1982); Robert F. Burk, *The Corporate State and the Broker State: The Du Ponts and American National Politics, 1925–1940* (1990); Keith Dix, *What's a Coal Miner to Do? The Mechanization of Coal Mining* (1988); Sidney Fine, *Sit-Down: The General Motors Strike of 1936–1937* (1969); Steven Fraser, *Labor Will Rule: Sidney Hillman and the Rise of American Labor* (1991); Philip J. Funigiello, *Toward a National Power Policy: The New Deal and the Electric Utility Industry, 1933–1941* (1973); Ellis Hawley, *The New Deal and the Problem of Monopoly: A Study in Economic Ambivalence* (1966); Dorothy Healey and Maurice Isserman, *Dorothy Healey Remembers: A Life in the Communist Party* (1990); James A. Hodges, *New Deal Labor Policy and the Southern Cotton Textile Industry, 1934–1941* (1986); Harvey Klehr, *The Heyday of American Communism: The Depression Decade* (1984); Roy Lubove, *The Struggle for Social Security, 1900–1935*, 2d ed. (1986); Thomas McCraw, *TVA and the Power Fight, 1933–1939*

(1971); Greg Mitchell, *The Campaign of the Century: Upton Sinclair's Race for Governor of California* (1992); Bruce Nelson, *Workers on the Waterfront: Seamen, Longshoremen, and Unionism in the 1930s* (1988); Nell Irvin Painter, *The Narrative of Hosea Hudson: His Life as a Negro Communist in the South* (1979); James T. Patterson, *Congressional Conservatism and the New Deal* (1967); Richard Polenberg, *Reorganizing Roosevelt's Government, 1936–1939* (1966); Vicki L. Ruiz, *Cannery Women, Cannery Lives: Mexican Women, Unionization, and the California Food Processing Industry* (1987).

The New Deal, Women, and Minority Groups

Dan T. Carter, *Scottsboro: A Tragedy of the American South,* rev. ed. (1979); William H. Chafe, *The American Woman: Her Changing Social, Economic, and Political Role, 1920–1970* (1972); Cletus E. Daniel, *Bitter Harvest: A History of California Farmworkers, 1870–1941* (1981); Sara M. Evans, *Born for Liberty: A History of Women in America* (1989); Suzanne Forrest, *The Preservation of the Village: New Mexico's Hispanics and the New Deal* (1989); Mario T. Garcia, *Mexican Americans: Leadership, Ideology, and Identity* (1989); Nancy L. Grant, *TVA and Black Americans: Planning for the Status Quo* (1990); William H. Harris, *Keeping the Faith: A. Philip Randolph, Milton P. Webster, and the Brotherhood of Sleeping Car Porters, 1925–1937* (1977); Abraham Hoffman, *Unwanted Mexican Americans in the Great Depression, Repatriation Pressures, 1929–1939* (1974); James H. Jones, rev. ed., *Bad Blood: The Tuskegee Syphilis Experiment, A Tragedy of Race and Medicine* (1992); Lawrence C. Kelly, *The Assault on Assimilation: John Collier and the Origins of Indian Policy Reform* (1983); Harry A. Kersey, Jr., *The Florida Seminoles and the New Deal, 1933–1942* (1989); Alice Kessler-Harris, *Out to Work: A History of Wage-Earning Women in the United States* (1982); Kenneth Philip, *John Collier's Crusade for Indian Reform, 1920–1954* (1977); Mark Reisler, *By the Sweat of Their Brow: Mexican Immigrant Labor in the United States, 1900–1940* (1976); Lois Scharf, *To Work and to Wed: Female Employment, Feminism, in the Great Depression* (1980); Susan Ware, *Beyond Suffrage: Women in the New Deal*

(1981); Nancy J. Weiss, *Farewell to the Party of Lincoln: Black Politics in the Age of FDR* (1983); Raymond Wolters, *Negroes and the Great Depression: The Problem of Economic Recovery* (1970); Robert L. Zangrando, *The NAACP Crusade Against Lynching, 1909–1950* (1980).

The New Deal in Decline

Alan Brinkley, *The End of Reform: New Deal Liberalism in Recession and War* (1995); Steve Fraser and Gary Gerstle, eds., *The Rise and Fall of the New Deal Order, 1930–1980* (1989); William E. Leuchtenburg, *The Supreme Court Reborn: The Constitutional Revolution in the Age of Roosevelt* (1995); Harvard Sitkoff, ed., *Fifty Years Later: The New Deal Evaluated* (1985).

Popular Culture During the Great Depression

Daniel Aaron, *Writers on the Left: Episodes in American Literary Communism* (1961); Andrew Bergman, *We're in the Money: Depression America and Its Films* (1971); Lizbeth Cohen, *Making a New Deal: Industrial Workers in Chicago* (1990); Richard H. Pells, *Radical Visions and American Dreams: Culture and Social Thought in the Depression Years* (1973); Gerald Weales, *Canned Goods as Caviar: American Film Comedy of the 1930s* (1985).

Biographies

John Barnard, *Walter Reuther and the Rise of the Auto Workers* (1983); David Burner, *Herbert Hoover* (1979); Melvyn Dubovsky and Warren Van Tine, *John L. Lewis* (1977); Steven Fraser, *Labor Will Rule: Sidney Hillman and the Rise of American Labor* (1991); Thomas Kessner, *Fiorella H. La Guardia and the Making of Modern New York* (1989); Joe Klein, *Woody Guthrie* (1980); Joseph Lash, *Eleanor and Franklin* (1971); Jim McJimsey, *Harry Hopkins* (1987); Arthur Schlesinger, Jr., *The Age of Roosevelt,* 3 vols. (1957–1960); Richard N. Smith, *An Uncommon Man: The Triumph of Herbert Hoover* (1984); Geoffrey C. Ward, *A First-Class Temperament: The Emergence of Franklin Roosevelt* (1989); T. Harry Williams, *Huey Long* (1969).

CHAPTER 25

The End of Isolation: America Faces the World, 1920–1945

DIPLOMACY BETWEEN THE WARS

American Diplomacy During the 1920s
United States Policy Toward Latin
 America
The Isolationist Mirage

THE COMING OF WORLD WAR II

Conflict in the Pacific
Italy
Germany
The American Response to Hitler
War Begins
"The Arsenal of Democracy"
A Collision Course in the Pacific
Pearl Harbor

AMERICA MOBILIZES FOR WAR

Mobilizing the Economy
Taming Inflation
Election of 1944
Molding Public Opinion

SOCIAL CHANGES DURING THE WAR

Women
African Americans
Mexican Americans
Fear of Enemy Aliens
Internment of Japanese Americans

THE WAR IN EUROPE

The Grand Alliance
Early Axis Victories
Stemming the German Tide
Liberating Europe
The Yalta Conference

THE WAR IN THE PACIFIC

Island Hopping
The Dawn of the Atomic Age
The Manhattan Project
Hiroshima and Nagasaki

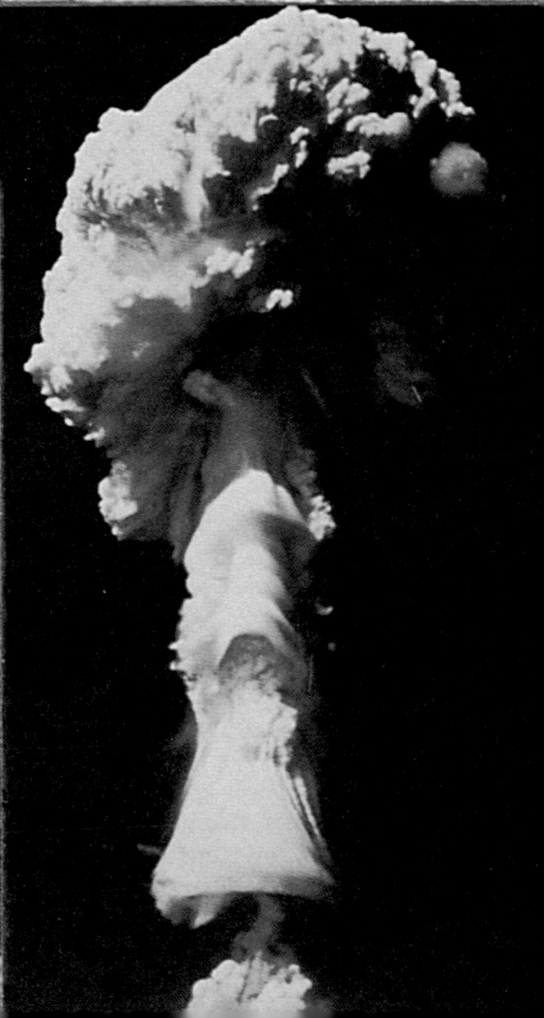

At 3 P.M., January 27, 1945, Russian troops of the 100th and 107th divisions entered Auschwitz, a village in southern Poland 30 miles west of Krakow. There, inside Auschwitz's concentration camps, they found 7600 inmates along with World War II's most terrible secret: the Holocaust. Two days later, the U.S. 7th Army liberated Dachau, another infamous Nazi death camp, located just outside Munich. The liberators could scarcely believe what they saw: starving prisoners, bones protruding from their skin, serial numbers tattooed on their arms; stacks of half-burned corpses, and piles of human hair.

Auschwitz was not the first Nazi concentration camp—that dubious distinction belonged to Dachau, which was set up in 1933—but it was the most infamous; 1.6 million people died there. Of the victims, 1.3 million were Jews and 300,000 were Gypsies, Polish Catholics, and Russian prisoners of war. Altogether, people from 28 nations lost their lives at Auschwitz, including the disabled, homosexuals, political prisoners, and others deemed unfit to live in Adolf Hitler's Third Reich.

Auschwitz had two main areas. "Auschwitz I" contained a gas chamber, a crematorium, housing for prisoners used in slave labor, and Dr. Josef Mengele's "medical research" station (where one experiment involved seeing how long babies could survive without food).

"Auschwitz II–Birkenau" contained only gas chambers and crematoria. It was here that cattle cars dumped their exhausted passengers, who then entered through a gate inscribed with the false promise "Work Will Make You Free." SS guards directed each new arrival to the left or the right. The healthy and strong went to the right. The weak, the elderly, and the very young went up a ramp to the left—to the gas chambers, disguised as showers. Inmates were told that the showers would be used to disinfect them, but there was no plumbing and the showerheads were fake. Guards injected a poison gas, Zyklon B, through openings in the ceilings and walls; when the deadly gas had done its work, the bodies were cremated. The ashes were used as road filler and fertilizer, or simply dumped into surrounding ponds and fields.

Auschwitz was a product of Adolf Hitler's belief that Germans constituted a master race that had a right to kill those they deemed inferior. "Nature is cruel, therefore we too may be cruel," Hitler stated in 1934. "If I can send the flower of the German nation into the hell of war . . . then surely I have a right to remove millions of an inferior race that breeds like vermin!"

In 1941 and 1942, the Nazi *Führer* (leader) initiated the "Final Solution to the Jewish Problem." The Nazis did their best to disguise their murderous scheme behind euphemisms and camouflage, but the truth sometimes slipped out. Heinrich Himmler, the official in charge of carrying out the final solution, explained to his top officers: "In public we will never speak of it. I am referring to the annihilation of the Jewish people. In our history, this is an unwritten and never-to-be written page of glory."

In the spring of 1944, four prisoners escaped from Auschwitz, carrying tangible proof of the Nazi's systematic program of mass murder. American and British leaders learned in mid-July what was happening at Auschwitz, but they rejected pleas to bomb the gas chambers or the roads and rail lines leading to the camps. Military officials opposed the bombing because it would divert "considerable air support essential to the success of our forces now engaged in decisive operations."

This was not the first time that western help had failed to come. During the 1930s, the U.S. State Department blocked efforts by Jewish refugees to migrate to the United States. Between 1933 and 1945, the United States allowed in only 132,000 Jewish refugees, just 10 percent of the quota allowed by law. This opposition to Jewish immigration reflected widespread anti-Semitism. As late as 1939, opinion polls indicated that 53 percent of Americans agreed with the statement "Jews are different and should be restricted." In the end, less than 500,000 Jews (out of 6.5 million) survived in Nazi-occupied Europe.

The Holocaust was an appalling and unique tragedy in human history. Never before had a sovereign state, with the cooperation of bureaucrats, industrialists, and civilians, sought to systematically exterminate an entire people. Yet many wonder whether Auschwitz's terrible lesson has been learned. Despite the establishment of the state of Is-

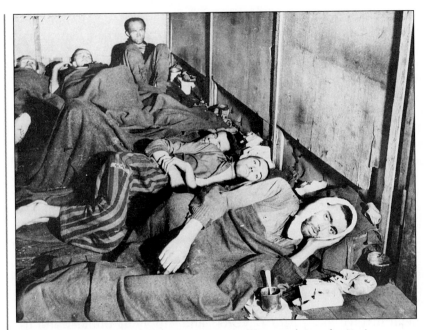

The scenes that greeted the troops who liberated Auschwitz in January 1945 almost defied belief. Perhaps as many as 12,000 people were slaughtered each day at Auschwitz.

rael, improved Christian-Jewish relations, and heightened sensitivity to racism, many Americans remain ignorant of the past. A 1995 opinion poll found that 5 percent of Americans denied that the Holocaust occurred and 10 percent express doubts or ignorance. More than half a century after the liberation of Auschwitz, "ethnic cleansing" and the persecution of religious, racial, and ethnic groups continues in Bosnia, China, Guatemala, India, Sri Lanka, Turkey, and elsewhere.

No war in history killed more people or destroyed more property than World War II. Altogether, 70 million people served in the armed forces during the war; of these, some 7.5 million Soviet troops died in World War II, along with 3.5 million Germans, 1.25 million Japanese, and 400,000 Americans. Civilian deaths were even higher. At least 19 million Soviet civilians, 10 million Chinese, and 6 million European Jews lost their lives during the war. All told, 17 million combatants—and an unknown number of civilians—lost their lives in the conflict.

More than any previous war in history, World War II was a total war. Some 70 nations took part in the war, and fighting took place on the continents of Europe, Asia, and Africa, as well as on the high seas. Entire societies participated, either as soldiers, war workers, or victims of occupation and mass murder. In the United States, the war had vast repercussions: it ended unemployment, brought millions of married women into the workforce, initiated sweeping changes in the lives of the nation's minority groups, and dramatically expanded government's presence in American life. Finally, World War II marked the beginning of the nuclear age.

DIPLOMACY BETWEEN THE WARS

World War I had left the public suspicious of foreign crusades. In 1936, eight Princeton undergraduates formed the Veterans of Future Wars. The organization demanded a bonus of $1000 for every man between the ages of 18 and 36—payable immediately, so that they could enjoy it before being forced to fight the "next war." A women's auxiliary, the Future Gold Star Mothers, demanded government pensions for women, so that they could afford to visit their sons' graves in Europe.

Americans wanted to retreat from foreign affairs. "The people have had all the war, all the taxation, and all the military service they want," declared President Calvin Coolidge in 1925. During the 1920s and much of the 1930s, the United States concentrated on improving its status in the Western Hemisphere and on avoiding European entanglements.

American Diplomacy During the 1920s

During the 1920s, Republican leaders debated joining and ultimately refused to join the League of Nations or the World Court. Such commitments, they feared, might involve the United States too deeply in global politics. Yet Washington remained keenly interested in preserving international stability and tried to promote world peace through diplomatic means.

In 1921 representatives of nine Asian and European nations met in Washington to discuss ways to ease tensions in the Pacific. Secretary of State Charles Evans Hughes stunned the meeting by making specific proposals for disarmament. He called for a ten-year moratorium on the construction of battleships, and an agreement that for every five naval vessels owned by the United States or Britain, Japan could have three, and France and Italy one and three-fourths. To win support for what the Japanese delegates called a ratio of "Rolls-Royce, Rolls-Royce, Ford," the United States and Great Britain agreed not to improve their fortifications in the Far East, especially in the Philippines. To appease Japanese resentment at its inferior position, the United States, Britain, and France also agreed in the Four-Party Treaty of 1922 to consult with Japan before going to war in Asia. Neither treaty, however, contained any provision for enforcement.

In 1928 the French foreign minister, Aristide Briand, and Secretary of State Frank B. Kellogg attempted to outlaw war. The Kellogg-Briand Pact, which was eventually signed by 62 nations, renounced war as an instrument for resolving international disputes. If attacked, however, the signatories could defend themselves by force. While it raised hopes for peace and earned Kellogg the Nobel Peace Prize, the Kellogg-Briand Pact had no chance of preventing future bloodshed, since it, too, lacked an enforcement mechanism. Cynics said the treaty had all the legal force of an "international kiss."

United States Policy Toward Latin America

Twenty times between 1898 and 1932, the United States intervened militarily in the Caribbean and Central America, suppressing popular uprisings in Nicaragua, seizing customs houses in Cuba, occupying Haiti (for 17 years), and supplying military and financial aid to friendly parties in the Mexican Revolution. Despite repeated American interventions, however, the region remained unstable.

During the 1920s Republican administrations inched away from gunboat diplomacy and tried to develop better relations with Latin America. Although progress was uneven and Washington's policies occasionally reverted to heavy-handed interventions, the thrust of Republican diplomacy during the 1920s clearly anticipated the shift toward improved relations with Latin America (dubbed the "Good Neighbor Policy" by the Democrats in the 1930s). In 1924, for example, the United States pulled the marines out of the Dominican Republic, and the following year American troops left Nicaragua, only to be sent back a few months later when a revolution broke out. But the real test of the United States' desire for improved relations came in Mexico.

Following Alvaro Obregón's election as president of Mexico in 1920, the Mexican government threatened to expropriate American-owned oil properties. The oil companies demanded government intervention, and in 1927 President Calvin Coolidge appointed Dwight Morrow, a partner in the firm of J. P. Morgan and Company, as ambassador. Mexicans expected the worst; one newspaper declared, "after Morrow come the marines." They were wrong. One of Morrow's first actions was to change the sign on the embassy to read "United States Embassy," rather than "American Embassy." It was a small gesture, but its significance was not lost on the Mexicans, who had long resented the United States' arrogance in appropriating a continental adjective. Morrow's diplomacy paid handsome dividends, and in 1927 Mexico once again recognized American-owned oil properties.

President Herbert Hoover continued the diplomacy of reconciliation. He announced plans to withdraw marines from Nicaragua and Haiti, and he resisted pressure from Congress to establish a customs receivership in El Salvador when the government there defaulted on its bonds. In 1930 Hoover approved a document written by Undersecretary of State J. Reuben Clark. The Clark Memorandum repudiated the Roosevelt Corollary to the Monroe Doctrine, which for 25 years had justified U.S. intervention in Latin America.

In his first inaugural address, President Franklin D. Roosevelt dedicated the United States "to the policy of the good neighbor." Secretary of State Cordell Hull stunned Latin America in December 1933 at the Seventh Pan-American Conference by declaring, "no state has the right to intervene in the international or external affairs of another." The marines left Nicaragua in 1933 and Haiti in 1934. The United States also nullified the Platt Amendment, thereby surrendering the right to intervene in the affairs of Cuba; and it gave Panama its political independence. Furthermore, when Mexico finally expropriated foreign oil properties in 1938, Roosevelt rejected calls to send in troops and let the action stand. The good-neighbor policy did not solve all the problems with Latin America, but it promoted better relations just when the United States needed hemispheric solidarity to meet the threat of global war.

The Isolationist Mirage

During the Great Depression, isolationist sentiment surged. In 1935, 150,000 college students participated in a nationwide Student Strike for Peace and half a million signed pledges saying that they would refuse to serve in the event of war. A public opinion poll indicated that 39 percent of college students would refuse to participate in any war, even if the country was invaded.

Antiwar sentiment was not confined to undergraduates. Disillusionment over World War I fed opposition to foreign entanglements. "We didn't win a thing we set out for in the last war," said Senator Gerald Nye of North Dakota. "We merely succeeded, with tremendous loss of life, to make secure the loans of private bankers to the Allies." The overwhelming majority of Americans agreed; an opinion poll in 1935 found that 70 percent of Americans believed that intervention in World War I had been a mistake.

Isolationist ideas spread through American popular culture during the mid-1930s. The Book-of-the-Month Club featured a volume entitled *Merchants of Death.* Its author contended that the United States had been drawn into the European war by international arms manufacturers, who had deliberately fomented conflict in order to market their products. From 1934 to 1936, a congressional committee, chaired by Senator Nye, investigated charges that false Allied propaganda and unscrupulous Wall Street bankers had dragged Americans into the European war. In April 1935—the eighteenth anniversary of America's entry into World War I—50,000 veterans held a peace march in Washington, D.C.

By 1938, however, pacifist sentiment was fading. A rapidly modernizing Japan was seeking to acquire raw materials and territory on the Asian mainland; a revived Germany was rebuilding its military power and grabbing land bloodlessly on its eastern borders; and Italy was trying to restore Roman glory through military might.

THE COMING OF WORLD WAR II

The modern world had never known a leader like Adolf Hitler. A charismatic and spellbinding orator, Hitler possessed a unique ability to articulate a nation's darkest fears and hatreds and then turn them to his own twisted purposes. Winston Churchill offered a profound truth when he described Hitler as the "monstrous product of former wrongs and shame."

Hitler exploited the psychological injuries inflicted on Germans by World War I. Rare indeed was the German who did not feel stunned by his country's sudden, unexpected defeat or who did not seethe with anger over the harsh peace imposed by the victors. Hitler's great genius (and history's great tragedy) was his ability to tap into his countrymen's anger and resentment. Exploiting the ugly strain of anti-Semitism in German culture, he claimed that the country's economic woes were the result of a conspiracy of German Jews. Hitler also attacked the Treaty of Versailles, telling his countrymen that they would regain their national honor only if they abrogated the treaty. Purged of so-called Jewish traitors, cleared of the blame for causing the war, freed from onerous reparation payments, and rescued from emasculating disarmament, Germany would rise anew and reclaim her position as a world leader.

The 1920s had prepared many Germans to embrace a leader who promised to restore national pride. The Treaty of Versailles had saddled Germany with a reparations bill of $34 billion in 1921. Unable to make the interest payments, let alone the principal, Germany staggered beneath the burden until its economy dissolved into severe unemployment and hyperinflation. Forty million marks were worth one cent. A newspaper cost 200 million marks.

Confronted by Germany's imminent economic collapse, the United States offered a measure of relief. In 1924 Charles Dawes, a prominent American banker, worked out a proposal (the Dawes Plan) that reduced the reparations bill and provided Germany with an American loan. With prodding from the United States, Great Britain and France cut reparations to $2 billion, but even that proved too much when the Great Depression struck. Germany entered the 1930s with its economy in shambles. Depression hardship in Germany provided fertile soil for Adolf Hitler.

Hitler's drive for political power began in 1919, when he joined the small National Socialist Workers' Party (later known as the Nazis), which demanded that all Jews be deprived of German citizenship and that all German-speakers be united in a single country. A brilliant propagandist and organizer, Hitler gave the Nazi movement a potent symbol, the swastika; raised party membership to 15,000 by 1923; and formed a private army, the storm troopers, to attack his political opponents. In the fall of 1923, Hitler engineered a revolt, the Beer-Hall Putsch, to overthrow Germany's five-year-old Weimar Republic. It was a dismal failure; the National Socialist Party was ordered dissolved and Hitler was imprisoned for nine months.

While in prison he wrote a book titled *Mein Kampf* (My Struggle), which laid out his beliefs and vision for Germany. He called on Germans to repudiate the Versailles Treaty, rearm, conquer countries with large German populations like Austria and Czechoslovakia, and seize *lebensraum* (living space) for Germans in Russia.

Following his release from prison, Hitler persuaded the German government to lift its ban on the National Socialist Party. In 1928, the Nazis polled just 810,000 votes in German elections, but by 1930, after the depression began, they polled 6½ million votes. Two years later Hitler ran for president. He lost, but received 13½ million votes, 37 percent of all votes cast. The Nazis had suddenly became the single largest party in the German parliament, and in January 1933, Germany's president appointed Hitler to the post of chancellor. A year and a half later Hitler was dictator of Germany.

Within months of becoming chancellor, Hitler's National Socialist government outlawed labor unions, imposed newspaper censorship, and outlawed all other political parties. The regime established a secret police force, the Gestapo, to suppress all opposition, and required all children ten years and older to join Nazi youth groups. By 1935, Hitler had transformed Germany into a fascist state, with the government exercising total control over all political, economic, and cultural activities.

Anti-Semitism was an integral part of Hitler's political program. The 1935 Nuremberg Laws forbade intermarriage between Jews and Germans, restricted Jewish property rights, and barred Jews from the civil service, the universities, and all professional and managerial occupations. On the night of November 9, 1939—a night now known as *Kristallnacht* (the night of the broken glass)—the Nazis imprisoned more than 20,000 Jews in concentration camps and destroyed more than 200 synagogues and 7500 Jewish businesses.

A reviving Germany was not the only threat to world peace. While Hitler busied himself with rearming Germany, occupying the Rhineland, annexing Austria, and seizing Czechoslovakia, Japan attacked China, and Italy attacked Ethiopia.

Conflict in the Pacific

Another major threat to international stability following World War I came in the Far East. Chronically short of raw materials, Japan was desperate to establish political

and cultural hegemony in Asia. In September 1931 Japan invaded Manchuria, reducing the Chinese province to a puppet state. President Hoover, a peaceful man, rejected American military intervention. He also refused to impose economic sanctions against Japan, fearing that such reprisals might hurt American exports or, worse yet, lead to war. Instead, Hoover applied the Stimson Doctrine, which revived the Wilsonian policy of refusing to recognize governments established by force.

Expecting bolder measures, Japan ignored America's slap on the wrist and concluded that the United States would not use military might to oppose Japan's designs on the Far East. In 1934, Japan terminated the Five-Power Naval Treaty of 1922, which had limited its naval power in the Pacific, and in 1937 invaded China. In response, the League of Nations sponsored a conference that same year in Brussels. As the delegates debated whether or not to impose economic sanctions against Japan, the United States announced it would not support sanctions. The conference adjourned after passing a report that mildly criticized Japanese aggression.

Any doubts regarding United States willingness to appease Japan vanished a few weeks later. In December 1937 Japanese aircraft bombed the *Panay*, a U.S. gunboat stationed on the Yangtze River near Nanking, killing three Americans. While the attack angered the public, few called for war as they had following the sinking of the *Maine* or the *Lusitania*. Secretary of State Cordell Hull sent sharply worded protests to Tokyo, but the United States quickly accepted Japan's "profound apology," which included indemnities for the injured and the relatives of the dead, promises against future attacks, and punishment of the pilots responsible for the bloodshed. In short, by the end of 1937, as one historian has noted, "America's Far Eastern Policy had retreated to inaction."

Italy

Mussolini's Italy posed another threat to world peace. Benito Mussolini, Italy's fascist

Axis Takeovers in Europe, 1936–1939

dictator from 1922 to 1943, promised to restore his country's martial glory. Surrounded by storm troopers dressed in black shirts, Mussolini delivered impassioned speeches from balconies, while crowds chanted "Duce! Duce!"

His opponents mocked him as the "Sawdust Caesar," but for a time his admirers included Winston Churchill and humorist Will Rogers. Cole Porter, the popular songwriter, referred to the Italian leader in one of his smash hits: "You're the top," he wrote, "you're Mussolini."

Mussolini invented a political philosophy known as fascism, extolling it as an alternative to socialist radicalism and parliamentary inaction. By fascism, he meant one-party government, strict government control of business and labor, and severe restrictions on personal liberty. Fascism, he promised, would end political corruption and labor strife while maintaining capitalism and private property. It would make trains run on time. Like Hitler's Germany, fascist Italy adopted anti-Semitic laws banning marriages between Christian and Jewish Italians, restricting Jews' right to own property, and removing Jews from positions in government, education, and banking.

One of Mussolini's goals was to create an Italian empire in North Africa. In 1912 and 1913, Italy conquered Libya. In 1935, Mussolini provoked war with Ethiopia, conquering the country in eight months. Two years later, Mussolini sent 70,000 Italian troops to Spain to help Francisco Franco defeat the republican government in the Spanish Civil War. His slogan was "Believe! Obey! Fight!"

Germany

The third threat to world peace came from a revived Germany. Hitler had vowed to reclaim Germany's position as a world leader. True to his vow to reclaim Germany's position as a world leader, Hitler pulled Germany out of the League of Nations and secretly began to rearm. In 1935 he publicly announced that he was building an air force and a 550,000-man-strong army. He also declared that Germany would have a peacetime draft, a clear violation of the Treaty of Versailles.

In 1936, Hitler concentrated on forging alliances with nations that shared Germany's taste for expansion and aggression. First he signed the Anti-Comintern Pact (forerunner of a full-scale military alliance) with Japan. Next, he formed the Rome-Berlin Axis with Italy. Finally, he reoccupied the Rhineland, the German-speaking region between the Rhine River and France. Once again, France and Great Britain did nothing to oppose Hitler's bold advance, for they believed (or wanted to believe) that the Rhineland would satisfy his expansionist ambitions.

But the Rhineland only whetted Hitler's appetite. Intent on reuniting all German-speaking peoples of Europe under the "Third Reich," Hitler annexed Austria in 1938 and imprisoned the country's chancellor. Once again, the British and the French acquiesced, hoping Austria would be Hitler's last stop. Later that year he demanded the Sudetenland, the German-speaking region of western Czechoslovakia.

This time France and Great Britain felt compelled to act. In September 1938 Edouard Daladier, the premier of France, and Neville Chamberlain, Britain's prime minister, met with Hitler in Munich, Germany, to ask whether he had further designs on Europe. Fearing that they could not count on each other to use force, British and French leaders eagerly accepted Hitler's promises not to seek additional territory in Europe. Upon arriving in England, Chamberlain told his anxious countrymen he had returned with an agreement that guaranteed "peace in our time." In less than a year, Munich would become synonymous with shameful appeasement and Chamberlain would be vilified for believing Hitler's lies.

By 1938, then, Hitler had kept his promise to avenge the humiliations Germans had suffered at Versailles. Germany's frontiers were larger than they had been in 1914, the country was rearmed, and German national pride had been restored. In addition, Germany had acquired powerful allies in Japan and Italy. All this had transpired virtually unopposed by the victors of World War I.

Benito Mussolini and Adolf Hitler share their diplomatic triumph over France and England in Munich in 1938, after the signing of the Munich Pact.

The member states of League of Nations had offered only feeble protests and failed to act. Their caution reflected the mood of a war-weary world. Everyone hoped the Germans, Italians, and Japanese would be satisfied with their acquisitions and stop their expansions. In retrospect, such hopes were clearly wrong, but at the time they did not appear unfounded. Western leaders assumed they were dealing with reasonable and responsible men; they had no way of knowing appeasement would only fuel the Axis dictators' appetites for expansion.

In late summer, Hitler took one further step. On August 24, 1939, Germany and the Soviet Union signed a nonaggression treaty. In exchange for the pact, Hitler agreed to grant the Soviet Union a sphere of influence over eastern Poland, Estonia, Latvia, Finland, and Bessarabia (northeastern Romania), while Stalin approved Germany's designs on western Poland and Lithuania. With his eastern front protected from attack, Hitler was now prepared for war.

The American Response to Hitler

The United States responded to Europe's turmoil with caution. Preoccupied with the Great Depression, President Roosevelt had little time or energy to deal with foreign affairs. Yet America's timidity also reflected the strength of its isolationist sentiment. Congress, not the president, played the dominant role in foreign affairs for much of the 1930s, and Congress was determined to keep the United States out of another European conflict.

Roosevelt's first diplomatic initiative involved the Soviet Union. Hoping to expand foreign trade and to use the Soviet Union to balance Japan in the Far East, he formally recognized the Soviet Union in 1933, provoking the wrath of isolationists and anti-Communists alike.

Privately, Roosevelt opposed the growth of isolationist sentiment in the United States during the early and mid-1930s. In his view, the United States, like it or not, had to play an important role in world affairs because it had become a major world power. But Roosevelt's freedom to act was severely limited by isolationists in Congress. Between 1935 and 1937, Congress passed three separate neutrality laws, which clamped an embargo on arms sales to belligerents, forbade American ships from entering war zones and prohibited them from being armed, and barred Americans from traveling on belligerent ships, respectively. Clearly, Congress was determined not to repeat what it regarded as the mistakes that had plunged the United States into World War I.

The neutrality laws troubled Roosevelt. Convinced that these laws posed a serious threat to presidential power, Roosevelt delivered a speech in October 1937 in which he spoke of the need to "quarantine the aggressors." But he immediately retreated into silence when it became clear the public did not support vigorous action. This was where matters stood when Hitler decided to take advantage of the world's indecisiveness.

War Begins

At daybreak on September 1, 1939, mechanized German forces poured across the Polish border, while German bombers and fighters attacked Polish railroads from the air. On

September 17, Russia attacked Poland from the east. Poland was overrun within three weeks.

The key to Germany's success was a new military strategy known as *blitzkrieg* ("lightning war"). Blitzkrieg stressed speed, force, and surprise; by closely coordinating air power and mechanized ground forces, Germany ripped through its adversary's defenses.

Britain and France declared war on Germany on September 3, 1939, two days after the German invasion began, but they did little while Poland fell. France moved its troops to its famous Maginot Line, a supposedly invincible line of defensive fortifications built to protect France's eastern border. No fighting took place in late 1939 and early 1940, leading some to call this a "phony war."

Then in April 1940, German freighters sailed secretly into Norway's major ports

Hitler's armies devastated Poland with their tremendous force and firepower. Here soldiers drive through a town battered by repeated bombings.

and the port of Copenhagen, Denmark's capital, their holds filled with German troops. The Danes, taken completely by surprise, surrendered in two hours; the Norwegians held out until June, when they, too, capitulated. British troops had tried to assist Norway, but were forced to retreat due to a lack of air support. Following the Norway debacle, British Prime Minister Neville Chamberlain was forced to resign. He was replaced by Winston Churchill, who, since 1932, had been warning about the danger Hitler posed. Upon becoming prime minister, Churchill told the British people that he had nothing to offer them but "blood, toil, tears, and sweat" in their fight to resist foreign aggression.

In May 1940, Hitler began his assault on western Europe. He outflanked France's Maginot Line by attacking Belgium, Luxembourg, and the Netherlands before driving his forces into France. Luxembourg surrendered in one day; Holland in five. A British expeditionary force rushed across the English Channel to try to stop the German offensive. But a German tank thrust forced the British to retreat to the French seaport of Dunkirk. With the British force nearly surrounded, Hitler had a chance to crush his opponents. But Britain's Royal Air Force held off German bombers long enough to allow a flotilla of yachts, ferries, and fishing boats to evacuate 338,000 Allied troops across the English Channel.

British forces had been driven from the continent. Worse yet, they had been forced to leave their weapons and tanks behind. Britain turned to the United States for help. President Roosevelt responded to the Dunkirk disaster by ordering U.S. military arsenals to send all available war materiel to Britain to replace the lost equipment.

During World War I, France held out against the Germans for four years. This time, French resistance lasted two weeks. Germany began its assault on France June 5; its troops entered Paris June 14; and on June 22, a new French government, made up of pro-German sympathizers, was set up at Vichy. In just six weeks, Germany had conquered most of continental Europe.

Convinced that Britain would negotiate with him (in order to keep control of its empire), Hitler decided against an immediate invasion of Britain. But Churchill refused to bargain. Defiantly, he told his people that he would resist any German assault: "We shall fight on the beaches . . . we shall fight in the streets . . . we shall never surrender."

Hitler was furious. First, he unleashed German submarines against British shipping. Then in July he sent his air force, the Luftwaffe, to destroy Britain from the air. At the time the assault began the Royal Air Force (RAF) had just 704 serviceable planes, while Germany had 2682 bombers and fighters ready for action. Throughout July and August the Luftwaffe attacked airfields and radar stationed on Britain's southern and eastern coast. Then, in September, Hitler shifted strategy and began to bomb civilian targets in London. These air raids, known collectively as the blitz, continued through the fall and winter. In May 1941, the blitz ended. The RAF, while outnumbered, had won the Battle of Britain. Churchill expressed his nation's gratitude with famous words: "Never in the field of human conflict was so much owed by so many to so few."

Having failed in his bid to destroy Britain with air power, Hitler again shifted strategy and invaded the Soviet Union. The attack, which began June 22, 1941, violated the German-Soviet nonaggression pact. Hitler's goal was to seize Soviet food, oil, and slave labor for Germany. At first, the Nazi war machine seemed invincible. By fall, Hitler's armies had overrun the grain fields of Ukraine and were approaching Moscow and Leningrad. But instead of pressing ahead toward Moscow, as his generals advised, Hitler instead decided to seize Leningrad and occupy the Ukraine. By the time he was ready to advance on Moscow, temperatures had plunged to 40 degrees below zero. In the frigid cold, German troops suffered frostbite and their equipment broke down.

The week between December 6 and 11, 1941, proved to be one of the most pivotal in the entire war. On December 6, Soviet forces repulsed the German attack on Moscow; it was Hitler's first military defeat. The next day, Japanese forces attacked the American naval base at Pearl Harbor, Hawaii, bringing the United States into the war. On December 11, Hitler declared war on the United States.

"The Arsenal of Democracy"

Like Wilson before him, Roosevelt responded to Europe's war by declaring America's neutrality. Unlike the idealistic Wilson, however, he did not ask his countrymen to be "neutral in thought as well as in action." After France fell, Roosevelt feared a German victory would threaten America's future security, and he resolved to save England at all costs—including war.

Before he could rescue Britain, however, Roosevelt first had to regain control of American foreign policy. Soon after Germany invaded Poland, he pushed a fourth neutrality act through Congress. It modified the earlier legislation by permitting belligerents to purchase war materials, provided they paid cash and carried the goods away in their own ships. This act was pro-British because England controlled the Atlantic. Acting on his own authority, Roosevelt then rushed thousands of planes and guns to Britain. In September 1940 he persuaded Congress to pass the first peacetime draft in American history and signed an executive agreement with Great Britain transferring 50 destroyers to England in exchange for 99-year leases on eight British bases in the Western Hemisphere. Most Americans supported the destroyers-for-bases deal.

Fearing Roosevelt was duplicating Wilson's mistakes, isolationists opposed the tilt toward Britain. Strongest in the Midwest, they represented the entire spectrum of political thought, including Republicans such as Senators Arthur Vandenberg of Michigan and Robert Taft of Ohio; Democrats such as Joseph Kennedy, ambassador to Great Britain; and progressives such as Wisconsin's Senator Robert La Follette. Their most powerful argument was that Europe's war did not threaten "fortress America." Germany had no designs on the Western Hemisphere, they insisted. The United States should therefore sit this war out.

The war dominated the election of 1940. Running for an unprecedented third term, Roosevelt handily defeated Republican challenger Wendell Willkie, 27 million votes to 22 million votes, and 449 electoral votes to 82. As New York City Mayor Fiorello La Guardia put it, Americans preferred "Roosevelt with his known faults to Willkie with his unknown virtues."

During the campaign, Willkie charged Roosevelt with maneuvering the United States into the European war. On the eve of the election, Roosevelt responded, offering these reassuring words to American parents: "I have said this before, but I shall say it again and again: your boys are not going to be sent into any foreign wars." In actuality, however, events were drawing the country closer to war.

After the election, Churchill informed Roosevelt that England had run out of money and could no longer purchase war supplies.

Consequently, the president replaced "cash and carry" with a "lend-lease" bill, which Congress passed after a bitter debate and Roosevelt signed in March 1941. With "this legislation," he declared, "our country has determined to do its full part in creating an adequate arsenal of democracy."

To cement the Anglo-American bond, Roosevelt met with Churchill in August 1941 on board the USS *Augusta* off the coast of Newfoundland. There they negotiated the Atlantic Charter, which pledged mutual support for democracy, freedom of the seas, arms reductions, and a just peace. In everything but name the United States and Great Britain were now allies.

While the public strongly supported aid for Great Britain, many Americans balked at helping the Russians, who had been invaded by Germany in June 1941. Roosevelt, however, immediately offered lend-lease aid to the Soviet Union, and in November 1941 the United States allocated $1 billion in aid to the Soviets. While critics denounced Roosevelt, Churchill, who knew wars often made strange

Kneeling in prayer near the Capitol in Washington, D.C., members of the "Mother's Crusade" against the lend-lease bill plead for Congress not to pass the measure.

bedfellows, supported the decision whole-heartedly. "If Hitler invaded Hell," declared Churchill, "I would make at least a favorable reference to the Devil in the House of Commons." By 1945 America's allies had received $50 billion, four times the amount loaned to the allies in World War I.

In April 1941 the United States went beyond financial assistance by constructing bases in Greenland and escorting convoys as far as Iceland to protect them from German submarines. The American navy started tracking German submarines and signaling their locations to British destroyers. After a German submarine attacked an American destroyer in September, Roosevelt ordered the navy to "shoot on sight" any German ships in the waters around Iceland. Yet the president stopped short of asking Congress for a formal declaration of war; for a few more months the United States maintained the fiction of neutrality.

A Collision Course in the Pacific

Thanks to the public's preoccupation with Europe, Roosevelt had a relatively free hand in the Far East, where Japan was seeking to acquire large parts of China and the western Pacific. Yet Japan's dream of expansion clashed with the two main pillars of America's Far Eastern policy—preserving the "Open Door" for trade, and protecting China's territorial integrity.

After Japan invaded China in 1937, relations between Washington and Tokyo deteriorated rapidly. The United States pressured Japan to withdraw, but Tokyo refused. In July 1939 Secretary of State Cordell Hull, aware that American exports fueled Japan's war machine, threatened to impose economic sanctions. Roosevelt, however, held back, fearing Japan would attack the Dutch East Indies to secure the oil it needed.

Events quickly forced Roosevelt's hand. In 1940 Japan occupied northern Indochina, an obvious step toward the Dutch East Indies. Late in September, Roosevelt placed an embargo on scrap iron and steel, hoping eco-

nomic sanctions would strengthen moderates in Japan who wished to avoid conflict with the United States.

When these actions failed to deter Japanese aggression, Roosevelt froze Japanese assets in the United States and cut off steel, oil, and aviation fuel exports to Japan. Hurt by these sanctions, Japan negotiated with the United States throughout 1941. Instead of compromising, however, the United States asked Japan to withdraw immediately from Indochina and China, concessions that would have ended Japan's dream of economic and military hegemony in Asia.

In a last-ditch effort to avoid war, Japan promised not to march further south, not to attack the Soviet Union, and not to declare war against the United States if Germany and America went to war. In return, Japan asked the United States to abandon China. Roosevelt refused. In October 1941 the Japanese government fell and General Hideki Tojo, the leader of the militants, seized power. War was imminent.

Most military experts expected Japan to attack the Dutch East Indies to secure oil and rubber. Before striking there, however, Japan moved to neutralize American naval power in the western Pacific.

Pearl Harbor

At 7:02 A.M., December 7, 1941, an Army mobile radar unit set up on Oahu Island in Hawaii picked up the tell-tale blips of approaching aircraft. The two privates operating the radar contacted the Army's General Information Center, but the duty officer there told them to remain calm; the planes were probably American B-17s flying in from California. In fact, they were Japanese aircraft that had been launched from six aircraft carriers 200 miles north of Hawaii.

At 7:55 A.M., the first Japanese bombs fell on Pearl Harbor, the main base of the U.S. Pacific Fleet. Moored in the harbor were more than 70 warships, including 8 of the fleet's 9 battleships. There were also 2 heavy cruisers, 29 destroyers, and 5 submarines.

Four hundred airplanes were stationed nearby.

Japanese torpedo bombers, flying just 50 feet above the water, launched torpedoes at the docked American warships. Japanese dive bombers strafed the ships' decks with machine gun fire, while Japanese fighters dropped high-explosive bombs on the aircraft sitting on the ground. Within half an hour, the U.S. Pacific Fleet was virtually destroyed. The U.S. battleship *Arizona* was a burning hulk. Three other large ships—the *Oklahoma*, the *West Virginia,* and the *California*—were sinking.

A second attack took place at 9 A.M., but by then the damage had already been done. Seven of the eight battleships were sunk or severely hit. Out of 400 aircraft, 188 had been destroyed and 159 were seriously damaged. The worst destruction occurred to the *Arizona*—a thousand of the ship's sailors drowned or burned to death. Altogether, 2403 Americans died during the Japanese attack on Pearl Harbor; another 1178 were wounded. Japan lost just 55 men.

Militarily it was not a total disaster. Japan had failed to destroy Pearl Harbor's ship-repair facilities, the base's power plant, and its fuel tanks. Even more important, three U.S. aircraft carriers, which had been on routine maneuvers, escaped destruction. But it was a devastating blow nonetheless. That same day, Japanese forces also launched other attacks throughout the Pacific, striking Guam, Hong Kong, Malaya, Midway Island, the Philippine Islands, and Wake Island.

The next day, President Roosevelt appeared before a joint session of Congress to ask for a declaration of war. He began his address with these famous words: "Yesterday, December 7, 1941—a date that will live in in-

In little more than an hour, the surprise attack at Pearl Harbor killed more than 2400 American sailors and damaged or sunk eight battleships, including the USS *Arizona,* pictured here.

famy—the United States of America was suddenly and deliberately attacked by naval and air forces of the Empire of Japan." Congress declared war on Japan, with only one dissenting vote.

AMERICA MOBILIZES FOR WAR

After Pearl Harbor, practically everyone agreed on what had to be done: jump-start the economy, raise an army, and win the war. Yet the economic challenges facing the United States were truly mind-boggling. New plants had to be built and existing ones expanded; raw materials had to be procured and distributed where needed; labor had to be kept on the job; production had to be raised; and all this had to be accomplished without producing soaring inflation.

Mobilizing the Economy

Following the declaration of war, Roosevelt easily made the switch from reformer to war leader, telling reporters that "Dr. New Deal" had to be replaced by "Dr. Win-the-War." Like Wilson before him, Roosevelt wished to avoid government controls. He, too, would fail. World War II created a huge (and apparently permanent) federal bureaucracy. In January 1942 Roosevelt created the War Production Board (WPB) to "exercise general responsibility" over the economy.

Business leaders responded coolly to the call for economic conversion. With profits already high because of the war in Europe, many industrialists did not wish to jeopardize their position in the domestic market by converting factories to military production. Others worried about getting stuck with inflated capacity after the war ended. As one executive cautioned, "Guns are not windshield wipers."

To gain their support, the government suspended competitive bidding, offered cost-plus contracts, guaranteed low-cost loans for retooling, and paid huge subsidies for plant construction and equipment. Lured by huge profits, the American auto industry began to produce war vehicles and construct new factories, like the huge Willow Run plant near Detroit, to build airplanes. In 1940, 6000 planes rolled off Detroit's assembly lines; by 1942 production had soared to 47,000, and by the end of the war it had exceeded 100,000, more than doubling Roosevelt's goal.

Consumer industries prospered, too. Robert W. Woodruff of Coca-Cola made his 5-cent drink the most widely distributed consumer product in the world by convincing the army that soldiers needed Coke to refresh their fighting spirit. Backed by government subsidies, Woodruff built an international network of plants, and then purchased them at a fraction of their cost after the war, ensuring Coca-Cola's postwar supremacy in the soft drink industry.

Most military contracts went to big businesses because large-scale production simplified buying. At Roosevelt's insistence the Justice Department stopped prosecuting antitrust violators, a policy that accelerated business consolidations. Overall, industrial profits doubled, but small industries, lacking the capital to convert to war production, got crowded away from the federal trough.

When he saw the production figures of American industry during World War II, Winston Churchill smiled broadly and exclaimed, "Nothing succeeds like excess!" Great Britain's bulldog of a prime minister was right: Allied armies won the decisive battles of World War II, but the Allied victory rested squarely on America's economic might. Within a year of the Japanese attack on Pearl Harbor, the output of the nation's war industries outstripped that of all the Axis countries combined; by 1944, it was twice as great. By the war's end, industrial production had soared an astonishing 96 percent, as Americans produced 80,000 airplanes, 60,000 tanks, 17.4 million rifles, and more than 4 million tons of artillery shells.

Government-sponsored research became a major new industry during World War II. To counter Germany's scientific and technological superiority, Roosevelt created the Office of Scientific Research and Development (OSRD) in 1942. Federal funds supported the development of radar, flame throwers, antiaircraft guns, rockets, and even new medicines. Thanks in large part to penicillin and new blood plasma techniques, the death rate of wounded soldiers who reached medical installations was half that of World War I. Antimalarial drugs and insecticides dramatically reduced the incidence of mosquito-carried diseases among troops in the Mediterranean and in the Pacific.

No less than industry, American agriculture performed impressively during World War II. To encourage production, Roosevelt allowed farmers to make large profits by setting crop prices at high levels. Good weather, mechanization, and a dramatic increase in the use of fertilizers did the rest. Cash income for farmers jumped from $2.3 billion in 1940 to $9.5 billion in 1945.

The distribution of profits in agriculture followed the same pattern as in industry: most went to large-scale operators who could afford expensive machinery and fertilizers. Many small farmers, saddled with huge debts from the depression, abandoned their farms for jobs in defense plants or the armed services. Over 5 million farm residents (17 percent of the total) left rural areas during the war.

Overall, the war brought unprecedented prosperity to Americans. Per capita income rose from $373 in 1940 to $1074 in 1945, and total personal income went from $81 billion to $182 billion during the same years. Workers never had it so good. The total income of families increased dramatically as large numbers of women joined the workforce, creating millions of two-income families. In fact, World War II brought Americans more money than they could spend, for the production of consumer goods could not keep pace with the new buying power. Everything from toasters to diapers was in short supply.

Taming Inflation

The shortages led to inflation. Prices rose 18 percent between 1941 and the end of 1942. Apples sold for ten cents apiece; the price of a watermelon soared to $2.50; and oranges reached an astonishing $1.00 a dozen.

Many goods were unavailable regardless of price. To conserve steel, glass, and rubber for war industries, the government halted production of cars in December 1941. A month later, production of vacuum cleaners, refrigerators, radios, sewing machines, and phonographs ceased. Altogether, production of nearly 300 items deemed nonessential to the war effort—including coat hangers, beer cans, and toothpaste tubes—was banned or curtailed.

Congress responded to surging prices by establishing the Office of Price Administration (OPA) in January 1942, with the power to freeze prices and wages, control rents, and institute rationing of scarce items. The OPA quickly rationed foodstuffs. Every month, each man, woman, and child in the country received two ration books—one for canned goods and one for meat, fish, and dairy products. Meat was limited to 28 ounces per person a week; sugar to 8 to 12 ounces; and coffee, a pound every 5 weeks. Rationing was soon extended to tires, gasoline, and shoes. Drivers were allowed a mere 3 gallons a week, while pedestrians were limited to two pairs of shoes a year. The OPA extolled the virtues of self-sacrifice, telling people to "Use it up, wear it out, make it do, or do without."

In addition to rationing, Washington attacked inflation by reducing the public's purchasing power. The administration encouraged the sale of war bonds, which not only

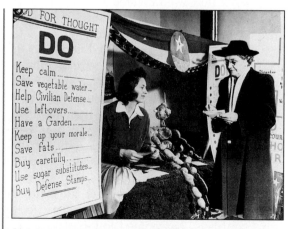

At a consumer conservation booth in West Dundee Township, Illinois, women offered "food for thought" in an attempt to help the war effort.

helped finance the war but also absorbed more than 7 percent of the real personal income of Americans. Taxation was also used to combat inflation. To cool off consumer purchasing power, Congress passed the Revenue Act of 1942, which raised corporate taxes, increased the excess profits tax, and levied a 5 percent withholding tax on anyone who earned more than $642 a year. Tax reforms forced citizens to pay more than 40 percent of the war's total cost as the war progressed, laying the foundation for postwar tax policies. Wage controls offered another tool for controlling inflation. The War Labor Board (WLB), established in 1942, had the power to set wages, hours, and working conditions.

These programs, working together, brought inflation under control. After 1942 the annual inflation rate did not exceed 1.5 percent. Still, the administration's methods pleased no one. Everyone groused about taxes; manufacturers and farmers denounced price controls as an attack on their profits; and labor officials condemned wage freezes as an assault on their incomes.

Yet American workers clearly reaped a bonanza from World War II. Because the war created 17 million new jobs at the exact moment when 15 million men and women entered the armed services, unemployment virtually disappeared. After Pearl Harbor, labor soared to an absolute premium, drawing into the workforce previously unemployed and underemployed groups such as women, teenagers, African Americans, senior citizens, and the handicapped. Under the benevolent hand of government protection, unions rebounded from their sharp decline of the 1920s and early 1930s. Union membership jumped from 10.5 million to 14.75 million during the war.

Despite these gains, labor unrest increased throughout the war. After Pearl Harbor union officials pledged not to strike until the war ended, but inflation and wage restrictions quickly eroded their goodwill. The number of work stoppages rose from 2960 in 1942 to 4956 in 1944, though most ended quickly and did not harm the war effort.

In contrast to the president, Congress took a hostile stand toward labor. Over Roosevelt's veto, Congress passed the Smith-Connally Act, which banned strikes in war industries, authorized the president to seize plants useful to the war effort, and limited political activity by unions. The Smith-Connally Act reflected a resurgence of conservatism, both in Congress and in the country at large. Though the Democrats continued to maintain a thin majority in both houses of Congress throughout the war, a coalition of Republicans and conservative Democrats after 1942 could defeat any measure.

Beginning in 1943 Roosevelt's opponents led a successful attack against the New Deal, refusing to fund the Civilian Conservation Corps, the Works Progress Administration, the National Youth Administration, and the National Resources and Planning Board. According to conservatives, these agencies had dangerously expanded federal power and deserved to die.

Election of 1944

With reform in retreat, the Republicans expected to win the election of 1944. Thomas E. Dewey, the dapper young governor of New York, won his party's nomination on the first ballot. While Dewey accepted the New Deal as part of American life, he opposed its expansion. No distance separated the two major candidates on foreign affairs.

Roosevelt easily captured his party's nomination for a fourth term. Because his health was deteriorating badly—he was suffering from hypertension and heart disease—his choice of a vice president was more important than usual. Roosevelt allowed the Democratic convention to select a nominee, and it picked Harry S Truman of Missouri, best known as leader of a Senate committee investigating corruption in defense spending.

The 1944 campaign revitalized Roosevelt. He unveiled plans for a "GI Bill of Rights," promising liberal unemployment benefits, educational support, medical care, and housing loans for veterans, which Congress approved overwhelmingly in 1944. Unwilling to switch leaders while at war, the public stuck with Roosevelt to see the crisis through. The president received 25,611,936 votes to Dewey's 22,013,372, and he won in the electoral college, 432 to 99.

Molding Public Opinion

Having witnessed the mistakes of World War I, Roosevelt did not want government propaganda to arouse or fuel false hopes. Shortly before Pearl Harbor, he created the Office of Facts and Figures under Archibald MacLeish, the Librarian of Congress. A poet, MacLeish became embroiled in bureaucratic struggles with government agencies, the armed services, and the Office of Strategic Services. By 1944 the government had all but abandoned its efforts to shape public opinion about the war.

Private enterprise filled the void. Movies, comic strips, newspapers, books, and advertisements reduced the war to a struggle between good and evil as the Allies engaged in mortal combat with Japan and Germany. The Japanese bore the brunt of the propaganda, especially during the first two years of fighting. Caricatured with thick glasses and huge buck teeth, public portraits of the Japanese grew more ugly and vicious as deeply ingrained racism fed the stereotypes, reviving old fears of the "yellow peril."

Germans, by contrast, elicited more complex attitudes in Americans, largely because passions were not inflamed by racism. At first, Americans blamed Hitler for the war. As eyewitness accounts of German atrocities began to filter back from the front, however, the public's views shifted. Americans gradually came to blame not just the Nazis, but all Germans, for the war.

Motion pictures emerged as the most important instrument of propaganda during World War II. After Pearl Harbor, Hollywood immediately enlisted in the war cause. The studios quickly copyrighted movie titles like "Yellow Peril" and "V for Victory." Hollywood's greatest contribution to the war effort was in the area of morale. Combat films produced during the war emphasized patriotism, group effort, and the value of sacrifice for a larger cause. They portrayed World War II as a peoples' war, typically featuring a group of men from diverse ethnic backgrounds who were thrown together, tested on the battlefield, and molded into a dedicated fighting unit. Wartime films also featured women serving as combat nurses, riveters, welders,

"Joe, yestiddy ya saved my life an' I swore I'd pay ya back. Here's my last pair of dry socks."

Bill Mauldin's cartoon characters, Willie and Joe, were popular not only at home but also among soldiers abroad.

and long-suffering mothers who kept the home fires burning.

Off-screen, leading actors and actresses led recruitment and bond drives and entertained the troops. Leading directors like Frank Capra and John Huston made documentaries to explain "why we fight" and to show civilians what actual combat looked like.

SOCIAL CHANGES DURING THE WAR

World War II produced important changes in American life, some trivial, others profound. One striking change involved fashion. To conserve wool and cotton, dresses became shorter, and vests and cuffs disappeared, as did double-breasted suits, pleats, and ruffles.

More significant was a tremendous increase in mobility. The war set families in motion, pulling them off farms and out of small towns, and packing them into large urban areas. Urbanization had virtually ceased during the depression, but the war saw the number of city dwellers leap from 46 to 53 percent.

War industries sparked the urban growth. Detroit's population exploded as the automotive industry switched to war vehicles. Washington, D.C., became another boomtown, as tens of thousands of new workers staffed the swelling ranks of the bureaucracy. The most dramatic growth occurred in California, however. Of the 15 million civilians who moved across state lines during the war, over 2 million went to California to work in defense industries.

Women

The war had a dramatic impact on women. Easily the most visible change involved the sudden appearance of large numbers of women in uniform. The military organized women into auxiliary units with special uniforms, their own officers, and, amazingly, equal pay. By 1945 more than 250,000 women had joined the Women's Army Corps (WAC),

the Army Nurses Corps, the Women Accepted for Voluntary Emergency Service (WAVES), the Navy Nurses Corps, the Marines, and the Coast Guard. Most women who joined the armed services either filled traditional women's roles, such as nursing, or replaced men in noncombat jobs.

Women also substituted for men on the home front. For the first time in history married working women outnumbered single working women as 6.3 million women entered the workforce during the war. The war challenged the conventional image of female behavior, as "Rosie the Riveter" became the popular symbol of women who abandoned traditional female occupations to work in defense industries.

Women paid a price for their economic independence, though. Outside employment did not free wives from domestic duties. The same women who put in full days in offices and factories went home to cook, clean, shop, and care for children. They had not one job, but two, and the only way they could fill both was to sacrifice relaxation, recreation, and sleep. Outside employment also raised the problem of child care. A few industries, such

During the war, a growing number of women not only joined the armed forces, but also helped out in the labor force at home by filling jobs normally held by men.

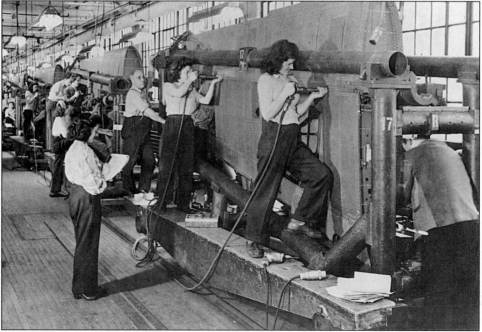

as Kaiser Steel, offered day-care facilities, but most women had to make their own informal arrangements.

Social critics had a field day attacking women. Social workers blamed working mothers for the rise in juvenile delinquency during the war, while other critics condemned women for their immodesty, self-indulgence, drinking, dress standards, and sexual promiscuity. "Choose any set of criteria you like," wrote the famous anthropologist Margaret Mead in 1946, "and the answer is the same: women and men are confused, uncertain and discontented with the present definition of women's place in America."

Amid this confusion, many women elected to cling to the familiar by embracing the traditional roles of housewives and mothers. Between 1941 and 1945, the marriage rate reached new heights: 105 marriages per every 1000 women between the ages of 17 and 29, well above 89.1, the rate during the "normal" years of 1925 to 1929. The birthrate increased, too, rebounding sharply from the all-time low of 18 to 19 per 1000 people during the depression. In 1943 the birthrate jumped to 22.7, and by 1946 it had reached 25, where it remained, with modest fluctuations, for the rest of the decade. Overall, the "baby boom" did not signal a return to large families; rather, the birthrate rose because women married at younger ages and had their families earlier in life.

Hasty marriages between young partners often proved brittle. Wartime separations forced newlyweds to develop new roles and become self-reliant, and many couples later found it difficult to reestablish their relationships. Rather than remain in unhappy marriages, they often opted for divorce. In 1946 the American courts granted a record 600,000 divorces. By 1950 the divorce rate stood at one-quarter of the marriages, well above the prewar levels.

Yet Americans had not given up on marriage. The divorce rate had been climbing steadily (except during the depression years when many people could not afford to get married or divorced) since 1900. Furthermore, most Americans who divorced during the 1940s promptly remarried. They had rejected their mates, not marriage.

African Americans

During World War II, African Americans waged battles on two fronts. They helped the country win the war overseas and pressed for equal rights at home. African Americans called this dual struggle for victory against fascism and discrimination the "Double V" campaign. They played many critical roles in the war effort. About a million African Americans served in the armed forces during World War II, about half serving overseas. The armed forces were segregated, and many African-American soldiers complained that they were treated like prisoners of war. Nevertheless, all-black units like the famous "Tuskegee Airmen" (the 99th Pursuit Squadron), which flew combat missions in Europe; the 92nd Division, which suffered 3161 casualties in campaigns in Italy; and the 761st Tank Battalion, which fought at the Battle of the Bulge, played pivotal battlefield roles.

World War II helped reshape the nation's race relations. In 1941, the overwhelming majority of the nation's African-American population—10 out of 13 million—lived in the South, primarily in rural areas. During the war, more than one million African Americans migrated to the North and West—twice the number during World War I—and more than two million found work in defense industries. Yet African Americans continued to be the last hired and the first fired, and other forms of discrimination remained blatant, especially in housing and employment.

African-American leaders fought discrimination vigorously. In the spring of 1941 (months before America entered the war), the president of the Brotherhood of Sleeping Car Porters, A. Philip Randolph, with strong backing from the National Association for the Advancement of Colored People (NAACP), called for 150,000 people to march on Washington to protest discrimination in defense industries. Embarrassed and concerned, Roosevelt issued an executive order prohibiting discrimination in defense industries and creating the Fair Employment Practices Commission (FEPC). But the FEPC's tiny staff lacked the power and resources to enforce its decisions. During the war the FEPC did not even process most complaints, and contractors ignored 35 of the 45 compliance orders the commission issued.

African Americans fared no better in the public sector. Most African Americans in the federal bureaucracy worked as janitors, and the armed services treated its African-American soldiers as second-class citizens. The marines excluded blacks; the navy used them as servants; and the army created separate black regiments commanded mostly by white officers. The Red Cross even segregated blood plasma.

Not surprisingly, racial tensions deepened during the war. The number of African-American GIs rose from 100,000 in 1941 to 700,000 in 1944. Many joined the armed services hoping to find social mobility. Instead, they encountered segregation and discrimination. They resented white officials who denounced Nazi racism but remained silent about discrimination at home. Northern African Americans stationed in the South found race relations shocking. Signs on buses in Charleston, South Carolina, read: "Avoid Friction. Be Patriotic. White passengers will be seated from front to rear, colored passengers from rear to front."

Conditions in the civilian sector were no better. As urban areas swelled with defense workers, housing and transportation shortages exacerbated racial tensions. In 1943 a riot broke out in Detroit in a federally sponsored housing project. Polish Americans wanted African Americans barred from the new apartments named, ironically, in honor of Sojourner Truth, the ex-slave abolitionist and poet. White soldiers from a nearby base joined the fighting, and other federal troops had to be brought in to disperse the mobs. The violence left 35 African Americans and 9 whites dead.

Similar conflicts erupted across the nation, exposing in each instance the same jarring contradiction: white Americans espoused equality abroad but practiced discrimination at home. One African-American soldier told Swedish social scientist Gunnar Myrdal, "just carve on my tombstone, here lies a black man killed fighting a yellow man for the protection of a white man." A 1942 survey showed that many African Americans sympathized with the Japanese struggle to expel white colonialists from the Far East. Significantly, the same survey revealed that a majority of white industrialists in the South preferred a German victory to racial equality in America.

Many African Americans responded to the rising tensions by joining civil rights organizations—during World War II, the NAACP, for example, intensified its legal campaigns against discrimination. Its membership grew from 50,000 to 500,000 as large numbers of African Americans and middle-class whites demanded racial equality.

Some African Americans, however, considered the NAACP too slow and too conciliatory. Rejecting legal action, the Congress of Racial Equality (CORE), founded in 1942, organized a series of "sit-ins." Civil disobedience produced a few victories in the North, but the South's response was brutal. In Tennessee, for example, angry whites savagely beat the civil rights leader Bayard Rustin for refusing to move to the back of the bus. While civil rights activists made few gains during World War II, they did forge new demands and tactics that would shape the civil rights movement after the war.

Federal officials did little to advance civil rights. Personally, Roosevelt sympathized with African Americans, but he feared losing the Solid South's support if he moved too rapidly on the race issue. Thus, while he admitted African-American leaders to the White House to hear their grievances, Roosevelt seldom took action. Eleanor Roosevelt remained the conscience of the administration, voicing her sympathy for civil rights at every juncture, but the president refused to take the political risks needed to end discrimination and promote racial equality.

Mexican Americans

World War II affected Mexican Americans no less than African Americans and women. Almost 400,000 Mexican Americans served in the armed forces during the war. As soldiers, they expanded their contacts with American society, for the first time visiting new parts of the country in which large groups of people held few prejudices against them. For Mexican Americans in the civilian sector, jobs in industry provided an escape hatch from the desperate poverty of migratory farm labor. In New Mexico, for example, about one-fifth of the rural Mexican American population left for war-related jobs.

The need for farm workers rose dramatically after Pearl Harbor. To meet the demand, the United States established the *bracero* (work hands) program in 1942; by 1945 several hundred thousand Mexican workers had immigrated to the Southwest. Commercial farmers welcomed them, but labor unions resented the competition, leading to animosity and discrimination against Mexicans and Mexican Americans alike.

In Los Angeles, ethnic tensions erupted into violence. White society both feared and resented newly formed Mexican-American youth gangs, whose members celebrated their ethnicity by wearing flamboyant "zoot suits" and by tattooing their left hands. In June 1943 hundreds of white sailors on liberty from nearby naval bases invaded downtown Los Angeles. Eager to put down the Mexican-American youths, they attacked the "zooters" and riots broke out for several nights. The local press blamed Mexican-American gangs, and the riots did not end until military police ordered sailors back to their ships.

Despite outbursts of violence and discrimination, World War II benefited the poor of all races. Thanks to full employment and progressive taxation, people at the bottom had income redistributed in their favor. Americans who occupied the top 5 percent economically saw their share of disposable income fall from 23 percent in 1939 to 17 percent in 1945. Before the war there were 12 families with an income under $2000 for every family with an income over $5000; after the war the ratio was almost even. Still, the gains made by poor people came from the state of the economy (the need for soldiers and workers), not from federal policies or the efforts of organized labor.

Fear of Enemy Aliens

On December 8, 1941, Roosevelt issued an executive order regarding enemy aliens. It suspended naturalization proceedings for Italian, German, and Japanese immigrants, required them to register, restricted their mobility, and prohibited them from owning items that might be used for espionage and sabotage, such as cameras and short-wave radios. In practice, however, the government did not accord enemy aliens the same treatment:

Location of Nazi Concentration and Death Camps

Italian and German aliens received lenient treatment, while Japanese aliens suffered gross injustices.

Approximately 600,000 Italian aliens lived in the United States in 1940. In general, the government treated them well throughout the war, administering the enemy alien laws with compassion. On Columbus Day, 1942 (just before the congressional elections), Roosevelt lifted the enemy alien designation for Italians and established simplified naturalization procedures. German aliens received similar treatment; though less numerous (264,000) and not as politically important to the Democrats, Roosevelt's administration treated them fairly throughout the war.

Jewish refugees complicated the German question. Reflecting a nasty strain of anti-Semitism, Congress in 1939 refused to raise immigration quotas to admit 20,000 Jewish children fleeing Nazi oppression. As the wife of the U.S. commissioner of immigration remarked at a cocktail party, "20,000 children would all too soon grow up to be 20,000 ugly adults."

Instead of relaxing immigration quotas, American officials worked in vain to persuade Latin American countries and Great Britain to admit Jewish refugees. Other officials, such as Assistant Secretary of State Breckinridge Long, the chief administrator for immigration policy, insisted that winning the war offered the best means for rescuing European Jews. Bitterly anti-Semitic in his private views, Long argued that any relaxation of the quota system would permit Nazi spies to slip into the country along with legitimate refugees.

While the futile debates dragged on, Hitler's death camps killed helpless victims at the rate of 2000 an hour. As late as 1944, American officials who knew the ghastly truth even publicly downplayed reports of genocide in the press. Air reconnaissance missions had taken scores of photographs of the death camp at Auschwitz, and military intelligence officers had learned the locations of several other concentration camps.

Finally, in January 1944, Secretary of the Treasury Henry Morgenthau, forced the issue. The only Jew in the Cabinet, Morgenthau presented to Roosevelt the "Report to the Secretary on the Acquiescence of this Government in the Murder of the Jews." Shamed into action, Roosevelt created the War Refugee Board, which, in turn, set up refugee camps in Italy, North Africa, and the United States. But America's response offered too little, too late. During the 18 months of the War Refugee Board's existence, Hitler killed far more Jews than the War Refugee Board saved.

Internment of Japanese Americans

Like Jews, Japanese Americans got a bitter taste of discrimination during World War II. Barred from migrating to the United States by the Immigration Act of 1924, they comprised only a tiny portion of the population in 1941—no more than 260,000 people; 150,000 lived in Hawaii, with the remaining 110,000 concentrated on the West Coast, where they worked mostly as small farmers or businesspeople serving the Japanese community. After Pearl Harbor, rumors spread about Japanese troops preparing to land in California, where they allegedly planned to link up with Japanese Americans and Japanese aliens poised to strike as a fifth column for the invasion.

On February 19, 1942, Roosevelt authorized the Department of War to designate military areas and to exclude any or all persons from them. Armed with this power, military authorities immediately moved against Japanese aliens. In Hawaii, where residents of Japanese ancestry formed a large portion of

the population and where the local economy depended on their labor, the military did not force Japanese Americans to relocate. On the West Coast, however, military authorities ordered the Japanese to leave, making no distinction between aliens and citizens. Forced to sell their

Location of Internment Camps for Japanese Americans

property for pennies on the dollar, most Japanese Americans suffered severe financial losses. Relocation proved next to impossible, as no other states would take them. The governor of Idaho, for example, opposed any migration, declaring: "The Japs live like rats, breed like rats and act like rats. We don't want them."

When voluntary measures failed, Roosevelt created the War Relocation Authority. It resettled 100,000 Japanese Americans in ten camps scattered across six western states and Arkansas called relocation camps. Resembling minimum security prisons, these concentration camps locked American citizens who had committed no crimes behind barbed wire. They were crowded into ramshackle wooden barracks where they lived one family to a room furnished with nothing but cots and bare light bulbs, forced to endure bad food, inadequate medical care, and poorly equipped schools.

Nearly 18,000 Japanese-American men won release from the camps to fight for the United States Army. Most served with the 100th Infantry Battalion and the 442nd Regimental Combat Team. In Italy, the 442nd sustained nearly 10,000 casualties, with 3600 Purple Hearts, 810 Bronze Stars, 342 Silver Stars, 123 divisional citations, 47 Distinguished Service Crosses, 17 Legions of Merit, 7 Presidential Unit Citations, and 1 Congressional Medal of Honor. In short, they fought heroically for the United States, emerging as the most decorated military unit in World War II. In one of the most painful scenes in American history, Japanese-American parents, still locked inside

Japanese Americans of all ages, tagged like pieces of luggage, await their relocation to one of ten detention camps in seven states. This family was from Hayward, California.

concentration camps, received posthumous Purple Hearts for their sons.

Japanese Americans protested their treatment, claiming numerous civil rights violations. Citing national security considerations, the Supreme Court backed the government, 6 to 3, in *Korematsu* v. *United States* (1944). But in a dissenting opinion, Frank Murphy admitted federal policy had fallen "into the ugly abyss of racism." On December 18, 1944, in the *Endo* case, the Supreme Court ruled that a civilian agency, the War Relocation Authority, had no right to incarcerate law-abiding citizens. Two weeks later the federal government began closing down the camps, ending one of the most shameful chapters in American history.

THE WAR IN EUROPE

The Grand Alliance

Following Pearl Harbor, the Axis Powers of Germany, Japan, and Italy faced the Grand Alliance, composed of the United States, Great Britain, Free France, and the Soviet

Union. Yet from the beginning the Grand Alliance was an uneasy coalition, born of necessity and racked with tension. Apart from the need to defeat the enemy, the Allies found it difficult to agree on anything.

Winston Churchill, Great Britain's prime minister, approached international affairs in spheres-of-influence, balance-of-power terms. He wanted to block Soviet expansion and was determined that Britain play a major role in postwar Europe. Furthermore, he wanted Britain to emerge form the war with its colonial empire intact.

France's goals reflected the vision of one man—General Charles de Gaulle, who after the fall of France in 1940 had established in London a French government-in-exile. Above all, de Gaulle wanted to restore France to greatness. By nature aloof and suspicious, he fought to retain his country's empire, and as the war progressed American officials came to regard de Gaulle as a political extremist. In policy disputes, he often sided with Britain to oppose American and Soviet demands.

Joseph Stalin spoke for the Soviet Union. The son of a cobbler, Stalin rose to power by crushing all political rivals during the turbulent years following the Bolshevik revolution. Iron-willed, deeply paranoid, and bold as a thief, "Uncle Joe" enjoyed a well-deserved reputation as a formidable negotiator. Throughout World War II, he pressed for a postwar settlement that would guarantee the Soviet Union's future security and open new lands for Communism. To protect the Soviet Union from future attacks, Stalin insisted upon Germany's total destruction. As additional insurance, he demanded parts of Poland and Finland and all of the Baltic states. Eastern Europe would then form a buffer against future aggression from the West, provide colonies for rebuilding the Soviet economy, and add new territory to the Communist world map.

Roosevelt had his own ideas about how the world should look after the war. In broad terms, he opposed colonialism and the spread of Communism; and he supported open markets, democratic elections to counter spheres of influence, and a new League of Nations to promote world peace. Among these objectives, anticolonialism and support for free markets were his top priorities, and both goals reflected Roosevelt's remarkable ability to join political principle with economic advantage.

No less than his counterparts, Roosevelt's personality shaped his policies. Because he disliked the rough and tumble of hard bargaining, he tried to avoid clashes with other leaders by postponing difficult decisions and by relying too heavily on his personal charm. In addition, Roosevelt's pragmatic approach to problem solving made him seek compromises whenever possible, which meant that he often sacrificed principles in order to preserve Allied cooperation.

From the outset, then, dissent riddled the Grand Alliance. In pursuit of its own national interests, each ally had a separate agenda, its own set of demands, and its own vision of the how the world map should look when the war ended. Given these conflicts, the Allies could look forward not to harmony but to clashes over military strategy throughout the war, bitter debates over peace terms at the war's end, and decades of international strife in the postwar era.

Early Axis Victories

For six months after Pearl Harbor, Japan looked unbeatable. Japanese forces captured Guam, Wake Island, the Philippines, Hong Kong, and Malaya and slashed deep into Burma. General Douglas MacArthur was driven from the Philippines in March 1942. In a matter of months Japanese troops had conquered a vast expanse of territory extending from the Gilbert Islands through the Solomons and from New Guinea to Burma, leaving India and Australia vulnerable to attack.

Nor did the Allied cause look any brighter in Europe. During the first ten months of 1942, German submarines sank over 500 American merchant ships. With its lend-lease supplies threatened, Great Britain stood in danger of collapsing before the United States could mobilize. On the Russian front, German troops pressed toward Stalingrad, and in North Africa, where German Field Marshal Erwin Rommel, the famous "Desert Fox," was sweeping toward the Suez Canal, the situa-

tion seemed equally bleak. In short, 1942 opened badly for the Allies. Axis victories in the Pacific, Europe, and Africa served notice the war would be long and costly.

Stemming the German Tide

Roosevelt decided to assign Germany top priority for two reasons: First, he doubted Hitler could be dislodged from Europe if Britain fell; and, second, Roosevelt wanted to placate Stalin, whose troops were bearing the brunt of the German war machine. As the Germans drove deep into Soviet territory in 1942, Stalin demanded a second front in France to force Germany to divide her armies, thereby relieving some of the pressure on the Soviet Union. As one observer remarked, Soviet Foreign Minister V. M. Molotov knew only four words of English: "yes," "no," and "second front."

By the autumn of 1942 the tide was beginning to turn on the eastern front. In September the Red Army won a key victory at Stalingrad. Then the Soviets launched a furious counterattack, beginning the long drive to push the Germans back across the Ukraine. Despite Soviet victories and Stalin's repeated pleas for a second front, the Allies, at Churchill's insistence, decided to attack the Germans in North Africa instead of France. Stalin saw this as a betrayal and his suspicions deepened.

Allied victories in Africa seemed to confirm Churchill's wisdom. British Field Marshal Sir Bernard Montgomery drove the Germans back to Tunis in October, and in November 1942 General Dwight D. Eisenhower led a force of 400,000 Allied soldiers in a full-scale invasion of North Africa. Complete victory in North Africa came on May 12, 1943, when the remnants of the Axis armies surrendered. Germany and Italy had both suffered a major defeat and Allied shipping could now cross the Mediterranean in safety.

Cheered by North African victories, Churchill and Roosevelt met in Casablanca, French Morocco, in January 1943. Stalin did not attend, explaining he could not leave the Soviet Union at this critical juncture of the war. Haunted by ghastly memories of World War I and fearing a premature invasion of

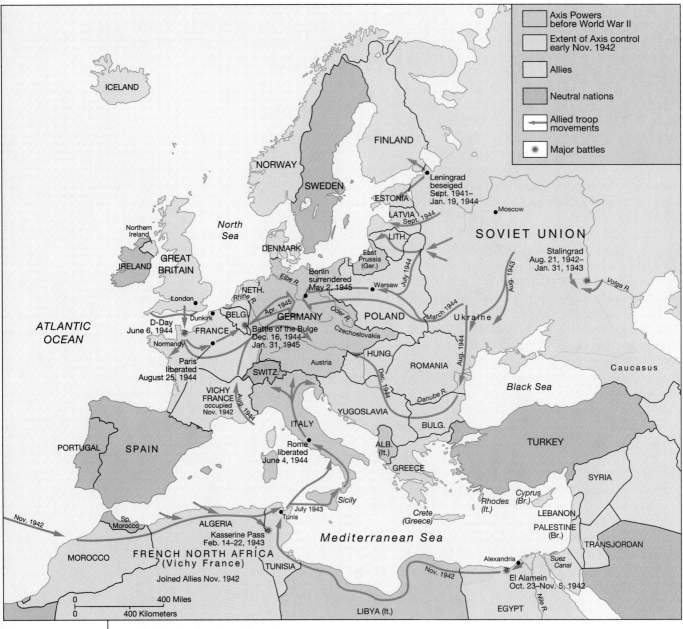

World War II, European Theater

France might bog down into trench-style warfare, Churchill pushed hard for an attack on Sicily and then Italy. The United States initially opposed the plan, arguing it would delay the invasion of France, but Churchill prevailed. As one American military adviser remarked at the time: "We came, we listened, and we were conquered." With the promised invasion of France again put on hold,

Churchill and Roosevelt moved to reassure Stalin. Vowing publicly to make peace with the Axis powers only on the basis of unconditional surrender, the two leaders also renewed their pledge to open a second front.

Sicily fell in August 1943 after a campaign of slightly more than a month. Victory in Italy, however, did not come cheaply. The terrain was mountainous, and the Germans offered savage resistance. Stalin deeply resented the commitment of Allied troops there, which further postponed the long-promised second front in France. Moreover, since Soviet troops had not fought in the Italian campaign, Roosevelt and Churchill did not allow Stalin to participate in organizing an occupation government there. The next time Stalin wanted a voice in a region he made certain to have his armies on site.

Liberating Europe

In November 1943 Roosevelt, Churchill, and Stalin held their first face-to-face conference, meeting in Teheran, the capital of Iran. Buoyed by military success, Stalin sounded conciliatory as they discussed a second front. The leaders set May 1944 as the target date for Operation OVERLORD, the code name for the invasion of France. To increase the odds for success, Stalin promised to coordinate Russia's spring offensive with the invasion.

Once the leaders turned to postwar issues, however, the conference dissolved into bitter controversy. Stalin demanded Soviet control over Eastern Europe and insisted Germany be divided into several weak states. Opposing both demands, Churchill proposed democratic governments for Eastern Europe, especially in Poland, for which England had gone to war, and argued that the balance of power in postwar Europe required a united Germany. Roosevelt, on the other hand, knew Stalin had the inside track in Eastern Europe. Convinced he could handle "Uncle Joe," Roosevelt decided to leave territorial questions to a postwar international organization dominated by the victors. Apart from reaching agreement on the second front, the Teheran Conference merely aired the leaders' conflicting demands.

In preparation for the invasion, the Allies instituted saturation bombing German territory. They dropped 2,697,473 tons of bombs, killing 305,000 civilians and damaging over 5.5 million homes. The air raids were supposed to wipe out the German war machine and break the people's will to resist, but missions such as the firebombing of Dresden,

which killed 100,000 people, convinced many Germans that Hitler's ravings about the evil Allies were true, and that stiffened their will to fight.

As the bombers pounded Germany the Allies prepared for the invasion of France, massing more than 3 million soldiers in England under the command of General Dwight D. Eisenhower. D-Day came on June 6, 1944. After two weeks of desperate fighting on the beaches of Normandy, the Allies began to push inland. A month later Allied troops were sweeping across Europe in a race for Berlin. They liberated Paris in August, and by mid-September Allied forces had crossed the German border. True to his word, Stalin synchronized his spring offensive with the invasion. Soviet troops engaged the Germans in furious combat all across Eastern Europe, tying up men and materials that otherwise could have been hurled against the Allies.

On December 16, 1944, German troops launched a massive counteroffensive. In the Battle of the Bulge, German armored divisions slashed 60 miles to the Franco-Belgian border before being defeated by General George Patton's Third Army. By January 1945 Soviet troops had captured Warsaw, and by February they were within 45 miles of Berlin.

The Yalta Conference

With victory in Europe at hand, Roosevelt, Churchill, and Stalin met in February 1945 at Yalta, on the Black Sea, to settle the shape of the postwar world. They concurred on the partition of Germany, but there the agreement stopped. Stalin wanted $20 billion in reparation payments from Germany, half of which would go to Russia. Churchill opposed him, rejecting any plan that would leave Germany financially prostrate after the war.

Eastern Europe was the most divisive issue at Yalta. Stalin had long insisted on Soviet control over the Baltic states (Estonia, Lithuania, and Latvia), as well as portions of Finland, Poland, and Romania. In October 1944 Stalin and Churchill met secretly in Moscow, where they agreed to divide Eastern Europe into British and Soviet spheres for the duration of the war. Consistent with these earlier demands, Stalin laid claim to eastern Poland at the Yalta Conference, reminding Churchill and Roosevelt that since he had not opposed their political decisions in Italy, he would not tolerate any interference in Eastern Europe. Under pressure from Roosevelt and Churchill, however, Stalin grudgingly agreed to hold free elections in Poland itself, promising that any new government formed there would include democratic elements. Yet as one of Roosevelt's chief military advisers warned the president, Stalin tacked so many amendments onto the Polish agreement that the Soviets "could stretch it all the way from Yalta to Washington without technically breaking it."

The remaining issues at Yalta proved less troublesome. Stalin pledged to enter the war against Japan within three months after Germany surrendered, and he renewed his promise to join the United Nations. Roosevelt considered both concessions to be important victories because he wanted Soviet help in defeating Japan and because he remained hopeful the United Nations could negotiate peaceful solutions to the disputes between the United States and the Soviet Union after the war.

Stalin, Roosevelt, and Churchill at their meeting at Yalta in February 1945 to discuss the state of the postwar world.

LANDINGS ON D-DAY
The Longest Day

FOR the Allies in World War II, the D-Day landing on June 6, 1944, was the long-planned, long-anticipated blow against Nazi Germany. Originally scheduled for 1942, it had been pushed back first to 1943 and finally to 1944. Although both the Soviet Union and impatient Americans had clamored for an earlier invasion, Prime Minister Winston Churchill of Great Britain, who remembered the difficulties of Dunkirk, counseled caution.

The cross-channel invasion was a risky proposition and an immense undertaking. During early 1944, the Allies moved thousands of aircraft, tanks, trucks, jeeps, and men into southeastern England, moving soldiers to joke that if the invasion was long postponed, England would tilt and sink into the Channel. Then there were the imponderables no amount of careful planning could predict: weather, visibility, the state of the Channel.

As much as possible General Dwight D. Eisenhower, who was the overall commander of the invasion, tried to deceive the Germans into believing that the invasion would take place at the Pas de Calais, around Boulogne, Calais, and Dunkirk. It appears that Hitler did believe that the Allies would strike there. Instead, Ike centered his attack further to the west, along the French coast between Cherbourg and Le Havre. Altogether, the Allies assaulted five beaches and dropped paratroopers and airborne infantry into three sites.

Further east, British paratroopers were given the task of securing the left flank by gaining control of the Orne River. American paratroopers were given the job of securing the right flank along the Merderet River. In between these two points, the Allies landed on five beaches: Sword (British), Juno (Canadian), Gold (British), Omaha (American), and Utah (American). All totaled, 2,876,000 soldiers, sailors, and airmen; 11,000 aircraft; and over 2000 vessels played a part in the invasion.

At several beaches, especially Utah, the Allies met little opposition. At others, notably Omaha, the story was much different and losses were heavy. More than 2000 Americans were killed or wounded securing Omaha beach on June 6. But by the end of that "longest day" the Allies had accomplished their goal. They were back in France and ready to move east toward Germany.

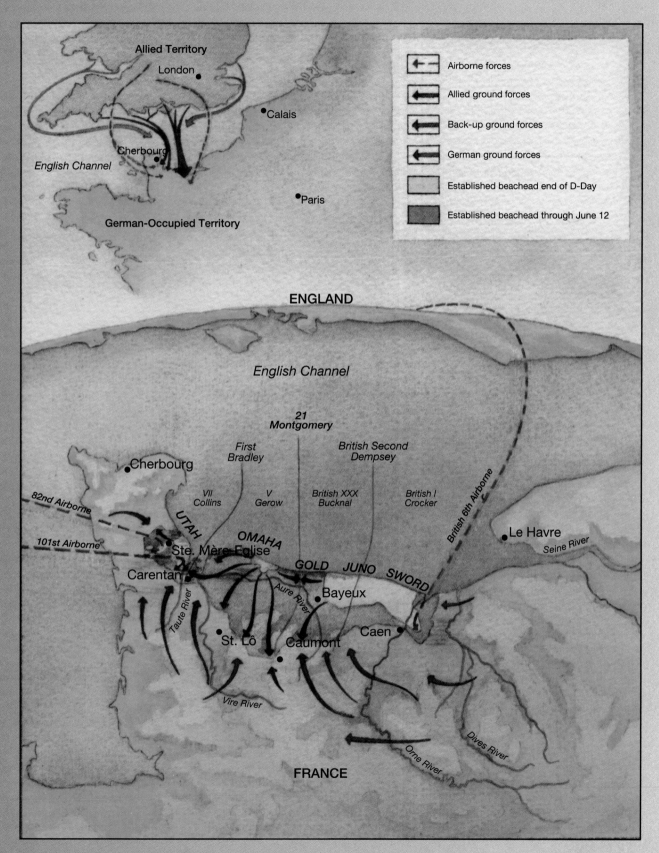

Airborne forces
Allied ground forces
Back-up ground forces
German ground forces
Established beachead end of D-Day
Established beachead through June 12

Allied Territory

London

Calais

Cherbourg

English Channel

German-Occupied Territory

Paris

ENGLAND

English Channel

21
Montgomery

First
Bradley

British Second
Dempsey

Cherbourg

82nd Airborne

VII
Collins

V
Gerow

British XXX
Bucknal

British I
Crocker

British 6th Airborne

Le Havre

Seine River

101st Airborne

UTAH

OMAHA

Ste. Mère-Eglise

GOLD   JUNO   SWORD

Carentan

Aure River

Bayeux

Taute River

Caen

St. Lô

Caumont

Vire River

Orne River

Dives River

FRANCE

Critics have denounced Roosevelt for his role at Yalta, insisting Stalin would have surrendered Eastern Europe had Roosevelt held firm. This argument seriously discounts Stalin's obsession with protecting his homeland from future attacks. The Soviet Union had paid a staggeringly high price for victory in World War II. When the war finally ended, the country had suffered approximately 18 million military and civilian deaths. More Soviets died at Stalingrad than the United States lost in all theaters of the war combined. Stalin's determination to maintain Soviet control of Eastern Europe was also bolstered by the fact that the Red Army occupied Eastern Europe in the spring of 1945. Stalin was not about to lose at the conference table what he had won on the battlefield.

Allied victories came rapidly after the Battle of the Bulge. On March 4, American troops reached the Rhine River, and in April they joined forces with the Soviet army 60 miles south of Berlin. After Roosevelt's death on April 12, however, Stalin immediately tested the new president, Harry S Truman. Stalin ordered the execution of democratic leaders in Eastern Europe and replaced them with Communist governments. Truman deplored Stalin's disregard for the Yalta agreements, but like Roosevelt he refused to fight the Soviets to save Eastern Europe. Instead, he followed General Eisenhower's advice about finishing off Germany. On April 22 Soviet troops reached Berlin and occupied the city after house-to-house fighting, and on April 30 Hitler committed suicide. Germany surrendered one week later. On May 8, 1945, the Allies celebrated V-E (Victory in Europe) Day.

THE WAR IN THE PACIFIC

On December 7, 1941, Japan had launched an offensive incredible in its scale. A thousand Japanese warships attacked an area comprising one-third of the earth's surface, including Guam, Hong Kong, Malaya, Midway Island, the Philippine Islands, and Wake Island. The offensive was a stunning success. Hong Kong was overrun in 18 days; Wake Island in two weeks; Singapore held out for two months. By May, the Japanese had also captured the islands of Borneo, Bali, Sumatra, and Timor. In addition, Japan had taken Rangoon, Burma's main port, and seized control of the rich tin, oil, and rubber resources of southeast Asia.

But by mid-summer of 1942, American forces had halted the Japanese advance. In May, a Japanese troop convoy was intercepted and destroyed by the U.S. Navy at Coral Sea, preventing a Japanese attack on Australia. In early June, at Midway Island in the Central Pacific, the Japanese launched an aircraft carrier offensive to cut American communications and isolate Hawaii to the east. In a three-day naval battle the Japanese lost three destroyers, a heavy cruiser, and four carriers. The Battle of Midway broke the back of Japan's navy.

Island Hopping

On August 7, 1942, the 1st Marine Division attacked Guadalcanal in the Solomon Islands; after six months of hard fighting they drove the Japanese troops into the sea, securing the Allied supply line to Australia. The victory also protected the Allies' eastern flank, enabling General Douglas MacArthur, commander of southwest Pacific forces, to seize the northern coast of nearby New Guinea in September 1943. Instead of assaulting Japanese strong points on the island, MacArthur leapfrogged up the coast. By capturing isolated positions, MacArthur cut Japanese supply lines and forced Japanese troops to abandon their fortifications. By July 1944 MacArthur's forces controlled all of New Guinea.

Meanwhile, Admiral Chester Nimitz's naval and marine forces in the Central Pacific were "island hopping" toward Japan, capturing important positions, building airstrips, and then moving on to the next island. After securing the Gilbert Islands and the Marshall Islands, Nimitz attacked Saipan, Tinian, and Guam, from which the Americans could strike the main Japanese islands with B-29 bombers. Determined to protect their homeland against air raids, Japanese commanders resolved to fight to the last man. In the battle for Saipan, 30,000 of the island's 32,000 Japan-

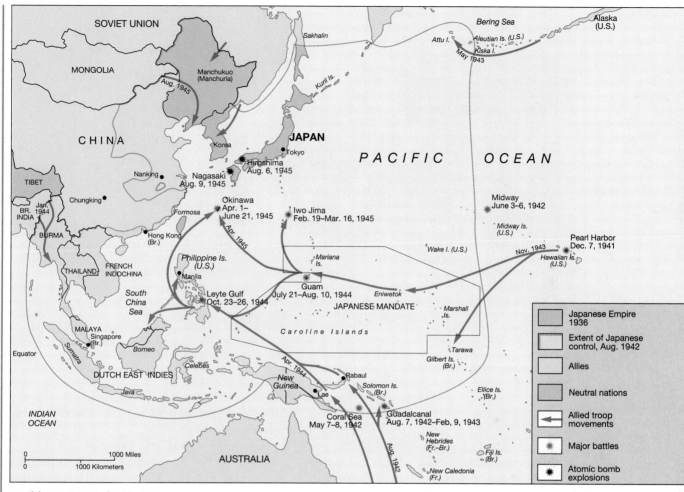

World War II, Pacific Theater

ese defenders died, and 6000 of the island's 12,000 Japanese civilians committed suicide rather than surrender. Tinian and Guam fell to the Americans in early August, and B-29s began regular bombing raids over Japan in November 1944.

On October 21, 1944, General MacArthur invaded the Philippines. That same month the navy won a stunning victory at the Battle of Leyte Gulf, where the Japanese lost virtually their entire remaining battle fleet. American submarines now controlled Pacific shipping lanes, sealing the Japanese Islands off from military and food supplies. In January, Allied forces invaded Luzon, the main island of the Philippines, and Allied troops claimed victory five months later.

While MacArthur was reclaiming the Philippines, the American island-hopping strategy was entering its final phase. By early March the island of Iwo Jima fell to U.S. marines. Its capture enabled fighter planes to link up with B–29s heading out of Saipan, providing escorts for their raids on Japan. On April 1, 1945, American troops attacked Okinawa, 350 miles southwest of Japan. Japanese resistance was fierce. Kamikaze attacks (suicide flights by Japanese pilots) rose dramatically. Okinawa fell in June, after 70,000 Japanese soldiers had died defending it. In the meantime, B-29s firebombed Japan, killing more than 330,000 civilians and cutting deeply into war production.

Confronted with certain defeat, many moderate leaders in Japan wanted to avoid an

On October 21, 1944, General Douglas MacArthur, commander of the Southeast Pacific forces, splashed ashore in the Philippines with the 96th division.

invasion, but strong factions within the military vowed to keep fighting. In an effort to save Japan, the Emperor switched his support to the peace party in February 1945. He then sent out peace feelers to Stalin, who in turn conveyed them to Truman at the Potsdam Conference in July 1945.

The Dawn of The Atomic Age

Few presidents have been asked to conduct diplomacy with less preparation than Harry S Truman. He had risen to power as a loyal machine politician in Kansas City. Both as vice president and former senator from Missouri he knew next to nothing about foreign affairs, especially since Roosevelt kept him in the dark, neither seeking his counsel nor confiding in him. When Roosevelt's death elevated him to the White House, Truman told reporters: "I felt like the moon, the stars, and all planets had fallen on me." Yet Truman brought certain assets to the challenge. A man who possessed the courage of his convictions, he fully intended to be a

strong president and to make decisions resolutely.

Truman's first test came at Potsdam, a suburb of Berlin, where the Allied leaders convened in July 1945 for their last wartime meeting. Though new to the job, Truman had been in office long enough to believe Roosevelt had been too soft on Stalin, whom he viewed as a liar and a bully. Yet like his predecessor Truman did not wish to risk a showdown over Eastern Europe, largely because his military advisers insisted the United States still needed the Soviet Union's help against Japan. The Potsdam Declaration of July 26 demanded immediate "unconditional surrender," warning that any other action would lead to "prompt and utter destruction."

During the Potsdam negotiations, Truman learned that American scientists had successfully tested the first atomic bomb. Hoping to impress Stalin, Truman told him in a conversation one evening the United States now possessed a new weapon of awesome power. Stalin blithely replied he trusted the United States would make good use of it against Japan.

The Manhattan Project

In 1939, Albert Einstein wrote a letter to President Roosevelt, warning him that the Nazis might be able to build a weapon with incredible destructive potential: an atomic bomb. The idea seemed impossible, and at first scientists worked on the project largely on their own. Then on December 2, 1942, Enrico Fermi, an Italian refugee, demonstrated that it was possible to produce a nuclear chain reaction. In an old squash court beneath the University of Chicago's football field, he built the world's first nuclear reactor. Fermi's reactor produced the first self-sustained, controlled nuclear chain reaction.

To ensure that the United States developed a bomb before Nazi Germany, the federal government started the Manhattan Project, a secret $2-billion program with 120,000 employees. At Los Alamos, New Mexico; Oak Ridge, Tennessee; and Hanford, Washington, the world's top physicists—including many Jewish refugees from Germany—worked in secrecy to develop the new weapon.

At dawn on July 16, 1945, in the New Mexico desert near Alamogordo, the Manhattan Project's scientists watched the first atomic bomb explode. There was a blinding flash of pink, blue, red, and yellow light. The heat generated by the bomb at that instant was ten thousand times hotter than the sun. The explosion broke windows 125 miles away. A military observer called the explosion "unprecedented, magnificent, beautiful, stupendous and terrifying."

President Harry S Truman had never heard of the Manhattan Project until he was sworn in. It was during the Potsdam negotiations that he learned that American scientists had tested the first atomic bomb. Many scientists who worked on the Manhattan Project, as well as several key political figures, pleaded with Truman not to use the bomb because they foresaw its implications for a postwar arms race with the Soviet Union. Others, arguing from a moral position, wanted the United States to warn the Japanese about the bomb's terrifying power, giving them a chance to surrender. Truman rejected these arguments and approved the use of the new weapon.

Hiroshima and Nagasaki

On the morning of August 6, 1945, the *Enola Gay,* a B-29 Superfortress, took off from a tiny Pacific atoll bound for Hiroshima, Japan's eighth-largest city. At 8:15 A.M., the plane released an atomic bomb nicknamed "Little Boy." The explosion when it hit began as a pinpoint of light that grew into a fireball half a mile across. A cloud of smoke rose upward, gradually assuming the shape of a giant mushroom 50,000 feet high.

On the ground, 4.4 square miles of central Hiroshima was obliterated. Buildings melted, steel bridges burned, the city's river caught fire. Peoples' shadows were photographed onto walls and sidewalks. Black rain containing radioactive dust fell on the city, leaving red splotches on the bodies it touched. Between 80,000 and 140,000 people were killed or fatally wounded.

Three days later, on August 9, another B-29, the *Bock's Car,* dropped a second bomb, this time on the city of Nagasaki. About 35,000 people were killed. The following day Japan sued for peace. On September 2, 1945, Japanese officials surrendered unconditionally to General Douglas MacArthur aboard the battleship U.S.S. *Missouri* in Tokyo Bay. World War II was over.

President Truman's decision to order the atomic bombings has been the subject of intense historical debate. Truman's defenders argue that the bombs ended the war quickly, avoiding the necessity of a costly invasion and the probable loss of tens of thousands of Americans lives and hundreds of thousands of Japanese lives. According to some intelligence estimates, an invasion might have cost 268,000 American casualties, with Japanese costs several times that figure.

Truman's defenders also argue that Hiroshima and Nagasaki were legitimate targets with both military bases and war industry, and their civilian populations had been showered with leaflets warning them to evacuate. Finally, they argue that two bombs were ultimately necessary to end the war. They note that even after the atomic bomb had fallen on Hiroshima, the Japanese war minister implored the nation's Supreme Council "for one

THE HUMAN TOLL OF COMBAT

HIROSHIMA AND NAGASAKI

ON July 16, 1945, the Atomic Age became reality. The place was Alamogordo Air Force Base in the southern desert region of New Mexico. The occasion was the first successful detonation of an atomic bomb. Observers witnessed "a blinding flash that lighted the entire northwestern sky." Next came "a huge billow of smoke," followed by "an enormous ball of what appeared to be fire and closely resembled a rising sun." Dr. J. Robert Oppenheimer, the chief scientist in charge of the team that designed the weapon, was so astonished by the scale of the blast that he recalled the Hindu quotation: "I am become death, shatterer of worlds."

Back in 1939 two brilliant scientists, Albert Einstein and Enrico Fermi, both of whom had fled fascism and anti-Semitism in Europe, warned President Roosevelt that German nuclear physicists under Adolf Hitler's control might well be trying to develop such a bomb. Roosevelt realized the implications, and he set in motion what became the "Manhattan Project," a top-secret effort involving civilian scientists and army engineers to apply the theory of nuclear fission to a bomb. Hitler's scientists never succeeded, but in July 1945, with the war over in Europe, the United States now had a weapon with the potential to threaten civilization itself. The question was whether the bomb would be used against Japan, the last of the Axis powers still at war.

The Japanese were a formidable foe. Since 1942 U.S. troops had been rolling back their empire, all the way to the shore of Japan and

69680A.C.

the Chinese mainland by the summer of 1945. The casualty toll was horrendous. Japanese soldiers fought with a sense of personal honor that struck Americans as fanatical. They would not surrender when beaten, but would fight to their death. To do otherwise would be to disgrace themselves, their families, and their emperor, whom they considered a god.

At first, in defending Pacific islands such as Guadalcanal (August 1942–February 1943), Japanese soldiers mounted suicidal *banzai* charges. They ran forward in waves at U.S. troops, inflicting massive damage before being shot down. Later, on islands such as Iwo Jima (February–March 1945), they used elaborate networks of underground bunkers to wreak havoc, so effectively that U.S. casualties started to reach the 50 percent range. By 1945 the Japanese were unleashing kamikaze raids in

which pilots sacrificed themselves for the glory of the empire by dive-bombing their planes into U.S. naval vessels. In the bloody battle of Okinawa (April–June 1945), kamikaze pilots flew some 2800 planes into American ships, inflicting 10,000 casualties and sinking 28 vessels and damaging 325 others.

American soldiers, as well as the U.S. public at large, neither understood nor respected Japanese martial values. Explained a Marine Corps general, to shoot "a Jap . . . was like killing a rattlesnake." A Guadalcanal veteran stated that the Japanese soldier "possessed considerable cleverness; he could not be classified as an intellectual. He was more of an animal. He could live on a handful of rice." Almost universally, Americans used terms of racial derision to describe an enemy that had not only mounted the "sneak attack" on Pearl Harbor but now refused to surrender when beaten.

Such attitudes affected the development of a comprehensive U.S. war plan, known as Operation DOWNFALL, that was constructed on the assumption that only a full-scale invasion of Japan would bring total victory in the Pacific. The first phase of the plan, called Operation OLYMPIC, involved an assault on Kyushu, the southernmost island of Japan, to begin in November 1945. The Joint Chiefs of Staff presented OLYMPIC to President Truman in June and stated that American casualties could reach 268,000 (out of 767,000 participants). The Japanese still had 2.3 million soldiers ready to fight and another 4 million citizens trained in the use of arms. If they battled to the death, as they had so far, American casualties, the Joint Chiefs predicted, would exceed 1 million by the time U.S. troops conquered the main island of Honshu in 1946 or 1947.

Because of the bloody price everyone expected to pay, high-ranking American officials were anxious to involve Russia—attacking through Manchuria and Korea—in the final crushing of Japan. At Yalta in February 1945 President Roosevelt secured pledges of Soviet assistance. Then at Potsdam in July, President Truman seemed much less interested. Having just learned of the test results in New Mexico, Truman told Joseph Stalin of "a new weapon of unusual destructive force." Stalin, however, would not be cast aside. He still wanted the territory (the lower half of Sakhalin Island, the Kurile Islands, and certain considerations in Manchuria) promised at Yalta. The Soviet leader thus "hoped" the United States "would make good use" of the weapon "against the Japanese," but the Russians would not be denied their part in the invasion or the promised territory.

Meanwhile, a committee of American scientists and military officers were working at selecting possible targets. Some advocated a demonstration at a preannounced neutral site as a way of cajoling the Japanese into surrender, but others feared what might happen should the bomb prove to be a dud—all leverage would then be lost. Finally, with great reluctance, these advisers agreed that there was "no acceptable alternative to direct military use" of the bomb.

In public, Truman never admitted to any qualms about the decision to employ the new weapon, but in private, he wondered how "we as the leader of the world for common welfare" could drop "this terrible bomb." Still, he accepted the responsibility for many reasons. He hoped to save thousands of American lives by avoiding a full invasion of Japan against soldiers who fought like "savages, ruthless, merciless, and fanatic." Likely, too, Truman and his advisers feared the expansionism of the Communist regime of Joseph Stalin. Using the bomb might prove a great point of leverage in dealing with the Soviets in the days ahead.

While Truman and others considered the alternatives, a select unit of the Army Air Force, flying B-29s, made a series of practice bomb runs over Japan. Since these planes did not attack, as they had so often before in firebombing cities like Tokyo, no one paid much attention. Then on August 6, 1945, at a few minutes past 8:00 A.M., three B-29s at 31,600 feet of altitude appeared over Hiroshima. Colonel Paul Tibbets, piloting the lead bomber, *Enola Gay*, turned the controls over to Major Thomas Ferebee, the bombardier officer, who completed the run. It took 45 seconds, as *Enola Gay* banked away quickly, for the atomic bomb to reach the ground. As the fireball erupted toward the sky, nearly 100,000 people, including thousands of soldiers at the headquarters of Japan's Second General Army just 2000 yards from ground zero, died instantly. Three days later, in the absence of a firm willingness of the Japanese to surrender, a second bomb flattened Nagasaki and killed about 35,000 people. Thousands more perished later from serious burns, radiation poisoning, and other devastating effects of the two bombings.

The dropping of the atomic bombs gave peace advocates in Japan the muscle they needed to overcome the militarists. When on August 10 Emperor Hirohito agreed to seek peace terms, the war faction reluctantly acceded, but only after General Anami Korechika, the war minister, upheld his honor on August 14 by committing suicide. He could not bear hearing Hirohito's proclamation of surrender.

When American troops training for Operation OLYMPIC heard about the surrender, they rejoiced. "We would not be obliged to run up the beaches near Tokyo assault-firing while being mortared and shelled," wrote one soldier. "We are going to live. We are going to grow up to adulthood after all." They did not realize how different the world would be with nuclear weapons in the hands of the two superpowers to emerge from World War II. For a moment, however, General Douglas MacArthur understood. After the Japanese surrender ceremony on September 2, 1945, he stated: "We have had our last chance. If we do not devise some greater and more equitable system, Armageddon will be at our door."

last great battle on Japanese soil—as demanded by the national honor. . . . Would it not be wondrous for this whole nation to be destroyed like a beautiful flower."

Truman's critics argue that the war might have ended even without the atomic bombings. They maintain that the Japanese economy would have been strangled by a continued naval blockade and forced to surrender by conventional firebombing. The revisionists also contend that the president had options apart from using the bombs. They believe that it might have been possible to induce a Japanese surrender by a demonstration of the atomic bomb's power or by providing a more specific warning of the damage it could produce or by guaranteeing the Emperor's position in postwar Japan.

The revisionists also believe that estimates of potential American casualties were grossly inflated after the war to justify the bombing. And finally, they argue that the bomb might have been dropped mainly to justify its cost or to scare the Soviet Union. The Soviet Union

entered the Japanese war August 8, and some revisionists charge that the bombings were designed to end the war before the Red army could occupy northern China.

CONCLUSION

Fifty years after the United States brought World War II to an end by dropping two atomic bombs on Japan, a major public controversy erupted over plans to exhibit the fuselage of the *Enola Gay* at the Smithsonian Institution's Air and Space Museum. As originally conceived, the exhibit, titled "The Last Act: The Atomic Bomb and the End of World War II," was designed to provoke debate about the decision to drop atomic bombs. Museum visitors would be encouraged to reflect on the morality of the bombing and to ask whether the bombs were necessary to end the war.

The proposal generated a firestorm of controversy. The part of the script that pro-

The bomb dropped on Hiroshima on August 6, 1945, marked the first use of a nuclear weapon in warfare. The bomb, carrying a destructive force equal to 20,000 tons of TNT, obliterated nearly 60 percent of the city.

THE ROAD TO WAR
WORLD WAR II

1939	Germany invades Poland	World War II begins.
	Neutrality Act of 1939	Allows the sale of arms to belligerents.
1940	Arms sales to Britain	The U.S. agrees to sell Britain surplus and outmoded arms.
	Destroyers for bases	The U.S. gives 50 American destroyers to Britain in exchange for British bases in the Western Hemisphere.
	Embargo imposed	President Roosevelt imposes an embargo on the export of scrap steel and iron to Japan.
	Draft instituted	The military draft goes into effect.
	"Arsenal of Democracy"	President Roosevelt announces that the U.S. will be the "arsenal of democracy."
1941	Lend-Lease	President Roosevelt signs the Lend-Lease Act empowering the president to lend war materiel to countries whose freedom is vital to U.S. interests.
	Assets frozen	President Roosevelt freezes assets of Germany, Italy, and Japan in the United States and closes German and Italian consulates.
	Pearl Harbor attacked	Japanese forces attack the naval base at Pearl Harbor, Hawaii, killing 2403 Americans, sinking or disabling 19 ships, and destroying some 150 planes.
	Declaration of war	Declaring December 7 "a date that shall live in infamy," President Roosevelt asks Congress to declare war against Japan. Germany declares war on the United States on December 11, 1941.

duced the most opposition stated: "For most Americans, this . . . was a war of vengeance. For most Japanese it was a war to defend their unique culture against Western imperialism." Another controversial section addressed the question: "Would the bomb have been dropped on the Germans?" The answer began "Some have argued that the United States would never have dropped the bomb on the Germans, because Americans were more reluctant to bomb 'white people' than Asians."

Veterans groups considered the proposed exhibit too sympathetic to the Japanese, that it portrayed them as victims of racist Americans hell-bent on revenge for Pearl Harbor. They called the exhibit an insult to the U.S. soldiers who fought and died during the war and com-

plained that it paid excessive attention to Japanese casualties and suffering and insufficient attention to Japanese aggression and atrocities. The U.S. Senate unanimously passed a resolution calling a revised version of the exhibit "unbalanced and offensive" and reminding the museum of "its obligation to portray history in the proper context of its time."

In the end, the Smithsonian decided to scale back the exhibit, displaying the *Enola Gay's* fuselage along with a small plaque. In announcing the decision, a Smithsonian official explained, "In this important anniversary year, veterans and their families were expecting, and rightly so, that the nation would honor and commemorate their valor and sacrifice. They were not looking for analysis and, frankly, we

CHRONOLOGY OF KEY EVENTS

1921	Washington Naval Conference places limits on construction of large warships
1922	Mussolini seizes power in Italy
1924	Dawes Plan to help Germany pay war reparations
1928	Kellogg-Briand Pact renounces war "as an instrument of national policy"; Clark Memorandum states that the United States does not have a right to intervene militarily in the affairs of Latin American nations
1931	Japan invades Manchuria
1932	Stimson Doctrine declares that the United States would not recognize Japanese territorial gains in China
1933	Adolf Hitler is appointed chancellor of Germany; Roosevelt announces Good Neighbor Policy, withdraws marines from Haiti, and nullifies Platt Amendment
1935	Neutrality Act allows president to bar arms sales to nations at war (is extended in 1936 to bar loans to belligerents and in 1937 to bar shipments of nonmilitary goods)
1936	German troops reoccupy the Rhineland; Spanish Civil War begins
1937	Japan invades China
1938	Germany annexes Austria; Munich Pact hands over a third of Czechoslovakia to Nazi Germany
1939	Soviet Union and Germany sign a nonaggression pact; World War II begins following Germany's invasion of Poland
1940	United States transfers 50 destroyers to Britain in exchange for bases in Newfoundland and the Caribbean; United States institutes first peacetime military draft; Roosevelt is elected to third term

1941	Lend-Lease Act allows United States to lend war materials to Britain; Roosevelt issues order prohibiting discrimination in defense industries; Germany invades USSR; United States sets embargo on scrap metal, oil, and fuel to Japan; Japan attacks Pearl Harbor, killing over 2400 U.S. soldiers and sailors; United States enters World War II
1942	Congress creates the Office of Price Administration to control prices and ration scarce goods; President Roosevelt authorizes internment of 112,000 West Coast Japanese Americans; Philippine Islands surrender to Japan; U.S. Navy wins a major victory at Midway Island in the central Pacific; British and U.S. forces land in French North Africa
1943	British and U.S. forces defeat Axis forces in North Africa; U.S. marines secure control of Guadalcanal in the Solomon Islands; Soviets halt German drive into Soviet Union; Allies invade Italy; Mussolini is overthrown and new Italian government surrenders to Allies
1943– 1944	U.S. marines and navy seize islands of Tarawa, Kwajelin, Wake, and Guam in central Pacific and New Guinea in South Pacific
1944	U.S. Supreme Court upholds legality of the forced relocation of Japanese Americans; D-Day—Allies launch amphibious invasion of northern France; U.S. forces begin an invasion of Philippine Islands and aerial attacks on Japan; Bretton Woods conference draws up plans for International Monetary Fund and International Bank to finance postwar economic recovery; Dumbarton Oaks conference makes plans for creation of United

(continued)

	Nations; German troops launch counteroffensive in the Ardennes Forest along Belgium-Luxembourg border		United Nations; Roosevelt dies; Harry S Truman becomes thirty-third president; Germany surrenders; Potsdam conference plans postwar settlement in Europe and final attack on Japan; United States drops atomic bombs on Hiroshima and Nagasaki; Japan surrenders
1945	At Yalta, Roosevelt, Churchill, and Stalin discuss Soviet entry into the war against Japan, the postwar division of Europe, and plans for the		

did not give enough thought to the intense feelings such an analysis would evoke."

World War II cost America one million casualties and over 300,000 deaths. In both domestic and foreign affairs, its consequences were far-reaching. It had an immediate and spectacular impact on the economy by ending the Great Depression. Fueled by government contracts, the economy expanded dramatically, soaring to full employment and astounding the world with its productivity. The war accelerated corporate mergers and the trend toward large-scale agriculture. Labor unions also grew during the war as the government adopted pro-union policies, continuing the New Deal's sympathetic treatment of organized labor.

Presidential power expanded enormously during World War II, anticipating the rise of what postwar critics termed the "imperial presidency." The Democrats reaped a political windfall from the war. Roosevelt rode the wartime emergency to unprecedented third and fourth terms, preserving the New Deal coalition so effectively that many people wondered if the Republicans would ever elect another president. Despite such victories, however, the reform spirit had waned, a victim, it seemed, of the country's unmistakable swing to the right in politics.

The war's social effects varied from group to group. For most people, it had a disruptive influence—separated families, overcrowded housing, and a shortage of consumer goods. The war also accelerated the movement from the countryside to the cities, and it challenged gender and racial roles, opening new opportunities for women and minority groups. Yet sexual and racial barriers remained, highlighting reforms left unfinished at home, even as American troops fought totalitarian forces abroad.

In foreign policy, the many disagreements between the Allies on military strategy and peace terms foreshadowed the major conflicts that dominated the postwar era. Gone forever was the notion of fortress America, isolated and removed from world affairs. In its place stood a strong internationalist state, determined to exercise power on a global scale. Second only to the victory the Allies won for freedom, the war's most important legacy was the end of isolation and the rise of America's commitment to international security.

SUGGESTIONS FOR FURTHER READING

Michael C. C. Adams, *The Best War Ever* (1994). Offers a succinct interpretation of the impact of World War II on American troops and the homefront.

P. M. H. Bell, *The Origins of the Second World War in Europe*, 2d ed. (1989). Examines the conflict's causes.

John Ellis, *Brute Force: Allied Strategy and Tactics in the Second World War* (1990). Discusses military strategy.

Akira Iriye, *The Origins of the Second World War in Asia and the Pacific* (1987). Analyzes the roots of war with Japan.

Geoffrey Perrett, *There's a War to Be Won* (1991). Investigates the combat experience.

William O'Neill, *A Democracy at War: America's Fight at Home and Abroad in World War II* (1993). Presents an excellent overview of American involvement in the conflict.

Allen M. Winkler, *Home Front U.S.A.* (1986). Explores the impact of the conflict on American society.

Overviews and Surveys

Selig Adler, *The Uncertain Giant: American Foreign Policy Between the Wars* (1969); Albert R. Buchanan, *The United States and World War II*, 2 vols. (1964); Sean Dennis Cashman, *America, Roosevelt, and World War II* (1989); Martha Hoyle, *A World in Flames: A History of World War II* (1970); Robert Leckie, *The Wars of America*, rev. ed., 2 vols. (1981); Gerald D. Nash, *The Crucial Era: The Great Depression and World War II*, 2d ed. (1992); Geoffrey Perret, *Days of Sadness, Years of Triumph, 1939–1945* (1973); Studs Terkel, ed., *"The Good War": An Oral History of World War Two* (1984); Russell F. Weigley, *The American Way of War: A History of United States Military Strategy and Policy* (1973); Gordon Wright, *The Ordeal of Total War, 1939–1945* (1968).

Diplomacy Between the Wars

Charles Chatfield, *For Peace and Justice: Pacifism in America, 1914–1941* (1971); Charles DeBenedetti, *Origins of the Modern American Peace Movement, 1915–1929* (1978); Warren Cohen, *Empire without Tears: American Foreign Relations, 1921–1933* (1987); Frank Costigliola, *Awkward Dominion: American Political, Economic, and Cultural Relations with Europe* (1984); Michael Dunne, *The United States and the World Court, 1920–1935* (1988); Robert H. Ferrell, *Peace in Their Time: Men Who Led Us In and Out of War, 1914–1945* (1953); Irwin F. Gellman, *Good Neighbor Diplomacy* (1979); Richard M. Ketchum, *The Borrowed Years, 1938–1941* (1989); Manfred Jonas, *Isolationism in America, 1935–1941* (1966); Joan Hoff-Wilson, *American Business and Foreign Policy, 1920–1933* (1971); John E. Wiltz, *In Search of Peace: The Senate Munitions Inquiry* (1963); Bryce Wood, *Making of the Good Neighbor Policy* (1961).

The Coming of World War II

Thomas A. Bailey and Paul B. Ryan, *Hitler vs. Roosevelt: The Undeclared Naval War* (1979); Robert J. Butow, *Tojo and the Coming of the War* (1961); Warren I. Cohen, *America's Response to China*, 3d ed. (1990); Wayne S. Cole, *America First: The Battle Against Intervention, 1940–1941* (1953), and *Roosevelt and the Isolationists* (1983); James V. Compton, *The Swastika and the Eagle: Hitler, the United States, and the Origins of World War II* (1967); Robert Dallek, *Franklin D. Roosevelt and American Foreign Policy, 1932–1945* (1979); Robert A. Divine, *Illusion of Neutrality* (1962), and *Second Chance: The Triumph of Internationalism During World War II* (1967); Herbert Feis, *The Road to Pearl Harbor* (1950); Robert Edwin Herzstein, *Roosevelt & Hitler: Prelude to War* (1989); Akira Iriye, *After Imperialism: The Search for a New Order in the Far East, 1921–1931* (1965); Warren F. Kimball, *The Most Unsordid Act: Lend-Lease, 1939–1941* (1982); Joseph P. Lash, *Roosevelt and Churchill, 1939–1941* (1976); Marvin V. Melosi, *The Shadow of Pearl Harbor: Political Controversy over the Surprise Attack* (1977); Gordon W. Prange, *At Dawn We Slept: The Untold Story of Pearl Harbor* (1981); David Reynolds, *The Creation of the Anglo-American Alliance: 1937–41* (1982); Bruce Russet, *No Clear and Present Danger: A Skeptical View of the United States Entry into World War II* (1972); Michael Schaller, *The U.S. Crusade in China 1938–1945* (1979); John E. Wiltz, *From Isolation to War: 1931–1941* (1968); Roberta Wohlstetter, *Pearl Harbor: Warning and Decision* (1962).

America Mobilizes for War

John Morton Blum, *V Was for Victory: Politics and American Culture During World War II* (1976); David Brinkley, *Washington Goes to War* (1988); Frank W. Fox, *Madison Avenue Goes to War* (1975); William K. Klingaman, *1941: Our Lives in a World on the Edge* (1988); Paul A. C. Koistinen, *The Hammer and the Sword: Labor, the Military, and Industrial Mobilization, 1920–1945* (1979); Clayton Koppes and Gregory Black, *Hollywood Goes to War: How Politics, Profits, and Propaganda Shaped World War II Movies* (1987); Nelson Lichtenstein, *Labor's War at Home: The CIO in World War II* (1982); Richard Lingeman, *Don't You Know There's a War On? The American Home Front, 1941–1945* (1970); Richard Polenberg, *The War and Society: The United States, 1941–1945* (1972); David R. Segal, *Recruiting for Uncle Sam: Citizenship and Military Manpower Policy* (1989); Harold G. Vatter, *The U.S. Economy in World War II* (1985); Gerald T. White, *Billions for Defense: Government Financing by the Defense Plant Corporation During World War II* (1980).

Social Changes During the War

Alison R. Bernstein, *American Indians and World War II* (1991); Karen Anderson, *Wartime Women: Sex Roles, Family Relations, and the Status of Women During World War II* (1981); Allan Berube, *Coming Out*

Under Fire: The History of Gay Men and Women in World War Two (1990); A. Russell Buchanan, *Black Americans in World War II* (1977); D'Ann Campbell, *Women at War with America: Private Lives in a Patriotic Era* (1984); Dominic J. Capeci, Jr., *Race Relations in Wartime Detroit* (1984); John Costello, *Virtue Under Fire: How World War II Changed Our Social and Sexual Attitudes* (1985); Richard M. Dalfiume, *Desegregation of the U.S. Armed Forces: Fighting on Two Fronts, 1939–1953* (1969); Roger Daniels, *Concentration Camps USA: Japanese Americans and World War* (1971), and *Prisoners Without Trial: Japanese Americans in World War II* (1993); Richard Drinnon, *Keeper of Concentration Camps: Dillon S. Myer and American Racism* (1987); Charity Adams Earley, *One Woman's Army: A Black Officer Remembers the WAC* (1989); Audrie Girdner and Alme Loftig, *The Great Betrayal: The Evacuation of the Japanese-Americans During World War II* (1969); Sherna Berger Gluck, *Rosie the Riveter Revisited: Women, the War, and Social Change* (1987); Anne Bosanko Green, *One Woman's War: Letters Home from the Women's Army Corps, 1944–1946* (1989); Chester W. Gregory, *Women in Defense Work During World War II: An Analysis of the Labor Problem and Women's Rights* (1974); Susan M. Hartmann, *The Home Front and Beyond: American Women in the 1940s* (1982); Peter H. Irons, *Justice at War: The Story of the Japanese American Internment Cases* (1983); George Lipsitz, *Rainbow at Midnight: Labor and Culture in the 1940s* (1989); Deborah E. Lipstadt, *Beyond Belief: The American Press and the Coming of the Holocaust* (1993); Mauricio Mazón, *The Zoot-Suit Riots: The Psychology of Symbolic Annihilation* (1984); August Meier and Elliot Rudwick, *CORE, 1942–1968* (1973); Gunnar Myrdal, *An American Dilemma* (1944); Robert Shogan and Thomas Craig, *The Detroit Race Riot: A Study in Violence* (1964); William M. Tuttle, Jr., *"Daddy's Gone to War": The Second World War in the Lives of America's Children* (1993); Neil Wynn, *The Afro-American and the Second World War* (1976).

The War in Europe

James MacGregor Burns, *Roosevelt: Soldier of Freedom* (1970); Diane Shaver Clemens, *Yalta* (1970); Michael D. Doubler, *Closing with the Enemy: How GIs Fought the War in Europe* (1994); Kent Roberts Greenfield, *American Strategy in World War II: A Reconsideration* (1963); Eric Larabee, *Commander in Chief: Franklin Delano Roosevelt, His Lieutenants, and Their War* (1987); Ronald Schaffer, *Wings of Judgment: American Bombing in World War II* (1985); Michael Sherry, *The Rise of American Air Power* (1987); Bradley F. Smith, *The Shadow Warriors: O.S.S. and the Origins of the C.I.A.* (1983); Gaddis Smith, *American Diplomacy During the Second World War, 1941–1945* (1965); John Snell, *Illusion and Necessity: The Diplomacy of Global War, 1939–1945* (1963); Mark A. Stoler, *The Politics of the Second Front: American Military Planning and Diplomacy in Coalition Warfare, 1941–1943* (1977).

The War in the Pacific

John Costello, *The Pacific War* (1981); John W. Dower, *War Without Mercy: Race and Power in the Pacific War* (1986); Roger Hilsman, *American Guerrilla: My War Behind Japanese Lines* (1990); Akira Iriye, *Power and Culture: The Japanese-American War* (1981); Gordon W. Prange, *Miracle at Midway* (1982); Ronald H. Spector, *Eagle Against the Sun: The American War with Japan* (1985).

The Dawn of the Atomic Age

Gar Alperovitz, *Atomic Diplomacy: Hiroshima and Potsdam*, rev. ed. (1985); Robert Butow, *Japan's Decision to Surrender* (1954); Herbert Feis, *The Atomic Bomb and the End of World War II* (1966); Gregg Herkin, *The Winning Weapon: The Atomic Bomb in the Cold War: 1945–1950* (1980); Robert Jungk, *Brighter than a Thousand Suns: A Personal History of the Atomic Scientists* (1958); Dan Kurzman, *Day of the Bomb: Countdown to Hiroshima* (1986); Martin J. Sherwin, *A World Destroyed: The Atomic Bomb and the Grand Alliance* (1975).

Biographies

Saul Alinsky, *John L. Lewis* (1949); Mark S. Foster, *Henry J. Kaiser: Builder in the Modern American West* (1989); Warren F. Kimball, *The Juggler: Franklin Roosevelt as Wartime Statesman* (1991); Michael Schaller, *Douglas MacArthur: The Far Eastern General* (1989); Barbara Tuchman, *Stilwell and the American Experience in China, 1911–45* (1971).

CHAPTER **26**
WAGING PEACE AND WAR

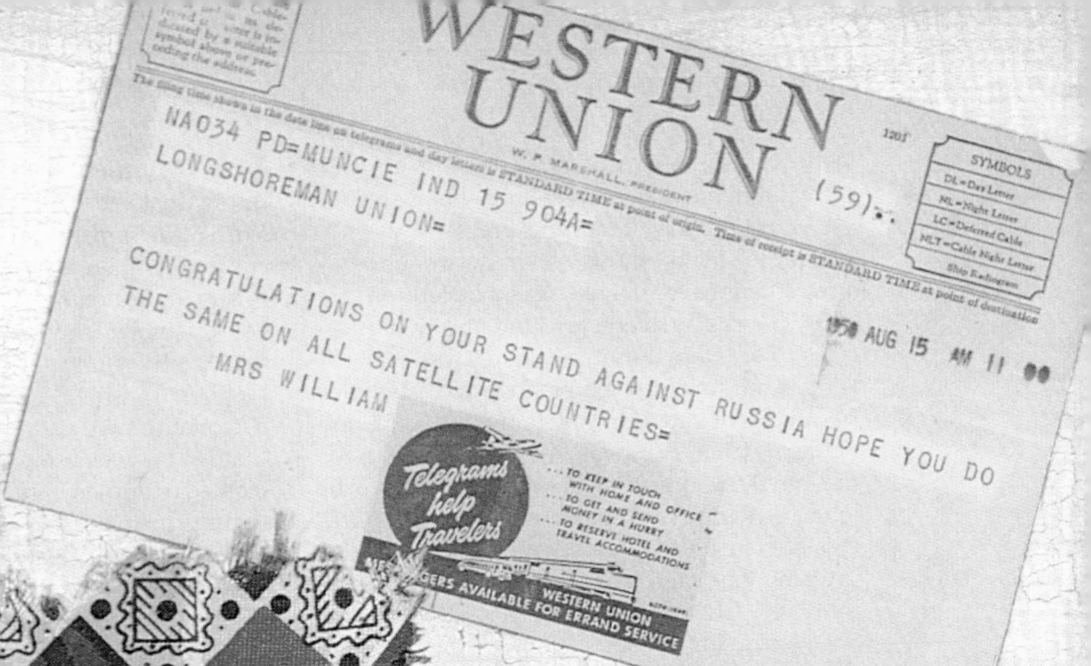

COMMUNIST PARTY ORGANIZATION U.S.A-FEB. 9, 1950

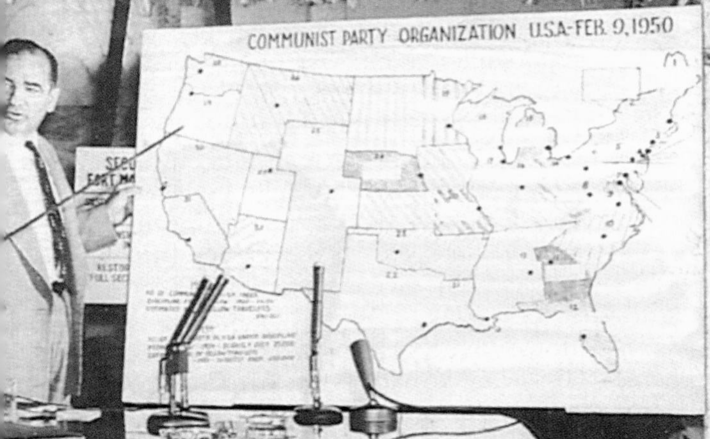

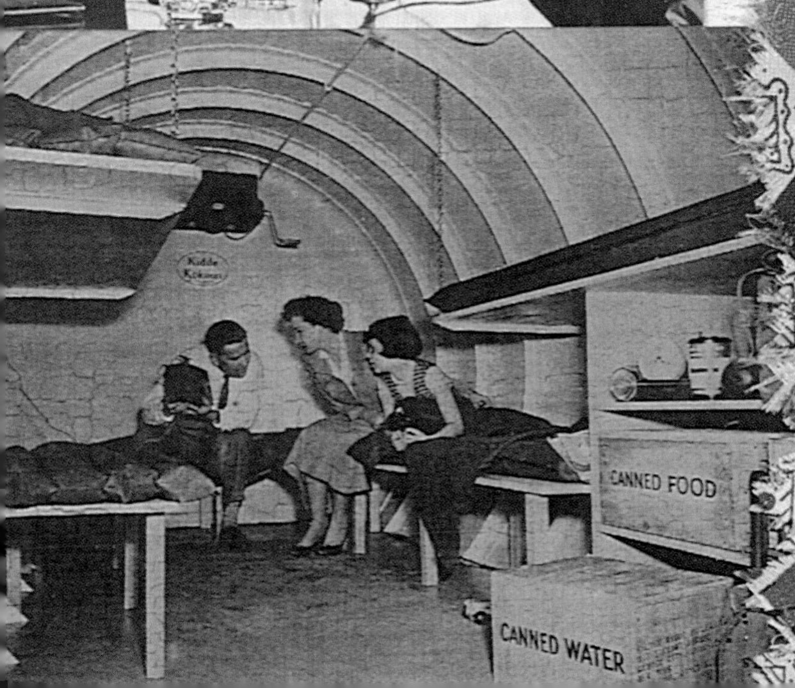

CONTAINING THE RUSSIAN BEAR
Origins of the Cold War
A World Divided
Tough Talk
The Truman Doctrine
The Marshall Plan: "Saving Western Europe"

THE CONTAINMENT POLICY
Berlin Test
Troubling Times
The Korean War

THE COLD WAR AT HOME
Adjusting to Peace
Confronting the Demands of Labor
Failure of the Fair Deal
Searching for the Enemy Within
The Rise and Fall of Joseph McCarthy

THE PARANOID STYLE
HUAC Goes to Hollywood
"What's Wrong with Our Kids Today?"

CANNED FOOD

CANNED WATER

It was Sunday, August 27, 1948. Whittaker Chambers appeared calm as he answered questions on "Meet the Press," a weekly radio news show. Chambers's appearance, like most of his life, was a deception. He knew he was on enemy ground and that questions were the ammunition of the war. "I sought not to let myself be crowded," he later recalled, "not to lose my temper during the baiting." Chambers was very still, waiting for the inevitable question. He didn't have to wait long. Edward T. Folliard, a reporter for the *Washington Post,* asked, "Are you willing to say now that Alger Hiss is or ever was a Communist?" Chambers paused a second before answering, for the answer could open him up to a slander or libel suit. Then came his terse, important reply: "Alger Hiss was a Communist and may be now."

The road to "Meet the Press" had begun for Chambers a generation before 1948. It was one paved with unhappiness. His father, Jay, had left his wife Laha for a time, returning after three years. He demonstrated no love or affection for his wife or children. Whittaker remembers that his father—who never allowed his children to call him "Papa"—dined alone and seldom spoke, except perhaps to say "don't." Home experiences left Chambers rebellious and feeling unwanted. After being forced to withdraw from Columbia for writing a mildly sacrilegious play, he flirted with radical political philosophies, moved through a succession of love affairs, and kicked about Europe. In 1926 his brother Richard committed suicide. It was the most painful event in Chambers's life, and for several months he was inconsolable. Almost as a form of therapy, he committed himself fully to another family—the Communist party. During his time of troubles, it gave his life a direction and a purpose.

During the late 1920s and early 1930s, as the United States sank deeper and deeper into the Great Depression, other Americans joined Chambers in the Communist party. Feeling betrayed by the capitalist order, they looked toward the Soviet Union for economic and political inspiration. The Soviet Union, under Joseph Stalin, appeared less affected by the depression than the capitalist West. Still more Americans joined the Communist party because only the Soviets seemed to be standing up against the Fascist threat posed by Hitler, Mussolini, and Franco. For Chambers and his comrades, then, the Red Star represented the future and the hope of the world.

Chambers met Alger Hiss in 1934, when they both belonged to the same Communist "cell" in Washington, D.C. In appearance and personality they were almost perfect opposites. Chambers was sloppy; his clothes always seemed rumpled, and his face had a sleepy, slightly disinterested cast. Hiss was cut from different cloth. Handsome and aristocratic-looking, Hiss's career was marked by ambition and achievement. He was an honors student at Johns Hopkins University and Harvard Law School; he was a favorite of future Supreme Court justice Felix Frankfurter; he clerked for the legendary Oliver Wendell Holmes. Popular with influential superiors and his co-workers, Hiss obviously seemed singled out as one of the best and brightest, as one who would succeed. And he did. He acted as a counsel for the Agricultural Adjustment Administration, worked for the Senate committee investigating the munitions industry, went to the Yalta Conference with President Roosevelt, helped to organize the United Nations, and served as president of the Carnegie Endowment for International Peace.

Through these years of his impressive career, Hiss worked with Whittaker Chambers for the Communist party. It was while Hiss served as a legal assistant for the Senate committee investigation of the munitions industry that he became close friends with Chambers. He allowed Chambers to use his Washington, D.C., apartment for two months, gave him an automobile, and even permitted him to stay in his home on several occasions. Although Hiss would later deny that he knew Chambers—and then admit that he knew him slightly under a different name—the evidence is clear on one point: the very different men had formed a close friendship. It was during that period of friendship in the mid-1930s, Chambers later testified, that Hiss began to give him secret government documents.

Like many of his American comrades, Chambers later, in the late 1930s, abandoned the ideology of communism and lost faith in

Bureaucrat Alger Hiss (left), accused of being a Communist spy by Whittaker Chambers (right), was convicted of perjury (in his second trial for perjury; the first ended in a hung jury). This episode helped heighten American fear of communism at home.

the Soviet Union. There were sound reasons for this break. For the true believers of the early 1930s, the Soviet Union was the light that failed. By 1938 news of Stalin's purges, which would eventually lead to the deaths of millions of Soviets, had reached the West. Such gross disregard for humanity shook many American Communists. In addition, in 1939 Stalin signed a nonaggression pact with Hitler's Germany. Once seen as the bulwark against Nazi expansion, the Soviet Union now joined Germany in dividing Poland. Although during World War II the United States and the Soviet Union were forced together as allies, Communist ideology ceased to attract many American followers.

Chambers not only quit the Communist party, he turned against it with vengeful wrath. As an editor for *Time* magazine, he openly criticized Communist tactics and warned about the evils of the Soviet Union. Time only increased his rage. Finally in 1948 he went before the House Un-American Activities Committee (HUAC) and told his life story, carefully naming all his former Communist party friends and associates. Of all the people he named, the one who attracted the most attention was the brilliant young New Dealer Alger Hiss.

Hiss of course denied Chambers's allegations. He too appeared before HUAC. Well-dressed and relaxed despite a too-tight collar, he testified, "I am not and never have been a member of the Communist party. . . . I have never followed the Communist party line, directly or indirectly. To the best of my knowledge, none of my friends is a Communist." As he smilingly answered questions, he confidently stood on his record of public service. Unlike his nervous, rumpled accuser, Hiss was the picture of placid truthfulness. His testimony satisfied most of the committee members, even the Republicans.

Not all were satisfied, however. After listening to both Chambers and Hiss, Republican Richard Nixon, a junior congressman from California, still was not sure Hiss was as innocent as he seemed. As one psychohistorian bluntly put it, Hiss "was everything Nixon was not." Nixon's background of struggle contrasted sharply with Hiss's career, and Nixon believed Hiss treated him "like dirt." At Nixon's insistence, Hiss and Chambers were brought together face to face before the HUAC. It was at that meeting that Chambers demonstrated his encyclopedic knowledge about Hiss—his family—and his life. He discussed the furniture in the other man's house and his hobbies. Chambers showed beyond any doubt that at one time he had been close to Hiss. For once Hiss's confident equanimity vanished. He challenged Chambers to make his accusations in public, where he would not be protected against a libel suit.

Chambers accepted the challenge, and on "Meet the Press" he repeated his charges. Hiss hesitated for a month and then sued Chambers for defamation. During the involved trials that followed, Chambers proved his case. He even produced a series of classified, microfilmed documents he had stored in a hollowed-out pumpkin on his Maryland farm. Experts testified that the classified documents had been written in Hiss's hand or typed on his Woodstock typewriter. Hiss was indicted for perjury by a federal grand jury. Although the first trial ended in a hung jury, the second trial was far less satisfactory for Hiss. In January 1950 he was found guilty of perjury and sentenced to five years in prison.

The Hiss-Chambers affair was one of the major episodes of the late 1940s. Those years were a time of momentous changes. America took an active and aggressive stand in world affairs and accepted the responsibilities and problems of world leadership. Across the globe it clashed with the Soviet Union over a series of symbolic and real issues in what was labeled the Cold War. These ideological and economic battles affected American domestic and foreign policy. During the late 1940s and early 1950s Americans attacked the Communist threat inside as well as outside the United States. In an atmosphere charged with fear, anxiety, paranoia, and hatred, the United States waged peace and war with equal emotional intensity.

CONTAINING THE RUSSIAN BEAR

During World War II, when the United States and the Soviet Union were allies, Joseph Stalin was known as Uncle Joe. The media portrayed him as a stern but fair leader and pictured communism as strikingly like capitalism. Even Hollywood cooperated in this image-making process. Warner Brothers' *Mission to Moscow* (1943), Sam Goldwyn's *North Star* (1943), MGM's *Song of Russia* (1943), and Frank Capra's *Battle of Russia* all emphasized pro-Soviet themes. *Mission to Moscow* was particularly kind to Stalin, who appeared on screen as a gentle, pipe-smoking, sad-eyed friend of America.

In reality Stalin was a determined, ruthless leader who, over the years, had systematically eliminated his actual and suspected political rivals. Between 1933 and 1938 he violently eliminated over 850,000 members of the Communist party, and perhaps one million more died in labor camps. He was apparently suspicious of almost everyone, inside and outside of the Soviet Union. If his attitude was extreme, it was not totally irrational. Twice in his lifetime Russia had been invaded from the West. Twice Germans had pushed into his country, killing millions upon millions of Russians. Russia suffered almost 4 million military and civilian deaths in World War I, and more than 20 million in World War II. For Stalin, the West, stood unalterably opposed to communism. He would take what he could from the West, but he would never trust westerners.

Stalin, however, was not the only suspicious world leader. The newest Western leader, President Harry Truman, was wary of Stalin but did not exactly regard him as the enemy, at least not in 1945—after all, the Soviet Union and America had been allies during World War II. When Truman took office on April 12, 1945, he assumed he could deal with Stalin. Advisers told him that Stalin was a tough, no-nonsense leader. These were characteristics that the tough, no-nonsense Truman could appreciate. His first meeting with Stalin at Potsdam confirmed his initial assessment of the Soviet leader. "I like Stalin," Truman wrote his wife Bess. "He is straightforward. Knows what he wants and will compromise when he can't get it."

Potsdam was the light before the long dark tunnel. Truman was overly optimistic about his ability to work with Stalin. Totally different backgrounds and philosophies separated the two leaders from the start, and the directions in which they led their countries drove them further apart. The United States and the Soviet Union emerged from World War II as the two most powerful countries in the world, even though the Soviet Union had suffered tremendous industrial, agricultural, and human losses during the war. Both countries were inexperienced as world leaders, but both knew exactly what they wanted, and what they wanted guaranteed future conflicts. The result was the Cold War.

The onset of the Cold War was due in part to the growing divergence between the United States and the Soviet Union after World War II. At Potsdam, Britain's Prime Minister Clement Attlee, President Truman, and Stalin tried unsuccessfully to decide the future of Poland and Germany.

Origins of the Cold War

For Western leaders and their diplomats, World War II had a successful but not neat ending. Too many questions were left unanswered, too many issues unresolved. At Yalta and then at Potsdam the leaders of the Soviet Union, Great Britain, and the United States discussed the future of Poland and Germany, but no firm conclusions were reached. Afraid of further straining the already uneasy wartime alliance, they decided to leave such thorny issues to the future. When the future arrived in August 1945 after America dropped two atomic bombs on Japan, the fates of Eastern Europe and Germany were as yet undetermined, as was the relationship between the United States and the Soviet Union.

When Germany had invaded Poland in early September 1939, England and France had come to the aid of Poland. The Soviet Union had not. Instead, the Soviets had invaded Poland from the east and gobbled up a large section of the country. In 1941, however, Germany invaded the Soviet Union and forced Stalin to join the Grand Alliance against Hitler. For the remainder of World War II, the Soviets had battled heroically against Germany on the eastern front. The West contributed weapons and supplies in this theater of the war, but it was the Red Army working alone that drove the Germans out of Eastern Europe. When the war ended, the Soviets controlled all of Eastern Europe from Stettin on the Baltic Sea to Trieste on the Adriatic Sea.

Had the Soviet Union liberated Eastern Europe, or simply replaced Germany as the master of the region? That was the crucial question of 1945. The debate centered on the fate of Poland: Truman insisted that the Soviets allow free and democratic elections in Poland. Certainly, Truman conceded, the Soviets had the right to expect any Polish government to be friendly toward the Soviet Union, but he expected Stalin to give Poland its complete freedom. Poland's fate was no abstract diplomatic issue to millions of Americans of Eastern European origins who pressed Truman to take a tough stand. Truman complied. He told Soviet Foreign Minister V. M. Molotov that America would not tolerate Poland being made into a Soviet puppet state. His speech was salted with profanity—"words of one syllable," Truman described them—and Molotov remarked, "I have never been talked to like that in my life."

Truman's mule-skinner language, however, did not impress Stalin. The Soviet leader had survived a harsh youth, a brutal prison term, a lonely exile, a revolution, and two world wars. He was not now about to give away Poland or any other territory the Red Army occupied simply because of Truman's colorful phrases. Twice during the twentieth century Germany had invaded Russia through Poland. Stalin was determined it would never happen again. As he had bluntly stated at Yalta, "For the Russian people, the question of Poland is not only a question of honor but also a question of security . . . of life and death for the Soviet Union."

Confronted by an inflexible opponent, Truman played his trump card. He threatened to cut off economic aid to the Soviet Union. Devastated by World War II, the Soviet Union needed the aid, but Stalin believed Poland was more important. Rather than abandon Poland, Stalin accepted the loss of American money. In the end, Truman was powerless. Americans would certainly not accept a war with the Soviet Union to reliberate Poland, and in 1945 the Soviet Union was not about to leave Poland voluntarily. Although there was no war, there was one important casualty: relations between America and the Soviet Union were strained to the breaking point.

A World Divided

The controversy over Poland indicated the direction of postwar Soviet-American relations. The two countries were divided by substantial issues, the most important of which was the degree of control they should and did have over other nations. At the end of the war both nations occupied large areas of land. America's control was based on the strength of its economy as much as its military position. Even as the country demobilized, American leaders were confident that they could use foreign aid to exert influence on the future development of the world. They were also confident that what was good for America would be good for the world. The Soviet Union's control in all of Eastern Europe—Hungary, Romania, Bulgaria, and Czechoslovakia, as well as Poland—depended on the physical presence of the Red Army. Stalin freely granted America and England their spheres of influence, but he wanted the West to recognize his own.

Truman refused. A believer in free trade, national self-determination, and the virtues of democracy, he opposed Stalin's use of military force as a diplomatic weapon. As he told Averell Harriman, America's ambassador to the Soviet Union, the United States might not expect to obtain 100 percent of what it wanted, but "we should be able to get eighty-five percent." The irony of the United States's position was clearly seen by political commentator Walter Lippmann: "While the British and the Americans held firmly . . . the whole position in Africa and the Mediterranean . . . and the whole of Western Germany . . . they undertook by negotiation and diplomatic pressure to reduce Russia's position in Eastern Europe."

Approaching the issues from different perspectives, the Soviet Union and America arrived at different conclusions. After World War II ended, they agreed on very little. The fate of Germany illustrates the basic conflict between the two powers. The Soviets wanted to punish Germany by stripping the country of its industry and imposing harsh reparation payments. Only a prostrate Germany, unarmed and unthreatening, would satisfy Stalin. As Truman lost confidence in the Soviet Union, he came to believe in the need for a strong Germany to act as a block against Soviet expansion. The result of these conflicting approaches was, literally, a divided Germany. Occupied by the Red Army, East Germany became a Soviet satellite. West Germany fell under the American, British, and French spheres of influence and soon became part of the post-

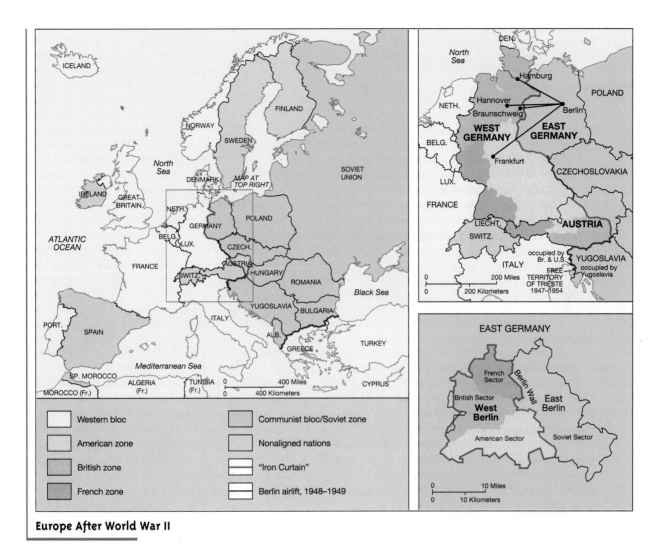

Europe After World War II

war democratic alliance. Not until the early 1990s would Germany again be united.

Control over atomic weapons also divided the two powers. America developed and used the first atomic bomb—demonstrating to the world that it possessed not only the scientific knowledge to construct the bomb but also the will to use the weapon. But, it also realized that future world safety depended on some plan to control its awesome potential. Publicly Truman seemed favorable to international control of the world's fissionable materials. Yet, privately, he used the threat of the bomb in his negotiations with the Soviet Union. America, Secretary of War Henry L. Stimson commented, wore the "weapon rather ostentatiously on our hip." Stalin reacted with suspi-

cion and bitterness to this contradictory policy, distrusting any atomic control plan that originated in the United States. Rather than make Stalin more manageable, America's atomic diplomacy stiffened his resolve and made him cling even more firmly to Eastern Europe as a buffer. At a high-level meeting in the Kremlin he announced his own plan: "A single demand of you, comrades: provide us with atomic weapons in the shortest possible time. You know that Hiroshima has shaken the whole world. The equilibrium has been destroyed. Provide the bomb. It will remove a great danger from us." The result: an atomic arms race, not international cooperation.

By early 1946 U.S.-Soviet relations were badly strained. In February of that year, Stalin warned all Soviet citizens that there would never be a lasting peace with the capitalistic West, economic sacrifices and perhaps more warfare lay ahead. Supreme Court Justice William Douglas labeled the speech "the declaration of World War III." The next month Winston Churchill traveled to Fulton, Missouri, to give a lecture of his own. With Truman by his side, he announced that "from Stettin in the Baltic to Trieste in the Adriatic, an iron curtain has descended across the continent"; only a combined Anglo-American effort could lift the curtain. Fortunately, Churchill emphasized, "God has willed" the atomic bomb to America. Dramatic words, ominous warnings, threats and counterthreats—the Cold War clearly had been declared.

Tough Talk

Although real issues divided America and the Soviet Union, the emotionally charged rhetoric and the emergence of Cold War myths hardened the battle lines. Truman lacked the skill and the language of a diplomat, and like leaders before and after him he was trying to avoid the mistakes of the immediate past. His advisers encouraged him to take a hard line toward the Soviet Union. Remembering how the British and the French had given in to Hitler at the Munich Conference of 1938, American foreign policy-makers were determined not to allow history to repeat itself. Equating Stalin's goals with Hitler's, however, was a grave mistake. Stalin was concerned more with security than expansion; he wanted to protect his country from a future attack, not initiate World War III. As George Kennan, America's leading expert on the Soviet Union, later observed, "The image of a Stalinist Russia poised and yearning to attack the West, and deterred only by our possession of atomic weapons, was largely a creation of the Western imagination."

The Munich example and the get-tough talk turned American public opinion against the Soviet Union. Leading American diplomat Dean Acheson warned, "I think it is a mistake to believe that you can, at any time, sit down with the Russians and solve problems." Comments of this sort were aired over and over in

public as the media began to build a new, more menacing image of Stalin. The pipe in hand and sad, soft eyes of Uncle Joe quickly faded in late 1945 and early 1946. News stories emphasized confrontation, conflict, and controversy. Talk turned no longer toward how to avoid an explosive conflict but rather how to win it. In the mind of the public, the Soviet Union soon became the once and future enemy of America.

The Truman Doctrine

America's rise as a world power was paralleled by Britain's decline. England, like much of the rest of Europe, suffered terribly during World War II. The war shattered its economy, and burned-out buildings and miles of fresh graves silently testified to the country's physical and human losses. By early 1947 Britain could no longer stand as the leader of the Western democracies. On Friday, February 21, 1947, England passed the torch to America. The British ambassador in Washington requested an emergency meeting with Secretary of State George C. Marshall. He had "a piece of blue paper" to deliver. The quaint phrase meant, in diplomatic parlance, a formal and important message. Simply put, the ambassador announced that Britain could no longer economically support Greece and Turkey in their fight against Communist rebels. If these two countries, which were vitally important because of their position between the Soviet Union and the Mediterranean and the Middle East, were to be kept as Western allies, the United States had to aid their cause. Emphasizing this point, the message concluded, "Unless urgent and immediate support is given to Greece, it seems probable that the Greek Government will be overthrown and a totalitarian regime of the extreme left will come into power."

Truman was prepared to assume the burden, but there were doubts whether the country was. Republicans had regained control of Congress in the November 1946 elections, and they were not anxious to shoulder expensive new foreign programs. In addition, rapid demobilization after World War II had drastically reduced the size and effectiveness of the

American military forces. Still, something had to be done. Truman's advisers and congressional leaders recommended that he speak directly to the American people. But as Republican Senator Arthur Vandenberg warned, to win public support the president would have to "scare the hell out of the American people."

On March 12, 1947, Truman appeared before a joint session of Congress and described the Greek and Turkish situations as battles between the forces of light and the legions of darkness. "At the present moment in world history nearly every nation must choose between alternative ways of life," he said. "One way of life is based upon the will of the majority, and is distinguished by free institutions, representative government, free elections, guarantees of individual liberty, freedom of speech and religion, and freedom from political oppression. The second way of life is based upon the will of a minority forcibly imposed upon the majority. It relies upon terror and oppression." Congress sounded its approval as Truman came to his climactic sentence: "I believe that it must be the policy of the United States to support free peoples who are resisting attempted subjugation by armed minorities or outside pressures." Labeled the Truman Doctrine, the statement set the course U.S. foreign policy would follow during the next generation.

Specifically, Truman called for economic and financial aid to "save" Greece and Turkey. Congress responded by appropriating $400 million. By later standards it was a paltry sum, but it was a significant beginning. In the future, America would send billions of dollars in economic and military aid to countries fighting communism, even though the leaders of some of those nations were themselves dictators. In Truman's morality play, however, "anti-Communists" and "free peoples" became synonymous.

Although Truman succeeded in getting aid for Greece and Turkey and in arousing the American public, a few foreign policy experts believed that his scare tactics did more harm than good. Diplomat George Kennan deplored the sweeping language of the Truman Doctrine, which placed U.S. aid to Greece "in the framework of a universal policy rather than in that of a specific decision addressed to a specific set of circumstances."

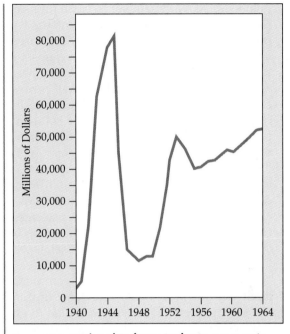

FIGURE 26.1 **National Defense Budgets, 1940–1964**

The Marshall Plan: "Saving Western Europe"

The millions of dollars sent to Greece and Turkey stabilized the pro-American governments of the two countries. But at the same time America was losing support in Western Europe, a far more vital region. Although the war had ended in the spring of 1945, Europe's problems continued. It lacked the money to rebuild its war-torn economies and scarred cities. To make matters worse, the winters of 1946 and 1947 were brutally cold. News reports from early 1947 told the sad story. Snow buried thousands of sheep in northern England; between December 1 and February 8, 40 residents of Berlin and 68 of Hamburg died from the cold; Holland was short of food; Italy was inundated by floods; and across the continent the weather report was always the same: "cold or very cold." The winter hardships were a boon to the Communist party, which made marked gains. American leaders assumed that economic distress would continue to breed political extremism. *New York Times* correspondent Anne O'Hare McCormick told Americans in the *Times:* "The extent to which democratic government survives on [the] continent depends on how far this country is willing to help it survive." Truman concurred, and so did his advisers. They were upset by the growth of anti-Americanism in Europe, an area that figured prominently in their postwar economic plans. The image of America had changed from that of loyal ally to selfish exploiter. Describing the typical occupation soldier in Germany, an army chaplain wrote, "There he stands in his bulging clothes, fat, overfed, lonely, a bit wistful, seeing little, understanding less—the Conqueror, with a chocolate bar in one pocket and a package of cigarettes in the other. . . . The chocolate bar and the cigarettes are about all that he, the Conqueror, has to give the conquered."

At the Harvard University commencement on June 5, 1947, Secretary of State George C. Marshall announced a plan to give Europe more. After describing the severe problems facing Europe, Marshall suggested that America could not afford to send a Band-Aid to cover the deep European wounds. "A cure rather than a mere palliative" was in order—Europe needed massive economic blood transfusions. He told his audience that the cost might seem high. Without America's help, however, "economic, social, and political deterioration of a very grave character" would result. And from a more selfish point of view, America needed a strong, democratic Europe to provide rich markets for American goods and to act as a check against Soviet westward expansion.

In early 1948 Congress appropriated $17 billion to be spent over the next four years for the European Recovery Program (ERP), more popularly called the Marshall Plan. The program put food in the mouths of hungry children, coal in empty furnaces, and money in near-empty banks. More importantly, it rebuilt the economic infrastructure of Western Europe and restored economic prosperity to the region. In the process it created stable markets for American goods. Americans were proud of the Marshall Plan, and Europeans were moved by it. Winston Churchill judged it "the most unsordid act in history." All told, the Marshall Plan greatly restored America's prestige abroad.

The Marshall Plan also fostered the economic integration of Western Europe by curbing nationalistic economic policies. American policy-makers believed that only by functioning as a single economic unit could Western Europe enjoy real prosperity. "A healthy Europe," John Foster Dulles remarked, could not be "divided into small compartments." Although the process toward economic integration was slow and occasionally painful, it did move forward. The European Payments Union was created in 1950, the European Coal and Steel Authority in 1951, and the European Economic Community (Common Market) in 1958. In the final analysis, the Marshall Plan served both America's Cold War strategy and plans for an economic internationalism.

THE CONTAINMENT POLICY

Money, even billions of dollars, could not substitute for a concrete foreign policy to guide U.S. actions: an explicit policy that mixed the international idealism of the Truman Doctrine and the economic realism of the Marshall Plan with the will to meet the real or perceived Soviet threat. The policy was not long in coming. In July 1947, the journal *Foreign Affairs* contained an article entitled "The Sources of Soviet Conduct" by "Mr. X." The article provided a blueprint for the policy of containment, which would influence American foreign policy for at least the next generation.

"Mr. X" was George Kennan, the government's foremost authority on the Soviet Union. Educated at Princeton University, Kennan had spent his adult life in the U.S. foreign service, where he carefully studied the Soviet scene. During World War II he was stationed in Moscow and was able to observe Soviet political behavior. Although he believed Russians were a "great and appealing people," he distrusted the Soviet government. In February 1946, he expressed his views of the Soviet Union in an 8000-word telegram to his superiors in Washington, and in the 1947 *Foreign Affairs* article, Kennan made his views public. He believed that Soviet communism was driven by two engines: the need for a repressive dictatorship at home and the belief there could never be any sense of community or true accord with the capitalist West. In fact, the Kremlin used the supposed threat from capitalism to justify its continued dictatorship. But, Kennan argued, Stalin and the leaders in the Kremlin were more interested in security than expansion. Soviets would only expand when allowed to by American weakness. It could be *contained* to its present borders by a politically, economically, and militarily active United States. What was needed was "the adroit and vigilant application of counter-force at a series of constantly shifting geographical and political points, corresponding to the shifts and maneuvers of Soviet policy." Kennan even suggested that if the United States was firm in its resolve to contain Soviet expansion, "the possibility remains . . . that Soviet power . . . bears within it the seeds of its own decay." In short, Kennan held out the hope of complete victory in the Cold War.

Although Kennan later remarked that he was talking about the political containment of a political threat, in 1947 his article was read as primarily a military blueprint. As such, it satisfied hard-liners but was challenged by many other politicians and respected political commentators. Walter Lippmann challenged Kennan's policy in a series of newspaper articles later published as *The Cold War: A Study in U.S. Foreign Policy* (1947). Containment, Lippmann commented, allowed the Soviet Union largely to decide when and where its battles against America would take place, and it promised to tie the United States to small unstable "client" countries that would be political, economic, and military drains on America. Seeing that the plan was primarily focused on Western European problems, Lippmann suggested that if followed it might well lead America into a land war in Asia, where the idea of victory would be a cruel delusion. America, Lippmann maintained, was not in the military, economic, or strategic position to implement containment. Lippmann found it "hard to understand how Mr. X could have recommended such a strategic monstrosity."

Containment involved confronting the spread of communism across the globe and as

Americans soon learned, its price was high. It meant supporting allies around the world with billions of dollars in military and economic aid, and it meant thousands of Americans dying in foreign lands. Since containment was a defensive policy, it involved a prolonged Cold War. Unlike World War I and World War II, the Cold War emphasized the doctrine of limited wars fought for limited goals. And in this arrangement, Kennan noted, "Man would have to recognize . . . that the device of military coercion would have . . . only relative—never an absolute—value in the pursuit of political objectives." It was a policy bound to breed frustration and anxiety—certain to influence domestic as well as foreign policy.

Pictured is diplomat George Kennan, whose analysis of United States-Soviet relations encouraged U.S. "containment" of the Russians and played a major role in the intensification of the Cold War.

Berlin Test

During the late 1940s containment seemed to fit American needs. American-Soviet tensions centered particularly on the future of Germany. The United States maintained that the economic revival of Western Europe depended on a reindustrialized and prosperous Germany. The Soviets believed that a reindustrialized Germany was a dangerous Germany. An early conflict over the two different viewpoints occurred in Berlin, a divided city located in the heart of East Germany, deep within the Soviet zone. Future Soviet Premier Nikita Khrushchev called democratic West Berlin a "bone in the throat" of Russia. In June 1948, Stalin decided to remove the bone by stopping all road and rail traffic between West Germany and Berlin. It was a crisis tailor-made for the containment policy. Stalin had picked the time and place. Now Truman had to decide upon a response.

He chose the sky. Stalin could close highways and railways, but he could not effectively close the skyways. For almost one year America and Britain kept West Berlin alive and democratic by a massive airlift. Food, coal, clothing, and all other essentials were flown daily into Berlin. It was a heroic feat, a triumph of technology. Western pilots logged 277,264 flights into West Berlin; they hauled in 2,343,315 tons of food, fuel, medicine, and clothing. Finally on May 12, 1949, Stalin lifted his blockade of West Berlin. For Stalin, the success of the airlift had become an embarrassment for the Soviet Union. In the West, containment had passed an important test.

Troubling Times

Truman scored a series of triumphs during 1947 and 1948. The Truman Doctrine, the Marshall Plan, and the Berlin Airlift strengthened his popularity at home and U.S. prestige abroad. In the election of 1948 Truman won a remarkable upset victory over Thomas E. Dewey. Then in 1949 eleven Western democracies joined the United States in signing the North Atlantic Treaty Organization (NATO) agreement, a mu-

During 1948 and 1949, an American and British airlift brought close to 7000 tons of food and fuel each day to Soviet-blockaded West Berlin.

tual defense pact. NATO signified America's position as the leader of the Western Alliance, and it conformed to the containment policy. But difficult times for Truman, containment, and America lay ahead. In late August 1949, American scientists detected traces of radioactive material in the Soviet atmosphere. The cause was as clear as a mushroom-shaped cloud. The Soviets had the bomb—a full decade before American intelligence expected it.

On September 22 Truman told the public: "We have evidence that an atomic explosion occurred in the USSR." Although the press tried to downplay the story, a wave of anxiety swept the country. Physicist Harold C. Urey told reporters, "There is only one thing worse than one nation having the atomic bomb— that's two nations having it."

Between 1945 and 1949 the threat of the bomb had given teeth to American policy. It was America's check on the Red Army, and U.S. policy-makers seldom allowed Soviet leaders to forget it. In 1945 Secretary of State James F. Byrnes told his Soviet counterpart V. M. Molotov, "If you don't cut out all this stalling and let us get down to work, I am going to pull an atomic bomb out of my hip pocket and let you have it." Now Molotov had one in his hip pocket. Truman responded by asking his scientists to accelerate the development of a hydrogen bomb; and Congress responded by voting appropriations for Truman's latest defense requests. Of such events and decisions are the humble origins of arms races.

On the heels of the Soviet bomb came more unwelcome news—the establishment of the Communist government in China after a bitter civil war. The war between Mao Tsetung (Mao Zedong) and Chou En-lai's (Zhou Enlai's) Communists and Chiang Kai-shek's (Jiang Jieshi's) Nationalists had been raging since the 1930s. The United States had strongly backed Chiang during the civil war, providing him with more than $3 billion in aid between 1945 and 1949. But the aid was unable to prop up a government that was structurally unsound, inefficient, and corrupt. In the first week of May 1949, Chiang fled across the Formosa Strait to Taiwan, and on September 21, Mao proclaimed Red China's sovereignty. With Chiang in Taiwan and Mao on the mainland, China became two countries.

The Truman administration tried to put the best face possible on the turn of events. Secretary of State Dean Acheson issued a thousand-page white paper explaining how Mao had won the civil war. It detailed the rampant corruption in the Nationalist government and Chiang's many mistakes. Assessing the role of the United States in the outcome of the conflict Acheson concluded, "Nothing that this country did or could have done within the reasonable limits of its capabilities could have changed that result. . . . it was the product of internal Chinese forces, forces which this country tried to influence but could not."

For the American public, however, that explanation was not good enough. The China most Americans knew, as one historian put it, was associated with novelist "Pearl Buck's peasants, rejoicing in the good earth . . . dependable, democratic, warm, and above all pro-American." It was an image that American missionaries confirmed during the 1920s and 1930s and one that journalists supported during World War II. Americans were told that there were two types of Asians—the good Chinese and the evil Japanese. In 1941 *Time* magazine even ran an article entitled "How to Tell Your Friends From the Japs." It confidently reported, "the Chinese expression is likely to be more placid, kindly, open; the Japanese more positive, dogmatic, arrogant."

Republicans and supporters of Chiang in America blamed Truman for "losing" China. Led by Henry Luce, the influential publisher of *Time* and *Life* who was the Chinese-born son of American missionaries, an informal group known as the China Lobby blasted the Truman administration. They claimed "egg-sucking phony liberals" had "sold China into atheistic slavery." The China Lobby believed that America had far more influence than it actually had, that a country that contained 6 percent of the earth's population could control the other 94 percent. They were wrong, but millions of Americans took their loud cries seriously.

"China lost itself," Acheson countered. "We picked a bad horse," Truman admitted. But given the political pressure at home, Truman was not about to change mounts in the middle of the race. Reversing America's traditional policy of recognizing de facto governments, Truman refused to recognize the Com-

The celebration of the first anniversary of Mao Tsetung's rule in 1950 brought many Chinese to the streets of Peking.

munist People's Republic of China. Instead he insisted that Chiang's Nationalist government on Taiwan was the legitimate government of China. It was an unrealistic policy, but one that future presidents found politically difficult to reverse. The United States and the People's Republic of China did not establish formal relations until 1979.

The Korean War

The rhetoric of the Truman administration tended to simplify complex issues, intensify the Cold War rivalry, and tie foreign policy to domestic politics. Failure abroad could have calamitous consequences for politicians at home. "If you can't stand the heat, get out of the kitchen," Truman often said. By 1950 the kitchen had become hotter. After "China fell," Truman was more determined than ever to contain communism.

The mood of the Truman administration is clearly evident in National Security Council Paper Number 68 (NSC-68), one of the most important documents of the Cold War. Completed in April 1950, it expressed the views of foreign-policy planners Paul Nitze and Dean Acheson that communism was a monolithic world movement directed from the Kremlin; it advocated "an immediate and large-scale build-up in our military and general strength of our allies with the intention of righting the power balance and in the hope that through means other than all-out war we could induce a change in the nature of the Soviet system." NSC-68 extended the Truman Doctrine and called for America to protect the world against the spread of communism. The cost would be great—NSC-68 estimated it at 20 percent of the gross national product, or over a 300-percent increase in military appropriations—but planners warned that without the commitment America faced the prospect of a world moving toward communism.

Truman realized that NSC-68 "meant a great military effort in time of peace. It meant doubling or tripling the budget, increasing taxes heavily, and imposing various kinds of economic controls." And he doubted whether Congress would accept such a peacetime buildup. He never got a chance to find out, for in June 1950 America went to war in Korea.

Korea, like Germany, was a divided country. When the Japanese surrendered its forces in Korea after World War II, Soviet troops accepted the surrender north of the 38th parallel,

American troops south of that line. With the deepening of the Cold War, the temporary division line became permanent. North of the 38th parallel, Communist Kim Il Sung governed North Korea. Supported by the Soviet Union, Kim forged a modern, disciplined army during the late 1940s. In South Korea, 75-year-old President Syngman Rhee, who received strong aid and support from the United States, opposed any reconciliation with Communist North Korea. But, as Secretary of State Acheson noted in an unfortunate speech before the National Press Club on January 12, 1950, South Korea lay outside America's primary "defense perimeter." As far as military security of South Korea was concerned, Acheson emphasized, should "an attack occur the initial resistance" must come from "the people attacked."

On June 25, 1950, the attack occurred. In an orderly, coordinated offensive, North Korea sent 90,000 men across the 38th parallel into South Korea. They faced a weak, disorderly South Korean army, aptly described as "little more than a constabulary." It was a mismatch

American occupation troops stationed in Japan joined South Korean allies in a retreat that ended up in the southeast area of Korea, where they managed to hold off the North Korean forces.

of epic proportions, and South Korean troops quickly mounted an all-out retreat. As the monsoon rains drenched the rice paddies and mountains, Korea moved swiftly toward unification under Kim's Communist government.

Why did North Korea attack? At the time, the Truman administration believed that the Soviets directed the assault. It regarded Kim as little more than a puppet whose strings were manipulated in Moscow. There is little evidence, however, to support this contention. More likely internal Korean politics dictated the course of events. Kim's position in North Korea was by no means secure. He faced organized opposition from a Democratic Front for the Unification of the Fatherland. The invasion of South Korea, therefore, may have been launched to undercut that movement. Certainly Kim informed Stalin of the impending invasion, but the idea and the timing were probably his own.

Truman had just finished a Saturday dinner in Independence, Missouri, when Acheson telephoned him with news of the invasion. His reaction was as rapid and as certain as North Korea's attack. Since both Koreas were technically wards of the United Nations, the Truman administration took the matter to the Security Council. With the Soviet Union absent (it was boycotting the United Nations over the refusal of the organization to seat the People's Republic of China), the Security Council by a 9 to 0 vote condemned the North Korean assault and demanded an immediate cease-fire. Encouraged by the United Nations's prompt action and without consulting Congress, Truman pledged American support to South Korea and strengthened the military position of the United States in Asia.

Truman termed the conflict a "UN police action" and, in fact, a number of UN members sent troops, but for all practical purposes it was a war that initially matched the United States and South Korea against North Korea. Air force advisers told Truman that they could stop the North Korean advance by bombing the Communist supply line. They convinced Truman that ground forces would not be needed. Truman's advisers seemed convinced that the Asians would turn and run at the first show of Western force. Although the bombs

destroyed miles of roads and bridges, they did not slow the North Korean advance.

On June 30, Truman took the fateful step of ordering American occupation troops stationed in Japan to proceed to Korea. They soon joined their South Korean allies in a headlong retreat. For six weeks the allies fell steadily back until they stabilized a perimeter in southeast Korea around the port city of Pusan. With their offensive halted, North Korean troops mounted a siege. To the surprise of the world, the Pusan perimeter held firm.

For American soldiers it had been a painful and disappointing two months. They were fighting in an unfamiliar country for an unsatisfactory objective. Truman's announced goal was simply to restore the 38th parallel as

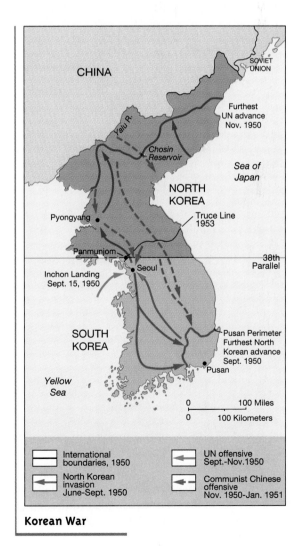

Korean War

the border between the two Koreas. Victory then was defined as a stalemate. Corporal Stephen Zeg of Chicago expressed the feeling of other soldiers when he commented, "I'll fight for my country, but I'll be damned if I see why I'm fighting to save this hellhole."

But fighting they were, and General Douglas MacArthur was determined to reverse the military situation of the war. A bold, even arrogant man, firmly fixed in his opinions and certain of his ability to command in battle, MacArthur decided to split his forces and launch a surprise attack against the North Ko-

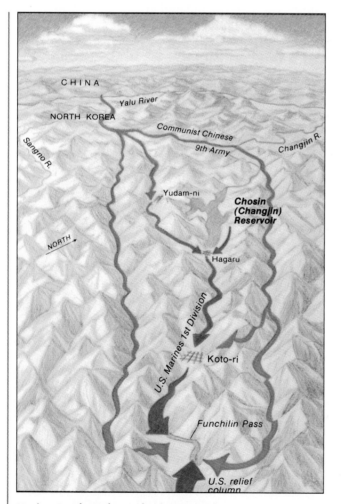

Marine Breakout from Chosin Reservoir
A Communist Chinese force of 100,000 had set a trap for the (20,000) marines at Chosin Reservoir. The marines doggedly fought their way out of the mountains in weather that ranged from −30°F at night to about 0° during the day.

rean's rear. On the morning of September 15, 1950, American marines began an amphibious attack on Inchon, a port city, wrote one historian, "about as large as Jersey City, as ugly as Liverpool, and as dreary as Belfast." MacArthur's military advisers warned him against the move, noting that Inchon possessed every natural and geographic handicap. MacArthur, however, was confident of victory. It was a bold, risky maneuver—a bold, risky, successful maneuver.

Faced with an enemy to their front and their rear, North Korean troops retreated across the border. By the beginning of October those North Korean soldiers who were not captured or killed were above the 38th parallel. Truman had achieved his stated objective. But the warrior in MacArthur wanted more—he wanted victory on the battlefield. And he said so, loudly and publicly. In private the Truman administration was moving toward MacArthur's position. Containment was giving way to a policy of liberation. After receiving MacArthur's reassurances at a private meeting on Wake Island, Truman decided to allow U.S. forces to move across the 38th parallel and "liberate" North Korea. Like MacArthur's Inchon landing, it was a bold plan, one predicated on the widely held American belief that China would not intervene in the conflict.

This time boldness failed. North Korea was a difficult country to invade. The American army had no reliable maps and mountainous terrain rendered traditional military tactics impossible. In addition, as MacArthur's forces moved recklessly north toward Manchuria, Chinese officials sent informal warnings to the United States that unless the advance stopped, their country would enter the fray. MacArthur ignored Chinese warnings and his own intelligence reports and kept moving.

Communist China struck in late November. Over 300,000 troops poured across the border and attacked unprepared American forces. An advance force of marines near the Chosin Reservoir was cut off from the main army. They made the best of a bad situation. "The enemy is in front of us, behind us, to the left of us, and to the right of us," Colonel Lewis B.

"Chesty" Puller told his regiment. "They won't escape *this* time." Puller's bravado, however, could not hide the terrible truth. The entry of Communist China into the conflict had radically altered the nature of the war.

Victory was now out of the question. Only MacArthur continued to talk about an absolute victory. If a nation was going to fight a war, he sermonized, it should fight to win. In Washington, however, the Truman administration was shifting back to the pre-Inchon policy of containment. When MacArthur publicly criticized the administration's newest approach, an angry Truman recalled him and replaced him with General Matthew B. Ridgway. In America Truman's sacking of "Mac" raised a firestorm of protest. An April 1951 Gallup poll reported that 66 percent of Americans disapproved of Truman's firing of the general, and then in October, 56 percent indicated that they believed the Korean conflict was a "useless war."

The Korean War dragged on until July 10, 1951, when formal peace negotiations began, but it proved to be a long, difficult process. While diplomats talked, American soldiers fought and died. Altogether, 34,000 Americans were killed and 103,000 wounded during the Korean War. When Truman left office in early 1953 the carnage was still continuing. Finally on July 26, 1953, the war officially ended, as it began, with North Koreans above the 38th parallel and South Koreans below it. It was a victory for Truman's containment policy, but for millions of Americans it somehow tasted like defeat.

THE COLD WAR AT HOME

Commie for a day. It was a theme idea. It answered the question, "What would it be like to live under a Soviet-type, communist dictatorship?" On May Day 1950, at Mosinee, Wisconsin, American Legionnaires disguised themselves as Soviet soldiers and staged a mock Communist takeover of their town. They arrested and summarily locked up the mayor and clergymen, nationalized all businesses, confiscated all firearms, and rid the library of rows of objectionable books. They even forced Mosinee residents to alter their eating habits. The local restaurants served only potato soup, dark bread, and black coffee, and only Young Communist Leaguers were permitted to eat candy. Eventually Mosinee patriots "liberated" their town, and at dusk a mass democratic rally was held amidst much patriotic music and the burning of Communist literature.

For most of Mosinee's citizens it was an edifying experiment. "We really learned about what 100 percent communism would be like," one resident observed. They concluded that life under communism was hardly worth living. Many found intolerable the lack of such basic freedoms as privacy, speech, press, religion, and decent food. One participant confessed, "I know some people who even drove to [neighboring] Wausau to get something to eat. In Russia I guess you wouldn't be able to get anything else anywhere."

Although there is an element of humor to Mosinee's Red May Day, behind the events was a national mood that was far from funny. As Truman waged the Cold War abroad, Cold War issues gradually came to dominate the American domestic scene. During the ensuing Red Scare, the fear of communism disrupted American life, and the freedoms that Americans took for granted came under attack. At home as well as abroad, Americans battled real and imagined Communist enemies.

Adjusting to Peace

Truman and his advisers approached the end of World War II with their eyes on the past. They were uneasy about the future: Memories of the Great Depression and the painful social and economic adjustment after World War I clouded their thinking. They knew that massive wartime spending, not the New Deal, had ended the Great Depression, and they worried that peace might bring more economic suffering. Peace with prosperity was their goal.

The solution to the problems of converting back to a peacetime economy, Truman believed, lay in the continuation, at least for a time, of wartime government economic controls. During the war, the Office of Price Administration (OPA) had controlled prices and held inflation in check. After Japan surrendered, Truman asked Congress to continue price controls and outlined a program for economic reconversion. To ensure future prosperity, Truman advocated such economic measures as a 65-cents-an-hour minimum wage, nationalization of the housing industry, and stronger fair employment practices legislation.

Congress responded half-heartedly, passing the Employment Act of 1946. Although it was less than Truman had requested, it did provide the institutional framework for more government control over the economy. The act created the Council of Economic Advisors to help "promote free competitive enterprise, to avoid economic fluctuations . . . and to maintain employment, production, and purchasing power." During the decades after 1946, the council exerted a powerful influence over economic policy.

On the other hand, Republicans and southern Democrats balked against a return to more "New Dealism." One influential congressman even accused Truman of "out-dealing the New Deal." Congress destroyed the OPA by relaxing its controls, a policy that created immediate inflation. Congress's refusal to pass Truman's economic package did not tumble America into another depression. In truth, the American economy was basically sound. Wartime employment and wartime saving had created a people whose money was burning holes in their pockets. They wanted peacetime goods—automobiles, houses, Scotch whiskey, nylon stockings, and red meat. Given the demand and the short supply, inflation was inevitable. In addition, the short supply of consumer goods increased black-market activities. Americans offered bribes for preferential treatment from car salesmen, butchers, and landlords, but as industries converted to peacetime production, consumer supplies rose to meet the new demands.

Confronting the Demands of Labor

The death of the OPA led to demands for higher wages as well as to higher prices. During the war labor unions had taken "no strike" pledges, and it was through their efforts that America became the "arsenal of democracy." Workers labored long and hard, agreeing to speedups and higher production quotas. Virtually no production time was lost to strikes.

The end of the war signaled the start of the strike season as workers demanded rewards for their wartime efforts and their loss of overtime pay. During 1946 over 4.5 million laborers struck, and 107,476,000 workdays were lost to strikes. If labor's cause was just, its timing was disastrous. After clashing repeatedly with an obstreperous Congress, Truman was in no mood to coddle labor. When two national railway brotherhoods threatened to disrupt the transportation system, Truman proposed to draft the workers. On national radio he announced, "The crisis at Pearl Harbor was the result of action by a foreign enemy. The crisis tonight is caused by a group of men within our country who place their private interests above the welfare of the nation." Confronted by hostile public opinion and an unsympathetic president, the brotherhoods went back to work.

Labor was angry. United Mine Workers leader John L. Lewis told reporters, "You can't mine coal with bayonets." As winter approached, Lewis took his men out on strike. The prospect of a cold winter created anxiety, and Truman reacted angrily threatening to take over the mines and lashing out publicly at the defiant Lewis. Finally Truman appealed directly to the miners, asking them to go back to work for the good and warmth of the nation. It worked. Lewis called off the strike. Truman's prestige and confidence soared.

Truman's gains were labor's losses. The congressional elections of 1946, which brought to power the conservative Republican-controlled Eightieth Congress, added to labor's problems. Led by Robert Taft, Congress pushed through the Labor-Management Relations Act of 1947 (better known as the Taft-Hartley Act), which was passed over Truman's veto. It outlawed the closed shop (a business or industry in which all the employees were required to join a union), gave presidents power to delay strikes by declaring a "cooling-off" period, and curtailed the political and economic power of organized labor. The act signified the conservative mood of the country.

It was a bad period for all workers, but for female workers it was especially hard. During the war they had filled a wide range of industrial jobs, but returning soldiers quickly displaced them. Some accepted the change and returned to their prewar occupations. Others resented the loss of their relatively high-paying jobs. What was worse, when new jobs opened up, employers hired and trained younger males rather than rehire the experienced females. Thus while male workers complained about the antilabor mood of the country, many unemployed women laborers lamented the antifemale prejudices among employers.

Failure of the Fair Deal

Political experts expected America to vote Republican in the 1948 presidential elections. Truman's policies had angered liberals, labor, Southerners, and most of Congress. Moreover, Democrats had occupied the White House since 1933. Republicans reasoned that it was time for a change. They nominated Thomas E. Dewey of New York, the GOP candidate in 1944. The Democrats stayed with Truman, even though large numbers of Southerners and liberals deserted the party to follow third-party movements. Southerners, angered by Truman's support of civil rights, formed the States' Rights Democratic party—better known as the Dixiecrats—and nominated Governor J. Strom Thurmond of South Carolina for president. Liberals joined with Communists to form the Progressive party, which nominated FDR's former vice president Henry A. Wallace for president.

An underdog from the start, Truman rolled up his sleeves and took his cause to the people by train, the 17-car "Presidential Special." The rear car was the *Ferdinand Magellan,* the bulletproof, steel-and-concrete-reinforced presidential car that had been made for Roo-

sevelt during the war. It weighed 285,000 pounds—heavy enough to crush every other car in the train had the engineer stopped suddenly. As it moved across the country, Truman blasted the "do-nothing" Eightieth Congress at each stop. "If you send another Republican Congressman to Washington, you're a bigger bunch of suckers than I think you are," he lectured. "Give 'em hell, Harry!" was the popular refrain. By contrast, Dewey sat tight, seemingly more concerned with his fastidious appearance than his bland speeches. His cold personality failed to move American voters. "I don't know which is the chillier experience—to have Tom ignore you or shake your hand," noted a Truman supporter. "You have to get to know Dewey to dislike him," added another.

By election day Truman had closed the gap. The old Roosevelt coalition—midwestern farmers, urban ethnics groups, organized labor, African Americans, and Southerners—remained sufficiently strong to send Truman back to the White House. Neither the Dixiecrats nor the progressives hurt Truman in any substantial way, since most Democrats chose to remain in the center of the party with Truman rather than drift toward the radical fringes. Truman's winning of the election was a testimony to the legacy of FDR as well as Truman's scrappiness, and to the often overlooked fact that Democrats outnumbered Republicans in the nation.

"Keep America Human With Truman," read one of his campaign posters. In 1949 he announced a plan to do just that. Known as the Fair Deal, the legislative package included an expansion of Social Security, federal aid to education, a higher minimum wage, federal funding for public housing projects, a national plan for medical insurance, civil rights legislation for minorities, and other measures to foster social and economic justice. As Truman explained, "I expect to give every segment of our population a fair deal." At the core of the Fair Deal was his belief that government-controlled economic expansion blunts extremism from the right and left and ensures prosperity.

Congress took Truman's package, stripped off the wrapping, threw away some

Most pollsters predicted that Republican candidate Thomas E. Dewey would win the 1948 presidential election, but in a stunning political upset the voters reelected President Truman.

of the contents, and sent it back to the president for his signature. Congress did extend Social Security, raise the minimum wage to 75 cents an hour, and further developed several New Deal programs. But the more original proposals of the Fair Deal—civil rights legislation, a national health insurance program, an imaginative farm program, and federal aid to education—were rejected by a Congress that opposed anything defined as "creeping socialism."

Truman, as well as Congress, contributed to the ultimate failure of the Fair Deal to achieve its objectives. Republicans and Southerners did join forces in opposition to civil rights and government spending programs, but Truman demonstrated an almost total inability to work with Congress on domestic issues. In addition, by 1949 foreign policy dominated the president's attention and claimed an increasing share of the federal budget.

Searching for the Enemy Within

While Congress removed the heart from Truman's Fair Deal, Cold War winds were chilling the country's political landscape. The tough diplomatic rhetoric of Truman, Acheson, and other policy-makers encouraged Americans to view the rivalry between the Soviet Union and the United States in simplistic terms. America became the "defender of free people," the Soviet Union the "atheistic enslaver of millions." Every time a world event did not go America's way, it was seen as a Soviet victory. In this world of black-and-white thinking, the suspicion that "enemies within" America were secretly aiding the Soviet cause took shape. Soon, talk of American "atomic spies" giving information to the Soviets and State Department officials sabotaging U.S. foreign policy became common.

Were spies working against American interests to further the Soviet cause? Unquestionably, yes. In 1945 Igor Gouzenko, a Soviet embassy official in Ottawa, defected to the West, carrying with him documents that detailed a Communist spy ring working in Canada and the United States. The evidence led to the arrests of two British physicists, Dr. Alan Munn May and Dr. Klaus Fuchs, who had worked on the Manhattan Project. Fuchs implicated a group of American radicals—Harry Gold, David Greenglass, Morton Sobell, and Julius and Ethel Rosenberg. Clearly these individuals had passed atomic secrets to the Soviets during the war. Whether or not this information helped the Soviet Union to develop an atomic bomb is largely conjecture.

The damage done by British spies Kim Philby, Guy Burgess, and Donald Maclean is more certain. The three men held high British diplomatic and intelligence posts and were privy to sensitive American CIA and British Secret Intelligence Service (SIS) information. In 1951 Burgess and Maclean defected to the Soviet Union, where they were joined by Philby in 1963. There is considerable circumstantial evidence that the information they passed to the Soviet Union severely compromised American Cold War intelligence and may have been influential in the Chinese intervention in the Korean War.

There were certainly spies; but the issue soon outgrew the question of mere espionage and became an instrument of partisan politics. Republicans accused Democrats of being "soft" on communism—in fact, of harboring spies in the State Department and other government agencies. Richard M. Nixon, who was elected to Congress in 1946, announced that Democrats were responsible for "the unimpeded growth of the communist conspiracy in the United States." As proof Republicans pointed to the "fall" of China, the atomic bomb in the Soviet Union, and Alger Hiss in the State Department.

Truman reacted to such criticism as early as 1947 by issuing Executive Order 9835, which established the Federal Employee Loyalty Program, authorizing the FBI to investigate all government employees. Although the search disclosed no espionage or treason, thousands of employees were forced to resign or were fired because their personal lives or past associations did not meet government inspection. Homosexuality, alcoholism, unpaid debts, contribution to left-wing causes, support of civil rights—all became grounds for dismissal.

Truman also used the anti-Communism issue to drum up support for his foreign policy. At the end of World War II public opinion polls revealed that few Americans regarded communism as a serious problem. Republican charges and Truman's loyalty program, however, encouraged citizens to profess 100 percent Americanism. In 1947 the president sent a special "Freedom Train" across the country to exhibit important national documents, including the Truman Doctrine. By 1950 communism had become a more visible issue at home as well as abroad.

Ethel and Julius Rosenberg paid the supreme price for being Communists. At least one may have been a spy, but the death penalty was not mandatory for their crime. Judge Irving R. Kaufman nevertheless made an example of them. Their "diabolical conspiracy to destroy a God-fearing nation," Kaufman charged, had given the Soviets the bomb "years before our best scientists predicted." He ordered the couple's execution for treason. On June 19, 1953, the Rosenbergs, parents of two young sons, died in the electric chair.

The Rise and Fall of Joseph McCarthy

More than any other person, Wisconsin Senator Joseph McCarthy capitalized on the anti-Communism issue. Although he did not start the crusade or even join it until 1950, the entire movement bears the name "McCarthyism." His career, which was the cause of so much suffering for so many, illuminated the price the country had to pay for temporarily placing anti-Communism above the Constitution.

Widespread protesting, both for and against Julius and Ethel Rosenberg, was common after their conviction for treason in 1951 and subsequent execution in 1953.

Elected to the Senate in 1946, McCarthy spent four years in relative obscurity, all the while demonstrating his incompetence and angering his colleagues. Then on February 9, 1950, he gave a Lincoln's Birthday address in Wheeling, West Virginia. Warning his audience about the threat of communism to America, he boldly announced, "While I cannot take the time to name all of the men in the State Department who have been named as members of the Communist Party and members of a spy ring, I have in my hand a list of 205 . . . a list of names that were known to the Secretary of State and who nevertheless are still working and shaping the policy of the State Department." McCarthy had no real list; he had no names. Simply put, he was lying. But within days he became a national sensation.

McCarthy dealt in simple solutions for complex problems. He told Americans that the United States could control the outcome of world affairs if it would get the Communists out of the State Department. It was those "State Department perverts," those "striped-pants diplomats" who "gave away" Poland, "lost" China, and allowed the Soviet Union to develop the bomb. It was the "bright young men who are born with silver spoons in their mouths" who were "selling the Nation out." His arguments found receptive ears among Catholics who had relatives in Eastern Europe, political outsiders who resented the power of the "Ivy League Eastern Establishment," supporters of Chiang, and pragmatic Republicans who wanted to return to the White House in 1952. And Joseph McCarthy's support grew with the outbreak of the Korean War in the early summer of 1950.

McCarthy's origins were humble; he worked his way through high school and a Catholic college and intentionally cultivated the image of a bull in a china shop. With his beetle brow, he looked the part of a movie villain. He was in all ways the opposite of Secretary of State Dean Acheson, whose Ivy League degrees, waxed mustache, and aristocratic accent were a flapping red flag to McCarthy. Throughout the early 1950s McCarthy bitterly attacked "Red Dean" and the State Department. But in the end, McCarthy ferreted out no Communists, espionage agents, or traitors.

McCarthy's basic tactic was never defend. Caught in a lie, he told another; when one case dissolved, he created another. He attacked Truman and Eisenhower, Acheson and Marshall, the State Department and the U.S. Army. No authority or institution frightened him. In 1954 his campaign against the army became so bitter that the Senate arranged special hearings. Televised between April 22 and June 17, the Army-McCarthy hearings attracted a high audience rating. It was the first time that most Americans saw McCarthy in action—the bullying of witnesses, the cruel innuendo, the tasteless humor. At one point he attempted to ruin a young lawyer's career in order to discredit the lawyer's associate, Joseph Welch, the army's chief counsel. Welch tried to stop McCarthy but couldn't. Appalled,

the chief counsel interrupted, "Until this moment, Senator, I think I never really gauged your cruelty or your recklessness. . . . If it were in my power to forgive you for your reckless cruelty, I would do so. I like to think I am a gentle man, but your forgiveness will have to come from someone other than me. . . . Have you no sense of decency, sir, at long last?"

He didn't, and a large television audience saw that he didn't. McCarthy's consequent downfall was as rapid as his rise. When the polls showed that his popularity had swung sharply downward, his colleagues mounted an offensive. On December 2, 1954, the Senate voted to "condemn" McCarthy for his unsenatorial behavior. Newspapers stopped printing his outlandish charges. He sank back into relative obscurity, and died on May 2, 1957.

The end of the Korean War and McCarthy's downfall signaled the end of the Red Scare. The Cold War remained, but most Americans soon realized that there was no significant domestic Communist threat. They learned that an occasional spy was part of the price that free societies pay for their personal freedom, and that "McCarthyism" can be the result of a curtailment of that freedom.

Senator Joseph McCarthy's downfall came about as a result of his unsubstantiated charges of Communist infiltration throughout the army.

THE KEFAUVER CRIME COMMITTEE

IN May 1950, at the very moment that Senator Joseph McCarthy was beginning his crusade against the domestic political threat posed by communism, the U.S. Senate created a special committee to investigate another "enemy within": organized crime. The nation appeared to be in the midst of an unprecedented wave of lawlessness. A memorandum to the president reported that a serious crime was committed in the United States every 18.7 seconds. Aggravated assault was up 68.7 percent over prewar averages; rape was up 49.9 percent. Burglary, murder, robbery, prostitution, gambling, and racketeering all were on the increase. Criminologists attributed the postwar crime wave to such factors as the wartime disruption of families, shortages of goods during and after the war, and a continuing public demand for illicit gambling. But journalists, citizen crime commissions, and the Federal Bureau of Narcotics identified another villain, organized crime.

Estes Kefauver, an ambitious 47-year-old first-term Tennessee Democratic senator, originally proposed a congressional investigation of organized crime in January 1949. The Truman administration, already rocked by charges of fiscal mismanagement, financial irregularities, and favors to businessmen, feared that any inquiry might link urban Democratic political machines to criminal activities. For a time, the administration succeeded in blocking a potentially embar-

rassing investigation. But on April 6, 1950, the bodies of two gangsters were found in a Kansas City, Missouri, Democratic political club under a photograph of President Truman. The Democratic-controlled Senate quickly authorized the investigation of organized crime.

For the next 15 months, the committee held hearings in 14 major cities and took testimony from more than 800 witnesses. The committee immediately attracted national attention by linking individuals close to Florida's Democratic governor, Fuller Warren, to a bookmaking syndicate controlled by Al Capone's mob in Chicago. Subsequent hearings in Kansas City and Chicago revealed widespread examples of political corruption and influence peddling.

Television made the Kefauver committee's hearings among the most influential in American history. While the Kefauver committee did not hold the first televised congressional hearings (it was actually the fifth congressional committee to allow TV cameras into a hearing room), it was the first to attract a massive number of viewers. As many as 20 to 30 million Americans watched spellbound as crime bosses, bookies, pimps, and hitmen

appeared on their television screens. They listened intently as the committee's chairman informed them that "there is a secret international government-within-a-government" in the United States, controlling gambling, vice, and narcotics traffic and infiltrating legitimate businesses, protected by corrupt police officers, prosecutors, judges, and politicians.

The high point of the investigation occurred in New York City, where the committee held televised hearings beginning on March 12, 1951, and lasting eight days. Over 50 witnesses testified before the committee, but public interest centered on the alleged boss of the New York underworld Frank Costello, alias Francisco Castaglia, alias Frank Severio. Costello was purportedly head of the organized crime family previously run by Vito Genovese and Charles Luciano.

In his initial appearance before the committee, Costello's lawyer objected to having his client's face televised. Technicians proceeded to focus the cameras on Costello's hands. The result was television at its most powerful. As committee counsel Rudolph Halley fired questions, Costello was seen nervously ripping sheets of paper to shreds, drumming his fingers on the table top, and clenching his fist.

During the New York hearings, daytime television audiences grew from a minuscule 1.5 percent of homes to a phenomenal 26.2 percent. In the New York metropolitan area an average of 86.2 percent of all individuals watching television watched the hearings, twice the number that had watched the World Series the previous October. The New York City electric company had to add a generator to supply power for all the television sets in use. Commented *Life* magazine: "The week of March 12, 1951, will occupy a special place in history. . . . [People] had suddenly gone indoors into living rooms, taverns and clubrooms, auditoriums and backoffices. There, in eerie half-light, looking at millions of small frosty screens, people sat as if charmed. . . . Never before had the attention of the nation been riveted so completely on a single matter."

The Kefauver committee failed to produce effective crime-fighting legislation, but it did heighten public awareness of the problem of political corruption and organized crime, and generated pressure to enforce existing law. In the aftermath of the committee's investigation, more than 70 local crime commissions were established. The Special Rackets Squad of the FBI launched 46,000 investigations, and by 1957, federal prosecutors had won 874 convictions and recovered $336 million. The committee's hearings were largely responsible for the defeat of proposals to legalize gambling in Arizona, California, Massachusetts, and Montana.

The investigation was important in one other respect. The Kefauver committee played a vital role in popularizing the myth that organized crime in the United States was an alien import, brought to the United States by Italian, and especially by Sicilian, immigrants in the form of the Mafia, a highly centralized, secret organization, that used violence and deceit to prey on the weaknesses and vices of the public. In its report, the committee asserted that much of the responsibility for gambling, loan sharking, prostitution, and narcotics trafficking lay in two major syndicates.

In fact, the committee's conclusion—that organized crime was rooted in a highly centralized ethnic conspiracy—was an error. Most organized crime in the United States is organized on a municipal and regional, rather than a national, basis. And despite the image portrayed in such epics as Mario Puzo's *The Godfather*, diverse ethnic groups have participated in such sophisticated crimes as large-scale gambling, loan sharking, narcotics trafficking, and labor racketeering.

Today, the power of the nation's traditional Mafia families appears to be dwindling. Since the mid-1980s, more than 100 top Cosa Nostra leaders have been sentenced to long prison terms. In Detroit, Kansas City, Milwaukee, New England, New Jersey, Philadelphia, and St. Louis, where Mafia gangs once influenced the construction, trucking, trash collection, and garment manufacturing industries, Mafia strength has sharply declined. The decline of the mob, however, does not mean the end of organized crime; rival crime groups have stepped in and taken over such activities as illegal gambling and drug trafficking.

THE PARANOID STYLE

The Cold War mentality left its imprint on politics and culture during the late 1940s and early 1950s. A certain "paranoid style" permeated the early Cold War years. Defining the term, historian Richard Hofstadter wrote:

It is, above all, a way of seeing the world and of expressing oneself. . . . The distinguishing thing about the paranoid style is . . . that its exponents see . . . a "vast" or "gigantic" conspiracy as *the motive force* in historical events. . . . The paranoid spokesman sees the fate of this conspiracy in apocalyptic terms—he traffics in the birth and death of whole worlds, whole political orders, whole systems of human values. . . . Since what is at stake is always a conflict between absolute good and absolute evil, the quality needed is not a willingness to compromise but the will to fight things out to the finish.

The nature of the fight against communism contributed to the paranoid style. Politicians warned Americans that communism silently and secretly destroyed a country from within. Although allegedly directed from Moscow, its aim was subversion through the slow destruction of a country's moral fiber. No one knew which institution it would next attack, or when. It might be the State Department or the YMCA; it might be the presidency, the army, the movie industry, or the Cub Scouts. Politicians counseled vigilance. They told Americans to watch for the unexpected, to suspect everyone and everything. As a result, between 1945 and 1955 a broad spectrum of institutions, organizations, and individuals came under suspicion. Whether it was the Mafia or the fluoridation of drinking water, Americans sought the answers to complex problems in the workings of conspiracies.

HUAC Goes to Hollywood

The House of Representatives had established the Un-American Activities Committee (HUAC) in the late 1930s to combat subversive right-wing and left-wing movements. Its history was less than distinguished. From the first it tended to see subversive Communists everywhere at work in American society.

HUAC even announced that the Boy Scouts were infiltrated by Communists. During the late 1940s and the early 1950s HUAC picked up the tempo of its investigations, which it conducted in well-publicized sessions. Twice during this period HUAC "traveled" to Hollywood to investigate Communist infiltration in the film industry.

HUAC first went to Hollywood in 1947. Although it didn't find the party line preached in the movies, it did call a group of radical screenwriters and producers into its sessions to testify. Asked if they were Communists, a group of leftist filmmakers known as the "Hollywood Ten" refused to answer questions about their political beliefs. As Ring Lardner, Jr., one of the ten, said, "I could answer . . . but if I did, I would hate myself in the morning." They believed that the First Amendment protected them. In the politically charged late 1940s, however, their rights were not protected. Those who refused to divulge their political affiliations were tried for contempt of Congress, sent to prison, and blacklisted.

HUAC went back to Hollywood in 1951. This time it called hundreds of witnesses from

The House Un-American Activities Committee conducted an investigation of Communist activities in Hollywood, in which testimony was given by such notable actors as Ronald Reagan.

both the political right and the political left. Conservatives told HUAC that Hollywood was littered with "Commies." Walt Disney even recounted attempts to have Mickey Mouse follow the party line. Of the radicals, some talked and others didn't. To cooperate with HUAC entailed "naming names"—that is, informing on one's friends and political acquaintances. Again, those who refused to name names found themselves unemployed and unemployable.

The HUAC hearings and blacklistings convinced Hollywood producers to make strongly anti-Communist films. Between 1947 and 1954 they released more than 50 such films. Most were second-rate movies, starring third-rate actors. The films assured Americans that Communists were thoroughly bad people—they didn't have children, they exhaled cigarette smoke too slowly, they murdered their "friends," and they went berserk when arrested. As one film historian has commented, the Communists in these anti-Communist films even looked alike; most were "apt to be exceptionally haggard or disgracefully pudgy," and there was certainly "something terribly wrong with a woman if her slip straps showed through her blouse."

The films may have been bad civics lessons, but they did have an impact. They seemed to confirm HUAC's position that Communists were everywhere, that subversives lurked in every shadow. They reaffirmed the paranoid style and helped to justify McCarthy's harangues and Truman's Cold War rhetoric.

"What's Wrong with Our Kids Today?"

At the same time as it was turning out films about serious but bumbling Communists, Hollywood was producing movies that contributed to the fear that something was terribly wrong with the youth of America. Films such as *The Wild One* (1954), *Blackboard Jungle* (1955), and *Rebel Without a Cause* (1955) portrayed adolescents as budding criminals, emerging homosexuals, potential fascists, and pathological misfits—everything but

Movies like *Rebel Without a Cause*, starring James Dean, depicted the futility and hopelessness of American youth in the 1950s.

perfectly normal kids. On close inspection, cultural critics concluded that something was indeed wrong with American youth, who, like Tony in *I Was a Teenage Werewolf* (1957), seemed closer to uncontrollable beasts than civilized adults. As Tony tells a psychiatrist, "I say things, I do things—I don't know why."

FBI reports and congressional investigations reinforced the theme of the moral decline of America's adolescents. J. Edgar Hoover, head of the FBI, linked the rise in juvenile delinquency to the decline in the influence of family, home, church, and local community institutions. Youths had moved away from benign authority toward the temptations of popular culture, which, Hoover said, "flout indecency and applaud lawlessness."

Frederic Wertham, a psychiatrist who studied the problem extensively, agreed, emphasizing particularly the pernicious influence of comic books. He believed that crime and horror comic books fostered racism, fascism, and sexism in their readers. In his book *Seduction of the*

Innocent (1954), Wertham even linked homosexuality to the reading of comics. Describing how the comic *Batman* could lead to homosexuality, Wertham quoted one of his male patients: "I remember the first time I came across the page mentioning the 'secret bat cave.' The thought of Batman and Robin living together and possibly having sex relations came to my mind, . . . I felt I'd like to be loved by someone like Batman or Superman." Far from being an unheard voice, Wertham's attack generated congressional investigations of and local attacks against the comic book industry. In response, the industry passed several self-regulatory codes designed to restrict the violent and sexual content of comic books.

For a number of critics, sports were an antidote to the ills of wayward youths. "Organized sport is one of our best weapons against juvenile delinquency," remarked J. Edgar Hoover. Youths who competed for championship trophies felt no inclination to compete for "wrist watches, bracelets and automobiles that belong to other people." Nor would they turn to Communism. As Senator Herman Welker of Idaho bluntly put it, "I never saw a ballplayer who was a Communist."

Given these widespread beliefs, the sports scandals of the early 1950s shocked the nation and raised fresh questions about the morality of American adolescents. In February 1951 New York authorities disclosed that players for the City College of New York (CCNY) basketball team had accepted money to fix games. By the time the investigations ended, Long Island University, New York University, Manhattan College, St. John's, Toledo, Bradley, and Kentucky were implicated in the scandal, which involved forging transcripts, paying players, and fixing games.

In August 1951 the scandal moved to football. This one involved academic cheating, not point shaving, and was confined to one school—the United States Military Academy at West Point. Altogether, academy officials dismissed 90 cadets, half of them football players, for violations of the school's honor code. "These acts," said Senator Harry F. Byrd of Virginia, "have struck a blow at the morals of the youth of the country which will last for a long time."

The West Point scandal, especially, struck at the nation's heart, for half a world away in Korea American soldiers were battling to contain communism. What of their moral fiber? They too had read comics, watched films written by left-wing screen writers, and been exposed to "subversive" influences. Did they have the "right stuff"? These questions swirled around the Korean prisoner-of-war (POW) controversy. Early reports suggested that American POWs in Korea were different from, and inferior to, those of World War II. Journalists portrayed them as undisciplined, morally weak, susceptible to "brainwashing," uncommitted to traditional American ideals, and prone to collaborate with their guards.

What was wrong? Who was corrupting the youth of America? The Republican *Chicago Tribune* blamed the New Deal. The Communist *Daily Worker* said it was the fault of Wall Street, bankers, and greedy politicians (the paranoid style, after all, had no party affiliation). Other Americans, without being too specific, simply felt that there was some ominous force working within America against America.

Adherents to the paranoid style dealt more in vague perceptions than concrete facts. They reacted more to what *seemed* to be true than to what actually was true. In fact, sociologists and historians have demonstrated that Korean POWs behaved in much the same way as POWs from earlier wars. Juvenile delinquency was not on an upswing during the late 1940s and 1950s. And alien subversive forces were not undermining American morality. In retrospect, we know this. But the rhetoric of the Cold War and McCarthyism created a political atmosphere that proved fertile for the paranoid style.

CONCLUSION

By 1953 and 1954 there were indications of a thaw in the Cold War. First came the death of Joseph Stalin, which was officially announced on March 5, 1953. Shortly thereafter Georgi Malenkov told the Supreme Soviet, the highest legislative body of the Soviet Union: "At the present time there is no disputed or unresolved question that cannot be settled peace-

CHRONOLOGY
OF KEY EVENTS

1938 House Un-American Activities Committee (HUAC) is created to investigate Fascist or Communist subversion

1945 United Nations is founded

1947 Truman Doctrine declares that the United States will provide military and economic aid to allies faced by external aggression or internal subversion; Truman establishes a federal program to investigate the loyalty of government employees; Marshall Plan provides $17 billion over four years to Western Europe to aid in its economic recovery; Taft-Hartley Act, passed over President Truman's veto, bans the closed shop, restricts union political contributions, and allows courts to delay strikes threatening health or safety; HUAC investigates Communist infiltration of the film industry

1948 State of Israel proclaimed; United States, Britain, and France merge their zones of occupation in Germany to form an independent nation, West Germany; Soviet Union blockades Berlin; ex-Communist Whittaker Chambers charges that former State Department official Alger Hiss gave him secret government documents

1949 NATO is founded; Berlin blockade ends; Mao Tse-tung's Communist forces win China's civil war; Soviet Union successfully tests an atomic bomb

1950 NSC–68 argues that the United States must commit itself to whatever military steps are necessary to stop the spread of Communism; Senator Joseph McCarthy claims he has the names of 205 State Department employees who were members of the Communist party; North Korean troops cross the 38th parallel, beginning the Korean War; UN forces invade North Korea; Chinese troops enter North Korea and force UN troops to retreat across the 38th parallel

1951 Negotiations to work out a cease-fire in Korea begin; HUAC conducts a second investigation of Communist subversion in Hollywood; Ethel and Julius Rosenberg are sentenced to death for espionage

1953 Dwight D. Eisenhower is inaugurated as the thirty-fourth president; cease-fire signed in Korean War

1954 Army-McCarthy hearings; U.S. Senate censures McCarthy for "conduct unbecoming a member"

fully by mutual agreement. . . . This applies to our relations with all states, including the United States of America." That summer the Korean War ended in a stalemate that allowed both the United States and the Communist forces to save face. In America, 1954 saw the fall of McCarthy. Certainly these events did not end the paranoid style in either America or the Soviet Union, but they did ease the tension.

In addition, by 1954 both the United States and the Soviet Union had become more comfortable in their positions as world powers.

Leaders in both countries had begun to realize that neither side could readily win the Cold War. Between 1945 and 1954 each side had carved out spheres of influence. The Soviet Union and its sometime-ally China dominated most of Eastern Europe and the Asian mainland. America and its allies controlled Western Europe, North and South America, most of the Pacific, and to a lesser extent Africa, the Middle East, and Southeast Asia. Throughout much of the Third World, however, emerging nationalistic movements would challenge both U.S. and Soviet influences.

In the United States, the containment policy was seldom even debated. The Truman Doctrine and muscular internationalism governed foreign policy decisions, but economic and political questions lingered. How much would containment cost? Where would the money come from? Which Americans would pay the most? Would it mean the end of liberal reform? Over the next decade American leaders would wrestle with these and other questions.

SUGGESTIONS FOR FURTHER READING

Gar Alperovitz, *Atomic Diplomacy*, rev. ed. (1985). Controversial study that ignited a serious second look at the reasons for America's use of atomic weapons.

Larry Ceplair and Steven Englund, *The Inquisition in Hollywood* (1980). Studies the impact of Washington on Hollywood and Hollywood's impact on America.

Stanley I. Kutler, *The American Inquisition: Justice and Injustice in the Cold War* (1982). A series of poignant studies of the human consequences of the domestic side of the Cold War.

Walter LeFeber, *America, Russia, and the Cold War*, 7th ed. (1993). The frequently updated story of the great rivalry of the second half of the twentieth century.

David McCullough, *Truman* (1992). Sprawling biography of Harry Truman and the world that made him.

David M. Oshinsky, *A Conspiracy So Immense: The World of Joe McCarthy* (1983). A fascinating biography of a man who gave his name to an age.

Allen Weinstein, *Perjury: The Hiss-Chambers Case* (1978). A detailed examination of Alger Hiss's guilt.

Daniel Yergin, *Shattered Peace* (1977). Well-written, balanced exploration of the origins of the Cold War.

Overviews and Surveys

Stephen E. Ambrose, *Rise to Globalism: American Foreign Policy Since 1938*, 5th ed. (1988); H. W. Brands, *Inside the Cold War* (1991); William H. Chafe, *The American Woman* (1972); Warren I. Cohen, *America in the Age of Soviet Power, 1945–1991* (1993); John Diggins, *The Proud Decades: America in War and Peace, 1941–1960* (1988); John Lewis Gad-dis, *The United States and the Cold War* (1992); Alonzo Hamby, *The Imperial Years* (1976); Godfrey Hodgson, *America in Our Time* (1976); R. W. Leopold, *The Growth of American Foreign Policy* (1962); William Leuchtenburg, *A Troubled Feast*, rev. ed. (1983); William Manchester, *The Glory and the Dream* (1974); Thomas J. McCormick, *America's Half-Century* (1989); Thomas G. Paterson and Robert J. McMahon, *The Origins of the Cold War*, 3d ed. (1991); Emily and Norman Rosenberg, *In Our Times*, 5th ed. (1995); Frederick F. Siegel, *A Troubled Journey* (1984); Lawrence Wittner, *Cold War America*, rev. ed. (1978); Randall B. Woods and Howard Jones, *Dawning of the Cold War* (1991); Howard Zinn, *Postwar America, 1945–1971* (1973).

Containing the Russian Bear and the Containment Policy

Terry H. Anderson, *The United States, Great Britain and the Cold War, 1944–1947* (1981); James Aronson, *The Press and the Cold War* (1970); Stanley D. Bachrack, *The Committee of One Million: "China Lobby" Politics, 1953–1971* (1976); Richard J. Barnet, *The Giants: Russia and America* (1977); Ronald J. Caridi, *The Korean War and American Politics* (1969); Gordon H. Chang, *Friends and Enemies: The United States, China, and the Soviet Union, 1948–1972* (1990); Bernard C. Cohen, *The Public's Impact on Foreign Policy* (1972); Frank Costigliola, *France and the United States: The Cold Alliance Since World War II* (1992); Bruce Cumings, *The Origins of the Korean War*, 2 vols. (1981–1990); Lynn Etheridge Davis, *The Cold War Begins: Soviet-American Conflict over Eastern Europe* (1974); A. W. DePorte, *Europe Between the Superpowers: The Enduring Balance*, 2d ed. (1986); Richard B. Finn, *Winners in Peace: MacArthur, Yoshida, and Postwar Japan* (1992); D. F. Fleming, *The Cold War and Its Origins*, 2 vols. (1961); Rosemary Foot, *A Substitute for Victory* (1990); John L. Gaddis, *The United States and the Origins of the Cold War, 1941–1947* (1972), and *Strategies of Containment: A Crucial Appraisal of Postwar American National Security Policy* (1982); Lloyd C. Gardner, *Architects of Illusion: Men and Ideas in American Foreign Policy, 1941–1949* (1970); Marshall I. Goldman, *Détente and Dollars: Doing Business with the Soviets* (1975); Michael Hogan, *The Marshall Plan* (1987); Akira Iriye, *The Cold War in Asia* (1974); Howard Jones, *A New Kind of War: America's Global Strategy and the Truman Doctrine in Greece* (1989); Burton Kaufman, *Trade and Aid* (1982); Joyce and Gabriel Kolko, *The Limits of*

Power: The World and U.S. Foreign Policy, 1945–1954 (1972); Bennett Kovrig, The Myth of Liberation: East-Central Europe in U.S. Diplomacy and Politics Since 1941 (1973); Bruce Kuklick, American Policy and the Division of Germany (1972); Melvyn P. Leffler, A Preponderance of Power: National Security, the Truman Administration, and the Cold War (1991), and The Specter of Communism: The United States and the Origins of the Cold War (1994); Ralph B. Levering, The Public and American Foreign Policy, 1918–1978 (1978), and The Cold War, 1945–1987, 2d ed. (1988); Louis Liebovich, The Press and the Origins of the Cold War, 1944–1947 (1988); Vojtech Mastny, Russia's Road to the Cold War, 1941–1945 (1979); Ernest R. May, The Truman Administration and China, 1945–1949 (1975); David Mayers, George Kennan and the Dilemmas of U.S. Foreign Policy (1993); Thomas Paterson, On Every Front: The Making and Unmaking of the Cold War, rev. ed. (1992); David Rees, Korea: The Limited War (1964); Martin Sherwin, A World Destroyed: The Atomic Bomb and the Grand Alliance (1975); John W. Spanier, The Truman-MacArthur Controversy and the Korean War (1959); Hugh Thomas, Armed Truce: The Beginnings of the Cold War (1986); Adam B. Ulam, Expansion and Coexistence: The History of Soviet Foreign Policy, 1917–73, 2d ed. (1974); William Welch, American Images of Soviet Foreign Policy (1970); Allen S. Whiting, China Crosses the Yalu: The Decision to Enter the Korean War (1960); Lawrence Wittner, American Intervention in Greece, 1943–1949 (1982).

The Cold War at Home

Edwin R. Bayley, Joe McCarthy and the Press (1981); H. W. Brands, The Devil We Knew: Americans and the Cold War (1993); Jeff Broadwater, Eisenhower and the Anti-Communist Crusade (1992); David Caute, The Great Fear: The Anti-Communist Purge under Truman and Eisenhower (1978); Richard Freeland, The Truman Doctrine and the Origins of McCarthyism (1972); Richard M. Fried, Men Against McCarthy (1976), and Nightmare in Red (1990); Walter Goodman, The Committee (1968); Robert Griffith, The Politics of Fear, 2d ed. (1987); Alonzo Hamby, Beyond the New Deal: Harry S. Truman and American Liberalism (1973); Susan M. Hartmann, Truman and the 80th Congress (1971); Fred Inglis, The Cruel Peace: Everyday Life and the Cold War (1991); Richard S. Kirkendall, Harry S. Truman, Korea, and the Imperial Presidency (1975); R. Alton Lee, Truman and Taft-Hartley (1966); Samuel Lubell, Future of American Politics, 2d ed. (1956); Maeva Marcus, Truman and the Steel Seizure Case (1977); Allen J. Matusow, Farm Policies and Politics in the Truman Years (1967); John H. Neville, The Press, the Rosenbergs, and the Cold War (1995); Michael Rogin, The Intellectuals and McCarthy (1967); Athan Theoharis, Seeds of Repression: Harry S. Truman and the Origins of McCarthyism (1971).

The Paranoid Style

Paul Boyer, By the Bomb's Early Light: American Thought and Culture at the Dawn of the Atomic Age (1994); Stephen Fox, Blood and Power: Organized Crime in Twentieth-Century America (1990); Eric Goldman, The Crucial Decade and After (1961); Richard Hofstadter, The Paranoid Style in American Politics and Other Essays (1965); William Howard Moore, The Kefauver Committee and the Politics of Crime (1974); Victor Navasky, Naming Names (1980); Nora Sayre, Running Time: Films of the Cold War (1982); Stephen J. Whitfield, The Culture of the Cold War (1991).

Biographies

Dean Acheson, Present at the Creation: My Years in the State Department (1969); Charles E. Bohlen, Witness to History, 1929–1969 (1973); Douglas Brinkley, Dean Acheson: The Cold War Years, 1953–1971 (1992); David Callahan, Dangerous Capabilities: Paul Nitze and the Cold War (1990); Clark Clifford with Richard Holbrooke, Counsel to the President, A Memoir (1991); Robert J. Donovan, Conflict and Crisis (1977), and Tumultuous Years (1982); Robert H. Ferrell, George C. Marshall (1966), and Harry S Truman and the Modern American Presidency (1983); Charles L. Fontenay, Estes Kefauver (1980); Gregory A. Fossedal, Our Finest Hour: Will Clayton, the Marshall Plan, and the Triumph of Democracy (1993); Joseph Bruce Gorman, Kefauver (1971); Walter L. Hixson, George F. Kennan (1989); Ronald McGlothlen, Controlling the Waves: Dean Acheson and U.S. Foreign Policy in Asia (1993); David S. McLellan, Dean Acheson (1976); Robert P. Newman, Owen Lattimore and the "Loss" of China (1992); James T. Patterson, Mr. Republican: A Biography of Robert A. Taft (1972); Thomas C. Reeves, The Life and Times of Joe McCarthy (1982); Edward L. and Frederick H. Schapsmeier, Prophet in Politics: Henry A. Wallace and the War Years, 1940–1965 (1971); Gaddis Smith, Dean Acheson (1972); Ronald Steel, Walter Lippmann and the American Century (1980); Anders Stephanson, Kennan and the Art of Foreign Policy (1989); Mark A. Stoler, George C. Marshall (1989); Harry S Truman, Memoirs, 2 vols. (1955–1956).

CHAPTER 27
IKE'S AMERICA

QUIET CHANGES
"I Like Ike"
"Dynamic Conservatism"
A Country on Wheels
Ike, Dulles, and the World
A New Face in Moscow
1956: The Dangerous Year
The Troubled Second Term
Sputnik and Sputtering Rockets
Third-World Challenges
Not with a Bang, But a Whimper

WE SHALL OVERCOME
Taking Jim Crow to Court
A Failure of Leadership
The Word from Montgomery

THE SOUNDS OF CHANGE
Father Knows Best
The Other Side of the Coin
The Meaning of Elvis
A Different Beat

The New York Times.

"All the News That's Fit to Print"   LATE CITY

VOL. CVII... No. X,XX.   NEW YORK, SATURDAY, OCTOBER 5, 1957

SOVIET FIRES EARTH SATELLITE INTO SPAC
IT IS CIRCLING THE GLOBE AT 18,000 M. P.
SPHERE TRACKED IN 4 CROSSINGS OVER

HOFFA IS ELECTED
TEAMSTERS' HEAD;
WARNS OF BATTLE

COURSE RECORDED

Navy Picks Up Radio
Signals—4 Report
Sighting Device

Device Is 8 Times Heavier
Than One Planned by U.S.

ARGENTINA TAKES
EMERGENCY STEPS

SATELLITE SIGNAL
BROADCAST HERE

Mose Wright stood and surveyed the courtroom. Most of the faces he saw were white. The two accused men were white. The 12 jurors were white. The armed guards were white. Slowly, Wright, a 64-year-old African-American sharecropper, extended his right arm. "Thar he," Wright answered, pointing at J. W. Milam. He then pointed at Roy Bryant, the second defendant. In essence, Wright was accusing the two whites of murdering Emmett Till, his 14-year-old nephew—accusing them in a segregated courtroom in Sumner, Mississippi. Wright later recalled that he could "feel the blood boil in hundreds of white people as they sat glaring in the courtroom. It was the first time in my life I had the courage to accuse a white man of a crime, let alone something as terrible as killing a boy. I wasn't exactly brave and I wasn't scared. I just wanted to see justice done."

Mose Wright and his three boys, seated in the "colored" section of the courtroom, attended the trial of Roy Bryant and J. W. Milam, accused of killing Emmett Till in Mississippi.

It was 1955, but the march of racial justice in the South had been painfully slow. In 1954 the Supreme Court of the United States, in the landmark *Brown* v. *Board of Education of Topeka* decision, had ruled that segregated schooling was "inherently unequal." News of the *Brown* decision drew angry comments and reactions from all corners of the Jim Crow South. Mississippi Senator James Eastland told his constituents that the decision destroyed the Constitution of the United States and counseled, "You are not obliged to obey the decisions of any court which are plainly fraudulent." Throughout Dixie, Klansmen burned crosses while other white leaders hastily organized Citizens' Councils. Self-proclaimed protectors of white America vowed "to make it difficult, if not impossible, for any Negro who advocates desegregation to find and hold a job, get credit, or renew a mortgage."

Into the racially charged atmosphere of August 1955 came Emmett Till. Taking a summer vacation from his home on the South Side of Chicago, he rode a train to visit relatives living near Money, Mississippi. Emmett had known segregation in Chicago, but nothing like what he discovered in Money, where shortly before his arrival an African-American girl had been "flogged" for "crowding white people" in a store.

Emmett's mother told him what to expect and how to act: "If you have to get on your knees and bow when a white person goes past, do it willingly." But Emmett had a mind and a mouth of his own. In Chicago, he told his cousins, he was friends with plenty of white people. He even had a picture of a white girl, *his* white girl, he said. "Hey," challenged a listener, "there's a [white] girl in that store there. I bet you won't go in there and talk to her."

Emmett accepted the challenge. He entered Bryant's Grocery and Meat Market, browsed about, and bought some bubble gum. As he left, he said, "Bye, Baby" to Carolyn Bryant and gave a "wolf call" whistle. Outside an old black man told Emmett to scat before the woman got a pistol and blew "his brains out." The advice sounded sage enough, so Emmett beat a hasty retreat.

A few days later Roy Bryant returned to Money after hauling shrimp from Louisiana to Texas. What his wife told him is unknown, but it was enough to make him angry. After midnight that Saturday night, he and his half-brother, J. W. "Big" Milam, drove to Mose Wright's unpainted cabin. They demanded the "boy who done the talkin'." Mose tried to explain that Emmett was from "up nawth," that he "ain't got good sense" and was unfamiliar with southern ways. The logic of the argument was lost on the two white men, one of whom told Mose that if he caused trouble he would never see his next birthday.

Various stories have been told about what happened during the next few hours. One thing is for certain: Emmett Till did not live much past daybreak. According to Milam and Bryant's account, they had only meant to scare the northern youth. But Emmett did not beg for mercy. Therefore they *had* to kill him. "What else could we do?" Milam asked. "He was hopeless. I'm no bully; I never hurt a nigger in my life. I like niggers in their place. I know how to work 'em. But I just decided it was time a few people got put on notice."

Three days later Emmett's badly beaten body was found in the Tallahatchie River. A gouged-out eye, crushed forehead, and bullet in his skull gave evidence to the beating he took. Around his neck, attached by barbed wire, was a 75-pound cotton gin fan. At the request of his mother, the local sheriff sent the decomposing body to Chicago for burial.

Mamie Bradley, Emmett's mother, grieved openly and loudly. Contrary to the wishes of Mississippi authorities, she held an open-casket funeral. Thousands of African-American Chicagoans attended the viewing, and the African-American press closely followed the episode. *Jet* magazine even published a picture of the mutilated corpse. In the African-American community the Till murder case became a cause célèbre. In a land that valued justice, would any be found in Mississippi?

In Money, white Southerners rallied to Bryant and Milam's side. Supporters raised a $10,000 defense fund, and southern editorials labeled the entire affair a "Communist plot" to destroy southern society. By the time the trial started, American interest seemed focused on Mississippi. Few people, however, expected that Bryant and Milam would be judged guilty because few expected any African Americans would testify against white men in Mississippi.

Mose Wright proved the folly of common wisdom. He dramatically testified against the white men. So did several other relatives of Emmett Till. But in his closing statement, John C. Whitten, one of the five white defense attorneys, told the all-white, all-male jury: "Your fathers will turn over in their graves if [Milam and Bryant are found guilty] and I'm sure that every last Anglo-Saxon one of you has the courage to free these men in the face of that [outside] pressure."

The jury returned a "not guilty" verdict in one hour and seven minutes. "If we hadn't stopped to drink a pop, it wouldn't have taken that long," one juror commented. On that day in 1955 there was no justice in Sumner, Mississippi. Michigan Congressman Charles Diggs, who sat with other African Americans in the rear section of the segregated courtroom, recalled, "I certainly was angered by the decision, [but] I was not surprised by it. And I was strengthened in my belief that something had to be done about the dispensation of justice in that state." Roy Wilkins of the NAACP remarked that "there is in the entire state no restraining influence of decency, not in the state capital, among the daily newspapers, the clergy, not among any segment of the so-called lettered citizens."

But if there was no justice that day, there were clear signs of change. An African-American man had demanded justice in white-controlled Mississippi. Soon—very soon—other voices would join Mose Wright's. Their peaceful but insistent cries would be heard over the surface quiet of Dwight Eisenhower's America. They would force America to come to terms with its own ideology. After a heroic struggle against fascism and during a cold conflict against communism, Americans no longer could ignore racial injustice and inequality at home.

It was time for change. During the late 1940s and the 1950s the process began. Slow, painful, poignant, occasionally uplifting—the march toward justice moved forward. It was part of other significant social and economic changes taking place in America. Against the backdrop of Eisenhower's calm assurances, a new country was taking shape.

QUIET CHANGES

Most white Americans during the late 1940s and the early 1950s were unconcerned about the struggles of their African-American compatriots. Perhaps some admired Jackie Robinson's efforts on the baseball field, but few made the connection between integration in sports and civil rights throughout society. Other concerns seemed more urgent. In November 1952 the Korean War was dragging into its third year, and the chances for a satisfactory peace were fading. Joseph McCarthy was still warning Americans about the Communist infiltration of the U.S. government. Political corruption had stained the Truman administration. At the polls Americans were ready to vote for change.

"I Like Ike"

Republicans certainly felt it was time for change. The Democrats had occupied the White House for the previous 20 years. In 1952 they ran Governor Adlai Stevenson of Illinois for the presidency. A political moderate and a vocal anti-Communist, the witty, sophisticated Stevenson was burdened by Truman's unpopularity. His Republican opponent was Dwight David Eisenhower, a moderate, anti-Communist war hero. The Republican campaign strategy was summarized in a formula—K_1C_2. Eisenhower promised that if elected he would first end the war in Korea then battle communism and corruption at home. The nation responded. Eisenhower was swept into office. He even carried several southern states and cut into the urban-ethnic coalition of the Democrats.

"I Like Ike" campaign buttons and posters captured the public sentiment. And there was much to like. Few people had advanced so far while making so few enemies. Ike's was the classic Horatio Alger success story. Although

born in Texas, he was raised in Abilene, Kansas, the northern terminus of the Chisholm Trail. An accomplished athlete and a good student, Ike earned an appointment to West Point, where he graduated in 1915 among "the class on which the stars fell." (Fifty-nine of the 164 graduates of the class would rise to the rank of brigadier general or higher.)

As an army officer, Eisenhower demonstrated rare organizational abilities and a capacity for complex detail work. If by 1939 he had only risen to the rank of lieutenant colonel, he had nonetheless impressed his superiors. With the outbreak of World War II, he was promoted with startling rapidity. In fact, in 1942 General George Marshall passed over 366 more senior officers to promote Eisenhower to major general and appoint him commander of the European Theater of Operations. It was Ike who planned and oversaw America's invasions of North Africa, Sicily, and Italy and who led the combined British-American D-Day invasion of France. By the end of the war, Ike was a four-star general and an international hero.

Ike's ability to win the loyalty of others and work with people of diverse and difficult temperaments would serve him well as a politician. But during the early postwar years, he expressed no interest in holding political office. "I cannot conceive of any set of circumstances that could drag out of me permission to consider me for any political post from dog catcher to Grand High Supreme King of the Universe," he told a reporter in 1946. And indeed there is no evidence that Ike had ever voted or had any party affiliation before running for the presidency on the Republican ticket in 1952.

Eisenhower did have strong beliefs concerning America's domestic and foreign policies. His fiscal conservatism led him to the Republican party, and his internationalism convinced him to run for the presidency. He did not want to see an isolationist Republican elected in 1952, and the early front-runner was isolationist Robert Alphonso Taft, the powerful Ohio senator. Once Ike had defeated Taft for the nomination, his victory over Stevenson was almost anticlimactic.

Almost overnight the image of Eisenhower was transformed from one of a master military organizer to one of mumbling, bumbling, smiling incomprehensibility. Reporters commented on his friendly smile, engaging blue eyes, and his mangled syntax. As a young officer Eisenhower had written striking speeches for Douglas MacArthur, and as a World War II general he had impressed reporters with the precision of his thought. Commenting on Ike's speaking style, FDR's press secretary said, "He knows his facts, he speaks freely and frankly, and he has a sense of humor, he has poise, and he has command."

Had Eisenhower somehow sunk into senility on taking office? Certainly not. He sensed that the country needed a rest from 20 years of active presidents. Rather than needing an earth-shaker, the country needed a "dirt smoother." The result was the "hidden-hand leadership" of Ike. In public he seemed everyone's favorite grandfather and golfing buddy, friendly, outgoing, quick to please, but only slightly interested in being president. Although he had read widely in both military history and the classics, he insisted publicly that he only read westerns, and those not too closely. But throughout his eight years in office, Eisenhower focused closely on his two major priorities: U.S.-Soviet relations and a balanced budget. These issues, not civil rights or other important social concerns, occupied most of his attention.

"Dynamic Conservativism"

Eisenhower brought the military chain of command system to the White House. He was in charge, and he kept the major decisions of his administration in his own hands. But he left the detail work and the political battling to his subordinates. The most important person after Eisenhower in this command structure was Sherman Adams, the former governor of New Hampshire who served as Ike's chief of staff. Adams determined who got to see the president and what issues were placed before him. Although forced to resign in 1958 for influence peddling (he had accepted an Oriental rug and a vicuña coat from a New England textile magnate), Adams pioneered modern White House administration.

Ike saw himself as a forward-looking Republican. He called himself a conservative, "but an extremely liberal conservative," one who was concerned with fiscal prudence but not at the expense of human beings. Ike termed his approach "modern Republicanism" and "dynamic conservativism," by which he meant, "conservative when it comes to money matters and liberal when it comes to human beings." In practice this approach led the Eisenhower administration to cut spending while not rolling back New Deal social legislation.

George Humphrey, a conservative Ohio industrialist, served as Eisenhower's treasury secretary. More conservative than Eisenhower, Humphrey believed that the federal government should shift more fiscal responsibilities to the state and private sectors. He did succeed in getting Congress to abolish the Reconstruction Finance Corporation (see Chapter 24) and turn over off-shore oil rights to the seaboard states. The *New York Times* called this latter piece of legislation, the Submerged Land Act, "one of the greatest and surely the most unjustified give-away programs in all the history of the United States." On the whole, however, Eisenhower's domestic programs were hardly reactionary.

During Ike's two terms the country made steady and at times spectacular economic progress. In 1955 the minimum wage was raised from 75 cents to $1 per hour, and during the 1950s the average family income rose 15 percent and real wages went up 20 percent. And work was plentiful. During the decade, unemployment averaged only 4.5 percent per year, a figure close to the magical 4 percent economists considered "full employment." Stable prices, full employment, and steady growth were the economic hallmarks of the 1950s. "American labor has never had it so good," AFL-CIO chief George Meany told his associates in 1955. Although the population increased by 28 million people, the country was on the whole better housed and fed than ever before. The output of goods and services rose 15 percent. Especially for white Americans, "modern Republicanism" seemed a viable alternative to New Dealism.

A Country on Wheels

If Eisenhower labored to curtail the role of the federal government in some areas, he expanded it in other places. As an expert on military logistics, Ike frequently expressed concern about the sad state of the American highway system. During World War II he had been impressed by Hitler's system of *Autobahnen,* which allowed the German dictator to deploy troops to different parts of Germany with incredible speed. From his first days in office, Eisenhower worked for legislation to improve America's highway network.

The highway lobby agreed. Following the philosophy that what was good for General Motors was good for the country, the highway lobby—a loose collection of pressure groups that included representatives from the automobile, trucking, bus, oil, rubber, asphalt, and construction industries—pushed for a new federally subsidized interstate highway system. Not only would such a project provide millions of new jobs, it would contribute to a safer America by making it easier to evacuate major cities in the event of a nuclear attack.

As a result of presidential and lobby pressure, in 1956 Congress passed the National

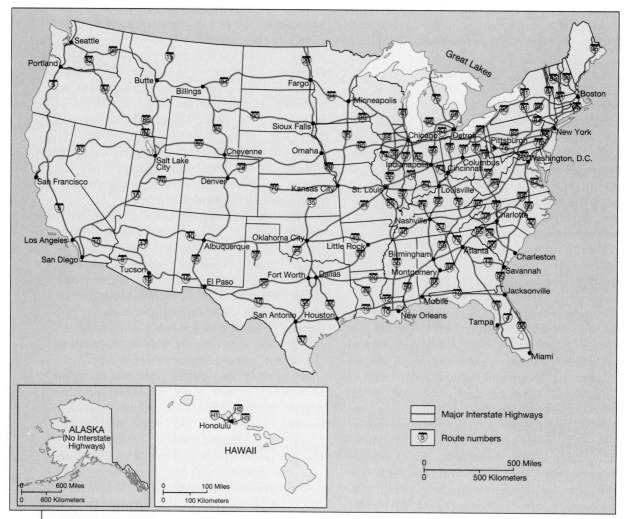

United States Interstate Highway System
The 1956 plan to create an interstate highway system drastically changed America's landscape and culture.

System of Interstate and Defense Highways Act, the most significant piece of domestic legislation enacted under Eisenhower. As planned, the system would cover 41,000 (later expanded to 42,500) miles, cost $26 billion, and take 13 years to construct. Although it took longer to complete and cost far more than Congress projected, it did provide the United States with the world's most extensive superhighway system. Secretary of Commerce Sinclair Weeks estimated that the act would create 150,000 new construction jobs and rank as "the greatest public works program in history."

More than any other piece of legislation, it also changed America. After Congress passed the 1956 bill, cultural critic Lewis Mumford wrote, "When the American people, through their Congress, voted . . . for a $26 billion highway program, the most charitable thing to assume is that they hadn't the faintest notion of what they were doing." Mumford realized that this commitment to internal combustion engines would alter the culture and landscape of America; and it has. It accelerated the decline of the inner city and the flight to the suburbs. The downtown portions of cities, once thriving with commerce and excitement, rapidly turned into ghost towns. As downtown businesses, hotels, and theaters closed, suburban shopping malls with multiscreen cinemas and roadside motels began to dot the American highway landscape. Drive-in theaters, gasoline service stations, mobile homes, and multicar garages signified the birth of a new extended society, one without center or focus. Indeed, highway construction was simply one expression of Americans' obsession with the automobile during the 1950s and 1960s. After being deprived of new cars during the war—when the maximum speed limit was 35 miles per hour—Americans adopted the new automobile philosophy of bigger is better and the biggest and fastest is the best. In 1952 over 52 million cars crowded American roads, and that number doubled during the next 20 years.

New home architecture exemplified America's mobile-minded culture. The garage, once separated from and located behind the house, achieved a new position. By the 1960s the average home devoted more space to the family automobiles than to individual family members. With access to the house itself—usually through the kitchen—the garage had become an integrated part of the house and the car an important member of the family. Home architects in the 1960s and 1970s showed the growing importance of the automobile by placing the garage in a prominent position in the front of the house.

America's commitment to highways and cars created numerous problems. Mass transportation suffered most conspicuously. Streetcars and commuter railroads languished, as did the country's major interstate railroads. Since highway construction was financed by a nondivertible gasoline tax, government often

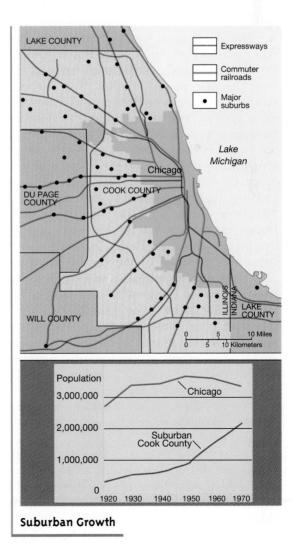

Suburban Growth

ignored mass transit. In the years since the end of World War II, 75 percent of government expenditures for transportation have gone for highways as opposed to 1 percent for urban mass transit. As a result, those not able to use automobiles—the old, the very young, the poor, the handicapped—became victims of America's automobile obsession.

Ike, Dulles, and the World

For Eisenhower, "modern Republicanism" was more than simply a domestic economic credo. It also implied an internationalist foreign policy. As with domestic policy, Ike preferred to operate behind the scenes in foreign policy. But he did make all major foreign policy decisions.

The point man for Ike's foreign policy was Secretary of State John Foster Dulles. When Eisenhower asked Dulles to head the State Department, he remarked, "You've been training yourself to be Secretary of State ever since you were nine years old." And so he had. An interest in foreign affairs was part of the Dulles heritage. Dulles's maternal grandfather had served as Benjamin Harrison's secretary of state, and one of his uncles, Robert Lansing, had occupied the same post under Woodrow Wilson. In 1919, as a young man, Dulles had been part of the American delegation to the Versailles Peace Conference, and later, as a member of the prestigious Wall Street law firm of Sullivan and Cromwell, he had represented clients with international interests. After World War II, he helped organize the United Nations and then served as a delegate. In addition, throughout his life Dulles was a careful student of foreign affairs and international politics. Eisenhower noted, there was "only one man I know who has seen *more* of the world and talked with more people and *knows* more than [Dulles] does—and that's me."

Dulles's experience and knowledge were somewhat offset by his rigidity and excessive moralism. If Americans felt comfortable calling President Eisenhower "Ike," not even close friends called Dulles "Jack." Plain and as unpolished as granite, Dulles took himself, his

Presbyterian religion, and the world seriously. "His face," commented an associate, "was permanently lined with an expression of unhappiness mingled with faint distaste—the kind of face that, on those rare occasions when it was drawn into a smile, looked as though it ached in every muscle to get back into its normal shape." One Washington correspondent described him as "a card-carrying Christian," and he frequently delivered lectures on the evils of "atheistic, materialistic Communism." He tended to see opposition to communism in religious terms. A friend recalled a conversation in which China's Chiang Kai-shek and South Korea's Syngman Rhee were criticized. Offended, Dulles announced: "No matter what you say about them, those two gentlemen are modern-day equivalents of the founders of the church. They are Christian gentlemen who have suffered for their faith."

Although Eisenhower and Dulles had strikingly different public styles, they shared a common vision of the world. Both were internationalists and cold warriors who believed that the Soviet Union was the enemy and that the United States was and should be the protector of the free world. Peace was their objective—but never a peace won by appeasement. To keep honorable peace, both were willing to consider the use of nuclear weapons and go to the brink of war. As Dulles said in 1956, "You have to take some chances for peace, just as you must take chances in war."

Occasionally Dulles's impassioned anti-Communist rhetoric obscured the actual policies pursued by the Eisenhower administration. In public Dulles rejected the containment doctrine as a "negative, futile and immoral policy" and advocated the "liberation" of Eastern Europe. It was time to "roll back" the Iron Curtain, he said, and if nuclear weapons were needed to achieve America's objectives—well, then, so be it. In public Dulles constantly flexed his—and America's—muscles.

In reality, Eisenhower's objectives were far more limited and his approach toward foreign policy much more cautious. Eisenhower supported containment, but not as practiced by Truman. In Eisenhower's eyes, Truman's approach was unorganized and far too expensive. Like political journalist Walter Lippmann in the late 1940s, Ike believed that the United States could not support every country that claimed to be fighting communism. As historian Charles C. Alexander noted, "The chief lesson Eisenhower and his associates drew from Korea was that limited wars, fought with conventional weaponry on the periphery of the Communist world, only drained the nation's resources and weakened its allies' resolve." If America continued Truman's shotgun policies, the costs would soon become higher than Americans would be willing to pay. A change, Ike maintained, was needed.

Eisenhower termed his adjustments of the containment doctrine the "New Look." Ike's program began with the idea of saving money. To do this he decided to emphasize nuclear weapons over conventional weapons, assuming that the next major war would be a nuclear conflict. This "more bang for the buck" program drew angry criticism. Congressional hawks claimed that Eisenhower was "putting too many eggs in the nuclear basket," and liberals suggested that the program would inevitably lead to nuclear destruction.

Whatever the criticisms, the New Look did save money. While air and missile forces were expanded, the army's budget was trimmed of all its fat and much of its bone. In fact, if Eisenhower had had his way, the army would have been completely reorganized. The results of Eisenhower's approach were dramatic. In 1953 defense cost $50.4 billion. By 1956 Eisenhower had reduced the defense budget to $35.8 billion. In addition, during the same period troop levels were reduced by almost one-third. Future presidents did not so much reverse Eisenhower's approach as enlarge it. They continued the nuclear buildup started by Eisenhower, and at the same time insisted on increased spending on conventional weapons. The result was an ever-escalating defense budget.

The New Look took an unconventional approach to conventional warfare. Ike had learned from Truman's mistakes in Korea. America could not send weapons and men to all corners of the world to contain communism. It was a costly, deadly policy. Instead, the New Look emphasized the threat of massive retaliation to keep order, and reinforced America's position with a series of foreign alliances that encouraged indigenous troops and peoples to resist Communist expansion. Finally, Eisenhower used the

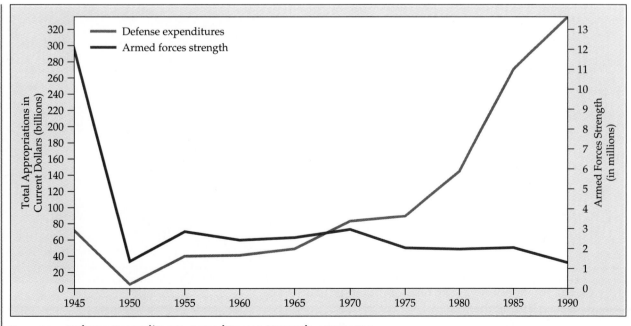

FIGURE 27.1 **Defense Expenditures, Armed Forces Strength, 1945–1990**

CIA as a covert foreign policy arm. Through timely assassinations and political coups engineered by the CIA, Eisenhower was able to prevent—or at least forestall—the emergence of anti-America regimes. While historians argue about the morality of the CIA's covert operations, they were very much a part of the New Look.

A New Face in Moscow

The world changed dramatically a few months after Eisenhower took office. On March 5, 1953, Joseph Stalin, the Soviet dictator whom Ike knew personally, died. Always fearful of rivals, Stalin did not groom a successor. The result was a power struggle within the Kremlin, from which Nikita Khrushchev emerged as the winner.

Khrushchev looked like a cross between a Russian peasant and Ike himself. Short, rotund, and bald, he had a warm smile and alert eyes. Unlike Stalin, Khrushchev enjoyed meeting people, making speeches, and traveling abroad. If occasionally he lost his temper and uttered belligerent remarks—he once even took off his shoe and pounded it on a table at the United Nations— Khrushchev did try to lessen the tensions between the Soviet Union and the United States.

Ike shared Khrushchev's dream for peaceful coexistence between the two world leaders. In fact, Eisenhower used Stalin's death as an opportunity to extend an olive branch. The Soviet Union peacefully responded. During 1955 the nations resolved several thorny issues: the Soviets repatriated German prisoners of war who had been held in the Soviet Union since World War II, established relations with Greece and Israel, and gave up claims to Turkish territory. The Soviet Union's most significant action was to withdraw from its occupation zone of Austria. Until the massive changes in Eastern Europe in 1990 and 1991, it was the only time that the Soviet Union withdrew from territory that it had seized during the war.

The cold winter of the Cold War seemed to be over. Khrushchev condemned Stalin's excesses, and Eisenhower talked guardedly about a new era of cooperation. In July 1955, the two leaders met in Geneva, Switzerland, for a summit conference. During the meeting, Eisenhower suggested that the United States and the Soviet Union allow aerial surveillance and photography of each other's nations to lessen the chance of a possible surprise attack. Khrushchev rejected this "open skies" proposal, calling it "a very transparent espionage device." Actually, although the meeting achieved few tangible results, the two leaders seemed to be working toward the same peaceful ends. Against Dulles's advice, Eisenhower even smiled when posing for pictures with the Soviets. "A new spirit of conciliation and cooperation" had been achieved, Ike announced. Unfortunately, "the Spirit of Geneva" would not survive the confrontations ahead.

1956: The Dangerous Year

Neither Eisenhower nor Khrushchev was completely candid. While working for "peaceful coexistence," both still had to satisfy critics at home. In Washington, Dulles continued to

A worker from the Kiev region greets Soviet Premier Nikita Khrushchev at the Twentieth Congress of the Communist party in the Soviet Union.

Before the crushing Soviet onslaught on November 4, 1956, Hungarian freedom fighters rush toward Budapest in an attempt to fight off Soviet forces.

call for the "liberation" of Eastern Europe and to hint that the United States would rally behind any Soviet-dominated country that struck a blow for freedom. In reality, Eisenhower was not about to risk war with the Soviet Union to come to the defense of Poland, Hungary, or Czechoslovakia.

At the same time, Khrushchev's speeches often promised more than he would or could deliver. On February 24, 1956, for example, Khrushchev delivered a remarkable speech before the Twentieth Party Congress. For four hours in his "Crimes of Stalin" speech, he condemned the former dictator's domestic crimes and foreign policy mistakes, endorsed "peaceful coexistence" with the West, and indicated that he was willing to allow greater freedom behind the "Iron Curtain." Although the speech was supposed to be secret, the CIA obtained copies and distributed them throughout Eastern Europe.

Poland took Khrushchev at his word and moved in a more liberal, anti-Stalinist direction. Wladyslaw Gomulka, who represented the nationalistic wing of the Polish Communist party, gained power in Poland and moved his country away from complete Soviet domination. Claiming that "there is more than one road to socialism," Gomulka announced that Poles would defend with their lives their new freedoms. Since Poland did not attempt to withdraw from the Soviet block, Khrushchev allowed Poland to move along its more liberal course.

What Poland had won, Hungary wanted—and perhaps a bit more. On October 23, 1956, students and workers took to the streets in Budapest loudly demanding changes. They knocked over a gigantic statue of Stalin and desecrated it with freedom slogans and graffiti. As in Poland, they forced a political change. Independent Communist Imre Nagy replaced a Stalinist leader. The Soviets peacefully recognized the new government. Pressing his luck, Nagy then announced that he planned to pull Hungary out of the Warsaw Pact—the Soviet-dominated defense community created in response to the signing of the NATO Pact—and allow opposition political parties.

Khrushchev sent Soviet tanks and soldiers into Budapest to crush what he now termed a "counterrevolution" and the work of "fascist reactionary elements." Students with bricks and hastily made Molotov cocktails were no match for the Red Army. The Soviets kidnapped Nagy (and later executed him), killed hundreds of demonstrators, and brutally restored their control over Hungary. All the while the Eisenhower administration just watched, demonstrating that the notion of "liberation" was mere rhetoric, not policy. Ike even refused a CIA request to parachute weapons and supplies to the Hungarian freedom fighters. Hungary, said Ike, was "as inaccessible to us as Tibet."

Actually, at the time of the Soviet move into Budapest, Eisenhower was more concerned with the troubled Western alliance. The source of the problem was Egypt, whose nationalistic leader, President Gamal Abdel Nasser, was struggling to remain neutral in the Cold War. The United States had attempted to win Nasser's favor by promising to finance the construction of the Aswan High Dam on the Nile. But when Nasser recognized the People's Republic of China and pursued amicable relations with the Soviet Union, the Eisenhower administration withdrew the proposed loan. Neither Dulles nor Eisenhower was happy with Nasser's fence-sitting diplomacy.

Nasser struck back. On July 26, he nationalized the Suez Canal, the waterway linking the oil-rich Gulf of Suez and the Mediterranean. Half of Western Europe's oil came through the Suez Canal, which Ike believed was essential to the security of Western Europe. "And it will be run by Egyptians," Nasser added in an emotional message to the world. If Eisenhower was upset, British and French leaders were outraged, loudly claiming that the seizure threatened their Middle Eastern oil supplies. Eisenhower counseled caution, but Britain, France, and Israel resorted to "drastic actions." On October 29, Israel invaded Egypt and Britain and France used the hostilities as a pretext to seize the Suez Canal.

Eisenhower was furious. He interrupted his reelection campaign to return to Washington. One observer reported, "The White House crackled with barracks-room language." Ike told Dulles to inform the Israelis that "goddamn it, we're going to apply sanctions, we're going to the United Nations, we're going to do everything that there is so we can stop this thing."

Eisenhower stood on the high ground, where he was uncomfortably aligned with the Soviet Union. Without law there can be no peace, he claimed, adding, "and there can be no law—if we were to invoke one code of international conduct for those who oppose us—and another for our friends." Cut off from American support and faced with angry Soviet threats, Britain, France, and Israel halted their operations on November 6, the same day Eisenhower overwhelmingly defeated Adlai Stevenson and was reelected for a second term.

Taken together, the Hungarian and the Suez crises strained America's relations with both the Soviet Union and Western Europe. "The spirit of Geneva" was being replaced by a more hostile mood. Nowhere was this better seen than in the 1956 Olympic Games, held in Melbourne, Australia, only two weeks after the November incidents. Egypt, Lebanon, and Iraq refused to take part in any Games that included Britain, France, and Israel. And in the water polo competition, a match between the Soviet Union and Hungary quickly deteriorated into a form of aquatic warfare. The pool ran red with blood and the contest had to be halted before its official end.

The Troubled Second Term

In foreign affairs, Eisenhower's second term was less successful than his first. Although he restrained military spending and shrewdly utilized information gathered by U-2 spy missions, his actions received more criticism at home and abroad. Age and health may have contributed to this turn of events. During his first four years in office, Ike suffered a heart attack and a bout with ileitis, which entailed a serious operation. During his second term, he was more apt to take vacations and play golf and bridge with his close friends. John Foster Dulles's health was also declining. During the Suez crisis doctors discovered that he had cancer. Acute physical pain punctuated his last years as secretary of state and he died in 1959.

Sputnik and Sputtering Rockets

More than ill health plagued Ike's foreign policy. Soviet technological advances created a mood of edginess in American foreign policy and military circles. In 1957 the Soviet Union successfully placed a tiny transmitter encased in a 184-pound steel ball into an orbit around earth. They called the artificial satellite *Sputnik*—Russian for "fellow traveler of Earth"—but the humor of the name was lost on most Americans, who were too concerned about Soviet rocket advances to laugh.

Less than one month later, the Soviet Union launched its second *Sputnik*, this one built on a larger and grander scale. It weighed 1120 pounds, contained instruments for scientific research, and carried a small dog named Laika who was wired with devices to gauge the effects of extragravitational flight on animal functions. If the first *Sputnik* demonstrated that the Soviets had gained the high ground, the second indicated that they intended to go higher and to place men in space.

Before the end of 1957, the United States tried to respond with a satellite launch of its own. Code-named *Vanguard*, the satellite was placed on the top of a three-stage navy rocket that was ignited on December 6. Describing the "blast off," a historian wrote, "It wobbled a few feet off the pad and exploded. The grapefruit-sized American rival to *Sputnik* fell to the ground and beeped its last amid geysers of smoke." It was the first of a series of highly publicized American rocket launches that ended with the sputtering sound of failure.

U.S. efforts to compete with the Soviet Union's space advances suffered a major setback when the *Vanguard* exploded two seconds after takeoff on December 6, 1957.

Sputnik forced Americans to question themselves and their own values. Had the country become soft and overly consumer oriented? While Soviet students were studying calculus, physics, and chemistry, had American students spent too much time in shop, home economics, and driver education classes? More importantly, did *Sputnik* give the Soviet Union a military superiority over the United States? If a Soviet rocket could put a thousand-pound ball in orbit could the same rocket armed with a nuclear warhead hit a target in the United States? Such questions disturbed ordinary Americans and U.S. policymakers alike.

In truth, Americans overrated the importance of *Sputnik*. It was not all that it seemed. As German-born Wernher von Braun, one of America's leading rocket scientists, would later demonstrate, launching a satellite was no great accomplishment. It simply took rockets with great thrust. Delivering a warhead to a specific target was quite another matter. That entailed sophisticated guidance systems, which the Soviet Union had certainly not developed.

Sputnik then did not demonstrate Soviet technological superiority. It did, however, indicate the willingness of Soviet leaders to place military advancement ahead of the physical well-being of their citizens. As a French journalist noted, the price of *Sputnik* was "millions of pots and shoes lacking." The Soviet Union lagged behind the West in diet, health care, education, housing, clothing, and transportation.

American policy-makers reacted to the illusion of Soviet success. Congress appropriated more money for "defense-related" research and funneled more dollars into higher education in the United States. In fact, *Sputnik*

was a tremendous boon for education. In an attempt to improve science and mathematics skills, Congress passed the National Defense Education Act (1958) to help finance the undergraduate and graduate educations of promising students. The Eisenhower administration jumped into the "space race," determined to be the swiftest. A leading historian of space measured the success of Eisenhower's effort by noting, "more new starts and technical leaps occurred in the years before 1960 than in any comparable span. Every space booster and every strategic missile in the American arsenal, prior to . . . the 1970s, date from these years."

Third-World Challenges

If *Sputnik* was largely an illusionary challenge, nationalist movements in the Third World created more serious problems. Eisenhower's response to such movements varied from case to case. On the one hand, he opposed Britain and France's efforts to use naked physical aggression to whip Egypt into line. On the other hand, Ike employed covert CIA operations to achieve his foreign policy goals. In 1953 the CIA planned and executed a coup d'état which replaced a popularly elected government in Iran with a pro-American regime headed by Shah Mohammad Reza Pahlavi. The reason for the coup was that the elected government had taken over Iranian oil resources that the British had been exploiting. One year later the CIA masterminded the overthrow of a leftist government in Guatemala and replaced it with an unpopular but strongly pro-American government.

To keep order in what he believed were areas vital to American interests, Eisenhower would even resort to armed intervention. In 1958, Lebanese Moslems backed by Egypt and Syria, threatened a revolt against the Beirut government dominated by the Christian minority. President Camille Chamoun appealed to Eisenhower for support. Concerned with Middle Eastern oil, Ike ordered marines from America's Sixth Fleet into Lebanon. Watching from the beaches of Beirut, sunbathers and

The U.S. reaction to *Sputnik* led to a proliferation of rocket and satellite launches in both the USSR and the United States in the late 1950s.

ice-cream vendors cheered the American show of force.

Once order was restored and Lebanese politicians had agreed on a successor to Chamoun, Ike withdrew American troops from Lebanon. But like the CIA activities in Guatemala and Iran, short-term benefits came with long-term costs. Increasingly, the United States became identified with unpopular, undemocratic, and intolerant right-wing regimes. Such actions tarnished America's image in the Third World.

The problems of Eisenhower's approach toward the Third World were clearly seen in his handling of the Cuban Revolution. In 1959, revolutionary Fidel Castro overthrew Fulgencio Batista, a right-wing dictator who had encouraged American investments in Cuba at the expense of the Cuban people. Before the revolution, in fact, American companies owned 90 percent of Cuban mining operations, 80 percent of its utilities, and 40 percent of its sugar operations. Castro quickly set about to change the situation. He confiscated land and properties in Cuba owned by Americans, executed former Batista officials, built hospitals and schools, ended racial segregation, improved workers' wages, and moved leftward. Before long, Castro had begun to jail writers and critics, hold public executions, postpone elections, and condemn the United States as the "vulture . . . feeding on humanity."

Instead of waiting for Cuba's anti-American feelings to subside, Eisenhower decided to move against Castro. He gave the CIA permission to plan an attack on Cuba by a group of anti-Castro exiles, a plan that would culminate with the disastrous Bay of Pigs invasion (see Chapter 29). As one of his last acts as president, in 1961 Eisenhower severed diplomatic relations with Cuba. Such actions only increased Castro's anti-American resolve and further drove him into the arms of the Soviet Union.

Ultimately, the Truman and Eisenhower brands of containment were unsuccessful in dealing with nationalistic independence movements. Such movements dominated the post–World War II world. Between 1944 and 1974, for example, 78 countries won their independence. These included more than one billion people, or close to one-third of the world's population. By using a political yardstick to evaluate these movements, American presidents since Truman have made critical mistakes that have lowered the image of the United States in the Third World and given ammunition to Third World politicians who have pandered to anti-American emotions.

Not with a Bang, But a Whimper

Going into his last year in office, Eisenhower hoped to improve on the foreign policy record of his second term. Since his last meeting with Khrushchev in Geneva, the Cold War had intensified. In particular, the Soviets were once again threatening to cut off Western access to West Berlin, an action Eisenhower feared might lead to a nuclear war. To solve the problem—or at least to neutralize it—Eisenhower invited Khrushchev to visit the United States. The Soviet leader toured Iowa farms, visited Hollywood, and was generally warmly received by the American people. His biggest disappointment was that for security reasons he could not visit Disneyland, but he did get a chance to meet and drink with John Wayne. Turning to politics, he spent two days in private talks with Eisenhower at Camp David, where the two agreed to a formal summit meeting set for May 1960 in Paris.

The two world leaders never again had serious talks. Just before the meeting the Soviets shot down an American U-2 spy plane over their territory. So sophisticated was the plane's surveillance equipment, it could read a newspaper headline from 10 miles above the earth's surface or take pictures of the earth's surface 125 miles wide and 3000 miles long. During the previous few years, U-2 missions had kept Eisenhower abreast of Soviet military developments and convinced him that *Sputnik* posed no military threat to the United States. Nevertheless, the existence of such planes was a military secret, and U-2 pilots had strict orders to self-destruct their planes rather than be forced down in enemy territory. (For crash landings in neutral countries, the pilots carried a silk banner with the same statement in 14 languages: "I bear no malice toward your people. If you help me you will be rewarded.")

Assuming that the pilot had followed orders, Eisenhower responded to the Soviet charges of spying by publicly announcing that the Soviets had shot down a weather plane that had blown off course. Unfortunately for Ike, the pilot, Francis Gary Powers, had not followed orders, and the Soviets had him and the wreckage of his plane. Trying to save the summit, Khrushchev offered Eisenhower a way to save face. The Soviet leader indicated that he was sure that Eisenhower had not known about the flights. Eisenhower, however, accepted full personal responsibility and refused to apologize for actions he deemed were in defense of America. Rather than appear soft himself, Khrushchev refused to engage in the Paris summit.

Eisenhower's presidency ended on this note of failure—a chance to improve Soviet-American relations had been lost. But this end to his presidency should not obscure his positive accomplishments. He had ended one war, kept America out of several others, limited military spending, and presided over seven and a half years of relative peace. Like George Washington, when Eisenhower left office he issued warnings to America about possible future problems. In particular, he noted, the "military-industrial complex"—an alliance between government and business—could threaten the democratic process in the country. As Eisenhower remarked early in his presidency, "Every gun that is made, every warship launched, every rocket fired signifies, in the final sense, a theft from those who hunger and are not fed, those who are cold and are not clothed."

WE SHALL OVERCOME

When Dwight Eisenhower took office in early 1953 almost everywhere in the United States racism—often institutionalized, sometimes less formal—was the order of the day. Below the Mason-Dixon line it reached its most virulent form in the Jim Crow laws that governed the everyday existence of southern blacks. Whites framed the Jim Crow laws to separate the races and to demonstrate to all the superiority of whites and the inferiority of African Americans. Jim Crow dictated that whites and blacks eat in separate restaurants, drink from separate water fountains, sleep in separate hotels, and learn in separate schools. In some states, the separate schoolbooks of black and white children were stored in separate closets so as to avoid contamination by touch.

Jim Crow subjected African Americans to daily degradation and soul-destroying humiliation. Blacks had to give way on sidewalks to whites, tip their hats, and speak respectfully. African Americans addressed whites of all ages as Mr., Mrs., or Miss; whites addressed African Americans of all ages by their first names. Although the underpinning of the Jim Crow laws was the "separate but equal" doctrine enunciated in *Plessy* v. *Ferguson* (1896), both blacks and whites realized that subjugation, not equality, was the object of the laws.

Soviet Premier Nikita Khrushchev visited the United States in September 1959, meeting with President Eisenhower and then touring the country. In Washington Khrushchev presented Eisenhower with a model of the sphere which a Soviet rocket landed on the moon.

Jim Crow even leaped over national boundaries. When a waitress at a Howard Johnson's in Dover, Delaware, refused to serve a glass of orange juice to the finance minister of Ghana, America's image abroad suffered.

Segregation affected whites as well as African Americans. Melton A. McLaurin, a historian who grew up in Wade, North Carolina, recalled that race relations in the South in the mid-1950s were much as they had been in the 1890s. Jim Crow etiquette touched all relations between both races. "Blacks who had to enter our house," McLaurin noted, "for whatever reason, came in the back door. Unless employed as domestic servants, blacks conducted business with my father or mother on the back porch or, on rare occasions, in the kitchen. Blacks never entered our dining or living areas . . . except as domestics. . . . When a black person approached a doorway at the same time as a white adult, the black stepped back and sometimes even held the door open for the white to enter. The message I received from hundreds of such signals was always the same. I was white; I was different; I was superior. It was not a message with which an adolescent boy was apt to quarrel."

North of Dixie the situation was not much better. To be sure, rigid Jim Crow laws did not exist, but, informally, blacks were excluded from the better schools, neighborhoods, and jobs. Whites argued that the development of ghettos was a natural process, not some sort of racist agreement between white realtors. Such, however, was not the case. William Levitt, the most famous post–World War II suburban housing developer, attempted to keep African Americans out of his developments. A passage in the New York Levittown covenant read: "No dwelling shall be used . . . by members of other than the Caucasian race, but the employment and maintenance of other than Caucasian domestic servants shall be permitted." Even after the courts struck down such restrictions, Levitt instructed his realtors not to sell to blacks. Indeed, *Shelley* v. *Kraemer* (1948), the court case that stated that state courts could not uphold housing restrictions, only declared such restrictions legally unenforceable; it did not outlaw such practices per se. To break a racially motivated housing re-

Jim Crow laws were not limited to restaurants or hotels in cities. This roadside sign shows that segregation was common in areas outside southern metropolitan locations.

striction, a black had to take the initiative and force a court test.

When Ike left office in 1961, segregation remained largely unchanged. In that year, John Howard Griffin's book *Black Like Me* gave white America a stark look at the daily life of millions of African Americans. After shaving his head and darkening his skin chemically, Griffin traveled about the South to experience what it was like to live as a black in Jim Crow America. He described the humiliating search for hotels, restaurants, and restrooms in a land where for blacks unequal facilities were a constant and no facilities always a real possibility. He also described how blacks came to each other's aid and support. A national best-seller

SPORTS AND LEISURE

INTEGRATION IN SPORTS

ON April 18, 1946, the sports world focused on a baseball field in Jersey City, an industrial wasteland on the banks of the Passaic River. It was the opening day for the Jersey City Giants of the International League. Their opponents were the Montreal Royals, the Brooklyn Dodgers' leading farm team. Playing second base for the Royals was Jackie Roosevelt Robinson, a pigeon-toed, highly competitive, marvelously talented African-American athlete. The stadium was filled with curious and excited spectators, and in the press box sportswriters from New York, Philadelphia, Baltimore, and cities further west fidgeted with their typewriters. It was not just another season-opening game. Professional baseball, America's national game, was about to be integrated.

Since the late nineteenth century professional baseball and most other professional team sports had prohibited interracial competition. White athletes played for the highest salaries, in the best stadiums, before the most spectators. During the same years black teams barnstormed the country playing where they could and accepting what was offered. For them, the pay was low, the stadiums rickety, and the playing conditions varied between bad and dangerous. The *Plessy* v. *Ferguson* ideal of "separate but equal" was a cruel joke.

During the period of forced segregation, whites stereotyped African-American athletes. Since colonial times whites had maintained that blacks were instinctive rather than thoughtful, physical rather than intellectual, complacent rather than ambitious. As athletes, whites believed blacks were physically gifted but lazy, undisciplined, and wholly lacking in competitive drive. Disregarding the success of black athletes in individual sports whites clung to the racist theory that nature had fashioned blacks to laugh and sing and dance and play, but not to sacrifice, train, work, compete, and win.

The most successful African-American athletes and teams catered to these stereotypes. The Harlem Globetrotters, for example, played the role of Sambo in sweats. Started in 1927 by white Chicago entrepreneur Abe Saperstein, the all-black Harlem Globetrotters basketball team presented African-American athletes as wide-eyed, toothy, camera-mugging clowns. White audiences loved their antics—Marques Haynes dribbling circles around his hopeless white opponents while the rest of the Trotters stretched out on the floor feigning sleep; Meadowlark Lemon hiding the basketball under his jersey and sneaking down the court to make a basket; Goose Tatum slam-dunking while reading a comic book; all of them cavorting around with deflated, lopsided, or balloon balls, throwing confetti-filled water buckets on an indulgent crowd, and deviously getting away with every conceivable infraction of the rules.

Saperstein insisted that "his boys" conform off as well as on the court. As a Trotter veteran told new teammate Connie Hawkins, "Abe don't care what you do with colored, but don't let him catch you with no white broads . . . And don't let him see you with a Cadillac. He don't stand for that either." Nor did Saperstein allow his players to contradict whites. He wanted only "happy darkies," not "uppity niggers," on his team.

The Indianapolis Clowns were the Harlem Globetrotters of baseball. They played in grass skirts and body paint and engaged in comedy as much as baseball. Pregame routines included acrobatics and dancing, exaggerated black English, minstrel slapstick, and grinning, always lots of grinning. How could any reasonable person expect major league performances out of people playing baseball in grass skirts and war paint?

Jackie Robinson came to bat in the first inning. His very presence had ended segregation in "organized baseball." Now he wanted to strike a blow against the racist stereotyping. Nervous, he later recalled that his palms seemed "too moist to grip the bat." He didn't even swing at the first five pitches. On the sixth pitch he hit a bouncing ball to the shortstop who easily threw him out. It was a start of sorts.

In the third inning Robinson took his second turn at bat. With runners on first and second, he lashed out at the first pitch and hit it over the left-field fence 330 feet away. In the press box Wendell Smith and Joe Bostic, two African-American reporters for the *Amsterdam News*, "laughed and smiled. . . . Our hearts beat just a little faster and the thrill ran through us like champagne bubbles." According to another account, among the white sportswriters "there were some very long faces."

Robinson wasn't through for the day. In the fifth inning he had a bunt single, stole second, advanced to third on a ground ball, and, faking an attempt to steal home, forced a balk and scored. It was a virtuoso performance. During the remainder of the game he had two more hits, another stolen base, and forced a second balk. In the field he was tough, intense, and smart, a reverse image of the stereotypical black athlete. It was a fine day for Robinson and his supporters. "Baseball took up the cudgel of democracy," Bostic wrote, "and an unassuming, but superlative Negro boy ascended the heights of excellence to prove the rightness of the experiment. And prove it in the only correct crucible for such an experiment—the crucible of white hot competition."

The success of Jackie Robinson in baseball led to the integration of the other major professional sports. In 1946 the Cleveland Rams moved their football franchise to Los Angeles, and to boost ticket sales they signed African Americans Kenny Washington and Woody Strode, both of whom had played football with Robinson at UCLA. Professional football thus became the next to be integrated. In 1950 the Boston Celtics of the National Basketball Association signed Chuck Cooper of Duquesne to a professional contract, and the New York Knicks signed Nat "Sweetwater" Clifton away from the Harlem Globetrotters, over Abe Saperstein's bitter protests. The same year, the United States Lawn Tennis Association allowed African Americans to compete at Forest Hills. In a relatively short time integration came to American professional sports.

The process was not without individual pain. Robinson especially became the object of hate mail, death threats, and racial slurs. Opposition runners spiked him and pitchers threw at him. Off the field he faced a life of segregated restaurants, clubs, theaters, and neighborhoods. Patient, witty, and quick to forgive, he endured extraordinary humiliation. He became an American hero, but he paid dearly. Throughout the 1946 and 1947 seasons Robinson was plagued by headaches, bouts of depression, nausea, and nightmares. Talking about the pressures on her husband, Rachel Robinson recalled, "There were the stresses of just knowing that you were pulling a big weight of a whole lot of people on your back . . . I think Jackie felt . . . that there would be serious consequences if he didn't succeed and that one of them would be that nobody would try again for a long time." Of course, other African-American players also confronted trials on and off the field, but as Robinson's teammate Roy Campanella said, "nothing compared to what Jackie was going through."

Integration in sports preceded integration in society at large. But in both sports and the civil rights movement, racial gains were paid for by individuals willing to risk serious hardships. Change seldom came easily and the struggle never ended quickly. In baseball, for example, as late as 1988 many white bureaucrats still resisted the idea of African-American managers, resorting to the same racial stereotyping that had plagued America for over 350 years.

that sold over five million copies, Griffin's tale shocked and shamed many whites who never realized—or even considered—the plight of black Americans.

During Eisenhower's years in office, however, African Americans did make some significant strides in their quest for civil rights. In particular, during the decade after 1954 African Americans won a series of legal victories that in theory if not always in practice buried Jim Crow. They were years of joy and years of sadness, when the best as well as the worst aspects of the American character were clearly visible.

Taking Jim Crow to Court

World War II underscored the yawning gap between the promise and reality of life in America. Fighting against Nazi racist theories helped to draw attention to real racial problems at home. At the start of the war, defense industry managers refused to hire African Americans, and the races were segregated in the armed services. The war and a threat by African-American leader A. Philip Randolph to organize a protest march on Washington led to some changes. Executive Order 8802 prohibited discrimination in the war industries. But the outbreak of the Detroit race riot during the hot summer of 1943 demonstrated that African Americans were dissatisfied with racial conditions at home. "Our war is not against Hitler and Europe," claimed one African-American columnist, "but against the Hitlers in America." Those drafted to fight against Japan foresaw the irony of many of their fates: "Here lies a black man killed fighting a yellow man for the glory of a white man."

After the war conditions improved at a snail's pace. With an eye on African-American Democratic northern voters, Truman established the President's Committee on Civil Rights, which issued a report that most white politicians ignored. While Truman called for "fair employment throughout the federal establishment" and ordered the racial desegregation of the armed services, southern politicians proclaimed the need to return to the embrace of Jim Crow. "No Negro will vote in

Georgia for the next four years," Eugene Talmadge promised after he was elected governor of Georgia. And in Congress, Southerners like Senator Theodore G. Bilbo railed against Truman's moderate racial reforms. Opposing Truman's plan for universal military training, Bilbo exhorted, "If you draft Negro boys into the army, give them three good meals a day and let them shoot craps and drink liquor around the barracks for a year, they won't be worth a tinker's dam thereafter."

By the late 1940s African Americans had realized that they would have to lead the fight against racial injustice. In the early years of the battle, the NAACP spearheaded the struggle. But the organization faced a number of problems, both within and outside the African-American community. For example, many believed the NAACP was racist and elitist. The organization was staffed by educated middle-class African Americans who seemed out of touch with the majority of their race. Worse yet, many African Americans charged that the NAACP was staffed by light-skinned blacks because it accepted the theory that mulattos were more aggressive, enterprising, and ambitious than their pure-blooded counterparts.

Outside of the African-American community, the NAACP encountered a hostile white society. In Congress, southern Democrats—there were few southern Republicans—opposed any assault on segregation—the prevailing form of institutionalized racism.

Given this racial climate, the NAACP moved cautiously. Instead of attacking segregation head-on and demanding full equality, the organization chose to chip away at the legal edges of Jim Crow. The separate but equal doctrine was particularly vulnerable. In *Missouri ex rel Gaines* (1938), *Sweatt* v. *Painter* (1950), and *McLaurin* v. *Board of Regents* (1950), the NAACP lawyers demonstrated the impossibility, even the absurdity, of applying the separate but equal yardstick to graduate education and law schools. In all three cases, the Supreme Court agreed. If, the court implied, separate but equal educational systems were to be continued, then states had to pay more than lip service to equality.

Some children attended segregated schools, but others, such as these African-American children in West Memphis, Arkansas, were crammed into the sanctuary of a church for their classes.

In grade school and high school education, just as in graduate education, the South translated separate but equal to read "separate and highly unequal." In South Carolina's Clarendon County, for example, 75 percent of the students were African American, but the white minority received 60 percent of the educational funds. On the average, the county spent $179 per year on each white student and $43 per year on each African-American student. Where were the separate but equal standards, asked NAACP lawyers.

Intellectual and financial considerations were not the only factors that precluded equality. Psychologists argued that segregation instilled feelings of inferiority among African-American children. Psychologist Kenneth Clark conducted a simple test with African-American children attending segregated schools. He showed the children two dolls, one black and the other white. In one case, of the 16 children tested, 10 said they liked the white doll better, 11 added that the black doll looked "bad," and 9 remarked that the white doll looked "nice." Recalling the tests, Clark noted, "The most disturbing question—and the one that really made me, even as a scientist, upset—was the final question: 'Now show me the doll that's most like you.' Many of the children became emotionally upset when they had to identify with the doll they had rejected. These children saw themselves as inferior, and they accepted the inferiority as part of reality." When asked that question, one child even smiled and pointed to the black doll: "That's a nigger. I'm a nigger."

It was inhumane to continue such psychological damage, the NAACP concluded. In 1952 the NAACP consolidated a series of cases under the name of the first case—*Brown* v. *Board of Education of Topeka*—which challenged the very existence of the separate but equal doctrine. The Supreme Court listened to the arguments and began its extended deliberation. Then in September 1953 Chief Justice Fred M. Vinson, who seemed to be leaning against ending segregation, died of a heart attack.

President Eisenhower named Earl Warren to take Vinson's place. It was a political, not an ideological, appointment. Formerly governor of California, Warren had helped Ike win the Republican nomination in 1952. Appointment as Chief Justice of the United States was a fine reward. On the surface, minorities had little reason to suspect that Warren would be on their side. During World War II he had been active in the relocation of 100,000 Japanese Americans into internment camps; but in the years after that action, Warren realized that his action had been a mistake. The *Brown* case offered him a second chance.

After working to achieve unanimity in the court, Warren read the Court's decision on May 17, 1954. "Does segregation of children in public schools solely on the basis of race, even though the physical facilities and other tangible factors may be equal, deprive children of the minority group of equal educational opportunities?" Warren asked. "We believe it does," he answered. "To separate them from others of similar age and qualifications solely because of their race generates a feeling of inferiority as to their status in the community that may affect their hearts and minds in a way very unlikely ever to be undone." In public education, he concluded, the "separate but equal" doctrine has no place. "Separate educational facilities are inherently unequal."

The *Chicago Defender* labeled the *Brown* decision "a second emancipation proclamation," and the *Washington Post* called it "a new birth of freedom." But such Court decisions have to be enforced. As Charles Houston, a leading NAACP lawyer, remarked, "Nobody needs to explain to a Negro the difference between the law in the books and the law in action."

A Failure of Leadership

A year after the *Brown* decision, the Supreme Court ruled that schools should desegregate "with all deliberate speed." It was a vague phrase, a cautious phrase, a legally meaningless phrase. Perhaps it was the price Warren had to pay for the previous year's unanimous

verdict. In any case, the second decision placed the burden of desegregation into the hands of local, state, and national leaders. If the process was to be accomplished with the minimum amount of conflict, those leaders would have to be firm in their resolve to see justice done. Such, however, would not be the case.

On the national level, Eisenhower moved uncomfortably and cautiously on the issue of civil rights and desegregation. Born in Texas and reared in the white Midwest, Ike spent most of his life in a segregated army. He did not see racism as a great moral issue, and he was unresponsive to the demand for equality. In truth, Eisenhower believed that the *Brown* decision had been a mistake, for which he blamed Earl Warren. He later asserted that the appointment of Warren had been the "biggest damn fool mistake" he had ever made. When questioned about the decision in 1954, he claimed, "I don't believe you can change the hearts of men with laws or decisions."

The brand of Ike's leadership and his ambitions for the Republican party further weakened his response. His behind-the-scenes approach—the "hidden-hand" style—led him to avoid speaking out clearly and forcefully on the subject. Moral outrage was not his style. In addition, he was popular in the South and harbored hopes of bringing that section of the country into the Republican party. Finally, his commitment to integration was lukewarm at best, and he placed controlling military spending above desegregating the South. Therefore, instead of deploring the killing of Emmett Till and other atrocities by southern whites, Eisenhower kept quiet.

In the South, Eisenhower's silence was often as deadly as bullets. If Eisenhower had acted decisively in support of the *Brown* v. *Board of Education* decision—if he had placed the full weight of his office behind desegregation—there is some evidence that the South would have complied peacefully with the verdict. By not acting forcefully, however, Eisenhower strengthened the position of Southerners who equated desegregation with death. "Ending segregation," Governor James F. Byrnes of South Carolina said, "would mark the beginning of the end of civilization in the South as we have known it."

The Little Rock crisis demonstrated the failure of national and state leadership. In 1957 in Little Rock, Arkansas, school officials were ordered to desegregate. As they prepared to do so, Governor Orval Faubus, locked in a reelection fight, intervened. Announcing that any integration attempt would disrupt public order, he sent in the National Guard to prevent black children from entering Central High. While Eisenhower quietly tried to maneuver behind the scenes, a crisis was brewing. On the morning of September 23, 1957, when black children attempted to attend school, they were inhospitably greeted by an angry mob chanting, "two, four, six, eight, we ain't going to integrate."

Television turned the ugly episode into a national drama. Millions of Americans for the first time witnessed violent racism, as angry whites moved around the defenseless children like hungry sharks. Television gave a face to racism, a concept that for many white Americans was still an abstraction. It showed the reality of hate and racism in the South. For the first but not last time, television aided the cause of civil rights by conveying the human suffering caused by racism.

To restore order, Eisenhower federalized the Arkansas National Guard and sent one thousand paratroopers from the 101st Airborne Division to Little Rock. It was the first time since Reconstruction that a president had ordered troops to the South. Although their presence desegregated Central High School in 1957, the following year Faubus closed Little Rock's public schools, declaring "I stand now and always in opposition to integration by force or at bayonet point." Taken together, Faubus's shortsighted political moves and Eisenhower's refusal to take action until public order had been disrupted created a crisis that more thoughtful leadership might have avoided.

The Word from Montgomery

This failure on the part of white leaders convinced African Americans that court orders would not magically produce equal rights. The fight would be difficult, the march long. Many realized this even before the Little Rock crisis. On a cold afternoon in 1955 in Montgomery, Alabama, Rosa Parks, a well-respected African-American seamstress who

Paratroopers escorted African-American students to and from school in Little Rock, Arkansas, after violence erupted when the schools were instructed to desegregate.

was active in the NAACP, took a significant stride toward equality. She boarded a bus and sat in the first row of the "colored" section. The white section of the bus quickly filled, and according to Jim Crow rules, African Americans were expected to give up their seats rather than force whites—male or female—to stand. The time came for Mrs. Parks to give up her seat. She stayed seated. When told by the bus driver to get up or he would call the police, she said, "You may do that." Later she recalled that the act of defiance was "just something I had to do." The bus stopped, the driver summoned the police, and Rosa Parks was arrested.

Rosa Parks's arrest (above) for refusing to move to the back of a bus led to citywide bus boycotts throughout 1956. (Below) Martin Luther King, Jr., was one of the first to ride the buses when the bus systems were integrated.

African-American Montgomery rallied to Mrs. Parks's side. Like her, they were tired of riding in the back of the bus, tired of giving up their seats to whites, tired of having their lives restricted by segregation laws. Local leaders decided to organize a boycott of Montgomery's white-owned and white-operated bus system. They hoped that economic pressure would force changes that court decisions could not. For the next 381 days, more than 90 percent of Montgomery's African-American citizens participated in a heroic and successful demonstration against racial segregation. Among African Americans, the common attitude toward the protest was voiced by an elderly woman when a black leader offered her a ride. "No," she replied, "my feets is tired, but my soul is rested."

To lead the boycott, Montgomery African Americans turned to the new minister of the Dexter Avenue Baptist Church, a young man named Martin Luther King, Jr. Reared in Atlanta, the son of a respected and financially secure minister, King had been educated at Morehouse College, Crozier Seminary, and Boston University, from which he earned a doctorate in theology. King was an intellectual, excited by ideas and deeply influenced by the philosophical writings of Henry David Thoreau and Mahatma Gandhi as well as by the teachings of Jesus, all of whom believed in the power of nonviolent, direct action.

King's words as well as his ideas stirred people's souls. At the start of the Montgomery boycott he told his followers:

There comes a time when people get tired. We are here this evening to say to those who have mistreated us so long that we are tired—tired of being segregated and humiliated, tired of being kicked about by the brutal feet of oppression . . . We've come here tonight to be saved from the patience that makes us patient with anything less than freedom and justice . . . If you protest courageously and yet with dignity and Christian love, in the history books that are written in future generations, historians will have to pause and say "there lived a great people—a black people—who injected a new meaning and dignity into the veins of civilization."

In King, civil rights had found a genuine spokesman, one who preached a doctrine of change guided by the Christian ideal of love and not by racial hatred. "In our protest," he observed, "there will be no cross burnings. No white person will be taken from his home by a hooded Negro mob and brutally murdered. There will be no threats and no intimidation."

The success of the Montgomery boycott inspired nonviolent protests elsewhere in the South. Increasingly, young African Americans took the lead. Violence and biased law enforcement did not stop the protesters. Indeed, within a few months of the successful conclusion of the Montgomery boycott, demonstrations erupted in 54 cities in 9 states. The protesters were arrested, jailed, beaten, and even knocked off their feet by high-pressure fire hoses, but still they pressed on.

The protests were widely reported in the country's newspapers and televised nightly on the news shows. Americans everywhere were confronted with the stark reality of segregation. Ignorance of the situation became an impossibility; and as the violence continued, national pressure mounted on white politicians to take decisive action. By the early 1960s the word from Montgomery had reinforced the *Brown* decision. It was time for freedom to become a reality. (See Chapter 30 for further discussion of civil rights.)

THE SOUNDS OF CHANGE

Beginning in the 1970s, American advertisers started to market a new commodity—the fifties. They marketed it as a Golden Decade, a carefree time before the assassination of John F. Kennedy, the Vietnam War, and Watergate. According to the popular myth, kids in the 1950s thought "dope" referred to a dull-witted person, parents married for life, and major family problems revolved around whether or not sis had a date for the prom. This image of the decade has taken different forms. *Happy Days* presented it on television; *American Grafitti* and *Diner* (set in the early sixties) detailed it on the silver screen. It was an age of innocence, tranquility, and static

charm. In truth, however, that carefully packaged Golden Decade never existed. Instead, the decade was alive with dynamic, creative tensions.

Father Knows Best

The stock television situation comedy (sitcom) of the 1950s centered on a white family with a happily married husband and wife and two— or sometimes three—well-adjusted children. Most often, the family lived in a white, two-story suburban home, from which the father ventured daily to his white-collar job. The wife did not work outside the house—there was no need since the husband made a comfortable living. In any case, the shows emphasized, wives were also mothers, and mothers were supposed to stay home and tend the children. *Father Knows Best* was the classic example of this genre. It ran from 1954 to 1962 and signaled an optimistic outlook through its title song, "Just Around the Corner There's a Rainbow in the Sky."

The picture these sitcoms presented of America was not entirely inaccurate. Starting after World War II, Americans moved steadily toward the suburbs, which during the 1950s grew six times faster than cities. Several factors contributed to this migration. The high

Television programs of the 1950s often centered around a happy, well-adjusted suburban family with two or three children.

Table 27.1 POPULATION OF METROPOLITAN AREAS, BY REGION, SIZE, AND RACE, 1950–1970

Year		Inner City	Suburbs	African-American Population as Percent of Inner City	African-American Population as Percent of Suburbs
1950	White	43,001,634	33,248,836		
	Black	6,194,948	1,736,521	12.5	4.9
	Other	216,210	102,531		
1970	White	49,430,443	71,148,286		
	Black	13,140,331	3,630,279	20.5	4.8
	Other	1,226,169	843,303		

Source: Data taken from *Historical Statistics of the United States*, Bicentennial Edition, vol. 1, p. 40.

price of urban real estate had driven industries out of the cities, and as always in American history, the population followed the jobs. By 1970 suburban areas had more manufacturing jobs than the central cities. In addition, developers were building abundant, inexpensive homes, which newly married couples, aided by VA and FHA loans, purchased. Of the 13 million homes constructed during the 1950s, 11 million were built in the suburbs.

Nor was the television image of predominantly white suburban families misleading. A far greater percentage of whites than African Americans moved to the suburbs. In 1950 African Americans comprised 12.5 percent of America's urban population and 4.9 percent of the country's suburban population. By 1970 the urban figure had climbed to 20.5 percent with the suburban number declining modestly to 4.8 percent. Housing and job restrictions worked to keep African Americans in the central cities while allowing whites to fill the suburban areas.

Even the image of the suburban housewife preoccupied with her husband and her family was socially sanctioned. American women in the 1950s had babies as never before. The population of the United States increased by under 10 million in the 1930s, 19 million in the 1940s, and a staggering 30 million in the 1950s. During the 1950s the nation's growth rate approached that of India. The best-sellers list indicated America's concern with children: between 1946 and 1976 the pocket edition of Dr. Benjamin Spock's *Baby*

and Child Care sold over 23 million copies, ranking it behind only the Bible and the combined works of Mickey Spillane and Dr. Seuss.

During that age of remarkable fertility, popular writers glorified the role of the mother. The best-seller *Modern Woman: The Lost Sex* went as far as to say that an independent woman was "a contradiction in terms." The ideal woman, writers observed, was content being a wife and a mother or, in a word, a homemaker. "Women must boldly announce," wrote novelist Sloan Wilson, "that no job is more exacting, more necessary, or more rewarding than that of housewife and mother." In the 1950s women married

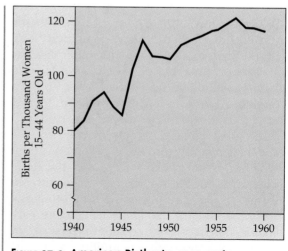

FIGURE 27.2 American Birthrate, 1940–1960

PRIMARY SOURCE ESSAY

EDWARD R. MURROW AND THE FUNCTION OF TELEVISION

During the 1940s and the 1950s, Edward R. Murrow (1908–1965) was the soul of radio and television news. His crisp, laconic style was as familiar to American listeners as his darting eyes and ever-present cigarette were to American viewers. Murrow entered the radio news business in the mid-1930s and he helped to determine its course and development. In 1938 when Hitler's determination to take the Sudetenland threatened war in Europe, Murrow and his roving reporter William L. Shirer brought the crisis to the American people with a series of special broadcasts. During World War II Murrow—with his familiar "This . . . is London"—broadcast reports from rooftops, streets, and air-raid shelters, amid falling bombs and flying debris. After the war Murrow took his professional news skills to television. In 1951 his "See It Now" aired for the first time. This weekly half-hour show probed the important issues, policies, and personalities of the day. In 1954 "See It Now" even took on Senator Joseph McCarthy. From 1953 to 1959 Murrow also hosted the popular "Person to Person," an entertainment program that featured interviews with Hollywood celebrities and world leaders. But Murrow was always first a journalist and only second an entertainer. He deplored the shift in television from education to entertainment. Defeated by the forces of escapism and profit, he left broadcasting in 1961.

Edward R. Murrow at the microphone of his CBS-TV program, September 1957. Murrow, who believed in the instructional value of television, deplored the fact that most televised entertainment insulated the viewing public from reality.

REPRINTED IN *THE REPORTER* (NOV. 13, 1958), PP. 32–36

OUR history will be what we make it. And if there are any historians about fifty or a hundred years from now, and there should be preserved the kinescopes for one week of all three networks, they will there find recorded in black-and-white, or color, evidence of decadence, escapism, and insulation from the realities of the world in which we live. I invite your attention to the television schedules of all networks between the hours of eight and eleven P.M. Eastern Time. Here you will find only fleeting and spasmodic reference to the fact that this nation is in mortal danger. There are, it is true, occasional informative programs presented in that intellectual ghetto on Sunday afternoons. But during the daily peak viewing periods, television in the main insulates us from the realities of the world in which we live. If this state of affairs continues, we may alter an advertising slogan to read: "Look Now, Pay Later." For surely we shall pay for using this most powerful instrument of communication to insulate the citizenry from the hard and demanding realities which must be faced if we are to survive. I mean the word—"survive"—literally. If there were to be a competition in indifference, or perhaps in insulation from reality, then Nero and his fiddle, Chamberlain and his umbrella, could not find a place on an early-afternoon sustaining show. If Hollywood were to run out of Indians, the program schedules would be mangled beyond all recognition. Then some courageous soul with a small budget might be able to do a documentary telling what, in fact, we have done—and are still doing—to the Indians in this country. But that would be unpleasant. And we must at all costs shield the sensitive citizens from anything that is unpleasant.

One of the basic troubles with radio and television news is that both instruments have grown up as an incompatible combination of show business, advertising, and news. Each of the three is a rather bizarre and demanding profession. And when you get all three under one roof, the dust never settles. The top management of the networks, with a few notable exceptions, has been trained in advertising, research, sales, or show business. But by the nature of the corporate structure, they also make the final and crucial decisions having to do with news and public affairs. Frequently they have neither the time nor the competence to do this. It is not easy for the same small group of men to decide whether to buy a new station for millions of dollars, build a new building, alter the rate card, buy a new Western, sell a soap opera, decide what defensive line to take in connection with the latest Congressional inquiry, how much money to spend on promoting a new program, what additions or deletions should be made in the existing covey or clutch of view-presidents, and at the same time—frequently on the same long day—to give mature, thoughtful consideration to the manifold problems that confront those who are charged with the responsibility for news and public affairs.

In 1958 the Radio-Television News Directors Association (RTNDA) invited Murrow to address their annual meeting. The organization did not care about the subject of his address; they wanted Murrow for his name, not for his thoughts on any particular subject. To the surprise of the organization, Murrow accepted the invitation. His speech "may do neither of us any good," he told RTNDA's program chairman. But he did have something that needed saying.

Murrow was the most famous television and radio journalist in America. No one else was even close. On CBS, "See It Now" had made as well as reported the news. In 1954 "See It Now" had courageously and successfully defended Lieutenant Milo Radulovich, an officer in the Air Force Reserve, who had been dismissed because of his associations with suspected radicals. The suspected radicals were his father and his sister. After Murrow's show on the case, the air force reinstated Radulovich. That same year, Murrow had taken on Joe McCarthy, and the show helped to break the grip of terror McCarthy had on America. Ending the show, Murrow told his viewers, "We proclaim ourselves—as indeed we are—the defenders of freedom, . . . but we cannot defend freedom abroad by deserting it at home. The actions of the junior Senator from Wisconsin have caused alarm and dismay amongst our allies abroad and given considerable comfort to our enemies, and whose fault is it? Not really his. He didn't create this situation of fear; he merely exploited it, and rather successfully. Cassius was right: 'The fault, dear Brutus, is not in the stars but in ourselves . . . ' "

But with fame came controversy and problems, especially with the management of CBS. Television is a commercial medium. It depends on advertising by sponsors for its revenues. And sponsors fear shows that generate controversy, for controversy can create a negative image that might defeat the objective of advertising itself. Alcoa, the sponsor of "See It Now," worried about the impact of the show, and this in turn concerned CBS president Frank Stanton and chairman of the board William S. Paley. In short, CBS was caught in the classic conflict of commercial television: programming freedom versus the demands of the sponsor. Murrow believed that the news division should not be constrained editorially by the profit motive. Stanton and Paley were not so sure. By 1958 Murrow could see that he was losing the fight, and he wanted to warn America before the contest was completely over.

Murrow's speech before RTNDA had a sense of urgency. "We are currently wealthy, fat, comfortable, and complacent," he said. "We have currently a built-in allergy to unpleasant or disturbing information. Our mass media reflect this. But unless we get up off our fat surpluses and recognize that television in the main is being used to distract, delude, amuse, and insulate us, then television and those who finance it, those who look at it and those who work at it, may see a totally different picture too late." He believed in the possibilities of television, but he knew that it could only be as good as the people who controlled the networks and stations: "This instrument can teach, it can illuminate, yes, it can even inspire. But it can do so only to the extent that humans are determined to use it to those ends. Otherwise it is merely wires and lights in a box."

Murrow lost the fight. In less than three years he was gone from CBS. But what he said is just as true today as it was in 1958. When asked why he criticized the industry that brought him fame and fortune, Murrow responded, "I've always been on the side of the heretics against those who burned them because the heretics so often proved right in the long run. Dead—but right." Murrow, the heretic, lost his electronic pulpit because he told the truth.

younger and had children sooner than they had in the previous two decades.

The Other Side of the Coin

Father Knows Best and other shows portrayed an ideal world where serious problems seldom intrude and where life lacks complexity. In fact, the move to suburbia and the changes in family life forced Americans to reevaluate many of their beliefs. Cultural critics, for example, claimed that life in suburbia fostered mindless conformity. Lewis Mumford described suburbs as "a multitude of uniform, unidentifiable houses, lined up inflexibly, at uniform distances, on uniform roads, in a treeless communal wasteland, inhabited by people of the same class, the same income, the same age group." And a popular song called the suburban homes:

Little boxes on the hillside,
Little boxes made of ticky tacky
Little boxes on the hillside,
Little boxes all the same.

Some writers feared the United States had become a country of unthinking consumers driven by advertisers to desire only the latest gadget. Americans bought automobiles, houses, and electrical appliances as never before. Thirty percent more Americans owned homes in 1970 than in 1940. Between 1945 and 1960 the number of cars in the country increased by 133 percent and the use of electricity tripled. Perhaps the ultimate symbol of this consumerism was the Barbie doll. Introduced to the American public in 1958, Barbie cost only $3 dollars, but her full wardrobe cost over $100. Indeed, the buying of homes, cars, televisions, and electrical appliances fueled the tremendous economic growth between 1945 and 1970. Clearly, buying was good for the American economy, but was it beneficial to the individuals who spent more and more of their time in their cars and watching their televisions? Cultural observers despaired.

Some women also expressed frustration about their roles as wives and mothers. One poll of the 1934 graduates of the best women's colleges reported that one out of every three women felt unfulfilled. Although many women worked, cultural stereotyping prevented most of them from rising to the higher-paying, more prestigious positions. In addition, Betty Friedan, a leader in the women's rights movement, noted that women who did place a career above marriage or family were regarded as abnormal.

The problems of suburban life were explored in numerous films, novels, articles, and advice books. The film *Invasion of the Body Snatchers* (1956) is an outstanding example of the perceived fear that suburbia had created a nation of conformists. In the movie, the inhabitants of the town of Santa Mira are turned into emotionless shells by giant pods from outer space. Like abusers of Miltown or Thorazine—the most popular adult drugs of the 1950s—the pod-people utterly lacked individuality. As one explains, podism means being "reborn into an untroubled world, where everyone's the same." In that world, "there is no need for love or emotion." For such cultural critics as David Riesman, author of *The Lonely Crowd* (1955), America's acceptance of conformity threatened to make podism a reality.

The critics, however, overreacted to the "suburban threat." If the houses looked the same, the people were individuals—even if they often banded together to try to form suburban communities. In the suburbs, white working-class families could afford for the first time to purchase homes and live middle-class lives. This was a real accomplishment. The problems that critics observed in the suburbs—the tendency toward conformity, cultural homogeneity, materialism, and anxiety over sex roles—were urban problems as well.

The Meaning of Elvis

The harshest critics of "suburban values" were American youths. Their criticism took different forms. Some of it was thoughtful and formalized, the result of the best efforts of young intellectuals. At other times it took a more visceral form, a protest that came from the gut rather than the mind. Of the second type, none was more widely embraced by youths—or roundly attacked by adults—than rock and roll.

Rock and roll was the bastard mulatto child of a heterogeneous American culture. It combined black rhythm and blues with white country music. It was made possible by the post–World War II demographic changes. The movement of southerners to the cities of the upper South and North threw together different musical traditions and forged an entirely new sound. Its lyrics and heavy beat challenged the accepted standards of "good taste" in music. Giving voice to this challenge, black rock-and-roll artist Chuck Berry sang:

Well, I'm gonna write a little letter, gonna mail it
    to my local D.J.
Yes, it's a jumpin' little record I want my jockey
    to play
Roll over Beethoven, I gotta hear it again today
You know my temp'rature's risin' and the juke-
    box blowin' a fuse
My heart's beatin' rhythm and my soul keeps sin-
    gin' the blues
Roll over Beethoven and tell Tchaikovsky the
    news.

Confronting conventional morality, rock and roll was openly vulgar. The very term—"rock 'n' roll"—had long been used in blues songs to describe lovemaking, and early black rock-and-roll singers glorified physical relationships. Little Richard sang:

Well, Long Tall Sally she's built for speed, she got
Everythin' that Uncle John needs.

And in another song, he boasted:

I'm gonna RIP IT UP!
I'm gonna rock it up!
I'm gonna shake it up. I'm gonna ball it up!
I'm gonna RIP IT UP and ball tonight.

From its emergence in the early 1950s, rock and roll generated anger and criticism. In the South, white church groups attacked it as part of an NAACP plot to corrupt the morals of southern youths and foster integration. In Hartford, Connecticut, Dr. Francis J. Braceland described rock and roll as "a communicable disease, with music appealing to adolescent insecurity and driving teenagers to do outlandish things . . . It's cannibalistic and tribalistic." Particularly between 1954 and 1958, there were numerous crusades to ban rock and roll from the airways.

Most of the criticism of rock and roll focused on Elvis Presley, who more than any other artist most fully fused country music with rhythm and blues. In his first record, he gave the rhythm-and-blues song "That's All Right Mama" a country feel and the country classic "Blue Moon over Kentucky" a rhythm-and-blues swing. It was a unique exhibition of genius. In addition, Presley exuded sexuality. When he appeared on the Ed Sullivan Show, network executives instructed cameramen to avoid shots of Elvis's suggestive physical movements. Finally, Presley upset segregationists by performing "race music." Head of Sun Records Sam Phillips had once claimed, "If I could find a white man who had the Negro sound and the Negro feel, I could make a million dollars." Presley was that white man.

Elvis Presley, one of the great pioneers of rock-and-roll music, was the target of much controversy throughout his life.

In the end, however, the protests implicit in Elvis Presley and rock and roll were largely co-opted by middle-class American culture. Record producers, most of whom were white, smoothed the jagged edges of rock and roll. Sexually explicit recordings were rewritten and rerecorded—a process known as "covering"—by white performers and then sold to white youths. African-American singer Joe Turner, for example, recorded "Shake, Rattle and Roll" for an African-American audience. Its lyrics ran:

Get out of that bed,
And wash your face and hands.
Get into the kitchen,
Make some noise with the pots and pans.
Well you wear low dresses,
The sun comes shinin' through.
I can't believe my eyes,
That all of this belongs to you.

The white group Bill Haley and the Comets "covered" the song for a white audience. The new version stated:

Get out in that kitchen,
And rattle those pots and pans.
Roll my breakfast
'Cause I'm a hungry man.
You wear those dresses,
Your hair done up so nice.
You look so warm,
But your heart is cold as ice.

In the second version all references to beds and bodies have been eliminated; by 1959 rock and roll had become an accepted part of mainstream American culture.

A Different Beat

Rock-and-roll artists never rejected the idea of success in America. If they challenged conventional sexual mores and tried to create a unique sound, they accepted the rewards of success in a capitalistic society. Elvis Presley translated success into a steady stream of Cadillacs and conventional, unchallenging films. Not all youth protests, however, were so easily absorbed into middle-class culture. The Beat movement, for example, questioned the values at the heart of that culture.

The Beat Generation extolled the very thing that conventional Americans abhorred, and they rejected what the others prized. Beats scorned materialism, traditional family life, religion, traditional sexuality, and politics. They renounced the American Dream. Instead, they valued spontaneity and intuition, searching for truth through Eastern mysticism and drugs. Although whites formed the rank and file of the Beat Generation, they glorified the supposedly "natural" life of African Americans, a life representing (at least for whites) pure instinctual drives. They adopted African-American music and the jive words of the black lexicon. Terms such as *cat, solid, chick, Big Apple, square,* were all absorbed into the Beat vocabulary.

Allen Ginsberg was the leading poet of the Beat Generation. A graduate of Columbia University, where he was influenced by the life-style of New York City lowlifes and artists, Ginsberg moved to San Francisco in the mid-1950s. There, surrounded by kindred souls, Ginsberg came to accept his homosexuality and preached a life based on experimentation. He also developed an authentic poetic voice. In 1955 he wrote "Howl," the prototypical Beat poem, while he was under the influence of drugs. "Howl" is a literary kaleidoscope, a breathless succession of stark images and passionate beliefs. In a unique but soon to be widely imitated style, Ginsberg declared,

Allen Ginsberg was educated at the University of California, Berkeley, and at Columbia University. His poetry expressed the Beat Generation's dissatisfaction with conventional middle-class values.

CHRONOLOGY OF KEY EVENTS

1944	GI Bill of Rights grants veterans financial aid for education and government loans for building houses and starting businesses			organize a bus boycott to protest segregation; Eisenhower and Khrushchev hold summit in Geneva, Switzerland
1947	25-year-old Jackie Robinson becomes the first black player in major league baseball		**1956**	Soviet troops crush Hungarian uprising; Suez crisis; United States begins interstate highway system
1948	President Truman bans segregation in armed forces		**1957**	Eisenhower sends troops to Little Rock, Arkansas, to enable black students to enroll in formerly all-white public schools; Soviet Union launches the first satellite, *Sputnik*
1953	Dwight D. Eisenhower becomes thirty-fourth president; Stalin dies; Nikita Khrushchev emerges as leader of the Soviet Union; CIA helps bring Shah Mohammad Reza Pahlavi to power in Iran		**1958**	U.S. marines intervene in Lebanon; Congress passes the National Defense Education Act to provide federal aid to schools and colleges
1954	CIA masterminds overthrow of leftist government of Guatemala; *Brown* v. *Board of Education of Topeka* decision holds that "separate educational facilities are inherently unequal"		**1959**	Fidel Castro leads Cuban Revolution against the regime of Fulgencio Batista
1955	Emmett Till murdered; black residents of Montgomery, Alabama,		**1960**	U–2 spy plane is shot down over the Soviet Union

I saw the best minds of my generation destroyed
    by madness, starving hysterically naked,
dragging themselves through the negro streets at
    dawn looking for an angry fix . . .

Ginsberg even questioned accepted Cold War beliefs. He wrote:

America you don't really want to go to war.
America it's them bad Russians.
Them Russians them Russians and them Chinamen. And them Russians.
Them Russians want to eat us alive.
America this is quite serious.
America this is the impression I get from looking
    in the television set.
America is this correct?

Ginsberg and Jack Kerouac, the leading Beat novelist, outraged adults but discovered followers on college campuses and in cities across America. They tapped an underground dissatisfaction with the prevailing blandness of conventional culture. In this, their appeal was similar to that of rock and roll. Both were scattering seeds that would bear fruit during the next decade.

CONCLUSION

Ike's America was both more and less than what it seemed. In foreign and domestic affairs, Eisenhower appeared to allow his subordinates to run the country, when in reality he made the important decisions. Whether it was national highways or the Middle East, Eisenhower's vision of order helped shape American policy. He was more influential than most Americans during the 1950s realized.

If Eisenhower was more active than he appeared, then the country was more dynamic than it seemed on the surface. Although critics railed against the conformity of suburban America, everywhere there were signs of change. During the 1950s African Americans quickened the pace of their struggle for equality, and youths experimented with alternatives to traditional behavior. And increasingly these two rebellions merged to form a distinct subculture. During the 1960s, the war in Vietnam would give a political edge to that subculture.

SUGGESTIONS FOR FURTHER READING

Taylor Branch, *Parting the Waters: America in the King Years, 1954–1963* (1988). Fascinating epic study of the first decade of the civil rights movement.

Robert A. Caro, *The Power Broker: Robert Moses and the Fall of New York* (1974). A long, detailed, intriguing look at power politics in New York City.

John D'Emilio and Estelle Freedman, *Intimate Matters: A History of Sexuality in America* (1988). An open look at an important topic normally ignored by historians.

David Garrow, *Bearing the Cross: Martin Luther King, Jr., and the Southern Christian Leadership Conference* (1986). A prize-winning biography of the most important civil rights leader.

Kenneth Jackson, *The Crabgrass Frontier: The Suburbanization of the United States* (1985). The reasons for, and the impact of, the suburb.

Richard Kluger, *Simple Justice: The History of* Brown v. Board of Education *and Black America's Struggle for Equality* (1976). A detailed and humane examination of one of the most important Supreme Court cases of the twentieth century.

Melton A. McLaurin, *Separate Pasts: Growing Up White in the Segregated South* (1987). A close look at everyday relations between the races.

Greil Marcus, *The Mystery Train*, 3d ed. (1990). This group of essays gives one of the best looks at the meaning of Elvis Presley.

Overviews and Surveys

Stephen E. Ambrose, *Rise to Globalism: American Foreign Policy Since 1938*, 5th ed. (1988); H. W. Brands, Jr., *Cold Warriors: Eisenhower's Generation and American Foreign Policy* (1988); William H. Chafe, *The Unfinished Journey*, 3d ed. (1995), and *The American Woman* (1972); Warren I. Cohen, *America in the Age of Soviet Power, 1945–1991* (1993); Alonzo Hamby, *The Imperial Years* (1976); Godfrey Hodgson, *America in Our Time* (1976); Walter LaFeber, *America, Russia, and the Cold War*, 7th ed. (1993); Emily and Norman Rosenberg, *In Our Times*, 5th ed. (1995); Frederick F. Siegel, *A Troubled Journey* (1984); Pauline Winand, *Eisenhower, Kennedy, and the United States of Europe* (1993); Lawrence Wittner, *Cold War America*, rev. ed. (1978).

Quiet Changes

Charles Alexander, *Holding the Line: The Eisenhower Era, 1952–1961* (1975); Chester L. Cooper, *The Lion's Last Roar: Suez, 1956* (1978); Robert A. Divine, *The Sputnik Challenge: Eisenhower's Response to the Soviet Satellite* (1993), and *Eisenhower and the Cold War* (1981); Tom Engelhardt, *The End of Victory Culture: Cold War America and the Disillusioning of a Generation* (1995); Fred I. Greenstein, *The Hidden-Hand Presidency: Eisenhower as Leader* (1982); Peter L. Hahn, *The United States, Great Britain, and Egypt, 1945–1956* (1991); Richard Immerman, *The CIA in Guatemala* (1982); Madeleine Kalb, *The Congo Cables: The Cold War in Africa— from Eisenhower to Kennedy* (1982); William R. Louis and Roger Owens, eds., *Suez 1956: The Crisis and the Consequences* (1989); Clay McShane, *Down the Asphalt Path: The Automobile and the American City* (1994); Richard Melanson and David Mayers, eds., *Reevaluating Eisenhower: American Foreign Policy in the 1950s* (1987); Stephen G. Rabe, *Eisenhower and Latin America: The Foreign Policy of Anti-Communism* (1988); John B. Rae, *The Road and the Car in American Life* (1971); Mark H. Rose, *Interstate: Express Highway Politics, 1939–1989*, rev. ed. (1990); Stephen Schlesinger and Steven Kinzer, *Bitter Fruit: The Untold Story of the American Coup in Guatemala* (1982); John W. Sloan, *Eisenhower and the Management of Prosperity* (1991); James Sundquist, *Politics and Policy: The Eisenhower, Kennedy, and Johnson Years* (1968); Richard Welch, Jr., *Response to Revolution: The United States and the Cuban Revolution, 1959–1961* (1985).

We Shall Overcome

Numan V. Bartley, *The Rise of Massive Resistance: Race and Politics in the South During the 1950s* (1969); Jack Bass, *Unlikely Heroes: The Dramatic Story of the Southern Judges of the Fifth Circuit* (1981); Sally Belfrage, *Freedom Summer* (1965); William Berman, *The*

Politics of Civil Rights in the Truman Administration (1970); Albert Blaustein and Clarence Clyde Ferguson, Jr., *Desegregation and the Law*, 2d ed. (1962); Robert F. Burk, *The Eisenhower Administration and Black Civil Rights* (1984); William H. Chafe, *Civilities and Civil Rights: Greensboro, North Carolina, and the Black Struggle for Equality* (1980); Robert Conot, *Rivers of Blood, Years of Darkness* (1967); Richard Dalfiume, *Desegregation of the U.S. Armed Forces: Fighting on Two Fronts, 1939–1953* (1969); John Dittmer, *Local People: The Struggle for Civil Rights in Mississippi* (1994); David Garrow, *Protest at Selma* (1978); Steven Lawson, *Black Ballots: Voting Rights in the South, 1944–1969* (1976), and *Running for Freedom: Civil Rights and Black Politics in America Since 1941* (1991); Manning Marable, *Race, Reform, and Rebellion: The Second Reconstruction in Black America, 1945–1990* (1991); Donald R. McCoy and Richard T. Ruetten, *Quest and Response: Minority Rights and the Truman Administration* (1973); August Meier and Elliott Rudwick, *CORE: A Study in the Civil Rights Movement, 1942–1968* (1973); Benjamin Muse, *The American Negro Revolution* (1968); Gunnar Myrdal, *An American Dilemma*, 2 vols. (1944); William L. O'Neill, *American High: The Years of Confidence, 1945–1960* (1986); James Peck, *Freedom Ride* (1962); Howell Raines, *My Soul Is Rested: Movement Days in the Deep South Remembered* (1977); Harvard Sitkoff, *The Struggle for Black Equality* (1981); Morton Sosna, *In Search of the Silent South: Southern Liberals and the Race Issue* (1977).

The Sounds of Change

Kent Anderson, *Television Fraud* (1978); Erik Barnouw, *Tube of Plenty*, 2d ed. (1990); Carl Belz, *The Story of Rock*, 2d ed. (1972); Paul A. Carter, *Another Part of the Fifties* (1983); William H. Chafe, *Women and Equality* (1977); Bruce Cook, *The Beat Generation* (1971); Marcus Cunliffe, *The Literature of the United States*, 4th ed. (1986); Scott Donaldson, *The Suburban Myth* (1969); James Flink, *The Car Culture* (1975);

Betty Friedan, *The Feminine Mystique* (1963); John Kenneth Galbraith, *The Affluent Society*, 4th ed. (1984); Herbert Gans, *The Levittowners* (1967); Charlie Gillett, *The Sound of the City: The Rise of Rock and Roll*, rev. ed. (1984); Michael Harrington, *The Other America: Poverty in the United States* (1962); Molly Haskell, *From Reverence to Rape: The Treatment of Women in the Movies*, 2d ed. (1987); Will Herberg, *Protestant, Catholic, Jew* (1955); Jerry Hopkins, *The Rock Story* (1970); Pauline N. Kael, *I Lost It at the Movies* (1965); Marcus Klein, comp., *The American Novel since World War II* (1969); W. T. Lhamon, Jr., *Deliberate Speed: The Origins of a Cultural Style in the American 1950s* (1990); David Marc, *Demographic Vistas: Television in American Culture* (1984); Douglas Miller and Marion Nowak, *The Fifties: The Way We Really Were* (1977); James T. Patterson, *America's Struggle Against Poverty, 1900–1980* (1981); Ned Polsky, *Hustlers, Beats, and Others* (1967); David M. Potter, *People of Plenty: Economic Abundance and the American Character* (1954); David Riesman, *The Lonely Crowd* (1950); Stephen M. Rose, *The Betrayal of the Poor: The Transformation of Community Action* (1972); Lynn Spigel, *Make Room for TV: Television and the Family Ideal in Postwar America* (1992); I. F. Stone, *The Haunted Fifties* (1963); Michael Wood, *America in the Movies* (1975).

Biographies

Stephen E. Ambrose, *Eisenhower*, 2 vols. (1983–1984); Jervis Anderson, *A. Philip Randolph* (1973); Robert J. Donovan, *Eisenhower* (1956); Peter Goldman, *The Death and Life of Malcolm X*, 2d ed. (1979); Alex Haley, *Autobiography of Malcolm X* (1965); Townsend Hoopes, *The Devil and John Foster Dulles* (1973); David L. Lewis, *King*, 2d ed. (1978); Peter Lyon, *Eisenhower: Portrait of the Hero* (1974); Anne Moody, *Coming of Age in Mississippi* (1968); Stephen B. Oates, *Let the Trumpet Sound: The Life of Martin Luther King, Jr.* (1982).

CHAPTER 28
POWER SHIFTS: THE EMERGENCE OF THE SOUTH AND WEST

THE EMERGENCE OF THE SOUTHERN RIM
From the Long Hot Summer to the Sunbelt
A Shift in Race Relations
The Business of the South Is Business

THE MYTH AND REALITY OF THE WEST
Packaging the West
Washington and the West
From Extraction to Diversification
The Problems and Benefits of Growth

POLITICS WESTERN STYLE
An Aberration or an Omen?
Shifting Party Loyalties
The Politics of Liberation

ROLINAARIZONALOUISIANAGEORGIAOKLAHOMAUTAHFLORIDAMISS

There was something about actor John Wayne that simply intrigued other people. He was like his country—oversized, powerful, and dramatic; part Daniel Boone, part Mike Fink, and all American. He was the Ringo Kid framed against a Monument Valley butte, holding a gun in one hand and a saddle in the other; he was Sergeant John M. Stryker telling his men to "Saddle up" before assaulting Iwo Jima; he was Thomas Dunson parting a sea of longhorns to get to Montgomery Clift; he was Captain Nathan Brittles reading the inscription on his "brand-new silver watch"; he was all those men on horseback or performing a service for their country or taking matters into their own hands—Captain Kirby York and Captain Rockwell Torrey, Pittsburgh Markham and Cole Thornton, Sean Thornton and Hondo Lane, Ethan Edwards and Tom Doniphon, George Washington McLintock and Rooster Cogburn—memorable characters from memorable films. Over the years he lost the smooth, fresh handsomeness of his youth. His hair fell out, his waist thickened, his face became lined and weathered. But the changes seemed to have made him even more appealing. His face seemed to take on a chiseled, Mount Rushmore quality, as if it had existed forever. Perhaps it was that quality, his granite sense of permanence, that attracted such awe. As much as any man of his century, he had become a symbol of America. As cultural critic Eric Bentley wrote, John Wayne was "the most important American of our time. . . . In the age when the image is the most important thing, Wayne is the principal image."

Yet during the late 1960s and 1970s no American seemed more out of step with the social and cultural changes in America than John Wayne. His critics charged that he was a political Neanderthal, a monument to such outmoded concepts as rugged individualism and sentimental patriotism. Since the 1920s he had starred in over 150 films in which he played varieties of the same character: the independent man of action who rode tall in the saddle, confronted evil on deserted streets at high noon, and protected innocent men and women. About his character—and indeed

Born Marion Michael Morrison in Winterset, Iowa, in 1907, John "Duke" Wayne came to symbolize the man of the West—honest, brave, upright, and true—in his movie roles. As cattleman Thomas Dunston in *Red River* (1948), he led his Texas longhorns on the 1000-mile long drive along the Chisholm Trail from San Antonio, Texas, to the railroad center at Abilene, Kansas.

himself—there was a certain surliness, a roughness about the edges that manifested itself in his coarse, blunt language and bull-in-a-china-closet behavior, yet no one who watched his films doubted what he stood for or where he would be when the trouble began.

But during the years of Lyndon Johnson's Great Society and protests against the war in Vietnam, John Wayne's simplistic attitudes and patriotism seemed naive. He preached individuality in an age of bureaucracy and *laissez-faire* in an era of social engineering. Liberal critics asserted that he was a dangerous superpatriot and attacked his 1968 film *The Green Berets,* which defended America's role in Vietnam. *New York Times* reviewer Renata Adler wrote that the film was "unspeakable, . . . stupid, . . . rotten and false"; another critic called it "immoral, in the deepest sense." The attacks confused Wayne. "I am an . . . honest-to-goodness, flag-waving patriot," he told reporters. "It's kind of a sad thing when a normal love of country makes you a superpatriot."

Wayne responded to his critics with his own scathing denunciation of liberalism. He could not abide freeloaders and reserved his sharpest barbs for what he felt were the weakest links in liberalism's chain of being—crime, welfare, and affirmative action. Perhaps his views on evil and justice had been shaped by his own Western movies, but he believed that some people were just badly flawed and incapable of even minimally acceptable social behavior except when the threat of swift punishment hung permanently over their heads. "I don't go along with . . . this new thing of genuflecting to the downtrodden," he told a reporter in 1969. "We ought to go back to praising the kids who get good grades, instead of making excuses for the ones who shoot the neighborhood groceryman." And he insisted that society had not only the right but the absolute duty to punish criminal behavior.

Just as he deplored coddling criminals, he opposed most welfare programs, which he claimed robbed clients of self-respect and personal responsibility. A firm believer in individual charity, he scoffed at the idea of government charity, especially when it was financed by his and his friend's money. "I don't want any handouts from a benevolent government," he explained in 1970. "I do not want the government to take away my human dignity and ensure me of anything more than normal security." To his way of thinking, entitlement programs were addictions, monkeys on the back of America and a terrible disservice to recipients. "You never do anybody a favor giving them something for nothing," he said. "You take away their survival instincts, their ambition, and their self-respect."

If liberals condemned Wayne's views, conservatives in the 1980s and 1990s embraced them. For millions of Americans John Wayne—tall, rugged, forthright, and independent—became the embodiment of the Ameri-

can ethos. President Jimmy Carter, against whom Wayne campaigned in 1976, said "John Wayne was "bigger than life. In an age of few heroes, he was the genuine article. But he was more than a hero; he was the symbol of many of the qualities that make America great . . . ." And Irish actress Maureen O'Hara remarked, "To the people of the world, John Wayne is not just an actor. . . . John Wayne is the United States of America. He is what they believe it to be. He is what they hope it to be. And he is what they hope it will always be." Finally, in 1995, sixteen years after his death, a Harris Poll listed Wayne as America's Leading Movie Star.

Certainly no American of the twentieth century is more identified with America than John Wayne. In his 1990 novel *The Golden Orange*, popular writer Joseph Wambaugh attested to the power of Wayne as a symbol and an idol. Wambaugh writes of a softball tournament held in Southern California where all the teams are encouraged to select "imaginative" names—the cruder the better. "And yet, the *only* caveat insofar as picking out a name is that no entrant can, in any way, denigrate the United States of America, or John Wayne. *That* is how profanity gets defined in *these* parts."

To America and to the world John Wayne was the embodiment of another ethos as well: the American West. Not only did he play western roles and live in Southern California, in so many ways he spoke for the West. In his films, easterners were often portrayed as corrupt and effete, men who controlled power to the detriment of "the people"; westerners were portrayed as freedom-loving, independent sorts who wanted only to escape the domination of eastern bankers and land agents. This resentment of the political and economic power of the East helped to shape twentieth-century western—as well as southern and southwestern—history. It helped explain Richard Nixon's sense that he was an outsider and the conservative political revolts led by Barry Goldwater and Ronald Reagan. Indeed, by the 1980s and 1990s the beliefs John Wayne espoused underlay a great power shift in the United States.

John Wayne won an Academy Award for his performance in *True Grit* (1969), but the Oscar may have honored as much all the heroic characters he played in his more than 150 films. Embodying the image of the rugged hero, Wayne played leading roles in all but 11 of the movies in which he appeared.

THE EMERGENCE OF THE SOUTHERN RIM

The central political, social, economic, and cultural fact of the second half of the twentieth century has been the gradual shift in power from the older industrial states and cities of the northeast and upper midwest to the southern and western rim of the United States. This rim—circling half the country from the Chesapeake region to Raleigh and Charlotte; south to Atlanta, Jacksonville, Miami, and Tampa; west to Birmingham, New Orleans, Houston, Dallas, San Antonio, Albuquerque, Phoenix, San Diego, and Los Angeles; then north up the coast of California to San Francisco Bay, to Oregon, and on to Seattle—has experienced the country's greatest growth and economic success. It has been and continues to be the destination for millions of immigrants from Asia, Mexico, and Central America, the spawning ground of new political ideas, and the most fertile area for cultural expression. Since 1964, all of the country's elected presidents—Lyndon Johnson, Richard Nixon, Jimmy Carter, Ronald Reagan, George Bush, and Bill Clinton—have either been born or claim residence in the South and West.

It is a region that defies hasty attempts at labeling. Is it the home of Ronald Reagan's conservatism or Jimmy Carter's liberalism? Merle Haggard's redneck revolt or San Francisco's Summer of Love? John Wayne's go-for-your-gun philosophy or Robert Redford's passion for the wilderness? It is all of these and more. But above anything else, this southern and western rim has defined itself by two measures: first, by its antithesis to the East; and second, by its concern for individual liberty. Like a John Wayne movie, the two go together. Running through much of southern and western political and cultural rhetoric is the idea that the East—especially the economic power of Wall Street and the political power of Washington—threatens individualism.

From The Long Hot Summer to the Sunbelt

When World War II ended, the South was the poorest, most economically backward section of the United States. Per capita income was barely one-half that of the national average, and income distribution was badly skewed. Pockets of the South in South Carolina, Georgia, Mississippi, and Louisiana seemed never to have recovered from the Civil War, and other regions in Appalachia had *never* had a prosperous time. Altogether, the South was the "Nation's No. 1" economic problem.

Changes since 1945 have been remarkable, though not uniform. Poverty still plagues much of the inner South, especially the rural sections of Alabama, Arkansas, Kentucky, Mississippi, and Tennessee. The South as a whole continues to lag behind the nation in funding for public education, high school graduation rates, health standards, working conditions, and hourly wages. But along the rim of the South—from the Chesapeake Bay down to Florida and over to Texas—and in the cities and suburbs of the Carolinas, Georgia, and Louisiana, prosperity has replaced poverty.

No one factor accounts for the changes. Technology, politics, and social and cultural shifts have aided the rise of the "New South." Perhaps it all began with the end of the long hot summer. If the Northeast and Midwest had cold winters, the South had uncomfortably hot, long summers, normally accompanied by high humidity, mosquitoes, and disease. In the areas closest to the Gulf of Mexico, summer conditions often began in April and lasted well into October. It was not a climate that encouraged immigration or industrial relocation.

Wealthy southerners tried to escape the oppressive heat and humidity by building houses with high ceilings, long breezeways, large windows, bedroom transoms, and broad awnings. With the invention in 1882 of the electric fan—or "whirligig" as it was called in the South—the urban middle class also found some relief from the heat if not the humidity. But the urban poor and rural dwellers lacking electric power found little comfort. During the first half of the twentieth century, however, engineers developed and refined the technology of "air-conditioning," an electrical system that simultaneously cooled, circulated, dehumidified, and cleansed air. First used in southern textile and tobacco industries, by the 1920s and 1930s air-conditioning had spread into the better hotels, first-run movie theaters, Pullman railroad cars, and some public buildings. By the end of the 1930s theater owners knew that they could vastly increase ticket sales by installing air-conditioning and putting up frost-covered signs advertising "20 DEGREES COOLER INSIDE."

But it was not until after World War II that most southerners felt the impact of air-conditioning. As one historian on the subject commented, "The air conditioner came to the South in a series of waves, and only with the wave of the 1950s was the region truly engulfed." Gradually air-conditioning spread to department stores, banks, government buildings, hospitals, schools, and, finally, homes and automobiles. Home air-conditioning soared after the introduction in 1951 of an inexpensive, efficient window unit. By 1960, 18 percent of all southern homes had either window units or central air-conditioning. That number topped 50 percent in 1970 and almost 75 percent by 1980. Still, there were limitations. In 1980, for example, 79.9 percent of urban houses had air-conditioning, compared to 59.2 percent of rural houses. For African Americans in the South the figures in 1980 were 58 percent of urban houses and 32.4 percent of rural houses.

"The South of the 1970s could claim air-conditioned shopping malls, domed stadiums, dugouts, green-houses, grain elevators, chicken coops, aircraft hangers, crane cabs, off-shore oil rigs, cattle barns, steel mills,

The advent of air-conditioning brought boom times to the South. Window units cooled limited spaces such as single rooms while larger central units cooled entire buildings, offering people a pleasant respite from the area's oppressive heat and humidity.

and drive-in movies and restaurants," wrote one historian. In Texas, the South's most air-conditioned state, even the Alamo has central air, and the annual cost for air-conditioning in Houston exceeded the gross national product of some Third World countries. The victory over heat also had great significance. It has helped to promote "the Americanization of Dixie" by removing one obstacle to the movement of people to the region. During the first half of the twentieth century more Americans moved out of the South than moved into the region. The exodus began to slow in the 1950s, and during the 1960s the trend reversed: more people moved into the South than left. The *New York Times* called the 1970 census "The Air-Conditioned Census." "The humble air-conditioner," a *Times* editorialist wrote, "has been a powerful influence in circulating people as well as air in this country."

The innovation also encouraged industries to relocate to the South, the history of which had been dominated by agriculture. At the time of Pearl Harbor, more than 40 percent of all southerners were farmers. Forty years later only 3 to 4 percent of southerners were farmers. The spread of industry southward has provided new sources of income and jobs. With the decline of heavy industry in the 1960s and 1970s, many manufacturers have relocated to the South where they could buy less expensive land, pay fewer taxes and lower wages, and avoid union difficulties.

If air-conditioning eased this industrial transition, it also opened the South to tourism. The reality of the long, hot summer gave way to the ideal of the Sunbelt—a vision of year-around golf, Christmas barbecues, and life without snow tires. Vacationers flocked to southern resorts, from Hilton Head, South Carolina, in the southeast to Scottsdale, Arizona, in the southwest. Older Americans moved to the South and West when they retired. Without air-conditioning such demographic shifts would have been difficult to imagine. "Can you conceive a Walt Disney World . . . in the 95-degree summers of central Florida without air-conditioned hotels, attractions and shops?" a newspapers editorialist asked. "Can you see a Honeywell or Sperry or anyone else opening a big plant where their workers would have to

spend much of their time mopping brows and cursing mosquitoes?"

Air-conditioning, however, was not without its critics. Some southern traditionalists insisted that forced, cool air had made the region more American and less southern. Large, high-ceiling southern plantation houses or even small, elevated, tin-roofed "cracker" houses gave way to tract homes, indistinguishable from similar tract homes in New York or Iowa. Similarly, critics argued that air-conditioning had reduced the tradition of "visiting," ended the practice of mid-day siestas, and dulled southerners' sense of place and history. In short, critics claimed that air-conditioning had turned Rebels into Yankees. Undoubtedly such claims were exaggerated, but air-conditioning—along with growing prosperity and migration to the South—had blurred the divisions between North and South.

A Shift in Race Relations

More than air-conditioning, however, accounted for the change in the South. Race relations, long the defining characteristic of the region, also underwent profound changes. Institutional racism, as characterized by a series of Jim Crow laws (see Chapter 19), died a slow death in Dixie. Throughout the 1940s white southerners ignored the stirring of racial progress taking place in the North, and even after the 1954 *Brown* v. *Board of Education of Topeka* decision, which delivered the most decisive blow to the concept of separate but equal, many white southerners refused to accept racial change. During the 1950s and early 1960s such southern politicians as Governor Lester Maddox of Georgia, Governor Ross Barnett of Mississippi, and Governor George Wallace of Alabama fought rear-guard actions against any change in the racial status quo. (See Chapters 27 and 30 for more detail on the quest for civil rights.)

But change did come. Civil rights acts in 1957, 1960, and 1964 struck down the legal basis of Jim Crow, and the Voting Rights Act of 1965 gave African Americans in the South (and elsewhere) the instrument to win even more changes. Such organizations as the Southern Christian Leadership Conference, the Congress for Racial Equality, and the Student Nonviolent Coordinating Committee struggled to ensure the reality of change. The end result was a new South—certainly not one where all racial problems had been solved or the distinction between black and white had been eliminated, but one that was at least confronting the question of race.

Perhaps Jimmy Carter from Plains, Georgia, best demonstrated the changes in the South. Carter grew up in a segregated South, in a county that resisted civil rights laws and all attempts to eradicate racial distinctions. Martin Luther King, Jr., had spent time in one of the county's jails, and in the 1960s white officials attempted to enforce illegal segregation statutes. In 1966 Carter ran for governor of Georgia but was defeated by Lester Maddox, who had become famous for announcing that he would use an axe handle to beat any demonstrators who tried to desegregate his restaurant. Carter ran again in 1970 and this time won. In his inaugural address he announced that the South had entered a new age: "I say to you quite frankly that the time for racial discrimination is over. ...No poor, rural, weak, or black person should ever have to bear the burden of being deprived of the opportunity of an education, a job, or simple justice." As a symbol of his fresh approach, he ordered a portrait of Martin Luther King, Jr., hung in the state capitol.

Advances against racism opened a new age of prosperity in the South. Attitudes expressed by Jimmy Carter and other politicians like him announced that the desire for progress in the South had finally overcome the desire for white supremacy. Since the 1870s proponents of the New South had called for southerners to stop living in the past, to renounce overt racism, and to accept industrialism. Only then, they argued, would the South enjoy the same material progress as the North. Though it took almost a century for the new ethos to emerge—aided by Supreme Court decisions and Congressional legislation—by the 1970s it had gained a firm foothold, especially in southern cities. It was no coincidence that urban business leaders became some of the most influential advocates of desegregation.

The Business of the South Is Business

Industry and economic development followed air-conditioning and civil rights into the South. Although talk of a New South—an economically diversified South—had begun almost as soon as the Civil War ended, it took almost one hundred years to make the transition from a fine idea to a reality. Before World War II, most of the talk about southern industrialism and prosperity was mere boosterism, and the profits from what little industry had developed usually flowed north. Thanks largely to the federal government, the southern economy did grow during the 1940s. During the war, Uncle Sam invested almost $9 billion in the South, mostly in defense-related activities. Although the government spent even more in other regions, the war provided the greatest infusion of cash and jobs in the South's history. At Oak Ridge, Tennessee, for example, where uranium was processed for atomic bombs, over 100,000 new jobs were created.

Throughout the region the story was much the same. Government shipyards in Newport News, Norfolk, Charleston, Tampa, Mobile, Pascagoula, New Orleans, and Houston provided hundreds of thousands of jobs. Aircraft, oil refinery, chemical, aluminum, and tin milling plants created many more. The

The temperate weather conditions of the South made possible unique construction designs such as the corn products refinery in Corpus Christi, Texas. The mill house of the refinery is wall-less, permitting the fresh night air to waft through the building.

South's industrial capacity increased by 40 percent, and per capita income tripled.

After the war the government closed some but not all of the bases and production facilities. As late as 1980, 24 of the Army's major American posts were located in the South, and almost half the soldiers in uniform were stationed below the Mason-Dixon line. In 1980 alone, the Department of Defense spent more than $50 billion in the South, or 39.5 percent of its budget. Together, the bases and plants gave the South a start from which to grow.

World War II provided the South with a modest takeoff period, but the late 1960s and 1970s witnessed spectacular growth. For investors, businesspeople, and industrialists, the South had certain natural advantages. Labor was cheaper and labor unions were weaker in the South than in the North. In addition, the South offered industry cheaper land, lower taxes, and fewer regulations—all of which meant reduced general operating costs. As industry in the Midwest declined—

the result of high taxes, labor strife, technological obsolescence, and government interference—the South became an attractive place for industrial resettlement. The Midwest became known as the Rustbelt, the South as the Sunbelt. Rust and Sun, decay and growth—Americans quickly responded to the images. By the 1960s the South had reversed its century-old problem of outmigration—more people were moving into the region than out. Professional baseball perhaps best symbolized the new trend. In 1966 the popular Braves baseball team departed Milwaukee for Atlanta. The justifications the Braves organization gave for the move: better ballpark, lower rent, tax breaks, and an outstanding television contract; in other words, more money.

The 1970s were boom years in the southern Sunbelt. Young, well-educated northerners moved into the region looking for economic opportunity, and middle-class retirees relocated to the Carolinas and Florida to take advantage of the sun and lower cost of living. At the same time, northern and foreign capital

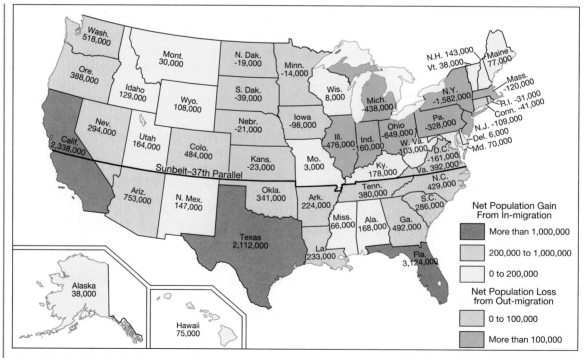

Migration to the Sunbelt, 1970–1981

poured into the South for industrial expansion. In the years immediately following World War II, Ford and General Motors built plants in Georgia; in the last third of the twentieth century Nissan and Saturn set up shop in Tennessee, Toyota in Kentucky, BMW in South Carolina, and Mercedes-Benz in Alabama. Critics of the southern automobile plants charged that state officials paid too high a price, that the subsidies and incentives offered the companies—including tax-free municipal bonds to subsidize construction and millions of dollars to train workers—negated the creation of new jobs. But the new plants *did* mean jobs; they *did* mean economic growth. While the wages and benefits in the new factories were below national averages, they were usually well above local averages.

Urbanization accompanied industrialization, and the South's traditional dependency on agriculture declined. As the percentage of southerners engaged in farming fell from 40 to 3 or 4 percent during the period from 1941 to 1981, the number of farms shrank from 2.9 million to 949,000. The transition from rural to urban, from farm to industry, brought with it a human toll of pain and suffering. Thousands of country music and blues songs lament the agony of transition. Songs like "Detroit City" and "Cotton Mill Colic" emphasize the coldness of factory towns and the numbing boredom of industrial work.

Progress, desegregation, and increasing industrialism have not cost the South its distinctiveness. Throughout the second half of the twentieth century, regional and sectional pride remained stronger below the Mason-Dixon line than above it. For example, in one sociological study about 90 percent of people living in North Carolina responded that they believed they lived in the "best state." In Massachusetts only about 40 percent of the residents so answered. Similarly, regional identifications—such as "southern" or "northern," "Dixie" or "Yankee"—in businesses remained much stronger in the South than the North. The popular magazine *Southern Living*, aimed at the southern middle class, illustrated the continued appeal of regional identity in its stories about southern football and tailgate parties, Bourbon advertisements, and recipes for wild game.

While many lament the passing of the traditional South, many more celebrate the new levels of prosperity. The South has become more like the rest of the country, a land where rich suburbs and pockets of poverty coexist, and strip mall and fast-food restaurants compete with older, family-run operations.

THE MYTH AND REALITY OF THE WEST

The West is an image and a bundle of myths firmly ingrained in the American imagination. It is a tactile image. It can be touched as well as seen, smelled as well as read. It has been portrayed in thousands of Westerns on movie and television screens, and in even more novels and short stories. And unlike tales about Puritan settlers or cotton planters, its appeal has not diminished with the end of the twentieth century.

Packaging the West

Advertisers understand the appeal of the West; they package the West to sell products. Consider the Marlboro Man and Marlboro Country. This figure of rugged independence, riding alone across a snow-covered high plateau or a dried-out range, his face tanned and weathered by work in the sun and exposure to the elements, became a fixture in American and world popular culture in the mid-twentieth century. In the minds of many consumers, the Marlboro Man was the essence of masculinity, and the advertising image itself became an icon. The history of the Marlboro Man, however, suggests just how potent images of the West are. In 1954, Marlboro was the name brand of a filtered cigarette produced by Philip Morris and sold primarily to women. The cigarettes came in a white soft pack, had a red "beauty tip" filter to camouflage lipstick, and sold under the slogan, "Mild as May." Considered effeminate cigarettes, Marlboros had less than one-quarter of one percent market share. "Men will never smoke cigarettes with filters," was the common advertising wisdom.

Then Chicago advertiser Leo Burnett took over the Marlboro account. He changed the woman's cigarette into a man's cigarette, in fact a man's man's cigarette. The white soft pack became a strong red and white hard, flip-top pack. The "beauty tip" bit the dust, as did the "Mild as May" slogan, replaced by the image of a cowboy with a tattoo on the back of one hand. The original photographer of the series later recalled, however, that he used pilots, not cowboys, for models "because pilots seem to have little wrinkles around the eyes." The combination of rustic masculinity and a western setting—Marlboro Man and Marlboro Country—had an immediate appeal, and Burnett's campaign became the most financially successful in advertising history.

More recently designer Ralph Lauren used the same marketing strategy. Born in New York City, the son of a Russian immigrant, Lauren is an American success story. After dropping out of the City College of New York, he got a job as a tie salesman. In 1967, he designed his own line of ties, and over the next two decades, expanded into menswear, women's wear, perfume, luggage and handbags, and home furnishings. By the mid-1980s, he had accumulated a personal fortune of a half-billion dollars. Part of his success was the result of appropriation of popular images, from polo players and British explorers to cowboys and Indians. The West provided fertile territory for Lauren. His rugged western wear line, including jeans, snap-button cowboy shirts, Indian design jackets, and Chaps cologne, was particularly profitable. Lauren's advertising followed the Marlboro Man pattern. His models rode horses and busted broncos; they epitomized hard-bitten masculinity. Commercials and advertisements for Chaps and Lauren's western wear stressed qualities of independence and strength by identifying with the iconography of the West.

Both Ralph Lauren's cowboys and the Marlboro Man sold images that Americans wanted to buy—in fact, had always wanted to buy. The West was America's great romance. In the nineteenth century, wealthy Americans bought the western paintings of Frederic Remington and Charles Russell, while their poorer countrymen purchased dime novels featuring the exploits of Billy the Kid, Doc Holliday, or the James Brothers. And they went to see William "Buffalo Bill" Cody's Wild West Show and thrilled at the Indian attacks and narrow escapes. By the end of the century, the West was a key element in American popular culture, and it seemed in the blood of the people.

The popular nineteenth-century, western formulas carried over into the twentieth century. In the pulp fiction, short stories, and novels of Zane Grey, Max Brand, Ernest Haycox, Alan Le May, and Louis L'Amour Americans received a steady supply of guns, guts, and grit. Grey's preachy western tales proved endlessly popular in the first half of the century, and no writer has had more films made of his works. L'Amour has been one of the biggest selling writers in the second half of the

One of the most widespread of the Western images in advertising was the Marlboro Man who invited smokers to "Come to Marlboro Country."

century. By the 1980s, his western novels had sold over 200 million copies.

If the West translated well to the printed page, it found its true medium on the silver screen. The marriage between Hollywood and the West has been a long one. Although it was filmed in New Jersey, *The Great Train Robbery* (1903) portrayed a train hold-up, the formation of a posse, a horseback chase, and dance hall scene; it was the earliest fiction western film. Thousands more followed. In the 1920s Broncho Billy Anderson, William S. Hart, Tom Mix, Harry Carey, and Hoot Gibson portrayed the western hero in scores of silent films. In the 1930s, during Hollywood's first decade of sound production, the "B" westerns of such actors as John Wayne, Tim McCoy, Bob Steele, Buck Jones, William Boyd, and Gene Autry were popular attractions in small theaters in the South, Midwest, and West. After the success of *Stagecoach* in 1939, "A" westerns began to dominate the biggest theaters in the nation's largest cities. The great western boom carried through World War II into the early decades of television in the 1950s and 1960s.

The millions of Americans who watched westerns every year received civic instruction along with their entertainment. The message of many of the westerns was that Washington and Wall Street, the seats of national political and economic power, could not be trusted. John Wayne's westerns, for example, told the story of a West besieged by evil—ruthless merchants, monopolistic land and water agents, greedy bankers, and corrupt government officials. Innocent people are shot at, beaten up, and left for dead; they are cheated, robbed, and chased off their land. Order is restored only by a tough, independent man with a gun. Although some films deal with the threat of Native Americans, the vast majority center on the dangers inherent in Washington bureaucrats and big-city bankers.

Washington and the West

For many real-life westerners, John Wayne's message and the circumstances of his films

were not that far from the truth. By the late nineteenth century the battles between U.S. settlers in the West and their Hispanic and Native American opponents had ended and the West had been conquered. But the new western leaders soon grew to resent the economic and political power of the East. Throughout the late nineteenth century and the twentieth century there were revolts against the entrenched power of the East. Populists fought against discriminatory railroad freight rates, a banking industry centralized east of the Mississippi, corporate greed, and high protective tariffs. In the 1930s, westerner and western historian Walter Prescott Webb observed, "Wherever I turn in the South and West I find people busily engaged in paying tribute to someone in the North." Talk of the "financial dictatorship" of Wall Street and the "Eastern corporate aristocracy" came easily to hard-pressed farmers and ranchers living in the West.

Yet at the same time that they were complaining about federal power, they received more than their share of federal dollars. The prosperity of the post–World War II West was largely financed and constructed by Washington, D.C. Although the federal government had always pumped money into the West, the investment steeply increased in the 1930s. Disappointed by fellow westerner President Herbert Hoover's agricultural and cattle programs, conservation policies, and opposition to federally funded public power, westerners, like most other Americans, turned against him in 1932 and supported Franklin D. Roosevelt. FDR did not disappoint them. His New Deal provided relief in the form of jobs, agricultural price supports, farm loans, and rural electrification.

But more importantly, Roosevelt enthusiastically supported western dam, power, and irrigation projects. In particular, he promoted the Central Valley Project on the Sacramento River to divert water from northern California to provide water, irrigation, and electric power for the rest of the state; the completion of the Hoover (Boulder) Dam on the Colorado River to provide water and electric power for southern California, the Imperial Valley, and the southwest; the Grand Coulee Dam on the Columbia River to provide electric power, irrigation, flood control, and navigational improvements in the northwest; and Colorado-Big Thompson Project to provide electric power in eastern Colorado.

The various dam projects helped to turn the West, in the words of historian Donald Worster, into "a modern *hydraulic society,* which is to say, a social order based on the intensive manipulation of water and its products in an arid setting." By 1978 the Census of Agriculture reported that the West had one-tenth of the world's irrigated land—43,668,834 acres—and nine of the top ten agriculturally productive counties in the United States. California, with eight of those counties, was the most agriculturally productive state in the country.

World War II accelerated the growth of the West at the same time that it created new bonds between Washington and the region. "Never in western history," wrote historian Richard White, "did changes come so quickly or have such far-reaching consequences as between 1941 and 1945. It was as if someone had tilted the country: people, money, and soldiers all spilled west. That tilt came from the federal bureaucracies, which devoted a disproportionate share of their enlarged resources to western development." During the war the federal government spent $70 billion in the western states and poured $40 billion more into factories, military bases, and capital improvements, over half of which was spent in California. The money provided more jobs, and the jobs lured newcomers to the region. In southern California alone, government orders created more than 250,000 new jobs in the aircraft and shipbuilding industries. Since the new industries were located in or near major cities, the urban population of the West soared. Many parts of the rural West, especially the states east of the Rockies, experienced population declines. Of the more than one million people who moved to California, most settled in the southern part of the state. Before the war, San Diego was a small city of

Water regulation projects often helped foster the tourist industry in the West. This view of the Shasta Dam and Reservoir, part of the Central Valley Project on the Sacramento River in California, is from a high point above the tourists' vista point overlooking the dam.

60,000 people; during the war, it grew to more than 250,000.

Defense industries spurred the growth and industrial expansion of the West. Probably more than any other person, industrialist Henry J. Kaiser epitomized the driving concern for defense and dollars. A central player in the development of the western infrastructure of roads, dams, bridges, and pipelines, Kaiser went into the shipbuilding business at the outbreak of war. He built steel works in Fontana, California, and shipyards in Richmond, Oakland, Sausalito, Vallejo, and San Pedro, California. Altogether, his industries employed close to 300,000 people, to whom they paid high wages and offered attractive medical and retirement benefits.

Others followed the trail Kaiser blazed. The Boeing plant in Seattle and the Douglas, Lockheed, North American, Northrop, and Hughes plants in southern California dominated the aircraft industry and provided several hundred thousand good-paying jobs.

Henry Kaiser epitomized the close relationship between government and industry in the West. Government loans financed Kaiser's shipyards and cost-plus government contracts guaranteed his profits.

The growth of the aircraft industry even threatened to overshadow the motion picture industry in southern California. Almost as a symbol of the emergence of the new industry, Warner Brothers Studios, located in Burbank near Lockheed and fearing an enemy attack, painted a 20-foot arrow on the roof of a sound stage with the message: LOCKHEED— THATAWAY. And Hollywood film stars complained that all the good chauffeurs, butlers, cooks, and maids had either enlisted or taken better-paying jobs in aircraft factories. One advertisement announced: "Maid wanted; will pay Lockheed wages."

The end result was the transformation of the West, and especially California, from a virtual colony of the East into the fastest growing, most economically booming section of the country. Once westerners had complained about the East's near monopoly over banks and financial institutions. By the end of the war, the largest bank in the world was the Bank of America, the San Francisco–based bank run by the Giannini family which had financed not only much of the growth of the film industry but the expansion of Bendix, Chrysler, Westinghouse, North American Aviation, and Northrop Aircraft Corporation. As G. P. Giannini observed in 1945: "The West has all the money to finance whatever it wants to; we no longer have to go New York for financing, and we're not at its mercy. Wall Street used to give a western enterprise plenty of rope, and when it broke, it took over." Now the West owned the rope.

From Extraction to Diversification

Walter O'Malley was once described as having "a face even Dale Carnegie would want to punch." In the mid-1950s, O'Malley, the owner of the Brooklyn Dodgers, was known for his penny-pinching concern for profits and his lack of humor. But in late 1957, many residents of Brooklyn added "traitor" to O'Malley's list of character flaws. In that year he announced his decision to move his Dodgers the following year from Brooklyn to Los Angeles, and for good measure, he convinced Horace Stoneham, owner of the New York Giants, to relocate his team to San Francisco. Dodger and Giant fans sent up a howl of betrayal. Journalist Arthur Daley wrote that some "teams were forced to move by apathy, or incompetence. The only word that fits the Dodgers is greed.... Baseball is a sport, eh? ... the crass materialism of O'Malley and Horace Stoneham of the Giants presents the disillusioning fact that it's big business, just another way to make a buck."

Actually, the Dodgers' move west was more complicated than the "disillusioning fact" suggests. O'Malley was concerned about the deterioration of the Brooklyn neighborhood that was the home of Ebbets Field. The quaint structure was located in an increasingly unsafe section of the city and it lacked parking facilities. O'Malley wanted to move to a new Brooklyn stadium, but his plans were blocked by New York power broker Robert Moses. In the end, O'Malley fled the labyrinthine politics and regulations of New York for the more generous political and cultural climate of Los Angeles.

The Dodgers' move west symbolized the new westward tilt of the country. Professional baseball teams were businesses, subject to the same market forces as other businesses. Chambers of Commerce throughout the country actively competed to bring new businesses to their communities. New businesses translated into more jobs and more money. Eager state and local governments used promises of low-interest loans, free land, cheap leases on city-built facilities, low property taxes or even property tax exemptions, and the building of county access roads to factory sites to attract new businesses. Certainly by the end of World War II, the West could boast that it was the land of sunshine and jobs.

In the half-century after World War II, the West completed the transition from being a land of extractive industries—mining, agriculture, ranching, oil, and logging—to being a region of vast economic diversification. By the 1970s, the newer electronic, aerospace, high-technology, and service industries had surpassed in financial importance the older eco-

Dodger players Pee Wee Reese and Don Zimmer acknowledge the sentiments of their fans who wanted to "Keep the Dodgers in Brooklyn." But the fans' outcry could not prevent the Dodgers from moving across the country to Los Angeles.

nomic staples of farming and ranching, coal and copper mining, and oil drilling and lumber operations. This economic leap led directly to millions of new jobs and accelerated the flow of emigrants into the West. Between 1945 and 1960, population west of the Mississippi River increased from 32 to 45 million people. The population of Arizona, one of the fastest growing states, grew by 163 percent. In 1960, California, which led the rest of the West in growth and prosperity, passed New York as the most populous American state. By the 1980s, the combined population of the West and the South for the first time exceeded the combined population of the Northeast and Midwest.

As it had during World War II, the federal government aided the growth of the West. Part of the reason lies in the fact that the federal government owned so much of the arid land of the West: more than 85 percent of Nevada, 63 percent of Idaho, 61 percent of Utah, and 50 percent of Wyoming. By 1960, close to one-third of all workers in the Los Angeles area worked for the defense industry, and that figure was well over two-thirds in San Diego. Up and down the West Coast it was more of the same. From the marine base at Camp Pendleton and the shipyards in San Diego to the nuclear complex at Hanford, Washington, and the shipyards in Seattle, the federal government's military spending helped to subsidize the boom in the West.

In the process, the West became the nuclear heartland of America, a development that rested uneasily on the minds of many people in the region. Offutt Air Force Base near Omaha, Nebraska, headquartered the country's Strategic Air Command; during the Cold War years the Hanford Reservation on the Columbia River manufactured and processed plutonium; Colorado's Cheyenne Mountain housed the Combat Operations Center of the North American Air Defense Command; the Black Hills and the Four Corners area supplied uranium; and New Mexico, where the first atomic bomb was tested, provided a home for various missile sites, military bases, and Sandia Laboratories, the Atomic Energy Commission's primary re-

search facility. In addition, the federal government assembled nuclear bombs in plants at Rocky Flats, Colorado, and Pantex, Texas; conducted extensive nuclear testing in Utah and Nevada; and dumped—or hoped to dump—nuclear waste in unoccupied western desert land.

Defense activity bred new industries and new jobs. Billions of dollars in federal and state grants went to researchers in western universities, enlarging the reputations of such schools as California Institute of Technology, the University of California at Berkeley, and the University of Washington. Private companies such as Martin-Marietta and General Dynamics contributed to western economies in the form of skilled, high-paying jobs. The aerospace industry, which blossomed in the West during World War II, remained largely in the West after the war. From Wichita, Kansas's line of smaller aircraft such as Learjet, Beach, and Cessna; to Los Angeles's and Fort Worth's line of larger jets such as Lockheed, Douglas, and North American; to Houston's Johnson Space Center—the skies belonged to the West.

The Problems and Benefits of Growth

Such development was not without troubles, however. As the West discovered, government money and government waste went hand-in-hand. Few people complained when the government paid too much for a lug nut or toilet seat, but waste and sloppiness in nuclear development had more dire consequences. Under the pressures of the Cold War, the government proceeded recklessly in the development of its nuclear capabilities. Test blasts probably showered many westerners with deadly radioactive fallout. In 1953, for instance, the Atomic Energy Commission detonated 11 atomic bombs in the dry lake bed of Yucca Flats, Nevada. Two of the bombs were especially "dirty" with strontium 90 and cesium 137 isotopes. The surrounding desert was covered with a fine gray ash, and an aberrant wind carried some of the fallout more than 150 miles to the east, blanketing St. George, Utah, and the Escalante Valley. In 1954, when the John Wayne movie *The Conqueror* was filmed in the area, the levels of radioactivity were still high. Over the next thirty-five years, 91 of the cast and crew of 220 people would develop cancer, a number three times higher than actuarial tables would predict. Similarly, cancer rates in and around St. George would be among the highest in the nation.

Dealing with the hundreds of thousands of gallons of nuclear waste compounded the problem. The simple truth was that the government gave far too little thought to the by-products of nuclear development, and it wasn't until the end of the Cold War that more attention was focused on the problem. The government might shut down the Hanford Reservation, but where could it store the left-over plutonium? While some nuclear waste experts suggested a Yucca Flats dumping ground, others argued that there was no safe way to bury "hot" material with isotopes that might remain active for a hundred thousand years. To a large degree, it is still a debate that is being conducted in the West by westerners.

Nuclear waste was not the only problem created by the rapid growth of the West. Led by the Bureau of Reclamation and the Corps of Engineers, who often worked at cross-purposes, government planners and wealthy westerners continued their helter-skelter dam building. "Every major river of the West came, to a greater or lesser extent, under the control of the dam builders and water pumpers," commented two authorities on the twentieth-century West. Never had any country created a more elaborate "hydraulic society." Water from the great western rivers—from the Columbia, the Snake, the Colorado, the South Platte, and the Rio Grande to the Red, the Missouri, and the Arkansas—was dammed, drained, and diverted to provide irrigation, electricity, shipping channels, and leisure activities. In the wild scramble for water, states and nations began quarreling. Arizona and Colorado complained that *their* water was being used

by Californians to fill their swimming pools and grow their crops; Mexico charged that the United States was monopolizing the Rio Grande. But throughout most of the late twentieth century, federal money flooded the West. By the early 1980s, the West boasted 41.3 million acres of the nation's 49 million acres of irrigated land.

The benefits of the damming of the West were many, though they were not equally distributed throughout western society. With the help of irrigation, the West became the new American breadbasket, and the billions of kilowatt-hours of electric power supported the needs of the region. But there were costs as well. Flood control was often illusionary; water accumulated salt and selenium; land suffered from siltation, erosion, and salt residues; dams threatened to collapse. Most of all, water supplies dwindled. By the 1980s, many Americans grew alarmed by the declining levels of the Ogallala Aquifer, which provided water for irrigation in Texas and the Great Plains states.

A final problem created by the economic growth of and emigration to the West was its dependence on the automobile. Unlike many eastern cities that developed before the advent of the internal combustion engine—indeed, before the development of any useful form of mass transportation—the West matured with automobiles. This mobility, coupled with the availability of inexpensive land for individual homes, resulted in the emergence of an extended society of suburbs, connected by miles of highways woven together by underpasses and overpasses. If Boston, New York, and Philadelphia were "walking cities," Los Angeles, Phoenix, Denver, Dallas, and Houston became "driving cities." This condition was made worse by the decline in railroads and urban mass transit. By the 1970s it became clear that western cities had developed twin dependencies: diverted water and gasoline.

The gasoline addiction had predictable, but long-ignored, results. In the 1930s the word "smog" had been coined to describe the chemical-laden fogs that fell like a blanket over Pittsburgh. By the 1940s smog had be-

Damming Western Waters

come a problem—albeit a small, acceptable one—in the land of sunshine. The winds—or, more precisely, the lack of winds—in the Los Angeles basin contributed to the problem. Unlike the areas to the north and south, Los Angeles normally has very still air. Even in the nineteenth century, it was a town where the smoke from campfires and, later, smudge pots lingered for hours in the atmosphere. But, as one historian commented, "The smog in Los Angeles had little to do with smoke and nothing to do with fog, and if the saffron blanket itself came as a shock, the discovery of its primary cause was equally sensational." It was the residue of unburned hydrocarbons, the by-product of running automobile engines. To make matters even worse, smog was not just an aesthetic eyesore; it was an actual eyesore and a serious health problem, capable of killing crops and trees and endangering the lives of humans and animals.

For most of the second half of the twentieth century, however, the benefits of western growth overshadowed the question of nuclear waste, the shrinking water supply, and the spread of smog. From 1945 to the early 1970s, almost every sector of the western economy leaped forward. With the development of the interstate highway system and less expensive commercial air travel, western tourism flourished. Millions of tourists visited the Badlands, the Grand Canyon, Monument Valley, Yellowstone National Park, or the other natural sites in the West. Millions more invaded the ski resorts at Vail, Aspen, Snowbird, Sundance, and Sun Valley. Las Vegas and Reno attracted tourists determined to have fun and make money. Disneyland and the beaches of southern California acted like a magnet for young people—and their parents—from all over the world. Increasingly, when Europeans and South Americans thought of the United States, their minds conjured visions of deep canyons and Mickey Mouse.

For a while, even the traditional western extractive industries—agriculture, ranching, mining, lumber, and petroleum—boomed. More than even before the war, farming and ranching became big businesses. Highly capitalized, heavily mechanized, often dependent

Bright lights and spectacular entertainments help lure millions of tourists to the gambling casinos in Las Vegas.

on federal price supports, both were fabulously productive. The same was true for mining, lumbering, and petroleum industries. Western copper, uranium, wood, and oil were in constant demand. But in the late 1960s and early 1970s those industries began to face difficult times. Foreign competition plagued all of them. Chilean copper, Canadian lumber, and Arab oil often undersold Americans even in their own markets. In addition, environmentalists and government regulatory agencies made it more difficult, and more expensive, for lumber interests, miners, and oil drillers to practice business as usual. By the 1990s, there were signs that the oil industry might regain some of its former profitability, but the outlook for agriculture, lumber operations, and mining was less optimistic.

The post–World War II West was too diversified, however, for the decline in the extractive industries to mean a collapse of the western economy. Manufacturing, tourism, service, and high-tech industries ensured that the West would continue to grow economically. The emergence of high-tech manufacturing in California's Silicon Valley, Austin,

Texas, and Seattle, Washington; the shipyards of Oakland and Long Beach in California; the banking and medical complex in Houston, Texas; and the defense-aerospace industries throughout the West prospered even while the national economy sagged. The age of the cowboy, the romantic man on horseback, had ended. Increasingly, Bill Gates, founder of Microsoft Corporation and America's wealthiest individual, sitting in front of his home computer screen in Seattle, Washington, symbolized the new West.

POLITICS WESTERN STYLE

In the early 1960s, Arizona Senator Barry Goldwater seemed out of step with most of his colleagues in Washington. In both parties eastern liberalism and style seemed the order of the day. Democratic President John F. Kennedy talked confidently, and eloquently, about a more active role for government in the quest for social justice. Republican politicians such as Nelson Rockefeller of New York,

Henry Cabot Lodge of Massachusetts, William Scranton of Pennsylvania, and George Romney of Michigan also advocated a more liberal domestic agenda, one more in accordance with Franklin D. Roosevelt's New Deal and Dwight Eisenhower's Modern Republicanism than the more conservative ideas of such former Republican leaders as Senator Robert Taft of Ohio. But Goldwater seemed unaffected by the charge toward liberalism.

Goldwater believed that the country's problem was not too little government activity but too much. In 1960 he wrote (or, more accurately, had ghost-written) a brief book outlining his beliefs, *The Conscience of a Conservative*. The 123-page volume quickly became a best-seller, selling 3.5 million copies of the book within four years. The most important theme of the book was freedom—for individuals and nations. As a conservative, Goldwater wrote that he was dedicated to "achieving the maximum amount of freedom for individuals that is consistent with the maintenance of social order." The enemy of individual freedom, he argued, was the federal government, which had become "a Leviathan, a vast national authority out of touch with the people, and out of control." He wanted to rein in the government, reduce its size, and restrict its activities to establishing order, maintaining defense, and administering justice.

In terms of concrete measures, Goldwater called for the end of all subsidies and price supports for farmers, the passage of right-to-work laws and the abolition of the closed shop, a new form of taxation (he called the federal income tax "confiscatory"), and a reduction of federal bureaucracy and spending. He opposed most forms of welfare and government spending on social, educational, public housing, and urban renewal programs. "I have little interest in streamlining government or making it more efficient, for I mean to reduce its size," he wrote. "I do not undertake to promote welfare, for I propose to extend freedom. My aim is not to pass laws, but to repeal them." As for foreign affairs, he called for a vigorous fight against communism and the defense of freedom throughout the world.

The Conscience of a Conservative inspired a new generation of Republican thinkers. Patrick Buchanan, who would later emerge as a powerful conservative spokesman, said, "*Conscience of a Conservative* was our new testament; it contained the core beliefs of our political faith, it told us why we had failed, what we must do. We read it, memorized it, quoted it.... For those of us wandering in the arid desert of Eisenhower Republicanism, it hit like a rifle shot."

An Aberration or an Omen?

Who was this new conservative marksman? Barry Goldwater was a product of the twentieth-century West. "My life," he wrote, "parallels that of twentieth-century America—raw energy amid boundless land and unlimited horizons." He was born in Arizona when it was still a territory and raised on tales of the men and women who settled in the West. "My mother spoke a lot about our country when we were kids—our heritage of freedom, the history of Arizona, how individual initiative had made the desert bloom." But, as a westerner, he was quite aware that the federal government restricted his freedom. Only 17 percent of his home state, he noted, was "in private hands," and often the capital needed for western development was in the hands of eastern bankers. In his successful 1952 race for the U.S. Senate, he attacked "America's new super state—burgeoning federal spending and a bloated bureaucracy."

Once in the Senate, Goldwater continued his attack on eastern power bases and leaders. As a westerner, he noted, "I had no qualms about taking on the Eastern establishment, whether it was Rockefeller, the banks, or the large corporations, because we had long been dominated by these interests. For a century, the West had been a colony of big Eastern money—a boom when they had invested and a bust when they had pulled out of various mining and other operations. We had been left with ghost towns and holes in the ground where gold, silver, and mineral deposits had been discovered." Goldwater

In his campaign appearances during the 1964 presidential race, Barry Goldwater drew crowds of well-wishers as well as detractors, who were often concerned that his aggressive stance against Communists might lead to nuclear war.

saw himself as an outsider and had no desire to become part of the inner circle of the Republican party. Instead, he articulated a political credo that aimed at taking power away from Washington and Wall Street and returning it to individual states. What he called for was a radical change in the Republican party that reflected the new realities of America, an "effort to move the party from the dominance of less than a dozen families and others in the East to hundred of thousands of small businessmen and others in the South, West, and elsewhere."

In 1964 Goldwater saw an opportunity. Attacking big government, deficit spending, high taxes, and social programs, he campaigned for the Republican nomination for president. "I will not change my beliefs to win a vote," he promised. "I will offer a choice, not an echo." Although the delivery of his speeches was often flat and his personal style wooden, his words were charged with outrage over a government that he believed had become too big, too fat, and too complacent. Throughout the winter and spring of 1964, he

stumbled toward the nomination, eliminating one Republican rival after another. At times, the political struggles became bitter. Rockefeller branded Goldwater as a wild-eyed radical who might lead the country into a nuclear war. "WHO DO YOU WANT IN THE ROOM WITH THE H-BOMB BUTTON?" asked a Rockefeller campaign flyer. Goldwater responded by criticizing Rockefeller's recent divorce. "Why are women for Goldwater?" asked Goldwater campaign literature. "Because he is a responsible family man . . . ." In a vicious fight for the nomination, Goldwater's opponents accused him of being trigger-happy and harboring racist beliefs; they even compared him to Adolph Hitler. But Goldwater won the battle. Reflecting the beliefs of their new candidate, the Republican platform called for spending cuts, reduced taxes, and a balanced budget; advocated stopping the flow of pornography through the mail and restoring school prayers; and demanded a foreign policy that aggressively confronted Communists.

In the 1964 presidential election Goldwater faced Lyndon Johnson and his well-oiled

Democratic machine. Johnson promised more government and more federal activity. Summarizing the Democratic agenda, Johnson said, "I just want to tell you this—we're in favor of a lot of things and we're against mighty few." On Johnson's side were prosperity and a substantial legislative record, which included the Civil Rights Act, the Wildlife Preservation Act, and the War on Poverty's Economic Opportunity Act. Looking toward the future, the Texas politician promised a Great Society, where want and suffering were eliminated. Medicare, Medicaid, regional redevelopment, urban renewal, and support for education—all were on Johnson's ambitious agenda. As several politicians suggested, criticizing Lyndon Johnson was like taking a shot at Santa Claus.

Not content just to say what they were for, Johnson and his campaign organizers made it clear what they were against. In two words: Barry Goldwater. In their public statements, television advertisements, and bumper stickers, they implied that if Goldwater was elected he might lead the nation into a nuclear war. "In your heart, you know he might" and "In your guts, you know he's nuts" were their constant refrains. In one television commercial, a young girl was shown picking the petals of a daisy in a sun-drenched field. As she plucked she counted, until her voice was drowned out by a stronger, military voice that commenced a military countdown, ending with the sight of a nuclear blast. The commercial ended with the voice of Lyndon Johnson: "These are the stakes. To make a world in which all of God's children can live, or go into the dark. We must either love each other, or we must die." To the end, the Democrats waged a bitter, effective campaign. Later in his life, Goldwater said, "I've often said that if I hadn't known Barry Goldwater in 1964 and I had to depend on the press and the cartoons, I'd have voted against the son of the bitch."

That is exactly what most Americans did. Goldwater lost big in 1964—43 million votes to 27 million votes. Johnson carried over 60 percent of the popular vote, something that few other presidential candidates had ever done. Newspaper and television commenta-

tors were quick to write off Goldwater and his conservative supporters as a political aberration. A *Time* magazine writer prophesied, "The conservative cause whose championship Goldwater assumed suffered a crippling setback. . . . The humiliation of their defeat was so complete that they will not have another shot at party domination for some time to come." Yet when conservatives began to study the returns, the defeat did not seem so absolute. Goldwater had run well in the Deep South, long considered sacred ground for the Democratic party. He had also attracted considerable support in the Southwest, the mountain states, southern California, and northeastern urban, ethnic-Catholic neighborhoods.

Taken as a whole, Republican strategist Kevin Phillips believed that the 1964 returns contained good news for the future of the Republican party and the conservative movement. In his book *The Emerging Republican Party* (1969), Phillips argued that an important shift in power was taking place in American politics. New Deal liberalism and the northeastern intellectual and media elite no longer expressed the needs and met the demands of

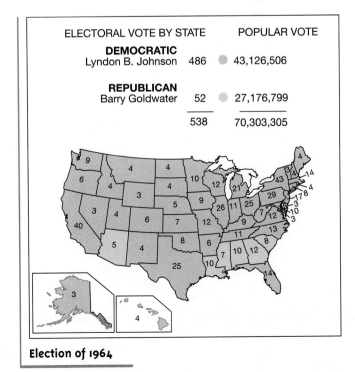

Election of 1964

most Americans, especially westerners and southerners. Deep in the South, out on the range, on the Sunbelt golf courses, and in working-class Catholic neighborhoods, a new ethos was taking shape. The political revolt, Phillips noted, would be led by people like Goldwater, men and women who wanted less government, less special-interest reforms, and more of their own paychecks. As one conservative Texan later said, "The '64 campaign was the Alamo before San Jacinto. . . . 1964 would prove a pivotal election, a beginning rather than an end."

Shifting Party Loyalties

Ultimately, Phillips was right. There was a political earthquake taking place in the United States, and its rumblings would be felt for the rest of the century. If Goldwater's defeat was not an obvious signpost, Republican Presidential and Congressional victories in 1968, 1972, 1980, 1984, 1988, and 1994 were. In 1968 and 1972, presidential candidate Californian Richard Nixon, though more moderate than Goldwater on social is-

sues, attacked liberal rulings by the Supreme Court, called for a return to "law and order," and appealed to the traditional values of hard work, religious faith, patriotism, and family. The South and West responded. In 1968, Nixon carried almost the entire West and most of the upper South (the Deep South went to American Independent candidate George Wallace). In his 1972 landslide victory, Nixon won every southern and western state. Eight years later, Ronald Reagan captured the presidency running on a platform that could have been written by Barry Goldwater's ghost writer. Reagan called upon American politicians to get tough on the Soviet Union, balance the federal budget, reduce the size of government, and support legislation to strengthen family values. Americans responded, sending him into office in 1980 and then overwhelmingly endorsing his first term in 1984. Texas Republican George Bush served two terms as vice president and then won the presidency in 1988. His victory united the same coalition that Goldwater and Nixon had built and Reagan had satisfied. Although Democrat Bill Clinton defeated Bush in 1992, his failure to satisfy southern and western conservatives resulted in a major defeat in the 1994 congressional elections (see Chapter 31).

The reasons for the shift in the center of political power from Northeast and Midwest to South and West and party alliances from Democrat to Republican had become clear by the 1990s. The power shift was largely the result of the movements of peoples. In the 1970s, for example, the decade in which the Republicans made their largest gains, millions of Americans relocated and immigrants moved to the South and West: the population of Florida increased by 3,124,000, California by 2,338,000, and Texas by 2,112,000; while New York's population declined by 1,582,000, Ohio by 649,000, and Illinois by 476,000. The same pattern was true for other states. Traditional industrial states—Massachusetts, Pennsylvania, Michigan, and Indiana—suffered sharp declines. Southern and western states—Virginia, North Carolina, Georgia, Arizona, Colorado, Oregon, and Washington—enjoyed equally sharp increases. By

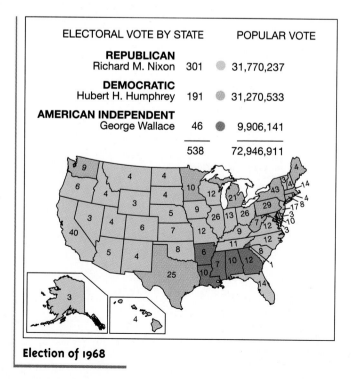

ELECTORAL VOTE BY STATE		POPULAR VOTE
REPUBLICAN Richard M. Nixon	301	31,770,237
DEMOCRATIC Hubert H. Humphrey	191	31,270,533
AMERICAN INDEPENDENT George Wallace	46	9,906,141
	538	72,946,911

Election of 1968

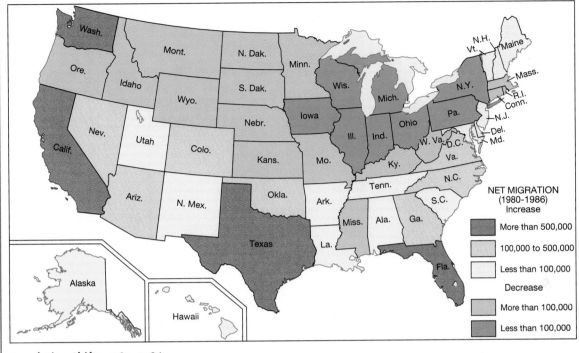

NET MIGRATION
(1980-1986)
Increase

More than 500,000

100,000 to 500,000

Less than 100,000

Decrease

More than 100,000

Less than 100,000

Population Shifts, 1980–1986

1980, for the first time in American history, the majority of the population lived in the South and West. Such population shifts bolstered the political power of the South and West and reduced the political clout of the Northeast and the Midwest.

The same decade saw a shift in party loyalties in the South. For nearly a century white Southerners had voted Democrat, or, more precisely, non-Republican. For them, the Republican party was the party of Lincoln, the Civil War, and military Reconstruction. Their Democratic party stood for limiting the size and power of the federal government and for allowing the states to take care of their own problems and exploit their own resources. Barry Goldwater, and then Richard Nixon, appealed directly to these issues. In *The Conscience of a Conservative*, Goldwater's condemnation of the growth in federal power was as much a defense of the constitutional principle of states' rights. He particularly attacked the idea that the federal government could demand the integration of southern public schools. Goldwater wrote, "I am firmly convinced—not only that integrated

schools are not required—but that the Constitution does not permit any interference whatsoever by the federal government in the field of education." Although Nixon did not go quite as far as Goldwater, he did succeed in limiting the role of the federal government in forced desegregation of southern public schools. In addition, he argued that the Supreme Court had enlarged the power of the federal government; he appointed justices who were committed to reversing that trend. By the time Reagan ran for the presidency in 1980, the Republican party had become "the new Grand Old Party" for much of the white South.

Unlike the South, the West had never had a strong tradition of party loyalties. The seats of both parties, they argued, were in the East, and both parties were dominated by eastern interests. As a result the West never developed the machine politics of the East and was more sensitive to democratic political innovations. Initiative, referendum and recall, and woman suffrage, for instance, were more quickly accepted in the West than in other sections of the country. Similarly, the West was

MEDICINE AND MORALITY

AIDS: A MODERN PLAGUE

AMERICANS have long debated what to do about sexually transmitted disease (STD). Health officials have insisted that STD is a medical problem that should be handled like any other communicable disease: through research, treatment, public education, and the vigorous application of modern techniques of epidemiology. Others have argued that STD is primarily a moral problem.

World War I brought the issue to a head. Army planners debated whether to concentrate on trying to prevent STD through educational propaganda against extramarital sex (accompanied by a crackdown on red-light districts), or whether to sanction the use of condoms and focus on medical treatment to cure infection. In the end, they elected to combine both approaches. Moreover, when the problem reappeared in World War II, the government promptly adopted the same solution: scary propaganda against extramarital sex, followed by condoms and treatment for soldiers who surrendered to temptation. Even the debate over treatment sounded like an echo. The discovery of penicillin precipitated another round of arguments over whether this new "wonder drug" should be given to soldiers who contracted STD. The dispute was settled exactly as it had been in World War I: Wayward souls received treatment.

Following World War II, public funding for STD work rose and

the number of cases fell. The victory over STD, however, proved to be short-lived, for infection rates tripled between 1950 and 1975. What happened? In part, health officials were victims of their own success. Given the power of new antibiotics, doctors stopped worrying as much about the social behavior that led to transmission, and they became less vigilant in their efforts to track down the partners of infected patients. Yet the doctors were not solely to blame. The public's apathy was reflected in reduced health budgets for STD work.

The lull ended in the 1980s with the appearance of acquired immune deficiency syndrome (AIDS), the most terrifying disease of modern times. As early as 1980, physicians began reporting a strange medical phenomenon among gay men. These patients were falling prey to fatigue, a puzzling combination of infections, a rare skin cancer known as Kaposi's

sarcoma, and eventual death. No one recovered from the disease.

After prolonged and ill-funded research, AIDS was finally linked to a retrovirus, which scientists named the "human immuno-deficiency virus," or HIV. Additional research soon revealed AIDS cases among heterosexuals, Haitians, hemophiliacs, and intravenous drug users, indicating that the disease was not limited to a single group; rather, it threatened everyone. But why did it take so long to mobilize research efforts and public awareness? The explanation lies in long-standing attitudes about STD.

First and foremost, AIDS was widely regarded at first as a "gay" disease, and homosexuals were a favorite target of the "new right" and the "moral majority," whose political clout had helped put Ronald Reagan in the White House. Patrick Buchanan, White House director of communications, proclaimed that homosexuals had "declared war on nature, and now nature is extracting an awful retribution." By the time the United States finally took notice of AIDS in 1987, more than 21,000 Americans had already died. Part of the reason lay in President Reagan's cutbacks in domestic programs: AIDS became another casualty of Reaganomics, another victim of the administration's hostility to social services. In the end, however, a series of shocking events forced the government to act: These included the discovery of AIDS-contaminated hospital blood supplies; the appearance of AIDS in heterosexuals; and the surprisingly bold anti-AIDS campaign of Surgeon General C. Everett Koop.

Koop recommended AIDS education for schoolchildren "at the earliest date possible," and he further advocated the promotion and use of condoms. Conservatives were outraged and charged the government with attempting to promote immorality. But Koop and other public health officials held firm. The government sponsored television and radio ads warning the public against "unsafe sex," and mailed an explicit brochure on AIDS to every household in America.

As public concern rose, various groups demanded that AIDS sufferers be quarantined. Though health authorities repeatedly stressed that casual contacts could not spread the disease, many people feared the worst. The objections of civil libertarians, who opposed quarantine, left most people cold, as did the arguments of those who rejected quarantine on practical grounds. (Where were tens of thousands of AIDS sufferers to be kept? Who was to pay for their care during this forced isolation?) While these arguments kept any serious movement for quarantine from developing, the public remained edgy. Some parents withdrew their children from schools where AIDS patients were enrolled, and AIDS sufferers found that many of their co-workers wanted them removed from their jobs.

Yet some of the reactions to AIDS within the gay community were no less extreme. Granted, most gay leaders struggled from the outset to publicize AIDS and to promote safe sex and monogamous relationships. But other gays reacted with denial. Some initially believed (or chose to believe) that AIDS was a heterosexual propaganda tactic designed to crush the nascent gay movement or that it reflected a secretly planned biological warfare against gay men by the CIA or some secret government cabal. To many, gay liberation meant not merely toleration of homosexuality but a celebration of sexuality, a reordering of values with greater emphasis on the long-suppressed pleasure principle. Multiple and unprotected contacts were the final necessary step to political freedom. Others proclaimed that AIDS could never hit them. And still others became resigned and carried on as usual—in the gay community they became known as Doris Days, after the actress famous for singing "Qué será, será" ("What Will Be, Will Be").

The end of the AIDS story is still to be written, for no one can predict the impact this deadly disease will have on American society. By 1995 more than 475,000 Americans had been diagnosed with the disease, more than 285,000 had died from it, and another 1 million are believed to be infected. With a cure nowhere in sight, medical authorities expect to be confronted by literally hundreds of thousands of AIDS patients by the turn of the century. Their care will be both protracted and expensive. Who will pay for it?

Despite such grim realities, sex researchers report few changes in the public's private behavior, especially in those groups that are at high risk for contracting the disease. Though hard data are lacking, the experts agree that "unsafe sex" remains a common practice among adolescents and young adults, and the same holds true for many like the progressives, many Americans today will no doubt continue to place their hopes on education and on the search for new medical advances with which to eradicate AIDS, debating all the while whether those who contract the disease should be pitied or condemned.

more receptive to left-wing and right-wing third-party movements. From the Populist movement in the 1890s and the Wobblies in the early part of the twentieth century to Francis Townsend's campaign in the 1930s and Barry Goldwater's revolt in the 1950s, the West had been more apt to swing toward political extremes.

The Politics of Liberation

The idea of individual freedom, as measured by less government and fewer restrictions, has characterized much of the political thinking of the post–1945 West. To be sure, individual freedom provided the core of the Goldwater and Reagan movements. It helps explain Goldwater's attack on the federal government and defense of a version of states' rights and Reagan's demands for deregulation. But the idea of individual freedom has also energized movements outside of Republican politics.

On the political left, the West Coast counterculture movement and such African-American liberation movements as the Black Panthers proclaimed a profound distrust of "government" solutions and federal bureaucracies. Ken Kesey, the novelist whose fictional heroes seemed to speak for many alienated youths, rejected the politics of party organizations and mass solutions. The heroes of his novels *One Flew Over the Cuckoo's Nest* (1962) and *Sometimes a Great Notion* (1964) are first and foremost individualists who battle more for individual dignity—the right to make individual decisions—than any sort of collective ideal. Similarly, Black Panther leaders struggled to gain control of their own communities and steered clear of traditional party politics.

Similarly, the West's most politically active religious minority, the Mormons, have a history of conflict with and distrust of the federal government. Across the high plains and deserts of Utah, Nevada, Idaho, southern California, western Wyoming, and northern Arizona, millions of Mormons nursed long memories of persecution at the hands of the federal government. During the nineteenth century,

anti-Mormon mobs, often with the cooperation of federal and state officials, had driven them out of Ohio, Missouri, and Illinois. When they settled in the desolate valley of the Great Salt Lake, seeking only to be left alone to practice their religion and build their communities, the federal government continued to hound them. In 1857, President James Buchanan had dispatched the first federal troops to force the observation of antibigamy laws, an issue that divided Mormons and the U.S. government for the next several decades. Federal judges convicted and jailed hundreds of Mormons for practicing plural marriages. More battles followed—over the status of Mormon lands and the right of Mormons to be elected to Congress. After 60 years of persecution, Mormons became convinced that the federal government was bent on their destruction.

During the twentieth century, animosities between Washington and the Mormons eased, but suspicions lingered in the intermountain West, occasionally erupting into full-blown controversies. Mormons had little faith in the federal government to solve social problems. Welfare was a case in point. Under the Mormon welfare system, recipients had to accept counseling and work assignments in return for aid. Many Mormons criticized federal welfare, which they considered a dole that would produce a generation of lazy, indolent recipients who expected entitlements. In the 1950s, when atomic bomb testing in Nevada produced high levels of radioactive fallout in Utah, thousands of Mormons saw it as a government conspiracy to destroy them. Finally, late in the 1970s, church leaders vigorously protested the federal government's decision to place MX missiles, armed with thermonuclear warheads, under Utah soil. They did not relish the idea that in the event of a nuclear war between the United States and the Soviet Union, Utah would be the first region of the country to be destroyed.

Yet it was on the political right where individualism and antifederal sentiment made their most important political impact. Often the battle was over the control of land and natural resources. With the downturn in the economy in the 1970s, Western developers and businesspeople began to complain about federal environmental legislation. The debate over "beneficial use" became the flash point. Environmentalist groups such as the Sierra Club and the Friends of the Earth charged that developers were willing to destroy the land and the ecosystem in their pursuit of profits. Loggers, ranchers, miners, and other Westerners who depended on inexpensive access to government lands argued that the mass of federal regulations made it impossible for them to hold their own in competitive world markets.

The Sagebrush Rebellion was the most dramatic example of the battle between state and federal governments over control of state land. In the late 1970s and early 1980s, some conservative Western politicians began to clamor for the federal government to cede its control of western land to the individual states. The idea was to develop some of the land, sell much of the rest, and promote Western growth and prosperity. (Other Westerners, liberal and conservative, saw the rebellion as an attempted land grab by miners, ranchers, and loggers, a sort of return to the most exploitive methods of the nineteenth century.)

Utah Senator Orrin Hatch introduced in 1979 legislation to return 544 million acres in 13 Western states from federal to state control; then-presidential-hopeful Ronald Reagan endorsed the proposal. But the rebellion failed. Arizona governor Bruce Babbitt summed it up as an attempt to "sell off the land into private ownership, lock the gates, post the no-trespassing sign, and proceed to use and abuse the land." In truth, though many Westerners had little faith in the wisdom of the federal government and resented federal regulation, they had even less faith in and more fear of their own developers. In the battle between developers and preservationists, most Westerners found themselves seeking middle ground.

The fight over Western lands, however, did not slow down the West's steady political drift to the right. Tax revolts were more successful than the Sagebrush Rebellion. If Westerners were content to allow the government to control a vast portion of their land, they steadfastly maintained that they should be able to control more of their own incomes. The tax rebellion was waged on state and federal fronts. In 1978 California passed Proposition 13, which demanded a 57 percent cut in

A variety of environmental groups have participated in the controversy over the use and control of Western lands and resources. Some groups, like the Sierra Club, focus on government policy; others, like the more radical Earth First! emphasize direct action.

CHRONOLOGY
OF KEY EVENTS

1951	Inexpensive, efficient window air conditioner unit introduced
1958	Dodgers and Giants professional baseball teams move from New York to California
1960	*The Conscience of a Conservative*, in which politician Barry Goldwater outlines his beliefs, is published; sells 3.5 million copies in four years; California surpasses New York as the nation's most populous state
1964	Barry Goldwater wins the Republican nomination for president; Democrat Lyndon Johnson defeats Goldwater in landslide victory
1966	Braves professional baseball team moves from Milwaukee to Atlanta
1968	Richard Nixon is elected nation's thirty-seventh president

1972	Nixon is elected to second term, winning every southern and western state
1978	California voters approve Proposition 13, which calls for a 57 percent reduction in state property taxes
1980	Ronald Reagan is elected fortieth president
1984	Reagan is reelected to second term
1988	George Bush, Reagan's vice president, is elected forty-first president
1992	Democrat Bill Clinton defeats Bush to become nation's forty-second president
1994	Democrats suffer overwhelming defeats in congressional and gubernatorial elections

state property taxes. The bill drained the state's treasury surplus and resulted in less services. In other states the rebellion was less extreme, but most Western state politicians had to move toward rigid fiscal conservatism to win election or to stay in office. In several cases, politicians—most notably Phil Gramm of Texas—even left the Democratic party and became Republicans.

CONCLUSION

The November 21, 1994, cover of *Time* magazine said it all without a word. A stampeding elephant, eyes fixed straight ahead in a pitiless stare, has trampled and killed a tiny donkey. The donkey is utterly flattened, its eyes and tongue forced out of its head. The off-year elections, the cartoon indicated, had resulted in a complete and total Republican victory. Before the election the Democratic party had

controlled the Senate 56 to 44, the House of Representative 256 to 178, and state governors' mansions 29 to 20. After the election, the Republican party controlled the Senate 53 to 47, the House 227 to 199, and governorships 30 to 17. It was a landslide rejection of President Bill Clinton's first two years in office and, according to many commentators, a generation of Democratic policy making. Putting the election into perspective, a *Newsweek* magazine writer noted, "Seventy-seven years ago, almost to the day, Bolsheviks in Petrograd raced into the Winter Palace in the name of communism. Last week in one of the most profound electoral routs in American history, Republicans won the right to occupy the Capitol and to mount what their more hyperbolic commanders think of as a counterrevolution: a full-scale attack on the notion that a central government should play a central role in the life of a nation."

The importance of the election, however, transcended party politics. It was not so much which party had won the election but which Republicans controlled the agenda that was crucial. The new Speaker of the House, and Republican lightning rod, was Newt Gingrich, a southern congressman who spoke the language of Barry Goldwater. Gingrich's "Contract With America" called for major budget cuts, tax cuts, and federal bureaucratic cuts. He promised to make the federal government cheaper and smaller, to return power to the states, and to reform government benefit programs. Sounding every bit a revolutionary, Gingrich said, "I will cooperate, but I won't compromise. . . . I may fail, we may fail. But this is real. I am who I seem to be."

Gingrich and his message underscored an important shift in American history. No longer were leaders from the biggest Eastern and Midwestern states. The new leaders in Washington came from the South and the West. Gingrich represented Georgia, Senate Majority Leader Robert Dole, Kansas; Phil Gramm, Texas. Their battle call was freedom. Criticizing President Clinton's comment that the election represented the wish by Americans for a government that "empowers" them, Gramm remarked, "He just doesn't get it. Government doesn't empower you. Freedom empowers you." It was a western credo he proclaimed, a doctrine that runs through a hundred John Wayne films. The question unanswered was: Is it a credo for the twenty-first century?

SUGGESTIONS FOR FURTHER READING

Carl Abbott, *New Urban America: Growth and Politics in the Sunbelt Cities of the South* (1981). A perceptive and knowledgeable analysis of regional demographics and politics.

Raymond Arsenault, *The End of the Long Hot Summer: The Air Conditioner and Southern Culture* (1984). Explores the social impact of air-conditioning in the South—a neglected but important aspect of the region's history.

William Cronon, George Miles, and Jay Gitlin, eds., *Under An Open Sky: Rethinking America's Western Past* (1992). Seeks to dislodge western history from its old moorings and point it in new directions.

Patricia Nelson Limerick, Clyde Millner II, and Charles Rankin, eds., *Trails: Toward a New Western History* (1991). Essays on the cutting edge of new historical interpretations of the West.

Richard Slotkin, *Gunfighter Nation: The Myth of the Frontier in Twentieth-Century America* (1992). Surveys the intersection between popular culture and the mythic American West.

Randy Roberts and James S. Olson, *John Wayne: American* (1995). Explores the life of an important Western icon, and examines his influence on national identity.

Richard White, *"It's Your Misfortune and None of My Own": A New History of the American West* (1991). A fresh perspective on the history of a region.

Donald Worster, *Rivers of Empire: Water, Aridity, and the Growth of the American West* (1985). How the West's most precious resource shaped regional identity.

Overviews and Surveys

Richard M. Bernard and Bradley R. Rice, eds., *Sunbelt Cities: Politics and Growth Since World War II* (1983); David R. Goldfield, *Cotton Fields and Skyscrapers, Southern City and Region, 1607–1980*, rev. ed. (1989); Roger Gottlieb and Peter Wiley, *Empires in the Sun: The Rise of the New American West* (1982); Bradford Luckingham, *The Urban Southwest* (1982); Michael P. Malone and Richard W. Etulain, *The American West: A Twentieth-Century History* (1989); Raymond A. Mohl, ed., *Searching for the Sunbelt: Historical Perspectives on a Region* (1990); Gerald Nash, *The American West in the Twentieth Century* (1973), *The American West Transformed: The Impact of the Second World War* (1985), and with Richard W. Etulain, eds., *The Twentieth-Century West: Historical Interpretations* (1989); David C. Perry and Alfred J. Watkins, eds., *The Rise of the Sunbelt Cities* (1977); Kirkpatrick Sale, *Power Shift: The Rise of the Southern Rim and Its Challenge to the Eastern Establishment* (1975); Bruce J. Schulman, *From Cotton Belt to Sunbelt: Federal Policy, Economic Development and the Transformation of the South, 1938–1980* (1991); Bernard L. Weinstein and Robert E. Firestine, *Regional Growth and Decline in the United States: The Rise of the Sunbelt and the Decline of the Northeast* (1978).

The Emergence of the Southern Rim

Shirley Abbott, *Womenfolks: Growing Up Down South* (1983); Jack Bass and Walter Devries, *The*

Transformation of Southern Politics (1976); Earl Black and Merle Black, *The Vital South: How Presidents Are Elected* (1992); James Cobb, *Industrialization and Southern Society, 1877–1984* (1984), and *Selling of the South* (1982); Albert E. Cowdrey, *This Land, This South: An Environmental Hobby* (1983); Carl Degler, *Place Over Time: The Continuity of Southern Distinctiveness* (1977); John Egerton, *The Americanization of Dixie: The Southernization of America* (1974); Flora Gill, *Economics and Black Exodus: An Analysis of Negro Emigration from the Southern United States, 1910–1970* (1979); Barbara Griffith, *The Crisis of American Labor: Operation Dixie and the Defeat of the CIO* (1988); Elizabeth Jacoway and David R. Colburn, eds., *Southern Businessmen and Desegregation* (1982); F. Ray Marshall, *Labor in the South* (1967); Lucy Randolph Mason, *To Win These Rights: A Personal Story of the CIO in the South* (1952); Merl E. Reed, Leslie S. Hough, and Gary M. Fink, eds., *Southern Workers and Their Unions, 1880–1975* (1981); Charles P. Roland, *The Improbable Era: The South Since World War II* (1975); Nannie May Tilley, *The R. J. Reynolds Tobacco Company* (1985).

The Myth and Reality of the West

Susan Armitrage and Elizabeth Jameson, eds., *The Women's West* (1987); Leonard J. Arrington and Anthony Cluff, *Federally Financed Industrial Plants Constructed in Utah During World War II* (1969); Robert G. Athearn, *The Mythic West in Twentieth-Century America* (1986); Howard Ball, *Justice Downwind: America's Atomic Testing Program in the 1950's* (1986); Scott L. Bottles, *Los Angeles and the Automobile: The Making of a Modern City* (1987); Patricia Janis Broder, *The American West: The Modern Vision* (1984); Jeni Calder, *There Must Be a Lone Ranger: The American West in Film and in Reality* (1975); John G. Cawelti, *The Six-Gun Mystique,* 2d ed. (1984); Richard O. Davies, *The Age of Asphalt: The Automobile, the Freeway, and the Condition of Metropolitan America* (1975); John M. Findlay, *Magic Lands: Western Cityscapes and American Culture After 1940* (1992); William H. Goetzmann and William N. Goetzmann, *The West of the Imagination* (1986); Donald E. Green, *Land of the Underground Rain: Irrigation on the Texas High Plains, 1910–1970* (1973); Lynton R. Hayes, *Energy, Economic Growth, and Regionalism in the West* (1980); Norris Hundley, Jr., *The Great Thirst: California and Water, 1770's–1990's* (1992); William Kahrl, *Water and Power: The Conflict over Los Angeles' Water Supply* (1982); Patricia Nelson Limerick, *The Legacy of Conquest: The Unbroken Past of the American West* (1987); Gerald D. Nash, *World War II and the West: Reshaping the Economy* (1990); Rita Parks, *The Western Hero in Film and Television: Mass Media Mythology* (1982); Donald J. Pisani, *From the Family Farm to Agribusiness: The Irrigation Crusade in California and the West* (1984); Earl Pomeroy, *The Pacific Slope* (1965); Marc Reisner, *Cadillac Desert: The American West and Its Disappearing Water* (1986); Elmo Richardson, *Dams, Parks, and Politics: Resource Development and Preservation in the Truman-Eisenhower Era* (1973); William W. Savage, Jr., *The Cowboy Hero: His Image in American History and Culture,* (1979); Richard Slotkin, *The Fatal Environment: The Myth of the Frontier in the Age of Industrialization* (1985); Duane Smith, *Mining America: The Industry and the Environment* (1987); Henry Nash Smith, *Virgin Land: The American West as Symbol and Myth* (1950); Jane Tompkins, *West of Everything: The Inner Life of Westerns* (1991); Jon Tuska, *The Filming of the West* (1976); Will Wright, *Six-guns and Society: A Structural Study of the Western* (1975); Daniel Yergin, *The Prize* (1991).

Politics Western Style

Daniel J. Elazar, *Cities of the Prairie: The Metropolitan Frontier and American Politics* (1970); Phillip O. Foss, *Politics and Grass: The Administration of Grazing on the Public Domain* (1960); Peter F. Galderisi, et al., eds, *The Politics of Realignment: Party Change in the Mountain West* (1987); William L. Graf, *Wilderness Preservation and the Sagebrush Rebellions* (1990); Samuel P. Hays, *Beauty, Health and Permanence: Environmental Politics in the United States, 1955–1985* (1987); Norris Hundley, *Water and the West: The Colorado River Compact and the Politics of Water in the American West* (1975); Frank H. Jonas, ed., *Western Politics* (1969); Robert L. Kelley, *Battling the Inland Sea: American Political Culture, Public Policy, and the Sacramento Valley, 1850–1986* (1989); Richard D. Lamm and Michael McCarthy, *The Angry West: A Vulnerable Land and Its Future* (1982); Gary D. Libecap, *Locking Up the Range: Federal Land Controls and Grazing* (1981); Roger W. Lotchin, *Fortress California, 1910–1961: From Warfare to Welfare* (1992); Carl J. Mayer and George A. Riley, *Public Domain, Private Domain: A History of Public Mineral Policy in America* (1985); Neil Morgan, *Westward Tilt: The American West Today* (1961); David F. Prindle, *Petroleum Politics and the Texas Railroad Commission* (1981); Roger Rapaport, *California Dreaming: The Political Odyssey of Pat and Jerry Brown* (1982); Clive S. Thomas, ed., *Politics and Public Policy in the Contem-*

porary American West (1991); A. Constandina Titus, Bombs in the Backyard: Atomic Testing and American Politics (1986).

Biographies

Robert A. Caro, The Years of Lyndon Johnson: The Path to Power (1982), and Means of Ascent (1990); Jimmy Carter, Keeping Faith (1982); Paul Conkin, Big Daddy from the Pedernales: Lyndon Baines Johnson (1986); Mark S. Foster, Henry J. Kaiser: Builder in the Modern American West (1989); Robert Alan Goldberg, Barry Goldwater (1995); Erwin Hargrove, Jimmy Carter as President (1989); John Keats, Howard Hughes (1966); Albert P. Heiner, Henry J. Kaiser, American Empire Builder: An Insider's View (1989); Gerald D. Nash, A. P. Giannini and the Bank of America (1992); Randy Shilts, The Mayor of Castro Street: The Life and Times of Harvey Milk (1982).

CHAPTER **29**
VIETNAM AND THE CRISIS OF AUTHORITY

THE ILLUSION OF GREATNESS
Television's President
The "Macho" Presidency
Something Short of Camelot
Cuba Libre Revisited

VIETNAM: AMERICA'S LONGEST WAR
A Small Corner of a Bigger Picture
Kennedy's Testing Ground
Texas Tough in the Gulf of Tonkin
Lyndon's War
To Tet and Beyond
The Politics of a Divided Nation

THE TORTUOUS PATH TOWARD PEACE
Outsiders on the Inside
Vietnamization: The Idea and the
  Process
A "Decent Interval"
The Legacy of the War

Ho Chi Minh was born roughly 9000 miles from America, but he might as well have come from a different planet. Ho was a tiny, frail, thin splinter of a man. He was gentle, and in public always deferential. Even after he had come to sole power in North Vietnam, he steadfastly avoided all the trappings of authority. Instead of uniforms or the white sharkskin suit of the mandarin, Ho favored the simple shorts and sandals worn by the Vietnamese peasants. He was sure of who he was—certain of his place in Vietnamese history—and he had no desire to impress others with his position. To his followers, he was "Uncle Ho," the kind, bachelor relative who treated all Vietnamese citizens like the children he never had. But in the pursuit of Vietnamese independence and the realization of a Communist nation, Ho could be cold-blooded and ruthless.

Ho was born in 1890 in a village in a central province of the French colony of Vietnam and was originally named Nguyen Sinh Cung. In 1912 he left Vietnam and began a generation-long world odyssey. Signing on as a sailor aboard a French freighter, he moved from one port to the next. For a time he stayed in the United States, visiting Boston, New York City, and San Francisco. He was amazed not only by America's skyscrapers but also by the fact that immigrants in the United States enjoyed the same legal rights as American citizens. He was also struck by the impatience of the American people, their expectations of immediate results. (Later, during the Vietnam War, Ho would say to his military leaders, "Don't worry, Americans are an impatient people. When things begin to go wrong, they'll leave.")

After three years of almost constant travel, Ho settled in London, where he worked at the elegant Carlton Hotel. His living quarters were squalid, and he quickly learned that poverty existed even in the wealthiest, most powerful countries. Then it was on to Paris, where he came in contact with the French left. As he studied there, his nationalist ambitions became tinged with revolutionary teachings. He was still in Paris when World War I ended and the world leaders came to Versailles for the Peace Conference. Inspired by Woodrow Wilson's call for national self-determination, Ho wrote that "all subject peoples are filled with hope by the prospect that an era of right and justice is opening to them." Ho wanted to meet Wilson; he wanted to plead for independence for his country. Wilson ignored his request; Vietnam remained France's colony. Ho moved on—farther east and further left.

Disillusioned with France and socialism, Ho traveled to Moscow, where Lenin had declared war against imperialism; there Ho embraced communism. In Communist ideology he saw a road to his ultimate goal, the liberation of Vietnam. By the early 1920s he was actively organizing Vietnamese exiles into a revolutionary force. He continued to travel—to Western Europe, back to Russia, to China, back to Russia, to Thailand, back to the West. He lived a life of secrecy, moving from place to place, changing his name, renouncing anything even remotely resembling a personal life. No wife, no children, few friends—only a cause. As he advised one Vietnamese returning to the homeland, "The colonialists will be on your trail. Keep away from our friends' homes and don't hesitate to pose as a degenerate if it will help put the police off the scent."

In 1941 Ho returned to Vietnam. The time was right, he believed, to free Vietnam from colonial domination. During the early part of World War II, the Japanese had won control of the country from the French; now Ho and his followers would force out the Japanese. Ho allied himself with the United States. Working alongside American Office of Strategic Services (OSS) agents, he proved his mettle. He impressed the agents with his bravery, intelligence, and unflagging devotion to his cause.

Ho Chi Minh was influenced as a young man by French socialism and Soviet communism in his goal to liberate Vietnam from the French.

On September 2, 1945, borrowing passages from the American Declaration of Independence, Ho declared Vietnamese independence.

The French, who returned to Vietnam after the war, had different plans for Vietnam, so Ho's struggle continued. In candid moments he admitted that he didn't expect to live to see Vietnam fully independent. Yet he knew that the struggle of others would eventually secure independence. Ho had patience. It was a quality that the West found difficult to understand.

That was only one of the qualities of Ho and of the Vietnamese that the West did not understand. A deep intellectual chasm divided Vietnam and the West. The latter viewed history as a straight line in which progress was the governing principle. Emphasizing technological advancements and material improvements, Westerners glorified change and prized individualism.

The Vietnamese were products of different beliefs. Notions of competition, individualism, and technological change were anathema to tradition-bound Vietnamese. For a thousand years they had survived using the same rice-cultivating methods. Often, however, the margin between survival and death was a razor's edge. Unlike the United States, Vietnam did not have fertile frontiers to settle. To make do with the land they had, the Vietnamese organized life around villages and practiced a cooperative existence. Rich people were considered selfish because their wealth *had* to be gained at the direct expense of others. As one authority explained, "the idea remains with the Vietnamese that great wealth is antisocial, not a sign of success but a sign of selfishness."

Like wealth, individualism threatened the corporate nature of village life, which was based on duties and social harmony, not individual rights and individual justice. Even their language excluded the idea of individualism. Vietnamese has no personal pronoun equivalent to the Western *I, je, ich.* A person speaks of oneself in relationship to the person being addressed—for example, as "your teacher," "your brother," "your wife."

Nor did Vietnamese believe in intellectual freedom, which fostered debate and dis-cord, rather than community stability. Americans considered Soviet communism evil because it discouraged the exchange of free ideas; Ho Chi Minh was drawn to the doctrine because it provided a set of answers not subject to questioning; he was the product of that closed world. America was the prophet of an open world. Motivated by the Cold War, during the period between 1954 and 1973, U.S. officials became convinced that they had to "save" Vietnam from Ho Chi Minh and his Communist brand of nationalism. Given Vietnamese leadership, traditions, and desire for independence, the American intervention in Vietnam was almost certain to fail.

THE ILLUSION OF GREATNESS

In the 1960 presidential race Kennedy challenged his Republican opponent, Richard M. Nixon, to a series of television debates. At the time, Kennedy faced an uphill battle. Young, handsome, and wealthy, Kennedy was considered by many too young, too handsome, and too wealthy to make an effective president. His undistinguished political record stood in stark contrast to Nixon's work in Congress and his eight years as Eisenhower's vice president. In addition, Kennedy was Catholic, and Americans had never elected a Catholic president. Behind in the polls, Kennedy needed a dramatic boost. Thus the challenge. Against the advice of his campaign manager, Nixon accepted.

Television's President

John Fitzgerald Kennedy was made for television. His tall, thin body gave him the strong vertical line that cameras love, and his weather-beaten good looks appealed to women without intimidating men. He had a full head of hair, and even in the winter he maintained a tan. Complementing his appearance was his attitude. He was always "cool" in public. This too was tailor-made for the "cool medium," television. Wit, irony, and understatement, all delivered with a studied nonchalance, translate well on television. Table-thumping, impassioned speech, and even earnest sincerity often just do not work on television.

The first debate was held in Chicago on September 26, 1960, only a little more than a month before the election. Nixon arrived looking ill and weak—during the previous six weeks he had banged his kneecap, which became infected, spent several weeks in the hospital, and then caught a bad chest cold that left him hoarse and weak. By the day of the debate he looked like a nervous corpse—pale, 20 pounds underweight, and haggard. Makeup experts offered to hide his heavy beard and soften his jowls, but Nixon accepted only a thin coat of Max Factor's "Lazy Shave," a pancake cosmetic.

Kennedy looked better, very much better. He didn't need makeup to appear healthy, nor did he need special lighting to hide a weak profile. He did, however, change suits. He believed that a dark blue rather than a gray suit would look better under the bright lights. Kennedy was right, of course, as anyone who watches a nightly news program realizes.

When the debate started, Kennedy spoke first. Although he was nervous, he intentionally slowed down his delivery. His face was controlled and cool. He smiled with his eyes and perhaps the corners of his mouth, and his laugh was a mere suggestion of a laugh. His body language was perfect. As for what he said, Kennedy disregarded the prearranged ground rules and shifted what was supposed to be a debate on domestic issues to one on foreign policy.

Nixon fought back. He perspired, scored debating points, produced memorized facts, and struggled to win; but his efforts were "hot"—bad television. Instead of hearing a knowledgeable candidate, viewers saw a nervous, uncertain man, one whose clothes did not fit and whose face looked pasty and white. In contrast, what Kennedy said sounded statesmanlike, and he *looked* right. Kennedy was the clear winner. Only later did Nixon realize that the telecast had been a production, not a debate.

When the polls on the results came out, Kennedy inched ahead of Nixon in a Gallup poll for the first time during the campaign. Republicans realized the impact of the debate—Republican Senator Barry Goldwater called it "a disaster." Most of the people who were undecided before watching the debate ended up voting for Kennedy. That proved to be the margin of victory: only one-tenth of one percent separated the two candidates. Perhaps the most important result of the election, however, was not Kennedy's victory but the demonstration of the power of television. The medium came into its own in 1960.

The "Macho" Presidency

In his inaugural address Kennedy issued threats and challenges as well as making promises. Proud to be the first American president born in the twentieth century, determined to be the torch-bearer for "a new generation," Kennedy wanted the world to know where he stood: "Let every nation know, whether it wishes us well or ill, that we shall pay any price, bear any burden, meet any hardship, support any friend, oppose any foe to assure the survival and the success of liberty." And who would pay, bear, meet, support, and oppose? On this point too Kennedy was clear: "And so, my fellow Americans: ask not what your country can do for you—ask what you can do for your country."

During the Kennedy-Nixon debates, John F. Kennedy demonstrated that for television politics, style was as important as substance.

After listening to the blandness and mangled syntax of Eisenhower's addresses, here was a speaker of rare ability, here were speeches beautifully phrased. Kennedy probably asked for more sacrifice and promised more rewards than any other president since Woodrow Wilson. Only years after his death did people begin to ask if he was serious or if he was more concerned with how he said something rather than with what he said. Indeed, he and his speech writers were attracted to verbal sleight-of-hand tricks: "If a free society cannot help the many who are poor, it cannot save the few who are rich. . . . Let us never negotiate out of fear, let us never fear to negotiate." Like the television debates, such statements emphasized style over substance.

Who was this speaker? Competition and an aggressively masculine view of the world ran through the life of John F. Kennedy. He was the son of a multimillionaire who demanded excellence of all his sons and who believed that as Boston Irish Catholics they had to try harder and be tougher than their Protestant neighbors. This was particularly difficult for John Kennedy, who suffered throughout his life from a series of illnesses and physical problems, including Addison's disease and chronic back trouble. His brother Bobby recalled, "At least one-half of the days that he spent on this earth were days of intense physical pain."

But he never used—and his father never accepted—pain as an excuse for inactivity. At Harvard University he played football, boxed, swam, and ran, and during vacations at the family home in Hyannisport he roughhoused with his brothers and sisters. Throughout his life, Kennedy maintained this physical view of life. To impress the Kennedys, one associate remembered, you had to "show raw guts, fall on your face now and then. Smash into the house once in a while going after a pass. Laugh off twisted ankles or a big hole torn in your best suit."

Kennedy's macho ethos extended to his attitude toward women. Like his father, he regarded sexual conquests as a sign of manhood. During his Washington years as a U.S. senator, he moved from one affair to the next.

He did not even bother to learn the names of his one-night-stands, referring to them by such generic names as "Kiddo" or "Sweetie." Nor did Kennedy's affairs end after he was married and elected president. When he wanted companionship and conversation he turned to his male friends.

Kennedy brought this masculine attitude to his presidency. He surrounded himself with advisers who shared his energetic approach to work and play. He seemed charged with a sense of urgency and was fond of the Churchill quote, "Come then—let us to the task, to the battle and toil—each to our part, each to our station. Let us go forward together in all parts of the [land]. There is not a week, nor a day, nor an hour to be lost."

In his own speeches Kennedy stressed the theme that America was entering a period of crisis: "In the long history of the world, only a few generations have been granted the role of defending freedom in its maximum danger. I do not shrink from this responsibility—I welcome it." Without crisis, Kennedy believed, no person could achieve greatness, and he desired greatness. As was expressed in his Pulitzer-Prize-winning *Profiles in Courage,* "Great crises produce great men, and great deeds of courage."

Something Short of Camelot

From the very first, journalists associated the Kennedy administration with Camelot. According to the popular legend, King Arthur and his Knights of the Round Table established in the realm of Camelot a period of unparalleled peace and prosperity. Although Kennedy himself enjoyed the Camelot comparisons, the record of his administration and personal behavior fell short of the ideal.

Several factors worked to limit the success of Kennedy's domestic programs. To begin with, Kennedy lacked both political support in Congress and a firm commitment to push for liberal reforms. Ideologically, he was a centrist Democrat. In addition, although his party held a solid majority in the House, 101 of 261 Democratic representatives came from

MY LAI AND THE QUESTION OF WAR ETHICS

THAT terrible day began early on the morning of March 16, 1968, with the *whop-whop-whop-whop* sound of helicopters carrying the men of Charlie Company to their designated battle stations for the Pinkville operation. Their goal, along with the rest of Task Force Barker, was to utterly destroy the 48th Local Force Battalion of the National Liberation Front, the elusive and deadly Vietcong unit operating in Quang Ngai Province. Slightly more than 100 men comprised Charlie Company of the United States Army's 1st Battalion, 20th Infantry. Most were young, between 18 and 22 years old, and most were nervous. Each hoped that he would live though the day, but nobody had any guarantees and they all expected that some members of their company would not see the sun set.

There were sound reasons for the gloomier expectations. Although they had been in Vietnam for less than three months and had yet to have a major confrontation with a Vietcong unit, the company had been bloodied on several occasions. Trudging through Quang Ngai, a beautiful stretch of land between the Annamese mountains and the white sandy beaches of the South China Sea—a quiltwork province of rice paddies dotted with bamboo and banana trees—soldiers in Charlie Company had lost legs, arms, and lives to Vietcong boobytraps. February 25,

1968, had been a particularly bad day. Part of the unit had wandered into the middle of a minefield. Although the officer in charge screamed "Freeze!", a few men panicked, moved, and detonated more mines. "Anyone who moved to try to help someone just got blown up themselves," recalled one GI. One soldier was split open from his crotch to his chest cavity "as if someone had taken a cleaver" to him. Three GIs were killed, another 12 badly injured, and everyone was shaken. One GI remembered thinking, "This is war, this is what it is all about, this is what happens to you."

The men of Charlie Company regarded the Pinkville operation as a chance for revenge—revenge for their friends who had died or been wounded, revenge for their uncomfortable patrols though hostile country, revenge for the fear they felt and a land they hated and a people they did not understand. One sergeant recalled that the central message at the briefing on the eve of the operation was: "This was a time for us to get even. A time for us to settle the score. . . . The order we were given was to kill and de-

stroy everything that was in the village. It was to kill the pigs, drop them in the wells; pollute the water supply; kill, cut down the banana trees; burn the village; burn the hootches as we went through it. It was clearly explained that there were to be no prisoners. The order that was given was to kill everything in the village. Someone asked if that meant women and children. And the order was: everyone in the village. Because those people that were in the village—the women, the kids, the old men—were VC. . . . It was quite clear that no one was to be spared in that village."

Thus when the men of Charlie Company climbed out of their helicopter transports near the tiny village designated My Lai 4, they expected to engage the enemy, and they expected to kill. The enemy, as so often had been the case, was gone. If they had been in Quang Ngai—and even that was doubtful—they had left. When the men moved into My Lai 4 and several subhamlets in the same general area, they encountered no enemy fire. The only people they met were villagers, mostly women, children, and old men. Unquestionably some were Vietcong supporters; Quang Ngai had long been regarded as VC country. But according to the rules of military engagement, the villagers were noncombatants, and U.S. soldiers were required to treat them accordingly.

On this day the rules of "civilized" warfare were not observed. From the very beginning, soldiers shot anything that moved, including unarmed villagers. Once the shooting began there was a chain reaction, as more and more soldiers discharged their weapons. They shot pigs, chickens, cows, ducks, and water buffalo in the fields. They shot old men sitting outside their homes, women holding babies, children searching for places to hide. A few soldiers raped women before they killed them. One group of children were shot as they reached their hands out toward a GI in the hope of receiving food or candy. At several points, scores of villagers were gathered into groups and executed. Altogether, the soldiers killed about 400 villagers.

Not every member of Charlie Company participated in the slaughter. Some only fired when they were given direct orders to fire, others simply refused to fire at all. Each man was presented with a difficult moral choice—follow what he believed were his orders or do what his conscience told him was right. At one point helicopter pilot Hugh Thompson, Jr., shocked by what he saw from his Plexiglass "bubble ship," landed his chopper to protect a group of defenseless villagers. He told the American sol-diers—his own countrymen—that if they shot the villagers he would turn his machine gun on them. He simply could not abide what he saw happening. And when he returned to base he reported what he had seen.

What had happened in those four hours the morning of May 16, 1968, was a spontaneous tragedy. Soldiers following orders, men out of control, the logical end result of a policy of free-fire zones and search and destroy missions and systematic body counts—all these explanations would later be employed to explain the massacre. There is no doubt that the GIs were given orders to shoot. Lieutenant William Calley, the ranking officer in My Lai, both ordered and participated in the worst executions, and he certainly believed that he was following the orders of his commander, Captain Ernest Medina. At one point, Calley told Medina that civilians were slowing the progress of Charlie Company; Medina "told Calley simply to get rid of them." In the mass confusion of the morning—in what one military strategist has called "the fog of war"—things happened that probably no one could have predicted.

But what happened after that morning was coldly calculated. A massacre, not a battle, had taken place—the signs of indiscriminate killing of civilians were apparent. Battles mean that your own men get killed and wounded; the only casualty in Charlie Company was one accidental, self-inflicted wound. Battles successfully waged mean the capture of enemy soldiers and weapons; the official account of the "battle" of My Lai listed 128 enemies killed but only 3 weapons recovered. Just looking at the numbers, any experienced officer could have guessed what had taken place. Thompson had reported the truth. But there was no serious investigation, only an unspoken coverup that reached up the chain of command from Captain Medina to Lieutenant Colonel Frank Barker to Colonel Oran Henderson to Major General Samuel Koster. As far as they were concerned, no infractions of the military code of engagement had occurred.

Later the world learned differently. On April 2, 1969, Ronald Ridenhour, a former soldier who had heard of the massacre while serving with several former members of Charlie Company, wrote letters to 31 leading United States senators and government officials, including President Richard Nixon and Secretary of Defense Melvin Laird, reporting what he had learned of the massacre. The letters led to several in-depth investigations, which ultimately resulted in charges against two generals, four full colonels, four lieutenant colonels, four majors, six captains, and eight lieutenants. Lieutenant General William Peers, head of the official military investigation, listed 224 serious violations of the military code. In the end, however, only one man, William Calley, was convicted of any wrongdoing, and he was pardoned three years after his conviction.

southern and border states, and they normally voted with conservative Republicans. Added to this problem was Kennedy's distaste for legislative infighting and his poor working relations with many senators. He limited his domestic agenda to such traditional Democratic proposals as a higher minimum wage, increased Social Security benefits, and modest housing and educational programs. In his inaugural address he did not even mention poverty or race. In the final analysis, Kennedy was so concerned with the "crises abroad" that he did not want to risk any of his political capital on unpopular domestic reforms. Nor, as one biographer of Kennedy has commented, was the electorate "crying out for social justice legislation in the early 1960s."

There were small successes. Congress raised the minimum wage, expanded Social Security, and appropriated a few billion dollars for public housing and aid to economically depressed areas. But such legislation hardly amounted to the "new frontier" Kennedy promised. These gains were offset by the setbacks, which Kennedy accepted perhaps too stoically. Congress defeated the president's plan for federal aid to education, a health insurance plan for the aged, and programs to help migrant workers, unemployed youths, and urban commuters.

African Americans were especially disappointed with Kennedy's performance. They had, after all, supplied Kennedy's margin of victory in the 1960 election. But once elected JFK was slow in using his office to further the cause of civil rights.

For African Americans, the early 1960s were difficult, violent years that tested their resolve. White segregationists confronted nonviolent desegregation efforts with unprovoked ferocity. Violence erupted in city after city. NAACP organizer Medgar Evers was shot down outside his home in Jackson, Mississippi. Four young African-American girls were killed when a Birmingham church was bombed. Police authorities sprayed civil rights protesters, including children, with high-pressure fire hoses and unleashed attack dogs on them. (See Chapter 30 for a fuller treatment of the fight for civil rights.)

Through his first two years in office, Kennedy remained largely silent. To win southern congressional support he even backed the nomination of a Mississippi jurist—who had once referred to African Americans as "chimpanzees"—for a seat on the federal bench. Although Attorney General Robert Kennedy aided protesters when federal laws were violated, JFK and the FBI staked out a conservative position. As one historian noted, "Civil rights workers were assaulted and shot at—systematically, often openly, frequently by law enforcement officials themselves. And through it all, in virtually every case, federal authorities did nothing."

In 1963 Kennedy changed his position. In part this about-face was the result of Robert Kennedy's prodding; in part it was the result of television, which daily showed shocking examples of brutality in the South and accelerated the demand for change. In late May 1963, Kennedy eloquently announced his new position. It should be possible, he said, "for American students of any color to attend any public institution without having to be backed up by troops. . . . But this is not the case. . . . We preach freedom around the world . . . but are we to say to the world . . . that we have no second-class citizens except Negroes, that we have no class or caste system, no ghettos, no master race except with respect to Negroes?"

Perhaps Kennedy was convinced that the time had come for "the nation to fulfill its promise." Perhaps, as his supporters claim, in 1963 Kennedy was beginning to fulfill his own promise. His death in late 1963 left questions unanswered, potential unrealized. Judged by his accomplishments, however, Kennedy's Camelot, like King Arthur's, existed largely in the realm of myth. Although he could inspire people to follow, too often on domestic issues he chose not to lead.

Cuba Libre Revisited

Foreign affairs consumed Kennedy's interest. Unlike domestic politics, international conflicts were more clear-cut, and the divisions between "us" and "them" more certain. Foreign affairs also allowed Kennedy to express his masculine view of the world. He could employ the Kennedy approach to difficult decisions, which he once described as: calculate the odds, make your choice, and "grab [your] balls and go."

In his approach to the world, Kennedy generally continued the essentially Cold War policies of Truman and Eisenhower. He accepted the strategy of containment and the notion that the Soviet Union would take advantage of any sign of weakness by the United States. He was also suspicious of conventional diplomatic channels, preferring to listen to his young advisers rather than seasoned State Department officials.

Kennedy's handling of Cuban relations revealed his bellicose tendencies. Like Eisenhower, Kennedy was dismayed by the success of Fidel Castro. Just as Americans during the 1890s had cried *Cuba Libre,*" on taking office Kennedy began to search for a way to "free" Cuba, this time from Castro's communism rather than Spain's colonialism. His desire to strike a blow against communism led him to embrace a CIA plan to overthrow Castro. If the CIA had successfully planned coups in Guatemala, Iran, and Laos, Kennedy reasoned, then perhaps it could do the job in Cuba.

The CIA plan, which was hatched during the Eisenhower administration, entailed both the assassination of Castro and the training and transporting of a force of Cuban exiles to Cuba, where they would launch a counterrevolution. It was a plan that even the joint chiefs of staff believed would probably fail. Even worse, the plan was one of the worst-kept secrets in the Western Hemisphere. As one historian noted, "Washington knew because the CIA had to drum up broad support in the government for it. Miami knew because the CIA had done everything but take out classified ads to get volunteers. Guatemala knew because the exile brigade was training there, as a local newspaper pointed out. And Castro knew because everyone else did—except the American people." Pierre Salinger, Kennedy's press secretary, later called the plan "the least covert military operation in history," and Kennedy bitterly complained before the invasion, "I can't believe what I'm reading! Castro doesn't need agents over here. All he has to do is read our papers. It's all laid out for him."

The invasion on April 17, 1961, at the Bay of Pigs was an unmitigated disaster. Several attempts to assassinate Castro failed, and the Cuban people did not rise up to join the invaders, who were trapped on the beaches. Nor would Kennedy authorize U.S. air support for the exile forces. As a result, all but 300 of the 1500 invaders were killed or captured. If anything, the Bay of Pigs fiasco strengthened Castro's position in Cuba.

The Bay of Pigs invasion, however, did not end Kennedy's problems with Cuba. In the fall of 1962 a more serious crisis arose when the Soviet Union began to install intermediate-range ballistic missiles (IRBMs) in Cuba. Instead of trying to work through proper diplomatic avenues—a process that would have taken time and might have hurt the Democrats in the upcoming election— Kennedy announced the alarming news to an anxious television audience. After showing the public the American cities that the missiles could destroy, Kennedy said he would not permit Soviet ships transporting the weapons to enter Cuban waters. "The people were assured," a scholar commented, "that he would run any risk, including thermonuclear war, on their behalf." Such assurances created a genuine mood of crisis in the country.

Behind the scenes, Kennedy and Soviet Premier Nikita Khrushchev searched for a way to defuse the crisis. During the entire affair Bobby Kennedy counseled level-headed restraint and Khrushchev eschewed any shoe-pounding antics. In the end, the world leaders achieved a solution. Khrushchev agreed to remove the missiles under United Nations inspection in return for an American pledge not to invade Cuba. The Kennedy administration interpreted the result as a victory. "We're eyeball to eyeball and I think the other fellow just blinked," Secretary of State Dean Rusk observed during the episode. And, indeed, the Soviet Union could hardly disagree. The missile crisis provided the ammunition to force Khrushchev out of power.

Shocked and saddened Americans everywhere shared the loss felt by President Kennedy's widow and two young children.

The two "superpowers" had stood at the brink, gazed into the abyss, and stepped back. And for what? "When all is said and done," observed one historian, "it seems that President Kennedy had risked ultimate disaster in service to a crisis that was more illusory than real, at least in military terms."

Again, the unsatisfactory "perhaps" reappeared. Perhaps Kennedy learned more from the Cuban missile crisis than he had from the Bay of Pigs invasion. Friends of Kennedy claimed that he reached maturity during the crisis and that it motivated him to move toward détente—an easing of tensions—with the Soviet Union. In several 1963 speeches he called for "not merely peace in our time but peace for all time" and a "world safe for diversity." And he did support a treaty banning all atmospheric testing of nuclear weapons. Perhaps Kennedy had come to a new maturity.

The tragedy is that nobody can ever know. On November 22, 1963, Lee Harvey Oswald assassinated President Kennedy in Dallas, Texas. (Later investigations questioned whether Oswald acted alone, although the most thorough study of the assassination concluded that he did.) The event moved the nation. Newsman Walter Cronkite cried on television, and millions of Americans cried in their homes. Once again, television gave the event a mythical quality—showing his grieving wife, his barely understanding children, his solemn funeral. Americans mourned together, eyes fixed on their television sets. And immediately commentators began to evaluate Kennedy's presidency in terms of not what had been but what might have been.

VIETNAM: AMERICA'S LONGEST WAR

How did it start? And when? Even while the war in Vietnam tore at the heart of America in the 1960s most Americans, including some foreign policy experts, were not exactly sure of the answers to such basic questions. Johnson said he was continuing Kennedy's policy, who had continued Eisenhower's, who had continued Truman's, who had acted as he believed Roosevelt would have acted. The answers stretch back into time.

A Small Corner of a Bigger Picture

Struggle, like a mighty river, runs through the history of the small country of Vietnam. Ironically, part of Vietnam's troubles were due to the richness of its own land. Its agricultural products (especially rice) and mineral deposits lured invaders from the North, East, and West. China, the giant to its north, came first. For almost 2000 years Vietnam battled against China for its independence. Next came the French. During the seventeenth, eighteenth, and nineteenth centuries, French traders and missionaries penetrated Vietnam, establishing their control over the country in the name of *la mission civilisatrice.* This "civilizing mission," however, robbed the Vietnamese of the wealth of their land and their independence. France's rules of governing Vietnam—described as "a lot of subjugation, very little autonomy, a dash of assimilation"—created discontent among the Vietnamese, some of whom welcomed the next invader, Japanese, who took over the country during World War II.

The Vietnamese declared their independence in 1945, but that same year the French returned, bent on the resubjugation of the country. The struggle continued, with the Communist Vietminh under Ho Chi Minh controlling the north of the country and the French in the south. Between 1945 and 1954 both sides suffered terrible losses in the bitter guerrilla struggle.

The United States faced a difficult decision over this struggle. During World War II, Franklin Roosevelt had favored Vietnamese independence and had aided Ho's fight against the Japanese. He recognized that the age of colonialism was doomed, and he wanted the United States identified with anticolonialism. At the same time, however, Roosevelt believed that a strong postwar Western Europe was essential to American security, and he did not want to alienate

Britain or France by pressing too hard for an end to empires.

On Roosevelt's death, Harry Truman inherited FDR's problems. Even more than his former boss, he advocated a strong Western Europe, even if that strength had to be based on the continuation of empires. It was a Cold War decision. The United States, Truman maintained, "had no interest" in "championing schemes of international trusteeship" that would weaken the "European states whose help we need to balance Soviet power in Europe."

Vietnam became a pawn in the game of Cold War politics. Truman wanted French support against the Soviet Union. France wanted Vietnam. Truman willingly agreed to aid France's ambitions in exchange for that country's support. The success of Mao Zedong's Communist revolution in China strengthened America's support of the French in Vietnam. Obsessed with the idea of an international Communist conspiracy, Truman and his advisers contended that Stalin, Mao, and Ho were united by the single ambition of world domination. They overlooked the historical rivalries that pulled Russia, China, and Vietnam apart. As Ho Chi Minh once told his people, "It is better to sniff French dung for a while than eat China's all our life."

By the late 1940s, the United States had assumed a large part of the cost of France's effort to regain its control over Vietnam, and the price escalated during the early 1950s. By 1952 the United States was shouldering roughly one-third of the cost of the war, and between 1950 and 1954 America contributed $2.6 billion to France's war effort. But it was not enough—France could not defeat Ho's Vietminh.

In 1954 the war reached a crisis stage. In an effort to lure the Vietminh into a major engagement, the leading French commander moved more than 13,000 soldiers to Dien Bien Phu, a remote outpost in a river valley in northwest Vietnam. The Vietminh surrounded the fort and moved artillery pieces to the hills above the French airstrip. From there they mounted a siege of the outpost. As the months passed, French manpower and prestige suffered punishing blows. Inside Dien

Vietnam and Southeast Asia

Bien Phu, latrines overflowed, food supplies ran out, water spoiled, and unburied bodies fouled the air. Finally, on May 7, 1954, the last French commander surrendered.

During the siege the French continually asked President Eisenhower for military support, but he refused to act without the consent of Congress and Britain. Neither favored American military intervention. Senator Lyndon Johnson of Texas expressed the majority view in Congress when he opposed "sending American G.I.s into the mud and muck of Indochina on a blood-letting spree to perpetuate colonialism and white man's exploitation in Asia." As a result, France gave up its attempt to recolonize Vietnam. At the peace talks in Geneva, the countries involved agreed to temporarily divide Vietnam at the 17th parallel into two countries and hold elections in the summer of 1956 to reunify Vietnam.

Eisenhower would not militarily aid France, but he quickly supported the independent government established in South Vietnam under the leadership of Ngo Dinh Diem. In America, where he spent several years in a Catholic seminary, Diem was known as an anti-Communist and a nationalist. In Vietnam, where he had not been for 20 years, he was hardly known at all. As a popular leader, he had no appeal. Imperious, often paranoid, overly reliant on his own family, Diem, a Catholic in an overwhelmingly Buddhist nation, suc-

The United States supported Ngo Dinh Diem because of his anti-Communist views, but he alienated the Vietnamese people, who rejected his rule.

cessfully alienated almost everyone who came into contact with him. Even United States intelligence sources rated his chances of establishing order in South Vietnam as "poor."

Diem, nevertheless, was America's man. Why? Because he was an anti-Communist and a nationalist, and, as John Foster Dulles said, "because we know of no one better." Lyndon Johnson put it more bluntly in 1961: "Diem's the only boy we got out there." Even Eisenhower supported Diem militarily and politically. Vietnam became a test case, an opportunity for the United States to battle communism in Asia with dollars instead of Americans. When the time came to hold the unification election, Diem, with American backing, refused. Instead, to show his popularity he held "free" elections in South Vietnam, where he received an improbable 98.2 percent of the popular vote. The dishonesty of the elections was underscored by the Saigon returns where Diem received 605,000 votes, although there were only 405,000 registered voters.

Diem's absolutist policies created problems. By the end of 1957, Vietminh guerrillas in South Vietnam—often called the Vietcong—were in open revolt. Two years later, North and South Vietnam resumed hostilities. The United States increased its aid, most of which went to improving the South Vietnamese military or into the pockets of corrupt officials. The United States spent little money on improving the quality of life of the peasants. Nor did the United States object strongly to Diem's dictatorial methods. Diem once said that the sovereign was "the mediator between the people and heaven," and he demanded absolute obedience.

By the end of Eisenhower's second term America had become fully committed to Diem and South Vietnam. To be sure, problems in Vietnam were not America's major concern. In fact, most Americans were unaware of their country's involvement there. More than anything, Vietnam was a small corner of a bigger picture. U.S. policy there was determined by larger Cold War concerns. America's presence in Vietnam, however, would soon be expanded.

Kennedy's Testing Ground

On taking office, John Kennedy reaffirmed his country's commitment to Diem and South Vietnam. He announced his intention to be even more aggressive than Truman or Eisenhower. In Vietnam Kennedy saw an opportunity to "prove" his nation's resolve and strength. Ultimately, however, South Vietnam as a country was less important to Kennedy than the challenge it presented.

Kennedy believed that the United States needed a fresh military approach. Eisenhower's "massive retaliation" was too limited. It was of no use in a guerrilla war like Vietnam. Kennedy labeled his approach "flexible response," and it entailed the development of conventional and counterinsurgency (antiguerrilla) forces as well as a nuclear response. Vietnam rapidly became the laboratory for counterinsurgency activities, a place for Special Forces (Green Berets) units to develop their own tactics. To achieve this end, Kennedy expanded the Special Forces from 2500 to 10,000 men.

To "win" in Vietnam, Kennedy realized that he would have to strengthen America's presence there. In November of 1961 he decided to deploy American troops to South Vietnam. By the end of 1961, 3205 American "advisers" were in Vietnam. Kennedy increased this force to 11,300 in 1962 and 16,300 in 1963. Although several of his advisers questioned this military escalation, arguing that once the United States committed troops it would be more difficult to pull out of the conflict, Kennedy remained firm in his desire to "save" South Vietnam.

As American involvement deepened, Diem's control over South Vietnam declined. He alienated peasants by refusing to enact meaningful land reforms and Buddhists by passing laws to restrict their activities. Responding to Diem's pro-Catholic policies, Buddhists began organized protests. They conducted hunger strikes and nonviolent protests. Several Buddhist monks engaged in self-immolation. In full view of American reporters and cameras, one burned himself to death on a busy, downtown Saigon intersection. Although the gruesome sight shocked Americans, Diem's sister-in-law, Madame Nhu, laughed at the "barbecues," offering gasoline and matches for more fiery deaths.

More deaths followed, and protests mounted. Diem exerted little influence outside of Saigon. Insightful American reporters such as David Halberstam, Neil Sheehan, Peter Arnett, and Stanley Karnow argued that the Diem regime was isolated and paranoid, that a stable democracy would never develop as long as Diem held power. Rather than talk with reporters, Diem would deliver five-, six-, even ten-hour monologues. One reporter recalled that during these sessions Diem's "face seemed to be focused on something beyond me.... The result was an eerie feeling that I was listening to a monologue delivered at some other time and in some other place—perhaps by a character in some allegorical play."

The Kennedy administration soon reached the conclusion that without Diem South Vietnam had serious problems, with Diem the country was doomed. In sum, Diem had to go. Behind the scenes, Kennedy encouraged Vietnamese generals to overthrow Diem. On November 1, 1963, Vietnamese army officers arrested and murdered Diem and his brother. Although Kennedy did not approve of the assassination, the United States quickly aided the new government.

Three weeks later Kennedy was assassinated in Dallas. Several of his friends have suggested that he had begun to reevaluate his Vietnam policy and that after the 1964 election he would have started the process of American disengagement. In a moment of insight, Kennedy himself had observed, "The troops will march in; the bands will play; the crowds will cheer; and in four days everyone will have forgotten. Then we will be told we have to send more troops. It's like taking a drink. The effect wears off, and you have to take another." But whatever Kennedy's future plans or insights, he still had increased U.S. involvement in Vietnam.

Unfortunately for Kennedy's successor, the prospects for South Vietnam's survival were less than they had been in 1961. By 1963 South Vietnam had lost the fertile Mekong Delta to the Vietcong and with it most of the country's rural population. From the peasants' perspective, the Saigon government stood for heavy taxes, no services, and military destruction; and increasingly they identified the United States with Saigon. Such was the situation Lyndon Johnson inherited.

Texas Tough in the Gulf of Tonkin

Lyndon Baines Johnson (LBJ) was a complex man—shrewd, arrogant, intelligent, sensitive, vulgar, vain, and occasionally cruel. He loved power, and he knew where it was, how to get it, and how to use it. "I'm a powerful sonofabitch," he told two Texas congressmen in 1958 when he was the most powerful legislator on Capitol Hill. Everything about Johnson seemed to emphasize or enhance his power. He was physically large and seemed even bigger, and he used his size to persuade people. The "Johnson treatment" involved "pressing the flesh"—a backslapping, hugging sort of camaraderie. He also used symbols of power adroitly, especially the telephone, which had replaced the sword and pen as the symbol of power. "No gunman," remarked one historian, "ever held a Colt .44 so easily" as Johnson handled a telephone.

A legislative genius, Johnson had little experience in foreign affairs. Reared in the poverty of the Texas hill country, educated at a small teachers' college, and concerned politically with domestic issues, before becoming president LBJ had expressed little interest in foreign affairs. "Foreigners are not like the folks I am used to," he often said, and whether it was a joke or not he meant it. He was particularly uncomfortable around foreign dignitaries and ambassadors, often receiving them in groups and scarcely paying attention to them. "Why do I have to see them?" he once asked. "They're [Secretary of State] Dean Rusk's clients, not mine."

Yet to say Johnson had little experience in foreign affairs is not to suggest that he did not have strong opinions on the subject. Like most politicians of the period, Johnson was an unquestioning Cold Warrior. In addition, along with accepting the domino theory—the idea that if Vietnam fell, other nations would also

fall to communism—and a monolithic view of communism, Johnson cherished a traditionally southern notion of honor and masculinity. It was his duty, he maintained, to honor commitments made by earlier presidents. "We are [in Vietnam] because . . . we remain fixed on the pursuit of freedom, a deep and moral obligation *that will not let us go.*" Leaving Vietnam, Johnson believed, would be a dishonorable act, dangerous for the nation's future. Raised in an area where the frontier was still visible, Johnson approached foreign policy like a Texas Ranger. To show weakness and back down was worse than cowardly—it was unmanly. As he often said, "If you let a bully come into your front yard one day, the next day he will be up on your porch and the day after that he will rape your wife in your own bed."

Furthermore, Johnson believed that any retreat from Vietnam would destroy him politically. Soon after becoming president, he told America's ambassador to Vietnam, "I am not going to be the President who saw Southeast Asia go the way China went." No, he would not "lose" Vietnam and allow Republican critics to attack him as they had Truman. "I knew," LBJ later noted, "that Harry Truman and Dean Acheson had lost their effectiveness from the day the communists took over China." Johnson was determined to win the war, to "nail the coonskin to the wall."

Before winning in Vietnam, however, he had to win in the United States. The presidential election in 1964 was his top priority. He was pitted against Barry Goldwater, the powerful Arizona senator from the Republican Right. "Extremism in the defense of liberty is no vice," Goldwater said, and if elected he promised to defend South Vietnam at any cost. He also preached against the welfare state, Social Security, the Nuclear Test Ban Treaty of 1963, and any rapprochement with the Soviet Union or China. Democrats transformed his campaign slogan "In Your Heart, You Know He's Right," to "In Your Heart, You Know He Might," by which they meant that Goldwater might start a nuclear war. Goldwater did little to discourage such thinking. In his campaign he labored to make "nukes" socially acceptable, even coining the uncomfortably comforting phrase "conventional nuclear weapon."

Johnson's campaign strategy was to appear as the thoughtful, strong moderate. He would not lose Vietnam, he told voters, but neither would he use nuclear weapons or "send American boys nine or ten thousand miles from home to do what Asian boys ought to be doing themselves." Johnson promised that if elected he would create a "Great Society" at home and honor American commitments abroad. As usual, he knew what the voters wanted to hear, and they rewarded him with a landslide victory in the November election.

Behind the scenes, however, the Johnson administration was maneuvering to obtain a free hand for conducting a more aggressive war in Vietnam. He did not want a formal declaration of war, which might frighten voters. Rather he desired a quietly passed resolution giving him the authority to deploy American forces. Such a resolution would allow him to act without the consent of Congress. Johnson and his advisers were planning to escalate American involvement in the Vietnam War, but they hoped it would go unnoticed.

Johnson used two reported North Vietnamese attacks on the American destroyer *Maddox* as a pretext for going before Congress to ask for the resolution. Actually, he was less than truthful about the circumstances of the attack. The first incident occurred in the Gulf of Tonkin in early August 1964 when the North Vietnamese suspected the *Maddox* of aiding a South Vietnamese commando raid into North Vietnam, a violation of that country's sovereignty. When North Vietnamese patrol boats approached the *Maddox*, the American ship and supporting navy jets opened fire, sinking one of the North Vietnamese ships and crippling two others. Although the North Vietnamese ships had launched several torpedoes, the *Maddox* was not hit and suffered only superficial machine-gun damage and a loss of ammunition. The second of the Gulf of Tonkin incidents probably never occurred. Assaulted by high waves, thunderstorms, and freak atmospheric conditions, the *Maddox*'s sonar equipment apparently malfunctioned registering 22 invisible enemy torpedoes. No enemy ships were visually sighted, and none

One of the most skilled politicians to serve as president, Lyndon Johnson was far more successful with domestic programs than in foreign affairs. Among the accomplishments of his "Great Society" agenda was passage of the 1965 Voting Rights Act.

of the electronically sighted torpedoes hit the *Maddox* or its accompanying ship the *C. Turner Joy.* Soon after the incident the commander of the *Maddox* reached the conclusion that no attack had ever taken place.

Johnson realized the dubious nature of the second attack. He told an aide, "Hell, those dumb stupid soldiers were just shooting at flying fish." Nevertheless, he went on national television and announced, "Aggression by terror against peaceful villages of South Vietnam has now been joined by open aggression on the high seas against the United States of America." Reassuring the country, he continued, "We know, although others appear to forget, the risks of spreading conflict. We seek no wider war." A few days later he pressed Congress for a resolution. American ships, he emphasized, had been repeatedly attacked, and he wanted authorization to "take all necessary measures" to repel attacks, prevent aggression, and protect American security. It was a broad resolution; Johnson said that it was "like Grandma's nightshirt—it covered everything." Almost without debate, the Senate passed the resolution on August 7 with only two dissenting votes, and the House of Representatives endorsed it unanimously. You "will live to regret it," Wayne Morse, who voted against it in the Senate, told the resolution's supporters. In the years that followed, as Johnson used his new powers to escalate the war, Morse's vote and prediction were vindicated, for the Gulf of Tonkin Resolution allowed Johnson to act in an imperial fashion.

Lyndon's War

Lyndon Johnson liked to personalize things. Once a military aide tried to direct Johnson to the correct helicopter, saying "Mr. President, that's not your helicopter." "Son, they're all my helicopters," Johnson replied. So it was with the Vietnam War. He did not start the war, but once reelected he quickly made it "his war." One authority on the war described Johnson's role:

He made appointments, approved promotions, reviewed troop requests, determined deployments, selected bombing targets, and restricted aircraft sorties. Night after night, wearing a dressing gown and carrying a flashlight, he would descend into the White House basement "situation room" to monitor the conduct of the conflict . . . often, too, he would doze by his bedside telephone, waiting to hear the outcome of a mission to rescue one of "my pilots" shot down over Haiphong or Vinh or Thai Nguyen. It was his war.

When he became president it was still a relatively obscure conflict for most Americans. Public opinion polls showed that 70 percent of the American public paid little attention to U.S. activities in Vietnam. At the end of 1963 only 16,300 U.S. military personnel were in Vietnam, with the number rising to 23,300 by the end of 1964. Most of the soldiers there, however, were volunteers. Only a few people strongly opposed America's involvement. All this would change dramatically over the next four years.

With the election behind him, Johnson started in early 1965 to reevaluate the position of the United States. In Saigon crisis followed crisis as one unpopular government gave way to the next. Something had to be done, and Johnson's advisers suggested two courses. The military and most of LBJ's foreign policy experts called for a more aggressive military presence in Vietnam, including bombing raids into North Vietnam and more ground troops. Other advisers, notably Under Secre-

In this photo, a North Vietnamese torpedo boat attacks the American destroyer USS *Maddox.* The attack took place in the Gulf of Tonkin on August 2, 1964, but the incident was not investigated fully until publication of the Pentagon Papers in 1971.

tary of State George Ball, believed the United States was making the same mistakes as the French. Ball believed that a land war in Indochina was not in America's best strategic interests and that bombing North Vietnam would only stiffen the resolve of the Communists. Escalation of the war could thus create serious problems. "Once on the tiger's back," Ball noted, "we cannot be sure of picking the place to dismount."

Johnson chose the first course, claiming it would be dishonorable not to come to South Vietnam's aid. In February 1965 Vietcong troops attacked the American base in Pleiku, killing several soldiers. Johnson used the assault as a pretext to commence air raids into the North. Code-named ROLLING THUNDER, the operation was designed to use American technological superiority to defeat North Vietnam. At first, Johnson limited U.S. air strikes to enemy radar and bridges below the 20th parallel. But as the war dragged on, he ordered "his pilots" to hit military targets in metropolitan areas. Between 1965 and 1973, American pilots flew more than 526,000 sorties and dropped 6,162,000 tons of bombs on enemy targets. (As a point of contrast, the total tonnage of explosives dropped in World War II by *all* belligerent countries was 2,150,000 tons.) Some of the landscape of South and North Vietnam began taking on a lunar look.

But the bombs did not lead to victory. Ironically, as Ball had predicted, the bombing missions actually strengthened the Communist government in North Vietnam. As a U.S. intelligence report noted, the bombing of North Vietnam "had no significantly harmful effects on popular morale. In fact, the regime has apparently been able to increase its control of the populace and perhaps even to break through the political apathy and indifference which have characterized the outlook of the average North Vietnamese in recent years."

The massive use of air power also undermined U.S. counterinsurgency efforts. Colonel John Paul Vann, an American expert on counterinsurgency warfare noted, "The best weapon 'for this type of war' . . . would be a knife. . . . The worst is an airplane. The next worst is artillery. Barring a knife, the best is a

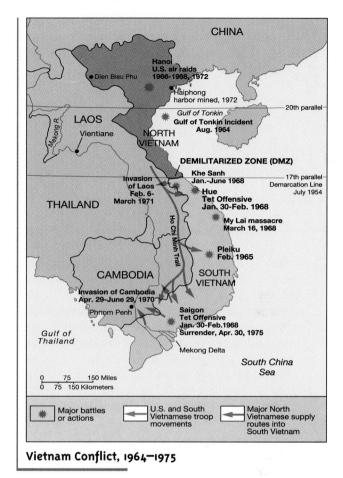

Vietnam Conflict, 1964–1975

rifle—you know who you're killing." By using bombing raids against the enemy in both the North and South, U.S. forces inevitably killed large numbers of civilians, the very people they were there to help. For peasants everywhere in Vietnam, U.S. jets, helicopters, and artillery "meant more bombing, more death, and more suffering."

A larger air war also led to more ground troops. As Johnson informed Ambassador Maxwell Taylor, "I have never felt that this war will be won from the air, and it seems to me what is much more needed and will be more effective is a larger and stronger use of rangers and special forces and marines." Between 1965 and 1968 the escalation of American forces was dramatic. When George Ball warned in 1965 that 500,000 American troops in Vietnam might not be able to win the war, other members of the Johnson administration laughed. By 1968 no one was laughing. Ball's prediction was painfully accurate. Escalation of American troops and deaths went hand in hand. The year-end totals for the United States between 1965 and 1968 were:

1965:	184,300 troops	636 killed.
1966:	385,300 troops	6644 killed.
1967:	485,600 troops	16,021 killed.
1968:	536,000 troops	30,610 killed.

But still there was no victory.

To Tet and Beyond

Throughout the escalation Johnson was less than candid with the American people. He argued that there had been no real change in American policy and that victory was in sight. Any reporter who said otherwise was roundly criticized. Increasingly he demanded unquestioning loyalty from his close advisers. Such demands led to an administration "party line." As the war ground on, the "party line" bore less and less similarity to reality.

In late 1967, General William Westmoreland returned to America briefly to assure the public that he could now see the "light at the end of the tunnel." In his annual report Westmoreland commented, "The year ended with the enemy increasingly resorting to desperation tactics; . . . and he has experienced only failure in these attempts." At the time, the American press focused most of its attention on the battle of Khe Sanh, and Westmoreland assured everyone that victory there was certain.

Then with a suddenness that caught all America by surprise, North Vietnam struck into the very heart of South Vietnam. On the morning of January 30, 1968, North Vietnam launched the Tet offensive. "Tet," the Vietnamese holiday that celebrates the lunar new year, traditionally is supposed to determine family fortunes for the rest of the year. Certainly the Tet offensive boded well for North Vietnam. A Vietcong suicide squad broke into the U.S. embassy in Saigon, and Vietnamese Communists mounted offensives against every major target in South Vietnam, including 5 cities, 64 district capitals, 36 provincial capitals, and 50 hamlets.

LOGISTICS IN A GUERRILLA WAR
The Longest War

THE Vietnam War, fought 9000 miles from America's shores, was a logistical nightmare for the United States. It had to ship hundreds of tons of supplies daily from the United States to bases in the Pacific and finally to fortified positions along the coast of Vietnam. Once the supplies were in Vietnam, they had to be protected from Vietcong guerrillas, who blended into the civilian population and often obtained jobs on U.S. bases. As a result, although American forces established defense perimeters around their bases, the areas were never totally secure. Bombs in U.S. movie theaters or even mess halls were haunting reminders of the unpredictability of guerrilla warfare.

North Vietnam sent much of its supplies south along the Ho Chi Minh Trail. Following a traditional series of trails through mountains and jungles from North Vietnam into Laos and Cambodia, finally emptying into South Vietnam, the Ho Chi Minh Trail was widened into a road capable of handling heavy trucks and thousands of troops. Along the Trail, support facilities, often built underground to escape American detection and air strikes, included operating rooms, fuel storage tanks, and supply coaches. Throughout the war, United States forces tried, but failed, to effectively disrupt the flow of supplies and soldiers south.

The Vietcong tunnel complex, another example of the unconventional war in Vietnam, created even more problems for American troops. The tunnels allowed Vietcong troops to appear and disappear almost by magic. The most famous tunnel complex was under Cu Chi, approximately 25 miles northeast of Saigon. It contained conference rooms, sleeping chambers, storage halls, and kitchens. U.S. forces bombed, gassed, and defoliated the Cu Chi area but failed to destroy the tunnels. "Tunnel rats"—South Vietnamese soldiers and short, wiry GI combat engineer SWAT teams—fought heroically in the tunnels, but they too were unable to destroy the complexes. In the end, it was the unconventional nature of the Vietnam War that guaranteed frustration and made it America's longest war.

Source: From *The Tunnels of Cu Chi* by Tom Mangold and John Penycate. Copyright © 1985 by Tom Mangold and John Penycate. Reprinted by permission of Random House, Inc.

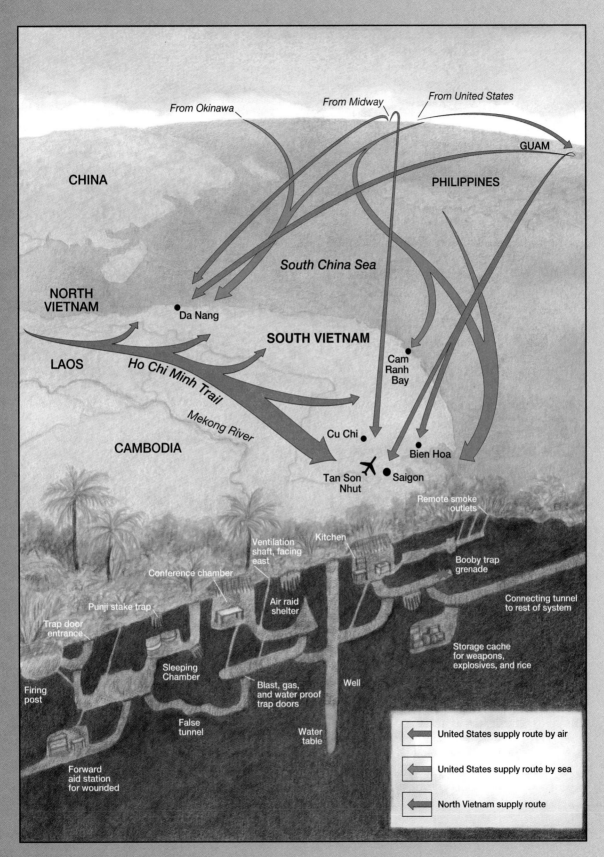

For what it was worth, the United States repelled the Tet offensive. For a few days the fighting was ferocious and bloody, as the rivals fought in highly populated cities and almost evacuated hamlets. In order to retake Hue, the ancient cultural center close to the border between North and South Vietnam where the fighting lasted for several weeks, allied U.S. and South Vietnamese troops had to destroy part of the city. One observer recorded that the city was left a "shattered, stinking hulk, its streets choked with rubble and rotting bodies." When the allied troops finally recaptured Hue, they discovered that North Vietnamese and Vietcong soldiers had killed several thousand political leaders, teachers, and other civilians, many of whom had been buried alive in one mass grave. In another village, where victory came at a high price, the liberating American general reported, "We had to destroy the town to save it." Both sides suffered terribly. But after the allies cleared the cities of enemy troops, General Westmoreland judged the episode a great allied victory. In the end, American and South Vietnamese troops recaptured lost areas and South Vietnamese civilians did not rally to the Vietcong cause. Indeed the Vietcong was so decimated by the Tet offensive that it never regained its full fighting strength.

If, technically speaking, the Tet offensive was a military defeat for North Vietnam, it was also a profound psychological victory. Johnson, his advisers, and his generals had been proclaiming that the enemy was on the run, almost defeated, tired of war, ready to quit. Tet demonstrated that the contrary was true. Upset and confused, CBS anchorman Walter Cronkite, the national voice of reason, expressed that attitude on his nightly newscast: "What the hell is going on? I thought we were winning the war?" The Tet offensive, more than any other single event, turned the media against the war and exposed the widening "credibility gap" between official pronouncements and public beliefs. NBC anchorman Frank McGee reported that the time had come "when we must decide whether it is futile to destroy Vietnam in the effort to save it."

After Tet, Americans stopped thinking about victory and turned toward thoughts of how best to get out of Vietnam. "Lyndon's planes" and "Lyndon's boys" had been unable to achieve Lyndon's objectives. For Johnson this fact was politically disastrous. His popularity plummeted, and in the New Hampshire primary Democratic peace candidate Eugene McCarthy received surprisingly solid support. On CBS's the *Smothers Brothers Comedy Hour* folk singer Pete Seeger openly criticized Johnson in the song "Waist Deep in the Big Muddy" about a "Big Fool [who] Says To Push On." Too intelligent a politician not to realize what was happening, on the night of March 31, 1968, LBJ went on television and made two important announcements. First, he said that the United States would limit its bombing of North Vietnam and would enter into peace talks any time and at any place. And second, Johnson surprised the nation by saying, "I will not seek, and I will not accept, the nomination of my party for another term as your President." A major turning point had been reached. The gradual escalation of the war was over. The period of deescalation had started. Even in official government circles, peace had replaced victory as America's objective in Vietnam.

The Politics of a Divided Nation

If Johnson's fall seemed remarkably swift, and if it seemed as if he were surrendering power without a fight, it was because he knew that his policies had badly divided the nation. LBJ honestly believed he had pursued the only honorable course in Vietnam, that he had had America's best interests at heart. His problem, however, was *not* that his intentions were dishonorable but that his *modus operandi*—the style of his leadership—involved great duplicity. Instead of fully committing the United States by calling up the reserves and National Guardsmen and by pushing for higher taxes to pay for the war, Johnson gambled that a slow, steady escalation would be enough to force North Vietnam to accept a negotiated peace. All during the buildup, LBJ assured the American people that he was not drastically changing policy and, besides, victory was in sight. But he could not fool all the people all the time, and after the Tet offensive he knew that he could not even fool most of the people any more.

Dissatisfaction with Johnson's policy surfaced first among the young, the very people who were being asked to fight and die for the cause. Most of the young men who were drafted did serve, and most served bravely. In the early years of "Lyndon's war," many soldiers sincerely believed that they were fighting—and dying—to preserve freedom and nourish democracy in Southeast Asia. One career soldier, who did his first tour in Vietnam in 1966, recalled the idealism of his experience. He talked enthusiastically about American contributions to the improvements in South Vietnamese village life. But by his last tour, in 1970, his idealism had died. As he told a friend, "I'm still ready to serve—any time. But as a killing machine, not a humanitarian."

As the war lengthened, an ever-growing number of soldiers shared in this disillusionment, which took different forms. Some soldiers turned to drugs to relieve the constant stress and fear that the war engendered. Journalist Michael Herr has written eloquently about the horrors of the war: "Satchel charges and grenades blew up jeeps and movie houses, the VC (Vietcong) got work inside all the camps as shoeshine boys and laundresses, . . . they'd starch your fatigues . . . then go home and mortar your area. Saigon and Cholan and Danang held such hostile vibes that you felt that you were being dry sniped every time someone looked at you." Drugs and sex helped some soldiers—many just boys away from home for the first time—to cope with the nature of a guerrilla war. One GI recalled that R&R—the traditional rest and recreation leave—was really I&I—"intoxication and intercourse." A 1969 Pentagon study estimated that nearly two of every three American soldiers in Vietnam were using marijuana and that one of every three or four had tried heroin. In 1970 CBS News televised a "smoke-in," in which GIs smoked marijuana through the barrel of a combat rifle . In such an atmosphere boys became men, fast. "How do you feel," Herr asked, "when a nineteen-year-old kid tells you from the bottom of his heart that he has gotten too old for this kind of shit?"

Other soldiers reacted by viewing *all* Vietnamese as the enemy. The nature of the war against the Vietcong caused this attitude in part. In a village of "civilians" any man, woman, or child *might* be the enemy. "Vietnam was a dark room full of deadly objects," wrote Herr, "and the VC were everywhere all at once like spider cancer." Tension and anxiety were as ever-present as olive drab.

Empty government phrases, however, also contributed to the problem. How could soldiers win the "hearts and minds" of villagers one day and rain napalm on them the next? Reacting to the surface idealism of U.S. policy, one experienced soldier commented, "All that is just a *load*, man. We're here to kill gooks, period." The My Lai massacre, in which American soldiers killed more than 100 (the official figure was 122 but it was probably many more) South Vietnamese civilians, was the sad extension of this attitude.

The morale of American soldiers plummeted. Desertion and absent-without-leave (AWOL) rates skyrocketed. The army desertion rate in 1966 had been 14.9 men per thousand; by 1971 it had risen to 73.5. In 1966 there were 57.2 AWOL incidents per thousand; that figure leaped to 176.9 in 1971. Even worse, "fragging"—the assassination of overzealous officers and noncommissioned officers (NCOs) by their own troops—increased at an alarming rate. The army claimed that at least 1011 officers and NCOs were killed or wounded by their own men during the Vietnam War.

At home, university students, most of whom were draft-exempt, also reacted to the war and Johnson's policies. The earliest and most vocal critics of the Vietnam War, they may have lacked a coherent ideology, but they were strong in numbers and energy. Between 1946 and 1970 enrollments in institutions of higher education had climbed from 2 to 8 million. Although not all students protested against the war, the most politically active ones did. As politicians they formed a curious breed—segregated from society as a whole, freed from adult responsibilities, bound to no real constituency, and encouraged by their teachers to think critically. Most student protesters were from upper middle-class families

In 1968, Democrat Eugene McCarthy ran for his party's presidential nomination as a peace candidate.

and could afford the intellectual luxury of being political idealists. (Youth culture as a whole will be discussed in greater detail in Chapter 30.)

Led by such leftist groups as Students for a Democratic Society (SDS), university students called for a more just society in which political life was governed by morality, not greed. During the early 1960s they focused on the civil rights movement, participating in freedom rides and voter registration drives. By the mid-1960s, however, they were increasingly shifting their attention to America's "unjust and immoral" war in Southeast Asia. With the shift their numbers swelled—only ten universities had SDS chapters in 1962, and each chapter had only a handful of members. By 1968 the organization could boast more than 100,000 members. By then, too, older voices had joined the student chorus of condemnation.

It was the older voices, energized by the idealism of youth, that led to Johnson's decision not to seek reelection in 1968. For many, it seemed as if the future of American politics belonged to the proponents of peace and morality. Students flocked to presidential candidate Gene McCarthy's peace cause. They cut their long hair, shaved their beards ("be clean for Gene"), put on coats and ties, and worked for McCarthy's campaign. McCarthy's success encouraged Robert Kennedy (RFK) to throw his hat into the ring. Although McCarthy supporters saw him as a political opportunist, Kennedy spoke eloquently for the cause of humanity and peace. When students at a Catholic university called for more bombings, RFK asked, "Do you understand

Although he was slow to declare his candidacy, Robert Kennedy soon became the darling of the antiwar movement.

At the Democratic convention in Chicago, police attacked thousands of unarmed, middle-class, antiwar college students in what was later termed a "police riot."

what that means? It means you are voting to send people, Americans and Vietnamese, to die. . . . Don't you understand that what we are doing to the Vietnamese is not very different than what Hitler did to the Jews?" Kennedy, who enjoyed midnight bull sessions on the meaning of existence and looked at ease with his tie loosened and his shirt sleeves rolled above his elbows, spoke a language that radical students understood. He exhibited the passion and commitment that McCarthy lacked. By the conclusion of the campaign, Kennedy had become the foremost peace candidate, and representative of young liberals.

At the celebration party after his narrow victory in the California primary, Kennedy said, "We are a great country, an unselfish country, and a compassionate country. I intend to make that my basis for running." Moments later a fanatic Palestinian shot him in the head. Along with Kennedy died the dreams of many Americans for a moral society. Columnist Murray Kempton spoke for many people: "I have liked many public men immensely, but I guess [RFK] is the only one I have ever loved." Although RFK had started in political life as a committed, aggressive anti-Communist and Cold Warrior, by the

time of his death he had radically reevaluated his earlier beliefs.

The Democratic party went to the Chicago convention without a candidate. There they battled among themselves—young and old; radical, liberal, and conservative. In the streets, outside the convention hall, police beat protesters in full view of television cameras. An official commission later termed it a "police riot." Inside the convention hall the fighting was largely verbal, but it was just as intense and bitter. Abraham Ribicoff, a senator from Connecticut, accused Chicago's mayor Richard Daley of allowing the police to use "Gestapo tactics" in the street; Daley accused Ribicoff of having unnatural relations with his mother. In the end, the Democratic party chose Hubert Humphrey, Johnson's liberal vice president, as their presidential candidate. Instead of change, the Democratic party chose a representative of the "old politics."

In a more tranquil convention in Miami, the Republican party endorsed Richard M. Nixon, who promised when elected to honorably end the Vietnam War, move against forced busing of black children to white schools, and restore "law and order." Calmer and more relaxed than ever before, the "new Nixon" claimed to speak for the great majority of Americans who obeyed the nation's laws, paid their taxes, regularly attended church, and loved their country. It was the same message Alabama's Governor George Wallace used as the foundation of his third-party candidacy. Running on the American Independent ticket, Wallace spoke for millions of working-class white Americans, young and old alike, who opposed forced integration of schools and neighborhoods, the activities of radical college students, and what they believed was the country's drift toward the left. Although Humphrey's finish in the campaign was strong, Nixon's and Wallace's appeal to traditional values had an undeniable attraction. And on election day, Nixon received 43.4 percent of the popular vote, Humphrey 42.7 percent, and Wallace 13.5 percent. Given the combined votes for Nixon and Wallace—57 percent—it was clear that the country was moving right rather than left.

THE TORTUOUS PATH TOWARD PEACE

During the presidential campaign of 1968, Richard Nixon expected the American voter to accept certain things on faith. First, he asked them to believe that he had a plan to honorably end the war in Vietnam. Second, he hoped that they would "buy" his new public image—the "new Nixon," experienced, statesmanlike, mature, secure, and ever so well adjusted. Most Americans probably did not believe either in the "new Nixon" or his pledge to "bring us together." On election day only 27 percent of eligible voters cast their ballot for him, but in 1968 that proved enough votes to win the election.

Outsiders on the Inside

If Nixon had developed "new" characteristics, those qualities had not forced out the "old." Richard Nixon still considered himself something of an outsider, a battler against an entrenched political establishment. Reared on the West Coast in humble circumstances, he had to overcome considerable obstacles in his

rise to power. In the process certain character traits emerged. He was a hard worker—careful, studious, with a tendency toward perfectionism; no detail was too small for his consideration. He also did not shy away from an unpopular task. During his years as Eisenhower's vice president, Nixon had proved particularly adept as a political hatchet man. He was also a loner—shy, introverted, humorless, uncomfortable in social situations. He was essentially a man of action, one who for most of his career carried a list of things to do in the inside pocket of his suit coat. Journalist Tom Wicker noted that the new Nixon was not very different from the old. Wicker observed: "He is, if anything, more reserved and inward, as difficult as ever to know, driven still by deep inner compulsion toward power and personal vindication, painfully conscious of slights and failures, a man who had imposed upon himself a self-control so rigid as to be all but visible."

As a restless outsider, Nixon harbored a heightened suspicion of political insiders. Throughout his career he had been an outspoken critic of State Department officials and other establishment bureaucrats. On taking office he therefore surrounded himself with close advisers who held noncabinet titles. Cabinet appointees, and particularly his secretary of state, William Rogers, had almost no voice in key decisions. Personal aides H. R. Haldeman and John Ehrlichman—called the "Germans" by the White House press corps—advised Nixon on domestic political issues. Vice President Spiro Agnew assumed the role of the administration's hatchet man so well that he became known as "Nixon's Nixon." He attacked the establishment with the ferocity of a professional wrestler verbally abusing an archival. The "sniveling, hand-wringing power structure," he said, "deserves the violent rebellion it encourages." As for foreign affairs, Nixon relied on his national security advisor, Henry Alfred Kissinger.

Most commentators regarded Kissinger as a strange ally for Nixon. Kissinger, after all, taught at Harvard, was a close associate of Nelson Rockefeller—Nixon's longtime Republican opponent—and had even offered to work for Nixon's Democratic opponent Hubert Humphrey. "Look," Kissinger said in 1968, "I've hated Nixon for years." Yet even while Kissinger was courting Humphrey, he was secretly working for Nixon's election. No matter who won in 1968, Kissinger would be on the victorious side. It was a piece of Machiavellian maneuvering that Nixon might have appreciated.

Beneath Kissinger's sophisticated exterior, he shared with Nixon fundamental characteristics and beliefs. Like Nixon, Kissinger's path to power was not a traditional one. A German Jew, he had lived for five years (between the ages of 10 and 15) in Nazi Germany; he had been verbally and physically abused by his Aryan classmates. He fled with the rest of his family to the United States during the late 1930s. After serving as an army translator-interrogator during World War II, he enrolled as a scholarship student at Harvard, from where he was graduated *summa cum laude* in 1950 and was awarded his Ph.D. in 1954. His dissertation, later published as *A World Restored*, examined the ideas and policies of the conservative world leaders and diplomats who reconstructed Europe after the social and political upheavals caused by the Napoleonic Wars. During the late 1950s and 1960s, Kissinger wrote, taught, and emerged as a leading expert on foreign affairs. Kissinger viewed himself as a political realist, and he resisted rigid ideological or moral stands. Successful diplomacy, he believed, demanded flexible and creative leaders.

Vain, irreverent, articulate, and intellectual, Kissinger shared Nixon's desire to alter the very nature of the country's foreign relations and to make history. Neither particularly enjoyed being part of a committee process, and the diplomacy of secrecy and intrigue attracted both. For all their surface differences, the shy politician and the flamboyant scholar were kindred spirits who combined to form an impressive team. As one historian observed, "each filled a vital gap in the other's abilities. Kissinger had no gift for American politics; he needed to serve a president who could manipulate the electorate into supporting his policies. Nixon benefited from Kissinger's good press contacts since his own were disastrous."

Vietnamization: The Idea and the Process

During his campaign Nixon had promised "peace with honor." He suggested that he had a secret plan to achieve those ends, but controversy surrounded just what that plan entailed. Several historians have suggested that Nixon's plan was an updated version of Eisenhower's plan to end the Korean War. In 1953 when Ike took office, he publicly called for peace while secretly sending a message to Chinese and North Korean leaders that if they stalled at the peace talks, he was prepared to use nuclear weapons to end the war. Nixon told his White House aide H. R. Haldeman that his plan was similar to Eisenhower's. He wanted North Vietnam to believe that he was a "madman." "I want the North Vietnamese to believe I've reached the point where I might do anything to stop the war," Nixon told Haldeman. "We'll just slip the word to them that 'for God's sakes, you know Nixon is obsessed about communists. We can't restrain him when he's angry—and he has his hand on the nuclear button'—and Ho Chi Minh himself will be in Paris in two days begging for peace." The "madman theory" helps to explain Nixon's dramatic shifts during his first four years in office as he moved between the poles of peacefully concluding the war and violently expanding the conflict.

One thing was certain, however. Nixon knew that he could not continue Johnson's policy. "I'm not going to end up like LBJ," he remarked, "holed up in the White House afraid to show my face on the street." The country needed something new. Whatever else he did, Nixon realized that to ensure some semblance of domestic tranquility he would have to begin to remove American troops from Vietnam. In May 1969 he announced, "The time is approaching when the South Vietnamese forces will be able to take over some of the fighting fronts now being manned by Americans." That summer he drummed harder on the idea of the South Vietnamese fighting their own war. In what has become known as the "Nixon Doctrine," the president insisted that Asian soldiers must carry more of the combat burden. Certainly the United States would continue to materially aid any anti-Communist struggle, but the aid would not include the wholesale use of American troops.

The Nixon Doctrine formed the foundation of Nixon's Vietnamization policy. Working from the questionable premise that the government of Nguyen Van Thieu was stable and prepared to assume greater responsibility for fighting the war, Nixon announced that he planned to gradually deescalate American military involvement. Increasingly, U.S. aid would be limited to war materiel, military advice, and air support. He coupled Vietnamization with a more strenuous effort to move along the peace talks.

Actually, the idea of Vietnamization was hardly new. In 1951 the French had called it *jaunissement,* or "yellowing." Advisers for Eisenhower, Kennedy, and Johnson had suggested one variation or another of the plan as the solution to the war. The major problem was that the South Vietnamese could not successfully fight the war—not in 1951, or 1961, or 1971. But faced with angry criticism at home, Nixon had no choice but to implement the policy.

At the same time as he extended the olive branch, he expanded the nature of the conflict. Hoping to slow down the flow of North Vietnamese supplies and soldiers into South Vietnam, Nixon ordered American B-52 pilots to bomb the Ho Chi Minh Trail both in Vietnam and in Cambodia. He kept this violation of Cambodian neutrality secret from the American public. It was a bold move, but not very productive. The bombs only reduced the flow of men and supplies by approximately 10 percent.

When both the increased bombing of North Vietnam and Kissinger's peace talks with North Vietnamese officials failed to end the war, Nixon resorted to harsher military efforts. After watching *Patton,* his favorite movie, on board the presidential yacht *Sequoia,* he decided to "go for all the marbles" and send American ground forces to Cambodia to destroy Communist supply bases. On the night of April 30, 1970, he went on television and told the American people of his plan.

Ignoring previous American violations of Cambodian neutrality, he said that U.S. policy had been "to scrupulously respect the neutrality of the Cambodian people," while North Vietnam had used the border areas for "major base camps, training sites, logistics facilities, weapons and ammunition factories, airstrips and prisoner-of-war compounds," as well as their chief military headquarters. As a result, Nixon announced a joint American and South Vietnamese "incursion" into Cambodia's border regions, to be limited to 60 days. In an attempt to rally American support, Nixon emphasized that the country's honor and even manhood were at stake: "We will not be humiliated, we will not be defeated. If when the chips are down the U.S. acts like a pitiful helpless giant, the forces of totalitarianism will threaten free nations and free institutions throughout the world. It is *not our power but our will* that is being tested tonight."

Militarily the "incursion" fell far short of success. Although American forces captured large stockpiles of weapons and supplies, the operation did not force North Vietnam to end the war. But the "incursion" had dangerously enlarged the battlefield. More importantly, the invasion of Cambodia reignited the fires of the peace movement at home. Throughout the country, colleges and universities shut down in protest. Students raged at what they believed was an "immoral, imperialist policy." At Kent State University in Ohio a volley of gunshots fired by Ohio National Guardsmen broke up a peaceful demonstration. The shots killed 4 students and wounded 9 others. Less than two weeks later, policemen shot 2 more innocent students at Jackson State University in Mississippi. Instead of victory or even peace, Nixon's efforts had further divided America.

As an effective policy for ending the war, Vietnamization was a failure. To be sure, the policy allowed Nixon to bring home American combat troops. When Nixon took office 540,000 American troops were in Vietnam; four years later only 70,000 remained. But American reductions were not accompanied by a marked improvement in the South Vietnamese army. This was clearly illustrated by the unsuccessful 1971 South Vietnamese invasion into Laos. If anything, South Vietnam became more depen-

In the spring of 1970, Ohio National Guardsmen fired into a group of protesting students at Kent State University, killing four students.

dent on the United States during the years of Vietnamization. By 1972 South Vietnam's only product and export was war, and even this commodity was of inferior quality.

A "Decent Interval"

By 1972 Nixon simply wanted to end the war with as little embarrassment as possible. As a viable country, South Vietnam was hopeless. Without an active U.S. military presence, the country's demise was a foregone conclusion. Negotiations presented the only way out. Nixon and Kissinger hoped to arrange for a peace that would permit the United States and South Vietnam to save face and allow a "decent interval" of time to ensue between the American departure and the collapse of the government in Saigon. In the pursuit of the goal, Nixon changed the character of American foreign policy.

The Soviet Union and the People's Republic of China aided and advised North Vietnam. Yet the two large Communist nations were hardly allies themselves. In fact, the Sino-Soviet split demonstrated to American leaders the fallacy of the old Cold War theme of a monolithic Communist movement. Nixon and Kissinger were astute enough to use the Sino-Soviet rift to improve U.S. relations with both countries. Improved relations, they believed, would move the United States several steps closer to an "honorable" peace in Vietnam. Unfortunately, Nixon and Kissinger greatly overestimated the influence of the Soviet Union and China on North Vietnam.

From his first days in office, Nixon had his eyes on the People's Republic of China, a nation that the United States had refused to recognize.

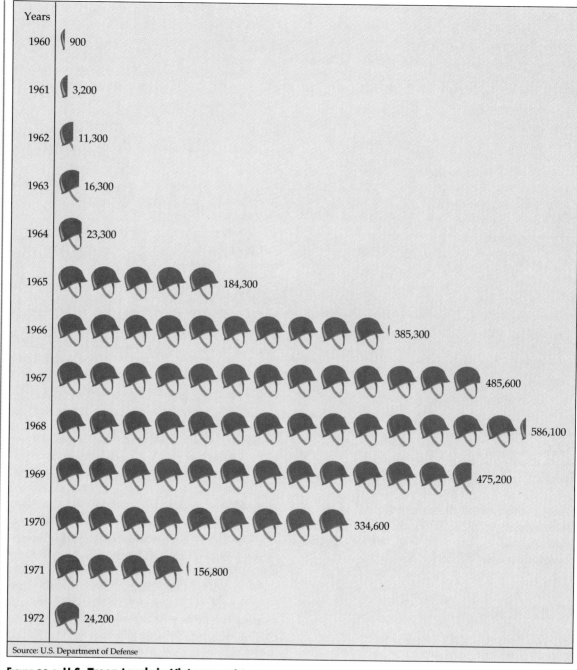

Years	
1960	900
1961	3,200
1962	11,300
1963	16,300
1964	23,300
1965	184,300
1966	385,300
1967	485,600
1968	586,100
1969	475,200
1970	334,600
1971	156,800
1972	24,200

Source: U.S. Department of Defense

FIGURE 29.1 **U.S. Troop Levels in Vietnam, 1960–1972**

One Nixon aide reported in 1969, "You're not going to believe this, but Nixon wants to recognize China." It seemed remarkable, since Nixon's Cold War record—his opposition to any concession to the Communists—was well known. But Nixon understood that his very record would protect him from public cries of being soft on communism; Nixon knew that unlike Truman, Kennedy, and Johnson, he did not have a Nixon to worry about.

Nixon approached China like a man holding a vase from the Ming dynasty, mixing caution with slow careful movements. In fact, both China and the United States walked on eggshells. Mao Tse-tung told reporter Edgar Snow that he "would be happy to talk with [Nixon] either as a tourist or as President." And Mao ended China's athletic isolation in 1971 by sending a table tennis team to the world championships in Nagoya, Japan, and then inviting an American team to compete in Beijing. Capitalizing on the success of Ping-Pong diplomacy, in the summer of 1971 Kissinger made a very secret trip to China. Kissinger's mission paved the way for Nixon's own very public trip to China in February 1972. American television cameras recorded Nixon's every move as he toured the Great Wall, the Imperial Palace, and the other sites of historic China. For the White House, one reporter noted, "It was the social event of the year." Constantly smiling and bubbling with excitement, Nixon thoroughly enjoyed the event, going so far as quoting Chairman Mao at an official toast and learning to eat with chopsticks. Although full diplomatic relations would not be established until 1979 under Jimmy Carter, Nixon's trip to China was the single most important event in the history of the relations between the United States and the People's Republic of China. It bridged, as Chinese foreign minister Chou En-lai remarked, "the vastest ocean in the world, twenty-five years of no communication."

In 1972 Richard Nixon visited China in an attempt to improve relations with that country. It was the first step toward achieving détente with the Soviet Union.

Concerned about the growing rapprochement between China and America, the Soviet Union sought to move closer to the United States. Once again, Nixon and Kissinger were pleased to oblige. In late May 1972, after many months of preparatory talks, Nixon traveled to Moscow to sign an arms control treaty with Soviet leader Leonid Brezhnev. The Strategic Arms Limitation Treaty of 1972 (SALT I) certainly did not preclude a future nuclear war between the superpowers. Although it froze intercontinental ballistic missile (ICBM) deployment, it did not alter the buildup of the more dangerous multiple independent reentry vehicles (MIRVs), which, according to one historian "was about as meaningful as freezing the cavalry of the European nations in 1938 but not the tanks." As so often has been the case during the Cold War, SALT I provided more of a warm breeze than the real heat wave necessary for a complete thaw of the Cold War. Both the United States and the Soviet Union hoped that SALT I would lead to other, more comprehensive, arms reductions treaties.

In other areas the United States and the Soviet Union made more substantial progress. American business forged inroads into the Soviet market. Pepsi-Cola executives, metallurgy and ammonia dealers, computer and machine tools traders, and electric gear and mining equipment salespersons all benefited from the improved relations between America and the Soviet Union. Some farmers also reaped significant rewards when disastrous harvests at home led the Soviet Union to purchase several billion dollars worth of American wheat, corn, and soybeans. And, of course, cultural and athletic exchanges and competition provided entertainment for millions of Americans and Soviets alike.

Thus, although Nixon had not been able to end the Vietnam War, his 1972 triumphs in the Soviet Union and China gave him more influence with North Vietnam's major allies. His visits to Beijing and Moscow also dazzled American voters. In 1972 Nixon easily defeated Democratic candidate George McGovern, capturing 61 percent of the popular vote and 521 of the 538 votes of the electoral college. Nixon's success with blue-collar workers, conservative Catholics, and Southerners signified the end of the New Deal coalition.

Once reelected, Nixon again focused on Vietnam. A month before the election, Kissinger had announced, "Peace is at hand," but no sooner was Nixon safely reelected than the peace talks broke down once again. Nixon's response was more and heavier bombing of North Vietnam. Starting on December 18 and continuing for the next ten days, the Christmas bombings—code-named Operation LINEBACKER II—attacked military targets in Hanoi and Haiphong and killed more than 1500 civilians, leveled a hospital, and destroyed large parts of Hanoi. Critics charged that Nixon was attempting to "wage war by tantrum" and that the bombings served no military purpose. Some even suggested that Nixon had become mentally unbalanced. Military authorities, however, maintained that the bombings quickened the pace of the peace process. When the bombings concluded, the warring nations resumed peace talks.

In a week North Vietnam and the United States had hammered out a peace, one that was strikingly similar to the October proposal. On January 27, 1973, America ended its active participation in the Vietnam War. The peace treaty provided for the release of all prisoners of war and America's military withdrawal from Vietnam. It also established a monitored cease-fire between North and South Vietnam and set up procedures aimed at solving the differences between the two countries. Nixon quickly claimed that he had won an honorable peace, that his "secret plan" had worked, even if it had taken four years and claimed the lives of 21,000 Americans, 107,000 South Vietnamese, and more than 500,000 North Vietnamese soldiers. And, of course, the lives of many thousands of Vietnamese civilians. Informing the American people of the peace, Nixon claimed, "South Vietnam has gained the right to determine its own future.... Let us be proud that America did not settle for a peace that would have betrayed our ally . . . that would have ended the war for us but continued the war for the fifty million people of Indochina." But as one historian commented, "In all likelihood, the peace accords that were finally signed in January 1973 could have been negotiated four years earlier. In the name of credibility, honor, and patriotism, hundreds of thousands of lives had been lost."

America left the war in 1973, but the war did not end then. All the peace provided for was a "decent interval" between America's withdrawal and North Vietnam's complete victory. When the South Vietnamese leader Nguyen Cao Ky heard Nixon's peace speech, he commented, "I could not stomach [it], so nauseating was its hypocrisy and self-delusion . . . there is no reason why they [the Communists] should stop now. . . . I give them a couple of years before they invade the South." He was right. Almost as soon as the ink on the "peace treaty" was dry, both North Vietnam and South Vietnam began to violate the treaty. Finally, in the spring of 1975 South Vietnamese forces collapsed. In March North Vietnam forces took Hue and Da Nang; by late April they were close to Saigon. On April 21 President Nguyen Van Thieu publicly lambasted the United States, resigned, and beat a hasty retreat from his country. On April 30 South Vietnam formally announced its unconditional surrender. Vietnam was finally unified. Free elections in 1956 might have accomplished the same results.

The Legacy of the War

Although America's active military participation in the Vietnam War ended in 1973, the controversy engendered by the war raged on long after the firing of the last shot. Much of the controversy centered on the returning veterans. Reports of drug use and fragging frightened many Americans who had come no closer to the war than their television sets. And veterans—most of whom had served their country faithfully and to the best of their abilities—were shocked by the cold, hostile reception they received when they returned to the United States. In *First Blood* (1982), John Rambo, played by Sylvester Stallone, captured the pain of the returning veterans: "Nothing is over. Nothing! You just don't turn it off. It wasn't my war—you asked me, I didn't ask you . . . and I did what I had to do to win. . . . Then I came back to the world and I see all those maggots at the airport, protesting me, spitting on me, calling me a baby-killer and all kinds of vile crap. . . . Back there I could fly a gunship, I could drive a tank, I was in charge of million-dollar equipment. Back here I can't even hold down a job parking cars. . . . Back here there's nothing!"

During the 1970s and 1980s the returning Vietnam War veteran loomed large in American popular culture. He was first portrayed as a dangerous killer, a deranged ticking time bomb that could explode at any time and in any place. He was Travis Bickle in *Taxi Driver* (1976), a veteran wound so tight that he seemed perpetually on the verge of snapping. Travis Bickle, wrote one film historian, "is the prototypical movie vet: in ways we can only imagine, the horror of the war unhinged him. He's lost contact with other human beings. . . . He's edgy: he can't sleep at night." He waits to explode. Or he was Colonel Kurtz in *Apocalypse Now* (1979), who adjusted to a mad war by going mad himself.

Not until the late 1970s did popular culture begin to treat the Vietnam War veteran as a victim of the war rather than a madman produced by the war. *Coming Home* (1978) and

The Vietnam War inspired a number of movies dealing with the conflict veterans faced on their return home. Some movies portrayed the veterans as victims of a tragic war; others like *Rambo: First Blood II* (shown here) made the veteran a hero and transformed the conflict into a noble crusade.

The Deer Hunter (1978) began the popular rehabilitation of the veteran, and such films as *First Blood* (1982), *Rambo: First Blood II* (1985), and *Missing in Action* (1984) transformed the veteran into a hero. On television, "Magnum, P.I.," "The A-Team," and "Air Wolf" also presented the veteran as a misunderstood hero.

The transformation of the veteran that took place in the late 1970s and 1980s indicated a fundamental shift in America's attitude toward the war. Millions of Americans began once again to see the war in terms of a noble crusade that could have been won. As John Rambo said in *Rambo: First Blood II*, "Do we get to win this time?" His former commander replied: "This time it's up to you." This message fit well with the political message of Ronald Reagan's America.

As American filmmakers "Ramboized" the conflict, Vietnam labored to reconstruct a viable nation out of the rubble of war. It was a difficult struggle. Roads and bridges, power plants and factories lay in ruins. Ports suffered from damage and neglect. Raw materials and investment capital were in short supply. If peace brought hope, it also brought the specter of economic ruin.

The recovery of the Socialist Republic of Vietnam was slow. One of the poorest countries in the world, it suffered from high inflation and unemployment, food shortages and starvation, and government inefficiency and corruption. In addition, military campaigns—such as the 1978 war against the Khmer Rouge in Kampuchea (formerly Cambodia)—siphoned off money needed to rebuild the country. Finally, the Soviet Union, Vietnam's closest ally, did not solve Vietnam's economic problems. "Americans without dollars," the Vietnamese have called the Soviets. One Vietnamese joke reflected the new relationship with the Soviet Union. After appealing to the Soviets for loans, Vietnam receives the cable: "Tighten your belts." Vietnam replies: "Send belts."

In 1986 Vietnam committed itself to radical change. A new generation of leaders turned to increased democracy and capitalism to solve their country's problems. They also turned to the West, and particularly the United States, for help. American leaders

CHRONOLOGY OF KEY EVENTS

1954	The French garrison at Dien Bien Phu falls to Vietnamese nationalists led by Ho Chi Minh; Geneva conference divides Vietnam into two regions with the promise to hold elections to reunify the country in 1956; North Vietnam is led by the Communist government of Ho Chi Minh and South Vietnam by the government of Ngo Dinh Diem
1956	South Vietnam refuses to participate in elections to unify the two Vietnams
1961	John F. Kennedy is inaugurated thirty-fifth president; Alliance for Progress pledges $20 billion in U.S. aid to Latin America over a ten-year period; Cuban exiles stage abortive invasion of Cuba at Bay of Pigs; East Germans erect Berlin Wall; Soviet Union breaks a three-year moratorium on nuclear tests
1962	Cuban missile crisis: In response to Khrushchev's decision to build missile bases in Cuba, President Kennedy imposes a naval blockade of Cuba, and Khrushchev orders the bases dismantled; President Kennedy increases the number of American advisers in South Vietnam to approximately 16,000
1963	United States and Soviet Union agree to ban nuclear tests in atmosphere; South Vietnamese army officers arrest and murder President Diem; President Kennedy is assassinated; Lyndon Johnson becomes thirty-sixth president
1964	North Vietnamese torpedo boats attack the U.S. destroyers *Maddox* and *C. Turner Joy* in the Gulf of Tonkin off the North Vietnamese coast; Congress passes Gulf of Tonkin Resolution, which gives the president authority to re-

	taliate against North Vietnamese aggression
1965	United States begins regular bombing missions over North Vietnam and sends first American ground combat troops into South Vietnam
1968	Tet offensive: During Tet, the Vietnamese lunar new year, the Vietcong stage attacks on major South Vietnamese cities; President Johnson suspends the bombing of North Vietnam and announces that he will not run for reelection; Democratic presidential candidate Robert F. Kennedy is assassinated; Richard M. Nixon is elected thirty-seventh president
1969	Nixon announces "Vietnamization" policy; South Vietnam to take increased responsibility for fighting the war
1970	32,000 U.S. troops join the South Vietnamese army in invading Cambodia; in antiwar protests, 4 students are killed and 9 injured at Kent State University in Ohio; and 2 students die and 12 are injured at Jackson State University in Mississippi; Congress repeals Gulf of Tonkin Resolution
1972	Nixon travels to China, ending 25 years of nonrecognition of the People's Republic of China; Strategic Arms Limitation Treaty with the Soviet Union freezes intercontinental ballistic missile deployment
1973	United States ends active participation in the Vietnam War
1975	North Vietnamese forces enter Saigon; North and South Vietnam are reunited; the former South Vietnamese capital is renamed Ho Chi Minh City

during the late 1980s and early 1990s, however, rejected Vietnam's pleas for aid. Although Vietnam had weakened its ties to the Soviet Union, withdrawn from Kampuchea, and tried to resolve the prisoners of war—missing in action (POW-MIA)—issue, official American policy continued to regard the Socialist Republic of Vietnam as a country untouchable. Vietnam may have won the war, but it had not won peace. Finally, however, in the summer of 1995, President Bill Clinton's administration extended diplomatic recognition to Vietnam. Ironically, Clinton's decision was based partially on his belief that recognition would finally resolve the MIA issue.

CONCLUSION

The Vietnam War confused and divided the nation. Tim O'Brien captured something of this confusion in his acclaimed novel *Going After Cacciato* (1978). After fighting in the war, his protagonist "didn't know who was right, or what was right; he didn't know if it was a war of self-determination or self-destruction, outright aggression or national liberation; he didn't know which speeches to believe, which books, which politicians; he didn't know if nations would topple like dominos or stand separate like trees, he didn't know who started the war, or why, or when, or with what motives; he didn't know if it mattered."

Richard Nixon promised in 1968 that if he were elected president, he would end the war honorably and bring Americans together again. Instead, he enlarged the scope of the war before ending it and further divided the country. So, too, Johnson had divided the nation. His vision of a better, more just society—the Great Society (see Chapter 30)—was dashed on the rocks of Vietnam. There was in Johnson's position the essence of tragedy. As he later explained to biographer Doris Kearns, "I knew from the start that I was bound to be crucified either way I moved. If I left the woman I really loved—the Great Society—in order to get involved with the bitch of a war on the other side of the world, then I would lose everything at home . . . but if I left that

war and let the communists take over South Vietnam, then I would be seen as a coward and my nation would be seen as an appeaser and we would both find it impossible to accomplish anything for anybody anywhere on the entire globe." In Johnson's view he was like a Puritan wrestling with the question of his own salvation:

Damned if you do,
Damned if you don't.
Damned if you will
Damned if you won't.

Of course, both Nixon and LBJ further injured their cause by being consciously deceptive in their dealings with the American people.

Vietnam, then, destroyed Johnson's presidency and it helped to undermine Nixon's. It was a war that left scars—on the people who fought in it and on the people who opposed and supported it; on Americans and on Vietnamese; and on U.S. foreign policy and its position in the world. For almost 35 years the United States had been actively involved in Indochina, but its influence in the region effectively ended in 1975. The Vietnam War, like the Communist victory in China in 1949, undercut America's position in Asia.

The most constructive outcome of the war was the lessons it taught. Congress learned that it had to take a more active role in foreign affairs. The War Powers Act (1973), which requires the president to account for his actions within 48 hours of committing troops in a foreign war, demonstrated that the Gulf of Tonkin Resolution had taught Congress a painful lesson. Ho Chi Minh's nationalism taught policy-makers that communism was not a monolithic movement and that not all small nations are dominoes. Perhaps politicians, policy-makers, and citizens alike even learned that national policy should be based on the realities of individual situations and not Cold War stereotypes.

SUGGESTIONS FOR FURTHER READING

Carl Bernstein and Robert Woodward, *All the President's Men* (1974). The study of how two men, following a story, helped bring down a presidency.

Michael Beschloss, *The Crisis Years, Kennedy and Krushchev, 1960–1963* (1992). A readable popular narrative that presents a case study in misunderstanding.

Robert Caro, *The Years of Lyndon Johnson* and *The Path to Power* (1982), and *Means of Ascent* (1990). The first two volumes read like an indictment of Lyndon Johnson but are fascinating nonetheless.

David Halberstam, *The Making of a Quagmire: America and Vietnam During the Kennedy Era*, rev. ed. (1988). Sprawling study of the reasons for America's failure in Vietnam.

Robert S. McNamara, *In Retrospect: The Tragedy and Lessons of Vietnam* (1995). A recent attempt by one of Kennedy's advisers to explain why and how America became mired in Vietnam.

Allen Matusow, *The Unraveling of America: A History of Liberalism in the 1960's* (1984). A hard look at the few successes and many failures of the 1960s.

Neil Sheehan, *A Bright Shining Lie: John Paul Vann and America in Vietnam* (1988). Uses the career of John Paul Vann to provide an in-depth look at the war in Vietnam.

Overviews and Surveys

Stephen E. Ambrose, *Rise to Globalism: American Foreign Policy Since 1938*, 5th ed. (1988); H. W. Brands, *The Wages of Globalism: Lyndon Johnson and the Limits of American Power* (1994); William H. Chafe, *The Unfinished Journey*, 3d ed. (1995), and *The American Woman: Her Changing Social, Economic, and Political Roles, 1920–1970* (1972); Warren I. Cohen and Nancy Bernkopf, eds., *Lyndon Johnson Confronts the World: American Foreign Policy, 1963–1968* (1994); Mario T. García, *Mexican Americans: Leadership, Ideology, Identity, 1930–1960* (1989); Juan Gómez-Quiñones, *Chicano Politics: Reality and Promise, 1940–1990* (1990); Walter LaFeber, *America, Russia, and the Cold War*, 7th ed. (1993); Kim McQuaid, *The Anxious Years: America in the Vietnam-Watergate Era* (1989); Matt Meier and Feliciano Rivera, *The Chicanos: A History of Mexican-Americans* (1972); James S. Olson and Randy Roberts, *Where the Domino Fell: America in Vietnam, 1945–1990* (1991); Julian Samora, *Los Mojados: The Wetback Story* (1971); Frederick F. Siegel, *A Troubled Journey* (1984); Ronald B. Taylor, *Chavez and the Farm Workers* (1975).

The Illusion of Greatness

Irving Bernstein, *Promises Kept: John F. Kennedy's New Frontier* (1991); James G. Blight and David A. Welch, *On the Brink: Americans and Soviets Reexamine the Cuban Missile Crisis* (1989); Carl M. Brauer, *John F. Kennedy and the Second Reconstruction* (1977); David Detzer, *The Brink: Cuban Missile Crisis, 1962* (1979); Herbert S. Dinerstein, *The Making of a Missile Crisis: October 1962* (1976); Louise FitzSimons, *The Kennedy Doctrine* (1972); Trumbull Higgins, *The Perfect Failure: Kennedy, Eisenhower, and the C.I.A. at the Bay of Pigs* (1987); Richard D. Mahoney, *JFK: Ordeal in Africa* (1983); Bruce Miroff, *Pragmatic Illusions: The Presidential Politics of JFK* (1976); Victor Navasky, *Kennedy Justice* (1971); Thomas G. Paterson, *Contesting Castro: The United States and the Triumph of the Cuban Revolution* (1994); Jack M. Schick, *The Berlin Crisis, 1958–1962* (1971); Richard Walton, *Cold War and Counterrevolution: The Foreign Policy of John F. Kennedy* (1972); Pascaline Winand, *Eisenhower, Kennedy, and the United States of Europe* (1993); Peter Wyden, *Bay of Pigs* (1979).

Vietnam: America's Longest War

David L. Anderson, *Trapped by Success: The Eisenhower Administration and Vietnam, 1953–1961* (1991); Christian G. Appy, *Working-Class War: American Combat Soldiers and Vietnam* (1993); David M. Barret, *Uncertain Warriors: Lyndon Johnson and His Vietnam Advisors* (1993); Larry Berman, *Planning a Tragedy: The Americanization of the War in Vietnam* (1982), and *Lyndon Johnson's War* (1989); Larry E. Cable, *Conflict of Myths: The Development of American Counterinsurgency Doctrine and the Vietnam War* (1986), and *Unholy Grail: The United States and the Wars in Vietnam* (1991); Harry Caudill, *Night Comes to the Cumberlands* (1963); Chester L. Cooper, *The Lost Crusade: America in Vietnam* (1970); Frances FitzGerald, *Fire in the Lake: The Vietnamese and the Americans in Vietnam* (1972); Todd Gitlin, *The Whole World Is Watching: Mass Media in the Making & Unmaking of the New Left* (1980); Sherry Gershon Gottlieb, *Hell No, We Won't Go: Evading the Draft During Vietnam* (1992); David Halberstam, *The Best and the Brightest* (1972); Michael Herr, *Dispatches* (1977); George C. Herring, *America's Longest War: The United States and Vietnam, 1950–1975*, 2d ed. (1986); Seymour Hersh, *My Lai 4: A Report on the Massacre and Its Aftermath* (1970); Stanley Karnow, *Vietnam, A History*, rev. ed. (1991); Christopher Lasch, *The Agony of the American Left* (1969); David Levy, *The Debate over Vietnam* (1991); Guenter Lewy, *America in Vietnam* (1978); Abraham Lowenthal, *The Dominican Intervention* (1972); Roger Morris, *Uncertain Greatness: Henry Kissinger and American Foreign Policy* (1977); Don Oberdorfer, *Tet!* (1971); George

Reedy, *The Twilight of the Presidency*, rev. ed. (1987); Ronald Spector, *After Tet: The Bloodiest War in Vietnam* (1992); Kathleen J. Turner, *Lyndon Johnson's Dual War: Vietnam and the Press* (1985); Brian Van-DeMark, *Into the Quagmire: Lyndon Johnson and the Escalation of the Vietnam War* (1991); Marilyn Young, *The Vietnam Wars: 1945–1990* (1991).

The Tortuous Path Toward Peace

John Dean, *Blind Ambition: The White House Years* (1976); John Hart Ely, *War and Responsibility: Constitutional Lessons of Vietnam and Its Aftermath* (1993); Fred Emery, *Watergate: The Corruption of American Politics and the Fall of Richard Nixon* (1994); Stephen Graubard, *Kissinger: Portrait of a Mind* (1973); Robert T. Hartmann, *Palace Politics: An Inside Account of the Ford Years* (1980); Seymour Hersh, *The Price of Power: Kissinger in the Nixon White House* (1983); Leon Jaworski, *The Right and the Power: The Prosecution of Watergate* (1976); J. Anthony Lukas, *Nightmare: The Underside of the Nixon Years* (1976); Keith Nelson, *The Making of Detente: Soviet-American Relations in the Shadow of Vietnam* (1994); Richard Nixon, *RN: The Memoirs of Richard Nixon*, 2 vols. (1978); Thomas Powers, *The Man Who Kept the Secrets: Richard Helms & the CIA* (1979); William Shawcross, *Sideshow: Kissinger, Nixon, and the Destruction of Cambodia,* rev. ed. (1987); Edward R. F. Sheehan, *The Arabs, Israelis, and Kissinger* (1976); Terry Terriff, *The Nixon Administration and the Making of U.S. Nuclear Strategy* (1995); Richard C. Thornton, *The Nixon-Kissinger Years: Reshaping America's Foreign Policy* (1989); Theodore H. White, *Breach of Faith: The Fall of Richard Nixon* (1975).

Biographies

Fawn M. Brodie, *Richard Nixon: The Shaping of His Character* (1981); David Burner, *John F. Kennedy and a New Generation* (1988); Warren Cohen, *Dean Rusk* (1980); Paul K. Conkin, *Big Daddy from the Pedernales: Lyndon Baines Johnson* (1986); Ronnie Dugger, *The Politician: The Life and Times of Lyndon Johnson* (1982); Henry Fairlie, *The Kennedy Promise: The Politics of Expectation* (1973); Eric Goldman, *The Tragedy of Lyndon Johnson* (1969); Joan Hoff, *Nixon Reconsidered* (1994); Doris Kearns, *Lyndon Johnson and the American Dream* (1976); Herbert S. Parmet, *Jack: The Struggles of John F. Kennedy* (1980), and *JFK: The Presidency of John F. Kennedy* (1983); Thomas C. Reeves, *A Question of Character: A Life of John F. Kennedy* (1991); Arthur Schlesinger, Jr., *A Thousand Days: John F. Kennedy in the White House* (1965); Tom Wicker, *One of Us: Richard Nixon and the American Dream* (1991).

CHAPTER 30
THE STRUGGLE FOR A JUST SOCIETY

LITTLE ROCK CENTRAL

THE STRUGGLE FOR RACIAL JUSTICE

Freedom Now
To the Heart of Dixie
"Bombingham"
Kennedy Finally Acts
The March on Washington
The Civil Rights Act of 1964
Voting Rights
Black Nationalism and Black Power
The Civil Rights Movement Moves
    North
The Great Society and the Drive for
    Equality
White Backlash
The Struggle Continues

THE YOUTH REVOLT

The New Left
The Making and Unmaking of a
    Counterculture

LIBERATION MOVEMENTS

Women's Liberation
Sources of Discontent
Feminism Reborn
Radical Feminism
The Growth of Feminist Ideology
The Supreme Court and Sex
    Discrimination
The Equal Rights Amendment
Impact of the Women's Liberation
    Movement
¡Viva La Raza!
The Native-American Power Movement
Gay and Lesbian Liberation
The Earth First

He has been called the nation's nag. He denounced soft drinks for containing excessive amounts of sugar (more than nine teaspoons a can). He warned Americans about the health hazards of red dyes used as food colorings and of nitrates used as preservatives in hot dogs. He even denounced high heels: "It is part of the whole tyranny of fashion, where women will inflict pain on themselves . . . for what, to please men." His name is Ralph Nader and since the mid-1960s he has been the nation's leading consumer advocate.

An extraordinarily frugal and committed crusader on behalf of the nation's consumers, Nader lived for years in an $80-a-month rooming house on about $15,000 a year. He eats in cheap restaurants, has never owned a car, has almost no social life, avoids all junk food, and dresses plainly. In 1983 he was still wearing shoes he had bought while he was in the army in 1959.

His parents came to the United States from Lebanon and settled in Winsted, Connecticut, where they ran a restaurant. Nader credits his parents with instilling the sense of justice and civic duty that has inspired his career.

He was born on February 27, 1934, and speaks at least six languages, including English, Arabic, Chinese, Portuguese, Spanish, and Russian. He received his bachelor's degree from Princeton (he once wore a bathrobe to class to protest conformity in dress) and earned a law degree at Harvard. At law school, he found his initial cause: automobile safety. After learning that auto accidents were the fourth leading cause of death (behind heart disease, cancer, and strokes), he launched a study of auto injury cases. His research convinced him that the law placed too much emphasis on driver mistakes and not enough on the unsafe design of cars.

In 1963, Nader hitchhiked from Hartford, Connecticut, where he had practiced law, to Washington, D.C., to devote his life to consumer protection. In 1965, he published a best-seller entitled *Unsafe at Any Speed,* which charged that automakers stressed styling, comfort, speed, power, and a desire to cut costs at the expense of safety. The book sold 60,000 copies in hardcover and 400,000 copies in paperback.

Nader gained public celebrity when the General Motors Corporation hired a detective to investigate his politics, religion, and sex life. General Motors's chairman was forced to apologize for this invasion of privacy before a Senate subcommittee, and eventually paid Nader a $425,000 settlement. Nader used the money to establish more than two dozen public interest groups. The people who work for these groups are known as "Nader's Raiders."

During the 1960s and 1970s, Nader was the driving force behind the passage of more than two dozen landmark consumer protection laws, including the National Traffic and Motor Vehicle Safety Act (which set up a federal agency to establish auto-safety standards and order recalls of cars that failed to meet them), the Occupational Safety and Health Act (which established another agency to set standards for on-the-job safety), the Consumer Products Safety Act, and the Freedom of Information Act (which allows citizens to request and see government records). His efforts have been instrumental in attaining job protection for whistle-blowers (employees who expose corrupt or abusive business practices), federal financing of presidential elections, and the creation of the Environmental Protection Agency. Few other Americans have ever compiled such a long and impressive list of legislative accomplishment.

His ultimate goal, however, was not simply to protect consumers from shoddy or dangerous products. It was to reinvigorate the nation's ideal of democracy by encouraging active grassroots citizen participation in politics. The best answer to society's problems, he believed, was for ordinary citizens to campaign for safer consumer products, better schools, a cleaner environment, and safer workplaces.

During the late 1970s and 1980s, his influence seemed to wane. In 1978, Congress defeated his proposal for a Consumer Protection Agency. Critics dismissed him as a "scold." Said *Newsweek* magazine: "An optimistic society wearies of his endless discontents." In a decade of deregulation, Nader's call for greater regulations seemed out of step with the beat of the times.

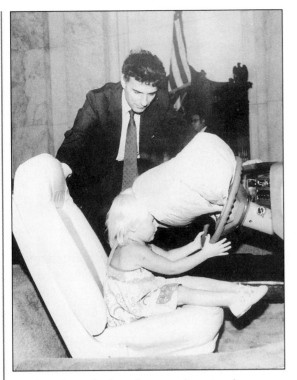

Ralph Nader is the best-known advocate of consumer protection laws in the United States. His group of attorneys, nicknamed "Nader's Raiders," have investigated such wide-ranging problems as automobile safety, the rights of the handicapped, tax reform, the environment, and public health. Here, Nader looks on during a demonstration showing the operation of an automobile airbag safety restraint.

As the 1980s ended and the 1990s began, however, it was clear that Nader was still a major force in American politics. He played a central role in passing a California initiative that rolled back the cost of auto insurance. He led a bitter fight against a proposed 51 percent congressional pay raise. And in his long campaign for auto safety he achieved an important breakthrough when the major automobile manufacturers agreed to install air bags in most of their cars.

Ralph Nader illustrates in vivid terms the difference that one person's life can make. His life also epitomizes the idealism and activism of the 1960s—a decade when hundreds of thousands of ordinary Americans gave new life to the nation's democratic ideals by pressing for racial justice, peace, and improvements in the quality of American life. African Americans used sit-ins, freedom rides, and protest marches to fight segregation, poverty, and unemployment. Feminists demanded equal employment opportunities and an end to sexual discrimination. Mexican Americans protested discrimination in voting, education, and employment. Native Americans demanded that the government recognize their land rights and the right of tribes to govern themselves. Gays and lesbians fought for the end of discrimination according to sexual preference. Environmentalists demanded legislation that controlled the amount of pollution released into the atmosphere.

Although consumerists, environmentalists, civil rights workers, feminists, and other grassroots activists seemed to fade from public view during the 1980s, they—like Ralph Nader—never abandoned their causes. Today they remain a powerful force in American life. Indeed, the very success of their efforts has led to a conservative grassroots reaction, one in which equally committed Americans have denounced busing, affirmative action, quotas, and abortion.

THE STRUGGLE FOR RACIAL JUSTICE

For African Americans in 1960 statistics were grim. Their average life span in 1960 was seven years less than that of white Americans. Their children had only half the chance of completing high school, only a third the chance of completing college, and a third the

Table 30.1 HIGH SCHOOL GRADUATES (PERCENTAGE OF POPULATION AGES 25–29)			
	1960	1966	1970
African Americans			
Male	36	49	54
Female	41	47	58
Whites			
Male	63	73	79
Female	65	79	76

Table 30.2 INCOME DISTRIBUTION OF AFRICAN AMERICANS, OTHER NONWHITES, AND WHITES 1960, 1969

	African Americans and Other Nonwhites (Percentage)		Whites (Percentage)	
	1960	1969	1960	1969
Under $3000	38	20	14	~8
$3000–4999	22	19	14	10
$5000–6999	16	17	19	12
$7000–9999	14	20	26	22
$10,000 and over	~9	24	27	49

chance of entering a profession, when they grew up. On average, African Americans earned half as much as white Americans and were twice as likely to be unemployed.

Despite a string of court victories during the late 1950s, many African Americans were still second-class citizens. Six years after the landmark *Brown* v. *Board of Education* decision, just 49 Southern school districts had desegregated and fewer than 1.17 percent of black schoolchildren in the 11 states of the old Confederacy attended public school with white classmates. Less than a quarter of the South's African-American voting-age population could vote, and in certain Southern counties African Americans could not vote, serve on grand juries and trial juries, or frequent all-white beaches, restaurants, and hotels.

In the North, too, African Americans suffered humiliation, insult, embarrassment, and discrimination. Many neighborhoods, businesses, and unions almost totally excluded them. Just as unemployment had increased in the South with the mechanization of cotton production, so too in northern cities unemployment soared as labor-saving technology eliminated many semiskilled and unskilled jobs that historically provided many African Americans with work. African-American families experienced severe strain; the proportion of families headed by women jumped from 8 percent in 1950 to 21 percent in 1960. "If you're white, you're right," a black folk saying went; "if you're brown stick around; if you're black, stay back."

During the 1960s, however, a growing hunger arose among African Americans for full equality. The Rev. Dr. Martin Luther King, Jr., gave voice to the new mood: "We're through with tokenism and gradualism and see-how-far-you've-comeism. We're through with we've-done-more-for-your-people-than-anyone-elseism. We can't wait any longer. Now is the time."

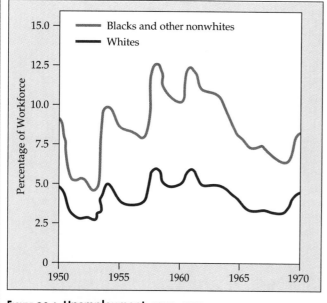

FIGURE 30.1 Unemployment, 1950–1970

Freedom Now

"Now is the time." These words became the credo and rallying cry for a generation. On

Monday, February 1, 1960, four African-American freshmen at North Carolina Agricultural and Technical College—Ezell Blair, Jr., Franklin McClain, Joseph McNeill, and David Richmond—walked into the F. W. Woolworth store in Greensboro, North Carolina, and sat down at the lunch counter. They asked for a cup of coffee. A waitress told them that she would only serve them if they stood.

Instead of walking away, the four college freshmen stayed in their seats until the lunch counter closed—giving birth to the "sit-in." The next morning, the four college students reappeared at Woolworth's, accompanied by 25 fellow students. By the end of the week protesters filled Woolworth's and other lunch counters in town. Now was their time, and they refused to end their nonviolent protest against inequality. Six months later, white city officials granted African Americans the right to be served in a restaurant.

Although the student protesters subscribed to King's doctrine of nonviolence, their opponents did not—assaulting the students both verbally and physically. When the police finally arrived, they arrested African-American protesters, not the whites who tormented them.

By the end of February, lunch counter sit-ins had spread to 30 cities in seven southern states. In Charlotte, North Carolina, a storekeeper unscrewed the seats from his lunch counter. Other stores roped off seats so that every customer had to stand. Alabama, Georgia, Mississippi, and Virginia hastily passed antitrespassing laws to stem the outbreak of sit-ins. Despite these efforts, the nonviolent student protests spread across the South. Students "attacked" segregated libraries, lunch counters, and other "public" facilities.

In April, 142 student sit-in leaders from 11 states met in Raleigh, North Carolina, and voted to set up a new group to coordinate the sit-ins, the Student Nonviolent Coordinating Committee (SNCC). The Rev. Dr. Martin Luther King, Jr., told the students that their willingness to go to jail would "be the thing to awaken the dozing conscience of many of our white brothers."

In the summer of 1960, sit-ins gave way to "wade-ins" at segregated public beaches. In Atlanta, Charlotte, Greensboro, and Nashville, African-American students lined up at white-only box offices of segregated movie theaters. Other students staged pray-ins (at all-white

Lunch counter sit-ins in 1960 sparked an advance in the crusade against Southern segregation. Such passive resistance tactics proved very effective.

churches), study-ins (at segregated libraries), and apply-ins (at all-white businesses). By the end of the year, 70,000 people had taken part in sit-ins in over 100 cities in 20 states. Police arrested and jailed more than 3600 protesters, and authorities expelled 187 students from college because of their activities. But the new tactic worked. On March 21, 1960, lunch counters in San Antonio, Texas, were integrated, and by August 1, lunch counters in 15 states had been integrated. By the end of the year, protesters had succeeded in integrating eating establishments in 108 cities.

The Greensboro sit-in initiated a new, activist phase in black America's struggle for equal rights. Fed up with the slow, legalistic approach that characterized the civil rights movement in the past, southern African-American college students began to attack Jim Crow directly. In the upper South, federal court orders and student sit-ins successfully desegregated lunch counters, theaters, hotels, public parks, churches, libraries, and beaches. But in three states—Alabama, Mississippi, and South Carolina—segregation in restaurants, hotels, and bus, train, and airplane terminals remained intact. In those states, young civil rights activists launched new assaults against segregation.

To the Heart of Dixie

In early May 1961 a group of 13 men and women, African American and white, set out from Washington, D.C., on two buses. They called themselves "freedom riders," and they wanted to demonstrate that despite a federal ban on segregated travel on interstate buses, segregation prevailed throughout much of the South. The freedom riders' trip was sponsored by the Congress of Racial Equality (CORE), a civil rights group dedicated to breaking down racial barriers through nonviolent protest. Inspired by the philosophy of Indian nationalist Mahatma Gandhi, the freedom riders were willing to endure jail and suffer beatings to achieve integration. "We can take anything the white man can dish out," said one African-American freedom rider, "but we want our rights . . . and we want them now."

In Virginia and North Carolina, the freedom riders met little trouble. African-American freedom riders were able to use white restrooms and sit at white lunch counters. But in Winnsboro, South Carolina, police arrested two African-American freedom riders, and outside Anniston, Alabama, a white hurled a bomb through one of the bus's windows, setting the vehicle on fire. Waiting white thugs beat the freedom riders as they tried to escape the smoke and flames. Eight other whites boarded the second bus and assaulted the freedom riders before police restrained the attackers.

In Birmingham, Alabama, another mob attacked the second bus with blackjacks and lengths of pipe. In Montgomery, a club-swinging mob of 100 whites attacked the freedom riders; and a group of white youths poured an inflammable liquid on one African-American man and ignited his clothing. Local police arrived ten minutes later, state police an hour later. Explained Montgomery's police commissioner: "We have no intention of standing police guard for a bunch of troublemakers coming into our city."

President Kennedy was appalled by the violence. He hastily deputized 400 federal marshals and Treasury agents and flew them to Alabama to protect the freedom riders' rights. The president publicly called for a "cooling-off period," but conflict continued. When freedom riders arrived in Jackson, Mississippi, 27 were arrested for entering a "white-only" washroom and were sentenced to 60 days on the state prison farm.

The threat of racial violence in the South led the Kennedy administration to pressure the Interstate Commerce Commission to desegregate air, bus, and train terminals. In more than 300 southern terminals, signs saying "white" and "colored" were taken down from waiting room entrances and lavatory doors.

Civil rights activists next aimed to open state universities to African-American students. Many Southern states integrated their universities without incident, but other states were stiff-backed in their opposition to integration. The depth of hostility to integration was apparent in an incident that took place in February 1956. A young woman named Autherine Lucy became the first African-

PRIMARY SOURCE ESSAY

MARTIN LUTHER KING, JR., AND THE "LETTER FROM BIRMINGHAM CITY JAIL"

It was during the Montgomery bus boycott that Martin Luther King, Jr. (1929–1968) first pricked the conscience of white America. Unjustly arrested, he walked out of jail to solemnly speak of the power of love. His house was bombed, and he calmed the angry crowd that had gathered and then faced the cameras to quietly assure reporters that no amount of violence could ever cause him to leave the path of peaceful protest. King's dignity and dedication impressed many people, but in 1955 he had not yet become the larger-than-life leader of later years. He was only 26 years old. He had not organized the boycott and had only reluctantly agreed to assume its leadership, but after the success of the Montgomery boycott, King received many invitations to speak and was invited to attend two conferences of southern ministers in 1957. As a result of those meetings the Southern Christian Leadership Conference (SCLC) was organized the following year in Atlanta, with King as its president. During this time, King was being legally harassed in both Alabama and Georgia. Especially after the student-led sit-in movement began in 1960, he and the SCLC mainly responded to calls for help from campaigns already underway. He joined movements in Atlanta and Albany, Georgia. He was jailed in both cities, but neither campaign met with the dramatic success of Montgomery. By 1963, King was seeking a site for a victory by nonviolent direct action.

Martin Luther King, Jr., came to Birmingham in 1963 at the request of the Reverend Fred Shuttlesworth. This time, however, King was to be involved in the movement from the start. He and his staff met with African-American leaders of the city to painstakingly plan every detail before launching sit-ins and demonstrations. Organization was thorough and successful. However, tactics employed by Police Commissioner Eugene "Bull" Connor prevented the movement from gaining national attention, thereby limiting its effectiveness. King decided he

Arrested during the Birmingham protests, Dr. King was held in the city jail for eight days, the first 24 hours of which were in solitary confinement.

must once again go to jail, and he was arrested on April 12. While there he received a newspaper containing a statement by eight white Alabama clergymen critical of King and the Birmingham campaign. They argued that King was an "outsider" and that the movement was ill-timed, lawless, extremist, and designed to provoke violence when negotiation was a better path.

In his jail cell King drafted a reply on the margins of the newspaper. He continued to write on scraps of toilet paper and scraps of other paper provided by a trustee until he finally got a pad of paper from his lawyers. Point by point he answered his fellow clergymen's charges. The result of his efforts was called the "Letter from Birmingham City Jail." It was later polished and reprinted in King's *Why We Can't Wait*. Like his "I Have a Dream" speech, the letter was an eloquent statement of his vision and was widely quoted.

LETTER FROM BIRMINGHAM CITY JAIL

WE know through painful experience that freedom is never voluntarily given by the oppressor, it must be demanded by the oppressed. Frankly I

have never yet engaged in a direct action movement that was "well timed," according to the timetable of those who have not suffered unduly from the disease of segregation. For years now I have heard the word "Wait!" It rings in the ear of every Negro with a piercing familiarity. This "wait" has almost always meant "never." It has been a tranquilizing Thalidomide, relieving the emotional stress for a moment, only to give birth to an ill-formed infant of frustration. We must come to see with the distinguished jurist of yesterday that "justice too long delayed is justice denied." We have waited for more than 340 years for our constitutional and God-given rights. The nations of Asia and Africa are moving with jetlike speed toward the goal of political independence, and we still creep at horse and buggy pace toward the gaining of a cup of coffee at a lunch counter.

I guess it is easy for those who have never felt the stinging darts of segregation to say wait. But when you have seen vicious mobs lynch your mothers and fathers at will and drown your sisters and brothers at whim; when you have seen hate-filled policemen curse, kick, brutalize, and even kill your black brothers and sisters with impunity; when you see the vast majority of your 20 million Negro brothers smothering in an airtight cage of poverty in the midst of an affluent society; when you suddenly find your tongue twisted and your speech stammering as you seek to explain to your six-year-old daughter why she can't go to the public amusement park that has just been advertised on television, and see the tears welling up in her little eyes when she is told that Funtown is closed to colored children, and see the depressing clouds of inferiority begin to form in her little mental sky, and see her begin to distort her little personality by unconsciously developing a bitterness toward white people; when you have to concoct an answer for a five-year-old son who is asking in agonizing pathos: "Daddy, why do white people treat colored people so mean?"; when you take a cross-country drive and find it necessary to sleep night after night in the uncomfortable corners of your automobile because no motel will accept you; when you are humiliated day in and day out by nagging signs reading "white" men and "colored"; when your first name becomes "nigger" and your middle name becomes "boy" (however old you are) and your last name becomes "John," and when your wife and mother are never given

---

Dr. King's message to white Alabama clergymen has been called 'a modern classic'

MY dear Fellow Clergymen,
While confined here in the Birmingham City Jail, I came across your recent statement calling our present activities "unwise and untimely." . . . since I feel that you are men of genuine goodwill and your criticisms are sincerely set forth, I would like to answer your statement in what I hope will be patient and reasonable terms.

I think I should give the reason for my being in Birmingham, since you have been influenced by the argument of "outsiders coming in." . . . I am here, along with several members of my staff, because we were invited here. I am here because I have basic organizational ties here.

Beyond this, I am in Birmingham because injustice is here. Just as the eighth century prophets left their little villages and carried their "thus saith the Lord" far beyond the boundaries of their home towns; and just as the Apostle Paul left his little village of Tarsus and carried the gospel of Jesus Christ to practically every hamlet and city of the Graeco-Roman world, I, too, am compelled to carry the gospel of freedom beyond my particular home town. Like Paul, I must constantly respond to the Macedonian call for aid. . . .

You deplore the demonstrations that are presently taking place in Birmingham. But I am sorry that your statement did not express a similar concern for the conditions that brought the demonstrations into being. . . . I would not hesitate to say that it is unfortunate that so-called demonstrations are taking place in Birmingham at this time, but I would say in more emphatic terms that it is even more unfortunate that the white power structure of this city left the Negro community with no other alternative.

In any nonviolent campaign there are four basic steps: 1) Collection of the facts to determine whether injustices are alive. 2) Negotiation. 3) Self-purification and 4) Direct Action. We have gone through all of these steps in Birmingham. There can be no gainsaying of the fact that racial injustice engulfs this community. Birmingham is probably the most thoroughly segregated city in the United States. Its ugly record of police brutality is known in every section of this country. Its unjust treatment of Negroes in the courts is a notorious reality. There have been more unsolved bombings of Negro homes and churches in Birmingham than any city in this nation. These are the hard, brutal and unbelievable facts. On the basis of these conditions Negro leaders sought to negotiate with the city fathers. But the political leaders consistently refused to engage in good faith negotiation.

Then came the opportunity last September to talk with some of the leaders of the economic community. In these negotiating sessions certain promises were made by the merchants—such as the promise to remove the humiliating racial signs from the stores. On the basis of these promises Rev. Shuttlesworth and the leaders of the Alabama Christian Movement for Human Rights agreed to call a moratorium on any type of demonstrations. As the weeks and months unfolded we realized that we were the victims of a broken promise. The signs remained. Like so many experiences of the past we were confronted with blasted hopes, and the dark shadow of a deep disappointment settled upon us. So we had no alternative except that of preparing for direct action, whereby we would present our very bodies as a means of laying our case before the conscience of the local and national community. We were not unmindful of the difficulties involved. So we

The "Letter from Birmingham City Jail," published in the August 1963 issue of *Ebony* magazine, stands as an eloquent statement of Dr. King's vision of racial equality and of his philosophy of nonviolent civil disobedience.

the respected title of "Mrs.", when you are harried by day and haunted by night by the fact that you are a Negro, living constantly at tip-toe stance, never quite knowing what to expect next, and plagued with inner fears and outer resentments; when you are forever fighting a degenerating sense of "nobodiness"—then you will understand why we find it difficult to wait. There comes a time when the cup of endurance runs over, and men are no longer willing to be plunged into an abyss of injustice where they experience the bleakness of corroding despair. I hope, sirs, you can understand our legitimate and unavoidable impatience.

Some of the letter answered criticisms specific to Birmingham. Most of it, however, explained the aspirations of African Americans and the doctrines of nonviolence and civil disobedience. Few of King's ideas were original. Because the letter was addressed to the clergy, he cited the Bible and theologians to make his points. The document was also intended for the American public, so King drew some examples from U.S. history. He noted the Boston Tea Party as an act of civil disobedience. To answer charges of extremism he listed others similarly accused: Jesus, Saint Paul, Martin Luther, John Bunyan, Abraham Lincoln, and Thomas Jefferson. In other words, he utilized widely believed and cherished ideals to define his movement. He sought to make whites understand and feel the frustrations of African Americans by recounting everyday experiences with which they could relate.

King had his human weaknesses. He did not single-handedly initiate, organize, or lead the civil rights movement. The real unsung heroes are probably the countless men and women in cities and small towns all over the South who risked everything to desegregate places like Winona, Mississippi. Nevertheless, King was the most effective propagandist of the civil rights movement. He served extremely well in the role of chief interpreter and translator of the movement to white America. It was a crucial role for which he has been justly honored.

American student admitted to the University of Alabama. A mob of 1000 greeted the young woman with the chant, "Keep 'Bama White!" Two days later, rioting students threw stones and eggs at the car she was riding to class. Lucy decided to withdraw from school, and for the next six years no African-American students attended the University of Alabama.

A major breakthrough occurred in September 1962, when a federal court ordered the state of Mississippi to admit James Meredith—a nine-year veteran of the air force—to the University of Mississippi in Oxford. Ross Barnett, the state's governor, promised on statewide television that he would "not surrender to the evil and illegal forces of tyranny" and would go to jail rather than permit Meredith to register for classes. Barnett flew into Oxford, named himself special registrar of the university, and ordered the arrest of federal officials who tried to enforce the court order.

James Meredith refused to back down. A "man with a mission and a nervous stomach," Meredith was determined to get a higher education. "I want to go to the university," he said. "This is the life I want. Just to live and breathe—that isn't life to me. There's got to be something more." He arrived at the Ole Miss campus in the company of police officers, federal marshals, and lawyers. Angry white students waited, chanting, "Two, four, six, eight—we don't want to integrate."

Four times James Meredith tried to register at Ole Miss. He finally succeeded on the fifth try, escorted by several hundred federal marshals. The ensuing riot left 2 people dead and 375 injured, including 166 marshals. Ultimately, President Kennedy sent 16,000 troops to put down the violence.

"Bombingham"

By the end of 1961, protests against segregation, job discrimination, and police brutality had erupted from Georgia to Mississippi and Tennessee to Alabama. Staunch segregationists responded by vowing to defend segregation. The symbol of unyielding resistance to integration was Alabama governor George C.

Wallace, a former state judge and a one-time state Golden Gloves featherweight boxing champion. Elected on an extreme segregationist platform, Wallace promised to "stand in the schoolhouse door" and go to jail before permitting integration. At his inauguration in January 1963, Wallace declared: "I draw the line in the dust and toss the gauntlet before the feet of tyranny, and I say segregation now, segregation tomorrow, segregation forever."

It was in Birmingham, Alabama, that civil rights activists faced the most determined resistance. A sprawling steel town of 340,000, Birmingham had a long history of racial acrimony. In open defiance of Supreme Court rulings, Birmingham had closed its 38 public playgrounds, 8 swimming pools, and 4 golf courses rather than integrate them. Calling Birmingham "the most thoroughly segregated city in the United States," the Rev. Dr. Martin Luther King, Jr., announced in early 1963 that he would lead demonstrations in the city until demands for fair hiring practices and desegregation were met.

Day after day, well-dressed and carefully groomed men, women, and children marched against segregation—only to be jailed for demonstrating without a permit. On April 12 King himself was arrested. While in jail he wrote his now-famous "Letter from Birmingham City Jail," a scathing response to a group of white clergymen who in a newspaper article had asked African Americans to wait patiently for equal rights. On pieces of toilet paper and newspaper margins, King wrote, "I am convinced that if your white brothers dismiss us as 'rabble rousers' and 'outside agitators'—those of us who are working through the channels of nonviolent direct action—and refuse to support our nonviolent efforts, millions of Negroes, out of frustration and despair, will seek solace and security in black nationalist ideologies, a development that will lead inevitably to a frightening racial nightmare."

For two weeks, all was quiet, but in early May demonstrations resumed with renewed vigor. On May 2 and again on May 3, more than a thousand of Birmingham's African-American youth marched for equal rights. In response, Birmingham's police chief,

Theophilus Eugene "Bull" Connor, unleashed police dogs on the children and sprayed them with fire hoses with 700 pounds of pressure. Watching the willful brutality on television, millions of Americans, white and African American, were shocked by this violent face of segregation.

Tension mounted as police arrested 2543 African Americans and whites between May 2 and May 7, 1963. Under intense pressure, the Birmingham Chamber of Commerce reached an agreement on May 9 with African-American leaders to desegregate public facilities in 90 days, hire African Americans as clerks and salespersons in 60 days, and release demonstrators without bail in return for an end to the protests.

Although King's goal was nonviolent social change, the short-term result of protest was violence and confrontation. On May 11, white extremists firebombed an integrated motel. That same night, a bomb destroyed the home of King's brother. Shooting incidents and racial confrontations quickly spread across the South. In June, an assassin armed with a Springfield rifle ambushed and killed 37-year-old Medgar Evers, the NAACP field representative in Mississippi, shooting him in the back. In September, segregationists planted 10 to 15 sticks of dynamite under the

steps of Birmingham's 50-year-old Sixteenth Street Baptist Church; the explosion killed 4 young African-American girls and injured 14 others. Elsewhere in the city that same day, a 16-year-old African-American Birmingham youth was shot from behind by a police shotgun, and a 13-year-old boy was shot while riding his bicycle. Ten people died during civil rights protests in 1963, 35 African-American homes and churches were firebombed, and 20,000 people were arrested.

Kennedy Finally Acts

The eruption of violence in Birmingham and elsewhere finally forced the Kennedy administration to act on civil rights. Twice before, in 1957 and 1960, the federal government had adopted weak civil rights acts designed to provide federal protection guaranteeing voting rights for African Americans. Now Kennedy responded to the racial violence by proposing a new, stronger civil rights bill that required the desegregation of public facilities, outlawed discrimination in employment and voting, and allowed the attorney general to initiate school desegregation suits.

Kennedy's record on civil rights inspired little confidence. He had voted against the 1957 Civil Rights Act, and in the 1960 campaign many African-American leaders, including former athlete and businessman Jackie Robinson, backed Richard Nixon even though Kennedy worked hard to court the African-American vote by promising new civil rights legislation and declaring that he would end housing discrimination with a "stroke of the pen." A few weeks before the 1960 election, Kennedy broadened his African-American support by helping to secure the release of Martin Luther King from an Atlanta jail, where he had been imprisoned for leading an antisegregation demonstration.

Once in office, however, Kennedy moved slowly on civil rights issues both because he feared alienating white Southern Democrats and because he had no real commitment to the cause. In both his inaugural address and his first State of the Union Address, he barely mentioned civil rights. And although

Police used dogs, high-pressure water hoses, clubs, and electric cattle prods to break up the nonviolent civil rights demonstration in Birmingham, Alabama, in May 1963. Scenes such as this one, televised to millions of viewers, aroused public indignation and sympathy for the civil rights movement.

Kennedy's administration filed 28 suits to protect African-American voting rights (compared to 10 suits filed during the Eisenhower years), it was not until November 1963, that Kennedy took steps to end housing discrimination with a "stroke of the pen"—after he had received hundreds of pens from frustrated civil rights leaders.

The March on Washington

The violence that erupted in Birmingham and elsewhere alarmed many veteran civil rights leaders. In December 1962, two veteran fighters for civil rights—A. Philip Randolph and Bayard Rustin—met at the office of the Brotherhood of Sleeping Car Porters in Harlem. Both men were pacifists, eager to rededicate the civil rights movement to the principle of nonviolence. Both men decided that a massive march for civil rights and jobs might provide the necessary pressure to prompt Kennedy and Congress to act.

On August 28, 1963, over 200,000 people gathered around the Washington Monument and marched eight-tenths of a mile to the Lincoln Memorial. The marchers carried placards reading: "Effective Civil Rights Laws—Now! Integrated Schools—Now! Decent Housing—Now!" and sang the civil rights anthem, "We Shall Overcome." Ten speakers addressed the crowd, but the event's highlight was an address by the Rev. Dr. Martin Luther King, Jr. After he finished his prepared text he launched into his legendary closing words. "I have a dream," he declared, "that one day on the red hills of Georgia the sons of former slaves and the sons of former slaveowners will be able to sit down together at the table of brotherhood. . . . I have a dream that one day even the state of Mississippi, a state sweltering with people's injustices, sweltering with the heat of oppression, will be transformed into an oasis of freedom and justice." As his audience roared their approval, King continued: "I have a dream that one day this nation will rise up and live out the true meaning of its creed: 'We hold these truths to be self-evident; that all men are created equal.' "

The Civil Rights Act of 1964

For seven months, debate raged in the halls of Congress. In a futile effort to delay the Civil Rights Bill's passage, opponents proposed over 500 amendments and staged a protracted filibuster in the Senate. On July 2, 1964—a little over a year after President Kennedy had sent it to Congress—the Civil Rights Act was enacted into law. It had been skillfully pushed through Congress by President Lyndon Johnson, who took office after Kennedy was assassinated in November 1963. As finally passed, the act prohibited discrimination in voting, employment, and public facilities such as hotels and restaurants, and it established the Equal Employment Opportunity Commission to prevent discrimination in employment on the basis of race, religion, or sex. Ironically, the provision barring sex discrimination had been added by opponents of the Civil Rights Act in an attempt to kill the bill.

Although most white Southerners accepted the new federal law without resistance, many violent incidents occurred as angry whites vented their rage in shootings and beatings. But despite such violent incidents, the Civil Rights Act was a success. In the first weeks after the act's passage, segregated restaurants and hotels across the South opened their doors to African-American patrons. Over the next ten years, the Justice Department brought legal suits against more than 500 school districts and more than 400 suits against hotels, restaurants, taverns, gas stations, and truck stops charged with racial discrimination.

Voting Rights

The 1964 Civil Rights Act prohibited discrimination in employment and public accommodations, but many African Americans were denied an equally fundamental constitutional right, the right to vote. The most effective barriers to voting were state laws requiring prospective voters to read and interpret sections of the state constitution. In Alabama, voters had to provide written answers to a 20-page test on the Constitution and state and local government. Questions included: "Where

On August 28, 1963, over 200,000 African Americans and whites gathered for a day-long rally at the Lincoln Memorial to demand an end to racial discrimination. The highlight of the event was Martin Luther King, Jr.'s inspiring "I Have a Dream" speech.

do presidential electors cast ballots for president?" "Name the rights a person has after he has been indicted by a grand jury."

In early 1965, in an effort to bring the issue of voting rights to national attention, Martin Luther King, Jr., launched a voter-registration drive in Selma, Alabama. Even though African Americans slightly outnumbered whites in the city of 29,500 people, Selma's voting rolls were 99 percent white and 1 percent African American. For seven weeks, King led hundreds of Selma's African-American residents to the county courthouse to register to vote. Nearly 2000 African American demonstrators, including King, were jailed by County Sheriff James

Clark for contempt of court, juvenile delinquency, and parading without a permit. After a federal court ordered Clark not to interfere with orderly registration, the sheriff forced African-American applicants to stand in line for up to five hours before being permitted to take a "literacy" test. Not a single African-American was added to the registration rolls.

When a young African-American man was murdered in nearby Marion, King responded by calling for a march from Selma to the state capitol of Montgomery, 50 miles away. On March 7, 1965, voting-rights demonstrators prepared to march. "I can't promise you that it won't get you beaten," King told them, "... but we must stand up for what is right!" As they crossed a bridge spanning the Alabama River, 200 state police with tear gas, night sticks, and whips attacked them. The march was temporarily halted. It resumed on March 21 with federal protection. The demonstrators chanted: "Segregation's got to fall . . . you never can jail us all." On March 25, a crowd of 25,000 gathered at the state capitol to celebrate the march's completion. Martin Luther King, Jr., addressed the crowd and called for an end to segregated schools, poverty, and voting discrimination. "I know you are asking today, 'How long will it take?' . . . How long? Not long, because no lie can live forever."

Within hours of the march's end, four Ku Klux Klan members shot and killed a 39-year-old white civil rights volunteer from Detroit named Viola Liuzzo. President Johnson expressed the nation's shock and anger. "Mrs. Liuzzo went to Alabama to serve the struggle for justice," the President said. "She was murdered by the enemies of justice who for decades have used the rope and the gun and the tar and the feather to terrorize their neighbors."

Two measures adopted in 1965 helped safeguard the voting rights of all Americans. On January 23, the states completed ratification of the Twenty-fourth Amendment to the Constitution barring a poll tax in federal elections. At the time, five Southern states still had a poll tax. On August 6, President Johnson signed the Voting Rights Act, which prohibited literacy tests and sent federal examiners to seven Southern states to register voters. Within a year, 450,000 Southern African Americans had registered to vote.

After nearly 2000 African Americans were arrested for trying to register to vote in Selma, Alabama, demonstrators (including Martin Luther King, Jr., center) began a protest march from Selma to Montgomery.

Black Nationalism and Black Power

At the same time that such civil rights leaders as Dr. Martin Luther King, Jr., fought for racial integration, other African-American leaders emphasized separatism and identification with Africa. Black nationalist sentiment was not something new. During the early nineteenth century, African-American leaders such as Paul Cuffe and Martin Delaney, convinced that African Americans could never achieve true equality in the United States, advocated migration overseas. At the turn of the century, Booker T. Washington and his followers emphasized racial solidarity, economic self-sufficiency, and African-American self-help, and at the end of World War I, millions of African Americans were attracted by Marcus Garvey's call to drop the fight for equality in America and instead "plant the banner of freedom on the great continent of Africa."

One of the most important expressions of the separatist impulse during the 1960s was the rise of the Black Muslims organization, which attracted 100,000 members. Founded in 1931, in the depths of the Depression, the Nation of Islam drew its appeal from among the growing numbers of urban African Americans living in poverty. The Black Muslims ele-

Table 30.3 Black Voter Registration Before and After the Voting Rights Act of 1965			
State	1960	1966	Percent Increase
Alabama	66,000	250,000	278.8
Arkansas	73,000	115,000	57.5
Florida	183,000	303,000	65.6
Georgia	180,000	300,000	66.7
Louisiana	159,000	243,000	52.8
Mississippi	22,000	175,000	695.4
North Carolina	210,000	282,000	34.3
South Carolina	58,000	191,000	229.3
Tennessee	185,000	225,000	21.6
Texas	227,000	400,000	76.2
Virginia	100,000	205,000	105.0

Source: U.S. Bureau of the Census, *Statistical Abstract of the United States: 1982–83* (103d edition) Washington, D.C., 1982.

vated racial separatism into a religious doctrine and declared that whites were doomed to destruction. "The white devil's day is over," leader Elijah Muhammad cried. "He was given six thousand years to rule. . . . He's already used up most trapping and murdering the black nations by the hundreds of thousands. Now he's worried, worried about the black man getting his revenge." Unless whites acceded to the Muslim demand for a separate territory for themselves, Muhammad said, "Your entire race will be destroyed and removed from this earth by Almighty God. And those black men who are still trying to integrate will inevitably be destroyed along with the whites."

The Black Muslims did more than vent anger and frustration. The organization was also a vehicle of African-American uplift and self-help. It called upon African Americans to "wake up, clean up, and stand up" in order to achieve true freedom and independence. To root out any behavior that conformed to racist stereotypes, the Muslims forbade eating pork and cornbread, drinking alcohol, and smoking cigarettes. Muslims also emphasized the creation of businesses.

The most controversial exponent of black nationalism was Malcolm X. The son of a Baptist minister who had been an organizer for Marcus Garvey's Universal Negro Improvement Association, he was born Malcolm Little in Omaha, Nebraska, but grew up in Lansing, Michigan. A reformed drug addict and criminal, Malcolm X learned about the Black Muslims in a maximum-security prison. After his release in 1952, he adopted the name Malcolm X to replace "the white slave-master name which had been imposed upon my paternal forebears by some blue-eyed devil." He quickly became one of the Black Muslims' most eloquent speakers, preaching a message of black nationalism and black pride. Condemned by some whites as a demagogue for such statements as "If ballots won't work, bullets will," Malcolm X gained widespread public notoriety by attacking Dr. Martin Luther King, Jr., as a "chump" and an Uncle Tom, by advocating self-defense against white violence, and by emphasizing black political power.

Malcolm X's main message was that discrimination led many African Americans to despise themselves. "The worst crime the white man has committed," he said, "has been to teach us to hate ourselves." Self-hatred, claimed Malcolm X, had caused many African Americans to lose their identity and become involved in crime, drug addiction, and alcoholism.

In March 1964 (after he violated an order from Elijah Muhammad and publicly rejoiced at the assassination of President John F. Kennedy), Malcolm X withdrew from Elijah Muhammad's organization and set up

Malcolm X, frustrated with moderate civil rights advocates, spoke sharply against racism and called for African-American self-defense against white violence. In 1964, he founded the Organization of Afro-American Unity, which was socialist in its philosophy.

the Organization of Afro-Americans. Less than a year later, his life ended in bloodshed. On February 21, 1965, in front of 400 followers, he was shot and killed, allegedly by followers of Black Muslim leader Elijah Muhammad, as he prepared to give a speech in New York City.

Inspired by Malcolm X's example, young black activists increasingly challenged the traditional leadership of the civil rights movement and its philosophy of nonviolence. The single greatest contributor to the growth of militancy was the violence perpetrated by white racists. One of the most publicized incidents took place in June 1964, when three young civil rights workers—two whites, Andrew Goodman and Michael Schwerner, and one African American, James Chaney—disappeared near Philadelphia, Mississippi. Six weeks after they were reported missing, their bodies were found buried under a dam; all three had been beaten, then shot. In December, the sheriff and deputy sheriff of Neshoba County, Mississippi, along with 19 others, were arrested on charges of violating the three men's civil rights, but just six days later the charges were dropped. David Dennis, a civil rights worker, spoke at James Chaney's funeral. He angrily declared, "I'm sick and tired of going to the funerals of black men who have been murdered by white men. . . . I've got vengeance in my heart."

In 1966 two key civil rights organizations—SNCC and CORE—embraced black nationalism. Stokely Carmichael, elected chairman of SNCC in May, proceeded to transform SNCC from an interracial organization committed to nonviolence and integration into an all-black organization committed to "black power." "Integration is irrelevant," declared Carmichael. "Political and economic power is what the black people have to have." Although Carmichael initially denied that "black power" implied racial separatism, he eventually called on African Americans to form their own separate political organizations. In July 1966—one month after James Meredith, the black air force veteran who had integrated the University of Mississippi, was ambushed and shot (but survived) while marching for voting rights in Mississippi—CORE also endorsed black power and repudiated nonviolence.

Of all the groups advocating racial separatism and black power, the Black Panther party received the widest publicity. Formed in October 1966, in Oakland, California, the Black Panther party was an armed revolutionary socialist organization advocating self-determination for urban ghettoes. "Black men," declared one party member, must unite to overthrow their white "oppressors," becoming "like panthers—smiling, cunning, scientific, striking by night and sparing no one!" The Black Panthers gained public notoriety by entering the gallery of the California State Assembly brandishing guns and by following police to prevent police harassment and brutality toward African Americans.

Separatism and black nationalism attracted no more than a small minority of African Americans. Public opinion polls indicated that only about 15 percent of African Americans identified themselves as separatists and that the overwhelming majority of African Americans considered Martin Luther King, Jr., their favored spokesperson. The older civil rights organizations such as the NAACP rejected separatism and black power, viewing it as an abandonment of the goals of nonviolence and integration.

Yet despite their relatively small following, black power advocates exerted a powerful and positive influence upon the civil rights movement. In addition to giving birth to a host of community self-help organizations, supporters of black power spurred the creation of black studies programs in colleges and universities and encouraged African Americans to take pride in their racial background and recognize that "black is beautiful." A growing number of African Americans began to wear "Afro" hairstyles and take African or Islamic surnames. Singer James Brown captured the new spirit: "Say it loud—I'm black and I'm proud."

In an effort to maintain support among more militant African Americans, civil rights leaders began to address the problems of the lower classes who lived in the nation's cities. By the mid-1960s Martin Luther King, Jr., had

A major achievement of the black power movement was an increase in educational opportunities for minorities in universities across the country; and it also spurred the creation of black studies programs in higher education.

The Civil Rights Movement Moves North

On August 11, 1965, five days after President Lyndon Johnson signed the Voting Rights Act, accusations of police brutality following the arrest of a 21-year-old for drunk driving ignited a riot in Watts, a predominantly black section of Los Angeles. The violence lasted five days and resulted in 34 deaths, 3900 arrests, and the destruction of over 744 buildings and 200 businesses in a 20-square-mile area. Rioters smashed windows, hurled bricks and bottles from rooftops, and stripped store shelves.

Over the next four summers, the nation's inner cities experienced a wave of violence and rioting. The worst violence occurred during the summer of 1967, when riots occurred in 127 cities. In Newark 26 persons lost their lives, over 1500 were injured, and 1397 were arrested. In Detroit 43 people died, $500 million in property was destroyed, and 14 square miles were gutted by fire. The last major wave occurred following the assassination of Martin Luther King, Jr., in Memphis, Tennessee, on April 4, 1968. Violence erupted in 168 cities, leaving 46 dead, 3500 injured, and $40 million worth of damage. In Washington, D.C., fires burned within three blocks of the White House.

In 1968 President Johnson appointed a commission to examine the causes of the race riots of the preceding three summers. Led by Illinois Governor Otto Kerner, the commission attributed racial violence to "white racism" and its heritage of discrimination and exclusion. Joblessness, poverty, a lack of political power, decaying and dilapidated housing, police brutality, and poor schools bred a sense of frustration and rage that had exploded into violence. The commission warned that unless major steps were taken, the United States would inevitably become "two societies, one black, one white—separate and unequal."

Until 1964 most white Northerners regarded race as a peculiarly Southern problem that could be solved by extending political and civil rights to Southern African Americans. Beginning in 1964 the nation learned that

begun to move toward the political left. He said it did no good to be allowed to eat in a restaurant if you had no money to pay for a hamburger. King denounced the Vietnam War as "an enemy of the poor," described the United States as "the greatest purveyor of violence in the world today," and predicted that "the bombs that [Americans] are dropping in Vietnam will explode at home in inflation and unemployment." He urged a radical redistribution of wealth and political power in the United States in order to provide medical care, jobs, and education for all of the country's people. And he spoke of the need for a second "March on Washington" by "waves of the nation's poor and disinherited," who would "stay until America responds ... [with] positive action." The time had come for radical measures "to provide jobs and income for the poor."

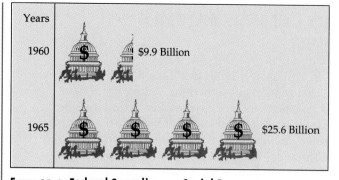

FIGURE 30.2 Federal Spending on Social Programs, Excluding Social Security

discrimination and racial prejudice were nationwide problems, that African Americans were demanding not just desegregation in the South but equality in all parts of the country. The nation also learned that resistance to demands for equal rights was not confined to the Deep South, but existed in the North as well.

In the North, African Americans suffered not from de jure (legal) segregation, but from de facto discrimination in housing, schooling, and employment—discrimination that lacked the overt sanction of law. "De facto segregation," wrote James Baldwin, "means that Negroes are segregated but nobody did it." The most obvious example of de facto segregation was the fact that the overwhelming majority of northern black schoolchildren attended predominantly black inner-city schools while most white children attended schools with a majority of whites. In 1968—14 years after the *Brown* v. *Board of Education* decision—federal courts began to order busing as a way to deal with de facto segregation brought about by housing patterns. In April 1971 in the case of *Swann* v. *Charlotte-Mecklenburg Board of Education,* the Supreme Court upheld "bus transportation as a tool of school desegregation."

The Great Society and the Drive for Equality

Lyndon B. Johnson had a vision for America. Believing that problems of housing, income, employment, and health were ultimately a fed-

eral responsibility, Johnson used the weight of the presidency and his formidable political skills to enact the most impressive array of reform legislation since the days of Franklin Roosevelt. He envisioned a society without poverty or discrimination, in which all Americans enjoyed equal educational and job opportunities. He called his vision the "Great Society."

A major feature of Johnson's Great Society was the "War on Poverty." The federal government raised the minimum wage and enacted programs to train poorer Americans for new and better jobs, including the 1964 Manpower Development and Training Act and the Economic Opportunity Act, which established such programs as the Job Corps and the Neighborhood Youth Corps. To assure adequate housing, in 1966 Congress adopted the Model Cities Act to attack urban decay, set up a cabinet-level Department of Housing and Urban Development, and began a program of rent supplements.

To promote education, Congress passed the Higher Education Act in 1965 providing student loans and scholarships, the Elementary and Secondary Schools Act of 1965 to pay for textbooks, and the Educational Opportunity Act of 1968 to help the poor finance college educations. To address the nation's health needs, the Child Health Improvement and Protection Act of 1968 provided for pre-

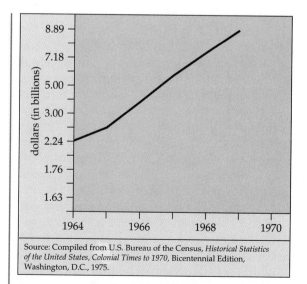

Source: Compiled from U.S. Bureau of the Census, *Historical Statistics of the United States, Colonial Times to 1970,* Bicentennial Edition, Washington, D.C., 1975.

FIGURE 30.3 Federal Aid to Education, 1964–1970

natal and postnatal care, the Medicaid Act of 1968 paid for the medical expenses of the poor, and Medicare, established in 1965, extended medical insurance to older Americans under the Social Security system.

Johnson also prodded Congress to pass a broad spectrum of civil rights laws, ranging from the Civil Rights Act of 1964 and the Voting Rights Act of 1965 to the 1968 Fair Housing Act barring discrimination in the sale or rental of housing. In 1965, LBJ issued an executive order requiring government contractors to ensure that job applicants and employees were not discriminated against. It required all contractors to prepare an "affirmative action plan" to achieve these goals.

Johnson broke many other color barriers. In 1966, he named the first black cabinet member and appointed the first black woman to the federal bench. In 1967 he appointed Thurgood Marshall to become the first African American to serve on the Supreme Court. The first southerner to reside in the White House in half a century, Johnson showed a stronger commitment to improving the position of African Americans than any previous president.

When President Johnson announced his Great Society program in 1964, he promised substantial reductions in the number of Americans living in poverty. When he left office, he could legitimately argue that he had delivered on his promise. In 1960, 40 million Americans, 20 percent of the population, were classified as poor. By 1969, their number had fallen to 24 million, 12 percent of the population. Johnson also pledged to qualify the poor for new and better jobs, to extend health insurance to the poor and elderly to cover hospital and doctor costs, and to provide better housing for low-income families. Here too Johnson delivered. Infant mortality among the poor, which had barely declined between 1950 and 1965, fell by one-third in the decade after 1965 as a result of expanded federal medical and nutritional programs. Before 1965, 20 percent of the poor had never seen a doctor; by 1970 the figure had been cut to 8 percent. The proportion of families living in houses lacking indoor plumbing also declined steeply, from 20 percent in 1960 to 11 percent a decade later.

Although critics argued that Johnson took a shotgun approach to reform and pushed

Prior to being named the first black Supreme Court justice in 1967, Thurgood Marshall had presented the legal arguments against school segregation before the Supreme Court that resulted in the *Brown* v. *Board of Education of Topeka* decision.

poorly thought-out bills through Congress, supporters responded that at least Johnson tried to move toward a more compassionate society. For African Americans during the 1960s median family income rose 53 percent; employment in professional, technical, and clerical occupations doubled; and average educational attainment increased by four years. The proportion of African Americans below the poverty line fell from 55 percent in 1960 to 27 percent in 1968. The unemployment rate fell 34 percent. The country had taken major strides toward extending equality of opportunity to African Americans. The number of whites below the poverty line also dropped dramatically, and such poverty-plagued regions as Appalachia made significant economic strides.

White Backlash

Ghetto rioting, the rise of black militancy, and resentment over Great Society social legislation combined to produce a backlash among many whites. Commitment to granting African Americans full equality declined. In the wake of the riots, many whites fled the nation's cities. The Census Bureau estimated that 900,000 whites moved each year from central cities to the suburbs between 1965 and 1970.

The 1968 Republican candidate Richard Nixon promised to eliminate "wasteful" federal antipoverty programs and to name "strict constructionists" to the Supreme Court. As president, Nixon moved quickly to keep his commitments. In an effort to curb Great Society social programs, Nixon did away with the Model Cities program and the Office of Economic Opportunity. "The time may have come," declared a Nixon aide, "when the issue of race could benefit from a period of benign neglect." The administration urged Congress not to extend the Voting Rights Act of 1965 and to end a fair housing enforcement program.

Nixon also made a series of Supreme Court appointments that brought to an end the liberal activist era of the Warren Court. During the 1960s, the Supreme Court greatly increased the ability of criminal defendants to defend themselves. In *Mapp* v. *Ohio* (1961), the high court ruled that evidence secured by the police through unreasonable searches must be excluded from trial. In *Gideon* v. *Wainwright* (1963), it declared that indigent defendants have a right to a court-appointed attorney. In *Escobedo* v. *Illinois* (1964), it ruled that suspects being interrogated by police have a right to legal counsel.

As president, Nixon promised to alter the balance between the rights of criminal defendants and society's rights. He selected Warren Burger, a moderate conservative, to replace Earl Warren as chief justice of the Supreme Court and then nominated two conservative white Southerners for a second court vacancy, only to have both nominees rejected (one for financial improprieties, the other for alleged insensitivities to civil rights). He eventually named four justices to the high court: Burger, Harry Blackmun, Lewis Powell, and William Rehnquist.

Under Chief Justice Burger and his successor William Rehnquist, the Supreme Court clarified the remedies that can be used to correct past racial discrimination. In 1974 the Court limited the use of school busing for purposes of racial desegregation by declaring that busing could not take place across school district lines. In the landmark 1978 case, *Bakke* v. *Regents of the University of California*, the Court held that educational institutions could take race into account when screening applicants but could not use rigid racial quotas. The following year, however, the court ruled that employers and unions could legally establish voluntary programs, including the use of quotas, to aid minorities and women in employment.

The Struggle Continues

Over the past quarter-century, African Americans have made impressive social and economic gains, yet full equality remains an unrealized dream. State-sanctioned segregation in restaurants, hotels, courtrooms, libraries, drinking fountains, and public washrooms was eliminated and many barriers to equal opportunity were shattered. In political representation, educational attainment, and representation in white collar and professional occupations, African Americans have made striking gains. Between 1960 and 1988 the number of African-American officeholders swelled from just 300 to nearly 6600 and the proportion of African Americans in professional positions quadrupled. African-American mayors have governed many of the nation's largest cities, including Chicago, Detroit, Los Angeles, Philadelphia, and Washington, D.C.

Respect for African-American culture has also grown. The number of African-American performers on television and in film has grown, though most still appear in comedies and crime shows. African Americans also compose and perform much of the country's popular music, but one particular form of musical expression—rap—provoked calls for censorship from those who believed that its lyrics espoused violence.

Nevertheless, millions of African Americans still do not share fully in the promise of American life. The proportion of lawyers who are black doubled between 1960 and 1990, but it has only gone from 1.3 percent to 3.2 percent. The percentage of physicians who are African American has dropped, from 4.4 percent to 3 percent.

According to census figures, African Americans still suffer twice the unemployment rate of whites and earn only about half as much. The poverty rate among black families is three times that of whites, the same ratio as in the 1950s, and black households earn only about $63 for every $100 a white household earns. More than 50 percent of black children are raised in homes headed by single mothers and almost half of all African-American children

Tom Bradley, the son of a sharecropper, became the first black mayor of Los Angeles in 1973, winning more than 56 percent of the total vote.

are born into families earning less than the poverty level (compared to 22 percent of the population as a whole).

Separation of the races in housing and schooling remains widespread. Nationally, less than a quarter of all African Americans live in integrated neighborhoods and only about 38 percent of African-American children attend racially integrated schools. And despite great gains in political clout, African Americans still do not hold political offices in proportion to their share of the population. In 1990 there were only 400 African-American legislators (state and federal), against 7335 white legislators, and altogether African Americans still make up less than 2 percent of the nation's officeholders.

Although the United States has eliminated many obstacles to progress in civil rights, reformers maintain that much remains to be done before the country attains Martin Luther King's dream of a nation where "all of God's children, black man and white man, Jew and Gentile, Protestant and Catholic, will be able to join hands and sing in the words of the old Negro spiritual, 'Free at Last, Free at Last, Thank God Almighty, I'm Free at Last.' "

THE YOUTH REVOLT

During the 1960s, one age group of Americans loomed larger than any other: youth. Their skepticism of corporate and bureaucratic authority, their strong emotional identification with the underprivileged, and their intense desire for stimulation and instant gratification shaped the nation's politics, dress, music, and film. Unlike their parents, who had grown up amid the hardships of the Depression and the patriotic sacrifices of World War II, young people of the 1960s grew up during a period of rapid economic growth. Feeling a deep sense of economic security, they sought personal fulfillment and tended to dismiss their parents' generation's success-oriented lives. "Never trust anyone over 30," went a popular saying.

Never before had young people been so numerous or so well-educated. During the

1960s, there was a sudden explosion in the number of teenagers and young adults. As a result of the depressed birthrates during the 1930s and the postwar baby boom, the number of young people aged 14 to 25 jumped 40 percent in a decade, until they constituted 20 percent of the nation's population. The nation's growing number of young people received far more schooling than their parents. Over 75 percent graduated from high school and nearly 40 percent went on to higher education.

At no earlier time in American history had the gulf between generations seemed so wide. Blue jeans, long hair, psychedelic drugs, casual sex, hippie communes, campus demonstrations, and rock music all became symbols of the distance separating youth from the world of conventional adulthood.

Tom Hayden (right) was a key figure in the student activism of the 1960s. Here Hayden and fellow activists Abbie Hoffman (left) and Jerry Rubin (center) address a crowd in Chicago on the day in 1969 that conspiracy indictments were handed down to the Chicago Seven.

The New Left

Late in the spring of 1962, five dozen college students gathered at a lakeside camp near Port Huron, Michigan, to discuss politics. For four days and nights the members of an obscure student group known as Students for a Democratic Society (SDS) talked passionately about such topics as civil rights, foreign policy, and the quality of American life. At 5 o'clock in the morning of June 16 the gathering ended when the participants agreed on a political platform that expressed their sentiments. This manifesto, one of the pivotal political documents of the 1960s, became known as the Port Huron Statement.

The goal set forward in the Port Huron Statement was the creation of a radically democratic political movement in the United States that rejected hierarchy and bureaucracy. In its most important paragraphs, the document called for "participatory democracy"—direct individual involvement in the decisions that affected their lives. This notion would become the battle cry of the student movement of the 1960s—a movement that came to be known as the New Left.

The Port Huron Statement's chief author was Tom Hayden. Born in 1939, in Royal Oak, Michigan, a predominantly Catholic working-class suburb of Detroit, he was, from an early age, unusually politically conscious and questioning of established authority. In high school, his idols were critics of conventional society, such as J. D. Salinger's Holden Caulfield and *Mad Magazine's* Alfred E. Neuman. He then attended the University of Michigan, read Jack Kerouac's beat novel *On the Road,* hitchhiked across the country, and witnessed student protests at the University of California at Berkeley. He spent much of 1961 in the South and was once badly beaten by local whites during civil rights protests in McComb, Mississippi.

During the 1960s, Tom Hayden became one of the key figures in the New Left. In 1968 he flew to North Vietnam as a protest against the Vietnam War. The next year he gained further notoriety as one of the "Chicago Seven" defendants who were acquitted of charges of conspiring to disrupt the 1968 Democratic presidential convention. Briefly, Hayden dropped out of politics, moved to Venice, California, and lived under a pseudonym. Later, he married actress Jane Fonda and became a member of the California legislature.

During the 1960s, thousands of young college students, like Tom Hayden, became politically active. The first issue to spark student radicalism was the impersonality of the modern university, which many students criticized for being too bureaucratic and impersonal. Students questioned university requirements, restrictions on student political activities, and dormitory rules limiting the hours that male and female students could socialize with each other. Restrictions on students handing out political pamphlets on university property led to the first campus demonstrations that broke out at the University of California at Berkeley and soon spread to other campuses.

Involvement in the civil rights movement in the South initiated many students into radical politics. In the early 1960s, many white students from northern universities began to participate in voter registration drives, freedom schools, sit-ins, and freedom rides in order to help desegregate the South. For the first time, many witnessed poverty, discrimination, and violence first-hand.

Student radicalism also drew inspiration from a literature of social criticism that flourished in the 1950s. During that decade, many of the most popular films, novels, and writings aimed at young people criticized conventional middle-class life. Popular films, like *Rebel Without a Cause,* and popular novels, like J. D. Salinger's *Catcher in the Rye,* celebrated

sensitive, directionless, alienated youths unable to conform to the conventional adult values of suburban and corporate America. Sophisticated works of social criticism by such maverick sociologists, psychologists, and economists as Herbert Marcuse, Norman O. Brown, Paul Goodman, Michael Harrington, and C. Wright Mills, documented the growing concentration of power in the hands of social elites, the persistence of poverty in a land of plenty, and the stresses and injustices in America's social order.

Above all, student radicalism owed its support to student opposition to the Vietnam War. In 1965 an SDS antiwar march attracted at least 15,000 protesters to Washington and commanded wide press attention. Over the next three years, opposition to the war brought thousands of new members to SDS; by 1968 the organization claimed at least 50,000 members. In addition to its antiwar activities, SDS also tried to organize a democratic "interracial movement of the poor" in northern city neighborhoods.

Many members of SDS quickly grew frustrated by the slow pace of social change and began to embrace violence as a tool to transform society. After 1968 SDS rapidly tore itself apart as an effective political force, and its final convention in 1969 degenerated into a

In the late summer of 1964 the first major student demonstrations took place at the University of California at Berkeley. Student protests against war, racism, and poverty continued throughout the country into the 1970s.

shouting match between radicals and moderates. That same year the Weathermen, a surviving faction of SDS, attempted to launch a guerrilla war in the streets of Chicago—an incident known as the "Days of Rage"—to "tear pig city apart." Finally, in 1970 three members of the Weathermen blew themselves up in a Greenwich Village brownstone trying to make a bomb out of a stick of dynamite and an alarm clock.

Throughout the 1960s, the SDS and other radical student organizations claimed to speak for the nation's youth, and in thousands of editorials and magazine articles, journalists accepted this claim. In fact, the SDS represented only a small minority of college students, who themselves composed a minority of the country's youth. Far more young Americans voted for George Wallace in 1968 than joined SDS, and most college students during the decade spent far more time studying and enjoying the college experience than protesting. Nevertheless, radical students did help to draw the nation's attention to the problem of racism in American society and the moral issues involved in the Vietnam War. In that sense, their impact far exceeded their numbers.

The Making and Unmaking of a Counterculture

The New Left had a series of heroes—ranging from Marx, Lenin, Ho, and Mao to Fidel, Che, and other revolutionaries. It also had its own uniforms, rituals, and music. Faded blue work shirts and jeans, wire-rimmed glasses, and work shoes were de rigueur even if the dirtiest work the wearer performed was taking notes in a college class. The proponents of the New Left emphasized their sympathy with the working class—an emotion that was seldom reciprocated—and listened to labor songs that once fired the hearts of unionists. The political protest folk music of Greenwich Village—of Phil Ochs, Bob Dylan, and their ilk—inspired the New Left.

But the New Left was only one part of youth protest during the 1960s. While the New Left labored to change the world and remake American society, other youths attempted to alter themselves and reorder consciousness. Variously labeled the counterculture, hippies, or flower children, they had their own heroes, music, dress, and approach to life.

In theory, supporters of the counterculture rejected individualism, competition, and capitalism. Adopting rather unsystematically ideas from oriental religions, they sought to become one with the universe. Rejection of monogamy and the traditional nuclear family gave way to the tribal or communal ideal, where members renounced individualism and private property and shared food, work, and sex. In such a community, love was a general abstract ideal rather than a focused emotion.

The quest for oneness with the universe led many youths to experiment with hallucinogenic drugs. LSD had a particularly powerful allure. Under its influence, poets, musicians, politicians, and thousands of other Americans claimed to have tapped into an all-powerful spiritual force. Timothy Leary, the Harvard professor who became the leading prophet of LSD, asserted that the drug would unlock the universe.

Although LSD was outlawed in 1966, use of the drug continued to spread. Perhaps some takers discovered profound truths, but by the late 1960s drugs had done more harm than good. The history of the Haight-Ashbury section of San Francisco illustrated the problems caused by drugs. In 1967 Haight was the center of the "counterculture," the home of the "flower children." In the "city of love" hippies ingested LSD, smoked pot, listened to "acid rock," and proclaimed the dawning of a new age. Yet the area was suffering from severe problems. High levels of racial violence, venereal disease, rape, drug overdoses, and poverty ensured more bad trips than good.

Even music, which along with drugs and sex formed the counterculture trinity, failed to alter human behavior. In 1969 journalists hailed the Woodstock Music Festival as a symbol of love. But a few months later a group of Hell's Angels violently interrupted the Altamont Raceway music festival. As Mick Jagger sang "Sympathy for the Devil" an Angel stabbed an African-American man to death.

Like the New Left, the counterculture fell victim to its own excesses. Sex, drugs, and rock and roll did not solve the problems facing the United States. And by the end of the 1960s the counterculture had lost its force.

LIBERATION MOVEMENTS

The struggle of African Americans for racial justice inspired a host of other groups to seek full equality. Women, Mexican Americans, Native Americans, and many other deprived groups protested against discrimination and organized to promote social change.

Women's Liberation

Hosted by Jack Bailey, a gravel-voiced former carnival barker, "Queen For a Day" was one of the most popular daytime television shows of the 1950s. Five times a week, three women, each with a hard-luck story, recited their tales of woe—diseases, retarded children, poverty—and the studio audience, with the aid of an applause meter, decided which woman was the most miserable, and she became "Queen for a Day." Bailey put a crown on her head, wrapped her in a mink coat (which she got to keep for 24 hours), and told her about the new Cadillac she would get to drive (also for the next 24 hours). And then came gifts for the queen: a year's supply of Helena Rubinstein cosmetics; a Clairol permanent and makeover by a Hollywood makeup artist; and the electric appliances thought to be necessary for female happiness—a toaster oven, automatic washer, automatic dryer, and an iron. Altogether, everything a woman needed to be a prettier and better housewife.

One woman in the television audience was Betty Friedan. A 1942 honors graduate of Smith College and former psychology Ph.D. candidate at the University of California at Berkeley, Friedan had quit graduate school, married, moved to the New York suburbs, and bore three children in rapid succession. American culture told her that husband, house, children, and electric appliances were

The popular television show "Queen for a Day" reinforced established female sex roles by providing winners with everything they needed to be better housewives. Here, host Jack Bailey crowns a "Queen for a Day."

true happiness. But Friedan was not happy. And she was not alone.

In 1957 Friedan sent out a questionnaire to fellow members of her college graduating class. The replies amazed her. Again and again, she found women suffering from "a sense of dissatisfaction." Over the next five years, Friedan interviewed other women at PTA meetings and suburban cocktail parties, and she repeatedly found an unexplainable sense of melancholy and incompleteness. "Sometimes a woman would say 'I feel empty somehow . . . incomplete.' Or she would say, 'I feel as if I don't exist.' "

Friedan was not the only observer to detect a widespread sense of discontent among American women. Doctors identified a new female malady, the housewife's syndrome, characterized by a mixture of frustration and exhaustion. CBS broadcast a television documentary entitled "The Trapped Housewife." *Newsweek* magazine noted that the nation's supposedly happy housewife was "dissatisfied with a lot that women of other lands can only dream of. Her discontent is deep, pervasive, and impervious to the superficial remedies which are offered at every hand." The *New York Times* editorialized, "Many young women . . . feel stifled in their homes." *Redbook* magazine ran an article entitled "Why Young Mothers Feel Trapped" and asked for examples of this problem. It received 24,000 replies.

Why, Friedan asked, were American women so discontented? In 1963 she published her answer in a book entitled *The Feminine Mystique.* This book, one of the most influential books ever written by an American, helped launch a new movement for women's liberation. The book touched a nerve, but the origins of the movement lay deeper, in the role of females in American society.

Sources of Discontent

During the 1950s, many American women reacted against the poverty of the Depression and the upheavals of World War II by placing renewed emphasis on family life. Young women married earlier than had their mothers, had more children, and bore them faster. The average marriage age of American women dropped to 20, a record low. The fertility rate rose 50 percent between 1940 and 1950—producing a population growth rate approaching that of India. Growing numbers of women decided to forsake higher education or a career outside the home and achieve emotional fulfillment as wives and mothers. A 1952 advertisement for Gimbel's department store expressed the prevailing point of view. "What's college?" the ad asked. "That's where girls who are above cooking and sewing go to meet a man so they can spend their lives cooking and sewing." By "marrying at an earlier age, rearing larger families," and purchasing a house in the suburbs, young women believed, in the words of *McCall's* magazine, that they could find their "deepest satisfaction."

Politicians, educators, psychologists, and the mass media all echoed the view that women would find their highest fulfillment managing a house and caring for children. Adlai Stevenson, the Democratic presidential nominee in 1952 and 1956, told the graduating women at Smith College in 1955 that their role in life was to "influence us, men and boys"

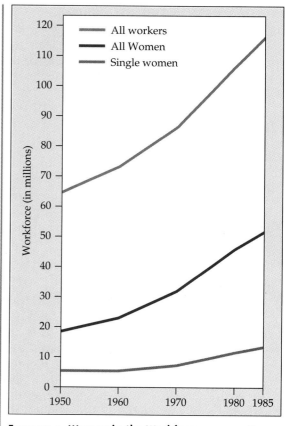

FIGURE 30.4 **Women in the Workforce, 1950–1985**

and "restore valid, meaningful purpose to life in your home." Many educators agreed with the president of Barnard College, who argued that women could not compete with men in the workplace because they "had less physical strength, a lower fatigue point, and a less stable nervous system." Women's magazines pictured housewives as happy with their tasks and depicted career women as neurotic, unhappy, and dissatisfied.

Already underway, however, were dramatic social changes that would contribute to a rebirth of feminism. A dramatic upsurge took place during the 1950s in women's employment and education. More and more married women entered the labor force, and by 1960 the proportion of married women working outside the home was one in three. The number of women receiving college degrees also rose. The proportion of bachelor's and master's degrees received by women rose from just 24 percent in 1950 to over 35 percent a decade later. Meanwhile, beginning in 1957 the birthrate began to drop as women elected to have fewer children. A growing discrepancy had begun to appear between the popular image of women as full-time housewives and mothers and the actual realities of many women's lives.

Feminism Reborn

In 1960 women played a limited role in American government. Although women comprised about half of the nation's voters, there were no female Supreme Court justices, federal appeals court justices, governors, cabinet officers, or ambassadors. Only 2 of 100 U.S. senators and 15 of 435 representatives were women. Of 307 federal district judges, 2 were women. Of 7700 members of state legislatures, 234 were women. Nor were these figures atypical. Only 2 American women had ever been elected governor, only 2 had ever served in a president's cabinet, and only 6 had ever served as an ambassador.

Economically, women workers were concentrated in low-paying service and factory jobs. The overwhelming majority worked as secretaries, waitresses, beauticians, teachers, nurses, and librarians. Only 3.5 percent of the nation's lawyers, 10 percent of the nation's scientists, and fewer than 2 percent of the nation's leading business executives were women.

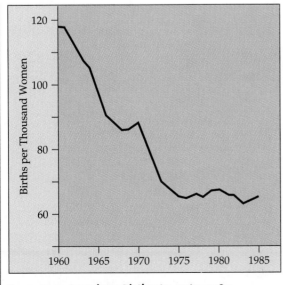

FIGURE 30.5 **American Birthrate, 1960–1985**

Lower pay for women doing the same work as men was commonplace. One out of every three companies had separate pay scales for male and female workers. A female bank teller typically made $15 a week less than a man with the same amount of experience, and a female laundry worker made 49 cents an hour less than her male counterpart. Altogether, the earnings of women working full-time averaged only about 60 percent of those of men.

In many parts of the country, the law discriminated against women. In three states—Alabama, Mississippi, and South Carolina—women could not sit on juries. Many states restricted married women's right to make contracts, sell property, engage in business, control their own earnings, and make wills. Six states gave fathers preference in the custody of young children after a divorce. In practically every state, men had a legal right to have intercourse with their wives whenever they chose to do so.

The mass media often portrayed women in an unrealistic and stereotyped way. Popular magazines like *Reader's Digest* and popular television shows like "I Love Lucy" often depicted women as stupid or foolish, jealous of other women, irresponsible about money, and overanxious to marry.

In December 1961 President John F. Kennedy placed the issue of women's rights on the national political agenda. Eager to fulfill a debt to women voters—he had not yet named a single woman to a policy-making position—Kennedy established a President's Commission on the Status of Women, the first presidential panel ever to examine the status of American women. Chaired by Eleanor Roosevelt, the commission issued its report in 1963, the year that Betty Friedan published *The Feminine Mystique*. The report's recommendations included a call for an end to all legal restrictions on married women's right to own property, to enter into business, and to make contracts; equal opportunity in employment; and greater availability of child-care services.

The most important reform to grow out of the commission's investigations was the 1963 Equal Pay Act, which required equal pay for men and women who performed the same jobs under equal conditions. The Equal Pay

CÉSAR CHÁVEZ AND *LA CAUSA*

IN early April 1962, a 35-year-old community organizer named César Estrada Chávez set out to single-handedly organize impoverished migrant farm laborers in the California grape fields. He, his wife, and their eight children packed their belongings into a dilapidated 9-year-old station wagon, and moved to Delano, California, a town of 12,000 that was the center of the nation's table-grape industry. Over the next two years, Chávez spent his entire lifetime savings of $1200 creating a small social service organization for Delano's field laborers; it offered immigration counseling, citizenship classes, funeral benefits, credit to buy cars and homes, assistance with voter registration, and a cooperative to buy tires and gasoline. As the emblem of his new organization, the National Farm Workers Association, Chávez chose a black Aztec eagle inside a white circle on a red background.

Chávez's sympathy for the plight of migrant farmworkers came naturally. He was born in Yuma, Arizona, in 1927, one of five children of Mexican immigrants. When he was 10 years old, his parents lost their small farm; he, his brothers and sisters, and his parents hoed beets, picked grapes, and harvested peaches and figs in Arizona and California. There were times when the family had to sleep in its car or camp under bridges. When young César was able to attend school (he attended more than 30 schools as a child), he was often shunted into special classrooms set aside for Mexican-American children.

In 1944, when he was 17, Chávez joined the navy, and served for two years on a destroyer escort in the Pacific. After World War II ended, he married and spent two and a half years as a sharecropper raising strawberries. That was followed by work in apricot and prune orchards and in a lumber camp. Then in 1952 his life took a fateful turn. He joined the Community Service Organization (CSO), which wanted to educate and organize the poor so that they could solve their own social and economic problems. After founding CSO chapters in Madera, Bakersfield, and Hanford, California, Chávez became the organization's general director in 1958. Four years later, he broke with the organization when it rejected his proposal to establish a farmworkers union.

Most labor leaders considered Chávez's goal of creating the first successful union of farmworkers in U.S. history an impossible dream. Not only did farm laborers suffer from high rates of illiteracy and poverty (average family earnings were just $2000 in 1965), they also experienced persistently high rates of unemployment (traditionally around 19 percent) and were divided into a variety of ethnic groups (Mexican, Arab, Filipino, and Puerto Rican). Making unionization even more difficult were the facts that farmworkers rarely remained in one locality for very long, and they were easily replaced by inexpensive Mexican day laborers, known as *braceros*, who were trucked into California and the Southwest at harvest time.

Moreover, farmworkers were specifically excluded from the protection of the National Labor Relations Act of 1935. Unlike other American workers, farmworkers were not guaranteed the right to organize, had no guarantee of a minimum wage, and had no federally guaranteed standards of work in the fields. State laws requiring toilets, rest periods, and drinking water in the fields were largely ignored.

In September 1965, Chávez was drawn into his first important labor controversy. The Filipino grape pickers went on strike. "All right, Chávez," said one of the Filipino grape pickers' leaders, "are you going to stand beside us, or are you going to scab against us?" Despite his fear that the National Farm Workers Association was not sufficiently well organized to support a strike (it had less than $100 in its strike fund), he assured the Filipino workers that members of his association would not go into the field as strikebreakers. *¡Huelga!*—the Spanish word for strike—became the grape pickers' battle cry.

Within weeks, the labor strike began to attract national attention. Unions, church groups, and civil rights organizations offered financial support for *La Causa*, as the farm workers' movement became known. In March 1966, Chávez led a 250-mile Easter march from Delano to Sacramento to dramatize the plight of migrant farm laborers. That same year, Chávez's National Farm Workers Association merged with an AFL-CIO affiliate to form the United Farm Workers Organizing Committee.

A staunch apostle of nonviolence, Chávez was deeply troubled by violent incidents that marred the strike. Some growers raced tractors along the roadside, covering the strikers with dirt and dust. Others drove spraying machines along the edges of their fields, spraying insecticide and fertilizer on the picketers. Local police officers arrested a minister for reading Jack London's definition of a scab ("a two-legged animal with a corkscrew soul, a water-logged brain, and a combination backbone made of jelly and glue"). Some strikers, in turn, intimidated strikebreakers by pelting them with marbles fired from slingshots and by setting fire to packing crates. One striker tried to drive a car into a group of growers.

In an effort to quell the escalating violence and to atone for the militancy of some union members, Chávez began to fast on February 14, 1968. For five days he kept the fast a secret. Then, in an hour-long speech to striking workers, he explained that continued violence would destroy everything the union stood for. He said that the "truest act of courage, the strongest act of manliness, is to sacrifice ourselves for others in a totally nonviolent struggle for justice." For 21 days he fasted; he lost 35 pounds and his doctor began to fear for his health. He finally agreed to take a small amount of bouillon and grapefruit juice and medication. On March 11, he ended his fast by taking communion and breaking bread with Senator Robert F. Kennedy.

The strike dragged on for three years. To heighten public awareness of the farmworkers' cause, Chávez in 1968 initiated a boycott of table grapes. It was the boycott that pressured many of the growers into settling the strike. An estimated 17 million American consumers went without grapes in support of the farmworkers' bargaining position. By mid-1970, two-thirds of California grapes were grown under contract with Chávez's union.

In the years following its 1970 victory, Chávez's union has been beset by problems from within and without. Union membership dwindled from a high of more than 60,000 in 1972 to a low of 5000 in 1974. (It has since climbed back to around 30,000). Meanwhile, public concern for the plight of migrant farmworkers declined.

Chávez died in 1993, at age 66. To commemorate his legacy, 25,000 people marched for more than two and a half hours to the spot where he had founded the United Farm Workers Union. As a result of Chávez's efforts, the most backbreaking tool used by farmworkers, the short hoe, was eliminated, and the use of many dangerous pesticides in the grape fields was prohibited. His efforts also brought about a 70 percent increase in real wages from 1964 to 1980, and establishment of healthcare benefits, disability insurance, pension plans, and standardized grievance procedures for farmworkers. He helped secure passage of the nation's first agricultural labor relations act in California in 1975, which prohibited growers from firing striking workers or engaging in bad-faith bargaining. Thanks to his efforts, migrant farm laborers won a right held by all other American workers: the right to bargain collectively.

Act was the first federal law to prohibit discrimination on the basis of gender.

The next year, Congress enacted a new weapon in the fight against gender discrimination. Title VII of the 1964 Civil Rights Act prohibited discrimination in hiring or promotion based on race, color, religion, national origin, or sex by private employers and unions. As originally proposed, the bill only outlawed racial discrimination, but in a futile effort to block the measure, Representative Howard Smith of Virginia amended the bill to prohibit discrimination on the basis of sex. Some liberals opposed the amendment on the grounds that it diverted attention from racial discrimination. But it passed in the House of Representatives 168 to 133. "We made it! God Bless America!" shouted a female voice from the House gallery when the amendment passed.

The Civil Rights Act made it illegal for employers to discriminate against women in hiring and promotion unless the employer could show that gender was a "bona fide occupational qualification" (for example, hiring a man as an attendant for a men's restroom). To investigate complaints of employment discrimination, the act set up the Equal Employment Opportunity Commission (EEOC).

At first, the EEOC focused its enforcement efforts on racial discrimination and largely ignored gender discrimination. To pressure the EEOC to enforce the law prohibiting sex discrimination, Betty Friedan and 300 other women formed the National Organization for Women (NOW) in 1966, with Friedan as president. The organization pledged "to take action to bring women into full participation in the mainstream of American society now, exercising all the privileges and responsibilities thereof in truly equal partnership with men." NOW filed suit against the EEOC "to force it to comply with its own government rules." It also sued the country's 1300 largest corporations for sex discrimination, lobbied President Johnson to issue an executive order that would include women within federal affirmative action requirements, and challenged airline policies that required stewardesses to retire after they married or reached the age of 32.

At its second national conference in November 1967, NOW drew up an eight-point bill of rights for women. It called for adoption of an Equal Rights Amendment (ERA) to the Constitution, prohibition of sex discrimination; provision for equal educational, job training, and housing opportunities for women; and repeal of laws limiting access to contraceptive devices and abortion.

Two proposals produced fierce dissension within the new organization. One source of disagreement was the Equal Rights Amendment. The amendment consisted of two dozen words: "Equality of rights under the law shall not be denied or abridged by the United States or by any state on account of sex." It had originally been proposed in 1923 to mark the seventy-fifth anniversary of the Seneca Falls Women's Rights Convention and was submitted to Congress at almost every session. For over 40 years, professional women, who favored the amendment, battled with organized labor and the Women's Bureau of the Labor Department, which opposed the amendment on the ground that it endangered "protective" legislation that set minimum wages and maximum hours for less-skilled women workers.

The other issue that generated controversy was the call for reform of abortion laws. In 1967 only one state—Colorado—had repealed nineteenth-century legal statutes that made abortion a criminal offense. Dissenters believed that NOW should avoid controversial issues that would divert attention away from economic discrimination.

Despite internal disagreements, NOW's membership grew rapidly, reaching 40,000 by 1974 and 175,000 by 1988. The group broadened its attention to include such issues as the plight of poor and minority women, domestic violence, rape, sexual harassment, the role of women in sport, and the rights of lesbians. The organization also claimed a number of achievements and victories, two of which were particularly important. In 1967, NOW persuaded President Lyndon Johnson to issue Executive Order 11375, which prohibited government contractors from discriminating on the basis of sex and required them to take "affirmative action" to ensure that women are properly represented in their workforce. The next year, the EEOC ruled that separate want ads

Women have been involved in protest movements throughout the years. Here women march in support of the Equal Rights Amendment. Failure to achieve ratification by the required three-fourths of states sent the amendment to its final defeat in 1982.

for men and women were a violation of Title VII of the 1964 Civil Rights Act.

Radical Feminism

Alongside NOW, other more radical feminist groups emerged during the 1960s among college students involved in the civil rights movement and the New Left. Women, within these organizations for social change often found themselves treated as "second-class citizens," responsible for kitchen work, typing, and serving "as a sexual supply for their male comrades after hours." "We were the movement secretaries and the shit-workers," one woman recalled; "we were the earth mothers and the sex-objects for the movement's men." In 1964 Ruby Doris Smith Robinson presented an indignant assault on the treatment of women civil rights workers in a paper entitled "The Position of Women in SNCC," to a SNCC staff meeting. Stokely Carmichael reputedly responded, "The only position for women in SNCC is prone."

In 1967 in cities across the country, independent women's groups sprouted up. In the fall, at the first national gathering of women's groups at the National Conference for New Politics, women demanded 51 percent of all committee seats in the name of minority rights. When men refused to meet their demand, the women walked out—signaling the beginning of a critical split between the New Left and the women's movement. The next year, radical women's groups appeared on the front pages of the nation's newspapers when they staged a protest of the Miss America pageant and provided a "freedom trash can," in which women could throw "old bras, girdles, high-heeled shoes, women's magazines, curlers, and other instruments of torture to women." They concluded their rally by crowning a sheep Miss America.

Over the next three years the number of women's liberation groups rapidly multiplied, bearing such names as the Redstockings, WITCH (the Women's International Terrorist Conspiracy from Hell), and the Feminists. By 1970 there were at least 500 women's liberation groups, including 50 in New York, 25 in Boston, 30 in Chicago, and 35 in San Francisco. Women's liberation groups established the first feminist bookstores, shelters for battered women, rape crisis centers, and abortion counseling centers. In 1971 Gloria Steinem and others published *Ms.*, the first national feminist magazine. The first 300,000 copies were sold out in eight days.

Radical new ideas began to fill the air. One women's liberation leader, Ti-Grace Atkinson, denounced marriage as "slavery," "legalized rape," and "unpaid labor." Meanwhile, a host of new words and phrases entered the language, such as "consciousness raising," "Ms.," "bra burning," "sexism," "male chauvinist pig."

On August 26, 1970, the fiftieth anniversary of the ratification of the Nineteenth Amendment, the women's liberation movement dramatically demonstrated its growing strength by mounting a massive Strike for Equality. In New York City, 50,000 women marched down Fifth Avenue; in Boston, 2000 marched; in Chicago, 3000. Members of virtually all feminist groups joined together in a display of unity and strength.

The Growth of Feminist Ideology

Feminists subscribe to no single doctrine or set of goals. All are united, however, by a belief that women have historically occupied a subordinate position in politics, education, and the economic system. Modern feminist thought traces its roots to a book published by French philosopher Simone de Beauvoir in 1949. Entitled *The Second Sex*, the book traced the assumptions, customs, educational practices, jokes, laws, and modes of speech that socialize young women to believe that they are inferior beings.

A decade and a half later, Betty Friedan made another important contribution to the development of feminist ideology. In *The Feminine Mystique*, she analyzed and criticized the role of educators, psychologists, sociologists, and the mass media in conditioning women to believe that they could only find fulfillment as housewives and mothers. By requiring women to subordinate their own individual aspirations to the welfare of their husbands and children, the "feminine mystique" prevented

women from achieving self-fulfillment, which inevitably left them unhappy.

In the years following the publication of *The Feminine Mystique*, feminists developed a large body of literature analyzing the economic, psychological, and social roots of female subordination. It was not until 1970, however, that the more radical feminist writings reached the broader reading public in the form of the publication of Shulamith Firestone's *The Dialectic of Sex*, Germaine Greer's *The Female Eunuch*, and Kate Millett's *Sexual Politics*. These books argued that gender distinctions structure virtually every aspect of individual lives, not only in such areas as law and employment, but also in personal relationships, language, literature, religion, and an individual's self-perceptions. Even more controversially, these works attributed female oppression to men and an ideology of male supremacy. "Women have very little idea how much men hate them," declared Greer. As examples of misogyny these authors cited pornography, grotesque portrayals of women in literature, sexual harassment, wife abuse, and rape.

Since 1970 feminist theory has exploded in many different directions. Today, there are more than 30 national feminist news and opinion magazines along with an additional 20 academic journals dealing with women's issues. Historians, feminist literary and film critics, and physical and social scientists have begun to take insights derived from feminism and ask new questions about women's historical experience, the sex and status differences between women and men, gender role socialization, economic and legal discrimination, and the depiction of women in literature.

The Supreme Court and Sex Discrimination

Despite its conservative image, the Supreme Court under chief justices Warren Burger and William Rehnquist has been active in the area of sex discrimination and women's rights. In contrast to the Warren Court, which ruled on only one major sex discrimination case—upholding a law that excluded women from serving on juries—the Burger and Rehnquist Courts have considered numerous cases involving women's rights.

The Burger Court issued its first important discrimination decision in 1971. In its landmark decision, *Griggs* v. *Duke Power Company,* the Court established the principle that regardless of an employer's intentions, any employment practice is illegal if it has a "disparate" impact on women or minorities and "if it cannot be shown to be related to job performance." In subsequent cases, the Court legitimized the use of statistics in measuring employment discrimination and approved the use of back pay in compensating discrimination victims.

In 1975 the Burger Court reversed the Warren Court by striking down a Louisiana statute calling for all-male juries. In subsequent decisions, the high court ruled against a Utah law setting different ages at which men and women became adults, and overturned an Alabama law setting minimum height and weight requirements for prison guards, standards that disqualified almost all women.

The Court has not yet set an absolute rule that laws and employment practices must treat men and women the same. In 1976 the Court adopted its current standard for sex discrimination. The Court's test is that to be constitutional, a policy that discriminates on the basis of sex must be "substantially related to an important government objective."

The Court's most controversial decision involving women's rights was delivered in 1973 in the case of *Roe* v. *Wade.* A single, pregnant Texas waitress, assigned the pseudonym Jane Roe in order to protect her privacy, brought suit against Dallas district attorney Henry Wade, to prevent him from enforcing a nineteenth-century Texas statute prohibiting abortion. The Court ruled on the woman's behalf and struck down the Texas law and all similar laws in other states. In its ruling, the Court declared that the decision to have an abortion is a private matter of concern only to a woman and her physician, and that only in the last three months of pregnancy could the government limit the right to abortion.

Many Americans—including many Catholic lay and clerical organizations—bitterly opposed the Supreme Court's *Roe* v. *Wade* decision and banded together to form the "right-to-life" movement. The major legislative success of the right-to-life movement was adoption by Congress of the so-called

Right-to-life groups, backed by Protestant fundamentalists, conservatives, and the Catholic church, scored a victory with the Hyde amendment. Prochoice groups, however, helped organize privately funded agencies and clinics to allow women a choice.

Hyde Amendment, which permitted states to refuse to fund abortions for indigent women.

The Equal Rights Amendment

In March 1972 Congress passed an Equal Rights Amendment (ERA) to the United States Constitution, prohibiting sex discrimination, with only 8 dissenting votes in the Senate and 24 in the House. Before the year was over, 22 state had legislatures ratified the ERA. Ratification by 38 states was required before the amendment would be added to the Constitution. Over the next five years, only 13 more states ratified the amendment—and 5 states rescinded their ratification. In 1978, Congress gave proponents of the amendment

39 more months to complete ratification, but no other state gave its approval.

The ERA had been defeated, but why? Initially, opposition came largely from organized labor, which feared that the amendment would eliminate state "protective legislation," that established minimum wages and maximum hours for women workers. Increasingly, however, resistance to the amendment came from women of lower economic and educational status, whose self-esteem and self-image were bound up with being wives and mothers and who wanted to ensure that women who devoted their lives to their families were not accorded lower status than women who worked outside the home.

The leader of the anti-ERA movement was Phyllis Schlafly, a Radcliffe-educated mother

Table 30.4 PERCENTAGE OF FEMALES IN SELECTED OCCUPATIONS

Occupation	1972 (Percentage)	1980 (Percentage)	1989 (Percentage)
Professional/technical	39.3	44.3	45.2
Accountants	21.7	36.2	48.6
Computer specialists	16.8	25.7	35.7
Engineers	0.8	4.0	7.6
Lawyers and judges	3.8	12.8	22.3
Life/physical scientists	10.0	20.3	26.9
Physicians/dentists	9.3	12.9	16.5
Professors	28.0	33.9	38.7
Engineering/science technicians	9.1	17.8	19.2
Writers/artists/entertainers	31.7	39.3	46.0
Sales	41.6	45.3	49.3
Real estate agents/brokers	36.7	50.7	51.0
Clerks, retail	68.9	71.1	81.8
Clerical	75.6	80.1	80.0
Bookkeepers	97.9	90.5	91.7
Clerical supervisors	57.8	70.5	58.2
Office machine operators	71.4	72.6	62.6
Secretaries	99.1	99.1	98.3
Crafts workers	3.6	6.0	8.6
Blue-collar supervisors	6.9	10.8	n/a*
Machinists and jobsetters	0.6	4.0	n/a*
Tool and die makers	0.5	2.8	n/a*
Mechanics (except automobile)	1.0	2.6	3.1

Source: U.S. Bureau of the Census, *Statistical Abstract of the United States: 1982–83* (103d edition), *1991* (111th edition), Washington, D.C., 1982, 1991.

*n/a = not available.

of six from Alton, Illinois. She earned a law degree at the age of 54, wrote nine books (including the 1964 bestseller *A Choice Not an Echo*), and created her own lobbying group, the Eagle Forum. Schlafly argued that the ERA was unnecessary because women were already protected by the Equal Pay Act of 1963 and the Civil Rights Act of 1964, which barred sex discrimination, and that the amendment would outlaw separate public restrooms for men and women and deny wives the right to financial support. She also raised the "women in combat" issue by suggesting that the passage of the ERA would mean that woman would have to fight alongside men during war.

Impact of the Women's Liberation Movement

Since 1960 women have made enormous social gains. Gains in employment have been particularly impressive. During the 1970s, the number of working women climbed 42 percent and much of the increase was in what traditionally was considered "men's" work and professional work. The percentage of lawyers who were women increased by 9 percentage points; the percentage of professors by 6 points; of doctors by 3.6 points. By 1986, women made up 15 percent of the nation's lawyers, 40 percent of all computer programmers, and 29 percent of the country's managers and administrators.

Striking gains have been made in undergraduate and graduate education. Today, for the first time in American history, women constitute a majority of the nation's college students and nearly as many women as men receive master's degrees. In addition, the number of women students receiving degrees from professional schools—including dentistry, law, and medicine—has shot upward, from just 1425 in 1966 to over 20,000 by the early 1990s. Women comprise nearly a third of the students attending law school and medical school.

Women have also made impressive political gains. In 1988 over two dozen women served in Congress, over 80 served as mayors of large cities, and over a thousand served in

state legislatures. In 1984, for the first time, a major political party nominated a woman, Geraldine Ferraro, for the vice presidency. Ten percent of the top appointed offices during the Reagan administration went to women, and Sandra Day O'Connor was named the first woman to sit on the Supreme Court. Three women held cabinet posts and a woman was appointed ambassador to the United Nations. By 1988 over 15,000 women held elective office.

In spite of all that has been achieved, however, problems remain. Most women today continue to work in a relatively small number of traditional "women's" jobs, and a full-time female worker earns only 68 cents for every $1 paid to men. Even more troubling is the fact that large numbers of women live in poverty. The "feminization of poverty" is a trend that has been growing since the 1970s. Today, nearly half of all marriages end in divorce and many others end in legal separation and desertion—and the economic plight of these women is often grave. Families headed by women are four and a half times as likely to be poor as families headed by males. Although female-headed families constitute only 15 percent of the U.S. population, they account for over 50 percent of the poor population.

¡Viva La Raza!

On election day, 1963, hundreds of Mexican Americans in Crystal City, Texas, the "spinach capital of the world," gathered near

Table 30.5 Ratio of Divorces to Marriages, 1890–1987

1890	1–17
1900	1–12
1910	1–11
1920	1–7
1930	1–5
1940	1–6
1950	1–4.3
1960	1–3.8
1970	1–3.5
1980	1–2
1987	1–2.1

a statue of Popeye the Sailor to do something that most had never done before: vote. Although Mexican Americans outnumbered whites two to one, whites controlled all five seats on the Crystal City council. For three years, organizers struggled to register Mexican-American voters. When the election was over, Mexican Americans had won control of the city council. "We have done the impossible," declared Albert Fuentes, who led the voter-registration campaign. "If we can do it in Crystal City, we can do it all over Texas. We can awaken the sleeping giant."

During the 1960s, a new Chicano movement suddenly burst onto the national stage. Epic struggles arose across the Southwest to register voters, organize farmworkers, and regain stolen lands. The Mexican-American struggle for political and civil rights has received far less attention than the struggles of other minority groups for social justice, but it is in fact only the most recent expression of a long tradition of Mexican-American labor and political activism.

At the beginning of the twentieth century, between 380,000 and 560,000 U.S.- and foreign-born Mexicans lived in the United States. Prior to the Mexican War, many Mexican-American farmers lived on land granted by Mexico or Spain. Following the war, these grants had to be legally confirmed. Fraud, protracted litigation, and onerous taxes deprived many Mexican Americans of their land; by the turn of the century most worked as tenant farmers or as farm laborers on lands owned by whites. Mexican Americans faced discrimination, disfranchisement, and even lynchings. Antimiscegenation laws prohibited intermarriage with whites.

Three major surges of immigration, punctuated by two large-scale efforts at deportation, shaped twentieth-century Mexican-American history. Between 1910 and 1930, nearly 700,000 Mexican immigrants entered the southwestern United States, pushed out of Mexico by revolutionary upheaval and economic instability and pulled into the Southwest's increasing demand for low-wage, unskilled physical labor. Mexican immigrants took jobs as migratory laborers or seasonal workers in mines and packing-houses and on commercial farms and ranches. But these jobs generally resulted in lives charac-terized by geographical isolation and physical mobility, with few opportunities for economic advancement. Most immigrants lived in segregated communities where Mexican culture and organizations prevailed.

Depression-era unemployment, however, reduced immigration to less than 33,000 during the 1930s. The United States and Mexico sponsored a "repatriation" program that returned half a million people to Mexico, about half of whom were American citizens. Although the program was supposed to be voluntary, many were pressured to leave.

Demand for Mexican-American labor resumed during World War II. In 1942, the United States and Mexico instituted the *bracero* program, which allowed Mexican contract laborers to work in the United States in seasonal agriculture and other sectors of the economy. Following the war, however, a new deportation effort sought to expel resident Mexicans who lacked American citizenship. During the 1960s, Mexican immigration rose rapidly, propelled by the rapid growth of Mexico's population—which had tripled in 50 years; by the higher wages to be found in the United States—at least six times higher than those in Mexico; and the unwillingness of the Mexican government to control immigration after the demise of the bracero program in 1964. Mexican immigration has continued to increase into the 1990s.

Beginning in the early twentieth century, Mexican Americans formed many organizations to address problems of poverty and discrimination. Among the earliest were self-help organizations known as *mutualistas,* which provided members with a broad range of benefits and services, including credit, insurance, funeral and disability benefits, and which often served as the basis for labor unions. During the 1920s, new kinds of organizations appeared, which sought to assimilate Mexican Americans into the mainstream of American society and combat discrimination in education, jobs, wages, and political representation. These organizations united in 1929 to form the League of United Latin American Citizens (LULAC). During the 1940s and 1950s, LULAC organized voter-registration drives and filed lawsuits to end school and job discrimination. World War II marked a major turning point in Mexican-American history. More than

300,000 Mexican Americans served in the armed forces, earning more military honors proportionately than any other ethnic group. Veterans formed new activist organizations, like the American G.I. Forum and the Mexican American Political Association, to fight discrimination and end segregation.

As the 1960s began, Mexican Americans shared problems of poverty and discrimination with other minority groups. The median income of a Mexican-American family was just 62 percent of the median income of the general population, and over a third of Mexican-American families lived on less than $3000 a year. Unemployment was twice the rate among non-Hispanic whites, and four-fifths of employed Mexican Americans were concentrated in semiskilled and unskilled jobs, a third in agriculture.

Educational attainment lagged behind other groups (Mexican Americans averaged less than nine years of schooling as recently as 1970), and Mexican-American pupils were concentrated in predominantly Mexican-American schools, less well staffed and supplied than non–Mexican-American schools, with few Hispanic or Spanish-speaking teachers. Gerrymandered election districts and restrictive voting legislation resulted in the political underrepresentation of Mexican Americans. In addition, they were underrepresented or excluded from juries by requirements that jurors be able to speak and understand English.

During the 1960s, there was a new surge of Mexican-American militancy. In 1962 César Chávez began to organize California farmworkers, and three years later, in Delano, California, he led his first strike. At the same time that Chávez led the struggle for higher wages, enforcement of state labor laws, and recognition of the farmworker union, Reies Lopez Tijerina fought to win compensation for the descendants of families whose lands had been seized illegally. In 1963 Tijerina founded the Alianza Federal de Mercedes (the Federal Alliance of Land Grants) in New Mexico to restore the legal rights of heirs to Spanish and Mexican land grants that had been guaranteed under the treaty ending the Mexican War.

In Denver, Rodolfo ("Corky") Gonzales formed the Crusade for Justice in 1965 to protest school discrimination, provide legal,

medical, and financial services and jobs for Chicanos; and foster the Mexican-American cultural heritage. La Raza Unida political parties arose in a number of small towns with large Mexican-American populations. On college campuses across the Southwest, Mexican Americans formed political organizations.

In 1968 Congress responded to the demand among Mexican Americans for equal educational opportunity by enacting legislation encouraging school districts to adopt bilingual education programs to instruct non–English speakers in both English and their native language. In a more recent action, Congress moved in 1986 to legalize the status of many immigrants, including many Mexicans, who entered the United States illegally. The Immigration Reform and Control Act of 1986 provided permanent legal residency to undocumented workers who had lived in the United States since before 1982, and prohibits employment of illegal aliens.

Since 1960 Mexican Americans have made impressive political gains. During the 1960s four Mexican Americans—Senator Joseph Montoya of New Mexico and representatives Eligio de la Garza and Henry B. Gonzales of Texas and Edward R. Roybal of California—were elected to Congress. In 1974 two Chicanos were elected governors—Jerry Apodaca in New Mexico and Raul Castro in Arizona—becoming the first Mexican-American governors since early in this century. In 1981 Henry Cisneros of San Antonio, Texas, became the first Mexican-American mayor of a large city.

Henry Cisneros, elected mayor of San Antonio in 1981, was interviewed by Walter Mondale in 1984 as a potential Democratic vice-presidential nominee.

Today, 14 million Mexican Americans live in the United States. This is a 60 percent increase over the number in 1980 and a fourfold increase over 1960, making Mexican Americans the country's youngest and fastest-growing minority group.

Because of Mexico's proximity, a continuous influx of new arrivals, and concentration in predominantly Mexican barrios and colonias, Mexican Americans are able to maintain ties with their ancestral culture to a degree not possible for other ethnic groups. An estimated 40 percent of all Hispanics (of which Mexican Americans make up almost two-thirds) are immigrants and another 30 percent are the children of immigrants. As a result, Mexican Americans, more than any other immigrant group, have evolved a bilingual, bicultural identity that combines Mexican and American elements. Today, half of all Mexican Americans speak Spanish at home.

While high birthrates and immigration have contributed to increased political power, Mexican Americans continue to lag behind other groups in political representation due to lower voting rates and the fact that many are not yet naturalized citizens. Mexican Americans are also less well off than other Americans in income, education, and home ownership rates. They are twice as likely to be poor as non-Hispanics and three times less likely to have completed college. Third-generation Mexican Americans average just 11 years of schooling, 2 years less than non-Hispanics. More than other groups, Mexican-American workers are concentrated in low-paying jobs in factories, warehouses, construction, and the service sector. Mexican-American teenagers are more likely to drop out of high school, often to help their families during periods of economic distress. Mexican Americans are less likely than any other ethnic group to have health insurance.

Today, many Americans worry about whether Mexican immigrants will assimilate into the mainstream of American life. Many fear that prospects for upward mobility—so vital for the assimilation of earlier immigrant groups—are eroding, and that the consequences are apparent in an increase in teenage pregnancy and single-parent households.

Others express anger about illegal immigration—an issue that has increasingly inflamed American politics. In 1994 California voters adopted Proposition 187, denying public services such as schooling and medical treatment to illegal aliens.

As the United States approaches the twenty-first century, many important political and socioeconomic issues face the country's largest immigrant group. For most European ethnic groups, ethnic background ceased to be an important factor in social or economic standing by the third generation. Will the same be true of Mexican Americans? Will Mexican Americans advance socially, economically, and politically as did European immigrants or will racism and discrimination consign many to an economic underclass? Will Mexican Americans follow the European immigrant path of movement out of distinct urban enclaves and intermarriage, or will they successfully maintain a distinct identity and cultural heritage?

The Native-American Power Movement

In November 1969, 200 Native Americans seized the abandoned federal penitentiary on Alcatraz Island in San Francisco Bay. For 19 months Indian activists occupied the island in order to draw attention to conditions on the nation's Indian reservations. Alcatraz, the Native Americans said, symbolized conditions on reservations: "It has no running water; it has inadequate sanitation facilities; there is no industry, and so unemployment is very great; there are no health care facilities; the soil is rocky and unproductive." The activists, who called themselves Indians of All Tribes, offered to buy Alcatraz from the federal government for "$24 in glass beads and red cloth."

On Thanksgiving Day, 1970, 350 years after the Pilgrims' arrival, Wampanoag Indians, who had taken part at the first Thanksgiving, held a National Day of Mourning at Plymouth, Massachusetts. A tribal representative declared, "We forfeited our country. Our lands have fallen into the hands of the aggressor. We have allowed the white man to keep us on our knees." Meanwhile, another group of Native Americans established a settlement at Mount Rushmore, to demonstrate Indian claims to the Black Hills.

During the late 1960s and early 1970s, a new spirit of political militancy arose among the first Americans, just as it had among African Americans, women, and Mexican Americans. No other group, however, faced problems more severe than Native Americans. Throughout the 1960s, Native Americans were the nation's poorest minority group, worse off than any other group according to virtually every socioeconomic measure. In 1970 the Indian unemployment rate was ten times the national average, and 40 percent of the Native-American population lived below the poverty line. In that year, Native-American life expectancy was just 44 years, a third less than that of the average American. In one Apache town of 2500 on the San Carlos reservation in Arizona, there were only 25 telephones and most homes had outdoor toilets and relied on wood-burning stoves for heat.

Conditions on many of the nation's reservations were not unlike those found in underdeveloped areas of Latin America, Africa, and Asia. The death rate among Native Americans exceeded that of the U.S. population as a whole by a third. Deaths caused by pneumonia, hepatitis, dysentery, strep throat, diabetes, tuberculosis, alcoholism, suicide, and homicide were 2 to 60 times higher than the entire U.S. population. Half a million Indian families lived in unsanitary dilapidated dwellings, many in shanties, huts, or even abandoned automobiles.

On the Navajo reservation in Arizona, which is roughly the size of West Virginia, most families lived in the midst of severe poverty. The birthrate was very high; two-and-a-half times the overall U.S. rate and the same as India's. Living standards were low; the average family's purchasing power was about the same as that of a family in Malaysia. The typical house had just one or two rooms; 60 percent of the reservation's dwellings had no electricity, and 80 percent had no running water or sewers. Educational levels were low. The typical resident had completed just five years of school, and fewer than one adult in six had graduated from high school.

During World War II Native Americans began to revolt against such conditions. In 1944 Native Americans formed the National Congress of American Indians (NCAI), the first major intertribal association. Among the group's primary concerns were protection of Native-American land rights and improved educational opportunities for Native Americans. When Congress voted in 1953 to allow states to assert legal jurisdiction over Native-American reservations without tribal consent, and the federal government sought to transfer federal responsibilities for a dozen tribes to the states (a policy known as "termination") and to relocate Native Americans into urban areas, the NCAI led opposition to these measures. "Self-determination rather than termination!" was the NCAI slogan. Earl Old Person, a Blackfoot leader, commented, "It is important to note that in our Indian language the only translation for termination is to 'wipe out' or 'kill off' ... how can we plan our future when the Indian Bureau threatens to wipe us out as a race? It's like trying to cook a meal in your tipi when someone is standing outside trying to burn the tipi down."

By the late 1950s a new spirit of Native-American nationalism had arisen. In 1959 the Tuscarora nation of upstate New York, successfully resisted efforts by the state power authority to convert reservation land into a reservoir. In 1961 a militant new Native-American organization appeared, the National Indian Youth Council, which began to use the phrase "Red Power" and sponsored demonstrations, marches, and "fish-ins" to protest state efforts to abolish Native-American fishing rights guaranteed by federal treaties. Native Americans in the San Francisco Bay area in 1964 established the Indian Historical Society to present history from the Indian point of view, while the Native American Rights Fund brought legal suits against states that had taken Indian land and abolished Indian hunting, fishing, and water rights in violation of federal treaties. Many Indian nations also took legal action to prevent strip mining or spraying of pesticides on Native-American lands.

The best known of all Indian Power groups was AIM, the American Indian

Movement, formed by a group of Chippewas in Minneapolis in 1966 to protest alleged police brutality. In the fall of 1972, AIM Native Americans led urban dwellers, traditionalists, and the young along the "Trail of Broken Treaties" to Washington, D.C., where they seized the offices of the Bureau of Indian Affairs and occupied them for a week in order to dramatize their grievances. In the spring of 1973, 200 heavily armed Native Americans took over the town of Wounded Knee, South Dakota, site of an 1890 massacre of 300 Sioux by the U.S. army cavalry. They occupied the town for 71 days.

Militant protests paid off. The 1972 Indian Education Act gave Indian parents greater control over their children's schools. The 1976 Indian Health Care Act sought to address deficiencies in health care, while the 1978 Indian

Members of AIM, the American Indian Movement, occupied the town of Wounded Knee, South Dakota, for over two months to focus attention on Native-American grievances.

Child Welfare Act gave tribes control over custody decisions involving Native-American children. A series of landmark Supreme Court decisions aided the cause of Native-American sovereignty and national self-government. The 1959 *Williams* v. *Lee* case upheld the authority of Native-American courts to make decisions involving non–Native Americans. The 1968 case of *Menominee Tribe* v. *United States* declared that states could not invalidate fishing and hunting rights Native Americans had acquired through treaty agreements.

Beginning in the 1970s, a number of nations initiated lawsuits to recover land illegally seized by whites. In 1980, the federal government agreed to pay $81.5 million to the Passamaquoddy and Penobscot of Maine, and $105 million to the Sioux in South Dakota. Court decisions also permitted tribal authorities to sell cigarettes, run gambling casinos, and levy taxes.

Native Americans are no longer a vanishing group of Americans. The 1990 census recorded a Native-American population of over 2 million, five times the number recorded in 1950. About half of these people live on reservations, which cover 52.4 million acres in 27 states, while most others live in urban areas. The largest Native-American populations are located in Alaska, Arizona, California, New Mexico, and Oklahoma. As the Native-American population has grown in size, individual Indians have claimed many accomplishments, including receipt of the Pulitzer Prize for fiction by N. Scott Momaday, a Kiowa.

Although Native Americans continue to face severe problems of employment, income, and education, they have decisively demonstrated that they will not abandon their tribal identity and culture or be treated as dependent wards of the federal government.

Gay and Lesbian Liberation

On June 27, 1969, New York City police staged an early morning raid on the Stonewall Inn, a Greenwich Village bar catering primarily to transvestites, gay men, and lesbians. Raids on gay or cross-dressers' bars were common at the time. State law threatened bars with the loss of their liquor licenses if they tolerated same-sex dancing or employed or served men who wore women's clothing. Instead of acquiescing passively in the raid, the bar's patrons fought back, battling the police with bricks, bottles, and shards of broken glass. Three days of civil disobedience followed.

This incident ushered in a new era for gays and lesbians in the United States: an era of pride, openness, and activism. It led many gays and lesbians to "come out of the closet" and publicly assert their sexual identity and to organize politically. In Stonewall's wake, activist organizations like the Gay Liberation Front transformed sexual orientation into a political issue, attacking customs and laws that defined homosexuality as a sin, a crime, or a mental illness.

Hostility toward homosexuality had deep roots in American society. State sodomy laws criminalized homosexual acts. Federal immigration laws excluded homosexual aliens. The 1873 Comstock Act permitted postal authorities to exclude homosexual publications from the mail, while Hollywood's "Production Code," adopted in 1934, prohibited the depiction of gay characters or open discussion of homosexuality in film. The American Psychiatric Association's diagnostic manual defined homosexuality as a psychopathology. During the McCarthy era, the charge that homosexuals were "moral perverts" and security risks led the government to adopt rules explicitly excluding them from federal jobs or military service. Police entrapment of homosexual men and harassment of gay bars were widespread; during the 1950s, in cities such as Philadelphia and Washington, D.C., police arrested 100 men a month on misdemeanor charges relating to homosexuality.

Although the emergence of the gay and lesbian liberation movement caught the general public by surprise, it did not emerge overnight. During the 1950s, a handful of advocacy groups, including the Mattachine Society and the Daughters of Bilitis, arose, opposing laws that prohibited and punished homosexuality. By the late 1960s, gay and lesbian subcultures and communities had grown in many of the nation's cities, complete with bars, cabarets, magazines, and restaurants.

At the same time, challenges to earlier legal and medical opinion about homosexuality appeared. Alfred Kinsey's studies of sexual behavior, published in 1948 and 1953, suggested that homosexual and lesbian behavior was far more prevalent than most Americans previously suspected. Kinsey estimated about 10 percent of men and 5 percent of women were sexually attracted primarily to members of their own sex. During the 1960s, reformers within the legal profession argued in favor of decriminalizing private, consensual adult homosexual relations, on the grounds that government should not regulate private morality. In 1961, Illinois became the first state to repeal its sodomy statutes. The next year the Supreme Court ruled that a magazine featuring photographs of male nudes was not obscene and therefore not subject to censorship. In 1973, the American Psychiatric Association removed homosexuality from its list of psychopathologies.

In recent years, homosexuality has become one of the most highly charged issues in American politics. In 1986 the Supreme Court upheld state sodomy laws, ruling that private acts of homosexuality were not protected by the Constitution. Gay advocacy groups responded to the decision by lobbying for passage of state and city civil rights acts that would ban discrimination on the basis of sexual orientation in employment and housing. As a result of the gay rights movement, two states—New York and Vermont—and several municipalities, extended health and dental insurance to the gay and lesbian domestic partners of public employees. A number of municipalities and states, including Colorado, responded to these initiatives by passing referenda prohibiting government from extending special rights to homosexuals. But state courts found these to be unconstitutional infringements on the right of gay and lesbian citizens to petition government. In 1993, a major controversy erupted after President Bill Clinton proposed allowing gays and lesbians to serve openly in the military. The policy that eventually emerged—nicknamed "don't ask, don't tell"—satisfied few, and federal courts refused to permit the expulsion of gays from the military.

The Earth First

In 1962, Rachel Carson, a marine biologist, published a book that would do more to awaken environmental consciousness than any other single work. Entitled *Silent Spring*, it described how DDT and other chemical pesticides contaminated nature's food chain, killing large numbers of birds and fish and causing human illnesses. This book helped initiate the most influential environmentalist movement in modern American history.

Modern environmentalism began at the end of the nineteenth century. In 1872, Congress created the first national park, Yellowstone. In 1891, the Forest Reserve Act gave the president the power to set up national forests. The next year saw the founding of the Sierra Club, the nation's first organization committed to protecting wilderness areas.

During the Progressive era, conflicting visions of the environment struggled for dominance. While some men, like Gifford Pinchot, the head of the U.S. Forest Service under Theodore Roosevelt, were primarily interested in using scarce natural resources more rationally and efficiently, others, like the naturalist John Muir, who was the Sierra Club's first president, were eager to preserve wilderness and wildlife for their own sake and prevent industrial development from despoiling nature's beauty.

Franklin Roosevelt's New Deal initiated a number of important conservation projects. The Civilian Conservation Corps put three million young men to work restoring national parks and forests. The Tennessee Valley Authority restored the region's forests by planting trees and controlling flooding, and provided cheap electricity by building dams. The Soil Conservation Service combatted the poor farming and ranching practices that contributed to the loss of topsoil during the Dust Bowl of the early 1930s.

It was during the 1960s, however, that environmentalism became a mass movement. A series of environmental horror stories broadened the environmentalist constituency from naturalists to include a majority of Americans. Cleveland's Cuyahoga River caught fire; toxic residues were discovered in mothers'

breast milk; acid rain destroyed lakes and streams. Americans became increasingly alarmed about "killer smog," the paving over of farmland, off-shore oil drilling, and the loss of wetlands.

Scientists played a critical role in arousing public awareness. Paul R. Erhlich, a Stanford ecologist and author of the 1968 best-seller *The Population Bomb,* warned that world population growth was outstripping the earth's supply of food, fresh water, and mineral resources. In *The Closing Circle,* Barry Commoner alerted Americans to the dangers of nuclear radiation and made them aware of the fragility of the natural environment.

The establishment of new organizations, like the Environmental Defense Fund founded in 1967, and the heightened interest in "organic farming" and "natural foods"—foods produced without using synthetic chemicals—testified to the growing public interest in environmental protection. The National Environmental Policy Act, passed in 1969, required preparation of environmental impact statements for all federally funded highways, dams, pipelines, and power plants. But it was the celebration of the first "Earth Day" that underscored public concern for the environment. On April 22, 1970, 20 million Americans gathered in parks, planted trees, and staged demonstrations to observe Earth Day.

In Earth Day's wake, Congress combined 15 federal pollution programs to create the Environmental Protection Agency to set and enforce pollution standards; passed the Clean Air and Clean Water Acts; and enacted the Endangered Species Act in 1973, protecting threatened species of wildlife. Since these initial measures were adopted, environmental concern has surged and ebbed. During the mid-1970s, when the United States experienced severe oil shortages and economic productivity dipped, fewer Americans were willing to sacrifice economic growth or a high standard of living for environmental protection. During his presidency, Ronald Reagan argued that the solution to environmental problems was to be found in the workings of the marketplace rather than in government regulation. But whenever news reports of environmental degradation appeared, public concern quickly resurfaced. In 1978 reports that dangerous chemicals had been buried beneath Love Canal in New York led Congress to create the "Superfund" to finance the clean-up of the nation's most dangerous toxic waste sites. Publicity over the dangers of "ozone depletion" led the United States and most other nations to negotiate a 1989 treaty cutting production of chlorofluorocarbons that destroy the atmosphere's protective ozone shield. Also in 1989, a U.S. tanker, the *Exxon Valdez*, spilled nearly 11 million gallons of crude oil into Alaska's Prince William Sound, sparking intense public concern.

The report card on the nation's environmental record offers a mixed picture. Contamination levels of DDT, lead, and cancer-causing polychlorinated biphenyls have declined sharply. By 1995, environmental regulations had reduced sulfur dioxide emissions by 53 percent; carbon monoxide by 57 percent; smoke and soot by 59 percent; and smog by 39 percent; and had made America's water supply the cleanest in the industrial world. Strict federal rules curbed automobile and industrial emissions, while increasing automobile mileage and the efficiency of appliances. As a result, while the American economy grew by 50 percent between 1970 and 1995, energy usage increased by only 10 percent.

Yet in spite of the regulation of power-plant smokestacks, aquatic life in 4000 lakes remains threatened by acid rain, and while automobile tailpipe emissions have been sharply curtailed, half the population lives in counties that violate federal clean air standards. Despite efforts to clean the nation's rivers and lakes, many freshwater fish contain dangerous levels of toxic chemicals. And as some older environmental hazards have been addressed, new concerns have arisen, such as global warming—the greenhouse effect caused by the buildup of carbon dioxide and other gases in the stratosphere—and the depletion of the earth's protective ozone shield. Ecopopulists warn about dangers posed by genetic engineering and electromagnetic radiation. Animal rights activists call on Americans to replace an "anthrocentric" perspective with an outlook respecting the value of all living things.

Public opinion polls indicate that Americans overwhelmingly support environmental protection and over three-quarters consider themselves environmentalists. Membership in environmental organization has increased sharply, and the national symbol, the bald eagle, once on the verge of extinction, has been reclassified as "threatened" rather than "endangered."

But whether a fundamental change has taken place in America's relationship to nature remains uncertain. Despite limited efforts at recycling, America remains a "throwaway" society that produces twice as much garbage as Europe. America also remains an extraordinarily mobile society relying on private cars for transportation. With just 2 percent of the world's population, the United States uses 24 percent of the world's energy—twice as much as Japan and Western Europe. And the United States remains a growth-oriented society that continues to absorb millions of acres of cropland each year for highways, tract housing, and office buildings. Each year the federal government continues to add 35 to 50 species to the list of endangered species.

CONCLUSION

During the 1960s, many groups, including African Americans, women, Mexican Americans, and Native Americans, struggled for equal rights. Early in the decade, college students, impatient with the slow pace of legal change, staged sit-ins, freedom rides, and protest marches to challenge legal segregation in the South. Passionately committed to a philosophy of nonviolent direct action, these students suffered beatings and went to jail to achieve integration. Their efforts led the federal government to pass the Civil Rights Act of 1964, prohibiting discrimination in public facilities and employment, and the Twenty-fourth Amendment to the Constitution and the Voting Rights Act in 1965, guaranteeing voting rights.

Despite significant legal gains, many African Americans felt a growing sense of frustration and anger. The violence perpetrated by

CHRONOLOGY
OF KEY EVENTS

1960 Four freshmen at North Carolina Agricultural and Technical College in Greensboro, North Carolina, stage the first sit-in to protest segregation; Student Nonviolent Coordinating Committee (SNCC) is founded

1961 Congress of Racial Equality (CORE) stages freedom rides to expose segregation in transportation; *Mapp* v. *Ohio* holds that evidence obtained by unreasonable searches must be excluded at trial

1962 James Meredith enrolls at the University of Mississippi; Students for a Democratic Society (SDS) issue Port Huron Statement; César Chávez begins to organize California farm workers

1963 George C. Wallace is inaugurated Alabama governor; Martin Luther King, Jr., leads demonstrations against segregation in Birmingham, Alabama; racial violence in the South leaves 10 people dead, 35 black homes and churches fire-bombed; Betty Friedan publishes *The Feminine Mystique,* helping launch a new feminist movement; Equal Pay Act, first federal law to prohibit sex discrimination, requires equal pay for identical work; *Gideon* v. *Wainwright* holds that indigent defendants have a right to a court-appointed attorney; March on Washington, D.C., for civil rights and jobs; John F. Kennedy is assassinated; Lyndon Johnson becomes thirty-sixth president

1964 President Johnson announces War on Poverty; Manpower Development and Training Act and Economic Opportunity Act establish the Job Corps and Neighborhood Youth Corps; in *Escobedo* v. *Illinois,* Supreme Court rules that sus-pects being interrogated by police have a right to legal counsel; Civil Rights Act prohibits discrimination in employment and public facilities; Twenty-fourth Amendment prohibits poll taxes in federal elections

1965 Malcolm X is assassinated; Martin Luther King, Jr., leads demonstrations in Selma, Alabama, to bring issue of voting rights to national attention; Voting Rights Act prohibits literacy tests and sends federal examiners to seven southern states to register black voters; riot in Watts, predominantly black section of Los Angeles, results in 34 deaths; Medicare extends medical insurance to older Americans; Executive Order 11246 requires government contractors to prepare affirmative action plans; Ralph Nader publishes *Unsafe at Any Speed*

1966 SNCC and CORE embrace black nationalism; Black Panther party is organized; National Organization for Women (NOW) is formed; Congress passes Model Cities Act to attack urban blight

1967 Riots take place in 127 cities

1968 Medicaid expanded to cover the medical expenses of the poor; assassination of Martin Luther King, Jr., in Memphis, Tennessee, is followed by riots in 168 cities

1969 Three days of civil disobedience follow a police raid on the Stonewall Inn in New York City, a gay and lesbian bar

1970 Twenty million Americans celebrate the first Earth Day; Congress creates the Environmental Protection Agency and passes the Clean Air and Clean Water Acts

1971 In *Swann* v. *Charlotte-Mecklenburg Board of Education,* U.S. Supreme

(continued)

| 1973 | Court upholds school busing as a tool of racial integration

Roe v. *Wade* decision legalizes abortion; the American Psychiatric Association removes homosexuality from its list of psychopathologies; Congress enacts the Endangered Species Act | 1986 | Immigration Reform and Control Act provides permanent legal residency to undocumented workers who have lived in United States since 1982 |
| | | 1993 | Gays and lesbians are permitted to serve in the military |

white racists and a growing white backlash against civil rights led black nationalists to downplay the goal of integration and instead emphasize political power, community control of schools, creation of businesses, and black pride. Frustration also grew in urban ghettoes, where a disproportionate number of African Americans faced problems of poverty, unemployment, and de facto segregation that were not addressed by civil rights legislation. In the summer of 1965, black frustration erupted into violence in Watts, a predominantly black district of Los Angeles, and over the next three years, over 150 major riots occurred.

In a far-reaching effort to reduce poverty, alleviate hunger and malnutrition, extend medical care, provide adequate housing, and enhance the employability of the poor, President Johnson launched his Great Society program in 1964. Although critics charged that federal public assistance food subsidies, health programs, and child care programs contributed to welfare dependence, family breakup, and an increase in out-of-wedlock births, the programs did succeed in cutting the proportion of families living in poverty in half.

The example of the civil rights movement inspired other groups to press for equal opportunity. The women's movement fought for passage of antidiscrimination laws, equal educational and employment opportunities, and a transformation of traditional views about women's place in society. Mexican Americans battled for bilingual education programs in schools, unionization of farm workers, improved job opportunities, and increased polit-

ical power. Native Americans pressed for control over their lands and resources, the preservation of native cultures, and tribal self-government. Gays and lesbians organized to end legal discrimination based on sexual orientation.

SUGGESTIONS FOR FURTHER READING

Rodolfo Acuña, *Occupied America*, 3d ed. (1988). Discusses the Mexican-American struggle for equality.

Taylor Branch, *Parting the Waters: America in the King Years* (1988). Recounts the history of the Civil Rights movement.

William H. Chafe, *The Unfinished Journey: America Since World War II*, 3d ed. (1995). Provides a comprehensive overview of the movements for gender and racial equality.

John D'Emilio, *Sexual Politics, Sexual Communities: The Making of a Homosexual Minority in the United States, 1940–1970* (1983). Traces the roots of the struggle for gay and lesbian liberation.

John Dittmer, *Local People: The Struggle for Civil Rights in Mississippi* (1994). Examines the Civil Rights movement in a specific state.

David G. Gutierrez, *Walls and Mirrors: Mexican Americans, Mexican Immigrants, and the Politics of Ethnicity* (1995). Analyzes the quest of Mexican Americans for equal rights.

Donald L. Parman, *Indians and the American West in the Twentieth Century* (1994). Examines the Native-American struggle to preserve tribal self-government and reassert control over resources.

Philip Shabecoff, *A Fierce Green Fire: The American Environmental Movement* (1993). Chronicles the growth of the American environmental movement.

Overviews And Surveys

David Farber, ed., *The Sixties: From Memory to History* (1994); Richard N. Goodwin, *Remembering America: A Voice from the Sixties* (1988); Godfrey Hodgson, *America in Our Time* (1976); Allen Matusow, *The Unraveling of America: A History of Liberalism in the 1960s* (1984); William O'Neill, *Coming Apart: An Informal History of America in the 1960s* (1971); David Steigerwald, *The Sixties and the End of Modern America* (1995).

The Struggle for Racial Justice

Sally Belfrage, *Freedom Summer* (1965); Michael Belknap, *Federal Law and Southern Order: Racial Violence and Constitutional Conflict in the Post-Brown South* (1987); Derrick Bell, *And We Are Not Saved: The Elusive Quest for Racial Justice* (1987); Jack Bloom, *Class, Race, and the Civil Rights Movement* (1987); Carl Brauer, *John F. Kennedy and the Second Reconstruction* (1977); Eric R. Burner, *And Gently He Shall Lead Them: Robert Purris Moses and Civil Rights in Mississippi* (1994); Clayborne Carson, *In Struggle: SNCC and the Black Awakening of the 1960s* (1981); Sean Dennis Cashman, *African Americans and the Quest for Civil Rights* (1991); William H. Chafe, *Civilities and Civil Rights* (1980); Vicki L. Crawford et al., eds., *Women in the Civil Rights Movement* (1990); Chandler Davidson and Bernard Grofman, *Quiet Revolution: The Impact of the Voting Rights Act in the South* (1994); Michael Eric Dyson, *Making Malcolm: The Myth and Meaning of Malcolm X* (1995); Adam Fairclough, *Martin Luther King, Jr.* (1990); Ronald P. Formisano, *Boston Against Busing: Race, Class, and Ethnicity in the 1960s and 1970s* (1991); David Garrow, *Bearing the Cross: Martin Luther King, Jr. and the Southern Christian Leadership Conference* (1986), and *The FBI and Martin Luther King* (1981); David R. Goldfield, *Black, White, and Southern: Race Relations and Southern Culture* (1990); Hugh Davis Graham, *The Civil Rights Era: The Origins and Development of National Policy* (1990); Vincent Harding, *There is a River: The Black Struggle for Freedom in America* (1981); Walter A. Jackson, *Gunnar Myrdal and America's Conscience: Social Engineering and Racial Liberalism* (1990); Richard Kluger, *Simple Justice: The History of Brown v. Board of Education and Black America's Struggle for Equality* (1975); Steven Lawson, *Black Ballots: Voting Rights in the South, 1944–1969* (1976), and *Running for Freedom: Civil Rights and Black Politics* (1991): Nicholas Lemann, *The Promised Land: The Great Black Migration and How It Changed America* (1991); Doug McAdam, *Freedom Summer* (1988); August Meier and Elliot Rudwick, *CORE: A Study in the Civil Rights Movement, 1942–1968* (1973); Stephen Oates, *Let the Trumpet Sound: The Life and Times of Martin Luther King, Jr.* (1982); Frank R. Parker, *Black Votes Count: Political Empowerment in Mississippi* (1990); Thomas R. Peake, *Keeping the Dream Alive: A History of the Southern Christian Leadership Conference* (1987); Armstead L. Robinson and Patricia Sullivan, eds., *New Directions in Civil Rights Studies* (1991); Bernard Schwartz, *Inside the Warren Court* (1983); Harvard Sitkoff, *The Struggle for Black Equality* (1981); Melvin I. Urofsky, *A Conflict of Rights: The Supreme Court and Affirmative Action* (1991), and *The Continuity of Change: The Supreme Court and Individual Liberties, 1953–1986* (1990); William L. Van Deburg, *New Day in Babylon: The Black Power Movement and American Culture* (1992); Nancy J. Weiss, *Whitney M. Young, Jr., and the Struggle for Civil Rights* (1989); John White, *Black Leadership in America*, 2d ed. (1990); Eugene Wolfenstein, *The Victims of Democracy: Malcolm X and the Black Revolution* (1980); C. Vann Woodward, *Strange Career of Jim Crow*, 3d ed. (1974).

The Youth Revolt

Terry H. Anderson, *The Movement and the Sixties* (1995); Paul Buhle, *History and the New Left* (1990); William H. Chafe, *Never Stop Running: Allard Lowenstein and the Struggle to Save American Liberalism* (1993); Morris Dickstein, *Gates of Eden: American Culture in the Sixties* (1977); Todd Gitlin, *The Sixties: Years of Hope, Days of Rage* (1993); Maurice Isserman, *. . . If I Had a Hammer: The Death of the Old Left and the Birth of the New Left* 1987); W. J. Rorabaugh, *Berkeley at War: The 1960s* (1989); Theodore Roszak, *The Making of a Counter Culture* (1969); Stanley Rothman and S. Robert Lichter, *Roots of Radicalism* (1982); Kirkpatrick Sale, *SDS* (1973); Jon Wiener, *Come Together: John Lennon in His Time* (1984).

Liberation Movements

Mary Jo Bane, *Here to Stay: American Families in the Twentieth Century* (1978); Mario Barrera, *Race and Class in the Southwest* (1979); Judith Barwick, *In Transition: How Feminism, Sexual Liberation, and the Search for Self-Fulfillment Have Altered America* (1979); Mary Frances Berry, *Why ERA Failed* (1986); Albert Camarillo, *Hispanics in a Changing Society* (1979); William H. Chafe, *Women and Equality* (1977); Andrew J. Cherlin, ed., *The Changing American Family and Public Policy* (1988); Margaret Cruikshank, *The Gay and Lesbian Liberation Movement* (1992); Sara Evans, *Personal Politics: The Roots of*

Women's Liberation in the Civil Rights Movement and the New Left (1979); Victor R. Fuchs, *How We Live* (1983); Mario T. García, *Mexican Americans: Leadership, Ideology and Identity* (1989); Juan Gómez-Quiñones, *Chicano Politics* (1990) and *Mexican American Labor* (1994); Hazel W. Hertzberg, *The Search for an American Identity* (1971); Bill Ong Hing, *Making and Remaking Asian America Through Immigration Policy* (1993); Judith Hole and Ellen Levine, *Rebirth of Feminism* (1971); Peter Iverson, *The Navajo Nation* (1981); Virginia Sánchez Korrol, *From Colonia to Community* (1983); Sar A. Levitan et al., *What's Happening to the American Family? Tensions, Hopes, Realities* (1988); Matt S. Meier and Feliciano Rivera, ed., *Mexican Americans/American Mexicans* (1993); Neil Miller, *Out of the Past: Gay and Lesbian History* (1995); Steven Mintz and Susan Kellogg, *Domestic Revolutions: A Social History of American Family Life* (1988); Joan Moore and Harry Pachon, *Hispanics in the United States* (1985); Roger Nichols, *The American Indian: Past and Present*, 3d ed. (1985); David Popenoe, *Disturbing the Nest: Family Change and Decline in Modern Societies* (1988); Roslind Rosenberg, *Divided Lives: American Women in the Twentieth Century* (1992); Leila Rupp and Verta Taylor, *Survival in the Doldrums: The American Women's Rights Movement, 1945 to the 1960s* (1987); George Sanchez, *Becoming Mexican American* (1993); Peter Skerry, *Mexican Americans: The Ambivalent Minority* (1993); William Wei, *The Asian American Movement* (1993).

Biographies

Carl Brauer, *John F. Kennedy and the Second Reconstruction* (1977); Eric R. Burner *And Gently He Shall Lead Them: Robert Purris Moses and Civil Rights in Mississippi* (1994); William H. Chafe, *Never Stop Running: Allard Lowenstein and the Struggle to Save American Liberalism* (1993); Adam Fairclough, *Martin Luther King, Jr.* (1990); David Garrow, *Bearing the Cross: Martin Luther King., Jr. and the Southern Christian Leadership Conference* (1986) and *The FBI and Martin Luther King* (1981); Walter A. Jackson, *Gunnar Myrdal and America's Conscience: Social Engineering and Racial Liberalism* (1990); Stephen Oates, *Let the Trumpet Sound: The Life and Times of Martin Luther King, Jr.* (1982); Nancy J. Weiss, *Whitney M. Young, Jr., and the Struggle for Civil Rights* (1989); Jon Wiener, *Come Together: John Lennon In in His Time* (1984); Eugene Wolfenstein, *The Victims of Democracy: Malcolm X and the Black Revolution* (1980).

CHAPTER 31
AMERICA IN OUR TIME

CRISIS OF POLITICAL LEADERSHIP
Restraining the Imperial Presidency
New-Style Presidents

WRENCHING ECONOMIC TRANSFORMATIONS
The Age of Inflation
Oil Embargo
Foreign Competition and
    Deindustrialization
Whipping Stagflation

A NEW AMERICAN ROLE IN THE WORLD
Détente
Foreign Policy Triumphs
No Island of Stability

THE REAGAN REVOLUTION
The Gipper
Reaganomics
The Celebration of Wealth
The Reagan Doctrine
A Remarkable Ideological Turnaround
The Reagan Revolution in Perspective

THE BUSH PRESIDENCY
A Kinder, Gentler Nation
Collapse of Communism
Economic and Foreign Policy
Enter Bill Clinton

A NEW COVENANT

Shortly after 1 A.M. on the morning of June 17, 1972, Frank Wills, a security guard at the Washington, D.C., Watergate office complex, spotted a strip of masking tape covering the lock of a basement door. He removed it. A short while later, he found the door taped open again. He called the police, who found two more taped locks, and a jammed door leading into the offices of the Democratic National Committee. Inside they discovered five men with cameras and electronic eavesdropping equipment.

At first, the Watergate break-in seemed like a minor incident. The identities of the burglars, however, suggested something more serious. One, James McCord, was chief security coordinator and electronics expert of the Committee for the Reelection of the President (CREEP). Others had links to the CIA. Two of the burglars carried papers bearing the name Howard Hunt, a special White House consultant, and $6500, which was traced to President Nixon's campaign committee.

Over the course of the next year, it became clear that the break-in was only one of a series of secret operations coordinated by the White House. Financed by illegal campaign contributions, these operations posed a threat to America's constitutional system of government and eventually forced Richard Nixon to resign the presidency.

The Watergate break-in had its roots in Richard Nixon's obsession with secrecy and political intelligence. To stop leaks of information to the press, in 1971 the Nixon White House assembled a team of "plumbers," consisting of former CIA operatives. This private police force, paid for in part by illegal campaign contributions, engaged in a wide range of criminal acts, including phone tapping and burglary, against those on its "enemies list."

In 1972 when President Nixon was running for reelection, his campaign committee authorized another series of illegal activities. It hired Donald Segretti to stage "dirty tricks" against potential Democratic candidates, which included mailing letters that falsely accused one candidate of homosexuality and fathering an illegitimate child. It considered a plan to use prostitutes to blackmail Democrats

at their national convention and to kidnap anti-Nixon radical leaders. The committee also authorized $250,000 for intelligence-gathering operations. Four times the committee sent burglars to break into Democratic headquarters.

Precisely what the campaign committee hoped to learn from these intelligence-gathering activities remains a mystery. It seems likely that it was seeking information about the Democratic party's campaign strategies and any information the Democrats had about illegal campaign contributions to the Republican party.

On June 23—six days after the botched break-in—President Nixon sought to impede the investigation of the Watergate break-in. He ordered aides to block an FBI investigation into White House involvement in the break-in on grounds that an investigation would endanger national security. He also counseled his aides to lie, under oath if necessary: "I don't give a [expletive deleted] what happens," he told his former attorney general, John Mitchell, who was then his campaign manager, "I want you all to stonewall it, let them plead the Fifth Amendment, cover-up, or anything else."

The Watergate break-in did not hurt Nixon's reelection campaign, since between the activities of the burglars and the president were layers of officials that had to be carefully peeled away, all of which took time. *Washington Post* reporters Bob Woodward and Carl Bernstein, sensing that the break-in was only part of a larger scandal, slowly pieced to-

The Watergate scandal led to the downfall of President Richard Nixon. Here the Senate Watergate Committee questions Nixon aide H. R. Haldeman.

On August 9, 1974, Richard Nixon resigned the presidency after the release of secret tapes revealed that he had been involved in a cover-up of the Watergate affair.

gether part of the story. Facing long jail terms, some of the burglars began to tell the truth, and the truth illuminated a path leading to the White House.

If Nixon had few political friends, he had legions of enemies. Over the years he had offended or attacked many Democrats—and a number of prominent Republicans. His detractors latched onto the Watergate issue with the tenacity of bulldogs.

The Senate appointed a special committee to investigate the Watergate scandal. Most of Nixon's top aides continued the cover-up. John Dean, the president's counsel, did not. Throughout the episode he had kept careful notes, and in a quiet precise voice he told the Senate Watergate Committee that the president was deeply involved in the cover-up. The matter was still not solved. All the committee had was Dean's word against the other White House aides.

On July 16, 1973, Alexander Butterfield, a former White House employee, dropped a bombshell by testifying that Nixon had recorded all Oval Office conversations. Whatever Nixon and his aides had said about Watergate in the Oval Office, therefore, was faithfully recorded on tape.

Nixon tried to keep the tapes from the committee by invoking executive privilege, insisting that a president had a right to keep confidential any White House communication, whether or not it involved sensitive diplomatic or national security matters. When Archibald Cox, a special prosecutor investigating violations of criminal law in the Watergate affair, persisted in demanding the tapes, Nixon ordered his attorney general, Elliot Richardson, to fire him; Richardson refused and resigned; Richardson's assistant, William Ruckelshaus also resigned. Ruckelshaus's assistant, Robert Bork, finally fired Cox, but Congress forced Nixon to name a new special prosecutor, Houston attorney Leon Jaworski. Ultimately, a unanimous Supreme Court ordered Nixon to turn over the tapes.

In the midst of the Watergate investigations, another scandal broke. Federal prosecutors accused Vice President Spiro Agnew of extorting payoffs from engineers and road building contractors while he was Maryland's governor and Baltimore County executive. In a plea bargain, Agnew pleaded no contest to a relatively minor charge—that he had falsified his income tax in 1967—in exchange for a $10,000 fine. Agnew resigned and Nixon appointed Gerald Ford to succeed Agnew as vice president.

The Watergate scandal gradually came to encompass not just the cover-up but a wide range of presidential wrongdoings, including political favors to business groups in exchange for campaign contributions; misuse of public funds; deceiving Congress and the public about the secret bombing of Cambodia in 1969 and 1970; authorization of illegal domestic political surveillance and espionage against dissidents, political opponents, and journalists; and attempts to use FBI investigations and income tax audits by the Internal Revenue Service to harass political enemies.

On July 24, 1974, the House Judiciary Committee recommended that the House of Representatives impeach Nixon for obstruction of justice, abuse of power, and refusal to relinquish the tapes. The end was near. On August 5 Nixon obeyed the Supreme Court ruling to release the tapes, which confirmed Dean's detailed testimony. Nixon had indeed been involved in a cover-up. On August 9, in a tearful farewell Nixon became the first American president to resign from office. The following day, Gerald Ford became the new president. "Our long national nightmare," he said, "is over."

CRISIS OF POLITICAL LEADERSHIP

The Vietnam War and the Watergate scandal had a profound effect on the presidency. The office suffered a dramatic decline in public respect, and Congress became increasingly unwilling to defer to presidential leadership. Congress enacted a series of reforms that would make future Watergate-type abuses of presidential authority less likely. In the process Congress recaptured constitutional powers that had been ceded to an increasingly dominant executive branch.

Restraining the Imperial Presidency

Over the course of the twentieth century, the presidency gradually supplanted Congress as the center of federal power. Presidential powers increased, presidential staff grew in size, and the executive branch gradually acquired a dominant relationship over Congress.

Beginning with Theodore Roosevelt, the president, and not Congress, established the nation's legislative agenda. Increasingly, Congress ceded its budget-making authority to the president. Lacking its own budget bureau to analyze specific funding needs, Congress was reluctant to depart from the budget put forward by the president and create its own priorities. Presidents even found a way to make agreements with foreign nations without congressional approval. After World War II, presidents moved away from treaty-making procedures, substituting executive agreements for treaties that require Senate approval. Even more important, presidents gained the power to wage undeclared war, despite the fact that Congress is the sole branch of government empowered by the Constitution to "declare" war.

No president went further than Richard Nixon in concentrating powers in the presidency. He refused to spend funds that Congress had appropriated; he claimed executive privilege against disclosure of information on administration decisions; he refused to allow key decision makers to be questioned before congressional committees; he reorganized the executive branch and broadened the authority of new cabinet positions without congressional approval. And during the Vietnam War, he ordered harbors mined and bombing raids launched without consulting Congress.

Watergate brought an end to the "imperial presidency" and the growth of presidential power. Over the president's veto, Congress enacted the War Powers Act (1973), which required future presidents to win specific authorization from Congress to engage U.S. forces in foreign combat for more than 90 days. Under the law, a president who orders troops into action abroad must report the reason for this action to Congress within 48 hours.

In the wake of Watergate, Congress enacted a series of laws designed to reform the political process. Disclosures during the Watergate investigations of money laundering, blatant influence peddling, and briefcases stuffed with $100 bills, led Congress to provide for public financing of presidential elections, public disclosure of sources of funding, limits on private campaign contributions and spending, and enforcement of campaign finance laws by an independent Federal Election Commission.

To make it easier to investigate crimes in the executive branch, Congress required the attorney general to appoint a special prosecutor to investigate accusations of illegal activities. To reassert its budget-making authority, Congress created a Congressional Budget Office and specifically forbade a president to impound funds without its approval. To open government to public scrutiny, Congress opened more committee deliberations and enacted the Freedom of Information Act, which allows the public and press to request declassification of government documents.

To reduce the authority of arbitrary and aging committee chairmen, the House of Representatives weakened the seniority system. In addition, the Senate modified the filibuster rule, allowing debate to be cut off with the consent of 60 senators instead of the previous requirement of two-thirds present and voting. The end result was to streamline the workings of Congress.

Some of the post-Watergate reforms have not been as effective as reformers anticipated. The War Powers Act has never been invoked and while various administrations have attempted to comply with the spirit of the law, no president has accepted its constitutional validity.

Campaign financing reform did not curb the power of special interests to curry favor with politicians or the ability of the very rich to outspend opponents. The Supreme Court struck down laws that forbade candidates to give more than $50,000 to their own presidential campaign and, more importantly, barred any limitations on unauthorized "independent expenditures" by individuals on behalf of a candidate.

Congress had somewhat more success in reining in the FBI and CIA. During the 1970s, congressional investigators discovered that the Federal Bureau of Investigation and the Central Intelligence Agency had, in defiance of their charters and federal law, broken into the homes, tapped the phones, and opened the mail of American citizens; illegally infiltrated antiwar groups and black radical organizations; and accumulated dossiers on dissidents. Investigators also found that the CIA had been involved in assassination plots against foreign leaders and had tested the effects of radiation, electric shock, and drugs (such as LSD) on unsuspecting citizens. Congress was outraged to learn that the CIA and organized crime plotted to assassinate Fidel Castro by supplying him with poison cigars, giving him drugs that would make his beard fall out, and shooting him with a weapon disguised as a pen.

As a result of these investigations, the government severely limited CIA operations in the United States and laid down strict guidelines for FBI activities. To tighten congressional control over the CIA, Congress established a joint committee to supervise CIA operations.

New-Style Presidents

In contrast to Nixon's abuses of presidential powers, the next two presidents, Gerald Ford and Jimmy Carter, cultivated reputations as modest, honest, forthright men. The first important public image of Ford's presidency was of Ford stepping outside his front door in his pajamas to pick up his newspaper. The first important image of Carter's presidency was of the new president carrying his own bags into the White House. Both men sought to project an image of ordinariness in order to symbolically reduce the presidency to a more human size. As Gerald Ford put it, "I am a Ford, not a Lincoln."

Both Ford and Carter were men of decency and integrity, but neither established reputations as strong, dynamic leaders. Although many Americans admired their honesty and sincerity, neither succeeded in winning the confidence of the American people. Moreover, neither administration had a clear sense of direction. Both Ford and Carter seemed to waffle on major issues of public policy. As a result, both came to be regarded as unsure, vacillating presidents.

As a 13-term congressman from Grand Rapids, Michigan, Ford had established a reputation as a moderate Republican who had voted against federal aid to education, Medicare, and antipollution programs and staunchly supported the Vietnam War. Upon becoming president, he dismissed the possibility of pardoning Richard Nixon for his Watergate misdeeds, then changed his mind. In the realm of economic policy, he began by urging tax increases but later called for a large tax cut. Similar indecision crippled his energy policy. At first, he tried to raise prices by imposing import fees on imported oil and ending domestic price controls; then he abandoned that position in the face of severe political pressure.

Carter, too, suffered from the charge that he modified his stances in the face of political pressure. A man of firm religious beliefs, who had grown up on a humble Georgia farm that lacked running water and electricity, Carter had served in the Navy's atomic submarine program before returning home to run his family's peanut business. During two terms as governor of Georgia, he spent months in states with early presidential primaries and caucuses in order to create the momentum he needed to win the Democratic presidential nomination. During his successful 1976 presidential campaign, Carter spoke of cutting military spending, abolishing nuclear weapons, and withdrawing American troops from South Korea. By the end of his term, however, Carter spoke of the need for sustained growth in defense spending, upgrading nuclear forces in Europe, and developing a new strategic bomber.

Both Ford and Carter were described as "passionless presidents" who failed to project a clear vision of where they wanted to lead the country. But in their defense, both faced serious problems, ranging from dealing with soar-ing oil prices to confronting third-world terrorists.

WRENCHING ECONOMIC TRANSFORMATIONS

He is the personification of American business. His autobiography stood on the top of the best-seller list for years. A thick, powerful slab of a man, Lee Iacocca is the picture of a successful, confident American businessman. The irony of the picture is, of course, that Lee Iacocca is also the most visible symbol of the American automobile industry, which is in turn the most prominent example of the failure of American industry to compete in a changing world economy.

At one time, the car makers in Detroit produced automobiles that mirrored America's strength and power. They were big, heavy, powerful cars, with such expensive options as power windows, power brakes, and power steering. When an engineer at Chrysler designed a smaller, low-slung car, K. T. Keller, the company's top executive, remarked in disgust, "Chrysler builds cars to sit in, not to piss over." So what if they weren't energy-efficient. So what if they only traveled 10 to 13 miles on a gallon of gas. Until 1973, gas was cheap; just 37 cents a gallon that year.

Detroit—the land of big cars, of General Motors, Ford, and Chrysler—was Iacocca's world. From 1946 to 1978 he worked for Ford, climbing the corporate ladder from salesman to zone manager, to district manager, to divisional head, to president of Ford. He was the driving force behind Ford's most popular car—the Mustang.

In 1978, Henry Ford II, the grandson of the company's founder, fired Iacocca. Iacocca lashed back: "Your timing stinks," he told Ford. "We've just made a billion eight for the second year in a row. That's three and a half billion in the past two years. But mark my words, Henry. You may never see a billion eight again. And do you know why? Because you don't know how the [expletive deleted] we made it in the first place!"

In Iacocca's angry words there was more truth than perhaps *he* even realized. In the late 1970s, the American automotive industry had crashed into new economic realities. Although Middle Eastern oil had been inexpensive during the period between 1945 and the early 1970s, economic realities dictated that the price must eventually rise dramatically. Each year more and more nations entered the industrial ranks; each year the consumption of oil increased; each year the limited supplies of oil decreased. These simple economic facts combined with emerging Arab nationalism and the solidarity of the Organization of Petroleum Exporting Countries (OPEC) were bound to drive up the price of oil. As the price of a gallon of gas charged toward the dollar mark, American drivers purchased smaller, better engineered, fuel-efficient cars from Japan and Europe. By 1982, Japanese cars had captured 30 percent of the U.S. market.

Men like Iacocca looked to the government for help. After being fired from Ford, Iacocca accepted the top position at Chrysler. With the help of a $1.2 billion loan from Washington, he put the ailing company on its feet again.

Since 1973, the American economy has undergone a series of wrenching economic transformations. Economic growth slowed; productivity flagged; inflation rose; and major industries faltered in the face of foreign competition. Despite a massive influx of women into the workforce, family wages stagnated. A quarter century of rapid post–World War II economic growth ended.

This economic slowdown was not confined to the United States; all major industrialized nations experienced slower economic growth. Annual growth in America's real national output per employed person averaged 1.8 percent between 1960 and 1973; it dropped to 0.1 percent between 1974 and 1978. Japan's rate fell from 8.9 percent during the first period to 3.2 percent in the second; West Germany's fell from 4.7 to 3 percent.

The causes of worldwide economic decline are hotly contested. It has been attributed to surges in world oil prices during the 1970s; to the growing expense of government policies designed to protect public health, safety, and the environment and to aid the poor; to alleged foreign "dumping" of products at prices below their cost of production; to demands of organized labor for higher wages; to low productivity increases in the expanding service sector; and to excessive government deficits.

If the causes of economic stagnation remain unclear, the social and political consequences have been profound—evident in a sharp influx of wives and mothers into the work force, tax revolts and demands for tax reform, and calls for protection of American industry.

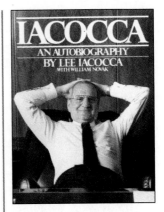

The cover of Lee Iacocca's autobiography portrays him as the consummate successful businessperson. Despite the decline in the American automobile industry, he put the ailing Chrysler company back on its feet—with the help of a large loan from the federal government.

The Age of Inflation

In 1967, the average price of a three-bedroom house was $17,000. A brand-new Cadillac convertible went for $6700 and a new Volkswagen for $1497. A portable typewriter cost $39 and a man's gray flannel suit $60. A Hershey chocolate bar sold for a nickel, a pound of sirloin for 89 cents, and a gallon of regular gasoline cost 39 cents. Two decades later, the prices of these products had quadrupled.

The upsurge in inflation started when Lyndon Johnson decided to fight the Vietnam War without raising taxes enough to pay for it. By 1968 the war was costing the United States $3 billion dollars a month, and the federal budget skyrocketed to $179 billion. With hundreds of thousands of Americans in the military service and even more working in defense-related industries, unemployment fell, wages rose, demand mushroomed, and government deficits increased. Inflation accelerated in the early 1970s as a result of a series of crop failures and sharp rises in commodities, especially oil.

High inflation had many negative effects on the American economy. It wiped out many families' savings. It provoked labor turmoil, as teachers, sanitation workers, auto workers, and others went on strike to try to win wage settlements ahead of inflation. It encouraged speculation in tangible assets—like art, antiques, precious metals, and real estate—rather than productive investment in new factories and technology. Above all, certain organized interest groups were able to keep up with inflation, while other less powerful groups, such as welfare recipients, saw the value of their benefits decline significantly.

Inflation reduced the purchasing power of most Americans. For over a decade, family wages remained flat. Yet inflation raised the prices of virtually all goods and services. Health care and housing, in particular, experienced price rises far above the inflation rate. The consequences were a sharp increase in the number of Americans unable to afford health insurance, and a dramatic increase in the cost of housing, which resulted in a sharp increase in homelessness.

Oil Embargo

Political unrest in the oil-rich Middle East contributed significantly to America's economic troubles. After suffering a humiliating defeat at the hands of Israel in the 1973 "Yom Kippur" war, Arab leaders unsheathed a new political weapon: oil. In order to pressure Israel out of territory conquered in the 1967 and 1973 wars, Arab nations cut oil production 25 percent and embargoed all oil exports to the United States. Leading the way was OPEC, which had been founded by Iran, Saudi Arabia, and Venezuela in 1960 to fight a reduction in prices by oil companies.

Because Arab nations controlled 60 percent of the proven oil reserves in the non-Communist world, they had the western nations over a barrel. Production cutbacks produced an immediate global shortage. The United States imported a third of its oil from Arab nations; western Europe imported 72 percent from the Middle East; Japan, 82 percent. Gas prices rose, long lines formed at gas pumps, some factories shortened the workweek, and some shopping centers restricted business hours.

The oil crisis brought to an end an era of cheap and ample energy. Americans had to learn to live with smaller cars and less heating and air-conditioning. But the crisis did have a positive side-effect. It increased public consciousness about the environment and stimu-

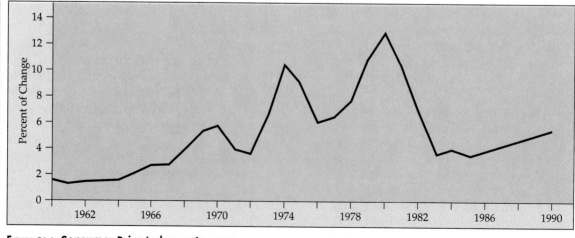

FIGURE 31.1 **Consumer Price Index, 1960–1990**

lated awareness of the importance of conservation. But for millions of Americans the lessons were painful.

Foreign Competition and Deindustrialization

It was January 17, 1949. Standing idly on the dock, waiting for work to begin, several longshoremen snickered in disbelief. The car looked ridiculously un-American. Tiny and ugly, it resembled half a walnut shell with wheels, or better yet, an insect, a "bug," a "beetle." Ben Pon, the official Volkswagen agent to the United States, was aboard the Dutch freighter *Westerdam* in New York Harbor, holding a press conference to introduce the VW to American consumers. He called the car the "Victory Wagon," but skeptical reporters dubbed it "Hitler's car." It was. A generation of American moviegoers remembered seeing it in 1930s newsreels touting Germany's economic recovery. But how could it ever appeal to Americans? The Volkswagen was slow, dull, small, and fuel-efficient, just when Americans were lusting after fins, scoop grilles, and chrome—lots of chrome. In 1949 Americans purchased 6,250,000 new automobiles. Two were VWs. The longshoremen were right, but not for long. They were laughing at the future.

In 1947, the United States was truly the world's factory. Half of all the world's manufacturing took place in the United States. Americans made 57 percent of the world's steel and 80 percent of the world's cars. It was inevitable that other countries would eventually challenge the dominance that American manufacturers had enjoyed in the aftermath of World War II. During the early 1960s, foreign manufacturers produced 6 percent of the cars purchased by Americans. That figure climbed to 20 percent in the late 1970s.

The foreign penetration extended far beyond the market for compact cars. Foreign countries began to dominate the highly profitable, technologically advanced fields, such as consumer electronics, luxury automobiles, and machine tools. Americans discovered that technologies their country had pioneered—such as semiconductors, color televisions, and

Declines in exports and increases in imports continue to trouble U.S. industry in the 1990s, leading many Americans to talk about the decline in the American automotive industry.

videocassette recorders—were now produced almost exclusively by foreign manufacturers. The decline in the American share of the market meant fewer jobs in the American automobile, steel, rubber, and electronics industries. In addition, American and even Japanese companies shifted low-skill production work to such places as Hong Kong, Indonesia, Singapore, South Korea, and Taiwan, where goods could be produced more cheaply because of lower wage scales.

Few economic developments aroused as much public concern during the 1970s as the loss of American jobs in basic industry. According to one estimate, 30 million jobs disappeared during the 1970s as the direct result of plant, store, and office shutdowns. Displaced workers saw their savings depleted, mortgages foreclosed, and health and pension benefits lost. Even when they found new jobs, they typically had to settle for wages substantially below what they had earned before. Plant shutdowns and closings had profound effects on entire communities, which lost their tax bases at the time that they needed to fund health and welfare services.

Whipping Stagflation

During the 1960s, the primary goal of economic policy was to encourage growth and keep unemployment low. Inflationary pressures were successfully tamed through "jawboning" industry leaders and unions to keep prices and wages stable. But by the early 1970s the economy started to suffer from stagflation—high unemployment and inflation coupled with stagnant economic growth. This presented economic policy-makers with a new and perplexing problem.

The problem with stagflation was the pain of its options. To attack inflation by reducing consumer purchasing power only made unemployment worse. The other choice was no better. Stimulating purchasing power and creating jobs also drove prices higher. Not surprisingly, economic policy during the 1970s was a nightmare of confusion and contradiction.

By 1971, pressures produced by the Vietnam War and federal social spending pushed the inflation rate to 5 percent and unemployment to 6 percent. President Richard Nixon responded by increasing federal budget deficits and devaluing the dollar. These policies were an attempt to stimulate the economy and to make American goods more competitive overseas. Nixon also imposed a 90-day wage and price freeze, followed by a mandatory set of wage-price guidelines, and then by voluntary controls. Inflation stayed at about 4 percent during the freeze, but once controls were lifted, inflation resumed its upward climb.

In 1974 during the first oil embargo, inflation hit 12 percent. Gerald Ford, the new president, initially attacked the problem in a traditional Republican fashion, tightening the money supply by raising interest rates and limiting government spending. In the end, his economic policy proved to be no more than a series of ineffectual wage and price guidelines monitored by the federal government. In the subsequent recession, unemployment reached 9 percent.

In January 1977, when Jimmy Carter took office, 7.4 percent of the workforce was unemployed. Carter responded with an ambitious spending program and called for the Federal Reserve (the Fed) to expand the money supply. Within two years, inflation had accelerated to 13.3 percent.

With inflation getting out of hand, the Federal Reserve Board announced in 1979 that it would fight inflation by restraining the growth of the money supply. Unemployment increased and interest rates moved to their highest levels in the nation's history. By November 1982, unemployment hit 10.8 percent, the highest since 1940. One out of every five American workers went some time without a job.

Along with high interest rates, the Carter administration adopted another weapon in the battle against stagflation: deregulation. Convinced that regulators too often protected the industries they were supposed to oversee, the Carter administration deregulated air and surface transportation and the savings and loan industry.

The effects of deregulation are hotly contested. Rural towns suffered cutbacks of bus, rail, and air service. Truckers and rail workers lost economic benefits of regulation. Travelers complained about rising airfares and congested airports. Cable TV viewers resented rising rates. Champions of deregulation argued that the policy increased competition, stimulated new investment, and forced inefficient firms either to become more efficient or shut down.

A NEW AMERICAN ROLE IN THE WORLD

In his inaugural address in 1961, John Kennedy stated that America would "pay any price, bear any burden, meet any hardship, support any friend or oppose any foe to assure the survival and the success of liberty." But by 1973, in the wake of the Vietnam War, American foreign policy-makers regarded Kennedy's stirring pledge as unrealistic.

The Vietnam War offered a lesson about the limits of American power. It underscored the need to distinguish between vital national interests and peripheral interests, and to balance America's military commitments with its limited resources. Above all, the Vietnam War appeared to illustrate the dangers of obsessive anti-Communism. Such a policy failed to recognize the fact that the world was becoming more complex, that power blocs were shifting, and that the interests of Communist countries and the United States could some-times overlap. Too often, American policy seemed to have driven nationalists and re-formers into Communist hands and to have led the United States to support corrupt, un-popular authoritarian regimes. The great challenge facing American foreign-policy-makers was how to preserve the nation's in-ternational prestige and influence in the face of declining defense budgets and mounting congressional opposition to direct overseas intervention.

Détente

As president, Richard Nixon radically rede-fined America's relationship with its two fore-most adversaries, China and the Soviet Union. In a remarkable turnabout from his record of staunch anti-Communism, he opened rela-tions with China and began strategic arms limitation talks with the Soviet Union. The goal of détente (the easing of tensions be-tween nations) was to continue to resist and deter Soviet adventurism while striving for "more constructive relations" with the Com-munist world.

Nixon and Henry Kissinger, the German-born former Harvard professor who served as assistant for national security affairs and later secretary of state, believed that it was necessary to curb the arms race, improve great power relationships, and learn to coex-ist with Communist regimes. The Nixon ad-ministration sought to use the Chinese and Soviet need for western trade and technology as a way to extract foreign policy conces-sions.

The new direction of American foreign policy was inaugurated in 1971 when the Nixon administration made the first overtures to China. Since 1949 U.S. policy recognized the Chiang Kai Shek regime on Taiwan as the legitimate government of China and refused to recognize the Chinese Communist govern-ment. In 1972 Nixon took part in a summit meeting in Beijing, walked the Great Wall, and slowly expanded American trade with China (see Chapter 29 for further discussion of Nixon's foreign policy).

Less dramatic, but no less important, was the beginning of a détente with the Soviet Union, culminating in a massive trade pact and strategic arms limitation talks. In a 1972 summit meeting in Moscow, the United States and Soviet Union vowed not to seek "unilat-eral advantages" against each other.

Recognizing that one of the legacies of Vietnam was a reluctance on the part of the American public to risk overseas interven-tions, Nixon and Kissinger also sought to build up regional powers that shared Ameri-can strategic interests, most notably China, Iran, and Saudi Arabia.

By the late 1970s, an increasing number of Americans believed that Soviet hard-liners viewed détente as a mere tactic to lull the West into relaxing its vigilance. Soviet Com-munist party chief Leonid Brezhnev rein-forced this view when he boasted of gains that his country had made at the United States' ex-pense—in Vietnam, Angola, Cambodia, Ethiopia, and Laos.

An alarming Soviet arms build-up con-tributed to the sense that détente was not working. By 1975, the Soviet Union had 50 percent more intercontinental ballistic mis-siles (ICBMs) than the United States, thirty times as many antiaircraft missile launchers, three times as many army personnel, three times as many attack submarines, and four times as many tanks. The United States con-tinued to have a powerful strategic deterrent, however, holding a 9000 to 3200 advantage in deliverable nuclear bombs and warheads. But the arms gap between the countries was narrowing.

Foreign Policy Triumphs

In the Middle East Jimmy Carter achieved a tremendous diplomatic success by negotiating peace between Egypt and Israel. Since the founding of Israel in 1948, Egypt's foreign policy had been built around destroying the Jewish state. In 1977, Anwar el-Sadat, the practical and farsighted leader of Egypt, de-cided to seek peace with Israel. To demon-strate that his intentions were sincere, he even traveled to Israel and spoke with the Israeli

Knesset. It was an act of rare political courage, for Sadat risked alienating Egypt from the rest of the Arab world without a firm commitment for a peace treaty with Israel.

Although both countries wanted peace, major obstacles had to be overcome. Sadat wanted Israel to retreat from the West Bank of the Jordan River and from the Golan Heights (which it had taken from Jordan in the 1967 war), recognize the Palestine Liberation Organization (PLO), provide a homeland for the Palestinians, relinquish its unilateral hold on the city of Jerusalem, and return the Sinai to Egypt. Such conditions were unacceptable to Israeli Prime Minister Menachem Begin, who refused to consider recognition of the PLO or the return of the West Bank. By the end of 1977, Sadat's peace mission had run aground.

Jimmy Carter broke the deadlock by inviting both men to Camp David, the presidential retreat in Maryland, for face-to-face talks. It was almost like a working holiday. For two weeks in September 1978 they hammered out peace accords. Although several important issues were left unresolved, Begin did agree to return the Sinai to Egypt. In return, Egypt promised to recognize Israel, and as a result became a staunch American ally. For Carter it was a proud moment. Unfortunately, the Camp David Accords were denounced by the rest of the Arab Middle East, and in 1981 Sadat paid for his vision with his life when anti-Israeli Egyptian soldiers assassinated him.

In 1978 Carter also pushed the Panama Canal Treaty through the Senate, which provided for the return of the Canal Zone to Panama and improved the image of the United States in Latin America. One year later, he extended diplomatic recognition to the People's Republic of China. Carter's successes in the international arena, however, would soon be overshadowed by the greatest challenge of his presidency—the Iranian hostage crisis.

No Island of Stability

One of the tragic unfortunate aspects of American foreign policy is that the United

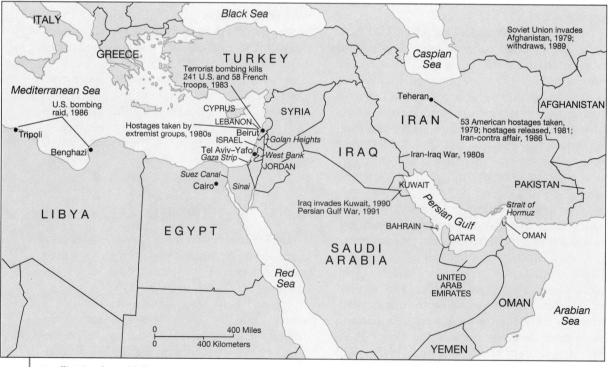

Conflict in the Middle East

Jimmy Carter's greatest triumph as president came with the signing of the Camp David Accords between Egypt and Israel.

States historically has supported many countries that hold power through murder, torture, and other violations of human rights. In the mid-1970s, U.S. allies Argentina, Brazil, Chile, El Salvador, Iran, Nicaragua, Paraguay, the Philippines, South Korea, and Uruguay engaged in torture.

During Jimmy Carter's presidency, the United States began to show a growing regard for the human rights practices of its allies. Carter was convinced that American foreign policy should embody the country's basic moral beliefs. In 1977 Congress began to require reports on human rights conditions in countries receiving American aid.

Of the nations accused of practicing torture, one of the most frequently cited was Iran. Estimates of the number of political prisoners in Iran ranged from 25,000 to 100,000. It was widely believed that most of them had been tortured by SAVAK, the secret police. Tortures included electric shock, beatings, insertions of bottles in the rectum, hanging

weights from the testicles, and rape. Writers, artists, and intellectuals were often targets of torture.

Since the end of World War II, Iran had been a valuable friend of the United States in the troubled Middle East. In 1953 the CIA had worked to ensure the power of the young Shah, Mohammad Reza Pahlavi. During the next 25 years, the Shah had often repaid the debt. He allowed the United States to establish electronic listening posts in northern Iran along the border of the Soviet Union, and during the 1973–1974 Arab oil embargo the shah continued to sell oil to the United States. The Shah also bought arms from the United States, which helped ease the American balance-of-payments problem. All things considered, few world leaders were more loyal to the United States.

Like his predecessors, Carter was willing to overlook the Shah's violations of human rights. To demonstrate America's support of the Shah, Carter visited Iran in late December 1977. He applauded Iran as "an island of stability in one of the most troubled areas of the world" and praised the Shah as a great leader who had won "the respect and the admiration and love" of his people.

The Shah was popular among wealthy Iranians and Americans. In the slums of the southern section of Teheran and in the poverty-stricken villages of Iran, however, there was little respect, admiration, or love for his regime. Led by a fundamentalist Islamic clergy and emboldened by want, the masses of Iranians turned against the Shah and his westernization policy.

In the early fall of 1978 the revolutionary surge in Iran gained force. The Shah, who had once seemed so powerful and secure, was paralyzed by indecision, alternating between ruthless suppression and attempts to liberalize his regime. In Washington, Carter also vacillated, uncertain whether to stand firmly behind the Shah or to cut losses and prepare to deal with a new government in Iran.

In January 1979, the Shah fled to Egypt. Exiled religious leader Ayatollah Ruholla Khomeini returned to Iran, preaching the doctrine that the United States was the "Great Satan" behind the Shah. Relations between

America and the new Iranian government were terrible, but Iranian officials warned that they would become infinitely worse if the Shah were admitted to the United States. Nevertheless, Carter permitted the Shah to come to the United States for treatment of lymphoma. "You're opening a Pandora's box," the Iranian prime minister remarked when he heard the news.

On November 4, 1979, Iranian supporters of Khomeini invaded the American embassy in Teheran and captured 66 Americans, 13 of whom were freed several weeks later. The rest were held hostage for 444 days and were the objects of intense political interest and media coverage. Between 1972 and 1977 the three major television networks had devoted only an average of five minutes per year to coverage of Iran; during the hostage crisis Iran coverage appeared every night.

Carter was helpless. Because Iran was not a stable country in any recognizable sense, it was impossible to pressure. Iran's demands—the return of the Shah to Iran and admission of U.S. guilt in supporting the Shah—were unacceptable. Carter devoted far too much attention to the almost insoluble problem. The hostages stayed in the public spotlight in part because Carter kept them there.

Carter's foreign policy problems mounted in December 1979, when the Soviet Union sent tanks into Afghanistan. In response, the Carter administration imposed an embargo on grain and high-technology exports to the USSR and boycotted the 1980 Olympics in Moscow. The Soviet Union gradually withdrew its troops from Afghanistan a decade later.

Some Carter advisers advocated the use of force to free the hostages in Iran. Although Carter disagreed at first, he eventually authorized a rescue attempt. It failed and his position became even worse. Negotiations finally brought the hostages' release, but in a final humiliation for Carter, the hostages were held until minutes after Ronald Reagan, Carter's successor, had taken the oath of office. Yet while the timing of the hostage release was seen as a humiliation, Carter had

After 444 days the Iranian hostage crisis ended, but not before it had virtually paralyzed Carter's administration and destroyed his chances for reelection.

played a pivotal role in negotiation that ended their captivity by agreeing to release frozen Iranian assets in exchange for their freedom.

When Carter left office in January 1981 many Americans judged his presidency a failure. Although in 1978 he had pushed through Congress the Panama Canal Treaty, which provided for the return of the Canal Zone to Panama and improved the image of the United States in Latin America, and although in 1979 he consummated the process of recognizing Communist China, the prolonged hostage crisis undermined his presidency. Instead of being remembered for the good he accomplished for the Middle East at Camp David, he was remembered for what he failed to accomplish. The Iranian hostage crisis had become emblematic of a perception that America's role in the world had declined.

THE REAGAN REVOLUTION

The traumatic events of the 1970s—Watergate, stagflation, the energy crisis, the defeat of South Vietnam, and the Iranian hostage crisis—produced a severe loss of confidence among the American people. Americans were deeply troubled by the relative decline of American strength in the world; the decline of the productivity and innovation in American industry; and the dramatic growth of lobbies and special-interest groups that seemed to have paralyzed the legislative process. Many worried that too much power had been stripped from the presidency, that political parties were so weakened and Congress so splintered that it was impossible to enact a coherent legislative program.

Ronald Reagan capitalized on this frustration. When he ran for the presidency against Carter in 1980, he asked Americans, "Are you better off than you were four years ago?" With inflation at 18 percent, the answer was obvious: "No." Reagan won a landslide victory, carrying 43 states and almost 51 percent of the popular vote compared to Carter's 41 percent. In addition, the Democrats lost the Senate for the first time since 1954.

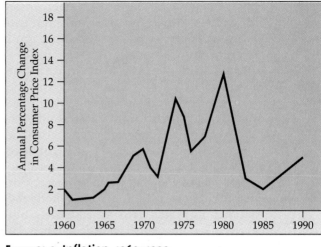

FIGURE 31.2 **Inflation, 1960–1990**

The Gipper

When he was elected president in 1980, Ronald Reagan was already well known to the American people as a movie actor and radio and television announcer. He had risen to celebrity status from extremely modest beginnings. Born in 1911, Reagan, the son of a shoe salesman, grew up in a succession of small Illinois towns. After a stint as a sportscaster at a radio station in Des Moines, he landed a Hollywood screen test in 1937. He went on to make 50 films, most of them B movies. Often remembered for his performance in *Knute Rockne, All American* (1940), Reagan played George Gipp, the Notre Dame halfback, whose dying words were "win one for the gipper." After World War II, he served as president of the Screen Actors Guild, and in 1954, he turned to television, hosting *GE Theater* and *Death Valley Days*.

In politics, he started out as a liberal, staunchly supporting Franklin D. Roosevelt and the New Deal. As head of the Screen Actors Guild, however, he became concerned about Communist infiltration of the labor movement in Hollywood. In 1952 and 1956, he voted for Dwight Eisenhower and in 1960 he led Democrats for Nixon.

Reagan was catapulted into the national political spotlight in 1964 when he gave an emotional television speech in support of Republican presidential nominee Barry Goldwater, denouncing big government, foreign aid, welfare, urban renewal, and high taxes. Two years later, Reagan successfully ran for governor of California, promising to cut state spending and crack down on student protesters.

In the 1980 presidential campaign, Reagan drew strong support from white Southerners, suburban Roman Catholics, evangelical Christians, and particularly the New Right, a confederation of disparate political and religious groups bound together by their concern over what they considered the erosion of values in America. In March 1981 an assassin's bullet nearly killed Reagan. He truly captured the nation's imagination by responding to the shooting with remarkable courage. From his hospital bed, he sent a message to his wife Nancy, "Honey, I forgot to duck."

Reaganomics

When President Reagan took office he promised to cut inflation, rebuild the nation's defenses, restore economic growth, and trim the size of the federal government by limiting its role in welfare, education, and housing. He pledged to end exorbitant union contracts to make American goods competitive again, to cut taxes drastically to stimulate investment and purchasing power, and to decontrol businesses strangled by federal regulation in order to restore competition. Despite his pledges, his policies trimmed little from the size of the federal government, failed to make American goods competitive in the world market, and led to increased consolidation rather than competition. Nevertheless, many Americans believed that he had improved the country's economic situation.

Reagan blamed the country's economic ills on declining capital investment and a tax structure biased against work and productive investment. To stimulate the economy, he persuaded Congress to slash tax rates. In 1981, he pushed a bill through Congress cutting taxes 5 percent in 1981 and 10 percent in 1982 and 1983. In 1986, the administration pushed through another tax bill, which substantially reduced tax rates for the wealthiest Americans to 28 percent, while closing a variety of tax loopholes.

In August 1981, Reagan dealt a devastating blow to organized labor by dismissing 15,000 striking air traffic controllers. Union leaders condemned the firings, but in an antiunion atmosphere most Americans backed Reagan. His popularity ratings soared.

To strengthen the nation's defenses, the Reagan administration doubled the defense budget, to more than $330 billion in 1987. Reagan believed that a militarily strong America would not have been humiliated by Iran and would have discouraged Soviet adventurism.

To "liberate free enterprise from fifty years of liberal Democratic restraints," Reagan expanded the Carter administration's efforts to decontrol and deregulate the economy. Congress deregulated the banking and natural gas industries and lifted ceilings on interest rates. Federal price controls on airfares were lifted as well. The Environmental Protection Agency relaxed its interpretation of the Clean Air Act; and the Department of the Interior opened up large areas of the federal domain, including offshore oil fields, to private development.

The results of deregulation were mixed. Bank interest rates became more competitive, but smaller banks found it difficult to hold their own against larger institutions. Natural gas prices increased, but so did production, easing some of the country's dependence on foreign fuel. Airfares on high-traffic routes between major cities dropped dramatically in the 1980s when price controls were lifted, but fares for short, low-traffic flights skyrocketed. Most critics agreed, however, that deregulation had restored some short-term competition to the marketplace. Yet in the long term, competition also led to increased business failures and consolidation.

Reagan's laissez-faire principles could also be seen in his administration's approach to social programs. Convinced that federal welfare programs promoted laziness, promiscuity, and moral decay, Reagan limited benefits to those he considered the "truly needy." His administration cut spending on a variety of social welfare programs, including Aid to Families with Dependent Children; food stamps; child nutrition; job training for young people; programs to prevent child abuse; and mental health services. The Reagan administration also eliminated cash welfare assistance for the working poor and reduced federal subsidies for child-care services for low-income families. A symbol of Reagan social service cuts was an attempt by the Agriculture Department in 1981 to allow ketchup to be counted as a vegetable in school lunches.

Reagan left office with the economy in the midst of its longest post–World War II expansion. The economy was growing faster, with less inflation, than any time since the mid-1960s. Adjusted for inflation, disposable personal income per person rose 20 percent after 1980. Inflation fell to less than 4 percent. Unemployment was down to around 5 percent. These figures compared favorably to January 1981, the month Reagan became president, when inflation was running at 13 percent a year and unemployment stood at 7.4 percent.

Reagan's critics, however, charged that Reagan had only created the illusion of prosperity. They denounced the massive federal budget deficit, which increased $1.5 trillion during the Reagan presidency, three times the debt accumulated by all 39 of Reagan's presidential predecessors. They decried the growing income gap between rich and poor, as well as the expensive consequences of reduced government regulation, such as cleaning up federal nuclear weapons facilities, and, especially, bailing out the nation's savings and loans industry.

The Celebration of Wealth

In 1981, the year Ronald Reagan was inaugurated as president, ABC television introduced the smash hit *Dynasty,* a show celebrating glamour and greed. It was, in the eyes of many social commentators, an appropriate beginning for the 1980s—a decade of greed, selfishness, and an anything-goes attitude. It was a decade when financier Ivan Boesky claimed, "Greed is not a bad thing. You shouldn't feel guilty"; when Nancy Reagan spent $25,000 on her inaugural wardrobe and $209,508 on new White House china; when the prime-time television soap opera about the super-rich, *Dallas,* reached number one in the ratings; and when Madonna had a pop music hit entitled "Material Girl." On television, advertisers told consumers, "Yes, you can have it all, you deserve it all, all for you, yes . . ." President Reagan's message was simi-

lar. Americans could have it all—low taxes, a strong defense, and middle-class entitlements.

Wall Street enthusiastically took part in the new celebration of wealth, as the Reagan years witnessed a corporate merger and takeover boom of unprecedented proportions. By using low-grade, risky "junk bonds" to finance corporate acquisitions, corporate raiders such as Michael Milken of Drexel Burnham Lambert purchased and dismantled companies for huge profits. In 1987, Milken earned $550 million by financing acquisitions.

During the 1980s, 100,000 Americans became millionaires every year. The average annual earnings of the bottom 20 percent, however, fell from $9376 to $8800. In addition, many of the new jobs created during the Reagan years were in the low-wage service industries.

By the early 1990s, there were signs that the time had come to pay for the financial excesses of the 1980s. Following a 508-point fall in the Dow Jones industrial average on October 19, 1987—a 22.6 percent plunge in stock values—many Wall Street stock brokerage firms began to lay off employees, cutbacks that continued despite the market's recovery. In 1989, Milken was indicted on charges of criminal racketeering and securities fraud. The next year, Drexel Burnham Lambert agreed to pay a fine of $650

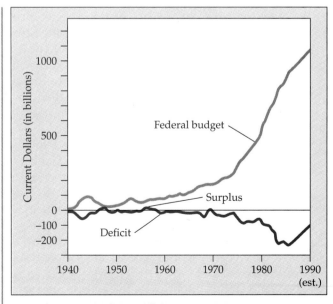

FIGURE 31.3 **U.S. Budget Deficits, 1940–1990**

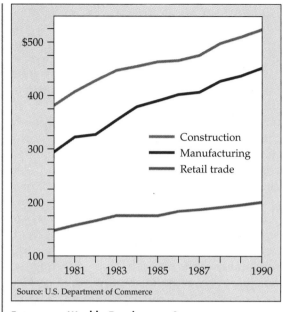

FIGURE 31.4 Weekly Earnings, 1980–1990

million and filed for bankruptcy. Wall Street speculator Ivan Boesky was fined $100 million for insider trading and sentenced to jail. Those Americans who had participated in the ambition, greed, vanity, and excess of the 1980s seemed to be getting their comeuppance.

The Reagan Doctrine

During the early years of the Reagan presidency, Cold War tensions between the Soviet Union and the United States intensified. Reagan entered office deeply suspicious of the Soviet Union. Reagan described the Soviet Union as "an evil empire" and called for a space-based missile defense system, derided by critics as "Star Wars."

Reagan and his advisers tended to view every regional conflict through a Cold War lens. Nowhere was this more true than in the Western Hemisphere, where Reagan was determined to prevent Communist takeovers. In October 1983 Prime Minister Maurice Bishop of Grenada, a small island nation in the Caribbean, was assassinated and a more radical Marxist government took power. Soviet money and Cuban troops came to Grenada, and when they began constructing an airfield capable of landing large military aircraft, the Reagan administration decided to remove the Communists and restore a pro-American regime. On October 25 American troops invaded Grenada, killed or captured 750 Cuban soldiers, and established a new government. The invasion sent a clear message throughout the region that the Reagan administration would not tolerate communism in its hemisphere.

In his 1985 state of the union address, President Reagan pledged his support for anti-Communist revolutions in what would become known as the "Reagan Doctrine." In Afghanistan, the United States was already providing aid to anti-Soviet freedom fighters, ultimately helping to force Soviet troops to withdraw. It was in Nicaragua, however, that the Reagan doctrine received its most controversial application.

In 1979 Nicaraguans revolted against the corrupt Somoza regime. A new junta took power, dominated by young Marxists known as Sandinistas. The Sandinistas insisted that they favored free elections, nonalignment, and a mixed economy, but once in power they postponed elections, forced opposition leaders into exile, and turned to the Soviet bloc for arms and advisers. For the Reagan administration, Nicaragua looked "like another Cuba," a Communist state that threatened the security of its Central American neighbors.

In his first months in office, President Reagan approved covert training of anti-Sandinista rebels (called "contras"), some of whom were former members of the Somoza National Guard. While the contras waged war on the Sandinistas from camps in Honduras, the CIA provided assistance, mining Nicaraguan harbors and issuing a manual offering ways of assassinating Sandinistas. In 1984 Congress ordered an end to all covert aid to the contras.

The Reagan administration circumvented Congress by soliciting contributions for the contras from private individuals and from foreign governments seeking U.S. favor. The president also permitted the sale of arms to Iran, with profits diverted to the contras. The arms sale and transfer of funds to the contras were handled surreptitiously through the CIA intelligence network, apparently with the full support of CIA director William Casey. Exposure of the Iran-contra affair in late 1986 provoked a major congressional investigation.

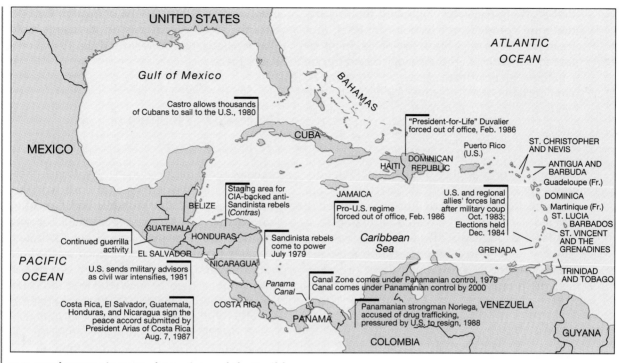

U.S. Involvement in Central America and the Caribbean

Map labels:
- UNITED STATES
- Gulf of Mexico
- ATLANTIC OCEAN
- Castro allows thousands of Cubans to sail to the U.S., 1980
- BAHAMAS
- CUBA
- "President-for-Life" Duvalier forced out of office, Feb. 1986
- Puerto Rico (U.S.)
- ST. CHRISTOPHER AND NEVIS
- MEXICO
- HAITI
- DOMINICAN REPUBLIC
- ANTIGUA AND BARBUDA
- Guadeloupe (Fr.)
- DOMINICA
- Martinique (Fr.)
- ST. LUCIA
- BARBADOS
- ST. VINCENT AND THE GRENADINES
- Staging area for CIA-backed anti-Sandinista rebels (Contras)
- BELIZE
- JAMAICA
- Pro-U.S. regime forced out of office, Feb. 1986
- U.S. and regional allies' forces land after military coup Oct. 1983; Elections held Dec. 1984
- GUATEMALA
- HONDURAS
- Caribbean Sea
- GRENADA
- Continued guerrilla activity
- EL SALVADOR
- Sandinista rebels come to power July 1979
- PACIFIC OCEAN
- NICARAGUA
- TRINIDAD AND TOBAGO
- U.S. sends military advisors as civil war intensifies, 1981
- Panama Canal
- Canal Zone comes under Panamanian control, 1979 Canal comes under Panamanian control by 2000
- VENEZUELA
- Costa Rica, El Salvador, Guatemala, Honduras, and Nicaragua sign the peace accord submitted by President Arias of Costa Rica Aug. 7, 1987
- COSTA RICA
- PANAMA
- Panamanian strongman Noriega, accused of drug trafficking, pressured by U.S. to resign, 1988
- GUYANA
- COLOMBIA

The scandal seriously weakened the influence of the president.

The American preoccupation with Nicaragua began to subside in 1987, after President Oscar Arias Sanchez of Costa Rica proposed a regional peace plan. In national elections in 1990, the Nicaraguan opposition routed the Sandinistas, bringing an end to ten turbulent years of Sandinista rule.

A Remarkable Ideological Turnaround

In 1982, 75-year-old Soviet party leader Leonid Brezhnev died. His regime had been marked by growing stagnation, corruption, and a huge military build-up. Initially, the post-Brezhnev era seemed to offer little change in U.S.-Soviet relations. KGB leader Yuri Andropov succeeded Brezhnev but died after only 15 months in power. He was replaced by another Brezhnev loyalist, Konstantin Chernenko, who died just a year later. His successor was Mikhail Gorbachev, a 54-year-old agricultural specialist with little formal ex-

perience in foreign affairs who pledged to continue the policies of his predecessors.

Within weeks, however, Gorbachev called for sweeping political liberalization—*glasnost*—and economic reform—*perestroika.* He allowed wider freedom of the press, assembly, travel, and religion. He persuaded the Communist party leadership to end its monopoly on power, created the Soviet Union's

Controversy and unrest arose in the Reagan administration when no one would accept responsibility for the Iran-contra affair.

first working legislature; allowed the first nationwide competitive elections in 1989; and freed hundreds of political prisoners. In an effort to boost the sagging Soviet economy, he legalized small private business cooperatives, won parliamentary approval for the leasing of lands to individuals with the right of inheritance, and approved foreign investment within the Soviet Union.

In foreign affairs, Gorbachev completely reshaped world politics. He cut the Soviet defense budget, withdrew Soviet troops from Afghanistan and eastern Europe, allowed a unified Germany to become a member of NATO, and agreed with the United States to destroy short-range and medium-range nuclear weapons. Most dramatically, Gorbachev actively promoted the democratization of for-

mer Soviet satellite nations in Eastern Europe. For his accomplishments in defusing Cold War tensions, he was awarded the 1990 Nobel Peace Prize.

The Reagan Revolution in Perspective

In the presidential election of 1984, Ronald Reagan and Vice President George Bush won in a landslide over Walter Mondale and Geraldine Ferraro, the first woman nominated for vice president on a major party ticket. Although Reagan's second term was plagued by the Iran-contra scandal, he left office after eight years more popular than he arrived. He could claim the distinction of being the first president to serve two full terms since Dwight Eisenhower.

Ronald Reagan could also point to an extraordinary string of accomplishments. He had dampened inflation, restored public confidence in government, and presided over the beginning of the end of the Cold War. He doubled the defense budget, named the first woman to the Supreme Court, launched a strong economic boom, and created a heightened sense of national unity. In addition, his supporters said that he restored vigor to the national economy and psyche, rebuilt America's military might, regained the nation's place as the world's preeminent power, restored American patriotism, and championed traditional family values.

On the other hand, his detractors criticized him for a reckless use of military power, and for circumventing Congress in foreign affairs. They accused Reagan of fostering greed and intolerance, and they charged that his administration, in its zeal to cut waste from government, ripped the social safety net and skimped on the government's regulatory functions. The administration, they further charged, was insensitive on racial issues.

Reagan's detractors were particularly concerned about his economic legacy. During the Reagan years the national debt tripled, from $909 billion to almost $2.9 trillion (the interest alone amounted to 14 percent of the federal budget), soaking up savings, causing in-

In order to stimulate the Soviet economy, Mikhail Gorbachev launched his program of *perestroika*, or economic restructuring, which welcomed foreign investment and encouraged joint ventures with foreign businesses. *Perestroika* permitted U.S. businesses, like this American pizzeria, to operate in Moscow.

terest rates to rise, depressing local economies, and forcing the federal government to shift more and more responsibilities onto the states. Corporate and individual debt also soared. During the early 1990s, the American people consumed $1 trillion more goods and services than they produced. The United States also became the world's biggest debtor nation, as a result of a weak dollar, a low level of exports, and the need to borrow abroad to finance budget deficits.

THE BUSH PRESIDENCY

In the 1988 presidential campaign the Republican candidate, Vice President George Bush, was said to have the best resumé in Washington. Winning the Distinguished Service Cross during World War II, Bush had made a fortune in the Texas oil business, and then went to Washington where he served as a Congressman, ambassador to the United Nations, envoy to China, and director of the CIA. His Democratic opponent, Massachusetts governor Michael Dukakis, was a serious, hardworking son of Greek immigrants.

Mudslinging and personal invective are nothing new in American politics, but the 1988 campaign was unusually vacuous and cynical. Real differences between the candidates' positions—over health care, housing policy, foreign policy, and defense spending—were submerged in a battle over character, abortion, prison furloughs, school prayer, and patriotism. The most emotional issue of the campaign involved the Pledge of Allegiance. Seizing on Governor Dukakis's veto of a 1977 Massachusetts bill requiring teachers to lead their classes in the pledge, Vice President Bush suggested that his opponent's liberalism led him to place civil liberties above patriotism. "Should public-school teachers be required to lead our children in the Pledge of Allegiance?" Bush asked his audience at the Republican convention. "My opponent says no—but I say yes."

The 1988 presidential campaign dramatized a development that had been reshaping American politics since the late 1960s: the growing power of media consultants and pollsters, who market candidates much as cigarette manufacturers or soap companies sell their products, by emphasizing imagery and symbolism. At the end of a race that saw both candidates use negative campaigning, Bush was elected the forty-first president of the United States, with 56 percent of the popular vote.

A Kinder, Gentler Nation

Presidents' inaugural addresses often set the tone for their entire terms in office. At his inauguration, Jimmy Carter stressed the limits of American power in the world. Ronald Reagan set an entirely different tone in his inaugural address, in which he voiced his desire to reduce government's social welfare role: "Government is not the solution to our problem; government is the problem."

In his inaugural address, Bush signaled a departure from the avarice and greed of the Reagan era by calling for a "new engagement in the lives of others." He promised to be more of a "hands-on" administrator than his predecessor, and he committed his presidency to creating a "kinder, gentler" nation, more sensitive and caring to the poor and disadvantaged.

During his first years in office, President Bush and the Democratic-controlled Congress addressed many issues ignored during the Reagan years. For the first time in eight years, the federal government raised the minimum wage—from $3.35 to $4.25 an hour. For the first time in 13 years, Congress amended federal air pollution laws in order to reduce noxious emissions from smokestacks and tailpipes and reduce acid rain. For the first time since 1971, Congress considered child-care legislation and ultimately voted to provide subsidies to low-income families to defray the costs of child care. In other actions, Congress prohibited job discrimination against the disabled, required nutrition labeling on processed foods, and expanded immigration into the United States.

In two areas critics accused President Bush of reneging on his promise of a "kinder, gentler" nation. He vetoed a new civil rights bill bolstering protections for minorities and women against job discrimination, on the grounds that it would lead to quotas, and he also vetoed a bill that would have provided up to six months of unpaid family leave for workers with newly born or adopted children or emergencies. In November 1991, however, Bush signed a compromise Civil Rights Act, which made it easier for workers to win antidiscrimination lawsuits.

Collapse of Communism

For 40 years Communist party leaders in Eastern Europe had ruled confidently. Although each year their countries fell further behind the West, they remained secure in the knowledge that the Soviet Union, backed by the Red Army, would always send in the tanks when the forces for change became too great. But they had not bargained on a liberal Soviet leader like Mikhail Gorbachev.

As Gorbachev moved toward reform within the Soviet Union and détente with the West, he pushed the conservative regimes of Eastern Europe outside his protective umbrella. By the end of 1989 the Berlin Wall had been smashed and across Eastern Europe citizens took to the streets, overthrowing 40 years of Communist rule. Like a series of falling dominos, Communist parties in Poland, East Germany, Hungary, Czechoslovakia, and Bulgaria fell from power.

Gorbachev, who had wanted to reform communism, had not anticipated the swift swing toward democracy in Eastern Europe. Nor had he fully foreseen the impact that democracy in Eastern Europe would have on the Soviet Union. By 1990 leaders of several Soviet republics began to demand independence or greater autonomy within the Soviet Union.

Gorbachev had to balance the growing demand for radical political change within the Soviet Union with the demand by Soviet hardliners that he dam the new democratic currents and turn back the clock. Faced with dangerous political opposition from the right and the left and with economic failure throughout the Soviet Union, Gorbachev tried to satisfy everyone and in the process satisfied no one.

In 1990, following the example of eastern Europe, the three Baltic states of Lithuania, Latvia, and Estonia announced their independence, and other Soviet republics demanded greater sovereignty. Nine of the 15 Soviet Republics agreed to sign a new union treaty, granting far greater freedom and autonomy to individual republics. But in August 1991, before the treaty could be signed, conservative communists tried to oust Gorbachev in a coup d'état. Boris Yeltsin, president of the Republic of Russia, and his supporters defeated the coup, which undermined support for the Communist party. Gorbachev fell from power. The Soviet Union ended its existence in December 1991, when Russia and most other republics formed the Commonwealth of Independent States.

In 1993, a new power struggle broke out, pitting Yeltsin against communists and nationalists in the Russian Parliament. In August, Yeltsin dissolved the Parliament, charging an "irreconcilable opposition" with blocking his reforms. Yeltsin ordered opposi-

For nearly three decades the Berlin Wall was the most visible symbol of the Cold War and of the division between East and West. The most dramatic incident marking the end of the Cold War was the destruction of the Wall in November 1989.

Lacking public and popular support, the attempted right-wing coup in the Soviet Union collapsed within days. Here, protesters cheer the soldiers who have withdrawn their tanks from the coup.

tion legislators, holed up in the Parliament building, to evacuate. Fierce street battles erupted between troops loyal to Yeltsin and thousands of armed communists and nationalists before the army crushed the uprising, attacked the building, and forced Yeltsin's opponents to surrender.

The struggles between reformers, nationalists, and communists persisted. The former Soviet Union remained beset by deep economic problems and severe ethnic and regional conflicts that showed little sign of abating.

Economic and Foreign Policy

Many Americans believed that the end of the Cold War would bring a huge peace dividend, which could be used to reduce the federal budget deficit and fund domestic social programs. Soon after Bush took office, however, Americans learned that much of the peace dividend would have to be spent to clean up nuclear wastes produced at federal facilities and to bail out the nation's troubled savings and loan industry.

The roots of the savings and loan crisis were planted during the presidency of Jimmy Carter, when high inflation and high interest rates threatened to bankrupt savings institutions, which could not compete with other financial institutions permitted to pay high interest rates. A 1980 law lifted limits on the interest rates savings institutions could pay and allowed them to make a limited amount of investments in commercial real estate. In 1982 and 1983, Congress broadened the institution's capacity to make unsecured commercial loans and investments in commercial real estate.

The savings and loan industry's problems began in the mid-1980s, when falling oil prices led to a collapse of land values, especially in the Southwest, creating huge losses for savings institutions invested in real estate. By the end of the decade these institutions began to fail in large numbers. The mounting bills for the savings and loan bailout propelled President Bush in 1990 to violate his 1988 "no new taxes" campaign pledge.

The first important foreign policy act of the Bush administration was an invasion of

THE END OF TWO ERAS

THE dates on the obituary read 1922 to 1991. When the death was duly recorded in newspapers and magazines throughout the world, only a handful of bureaucrats mourned the corpse. That body—the Union of Soviet Socialist Republics (USSR)—was the light that failed. Born in the cold and ice of a late Russian December, the USSR promised equality and justice. Driven by the belief in communism, Vladimir Lenin, the leader of the Bolsheviks who came to power in Russia in 1917 and founded the USSR five years later, announced that Russia was only the first step. Eventually, he said, communism would free the entire world and introduce a new epoch of peace, prosperity, and happiness for all people. The epoch never arrived. It remained only in the minds of the true believers. Instead of liberating the world, Soviet leaders suppressed freedom inside the Soviet Union. As one journalist noted in his obituary of the Soviet Union, "There is no reason to mourn the death of a country that killed millions of its own citizens in the collectivization campaign, the purges and the famines that were used as an instrument of government policy."

Born in a brutal Russian winter, the USSR died in an equally severe winter. About the death there was a singular note of irony. The Soviet leader who had done the most to reform and humanize the country caused its death. Mikhail Gorbachev became the leader of the Soviet Union in 1985. He was relatively young—in 1980 he had become the youngest full member of the Politburo, the ruling body in the USSR—and very well educated. He knew that every year his country was falling further and further behind the West in every material sense. Determined to correct the slide, he introduced measures to restructure the Soviet economy (*perestroika*) and to create a new political openness (*glasnost*). His economic measures never worked, but his political initiatives worked all too well.

First, Eastern Europe used the new openness to break away from the Soviet orbit. Then, the USSR's Baltic republics of Lithuania, Latvia, and Estonia demanded and received independence. Finally, the remaining 12 republics of the Soviet Union decided that the union was unworkable and undesirable. Gorbachev attempted to hold the republics together but failed. On Christmas Day, 1991, he faced the reality that the Soviet Union no longer existed and resigned from office.

The Soviet newspaper *Izvestia* commented that Gorbachev "did all he could." Perhaps no leader could have kept the Soviet Union from breaking apart once liberalization had started. Political freedom was singularly out of step with Soviet political traditions. But Gorbachev did fail in several areas. A man who had risen through the Soviet bureaucracy, Gorbachev failed to significantly reform or abolish that bureaucracy even though it became clear that that very bureaucracy was the primary obstacle to *perestroika*. In addition, he never devised a plan to allow enough freedom in the individual republics, and he even tacitly permitted Soviet security forces to use tanks and guns to suppress the Baltic independence movements. But most importantly, Gorbachev's *perestroika* did not work because it did not bring a new era of prosperity to the Soviet Union. Gorbachev admitted that "the old system fell apart even before the new system began to work," but as one authority commented, "there was no new system." Like every Soviet leader since Lenin, Gorbachev had promised far more than he delivered.

The death of the Soviet Union posed immense problems both for the newly independent republics and the United States. Even before Gorbachev's resignation, 11 of the 12 remaining republics—only the republic of Georgia was excluded—joined together into a new confederation called the Commonwealth of Independent States. Led by the republics of Russia, Belorussia, and Ukraine, the new entity was more an alliance than a state. The republics agreed to cooperate in economic reforms aimed at moving them toward a free enterprise system and maintain at least temporarily the ruble as the common currency. Further, and without being very specific, they announced that the Commonwealth would coordinate economic, military, and foreign policies of its independent members. Central to the Commonwealth, however, was the idea that each member was and remained a sovereign nation. To underscore this idea, the Commonwealth located its capital in Minsk rather than Moscow, the seat of Soviet power, or St. Petersburg, the capital of czarist Russia.

From the first, the Commonwealth faced a difficult task. Disputes quickly arose over how to divide the military and economic resources of the old Soviet Union. The sovereign republics had to decide how to divide the forces and equipment of the Red Army and the Soviet Navy as well as the Soviet state treasury, central television network, space infrastructure, and the hundreds of other assets once controlled by the Soviet Union. As a symbol of the great change, in February 1992 the Commonwealth Olympic team competed in the Albertville Winter Games under the Olympic flag and their victories were marked by the playing of the Olympic anthem.

Even more pressing than the decision on how to divide Soviet property was the conversion to a limited free-market system. In early 1992 the Commonwealth lifted most price controls and the cost of goods shot upward. The prices of such basic commodities as bread and gasoline, over which some controls still existed, tripled or quadrupled literally overnight. The prices of noncontrolled items increased much more. A kilo of kielbasa sausages was 2.20 rubles in January 1991; the price rose to 43.75 rubles (and as high as 200 rubles in particularly hard-pressed St. Petersburg) in January 1992. The ruble itself experienced the shock. The official exchange used to be 1.8 per dollar; in January 1992 the exchange rate rose to well over 100 rubles per dollar. The economic changes created severe hardships for people whose monthly income averaged 400 rubles. Many citizens of the Commonwealth considered the winter of 1992 as the worst in their lives.

The death of the Soviet Union also had a profound effect on the United States. On one level the United States had to redirect its foreign policy. The era of the Cold War was over. The Soviet Union, America's Cold War rival, no longer existed. President George Bush responded to the changes by announcing victory in the Cold War, recognizing the new independent republics, and sending aid to the beleaguered members of the Commonwealth. Although Americans continued to worry about who controlled the Commonwealth's nuclear weapons, there was no longer the fear of war between the Soviet Union and the United States.

On another level, the end of the Cold War undermined one of the organizing principles of American culture. American mass culture in particular revolved around the idea of "us" and "them." Throughout the Cold War era Hollywood made successful movies that played, on this theme. From such movies as *I Was a Communist for the FBI, My Son John, Dr. Strangelove,* *Fail Safe, Red Alert,* and *On the Beach* to the James Bond action pictures and John Wayne westerns, Cold War issues provided the explicit or implicit basis for the films. Not to be outdone, popular writers capitalized on Cold War themes. John Le Carré, William F. Buckley, Jr., and Tom Clancy wrote bestsellers that centered on Cold War plots. Television also pitted "us" against "them" on numerous programs. During the 1960s *The Man from U.N.C.L.E., Mission Impossible,* and *I Spy* were popular programs that featured Cold War storylines. Even sports were influenced by the Cold War. In particular, the Olympic Games reflected Cold War tension and anxieties. American cheers of "USA, USA" at Olympic events became ritualistic Cold War chants.

American education and science similarly were partial hostages to the Cold War. After the success of the Soviet *Sputnik* in 1957, Congress appropriated funds for the establishment of the National Aeronautics and Space Administration (NASA) and passed the National Defense Education Act. In the Cold War the space race and education became highly political issues. President John F. Kennedy's decision to push America's space program toward putting a person on the moon—a decision that many of America's leading scientists opposed—was more a response to the Cold War than the needs of science. And Neil Armstrong's July 21, 1969, moon walk was confirmation of America's victory in the space race.

The death of the Soviet Union, then, ended two eras. How citizens of both the United States and the Commonwealth of Independent States will respond to that death will be one of the most important issues in the remainder of the 1990s and the twenty-first century.

Panama, which the Pentagon called Operation JUST CAUSE. The origins of the conflict stretched back to 1987 when a high Panamanian military official accused strong-man General Manuel Antonio Noriega of committing fraud in the 1984 presidential election and of drug trafficking. Violent street demonstrations broke out in Panama. Angry Panamanians called for Noriega's overthrow. Noriega responded by declaring a state of emergency. The crisis escalated when two Florida grand juries indicted the general on charges that he protected and assisted the Colombian drug cartel.

U.S.-Panamanian relations deteriorated further when Noriega voided results of the 1989 presidential election and sent paramilitary forces into the streets of Panama City where they beat up opposition candidates. Conflict grew imminent when Noriega declared his country in a "state of war" against the United States. A day later Panamanian troops fired on four unarmed American military personnel at a roadblock, killing one. Bush dispatched a force of 10,000 troops to safeguard the lives of Americans and protect the integrity of the Panama Canal treaties. It is estimated that between 300 and 800 Panamanian civilians and military personnel died during the invasion. There were 23 American casualties. In the end, however, Noriega was forced out of power and deported to the United States to stand trial for drug trafficking.

A much more serious test of Bush's foreign policy occurred in the Middle East. At 2 A.M. on August 2, 1990, Iraqi troops invaded and occupied Kuwait, a small, oil-rich emirate on the Persian Gulf. Iraq's leader, Saddam Hussein, justified the invasion on the grounds that Kuwait, which he accused of intentionally depressing world oil prices, was historically a part of Iraq.

Iraq's invasion of Kuwait caught the United States off-guard. Hussein's regime was a brutal military dictatorship that ruled by secret police and used poison gas against Iranians, Kurds, and Shiite Muslims. During the 1970s and 1980s the United States—and Britain, France, the Soviet Union, and West Germany—sold Iraq an awesome arsenal of weapons, including missiles, tanks, and the equipment needed to produce biological, chemical, and nu-

THE FIRST CRISIS OF THE POST–COLD WAR ERA

The Persian Gulf War

IN August 1990, with Iraqi forces poised near the Saudi Arabian border, the Bush administration dispatched 180,000 troops to protect the Saudi kingdom. The crisis took a dramatic turn in November 1990 when Bush doubled the number of American troops deployed in the Persian Gulf. Iraqi forces in Kuwait had climbed to 430,000 and coalition forces had to increase if Iraq was to be ejected from Kuwait by force. The president went to the United Nations for a resolution permitting the use of force against Iraq if it did not withdraw by January 15, 1991. After a heated debate, Congress also gave the president authority to wage war.

The 545,000-strong Iraqi army, the world's fourth largest, was equipped with antiship Exocet missiles, top-of-the-line Soviet T–72 tanks, and long-range artillery capable of firing nerve gas. Hussein tried to bring Israel into the war by launching Scud missiles at Israeli cities, a strategy thwarted when the United States sent Patriot antimissile missiles to Israel. A month of allied bombing gave the coalition forces air supremacy and destroyed thousands of Iraqi tanks and artillery pieces, supply routes and communications lines, command-and-control bunkers, and limited Iraq's ability to produce nuclear, chemical, and biological weapons. Iraqi troop morale suffered so badly during the bombing that an estimated 30 percent of Baghdad's forces deserted before the ground campaign even started.

The allied ground campaign relied on deception, mobility, and overwhelming air superiority to defeat a larger Iraqi army. The allied strategy was to mislead the Iraqis into believing that the allied attack would occur along the Kuwaiti coastline and Kuwait's border with Saudi Arabia. Meanwhile, General H. Norman Schwarzkopf, U.S. commander of the coalition forces, shifted more than 300,000 U.S., British, and French troops into western Saudi Arabia, allowing them to strike deeply into Iraq and trap Iraqi forces deep in southern Iraq and Kuwait. Only 100 hours after the ground war started, the war ended.

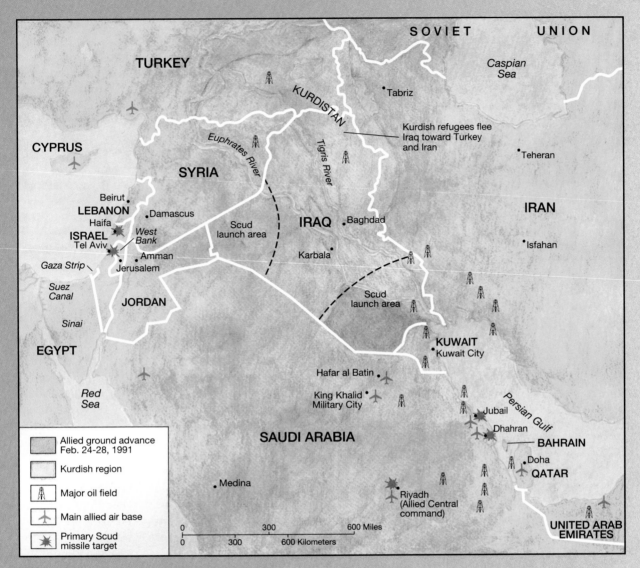

Major Action in the Persian Gulf

Legend:
- Allied ground advance Feb. 24-28, 1991
- Kurdish region
- Major oil field
- Main allied air base
- Primary Scud missile target

Map labels:
SOVIET UNION
TURKEY
Caspian Sea
Tabriz
KURDISTAN
Kurdish refugees flee Iraq toward Turkey and Iran
Teheran
CYPRUS
Euphrates River
Tigris River
SYRIA
IRAN
Beirut
LEBANON
Damascus
Haifa
West Bank
Scud launch area
IRAQ
Baghdad
Isfahan
ISRAEL
Tel Aviv
Amman
Karbala
Gaza Strip
Jerusalem
Suez Canal
JORDAN
Scud launch area
Sinai
EGYPT
KUWAIT
Kuwait City
Hafar al Batin
Red Sea
Persian Gulf
King Khalid Military City
Jubail
SAUDI ARABIA
Dhahran
BAHRAIN
Doha
QATAR
Medina
Riyadh (Allied Central command)
UNITED ARAB EMIRATES

Scale:
0   300   600 Miles
0   300   600 Kilometers

United States troops patrol the streets of Panama City during the U.S. invasion of Panama in December 1989.

clear weapons in an attempt to encourage Hussein to moderate his rule. During Baghdad's eight-year-long war with Iran, the United States, which opposed the growth of Muslim fundamentalist extremism, tilted toward Iraq.

President Bush's decision to first resist and then to reverse Iraqi aggression reflected his assessment of vital national interests. The invasion had given Hussein direct control over a significant portion of the world's oil supply. It had also disrupted the balance of power in the Middle East and placed Saudi Arabia and the Persian Gulf emirates in jeopardy. Iraq's battle-hardened war machine—consisting of 545,000 troops, 5000 tanks, 500 fighter aircraft, and chemical and biological weapons—threatened the security of such valuable U.S. allies as Egypt and Israel.

In a sharp departure from American foreign policy during the Reagan presidency, Bush organized an international coalition against Iraq, convincing Turkey and Syria to close Iraqi oil pipelines, winning Soviet support for an arms embargo, and establishing a multinational army to protect Saudi Arabia, with contingents from Western and Arab nations. The administration also persuaded the Security Council of the United Nations to adopt a series of resolutions condemning the Iraqi invasion, demanding restoration of the Kuwaiti government, and imposing an economic blockade.

Bush's decision to liberate Kuwait was an enormous political and military gamble, and

the allied victory in the Persian Gulf War did not mean the end of hostilities. Saddam Hussein remained in power, and in the war's aftermath, he brutally suppressed independence movements by two minority groups—the Kurds and the Shiites—in his own country. Still, his ability to control events in the region was dramatically curtailed.

The Persian Gulf War was the most popular American war since World War II. It restored American confidence in its position as the world's sole superpower and helped exorcise the ghost of Vietnam that had haunted American foreign policy debates for nearly two decades. The doubt, drift, and demoralization that began with the Vietnam war appeared to have ended.

Enter Bill Clinton

In January 1991 *Time* magazine placed George Bush on its cover. It pictured him with two faces, because his presidency seemed to have two very different images. "One was a foreign policy profile that was a study in resoluteness," the magazine said, "the other a domestic visage just as strongly marked by wavering and confusion."

In the Persian Gulf War, Bush acted from clear, unequivocal principles. Convinced that it was necessary to humiliate Saddam Hussein and prove that America would resist aggression, Bush demonstrated that a determined and skillful president has the power to move a reluctant nation to support his policies.

In domestic affairs, on the other hand, Bush's leadership was less decisive. On such issues as taxes, abortion, and civil rights, he adopted a flexible, pragmatic approach that led some critics to describe him as a political chameleon. Unlike Ronald Reagan, who brought a series of fixed philosophical principles to domestic issues, Bush appeared less interested in domestic affairs and more willing to renege on his pledge not to raise taxes.

Bush's failure to alter the downward slide of the American economy played the crucial role in the 1992 presidential election. In a bitter three-way contest, marked by intense assaults on both the candidates' records and their characters, Arkansas Governor Bill Clinton defeated George Bush and Texas business-man Ross Perot to become the first Democratic president in 12 years. President Bush, whose popularity soared to 90 percent after the Persian Gulf War, received 38 percent of the vote, to Clinton's 43 percent and Perot's 19 percent.

The central issue in the election was the nation's sluggish economy. During the Bush presidency, fewer new jobs were created than in any other presidential term since World War II. Indeed, fewer Americans were on private payrolls at the end of his term than when he took office. Unemployment reached the highest level in eight years; personal incomes stagnated; businesses failed in record numbers; the federal debt surpassed $4 trillion; and medical care absorbed 15 percent of the nation's output, while a quarter of the population lacked health insurance. Poverty rose to the highest rate in over two decades—a fact dramatically underscored by the outbreak of the deadliest riot in America's history, in Los Angeles in April 1992.

A NEW COVENANT

President Clinton pledged a "new covenant" for America: a new approach to government between the unfettered free market championed by the Republicans and the welfare state economics that the Democratic party had represented in the past. Promising to focus like a laser beam on the economy, he strove to reduce the federal budget deficit by raising taxes on the wealthiest Americans and cutting government spending. To create jobs he sought to stimulate world trade. In late 1993 he convinced Congress to pass the North American Free Trade Agreement (NAFTA), eliminating trade barriers between Canada, Mexico, and the United States, and also completed negotiations on the General Agreement on Trade and Tariffs (GATT), reducing global trading barriers.

Clinton committed his administration to ending 12 years of "legislative gridlock" and "social neglect." To aid working parents, he

Bill Clinton won the 1992 presidential election with a campaign that centered on economic issues and reform of the nation's health care system. After election he appointed Hillary Rodham Clinton, his wife, to head the task force preparing the plan for health care reform. Powerful opposition from anti-Clinton forces in Congress, commercial operations, and national organizations, all of whom objected to all or part of the plan, thwarted passage of a health care reform bill.

signed parental leave legislation, allowing parents to take unpaid job leaves during family emergencies. To combat violent crime, he persuaded Congress to enact a waiting period for handgun purchases and a ban on the sale of assault weapons. He also revised policies that had excluded homosexuals from the military and pledged to eliminate "welfare as we know it," by replacing welfare dependency with programs emphasizing education and job training.

The centerpiece of Clinton's legislative agenda was a program of universal health care coverage—the largest federal social welfare initiative since Social Security during the Great Depression. Despite the fact that his political party controlled both houses of Congress, his proposal to guarantee lifelong care to the millions of Americans without health insurance was defeated in 1994.

In foreign policy, his administration witnessed the end of apartheid in South Africa and the replacement of white rule with a multiracial democracy. It also saw the Israeli transfer of control over the Gaza Strip and portions of the West Bank to the Palestine Liberation Organization. In addition, the Clinton administration ended a long-standing U.S. trade embargo with Vietnam, sent troops to Haiti to restore a democratically elected government, and dispatched peacekeepers to Bosnia, helping to end a conflict that had been Europe's most violent since World War II.

In the 1994 off-year elections, the Democratic party suffered shocking losses as Republicans gained 11 state governorships and control of both houses of Congress for the first time in four decades. Many voters, anxious about their economic well-being, threw their support to the Republican party and its "Contract with America," which called for balanced budgets, tax cuts, and reductions in the size of government. The Republican party received its first Senate majority in eight years and its first control of the House of Representatives since 1954.

Twice, the federal government was forced to partially shut down when President Clinton and the Republican-controlled Congress failed to agree on a federal budget. Early in 1996, however, the president and Congress achieved a temporary budget agreement. Nevertheless, economic anxieties—fueled by corporate layoffs and stagnating family incomes—continued to weigh heavily on American voters.

CONCLUSION

As the twentieth century draws to a close, America's ideals of democracy and personal freedom are ascendant across the world. From Tiananmen Square—where Chinese students erected a goddess of liberty modeled on the Statue of Liberty—to the Philippines, popular protests and demonstrations have called for "government of the people, for the people, and by the people." In Eastern Europe, the former Soviet Union, and across Latin America, people demand free speech, freedom of religion, freedom of the press, and free markets.

Yet paradoxically, as American ideals and values flourish abroad, Americans are anxious about their economy and their country's future. Many are angry, expressing cynical contempt toward their government. And while the American economy remains the world's most productive, many fear that American competitiveness and inventiveness are declining.

Other nations, such as Japan and Germany, save more and invest more than the United States, and are increasing the productivity of their industries faster. Except for a few areas of trade—such as high-tech products, financial services, and aircraft—foreign countries dominate the most technologically advanced fields, such as consumer electronics, luxury automobiles, and machine tools. No longer does the United States possess the world's highest level of per capita income. Particularly troubling are the national debt and federal deficit, which stand at record levels.

Americans also worry about crime, the state of their central cities, and the level of health and education in their society. The level of crime and violence in the United States is the highest in the industrialized world, as are America's rates of drug use, juvenile delinquency, teenage pregnancy, and teen suicide.

At the end of World War II, many commentators referred to the twentieth century as

CHRONOLOGY
OF KEY EVENTS

1971 A secret tape-recording system is installed in the White House; Nixon authorizes establishment of a plumbers unit to "stop security leaks and investigate other sensitive matters"

1972 Five burglars arrested breaking into Democratic national headquarters at Washington's Watergate office complex; President Nixon takes part in summit in China; President Nixon is reelected with 61 percent of the vote

1973 Televised Senate hearings on Watergate begin; Spiro Agnew pleads no contest to a charge of income tax evasion and resigns as vice president

1974 Federal grand jury indicts Nixon aides for perjury and obstruction of justice and names the president as an unindicted co-conspirator; House Judiciary Committee adopts three articles of impeachment against President Nixon; Nixon becomes the first president to resign from office; Ford becomes thirty-eighth president; Federal Campaign Reform Act sets limits on private campaign contributions and provides tax funds to presidential candidates

1976 Jimmy Carter is elected thirty-ninth president

1978 President Carter mediates Egyptian-Israeli peace settlement; Iranian revolution begins

1979 United States formally recognizes China; Iranian militants seize American hostages; Soviet Union invades Afghanistan; Somoza regime in Nicaragua is overthrown, Sandinistas take power

1980 Ronald Reagan is elected fortieth president

1981 American hostages are released from Iran; Reagan is shot in assassination attempt; Reagan approves covert training of anti-Sandinista contras; Reagan tax cuts are approved

1982 Congress deregulates banking industry and lifts controls on airfares

1983 Reagan proposes "Star Wars" missile defense system; United States topples Communist government on the Caribbean island of Grenada

1984 Congress orders an end to all covert aid to Nicaraguan contras

1985 United States begins secret arms-for-hostages negotiations with Iran; Mikhail Gorbachev becomes leader of the Soviet Union

1986 Profits from Iranian arms sales are diverted to Nicaraguan contras

1987 Iran-contra hearings; stock market plunges 508 points in a single session

1988 George Bush is elected forty-first president

1989 Opposition defeats Sandinistas in Nicaraguan elections; Communist regimes collapse in Eastern Europe

1990 Iraqi troops invade and occupy Kuwait

1991 U.S., Western, and Arab forces eject Iraq from Kuwait by force; failed coup in Soviet Union results in a shift in power to the Soviet republics and in independence for Lithuania, Latvia, and Estonia

1992 Bill Clinton is elected forty-second president

1993 Congress passes North American Free Trade Agreement (NAFTA), eliminating trade barriers between Canada, Mexico, and the United States; General Agreement on Trade and Tariffs (GATT) passed, reducing global trading barriers

1994 Congress defeats Clinton's health-care plan

the "American century." Today, the United States remains the mightiest, most productive nation in the world, a model of freedom and pluralism that people across the globe still strive to emulate. The great question to be asked as the century comes to an end is whether the people who have reached the moon have the commitment and will to solve the down-to-earth problems that confront their cities, their schools, and their physical environment.

SUGGESTIONS FOR FURTHER READING

William C. Berman, *America's Right Turn: From Nixon to Bush* (1994). Presents an incisive interpretation of recent American political history.

William H. Chafe, *The Unfinished Journey: America Since World War II*, 3d ed. (1995). Offers a concise synthesis of recent scholarship.

Paul Gottfried, *The Conservative Movement*, rev. ed. (1993). Gives an acute analysis of the growth of political conservatism.

Stanley I. Kutler, *The Wars of Watergate: The Last Crisis of Richard Nixon* (1990), and Michael Schudson, *Watergate in American Memory* (1992). Dissect the historical legacy of the Watergate scandal.

Overviews And Surveys

Michael Barone, *Our Country: The Shaping of America from Roosevelt to Reagan* (1990); Peter N. Carroll, *It Seemed Like Nothing Happened: The Tragedy and Promise of the 1970s* (1990); Frederick F. Siegel, *Troubled Journey: From Pearl Harbor to Ronald Reagan* (1984).

Crisis of Political Leadership

Terry Deibel, *Presidents, Public Opinion, and Power: The Nixon, Carter, and Reagan Years* (1986); John Robert Greene, *The Presidency of Gerald R. Ford* (1995); J. Anthony Lukas, *Nightmare: The Underside of the Nixon Years* (1976); Kim McQuaid, *The Anxious Years: America in the Vietnam-Watergate Era* (1989); Richard E. Neustadt, *Presidential Power and Modern Presidents*, rev. ed. (1990); James Reichley, *Conservatives in an Age of Change: The Nixon and Ford Administrations* (1981); Edward L. and Frederick H.

Schapsmeier, *Gerald R. Ford's Date with Destiny: A Political Biography* (1989); Jonathan Schell, *The Time of Illusion* (1975); Arthur M. Schlesinger, Jr., *The Imperial Presidency* (1973).

Wrenching Economic Transformations

Michael A. Bernstein and David E. Adler, eds., *Understanding American Economic Decline* (1994); Barry Bluestone and Bennett Harrison, *The Deindustrialization of America* (1982); David Calleo, *The Imperious Economy* (1982); Emmett Dedmon, *Challenge and Response: A Modern History of the Standard Oil Company* (1984); Thomas Edsall, *The New Politics of Inequality* (1984); Michael Goldfield, *The Decline of Organized Labor in the United States* (1987); Frank Levy, *Dollars and Dreams: The Changing American Income Distribution* (1987); Martin V. Melosi, *Coping with Abundance: Energy and Environment in Industrial America* (1985); Norman E. Nordhauser, *The Quest for Stability: Domestic Oil Regulation* (1979); Bernard Nossiter, *Fat Years and Lean Years: The American Economy Since Roosevelt* (1990); Michael Piore, *The Second Industrial Divide* (1984); Stephen G. Rabe, *The Road to OPEC* (1982); Herbert Stein, *Presidential Economics: The Making of Economic Policy from Roosevelt to Reagan*, 2d ed. (1988); Michael Stoff, *Oil, War, and Security* (1980); Daniel Yergin, *The Prize: The Epic Quest for Oil, Money, and Power* (1990).

A New American Role in the World

James A. Bill, *The Eagle and the Lion: The Tragedy of American-Iranian Relations* (1988); H. W. Brands, *The Wages of Globalism: Lyndon Johnson and the Limits of American Power* (1995); Gordon H. Chang, *Friends and Enemies: The United States, China, and the Soviet Union* (1990); Mark Gasiorowski, *U.S. Foreign Policy and the Shah* (1991); J. Michael Hogan, *The Panama Canal in American Politics* (1986); Nikki R. Keddie, *Iran, the United States, and the Soviet Union* (1991); Walter LaFeber, *The Panama Canal*, rev. ed. (1989); Joseph Lepgold, *The Declining Hegemony: The United States and European Defense, 1960–1990* (1990); Richard A. Melanson, *Reconstructing Consensus: American Foreign Policy Since the Vietnam War* (1990); Keith L. Nelson, *The Making of Détente: Soviet-American Relations in the Shadow of Vietnam* (1995); Kuross A. Samii, *Involvement by Invitation: American Strategies of Containment in Iran* (1987); Robert D. Schulzinger, *Henry Kissinger* (1989); Melvin Small, *Democracy and Diplomacy: The Impact of Domestic Politics on U.S. Foreign Policy* (1995); Gaddis Smith, *Morality, Reason and Power: American Diplomacy in the Carter Years* (1986); Seth Tillman, *The United States in the Middle East* (1982); Marvin Zonis, *Majestic Failure: The Fall of the Shah* (1991).

The Reagan Revolution

Norman C. Amaker, *Civil Rights and the Reagan Administration* (1988); Cynthia J. Arnson, *Crossroads: Congress, the Reagan Administration, and Central America* (1989); Coral Bell, *The Reagan Paradox: American Foreign Policy in the 1980s* (1989); Sidney Blumenthal, *Our Long National Daydream: A Political Pageant of the Reagan Era* (1988); Paul Boyer, ed., *Reagan as President* (1990); Lou Cannon, *President Reagan: The Role of a Lifetime* (1991); Robert Dallek, *Ronald Reagan: The Politics of Symbolism* (1984); Theodore Draper, *A Very Thin Line: The Iran-Contra Affair* (1991); Thomas Ferguson and Joel Rogers, *Right Turn: The Decline of the Democrats and the Future of American Politics* (1986); Steve Fraser and Gary Gerstle, *The Rise and Fall of the New Deal Order* (1990); Fred Halliday, *From Kabul to Managua: Soviet-American Relations in the 1980s* (1989); J. David Hoeveler, Jr., *Watch on the Right: Conservative Intellectuals in the Reagan Era* (1991); Haynes Johnson, *Sleepwalking Through History: America in the Reagan Years* (1991); David E. Kyvig, ed., *Reagan and the World* (1990); Jane Mayer and Doyle McManus, *Landslide: The Unmaking of the President, 1984–1988* (1988); John L. Palmer, ed., *Perspectives on the Reagan Years* (1986); Robert Pastor, *Condemned to Repetition: The United States and Nicaragua* (1987); Martin Wattenberg, *The Decline of American Political Parties, 1952–1988* (1990), and *The Rise of Candidate-Centered Politics: Presidential Elections of the 1980s* (1991); Garry Wills, *Reagan's America* (1987).

The Bush Presidency

Sidney Blumenthal, *Pledging Allegiance: The Last Campaign of the Cold War* (1990); Kevin Buckley, *Panama: The Whole Story* (1991); Jill Crystal, *Oil and Politics in the Gulf* (1990); E. J. Dionne, Jr., *Why Americans Hate Politics* (1991); Alan Ehrenhalt, *The United States of Ambition: Politicians, Power, and the Pursuit of Office* (1991); Robert O. Freedman, *Moscow and the Middle East* (1991); Moshe Lewin, *The Gorbachev Phenomenon* (1991); Martin Mayer, *The Greatest Ever Bank Robbery: The Collapse of the Savings and Loan Industry* (1990); Henry R. Nau, *The Myth of America's Decline* (1990); William Pfaff, *Barbarian Sentiments: How the American Century Ends* (1989); Stephen Pizzo, et al., *Inside Job: The Looting of America's Savings and Loans* (1989); Gail Sheehy, *The Man Who Changed the World: The Lives of Mikhail S. Gorbachev* (1990); Lawrence J. White, *The S&L Debacle* (1991); Garry Wills, *Under God: Religion and American Politics* (1990); Bob Woodward, *The Commanders* (1991).

Biographies

Stephen E. Ambrose, *Nixon* (1987); Dan Carter, *The Politics of Rage: George Wallace, the Origins of the New Conservatism, and the Transformation of American Politics* (1995); Steven M. Gillon, *The Democrats' Dilemma: Walter F. Mondale and the Liberal Legacy* (1992); Burton Ira Kaufman, *The Presidency of James Earl Carter, Jr.* (1993); David Maraniss, *First in His Class: A Biography of Bill Clinton* (1995); Roger Morris, *Richard Milhous Nixon: The Rise of an American Politician* (1990); Herbert S. Parmet, *Richard Nixon and His America* (1990); Tom Wicker, *One of Us: Richard Nixon and the American Dream* (1991); Garry Wills, *Nixon Agonistes* (1970), and *Reagan's America* (1988).

Appendix

THE DECLARATION OF INDEPENDENCE

THE CONSTITUTION OF THE UNITED
STATES OF AMERICA

AMENDMENTS TO THE CONSTITUTION

PRESIDENTIAL ELECTIONS

VICE PRESIDENTS AND CABINET
MEMBERS BY ADMINISTRATION

SUPREME COURT JUSTICES

ADMISSION OF STATES TO THE UNION

U.S. POPULATION, 1790–1990

REGIONAL ORIGINS OF IMMIGRATION

THE DECLARATION OF INDEPENDENCE

In Congress, July 4, 1776

The Unanimous Declaration of the Thirteen United States of America

When, in the course of human events, it becomes necessary for one people to dissolve the political bonds which have connected them with another, and to assume, among the powers of the earth, the separate and equal station to which the laws of nature and of nature's God entitle them, a decent respect to the opinions of mankind requires that they should declare the causes which impel them to the separation.

We hold these truths to be self-evident: That all men are created equal; that they are endowed by their Creator with certain unalienable rights; that among these are life, liberty, and the pursuit of happiness; that, to secure these rights, governments are instituted among men, deriving their just powers from the consent of the governed; that whenever any form of government becomes destructive of these ends, it is the right of the people to alter or to abolish it, and to institute new government, laying its foundation on such principles, and organizing its powers in such form, as to them shall seem most likely to effect their safety and happiness. Prudence, indeed, will dictate that governments long established should not be changed for light and transient causes; and accordingly all experience hath shown that mankind are more disposed to suffer, while evils are sufferable, than to right themselves by abolishing the forms to which they are accustomed. But when a long train of abuses and usurpations, pursuing invariably the same object, evinces a design to reduce them under absolute despotism, it is their right, it is their duty, to throw off such government, and to provide new guards for their future security. Such has been the patient sufferance of these colonies; and such is now the necessity which constrains them to alter their former systems of government. The history of the present King of Great Britain is a history of repeated injuries and usurpations, all having in direct object the establishment of an absolute tyranny over these states. To prove this, let facts be submitted to a candid world.

He has refused his assent to laws, the most wholesome and necessary for the public good.

He has forbidden his governors to pass laws of immediate and pressing importance, unless suspended in their operation till his assent should be obtained; and, when so suspended, he has utterly neglected to attend to them.

He has refused to pass other laws for the accommodation of large districts of people, unless those people would relinquish the right of representation in the legislature, a right inestimable to them, and formidable to tyrants only.

He has called together legislative bodies at places unusual, uncomfortable, and distant from the depository of their public records, for the sole purpose of fatiguing them into compliance with his measures.

He has dissolved representative houses repeatedly, for opposing, with manly firmness, his invasions on the rights of the people.

He has refused for a long time, after such dissolutions, to cause others to be elected; whereby the legislative powers, incapable of annihilation, have returned to the people at large for their exercise; the state remaining, in the mean time, exposed to all the dangers of invasions from without and convulsions within.

He has endeavored to prevent the population of these states; for that purpose obstructing the laws for naturalization of foreigners; refusing to pass others to encourage their migration hither, and raising the conditions of new appropriations of lands.

He has obstructed the administration of justice, by refusing his assent to laws for establishing judiciary powers.

He has made judges dependent on his will alone, for the tenure of their offices, and the amount and payment of their salaries.

He has erected a multitude of new offices, and sent hither swarms of officers to harass our people and eat out their substance.

He has kept among us, in times of peace, standing armies, without the consent of our legislatures.

He has affected to render the military independent of, and superior to, the civil power.

He has combined with others to subject us to a jurisdiction foreign to our constitution, and unacknowledged by our laws, giving his assent to their acts of pretended legislation:

For quartering large bodies of armed troops among us;

For protecting them, by a mock trial, from punishment for any murder which they should commit on the inhabitants of these states;

For cutting off our trade with all parts of the world;

For imposing taxes on us without our consent;

For depriving us, in many cases, of the benefits of trial by jury;

For transporting us beyond seas, to be tried for pretended offenses;

For abolishing the free system of English laws in a neighboring province, establishing therein an arbitrary government, and enlarging its boundaries, so as to render it at once an example and fit instrument for introducing the same absolute rule into these colonies;

For taking away our charters abolishing our most valuable laws, and altering fundamentally the forms of our governments;

For suspending our own legislatures, and declaring themselves invested with power to legislate for us in all cases whatsoever.

He has abdicated government here, by declaring us out of his protection and waging war against us.

He has plundered our seas, ravaged our coasts, burned our towns, and destroyed the lives of our people.

He is at this time transporting large armies of foreign mercenaries to complete the works of death, desolation, and tyranny already begun with circumstances of cruelty and perfidy scarcely paralleled in the most barbarous ages, and totally unworthy the head of a civilized nation.

He has constrained our fellow-citizens, taken captive on the high seas, to bear arms against their country, to become the executioners of their friends and brethren, or to fall themselves by their hands.

He has excited domestic insurrection among us, and has endeavored to bring on the inhabitants of our frontiers the merciless Indian savages, whose known rule of warfare is an undistinguished destruction of all ages, sexes, and conditions.

In every stage of these oppressions we have petitioned for redress in the most humble terms; our repeated petitions have been answered only by repeated injury. A prince, whose character is thus marked by every act which may define a tyrant, is unfit to be the ruler of a free people.

Nor have we been wanting in our attentions to our British brethren. We have warned them, from time to time, of attempts by their legislature to extend an unwarrantable jurisdiction over us. We have reminded them of the circumstances of our emigration and settlement here. We have appealed to their native justice and magnanimity; and we have conjured them, by the ties of our common kindred, to disavow these usurpations, which would inevitably interrupt our connections and correspondence. They, too, have been deaf to the voice of justice and of consanguinity. We must, therefore, acquiesce in the necessity which denounces our separation, and hold them, as we hold the rest of mankind, enemies in war, in peace friends.

We, therefore, the representatives of the United States of America, in General Congress assembled, appealing to the Supreme Judge of the world for the rectitude of our intentions, do, in the name and by the authority of the good people of these colonies, solemnly publish and declare, that these United Colonies are, and of right ought to be, FREE AND INDEPENDENT STATES; that they are absolved from all allegiance to the British crown, and that all political connection between them and the state of Great Britain is, and ought to be, totally dissolved; and that, as free and independent states, they have full power to levy war, conclude peace, contract alliances, establish commerce, and do all other acts and things which independent states may of right do. And for the support of this declaration, with a firm reliance on the protection of Divine Providence, we mutually pledge to each other our lives, our fortunes, and our sacred honor.

JOHN HANCOCK

BUTTON GWENNETT
LYMAN HALL
GEO. WALTON
WM. HOOPER
JOSEPH HEWES
JOHN PENN
EDWARD RUTLEDGE
THOS. HEYWARD, JUNR.
THOMAS LYNCH, JUNR.
ARTHUR MIDDLETON
SAMUEL CHASE
WM. PACA
THOS. STONE
CHARLES CARROLL OF CARROLLTON
GEORGE WYTHE
RICHARD HENRY LEE
TH. JEFFERSON
BENJA. HARRISON

THS. NELSON, JR.
FRANCIS LIGHTFOOT LEE
CARTER BRAXTON
ROBT. MORRIS
BENJAMIN RUSH
BENJA. FRANKLIN
JOHN MORTON
GEO. CLYMER
JAS. SMITH
GEO. TAYLOR
JAMES WILSON
GEO. ROSS
CAESAR RODNEY
GEO. READ
THO. M'KEAN
WM. FLOYD
PHIL. LIVINGSTON
FRANS. LEWIS
LEWIS MORRIS

RICHD. STOCKTON
JNO. WITHERSPOON
FRAS. HOPKINSON
JOHN HART
ABRA. CLARK
JOSIAH BARTLETT
WM. WHIPPLE
SAML. ADAMS
JOHN ADAMS
ROBT. TREAT PAINE
ELBRIDGE GERRY
STEP. HOPKINS
WILLIAM ELLERY
ROGER SHERMAN
SAM'EL. HUNTINGTON
WM. WILLIAMS
OLIVER WOLCOTT
MATTHEW THORNTON

The Constitution of the United States of America

PREAMBLE

We the People of the United States, in Order to form a more perfect Union, establish Justice, insure domestic Tranquility, provide for the common defence, promote the general Welfare, and secure the Blessings of Liberty to ourselves and our Posterity, do ordain and establish this Constitution for the United States of America.

ARTICLE I.

Section 1 All legislative Powers herein granted shall be vested in a Congress of the United States, which shall consist of a Senate and House of Representatives.

Section 2 The House of Representatives shall be composed of Members chosen every second Year by the People of the several States, and the Electors in each State shall have the Qualifications requisite for Electors of the most numerous Branch of the State Legislature.

No Person shall be a Representative who shall not have attained to the Age of twenty five Years, and been seven Years a Citizen of the United States, and who shall not, when elected, be an inhabitant of that State in which he shall be chosen.

Representatives and direct Taxes shall be apportioned among the several States which may be included within this Union, according to their respective Numbers, *which shall be determined by adding to the whole Number of free Persons, including those bound to Service for a Term of Years, and excluding Indians not taxed, three fifths of all other Persons.** The actual Enumeration shall be made within three Years after the first Meeting of the Congress of the United States, and within every subsequent Term of ten Years, in such Manner as they shall by Law direct. The Number of Representatives shall not exceed one for every thirty Thousand, but each State shall have at Least one Representative; *and until such enumeration shall be made, the State of New Hampshire shall be entitled to chuse three, Massachusetts eight, Rhode-Island and Providence Plantations one, Connecticut five, New York six, New Jersey four, Pennsylvania eight, Delaware one, Maryland six, Virginia ten, North Carolina five, South Carolina five, and Georgia three.*

When vacancies happen in the Representation from any State, the Executive Authority thereof shall issue Writs of Election to fill such Vacancies.

The House of Representatives shall choose their Speaker and other Officers; and shall have the sole Power of Impeachment.

Passages no longer in effect are printed in italic type.

*Section 3 The Senate of the United States shall be composed of two Senators from each State, *chosen by the Legislature thereof,* for six Years; and each Senator shall have one Vote.

Immediately after they shall be assembled in Consequence of the first Election, they shall be divided as equally as may be into three Classes. The Seats of the Senators of the first Class shall be vacated at the Expiration of the second Year, of the second Class at the Expiration of the fourth Year, and of the third Class at the Expiration of the sixth Year so that one third may be chosen every second Year; *and if Vacancies happen by Resignation, or otherwise, during the Recess of the Legislature of any state, the Executive thereof may make temporary Appointments until the next Meeting of the Legislature, which shall then fill such Vacancies.*

No Person shall be a Senator who shall not have attained to the Age of thirty Years, and been nine Years a Citizen of the United States, and who shall not, when elected, be an Inhabitant of that State for which he shall be chosen.

The Vice President of the United States shall be President of the Senate, but shall have no Vote, unless they be equally divided.

The Senate shall choose their other Officers, and also a President *pro tempore,* in the Absence of the Vice President, or when he shall exercise the Office of President of the United States.

The Senate shall have the sole Power to try all Impeachments. When sitting for that Purpose, they shall be on Oath or Affirmation. When the President of the United States is tried the Chief Justice shall preside: And no Person shall be convicted without the Concurrence of two thirds of the Members present.

Judgment in Cases of Impeachment shall not extend further than to removal from Office, and disqualification to hold and enjoy any Office of honor, Trust or Profit under the United States: but the Party convicted shall nevertheless be liable and subject to Indictment, Trial, Judgment and Punishment, according to Law.

Section 4 The Times, Places and Manner of holding Elections for Senators and Representatives, shall be prescribed in each State by the Legislature thereof; but the Congress may at any time by Law make or alter such Regulations, except as to the Places of choosing Senators.

The Congress shall assemble at least once in every Year, and such Meeting shall be on the first Monday in December, unless they shall by Law appoint a different Day.*

Section 5 Each House shall be the Judge of the Elections, Returns and Qualifications of its own Members, and a Majority of each shall constitute a Quorum to do Business; but a smaller Number may adjourn from day to day, and may be authorized to compel the Attendance of absent Members, in such Manner, and under such Penalties as each House may provide.

Each House may determine the Rules of its Proceedings, punish its Members for disorderly Behaviour, and, with the Concurrence of two thirds, expel a Member.

Each House shall keep a Journal of its Proceedings, and from time to time publish the same, excepting such Parts as may in their Judgment require Secrecy; and the Yeas and Nays of the Members of either House on any question shall, at the Desire of one fifth of those Present, be entered on the Journal.

Neither House, during the Session of Congress, shall, without the Consent of the other, adjourn for more than three days, nor to any other Place than that in which the two Houses shall be sitting.

Section 6   The Senators and Representatives shall receive a Compensation for their Services, to be ascertained by Law, and paid out of the Treasury of the United States. They shall in all Cases, except Treason, Felony and Breach of the Peace, be privileged from Arrest during their Attendance at the Session of their respective Houses, and in going to and returning from the same; and for any Speech or Debate in either House, they shall not be questioned in any other Place.

No Senator or Representative shall, during the Time for which he was elected, be appointed to any civil Office under the Authority of the United States, which shall have been created, or the Emoluments whereof shall have been encreased during such time, and no Person holding any Office under the United States, shall be a Member of either House during his Continuance in Office.

Section 7   All Bills for raising Revenue shall originate in the House of Representatives; but the Senate may propose or concur with Amendments as on other Bills.

Every Bill which shall have passed the House of Representatives and the Senate, shall, before it become a Law, be presented to the President of the United States; If he approve he shall sign it, but if not he shall return it, with his Objections to the House in which it shall have originated, who shall enter the Objections at large on their Journal, and proceed to reconsider it. If after such Reconsideration two thirds of that House shall agree to pass the Bill, it shall be sent, together with the Objections, to the other House, by which it shall likewise be reconsidered, and if approved by two thirds of that House, it shall become a Law. But in all such Cases the Votes of both Houses shall be determined by yeas and Nays, and the Names of the Persons voting for and against the Bill shall be entered on the Journal of each House respectively. If any Bill shall not be returned by the President within ten Days (Sundays excepted) after

it shall have been presented to him, the Same shall be a Law, in like Manner as if he had signed it, unless the Congress by their Adjournment prevent its Return, in which Case it shall not be a Law.

Every Order, Resolution, or Vote to which the Concurrence of the Senate and House of Representatives may be necessary (except on a question of Adjournment) shall be presented to the President of the United States; and before the Same shall take Effect, shall be approved by him, or being disapproved by him, shall be repassed by two thirds of the Senate and House of Representatives, according to the Rules and Limitations prescribed in the Case of a Bill.

Section 8   The Congress shall have Power To lay and collect Taxes, Duties, Imposts and Excises, to pay the Debts and provide for the common Defence and general Welfare of the United States; but all Duties, Imposts and Excises shall be uniform throughout the United States;

To borrow Money on the credit of the United States;

To regulate Commerce with foreign Nations, and among the several States, and with the Indian Tribes;

To establish an uniform Rule of Naturalization, and uniform Laws on the subject of Bankruptcies throughout the United States;

To coin Money, regulate the Value thereof, and of foreign Coin, and fix the Standard of Weights and Measures;

To provide for the Punishment of counterfeiting the Securities and current Coin of the United States;

To establish Post Offices and post Roads;

To promote the Progress of Science and useful Arts, by securing for limited Times to Authors and Inventors the exclusive Right to their respective Writings and Discoveries;

To constitute Tribunals inferior to the supreme Court;

To define and punish Piracies and Felonies committed on the high Seas, and Offences against the Law of Nations;

To declare War, grant Letters of Marque and Reprisal, and make Rules concerning Captures on Land and Water;

To raise and support Armies, but no Appropriation of Money to that Use shall be for a longer Term than two Years;

To provide and maintain a Navy;

To make Rules for the Government and Regulation of the land and naval Forces;

To provide for calling forth the Militia to execute the Laws of the Union, suppress Insurrections and repel Invasions;

To provide for organizing, arming, and disciplining the Militia, and for governing such Part of them as may be employed in the Service of the United States, reserving to the States respectively, the Appointment of the Officers, and the Authority of training the Militia according to the discipline prescribed by Congress;

To exercise exclusive Legislation in all Cases whatsoever, over such District (not exceeding ten Miles square) as may, by Cession of particular States, and the Acceptance of Congress, become the Seat of the Government of the United States, and to exercise like Authority over all Places purchased by the Consent of the Legislature of the State in which the Same shall be, for the Erection of Forts, Magazines, Arsenals, dock-Yards, and other needful Buildings;-And

To make all Laws which shall be necessary and proper for carrying into Execution the foregoing Powers, and all other Powers vested by this Constitution in the Government of the United States, or in any Department of Officer thereof.

Section 9   The Migration or Importation of such Persons as any of the States now existing shall think proper to admit, shall not be prohibited by the Congress prior to the Year one thousand eight hundred and eight, but a Tax or duty may be imposed on such Importation, not exceeding ten dollars for each Person.

The Privilege of the Writ of Habeas Corpus shall not be suspended, unless when in Cases of Rebellion or Invasion the public Safety may require it.

No Bill of Attainder or ex post facto Law shall be passed.

No Capitation, or other direct, Tax shall be laid, unless in Proportion to the Census or Enumeration herein before directed to be taken.

No Tax or Duty shall be laid on Articles exported from any State.

No Preference shall be given by any Regulation of Commerce or Revenue to the Ports of one State over those of another: nor shall Vessels bound to, or from, one State, be obliged to enter, clear, or pay Duties in another.

No Money shall be drawn from the Treasury, but in Consequence of Appropriations made by Law; and a regular Statement and Account of the Receipts and Expenditures of all public Money shall be published from time to time.

No Title of Nobility shall be granted by the United States: And no Person holding any Office of Profit or Trust under them, shall, without the Consent of the Congress, accept of any present, Emolument, Office, or Title, of any kind whatever, from any King, Prince, or foreign State.

Section 10   No State shall enter into any Treaty, Alliance, or Confederation; grant Letters of Marque and Reprisal; coin Money; emit Bills of Credit; make any Thing but gold and silver Coin a Tender in Payment of Debts; pass any Bill of Attainder, ex post facto Law, or

Law impairing the obligation of Contracts, or grant any Title of Nobility.

No State shall, without the Consent of the Congress, lay any Imposts or Duties on Imports or Exports, except what may be absolutely necessary for executing its inspection Laws: and the net Produce of all Duties and Imposts, laid by any State on Imports or Exports, shall be for the Use of the Treasury of the United States; and all such Laws shall be subject to the Revision and Control of the Congress.

No State shall, without the Consent of Congress, lay any Duty of Tonnage, keep Troops, or Ships of War in time of Peace, enter into any Agreement or Compact with another State, or with a foreign Power, or engage in War, unless actually invaded, or in such imminent Danger as will not admit of delay.

ARTICLE II.

Section 1   The executive Power shall be vested in a President of the United States of America. He shall hold his Office during the Term of four Years, and, together with the Vice President, chosen for the same Term, be elected, as follows:

Each State shall appoint, in such Manner as the Legislature thereof may direct, a Number of Electors, equal to the whole Number of Senators and Representatives to which the State may be entitled in the Congress: but no Senator or Representative, or Person holding an Office of Trust or Profit under the United States, shall be appointed an Elector.

The Electors shall meet in their respective States, and vote by Ballot for two Persons, of whom one at least shall not be an Inhabitant of the same State with themselves. And they shall make a List of all the Persons voted for, and of the Number of Votes for each; which List they shall sign and certify, and transmit sealed to the Seat of the Government of the United States, directed to the President of the Senate. The President of the Senate shall, in the Presence of the Senate and House of Representatives, open all the Certificates, and the Votes shall then be counted. The Person having the greatest Number of Votes shall be the President, if such Number be a Majority of the whole number of Electors appointed; and if there be more than one who have such Majority, and have an equal Number of Votes, then the House of Representative shall immediately choose by Ballot one of them for President; and if no Person have a Majority, then from the five highest on the List the said House shall in like Manner choose the President. But in choosing the President, the Votes shall be taken by States, the Representation from each State having one Vote; A quorum for this Purpose shall consist of a Member or Members from two thirds of the States, and a Majority of all the States shall be necessary to a Choice. In every Case, after the Choice of the President, the Person having the greatest Number of Votes of the Electors shall be the Vice President. But if there should remain two or more who have equal

Votes, the Senate shall choose from them by Ballot the Vice President.

The Congress may determine the time of choosing the Electors, and the Day on which they shall give their Votes; which Day shall be the same throughout the United States.

No person except a natural born Citizen, *or a Citizen of the United States, at the time of the Adoption of this Constitution,* shall be eligible to the Office of President; neither shall any Person be eligible to that Office who shall not have attained to the Age of thirty five Years, and been fourteen Years a Resident within the United States.

In Case of the Removal of the President from Office, or of his Death, Resignation, or Inability to discharge the Powers and Duties of the said Office, the Same shall devolve on the Vice President, and the Congress may by Law provide for the Case of Removal, Death, Resignation or Inability, both of the President and Vice President, declaring what Officer shall then act as President, and such Officer shall act accordingly, until the Disability be removed, or a President shall be elected.

The President shall, at stated Times, receive for his Services, a Compensation, which shall neither be encreased nor diminished during the Period for which he shall have been elected, and he shall not receive within that period any other Emolument from the United States, or any of them.

Before he enter on the Execution of his Office, he shall take the following Oath or Affirmation:-"I do solemnly swear (or affirm) that I will faithfully execute the Office of President of the United States, and will to the best of my Ability, preserve, protect and defend the Constitution of the United States."

Section 2   The President shall be Commander in Chief of the Army and Navy of the United States, and of the Militia of the several States, when called into the actual Service of the United States; he may require the Opinion, in writing, of the principal Officer in each of the executive Departments, upon any Subject relating to the Duties of their respective Offices, and he shall have Power to grant Reprieves and Pardons for Offences against the United States, except in Cases of Impeachment.

He shall have Power, by and with the Advice and Consent of the Senate, to make Treaties, provided two thirds of the Senators present concur; and he shall nominate, and by and with the Advice and Consent of the Senate, shall appoint Ambassadors, other public Ministers and Consuls, Judges of the supreme Court, and all other Officers of the United States, whose Appointments are not herein otherwise provided for, and which shall be established by Law: but the Congress may by Law vest the Appointment of such infe-

rior Officers, as they think proper in the President alone, in the Courts of Law, or in the Heads of Departments.

The President shall have Power to fill up all Vacancies that may happen during the Recess of the Senate, by granting Commissions which shall expire at the End of their next Session.

Section 3   He shall from time to time give to the Congress Information of the State of the Union, and recommend to their Consideration such Measures as he shall judge necessary and expedient; he may, on extraordinary Occasions, convene both Houses, or either of them, and in Case of disagreement between them, with Respect to the Time of Adjournment, he may adjourn them to such Time as he shall think proper; he shall receive Ambassadors and other public Ministers; he shall take Care that the Laws be faithfully executed, and shall Commission all the officers of the United States.

Section 4   The President, Vice President and all civil Officers of the United States, shall be removed from Office on Impeachment for, and Conviction of, Treason, Bribery or other high Crimes and Misdemeanors.

ARTICLE III.

Section 1   The judicial Power of the United States, shall be vested in one supreme Court, and in such inferior Courts as the Congress may from time to time ordain and establish. The Judges, both of the supreme and inferior Courts, shall hold their offices during good Behaviour, and shall, at stated Times, receive for their Services, a Compensation, which shall not be diminished during their Continuance in Office.

Section 2   The judicial Power shall extend to all Cases, in Law and Equity, arising under this Constitution, the Laws of the United States, and Treaties made, or which shall be made, under their Authority;—to all Cases affecting Ambassadors, other public Ministers and Consuls;—to all Cases of admiralty and maritime Jurisdiction;—to Controversies to which the United States shall be a Party;—to Controversies between two or more States;—between a State and Citizens of another State;—between Citizens of different States,—between Citizens of the same State claiming Lands under Grants of different States, and between a State, or the Citizens thereof, and foreign States, Citizens or Subjects.

In all Cases affecting Ambassadors, other public Ministers and Consuls, and those in which a State shall be Party, the supreme Court shall have original Jurisdiction. In all the other Cases before mentioned, the supreme Court shall have appellate Jurisdiction, both as to Law and Fact, with such Exceptions, and under such Regulations as the Congress shall make.

The Trial of all Crimes, except in Cases of Impeachment, shall be by Jury; and such Trial shall be held in the State where the said Crimes shall have been committed, but when not committed within any State, the Trial shall be at such Place or Places as the Congress may by Law have directed.

Section 3 Treason against the United States, shall consist only in levying War against them, or in adhering to their Enemies, giving them Aid and Comfort. No person shall be convicted of Treason unless on the Testimony of two Witnesses to the same overt Act, or on Confession in open Court.

The Congress shall have Power to declare the Punishment of Treason, but no Attainder of Treason shall work Corruption of Blood, or Forfeiture except during the Life of the Person attainted.

ARTICLE IV.

Section 1 Full Faith and Credit shall be given in each State to the public Acts, Records, and judicial Proceedings of every other State. And the Congress may be general Laws prescribe the Manner in which such Acts, Records and Proceedings shall be proved, and the Effect thereof.

Section 2 The Citizens of each State shall be entitled to all Privileges and Immunities of Citizens in the several States.

A Person charged in any State with Treason, Felony, or other Crime, who shall flee from Justice, and be found in another State, shall on Demand of the executive Authority of the State from which he fled, be delivered up, to be removed to the State having Jurisdiction of the Crime.

*No Person held to Service or Labour in one State, under the Laws thereof, escaping into another, shall, in Consequence of any Law or Regulation therein, be discharged from such Service or Labour, but shall be delivered up on Claim of the Party to whom such Service or Labour may be due.**

Section 3 New States may be admitted by the Congress into this Union; but no new State shall be formed or erected within the Jurisdiction of any other State; nor any State be formed by the Junction of two or more States, or Parts of States, without the Consent of the Legislatures of the States concerned as well as of the Congress.

The Congress shall have Power to dispose of and make all needful Rules and Regulations respecting the Territory or other Property belonging to the United States; and nothing in this Constitution shall be so construed as to Prejudice any Claims of the United States, or of any particular States.

Section 4 The United States shall guarantee to every State in this Union a Republican Form of Government, and shall protect each of them against Invasion; and on Application of the Legislature, or of the Executive (when the Legislature cannot be convened) against domestic violence.

ARTICLE V.

The Congress, whenever two thirds of both Houses shall deem it necessary, shall propose Amendments to this Constitution, or, on the Application of the Legislatures of two thirds of the several States, shall call a Convention for proposing Amendments, which, in either Case, shall be valid to all Intents and Purposes, as Part of this Constitution, when ratified by the Legislatures of three fourths of the several States, or by Conventions in three fourths thereof, as the one or the other Mode of Ratification may be proposed by the Congress; Provided *that no Amendment which may be made prior to the Year One thousand eight hundred and eight shall in any Manner affect the first and fourth Clauses in the Ninth Section of the first Article;* and that no State without its Consent, shall be deprived of its equal Suffrage in the Senate.

ARTICLE VI.

All Debts contracted and Engagements entered into, before the Adoption of this Constitution, shall be as valid against the United States under this Constitution, as under the Confederation.

This Constitution, and Laws of the United States which shall be made in Pursuance thereof; and all Treaties made, or which shall be made, under the Authority of the United States, shall be the supreme Law of the Land; and the Judges in every State shall be bound thereby, any Thing in the Constitution or Laws of any State to the Contrary notwithstanding.

The Senators and Representatives before mentioned, and the Members of the several State Legislatures, and all executive and Judicial Officers, both of the United States and of the several States, shall be bound by Oath or Affirmation, to support this Constitution; but no religious Test shall ever be required as a Qualification to any Office of public Trust under the United States.

ARTICLE VII.

The Ratification of the Conventions of nine States, shall be sufficient for the Establishment of this Constitution between the States so ratifying the Same.

Done in Convention by the Unanimous Consent of the States present the Seventeenth Day of September in the Year of our Lord one thousand seven hundred and Eighty seven and of the Independence of the United States of America the Twelfth* IN WITNESS whereof We have hereunto subscribed our Names,

GEORGE WASHINGTON,
President and Deputy from Virginia

New Hampshire
JOHN LANGDON
NICHOLAS GILMAN

Massachusetts
NATHANIEL GORHAM
RUFUS KING

Connecticut
WILLIAM S. JOHNSON
ROGER SHERMAN

New York
ALEXANDER HAMILTON

New Jersey
WILLIAM LIVINGSTON
DAVID BREARLEY
WILLIAM PATERSON
JONATHAN DAYTON

Pennsylvania
BENJAMIN FRANKLIN
THOMAS MIFFLIN
ROVERT MORRIS
GEORGE CLYMER
THOMAS FITZSIMONS
JARED INGERSOLL
JAMES WILSON
GOUVERNEUR MORRIS

Delaware
GEORGE READ
GUNNING BEDFORD, JR.
JOHN DICKINSON
RICHARD BASSETT
JACOB BROOM

Maryland
JAMES MCHENRY
DANIEL OF ST. THOMAS JENIFER
DANIEL CARROLL

Virginia
JOHN BLAIR
JAMES MADISON, JR.

North Carolina
WILLIAM BLOUNT
RICHARD DOBBS SPRAIGHT
HU WILLIAMSON

South Carolina
J. RUTLEDGE
CHARLES C. PINCKNEY
PIERCE BUTLER

Georgia
WILLIAM FEW
ABRAHAM BALDWIN

Amendments to the Constitution

*The first ten amendments (the Bill of Rights) were adopted in 1791.

AMENDMENT I

Congress shall make no law respecting an establishment of religion, or prohibiting the free exercise thereof; or abridging the freedom of speech, or of the press; or the right of the people peaceably to assemble, and to petition the Government for a redress of grievances.

AMENDMENT II

A well regulated Militia being necessary to the security of a free State, the right of the people to keep and bear Arms, shall not be infringed.

AMENDMENT III

No Soldier shall, in time of peace be quartered in any house, without the consent of the Owner, nor in time of war, but in a manner to be prescribed by law.

AMENDMENT IV

The right of the people to be secure in their persons, houses, papers, and effects, against unreasonable searches and seizures, shall not be violated, and no Warrants shall issue, but upon probable cause, supported by Oath or affirmation, and particularly describing the place to be searched, and the persons or things to be seized.

AMENDMENT V

No person shall be held to answer for a capital, or otherwise infamous crime, unless on a presentment or indictment of a Grand Jury, except in cases arising in the land or naval forces, or in the Militia, when in actual service in time of War or public danger; nor shall any person be subject for the same offense to be twice put in jeopardy of life or limb; nor shall be compelled in any criminal case to be a witness against himself, nor be deprived of life, liberty, or property, without due process of law; nor shall private property be taken for public use, without just compensation.

AMENDMENT VI

In all criminal prosecutions, the accused shall enjoy the right to a speedy and public trial, by an impartial jury of the State and district wherein the crime shall have been committed, which district shall have been previously ascertained by law, and to be informed of the nature and cause of the accusation; to be confronted with the witnesses against him; to have compulsory process for obtaining witnesses in his favor, and to have the Assistance of Counsel for his defence.

AMENDMENT VII

In Suits at common law, where the value in controversy shall exceed twenty dollars, the right of trial by jury shall be preserved, and no fact trial by a jury, shall be otherwise re-examined in any Court of the United States, than according to the rules of the common law.

AMENDMENT VIII

Excessive bail shall not be required, nor excessive fines imposed, nor cruel and unusual punishments inflicted.

AMENDMENT IX

The enumeration in the Constitution, of certain rights, shall not be construed to deny or disparage others retained by the people.

AMENDMENT X*

The powers not delegated to the United States by the Constitution, nor prohibited by it to the States, are reserved to the States respectively, or to the people.

AMENDMENT XI

[Adopted 1798]

The Judicial power of the United States shall not be construed to extend to any suit in law or equity, commenced or prosecuted against one of the United States by Citizens of another State, or by Citizens or Subjects of any Foreign State.

AMENDMENT XII

[Adopted 1804]

The Electors shall meet in their respective states, and vote by ballot for President and Vice-President, one of whom, at least, shall not be an inhabitant of the same state with themselves; they shall name in their ballots the person voted for as President, and in distinct ballots the person voted for as Vice-President, and they shall make distinct lists of all persons voted for as President, and of all persons voted for as Vice-President, and of the number of votes for each, which lists they shall sign and certify, and transmit sealed to the seat of the government of the United States, directed to the President of the Senate;—The President of the Senate shall, in the presence of the Senate and House of Representatives, open all the certificates and the votes shall then be counted;—The person having the greatest number of votes for President, shall be the President, if such number be a majority of the whole number of Electors appointed; and if no person have such majority, then from the persons having the highest numbers not exceeding three on the list of those voted for as President, the House of Representatives shall choose immediately, by ballot, the President. But in choosing the President, the votes shall be taken by states, the representation from each state having one vote; a quorum for this purpose shall consist of a member or members from two-thirds of the states, and a majority of all the states shall be necessary to a choice. And if the House of Representatives shall not choose a President whenever the right of choice shall devolve upon them, before *the fourth day of March* next following, then the Vice-President shall act as President, as in the case of the death or other constitutional disability of the President.—The person having the greatest number of votes as Vice-President, shall be the Vice-President, if such number be a majority of the whole number of Electors appointed, and if no person have a majority, then from the two highest numbers on the list, the Senate shall choose the Vice-President; a quorum for the purpose shall consist of two-thirds of the whole number of Senators, and a majority of the whole number shall be necessary to a choice. But no person constitutionally ineligible to the office of President shall be eligible to that of Vice President of the United States.

AMENDMENT XIII

[Adopted 1865]

Section 1   Neither slavery nor involuntary servitude, except as a punishment for crime whereof the party shall have been duly convicted, shall exist within the United States, or any place subject to their jurisdiction.

Section 2   Congress shall have power to enforce this article by appropriate legislation.

AMENDMENT XIV

[Adopted 1868]

Section 1   All persons born or naturalized in the United States, and subject to the jurisdiction thereof, are citizens of the United States and of the State wherein they reside. No State shall make or enforce any law which shall abridge the privileges or immunities of citizens of the United States; nor shall any State deprive any person of life, liberty, or property, without due process of law; nor deny to any person within its jurisdiction the equal protection of the laws.

Section 2   Representatives shall be apportioned among the several States according to their respective numbers, counting the whole number of persons in each State, excluding Indians not taxed. But when the right to vote at any election for the choice of electors for President and Vice-President of the United States, Representatives in Congress, the Executive and Judicial officers of a State, or the members of the Legislature thereof, is denied to any of the male inhabitants of such State, being twenty-one years of age, and citizens of the United States, or in any way abridged, except for participation in rebellion, or other crime, the basis of representation therein shall be reduced in the proportion which the number of such male citizens shall bear to the whole number of male citizens twenty-one years of age in such State.

Section 3   No person shall be a Senator or Representative in Congress, or elector of President and Vice-President, or hold any office, civil or military, under the United States, or under any State, who, having previously taken an oath, as a member of Congress, or as an officer of the United States, or as a member of any State legislature, or as an executive or judicial officer of any State, to support the Constitution of the United States, shall have engaged in insurrection or rebellion against the same, or given aid or comfort to the enemies thereof. But Congress may be a vote of two-thirds of each House, remove such disability.

Section 4   The validity of the public debt of the United States, authorized by law, including debts incurred for payment of pensions and bounties for services in suppressing insurrection or rebellion, shall not be questioned. But neither the United States nor any State shall assume or pay any debt or obligation incurred in aid of insurrection or rebellion against the United States, or any claim for the loss or emancipation of any slave; but all such debts, obligations and claims shall be held illegal and void.

Section 5   The Congress shall have power to enforce, by appropriate legislation, the provisions of this article.

AMENDMENT XV

[Adopted 1879]

Section 1   The right of citizens of the United States to vote shall not be denied or abridged by the United States or by any State on account of race, color, or previous condition of servitude.

Section 2   The Congress shall have power to enforce this article by appropriate legislation.

AMENDMENT XVI

[Adopted 1913]

The Congress shall have power to lay and collect taxes on incomes, from whatever source derived, without apportionment among the several States, and without regard to any census or enumeration.

AMENDMENT XVII

[Adopted 1913]

The Senate of the United States shall be composed of two Senators from each State, elected by the people thereof, for six years; and each Senator shall have one vote. The electors in each State shall have the qualifications requisite for electors of the most numerous branch of the State legislatures.

When vacancies happen in the representation of any State in the Senate, the executive authority of such State shall issue writs of election to fill such vacancies: *Provided,* That the legislature of any State may empower the executive thereof to make temporary appointments until the people fill the vacancies by election as the legislature may direct.

This amendment shall not be so construed as to affect the election or term of any Senator chosen before it becomes valid as part of the Constitution.

AMENDMENT XVIII

[Adopted 1919; Repealed 1933]

Section 1   After one year from the ratification of this article the manufacture, sale, or transportation of intoxicating liquors within, the importation thereof into, or the exportation thereof from the United States and all territory subject to the jurisdiction thereof for beverage purposes is hereby prohibited.*

Section 2   The Congress and the several States shall have concurrent power to enforce this article by appropriate legislation.

Section 3   This article shall be inoperative unless it shall have been ratified as an amendment to the Constitution by the legislatures of the several States, as provided in the Constitution, within seven years from the date of the submission hereof to the States by the Congress.

AMENDMENT XIX

[Adopted 1920]

Section 1   The right of citizens of the United States to vote shall not be denied or abridged by the United States or by any State on account of sex.

Section 2   Congress shall have power to enforce this article by appropriate legislation.

AMENDMENT XX

[Adopted 1933]

Section 1   The terms of the President and Vice-President shall end at noon on the 20th day of January, and the terms of Senators and Representatives at noon on the 3d day of January, of the years in which such terms would have ended if this article had not been ratified and the terms of their successors shall then begin.

Section 2   The Congress shall assemble at least once in every year, and such meeting shall begin at noon on the 3d day of January, unless they shall by law appoint a different day.

Section 3   If, at the time fixed for the beginning of the term of the President, the President elect shall have died, the Vice-President elect shall become President. If a President shall not have been chosen before the time fixed for the beginning of his term, or if the President elect shall have failed to qualify, then the Vice-President elect shall act as President until a President shall have qualified; and the Congress may by law provide for the case wherein neither a President elect nor a Vice-President elect shall have qualified, declaring who shall then act as President, or the manner in which one who is to act shall be selected, and such person shall act accordingly until a President or Vice-President shall have qualified.

Section 4   The Congress may by law provide for the case of the death of any of the persons from whom the House of Representatives may choose a President whenever the right of choice shall have devolved upon them, and for the case of the death of any of the persons from whom the Senate may choose a Vice-President whenever the right of choice shall have devolved upon them.

Section 5   Sections 1 and 2 shall take effect on the 15th day of October following the ratification of this article.

Section 6   This article shall be inoperative unless it shall have been ratified as an amendment to the Constitution by the legislatures of three fourths of the several States within seven years from the date of its submission.

AMENDMENT XXI

[Adopted 1933]

Section 1   The eighteenth article of amendment to the Constitution of the United States is hereby repealed.

Section 2   The transportation or importation into any State, Territory, or possession of the United States for delivery or use therein of intoxicating liquors in violation of the laws thereof, is hereby prohibited.

Section 3   This article shall be inoperative unless it shall have been ratified as an amendment to the Constitution by conventions in the several States, as provided in the Constitution, within seven years from the date of the submission hereof to the States by the Congress.

AMENDMENT XXII

[Adopted 1951]

Section 1   No person shall be elected to the office of the President more than twice, and no person who has held the office of President, or acted as President, for more than two years of a term to which some other person was elected President shall be elected to the office of the President more than once. But this Article shall not apply to any person holding the office of President when this Article was proposed by the Congress, and shall not prevent any person who may be holding the office of President, or acting as President, during the term within which this Article becomes operative from holding the office of President or acting as President during the remainder of such term.

Section 2 This article shall be inoperative unless it shall have been ratified as an amendment to the Constitution by the legislatures of three-fourths of the several States within several years from the date of its submission to the States within seven years from the date of its submission to the States by the Congress.

AMENDMENT XXIII

[Adopted 1961]

Section 1 The District constituting the seat of Government of the United States shall appoint in such manner as the Congress shall direct:

A number of electors of President and Vice-President equal to the whole number of Senators and Representatives in Congress to which the District would be entitled if it were a State, but in no event more than the least populous State; they shall be in addition to those appointed by the States, but they shall be considered, for the purposes of the election of President and Vice-President, to be electors appointed by a State; and they shall meet in the District and perform such duties as provided by the twelfth article of amendment.

Section 2 The Congress shall have power to enforce this article by appropriate legislation.

AMENDMENT XXIV

[Adopted 1944]

Section 1 The right of citizens of the United States to vote in any primary or other election for President or Vice-President, for electors for President or Vice-President, or for Senator or Representative in Congress, shall not be denied or abridged by the United States or any state by reason of failure to pay any poll tax or other tax.

Section 2 The Congress shall have the power to enforce this article by appropriate legislation.

AMENDMENT XXV

[Adopted 1967]

Section 1 In case of the removal of the President from office or his death or resignation, the Vice-President shall become President.

Section 2 Whenever there is a vacancy in the office of the Vice-President, the President shall nominate a Vice President who shall take the office upon confirmation by a majority vote of both houses of Congress.

Section 3 Whenever the President transmits to the President pro tempore of the Senate and the Speaker of the House of Representatives his written declaration that he is unable to discharge the powers and duties of his office, and until he transmits to them a written declaration to the contrary, such powers and duties shall be discharged by the Vice-President as Acting President.

Section 4 Whenever the Vice-President and a majority of either the principal officers of the executive departments or of such other body as Congress may by law provide, transmit to the President pro tempore of the Senate and the Speaker of the House of Representatives their written declaration that the President is unable to discharge the powers and duties of his office, the Vice-President shall immediately assume the powers and duties of the office as Acting President.

Thereafter, when the President transmits to the President pro tempore of the Senate and the Speaker of the House of Representatives his written declaration that no inability exists, he shall resume the powers and duties of his office unless the Vice-President and a majority of either the principal officers of the executive department or of such other body as Congress may by law provide, transmit within four days to the President pro tempore of the Senate and the Speaker of the House of Representatives their written declaration that the President is unable to discharge the powers and duties of his office. Thereupon Congress shall decide the issue, assembling within 48 hours for that purpose if not in session. If the Congress, within 21 days after receipt of the latter written declaration, or, if Congress is not in session, within 21 days after Congress is required to assemble, determines by two-thirds vote of both houses that the President is unable to discharge the powers and duties of his office, the Vice-President shall continue to discharge the same as Acting President; otherwise, the President shall resume the powers and duties of his office.

AMENDMENT XXVI

[Adopted 1971]

Section 1 The right of citizens of the United States, who are 18 years of age or older, to vote shall not be denied or abridged by the United States or any state on account of age.

Section 2 The Congress shall have the power to enforce this article by appropriate legislation.

AMENDMENT XXVII

[Adopted 1992]

No law varying the compensation for the services of the Senators and Representatives shall take effect, until an election of Representatives shall have intervened.

PRESIDENTIAL ELECTIONS

Year	Candidates	Parties	Popular Vote	Electoral Vote	Voter Participation
1789	**GEORGE WASHINGTON**		*	69	
	John Adams			34	
	Others			35	
1792	**GEORGE WASHINGTON**		*	132	
	John Adams			77	
	George Clinton			50	
	Others			5	
1796	**JOHN ADAMS**	Federalist	*	71	
	Thomas Jefferson	Democratic-Republican		68	
	Thomas Pinckney	Federalist		59	
	Aaron Burr	Dem.-Rep.		30	
	Others			48	
1800	**THOMAS JEFFERSON**	Dem.-Rep.	*	73	
	Aaron Burr	Dem.-Rep.		73	
	John Adams	Federalist		65	
	C. C. Pinckney	Federalist		64	
	John Jay	Federalist		1	
1804	**THOMAS JEFFERSON**	Dem.-Rep.	*	162	
	C. C. Pinckney	Federalist		14	
1808	**JAMES MADISON**	Dem.-Rep.	*	122	
	C. C. Pinckney	Federalist		47	
	George Clinton	Dem.-Rep.		6	
1812	**JAMES MADISON**	Dem.-Rep.	*	128	
	De Witt Clinton	Federalist		89	
1816	**JAMES MONROE**	Dem.-Rep.	*	183	
	Rufus King	Federalist		34	
1820	**JAMES MONROE**	Dem.-Rep.	*	231	
	John Quincy Adams	Dem.-Rep.		1	
1824	**JOHN Q. ADAMS**	Dem.-Rep.	108,740 (30.5%)	84	26.9%
	Andrew Jackson	Dem.-Rep.	153,544 (43.1%)	99	
	William H. Crawford	Dem.-Rep.	46,618 (13.1%)	41	
	Henry Clay	Dem.-Rep.	47,136 (13.2%)	37	
1828	**ANDREW JACKSON**	Democratic	647,286 (56.0%)	178	57.6%
	John Quincy Adams	National Republican	508,064 (44.0%)	83	
1832	**ANDREW JACKSON**	Democratic	687,502 (55.0%)	219	55.4%
	Henry Clay	National Republican	530,189 (42.4%)	49	
	John Floyd	Independent		11	
	William Wirt	Anti-Mason	33,108 (2.6%)	7	
1836	**MARTIN VAN BUREN**	Democratic	765,483 (50.9%)	170	57.8%
	W. H. Harrison	Whig		73	
	Hugh L. White	Whig	739,795 (49.1%)	26	
	Daniel Webster	Whig		14	
	W. P. Magnum	Independent		11	
1840	**WILLIAM H. HARRISON**	Whig	1,274,624 (53.1%)	234	80.2%
	Martin Van Buren	Democratic	1,127,781 (46.9%)	60	
	J. G. Birney	Liberty	7069	—	
1844	**JAMES K. POLK**	Democratic	1,338,464 (49.6%)	170	78.9%
	Henry Clay	Whig	1,300,097 (48.1%)	105	
	J. G. Birney	Liberty	62,300 (2.3%)	—	

Year	Candidates	Parties	Popular Vote	Electoral Vote	Voter Participation
1848	**ZACHARY TAYLOR**	Whig	1,360,967 (47.4%)	163	72.7%
	Lewis Cass	Democratic	1,222,342 (42.5%)	127	
	Martin Van Buren	Free-Soil	291,263 (10.1%)	—	
1852	**FRANKLIN PIERCE**	Democratic	1,601,117 (50.9%)	254	69.6%
	Winfield Scott	Whig	1,385,453 (44.1%)	42	
	John P. Hale	Free-Soil	155,825 (5.0%)	—	
1856	**JAMES BUCHANAN**	Democratic	1,832,955 (45.3%)	174	78.9%
	John C. Frémont	Republican	1,339,932 (33.1%)	114	
	Millard Fillmore	American	871,731 (21.6%)	8	
1860	**ABRAHAM LINCOLN**	Republican	1,865,593 (39.8%)	180	81.2%
	Stephen A. Douglas	Democratic	1,382,713 (29.5%)	12	
	John C. Breckinridge	Democratic	848,356 (18.1%)	72	
	John Bell	Union	592,906 (12.6%)	39	
1864	**ABRAHAM LINCOLN**	Republican	2,213,655 (55.0%)	212	73.8%
	George B. McClellan	Democratic	1,805,237 (45.0%)	21	
1868	**ULYSSES S. GRANT**	Republican	3,012,833 (52.7%)	214	78.1%
	Horatio Seymour	Democratic	2,703,249 (47.3%)	80	
1872	**ULYSSES S. GRANT**	Republican	3,597,132 (55.6%)	286	71.3%
	Horace Greeley	Democratic; Liberal Republican	2,834,125 (43.9%)	66	
1876	**RUTHERFORD B. HAYES**	Republican	4,036,298 (48.0%)	185	81.8%
	Samuel J. Tilden	Democratic	4,300,590 (51.0%)	184	
1880	**JAMES A. GARFIELD**	Republican	4,454,416 (48.5%)	214	79.4%
	Winfield S. Hancock	Democratic	4,444,952 (48.1%)	155	
1884	**GROVER CLEVELAND**	Democratic	4,874,986 (48.5%)	219	77.5%
	James G. Blaine	Republican	4,851,981 (48.2%)	182	
1888	**BENJAMIN HARRISON**	Republican	5,439,853 (47.9%)	233	79.3%
	Grover Cleveland	Democratic	5,540,309 (48.6%)	168	
1892	**GROVER CLEVELAND**	Democratic	5,556,918 (46.1%)	277	74.7%
	Benjamin Harrison	Republican	5,176,108 (43.0%)	145	
	James B. Weaver	People's	1,041,028 (8.5%)	22	
1896	**WILLIAM McKINLEY**	Republican	7,104,779 (51.1%)	271	79.3%
	William J. Bryan	Democratic People's	6,502,925 (47.7%)	176	
1900	**WILLIAM McKINLEY**	Republican	7,207,923 (51.7%)	292	73.2%
	William J. Bryan	Dem.-Populist	6,358,133 (45.5%)	155	
1904	**THEODORE ROOSEVELT**	Republican	7,623,486 (57.9%)	336	65.2%
	Alton B. Parker	Democratic	5,077,911 (37.6%)	140	
	Eugene V. Debs	Socialist	402,283 (3.0%)	—	
1908	**WILLIAM H. TAFT**	Republican	7,678,908 (51.6%)	321	65.4%
	William J. Bryan	Democratic	6,409,104 (43.1%)	162	
	Eugene V. Debs	Socialist	420,793 (2.8%)	—	
1912	**WOODROW WILSON**	Democratic	6,293,454 (41.9%)	435	58.8%
	Theodore Roosevelt	Progressive	4,119,538 (27.4%)	88	
	William H. Taft	Republican	3,484,980 (23.2%)	8	
	Eugene V. Debs	Socialist	900,672 (6.0%)	—	
1916	**WOODROW WILSON**	Democratic	9,129,606 (49.4%)	277	61.6%
	Charles E. Hughes	Republican	8,538,221 (46.2%)	254	
	A. L. Benson	Socialist	585,113 (3.2%)	—	
1920	**WARREN G. HARDING**	Republican	16,152,200 (60.4%)	404	49.2%
	James M. Cox	Democratic	9,147,353 (34.2%)	127	
	Eugene V. Debs	Socialist	919,799 (3.4%)	—	

Year	Candidates	Parties	Popular Vote	Electoral Vote	Voter Participation
1924	**CALVIN COOLIDGE**	Republican	15,725,016 (54.0%)	382	48.9%
	John W. Davis	Democratic	8,386,503 (28.8%)	136	
	Robert M. La Follette	Progressive	4,822,856 (16.6%)	13	
1928	**HERBERT HOOVER**	Republican	21,391,381 (58.2%)	444	56.9%
	Alfred E. Smith	Democratic	15,016,443 (40.9%)	87	
	Norman Thomas	Socialist	267,835 (0.7%)	—	
1932	**FRANKLIN D. ROOSEVELT**	Democratic	22,821,857 (57.4%)	472	56.9%
	Herbert Hoover	Republican	15,761,841 (39.7%)	59	
	Norman Thomas	Socialist	881,951 (2.2%)	—	
1936	**FRANKLIN D. ROOSEVELT**	Democratic	27,751,597 (60.8%)	523	61.0%
	Alfred M. Landon	Republican	16,679,583 (36.5%)	8	
	William Lemke	Union	882,479 (1.9%)	—	
1940	**FRANKLIN D. ROOSEVELT**	Democratic	27,244,160 (54.8%)	449	62.5%
	Wendell L. Willkie	Republican	22,305,198 (44.8%)	82	
1944	**FRANKLIN D. ROOSEVELT**	Democratic	25,602,504 (53.5%)	432	55.9%
	Thomas E. Dewey	Republican	22,006,285 (46.0%)	99	
1948	**HARRY S TRUMAN**	Democratic	24,105,695 (49.5%)	304	53.0%
	Thomas E. Dewey	Republican	21,969,170 (45.1%)	189	
	J. Strom Thurmond	State-Rights Democratic	1,169,021 (2.4%)	38	
	Henry A. Wallace	Progressive	1,156,103 (2.4%)	—	
1952	**DWIGHT D. EISENHOWER**	Republican	33,936,252 (55.1%)	442	63.3%
	Adlai E. Stevenson	Democratic	27,314,992 (44.4%)	89	
1956	**DWIGHT D. EISENHOWER**	Republican	35,575,420 (57.6%)	457	60.6%
	Adlai E. Stevenson	Democratic	26,033,066 (42.1%)	73	
	Other	—	—	1	
1960	**JOHN F. KENNEDY**	Democratic	34,227,096 (49.9%)	303	62.8%
	Richard M. Nixon	Republican	34,108,546 (49.6%)	219	
	Other	—	—	15	
1964	**LYNDON B. JOHNSON**	Democratic	43,126,506 (61.1%)	486	61.7%
	Barry M. Goldwater	Republican	27,176,799 (38.5%)	52	
1968	**RICHARD M. NIXON**	Republican	31,770,237 (43.4%)	301	60.6%
	Hubert H. Humphrey	Democratic	31,270,533 (42.7%)	191	
	George Wallace	American Indep.	9,906,141 (13.5%)	46	
1972	**RICHARD M. NIXON**	Republican	47,169,911 (60.7%)	520	55.2%
	George S. McGovern	Democratic	29,170,383 (37.5%)	17	
	Other	—	—	1	
1976	**JIMMY CARTER**	Democratic	40,828,587 (50.0%)	297	53.5%
	Gerald R. Ford	Republican	39,147,613 (47.9%)	241	
	Other	—	1,575,459 (2.1%)	—	
1980	**RONALD REAGAN**	Republican	43,901,812 (50.7%)	489	52.6%
	Jimmy Carter	Democratic	35,483,820 (41.0%)	49	
	John B. Anderson	Independent	5,719,722 (6.6%)	—	
	Ed Clark	Libertarian	921,188 (1.1%)	—	
1984	**RONALD REAGAN**	Republican	54,455,075 (59.0%)	525	53.3%
	Walter Mondale	Democratic	37,577,185 (41.0%)	13	
1988	**GEORGE H. W. BUSH**	Republican	48,886,000 (53.4%)	426	57.4%
	Michael S. Dukakis	Democratic	41,809,000 (45.6%)	111	
1992	**BILL CLINTON**	Democratic	43,728,375 (43%)	370	55.0%
	George H. W. Bush	Republican	38,167,416 (38%)	168	
	Ross Perot	—	19,237,247 (19%)	—	

*Electors selected by state legislatures.

Vice Presidents and Cabinet Members by Administration

The Washington Administration (1789–1797)

Vice President	John Adams	1789–1797
Secretary of State	Thomas Jefferson	1789–1793
	Edmund Randolph	1794–1795
	Timothy Pickering	1795–1797
Secretary of Treasury	Alexander Hamilton	1789–1795
	Oliver Wolcott	1795–1797
Secretary of War	Henry Knox	1789–1794
	Timothy Pickering	1795–1796
	James McHenry	1796–1797
Attorney General	Edmund Randolph	1789–1793
	William Bradford	1794–1795
	Charles Lee	1795–1797
Postmaster General	Samuel Osgood	1789–1791
	Timothy Pickering	1791–1794
	Joseph Habersham	1795–1797

The John Adams Administration (1797–1801)

Vice President	Thomas Jefferson	1797–1801
Secretary of State	Timothy Pickering	1797–1800
	John Marshall	1800–1801
Secretary of Treasury	Oliver Wolcott	1797–1800
	Samuel Dexter	1800–1801
Secretary of War	James McHenry	1797–1800
	Samuel Dexter	1800–1801
Attorney General	Charles Lee	1797–1801
Postmaster General	Joseph Habersham	1797–1801
Secretary of Navy	Benjamin Stoddert	1798–1801

The Jefferson Administration (1801–1809)

Vice President	Aaron Burr	1801–1805
	George Clinton	1805–1809
Secretary of State	James Madison	1801–1809
Secretary of Treasury	Samuel Dexter	1801
	Albert Gallatin	1801–1809
Secretary of War	Henry Dearborn	1801–1809
Attorney General	Levi Lincoln	1801–1805
	Robert Smith	1805
	John Breckinridge	1805–1806
	Caesar Rodney	1807–1809
Postmaster General	Joseph Habersham	1801
	Gideon Granger	1801–1809
Secretary of Navy	Robert Smith	1801–1809

The Madison Administration (1809–1817)

Vice President	George Clinton	1809–d. 1812
	Elbridge Gerry	1813–d. 1814
Secretary of State	Robert Smith	1809–1811
	James Monroe	1811–1817
Secretary of Treasury	Albert Gallatin	1809–1813
	George Campbell	1814
	Alexander Dallas	1814–1816
	William Crawford	1816–1817
Secretary of War	William Eustis	1809–1812
	John Armstrong	1813–1814
	James Monroe	1814–1815
	William Crawford	1815–1817
Attorney General	Caesar Rodney	1809–1811
	William Pinkney	1811–1814
	Richard Rush	1814–1817
Postmaster General	Gideon Granger	1809–1814
	Return Meigs	1814–1817
Secretary of Navy	Paul Hamilton	1809–1813
	William Jones	1813–1814
	Benjamin Crowninshield	1814–1817

The Monroe Administration (1817–1825)

Vice President	Daniel Tompkins	1817–1825
Secretary of State	John Quincy Adams	1817–1825
Secretary of Treasury	William Crawford	1817–1825
Secretary of War	George Graham	1817
	John C. Calhoun	1817–1825
Attorney General	Richard Rush	1817
	William Wirt	1817–1825
Postmaster General	Return Meigs	1817–1823
	John McLean	1823–1825
Secretary of Navy	Benjamin Crowninshield	1817–1818
	Smith Thompson	1818–1823
	Samuel Southard	1823–1825

The John Quincy Adams Administration (1825–1829)

Vice President	John C. Calhoun	1825–1829
Secretary of State	Henry Clay	1825–1829
Secretary of Treasury	Richard Rush	1825–1829
Secretary of War	James Barbour	1825–1829
	Peter Porter	1828–1829
Attorney General	William Wirt	1825–1829
Postmaster General	John McLean	1825–1829
Secretary of Navy	Samuel Southard	1825–1829

The Jackson Administration (1829–1837)

Vice President	John C. Calhoun	1829–1832
	Martin Van Buren	1833–1837
Secretary of State	Martin Van Buren	1829–1831
	Edward Livingston	1831–1833
	Louis McLane	1833–1834
	John Forsyth	1834–1837

Secretary of Treasury	Samuel Ingham	1829–1831
	Louis McLane	1831–1833
	William Duane	1833
	Roger B. Taney	1833–1834
	Levi Woodbury	1834–1837
Secretary of War	John H. Eaton	1829–1831
	Lewis Cass	1831–1837
	Benjamin Butler	1837
Attorney General	John M. Berrien	1829–1831
	Roger B. Taney	1831–1833
	Benjamin Butler	1833–1837
Postmaster General	William Barry	1829–1835
	Amos Kendall	1835–1837
Secretary of Navy	John Branch	1829–1831
	Levi Woodbury	1831–1834
	Mahlon Dickerson	1834–1837

The Van Buren Administration (1837–1841)

Vice President	Richard M. Johnson	1837–1841
Secretary of State	John Forsyth	1837–1841
Secretary of Treasury	Levi Woodbury	1837–1841
Secretary of War	Joel Poinsett	1837–1841
Attorney General	Benjamin Butler	1837–1838
	Felix Grundy	1838–1840
	Henry D. Gilpin	1840–1841
Postmaster General	Amos Kendall	1837–1840
	John M. Niles	1840–1841
Secretary of Navy	Mahlon Dickerson	1837–1838
	James Paulding	1838–1841

The William Harrison Administration (1841)

Vice President	John Tyler	1841
Secretary of State	Daniel Webster	1841
Secretary of Treasury	Thomas Ewing	1841
Secretary of War	John Bell	1841
Attorney General	John J. Crittenden	1841
Postmaster General	Francis Granger	1841
Secretary of Navy	George Badger	1841

The Tyler Administration (1841–1845)

Vice President	None	
Secretary of State	Daniel Webster	1841–1843
	Hugh S. Legaré	1843
	Abel P. Upshur	1843–1844
	John C. Calhoun	1844–1845
Secretary of Treasury	Thomas Ewing	1841
	Walter Forward	1841–1843
	John C. Spencer	1843–1844
	George Bibb	1844–1845
Secretary of War	John Bell	1841
	John C. Spencer	1841–1843
	James M. Porter	1843–1844
	William Wilkins	1844–1845

Attorney General	John J. Crittenden	1841
	Hugh S. Legaré	1841–1843
	John Nelson	1843–1845
Postmaster General	Francis Granger	1841
	Charles Wickliffe	1841
Secretary of Navy	George Badger	1841
	Abel P. Upshur	1841
	David Henshaw	1843–1844
	Thomas Gilmer	1844
	John Y. Mason	1844–1845

The Polk Administration (1845–1849)

Vice President	George M. Dallas	1845–1849
Secretary of State	James Buchanan	1845–1849
Secretary of Treasury	Robert J. Walker	1845–1849
Secretary of War	William L. Marcy	1845–1849
Attorney General	John Y. Mason	1845–1846
	Nathan Clifford	1846–1848
	Isaac Toucey	1848–1849
Postmaster General	Cave Johnson	1845–1849
Secretary of Navy	George Bancroft	1845–1846
	John Y. Mason	1846–1849

The Taylor Administration (1849–1850)

Vice President	Millard Fillmore	1849–1850
Secretary of State	John M. Clayton	1849–1850
Secretary of Treasury	William Meredith	1849–1850
Secretary of War	George Crawford	1849–1850
Attorney General	Reverdy Johnson	1849–1850
Postmaster General	Jacob Collamer	1849–1850
Secretary of Navy	William Preston	1849–1850
Secretary of Interior	Thomas Ewing	1849–1850

The Fillmore Administration (1850–1853)

Vice President	None	
Secretary of State	Daniel Webster	1850–1852
	Edward Everett	1852–1853
Secretary of Treasury	Thomas Corwin	1850–1853
Secretary of War	Charles Conrad	1850–1853
Attorney General	John J. Crittenden	1850–1853
Postmaster General	Nathan Hall	1850–1852
	Samuel D. Hubbard	1852–1853
Secretary of Navy	William A. Graham	1850–1852
	John P. Kennedy	1852–1853
Secretary of Interior	Thomas McKennan	1850
	Alexander Stuart	1850–1853

The Pierce Administration (1853–1857)

Vice President	William R. King	1853–d. 1853
Secretary of State	William L. Marcy	1853–1857
Secretary of Treasury	James Guthrie	1853–1857
Secretary of War	Jefferson Davis	1853–1857
Attorney General	Caleb Cushing	1853–1857

Postmaster General	James Campbell	1853–1857
Secretary of Navy	James C. Dobbin	1853–1857
Secretary of Interior	Robert McClelland	1853–1857

The Buchanan Administration (1857–1861)

Vice President	John C. Breckinridge	1857–1861
Secretary of State	Lewis Cass	1857–1860
	Jeremiah S. Black	1860–1861
Secretary of Treasury	Howell Cobb	1857–1860
	Philip Thomas	1860–1861
	John A. Dix	1861
Secretary of War	John B. Floyd	1857–1861
	Joseph Holt	1861
Attorney General	Jeremiah S. Black	1857–1860
	Edwin M. Stanton	1860–1861
Postmaster General	Aaron V. Brown	1857–1859
	Joseph Holt	1859–1861
	Horatio King	1861
Secretary of Navy	Isaac Toucey	1857–1861
Secretary of Interior	Jacob Thompson	1857–1861

The Lincoln Administration (1861–1865)

Vice President	Hannibal Hamlin	1861–1865
	Andrew Johnson	1865
Secretary of State	William H. Seward	1861–1865
Secretary of Treasury	Samuel P. Chase	1861–1864
	William P. Fessenden	1864–1865
	Hugh McCulloch	1865
Secretary of War	Simon Cameron	1861–1862
	Edwin M. Stanton	1862–1865
Attorney General	Edward Bates	1861–1864
	James Speed	1864–1865
Postmaster General	Horatio King	1861
	Montgomery Blair	1861–1864
	William Dennison	1864–1865
Secretary of Navy	Gideon Welles	1861–1865
Secretary of Interior	Caleb B. Smith	1861–1863
	John P. Usher	1863–1865

The Andrew Johnson Administration (1865–1869)

Vice President	None	
Secretary of State	William H. Seward	1865–1869
Secretary of Treasury	Hugh McCulloch	1865–1869
Secretary of War	Edwin M. Stanton	1865–1867
	Ulysses S. Grant	1867–1868
	Lorenzo Thomas	1868
	John M. Schofield	1868–1869
Attorney General	James Speed	1865–1866
	Henry Stanbery	1866–1868
	William M. Evarts	1868–1869
Postmaster General	William Dennison	1865–1866
	Alexander Randall	1866–1869
Secretary of Navy	Gideon Welles	1865–1869

Secretary of Interior	John P. Usher	1865
	James Harlan	1865–1866
	Ovrille H. Browning	1866–1869

The Grant Administration (1869–1877)

Vice President	Schuyler Colfax	1869–1873
	Henry Wilson	1873–d. 1875
Secretary of State	Elihu B. Washburne	1869
	Hamilton Fish	1869–1877
Secretary of Treasury	George S. Boutwell	1869–1873
	William Richardson	1873–1874
	Benjamin Bristow	1874–1876
	Lot M. Morrill	1876–1877
Secretary of War	John A. Rawlins	1869
	William T. Sherman	1869
	William W. Belknap	1869–1876
	Alphonso Taft	1876
	James D. Cameron	1876–1877
Attorney General	Ebenezer Hoar	1869–1870
	Amos T. Ackerman	1870–1871
	G. H. Williams	1871–1875
	Edwards Pierrepont	1875–1876
	Alphonso Taft	1876–1877
Postmaster General	John A. J. Creswell	1869–1874
	James W. Marshall	1874
	Marshall Jewell	1874–1876
	James N. Tyner	1876–1877
Secretary of Navy	Adolph E. Borie	1869
	George M. Robeson	1869–1877
Secretary of Interior	Jacob D. Cox	1869–1870
	Columbus Delano	1870–1875
	Zachariah Chandler	1875–1877

The Hayes Administration (1877–1881)

Vice President	William A. Wheeler	1877–1881
Secretary of State	William M. Evarts	1877–1881
Secretary of Treasury	John Sherman	1877–1881
Secretary of War	George W. McCrary	1877–1879
	Alex Ramsey	1879–1881
Attorney General	Charles Devens	1877–1881
Postmaster General	David M. Key	1877–1880
	Horace Maynard	1880–1881
Secretary of Navy	Richard W. Thompson	1877–1880
	Nathan Goff, Jr.	1881
Secretary of Interior	Carl Schurz	1877–1881

The Garfield Administration (1881)

Vice President	Chester A. Arthur	1881
Secretary of State	James G. Blaine	1881
Secretary of Treasury	William Windom	1881
Secretary of War	Robert T. Lincoln	1881
Attorney General	Wayne MacVeagh	1881
Postmaster General	Thomas L. James	1881
Secretary of Navy	William H. Hunt	1881
Secretary of Interior	Samuel J. Kirkwood	1881

The Arthur Administration (1881–1885)

Vice President	None	
Secretary of State	F. T. Frelinghuysen	1881–1885
Secretary of Treasury	Charles J. Folger	1881–1884
	Walter Q. Gresham	1884
	Hugh McCulloch	1884–1885
Secretary of War	Robert T. Lincoln	1881–1885
Attorney General	Benjamin H. Brewster	1881–1885
Postmaster General	Timothy O. Howe	1881–1883
	Walter Q. Gresham	1883–1884
	Frank Hatton	1884–1885
Secretary of Navy	William H. Hunt	1881–1882
	William E. Chandler	1882–1885
Secretary of Interior	Samuel J. Kirkwood	1881–1882
	Henry M. Teller	1882–1885

The Cleveland Administration (1885–1889)

Vice President	Thomas A. Hendricks	1885–d. 1885
Secretary of State	Thomas F. Bayard	1885–1889
Secretary of Treasury	Daniel Manning	1885–1887
	Charles S. Fairchild	1887–1889
Secretary of War	William C. Endicott	1885–1889
Attorney General	Augustus H. Garland	1885–1889
Postmaster General	William F. Vilas	1885–1888
	Don M. Dickinson	1888–1889
Secretary of Navy	William C. Whitney	1885–1889
Secretary of Interior	Lucius Q. C. Lamar	1885–1888
	William F. Vilas	1888–1889
Secretary of Agriculture	Norman J. Colman	1889

The Benjamin Harrison Administration (1889–1893)

Vice President	Levi P. Morton	1889–1893
Secretary of State	James G. Blaine	1889–1892
	John W. Foster	1892–1893
Secretary of Treasury	William Windom	1889–1891
	Charles Foster	1891–1893
Secretary of War	Redfield Proctor	1889–1891
	Stephen B. Elkins	1891–1893
Attorney General	William H. H. Miller	1889–1891
Postmaster General	John Wanamaker	1889–1893
Secretary of Navy	Benjamin F. Tracy	1889–1893
Secretary of Interior	John W. Noble	1889–1893
Secretary of Agriculture	Jeremiah M. Rusk	1889–1893

The Cleveland Administration (1893–1897)

Vice President	Adlai E. Stevenson	1893–1897
Secretary of State	Walter Q. Gresham	1893–1895
	Richard Olney	1895–1897
Secretary of Treasury	John G. Carlisle	1893–1897
Secretary of War	Daniel S. Lamont	1893–1897
Attorney General	Richard Olney	1893–1895
	James Harmon	1895–1897
Postmaster General	Wilson S. Bissell	1893–1895
	William L. Wilson	1895–1897
Secretary of Navy	Hilary A. Herbert	1893–1897
Secretary of Interior	Hoke Smith	1893–1896
	David R. Francis	1896–1897
Secretary of Agriculture	Julius S. Morton	1893–1897

The McKinley Administration (1897–1901)

Vice President	Garret A. Hobart	1897–d. 1899
	Theodore Roosevelt	1901
Secretary of State	John Sherman	1897–1898
	William R. Day	1898
	John Hay	1898–1901
Secretary of Treasury	Lyman J. Gage	1897–1901
Secretary of War	Russell A. Alger	1897–1899
	Elihu Root	1899–1901
Attorney General	Joseph McKenna	1897–1898
	John W. Griggs	1898–1901
	Philander C. Knox	1901
Postmaster General	James A. Gary	1897–1898
	Charles E. Smith	1898–1901
Secretary of Navy	John D. Long	1897–1901
Secretary of Interior	Cornelius N. Bliss	1897–1899
	Ethan A. Hitchcock	1899–1901
Secretary of Agriculture	James Wilson	1897–1901

The Theodore Roosevelt Administration (1901–1909)

Vice President	Charles Fairbanks	1905–1909
Secretary of State	John Hay	1901–1905
	Elihu Root	1905–1909
	Robert Bacon	1909
Secretary of Treasury	Lyman J. Gage	1901–1902
	Leslie M. Shaw	1902–1907
	George B. Cortelyou	1907–1909
Secretary of War	Elihu Root	1901–1904
	William H. Taft	1904–1908
	Luke E. Wright	1908–1909
Attorney General	Philander C. Knox	1901–1904
	William H. Moody	1904–1906
	Charles J. Bonaparte	1906–1909
Postmaster General	Charles E. Smith	1901–1902
	Henry C. Payne	1902–1904
	Robert J. Wynne	1904–1905
	George B. Cortelyou	1905–1907
	George von L. Meyer	1907–1909
Secretary of Navy	John D. Long	1901–1902
	William H. Moody	1902–1904
	Paul Morton	1904–1905
	Charles J. Bonaparte	1905–1906
	Victor H. Metcalf	1906–1908
	Truman H. Newberry	1908–1909
Secretary of Interior	Ethan A. Hitchcock	1901–1907
	James R. Garfield	1907–1909
Secretary of Agriculture	James Wilson	1901–1909
Secretary of Labor and Commerce	George B. Cortelyou	1903–1904
	Victor H. Metcalf	1904–1906

| | Oscar S. Straus | 1906–1909 |
| | Charles Nagel | 1909 |

The Taft Administration (1909–1913)

Vice President	James S. Sherman	1909–d. 1912
Secretary of State	Philander C. Knox	1909–1913
Secretary of Treasury	Franklin MacVeagh	1909–1913
Secretary of War	Jacob M. Dickinson	1901–1911
	Henry L. Stimson	1911–1913
Attorney General	George W. Wickersham	1909–1913
Postmaster General	Frank H. Hitchcock	1909–1913
Secretary of Navy	George von L. Meyer	1909–1913
Secretary of Interior	Richard A. Ballinger	1909–1911
	Walter L. Fisher	1911–1913
Secretary of Agriculture	James Wilson	1909–1913
Secretary of Labor and Commerce	Charles Nagel	1909–1913

The Wilson Administration (1913–1921)

Vice President	Thomas R. Marshall	1913–1921
Secretary of State	Williams J. Bryan	1913–1915
	Robert Lansing	1915–1920
	Bainbridge Colby	1920–1921
Secretary of Treasury	William G. McAdoo	1913–1918
	Carter Glass	1918–1920
	David F. Houston	1920–1921
Secretary of War	Lindley M. Garrison	1913–1916
	Newton D. Baker	1916–1921
Attorney General	James C . McReyolds	1913–1914
	Thomas W. Gregory	1914–1919
	A. Mitchell Palmer	1919–1921
Postmaster General	Albert S. Burleson	1913–1921
Secretary of Navy	Josephus Daniels	1913–1921
Secretary of Interior	Franklin K. Lane	1913–1920
	John B. Payne	1920–1921
Secretary of Agriculture	David F. Houston	1913–1920
	Edwin T. Meredith	1920–1921
Secretary of Commerce	William C. Redfield	1913–1919
	Joshua W. Alexander	1919–1921
Secretary of Labor	William B. Wilson	1913–1921

The Harding Administration (1921–1923)

Vice President	Calvin Coolidge	1921–1923
Secretary of State	Charles E. Hughes	1921–1923
Secretary of Treasury	Andrew Mellon	1921–1923
Secretary of War	John W. Weeks	1921–1923
Attorney General	Harry M. Daugherty	1921–1923
Postmaster General	Will H. Hays	1921–1922
	Hubert Work	1922–1923
	Harry S. New	1923
Secretary of Navy	Edwin Denby	1921–1923
Secretary of Interior	Albert B. Fall	1921–1923
	Hubert Work	1923

Secretary of Agriculture	Henry C. Wallace	1921–1923
Secretary of Commerce	Herbert C. Hoover	1921–1923
Secretary of Labor	James J. Davis	1921–1923

The Coolidge Administration (1923–1929)

Vice President	Charles G. Dawes	1925–1929
Secretary of State	Charles E. Hughes	1923–1925
	Frank B. Kellogg	1925–1929
Secretary of Treasury	Andrew Mellon	1923–1929
Secretary of War	John W. Weeks	1923–1925
	Dwight F. Davis	1925–1929
Attorney General	Henry M. Daugherty	1923–1924
	Harlan F. Stone	1924–1925
	John G. Sargent	1925–1929
Postmaster General	Harry S. New	1923–1929
Secretary of Navy	Edwin Derby	1923–1924
	Curtis D. Wilbur	1924–1929
Secretary of Interior	Hubert Work	1923–1928
	Roy O. West	1928–1929
Secretary of Agriculture	Henry C. Wallace	1923–1924
	Howard M. Gore	1924–1925
	William M. Jardine	1925–1929
Secretary of Commerce	Herbert C. Hoover	1923–1928
	William F. Whiting	1928–1929
Secretary of Labor	James J. Davis	1923–1929

The Hoover Administration (1929–1933)

Vice President	Charles Curtis	1929–1933
Secretary of State	Henry L. Stimson	1929–1933
Secretary of Treasury	Andrew Mellon	1929–1932
	Ogden L. Mills	1932–1933
Secretary of War	James W. Good	1929
	Patrick J. Hurley	1929–1933
Attorney General	William D. Mitchell	1929–1933
Postmaster General	Walter F. Brown	1929–1933
Secretary of Navy	Charles F. Adams	1929–1933
Secretary of Interior	Ray L. Wilbur	1929–1933
Secretary of Agriculture	Arthur M. Hyde	1929–1933
Secretary of Commerce	Robert P. Lamont	1929–1932
	Roy D. Chapin	1932–1933
Secretary of Labor	James J. Davis	1929–1930
	William N. Doak	1930–1933

The Franklin D. Roosevelt Administration (1933–1945)

Vice President	John Nance Garner	1933–1941
	Henry A. Wallace	1941–1945
	Harry S Truman	1945
Secretary of State	Cordell Hull	1933–1944
	Edward R. Stettinius, Jr.	1944–1945
Secretary of Treasury	William H. Woodin	1933–1934
	Henry Morgenthau, Jr.	1934–1945

Secretary of War	George H. Dern	1933–1936
	Henry A. Woodring	1936–1940
	Henry L. Stimson	1940–1945
Attorney General	Homer S. Cummings	1933–1939
	Frank Murphy	1939–1940
	Robert H. Jackson	1940–1941
	Francis Biddle	1941–1945
Postmaster General	James A. Farley	1933–1940
	Frank C. Walker	1940–1945
Secretary of Navy	Claude A. Swanson	1933–1940
	Charles Edison	1940
	Frank Knox	1940–1944
	James V. Forrestal	1944–1945
Secretary of Interior	Harold L. Ickes	1933–1945
Secretary of Agriculture	Henry A. Wallace	1933–1940
	Claude R. Wickard	1940–1945
Secretary of Commerce	Daniel C. Roper	1933–1939
	Harry L. Hopkins	1939–1940
	Jesse Jones	1940–1945
	Henry A. Wallace	1945
Secretary of Labor	Frances Perkins	1933–1945

The Truman Administration (1945–1953)

Vice President	Alben W. Barkley	1949–1953
Secretary of State	Edward R. Stettinius, Jr.	1945
	James F. Byrnes	1945–1947
	George C. Marshall	1947–1949
	Dean G. Acheson	1949–1953
Secretary of Treasury	Fred M. Vinson	1945–1946
	John W. Snyder	1946–1953
Secretary of War	Robert P. Patterson	1945–1947
	Kenneth C. Royall	1947
Attorney General	Tom C. Clark	1945–1949
	J. Howard McGrath	1949–1952
	James P. McGranery	1952–1953
Postmaster General	Frank C. Walker	1945
	Robert E. Hannegan	1945–1947
	Jesse M. Donaldson	1947–1953
Secretary of Navy	James V. Forrestal	1945–1947
Secretary of Interior	Harold L. Ickes	1945–1946
	Julius A. Krug	1946–1949
	Oscar L. Chapman	1949–1953
Secretary of Agriculture	Clinton P. Anderson	1945–1948
	Charles F. Brannan	1948–1953
Secretary of Commerce	Henry A. Wallace	1945–1946
	W. Averell Harriman	1946–1948
	Charles W. Sawyer	1948–1953
Secretary of Labor	Lewis B. Schwellenbach	1945–1948
	Maurice J. Tobin	1948–1953
Secretary of Defense	James V. Forrestal	1947–1949
	Louis A. Johnson	1949–1950
	George C. Marshall	1950–1951
	Robert A. Lovett	1951–1953

The Eisenhower Administration (1953–1961)

Vice President	Richard M. Nixon	1953–1961
Secretary of State	John Foster Dulles	1953–1959
	Christian A. Herter	1959–1961
Secretary of Treasury	George M. Humphrey	1953–1957
	Robert B. Anderson	1957–1961
Attorney General	Herbert Brownell, Jr.	1953–1958
	William P. Rogers	1958–1961
Postmaster General	Arthur E. Summerfield	1953–1961
Secretary of Interior	Douglas McKay	1953–1958
	Fred A. Seaton	1956–1961
Secretary of Agriculture	Ezra T. Benson	1953–1961
Secretary of Commerce	Sinclair Weeks	1953–1958
	Lewis L. Strauss	1958–1959
	Frederick H. Mueller	1959–1961
Secretary of Labor	Martin P. Durkin	1953
	James P. Mitchell	1953–1961
Secretary of Defense	Charles E. Wilson	1953–1957
	Neil H. McElroy	1957–1959
	Thomas S. Gates, Jr.	1959–1961
Secretary of Health, Education, and Welfare	Oveta Culp Hobby	1953–1955
	Marlon B. Folsom	1955–1958
	Arthur S. Flemming	1958–1961

The Kennedy Administration (1961–1963)

Vice President	Lyndon B. Johnson	1961–1963
Secretary of State	Dean Rusk	1961–1963
Secretary of Treasury	C. Douglas Dillon	1961–1963
Attorney General	Robert F. Kennedy	1961–1963
Postmaster General	J. Edward Day	1961–1963
	John A. Gronouski	1963
Secretary of Interior	Stewart L. Udall	1961–1963
Secretary of Agriculture	Orville L. Freeman	1961–1963
Secretary of Commerce	Luther H. Hodges	1961–1963
Secretary of Labor	Arthur J. Goldberg	1961–1962
	W. Willard Wirtz	1962–1963
Secretary of Defense	Robert S. McNamara	1961–1963
Secretary of Health, Education, and Welfare	Abraham A. Ribicoff	1961–1962
	Anthony J. Celebrezze	1962–1963

The Lyndon Johnson Administration (1963–1969)

Vice President	Hubert H. Humphrey	1965–1969
Secretary of State	Dean Rusk	1963–1969
Secretary of Treasury	C. Douglas Dillon	1963–1965
	Henry H. Fowler	1965–1969
Attorney General	Robert F. Kennedy	1963–1964
	Nicholas Katzenbach	1965–1966
	Ramsey Clark	1967–1969
Postmaster General	John A. Gronouski	1963–1965
	Lawrence F. O'Brien	1965–1968
	Marvin Watson	1968–1969
Secretary of Interior	Stewart L. Udall	1963–1969

Secretary of Agriculture	Orville L. Freeman	1963–1969
Secretary of Commerce	Luther H. Hodges	1963–1964
	John T. Connor	1964–1967
	Alexander B. Trowbridge	1967–1968
	Cyrus R. Smith	1968–1969
Secretary of Labor	W. Willard Wirtz	1963–1969
Secretary of Defense	Robert F. McNamara	1963–1968
	Clark Clifford	1968–1969
Secretary of Health, Education, and Welfare	Anthony J. Celebrezze	1963–1965
	John W. Gardner	1965–1968
	Wilbur J. Cohen	1968–1969
Secretary of Housing and Urban Development	Robert C. Weaver	1966–1969
	Robert C. Wood	1969
Secretary of Transportation	Alan S. Boyd	1967–1969

The Nixon Administration (1969–1974)

Vice President	Spiro T. Agnew	1969–1973
	Gerald R. Ford	1973–1974
Secretary of State	William P. Rogers	1969–1973
	Henry A. Kissinger	1973–1974
Secretary of Treasury	David M. Kennedy	1969–1970
	John B. Connally	1971–1972
	George P. Shultz	1972–1974
	William E. Simon	1974
Attorney General	John N. Mitchell	1969–1972
	Richard G. Kleindienst	1972–1973
	Elliot L. Richardson	1973
	William B. Saxbe	1973–1974
Postmaster General	Winton M. Blount	1969–1971
Secretary of Interior	Walter J. Hickel	1969–1970
	Rogers Morton	1971–1974
Secretary of Agriculture	Clifford M. Hardin	1969–1971
	Earl L. Butz	1971–1974
Secretary of Commerce	Maurice H. Stans	1969–1972
	Peter G. Peterson	1972–1973
	Frederick B. Dent	1973–1974
Secretary of Labor	George P. Shultz	1969–1970
	James D. Hodgson	1970–1973
	Peter J. Brennan	1973–1974
Secretary of Defense	Melvin R. Laird	1969–1973
	Elliot L. Richardson	1973
	James R. Schlesinger	1973–1974
Secretary of Health, Education, and Welfare	Robert H. Finch	1969–1970
	Elliot L. Richardson	1970–1973
	Caspar W. Weinberger	1973–1974
Secretary of Housing and Urban Development	George Romney	1969–1973
	James T. Lynn	1973–1974

Secretary of Transportation	John A. Volpe	1969–1973
	Claude S. Brinegar	1973–1974

The Ford Administration (1974–1977)

Vice President	Nelson A. Rockefeller	1974–1977
Secretary of State	Henry A. Kissinger	1974–1977
Secretary of Treasury	William E. Simon	1974–1977
Attorney General	William B. Saxbe	1974–1975
	Edward Levi	1975–1977
Secretary of Interior	Rogers Morton	1974–1975
	Stanley K. Hathaway	1975
	Thomas Kleppe	1975–1977
Secretary of Agriculture	Earl L. Butz	1974–1976
	John A. Knebel	1976–1977
Secretary of Commerce	Frederick B. Dent	1974–1975
	Rogers Morton	1975–1976
	Elliot L. Richardson	1976–1977
Secretary of Labor	Peter J. Brennan	1974–1975
	John T. Dunlop	1975–1976
	W. J. Usery	1976–1977
Secretary of Defense	James R. Schlesinger	1974–1975
	Donald Rumsfeld	1975–1977
Secretary of Health, Education, and Welfare	Caspar W. Weinberger	1974–1975
	Forrest D. Mathews	1975–1977
Secretary of Housing and Urban Development	James T. Lynn	1974–1975
	Carla A. Hills	1975–1977
Secretary of Transportation	Claude S. Brinegar	1974–1975
	William T. Coleman	1975–1977

The Carter Administration (1977–1981)

Vice President	Walter F. Mondale	1977–1981
Secretary of State	Cyrus R. Vance	1977–1980
	Edmund Muskie	1980–1981
Secretary of Treasury	W. Michael Blumenthal	1977–1979
	G. William Miller	1979–1981
Attorney General	Griffin Bell	1977–1979
	Benjamin R. Civiletti	1979–1981
Secretary of Interior	Cecil D. Andrus	1977–1981
Secretary of Agriculture	Robert Bergland	1977–1981
Secretary of Commerce	Juanita M. Kreps	1977–1979
	Philip M. Klutznick	1979–1981
Secretary of Labor	F. Ray Marshall	1977–1981
Secretary of Defense	Harold Brown	1977–1981
Secretary of Health Education, and Welfare	Joseph A. Califano	1977–1979
	Patricia R. Harris	1979
Secretary of Health and Human Services	Patricia R. Harris	1979–1981
Secretary of Education	Shirley M. Hufstedler	1979–1981

Secretary of Housing and Urban Development	Patricia R. Harris	1977–1979
	Moon Landrieu	1979–1981
Secretary of Transportation	Brock Adams	1977–1979
	Neil E. Goldschmidt	1979–1981
Secretary of Energy	James R. Schlesinger	1979–1979
	Charles W. Duncan	1979–1981

The Reagan Administration (1981–1989)

Vice President	George Bush	1981–1989
Secretary of State	Alexander M. Haig	1981–1982
	George P. Shultz	1982–1989
Secretary of Treasury	Donald Regan	1981–1985
	James A. Baker, III	1985–1988
	Nicholas Brady	1988–1989
Attorney General	William F. Smith	1981–1985
	Edwin A. Meese, III	1985–1988
	Richard Thornburgh	1988–1989
Secretary of Interior	James Watt	1981–1983
	William P. Clark, Jr.	1983–1985
	Donald P. Hodel	1985–1989
Secretary of Agriculture	John Block	1981–1986
	Richard E. Lyng	1986–1989
Secretary of Commerce	Malcolm Baldridge	1981–1987
	C. William Verity, Jr.	1987–1989
Secretary of Labor	Raymond Donovan	1981–1985
	William E. Brock	1985–1988
	Ann Dore McLaughlin	1988–1989
Secretary of Defense	Caspar W. Weinberger	1981–1988
	Frank Carlucci	1988–1989
Secretary of Health and Human Services	Richard Schweiker	1981–1983
	Margaret Heckler	1983–1985
	Otis R. Bowen	1985–1989
Secretary of Education	Terrel H. Bell	1981–1985
	William J. Bennett	1985–1988
	Lauro F. Cavazos	1988–1989
Secretary of Housing and Urban Development	Samuel Pierce	1981–1989
Secretary of Transportation	Drew Lewis	1981–1983
	Elizabeth Dole	1983–1987
	James L. Burnley, IV	1987–1989
Secretary of Energy	James Edwards	1981–1982
	Donald P. Hodel	1982–1985
	John S. Herrington	1985–1989

The Bush Administration (1989–1993)

Vice President	J. Danforth Quayle	1989–1993
Secretary of State	James A. Baker, III	1989–1992
	Lawrence Eagleburger	1992–1993
Secretary of Treasury	Nicholas F. Brady	1988–1993
Attorney General	Richard Thornburgh	1989–1991
	William Barr	1991–1992
Secretary of Interior	Manuel Lujan, Jr.	1989–1993
Secretary of Agriculture	Clayton K. Yeutter	1989–1991
	Edward Madigan	1991–1993
Secretary of Commerce	Robert A. Mosbacher	1989–1991
	Barbara Hackman Franklin	1992–1993
Secretary of Labor	Elizabeth H. Dole	1989–1990
	Lynn Morley Martin	1991–1993
Secretary of Defense	Richard Cheney	1989–1993
Secretary of Health and Human Services	Louis W. Sullivan	1989–1993
Secretary of Education	Lauro F. Cavazos	1989–1990
	Lamar Alexander	1991–1993
Secretary of Housing and Urban Development	Jack F. Kemp	1989–1993
Secretary of Transportation	Samuel K. Skinner	1989–1992
	Andrew H. Card, Jr.	1992–1993
Secretary of Energy	James D. Watkins	1989–1993
Secretary of Veterans Affairs	Edward J. Derwinski	1989–1992

The Clinton Administration (1993–   )

Vice President	Albert Gore, Jr.	1993
Secretary of State	Warren M. Christopher	1993
Secretary of the Treasury	Lloyd Bentsen,	1993–1995
	Robert Rubin	1995–
Attorney General	Janet Reno	1993
Secretary of the Interior	Bruce Babbitt	1993
Secretary of Agriculture	Mike Espy	1993–1995
	Dan Glickman	1995–
Secretary of Commerce	Ronald H. Brown	1993–1996
	Mickey Kantor	1996–
Secretary of Labor	Robert B. Reich	1993
Secretary of Defense	Les Aspin,	1993–1994
	William Perry	1994–
Secretary of Health and Human Services	Donna E. Shalala	1993
Secretary of Education	Richard W. Riley	1993
Secretary of Housing and Urban Development	Henry G. Cisneros	1993
Secretary of Transportation	Frederico F. Peña	1993
Secretary of Energy	Hazel R. O'Leary	1993
Secretary of Veteran's Affairs	Jesse Brown	1993

SUPREME COURT JUSTICES

Name	Terms of Service[1]	Appointed by
John Jay	1789–1795	Washington
James Wilson	1789–1798	Washington
John Rutledge	1790–1791	Washington
William Cushing	1790–1810	Washington
John Blair	1790–1796	Washington
James Iredell	1790–1799	Washington
Thomas Johnson	1792–1793	Washington
William Paterson	1793–1806	Washington
John Rutledge[2]	1795	Washington
Samuel Chase	1796–1811	Washington
Oliver Ellsworth	1796–1800	Washington
Bushrod Washington	1799–1829	J. Adams
Alfred Moore	1800–1804	J. Adams
John Marshall	1801–1835	J. Adams
William Johnson	1804–1834	Jefferson
Brockholst Livingston	1807–1823	Jefferson
Thomas Todd	1807–1826	Jefferson
Gabriel Duvall	1811–1835	Madison
Joseph Story	1812–1845	Madison
Smith Thompson	1823–1843	Monroe
Robert Trimble	1826–1828	J. Q. Adams
John McLean	1830–1861	Jackson
Henry Baldwin	1830–1844	Jackson
James M. Wayne	1835–1867	Jackson
Roger B. Tanay	1836–1864	Jackson
Philip P. Barbour	1836–1841	Jackson
John Cartron	1837–1865	Van Buren
John McKinley	1838–1852	Van Buren
Peter V. Daniel	1842–1860	Van Buren
Samuel Nelson	1845–1872	Tyler
Levi Woodbury	1845–1851	Polk
Robert C. Grier	1846–1870	Polk
Benjamin R. Curtis	1851–1857	Fillmore
John A. Campbell	1853–1861	Pierce
Nathan Clifford	1858–1881	Buchanan
Noah H. Swayne	1862–1881	Lincoln
Samuel F. Miller	1862–1890	Lincoln
David Davis	1862–1877	Lincoln
Stephen J. Field	1863–1897	Lincoln
Salmon P. Chase	1864–1873	Lincoln
William Strong	1870–1880	Grant
Joseph P. Bradley	1870–1892	Grant
Ward Hunt	1873–1882	Grant
Morrison R. Waite	1874–1888	Grant
John M. Harlan	1877–1911	Hayes
William B. Woods	1881–1887	Hayes
Stanley Matthews	1881–1889	Garfield
Horace Gray	1882–1902	Arthur
Samuel Blatchford	1882–1893	Arthur

Name	Terms of Service	Appointed by
Lucious Q. C. Lamar	1888–1893	Cleveland
Melville W. Fuller	1888–1910	Cleveland
David J. Brewer	1890–1910	B. Harrison
Henry B. Brown	1891–1906	B. Harrison
George Shiras, Jr.	1892–1903	B. Harrison
Howell E. Jackson	1893–1895	B. Harrison
Edward D. White	1894–1910	Cleveland
Rufus W. Peckham	1896–1909	Cleveland
Joseph McKenna	1898–1925	McKinley
Oliver W. Holmes	1902–1932	T. Roosevelt
William R. Day	1903–1922	T. Roosevelt
William H. Moody	1906–1910	T. Roosevelt
Horace H. Lurton	1910–1914	Taft
Charles E. Hughes	1910–1916	Taft
Willis Van Devanter	1911–1937	Taft
Joseph R. Lamar	1911–1916	Taft
Edward D. White	1910–1921	Taft
Mahlon Pitney	1912–1922	Taft
James C. McReynolds	1914–1941	Wilson
Louis D. Brandels	1916–1939	Wilson
John H. Clarke	1916–1922	Wilson
William H. Taft	1921–1930	Harding
George Sutherland	1922–1938	Harding
Pierce Butler	1923–1939	Harding
Edward T. Sanford	1923–1930	Harding
Harlan F. Stone	1925–1941	Coolidge
Charles E. Hughes	1930–1941	Hoover
Owen J. Roberts	1930–1945	Hoover
Benjamin N. Cardozo	1932–1938	Hoover
Hugo L. Black	1937–1971	F. Roosevelt
Stanley F. Reed	1938–1957	F. Roosevelt
Felix Frankfurter	1939–1962	F. Roosevelt
William O. Douglas	1939–1975	F. Roosevelt
Frank Murphy	1940–1949	F. Roosevelt
Harlan F. Stone	1941–1946	F. Roosevelt
James F. Byrnes	1941–1942	F. Roosevelt
Robert H. Jackson	1941–1954	F. Roosevelt
Wiley B. Rutledge	1943–1949	F. Roosevelt
Harold H. Burton	1945–1958	Truman
Frederick M. Vinson	1946–1953	Truman
Tom C. Clark	1949–1967	Truman
Sherman Minton	1949–1956	Truman
Earl Warren	1953–1969	Eisenhower
John Marshall Harlan	1955–1971	Eisenhower
William J. Brennan, Jr.	1956–1990	Eisenhower
Charles E. Whittaker	1957–1962	Eisenhower
Potter Stewart	1958–1981	Eisenhower
Byron R. White	1962–	Kennedy
Arthur J. Goldberg	1962–1965	Kennedy

Name	Terms of Service	Appointed by	Name	Terms of Service	Appointed by
Abe Fortas	1965–1970	Johnson	Sandra Day O'Connor	1981–	Reagan
Thurgood Marshall	1967–1991	Johnson	**William H. Rehnquist**	1986–	Reagan
Warren E. Burger	1969–1986	Nixon	Antonin Scalia	1986–	Reagan
Harry A. Blackmun	1970–1994	Nixon	Anthony Kennedy	1988–	Reagan
Lewis F. Powell, Jr.	1971–1988	Nixon	David H. Souter	1990–	Bush
William H. Rehnquist	1971–1986	Nixon	Clarence Thomas	1991–	Bush
John Paul Stevens	1975–	Ford	Ruth Bader Ginsburg	1993–	Clinton
			Stephen Breyer	1994–	Clinton

Chief Justices in bold type

[1]The date on which the justices took their judicial oath is here used as the date of the beginning of their service, for until that oath is taken they are not vested with the prerogatives of their office. Justices, however, receive their commissions ("letters patent") before taking their oath—in some instances, in the preceding year.

[2]Acting Chief Justice; Senate refused to confirm appointment.

ADMISSION OF STATES TO THE UNION

State	Date of Admission	State	Date of Admission
1. Delaware	December 7, 1787	26. Michigan	January 26, 1837
2. Pennsylvania	December 12, 1787	27. Florida	March 3, 1845
3. New Jersey	December 18, 1787	28. Texas	December 29, 1845
4. Georgia	January 2, 1788	29. Iowa	December 28, 1846
5. Connecticut	January 9, 1788	30. Wisconsin	May 29, 1848
6. Massachusetts	February 6, 1788	31. California	September 9, 1850
7. Maryland	April 28, 1788	32. Minnesota	May 11, 1858
8. South Carolina	May 23, 1788	33. Oregon	February 14, 1859
9. New Hampshire	June 21, 1788	34. Kansas	January 29, 1861
10. Virginia	June 25, 1788	35. West Virginia	June 20, 1863
11. New York	July 26, 1788	36. Nevada	October 31, 1864
12. North Carolina	November 21, 1789	37. Nebraska	March 1, 1867
13. Rhode Island	May 29, 1790	38. Colorado	August 1, 1876
14. Vermont	March 4, 1791	39. North Dakota	November 2, 1889
15. Kentucky	June 1, 1792	40. South Dakota	November 2, 1889
16. Tennessee	June 1, 1796	41. Montana	November 8, 1889
17. Ohio	March 1, 1803	42. Washington	November 11, 1889
18. Louisiana	April 30, 1812	43. Idaho	July 3, 1890
19. Indiana	December 11, 1816	44. Wyoming	July 10, 1890
20. Mississippi	December 10, 1817	45. Utah	January 4, 1896
21. Illinois	December 3, 1818	46. Oklahoma	November 16, 1907
22. Alabama	December 14, 1819	47. New Mexico	January 6, 1912
23. Maine	March 15, 1820	48. Arizona	February 14, 1912
24. Missouri	August 10, 1821	49. Alaska	January 3, 1959
25. Arkansas	June 15, 1836	50. Hawaii	August 21, 1959

U.S. Population, 1790–1990

Year	Population	Percent Increase	Population Per Square Mile	Sex (rounded to nearest milion) Male	Female	Median Age
1790	3,929,214		4.5	NA	NA	NA
1800	5,308,483	35.1	6.1	NA	NA	NA
1810	7,239,881	36.4	4.3	NA	NA	NA
1820	9,638,453	33.1	5.5	5	5	16.7
1830	12,866,020	33.5	7.4	7	6	17.2
1840	17,069,453	32.7	9.8	9	8	17.8
1850	23,191,876	35.9	7.9	12	11	18.9
1860	31,443,321	35.6	10.6	16	15	19.4
1870	39,818,449	26.6	13.4	19	19	20.2
1880	50,155,783	26.0	16.9	26	25	20.9
1890	62,947,714	25.5	21.2	32	31	22.0
1900	75,994,575	20.7	25.6	39	37	22.9
1910	91,972,266	21.0	31.0	47	45	24.1
1920	105,710,620	14.9	35.6	54	52	25.3
1930	122,775,046	16.1	41.2	62	61	26.4
1940	131,669,275	7.2	44.2	66	66	29.0
1950	150,697,361	14.5	50.7	75	76	30.2
1960	179,323,175	18.5	50.6	88	91	29.5
1970	203,302,031	13.4	57.4	99	104	28.0
1980	226,545,805	11.4	64.0	110	116	30.0
1985	237,839,000	5.0	64.0	117	123	31.3
1990	249,975,000	1.1	70.3	121	127	32.6

NA = Not available.

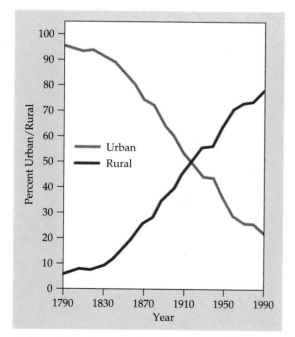

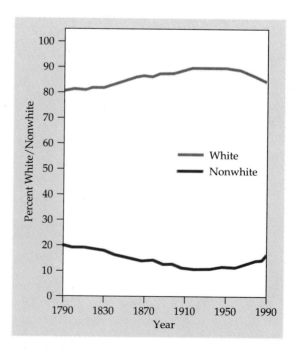

REGIONAL ORIGINS OF IMMIGRATION

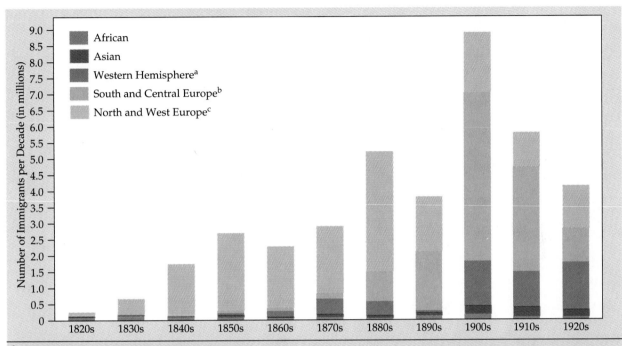

^aCanada and all countries in South America and Central America.

^bItaly, Spain, Portugal, Greece, Germany (Austria included, 1938–1945), Poland, Czechoslovakia (since 1920), Yugoslavia (since 1920), Hungary (since 1861), Austria (since 1861, except 1938–1945), U.S.S.R. (excludes Asian U.S.S.R. between 1931 and 1963), Latvia, Estonia, Lithuania, Finland, Bulgaria, Turkey (in Europe), and other European countries not classified elsewhere.

^cGreat Britain, Ireland, Norway, Sweden, Denmark, Iceland, Netherlands, Belgium, Luxembourg, Switzerland, France.

Source: Stephan Thernstrom, ed., *Harvard Encyclopedia of American Ethnic Groups* (1980), p. 480; and U.S. Bureau of the Census, *Statistical Abstract of the United States, 1984* (1983), p. 9.

CREDITS

Unless otherwise acknowledged, all photographs are the property of Scott-Foresman/Addison Wesley Longman. Page abbreviations are as follows: (T)top, (C)center, (B)bottom, (L)left, (R)right, (Ins)inset.

Back cover of single volume edition, front cover for volume 2, left page of title page spread all volumes: Suffragettes: Culver, Family photo: Collection of Michael Staats, FDR: Corbis/Bettmann, Nat Love: Library of Congress.

Front cover single volume edition, front cover volume 1, and right page of title page spread: Tom Torlino (2): Arizona Historical Society, Sojourner Truth: Sophia Smith Collection, Smith College, Northampton, MA, Drake Oil Well: Drake Oil Well Museum, Space shuttle: NASA, "Progress of Cotton": Copyright The Yale University Art Gallery, Mabel Brady Garvan Collection, detail of Harrison campaign handkerchief: New York Historical Society, Cotton gin: Corbis/Bettmann.

CHAPTER OPENERS

Chapter 1 (pages 2–3) Spanish in New World and European War Dogs: Theodor deBry, *America*, 1617/ Laudonnnie with Indian Chief: Print Collection/Miriam & Ira D. Wallach Division of Arts, Prints & Photography/New York Public Library, Astor, Lenox & Tilden Foundations / Ad for Virginia Settlers: New York Public Library, Astor Lenox & Tilden Foundations, Sugar Plantation: Theodore deBry, *America*, 1595, New York Public Library, Astor, Lenox & Tilden Foundations **Chapter 2 (pages 38–39)** Johnson Treaty with the Iroquois: New York Historical Society / View of New Amsterdam, Quaker Synod: New York Public Library, Astor, Lenox & Tilden Foundations / Metacomet: Shelburne Museum, Shelburne, VT., Photo: Ken Burris **Chapter 3 (pages 74–75)** Alexander de Batz, "Members of the Illinois Tribe": Peabody Museum/Harvard University / John Singleton Copley, "Head of a Negro": From the Collection of the Detroit Institute of Arts, Founders Society/Gibbs-Williams Fund / Benjamin West, "Penn's Treaty with the Indians": Pennsylvania Academy of the Fine Arts / Benjamin Franklin: Historical Society of Pennsylvania **Chapter 4 (pages 114–115)** Act newspaper: *Pennsylvania Journal*, October 31, 1765 / Boston Long Wharf: Courtesy Henry Francis duPont Winterthur Museum / George Washington at Trenton: Library of Congress / Map of Fort Clinton: New York Historical Society, George III: Colonial Williamsburg Foundation **Chapter 5 (pages 146–147)** Boston Long Wharf: Courtesy Henry Francis duPont Winterthur Museum / Navigation Treaty: New York Historical Society / James Madison portrait: Gilcrease Museum / *Common Sense*: Library of Congress / Washington at Valley Forge: Courtesy Valley Forge Historical Society / George Washington: Frick Collection, NY / Joseph Brant: New York Public Library, Astor, Lenox & Tilden Foundation **Chapter 6 (pages 182–183)** Continental currency: Smithsonian Institution / "Fairview Inn": Maryland Historical Society / New Cleared Farm in the New World: New York Public Library, Astor, Lenox & Tilden Foundations / George Washington: The Metropolitan Museum of Art, Bequest of Grace Wilkes, 1922 / Stagecoach: Library of Congress / "Signing of the Constitution": National Historical Park Collections, Eastern National Parks & Monuments Association **Chapter 7 (pages 216–217)** Benjamin West, "Conference of theTreaty of Paris": Courtesy the Henry Francis du Pont Winterthur Museum / Alexander Hamilton: Copyright Yale University Art Gallery / John Quincy Adams: Historical Society of Pennsylvania **Chapter 8 (pages 242–243)** "Burning of New York": Library of Congress / Dolly Madison: Pennsylvania Academy of the Fine Arts / Thomas Jefferson: Metropolitan Museum of Art, Bequest of Cornelia Crugar / Jefferson campaign broadside: New York Historical Society / James Madison: Gilcrease Museum / Tenskwatawa (the Prophet): Library of Congress **Chapter 9 (pages 268–269)** Cotton gin: Corbis/Bettmann Archive / Robert Fulton: Collection of Michael Staats / Lowell Offering: Lowell Historical Society / Cotton mill: Library of Congress / "Mississippi River at St. Louis": St. Louis Museum of Art, Collec-

tion of Arthur Ziern, Jr. **Chapter 10 (pages 298–299)** Harrison campaign handkerchief: New York Historical Society / Manchester factory: Library of Congress / Currier & Ives, "Preparing for Market": Copyright Yale University Art Gallery / Mabel Brady Garvan Collection / "Cherokee Phoenix": American Antiquarian Society / "Rafting Down stream": Indiana University Art Museum, Transfer from IU Collections to Museum / Andrew Jackson: Brooks Memorial Art Gallery **Chapter 11 (pages 330–331)** Asher B. Durand, "In the Catskills": Walters Art Gallery / Edgar Allan Poe: Manuscripts Dept./Lilly Library, Indiana University, Bloomington, IN / Harriet Tubman, Frederick Douglass: Library of Congress **Chapter 12 (pages 374–375)** Sugar Plantation, Steamboats on the Mississippi: Historic New Orleans Collection, Rochester, NY: George Eastman House, International Museum of Photography / Women working in cotton mill, Freed blacks in Richmond: Library of Congress / Slave Sale Poster: Picture Collection/New York Public Library / Lucretia Mott, Elizabeth Cady Stanton: Sophia Smith Collection, Smith College, Northampton, MA / Sharecroppers & overseer: Brown Brothers **Chapter 13 (pages 412–413)** Daguerreotype of two girls, Tintype of man with derby: Collection of Michael Staats / Illinois Central Railroad poster: Newberry Library / Plow ad: Courtesy, John Deere Company / Miners: California State Library / Chief Joseph: Library of Congress / Mormons sitting in front of their covered wagons: Western History Department/Denver Public Library / William S. Jewett, "The Promised Land-The Grayson Family": Berry-Hill Galleries, NY **Chapter 14 (pages 448–449)** Civil War soldier, Abraham Lincoln / Northern supplies: Library of Congress / Harriet Beecher Stowe: Stowe Day Foundation / Anti-Slave-Catchers' poster: New York Public Library, Astor, Lenox & Tilden Foundations / "Monitor & Merrimac": Chicago Historical Society **Chapter 15 (484–485)** Ulysses S. Grant, Robert E. Lee, Abraham Lincoln, Northern supplies / "Storming of Fort Wagner": Library of Congress / Battery A, 2nd Colored Artillery: Chicago Historical Society **Chapter 16 (pages 524–525)** Black Elk: Smithsonian Institution / Geronimo: National Archives / Carpetbagger: Culver Pictures Inc. / Black schoolroom, Ruins of Richmond, Nat Love: Library of Congress / sharecroppers: Valentine Museum, Richmond, VA **Chapter 17 (pages 562–563)** Benjamin Reinhart, "Stopping for the Night": Corcoran Gallery of Art, gift of Mr. and Mrs. Landsell Christie / Geronimo and Buffalo Bill: Culver Pictures / Alexander Graham Bell: Brown Brothers / Cattle drive: Kansas State Historic Site/United States Department of the Interior / Classroom, Tuskegee: Corbis/Bettmann **Chapter 18 (pages 604–605)** Department store: Corbis/Bettmann / King Oliver's Jazz Band: Hogan Jazz Archive/Tulane University / Trolley: Library of Congress / Aerial photo of New York City, Family photo: Collection of Michael Staats **Chapter 19 (pages 646–647)** Granger Poster, Railroad crew: Library of Congress / Union Label, Search-Light pamphlet: Collection of Michael Staats **Chapter 20 (pages 680–681)** William Randolph Hearst: Corbis/Bettmann / Queen Liluokalani: Hawaii State Archives / Map of Havana Harbor, 1901, Fern wallpaper: Collection of Michael Staats / "Sinking of the Maine": Chicago Historical Society / Theodore Roosevelt and Rough Riders: Library of Congress **Chapter 21 (pages 716–717)** Theodore Roosevelt and Rough Riders, Suffragettes: Library of Congress / Women's Union march: Brown Brothers / College women in chemistry class: Corbis/Bettmann / Football game: Culver Pictures, / Linoleum: Collection of Michael Staats / Marines in Vera Cruz: Granger Collection / Child laborer in mill: George House Eastman, International Museum of Photography **Chapter 22 (pages 756–757)** Harry Truman during WWI: Culver Pictures / Women welders: Granger Collection / Women repairing car: National Archives / 369th Infantry: Library of Congress /WWI medics: U.S. Signal Corps, The National Archives, Office of the Chief Signal Officer / Traffic jam, Chicago: Chicago Historical Society **Chapter 23 (pages 790–791)** Harding and Coolidge: Corbis/UPI/Bettmann / Family on porch: Collection of Michael Staats / Breaker boys: Records of the Children's Bureau / KKK: Library of Congress / Marcus Garvery: Brown Brothers / Agents col-

AP/Wide World **732** NAACP **735** UPI/Corbis/Bettmann **740** Brown Brothers **741L** Library of Congress **741R** State Historical Society of Wisconsin **743** Brown Brothers **751** Library of Congress

CHAPTER 22

759T The Granger Collection, New York **759B** UPI/Corbis/Bettmann **761** Imperial War Museum, London **764** Imperial War Museum, London **766** UPI/Corbis/Bettmann **771** The Archives of Labor and Urban Affairs, Wayne State University **773** New York Public Library, Astor, Lenox and Tilden Foundations **775L** UPI/Corbis/Bettmann **775R** The National Archives **776** The National Archives **779** Robert Hunt Library **783** Brown Brothers **786** *Chicago Tribune*-N.Y. News Syndicate

CHAPTER 23

792 Culver Pictures **800L** Brown Brothers **800R** UPI/Corbis/Bettmann **801L** *Vanity Fair* photograph by Breaker/Copyright © l928, 1956 by Condé Nast Publications, Inc. **801R** Brown Brothers **802** The Granger Collection, New York **804** Culver Pictures **807** Rollin Kirby, *New York World*, May 19, 1925 **809** Brown Brothers **810** AP/Wide World **811** Hampton University Museum, Hampton, Va. **813** *Life*, June 8, 1920 **814** U.S. Bureau of Printing and Engraving **816** *New York Times*, Oct. 25, 1929

CHAPTER 24

824 Culver Pictures **829** UPI/Corbis/Bettmann **830** AP/Wide World **831** Library of Congress **833** Brown Brothers **834** The Franklin D. Roosevelt Library **839** Corbis/ Bettmann **840** AP/Wide World **841** Culver Pictures **844** © 1938 by Esquire, Inc. **845** UPI/Corbis/Bettmann **846** Courtesy Lou Erikson

CHAPTER 25

859 Archive Photos **865** UPI/Corbis/Bettmann **866** UPI/Corbis/Bettmann **868** UPI/Corbis/Bettmann **870** Official U.S. Navy Photograph **872** AP/Wide World **874** *Up front* by Bill Mauldin, published by Henry Holt & Co. **875L** Library of Congress **875R** Baker Library, Harvard Business School **880** The National Archives/War Relocation Authority **884** The Franklin D. Roosevelt Library **888** UPI/Corbis/Bettmann **890** Official U.S. Air Force Photo **892** Official U.S. Air Force Photo

CHAPTER 26

901L James Whitmore/*Life* Magazine, Time Warner Inc. **901R** Thomas D. McAvoy **903** Acme/UPI/Corbis/Bettmann **909** UPI/Corbis/Bettmann **910** Ferro Jacobs/Black Star **911** Eastfoto/SOVFOTO **912** UPI/Corbis/Bettmann **918** UPI/ Corbis/Bettmann **920(both)** Elliot Erwitt/Magnum Photos **921** UPI/Corbis/Bettmann **922** Alfred Eisenstaedt/*Life* Magazine, Time Warner Inc. **924** AP/Wide World **925** Film Stills Archive/The Museum of Modern Art, New York

CHAPTER 27

932 AP/Wide World **940** SOVFOTO **941** UPI/Corbis/Bettmann **943** UPI/Corbis/Bettmann **944** Cornell Capa/Magnum **946** AP/Wide World **947** Costa Manos/Magnum **948** UPI/Corbis/Bettmann **951** © l949, Ed Clark/*Life* Magazine, Time Warner Inc. **953** AP/Wide World **954(both)** AP/Wide World **955** *Life* Magazine, Time Warner Inc. **957** Brown Brothers **961** Don Wright/*Life* Magazine, Time Warner Inc. **962** UPI/Corbis/Bettmann

CHAPTER 28

968 Everett Collection **970** Photofest **971** Corbis/Bettmann **973** Acme/UPI/Corbis/Bettmann **976** Gaslight Antiques **978** Bureau of Reclamation **979** Culver Pictures **980** UPI/Corbis/Bettmann **984**

Superstock **986** UPI/Corbis/Bettmann **990** Jeffrey Markowitz/Sygma **993** Stephen Ferry/Gamma-Liaison

CHAPTER 29

1000 UPI/Corbis/Bettmann **1002** UPI/Corbis/Bettmann **1004** Ron Haeberle/ *Life* Magazine, Time Warner Inc. **1008** *New York Daily News* Photo **1010** UPI/Corbis/Bettmann **1013** Lyndon Baines Johnson Library **1014** AP/Wide World **1020T** Roger Falconer/Black Star **1020B** Steve Schapiro/ Black Star **1021** Paul Sequeira **1025** Kent State University News Service **1027** Magnum Photos **1029** Kobal Collection

CHAPTER 30

1037 AP/Wide World **1039** UPI/Corbis/Bettmann **1041** Charles Moore/Black Star **1045** Charles Moore/Black Star **1047** Fred Ward/Black Star **1048** Bob Adelman/Magnum Photos **1049** John Launois/Black Star **1051** Constantine Manos/Magnum Photos **1053** Yoichi Okomoto/Photo Researchers **1055** Lisa Quinones/Black Star **1056** Nacio Jan Brown/Black Star **1057** Wayne Miller/Magnum Photos **1059** PhotoFest **1062** Bob Fitch/Black Star **1065** Arthur Grace/Magnum **1067T** Rick Friedman/Black Star **1067B** Ira Wyman/Sygma **1071** Herman Kokojan/Black Star **1074** AP/Wide World

CHAPTER 31

1084 Mark Godfrey/Archive Pictures Inc. **1085** Alex Webb/Magnum Photos **1089** Anthony Loew © 1984 **1091** Locher/Reprinted by permission: Tribune Media Services **1095** Bill Fitzpatrick/The White House **1096** Special Features/SIPA-Press **1101** Jack Higgins/with permission of the Chicago Sun-Times, Inc. **1102** Laski/SIPA-Press **1104** R. Bossu/Sygma **1105** Klaus Reisinger/Black Star **1106** Le Segretain/Sygma **1110** Timothy Ross/JB Pictures **1111** *U.S. News & World Report*

FIGURE, MAP, AND LITERARY CREDITS

356 Thoreau, Henry David, *Walden*. Boston: Ticknor and Fields, 1854. **463** Stowe, Harriet Beecher, *Uncle Tom's Cabin*. Boston: Houghton Mifflin Company, 1896. **801**, **Tab1e 22.2** From G. M. Gathorne-Hardy, *The Fourteen Points and the Treaty of Versailles*, Oxford Pamphets on World Affairs, No. 6, 1939, and Thomas G. Paterson et al., *American Foreign Policy: A History Since 1900*, 2d ed., Vol. 2. **814** From *Chicago: Growth of a Metropolis* by Harold M. Mayer and Richard C. Wade. Copyright © 1969 by the University of Chicago. Reprinted by permission of the University of Chicago Press. **852**, **Figure 24.2** From *American Bank Failures* by C. D. Bremer. Copyright © 1935 by Columbia University Press. Reprinted with permission of the publisher. **980** From "Little Boxes," words and music by Malvina Reynolds. Copyright © 1962 by Schroder Music Co. (ASCAP). Used by permission. All rights reserved. **981** From "Long Tall Sally" by Richard Penniman, Enntris Johnson, and Robert A. Blackwell and "Rip It Up" by Robert A. Blackwell and John S. Marascalo. Copyright © 1956, renewed 1984 by Venice Music Inc. All rights controlled and administered by SBK Blackwood Music Inc. under license from ATV Music (Venice). All rights reserved. International copyright secured. Used by permission. From "Roll Over Beethoven" by Chuck Berry. Used by permission of Isalee Music Company. **982** From "Shake, Rattle and Roll" words and music by Charles Calhoun. Copyright © 1954 (renewed) Unichappell Music Inc.(BMI). All rights reserved. Used by permission of Warner Bros. Publications U.S. Inc., Miami, FL 33014. **983** "HOWL" (5 lines) from *Collected Poems 1947–1980* by Allen Ginsberg. Copyright © 1955 by Allen Ginsberg. "America" from *Collected Poems 1947–1980* by Allen Ginsberg. Copyright © 1955, 1959 by Allen Ginsberg. Reprinted by permission of HarperCollins Publishers. **1061–1063** Martin Luther King, Jr., *Why We Can't Wait* (New York: Harper & Row, 1963, 1964).

Index

Abenaki Indians, 76

Abolitionism, 204, 205, 332, 342–346. *See also* Slavery; decline of, in the South, 396–397; division within, 345–346; early efforts, 342–343; and the Emancipation Proclamation, 507; literature and, 460–464; mob violence and, 388; in the North, 343–344; public reaction to, 344–345; and utopian communities, 350; and women's rights, 348–349

Abortion, 203, 792, 802, 803, 1064, 1067

Abrams v. *United States*, 774

Accounting, 577–578

Acheson, Dean, 906, 911–913, 918, 921, 1012

Act of Religious Toleration, 46

Act of Supremacy, 23

Adams, Abigail, 200, 234

Adams, Charles Francis, 504

Adams, Henry, 669

Adams, John, 154, 160, 178, 200, 233–237, 247–248, 254, 285; Alien and Sedition Acts, 236–237; election to presidency, 233; as foreign minister, 194; and move of Capitol to Washington, D.C., 234–235; and revolution of 1800, 237–239; as Vice President, 245; XYZ affair and, 235–236

Adams, John Quincy, 272, 273, 279, 295, 305, 306–310, 324, 430, 432; election to presidency, 306–307; foreign policy, 307–308; Indian policies, 307; and the Tariff of Abominations, 308

Adams, Rachel, 308, 317

Adams, Samuel, 127, 129, 132, 134, 137–141, 151, 152, 154, 158, 186, 189, 210; as Antifederalist, 210; father's business, 116–117, 122; resistance to British, 124–125

Adams, Sherman, 935

Adamson Act, 744, 750

Adams-Onis Treaty, 279

Addams, Jane, 708, 724, 729–730, 767

Adder's Den, The (Dye), 450–451

Adler, Renata, 968–969

Administration of Justice Act, 139, 140

Adventures of Huckleberry Finn, The (Twain), 625

Advertising, 796, 797, 874, 955, 975–976

Aero Club of America, 732

Afghanistan, 1096

Africa: German colonies in, 762; Italy in, 864; slave trade with, 15, 66–67, 69, 91

African Americans. *See also* Civil rights movement; Segregation; Slavery: in the abolitionist movement, 345–346; in the Alliance movement, 666; in the American Revolution, 166–167; Black Codes, 535–537; in the Civil War, 510–511; in the colonies, 40–41; and

colonization movement, 343–344, 346, 396, 506; cultural expression of, 360, 404, 548–549; education of, 205, 341, 342, 529, 544, 546, 548, 662, 731, 950–952; in the 1890s, 671–672; and Filipino freedom, 710; free blacks, 204, 294, 343–344, 345, 405–407, 457–460, 526–527, 528–530, 532–533, 535–537, 547–549; in the Great Depression, 827, 845–848; as indentured servants, 40; institutions of, 205, 292–293, 336, 548–549; literature of, 360, 404, 810–811; lynchings, 671–672, 779; in the middle class, 729; migration to cities, 616, 775–777, 794–795; New Negro, 810; population growth, 343; in the Progressive era, 719, 730–732, 736, 751–753; in the Spanish-American War, 700; and sports, 636, 948–949; and Tuskegee syphilis study, 846–847; voting rights of, 303, 540–543, 550, 661–662, 672, 674–675, 950, 972–973, 1046–1048, 1051; and westward expansion, 583–584; in World War I, 776, 809; in World War II, 876–877

African Methodist Episcopal Church, 205, 292, 336, 548

Age of Reason, 95–104, 168, 202, 333–334

Age of Romanticism, 727

Agnew, Spiro, 1022, 1085–1086

Agrarian movement, 664–668

Agricultural Adjustment Act (AAA), 836, 838, 845, 849

Agriculture: agrarian movement, 664–668; cooperatives, 665–666, 838; declining prices, 317, 656, 663–664, 667, 687; *encomienda* system, 20; and Grange movement, 659–660, 665–666, 687; in the Great Depression, 817, 836–838; innovation in, 285–286, 376, 586, 587–590; migrant workers in, 1062–1063; Native Americans and, 6–7, 8–9; and overcrowding, 12; production versus subsistence, 378, 380; railroads and, 586–587, 659–661; in the South, 43, 392–393, 587–590. *See also* Slavery; in westward expansion, 584–587; in World War I, 770–771; during World War II, 872

Agriculture Department, U.S., 665, 740, 1099

Aguinaldo, Emilio, 709–710

AIDS, 990–991

Aid to Families with Dependent Children (AFDC), 1098–1099

AIM (American Indian Movement), 1073–1074

Alabama: Montgomery bus boycott, 675; in the Reconstruction, 548; secession of, 489

Alabama (ship), 501

Alabama Indians, 8

Alamo, the, 428–430

Alaska, 685

Albany (Fort Orange), 33

Albany Plan of Union, 108, 142

Albany Regency, 305

Albert, King of Belgium, 761

Alcott, Abba, 358

Alcott, Bronson, 352, 354, 358

Alcott, Louisa May, 352, 354

Aldrich, Nelson W., 741

Alexander, Charles C., 939

Alexander II, Czar of Russia, 610

Alexander VI, Pope, 16

Alger, Horatio, 254, 571

Alianza Federal de Mercedes (the Federal Alliance of Land Grants), 1071

Alien Act, 236

Alien and Sedition Acts, 236–237

Alien Enemies Act, 236

Allen, Charles, 465

Allen, Ethan, 158

Allen, Frederick Lewis, 819

Allen, Richard, 205

Allerton, Mary Norris, 62

Alliance movement, 665–667

Altgeld, John, 670

Amalgamated Clothing Workers, 842

American Anti-Boycott Association, 732, 749

American Anti-Slavery Society, 348, 368

American Civil Liberties Union (ACLU), 774

American Colonization Society, 343, 396

American Commonwealth, The (Bryce), 650

American Federation of Labor (AFL), 599, 673, 676, 771, 772, 780, 805, 842

American Graffiti (film), 955

American Historical Association, 725

American Independent party, 464

American Indian Movement (AIM), 1073–1074

American Medical Association (AMA), 725, 728

American Missionary Association, 529, 548

American Office of Strategic Services (OSS), 1000–1001

American (Know Nothing) party, 464–466, 469–470, 473, 488, 652

American Peace Commission, 782

American Philosophical Society, 98

American Plague, 622

American Protective Association, 732

American Psychiatric Association, 1075

American Public Health Association, 622

American Railway Union (ARU), 670

American Red Cross, 518, 775, 819, 877

American Revolution: British military buildup, 162–164; British seizure of

American Revolution *(Continued)*
Philadelphia, 169; composition of Army, 166–168; Declaration of Independence, 159–162, 164, 260, 333, 343–344, 361, 475, 506, 557; events leading to, 117–144; expansion of, 158–159; financial issues following, 191–192, 222–225; first shots in, 151–154; France and, 168–169, 172, 174, 176–178, 194; Lexington and Concord, 151–152, 162; moderate versus radical views of, 154–158, 159–162; New York campaign, 164–165; northern theater, 156–157, 158, 162–167; reworking of British strategy in, 172–175; Saratoga capture, 169–172; southern theater, 158–159, 160, 172–175; Spain and, 168–169, 172, 178, 194; as subject of art, 361; Treaty of Paris, 117, 178, 193, 705, 709; Trenton campaign, 165–166; in Valley Forge, 148–149, 166–167, 172; Yorktown victory, 176–178
American Society for the Promotion of Temperance, 338
American System, 273, 307–308, 325
American system of production, 280, 285, 320
American Tin Plate Company, 564
American Tobacco Company, 749
American Woman Suffrage Association (AWSA), 541, 655
Amherst, Jeffrey, 109
Amusement parks, 637–638
Anaconda Plan, 497–498
Anderson, Broncho Billy, 977
Anderson, Marian, 845
Anderson, Robert, 491, 520
Andropov, Yuri, 1101
Andros, Edmund, 86–87
Anglican (English) church, 23, 48, 52, 55, 89
Anne, Queen of England, 105
Anthony, Susan B., 507, 541, 655, 802
Anti-Comintern Pact, 864
Antietam, battle of, 486, 487, 507, 508
Antifederalist party, 209–211, 221
Anti-Masonic party, 304, 321, 324, 464
Antinomianism, 56
Anti-Saloon League, 728
Anti-Semitism, 612, 613; and the Holocaust, 858–859, 862, 864, 878–879
Antislavery movement. *See* Abolitionism
Antiwar movement: for Mexican-American War, 438–440; for Vietnam War, 1018–1022, 1024, 1057
Antiwar sentiment, 861
Apache Indians, 417, 419, 552, 1073
Apartheid, 1112
Apes, William (Pequod), 360
Apocado, Jerry, 1071
Apocalypse Now (film), 1029
Appliances, 796, 798, 960, 971–972
Arapaho Indians, 9, 553, 554
Arawak Indians, 16
Arbella (ship), 53
Architecture, 618–619, 793, 851, 937

Argentina, 825, 1095
Aristotle, 93
Arizona, 981; colonization of, 415
Arizona (ship), 870
Arizona Territory, 441
Arkansas, 294; in the Reconstruction, 531; secession of, 491
Armstrong, Louis, 629, 798
Armstrong, Neil, 1107
Army, U.S.: in the Korean War, 911–915, 921, 934; post-Civil War reduction of, 684–685; presidential powers over, 540, 1031, 1086, 1087; in the Vietnam War, 1008–1019, 1024, 1057, 777–778; in World War I, 776, 777–778; in World War II, 871–874, 880–892
Army Appropriation Bill, 705
Army Corps of Nurses, 775
Army of the Commonwealth of Christ, 671
Arnett, Peter, 1011
Arnold, Benedict, 126–127, 158, 171, 175, 176
Arnold, Thurman, 836
Art: Ashcan school, 627–628, 722; Hudson River school, 361; of nineteenth century, 361–362; pre-Raphaelite school, 727
Arthur, Chester A., 657–659, 688; as successor to Garfield, 657–658
Articles of Confederation, 188–192, 206, 210, 220, 222; drafting of, 188–189; and the Great Compromise, 207–208; ratification of, 189–191; and taxation, 191
Artisan system, 379–382
Ashcan school, 627–628, 722
Asiento agreement, 105, 106
As I Lay Dying (Faulkner), 851
Assembly lines, 578–579, 795
Assimilation, 312–313, 556–557, 608
Association for the Study of Negro Life and History, 811
Astor, John Jacob, 431
Asylums, 342
Atahualpa (Inca), 19
Atkinson, Edwin, 599
Atkinson, Ti-Grace, 1066
Atlanta, capture of, 517–518
Atlanta Compromise, 587–588, 672, 674
Atlantic Charter, 868
Atomic Energy Commission, 981
Atomic weapons, 888–892. *See also* Cold War; bombing of Japan, 889–892; development of, 889, 890–891, 919, 981–982, 992; Manhattan Project, 889, 890–891, 919; Nuclear Test Ban Treaty, 1012; of Soviet Union, 910
Attucks, Crispus, 135
Auburn Prison, 339–340
Augusta (ship), 868
Auschwitz, 858, 859, 879
Austin, Moses, 426
Austin, Stephen F., 426–427, 429
Austria, 106, 864
Austria-Hungary, 759–760, 762, 778
Autobiography (Franklin), 101–103
Automobiles, 795–796, 850, 871, 936–938,

960, 982–983, 1036, 1037, 1088–1089, 1091
Autry, Gene, 977
Avilés, Pedro Menéndez de, 24
Aztecs, 7, 17–18, 19

Babbitt (Sinclair), 801
Babbitt, Bruce, 993
Babbitt, Irving, 850
Babcock, Orville, 682
Baby and Child Care (Spock), 956
Baby boom, 608, 876, 956–960, 1056
Bachelor subculture, 630
Backcountry fights, 364–365
Backus, Isaac, 100
Bacon, Nathaniel, 85
Bacon's Rebellion, 85–86
Baer, George F., 718
Baez, Buenaventura, 682
Bailey, Jack, 1059
Baker, Ray Stannard, 724–725, 736
Bakke v. *Regents of the University of California*, 1054
Balboa, Vasco Nuñez de, 16–17
Baldwin, James, 1052
Baldwin, Luther, 236
Ball, George, 1014–1016
Ballard, Martha, 63
Ballinger, Richard A., 741
Baltimore (ship), 692
Baltimore and Ohio Railroad, 595
Bandidos, 414
Banking: Federal Reserve System, 743, 750, 817–818, 832, 835, 836, 1092; Great Depression and, 832–836; National Banking acts, 504
Bank of America, 979
Bank of the United States: first, 223–224, 247; second, 272, 274, 275, 276, 277, 290, 318–319
Banneker, Benjamin, 205
Baptists, 100, 104, 196–197, 205, 336, 396, 398, 433, 570, 571
Barbados, 47, 67
Barbary pirates, 250–251, 278
Barbie doll, 960
Barbour, Charlie, 533
Barker, Frank, 1005
Barnard College, 1060
Barnett, Ross, 972, 1044
Barnum, P. T., 366
Barré, Isaac, 123
Barrow, Bennet H., 401–402
Bartholdi, Frederic Auguste, 607
Bartolomeo Vanzetti and Nicola Sacco (painting), 808
Barton, Clara, 518
Bartram, John, 98
Baruch, Bernard M., 770
Baseball, 630–634, 636, 652, 799, 934, 948–949, 974, 979–980
Basketball, 926, 948
Batista, Fulgencio, 945
Battle of Russia (film), 902
Baum, L. Frank, 556
Bayard, Thomas F., 691
Bay of Pigs invasion, 945, 1007–1008
Beadle, Erastus, 363

Beard, Charles A., 758
Bear Flag Revolt, 438
Beat Generation, 962–963
Beaumarchais, Pierre-Augustin Caron de, 168–169
Beauregard, P. G. T., 491, 496, 500
Beauvoir, Simone de, 1066
Bechet, Sidney, 629
Becknell, William, 422–423
Beckwourth, Jim, 422
Beecher, Catharine, 347
Beecher, Henry Ward, 471, 571
Beecher, Lyman, 388, 462
Begin, Menachem, 1094
Behaim, Martin, 13
Beiderbecke, Bix, 630
Belgium: and World War I, 761, 763, 764; in World War II, 866
Bell, Alexander Graham, 567, 568
Bell, John, 488
Bellamy, Edward, 721
Bellows, George, 627
Bemis, Edward W., 614
Bennett, James Gordon, 363
Bennett, Rolla, 293
Bentley, Eric, 968
Benton, Thomas Hart, 315–316
Berger, Victor, 780
Bering Straits, 5
Berkeley, John (Lord Berkeley), 80–81
Berkeley, William, 84–85
Berkman, Alexander, 669
Berle, Adolph, 836
Berlin Wall, 1104
Bermuda, 42
Bernard, Francis, 124, 125, 132–133
Bernays, Edward, 797
Bernstein, Carl, 1084–1085
Berry, Chuck, 961
Bessarabia, 865
Bethune, Mary McLeod, 848
Beveridge, Albert J., 686, 689–690, 699
Bibb, Henry, 403
Biddle, Nicholas, 319
Bidwell, John, 424
Bierstadt, Albert, 361, 627
Big business, 574–580; assembly lines and, 578–579, 795; and consumer economy, 795–797; and control of competition, 564–565, 574–577; Harding and, 812; Harrison and, 661; managerial styles in, 577–578; mass marketing and, 578; power of, 579–580; and retreat of progressivism, 813; and robber barons, 597
Big Stick Diplomacy, 744–746
Bilbo, Theodore G., 950
Billion-Dollar Congress, 662
Bill of Rights, 211, 221, 256, 475, 537
Billy the Kid, 583
Bimetallic standard, 656
Bird, Robert Montgomery, 363
Birmingham demonstrations, 1041–1044
Birney, James G., 345, 396
Birth control, 202–203, 348, 792–793, 802, 803
Bishop, Maurice, 1100
Bismarck, Otto von, 691

Bissell, George, 566
Black Bart (Charles E. Boles), 583
Blackboard Jungle (film), 925
Black Codes, 535–537
Black Death, 12
Blackfoot Indians, 1073
Black Hawk (Sauk), 314, 360
Black Hawk War, 314, 360, 424, 477, 495
Black Legend, 29
Black Like Me (Griffin), 947, 950
Blackmun, Harry, 1054
Black Muslims, 1048–1051
Black Panther party, 675, 992, 1050–1051
Black Republicans, 486, 489, 507
Blackwell, Elizabeth, 348
Blaine, James G., 652–653, 655, 659, 688, 692
Blair, Ezell, Jr., 1039
Blair Education Bill, 662
Blake (Delany), 360
Bland-Allison Act, 657, 661
Blithedale Romance, The (Hawthorne), 354
Blitzkrieg, 866–867
Blockades, 118, 497
Blount, James H., 693
Blue laws, 802
Blues, 629–630, 798, 975
Board of Trade and Plantations, 89, 106
Boaz, Franz, 758
Boesky, Ivan, 1099, 1100
Bolden, Buddy, 629
Boles, Peter, 126–127
Boleyn, Anne, 23
Bolshevik Revolution, 615, 759, 762, 769, 782–784, 825
Bon Homme Richard (ship), 178
Bonsel, Stephen, 710
Bonus Army, 831
Bonvouloir, Achard de, 168
Book of Mormon, 433, 435
Boone, Daniel, 197–198
Booth, John Wilkes, 520, 534
Booth, Sherman M., 460
Bootlegging, 806
Borden, Andrew, 606–607
Borden, Hannah, 383
Borden, Lizzie, 606–607
Bork, Robert, 1085
Bosnia, 1112
Boss spirits, 10
Boss Tweed Ring scandal, 547
Bostic, Joe, 949
Boston, population growth, 289–290
Boston Brahmins, 351–352
Boston Manufacturing Company, 271
Boston Massacre, 134–135, 136, 137
Boston Port Bill, 139
Boston Tea Party, 139
Boudinot, Elias, 291
Bourbons, 676–677
Bourne, Randolph S., 758–759, 767, 768, 770, 772, 773–774, 787
Bowdoin College, 358
Bowie, Jim, 428–430
Boxer Rebellion, 712
Boxing, 634–635, 636, 695
Boyce, John, 361
Boyd, William, 977

Boy Scouts of America, 732
Braceland, Francis J., 961
Bracero program, 878, 1062–1063, 1070
Braddock, Edward, 108–109
Bradford, William, 5, 48–52, 55
Bradley, Mamie, 933
Bradstreet, Anne, 60, 62
Brand, Max, 976
Brandeis, Louis D., 723, 724, 738, 744
Brant, Joseph (Thayendanegea; Mohawk), 171
Braun, Wernher von, 943
Brazil, 17, 67, 454, 1095
Breckinridge, John C., 488
Brent, Margaret, 64
Brezhnev, Leonid, 1027, 1093, 1101
Briand, Aristide, 860
Britain, 825; and the American Revolution. *See* American Revolution; anti-Spanish sentiment, 106; and the Civil War, 501; and colonial resistance to imperialism, 123–144; colonial rupture with, 136–140; colonies of, 4–5, 31–32, 40–70, 76–79, 81–104; English Civil War, 53, 81; Glorious Revolution, 86–87, 89; and Ireland, 26, 762; as nation-state, 14, 16; in the New World, 21–22, 25–26; and the Old Northwest, 230–232, 259; ousting from colonies, 159–162; and the Pacific Northwest, 278–279, 431–433; and the Panic of 1837, 319–320, 324, 384–385; pre-World War II, 864; Puritans in, 24, 52–53, 65; slavery and, 453, 454; and South American border disputes, 694, 695; taxes on the colonies, 85–86, 117, 121, 122–131, 191; and Treaty of Utrecht, 105–106; and the Treaty of Versailles, 782; and Truman Doctrine, 906; and War of 1812, 256–264, 306; and World War I, 761, 762–766; and World War II, 866, 880, 881; XYZ affair and, 235–236
Britain, battle of, 867
British Guiana, 694
British West Indies, 307
Brontë, Emily, 727
Brook Farm, 354, 358
Brooks, Preston, 472–473
Brotherhood of Sleeping Car Porters, 1046
Brown, Albert Gallatin, 452
Brown, Henry "Box," 360
Brown, James, 1050
Brown, John, 473, 478–480
Brown, Morris, 292
Brown, Moses, 382
Brown, Norman O., 1057
Brown, William Wells, 360
Brownson, Orestes, 352
Brownsville, Texas incident, 751
Brown v. Board of Education of Topeka, 932, 951–952, 972, 1038, 1052
Bryan, William Jennings, 641, 708, 710, 815; in the election of 1896, 648–649, 672–673, 677, 720; in the election of 1908, 740; in the Scopes trial, 807; as Secretary of State, 763, 766–767; Treaty of Paris and, 709

Bryant, Carolyn, 932
Bryant, Roy, 932–933
Bryce, James, 650, 653
Buchanan, James, 467, 473–475, 992; election to presidency, 450–451, 473–474; and the Lecompton Constitution, 475–476, 477; and the Morrill Tariff, 572
Buchanan, Patrick, 985, 990–991
Buck, Eliza, 462
Buckley, William F., Jr., 1107
Buell, Don Carlos, 497, 500
Buena Vista, battle of, 438
Buffalo, 552–553, 555, 581
Bulge, battle of, 883, 886
Bull Moose party, 742
Bullocke, James, 97
Bull Run, battles of, 496–497, 499–500
Bunau-Varilla, Philippe, 745
Bunker Hill, battle of, 156–157, 158, 361
Buntline, Ned, 363
Bunyan, John, 724
Burden, Janet, 727
Bureau of Corporations, 738, 744
Bureau of Indian Affairs, 1074
Bureau of Labor Statistics, 595
Bureau of Land Management, 584
Bureau of Reclamation, 982
Burger, Warren, 1054, 1066–1067
Burgess, Guy, 919
Burgoyne, John ("Gentleman Johnny"), 151, 156–157, 158, 168–169, 170–171
Burke Act, 557
Burlingame Treaty, 614
Burnett, Leo, 976
Burns, Anthony, 460
Burnside, Ambrose E., 486, 508, 511
Burr, Aaron, 238, 252–254; duel with Hamilton, 244–245, 252–253; treason proceedings, 253–254
Burroughs, Edgar Rice, 799
Bush, George, 970, 988, 1102, 1103–1111; domestic policy, 1103–1104, 1105; election to presidency, 1103; invasion of Panama, 1105–1108; and the Persian Gulf War, 1108–1110
Bushnell, David, 285
Butler, Andrew, 472
Butler, Pierce, 208
Butterfield, Alexander, 1085
Buttrick, John, 152
Buxtun, Peter, 847
Byrd, Harry F., 926
Byrd, Lucy Parke, 65
Byrd, William, II, 47, 65–66
Byrne, Eugene, 633
Byrnes, James F., 910, 952

C. Turner Joy (ship), 1014
Cabeza de Vaca, Alvar Núñez, 19
Cabinet, 221
Cable cars, 618
Cabot, John (Giovanni Caboto), 21
Cabral, Pedro Alvares, 16
Cabrillo, Juan Rodríguez, 19
Cahan, Abraham, 639
Calhoun, John C., 272–273, 276, 279, 290, 305, 306, 395, 431, 440, 450–451, 489;

and nullification doctrine, 308, 316–317; and threat of Southern secession, 456
Calhoun, William J., 697–698
California, 981; annexation to the United States, 437; anti-Mexican sentiment in, 441; application for statehood, 452, 455, 457; Chinese immigrants in, 614; colonization of, 415; federal projects in, 978–979, 981–982; Gold Rush, 441, 442–444, 451, 565–566; and the Mexican-American War, 436–437, 438; mission system in, 416, 417; Native Americans in, 417; overland trail to, 419–420, 422–423; settlement of, 423–424; and slavery, 451–452
California (ship), 870
Callender, James Thomson, 218, 232
Calley, William, 1005
Call It Sleep (Roth), 851
Calvert, Cecilius (Second Lord Baltimore), 45–46
Calvert, George (First Lord Baltimore), 45
Calvert, Leonard, 64, 67
Calvin, John, 23, 52
Cambodia (Kampuchea), 1024, 1029, 1086
Cambridge Agreement, 53
Camden, battle of, 174–175
Camera, 568
Campanella, Roy, 949
Camp David Accords, 1093–1094, 1097
Canada, 104–105, 688, 825; in the American Revolution, 158; Quebec Act, 140; in the War of 1812, 259, 260, 264; Webster-Ashburton Treaty, 431
Canals, 275–276, 280, 281–282
Cannibalism, 32, 419–420
Canning, George, 279
Cannon, "Uncle Joe," 741
Capital formation, 573–574, 589
Capitalism, 30–31, 553, 598, 666, 781
Capital punishment, 340
Capone, Al, 806, 922
Capra, Frank, 851, 874, 902
Cardoza, Francis, 544
Carey, Harry, 977
Carey, Matthew, 290, 380–381
Carmichael, Stokely, 1050, 1065
Carnegie, Andrew, 504, 564–566, 570–571, 572, 574, 576, 596, 599, 651, 669, 708–709, 710, 720
Carnegie Foundation, 571
Carnegie Steel Company, 564
Carney, William H., 510
Carolina colonies, 76–77
Carolinas, 46–47. *See also* North Carolina; South Carolina
Caroline (ship), 431
Carpenter, Alice, 49
Carpetbaggers, 543–544, 545, 549
Carranza, Venustiano, 747
Carson, "Fiddlin' John," 798
Carson, Rachel, 1076
Carter, Jimmy, 969, 970, 973, 1087–1088, 1092, 1094–1098, 1103; Camp David Accords, 1093–1094, 1097; China and,

1027; and human rights, 1095; and Iran hostage crisis, 1095–1096; Panama Canal Treaty, 1094, 1097
Carter, Landon, 459
Carteret, George, 80–81
Cartier, Jacques, 21, 28
Cartwright, Alexander J., Jr., 631
Cartwright, Samuel W., 459
Caruthers, William Alexander, 463
Carver, George Washington, 588
Carver, John, 49
Casey, William, 1100
Cass, Lewis, 455
Cassidy, Butch, 583
Castro, Fidel, 945, 1007, 1087
Castro, Raul, 1071
Catcher in the Rye (Salinger), 1057
Cather, Willard, 361
Catherine of Aragon, 23
Catholics and Catholicism: Catholic schools, 341; and the Crusades, 12–13; hostility toward, 465; Irish, 26; in the Middle Ages, 11–12; mission system, 416, 417; in New Spain, 20–21; and New World exploration, 16; and Protestant Reformation, 22–24, 52, 53; and religious freedom, 336; and slavery, 20
Cato's Letters (Trenchard and Gordon), 136
Catt, Carrie Chapman, 730, 775
Cattle, 578–579, 581–584, 837
Cavelier, René-Robert (Sieur de La Salle), 104
Cayuga Indians, 10, 171
Cayuse Indians, 432
Censorship, 639, 772–773, 851, 1075
Census, 219–220
Census Bureau, 1054
Census of Agriculture, 978
Central Intelligence Agency (CIA), 939–940, 941, 944, 945, 1007, 1084, 1087, 1095, 1100–1101
Central Pacific railroad, 572, 610
Central Valley Project, 977–978
Chain stores, 797
Chamberlain, Neville, 864, 866
Chambers, Whittaker, 900–902
Chamoun, Camille, 944–945
Champlain, Samuel de, 4, 34
Chancellorsville, battle of, 512
Chandler, Raymond, 850
Chaney, James, 1050
Channing, William Ellery, 334
Chaplin, Charlie, 799
Charles, Robert, 675
Charles I, King of England, 44–46, 53, 65
Charles II, King of England, 46, 56, 77–80, 82, 84, 85–86
Charles River Bridge v. *Warren Bridge*, 321
Charleston, South Carolina: in the American Revolution, 174; Barbadians in, 47; nullification controversy in, 317–318; Vesey Conspiracy, 292–293
Charlotte Temple (Rowson), 363
Charter of Liberties, 84
Chase, Salmon P., 470, 504
Chase, Samuel, 249–250

Chávez, César Estrada, 1062–1063, 1071
Chernenko, Konstantin, 1101
Cherokee Indians, 9, 110, 174, 198, 229, 275, 312, 313–315, 360, 554
Cherokee Nation v. *Georgia*, 313
Cherokee War, 110
Chesapeake (ship), 255
Chesapeake colonies, 58–60, 61, 65–68, 85–86
Chestnut, Charles, 810
Chew, Lee, 614
Cheyenne Indians, 417, 418, 419, 552, 553, 554, 555
Chiang Kai-shek (Jiang Jieshi), 910–911, 938, 1093
Chicago: Haymarket Square riot, 596–597, 598–599, 668, 687, 740; meatpacking business, 578–579, 594
Chicago White Sox, 799
Chicano movement, 1070
Chickamauga, battle of, 516
Chickasaw Indians, 9, 110, 174, 198, 229, 275, 312
Childbirth, in colonial era, 62–63
Child Health Improvement and Protection Act, 1052–1053
Child labor, 382, 385, 724, 729, 735, 744, 750, 838–839
Child Labor Act, 750
Chile, 691–692, 695, 1095
China, 911, 913, 942, 1094; Boxer Rebellion, 712; Carter and, 1027; division of, 910–911; Germany and, 784; immigrants from, 583, 610, 613, 614–615, 662; Nixon and, 1025–1027; Open Door Policy, 711–713, 869; Marco Polo in, 14; recognition of, 1096–1097; and Vietnam, 1009–1010
China Lobby, 911
Chinese Exclusion Act, 614, 662
Chinook Indians, 9
Chippewa Indians, 119, 230
Chivington, J. M., 554
Choctaw Indians, 8, 9, 110, 174, 261, 275, 312, 313
Choice Not an Echo, A (Schlafly), 1069
Choiseul, Duc de, 168
Cholera epidemic, 322–323
Chou En-lai (Zhou Enlai), 910, 1027
Christian, Archer, 632–633
Chrysler Building, 793
Chrysler Corporation, 1088, 1089
Church, Frederick, 361
Church, Rob, 707
Churchill, Winston, 862, 864, 866–867, 868–869, 871, 880–884, 906, 908, 1003
Church of England, 23, 48, 52, 55, 89
Church of Jesus Christ of Latter Day Saints, 433–435
Cigarette industry, 588, 806
Cincinnati Red Stockings, 631
Circus, 366
Cisneros, Henry, 1071
Cities, 615–641. *See also specific cities*; architecture of, 618–619, 793, 851, 937; beautification movements, 361–362, 637; crime and, 333, 339, 389, 620; culture in, 623–641; early nineteenth-century, 287–290; ghettoes, 619–620, 794–795; health problems, 226–227, 322–323, 622–623; housing in, 289–290, 619–622, 794–795; migration to, 616, 775–777, 794–795; population growth, 287–290, 615–623, 776–777, 793–795; problems of growth, 226–227, 322–323, 620–623; progressivism in, 733–734; residential segregation in, 289–290, 619–620, 794–795; sanitation problems, 322–323, 622; in the South, 975; sports and, 630–637; transportation technology and, 616–618, 622, 623, 795
Citizen Genêt Affair, 229
Citizens' Councils, 932
Citizenship, 474–475, 477, 478, 530, 537, 538
Citizen virtue, 192
City planners, 795
Civilian Conservation Corps (CCC), 839, 845, 848, 873, 1076
Civil Rights Act (1866), 537
Civil Rights Act (1875), 557
Civil Rights Act (1957), 972–973, 1045
Civil Rights Act (1960), 972–973
Civil Rights Act (1964), 972–973, 987, 1046, 1053, 1064–1065, 1069, 1077
Civil rights movement, 810, 876–877, 946–955, 1006, 1020, 1037–1055; background of, 1037–1038; Birmingham demonstrations, 1041–1045; and black nationalism, 1050–1051, 1079; and black power, 1048–1049; Detroit race riot, 950; early protests, 675, 1038–1040; freedom riders, 1040–1044; Greensboro sit-in, 1039–1040; Kennedy and, 1040, 1045–1046; legacy of, 1054–1055; legislation, 972–973; Little Rock crisis, 953; march on Washington, 1046; Montgomery bus boycott, 675, 953–955, 1041; in the North, 1051–1052; and school desegregation, 951–952; Selma demonstrations, 1047–1048; and voting rights, 1046–1048; white backlash, 1054; youth movement and, 1057
Civil Service Commission, 658–659
Civil War, 486–521. *See also* Reconstruction; Slavery; Confederate resistance in, 511–518; Confederate shortages in, 501–503; Confederate surrender at Appomattox, 520; Confederate victories in, 495–496, 498–500, 500, 511–512; and the Emancipation Proclamation, 487, 500, 506–511, 532–533; events leading to, 492; financial issues following, 534, 656; Fort Sumter insurrection, 487, 491; postwar conditions and issues, 527–531, 586, 589; resources of warring factions, 491–495; surrender of Confederacy in, 518–520; Union offensive in, 496–498; Union victories in, 487–488, 497–498, 500–501, 507, 508, 512–520; Union war effort, 503–506
Civil Works Administration (CWA), 839
Claim-jumpers, 425

Clancy, Tom, 1107
Clark, Champ, 777
Clark, J. Reuben, 861
Clark, James, 1047
Clark, Kenneth, 951
Clark, William, 252, 421
Clarke, Edward Young, 808
Clark Memorandum, 861
Classical economics, 722–723
Clay, Henry, 257, 272–273, 279, 306, 307, 315, 345; American System, 273, 307–308, 325; Compromise of 1850 and, 455–457; Missouri Compromise and, 294, 317; nullification crisis and, 317; second Bank of the United States and, 318
Clayton Antitrust Act, 744, 749
Clean Air Act, 1076, 1098
Clean Water Act, 1076
Clemenceau, Georges, 782, 784
Clement VII, Pope, 23
Clermont (ship), 281, 284
Cleveland, Grover, 607, 651, 653, 659–662, 670, 690, 691, 698; in the election of 1896, 648; election to presidency, 659, 669; foreign policy of, 693–694, 697; and immigration restrictions, 614; railroads and, 659–661; rebuilding of Navy and, 688–689
Cliff Dwellers (Bellows), 627
Clifton, Nat "Sweetwater," 949
Clinton, Bill, 970, 988, 994, 995, 1075, 1110–1112; new covenant, 1111; and Vietnam, 1031
Clinton, DeWitt, 281–282
Clinton, Henry, 151, 156–157, 158, 169, 173–174, 176–177
Closing Circle, The (Commoner), 1076
Clotel (Brown), 360
Clothing, 796–797
Coal mining, 595, 718–719, 738, 749–750
Cobb, Ty, 799
Coca-Cola, 640, 871
Cocaine, 640–641
Cody, William ("Buffalo Bill"), 976
Coercive Acts, 139–140, 141, 142
Coinage Act, 656
Coin's Financial School (Harvey), 672
Cold War, 902; Berlin airlift, 909–910; containment policy in, 908–910, 938–946; Cuba and, 1006–1008; détente, 1008, 1093, 1104; Eisenhower and, 938–946; end of, 1101–1102, 1104–1105, 1106–1107; inside the United States, 915, 918–925; Nixon and, 1024–1027, 1093; origins of, 902–908; and paranoid style, 924, 926; under Reagan, 1100–1101, 1102; Vietnam and, 1009, 1021, 1025
Cold War, The (Lippmann), 909
Cole, Thomas, 361, 627
Colfax, Schuyler, 551
Collier, John, 848
Collier's, 724
Colombia, 745
Colonization, African American, 343–344, 346, 396, 506

Colorado-Big Thompson Project, 978
Colorado Territory, 441, 554
Colored Alliance, 666
Columbus, Christopher, 4, 14, 15–16
Comanche Indians, 419
Comic books, 850, 925–926
Comic strips, 874
Coming Home (film), 1029
Command of the Army Act, 540
Committee of Industrial Organizations (CIO), 842
Committee on Public Information (CPI), 772–773
Committee to Reelect the President (CREEP), 1084
Commodity Credit Corporation, 838
Commoner, Barry, 1076
Common Sense (Paine), 160
Commonwealth of Independent States (CIS), 1104–1105, 1107
Commonwealth v. *Hunt*, 384
Communications, nineteenth-century, 283, 567, 568
Communism. *See also* Cold War: Bolshevik Revolution, 615, 759, 762, 782–784, 825; in China, 910, 914–915, 1009, 1025–1027; and collapse of Soviet Union, 1104–1105, 1106–1107; Cuba and, 1006–1008; Alger Hiss case, 900–902, 919; in Hollywood, 924–925; and the Korean War, 911–915, 921, 934; McCarthyism, 919–921, 1075, 1097; Nixon's recognition of China, 1025–1027; popular culture and, 902; Red Scare, 780–781, 805, 900–902, 918–925; Soviet, 825, 1104–1105; and the Vietnam War, 1000–1001, 1009–1010, 1092–1093
Community Chest, 819
Complex marriage, 350–351
Compromise of 1820, 208, 480–481
Compromise of 1850, 208, 455–457, 464, 481
Compromise of 1877, 558
Compromise Tariff of 1832, 456
Compulsory education, 662
Comstock, Anthony, 802–803
Comstock, William A., 833
Comstock Act, 1075
Concentration camps, 858, 859, 863, 878–879, 879–880
Coney Island, New York, 637–638
Confederate States of America: Civil War and, 491–521; formation of, 489–491
Confession magazines, 799–800
Confiscation Act, 506
Congregationalists, 88–89, 99, 100, 104, 197, 294
Congress, U.S.: debates on slavery, 291–295, 305–306, 469–470; in the election of 1994, 994–995, 1112; establishment of government by, 221; and Indian policy, 556–557; isolationism of, 683–685; and power of president, 208–209, 311–312, 540; Progressive-era legislation, 739, 749–751; and the

Reconstruction, 537–543; and Revolutionary War debt, 223–224
Congressional Government (Wilson), 743
Congress of Racial Equality (CORE), 877, 973, 1040, 1050
Conkling, Roscoe, 542, 651, 652–654
Connecticut: colonization of, 57, 86, 129; state constitution, 186
Connecticut Yankee in King Arthur's Court, A (Twain), 625
Connor, Theophilus Eugene "Bull," 1041, 1044–1045
Conqueror, The (film), 982
Conquistadores, 16–19
Conscience of a Conservative, The (Goldwater), 985, 989
Conscription, 511, 777
Conscription Act, 511
Conservation, 738, 741, 750, 993, 1076–1077
Consolidation, 576–577
Constitution, U.S., 206–211; Bill of Rights, 211, 221, 256, 475, 537; compromise in, 206–209; Eighteenth Amendment, 774; Fifteenth Amendment, 538, 541, 558, 672; Fifth Amendment, 475; First Amendment, 774, 924; Fourteenth Amendment, 537, 538, 541, 542, 557, 558, 573, 589, 651, 672; framers of, 206; implementing, 220–225; Nineteenth Amendment, 775, 804–805, 1066; post-Civil War issues, 530–531; and the presidency, 208–209, 221–222; ratification struggle, 209–211; Seventeenth Amendment, 734, 741; Sixteenth Amendment, 741, 743; slavery and, 207–208; Tenth Amendment, 221; Thirteenth Amendment, 528, 535, 538, 541; Twelfth Amendment, 239, 306; Twenty-fourth Amendment, 1048, 1077
Constitutional Convention, 77, 103, 206, 256
Constitutional Union party, 488
Consumer credit, 796, 797, 817
Consumer economy, 795–797
Consumer movement, 1036–1037
Consumer Products Safety Act, 1036
Consumer Protection Agency, 1036
Continental Association, 142
Continental Congress: First, 140–142; Second, 149–151, 154–155, 164–165, 166, 169, 170, 186, 188, 191, 206, 208
Continentals, 191–192
Continental System, 254
Contract with America, 995
Convention of Aranjuez, 172
Convention of 1800, 236
Conwell, Russell, 571
Coode, John, 87
Coolidge, Calvin, 812–813, 860
Cooper, Anthony Ashley, 46
Cooper, Chuck, 949
Cooper, James Fenimore, 352, 362, 627
Cooperatives, agricultural, 665–666, 838
Copland, Aaron, 801
Copley, John Singleton, 361

Copper, 566
Copperheads, 505–506
Corbett, James J. ("Gentleman Jim"), 635
Corbin, Margaret ("Dirty Kate"), 167
CORE (Congress of Racial Equality), 877, 973, 1040, 1050
Corn (maize), 5
Cornwallis, Charles (Lord Cornwallis), 165, 174–177
Coronado, Francisco Vásquez de, 19
Corporations, 573–574, 734. *See also* Big business
Corps of Engineers, 982
Cortés, Hernán, 17–18
Cortina, Juan Nepomuceno, 414
Corwin, Thomas, 439
Cós, Martín Perfecto de, 428
Cost accounting, 577–578
Costa Rica, 1101
Costello, Frank, 922–923
Cotton, 286–287, 290, 317, 376, 393, 437, 501, 502, 588–589, 689, 776, 838
Cotton, John, 54
Cotton gin, 285, 286, 376
Cotton Kingdom, 343, 454
Coughlin, Father Charles, 841–842, 844
Council for the Indies, 19
Council of Economic Advisors, 916
Counterculture, 992, 1058–1059
Country music, 961, 975
Coverture, 60, 64
Cox, Archibald, 1085
Cox, James M., 786, 830
Coxey, Jacob S., 670–671
Coxey's Army, 671
Craft, Ellen, 360
Craft, William, 360
Crandall, Prudence, 341
Crane, Hart, 800
Crane, Stephen, 626
Crawford, William, 306
Credit agencies, 796
Credit Mobilier scandal, 551
Creek Indians, 8, 9, 110, 174, 260–261, 275, 307, 312, 313
Creek War, 261
Creel, George W., 772
Crime, 1112; and growth of cities, 333, 339, 389, 620; Nixon and, 1054; organized, 612, 806, 922–923; and public transportation, 617; and reform movements, 333, 338–340; and the Wild West, 582–583, 584; women and, 606–607
Crisis, The (journal), 732
Crittenden, John J., 490
Crittenden Compromise, 490
Croatoan Indians, 27
Crockett, Davy, 366, 428–430
Cromwell, Oliver, 46, 77, 79, 82
Cronkite, Walter, 1008, 1018
Crusade for Justice, 1071
Crusades, 12–13
Cuba, 467, 690, 744, 860, 861, 1006–1008, 1100; annexation of, 705; Bay of Pigs invasion, 945, 1007–1008; Columbus in, 16; independence from Spain, 698–699, 704; independence from

the United States, 705; *Maine* incident, 698, 701–703; missile crisis, 1007–1008; slavery and, 398, 454
Cuban Revolution, 695–699, 945
Cuffe, Paul, 1048
Cullen, Countee, 800, 811
Culley, Johnston, 414
Cult of domesticity, 636–637, 792, 796, 1059–1060
cummings, e. e., 800
Cummins, Maria, 366
Currency Act, 122
Curtis Act, 556
Custer, George A., 555
Czechoslovakia, 784, 941
Czolgosz, Leon, 613, 736

Dachau, 858
Dakota Apartments, 621, 641
Daladier, Edouard, 864
Dale, Thomas, 43
Daley, Arthur, 980
Daley, Richard, 1021
Dalhart, Vernon, 798
Dame aux Camelias, La (Dumas), 727
Dam projects, 977–978, 982
Dana, Richard Henry, Jr., 363
Daniels, Josephus, 836
Dare, Virginia, 27
Darrow, Clarence, 807
Dartmouth (ship), 138–139
Dartmouth v. *Woodward*, 277
Darwin, Charles, 570, 626, 686, 806
Daugherty, Harry, 812
Daughters of Bilitis, 1075
Davenport, John, 57
David Copperfield (Dickens), 727
Davies, Samuel, 104
Davis, David, 558
Davis, Jefferson, 399, 487–488; imprisonment of, 542; as president of Confederacy, 489, 494–495, 499, 501, 502, 512, 516
Davis, John W., 812
Davis, Joseph, 399
Davis, Richard H., 704, 707
Dawes, Charles, 556–557, 862
Dawes, William, 151
Dawes Plan, 862
Dawes Severalty Act, 556, 557, 662, 848
Day, Benjamin H., 362
Day of Jubilo, 532–533
D-Day, 883, 884, 934
Dead Indian Act, 556–557
Dean, John, 1085, 1086
Deane, Silas, 168–169
Death Comes to the Archbishop (Cather), 361
Debs, Eugene V., 670, 742, 767, 774, 786
Debtor prisons, 340
Decatur, Stephen, 278
Declaration of Colonial Rights and Grievances, 141
Declaration of Independence, 159–162, 164, 186, 246, 260, 333, 343–344, 361, 475, 506, 557
Declaration of Rights, 86
Declaration of Sentiments, 348–349

Declaration of the Causes and Necessity for Taking up Arms, 155
Declaratory Act, 131
Declension, 64–65
Deer Hunter, The (film), 1029
Defense Department, U.S., 974
Defense industries, 978–979, 981
Defense of the Seven Sacraments (Henry VIII), 22
de Gaulle, Charles, 880
Deindustrialization, 1091
Deism, 98, 336
Delany, Martin, 346, 360, 1048
Delaware: as border state, 491, 528; colonization of, 82; slave trade in, 204–206; state constitution, 187
Delaware and Hudson Canal Company, 282
Delaware Indians, 83, 119, 199, 230
De La Warr, 43
DeLeon, Daniel, 670
Delmonico, Lorenzo, 624
de Lôme, Enrique Dupuy, 698
DeMille, Cecil B., 799
Democratic party: in the election of 1860, 487, 488; in the election of 1994, 994–995, 1112; in the Gilded Age, 648–655; Gold Democrats, 648; and the Know Nothing party, 464; Lincoln-Douglas debates, 476–478; Redeemers, 671; rise of, 321, 442, 464, 473; split in, 451, 467, 469, 487; and the Watergate break-in, 1084–1086
Democratic republicanism, 311
Demographic transition, 202
Dempsey, Jack, 799
Demuth, Charles, 800
Denmark, 685, 866
Dennis, David, 1050
Department stores, 624, 641
Depression. *See also* Great Depression: of the 1890s, 668–672, 687
Deregulation, 1098
Dermer, Thomas, 4
Descent of Man, The (Darwin), 686
Desert Land Act, 584
Deslondes, Charles, 405
De Soto, Hernando, 19, 28–29
Détente, 1008, 1093, 1104
Detroit race riot, 950
Dewey, George, 700
Dewey, John, 722, 723, 735, 758, 770
Dewey, Thomas E., 709, 873, 910, 917
Dewson, Molly, 845
Dialectic of Sex, The (Firestone), 1066
Dias, Bartholomeu, 15
Díaz, Porfirio, 746–747
Dickens, Charles, 281, 363, 727
Dickinson, John, 132, 155, 159–161, 188–189, 206
Dickson, William K. L., 638
Diem, Ngo Dinh, 1010–1011
Diggs, Charles, 933
Dime novels, 363, 976–977
Diner (film), 955
Dingley Tariff, 677
Dinwiddie, Robert, 108
Direct democracy, 733, 734, 749, 1056

Direct election, 667
Dirt, Andrew, 401
Disarmament, 860
Discourse of Western Planting (Hakluyt), 25–26
Discovery (ship), 30
Disney, Walt, 925
Disneyland, 983
Divine right theories of kingship, 45, 46
Division of labor, 381
Dix, Dorothea, 342, 518
Dixon, George, 636
Dodds, Robert "Baby," 629
Dole, Robert, 995
Dole, Sanford B., 694
Dollar Diplomacy, 746
Dominican Republic, 682–683, 685, 746, 860
Dominion of New England, 86–87
Doniphan, A. W., 438
Donner, George, 419
Donner party, 419–420
Dorais, Charley, 633
Dorr, Thomas W., 303
Dorr War, 303
Dos Passos, John, 851
Doubleday, Abner, 631
Douglas, Frederick, 346
Douglas, Stephen A., 455, 472, 475, 480, 481; and the Compromise of 1850, 457; debates with Lincoln, 476–478; in the election of 1860, 488–489; and Kansas-Nebraska Act, 467–469
Douglas, William, 906
Douglass, Frederick, 293, 332, 349, 360, 462, 478, 508, 528, 541
Dow, Lorenzo, 663
Dr. Jekyll and Mr. Hyde (Stevenson), 641
Dragging Canoe (Chincohacina; Cherokee), 174
Drake, Edwin L., 566
Drake, Francis, 24, 27
Drake's folly, 566–567
Dreiser, Theodore, 626, 627, 758
Drug use, 640–641, 743–744, 960, 1019, 1028, 1058
Dubinsky, David, 842
Du Bois, W. E. B., 544, 730–732, 753, 775–776, 810
Duchamp, Marcel, 627–628
Dudingston, William, 137
Dukakis, Michael, 1103
Duke, James B., 588
Dulles, John Foster, 908, 938, 940–941, 942–943, 1010
Dumas, Alexander, 727
Dumbell tenements, 621–622
Dunbar, Paul Lawrence, 810
Dunkirk disaster, 866
Dunne, Finley Peter, 741
Dustan, Hannah, 76–77, 105
Dust Bowl, 824, 837, 1076
Dutch, the: and the American Revolution, 172, 194; colonial, 29, 33–34, 79–80; in the New World, 29, 32–34, 78, 79–80, 84; in World War I, 763; in World War II, 866
Dutch East Indies, 869

Dutch West India Company, 34, 79
Dwight, Timothy, 238
Dye, John Smith, 450–451
Dyer, Mary, 82
Dynamic Sociology (Taylor), 723

Eagle (ship), 285
Eagle Forum, 1069
Eakins, Thomas, 627
Earl Old Person (Blackfoot), 1073
Earp, Wyatt, 583
Earth Day, 1076
East India Company, 138–139
Eastland, James, 932
Eastman, George, 568
Eaton, John H., 317
Eaton, Peggy, 317
Eaton, William, 250
Economic growth. *See also* Industrialization: consumer economy in, 795–797; of Germany, 1089, 1112; of Japan, 1089, 1112; in the North, 564–580; post-Revolution, 219–220; post-War of 1812, 274, 280–290; post-World War II, 935–936; private firms and, 284; under Reaganomics, 1098–1100; and search for new markets, 687–689; twentieth-century, 1088–1092, 1098–1100; in the West, 581–587, 979–984; World War II and, 871–873
Economic Opportunity Act, 987, 1052
Edison, Thomas, 568, 623, 638–639, 720, 798
Edison General Electric Company, 568
Education: of African Americans, 205, 341, 342, 529, 544, 546, 548, 662, 731, 950–952; and college foundings, 100, 104; compulsory, 662; evolutionism in, 807; Jefferson and, 340, 398; of Mexican Americans, 1071, 1072; Progressive, 722, 723, 735, 770; public schools, 340–341, 662; school segregation, 932, 951–952, 972, 1038, 1052; in the South, 394, 398; and technological innovation, 284; of women, 200–201, 202, 341–342, 347, 722, 1060–1061, 1069
Educational Opportunity Act, 1052
Edwards, Jonathan, 99
Egypt, 944; and Camp David Accords, 1093–1094, 1097; and the Persian Gulf War, 1110; Suez Canal, 942
Ehrlich, Paul R., 1076
Ehrlichman, John, 1022
Eighteenth Amendment, 774
Einstein, Albert, 889, 890
Eisenhower, Dwight D., 883, 884, 886, 921, 934–940, 942, 944–947, 952–953, 963, 1097; and containment policy, 944–945; and dynamic conservatism, 935; election to presidency, 934–935; and Jim Crow laws, 946–955; and the New Look, 939–940; reelection, 942–943; and U.S.-Soviet relations, 938–946; and Vietnam, 1010, 1011; in World War II, 881, 934
Electoral system, 233, 238–239, 301, 305–306, 474, 558, 656, 667, 1087

Electricity, 285, 567, 568, 618, 623–624, 796, 837
Elementary and Secondary Education Act, 1052
Eliot, Charles W., 632, 708
Eliot, John, 57
Eliot, T. S., 801
Elizabeth I, Queen of England, 23–27, 30
Elkins Act, 738
Ellington, Duke, 798
Ellis, Edith, 803
Ellis, Havelock, 803
Ellison, William, 406
Elmer Gantry (Sinclair), 801
El Salvador, 861, 1095
Emancipation Proclamation, 487, 500, 506–511, 532–533
Embargo Act, 255–256
Emergency Banking Relief Act, 832
Emergency Quota Act, 615
Emergency Relief Appropriation Act, 839
Emerging Republican Party, The (Phillips), 987–988
Emerson, Ralph Waldo, 351–353, 355, 357–359, 367, 394, 441, 480, 726
Emmett, Dan D., 392
Empire Building State, 793
Employment Act of 1946, 916
Empress of China (ship), 194
Encomienda system, 20
Endangered Species Act, 1076
Enforcement Acts, 550
England. *See* Britain
English Civil War, 53, 81
Enlightenment, 95–104, 168, 202, 333–334
Enola Gay (plane), 889–895
Entail, 31, 197
Environmental Defense Fund, 1076
Environmentalism, 1076–1077
Environmental Protection Agency (EPA), 1036, 1076, 1098
Episcopalians, 197, 205, 398
Equal Employment Opportunity Commission (EEOC), 1046, 1064
Equal Pay Act, 1061–1064, 1069
Equal Rights Amendment (ERA), 730, 805, 1064, 1068–1069
Equiano, Olaudah, 67
Era of Good Feelings, 271–295
Eratosthenes, 13
Ericson, Leif, 11
Eric the Red, 11
Erie Canal, 281–282
Escobedo v. *Illinois*, 1054
Esparza, Gregorio, 428–429
Espionage Act, 773, 774
Essay Concerning Human Understanding (Locke), 95
Estonia, 784, 865, 883, 1104, 1106
Ethiopia, 864
Ethnic cleansing, 859
Eugenics, 351
European Coal and Steel Authority, 908
European Economic Community (Common Market), 908
European Payments Union, 908
European Recovery Program (ERP), 908

Evangelical revivals, 334–335
Evans, Oliver, 284, 285
Evarts, William, 688
Evers, Medgar, 1006, 1045
Evolution, 806–807
Ewing, Finis, 434–435
Executive branch, 221, 222. *See also* Presidency, U.S.
Executive Order 11375, 1064
Existentialism, 801
Expansionism, 682, 685–694; and exceptionalism, 686–687
Ex Parte Merryman, 504–505
Exxon Valdez disaster, 1077

Factory system, 220, 382–383, 591, 593–594
Fair Deal, 917–918
Fair Employment Practices Commission (FEPC), 876–877
Fair Housing Act, 1051, 1053
Falaba (ship), 766
Fall, Albert B., 812
Fallen Timbers, battle of, 230, 231, 262
Fannin, James, 430
Farewell to Arms, A (Hemingway), 801
Farm Credit Administration, 837–838
Farming. *See* Agriculture
Farm Security Agency (FSA), 840, 848
Farragut, David G., 497, 500
Farrell, James T., 851
Fascism, 759, 825, 863–864
Faubus, Orval, 953
Faulkner, William, 800, 851
Favourite (ship), 264–265
Fawkes, Guy, 125
Federal Bureau of Investigation (FBI), 780, 925, 1084, 1086, 1087
Federal Council of Churches of Christ in America, 728
Federal court system, 221
Federal Deposit Insurance Corporation (FDIC), 836
Federal Election Commission, 1087
Federal Emergency Relief Act, 832–836
Federal Employee Loyalty Program, 919
Federal Farm Loan Act, 744
Federal Highway Act, 795
Federal Home Loan Bank System (FHLBS), 829
Federal Housing Authority (FHA), 845
Federalist Papers, The (Madison, Hamilton and Jay), 209–210, 222
Federalist party: collapse of, 264, 272, 305; and the elections of 1800, 237–239; and the Embargo Act, 255–256; and the judiciary, 248–250; origin of, 209–211, 225, 304–305; and patronage, 228, 248; and republican government, 245–246, 247–248; Sedition Act, 218; South and, 377; and the War of 1812, 256–257, 264
Federal Reserve Act, 743
Federal Reserve Board, 1092
Federal Reserve System, 743, 750, 817–818, 832, 835, 836, 1092
Federal Trade Commission (FTC), 744, 749
Female Eunuch, The (Greer), 1066

Feminine Mystique, The (Friedan), 1060, 1061, 1066

Feminism, 541, 729–730. *See also* Women's liberation movement; birth of, 347–349; in early novels, 366; growth of ideology, 1066; radical, 1065–1066; rebirth of, 1061–1065; split in, 805; as term, 350

Feminization of poverty, 1069

Fenno, John, 228

Ferdinand, Archduke Franz, Crown Prince of Austria, 759–760

Ferdinand, King of Spain (Ferdinand of Aragon), 14–16

Ferebee, Thomas, 891

Ferguson, Patrick, 175

Fermi, Enrico, 889, 890

Ferraro, Geraldine, 1069, 1102

Feudalism, 11–12, 14

Field, James G., 667

Field, Marshall, 624, 641

Fields, W. C., 851

Fifteenth Amendment, 538, 541, 558, 672

Fifth Amendment, 475

Fifty Million Bill, 698

Filibuster rule, 1087

Fillmore, Millard, 465; in the election of 1856, 473–474; as successor to Taylor, 450, 456–457

Films. *See* Movie industry

Finland, 784, 865, 883

Finney, Charles G., 335, 341, 350

Firestone, Shulamith, 1066

First Amendment, 774, 924

First Blood (film), 1028–1029

First Frame of Government, 82

Fish, Hamilton, 688, 832

Fisher, Irving, 815

Fishing rights, 178

Fiske, John, 686

Fitch, John, 220

Fitch, Samuel, 284

Fithian, Philip Vickers, 365

Fitzgerald, F. Scott, 798, 799, 800, 801

Fitzhugh, George, 379, 395

Five Nations of Iroquois, 10, 80, 85, 108. *See also* Cayuga Indians; Mohawk Indians; Oneida Indians; Onondaga Indians; Seneca Indians

Five-Power Naval Treaty, 863

Flathead Indians, 419, 432

Fletcher v. *Peck,* 277

Florida: British expedition against, 106; land speculation in, 814–815; Ponce de Leon and, 17; in the Reconstruction, 550; secession of, 489; Spain and, 24, 104, 178, 264, 279, 306; St. Augustine, 24, 105

Florida (ship), 501

Foch, Ferdinand, 778

Folk songs, 850

Folktales, 404

Folliard, Edward T., 900

Following the Color Line (Baker), 724–725

Fonda, Jane, 1056

Food Administration, 770–771

Food processing, 578–579, 594, 725, 738, 740, 750, 797

Football, 632–633, 695, 799, 926, 949

Foote, Andrew H., 500

Force Act, 317

Ford, Gerald, 1086–1088, 1092; pardon of Nixon, 1088

Ford, Henry, 795–796, 850

Ford, Henry, II, 1088

Ford, Sarah, 533

Ford Motor Company, 1088–1089

Fordney-McCumber Tariff, 818

Foreign Miners' Tax, 441

Foreign policy: under John Quincy Adams, 307–308; aggression in, 690–695; under Bush, 1105–1110; under Carter, 1093–1097; China and, 1025–1027; under Cleveland, 693–694, 697; expansionist, 682–683, 685–694; under Benjamin Harrison, 689, 690–693; isolationist, 683–685, 861, 865, 867, 934; under Jefferson, 250–264; under Kennedy, 1006–1008, 1011, 1092; under Monroe, 278; nationalism and, 278–280; under Nixon, 1025–1029, 1093; post-War of 1812, 278–280; progressivism in, 744–748; under Reagan, 1100–1101; Reconstruction-era, 683–690; under Theodore Roosevelt, 744–746; under Taft, 746; between World Wars, 859–861

Forest Reserve Act, 1076

Forty-niners, 443

Foster, Stephen, 367–368

Fourier, Charles, 350

Four-Party Treaty, 860

Fourteen Points, 781–782, 784, 785

Fourteenth Amendment, 537, 538, 541, 542, 557, 558, 573, 589, 651, 672

Fox, George, 81–82

Fox Indians, 230, 314, 424

Fragging, 1019, 1028

France, 825; and the American Revolution, 168–169, 172, 174, 176–178, 194; Catholicism in, 24; Citizen Genêt Affair, 229; French Revolution, 227–229; and fur trade, 108; and the Louisiana Purchase, 251–254; as nation-state, 14, 16; and Native Americans, 105, 109, 110, 119; in the New World, 21–22, 24, 32–34, 104–105, 109, 123; pre-World War II, 864; quasi war with, 235–236; slavery and, 454; and the Treaty of Versailles, 782, 784; and Vietnam, 1000–1001, 1009–1010; and World War I, 760, 761, 762, 766; and World War II, 866, 880; XYZ affair, 235–236

Francis I, King of France, 21

Franco, Francisco, 864, 900

Frank, Leo, 613

Frankfurter, Felix, 900

Franklin, Benjamin, 77, 92, 99, 140, 173, 202, 204; and Albany Plan of Union, 108; *Autobiography*, 101–103; and the Constitution, 206, 207, 209; in England, 131–132; in Paris, 169; and secular learning, 98

Franklin, Josiah, 101

Franklin, William, 103

Fredericksburg, battle of, 487, 511

Frederick the Great, King of Prussia, 109

Free blacks, 204, 294, 343–344, 345, 405–407, 457–460, 526–527, 528–530, 532–533, 535–537, 547–549

Freedmen's Bureau, 528–530, 537, 542, 543, 548

Freedom of Information Act, 1036, 1087

Freedom riders, 1040–1044

Freedom Train, 919

Free enterprise, 571–573

Freemasons, 304, 321, 324, 464

Freemen, 53, 54

Free Soil party, 345, 442, 452, 457–460, 478; and Bleeding Kansas, 470–473, 476

Frelinghuysen, Frederick T., 688

Frelinghuysen, Theodorus, 99

Frémont, John C., 422, 438; Civil War and, 506; in the election of 1856, 473–474

French and Indian War, 109, 110

French Revolution, 227–229

Freneau, Philip, 228

Freud, Sigmund, 626, 803, 804

Frick, Henry Clay, 669

Friedan, Betty, 960, 1059–1060, 1064, 1066

Friends of the Earth, 993

Fries, John, 237

Fries Rebellion, 237

Fruitlands, 354–358

Fuchs, Klaus, 919

Fuel Administration, 770

Fuentes, Albert, 1070

Fugitive Slave Law, 457–464, 477

Fugitive slaves, 346, 457–464, 477

Fulk, Joseph R., 639

Fuller, Margaret, 352, 354

Fuller, R. Buckminster, 851

Fulton, Robert, 281, 284, 285

Fulton's folly, 281

Fur trade, 33–34, 108, 199, 230–231, 422, 431–432

Gadsden, James, 467

Gadsden Purchase, 467, 469

Gadsen, Christopher, 134

Gage, Thomas, 139–140, 142, 151–152, 154, 156–157, 158, 163

Gag Rule, 324

Gall, Franz, 368

Gallatin, Albert, 247, 275–276, 652

Gallaudet, Thomas Hopkins, 342

Galloway, Charlie "Sweet Loving'," 629

Galloway, Joseph, 140, 142

Gálvez, Bernardo de, 178

Gama, Vasco da, 15

Gandhi, Mahatma, 954, 1040

Garbo, Greta, 799

Garden, Alexander, 98

Gardoqui, Diego de, 194

Garfield, James A.: assassination of, 657, 688; in the election of 1880, 657; presidency of, 650

Garies and Their Friends (Webb), 360

Garrison, William Lloyd, 343–346, 439, 478, 480, 802

Garter, Robert, 459

Garvey, Marcus, 810, 1048, 1049

Gary, Elbert, 564

Garza, Eligio de la, 1071

Gaspeé affair, 137

Gates, Bill, 984

Gates, Horatio, 170, 171, 174–175, 192–193

Gates, Thomas, 43

Gatling, Richard J., 764

Gatling gun, 764

Gay and lesbian liberation, 1074–1075

Gay Liberation Front, 1075

Gazette of the United States, 228

Gell, Monday, 293

General Agreement on Trade and Tariffs (GATT), 1111

General Federation of Women's Clubs, 728

General Motors Corporation, 796, 842–843, 1036, 1088

Genêt, Edmond Charles, 229

Geneva Conference, 940

Genovese, Vito, 922

George, Henry, 721

George, Milton, 665

George II, King of England, 106, 109

George III, King of England, 118, 119, 130, 131, 136, 139, 142, 151, 158, 161–163, 196, 277

Georgia: colonization of, 106; free blacks in, 204; secession of, 489; state constitution, 187; and westward expansion, 229

Germain, George (Lord Germain), 162, 169, 173

Germany: African colonies, 762, 881; and the American Revolution, 163, 164; Berlin airlift, 909–910; economic growth of, 1089, 1112; immigrants from, 92–93, 387–390, 465, 878; invasion of Poland, 865–867, 883, 903; invasion of Soviet Union, 867, 868, 881; Nazi party, 825, 861–862, 864–865, 874; post–World War I, 1091; post-World War II, 903, 904–905; pre-World War II, 861–862, 864–865; reparations bill, 862; in Samoa, 690–691, 695; and Treaty of Versailles, 781, 783, 784; and World War I, 759, 760–762, 763, 764–765, 766–767, 768, 769, 778; and World War II, 874, 880–886

Gerrymandering, 478, 1071

Gershwin, George, 801

Gestapo, 862

Gettysburg, battle of, 512–513, 514–515, 657

Ghettoes, 619–620, 794–795

Ghost Dance, 555

Giannini, G. P., 979

Gibbons v. *Ogden*, 277

GI Bill of Rights, 873

Gibraltar, 172, 178

Gibson, Hoot, 977

Gideon v. *Wainwright*, 1054

Gilbert, Humphrey, 26

Gilded Age, 650–677, 720, 721, 723

Gillespie, Archibald H., 437

Gingrich, Newt, 995

Ginsberg, Allen, 962–963

Glasnost, 1101

Glass-Steagall Act, 836

Glorious Revolution, 86–87, 89

Glover, Joshua, 460

Godey's Ladies Book, 347

Godfather, The (Puzo), 923

Godkin, Edwin L., 632, 658, 692, 708

Godspeed (ship), 30

Godwin, William, 202

Going After Cacciato (O'Brien), 1031

Gold, 656–657

Gold, Harry, 919

Gold Democrats, 648

Golden Orange, The (Wambaugh), 969

Goldman, Emma, 767

Gold Rush, 441, 442–444, 451, 565–566

Gold Standard Act, 677

Goldstein, Robert, 774

Goldwater, Barry, 969, 984–989, 992, 995, 1002, 1012–1013, 1097–1098

Goldwyn, Samuel, 639, 902

Golf, 636

Gomez, Maximo, 696

Gompers, Samuel, 599, 613–614, 673, 676, 708, 732

Gomulka, Wladyslaw, 941

Gone With the Wind (film), 392

Gonzales, Henry B., 1071

Gonzales, Rodolfo ("Corky"), 1071

González, Pablo, 747

Goodman, Andrew, 1050

Goodman, Benny, 798

Goodman, Paul, 1057

Good Neighbor Policy, 860–861

Goodyear, Charles, 203

Goold, Margerie, 61

Gorbachev, Mikhail, 1101–1102, 1104, 1106–1107

Gordon, Thomas, 136

Gore, Thomas, 768

Gorky, Maxim, 638

Gosiute Indians, 417, 419

Gospel of Wealth, 570–571, 721

Gouging matches, 364–365

Gouzenko, Igor, 919

Grady, Henry W., 587–588

Graham, Martha, 850–851

Gramm, Phil, 994, 995

Grand Canyon, 19

Grand Coulee Dam, 978

Grand State Alliance, 666

Grange, Harold "Red," 799

Grangers, 659–660, 665–666, 687

Grant, Madison, 612

Grant, Ulysses S., 435, 713; and black suffrage, 540–543; Civil War and, 494, 500, 501, 513, 516, 520; in the election of 1880, 657; election to presidency, 540, 551; expansionism of, 682–683; and the Reconstruction, 540, 551; re-election, 551

Grapes of Wrath (Steinbeck), 851

Gray, John, 134

Gray, Samuel, 135

Gray, Simon, 401

Great American Desert, 422, 581

Great Awakening, 90, 99–104, 397; second, 334–335

Great Basin, 417, 419

Great Britain. *See* Britain

Great Compromise, 207–208

Great Depression, 818–819, 824–851, 862, 865, 900; as global phenomenon, 975–876; Hoover and, 828–829; human toll of, 826–828; impact of, 825–828; New Deal programs, 836–849; reasons for, 816–819; Roosevelt and, 830–850; unemployment in, 825, 826, 827, 829, 839, 1070

Great Gatsby, The (Fitzgerald), 801

Great Migration, 53, 776–777

Great Society, 968, 987, 1013, 1031, 1052–1054, 1079

Great Strike of 1877, 595–596, 597

Great Train Robbery, The (film), 639, 977

Great War. *See* World War I

Great White Fleet, 745

Greece, 906, 907

Greeley, Horace, 354, 385, 424, 489–490, 507, 542, 551

Greenback party, 656, 657, 667

Greenbacks, 504, 551–552, 656–657

Green Berets, 1011

Green Berets, The (film), 968–969

Greene, Catharine, 376

Greene, Nathanael, 165, 175–176

Greenfield Village, 850

Greenglass, David, 919

Greenhouse effect, 1077

Greenland, 11, 869

Greensboro sit-in, 1039–1040

Green Spring faction, 84–85

Greer, Germaine, 1066

Grenada, 454, 1100

Grenville, George, 119–124, 130, 136

Gresham, Walter Q., 689

Grey, Edward, 763

Grey, Zane, 799, 976

Gridley, Richard, 156

Griffin, John Howard, 947, 950

Griggs v. *Duke Power Company*, 1067

Grimké, Angelina, 348

Grimké, Sarah, 348

Grinnell, Josiah B., 424

Guadalcanal, battle of, 886, 890

Guam, 690, 704, 705, 870, 886, 887

Guatemala, 944, 945, 1007

Guiteau, Charles, 657

Gulf of Tonkin Resolution, 1013–1014, 1031

Gunboat diplomacy, 860

Gutenberg, Johannes, 14

Guthrie, Woody, 824, 827, 840, 850

Guyana, 453

Gwynn, Nell, 79

Haciendas, 20, 21

Hague Conference, 760

Haiti, 251–252, 293, 746, 860, 861, 1112

Hakluyt, Richard, 25–26

Halberstam, David, 1011

Haldeman, H. R., 1022, 1023

Hale, Eugene, 689

Hale, Sarah J., 347
Haley, Bill, 962
Half-Breeds, 652–653, 657
Half-Way Covenant, 64–65
Hall, G. Stanley, 803
Halleck, Henry W., 494, 497, 500, 511
Halley, Rudolph, 922
Hamilton, Alexander, 191–192, 227, 231, 233, 236, 252, 254, 325, 380; and the Constitution, 206; duel with Burr, 244–245, 252–253; and the *Federalist Papers*, 209–210; financial program, 218, 222–225, 228, 229, 245, 247, 572; and patronage, 227–228; and yellow fever, 227
Hamlet, James, 460
Hammett, Dashiell, 850
Hammond, William, 640
Hancock, John, 132, 151, 152
Hancock, Winfield Scott, 515, 657
Handsome Lake (Seneca), 230
Hanna, Mark, 673, 732, 736
Hardin, John Wesley, 583
Harding, Warren G., 788; and big business, 812; in the election of 1920, 786
Harlem Globetrotters, 948, 949
Harlem Renaissance, 810–811
Harper's Ferry raid, 478–480
Harriman, Averell, 904
Harrington, Michael, 1057
Harris, George Washington, 366
Harrison, Benjamin, 582, 650, 654, 669; and big business, 661; election to presidency, 661; foreign policy of, 689, 690–693
Harrison, William Henry, 258, 262–263, 264, 431, 624; in the Battle of Tippecanoe, 260, 262–263, 300, 324; death, 324, 450–451; in the election of 1836, 324; election to presidency, 300–301, 324
Harrison Anti-Narcotic Act, 640
Harrison Narcotic Act, 744
Hart, William S., 977
Harte, Bret, 366, 625, 706
Hartford Convention, 264
Harvard, 55, 100, 116, 124, 284, 351, 354, 398, 632, 633
Harvey, John, 45
Harvey, William H., 672
Hat Act, 89
Hatch, Orrin, 993
Hatch Act, 586
Hawaii, 688, 690, 705; annexation controversy, 693–694; expansionism and, 692–694; Japanese in, 879; Pearl Harbor attack, 867, 869–871; in Young America policy, 466
Hawkins, Connie, 948
Hawkins, John, 24
Hawley-Smoot Tariff, 818
Hawthorne, Nathaniel, 351, 352, 354, 358–359, 363
Hay, John, 689–690, 704, 711–712, 745
Hay-Bunau-Varilla Treaty, 745
Haycox, Ernest, 976
Hayden, Tom, 1056
Hayes, Lucy, 656

Hayes, Rutherford B., 595–596, 650, 656–658, 684, 688; election to presidency, 557–558, 656
Hay-Herrán Treaty, 745
Haymarket Square riot, 596–597, 598–599, 668, 687, 740
Hayne, Robert Y., 316
Haynes, Marques, 948
Haywood, "Big Bill," 767
Head rights, 43
Hearst, William Randolph, 696–697, 698, 701–703, 843
Heenan, James C., 634
Hell's Angels, 1058
Helper, Hinton Rowan, 407–408
Hemings, Sally, 218
Hemingway, Ernest, 800, 801
Henderson, Fletcher, 798
Henderson, Oran, 1005
Hennessy, David, 612
Henri, Robert, 627
Henry, John, 140
Henry, Patrick, 129, 140–141, 201, 210
Henry, Prince of Portugal ("the Navigator"), 14, 15, 66
Henry VII, King of England (Henry Tudor), 14, 21
Henry VIII, King of England, 22–23
Henson, Josiah, 360, 402, 462
Hepburn Act, 749
Herkimer, Nicholas, 171
Herr, Michael, 1019
Herrera, José, 437
Herschel, John, 363
Hester Street (painting), 627
Heth, Joice, 366
Hickock, Wild Bill, 583
Hidalgo y Costilla, Miguel, 416
Higginson, Thomas Wentworth, 508
Higher Education Act, 1052
Highways, 796, 936–938, 983
Hill, James J., 738
Hill, Lucille Eaton, 637
Hill, Wills (Lord Hillsborough), 132–133
Hillbilly music, 798
Hillman, Sidney, 842
Himmler, Heinrich, 858
Hirohito, Emperor of Japan, 891
Hispaniola, 16, 79
Hiss, Alger, 900–902, 919
History of Massachusetts Bay (Hutchinson), 51
History of Plymouth Plantation (Bradford), 49–52
Hitler, Adolf, 825, 858, 861–863, 864–867, 869, 874, 884, 886, 890, 900, 906
Hoar, George Frisbie, 708
Hobbes, Thomas, 364
Ho Chi Minh, 1000–1001, 1009, 1023, 1031
Hofstadter, Richard, 924
Hogan, James J., 632
Holbrook, Josiah, 367
Holland. *See* Dutch, the
Holliday, Doc, 583
Hollywood. *See* Movie industry
Hollywood Ten, 924–925
Holmes, Oliver Wendell, 723, 774, 780, 900

Holocaust, 858–859, 862, 864, 878–879
Home Insurance Building, 618
Homeowners Loan Act, 836
Homer, Winslow, 627
Homestead Act, 504, 572, 584–585
Homestead strike, 669, 695
Homosexuality, 926; and AIDS, 990–991; gay and lesbian liberation, 1074–1075
Honduras, 398, 466–467, 746, 1100
Hong Kong, 870, 886
Hood, James Walker, 544
Hood, Zachariah, 129
Hooker, Joseph ("Fighting Joe"), 494, 511–512
Hooker, Thomas, 57
Hoover, Herbert, 812–815, 826, 831, 861, 863, 977; in the election of 1928, 813–814; election to presidency, 814; and the Great Depression, 828–829; as head of Food Administration, 770–771
Hoover, J. Edgar, 780, 925–926
Hoover (Boulder) Dam, 977
Hoovervilles, 826, 829
Hope, John, 674
Hopi Indians, 9, 417, 552
Hopkins, Elizabeth, 62
Hopkins, Harry, 839–840, 851
Hopkins, Oceanus, 62
Hopkins, Stephen, 123–124
Horse-drawn omnibus, 617–618, 623
Horses, 34
Horseshoe Bend, battle of, 261
House, Edward, 763
Household industries, 379–382
House Un-American Activities Committee (HUAC), 901–902, 924–925
Housing: Hoovervilles, 826, 829; post-World War II, 947; public, 813; in the suburbs, 795, 937, 947, 955–956, 960, 982; urban, 289–290, 619–622, 794–795; during World War II, 877
Housing and Urban Development, Department of, 1052
Houston, Charles, 952
Houston, Sam, 427–430, 431
Howard, Oliver O., 528
Howe, David, 219
Howe, Frederick, 779
Howe, Julia Ward, 342, 655
Howe, Richard (Lord Howe), 163–165
Howe, Samuel Gridley, 342
Howe, William, 148, 151, 156–158, 163–166, 169, 171, 173
Howells, William Dean, 621, 626, 708
How the Other Half Lives (Riis), 613
Hudson, Henry, 32–33
Hudson River school, 361
Hudson's Bay Company, 431, 432
Huerta, Victoriano, 747–748, 783
Hughes, Charles Evans, 744, 768, 780, 860
Hughes, John, 465
Hughes, Langston, 800, 811
Huguenots, 23–24
Huitzilopochtli, 7
Hulbert, William A., 631
Hull, Cordell, 861, 863, 869

Hull House, 729
Human rights, 184–185, 196–206, 1095
Humor, 366
Humphrey, George, 935
Humphrey, Hubert, 1021–1023
Huneker, James Gibbons, 638
Hungary, 941–942
Hunt, Henry J., 514–515
Hunt, Howard, 1084
Hunt, Thomas, 4
Huron Indians, 119
Hurston, Zora Neale, 811
Hussein, Saddam, 1108
Huston, John, 874
Hutchinson, Anne, 55–56, 81, 351
Hutchinson, Thomas, 51, 108, 116–117, 122, 124–125, 127, 128, 129, 136, 138–139
Hyde Amendment, 1067–1068

Iacocca, Lee, 1088–1089
Ice age, 5
Iceland, 869
Ickes, Harold, 839
Ickes, Harry, 848
Immigration, 607–615; Chinese, 583, 610, 613, 614–615, 662; colonial, 91–93; and the film industry, 639–640; German, 92–93, 387–390, 465, 878; and growth of cities, 616, 619–620, 794; Irish, 92, 361, 386–387, 465, 595; Italian, 609–610, 612, 613, 878, 923; Japanese, 878, 879–880; Jewish, 610–611, 612, 613, 678–679; and Know Nothing party, 464–466, 652; Mexican, 877–878, 1072; migrant workers, 609–610, 1062–1063; nativism and, 611–615, 807–808; new immigrants, 607–615, 652, 808; nineteenth-century, 386; old immigrants, 608; permanent immigrants, 610–611; Polish, 610, 611; in the Progressive era, 732; quota system, 615, 808, 878–879; restrictions on, 614, 615, 808, 817, 858, 878–879; Russian, 610–611, 612; sports and, 630, 652; temperance and, 338; and urban segregation, 619–620; World War II and, 878–880; xenophobia and, 807–808
Immigration Act of 1924, 879
Immigration Reform and Control Act, 1071
Immigration Restriction League, 614
Impending Crisis of the South, The, 407–408
Imperialism, 682–713; and Alaska, 685; and Chile, 691–692; Congress and, 683–685; and Cuba, 690, 695–705, 706–707, 745; and the Dominican Republic, 682–683, 685, 746; exceptionalism and, 686–687; and Guam, 690; and Hawaii, 690, 692–694; New Navy and, 688–690, 691, 692; and the Philippines, 690, 705–711; and Samoa, 690–691; and Wake Island, 690; white man's burden and, 686–688; yellow press and, 689–690, 696–699, 701–703

Imperial Valley, 977–978
Imperial wars, 104–109
Impost Plan, 192, 193
Impressment, 254–255, 256
Incas, 7, 19
Indentured servants, 40, 42–43, 59, 61–64, 67, 220
Indianapolis Clowns, 948–949
Indian Appropriations Act, 314
Indian Child Welfare Act, 1074
Indian Education Act, 1074
Indian Emergency Conservation Program (IECP), 848
Indian Health Care Act, 1074
Indian Historical Society, 1073
Indian Peace Commission, 554
Indian Reorganization Act, 848
Indians of All Tribes, 1072
Indigo, 77, 90
Industrialization: big business and, 574–580; and capital formation, 573–574; and deindustrialization, 1091; early nineteenth-century, 285–287; and laissez-faire economics, 571–573, 584, 624, 651, 663, 719, 721, 722; mineral resources and, 565–567, 575–576, 581; in the New South, 587–590, 972, 973–975; in the North, 377–385, 390–391; railroads and, 565, 568–569, 572–573, 575, 577, 578, 580; social class and, 385–386, 390–391; Social Darwinism and, 570–571, 612, 651; technological change and, 567–568; in the twentieth century, 564–580; workers and, 590–599
Industrial Revolution, 378–379, 387
Industrial Workers of the World (IWW; Wobblies), 767, 771–772, 774, 780
Infant mortality, 1051
Inflation, 25, 656–657; under Reaganomics, 1098–1100, 1102; stagflation, 1091–1092; and the Vietnam War, 1089–1090, 1092; during World War II, 872–873, 916
Influence of Sea Power upon History, The (Mahan), 689
Ingersoll, Jared, 129
Initiatives, 667, 749
Installment credit, 797, 817
Instinct of Workmanship, The (Veblen), 722–723
Institutes of the Christian Religion (Calvin), 23
Institutional economists, 722–723
Institutional racism, 972
Intercontinental ballistic missiles (ICBMs), 1027, 1093
Intermediate-range ballistic missiles (IRBMs), 1007–1008
Internal Revenue Service, 1086
International Harvester Corporation, 592
International Ladies' Garment Workers, 842
Interstate commerce, 206
Interstate Commerce Act, 660, 661
Interstate Commerce Commission (ICC), 572, 660, 738–740, 741, 749, 1040
Invasion of the Body Snatchers (film), 960

Iowa: admitted as free state, 452; settlement of, 424–425
Iran, 944, 945, 1007, 1090, 1095; hostage crisis, 1095–1096
Iran-contra affair, 1100–1101, 1102
Iraq, 942; and the Persian Gulf War, 1108–1110
Ireland: English raids on, 26; immigrants from, 92, 361, 386–387, 465, 595; independence of, 762; Irish Rebellion, 762, 763; potato famine, 386
Iron Act, 89
Iron Curtain, 906, 941
Iron plows, 286
Iroquois, 10, 33–34, 80, 85, 108, 110, 171, 174, 199. See also Five Nations of Iroquois; Six Nations of Iroquois
Iroquois Confederacy, 10, 80, 85, 108, 110, 171
Irrigation, 584
Irving, Washington, 351
Isabella, Queen of Spain (Isabella of Castile), 14–16
Isolationism, 683–685, 861, 865, 867, 934
Israel: and Camp David Accords, 1093–1094, 1097; and the Persian Gulf War, 1110; Yom Kippur War, 1090
Italy: Black Death in, 12; fascism in, 759, 825; immigrants from, 609–610, 612, 613, 878, 923; and Mediterranean trade, 13; pre-World War II, 863–864, 865; Renaissance in, 13; during World War II, 880, 882–883, 884
Ives, Charles, 801
I Was a Teenage Werewolf (film), 925
Iwo Jima, battle of, 887

Jackson, Andrew, 260–261, 264, 273, 306–321, 326–327, 340, 427; assassination attempt, 450, 451; Battle of New Orleans and, 261, 264, 271, 280; egalitarianism and, 310–311; in the election of 1824, 306; election to presidency, 308–310; and expanding powers of presidency, 311–312; Indian policy, 312–315, 321, 554; judicial appointments, 320–321; legacy of, 321; and public land disputes, 315–316; reelection, 318–319; and second Bank of the United States, 318–319; and Seminoles of Florida, 279; tariffs under, 316–318; and Texas question, 430
Jackson, Thomas J. ("Stonewall"), 435–436, 496, 499, 508, 512
Jackson, Tony, 629
Jackson State University, 1024
Jacob, Kathryn Allamong, 607
Jacobs, Harriet, 360
Jagger, Mick, 1058
Jamaica, 79, 405, 453
James, Frank, 583
James, Henry, 618–619, 727
James, Jesse, 583
James, William, 710, 723
James I, King of England (James Stuart), 30, 41, 44–45, 52–53

James II, King of England (Duke of York), 80–81, 86–87
Jamestown, 31–32, 40–45
Japan: attack on Pearl Harbor, 867, 869–871; bombing of, 889–892; economic growth of, 1089, 1112; immigrants from, 878, 879–880; invasion of Manchuria, 825, 863, 869; isolationism of, 466; militarism in, 825; and the Philippines, 860; pre-World War II, 863, 864, 865; Russo-Japanese War, 744–745; Stimson Doctrine, 863; and the Treaty of Versailles, 782; and Vietnam, 1009; during World War II, 880, 881, 886–892
Jaworski, Leon, 1085
Jay, John, 140, 178, 222, 231; and the *Federalist Papers*, 209–210; as secretary of foreign affairs, 194
Jay's Treaty, 231–232, 235
Jazz, 629, 630, 798, 801
Jazz Age, 798, 799
Jefferson, Martha, 218
Jefferson, Thomas, 116, 189, 196–197, 199, 228–229, 236–239, 245–252, 254–256, 274, 275, 281, 285, 294–295, 306, 307, 325, 360; and Barbary pirates, 250–251; and Declaration of Independence, 160–162, 186, 246; and education, 340, 398; in the election of 1796, 233; election to presidency, 245–246; Embargo Act, 255–256; on the French Revolution, 228; and the judicial branch, 248–250; Lewis and Clark expedition, 252, 421; and Louisiana Purchase, 251–254, 421; and Native American policy, 312; on North versus South, 391; reelection, 254; and religious freedom, 196–197; and republican government, 245–246, 247–248; and revolution of 1800, 237–239; as secretary of state, 222–225; and slavery, 204–205, 218, 246, 291, 305, 398–399, 459; and War of 1812, 258; and Whiskey Rebellion, 229, 237
Jeffersonian Republicans. *See* Republican party (Jeffersonian)
Jenkins, Robert, 106
Jenney, William LeBaron, 618
Jeremiads, 65, 85
Jews: and Anti-Semitism, 612, 613; and the film industry, 639–640; and the Holocaust, 858–859, 862, 864, 878–879; immigration of, 610–611, 612, 613, 878–879; population growth of, 336
Jiang Jieshi (Chiang Kai-shek), 910–911, 938, 1093
Jim Crow laws, 628–629, 636, 674–675, 700, 736, 753, 946–955, 1040. *See also* Civil rights movement
Jingoism, 692, 695
Job Corps, 1052
Joffre, Joseph, 765
John Brown's Raid, 478–480
John I, King of Portugal, 14
John II, King of Portugal, 15

Johnson, Andrew, 517, 685; impeachment threat, 540; and the Reconstruction, 530, 534–540; as successor to Lincoln, 534–535
Johnson, Anthony, 40
Johnson, Bunk, 629
Johnson, Guy, 170
Johnson, Hugh, 838
Johnson, James Weldon, 810
Johnson, Lyndon B., 970, 1008–1009, 1046, 1048, 1078; and civil rights movement, 1051–1054; in the election of 1964, 986–987; election to presidency, 987, 1012; Great Society programs, 968, 987, 1013, 1031, 1052–1054; as successor to Kennedy, 1013–1014; and Vietnam, 968, 1008–1009, 1013–1018, 1031, 1089–1090; and women's rights, 1064–1065
Johnson, Tom L., 733
Johnston, Albert Sidney, 494, 500
Johnston, Augustus, 129
Johnston, Joseph E., 494, 499, 516
Joint-stock trading companies, 30, 79, 138–139
Jones, Buck, 977
Jones, John Paul, 178
Jones, Samuel "Golden Rule," 733
Joplin, Scott, 629–630
Jordan, 1094
Jordan, David Starr, 708
Joseph (Nez Percé), 553
Joseph, William, 87
Journal Intime (Thoreau), 726–727
Journalism: muckraking, 218–219, 724–725, 728, 740; public opinion and, 689–690; yellow press, 689–690, 696–699, 701–703
Judicial branch, 221, 651. *See also* Supreme Court, U.S.; Jefferson and, 248–250; post-War of 1812, 277–278
Judicial review, 249
Judiciary Act of 1789, 221, 248
Judiciary Act of 1801, 248, 249–250
Judiciary Act of 1802, 248
Julian, George, 543
Jungle, The (Sinclair), 725, 740
Junk bonds, 1099–1100
Justice Department, U.S., 661, 774, 871

Kaiser, Henry J., 979
Kamikaze attacks, 887, 890
Kampuchea (Cambodia), 1024, 1029, 1086
Kansas: Bleeding, 470–473; Kansas-Nebraska Act, 467–470, 473, 477, 478, 481; Lecompton Constitution, 475–476, 477; and the Populist party, 667; sack of Lawrence, 471–472; and slavery, 467–473, 475–476, 477, 478, 481
Kansas-Nebraska Act, 467–470, 473, 477, 478, 481
Karankawa Indians, 419
Karnow, Stanley, 1011
Kasson, John A., 687
Kaufman, Irving R., 919

Kearns, Doris, 1031
Kearny, Stephen, 438
Keating-Owen Child Labor Act, 744
Keaton, Buster, 799
Keats, John, 727
Kefauver, Estes, 922
Kefauver Crime Committee, 922–923
Keller, K. T., 1088
Kellogg, Frank B., 860
Kellogg, Will K., 728
Kellogg-Briand Pact, 860
Kelly, Florence, 729
Kempton, Murray, 1021
Kendall, Amos, 308–309
Kennan, George, 906–907, 908–909
Kennedy, John F., 246, 984, 1001–1003, 1006–1008, 1063, 1092, 1107; assassination, 1008, 1011, 1049; civil rights movement and, 1040, 1045–1046; Cuba and, 1006–1008; debates with Nixon, 1001–1002; domestic policy, 1003–1006; election to presidency, 1002–1003; and Vietnam, 1011; and women's rights, 1061
Kennedy, John Pendleton, 392, 463
Kennedy, Joseph, 867–868
Kennedy, Robert, 1003, 1006, 1007, 1020–1021
Kenton, Simon, 198
Kent State University, 1024
Kentucky: as border state, 491, 528; and westward expansion, 198, 229; Wilderness Road, 198
Kerner, Otto, 1051
Kerouac, Jack, 963, 1056
Kesey, Ken, 992
Keteltas, William, 233
Kettle Hill, battle of, 707
Key, Ellen, 803
Key, Francis Scott, 260–261
Khe Sanh, battle of, 1016
Khomeini, Ayatollah Ruholla, 1095
Khrushchev, Nikita, 909, 940–942, 945–946, 1007
Kickapoo Indians, 230, 274
Kieft, William, 80
Kilrain, Jake, 635
Kilroy, Mathew, 134–135
Kim Il Sung, 912–913
Kinetophonograph, 638–639
King, Martin Luther, Jr., 461, 954–955, 973, 1038–1039, 1044–1051, 1055; assassination, 1051; in the Birmingham demonstrations, 1041–1044
King, Rufus, 293
King George's War, 106
King Philip's War, 58
Kings Mountain, battle of, 175
King William's War, 105
Kinsey, Alfred, 804, 1075
Kiowa Indians, 419, 1074
Kissinger, Henry, 1022–1023, 1025, 1027, 1028, 1093
Knights of the Golden Circle, 398
Know Nothing (American) party, 464–466, 469–470, 473, 488, 652
Knox, Henry, 222
Knox, John, 23, 52

Knox, Philander C., 718
Knute Rockne, All American (film), 1097
Koch, Robert, 322, 726
Koop, C. Everett, 991
Korean War, 911–915, 921, 934
Korechika, Anami, 891
Korematsu v. *United States*, 880
Koster, Samuel, 1005
Kristallnacht, 863
Ku Klux Klan, 549–550, 682, 808–809, 812, 1048
Kuwait, and the Persian Gulf War, 1108–1110

Labor Department, U.S., 1064
Labor unions. *See also* Work force: after World War II, 916–917; early, 597–599; forerunners of, 383–384; formation of, 595; and length of work day, 384, 592–593; and nativism, 807–808; post-World War I, 779–781; and social class, 385–386; strikes, 595–596, 597–599, 669–670, 687, 694, 695, 718, 736, 738, 774, 779–781, 839, 842–843; in World War I, 771–772, 774
La Causa, 1063
Ladies Magazine, 347
LaFarge, John, 627
Lafayette, Marquis de, 148
La Follette, Robert, 734, 741, 812–813, 867–868
La Guardia, Fiorello, 868
Laird, Melvin, 1005
Laissez-faire economics, 571–573, 584, 624, 651, 663, 719, 721, 722
Lake Erie, battle of, 259–260
L'Amour, Louis, 976–977
Lamy, Jean-Baptiste, 360
Land: and conservation movement, 738; Florida land boom, 814–815; Indian policy and, 198–199, 312–315, 553–557, 662, 1074; legislation regarding, 504, 572, 584, 586; and Mexican Americans, 1071; Northwest Ordinance, 199, 208, 291; post-Civil War distribution of, 529–530, 535, 542; public, disputes over, 315–316; and railroads, 572–573; and squatters, 425
Land banks, 116, 117, 122
Landon, Alfred M., 844
Land tenure, 303–304
Land warrant certificates, 197
Lane, Ralph, 27
Lansing, Robert, 763, 938
Laos, 1007
La Raza Unida, 1071
Larcom, Lucy, 382–383
Lardner, Ring, Jr., 924
Large policy, 690
Las Casas, Bartolomé de, 20–21
Latrobe, Benjamin, 234
Latvia, 784, 865, 883, 1104, 1106
Laud, William, 53
Laulewasika (Tenskwatawa; Shawnee), 258, 262–263
Lauren, Ralph, 976
Laurie, Walter, 152

Lawes Divine, Moral, and Martiall (Dale), 43
Lawrence (ship), 260
Lawrence, Richard, 340, 450
Lawrence, T. E., 762
Lawrence, William, 571
League of Nations, 781, 782, 784, 785, 787, 860, 863, 864, 865, 880
League of United Latin American Citizens (LULAC), 1070–1071
Leary, Timothy, 1058
Lease, Mary E., 663, 666
Leaves of Grass (Whitman), 359–360
Lebanon, 942, 944–945
Lebensraum, 862
Le Carré, John, 1107
Lecompton Constitution, 475–476, 477
Lee, Ann, 349
Lee, Arthur, 169
Lee, Daniel, 432
Lee, Jason, 432
Lee, Richard Henry, 160–161, 210, 240
Lee, Robert E., 435, 508; Civil War and, 486, 491, 493, 494, 499–500, 511–516, 520; and Harpers Ferry raid, 479–480
Legal system, 283–284. *See also* Judicial branch; capital punishment, 340; prisons in, 339–340
Legislative branch, 222. *See also* Congress, U.S.
Leisler, Jacob, 87, 89
Le May, Alan, 976
Lemon, Meadowlark, 948
Lend-lease bill, 868–869
Lenin, V. I., 762, 783–784, 1106
Lenorson, Samuel, 76
Leopard (ship), 255
Leo XIII, Pope, 640, 724
Lettered citizens, 933
Letters from a Farmer in Pennsylvania (Dickinson), 132
Letters on the Condition of Women and the Equality of the Sexes (Grimké), 348
Levitt, William, 947
Levittown, 947
Lewis, Isham, 398
Lewis, John L., 842, 916
Lewis, Lilburne, 398–399
Lewis, Meriwether, 252, 421
Lewis, Sinclair, 801
Liberal Republicans, 551
Liberation politics, 992–994, 1059–1077
Liberator, The, 344, 368, 439
Liberia, 343, 506
Liberty (ship), 132–133
Liberty party, 345, 442
Liberty Tree, 125, 127
Libya, 864
Life and Adventures of Joaquin Murieta, The (Ridge), 360
Life of Ma-Ka-Tai-Me-she-kia-Kiak or Black Hawk (Black Hawk), 360
Liliuokalani, Queen of Hawaii, 693–694
Limited liability doctrine, 573
Lincoln, Abraham, 246–247, 273, 388, 464, 469, 470, 475, 480, 488–491, 495–500, 736; assassination, 520, 534; Civil War and, 503–508, 511–513, 516,

530–531; debates with Douglas, 476–478; in the election of 1864, 517–518; election to presidency, 488–489; Emancipation Proclamation and, 487, 500, 506–511, 532–533; on the Know Nothing party, 466; and the Mexican-American War, 439; and the Reconstruction, 531–534; and secession of Southern states, 489–491
Lincoln, Benjamin, 174, 196
Lindbergh, Charles, 798
Lippard, George, 363
Lippmann, Walter, 723, 904, 909, 938–939
List, Friedrich, 284–285
Literacy tests, 614–615, 672
Literature: of abolitionism, 460–464; African American, 360, 404, 810–811; Beat Generation, 962–963; feminist, 1066; in the Great Depression, 850–851; Harlem Renaissance, 810–811; Mexican American, 360–361; Native American, 360; of the nineteenth century, 351–352, 355–357, 358–361, 460–464, 571; realism in, 624–626; of the twentieth century, 624–626, 800, 801, 810–811, 850–851
Lithuania, 784, 865, 883, 1104, 1106
Little Bighorn, battle of, 555
Little Men (Alcott), 354
Little Richard, 961
Little Women (Alcott), 354
Liuzzo, Viola, 1048
Livingston, Henry Beekman, 184
Livingston, Robert, 251
Lloyd George, David, 782, 784
Lochner v. *New York*, 723
Locke, John, 46, 95
Lodge, Henry Cabot, 614, 662, 683, 689–690, 694, 709, 720, 782, 785, 985
Lodge Bill, 662
Logan, James, 98
Lomax, Alan, 850
London, Jack, 1063
Lonely Crowd, The (Riesman), 960
Long, Breckinridge, 878–879
Long, Crawford, 285
Long, Huey, 841, 844
Long, Stephen H., 422
Longfellow, Henry Wadsworth, 351–352, 480
Longstreet, James, 514
Looking Backward (Bellamy), 721
Louisiana: colonization of, 104–105; in the Reconstruction, 531, 547, 550; secession of, 489
Louisiana Purchase, 251–254, 294, 421–422, 468
Louis IV, King of France, 105
Louis XI, King of France, 14
Louis XVI, King of France, 104, 168, 169, 172, 228
L'Ouverture, Toussaint, 252
Love Canal, 1077
Lovejoy, Elijah, 345
Lowell, Francis Cabot, 270
Lowell, James Russell, 355, 437, 625
Loyalists, 142
Loyal Nine, 125

Lucas, Eliza (Eliza Lucas Pinckney), 76, 77, 90
Lucas, George, 77
Lucas, James, 533
Luce, Henry, 911
Luciano, Charles, 922
Lucy, Autherine, 1040–1041
Luftwaffe, 867
Luks, George, 627
Lusitania (ship), 767
Luther, Martin, 22
Luxembourg, 866
Lyceum movement, 367
Lynching, 671–672, 779
Lyon, Mary, 341

MacArthur, Douglas, 881, 886–888, 889, 891, 935; and the Bonus Army, 831; Korea and, 914–915
Macaulay, Thomas Babington, 96
Macdonough, Thomas, 260
Macfadden, Bernard, 695
Machine guns, 762, 764
Mackintosh, Ebenezer, 125, 128, 135, 139
Maclean, Donald, 919
MacLeish, Archibald, 874
Macon's Bill No. 2, 256
Macune, Charles W., 666
Macy, Rowland H., 624, 641
Maddox (ship), 1013–1014
Maddox, Lester, 972, 973
Madero, Francisco I., 747
Madison, Dolley, 260
Madison, James, 191, 223, 228, 237, 248, 259, 260, 272, 276, 281, 305, 540; and the Constitution, 206, 207; election to presidency, 256; and the *Federalist Papers*, 209–210; reelection, 258; and War of 1812, 256–264
Madonna, 1099
Mafia, 612, 922–923
Magazines, 347, 363, 799–800, 851
Magellan, Ferdinand, 21
Maggie (Crane), 626
Maginot Line, 866
Magnalia Christi Americana (Mather), 51
Mahan, Alfred Thayer, 689
Mahican Indians, 9
Mail delivery, 677
Maine, 294, 431
Maine incident, 698, 701–703
Maine laws, 338
Main Street (Sinclair), 801
Makino, Nobuaki, 782
Malaeska, The Indian Wife (Beadle), 363
Malaya, 870, 886
Malcolm X (Malcolm Little), 1049–1050
Malenkov, Georgi, 926
Malthus, Thomas Robert, 202
Managerial styles, 577–578
Manchuria, 825, 863, 869, 914
Manhattan Project, 889, 890–891, 919
Manifest Destiny, 426–435, 747
Manitou, 10
Mann, Horace, 341
Mann Act, 741, 803
Mann-Elkins Act, 741

Manpower Development and Training Act, 1052
Manufacturing, 270–271; American system of production, 280, 285, 320; artisans in, 379–382; assembly lines in, 578–579, 795; decline of United States, 1091; early nineteenth-century, 285–287; factory system in, 220, 382–383, 591, 593–594; foreign competition in, 1091; growth of, 224–225; mass production in, 285, 578–579; post-War of 1812, 274, 280; and technological innovation, 284–285; in World War I, 770–772, 776–777
Manumission, 205
Mao Tse-tung (Mao Zedong), 910–911, 1009, 1027
Mapp v. *Ohio*, 1054
Marbury, William, 248–249
Marbury v. *Madison*, 249, 277, 475
Marcuse, Herbert, 1057
Marcy, William, 312
Mardi (Melville), 359
Marian exiles, 23, 24
Maria Theresa, Queen of Austria, 106
Marin, John, 627
Marion, Francis, 175
Marlboro Man, 975–976
Marne, battle of, 761
Marshall, George, 906, 908, 921, 934
Marshall, James W., 442–443, 445
Marshall, John, 248–249, 254, 277–278, 313, 320
Marshall, Thurgood, 1053
Marshall Plan, 907–908
Martin, Bradley, 579
Martin, Joseph Plumb, 148–149, 166, 179
Martínez, Antonio José, 360
Martin v. *Hunter's Lessee*, 277
Marx, Karl, 626
Marx Brothers, 851
Mary, Queen of Scots (Mary Stuart), 25
Mary I, Queen of England ("Bloody Mary"), 23
Mary II, Queen of England, 86–88
Maryland: as border state, 491; and ratification of Articles of Confederation, 189; slave trade in, 204–206; state constitution, 187
Maryland colony, 41, 45–47, 87, 89, 129, 167
Mason, George, 196
Mason, James M., 503
Mason-Dixon line, 280, 291, 377, 474, 546, 974, 975
Massachusetts: end of slavery in, 204; and ratification of the Constitution, 210, 211; Shays's Rebellion, 194–196, 206; state constitution, 159, 186
Massachusetts Bay colony, 52–58, 61, 64–65, 116–117; American Revolution in, 151–154, 156–157; Boston Massacre, 134–135, 136, 137; Boston Tea Party, 139; Coercive Acts, 139–140, 141, 142; Glorious Revolution, 86–87, 89; pastimes in, 96–97; witchcraft hysteria, 87–88
Massachusetts Government Act, 139

Massachusetts Land Bank, 116, 122
Massasoit (Wapanoag), 58
Mass production, 285, 578–579
Masterson, Bat, 583, 635
Mather, Cotton, 51, 62, 76–77, 96, 98
Mathews, Shailer, 633
Mattachine Society, 1075
Matthews, Robert (Matthias), 332
Maverick, Samuel, 135
Maxim, Hiram, 764
May, Alan Munn, 919
Mayas, 6–7
Mayflower (ship), 48, 49–51, 62
Mayflower Compact, 48
McCallum, Daniel, 577
McCarthy, Eugene, 1018, 1020
McCarthy, Joseph, 919–921, 922, 934, 957–958
McCarthyism, 919–921, 1075, 1097
McCauly, Mary Ludwig Hays, 200
McClain, Franklin, 1039
McClellan, George B., 436, 486–487, 494, 498–500, 507, 508, 511, 517, 518
McClure's, 632, 724
McCord, James, 1084
McCormick, Anne O'Hare, 907–908
McCormick Harvester Machine Company, 596
McCoy, Joseph G., 581
McCoy, Tim, 977
McCrea, Jane, 171
McCulloch v. *Maryland*, 277
McDowell, Irvin, 496, 498
McFeaing, John, 385
McGee, Frank, 1018
McGillivray, Alexander, 174, 229
McGovern, George, 1027
McKay, Claude, 811
McKinley, William, 703, 704, 710, 713; assassination, 613, 736; Cuba and, 697–705; in the election of 1896, 648–649, 672–673, 720; election to presidency, 677; Philippines and, 705–711; reelection, 736
McKinley Tariff, 661, 662, 669, 693
McLaurin, Melton A., 947
McLaurin v. *Board of Regents*, 950
McLemore, Jeff, 768
McNeill, Joseph, 1039
McParlan, James, 595
McPartland, Jimmy, 798
Mead, Margaret, 876
Meade, George G., 440, 494, 512–513, 516
Means, Gardiner, 836
Meany, George, 935
Meat Inspection Act, 740, 750
Meat-packing business, 578–579, 594, 725, 738, 740, 750
Mechaca, José Antonio, 361
Medicaid Act, 1053
Medical care: and AIDS, 990–991; for childbirth, 62–63; and cholera, 322–323; in the Civil War, 518–520; and gay rights, 1075; in the Progressive era, 725–728; for slaves, 458–459; and tuberculosis, 726–727; and Tuskegee syphilis study, 846–847; and yellow fever, 226–227, 622

Medicare, 1053
Medina, Ernest, 1005
Mein Kampf (Hitler), 862
Melodramas, 366–367
Melville, Herman, 358, 359, 438
Mencken, H. L., 96, 622, 801
Mengele, Josef, 858
Menominee Tribe v. *United States*, 1074
Mental testing, 777–778
Mercantilism, 78–79
Merchant capitalists, 30–31
Meredith, James, 1044, 1050
Merrimack (ship), 502
Merryman, Ex Parte, 504–505
Merryman, John, 505
Mesmerism, 368
Metacomet ("King Philip"; Wapanoag), 58
Methodists, 205, 292, 336, 396, 398, 432, 433
Metropolitan Life Insurance Building, 793
Mexican Americans: *bandidos*, 414; and the *bracero* program, 878, 1062–1063, 1070; in the Great Depression, 817, 827–828, 848, 1070; and liberation politics, 1062–1063, 1069–1072; literature of, 360–361; and the Mexican-American War, 440–441; and westward expansion, 414–417, 583–584; in World War II, 877–878, 1070–1071
Mexican-American War, 325, 435–442, 747, 1070; aftermath of, 440–441; anti-war protests, 438–440; Mexican-Americans and, 440–441; reasons for, 435–437; siege of the Alamo, 428–430; significance of, 441–442; Treaty of Guadalupe Hidalgo, 440, 441
Mexican Revolution, 416–417, 860
Mexico, 746–748, 783, 860–861; early Native Americans, 6–7, 17–18, 19; and Germany, 769; immigrants from, 877–878, 1072; invasion of Veracruz, 747; Mexican-American War, 435–442; Spain in, 415–417; and Texas, 426–430
Miami Indians, 199, 274
Micmac Indians, 9, 28–29
Microsoft Corporation, 984
Middle Ages, 11–12
Middle class: African American, 729; conditions at turn of century, 720; middle management and, 577–578; move to the suburbs, 795; in the Progressive era, 725–726, 733; women of, 728–729
Midway, battle of, 886
Midway Island, 685, 870, 886
Mier y Térán, Manuel de, 427
Migrant workers, 609–610, 1062–1063
Milam, J. W., 932–933, 933
Miles, Nelson A., 704
Militarism, 825
Military Reconstruction Act, 538, 539
Milken, Michael, 1099
Millay, Edna St. Vincent, 800
Millett, Kate, 1066

Milligan, Ex parte, 540
Millin, Margrett, 533
Mills, C. Wright, 1057
Mingo Indians, 119
Mining, 565–566, 595, 749–750
Minor, Virginia, 655
Minority groups. *See also specific minority groups*: in the 1890s, 671–672; in the Great Depression, 844–848; legislation concerning, 661–662; and sports, 630, 635–637, 948–949; working conditions of, 591; in World War II, 876–880
Minstrel shows, 367–368
Minutemen, 152
Miss America pageant, 1065
Missing in Action (film), 1029
Missionaries, 432
Missionary Diplomacy, 746–748
Mission system, 416, 417
Mission to Moscow (film), 902
Mississippi: poll taxes, 672; in the Reconstruction, 535, 536, 550; secession of, 489
Mississippian peoples, 8
Mississippi Plan, 672
Mississippi River, 178, 194, 232, 251, 264
Missouri, as border state, 491
Missouri (ship), 889
Missouri Compromise, 291–295, 317, 318, 452, 455, 456, 468, 475, 490
Missouri ex rel Gaines, 950
Mitchell, John, 718, 1084
Mix, Tom, 977
Mob violence, 388–389
Moby Dick (Melville), 359
Model Cities Act, 1052, 1054
Mohawk Indians, 10, 33, 171, 229
Molasses Act, 89, 121
Molly Maguires, 595, 597
Molotov, V. M., 881, 904, 910
Momaday, N. Scott (Kiowa), 1074
Mondale, Walter, 1102
Money question, 656
Monitor (ship), 502
Monmouth Court House, battle of, 200
Monroe, James, 251, 270–272, 278–279, 295, 312–313, 683; financial programs of, 272–274; foreign policy of, 278; Missouri Compromise, 291–295; Monroe Doctrine, 279–280; reelection, 301; second term, 301, 305–306; in the War of 1812, 272
Monroe Doctrine, 279–280, 306, 683, 694, 699, 784; Roosevelt Corollary, 746, 861
Montezuma II (Aztec emperor), 18
Montgomery, Bernard, 881
Montgomery, Richard, 158
Montgomery bus boycott, 675, 953–955, 1041
Montoya, Joseph, 1071
Montserrat, 454
Moral reform, 337–338
Moravians, 397
More, Paul Elmer, 850
Morgan, Daniel, 176

Morgan, J. P., 564–565, 568, 574–575, 576–577, 669, 718, 738, 740, 742, 750
Morgan, J. P., Jr., 780
Morgan, William, 304
Morgenthau, Henry, 850, 879
Mormons, 433–435
Morrill Land Grant Act, 504, 572, 586
Morrill Tariff, 572
Morris, Gouverneur, 191, 206, 208
Morris, Robert, 191–193, 206
Morrissey, John, 634
Morrow, Dwight, 860–861
Morse, Jedidiah, 284
Morse, Samuel F. B., 283, 285
Morse, Wayne, 1014
Morton, Ferdinand "Jelly Roll," 629–630
Morton, Thomas, 52
Mosby, John S., 632–633
Mosby's Raiders, 632
Moses, Robert, 980
Mott, Lucretia, 348
Mound Builders (Mississippian peoples), 8
Mountain men, 422
Mount Holyoke College, 341–342
Movie industry: censorship in, 639, 772–773, 851, 1075; Cold War and, 902, 1107; Great Depression and, 851; Jews in, 639–640; origins of, 638–640; propaganda and, 772–773, 874; Red Scare and, 902, 925; studio system, 798–799; Vietnam and, 968–969, 1028–1029; West and, 968, 977, 979; World War I and, 772–773; World War II and, 979; youth in, 925, 1057
Moyne, Jean Baptiste le (Sieur de Bienville), 104
Ms. magazine, 1066
Muckraking journalism, 218–219, 724–725, 728, 740
Mugwumps, 653, 658, 659
Muhammad, Elijah, 1049–1050
Muir, John, 738, 1076
Mulatto class, 20
Muller v. *Oregon*, 723
Mumford, Lewis, 621, 850, 937, 960
Munich Conference, 906
Munn v. *Illinois*, 660
Murieta, Joaquín, 414
Murphy, Edgar Gardner, 729
Murphy, Frank, 880
Murphy, Isaac, 636
Murray, John (Lord Dunmore), 158–159, 160, 201
Murray, Judith Sargent, 201
Murrow, Edward R., 957–959
Muscovy Company, 30
Music, 628–630, 773, 850, 960–962, 975, 1055, 1058; nineteenth century, 367–368; twentieth century, 798, 800–801, 824
Muslims: and the Crusades, 12–13; scientific knowledge of, 14; in Spain, 14
Mussolini, Benito, 825, 863–864, 900
My Lai massacre, 1004–1005, 1019
Myrdal, Gunnar, 877
Mysteries and Miseries of New York, The (Buntline), 363

Nader, Ralph, 1036–1037
Nader's Raiders, 1036
Nagy, Imre, 941–942
Napoleon Bonaparte, 252, 254, 256, 259–260, 264, 695, 696, 760
Napoleonic Wars, 258, 271, 279, 695, 696, 760
Narragansett Indians, 55, 57
Narváez, Pánfilo de, 19
Nashoba Colony, 350
Nashville (ship), 745
Nasser, Gamal Abdel, 942
Natchez Indians, 8
National Aeronautics and Space Administration (NASA), 1107
National American Woman Suffrage Association (NAWSA), 655, 730
National Anti-Cigarette League, 806
National Association for the Advancement of Colored People (NAACP), 732, 751, 776, 809–810, 876, 877, 933, 950–952, 1050
National Association of Colored Women, 729
National Association of Manufacturers, 732
National Association Opposed to Woman Suffrage, 730
National Banking acts, 504
National Birth Control League, 732
National Child Labor Committee, 729, 735
National Civic Federation, 732
National Collegiate Athletic Association, 732
National Conference for New Politics, 1065
National Congress of American Indians (NCAI), 1073
National Conservation Congress, 738
National Consumers League, 729
National debt, 223
National Defense Education Act, 944, 1107
National domain, 189, 191
National Environmental Policy Act, 1076
National Farm Workers Association, 1062–1063
National Gazette, 228
National Guard, 953, 1024
National Indian Youth Council, 1073
National Industrial Recovery Act (NIRA), 836, 838–839, 853
Nationalism: Black, 1048–1051, 1079; of the 1890s, 695; and industrialization process, 573; judicial, 277–278, 290; Native American, 1073–1074; post-War of 1812, 271–280; in the South, 395–396, 397–398; Third World, 944–945; Vietnamese, 1000–1001, 1009, 1010
Nationalists, 189, 191, 193, 209, 210
National Labor Relations Act (Wagner Act), 842–843, 849, 853, 1063
National Labor Relations Board, 842
National Labor Union (NLU), 598, 599
National League, 631–634

National Organization for Women (NOW), 1064–1065
National Origins Act, 615, 808
National parks, 738, 1076
National Recovery Administration (NRA), 838–839, 845, 849
National Republicans, 307, 321, 325
National Resources and Planning Board, 873
National Road, 276
National Security League, 767
National Socialist Workers' Party (Nazis), 862
National System of Interstate and Defense Highways, 936–937
National Trades' Union, 384
National Traffic and Motor Vehicle Safety Act, 1036
National Union for Social Justice, 842
National Union party, 517
National War Labor Board (NWLB), 771
National Woman's party, 730, 774–775
National Woman Suffrage Association (NWSA), 541, 655
National Women's Trade Union League, 729–730
National Youth Administration (NYA), 848, 873
Nation-states, emergence of, 14–16
Native American Rights Fund, 1073
Native Americans, 4–11. *See also names of specific tribes*; in the American Revolution, 169–171, 174, 178; assimilation policy, 312–313, 556–557; Cherokee War, 110; *conquistadores* and, 16–19; and European diseases, 4, 18, 57; and France, 105, 109, 110, 119; and fur trade, 422; in the Great Depression, 817, 848; King Philip's War, 58; lands of, 198–199, 312–315, 553–557, 662, 1074; languages of, 9; and liberation politics, 1072–1074; literature of, 360; and Ohio country, 229–230, 262–263; paleo-Indians, 5; Pilgrims and, 4–5; political militancy of, 1072–1073; Pontiac's uprising, 119–121; population growth, 8–9; Powhatan's Confederacy, 31–32, 43–44; removal policy, 229–230, 307, 312–315, 554–557; and scalping, 28–29, 76–77; slavery and, 20; values of, 9–10, 418–419; in the War of 1812, 259, 260, 262–263; and westward expansion, 229–230, 307, 312–315, 417–419, 552–557, 582–583; and the Wild West, 582–583
Native Son (Wright), 851
Nativism, 465, 611–615, 777, 807–808
Naturalization Act, 236
Navajo Indians, 417, 552, 1073
Naval science, 13–14
Navigation Acts, 78–79, 86, 89
Navigation System, 78, 79, 84, 193
Navy, U.S.: in the Civil War, 497, 501–502; Five-Power Naval Treaty, 863; Great White Fleet, 745; New Navy, 688–690, 691, 692; Pearl Harbor attack on, 867, 869–871; post-Civil War reduction of, 684; rebuilding of,

688–690, 692; and the Spanish-American War, 699–704; in World War I, 777; in World War II, 867, 869–871, 886–892
Nazi party, 825, 861–862, 864–865, 874
Nebraska: and free silver, 648; Kansas-Nebraska Act, 467–470, 473, 477, 478, 481; and the Populist party, 667, 668
Needham, Henry Beach, 632
Neff, Mary, 76
Neighborhood Youth Corps, 1052
Neo-Hamiltonianism, 272–273
Neolin (Delaware), 119
Netherlands. *See* Dutch, the
New Amsterdam, 29, 33, 80
Newbold, Charles, 286
Newburgh Conspiracy, 192–193
New Deal, 750, 836–849, 916, 918, 926, 977, 1076; decline of, 848–849; second, 842–844; women and minorities in, 844–849
New England Emigrant Aid Company, 470–471
New England Non-Resistance Society, 345
New Era politics, 812, 814
Newfoundland, 45
New France, 34, 104–105, 109
New Freedom, 742, 743, 749
New Frontier, 1006
New Guinea, 886
New Hampshire: in the American Revolution, 171; colonization of, 56; and ratification of the Constitution, 211; state constitution, 159, 187
New Harmony, Indiana, 349–350
New Humanists, 850
New Jersey: in the American Revolution, 165–166; colonization of, 80–81; state constitution, 187
New Jersey Plan, 207
Newlands Reclamation Act, 738
New Left, 1056–1058, 1065
New Look, 939–940
New Mexico: anti-Mexican sentiment in, 441; colonization of, 415; in the Mexican-American War, 438; mission system in, 416; Pueblo revolt, 440–441; slavery and, 455–456, 457
New Nationalism, 742
New Navy, 688–690, 691, 692
New Negro, 810
New Netherland, 29, 33–34, 79–80
New Orleans, 232, 261; battle of, 261, 264, 271, 280; Citizen Genêt Affair, 229; in the Civil War, 497, 500; founding of, 104; Storyville, 629–630
New Panama Canal Company, 745
Newport, Christopher, 30
New Right, 1098
New South, 587–590, 971–975
New Spain, 19–21, 22, 24–25, 32, 79, 82, 106, 279
Newspapers, 362–363, 874
Newton, Isaac, 95
New woman, 804–805
New World: England in, 4–5, 21–22, 25–26, 31–32, 40–70, 76–79, 81–104;

New World (Continued)
France in, 21–22, 24, 32–34, 104–105, 109, 123; Holland in, 29, 32–34, 78, 79–80, 84; Native Americans in, 5–11; slavery in, 453–454; Spain in, 19–21, 22, 24–25, 32, 79, 82, 106, 279
New York (Lippard), 363
New York (state): in the American Revolution, 164–165; colonization of, 80–81, 89; Erie Canal, 281–282; and ratification of the Constitution, 210, 211; repeal of Prohibition, 806; state constitution, 187; and westward expansion, 229
New York City: in the American Revolution, 164–165, 173, 174, 175, 177; Ashcan school, 627–628, 722; Boss Tweed Ring scandal, 547; cholera epidemic, 322–323; crime in, 333, 339, 389; electricity in, 623–624; Harlem, 794–795, 810–811; labor protests in, 383–384; Lower East Side, 620, 621; as New Amsterdam, 29, 33, 80; and Newburgh Conspiracy, 192, 193; parks in, 637–638; population growth, 287; public transportation in, 618; slums, 289–290, 619–620; Stamp Act Congress, 130; Stonewall Inn raid, 1074–1075; Tammany Hall machine, 733; urban segregation in, 289–290, 619–620
New York Giants, 979–980
New York Herald, 363, 542
New York Journal, 696–697, 701–703
New York Moral Reform Society, 337
New York Stock Exchange, 815
New York Sun, 362, 762
New York Tribune, 354, 385, 475, 476, 477, 489–490, 507, 551, 689
New York World, 696–697
Nez Percé Indians, 419, 432, 553
Ngo Dinh Diem, 1010–1011
Nguyen Cao Ky, 1028
Nguyen Van Thieu, 1024, 1028
Nhu, Madame, 1011
Niagara Movement, 731
Nicaragua, 398, 466–467, 746, 860, 861, 1095, 1100–1101
Nicholas II, Czar of Russia, 762
Nicholson, Francis, 87
Nicolls, Richard, 80–81
Nimitz, Chester, 886
Niña (ship), 15
Nineteenth Amendment, 775, 804–805, 1066
"Ninety-Five Theses" (Luther), 22
Nitze, Paul, 911–912
Nixon, Richard M., 919, 969, 970, 988, 989, 1005, 1045, 1054, 1097; and China, 1025–1027; debates with Kennedy, 1001–1002; and détente, 1093; in the election of 1968, 1021–1023; and Alger Hiss case, 901; and incursions into Cambodia, 1024, 1029, 1086; inflation and, 1092; as outsider, 1022–1023; and Oval Office recordings, 1085; pardoned by Ford, 1088; reelection, 1027–1028; resigna-

tion from presidency, 1086; and the Soviet Union, 1027, 1093; and Vietnam, 1021–1028, 1031, 1086; and the Watergate scandal, 1084–1087
Nixon Doctrine, 1023–1025
Noble and Holy Order of the Knights of Labor, 598–599
Non-Intercourse Act, 256
Noriega, Manuel Antonio, 1108
Normandy, 883
Norris, Frank, 568–569, 624–626
Norris, George, 741, 813
North, Frederick (Lord North), 136, 138–140, 142, 143, 162, 178
North, the: abolitionism in, 343–344; civil rights movement in, 1051–1052; economic growth in, 564–580; free blacks in, 332–333, 406–407, 457–460; industrialization in, 377–385, 390–391; Reconstruction in, 550–552; slavery in, 204; South versus, 377, 391–392
North American Free Trade Agreement (NAFTA), 1111
North Atlantic Treaty Organization (NATO), 910, 941–942
North Carolina: colonial, 47; and the Constitution, 220; in the Reconstruction, 535, 544; secession of, 491; state constitution, 187
Northern Confederacy, 252
Northern Securities Company, 738
Northrup, Solomon, 401
North Star (film), 902
North Star, The (newspaper), 346
Northwest Ordinance, 199, 208, 291
Northwest Passage, search for, 21–22, 26, 31, 32–33, 421
Norway, 866
Notes on the State of Virginia (Jefferson), 204
Notre Dame, 633
Novels, 363–366, 976–977
NOW (National Organization for Women), 1064–1065
Noyes, John Humphrey, 350–351
Nuclear Test Ban Treaty, 1012
Nude Descending a Staircase (painting), 628
Nullification, 308, 316–318, 456
Nuremberg Laws, 863
Nye, Gerald, 861

Oberlin College, 341, 342
Obregón, Alvaro, 747, 860
O'Brien, Tim, 1031
Occupational Safety and Health Act, 1036
O'Connor, Sandra Day, 1069
Office of Economic Opportunity, 1054
Office of Price Administration (OPA), 872, 916
Office of Scientific Research and Development (OSRD), 871–872
Oglethorpe, James, 106
O'Hara, Maureen, 969
O'Hare, Kate Richards, 774
Ohio, and westward expansion, 229
Ohio Company, 108

Ohio country, Native Americans and, 229–230, 262–263
Ohio Gang, 812
Oil, 566–567, 575–576, 812, 860–861, 935, 942, 984, 1089, 1090–1091, 1092, 1095
O'Keeffe, Georgia, 800
Okinawa, battle of, 887, 890
Oklahoma, 294
Oklahoma (ship), 870
Old Northwest, 189, 198–199; Britain and, 230–232, 259; removal policy in, 314; slavery and, 343
Olive Branch petition, 155, 158
Oliver, Andrew, 124–125, 128, 136, 144
Oliver, Joe "King," 629
Oliver, Peter, 124, 125
Olmsted, Frederick Law, 637
Olney, Richard, 660, 670, 694, 698
Olympic Games, 636, 942, 1096, 1107
O'Malley, Walter, 979–980
Omoo (Melville), 359
One Flew Over the Cuckoo's Nest (Kesey), 992
Oneida Community, 350–351
Oneida Indians, 10, 171
O'Neill, Bucky, 706–707
O'Neill, Eugene, 800
Only Yesterday (Allen), 819
Onondaga Indians, 10
On the Road (Kerouac), 1056
Opechancanough, 29, 44
Open Door Policy, 711–713, 869
Oppenheimer, J. Robert, 890
Orange, William of, 86–88
Oratory, 367
Oregon: Britain and, 278–279, 431–433; settlement of, 423–424; Spain and, 432
Oregon Trail, 422–423, 425–426, 432
Oregon Trail, The (Parkman), 363
Organization of Petroleum Exporting Countries (OPEC), 1089, 1090
Organized crime, 612, 806, 922–923
Oriskany, Battle of, 171
Orlando, Vittorio, 782
Osceola (Seminole), 314
Osgood, Samuel, 222
Ostend Manifesto, 467
O'Sullivan, John L., 426
Oswald, Lee Harvey, 1008
Otis, James, Jr., 124–125, 130
Otis, James, Sr., 124
Ottawa Indians, 230
Our Country (Strong), 687
Our Nig (Jacobs), 360
Owen, Robert, 349–350, 399
Ozone depletion, 1077

Pacific Northwest: Britain and, 278–279, 431–433; Native Americans and, 417–418, 419
Pacific Railway Act, 504
Padrones, 609
Page, Walter Hines, 763
Pahlavi, Mohammad Reza (Shah of Iran), 944, 1095–1096
Paine, Thomas, 160, 166, 189
Paiute Indians, 417, 419
Pale of Settlement, 610, 611

Paleo-Indians, 5
Palestine Liberation Organization (PLO), 1094, 1112
Paley, William S., 958
Palmer, A. Mitchell, 780–781
Palmer, Phoebe, 348
Panama, 106, 861; Balboa in, 16–17; invasion of, 1105–1108
Panama Canal, 745
Panama Canal Treaty, 1094, 1097
Panay (ship), 863
Panic of 1819, 290–291, 294, 302, 311, 318
Panic of 1837, 319–320, 324, 384–385
Panic of 1873, 551, 552, 656
Panic of 1893, 668–669
Panic of 1907, 743
Paper money, 116, 122, 191–192, 222, 324, 504, 551–552, 656
Paraguay, 1095
Paredes y Arrillaga, Mariano, 437
Paris Peace Conference, 705, 709
Park cemeteries, 361–362
Parke-Davis Company, 640
Parker, Alton B., 738
Parker, Dorothy, 801
Parker, John, 152
Parker, Theodore, 456
Parkman, Francis, 363
Parks, 637–638; national, 738, 1076; urban, 361–362, 637
Parks, Rosa, 953–954
Parlor games, 799
Parsons, Lawrence, 152
Participatory democracy, 1056
Party system. *See also names of specific parties*: disintegration of, 464–470; electoral system and, 233, 238–239, 301, 305–306, 474, 558, 656, 667, 1087; federal government and, 649–651; in the Gilded Age, 648–655; nominating conventions in, 303; origins of, 225–232; and party loyalty, 651–653; and party organization, 653–655; rebirth of, 301, 304–306; and shifting of party loyalties, 988–992
Passamaquoddy Indians, 1074
Pastorius, Francis Daniel, 82
Paterson, William, 207
Patriarchal values, 60–64, 197
Patronage, 227–228, 248, 305, 311–312, 321, 650, 652–653, 657–659
Patrons of Husbandry (Grangers), 659–660, 665–666, 687
Patroons, 80
Patton (film), 1024
Patton, George, 883
Patuxet Indians, 4–5, 10, 48
Paul, Alice, 730, 774–775
Paul, Cuffe, 343
Paulding, James Kirk, 366, 392
Pawnee Indians, 9, 552
Payne-Aldrich Tariff, 741
Peabody, Elizabeth, 352
Peace Democrats, 505–506
Peale, Charles Willson, 361
Pearl Harbor attack, 867, 869–871
Peck, Everard, 381
Peel, Robert, 389

Peers, William, 1005
Pemberton, John C., 513
Pendleton Act, 658
Penicillin, 847, 872, 990
Penn, William, 82–84
Pennsylvania: antislavery law, 204; colonization of, 81–84; and ratification of the Constitution, 211; state constitution, 187
Pennsylvania Evening Post, 362
Pennsylvania State University, 632
Penny press, 362
Penobscot Indians, 1074
Pentecostalism, 806–807
Pepperrell, William, 106
Pequot Indians, 29, 57, 360
Perceval, Spencer, 256
Percy, Hugh (Lord Percy), 152
Perestroika, 1101, 1106
Perkins, Frances, 845
Perot, Ross, 1111
Perry, Matthew, 466
Perry, Oliver Hazard, 259–260
Pershing, John J., 748, 777, 778
Persian Gulf War, 1108–1110
Peru, early Native Americans, 7, 19
Peters, John, 185
Petroleum. *See* Oil
Phagan, Mary, 613
Philadelphia: Constitutional Convention in, 77, 103, 206; Continental Congress in, 140–142, 149–151; founding of, 82–83; German immigrants in, 92–93; seizure of, in the American Revolution, 169; yellow fever epidemic of 1793, 226–227
Philadelphia (ship), 250
Philby, Kim, 919
Philip, John, 40
Philip II, King of Spain, 24–25
Philippines, 690, 705–711, 740, 744, 860, 870, 1095; annexation to the United States, 705; independence movement, 709–711; during World War II, 881, 886, 887
Phillips, David Graham, 724
Phillips, Kevin, 987–988
Phillips, Sam, 961
Phips, William, 88
Phonograph, 798
Phrenology, 368
Pickering, John, 249
Pickett, George E., 512, 514–515
Pickett's Charge, 512, 514–515
Picou, Alphonse, 629
Pierce, Franklin, 450–451, 473; election to presidency, 466–467; and Kansas, 471; Young America policy, 359, 466–467
Pigot, Robert, 157
Pike, Zebulon, 421–422
Pilgrims, 4–5, 29, 47–52
Pilgrim's Progress, The (Bunyan), 724
Pinchback, P. B. S., 545, 811
Pinchot, Gifford, 738, 741, 1076
Pinckney, Charles C., 77, 254
Pinckney, Eliza (Eliza Lucas), 76, 77, 90
Pinckney, Thomas, 77, 233, 238, 526

Pinckney's Treaty, 77, 232
Ping-Pong diplomacy, 1027
Pinta (ship), 15
Pioneers, The (Cooper), 352
Pirates, 250–251, 278
Pitt, William (Earl of Chatham), 109, 118, 130–131, 136
Pittsburgh, 108; population growth, 288–289
Pizarro, Francisco, 18–19
Plague, 12
Plantation system, 43, 392–393
Platt Amendment, 705, 745, 861
Players' League, 634
Plessy v. *Ferguson*, 589, 636, 672, 736, 946, 948
Plows, iron, 286
Plymouth colony, 4–5, 31, 48–52, 55
Pocahontas, 43–44
Poe, Edgar Allen, 354, 358
Poems on Various Subjects, Religious and Moral (Wheatley), 184
Pokanoket Indians, 5
Poland, 784, 858, 884, 901; German invasion of, 865–867, 883, 903; immigrants from, 610, 611; post-World War II, 903, 904, 941
Police departments, 388–389, 596–597, 620, 675, 1074–1075
Political parties. *See* Party system; *names of specific parties*
Polk, James K., 431, 432–438, 440, 442; election to presidency, 432; and the Mexican-American War, 436–440; and Oregon, 432–433; and the Walker Tariff, 442
Polk, Leonidas L., 663
Pollock v. *The Farmer's Loan and Trust Co.*, 669
Polo, Marco, 14
Polygamy, 435
Polygyny, 435
Pon, Ben, 1091
Ponce de Léon, Juan, 17
Pontiac (Ottawa), 119–121
Ponzi, Charles, 814–815
Pools, 564, 575
Popé, 21
Pope, John, 499
Popular culture. *See also* Sports: civil rights movement in, 1055; and the Cold War, 902; Communism in, 1107; during the Great Depression, 850–851; mid-twentieth century, 955–963; modern, 797–804; of the nineteenth century, 362–368; Vietnam War in, 1028–1029; westward expansion in, 366, 414–415, 582–583, 584, 968–969, 975–977; and World War I, 773; and World War II, 874
Popular sovereignty, 219, 455, 468, 469, 475, 478
Population Bomb, The (Ehrlich), 1076
Population growth. *See also* Immigration: African American, 343; and birth control, 202–203, 348, 792–793, 802, 803; in Britain, 25; of cities, 226–227, 287–290, 615–623, 776–777, 793–795;

Population growth (Continued)
  colonial, 58, 90–93; Jewish, 336; in the Middle Ages, 11–12; Native American, 8–9; post-Revolution, 219–220; in the South, 988–989; in the West, 980–981, 988
Populism, 662–668, 672–677, 695, 733, 734
Populist party, 464, 667–668, 671, 672–677
Pork barrel legislation, 304
Pornography, 802–803
Porter, Cole, 864
Porter, Edwin S., 639
Port Huron Statement, 1056
Portugal: Catholicism in, 24; as nation-state, 14, 15; and Treaty of Tordesillas, 16, 21, 22
Post roads, 281
Potawatomi Indians, 119, 230
Potsdam Conference, 888, 889, 891, 902
Potter, David, 530
Pound, Dean Roscoe, 723
Poverty: feminization of, 1069; welfare programs, 987, 1052–1054, 1098–1099; of working poor, 385–386
Poverty line, 1054
Powderly, Terence V., 598–599
Powell, Lewis, 1054
Powers, Francis Gary, 946
Powhatan (Pamunkey), 31–32, 42, 43–44
Powhatan's Confederacy, 31–32, 43–44
Poyas, Ned, 293
Poyas, Peter, 292–293
Praeger, Robert Paul, 773
Pragmatism, 723
Pratt, Richard, 556
Preemption Bill, 425
Pre-Raphaelite school, 727
Presbyterians, 23, 52, 92, 104, 197, 205, 294, 336, 396, 433, 743
Prescott, William, 156–157
Presidency, U.S.: and the Constitution, 208–209, 221–222; expanding powers of, 208–209, 311–312, 540, 895, 1086; and the Reconstruction, 531–537, 540; restraining powers of, 1086–1087
President's Commission on the Status of Women, 1061
Presley, Elvis, 961–962
Preston, Thomas, 135
Price, George M., 610–611
Price Revolution, 25
Prigg v. Pennsylvania, 457
Primogeniture, 31, 197
Princeton University, 633, 743
Princip, Gavrilo, 759
Principia Mathematica (Newton), 95
Prioleau, George W., 700
Prisons, 339–340
Pritchard, Jack, 293
Proclamation of 1763, 120–121, 189
Proclamation of Amnesty and Reconstruction, 531
Proctor, Jenny, 533
Proctor, Renfield, 696
Profiles in Courage (Kennedy), 1003
Progress and Poverty (George), 721

Progressive party, 742, 812–813
Progressivism, 718–753, 779, 1076; in cities, 733–734; factors leading to, 719–725; impact of, 748–753; influence on the New Deal, 836; at international level, 744–748; moral, 743–744; at national level, 736–744; organizing drive, 725–732; at state level, 734–736; twilight of, 813
Prohibition, 728–729, 735, 743–744, 774, 805–806. See also Temperance movement
Propaganda, 772–773, 874, 925
Property rights, 197–199, 302–303. See also Land; land tenure, 303–304; of women, 60, 64, 349, 546
Proprietary estates, 45
Prosser, Gabriel, 405
Prostitution, 728, 741, 802, 803
Protestant fundamentalism, 728, 735
Protestant Reformation, 22–24, 52, 53
Protestant Wind, 25
Provenzano, Joe, 612
Provenzano, Pete, 612
Ptolemy, 13
Public Health Service, 846–847
Public Utility Holding Company Act, 843
Public virtue, 186
Public Works Administration (PWA), 839
Pueblo Indians, 21, 418, 440–441
Puerto Rico, 79, 454, 704, 705
Pulitzer, Joseph, 696–698
Puller, Lewis B., 914–915
Pullman strike, 670, 687, 694, 695, 718, 736
Pulp fiction, 799
Punch, John, 40, 41
Pure Food and Drug Act, 740, 750
Puritans, 46, 47, 52–54; colonial pastimes, 96–97; community control and, 54–55; in England, 24, 52–53, 65; family roles among, 60–64; and the Glorious Revolution, 86–87, 89; Half-Way Covenant, 64–65; health of, 59; Long Island, 80, 87; and Native Americans, 57–58; public schools of, 340; witchcraft hysteria, 87–88
Purity Congress, 728
Purity Crusade, 802–803
Pushmataha (Choctaw), 313
Puzo, Mario, 923

Quakers, 81–84, 204, 230, 341, 396, 397
Quartering Act, 140
Quay, Matt, 654, 661
Quebec Act, 140
Queen Anne's War, 105
Queensberry Rules, 635
Quigley, Hugh, 361
Quinn, John, 628
Quitrents, 303–304
Quivers, Emanuel, 401

Radical feminism, 1065–1066
Radical Republicans, 530, 531, 534–535, 537–542, 557

Radio, 798, 850
Radulovich, Milo, 958
Ragtime, 629–630
Railroads, 280, 282–283, 610, 937; agriculture and, 586–587, 659–661; commuter, 617; competition and, 575; growth of, 568–569, 572–573, 584; and industrialization, 565, 568–569, 572–573, 575, 577, 578, 580; interstate commerce and, 659–661, 738–740; labor protests, 595–596, 669–670, 687, 694, 718, 736; land grants to, 572–573; and the meat-packing business, 578–579; power of, 580; regulation of, 734, 749; in the South, 397–398, 588, 589; transcontinental, 504, 558, 567, 569, 572, 581
Rainey, Ma ("Mother of the Blues"), 798
Raleigh, Walter, 27, 30
Rall, Johann, 165
Rambo: First Blood II (film), 1029
Ranching, 581–585
Randolph, A. Philip, 810, 876, 950, 1046
Randolph, Edmund, 207, 222, 232
Randolph, Edward, 86
Randolph, John, 257, 291, 308, 310
Rankin, Jeannette, 734
Rap, 1055
Raskob, John Jacob, 815
Rationalism, 95
Rational planning, 723
Rauschenbusch, Walter, 724
Reagan, Nancy, 1099
Reagan, Ronald, 969, 970, 988, 989, 990, 992, 993, 1076, 1096–1101, 1103, 1110; assassination attempt, 1098; Cold War and, 1100–1101, 1102; domestic policy, 1098–1100, 1102–1103; in election of 1964, 1097–1098; election to presidency, 1097; Iran-contra affair, 1100–1101, 1102
Reagan Doctrine, 1100–1101
Realism, 624–626
Rebel Without a Cause (film), 925, 1057
Reconstruction, 526–560, 652; black, 545; congressional, 537–543; final retreat from, 557–558; foreign policy, 683–690; in the North, 550–552; postwar conditions and issues, 527–531; presidential, 531–537; Radical, 538–540; in the South, 535–537, 543–550; in the West, 552–557; white resistance to, 549–550
Reconstruction Acts, 545
Reconstruction Finance Corporation (RFC), 829, 835, 935
Red Cross, 518, 775, 819, 877
Redeemer Democrats, 671
Red Power, 1073–1074
Red River (film), 968
Red Scare, 780–781, 805, 900–902, 918–925
Reed, Esther DeBerdt, 200
Reed, Walter, 622
Referenda, 667, 749
Reformation, 22–24, 52, 53
Reform Darwinists, 723

Reform movements, 333–351; moral, 337–338; radical, 342–351; religious, 334–336; social. *See* Social reform
Reform Municipal Voters League, 732
Rehnquist, William, 1054, 1066–1067
Reid, Whitelaw, 689
Religious freedom, 55, 56, 99, 196–197, 336
Religious toleration, 55
Relocation camps, 879–880
Remington, Frederic, 697, 976
Removal policy, 229–230, 307, 312–315, 554–557
Renaissance, 13
Rendezvous system, 422
Report on Manufactures (Hamilton), 224
Republicanism, 186, 200, 245–246, 247–248, 311
Republican party (Jeffersonian): decline of, 304–305; and the elections of 1800, 237–239; and French, 227; origins of, 225, 231, 256; and the War of 1812, 272
Republican party (modern): in the election of 1860, 488; in the election of 1994, 994–995, 1112; in the Gilded Age, 648–655; Half-Breeds, 652–653, 657; Liberal, 551; Mugwumps, 653, 658, 659; National Republicans, 307, 321, 325; origins of, 306–307, 467, 473–474; Radical, 530, 531, 534–535, 537–542, 557; restoration of, 811–814; Stalwarts, 652–653, 657; Union, 534; and the Watergate breakin, 1084–1086
Residency requirements, 672
Restrictive covenants, 794, 810, 947
Resumption Act, 552, 656
Revels, Hiram, 544
Revenue Act of 1764, 121
Revenue Act of 1942, 873
Revere, Paul, 141, 151
Revolutionary War. *See* American Revolution
Reynolds, Maria, 218
Rhee, Syngman, 912, 938
Rhineland, 863, 864
Rhode Island: colonization of, 55, 56, 86, 129; and the Constitution, 220; independence from Britain, 160, 166; and interstate commerce, 206; and religious tolerance, 55, 56, 197; state constitution, 186; and taxation, 192; voting rights, 303
Rhythm and blues, 961–962
Ribicoff, Abraham, 1021
Rice, 78
Richardson, Ebenezer, 127
Richardson, Elliot, 1085
Richmond, David, 1039
Rickover, Hyman G., 698
Ridenhour, Ronald, 1005
Riders of the Purple Sage (Grey), 799
Ridge, John Rollin (Cherokee), 360
Ridgeway, Matthew B., 915
Riesman, David, 960
Rights of Colonies, The (Hopkins), 123–124
Right-to-life movement, 1067–1068
Riis, Jacob, 613

Riots, 388–389
Ripley, George, 352, 354
Ritchie, Thomas, 308–309
Roads, 275–276, 281, 670–671, 796
Roanoak Indians, 27
Roanoke Island disaster, 26–27
Roaring Twenties, 816
Robber barons, 597
Robinson, Frederick, 325
Robinson, Jackie, 934, 948–949, 1045
Robinson, Rachel, 949
Robinson, Ruby Doris Smith, 1065
Rochambeau, Comte de, 175, 177
Rock and roll, 961–962
Rockefeller, John D., 504, 567, 570, 573–576, 596, 780
Rockefeller, Nelson, 984–986, 1022
Rockingham, Marquis of, 130
Rockne, Knute, 633, 799
Rocky Mountain Fur Company, 422
Roe, Jane, 1067
Roe v. *Wade*, 1067
Rogers, Mary, 389
Rogers, Will, 651, 864
Rogers, William, 1022
Rolfe, John, 32, 40, 41, 43–44
Romania, 883
Romanticism, 727
Rommel, Erwin, 881
Romney, George, 985
Roosevelt, Eleanor, 844–845, 877, 1061
Roosevelt, Franklin D., 824, 830–844, 848–851, 861, 865–874, 877–884, 888–891, 895, 1097; brain trust, 836; court packing scheme, 849–850; critics of, 840–842; death, 886, 888; and the depression of 1937, 850; in the election of 1920, 786; in the election of 1932, 830–831, 977; election to presidency, 831; Fireside Chats, 832–835; first 100 days, 832–836; New Deal, 750, 836–849, 1076; recognition of the Soviet Union, 865; reelections, 844, 848–849, 868, 895; as undersecretary of the Navy, 836; and Vietnam, 1009; World War II and, 867–874
Roosevelt, Theodore, 415, 554, 633, 689–690, 692, 695, 724, 740, 741–743, 749–751, 777; Big Stick diplomacy, 744–746; coal miners' strike and, 718–719; in the election of 1912, 742; and New Nationalism, 742; progressivism and, 736–740, 741, 742, 751, 1076; Rough Riders and, 706–707; as secretary of the navy, 700; Square Deal, 738; as successor to McKinley, 736–738; and World War I, 767–768
Rosenberg, Ethel, 919
Rosenberg, Julius, 919
Ross, Edward Alsworth, 612
Rossetti, Gabriel, 727
Rotary Club, 732
Roth, Henry, 851
Rough Riders, 706–707
Rough Riders, The (Roosevelt), 706
Rowing, 636
Rowson, Susanna, 363
Royal African Company, 68

Roybal, Edward R., 1071
Ruckelshaus, William, 1085
Rural Electrification Administration (REA), 837
Rush, Benjamin, 226–227
Rush-Bagot Agreement, 279
Rushin, Thomas Jefferson, 486
Rusk, Dean, 1007, 1012
Russell, Charles, 976
Russell, John, 503
Russia, 279; and Alaska, 685; Bolshevik Revolution, 615, 759, 762, 769, 782–784, 825; immigrants from, 610–611, 612; in the Pacific Northwest, 431–432; Russo-Japanese War, 744–745; and the Treaty of Versailles, 782–783; and World War I, 760, 762; and World War II, 881
Russo-Japanese War, 744–745
Rustbelt, 974–975
Rustin, Bayard, 877, 1046
Ruth, George Herman ("Babe"), 799
Ryan, John A., 724

Sacco, Nicola, 808
Sadat, Anwar el-, 1093–1094
Sadlier, Mary Anne, 361
Sagebrush Rebellion, 993
St. Leger, Barry, 170–171
Saint Lucia, 453
Saint Vincent, 453
Saipan, 886–887
Salem witch hysteria, 87–88
Salinger, J. D., 1056, 1057
Salinger, Pierre, 1007
Salisbury (Lord), 694
Salisbury Cotton Mills, 588
Salvation Army, 828
Samoa, 688, 690–691, 695, 705
Samoset, 5
Sanchez, Oscar Arias, 1101
Sand Creek massacre, 554
Sandinistas, 1100, 1101
Sandow, Eugene, 636
Sandys, Edwin, 43, 44
Sanger, Margaret, 792
Sanger, William, 792
San Jacinto (ship), 503
San Jacinto, battle of, 429–430, 436
San Juan Hill, battle of, 707
San Salvador, 16
Santa Anna, Antonio López de, 427–430, 440
Santa Clara County v. *The Southern Pacific Railroad*, 573
Santa Fe Trail, 422–423, 426
Santa María (ship), 15
Saperstein, Abe, 948–949, 949
Sargent, Dudley A., 637
Satellites, 943–944
Saudi Arabia, 1090, 1110
Sauk Indians, 230, 314, 360, 424
Savings and loan crisis, 1105
Scalawags, 543, 544, 545, 550
Scalping, 28–29, 76–77
Scarlet Letter, The (Hawthorne), 358
Schechter Poultry Corporation v. *United States*, 849

Schenck, Charles T., 774
Schenck v. *United States*, 774
Schlafly, Phyllis, 1068–1069
Schlieffen, Alfred von, 761
Schurz, Carl, 528
Schuyler, Philip, 170
Schwab, Charles, 564
Schwarzkopf, H. Norman, 1108
Schwerner, Michael, 1050
Science: in the Enlightenment, 98; and pseudoscience, 368; in the Renaissance, 14; and technological innovation, 284–285
Scientific management, 594
Scopes, John, 807
Scopes trial, 806–807
Scotland, 23, 92
Scott, Dred, 474–475, 477, 478, 530
Scott, Winfield, 325, 438–439, 440, 494, 497, 499
Scranton, William, 985
Scriven, Abream, 402–403
Secession, of southern states, 489–491
Second Sex, The (Beauvoir), 1066
Secret ballots, 733, 734
Sedgwick, Catharine, 366
Sedition Act, 218, 236, 247, 773
Seduction of the Innocent (Wertham), 925–926
Seeger, Pete, 850, 1018
Segregation, 549, 628–629, 672; de jure versus de facto, 1052; educational, 932, 951–952, 972, 1038, 1052; and the Fourteenth Amendment, 537, 538, 541, 542, 557, 558, 573, 589, 651, 672; and Jim Crow laws, 628–629, 636, 674–675, 700, 736, 753, 946–955, 1040; Progressivism and, 736; residential, in cities, 289–290, 619–620
Segretti, Donald, 1084
Séguin, Erasmo, 428–429
Séguin, Juan, 361, 428–429
Seider, Christopher, 127
Selective Service Act, 777
Selma demonstrations, 1047, 1048
Seminole Indians, 9, 279
Seneca Falls Women's Rights Convention, 348–349, 1064
Seneca Indians, 10, 108, 171, 229–230
Sequoyah, 312
Serapis (ship), 178
Serbia, 759–760
Settlement houses, 729, 735
Seven Days, battle of, 499
Seven Pines, battle of, 499
Seventeenth Amendment, 734, 741
Seven Years' War, 109, 110, 116–118, 155, 174
Sewall, Arthur, 673
Sewall, Samuel, 63
Seward, William H., 456, 469–470, 476, 488, 490, 503–504, 552, 685, 688
Sewer systems, 622–623
Sewing machines, 285
Sex discrimination: and equal pay, 1061–1064, 1069; and the Supreme Court, 1066–1068
Sexually transmitted diseases (STDs),

846–847, 990–991
Sexual Politics (Millett), 1066
Sexual revolution of early twentieth century, 801–804
Shafter, William R., 704
Shahn, Ben, 808
Shakers, 349
Shakespeare, Joseph, 612
Shamans, 10
Shame of the Cities, The (Steffens), 725
Sharecropping, 548, 549, 589, 591, 837, 838
Sharpsburg, battle of, 486, 487
Shasta Indians, 419
Shaw, Anna Howard, 775
Shaw, Robert Gould, 508, 510
Shawnee Indians, 119, 198, 199, 229, 230, 258, 262–263
Shays, Daniel, 195–196, 210
Shays's Rebellion, 194–196, 206
Sheehan, Neil, 1011
Shelley v. *Kraemer*, 947
Sheppard, Horatio David, 362
Sheridan, Philip, 528
Sherman, William T., 436, 494, 516, 517–518, 520, 527, 529
Sherman Antitrust Act, 661, 720, 738, 744
Sherman Silver Purchase Act, 661, 669
Shiloh (Pittsburgh Landing), battle of, 500
Shipbuilding, 78
Shipley, Jonathan, 103
Shippen, Nancy, 184–185, 200
Shippen, William, 184
Shipping Board, 770
Shirer, William L., 957
Sierra Club, 738, 993, 1076
Sigourney, Lydia, 363
Sigsbee, Charles D., 702
Silent Spring (Carson), 1076
Silver, 25, 648, 656–657, 661, 668, 669
Simmons, William Joseph, 808
Simms, William Gilmore, 363, 392, 398, 463
Simpson, "Sockless" Jerry, 663
Sinclair, Upton, 725, 740
Singapore, 886
Single tax, 721
Sioux Indians, 230, 417, 552, 553, 555, 1074
Sister Carrie (Dreiser), 626
Sit-ins, 1039–1040
Sitting Bull (Sioux), 555
Six Nations of Iroquois, 110, 171
Sixteenth Amendment, 741, 743
Skelly, Jack, 636
Skyscrapers, 618–619, 793
Slader, Mathew, 97
Slater, Samuel, 220, 382
Slavery, 4, 40, 398–405, 451–464; abolitionism. *See* Abolitionism; Black Codes, 535–537; and Compromise of 1850, 208, 455–457, 464, 481; congressional debates on, 291–295, 305–306, 469–470; and the Constitution, 207–208; decline of antislavery sentiment, 396–397; and Dye's conspiracy theory, 450–451; and the Emancipa-

tion Proclamation, 487, 500, 506–511, 532–533; expansion in the South, 376–377; extent of, 392–393; fugitive slaves, 346, 457–464, 477; impact on Southern economy, 393–394; and Jefferson, 204–205, 218, 246, 291, 305, 398–399, 459; and Kansas, 467–473, 475–476, 477, 478, 481; lifetime, 41; and Lincoln-Douglas debates, 476–478; and manumission, 205; and the Missouri Compromise, 291–295, 317, 318, 452, 455, 456, 468, 475, 490; Native American, 20; in New Spain, 20; in the North, 204; origins of American, 66–70; post-Revolution, 201–206, 225; and the Reconstruction, 526–527, 528–530, 532–533, 535–537, 547–549; reforming from within, 397; resistance of slaves, 251–252, 292–293, 404–405; shifting to, in Chesapeake colonies, 67–68; slave codes, 400–401; slave conspiracy of 1822, 292–293; and slave trade, 15, 66–67, 69, 91; and the Texas question, 430–431, 452; and three-fifths compromise, 208, 264, 291, 531; and the Wilmot Proviso, 442, 453; and world of slaves, 68–70, 401–404, 458–459
Slidell, John, 436, 503
Sloan, Alfred, 795–796
Sloat, John D., 438
Sloughter, Henry, 89
Smallpox, 622
Smith, Adam, 571
Smith, Alfred E., 724, 734, 813–814
Smith, Andrew, 632
Smith, Bessie, 798
Smith, Francis, 151–152
Smith, Hoke, 675, 734
Smith, Howard, 1064
Smith, Jacob H., 710
Smith, James L., 458
Smith, Jedediah, 422
Smith, John, 4, 32
Smith, Joseph, Jr., 433–434
Smith, Lucy Wilmot, 729
Smith, Mamie, 798
Smith, Wendell, 949
Smith College, 1059, 1060
Smith-Connally Act, 873
Smog, 983
Smythe, Thomas, 42, 43
Snake Indians, 419
Snow, Edgar, 1027
Snyder Act, 557
Sobell, Morton, 919
Social class: in colonial period, 93–95; and concentration of wealth, 579–580; and income distribution, 817, 970–972; and industrialization, 385–386, 390–391; inequality and, 720; and labor unions, 385–386; middle class. *See* Middle class; poverty and, 385–386, 1069, 1098–1099; and property rights, 197–199; in the Reagan era, 1099–1100; and Social Darwinism, 570–571; special privileges and, 303–304; and sports, 635–637; and

urban segregation, 619–620; working poor, 385–386

Social Darwinism, 570–571, 612, 651, 663, 686, 721, 723, 725

Social engineering, 723

Social Gospel movement, 724

Socialism, 667, 670, 733, 767, 774

Socialist Labor party, 670

Socialist Party of America, 670

Social reform, 338–342. *See also* Liberation politics; asylums, 342; crime and, 338–340; education, 340–341; in the Progressive era, 718–744, 748–753; during World War I, 774–775

Social Security Act, 843–844, 845, 853, 1006

Society of Friends. *See* Quakers

Sociological jurisprudence, 723

Soil Conservation Service, 837, 1076

Solomon Islands, 886

Sometimes a Great Notion (Kesey), 992

Somme, battle of, 764–765, 778

Somohalla (Wanapaun), 553

Song of Russia (film), 902

Sonntag, W. Louis, Jr., 618

Sons of Liberty, 125, 128, 129

Souls of Black Folks, The (Du Bois), 730–731

Sousa, John Philip, 695, 696

South, the. *See also* Civil War; Slavery: agriculture in, 43, 392–393, 587–590; anti-Semitism in, 613; distinctive identity of, 391–393, 395–396; education in, 394, 398; expansion of slavery in, 376–377; free blacks in, 405–407; nationalism in, 395–396, 397–398; New South, 587–590, 971–975; North versus, 377, 391–392; population growth in, 988–989; populism and, 662–668; radicalism of, 398; railroads in, 397–398, 588, 589; Reconstruction in, 535–537, 543–550; and westward expansion, 430–431, 451–453

South Africa, 1112

South Carolina: colonial, 47, 77, 105; free blacks in, 204; in the Reconstruction, 535, 544, 545, 546, 547, 550; secession of, 489; state constitution, 187; and the Tariff of Abominations, 308

Southern Agrarians, 850

Southern Christian Leadership Conference (SCLC), 973, 1041

Southern Pacific Railroad, 826

South Korea, 1095

Sovereignty, 186. *See also* Popular sovereignty

Soviet Union. *See also* Cold War: collapse of, 1104–1105, 1106–1107; Cuban missile crisis, 1007–1008; Eisenhower and, 938–946; German invasion of, 867, 868, 881; in the Gorbachev era, 1101–1102; Great Purge, 825, 901; invasion of Afghanistan, 1096; under Khrushchev, 940–942; Nixon and, 1027, 1093; Reagan and, 1100; recognition of, 865; space exploration, 943–944; during World War II, 880

Space exploration, 943–944, 1107

Spain: and the American Revolution, 168–169, 172, 178, 194; and the Cuban Revolution, 695–699; and Florida, 24, 104, 178, 264, 279, 306; and the Louisiana Purchase, 251–254; Mexican Revolution, 416–417; as nation-state, 14, 78; New Spain, 19–21, 22, 24–25, 32, 79, 82, 106, 279; and New World exploration, 4, 15–21; in the Pacific Northwest, 431–432; Philippines and, 705–711; post-War of 1812, 279; slavery and, 453; and Treaty of Tordesillas, 16, 21, 22; and the War of 1812, 261

Spanish-American War, 690, 699–713, 744

Spanish Armada, 25

Spanish Inquisition, 14

Spargo, John, 724

Specie Circular, 319

Spencer, Herbert, 570, 686

Spies, August, 596–597

Spirit of '76, The (film), 774

Spock, Benjamin, 956

Spoils system, 311–312, 658

Spooner, John C., 698–699

Sports, 630–637, 695, 799, 926, 934, 948–949, 974, 979–980. *See also specific sports*; backcountry fights, 364–365; colonial, 96–97; minority groups and, 630, 635–637, 948–949

Sprague, Frank, 618

Sputnik, 943–944, 1107

Spy, The (Cooper), 352

Squanto (Tisquantum), 4–5, 10, 48

Square Deal, 738

Squatters, 425

Stag at Starkey's (Bellows), 627

Stagecoach, 280–281

Stagecoach (film), 977

Stagflation, 1091–1092

Stalin, Joseph, 825, 880–884, 886, 888, 891, 902–906, 909–910, 913, 926, 940, 1009

Stallone, Sylvester, 1028

Stalwarts, 652–653, 657

Stamp Act, 122–131, 133, 136

Stamp Act Congress, 130

Standard Oil Company, 567, 575–576, 725, 749

Standish, Miles, 29, 52

Stanton, Edwin M., 508, 540

Stanton, Elizabeth Cady, 348, 507, 541, 655

Stanton, Frank, 958

Stark, John, 171

Starr, Belle, 583

"Star Spangled Banner, The," 260

Star Wars, 1100

State-chartered banks, 318

State Department, U.S., 221, 683–684, 688, 858

State governments, 186–188

States' rights, 236–237, 273, 316–317, 530

Steamboats, 277–278, 280

Steam engines, 284, 285, 287

Steaming Streets (Bellows), 627

Steamships, 281, 285

Steele, Bob, 977

Steel industry, 564–566, 576, 669, 779, 842–843

Steffens, Lincoln, 708, 725

Stein, Gertrude, 801

Steinbeck, John, 851

Steinem, Gloria, 1066

Stella, Joseph, 800

Stephens, Alexander H., 535

Sterns, Charles, 542

Steuben, Baron Friedrich von, 172

Stevens, Edward, 227

Stevens, John L., 693

Stevens, Thaddeus, 506, 530, 531, 557, 685

Stevens, Wallace, 800

Stevenson, Adlai, 934, 942, 1060

Stevenson, Robert Louis, 641

Stewart, A. T., 641

Stieglitz, Alfred, 627

Stimson, Henry L., 905

Stimson Doctrine, 863

Stock market: crash of 1929, 814–819; crash of 1987, 1099–1100

Stockton, Robert F., 438

Stoddard Solomon, 99

Stone, Lucy, 541, 655

Stoneham, Horace, 979–980, 980

Stonewall Inn raid, 1074–1075

Storytelling, 404

Stowe, Calvin, 462

Stowe, Harriet Beecher, 203, 358, 388, 402, 460–464

Stoyer, Jacob, 403

Strategic Arms Limitation Treaty (SALT I), 1027

Streetcars, 795

Strike for Equality, 1066

Strikes, 595–596, 597–599, 669–670, 687, 694, 695, 718, 736, 738, 774, 779–781, 839, 842–843

Strode, Woody, 949

Strong, Josiah, 687

Stuart, Gilbert, 361

Stuart, J. E. B., 479

Stuart, John, 174

Stubbes, Philip, 96

Student Nonviolent Coordinating Committee (SNCC), 973, 1039, 1050, 1065

Students for a Democratic Society (SDS), 1020, 1056

Student Strike for Peace, 861

Studs Lonigan (Farrell), 851

Stuyvesant, Peter, 80

Submarines: development of, 285; in World War I, 761, 766–767, 768–770; in World War II, 867, 869

Submerged Land Act, 935

Suburbs, 795, 937, 947, 955–956, 960, 982

Suez Canal, 942

Suffrage movement, 187, 303, 347, 541, 655

Sugar, 78, 693

Sugar Act, 121, 123, 124

Sullivan, Bridget, 606–607

Sullivan, John L., 171, 634–635, 636, 695

Sumner, Charles, 506, 531, 541, 557, 685; on Senate Foreign Relations committee, 682; and slavery, 472–473, 474

Sumner, William Graham, 570, 651
Sun Also Rises, The (Hemingway), 801
Sunbelt, 972, 974, 988
Sundance Kid, 583
Supreme Court, U.S.: citizenship and, 474–475, 477, 478, 530; civil rights and, 1054; court packing scheme, 849–850; establishment of, 221, 222; and gay rights, 1075; and the Interstate Commerce Commission, 660; Jackson appointments to, 320–321; nationalism and, 277–278, 290; Reconstruction and, 540; and segregation, 932, 951–952, 972, 1038, 1052; and sex discrimination, 1066–1068; slavery and, 474–475, 477, 478
Susan Constant (ship), 30
Sussex (ship), 767
Sutter, John A., 442
Swanberg, W. A., 703
Swann v. *Charlotte-Mecklenburg Board of Education*, 1052
Sweatt v. *Painter*, 950
Swift, Gustavus, 578, 596
Swift, Henry, 125
Switzerland, 23
Syphilis, 846–847
Syria, 1110

Taft, Robert A., 867–868, 916, 934
Taft, William Howard, 634, 747, 753, 812; Dollar Diplomacy, 746; election to presidency, 740–742; and immigration restrictions, 614
Taft-Hartley Act (Labor-Management Relations Act), 916–917
Taiwan, 910, 911, 1093
Talented Tenth, 731
Talleyrand, Charles Maurice de, 235
Tallmadge, James, 291
Tallmadge Amendment, 291, 294
Tall tales, 366
Talmadge, Eugene, 950
Tammany Hall, 733
Taney, Roger B., 320, 475, 504–505
Tappan, Arthur, 345
Tappan, Lewis, 345
Tarbell, Ida, 725
Tariff of Abominations, 308
Tariffs: and the American System, 273, 307–308; and the Cleveland administration, 660–661; Compromise Tariff of 1832, 456; Fordney-McCumber Tariff, 818; Hawley-Smoot Tariff, 818; McKinley Tariff, 661, 662, 669, 693; Morrill Tariff, 572; Payne-Aldrich Tariff, 741; post-Revolution, 221, 224; Tariff of 1828, 317; Tariff of 1832, 317; tariff reduction, 660; Underwood Tariff, 743, 749; Walker Tariff, 442; and the War of 1812, 273, 276; Wilson-Gorman Tariff, 669
Tarzan of the Apes (Burroughs), 799
Tatum, Goose, 948
Taxes: under Articles of Confederation, 191; and Bacon's Rebellion, 85–86; on the colonies, 85–86, 117, 121, 122–131, 191; education and, 200–201; Fries Rebellion, 237; Proposition 13 tax rebellion, 993–994; and the Reconstruction, 546–547; Shays's Rebellion, 194–196, 206; single tax, 721; Stamp Act, 122–131, 133, 136; and voting rights, 301–303; Whiskey Rebellion, 229, 237; during World War I, 772; during World War II, 873, 878
Taxi Driver (film), 1029
Taylor, Frederick W., 594, 723
Taylor, Marshall W. "Major," 636
Taylor, Maxwell, 1015
Taylor, William Graham, 724
Taylor, Zachary, 325, 345, 437, 438–439; and the Compromise of 1850, 456; death, 450, 451, 456; election to presidency, 325, 442
Tea Act, 138–139
Teague, Walter Dorwin, 851
Teapot Dome scandal, 812
Technics and Civilization (Mumford), 850
Technology: agricultural, 285, 286, 376, 586, 587–590; of cities, 616–618, 622, 623; nineteenth-century, 284–285, 567–568, 586–587
Tecumseh (Shawnee), 260, 263
Teheran Conference, 883
Telegraph, 283, 285
Telephones, 567, 568, 796
Television, 921, 922, 923, 955–960, 977, 1001–1002, 1006, 1055, 1107
Teller Amendment, 698–699, 705
Temperance movement, 332, 338, 728. *See also* Prohibition
Tenant farming, 837, 838
Ten Commandments (film), 799
Tenement Reform Law, 621–622, 728–729
Tennent, Gilbert, 99, 100
Tennessee, 198; in the Reconstruction, 531, 537, 538, 549–550; secession of, 491; and westward expansion, 229
Tennessee Valley Authority (TVA), 836, 837, 1076
Tennis, 949
Tenochtitlán, 7, 18
Tenskwatawa (Shawnee), 258, 262–263
Tenth Amendment, 221
Tenure of Office Act, 539–540, 540
Ten Years' War, 696
Terry, Eli, 285
Tesla, Nikola, 568
Test Act, 92
Texas, 279, 307, 426–431; annexation to the United States, 430–431, 436, 437; anti-Mexican sentiment in, 441; colonization of, 415; Mexico and, 426–430; secession of, 489; settlement of, 426–428; siege of the Alamo, 428–430; and slavery, 430–431, 452
Texas Revolution, 429–430
Texas v. *White*, 540
Textile industry, 270–271, 382–383, 549, 588–589, 779–780
Thanksgiving, 4, 5, 51, 1072–1073
Thayer, Eli, 470
Theatrical entertainment, 366–367

Theory of the Leisure Class (Veblen), 722–723
Third Reich, 864
Third World, nationalist movements in, 944–945
Thirteenth Amendment, 528, 535, 538, 541
Thomas, Lorenzo, 540
Thompson, Hugh, Jr., 1005
Thompson, Hugh Miller, 622
Thompson, Richard W., 684
Thomson, Charles, 141–142
Thoreau, Henry David, 352, 353–354, 355–357, 726–727, 954
Thorpe, Jim, 636
Three-fifths compromise, 208, 264, 291, 531
Thurmond, J. Strom, 917
Tibbets, Paul, 891
Tijerina, Reies Lopez, 1071
Tilden, Samuel J., 557, 656
Till, Emmett, 932–933, 952
Tillman, "Pitchfork Ben," 666, 708
Timber, 584, 589–590
Timber and Stone Act, 584
Timber Culture Act, 584
Time, concept of, 592, 594
Time zones, 580
Tinian, 887
Tippecanoe, battle of, 260, 262–263, 300, 324
Tisquantum (Squanto), 4–5, 10, 48
Tituba, 88
Tobacco, 8, 32, 40, 41–45, 47, 59, 78–79, 84, 85, 376, 588–589, 749, 806, 975–976
Tobago, 450
Tocqueville, Alexis de, 283, 336
Tojo, Hideki, 869
Toll roads, 281
Toltecs, 7
Tompkins, Sally L., 520
Tonkin Gulf Resolution, 1012–1014, 1031
Toombs, Robert, 452
Toomer, Jean, 811
Tories, 142
Tourism, 983
Townsend, Francis, 841–842, 844
Townshend, Charles ("Champagne Charlie"), 131–132, 136
Townshend Duties, 127, 131–132, 135–136, 138, 139
Tracy, Benjamin F., 689
Trade. *See also* Tariffs: and Barbary pirates, 250–251, 278; colonial, 78–79, 86, 89, 90; and the Crusades, 12–13; Embargo Act, 255–256; European Coal and Steel Authority, 908; fur, 33–34, 108, 199, 230–231, 422, 431–432; and Jamestown colony, 30–32; Macon's Bill No. 2, 256; mercantilism and, 78–79; in the Middle Ages, 12–13; and nation-states, 14–16; and Navigation Acts, 78–79, 86, 89, 193; Non-Intercourse Act, 256; post-Revolution, 194; and Townshend Duties, 127, 131–132, 135–136, 138, 139; XYZ affair and, 235–236
Trade associations, 812

Trade unions. *See* Labor unions
Trafalgar, battle of, 254
Trail of Tears, 312–315
Trainmen's Union, 595
Transcendentalism, 352–358, 726
Transportation. *See also specific modes of transportation*: cities and, 616–618, 622, 623, 795; nineteenth century, 275–276, 280–281; post-World War II, 936–938
Travis, Joseph, 405
Travis, William Barret, 428–430
Treason, 254
Treasury Department, U.S., 221
Treaty of Aix-la-Chapelle, 107–108
Treaty of Alliance, 172
Treaty of Amity and Commerce, 172
Treaty of Ghent, 264
Treaty of Greenville, 230
Treaty of Guadalupe Hidalgo, 440, 441
Treaty of Kanagawa, 466
Treaty of Paris, 117, 178, 193, 705, 709
Treaty of Ryswick, 105
Treaty of San Lorenzo, 232
Treaty of Tordesillas, 16, 21, 22
Treaty of Utrecht, 105–106
Treaty of Versailles, 781–786, 862, 864, 1000; disagreement in, 782–784; Fourteen Points, 781–782, 784, 785; League of Nations and, 781, 782, 784, 785, 787; ratification of, 784–786
Trenchard, John, 136
Trench warfare, 761, 762, 764–765
Trent affair, 503–504
Trevelyan, Charles Philips, 620
Triangle Shirtwaist Company, 734–735
Trinidad, 453
Tripoli, 250–251
Trist, Nicholas, 440
Trolleys, 618, 622, 623, 795
Trotter, William Monroe, 731
True Grit (film), 970
Truman, Harry S, 873, 891, 902–908, 910–919, 921, 1012; and bombing of Japan, 889–892; and containment policy, 938–939; Fair Deal, 917–918; Korean War, 911–915; Marshall Plan, 907–908; racial reforms, 950; Stalin and, 902, 904, 906; as successor to Roosevelt, 886, 888; Truman Doctrine, 906–907, 912, 919; and Vietnam, 1009
Truman Doctrine, 906–907, 912, 919
Trumbull, John, 361
Trusts, 576, 661, 720, 738
Truth, Sojourner, 332–333, 877
Tuberculosis (TB), 726–727
Tubman, Harriet, 346
Tucker, George, 392
Tucker, Nathaniel Beverly, 398
Tugwell, Rexford, 836
Turkey, 759, 906, 907, 1110
Turner, Joe, 962
Turner, Nat, 396, 405
Turnpikes, 281
Turtle (submarine), 285
Tuscarora Indians, 1073
Tuscaroras (Six Nations), 171

Tuskegee Airmen, 876
Tuskegee Institute, 587–588, 731, 827, 846–847
Twain, Mark (Samuel Clemens), 365, 366, 424, 625, 630–631, 650, 658, 708–710
Tweed Ring scandal, 547
Twelfth Amendment, 239, 306
Twenty-fourth Amendment, 1048, 1077
Twice-Told Tales (Hawthorne), 358
Twiller, Wouter van, 80
Two Years Before the Mast (Dana), 363
Tyler, Elizabeth, 808
Tyler, John: presidency of, 430–431; as successor to Harrison, 324–325, 430, 450; and Texas question, 431
Typee (Melville), 359

Ukraine, 867
Uncle Tom's Cabin, 460–464
Underground railroad, 460
Underwood Tariff, 743, 749
Unemployment, 1054, 1055; Depression-era, 825–827, 1070; in the Great Depression, 825, 826, 827, 829, 839, 1070
Unemployment insurance, 819, 843
Unionist Democratic party, 488
Union Pacific railroad, 572
Unions. *See* Labor unions
Unitarianism, 334, 336, 352–353
United Farm Workers, 1063
United Mine Workers (UMW), 718, 749–750, 780, 842, 916
United Nations, 884, 913, 1110
United States Railroad Administration, 770
United States Steel Corporation, 564–565, 576–577, 741–742
United States. v. *Debs*, 774
United States v. *E. C. Knight Co.*, 661
United Steelworkers of America, 842–843
Universalism, 336, 396, 433
Universal Negro Improvement Association (UNIA), 810
Universal white manhood suffrage, 302–303
University of Chicago, 723
University of Michigan, 632
University of Virginia, 398, 632–633
Unsafe at Any Speed (Nader), 1036
Urban League, 809, 810
Urban parks, 361–362, 637
Urey, Harold C., 910
Uruguay, 1095
U.S.A. (Dos Passos), 851
U–2 spy plane incident, 945–946
Utah: application for statehood, 455–456; slavery and, 455–456, 457
Utilities: public ownership of, 733; regulation of, 734, 843
Utopian communities, 349–351, 354–358

Vagrancy, 826
Valentino, Rudolph, 799
Vallandigham, Clement L., 505–506
Van Buren, Martin, 304, 305, 308–309, 312, 319–321, 442, 624; in the election

of 1840, 300; election to presidency, 319, 324
Vandenberg, Arthur, 867–868, 907
Vanderbilt, Cornelius, 575, 580
Van Devanter, Willis, 849
Vann, John Paul, 1015
Vanzetti, Bartolomeo, 808
Vardaman, James K., 734, 736
Vassar College, 347
Vause, Agatha, 64
Veblen, Thorstein, 722–723
V-E (Victory in Europe) Day, 886
Venezuela, 1090
Venezuela crisis, 694, 695
Verdun, battle of, 762
Vergennes, Comte de, 168–169, 172
Vermont, antislavery law, 204
Verrazzano, Giovanni da, 21
Vertical integration, 576
Very Brief Relation of the Destruction of the Indies, A (Las Casas), 21
Vesey, Denmark, 292–293, 318, 405
Vesey, Joseph, 292
Vesey Conspiracy, 292–293
Vespucci, Amerigo, 16
Vickers, George, 541
Vicksburg, battle of, 513, 516
Victoria, Queen of England, 501
Vietnam War, 968, 1008–1031; antiwar movement, 1018–1022, 1057; background of, 1000–1001, 1009–1010; guerrilla tactics in, 1016; Gulf of Tonkin Resolution, 1013–1014, 1031; inflation and, 1089–1090, 1092; Johnson and, 968, 1008–1009, 1010, 1013–1018, 1031, 1089–1090; legacy of, 1028–1031, 1092–1093; My Lai massacre, 1004–1005, 1019; Nixon and, 1021–1026; peace treaty, 1028; Tet offensive, 1016–1018; United States aid to, 1010; veterans of, 1029; and Vietnamization, 1023–1025
Vigilantism, 583, 671–672, 780
Villa, Pancho, 747–748
Vinson, Fred M., 951–952
Virginia: and ratification of Articles of Confederation, 189–190; and ratification of the Constitution, 210, 211; in the Reconstruction, 550; secession of, 491; slave trade in, 204–206; state constitution, 187
Virginia (ship), 502
Virginia colony, 40–45, 108, 167
Virginia Company, 30, 41–45, 48
Virginia Declaration of Rights, 196–197
Virginia dynasty, 305–306
Virginia Plan, 207
Virginia Resolutions, 129, 130
Virtual representation, 122–123
Volkswagen, 1091
Volstead Act, 774
Voting rights, 187, 301–303; of African Americans, 303, 540–543, 550, 661–662, 672, 674–675, 950, 972–973, 1046–1048, 1051; colonial, 85; of women, 187, 303, 347, 541, 655, 730, 734, 774–775, 804–805

Voting Rights Act (1965), 972, 1046–1048, 1051, 1053, 1054, 1077

Wabash, St. Louis & Pacific Railway Company v. *Illinois*, 660
Wade, Benjamin, 506, 534
Wade, Henry, 1067
Wade-Davis Bill, 531–534
Wagner, Robert F., 724
Wagner Act (National Labor Relations Act), 842–843, 849, 853, 1063
Wake Island, 690, 870, 886, 914
Walden (Thoreau), 355–356
Walker, David, 343
Walker, Freeman, 291
Walker, Patrick, 134
Walker, Quok, 203
Walker, William, 398
Walker Tariff, 442
Wallace, George, 464, 972, 988, 1022, 1044, 1058
Wallace, Henry, 838, 917
Wambaugh, Joseph, 969
Wampanoag Indians, 1072–1073
Wanamaker, John, 624, 641
Wanapaun Indians, 553
Ward, Artemus, 366
Ward, John Montgomery, 634
Ward, Lester Frank, 723
War Department, U.S., 221, 777, 805, 879
War dogs, 29
Ward system, 733
War Hawks, 257, 273
War Industries Board (WIB), 770
War Labor Board (WLB), 873
Warmouth, Henry C., 547
Warner, Charles Dudley, 650, 658
Warner, Susan, 363, 366
Warner Brothers Studies, 979
War of 1812, 256–264, 306; and decline of party system, 264, 272, 305; economic impact of, 274, 280–291; financial programs following, 272–274; nationalism following, 271–280; significance of, 261–264
War of Jenkins's Ear, 106
War of the Austrian Succession, 106
War of the League of Augsburg, 87, 105
War of the Spanish Succession, 105, 172
War on Poverty, 987, 1052–1054
War Powers Act, 1031, 1086, 1087
War Prayer, The (Twain), 710
War Production Board (WPB), 871
War Refugee Board, 879
War Relocation Authority, 879, 880
Warren, Earl, 952
Warren, Fuller, 922
Warren, Joseph, 137, 141, 151, 157, 158
Warren, William, 134–135
Warsaw Pact, 941–942
Wars of the Roses, 14–15
War Trade Board, 770
Washington, Booker T., 587–588, 589, 674, 730–731, 751, 809, 827, 1048
Washington, D.C.: abolition of slavery in, 456, 457; Capitol moves to, 234–235; civil rights march on, 1046;

Coxey's Army and, 671; in the War of 1812, 259, 260
Washington, George, 110, 140, 175, 177, 184, 196, 228–234, 247–248, 305, 683; and the Citizen Genêt Affair, 229; as commanding general of the army, 236; and the Constitution, 206, 208–209, 211; death, 239–240, 283; Farewell Address, 225, 246, 305, 683, 762; at Fort Duquesne, 108–109; and the French Revolution, 228–229; and Jay's Treaty, 230–232; and manumission, 204, 205; Newburgh Conspiracy and, 192–193; and Ohio country settlements, 229–230; presidency of, 221–225; retirement from presidency, 232; in the Revolutionary War, 148–149, 155, 164–166, 172; and the Whiskey Rebellion, 229
Washington, Kenny, 949
Washington, Martha, 239
Washington Post, 1084–1085
Water: dam projects, 977–978, 982; and westward expansion, 584, 585–586
Watergate scandal, 1084–1087
Watson, Elkanah, 97
Watson, John B., 797
Watson, Tom, 613, 668, 671, 672–673, 676
Watts riots, 1051
Wayles, John, 218
Wayne, Anthony, 230, 231, 262
Wayne, John, 968–969, 977, 982
Wealth of Nations, The (Smith), 571
Weathermen, 1057
Weaver, James B., 657, 667, 668
Webb, Frank, 360
Webb, Walter Prescott, 977
Webb-Kenyon Act, 743–744
Webster, Daniel, 272–273, 316, 367, 439, 455–456; in the election of 1836, 321; and second Bank of the United States, 318
Webster, Noah, 284
Webster-Ashburton Treaty, 431
Weed, Thurlow, 304
Week on the Concord and Merrimack Rivers, A (Thoreau), 355
Weeks, Sinclair, 937
Welch, Joseph, 921
Weld, Theodore, 344
Welfare capitalism, 825
Welker, Herman, 926
Welles, Gideon, 497
Wells, H. G., 618
Wells-Barnett, Ida, 672, 675, 729, 731
Wertham, Frederic, 925–926
Wesley, John, 99
West, Mae, 851
West, the, 975–994; in advertising, 975–976; economic diversification in, 581–587, 979–984; federal projects in, 977–979, 992–993; nineteenth-century visions of, 976–977; politics of, 984–994; in popular culture, 968–969, 975–977; population growth in, 980–981, 988; populism and, 662–668; Reconstruction in, 552–557
Westerdam (ship), 1091

Westinghouse, George, 568
Westmoreland, William, 1016, 1018
Weston, Thomas, 48, 52
West Point Military Academy, 494–495, 926
West Virginia (ship), 870
Westward expansion, 414–445; economic growth and, 581–587; Europe and, 11–34; exploration in, 421–422; farming in, 584–587; Far West, 419–435; fur trade and, 422; Hispanic Americans and, 414–417; and land rights, 197–199; and Manifest Destiny, 426–435; Native Americans and, 229–230, 307, 312–315, 417–419, 552–557, 582–583; Ohio country, 229–230, 262–263; and Oregon Trail, 422–423, 425–426, 432; overland trail to California, 419–420, 422–423; in the Pacific Northwest, 431–433; post-Civil War, 552–557; post-War of 1812, 274–276; public lands in, 315–316; ranching and, 581–585; slavery and, 430–431, 451–453, 469–480; and Texas, 426–431; Wild West and, 582–583, 584
Weyler y Nicolau, Valeriano, 696–697
Wheatley, Phillis, 184–185, 201, 204, 205
Wheatley, Susannah, 184
Wheelock, Eleazar, 104
Wheelwright, John, 56
Whig party, 477; collapse of, 451, 464–466, 467, 469, 473, 488; in the election of 1836, 321–324; in the election of 1840, 300; in England, 136, 442; and the Mexican-American War, 439; origins of, 304, 321; principles of, 325, 545
Whipper, William, 546
Whiskey Rebellion, 229, 237
Whistle-blowers, 1036
White, Hugh Lawson, 321
White, John, 27
White, Peregrine, 62
White, Richard, 978
White, Susanna, 62
White, William Allen, 724, 734
White Cap movement, 583
Whitefield, George, 99–100, 101–102, 103
White Squadron, 688–689, 691
White supremacy, 549–550, 552, 589, 652, 671–672, 753, 808–809
Whitman, Marcus, 432
Whitman, Narcissa Prentiss, 432
Whitman, Walt, 358, 359–360, 565, 568
Whitney, Eli, 285, 286, 376
Whitney, William, 688
Whittemore, Dexter, 379
Whitten, John C., 933
Why We Can't Wait (King), 1041
Wicker, Tom, 1022
Wide, Wide World, The (Warner), 363
Wild, Elizabeth, 61
Wilde, Oscar, 688
Wilderness, battle of the, 516
Wilderness Road, 198
Wildlife Preservation Act, 987
Wild One, The (film), 925

Wild West Show, 976
Wiley, Harvey W., 740
Wilkins, Roy, 933
Wilkinson, James, 253–254
Willard, Emma Hart, 341
Willard, Frances, 728
Willard, Samuel, 60
William and Mary, 100
Williams, Eugene, 779
Williams, Roger, 55–56, 197
Williams v. *Lee*, 1074
Williams v. *Mississippi*, 672
Willis, Albert S., 693–694
Willkie, Wendell, 868
Wills, Frank, 1084
Wilmot, David, 442, 455
Wilmot Proviso, 442, 453
Wilson, Edith Bolling, 785
Wilson, Sloan, 956
Wilson, Woodrow, 247, 619, 742–744,
   753, 758–759, 766–772, 775, 777, 779,
   830, 1000; declaration of neutrality,
   762–763; in the election of 1912, 742;
   in the election of 1920, 786; election to
   presidency, 742; and immigration re-
   strictions, 614–615; Missionary Diplo-
   macy, 746–748; and New Freedom,
   742, 743, 749; reelection, 768; Treaty
   of Versailles and, 781–786, 1000; and
   World War I, 769–778
Wilson-Gorman Tariff, 669
Winning of the West, The (Roosevelt), 415
Winthrop, John, 53–56, 57
Wisconsin, admitted as free state, 452
Wisconsin glaciation, 5
Witchcraft hysteria, 87–88
Wizard of Oz, The (Baum), 556
Wobblies (Industrial Workers of the
   World; IWW), 767, 771–772, 774, 780
Wolfe, James, 109, 110–111, 123
Wolfe, Thomas, 800
Woman in the Nineteenth Century (Fuller),
   354
Woman's Christian Temperance Union,
   728
Woman's Loyal National League, 507
Women: and abortion, 203, 792, 802, 803,
   1064, 1067; in the American Revolution, 167; and birth control, 202–203,
   348, 792–793, 802, 803; and childbirth,
   62–63; in the Civil War, 518–520;
   colonial, 59–64; crime and, 606–607;
   and the cult of domesticity, 636–637,
   792, 796, 1059–1060; education of,
   200–201, 202, 341–342, 347, 722,
   1060–1061, 1069; employment of,
   382–383, 593, 720, 728, 729–730, 775,
   805, 813, 826, 875–876, 917, 1069; in
   the Great Depression, 845; and human rights, 184–185, 200–201; Native
   American, 10; as novelists, 363–366;
   and patriarchal values, 60–64, 197; in
   the Progressive era, 728–730; property rights of, 60, 64, 349, 546; and

sexual revolution of early twentieth
   century, 801–804; slave, 403–404; in
   the South, 393; sports and, 636–637;
   voting rights of, 187, 303, 347, 541,
   655, 730, 734, 774–775, 804–805; in
   World War I, 775; during World War
   II, 875–876
Women's Bureau, 1064
Women's liberation movement, 960,
   1059–1069. *See also* Feminism; aboli-
   tionism and, 348–349; and the Equal
   Rights Amendment (ERA), 730, 805,
   1064, 1068–1069; impact of, 1069;
   sources of discontent in, 1060–1061;
   split in, 805; and the Supreme Court,
   1066–1068
Women's Loyal League, 541
Women's movement, 541
Wood, Jethro, 286
Wood, Leonard, 705, 767
Woodmason, Charles, 364
Woodruff, Robert W., 871
Woodson, Carter, 810–811
Woodstock Music Festival, 1058
Woodward, Bob, 1084–1085
Woolen Act, 89
Woolworth, Frank, 619
Woolworth Building, 619, 641, 793
Worcester v. *Georgia*, 313
Work force. *See also* Labor unions: after
   World War II, 916–917; child labor
   and, 382, 385, 724, 729, 736, 744, 750,
   838–839; discontent of, 593–595,
   669–671; in the Great Depression,
   838–840; industrialization and, 592–
   599; migrant workers in, 609–610,
   1062–1063; nativism and, 612–615;
   preindustrial, 590–593; resistance of,
   592, 594–597, 669–671; and violent
   conflict, 595–597; wages of, 590, 591,
   593, 595–596; women in, 382–383,
   593, 720, 728, 729–730, 775, 805, 813,
   826, 875–876, 917, 1069; working conditions and, 590–595
Workingmen's Benevolent Association
   (WBA), 595
Working Men's party, 384
Workmen's compensation, 734–735, 744,
   750
Works Progress Administration (WPA),
   839–840, 848, 873
World Anti-Slavery Convention, 348
World Court, 860
World Restored, A (Kissinger), 1023
World War I, 758–788; Allied violations
   of neutrality in, 763–766; Armistice,
   779; consequences of, 759; events
   leading to, 759–760; financing, 772;
   German defeat in, 778; German first
   strike, 760–762; neutrality ends,
   768–770; neutrality of United States
   in, 762–763; preparedness campaign,
   767–768; repression in, 772–774; social
   unrest following, 779–781; submarine

warfare, 761, 766–767, 768–770; Treaty
   of Versailles, 781–786, 862, 864, 1000;
   trench warfare, 761, 762, 764–765;
   United States in, 769–778; voluntarism in, 770, 772; World War II: beginning of, 865–867; bombing of
   Japan, 889–892; D-Day, 883, 884, 934;
   European theater, 865–868, 880–886;
   events preceding, 861–865; inflation
   during, 872–873, 916; mobilization of
   United States for, 871–874; neutrality
   of United States in, 867–869; Pa-
   cific theater, 869–871, 886–892; Pearl
   Harbor attack, 867, 869–871; social
   changes during, 874–880; Yalta Con-
   ference, 883–886, 903
Worster, Donald, 978
Wounded Knee, battle of, 555–556, 1074
Wright, Carroll D., 590–591
Wright, Frances (Fanny), 348, 350
Wright, Harry, 631
Wright, Mose, 932–933
Wright, Richard, 851
Writs of assistance, 124–125
Wuthering Heights (Brontë), 727
Wyandot Indians, 274

XYZ affair, 235–236

Yachting, 635–636
Yale, 100, 632
Yalta Conference, 883–886, 903, 904
Yancey, William L., 488, 503
Yellow fever, 226–227, 622
Yellow peril, 874
Yellow press, 689–690, 696–699, 701–703
Yellowstone National Park, 1076
Yeltsin, Boris, 1104–1105
Yeoman farmers, 25, 549
Yerkes, Robert M., 777–778
Yidn in America (Price), 611
Yom Kippur War, 1090
Yosemite National Park, 738
Yost, Fielding H., 632
Young, Brigham, 435
Young America movement, 359, 466–467
Young Communist League, 915
Young Men's Christian Association
   (YMCA), 803
Young Women's Christian Association
   (YWCA), 728
Youth movement, 1018–1022, 1055–1059
Ypres, battle of, 761–762
Yucatan (ship), 706
Yugoslavia, 784

Zapata, Emiliano, 747
Zeg, Stephen, 914
Zeppelin, 762
Zhou Enlai (Chou En-Lai), 910, 1027
Zimmerman, Arthur, 769
Zimmermann telegram, 769
Zoning, 623, 794
Zuni Indians, 9, 417, 552

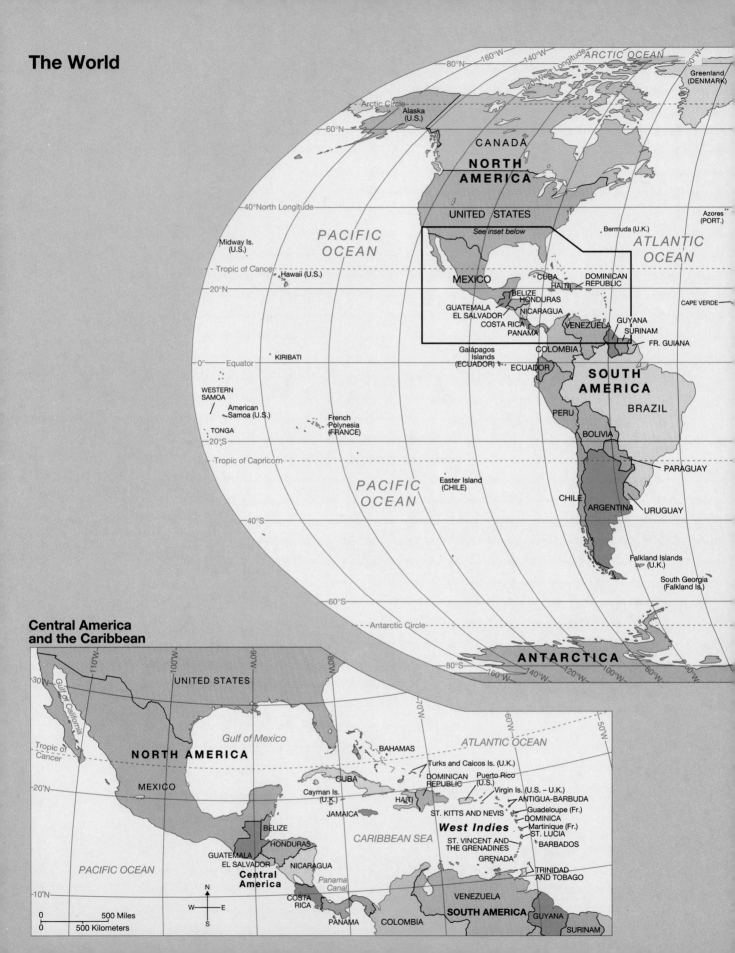

The World

Arctic Circle
Alaska (U.S.)
CANADA
NORTH AMERICA
Greenland (DENMARK)
80°N
160°W
140°W
120°W West Longitude
ARCTIC OCEAN
60°W
60°N
40°North Longitude
UNITED STATES
See inset below
Azores (PORT.)
Bermuda (U.K.)
ATLANTIC OCEAN
Midway Is. (U.S.)
PACIFIC OCEAN
Hawaii (U.S.)
Tropic of Cancer
MEXICO
CUBA
HAITI
DOMINICAN REPUBLIC
20°N
BELIZE
HONDURAS
GUATEMALA
EL SALVADOR
NICARAGUA
COSTA RICA
PANAMA
VENEZUELA
GUYANA
SURINAM
FR. GUIANA
CAPE VERDE
KIRIBATI
Galápagos Islands (ECUADOR)
COLOMBIA
0° Equator
ECUADOR
SOUTH AMERICA
WESTERN SAMOA
American Samoa (U.S.)
PERU
BRAZIL
TONGA
French Polynesia (FRANCE)
BOLIVIA
20°S
Tropic of Capricorn
PARAGUAY
PACIFIC OCEAN
Easter Island (CHILE)
CHILE
ARGENTINA
URUGUAY
40°S
Falkland Islands (U.K.)
South Georgia (Falkland Is.)
60°S
Antarctic Circle
ANTARCTICA
80°S
160°W
140°W
120°W
100°W
80°W
60°W

Central America and the Caribbean

30°N
110°W
100°W
90°W
80°W
UNITED STATES
Gulf of California
Gulf of Mexico
70°W
60°W
50°W
ATLANTIC OCEAN
NORTH AMERICA
BAHAMAS
Turks and Caicos Is. (U.K.)
Tropic of Cancer
MEXICO
CUBA
DOMINICAN REPUBLIC
Puerto Rico (U.S.)
Virgin Is. (U.S. – U.K.)
ANTIGUA-BARBUDA
20°N
Cayman Is. (U.K.)
HAITI
Guadeloupe (Fr.)
DOMINICA
Martinique (Fr.)
ST. LUCIA
JAMAICA
ST. KITTS AND NEVIS
West Indies
CARIBBEAN SEA
ST. VINCENT AND THE GRENADINES
BARBADOS
BELIZE
HONDURAS
GUATEMALA
EL SALVADOR
NICARAGUA
GRENADA
Central America
Panama Canal
TRINIDAD AND TOBAGO
10°N
COSTA RICA
PANAMA
VENEZUELA
COLOMBIA
SOUTH AMERICA
GUYANA
SURINAM
0 500 Miles
0 500 Kilometers
N W E S

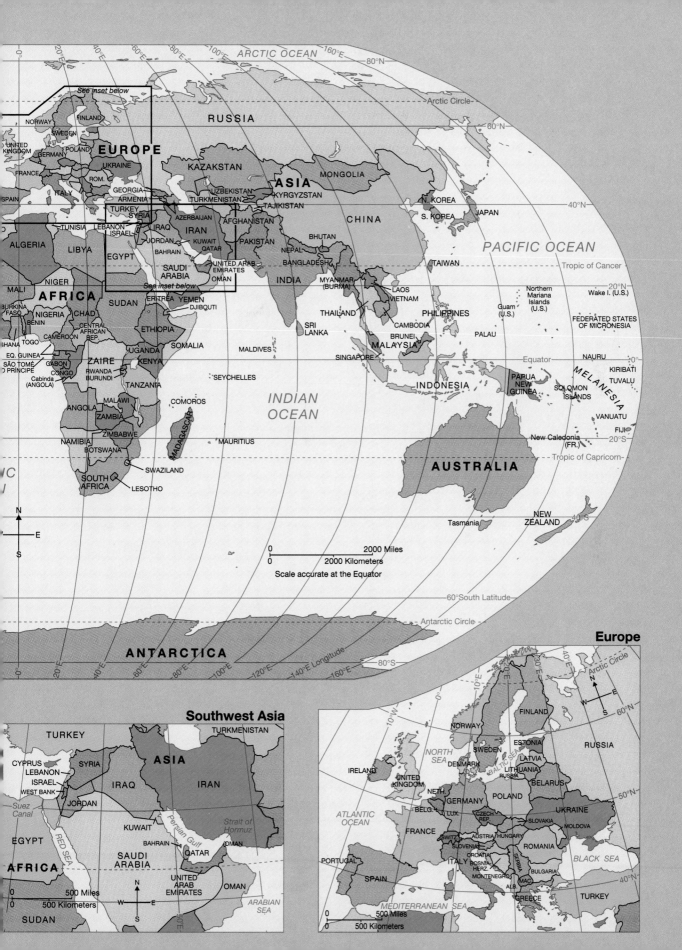